Canadian Tort Law
Cases, Notes & Materials

Eleventh Edition

Allen M. Linden
A Justice of The Federal Court of Canada

Lewis N. Klar
B.A., B.C.L., LL.M.
Dean
Faculty of Law, University of Alberta

Butterworths

Toronto and Vancouver

Canadian Tort Law: Cases, Notes & Materials

April 1999

The Butterworth Group of Companies

Canada
75 Clegg Road, MARKHAM, Ontario L6G 1A1
and
1721-808 Nelson St., Box 12148, VANCOUVER, B.C. V6Z 2H2
Australia
Butterworths Pty Ltd., SYDNEY
Ireland
Butterworths (Ireland) Ltd., DUBLIN
Malaysia
Malayan Law Journal Sdn Bhd, KUALA LUMPUR
New Zealand
Butterworths of New Zealand Ltd., WELLINGTON
Singapore
Butterworths Asia, SINGAPORE
South Africa
Butterworth Publishers (Pty.) Ltd., DURBAN
United Kingdom
Butterworth & Co. (Publishers) Ltd., LONDON
United States
Michie, CHARLOTTESVILLE, Virginia

Canadian Cataloguing in Publication Data

Linden, Allen M., 1934-
Canadian tort law

11th ed.
First four eds. published under the title: Cases on the law of torts.
9th ed. Canadian tort law: cases, notes and materials/by Cecil A. Wright, Allen M. Linden and Lewis N. Klar.
Includes index.
ISBN 0-433-41539-8

1. Torts — Canada — Cases. I. Klar, Lewis, 1946- . II. Wright, Cecil A., 1904–1967. Cases on the law of torts. III. Title.

KE1232.L57 1999 346.7103 C99-930424-0
KF1250.L57 1999

Printed and bound in Canada.

PREFACE

Like its predecessors, this casebook is meant to furnish a basis for an introductory course in the law of torts. Because the book is used primarily in Canadian law schools, the bulk of the material is Canadian. Much of this new Canadian material is exciting, for it reflects a vitality and vibrancy in our judges and scholars that matches the spirit of modern Canada. As we will see in this edition, Canadian tort law is in fact becoming increasingly more distinctive, differing often from the tort law of our fellow Commonwealth countries. Nowhere is this more true than in our approach to the liability of public authorities and the recovery of economic losses. In other areas as well, we have developed our own thinking about difficult legal issues, which others might learn from and even borrow. We do not neglect, however, the leading English cases, since understanding the sources of our law allows us to appreciate better the current law.

As in our previous editions, we have tried to ask questions more than provide answers. We do this for two reasons: (1) because it is much more stimulating to teach and to study torts by thinking about the as yet unanswered possibilities; and (2) because definitive answers to many fundamental questions is not a feature of modern and ever-changing tort law.

Although we have in this edition retained some of the basic organization adopted by Dean Wright in his first editions and followed by us in subsequent ones, some changes will be apparent in this edition. We have retained the basic flow of the material, starting off with the intentional torts, moving then into negligence, and finally examining strict liability and a series of specific other tort actions, but the structure within some of the sections has changed. One might note in this edition, for example, some rearrangement of the negligence material. Some introductory material on causation and damage is introduced earlier in Chapter 4. Chapter 6, "Proof" has been rearranged in the light of the "expiry" of *res ipsa loquitur* in *Fontaine v. I.C.B.C.* There is a new section on constitutional torts in Chapter 11, dealing with governmental liability. Perhaps most importantly there is included a new Chapter 10, "Economic Losses", incorporating the Supreme Court of Canada's new approach based on Professor Feldthusen's analysis.

The debate about tort law's relevance, especially in automobile accident compensation, continues. It has now been 25 years since New Zealand abolished the tort suit as a remedy for accidental injury and established in its place, a comprehensive, government-operated, compensation scheme. Although no other jurisdiction has attempted such a major reform, several have brought in no-fault schemes for auto-accident cases. We continue to debate the meaning and purposes of tort. Does tort deter, educate, restrain the abuse of power, and provide psychological benefits to victims? We see, for example the apparent rise of the use of tort for sexual assault victims. What does this tell us about our justice system? We also see competing theories of tort, some of which focus on the instrumentalist goals of tort and others on its ideological and philosophical basis. Whatever we conclude, however, there is no doubt about one thing; tort law continues to intrigue and fascinate; it is dynamic and it is alive.

Justice Linden wishes to thank his law clerks, Andrew Auerbach and Kathryn Turner, who assisted him in the preparation of this edition, as well as his talented and dedicated colleague, Aija Carisse, who prepared the manuscript. He would like to express his appreciation to Dean Lynn and former Dean Phillips of the Pepperdine University School of Law, for allowing him to use their fine library during the summer. Justice Linden also owes an enormous debt of gratitude to his wife Marjorie, who has time and again proved herself to be "tried, tested and true". He dedicates his part of this edition to his grandchildren, Adam, Sarah, Benjamin, Danya and Julia — the future.

Dean Klar wishes to thank his student assistant, Mr. Wade Clark, for his work on this edition. In addition, Ms. Sheila Parr, the Dean's executive assistant, has been, as always, an invaluable help. The continued support and encouragement of the Faculty of Law have allowed the Dean to continue to work on this text despite the ever increasing demands of administration, and for this he is grateful. Dean Klar dedicates this edition to Irene, Noah and Samara, who continue to provide inspiration and love.

We also thank our students and our colleagues, for improving our work with their thoughtful and insightful suggestions. We are indebted to the people at Butterworths for their editorial assistance, especially Emily Ferguson, Jane Long, Corinne Wolfe-Betz, Caryl Young and Janine Denney-Lightfoot.

Allen M. Linden
Lewis N. Klar
April 1999

ACKNOWLEDGEMENTS

A casebook on such a wide subject necessarily contains a great deal of references to the work of others. The authors and publishers of these articles and textbooks have been most generous in giving permission for the reproduction of works already in print. All footnotes and endnotes have been omitted from the body of excerpts reproduced in this text. References, of course, appear where necessary and possible in the text. It is convenient for us to list below, for the assistance of the reader, the publishers and authors for whose courtesy we are most grateful. The following is organized by author in alphabetical order.

American Bar Association Special Committee on Automobile Insurance Legislation, *Automobile No-Fault Insurance: A Study* (1978). © 1978 by the American Bar Association. Reprinted with permission.

The American Law Institute, *Restatement of Torts, Second,* §8A, §13, §21, §46, §283B, §402A, §519, §568, §578. © 1965 by The American Law Institute. Reprinted with permission.

Atiyah, *Accidents, Compensation and the Law* (5th ed.) (London: Butterworths, 1995).

Atiyah, "Thinking the Unthinkable" in Birks (ed.), *Wrongs and Remedies in the Twenty-First Century* (Oxford: Oxford University Press, 1996). By permission of Oxford University Press.

Bender, "A Lawyer's Primer in Feminist Theory and Tort" (1989), 38 J. of Legal Educ. 3 at 31. By permission of University of Iowa, Department of Law, Association of American Law Schools.

Birks, *Wrongs and Remedies in the Twenty-First Century* (Oxford: Oxford University Press, 1996). By permission of Oxford University Press.

Blum and Kalven, "Public Perspectives on a Private Law Problem — Auto Compensation Plans (1965)" (1964), 31 U. Chi. L. Rev. 646.

Calabresi, "Fault, Accidents and the Wonderful World of Blum and Kalven" (1965), 75 Yale L.J. 216. Reproduced by permission of The Yale Law Journal Company and Fred B. Rothman & Company from The Yale Law Journal, Vol. 75, pp. 216-238.

Calabresi, "The Decision for Accidents: An Approach to Non-Fault Allocation of Costs" (1965), 78 Harv. L. Rev. 713.

Don DeWees, *Exploring the Domain of Accident Law: Taking the Facts Seriously.* Copyright © 1996 by Oxford University Press, Inc. Used by permission of Oxford University Press, Inc.

Fine, Sean, "Rape victim knew of neighbourhood assaults, court told", *The Globe & Mail*, September 17, 1997. Reprinted with permission from *The Globe and Mail.*

Fleming, The Law of Torts (9th ed.) (Sydney: The Law Book Company, 1998). Reproduced with the express permission of LBC Information Services.

Haines, "The Medical Profession and the Adversary Process" (1973), 11 Osgoode Hall L.J. 41.

Henderson, "Expanding the Negligence Concept: Retreat from the Rule of Law" (1976), 51 Ind. L.J. 467. © Trustees of Indiana University and Fred B. Rothman & Co.

Hodson-Walker, "The Value of Safety Belts: A Review" (1970), 102 Can. Med. Ass. J. 391. Reprinted from, by permission of the publisher, CMAJ, Vol. 102, 1970.

Honey, Kim, "Police failed rape victim, judge rules", *The Globe & Mail*, July 4, 1998. Reprinted with permission from *The Globe and Mail*.

Honoré, "Law, Morals and Rescue" in Ratcliffe, *The Good Samaritan and the Law* (Doubleday, 1966). By permission of Honoré and Doubleday.

Insurance Council of Canada, "Compulsory *Minimum* Insurance for Private Passenger Vehicles" in *Automobile Insurance Facts* (1999).

Ison, "Tort Liability and Social Insurance" (1969), 19 U. Toronto L.J. 614. By permission of University of Toronto Press.

Keeton and O'Connell, *Basic Protection for the Traffic Victim* (Boston: Little, Brown & Co., 1965 and 1969).

Klar, "Downsizing Tort" in *Torts Tomorrow: A Tribute to Professor John G. Fleming* (Sydney: The Law Book Company, 1998). Reproduced with the express permission of LBC Information Services.

Klar, "Defences to Trespass and Intentional Interferences" in *Tort Law* (2nd ed.) (Toronto: Carswell), pp. 113-114. Reprinted by permission of Carswell — a division of Thomson Canada Limited. Footnotes omitted.

Linden, "Empowering the Injured" in *Torts Tomorrow: A Tribute to Professor John G. Fleming* (Sydney: The Law Book Company, 1998). Reproduced with the express permission of LBC Information Services.

Linden, "Forseeability in Negligence Law" in Special Lectures of the Law Society of Upper Canada on New Developments in the Law of Torts (1973).

Linden, "Strict Liability, Nuisance and Legislative Authorization" (1966), 4 Osgoode Hall L.J. 196.

Linden, "Tort Law as Ombudsman" (1973), 51 Can. Bar Rev. 155.

Linden and Sommers, "The Civil Jury in the Courts of Ontario: A Postscript to the Osgoode Hall Study" (1968), 6 Osgoode Hall L.J. 252 at 254

Picard and Robertson, "The Future" in *Legal Liability of Doctors and Hospitals in Canada* (3rd ed.) (Toronto: Carswell), pp. 421-422. Reprinted by permission of Carswell — a division of Thomson Canada Limited. Footnotes omitted.

Posner, "The Economic Approach to Law" (1975), 53 Texas L. Rev. 757.

Prichard Commission, "Liability and Compensation in Health Care" (1990) (Prichard Commission for the Conference of Deputy Ministers of Health of the Federal, Provincial and Territorial Governments). © J. Robert S. Prichard.

Prosser, "The Nature of Conversion" (1957), 42 Cornell L. Rev. 168. By permission of Fred B. Rothman & Co.

Prosser and Keeton, *Handbook of the Law of Torts* (5th ed.) (West Publishing Co., 1984).

Salmond, *The Law of Torts* (21st ed.) (London: Sweet & Maxwell, 1996).

Schwartz, "Mixed Theories of Tort Law: Affirming Both Deterrence and Corrective Justice." Published originally in 75 *Texas Law Review* 1801 (1977). Copyright 1977 by the Texas Law Review Association. Reprinted by permission.

Smith, "The Mystery of Duty" in Klar (ed.), *Studies in Canadian Tort Law* (1977), p. 1; also in Smith, *Liability in Negligence* (1984).

Weinrib, "Two Conceptions of Tort Law" in Devlin, ed., *Canadian Perspectives on Legal Theory* (Toronto: Emond Montgomery, 1991).

Williams, "The Aims of the Law of Tort" (1951) Current Legal Problems 137. (London: Sweet & Maxwell, 1951).

TABLE OF CONTENTS

Preface iii
Acknowledegments v
Table of Cases xvii

Chapter 1: Introduction: The Nature and Function of Tort Law
Linden, *Canadian Tort Law* 1
Wright, *Introduction to Cases on the Law of Torts* 1
Salmond, *The Law of Torts* 2
Holmes, *The Common Law* 4
Prosser, *Handbook of the Law of Torts* 5
Fleming, *The Law of Torts* 9
Calabresi, "Fault, Accidents and the Wonderful World of Blum and Kalven" 11
Weinrib, "Two Conceptions of Tort Law" 12
Williams, "The Aims of the Law of Tort" 15
Linden, "Tort Law as Ombudsman" 22

Chapter 2: Trespass and Intentional Interferences with Persons, Property, and Chattels
A. The Historical Context 33
Klar, *Tort Law* 33
Goshen v. Larin 35
B. Accidental, Negligent, and Intentional Conduct 38
Klar, *Tort Law* 38
Garratt v. Dailey 39
Restatement of Torts, Second 39
Carnes v. Thompson 40
Basley v. Clarkson 41
C. Volition and Capacity 42
Smith v. Stone 42
Tillander v. Gosselin 43
Lawson v. Wellesley Hospital 45
D. Assault 48
I. De S. & Wife v. W. De S. 48
Stephens v. Myers 49
Tuberville v. Savage 49
Bruce v. Dyer 51
Restatement of Torts, Second 53
Criminal Code of Canada 53
E. Battery 53
Cole v. Turner 53
Restatement of Torts, Second 54

Bettel et al. v. Yim 55
F. Sexual Wrongdoing 59
G. Intentional Infliction of Mental Suffering 61
Wilkinson v. Downton 61
Restatement of Torts, Second 65
H. False Imprisonment 66
Bird v. Jones 66
Chaytor et al. v. London, New York and Paris Association of Fashion Ltd. and Price 68
I. Trespass to Land 73
Entick v. Carrington 73
Atlantic Aviation v. Nova Scotia Light & Power Co. Ltd. 80
J. Interference with Chattels 83
1. Trespass to Goods 83
Everitt v. Martin 83
2. Detinue 84
3. Conversion 85
Prosser, *The Nature of Conversion* 85
Hollins v. Fowler 85
Steiman v. Steiman 88
K. Invasion of Privacy 90
Roth v. Roth 90
Atrens, "Intentional Interference with the Person" 98

Chapter 3: Defences to Trespass and Intentional Interferences
A. Consent 101
1. The Nature of Consent 101
O'Brien v. Cunard S.S. Co. 101
Norberg v. Wynrib 103
2. Consent in the Sporting Context 112
3. Consent in the Medical Context 115
Malette v. Shulman 115
Marshall v. Curry 120
B. Self-Defence 127
Cockcroft v. Smith 127
C. Defence of Property 131
Green v. Goddard 131
Bird v. Holbrook 132
D. Necessity 134
Dwyer v. Staunton 134
Vincent v. Lake Erie Transportation Co. 136
Southwark London Borough Council v. Williams and Anderson 140
E. Legal Authority 141
Klar, *Tort Law* 141
Criminal Code of Canada 142
Reynen v. Antonenko et al. 150

Chapter 4: Introduction to Negligence: Damage and Causation
A. Damage 156
1. Limitation Periods 157
B. Causation 158

Kauffman v. T.T.C. 159
1. Multiple Causes 160

Chapter 5: The Standard of Care
A. Unreasonable Risk 163
Bolton & Others v. Stone 163
Priestman v. Colangelo and Smythson 168
B. The Reasonable Person 175
Vaughn v. Menlove 175
Blyth v. Birmingham Water Works Co. 177
C. Custom 181
Waldick v. Malcolm 181
D. Statutory Standards 184
R. in Right of Canada v. Saskatchewan Wheat Pool 184
1. Limitations on Statutory Use 198
Gorris v. Scott 198
2. Compliance with Statute 202
Ryan v. Victoria (City) 202
E. Mental and Physical Disabilities 207
Wenden v. Trikha 207
F. The Young 211
1. Liability of the Young 211
Heisler v. Moke 211
G. Professional Negligence 216
1. Doctors 216
Challand v. Bell 216
Reibl v. Hughes 223
2. Lawyers 240
Brenner v. Gregory 240

Chapter 6: Proof
A. The Onus of Proof of Negligence 247
Wakelin v. The London & S.W. Ry. Co. 247
B. Inferring Negligence 249
Byrne v. Boadle 250
Fontaine v. Insurance Corporation of British Columbia 251
C. Multiple Defendants 255
Leaman v. Rea 255
D. Statutory Onus Shift in Proving Negligence 260
Highway Traffic Act 260
E. Inferring Causation 262
Snell v. Farrell 262
F. Multiple Causes: Two Negligent Defendants But Only One Cause of Accident 267
Cook v. Lewis 267
G. Market Share Liability 270
Sindell v. Abbott Laboratories et al. 270
Negligence Act 274

Chapter 7: Duty
A. The Concept of Duty Generally 277
M'Alister (or Donoghue) v. Stevenson 277

Smith, "The Mystery of Duty" ... 285
B. The Unforseeable Plaintiff ... 290
Hay (or Bourhill) v. Young ... 290
C. Failure to Act ... 296
1. "Nonfeasance" and "Misfeasance" ... 297
The Holy Bible, Luke 10:30-10:37 ... 297
Horsley et al. v. Maclaren et al.: "The Ogopogo" ... 298
2. Relationships Requiring Rescue ... 301
Jordan House Ltd. v. Menow and Honsberger ... 301
Klar, *Tort Law* ... 307
Oke v. Weide Transport Ltd. and Carra ... 308
Zelenko v. Gimbel Bros. ... 310
The Emergency Medical Aid Act ... 312
O'Rourke v. Schacht ... 314

Chapter 8: Remoteness
A. The General Principle ... 321
The Wagon Mound (No. 1) Overseas Tankship (U.K.) Ltd. v. Morts Dock & Engineering Co. Ltd. ... 321
B. Retreat from The Wagon Mound (No. 1) ... 327
1. The Thin-Skull Problem ... 327
Smith v. Leech Brain & Co. ... 327
2. Type of Damage ... 331
Hughes v. Lord Advocate ... 331
3. Possibility of Damage ... 337
The Wagon Mound (No. 2) Overseas Tankship (U.K.) Ltd. v. The Miller S.S. Co. Pty. Ltd. ... 337
Palsgraf v. Long Island Railroad Co. ... 343
Linden, "Forseeability in Negligence Law" ... 349
C. Intervening Forces ... 351
Harris v. T.T.C. and Miller ... 351
D. Recurring Situations ... 355
1. Rescue ... 355
Horsley et al. v. Maclaren et al.: "The Ogopogo" ... 355
2. Second Accident ... 367
Weiland v. Cyril Lord Carpets Ltd. ... 367
McKew v. Holland et al. ... 369
E. Intermediate Inspection ... 373
Ives v. Clare Brothers Ltd. et al. ... 373
F. Warnings and the Learned Intermediary ... 378
Hollis v. Dow Corning Corp. ... 379

Chapter 9: Defences to the Negligence Action
A. Contributory Negligence ... 383
Butterfield v. Forrester ... 383
Davies v. Mann ... 384
Negligence Act ... 386
Linden and Sommers, "The Civil Jury in the Courts of Ontario: A Postscript to the Osgoode Hall Study" ... 395
B. The Seat Belt Defence ... 396
Glaske v. O'Donnell ... 396
C. Voluntary Assumption of Risk ... 406

Hambley v. Shepley 406
D. Illegality 410
Hall v. Hebert 410

Chapter 10: Economic Losses
A. Liability for Negligent Statements 415
Queen v. Cognos Inc. 417
Hercules Management v. Ernst & Young 421
1. Contract and Tort 432
BG Checo International Inc. v. B.C. Hydro & Power Authority 433
B. Negligent Performance of Services 438
B.D.C. Ltd. v. Hofstrand Farms Ltd. 439
C. Economic Losses Caused by Defective Products and Structures 442
Winnipeg Condominium Corp. No. 36 v. Bird Construction Co. 442
D. Relational Economic Losses 451
Bow Valley Husky (Bermuda) Ltd. et al. v. Saint John Shipbuilding Ltd. 454

Chapter 11: Tort Liability of Public Authorities
A. Proceedings Against the Crown 467
Proceedings Against the Crown Act 467
B. What is the Duty Owed? 469
Just v. British Columbia 469
C. Constitutional Torts 484
Jane Doe v. Board of Police Commissioners for the Municipality of Metropolitan Toronto 484

Chapter 12: Strict Liability
A. Origin and Scope 489
Rylands v. Fletcher 489
1. Non-natural User 494
Rickards v. Lothian 494
Linden, "Whatever Happened to *Rylands v. Fletcher*?" 499
2. Escape 501
Read v. J. Lyons & Co. Ltd. 501
B. Defences 507
Peters v. Prince of Wales Theatre (Birmingham) Ltd. 507
Hale v. Jennings Brothers 510
Northwestern Utilities Ltd. v. London Guarantee & Accident Co. Ltd. 511
Greenman v. Yuba Power Products Inc. 522

Chapter 13: Nuisance
McLaren, "Nuisance in Canada" 531
A. Public Nuisance 532
Hickley v. Electric Reduction Co. of Canada 532
Mint v. Good 539
B. Private Nuisance 543
Pugliese v. National Capital Commn. 543

Tock v. St. John's Metropolitan Area Bd. 545
Russell Transport Ltd. v. Ontario Malleable Iron Co. Ltd. 546
Nor-Video Services Ltd. v. Ontario Hydro 550
Appleby v. Erie Tobacco Co. 556
Tock v. St. John's Metropolitan Area Bd. 562
C. An Economic Analysis of Nuisance 570

Chapter 14: Occupiers' Liability
A. The Common Law 575
Linden, "Canadian Tort Law" 575
Linden, "Canadian Tort Law", continued 576
Linden, "Canadian Tort Law", continued 578
B. Statutory Reform 582
Waldick v. Malcolm 582

Chapter15: Business Torts
A. Deceit 589
Derry v. Peek 589
Young v. McMillan et al. 591
B. Inducing Breach of Contract 595
1. Direct Inducement 595
Lumley v. Gye 595
2. Indirect Inducement 597
D.C. Thomson & Co. v. Deakin et al. 597
3. Interferences Short of Breach 599
Torquay Hotel Co. Ltd. v. Cousins et al. 599
4. Justification 602
Brimelow v. Casson 602
5. Extension to Negligence 604
Nicholls v. Township of Richmond 604
C. Intimidation 606
Rookes v. Barnard 606
D. Conspiracy 611
Canada Cement LaFarge Ltd. v. British Columbia Lightweight Aggregate Ltd. 611
E. Interference with Advantageous Business Relations 615
Tuttle v. Buck 615

Chapter 16: Defamation
Klar, *Tort Law* 621
A. The Values at Stake 621
Hill v. Church of Scientology of Toronto 621
B. What is Defamatory? 625
Murphy v. LaMarsh et al. 625
C. Libel or Slander? 637
Herbert, *The Uncommon Law (1935)*: *Chicken v. Ham* 637
Meldrum v. Australian Broadcasting Co. Ltd. 637
D. Publication 642
McNichol v. Grandy 642
E. Basis of Liability 645
E. Hulton & Co. v. Jones 645
Cassidy v. Daily Mirror Newspapers Ltd. 648
Vizetelly v. Mudie's Select Library Ltd. 650

F. Defences 655
1. Truth 655
Fleming, *The Law of Torts* 655
2. Absolute Privilege 656
3. Qualified Privilege 659
Sun Life Assurance Co. of Canada v. Dalrymple 659
Bereman v. Power Publishing Co. 663
Watt v. Longsdon 666
The Globe & Mail Ltd. v. Boland 669
4. Fair Comment 672
McQuire v. Western Morning News Co. 673

Chapter 17: Damages
A. The Purpose of Damages 679
Charles, "Justice in Personal Injury Awards" 679
B. General Principles 682
1. The Heads of Damage 682
Charles, "Justice in Personal Injury Awards", continued 682
2. The Role of the Jury 684
3. Lump Sum or Periodic Payments? 685
Charles, "Justice in Personal Injury Awards", continued 685
C. The Assessment of General Damages for Personal Injuries 689
Andrews v. Grand & Toy Alberta Ltd. et al. 689
D. A Note on Collateral Sources 709
E. Post-Accident Events 711
Jobling v. Associated Dairies Ltd. 711
F. Fatal Accidents 716
Trustee Act 716
Family Law Act 716
Keizer v. Hanna et al. 718

Chapter 18: Alternatives to Tort Law: Automobile Accident Compensation and Beyond
A. Automobile Accident Compensation: The Debate Over No-Fault 728
Duff and Trebilcock, *Exploring the Domain of Accident Law* 728
Keeton and O'Connell, *Basic Protection for the Accident Victim* 728
Blum and Kalven, "Public Law Perspectives on a Private Law Problem – Auto Compensation Plans" 732
American Bar Association, *Automobile No-Fault Insurance, A Study by the Committee on Automobile Insurance Legislation* 736
B. Are the Victims of Auto Accidents Different? 740
Linden, "Peaceful Coexistence and Automobile Accident Compensation" 740
Ison, "Tort Liability and Social Insurance" 740
Blum and Kalven, "Public Law Perspectives on a Private Law Problem – Auto Compensation Plans" 741
Blum and Kalven, "Public Law Perspectives on a Private Law Problem – Auto Compensation Plans", continued 742

C. Who Should Pay the Costs of Auto Accidents? 744
Calabresi, "The Decision for Accidents: An Approach to Non-Fault Allocation of Costs" 744
Calabresi, *The Costs of Accidents* 746
Keeton and O'Connell, *Basic Protection for the Traffic Victim* 747
D. New Schemes: The Reduction or Elimination of Tort Rights 749
Table 1: Canadian Automobile Insurance Plans – Compulsory Minimum Insurance Coverage for Private Passenger Vehicles 754

Index 759

TABLE OF CASES

[A page number in boldface type indicates that a case has been excerpted in the text.]

384238 Ontario Ltd. v. R. in Right of Canada, 87
473759 Alberta Ltd. v. Heidelberg Canada Graphic Equipment Ltd., 594

A

A. (D.A.) v. B. (D.K.), 60
A. (C.) v. C. (J.W.), 520
A.-G. of Manitoba et al. v. Campbell, 561
A.U.P.E. v. The Edmonton Sun, 632
Abbott et al. v. Kasza, 341, 348, 350
Abel v. McDonald, 592
Abramzik v. Brenner, 296
Abromovic v. C.P. Ltd., 464
Acheson v. Dory, 517
Ackerman v. Wascana Centre Authority, 582
ACL Holdings Ltd. v. St. Joseph's Hospital of Estevan, 606
Adam v. Ward, 659, 661, 668
Admiralty Commrs. v. S.S. Amerika, 717
Agar v. Canning, 112
Alaffe v. Kennedy, 157
Albrecht v. Burkholder, 632
Alcock v. Chief Constable of South Yorkshire Police, 296
Alcorn v. Mitchell, 55
Aldridge v. Van Patter, Martin and Western Fair Assoc., 506
Alexander v. Jenkins, 641
Alexandroff v. R. in Right of Ontario, 683, 685
Allan v. Bushnell T.V. Co. Ltd., 653
Allan v. New Mount Sinai Hospital et al., 102, 119
Allcock Laight & Westwood v. Patten, 276
Allen v. Flood, 596
Allen v. Gulf Oil Refining Ltd., 569
Allen v. Hannaford, 50
Allison v. Rank City Wall Canada, 355
Amar Cloth House Ltd. v. La Van & Co., 331, 682
Amos v. Vawter, 97
Anderson v. Chasney, 223
Anderson v. Skender, 78
Anderson v. Somberg, 259
Anderson v. Stevens, 393
Andreae v. Selfridge & Co. Ltd., 558
Andrews v. Grand & Toy Alberta Ltd. et al., 681, 686, **689**, 703
Angus v. Sun Alliance Insce. Co., 3
Anns v. Merton London Borough Council, 282, 283, 437, 475, 476, 479
Appleby v. Erie Tobacco Co., 556
Archer v. Catton & Co. Ltd, 157
Arendale et al. v. Canada Bread Company Ltd., 526
Arland and Arland v. Taylor, 178, 179
Arm River Enterprises v. McIvor, 541
Armstrong v. Mac's Milk, 519
Arnault v. Prince Albert (City) Board of Police Commissioners, 173
Arndt v. Smith, 233, 295
Arneil v. Paterson, 161
Arnold v. Teno; J.B. Jackson v. Teno, 681, 703
Ashby v. White, 317
Ashland Dry Goods Co. v. Wages, 67
Atcheson v. College of Physicians & Surgeons (Alberta), 597, 604
Athans v. Canadian Adventure Camps, 93
Athey v. Leonati, 160, 162, 330, 716
Atlantic Aviation v. Nova Scotia Light & Power Co. Ltd., 80
Attorney-General for Canada v. Diamond Waterproofing Ltd., 504
Attorney-General for Ontario v. Crompton, 342
Aust. Safeway Stores v. Zaluzna, 581
Austin v. Gendis Inc., 581
Aynsley et al. v. Toronto General Hospital (*sub nom.* Toronto General Hospital v. Matthews), 520
Aziz v. Adamson, 318

B

B. (D.) v. C.A.S. of Durham Region, 487
B. (P.A.) v. Curry, 60, 519, 520
B. (D.C.) v. Arkin, 45
B.C. Ferry Corp. v. Invicta Security Services Corp., 519
B.D.C. Ltd. v. Hofstrand Farms Ltd., 439
B.G. Ranches v. Manitoba Agricultural Lands Protection Board, 195, 468
Baart v. Kumar and Kumar, 683
Babcock v. Carr; Babcock v. Archibald, 603
Bacon v. Ryan, 517
Bahher v. Marwest Hotel Co. Ltd. et al., 148
Baird v. R. in Right of Canada, 194
Baker v. Bolton, 717

Baker v. Hopkins, 364
Baker v. Market Harborough, 258
Baker v. Willoughby, 715
Balabanoff v. Fossani, 652
Baldinger v. Banks, 44
Bank of British Columbia v. Canadian Broadcasting Corp., 654, 670
Banks v. Campbel, 96
Banks v. The Globe and Mail Ltd., 670
Barisic v. Devenport, 394
Barltrop v. C.B.C., 678
Barnett v. Chelsea & Kensington Hospital Management Committee, 160, 310
Barnett v. Cohen, 157
Barratt v. The Corporation of the District of North Vancouver, 479
Barrett v. Enfield London Borough Council, 314
Barrett v. Lorette and Ross, 153
Barthropp v. Corp. of Dist. of West Vancouver, 95
Basely v. Clarkson, 41
Bassett Realty v. Lindstrom, 197
Battistoni v. Thomas, 519
Baumeister v. Drake, 306
Bd. of Governors of Seneca College of Applied Arts and Technology v. Bhadauria, 318
Beauchamp v. Ayotte et al, 200
Beaudesert Shire Council v. Smith, 619
Beaver v. Crowe, 405
Bechard v. Haliburton Estate, 296
Beecham v. Henderson, 270
Beim v. Goyer, 173
Bell Canada v. Bannermount Ltd, 38
Bell Canada v. Cope (Sarnia) Ltd., 38, 261, 388, 392
Bell Canada v. The Ship "Mar-Tirenno", 139
Bell-Ginsburg v. Ginsburg, 111
Benning v. Wong, 505, 514
Bereman v. Power Publishing Co., 663
Berkoff v. Burchill, 628
Berns v. Campbell, 162, 715
Berntt v. Vancouver (City), 130, 393, 413
Besse v. Thorn, 153
Bettel et al. v. Yim, 55
BG Checo International Ltd. v. B.C. Hydro & Power Authority, 433
Bhadauria v. Bd. of Governors of the Seneca College of Applied Arts and Technology, 317
Bielitski v. Obadiak, 63
Big Point Club v. Lozon, 79
Bigcharles v. Merkel et al., 131
Binda v. Waters Const. Co, 259
Bird v. Holbrook, 132, 299
Bird v. Jones, 66
Bittner v. Tait-Gibson Optometrists Ltd., 172
Black v. Canadian Copper Co. (*sub nom.* Taillifer v. Canadian Nickel Co.), 560
Black v. New York, New Haven & Hartford Ry. Co., 305
Blair and Sumner v. Deakin, 161
Blake v. Barnard, 50
Block v. Cole, 517
Blyth v. Birmingham Water Works Co., 177
Boarelli v. Flannigan, 710
Boehringer v. Montalto, 83
Boland v. The Globe and Mail Ltd., 670
Bolton & Others v. Stone, 163, 173, 340
Bonte v. Bonte, 293
Boomer v. Atlantic Cement Co., 560
Boomer v. Penn, 210
Booth v. B.C. Television Broadcasting Systems, 633
Booth v. Toronto General Hospital, 125
Boothman v. R, 65
Bordeaux v. Jobs, 668
Bordeleau v. Bonnyville, 631
Botiuk v. Toronto Free Press Publications Ltd., 645
Botting v. B.C., 165
Bottomley v. F. W. Woolworth & Co. Ltd., 652
Boudreau v. Benaiah, 244
Bourhill v. Young, 292, 295
Bourque v. Wells, 715
Bow Valley Husky (Bermuda) Ltd. et al v. Saint John Shipbuilding Ltd., 387, 463, **454**, 476, 529
Boyachyk v. Dukes, 657
Braddock v. Bevins, 666
Bradford v. Pickles. *See* Mayor, Aldermen and Burgesses of the Borough of Bradford v. Pickles
Bradford v. Kanellos, 353
Brady v. Bank of Nova Scotia, 73
Brady v. Schatzel, 50
Braun v. Armour & Co., 630
Breitkreutz v. Public Trustee, 97
Brenner v. Gregory, 240
Brewer Brothers v. Canada (A.G.), 474
Brewer v. Saunders, 517
Briggs v. Laviolette, 147
Brimelow v. Casson, 602
British Columbia (Attorney General) v. Couillard, 537
Bromage v. Prosser, 647
Broome v. Cussell & Co. Ltd., 96
Brown v. British Columbia (Minister of Transportation and Highways), 474
Brown v. Rolls Royce Ltd., 184
Brown v. Shyne, 202
Brown v. University of Alberta Hospital, 221, 308
Brown v. Waterloo Regional Bd. of Com'rs of Police, 96
Browne v. D.C. Thomson & Co., 632
Bruce v. Dyer, 51, 129
Bruce v. McIntyre, 195
Buch v. Amory Manufacturing Co., 299
Buchan v. Ortho Pharmaceutical (Canada) Ltd., 378, 382
Buckley and T.T.C. v. Smith Transport Ltd, 209
Buckner v. Ashby and Horner Ltd., 375
Bunyan v. Jordan, 41
Bureau v. Campbell, 666
Burgess v. M/V Tamano, 536
Burmah Oil Co. v. Lord Advocate, 136
Burnett v. R., 92

Burnie Port Authority v. General Jones Pty. Ltd., 515
Burnie v. Port Authority, 505
Burton v. Crowell Publishing Co., 630
Buthmann v. Balzer, 450
Butterfield v. Forrester, 383
Byrne v. Boadle, 249, **250**
Byrne v. Deane, 630, 644

C

C. (L.G.) v. C. (V.M.), 666
C. (P.) v. C. (R.), 60
C. (T.L.) v. Vancouver (City), 413
C. v. City of Vancouver, 173
C.N.R. Co. v. di Domenicantonia, 96
C.N.R. Co. v. Norsk Pacific Steamship Co. Ltd., 282, 451, 453, 454, 463
C.N.R. v. Bakty, 364
C.P.R. v. Frechette, 407
C.P.R. v. Lockhart, 519
C.R.F. Holdings Ltd. et al. v. Fundy Chemical Intl. Ltd. et al., 593, 594
Cabral v. Gupta, 267
Caldwell v. McBride, 630
Calgary (City) v. Yellow Submarine Deli Inc., 498
Cambridge Water Co. Ltd. v. Eastern Counties Leather plc., 497, 505, 556
Caminer v. Northern and London Investment Trust Ltd., 179
Campbell Estate v. Calgary Power Ltd., 394
Campbell et al. v. Bartlett (No. 2), 274
Campbell v. Read, 96
Campbell v. S.S. Kresge Co. Ltd, 70
Campbell-Fowler v. Royal Trust Co, 60
Canada Cement Lafarge Ltd. v. British Columbia Lightweight Aggregate Ltd., 611
Canada v. Lukasic, 73, 657
Canadian Laboratory Supplies Ltd. v. Engelhard Industries of Canada Ltd., 87
Canadian Shredded Wheat Co. Ltd. v. Kellogg Co. of Canada Ltd., 618
Canadian Tire Co. Ltd. v. Desmond, 618
Canadian Western Natural Gas Co. Ltd. v. Pathfinder Surveys Ltd., 394
Candler v. Crane, Christmas & Co., 415, 416
Caners v. Eli Lilly Canada Inc., 393
Canphoto Ltd. et al. v. Aetna Roofing (1965) Ltd. et al., 354
Canson Enterprises Ltd. v. Boughton & Co., 592
Cant v. Cant, 65
Capan v. Capan, 92
Car & General Insurance Corp. Ltd. v. Seymour & Maloney, 408
Carnes v. Thompson, 40
Carpenter v. MacDonald, 149
Carroll and Carroll v. Chicken Palace Ltd, 179
Cashin v. Mackenzie, 157
Cassidy v. Daily Mirror Newspapers, Ltd., 634, **648**
Cataford v. Moreau, 724
Central Canada Potash Co. Ltd. v. Attorney-General for Saskatchewan, 609
Central Eastern Trust Co. v. Rafuse, 157, 242, 432, 437
Century Insurance Co. v. Northern Ireland Road Transport Bd., 520
Challand v. Bell, 216, 219
Chamerland v. Fleming, 406
Chapman v. Hearse, 364
Chapman v. Lord Ellesmere et al., 665
Charing Cross Electricity Supply Co. v. Hydraulic Power Co., 506
Charles R. Bell Ltd. v. City of St. John's, 513
Chartier v. Attorney-General of Quebec, 483
Chatterton v. Secretary of State for India, 658
Chaytor et al. v. London, New York and Paris Association of Fashion Ltd. and Price, 68
Check v. Andrews Hotel Co. Ltd. et al., 129, 130
Cherneskey v. Armadale Publishers Ltd., 635, 675
Cherry (Guardian) v. Borsman, 294, 295, 724
Chessie v. J.D. Irving Ltd., 542
Cheticamp Fisheries Co-op. v. Canada, 619
Child and Family Services of Central Manitoba v. Lavallee, 120
Chrispen v. Kalinowski, 488
Chrispen v. Novack, 668
Christie and Another v. Leachinsky, 145
Christie v. Geiger, 635
Church & Dwight Ltd. v. Sifto Canada Inc., 636
Ciarlariello v. Schacter, 233
City of Kamloops v. Nielsen, 450, 476
City of Prince George v. B.C. Television, 635
City of Vancouver v. Burchill, 201
Clark v. C.N.R., 195
Clark v. Canada, 65
Clarke v. Dickson, 592
Clarke v. Norton, 672
Cleary v. Hansen, 366
Clendenning and Bd. of Police Commrs of City of Belleville, Re, 244
Clyke v. Blenkhorn, 394
Coates v. The Citizen, 635, 654
Cockcroft v. Smith, 127
Coderre v. Ethier; Gachot v. Ethier, 175
Cohen v. S. McCord, 275
Colby v. Schmidt, 114
Cole v. Turner, 53
Collins v. General Service Transport, 201
Collins v. Wilcock, 54
Colonial Coach Lines Ltd. v. Bennett and C.P.R. Co., 316, 394
Comeau's Sea Foods Ltd. v. Canada (Minister of Fisheries and Oceans), 483
Committee for the Commonwealth of Canada v. Canada, 77
Comstock v. General Motors Corp, 377
Cone v. Welock, 179
Connell v. Prescott, 364

Consumers' Gas Co. v. Fenn. *See* Fenn v. Corporation of the City of Peterborough; Peterborough Utilities Commission et al. (Third Parties)
Consumers Glass Co. v. Foundation Co. of Canada, 156
Conyd v. Brekelmans, 641
Cook v. Lewis, 38, **267**, 270
Cooke v. Wildes, 668
Cooper v. Crabtree, 74
Cooper v. Hoeglund, 200
Co-operators Insurance Association v. Kearney, 519
Corey v. Havener, 161
Cormier et al. v. Blanchard, 537
Corothers et al. v. Slobodian et al., 366
Corp. of District of Surrey v. Carroll-Hatch and Associates Ltd, 276
Corrigan v. Bobbs-Merrill Co., 647
Costello v. Blakeson, 373
Costello v. Calgary (City), 41
Cosyns v. Smith, 276
Coughlin v. Kuntz, 96
County of Parkland v. Stetar, 274, 275
Covell v. Laming, 34
Cowan v. Duke of Buccleuch, 161
Cowan v. Harrington, 540
Coward v. Baddeley, 54
Cowper v. Studer, 198
Cox v. Glue, 82
Crane v. Worwood, 684
Cresswell v. Sirl, 134
Cristovao v. Doran's Beverages Inc., 275
Crocker and Sundance Northwest Resorts Ltd., 306, 307, 407, 413, 707
Cromwell v. Dave Buck Ford Lease Ltd., 718
Crosby v. O'Reilly, 709
Crossley v. Rawlinson, 351
Crossman v. R., 487
Crossman v. Stewart, 221
Crowe v. Noon, 147
Crown Diamond Paint Co. Ltd. v. Acadia Holding Realty Ltd., 507
Crozman v. Ruesch, 594
Cruise v. Niessen, 498
Cryderman v. Ringrose, 295, 724
Cunningham v. Moore, 197
Cunningham v. Wheeler, 710, 711
Curll v. Robin Hood Multifoods, 196
Curtis Publishing v. Butts, 671
Curtis v. Curtis, 641
Cussell & Co. Ltd. v. Broome, 96

D

D. (A Minor), Re, 127
"D" and the Council of the College of Physicians and Surgeons of B.C., Re, 125
D & F Estates Ltd. v. Church Comm'rs. for England, 450
D.C. Thomson & Co. Ltd. v. Deakin et al., 597
D.P.P. v. Beard, 42
Dabous v. Zuliani, 276
Dahlberg v. Naydiuk, 34, 37, 38, 261
Daishowa Inc. v. Friends of the Lubicon, 618
Dale v. Munthali, 221
Dallison v. Caffery, 147
D'Amato v. Badger, 453, 463
Danku v. Fort Frances (Town), 497, 499
Dart v. Pure Oil Co., 392
Davey et al. v. McManus Petroleum Ltd. (*sub nom.* Donnelly v. McManus Petroleum Ltd.), 685
Davey v. Greenlaw, 200
Davidson v. Connaught Laboratories, 160
Davies and Davies Ltd. v. Kott, 662
Davies v. Mann, 384
Davies v. Swan Motor Co. (Swansea) Ltd., 386
de la Giroday v. Brough, 267
De Meza and Stuart v. Apple, Van Straten, Shena and Stone, 275
Dellwo v. Pearson, 214
Delta Hotels Ltd. v. Magrum, 95
Demarco v. Ungaro et al, 242
Demeter v. Occidental Insurance Co. of California, 58
Dendekker v. F. W. Woolworth Co, 73, 147
Dennison et al. v. Sanderson et al., 630
Dept. of the Environment v. Thomas Bates & Son (New Towns Commn.), 450
Depue v. Flatau, 133
Derry v. Peek, 589, 591
Deshane v. Deere & Co., 378
Devoe v. Long, 134
Devon Lumber Co. Ltd. v. MacNeill, 555, 556
Deyo v. Kingston Speedway Ltd., 505
Dickhoff v. Armadale Communications Ltd., 644
Didow v. Alberta Power Ltd, 78, 79
Dillon v. Twin State Gas & Electric Co., 715
Dingwall v. Lax, 658
Diversified Holdings Ltd. v. R. in Right of British Columbia, 518
Dixon v. Deacon Morgan, 595
Dobson (Litigation Guardian of) v. Dobson, 293
Dodge v. Bridger, 152
Doern v. Phillips Estate, 174
Doiron v. Orr, 295, 724
Dokuchia v. Domansch, 506
Dolby v. McWhirter, 409
Dominey v. Sangster and Sangster, 682
Dominion Chain v. Eastern Constr. (*sub nom.* Giffels Associates Ltd. v. Eastern Const. Co.), 275
Dominion Securities Ltd. v. Glazerman, 89
Dominion Tape of Canada v. L.R. McDonald & Sons Ltd., 451
Donoghue v. Stevenson, 279, 280, 281, 282, 283, 415, 416, 437, 441, 450, 451
Doughty v. Turner Manufacturing Co. Ltd., 333
Douglas v. Tucker, 661
Draper v. Hotter, 517
Dredger Liesbosch v. S.S. Edison (Owners), 331
Drewry v. Towns, 183
Duce v. Rourke, 371
Ducharme v. Davies, 216, 307
Dudek v. Brown, 515, 516

Duemler v. Air Canada, 181
Duke of Brunswick v. Harmer, 644
Duncan Estate v. Baddeley, 718
Dunn v. Dominion Atlantic Ry. Co., 306
Dunne et al. v. North Western Gas Board et al., 514
Dupuis v. New Regina Trading Post, 364
Duquette v. Belanger, 657
Dutton v. Bognor Regis U.D.C., 375
Duval v. Séguin (*sub nom.* Duval v. Blais), 292, 293
Duwyn v. Kaprielian, 295, 330, 350
Dwyer v. Staunton, 134, 139
Dyck v. Manitoba Snowmobile Assn., 407
Dye v. McGregor, 197
Dziver et al. v. Smith, 684
Dziwenka v. The Queen in Right of Alberta, 179

E

E. Hulton & Co. v. Jones, 645
Eastwick v. New Brunswick, 578
Eccles v. Bourque et al., 152
Economopoulos v. A.G. Pollard Co., 644
Ed Miller Sales & Rentals Ltd. v. Caterpillar Tractor Co., 596
Edgeworth Const. Ltd. v. N.D. Lea & Associates Ltd., 437, 521
Edwards v. Smith, 179
Edwin Hill & Partners v. First National Finance Corp. Plc., 603
Egginton v. Reader, 519
Eisener v. Maxwell, 34
Ekstrom v. Deagon and Montgomery, 507
Elcano Acceptance Ltd. v. Richmond, Richmond, Stambler & Mills, 242
Elliot v. Amphitheatre Ltd., 409
Elliott v. Canadian Broadcasting Corp., 633
Ellis v. Johnstone, 517
Ellis v. Loftus Iron, 79
Ellison v. Rogers, 34, 37
Emeny v. Butters, 682
Engel v. Kam-Ppelle, 682
Entick v. Carrington, 73
Epstein v. Cressey Development Corp, 74
Escola v. Coca Cola Bottling Co. of Fresno, 523
Esso Petroleum v. Southport Corp., 536
Evans v. Bradburn, 129
Evans v. Canada, 195
Eve v. Mrs. E, 127
Everett v. Paschall, 558
Everitt v. Martin, 83
Eyers v. Gillis & Warren Ltd, 179
Eyre v. Garlick, 640

F

F., Re, 127
Fagan v. Atlantic Coast Line Ry. Co., 306
Falkenham v. Zwicker, 336
Farrington v. Thompson, 483
Farrugia v. Great Western Ry, 292
Fasken v. Time/System International APS, 73
Federic v. Perpetual Investments Ltd. et al., 509
Feener v. McKenzie, 202
Feng v. Graham, 684
Fenn v. Corporation of the City of Peterborough; Peterborough Utilities Commission et al. (Third Parties) (*sub nom.* Consumers' Gas Co. v. Fenn), 513
Fennellow v. Falez, 405
Fenwick v. Staples, 97
Ferguson v. McBee Technographics Inc., 636
Field v. Supertest Petroleum Corp., 201
Fillipowich v. Nahachewsky, 129
Fink v. Greeniaus, 409
Firemen's Fund v. Knobbe, 260
Fisher v. Carrousel Motor Hotel, 54
Fitzgerald v. Lane, 394
Flaman Wholesale Ltd. v. Firman et al., 636
Flame Bar-B-Q Ltd. v. Hoar, 95, 97
Fleischmann v. Grossman Holdings, 197
Fleming v. Atkinson, 518
Fletcher v. Collins, 147
Fletcher v. Manitoba Public Insurance Co., Re, 421, 441
Fletcher-Gordon v. Southam Inc., 671
Fobel v. Dean, 708
Foltz v. Moore-McCormack Lines Inc., 671
Fontaine v. Insurance Corporation of British Columbia, 249, **251**, 255, 258
Ford Motor Co. v. Wagoner, 377
Foth v. O'Hara, 73
Fouldes v. Willoughby, 87
Fowler v. Lanning, 37, 38
Frame v. Smith, 64, 65, 195, 614
France v. Parkinson, 258
Franks v. Sanderson, 515, 516
Fraser v. Sykes, 629, 632
Fraser v. U-Need A-Cab Ltd., 195
Freeman v. Sutter, 222
French (Elizabeth) v. Smith, 641
French (Oscar) v. Smith, 630, 641
Fulton v. The Globe and Mail, 672
Fuson v. Fuson, 671

G

G. (R). v. Christison, 614, 658
Gachot v. Ethier. *See* Coderre v. Ethier
Gagnon v. Beaulieu, 404
Galaske v. O'Donnell, 216, **396**, 406
Gallant et al. v. Boklaschuk et al., 718
Gallant v. Beitz; Nissan Automobile Co. (Canada) Ltd., 341, 350
Galts v. Ultra Care Inc., 587
Gambino v. DiLeo, 216
Gambriell v. Caparelli, 130
Gardiner v. John Fairfax & Sons Pty. Ltd., 629
Garratt v. Dailey, 39
Garry v. Sherritt Gordon Mines Ltd., 601
Gaul v. King, 197
Gazette Printing Company v. Shallow, 657
Geddis v. Proprietors of Bann Reservoir, 513, 514
Genik v. Ewanylo, 404
Genner v. Sparkes, 70
Gerigs v. Rose, 47
Gerrard v. Crowe, 139

Gershman v. Manitoba Vegetable Producers' Marketing, 610, 619
Gertsen v. Municipality of Metropolitan Toronto et al., 498
Gertz v. Robert Welch Inc., 653, 671
Gerula v. Flores, 42
Getty v. Calgary Herald, 636
Gilbert v. Stone, 42
Gill v. C.P.R. (*sub nom.* Canadian Pacific Ltd. v. Gill), 710
Gillen v. Noel, 393
Gillick v. West Norfolk & Wisbech Area Health Authority, 125
Gilson v. Kerrier R.D.C., 509
Gives v. C.N.R., 386
Glass v. Avenue Dodge Chrysler, 275
Globe and Mail Ltd. v. Boland. *See* The Globe and Mail Ltd. v. Boland
Godfrey v. Cooper, 201
Goldman v. Hargrave, 515
Golnik v. Geissinger, 129
Good v. North Delta-Surrey Sentinel, 653
Good-Wear Treaders Ltd. v. D. & B. Holdings Ltd., 376
Gordon v. Wallace, 210
Gorris v. Scott, 198, 200, 317
Goshen v. Larin, 34, **35**
Gosselin v. Moose Jaw (City), 474
Gould Estate v. Stoddart Publishing Co., 93
Gouzenko v. Harris et al., 629
Graham v. R., 392
Grand Restaurants of Canada Ltd. v. City of Toronto, 420
Grand Trunk Pacific Railway v. Earl, 386
Grant v. Reader's Digest Assoc. Inc., 629
Gray v. Alanco Developments Ltd., 684
Green v. Goddard, 131
Green v. Minnes, 92
Greenman v. Yuba Power Products Inc., 522, 523
Griggs v. Southside Hotel Ltd. & Berman, 519
Grossman v. R., 311
Grosvenor Park Shopping Centre Ltd. v. Waloshin, 78
Groves-Raffin Const. Ltd. v. Bank of Nova Scotia (*sub nom.* Groves-Raffin Const. Ltd. v. Can. Imperial Bank of Commerce), 275
Guilford Industries Ltd. v. Hankinson Management Services Ltd., 618
Guise v. Kouvelis, 665
Gunn v. Barr, 603
Gutsole v. Mathers, 640

H

H. (R.) v. Hunter, 724
H. R. Moch Co. v. Rensselaer Water Co., 311, 312
H. West & Son Ltd. v. Shephard, 706
H.B. Nickerson v. Wooldrige & Sons Ltd, 421
Hackshaw v. Shaw, 577, 581
Hagen v. Goldfarb, 541
Hagerman v. City of Niagara Falls, 409
Haig v. Bamford, 440, 591
Haines v. Bellisimo, 221
Hale v. Jennings Brothers, 510
Hale v. Westfair Foods Ltd., 581
Haley v. London Electricity Bd., 179
Haley v. Richardson (*sub nom.* McRae v. Richardson), 405
Hall v. Hebert, 19, 310, **410**, 413
Hallick v. Doroschuk, 515
Halls v. Mitchell, 641, 656
Halushka v. University of Sask., 233
Hambley v. Shepley, 102, **406**
Hankins v. Papillon, 233
Hannigan v. City of Edmonton, 275
Hardcastle v. South Yorkshire Ry., 540
Harland v. Fancsali, 595
Harris v. Law Society of Alberta, 483
Harris v. T.T.C. and Miller, 216, **351**, 353
Harris v. Wong, 133
Harrison v. British Railways Bd., 364
Harrison v. Carswell, 76, 78
Harrold v. Watney, 540
Hartlen v. Chaddock, 114
Hartmann v. Time, Inc., 645
Haswell v. Enman, 258
Hatch v. Ford Motor Co., 200
Hatfield v. Pearson, 353
Hatton v. Webb, 34
Hawryluk v. Otruba, 44
Hay (or Bourhill) v. Young, 290
Hayden v. Hasbrouck, 665
Haynes v. Harwood, 364
Hayward v. F. W. Woolworth Co. Ltd., 147
Hebditch v. MacIlwaine, 672
Hedgepeth v. Coleman, 644
Hedley Byrne & Co. Ltd. v. Heller & Partners Ltd., 282, 415, 416, 420, 432, 437, 440, 441, 451, 591
Heimler v. Calvert Caterers Ltd., 196, 526
Heisler v. Moke, 211, 214
Hellenius v. Lees, 255
Hemmings & Wife v. Stoke Pages Golf Club Ltd, 134
Hempler v. Todd, 309
Hendricks v. R., 311
Henningsen v. Bloomfield Motors Inc. et al., 524
Herbert v. Misuga, 53
Hercules Managements Ltd. v. Ernst & Young, 420, **421**, 432, 463, 476
Herd v. Weardale Steel Coal & Coke Co. Ltd., 72
Herman v. Graves, 52
Herring v. Boyle, 72
Herrington, 578
Hewson v. City of Red Deer, 201, 353
Hickerson v. Masters, 641
Hickey v. Electric Reduction Co. of Canada, 532
Hicks v. Cooper; Hicks v. Can. Petrofina Ltd., 715
Hill v. British Columbia, 68, 488
Hill v. Chief Constable of West Yorkshire, 314, 316

Hill v. Church of Scientology of Toronto, 94, **621**, 636, 654
Hills v. O'Bryan, 644
Hoar v. Wallace, 519
Hodgins v. Banting, 237
Hoffer v. School District of Assiniboine South, 340
Hoffman v. Jones, 387
Hogan et al v. McEwan et al; Royal Ins. Co. et al., (Third Parties), 174
Holcombe v. Whittaker, 50
Holinaty v. Hawkins, 509
Hollebone v. Barnard, 392, 393
Hollins v. Fowler, 85, 87
Hollinsworth v. BCTV, 94
Hollis v. Dow Corning Corp., 378, **379**, 382, 529
Hollywood Silver Fox Farm Ltd. v. Emmett, 561
Holt v. Sun Publishing Co., 635, 678
Holt v. Verbruggen, 130
Home Office v. Dorset Yacht Co. Ltd, 281, 282
Hopwood v. Muirson, 641
Horsley et al. v. Maclaren et al.: "The Ogopogo", 298, 355
Horsley v. MacLaren (*sub nom.* Matthews v. MacLaren), 160, 312, 364
Hoston v. East Berkshire Health Area Authority, 266
Houle v. City of Calgary; Houle (Thivierge) et al. (Third Parties), 707
Houseman v. Coulson (*sub nom.* X. v. Y.), 641, 644
Howe v. Lees, 668
Howe v. Niagara St. Catharines and Toronto Ry. Co., 306
Howes v. Crosby, 684
Hubbard v. Pitt, 618
Hudson v. Riverdale Colony, 516
Hudson's Bay Co. v. White, 20
Hughes v. Lord Advocate, 331, 334, 336
Humphries v. Connor, 152
Hunter v. Canary Wharf Ltd., 554, 555
Hunter v. Southam Inc., 94
Hurley v. Moore, 130
Husky Oil. *See* Bow Valley Husky (Bermuda) Ltd. et al. v. Saint John Shipbuilding Ltd.
Hutchings v. Nevin, 209
Hutterly v. Imperial Oil, 364
Hyett v. Great Western Ry., 364

I

I. De S. & Wife v. W. De S., 48
I.C.B.C. v. City of Vancouver, 174
Inglis Ltd. v. South Shore Sales & Service Ltd., 275, 376
Ippolito v. Janiuk et al., 682
Isaacs (M.) & Sons Ltd. v. Cook, 658
Ives v. Clare Brothers Ltd. et al., 373, 527

J

J. (A.) v. Cairnie Estate, 158
J.B. Jackson v. Teno. *See* Arnold v. Teno
J.R. Paine & Associates Ltd. v. Strong, Lamb & Nelson Ltd., 275
J.S.C. and C.H.C. v. Wren, 125
J.T. Stratford & Son Ltd. v. Lindley, 608, 619
Jackson v. Drury Construction Co., 507, 559
Jackson v. Magrath, 658
Jackson v. Staley, 644
Jackson v. Trimac Industries Ltd., 604
James St. Hardware v. Spizziri, 194
Jane Doe v. Board of Police Commissioners for the Municipality of Metropolitan Toronto, 316, 319, 355, **484**, 487
Janvier v. Sweeney, 63
Jennings v. C.N.R., 519
Jinks v. Cardwell, 64, 296
Jobling v. Associated Dairies Ltd., 711, 715
John Bosworth Ltd. v. Professional Syndicated Developments Ltd., 420
John Lewis & Co. Ltd. v. Tims, 147
Johnson et al. v. B.C. Hydro and Power Authority, 79
Johnson v. Lambotte, 210
Johnson v. Royal Can. Legion Grandview Branch No. 174, 114
Johnson v. Sorochuk, 201
Johnston v. A.G. of Canada, 194
Johnston v. Wellesley Hospital, 124
Jones v. Bennett, 670, 671, 672
Jones v. Brooks, 658
Jones v. Manchester Corp., 221
Jones v. Skelton, 673
Jordan House Ltd. v. Menow and Honsberger, 301, 306, 307, 413
Joseph Brant Memorial Hospital v. Koziol. *See* Kolesar v. Jeffries
Joyal v. Starreveld, 222
Junior Books Ltd. v. The Veitchi Co. Ltd., 448, 450
Just v. British Columbia, 469, 472, 473, 474, 475, 476, 480
Justus v. Wood, 201

K

K. (W.) v. Pornbacher, 60, 97, 520
Kahn v. Gt. Northwestern Telegraph Co., 653
Kamloops (City) v. Nielsen, 157, 282, 451, 472, 479, 480
Karderas v. Clow, 183
Karras v. Richter, 517
Kask v. Tam, 710
Katapodis v. Brooklyn Spectator, 630
Kathleen K. v. Robert B., 55, 111
Katko v. Briney, 132
Kauffman v. T.T.C., 159, 183
Kealey v. Berezowski, 295, 724
Keating v. Elvan Reinforced Concrete Co. Ltd. et al., 200
Keeble v. Hickeringill, 617, 619
Keep v. Quailman, 129
Keizer v. Hanna et al., 681, **718**, 722
Kelley v. R.G. Industries, 377
Kelliher (Village) v. Smith, 407

Kelly v. Gwinnell, 306
Kelly v. Hazlett, 102, 127
Kelly v. Henry Muhs Co., 200
Kelly v. Hoffman, 652
Kelsen v. Imperial Tobacco, 78
Kemsley v. Foot, 672
Kenmuir v. Huetzelmann, 97
Kennaway v. Thompson, 560
Kennedy v. Hughes Drug (1969) Inc., 335
Kent, 312
Keough v. Royal Canadian Legion, Henderson Highway Branch, 388
Kerr v. Davison, 672
Kerr v. Kennedy, 641
Kilgannon v. Sharpe Bros., 260
Kilgollan v. William Cooke & Co. Ltd., 200
Kines Estate v. Lychuk Estate, 222
King v. Redlich, 409
King v. Stolberg et al., 183
Kingu et al. v. Walmar Ventures Ltd, 420
Kinsella v. St. John Commercial Developers Ltd., 582
Kirk v. Trerise, 517
Knupffer v. London Express Newspaper, 633
Knutson v. Farr, 706
Koechlin v. Waugh, 143
Koerber v. Kitchener-Waterloo Hospital, 238
Kohler v. City of Calgary, 576
Kolesar v. Jeffries (*sub nom.* Joseph Brant Memorial Hospital et al. v. Koziol et al.), 269, 372
Korach v. Moore, 663
Kovacs v. Ontario Jockey Club, 70
Kroeker v. Jansen, 684
Krouse v. Chrysler Canada Ltd., 92, 93
Kubach v. Hollands, 375

L

Lacarte v. Board of Education of Toronto, 668
Lachambre v. Nair, 521
Lacroix v. The Queen, 82
Laferiere v. Lawson, 265
Lagasse et al. v. Rural Municipality of Ritchot et al., 407
Lajoie v. Kelly, 60
Lake v. Callison Outfitters Ltd., 519
Lamb v. Camden London Borough Council, 351
Lambert v. Lastoplex Chemicals Co. Ltd., 378, 382
Lambton v. Mellish, 161
Lan v. Wu, 707
Landry v. Patterson, 130
Lane v. Holloway, 130
Lange v. Bennett, 270
Lapointe v. Hopital Le Gardeur, 220
Lapointe v. Le Roi, 483
Laporte v. The Queen, 151
Laurentide Motels Ltd. v. Beauport (City), 479
Lauritzen v. Barstead, 334
Laviolette v. C.N.R., 577
Lavoie v. Lavoie, 576
Law Estate v. Simice, 175
Law v. Visser, 292
Lawrence v. Finch, 639
Lawrysyn v. Town of Kipling, 514
Laws v. Florinplace Ltd., 558
Lawson v. Wellesley Hospital, 45, 47, 210
Le Lievre v. Gould, 277
Leadbetter v. Brand, 237
Leaman v. Rea, 255, 258, 269
Lebrun v. High-Low Foods, Ltd., 143
Ledingham v. Di Natale, 710
Lee v. Wilson and MacKinnon, 647
Leenstra v. Miller, 708
Lehnert v. Stein, 408
Leischner v. West Kootenay Power, 394
Leonard v. Knott et al., 341
Lepp v. Hopp, 120
Leroux v. City of Lachine, 483
Letang v. Cooper, 37, 38
Letnik v. Metro Toronto, 262
Leverman v. Campbell Sharp Ltd., 672
Levi v. Charters of Canada Inc., 604
Levitz v. Ryan, 152
Lew v. Mount Saint Joseph Hospital Society, 296
Lewis (Guardian ad Litem of) v. B.C., 472, 521
Lewis v. Oeming, 516
Lewis v. Todd et al.; Canadian Provincial Insurance Co. (Third Party), 704
Lewis v. Town of St. Stephen, 556
Lewvest Ltd. v. Scotia Towers Ltd, 83
Lim Poh Choo v. Camden and Islington Area Health Authority, 686
Lim v. Titov, 83
Lindal v. Lindal, 704
Lindstrom v. Bassett Realty, 197
Lipiec v. Borsa, 92
Lister v. Romford Ice & Cold Storage Co. Ltd., 519
Littleton v. Hamilton, 672
Lloyd v. Grace, Smith & Co., 519
Loedel v. Eckert, 58, 97
London Assoc. for Protection of Trade v. Greenlands Ltd., 668
London Drugs Ltd. v. Kuehne & Nagel (Int.) Ltd., 283, 437, 438, 521, 522
Long v. Gardner et al, 130
Long v. Toronto Railway Company; B.C. Electric Ry. Co. Ltd. v. Loach, 386
Lonhro plc v. Fayed, 614
Lonrho Ltd. v. Shell Petroleum Co. Ltd. (No. 2), 613, 619
Loomis v. Rohan, 97
Loos v. Robbins, 671
Lougheed v. C.B.C., 635
Loveday v. Sun Newspaper, 661
Lucas v. Juneau, 370
Lumley v. Gye, 595, 596
Lumley v. Wagner, 596
Lusignan v. Concordia Hospital, 681
Lynch v. Lynch, 293
Lyon v. Village of Shelburne; Triton Engineering Services Ltd. et al. (Third Parties), 499
Lyth v. Dagg, 110

M

M. (F.W.) v. Mombourquette, 520
M. (K.) v. M. (H.), 60, 158
M. (M.) v. F. (R.), 60
M. (M.) v. K. (K.), 110
Ma Wai Kay et al. v. McGay Ltd., 276
MacDonald v. Alderson et al., 705
MacDonald v. Desourdy Construction Ltée, 270
MacDonald v. Hees, 128, 131
MacDonald v. Woodard, 260
MacDonald v. York County Hospital, 221
Macintosh v. Dun, 668
MacIssac and Beretanos, Re, 197
Mack v. Enns, 413
MacKenzie v. McArthur, 657
MacLeod v. Rowe, 183
Mahon v. Osborne, 255
Maitland v. Drozda, 708
Maitland v. Raisbeck and Hewitt, 541
Malat et al. v. Bjornson, 341
Malcolm v. Broadhurst, 329
Malette v. Shulman, 115, 119, 123
M'Alister (or Donoghue) v. Stevenson, 277
Manchester Corp. v. Farnworth, 514
Mandrake Management Consultants Ltd. v. T.T.C., 569
Manitoba (Attorney General) v. Adventure Flight Centres Ltd., 537
Mann v. Balaban, 129
Manor & Co. Ltd. v. M. V. "Sir John Crosbie", 139
Marconato et al. v. Franklin, 330
Marentille v. Oliver, 84
Maron et al. v. Baert & Siguaw Devs. Ltd., 516
Marshall v. Curry, 120, 123, 124, 295
Marshall v. Lionel v. Lionel Enterprises Inc., 295
Martin v. Berends, 72
Martin v. Houck, 70
Martin v. Perrie, 158
Mason v. Forgie, 233
Mason v. Sears and Cruikshank, 130
Masters v. Fox, 673
Matheson v. Governors of Dalhousie University and College, 113
Matthews v. McLaren. *See* Horsley v. McLaren
Mauney v. Gulf Refining Co., 354
Mawe v. Pigott, 630
Mayfair Ltd. v. Pears, 58
Maynes v. Galicz, 196, 516
Mayor, Aldermen and Burgesses of the Borough of Bradford v. Pickles, 560
Mazatti v. Acme Products Ltd., 631
Mazurkewich v. Ritchot, 114
McC v. Mullan, 244
McCabe v. Westlock Roman Catholic Separate School District No. 110, 708
McClelland v. Symons, 129
McCormick v. Marcotte, 221
McEllistrum v. Etches, 214, 215
McErlean v. Sarel, 213, 215, 578
McGee v. National Coal Board, 262, 265
McGillivray v. Kimber, 483
McGrath v. Pendergras, 685
McHale v. Watson, 214
McIntire v. McBean, 672
McKeachie v. Alvarez, 221
McKenzie et al. v. Hyde et al., 340, 341
McKenzie v. Robar, 201
McKew v. Holland et al., 369, 370
McKie v. The K.V.P. Co. Ltd., 560
McKinnon v. F.W. Woolworth Co. Ltd. et al., 614
McLaren v. B.C. Institute of Technology, 606
McLaren v. Schwalbe, 708
McLean v. Weir, 222
McLeod v. Palardy, 707
McLoughlin v. Kutasy, 662
McNeill v. Hill, 128
Mcnichol v. Grandy, 642
Mcquire v. Western Morning News Co., 673
McRae v. Richardson. *See* Haley v. Richardson
Mee v. Gardiner, 79
Meering v. Grahame-White Aviation Co, 71
Meldrum v. Australian Broadcasting Co., Ltd., 637
Memphis School District v. Stachura, 488
Menear v. Miguna, 644, 652
Mercer v. Commrs. for Road Transport & Tramways, 183
Mercer v. Gray, 371, 372
Mercer v. S.E. & C. Ry. Co., 310
Mersey Docks Harbour Bd. v. Coggins, 520
Metropolitan Railway Co. v. Jackson, 249
Metson v. R. W. De Wolfe Ltd., 511
Meyerson v. Hurlburt, 630
Michael v. Pennsylvania, 210
Mihalchuk v. Ratke, 498
Miles v. Judges, 221
Milgaard v. Saskatchewan (Minister of Justice), 671
Miller and another v. Jackson and another, 166
Miller v. Decker, 408
Miller v. Guardian Insurance Co. of Canada, 441
Miller v. Jackson, 559, 560
Millette v. Coté et al. (*sub nom.* R. v. Coté; Millette v. Kalogeropoulos), 316
Mills v. Moberg, 181
Mint v. Good, 539, 542
Minter v. Priest, 656
Mintuck v. Valley River Band No. 63A, 601, 610, 619
Miska v. Sivec, 129
M-Jay Farms Enterprises Ltd. v. Canadian Wheat Board, 474
M'Naghten, 46, 209
Mochinski v. Trendline Industries Ltd., 472, 521
Moddejonge et al. v. Huron County (Bd. of Education) et al., 364
Moffat v. Witelson, 221
Moises v. Canadian Newspaper Co., 654
Molson v. Squamish Transfer Ltd., 175
Monson v. Tussauds, Ltd., 640
Moody v. Toronto (City), 587
More v. Weaver, 656
Morgan v. Fry et al., 608

Morgan v. Loyacomo, 54
Morgan v. Odham's Press, 632
Morgans v. Launchbury et al., 11, 520
Morier v. Rivard, 244
Morris v. Platt, 129
Morrison v. Ritchie & Co., 634, 647
Morriss v. Marsen, 210
Morsillo v. Migliano, 517
Mortimer v. Cameron, 479, 587
Motherwell v. Motherwell, 92, 555, 561
Mowlds v. Fergusson, 661
Muir v. The Queen in Right of Alberta, 127
Muirhead v. Timber Bros. Sand & Gravel Ltd., 558
Mulcahy v. Ministry of Defence, 313
Mulholland v. Mitchell, 708
Mulloy v. Hop Sang, 119
Munro v. Toronto Sun Publishing Corp., 635, 653
Murphy v. Brentwood District Council, 282, 450, 451, 475, 476
Murphy v. Lamarsh et al., 625
Murphy v. McCarthy, 331
Murphy v. Plasterers' Union, 630
Murphy v. Steeplechase Amusement Co., 408
Murray Alter's Talent Associates Ltd. v. Toronto Star Newspapers Ltd., 632
Murray v. Bitango, 587
Murray v. McMurchy, 123
Murray v. Ministry of Defence, 72
Musgrove v. Pandelis, 504, 515
Mutual Life & Citizens Assur. Co. v. Evatt, 420

N

Nancy B. v. Hôtel-Dieu de Québec, 120
Nantel v. Parisien, 94
Napier v. Ferguson, 134
National Harbours Board v. Hildon Hotel (1963) Ltd., 537
Natonson v. Lexier, 97
Negretto v. Sayers, 329
Neiman-Marcus v. Lait, 632
Nelles v. Ontario, 73
Nelson Lumber Co. Ltd. v. Koch, 420
Nespolon v. Alford et al, 215
Nettleship v. Weston, 11, 179, 408
Netupsky v. Craig, 662
Neufeld v. Landry, 175
New York Times v. Sullivan, 653, 654, 671
Newell v. Smith, 542
Newstead v. London Express Newspaper Ltd., 647
Nicholls v. Township of Richmond, 604
Nickerson v. Forbes, 157
Nilsson Bros. Inc. v. McNamara Estate, 87
Nixon v. O'Callaghan, 656
Nolan v. Standard Publishing Co., 629
Norberg v. Wynrib, 59, **103**, 239
Normart Management Ltd. v. West Hill Redevelopment Co., 614
North Western Utilities, Ltd. v., 511
North York (Municipality) v. Kert Chemical Industries Inc., 507
Northern Helicopters Ltd. v. Vancouver Soaring Association et al., 196
Nor-Video Services Ltd. v. Ontario Hydro, 550, 555, 556
Nova Mink v. Trans-Canada Airlines, 284
Nova Scotia (Attorney General) v. Beaver, 538
Nowark v. Maguire, 641
Nunes Diamonds Ltd. v. Dominion Electric Protection Co, 432
Nuyen v. Slater, 671

O

Oakley v. Webb, 558
O'Brien v. Cunard S.S. Co., 101
O'Connor v. South Australia, 181
O'Connor v. Waldron, 656
Odlum and Sylvester v. Walsh, 201
Ogden v. Association of U.S. Army, 645
Ogwo v. Taylor, 367
Oke v. Weide Transport Ltd. and Carra (*sub nom.* Oke v. Gov't. of Man.), **308**, 334
Oll Ltd. v. Sect. of State for Transport, 314
Olutu v. Home Office, 488
Ontario (Attorney-General) v. Dieleman, 92, 538, 614, 628, 632, 629
Ontario Hospital Services Commn. v. Borsoski, 309
Oosthoek v. Thunder Bay (City), 480
O'Regan v. Bresson, 555
O'Rourke v. Schacht, 314
Ortenberg v. Plamondon, 632
Osborn v. Thomas Boulter & Son, 644
Osburn v. Mohindra and St. John Hospital, 521
Ostash v. Aiello. *See* Ostash v. Sonnenberg et al.
Ostash v. Sonnenberg et al, 196, 375
Ostrowe v. Lee, 639
Otto v. J. Grant Wallace, 73
Ottosen v. Kasper, 394

P

Page v. Smith, 296
Palek v. Hansen, 403
Palmer v. N.S. Forest Industries, 195
Palmer v. Solmes, 641
Palsgraf v. Long Island Railroad Co., 291, **343**
Papantonakis v. Australian Telecommunications Commn, 581
Papp v. Leclerc, 371
Paquette et al. v. Batchelor (*sub nom.* Batchelor v. Brown), 275
Paris v. Stepney Borough Council, 166
Parks West Mall Ltd. v. Jennett, 597
Parlett v. Robinson, 671
Patten v. Silberschein, 371
Pattison v. Prince Edward Region Conservation Authority, 509
Paulsen v. C.P.R, 200
Payne v. Lane, 201
Payne v. Maple Leaf Gardens, 409
Peacock v. Stephens, 201
Pearlman v. C.B.C., 631

Peck v. Tribune Co., 629
Pedlar v. Toronto Power Co, 157
Peek v. Gurney, 591
Peeters v. Canada, 97
Peixeiro v. Haberman, 158
Pellizzari v. Miller, 518
Penfold Wines Proprietary Ltd. v. Elliott, 84, 88
Penner v. Mitchell, 162, 715
Penso v. Solowan and Public Trustee, 707
Penton v. Calwell, 629, 661
Performing Right Society Ltd. v. Mitchell & Booker (Palais de Danse) Ltd., 519
Perka v. The Queen, 141
Perry v. Fried et al., 149
Perry v. Heatherington, 657
Perry v. Kendricks Transport Ltd., 504, 510
Peter v. Anchor Transit Ltd., 406
Peters v. Prince of Wales Theatre Birmingham) Ltd., 507
Peters-Brown v. Regina District Health Board, 94, 665
Pettersson v. Royal Oak Hotel Ltd., 519
Pfiefer v. Morrison, 156
Philip v. Hironaka, 403
Phillips v. Murray, 134
Phillips v. Robinson, 517
Phillips v. Soloway, 46, 47
Pigney v. Pointers Transport Services Ltd., 373
Pindling v. National Broadcasting Corp., 636
Pitman Estate v. Bain, 239
Pleau v. Simpson-Sears Ltd., 661
Polemis and Furness, Withy & Co. Ltd., Re, 321, 334, 340, 373
Police v. Greaves, 50
Pollock v. Winnipeg Free Press, 629
Portree v. Woodsmill, 587
Potter v. The Mercantile Bank of Canada, 388
Poupart v. Lafortune, 174
Powell v. Phillips, 198
Prasad v. Frandsen, 179
Price v. Milawski, 341, 372
Price v. South Metropolitan Gas Co., 513
Priestley v. Gilbert, 370
Priestman v. Colangelo and Smythson, 168
Prior v. McNab, 130
Pritchard v. Liggett & Myers Tobacco, 160
Privest Properties Ltd. v. Foundation Co. of Canada Ltd., 448
Provender Millers Ltd. v. Southampton County Council, 514
Pugliese et al. v. National Capital Commn., 543
Pullman v. Hill & Co., 644
Purcell v. Taylor, 517
Purdy v. Woznesensky, 64

Q

Q v. Minto Mgt., 355
Queen v. Cognos Inc., 417, 420, 436
Queensway Tank Lines v. Moise, 194
Quinn v. Leathem, 596
Quinn v. Scott, 179
Quintal v. Datta, 684

R

R. in Right of Canada v. Saskatchewan Wheat Pool, 184, 194, 195, 196, 197
R. in Right of the Province of Ontario v. Jennings, 706
R. v. Biron, 149
R. v. Brezack, 151
R. v. Buchinsky, 463
R. v. Burko, 76
R. v. Cey, 112
R. v. Coté, 336
R. v. Cuerrier, 111
R. v. Dudley, 139
R. v. Foundation Co. of Canada (*sub nom.* Foundation Co. of Canada Ltd. v. Canada), (*sub nom.* R. v. Thomas Fuller Const. Co. (1958) Ltd.), 275
R. v. Georgia Straight Publishing Ltd., 635
R. v. Hussey, 129
R. v. King, 210
R. v. Leclerc, 112
R. v. McGillivary, 487
R. v. Nord-Deutsche et al., 311
R. v. Peters, 78
R. v. Rule, 671
R. v. Salituro, 655
R. v. Saskatchewan Wheat Pool. *See* R. in Right of Canada v. Saskatchewan Wheat Pool
R. v. Smith, 129
R. v. St. George, 50
R. v. The Ship "Sun Diamond" et al., 537
R. v. Whitfield, 70
R. v. Zelensky, 59
Radovskis v. Tomm, 97
Rae v. T. Eaton Co. Maritimes Ltd., 526
Rahemtulla v. Vanfed Credit Union, 64
Rainbow Industrial Caterers Ltd. v. C.N.R., 436
Raleigh-Fitkin-Paul Morgan Mem. Hospital v. Anderson, 127
Ralston v. Fomich, 631
Ranson v. Kitner, 41, 129
Rapp v. McClelland & Stewart Ltd., 631
Ratych v. Bloomer, 710, 711
Razzell v. Edmonton Mint Ltd., 657
Read v. Coker, 50
Read v. J. Lyons & Co. Ltd., 501, 504
Reed v. Ellis, 160
Reese v. Coleman (No. 1), 181
Reibl v. Hughes, 120, 127, **223**, 230, 232, 233, 234, 235
Reynen v. Antonenko et al., 150
Reynoldson v. Simmons, 518
Rhodes v. C.N.R. Co., 296
Richards v. State of Victoria, 308
Rickards v. Lothian, 494, 510
Rieger v. Burgess, 684
Rigby v. Chief Constable of Northamptonshire, 507
Riske v. Canadian Wheat Board, 474
Rivtow Marine Ltd. v. Washington Iron Works, 378, 442
RJR-Macdonald Inc. v. Canada (Attorney General), 488

Robbins v. C.B.C, 92
Roberts v. Morana, 706, 707
Roberts v. Ramsbottom, 210
Roberts v. Read, 157
Robertson v. Stang, 88
Robinson v. Balmain New Ferry Co, 72
Robinson v. Dun, 668
Robitaille v. Vancouver Hockey Club Ltd., 95, 96
Robshaw v. Smith, 668
Robson v. Ashworth, 373
Rochester Gas & Electric Corp. v. Dunlop, 83
Rodriguez v. B.C. (A.G.), 120
Roe v. Ministry of Health, 260, 348
Rollinson v. R., 331, 487, 682
Romney Marsh v. Trinity House, 139
Roncarelli v. Duplessis, 481
Rondel v. Worsley, 242
Rookes v. Barnard, 96, **606**, 609, 610
Rose v. Ford, 709
Ross et al. v. Wall et al., 542
Ross v. Caunters, 244, 441
Ross v. Hartman, 201
Roth v. Roth, 90
Rothfield v. Manolakos, 479
Rothwell v. Raes, 521
Roy Swail Ltd. v. Reeves, 202
Royal Aquarium and Summer & Winter Garden Society v. Parkinson, 656
Royal Aquarium v. Parkinson, 658
Royal Bank v. Wilton, 597
Rozon v. Patenaude, 518
Ruckheim v. Robinson, 517
Russell Transport Ltd. v. Ontario Malleable Iron Co. Ltd., 546
Russen v. Lucas, 70
Russo v. Ontario Jockey Club, 78
Ryan v. Hickson, 215, 216
Ryan v. Victoria (City), 202, 432, 541, 568, 569
Rylands v. Fletcher, 489, 494, 496, 497, 498, 499, 504, 505, 507, 509, 510, 513, 514, 515, 516, 527, 559

S

S. et al. v. Clement et al., 487
S. v. M., 60
Saccardo v. City of Hamilton, 375, 498
Saconne v. Orr, 92
Saif Ali v. Sydney Mitchell & Co., 242
Samms v. Eccles, 60
Sandison v. Rybiak, 146
Sandy Ridge Sawing Ltd. v. Norrish, 611
Satterlee v. Orange Glenn School District, 194
Savickas v. City of Edmonton, 183
Sayers v. Harlow Urban District Council, 365
Scarff v. Wilson, 707
Schenck et al. v. R. in Right of Ontario, 570
Schilling v. C.G.A. Ass'n. of B.C., 313
Schmidt, Re. *See* Thornborrow v. MacKinnon), 157
Schneider v. Eisovitch, 295
Schneider v. Royal Wayne Motel Ltd., 558
Schofield v. Town of Oakville, 201
School Division of Assiniboine South, No. 3 v. Hoffer and Greater Winnipeg Gas Co. Ltd., 335
Schrump v. Koot, 708
Schwebel v. Telekes, 156
Schweitzer v. Central Hospital, 102
Scott v. R., 151
Scott v. Shepherd, 35
Seaboard Life Insurance Co. v. Babich, 463
Sealand v. McHaffie, 438
Seale v. Perry, 244
Searle v. Wallbank, 517, 518
Seaway Hotels Ltd. v. Consumers Gas Co., 451
SEDCO v. William Kelly Hldg. Ltd., 450
Segal v. Derrick Golf & Winter Club, 558
Seneca College, 318, 488
Seneka v. Leduc, 511
Seney v. Crooks, 240
Service Fire Insurance v. Larouche, 201
Sevidal v. Chopra, 593
Seymour v. Winnipeg Electric Ry, 364
Sforza v. Green Bus Lines, 210
Sgro et al. v. Verbeek, 406, 517
Shandloff v. City Dairy Ltd. et al., 525, 526
Shaw v. Gorter, 130
Shaw v. Lord, 129
Shea v. Noseworthy, 79
Sheffill v. Van Densen, 644
Shields v. Hobbs Mfg., 376
Shiffman v. Order of St. John, 498
Shirt v. Wyong Shire Council, 341
Shuttleworth v. Vancouver General Hospital, 558
Shwemer v. Odeon Morton Theatres Ltd., 576
Sidhu Estate v. Bains, 592, 594
Silva v. Winnipeg (City), 587
Silver v. Dominion Telegraph Co., 630, 653
Sim v. H.J. Heinz Co. Ltd., 92
Sim v. Stretch, 629
Simons v. Carr & Co., 644
Sindell v. Abbott Laboratories et al., 270
Sirros v. Moore, 244
Slattery v. Haley, 210
Slayter v. Daily Telegraph, 629
Slim v. Daily Telegraph, 678
Slocinski v. Radwan, 665
Smith Brothers & Co. v. W.C. Agee & Co., 665
Smith v. Hudzik Estate, 577
Smith v. Inglis Ltd., 375
Smith v. Leech Brain & Co., 327
Smith v. Maximovitch, 331
Smith v. Rae, 237, 311
Smith v. Stone, 42
Smith v. Widdicombe, 516
Snell v. Farrell, 159, 265, **262**, 266
Snider v. Calgary Herald, 653
Snitzer v. Becker Milk Co. Ltd., 576
Snyder v. Montreal Gazette, 635
Soldwisch v. Toronto Western Hospital, 237
Soon v. Jong et al., 54, 55
Sorenson and Sorenson v. Kaye Holdings, 593
Soroka v. Skjoth, 597
Soulsby v. City of Toronto, 310

Southern Portland Cement Ltd. v. Cooper, 166, 180
Southwark London Borough Council v. Williams and Anderson, 140
Spagnolo v. Margesson's Sports Ltd., 353
Spectra Architectural Group Ltd. v. Eldred Sollows Consulting Ltd., 603
Speed and Speed Ltd. v. Finance America Realty Ltd., 393
Speilberg v. A. Kuhn & Bros., 665
Spinks v. Canada, 421
Spivey v. Battaglia, 54
Spur Industries Inc. v. Del E. Webb Development Co., 560
Squittieri v. de Santis, 47
St. Amand v. St. John Propane Gas Co., 376
St. Anne's Well Brewery Co. v. Roberts, 498
St. Pierre v. Ontario, 556
Stachniewicz v. Mar-Cam Corp., 200
Stanley v. Hayes, 47
Stansbie v. Troman, 354, 371
Stark v. Auerbach et al., 657
State ex. rel. Smith v. Weinstein, 371
State Rubbish Collectors Assoc. v. Silznoff, 64
Stavast v. Ludwar, 201
Steiman v. Steiman, 88
Stein and Tessler v. Gonzales, 538
Stephens v. Myers, 49
Sterling Trusts v. Postma et al., 194
Stermer v. Lawson, 309, 353
Stewart v. Pettie, 20, 178, 306, 307
Stewart v. Stonehouse, 54
Stickney v. Trusz, 58
Stokes v. Carlson, 42
Stopforth v. Goyer, 671
Stovin v. Wise, 314
Strehlke v. Camenzind et al., 214
Stuart v. Canada, 581
Sturges v. Bridgman, 573
Suite v. Cooke, 295
Sulisz v. Flin Flon, 79
Sullivan v. Sullivan, 644
Summit Hotel Co. v. N.B.C., 652
Sun Life Assurance Co. of Canada et al. v. Dalrymple, 659
Supt. of Fam. & Child Service and Dawson et al.; Russell et al. and Supt. of Fam. & Child Service et al., Re, 126
Swami v. Lo (No. 3), 373
Swansburg v. Smith, 144
Swanson & Peever v. Canada, 473
Swanson v. Mallow, 35
Swinamer v. Nova Scotia (Attorney General), 474
Swinney v. Chief Constable of Northumbria Police Force, 314
Sycamore v. Ley, 134
Sylvester v. Crits, 222
Syms v. Warren, 658
System Contractors Ltd. v. 2349893 Manitoba Ltd., 594

T

T. (G.) v. Griffiths, 520
T. (L.) v. T. (R.W.), 60, 520
T.G. Bright Co. Ltd. v. Kerr, 519
T.J. (G.) v. Griffiths, 60
Tabor v. Scobee, 123
Taggard v. Innes, 47
Tait v. New Westminister Radio, 653
Tanner v. Norys, 153
Tarasoff v. Regents of U.C., 222
Tarjan v. Rockyview No. 44, 480, 481
Tarleton v. M'Gawley, 617
Taylor v. Asody, 387
Taylor v. Ginter, 95
Taylor v. Gray, 222
Taylor v. McGillivray, 59, 110, 240
Taylor v. Rover Co. Ltd., 375
Teece et al. v. Honeybourn et al., 38, 393
Telegraph Newspaper v. Bedford, 665
Temperton v. Russell, 617
Tenning v. Govt. of Manitoba, 319
Teno v. Arnold, 216, 307
ter Neuzen v. Korn, 219, 685, 706
Terracino v. Etheridge, 708
The Globe and Mail Ltd. v. Boland, 669
The King's Prerogative in Saltpetre, 136
The Liesboch v. The Edison, 682
The Pas (Town) v. Porky Packers Ltd., 421
The Wagon Mound (No. 1) Overseas Tankship (U.K.) Ltd. v. Morts Dock & Engineering Co. Ltd., 321, 326, 327, 329, 333, 334, 335, 336, 340, 341, 373
The Wagon Mound (No. 2) Overseas Tankship (U.K.) Ltd. v. The Miller S.S. Co. Pty. Ltd., 283, **337**, 340, 341
Thermo King Corp. v. Provincial Bank of Canada, 603
Thomas v. Sawkins, 152
Thompson v. Adelberg and Berman, 630
Thompson v. Amos, 665
Thompson v. Fox, 372
Thompson v. Toorenburgh, 371
Thompson-Schwab v. Costaki, 558
Thomson v. Lambert, 645
Thordarson v. Zastre, 200
Thorn v. James, 364
Thornborrow v. MacKinnon (*sub nom.* Re Schmidt; Thornborrow v. MacKinnon), 157, 723, 724
Thornton v. Board of School Trustees of School District No. 57 (Prince George) et al., 681, 703
Thorvaldson v. Saskatchewan, 602
Thurmond v. Pepper, 175
Tillander v. Gosselin, 43
Tindale v. Tindale, 47
Tock v. St. John's Metropolitan Area Bd., 496, 497, 498, 514, **545, 562**, 568
Todd v. Dun, 668
Tompkins Hardware Ltd. v. North Western Flying Services Ltd., 376, 393
Toneguzzo-, Norvell v. Burnaby Hospital, 708
Toogood v. Spyring, 659, 668

Torino Motors Ltd. v. City of Kamloops, 570
Toronto Railway v. Toms, 329
Torquay Hotel Co. Ltd. v. Cousins et al., 599, 601, 619
Town v. Archer, 221
Townsview Properties Ltd. v. Sun Construction & Equipment Co., 74
Toy v. Argenti, 364
Trache v. Can. Nor. Ry., 683
Tremain v. Pike, 335
Troppi v. Scarf, 725
Truman v. Sparling Real Estate Ltd., 275
Tuberville v. Savage, 49
Turner v. Thorne, 79
Turton v. Buttler, 92
Tuttle v. Buck, 615, 619

U

Ultramares v. Touche Niven & Co., 415
Ungaro v. Toronto Star Newspapers Ltd., 671
Unident Ltd. v. DeLong et al., 601
United States v. Caltex (Philippines) Inc., 136
United States v. Carroll Towing Co., 166, 405
United States v. Holmes, 140
Unruh v. Webber, 114
Unsworth v. Mogk, 196
Unterreiner v. Wilson, 244
Urbanski v. Patel, 366
Urquhart v. Hatt et al., 276

V

Valderhauq v. Libin, 73
Vale v. Intl. Longshoremen's & Warehousemen's Union, Local 508, 601
Valleyview Hotel Ltd. v. Montreal Trust Co., 260
Vana v. Tosta, 722
Vancouver General Hospital v. Fraser, 221
Vander Zalm v. Times Publishers et al., 629
Varner v. Morton, 640
Vaughan v. Menlove, 175, 178
Veinot v. Veinot, 129
Venning v. Chin, 38
Verbrugge v. Bush, 393
Videto v. Kennedy, 232, 233
Vile v. Von Wendt, 157
Vincent v. Lake Erie Transportation Co., 136
Vizetelly v. Mudie's Select Library, Ltd., 650, 652
Vlchek v. Koshel, 96
Volenti, 320
Volkswagen Canada Ltd. v. Spicer, 618
Voratovic v. L.S.U.C., 313
Vorvis v. I.C.B.C, 96
Vosburg v. Putney, 58
Vulcan Metals Co. v. Simmons Manufacturing Co., 592

W

W.J. Christie & Co. Ltd. v. Greer et al., 619
Wade v. Martin, 114
Wagner v. International Railway Co., 363
Wakelin v. The London & S.W. Ry. Co., 247
Waldick v. Malcolm, 181, 582
Walker Estate v. York-Finch Hospital, 239
Walker v. CFTO, 96
Wallace Construction Specialities Ltd. v. Manson Insulation Inc., 614
Ward v. James, 684
Ward v. Magna International Inc., 560
Ware v. Garston Haulage Co., 541
Warner v. Riddiford, 70
Warren v. Camrose (City), 183
Warren v. Green, 628
Watkins v. Olafson, 688, 707
Watson v. Kang, 405
Watson v. M'Ewan, 656
Watt v. Hertfordshire County Council, 172
Watt v. Longsdon, 666
Webb v. Attewell, 78
Webb v. Beavan, 641
Webster v. Chapman, 688
Wechsel v. Stutz, 244
Weiner v. Zoratti, 335
Wei's Western Wear Ltd. v. Yui Holdings Ltd., 498
Welbridge Holdings Ltd. v. Metropolitan Corp. of Greater Winnipeg, 480, 481
Wells v. Russell, 394
Wenden v. Trikha, 207, 209
Wentzell v. Veinot, 134
Westbank Band of Indians v. Tomat, 655
Western Fair Assoc., 506
Westlake v. R., 468
Whalley v. Lancashire and Yorkshire Ry., 139
Whipple v. Grandchamp, 202
White v. Conolly, 129
White v. Jones, 441
White v. Mellin, 618
White v. Turner, 221, 229, 230, 235
Whitehouse v. Jordan, 220
Whittingham v. Crease & Co., 244, 440
Wickberg v. Patterson, 389
Wieland v. Cyril Lord Carpets Ltd., 367, 370
Wild Rose Mills Ltd. v. Ellison Milling Co., 195
Wildwood Mall Ltd. v. Stevens, 78
Wiley v. Toronto Star Newspapers Ltd., 653
Wiley v. Tymar Mgmt., 587
Wilhocks v. Howell, 656
Wilkinson v. Downton, 61
Willis v. F.M.C. Machinery & Chemicals Ltd., 527
Wilsher v. Essex Area Health Authority, 221, 262, 265
Wilson v. Pringle, 54
Wilson v. Vancouver Hockey Club, 519
Windrim v. Wood, 716
Windsor Motors Ltd. v. District of Power River, 481
Winnipeg Child and Family Services v. G. (D.F.), 294
Winnipeg Condominium Corp. No. 36 v. Bird Construction Co., 442, 476
Winnipeg Electric Co. v. Geel, 261
Winrod v. Time, Inc., 645

Winterbottom v. Wright, 280
Wolfe v. Dayton, 517
Wong v. Arnold, 516
Woodgate v. Watson et al., 405
Woodward v. Begbie et al., 173, 270
Woollerton v. Costain, 79
Wormald v. Cole, 79
Wotta v. Haliburton Oil Well Cementing Co. Ltd., 258
Wright Estate v. Davidson, 373
Wright v. McLean, 113
Wright v. Ruckstull, 201
Wyant v. Crouse, 79

Y

Ybarra v. Spangard, 259, 260
Yellow Submarine Deli v. AGF Hospitality Associates Inc., 597
Yepremian v. Scarborough General Hospital et al., 520, 688
Young v. McMillan et al., 591
Youssoupoff v. Metro-Goldwyn-Mayer Pictures Ltd. (*sub nom.* Princess Alexandrovna v. Metro-Goldwyn-Mayer Pictures Ltd.), 628, 632, 639
Yuan v. Furstad, 405

Z

Zapf v. Muckalt, 114, 409
Zbyszko v. New York American, 630
Zelenko v. Gimbel Bros., 310
Zeppa v. Coca Cola Ltd., 255
Zervobeakos v. Zervobeakos, 354

CHAPTER 1

INTRODUCTION: THE NATURE AND FUNCTIONS OF TORT LAW

LINDEN, CANADIAN TORT LAW
6th ed. (1997)

The law of torts hovers over virtually every activity of modern society. The driver of every automobile on our highways, the pilot of every aeroplane in the sky, and the captain of every ship plying our waters must abide by the standards of tort law. The producers, distributors and repairers of every product, from bread to computers, must conform to tort law's counsel of caution. No profession is beyond its reach: a doctor cannot raise a scalpel, a lawyer cannot advise a client, nor can an architect design a building without being subject to potential tort liability. In the same way, teachers, government officials, police, and even jailers may be required to pay damages if someone is hurt as a result of their conduct. Those who engage in sports, such as golfers, hockey-players, and snowmobilers, may end up as parties to a tort action. The territory of tort law encompasses losses resulting from fires, floods, explosions, electricity, gas, and many other catastrophies that may occur in this increasingly complex world. A person who punches another person in the nose may have to answer for it in a tort case as well as in the criminal courts. A person who says nasty things about another may be sued for defamation. Hence, any one of us may become a plaintiff or a defendant in a tort action at any moment. Tort law, therefore, is a subject of abiding concern not only to the judges and lawyers who must administer it, but also the public at large, whose every move is regulated by it.

WRIGHT, INTRODUCTION TO CASES ON THE LAW OF TORTS
4th ed. (1967)

While no definition of a "tort" has yet been made that affords any satisfactory assistance in the solution of the problems we shall encounter, the purpose, or function, of the law of torts can be stated fairly simply. Arising out of the various and ever increasing clashes of the activities of persons living in a common society, carrying on business in competition with fellow members of that society, owning property which may in any of a thousand ways affect the person or property of others — in short doing all the things that constitute modern living — there must of necessity be losses, or injuries of many kinds sustained as a result of the activities of others. The purpose of the law of torts is to adjust these losses and to afford compensation for injuries sustained by one person as the result of the conduct of another. Such a statement of the problem indicates that the law of torts must constantly be in a state of flux, since it must be ever ready to recognize and consider new losses arising in novel ways. The introduction of printing, by facilitating the manner in which a man's reputation might be injured by the dissemination of the printed word, had a tremendous effect on the law of defamation; the radio of today presents even more serious problems, as do also the aeroplane and the modern motor car.

The study of the law of torts is, therefore, a study of the extent to which the law will shift the losses sustained in modern society from the person affected to the shoulders of him who caused the loss or, more realistically in many fields, to the insurance companies who are increasingly covering the many risks involved in the conduct of business and individual activities.

SALMOND, THE LAW OF TORTS

21st ed., Heuston and Chambers (eds.) (1996)

Tort and Crime

A tort is a species of civil injury or wrong. The distinction between civil and criminal wrongs depends on the nature of the appropriate remedy provided by law. A civil wrong is one which gives rise to civil proceedings — proceedings, that is to say, which have as their purpose the enforcement of some right claimed by the plaintiff as against the defendant. Criminal proceedings, on the other hand, are those which have for their object the punishment of the defendant for some act of which he is accused. It is often the case that the same wrong is both civil and criminal — capable of being made the subject of proceedings of both kinds. Assault, libel, theft and malicious injury to property, for example, are wrongs of this kind. Speaking generally, in all such cases the civil and criminal remedies are not alternative but concurrent, each being independent of the other. The wrongdoer may be punished criminally by imprisonment or otherwise, and also compelled in a civil action to make compensation or restitution to the injured person. . . .

Tort and Contract

The distinction between tort and contract is that the duties in the former are primarily fixed by the law, while in the latter they are fixed by the parties themselves. Further, in tort the duty is towards persons generally; in contract it is towards a specific person or persons. . . .

Tort and Equity

No civil injury is to be classed as a tort if it is only a breach of trust or some other merely equitable obligation. The reason for this exclusion is historical only. The law of torts is in its origin a part of the common law, as distinguished from equity, and it was unknown to the Court of Chancery. . . .

We may accordingly define a tort as *a civil wrong for which the remedy is a common law action for unliquidated damages, and which is not exclusively the breach of a contract or the breach of a trust or other merely equitable obligation.*

NOTES

1. Winfield and Jolowicz, *Tort*, 14th ed., Rogers (ed.) (1994), defined tortious liability as that which "arises from the breach of a duty primarily fixed by the law; this duty is towards persons generally and its breach is redressible by an action for unliquidated damages".

2. The late Professor John G. Fleming, in his *Law of Torts* (9th ed. 1998), the most influential book on tort law in the Commonwealth, explained that the word *tort* derives from the Latin *tortus*, meaning twisted or crooked, and early found its way into the English language as a general synonym for the word "wrong". In general terms, Fleming concludes that a tort is a "civil wrong other than a breach of contract, which the law will redress with damages". Fleming is unhappy with defining tort law, preferring instead to "describe it in terms of the policies which have brought it into existence and contrast these with the policies underlying other forms of liability".

3. To describe a tort as a civil wrong explains nothing about which wrongs the common law will consider to be actionable as torts. This was noted by Mr. Justice La Forest in *Angus v. Sun Alliance Insce. Co.* (1988) 52 D.L.R. (4th) 192, at 199, [1988] 2 S.C.R. 256, where His Lordship stated:

> A tort is a legal construct and is not to be confused with a wrong in the general sense. It only exists where the law says it exists, *i.e.*, where the law provides a remedy.

4. It should be stressed that tort law is not one dimensional; it serves several different functions depending upon the area of tort law under review. Tort law's primary area in contemporary society is personal injury and property damage caused by accidents, for example, automobile accidents. Tort law, however, concerns many other areas, for example, protection of the environment, reputations, and business interests.

   The American Bar Association Report, *Towards a Jurisprudence of Injury: The Continuing Creation of a System of Substantive Justice in American Tort* Law (1984), describes the pluralistic nature of tort law in the following terms:

> . . . the most sensible approach is to regard tort law from a pluralistic viewpoint, viewing it as a multifaceted response to a very varied set of problems. If one sought a natural metaphor, it might not be that of one large tree, but rather that of a densely packed forest area, where trees of different sizes and species grow together, with many sorts of vegetation. This area would be seen to run into other forest areas, which might be viewed as representing statutory compensation and regulation schemes and other parts of the common law.

5. The purpose of this chapter is to identify the main aims of modern tort law in a preliminary and tentative way. It will be seen that not all of its goals are harmonious, indeed some may be in conflict with others. It will also be noticed that not all the purposes of tort law are expressed openly in the case law. On the contrary, some of them are totally unrecognized or dimly perceived, or even vehemently denied. In sum, tort law serves a potpourri of objectives, some conscious and some unintended.

   See generally Linden, *Canadian Tort Law*, 6th ed. (1997), p. 2.

6. Professor Weinrib opines that "goals have nothing to do with tort law". He insists that tort law, like love, has no ulterior ends. In his article "Understanding Tort Law" (1989), 23 Valp. L.J. 485, at 526, he wrote:

> Explaining love in terms of ulterior ends is necessarily a mistake, because a loving relationship has no ulterior end. Love is its own end. In that respect, tort law is just like love.

To this Justice Linden, in *Canadian Tort Law*, 6th ed. (1997), p. 3, responded:

> It is true that tort law, like love, is valuable for its own sake, but there are many aspects of love and many facets of tort law. Professor Weinrib, by maintaining that there are no pragmatic ends of love and of torts, undervalues them both. There is more to love and to torts than just their intrinsic unpolluted merit, however splendid that may be. Neither should be sold short. True, the greatest thing about love is love itself, but love also inspires song, animates poetry, builds new families, encourages new enterprises, etc. Love can take credit for some of the good things that happen in our world, even though lovers may not start out with these effects in mind. Similarly, tort law may achieve beneficial effects, without necessarily setting out to do so, things like compensation, deterrence and education. Thus, whether by design or not, tort law, like love, is valuable not only intrinsically, but also for its other contributions to a better world.

HOLMES, THE COMMON LAW
(1881)

A man need not, it is true, do this or that act — the term "act" implies a choice — but he must act somehow. Furthermore, the public generally profits by individual activity. As action cannot be avoided, and tends to the public good, there is obviously no policy in throwing the hazard of what is at once desirable and inevitable upon the actor.

The state might conceivably make itself a mutual insurance company against accidents, and distribute the burden of its citizens' mishaps among all its members. There might be a pension for paralytics, and state aid for those who suffered in person or estate from tempest or wild beasts. As between individuals it might adopt the mutual insurance principle *pro tanto*, and divide damages when both were in fault, as in the *rusticum judicium* of the admiralty, or it might throw all loss upon the actor irrespective of fault. The state does none of these things, however, and the prevailing view is that its cumbrous and expensive machinery ought not to be set in motion unless some clear benefit is to be derived from disturbing the *status quo*. State interference is an evil, where it cannot be shown to be a good. Universal insurance, if desired, can be better and more cheaply accomplished by private enterprise. The undertaking to re-distribute losses simply on the ground that they resulted from the defendant's act would not only be open to these objections, but, as it is hoped the preceding discussion has shown, to the still graver one of offending the sense of justice. Unless my act is of a nature to threaten others, unless under the circumstances a prudent man would have foreseen the possibility of harm, it is no more justifiable to make me indemnify my neighbor against the consequences, than to make me do the same thing if I had fallen upon him in a fit, or to compel me to insure him against lightning. . . .

The general principle of our law is that loss from accident must lie where it falls, and this principle is not affected by the fact that a human being is the instrument of misfortune. But relatively to a given human being anything is accident which he could not fairly have been expected to contemplate as possible, and therefore to avoid.

PROSSER, HANDBOOK OF THE LAW OF TORTS
4th ed. (1971) now Prosser and Keeton, 5th ed. (1984)

Perhaps more than any other branch of the law, the law of torts is a battle ground of social theory. Its primary purpose, of course, is to make a fair adjustment of the conflicting claims of the litigating parties. But the twentieth century has brought an increasing realization of the fact that the interests of society in general may be involved in disputes in which the parties are private litigants. The notion of "public policy" involved in private cases is not by any means new to tort law, and doubtless has been with us ever since the troops of the sovereign first intervened in a brawl to keep the peace; but it is only in recent decades that it has played a predominant part. Society has some concern even with the single dispute involved in a particular case; but far more important than this is a system of precedent on which the entire common law is based, under which a rule once laid down is to be followed until the courts find good reason to depart from it, so that others now living and even those yet unborn may be affected by a decision made today. There is good reason, therefore, to make a conscious effort to direct the law along lines which will achieve a desirable social result, both for the present and for the future.

Individuals have many interests for which they claim protection from the law, and which the law will recognize as worthy of protection. Various interesting attempts have been made to classify these interests into categories, which of course have no virtue in themselves, and only serve to suggest the wide extent to which the law is concerned with human welfare. [People] wish to be secure in their persons against harm and interference, not only as to their physical integrity, but as to their freedom to move about and their peace of mind. They want food and clothing, homes and land and goods, money, automobiles and entertainment, and they want to be secure and free from disturbance in the right to have these things, or to acquire them if they can. They want freedom to work and deal with others, and protection against interference with their private lives, their family relations, and their fellow men. The catalogue of their interests might be as long as the list of legitimate human desires; and not the least of them is the desire to do what they please, without restraint and without undue consideration for the interests and claims of others.

In any society, it is inevitable that these interests shall come into conflict. When they do, the primitive man determines who shall prevail with sword and club and tomahawk; and there is recent melancholy evidence that the law of the jungle is not yet departed from the affairs of nations. But in a civilized community, it is the law which is called upon to act as arbiter.

The administration of the law becomes a process of weighing the interests for which the plaintiff demands protection against the defendant's claim to untrammeled freedom in the furtherance of his own desires, together with the importance of those desires themselves. When the interest of the public is thrown into the scale and allowed to swing the balance for or against the plaintiff, the result is a form of "social engineering" that deliberately seeks to use the law as an instrument to promote that "greatest happiness of the greatest number" which by common consent is the object of society. This process of "balancing the interests" is by no means peculiar to the law of torts, but it has been carried to its greatest lengths and has received its most general conscious recognition in this field. . . .

The process is not a simple one, and the problems which arise are complex, and seldom easy of solution. It is usually far easier to describe what has been done than to give a clear reason for it, and harder still to predict what the future may hold. It is a simple matter to say that the interests of individuals are to be balanced against one another in the light of those of the general public, but far more difficult to say where the public interest may lie. Most of the writers who have pointed out the process have stopped short of telling us how it is to be done. It is easy to say that the law will require of every [person] reasonable conduct not unduly harmful to his neighbors; but what is reasonable, and what is undue harm? In determining the limits of the protection to be afforded by the law, the courts have been pulled and hauled by many conflicting considerations, some of them ill defined and seldom expressed at all, no one of which can be said always to control. Often they have had chiefly in mind the justice of the individual case, which may not coincide with the social interest in the long run. If we are to have general rules, and the law is to have no favorites, occasional injustice is inevitable to someone who does not fit into the rule; and the constant struggle is to make the rule sufficiently flexible to allow for the particular circumstances, and yet so rigid that lawyers may predict what the decision may be, and men may guide their conduct by that prediction. It is only by a slow, halting, confused, and often painful progress that any agreement is reached as to the best general rule. Ultimately the law must coincide with public opinion, and cannot stand against it; but when the opinion is in a state of division and flux, it is not surprising that the courts' decisions reflect the battle which is raging about them. . . .

Factors Affecting Tort Liability

Among the many considerations affecting the decision as to which of the conflicting interests is to prevail, a few may be singled out for special mention, with the repeated caution that no one of them is of such supervening importance that it will control the decision of every case in which it appears.

Moral Aspect of Defendant's Conduct. One such factor is the moral aspect of the defendant's conduct — or in other words, the moral guilt or blame to be attached in the eyes of society to his acts, his motives, and his state of mind. Personal morals are of course a matter on which there may be differences of opinion; but it may be assumed that in every community there are certain acts and motives which are generally regarded as morally right, and others which are considered morally wrong. Of course such public opinion has its effect upon the decisions of the courts. The oppressor, the perpetrator of outrage, the knave, the liar, the scandal-monger, the [person] who does spiteful harm for its own sake, the egotist who deliberately disregards and overrides the interests of his neighbors, may expect to find that the courts of society condemn him no less than the opinion of society itself. In a very vague general way, the law of torts reflects current ideas of morality, and when such ideas have changed, the law has kept pace with them. . . .

[T]here are still many immoral acts which do not amount to torts, and the law has not yet enacted the golden rule. It is impossible to afford a lawsuit for every deed of unkindness or betrayal, and there is much evil in the world which must necessarily be left to other agencies of social control. The basest ingratitude is not a tort, nor is a cruel refusal of kindness or courtesy, or a denial of aid. The rich [person] is under no compulsion to feed his starving neighbor, and it is still the law that the owner of a boat who sees another drowning before his eyes may rest on his oars and let him drown — although per haps in so extreme a case it is a reproach to the law that it is so. Petty insults, threats, abuse and lacerated feelings must be endured in a society not many centuries removed from the law of the club. To what extent the moral ideas of a future day may yet create new torts to deal with such misconduct, it is now impossible to say.

In short, it is undoubtedly true that in the great majority of the cases liability in tort rests upon some moral delinquency on the part of the individual. But quite often it is based upon considerations of public policy which have little connection with private morals. The ethical principles which underlie the law are "not the moral code of popular speech, but an artificial and somewhat sublimated morality, which is formulated by the law and is called morality only by a use of that term which is almost metaphorical"....

Historical Development. The shadow of the past still lies rather heavily on the law of torts. When the common law first emerged, its forms of procedure were rigidly prescribed, and the plaintiff could have no cause of action unless he could fit his claim into the form of some existing and recognized writ. These "forms of action we have buried, but they still rule us from their graves". At the beginning of the nineteenth century they still existed although somewhat blurred in their outlines, as the core of common law procedure. By the middle of the century they began to be modified, liberalized, and at last replaced to a great extent by the modern procedural codes. The old attitude still persisted, however, that the substance of the plaintiff's right is determined and limited by the possibility of a remedy under the common law forms. Thus even today, we find courts holding that blasting operations which cast rocks onto the plaintiff's land may be actionable where those which merely shake his house to pieces are not, on the basis of the old distinction between the action of trespass and the action on the case. Added to this is the devotion to precedent and the distrust of new ideas, which is by no means peculiar to the law but for which it often is reproached, and which has made it change slowly. There are not many rules in tort law as to which one may say that there is no better reason for their existence than that they were laid down by Lord Mildew three centuries since, at a time when the world was a very different place, but they do exist.

Nevertheless, change and development have come, as social ideas have altered, and they are constantly going on. The law of deceit has progressed from a point where it was assumed as a matter of course that every seller of goods will lie; the law of slander at one time held that mere "brabbling words" imputing harlotry to a woman were not actionable; and the same evolution is to be traced in the law of seduction, the right of privacy, and interference with contractual relations. More recently courts have recognized for the first time an action for prenatal injuries, a recovery by a wife for personal injury at the hands of her husband, new tort liabilities of municipal corporations, and a whole new field of actions for nervous shock and mental suffering. This process of development, of course, is not ended, and continues every year....

Convenience of Administration. It does not lie within the power of any judicial system to remedy all human wrongs. The obvious limitations upon the time of the courts, the difficulty in many cases of ascertaining the real facts or of providing any effective remedy, have meant that there must be some selection of those more serious injuries which have the prior claim to redress and are dealt with most easily. Trivialities must be left to other means of settlement, and many wrongs which in themselves are flagrant — ingratitude, avarice, broken faith, brutal words, and heartless disregard of the feelings of others — are beyond any effective legal remedy, and any practical administration of the law.

The courts always have stood more or less in dread of a "flood of litigation" involving problems which they are not prepared to deal with. At one time they refused to permit any inquiry as to the state of a man's knowledge, or his belief or intentions, upon the ground that "they cannot be known". For many years they denied all recovery in cases of "mental suffering" involving fright or shock without physical impact, for fear it would "open a wide door for unjust claims, which cannot successfully be met". The refusal to extend the obligation of a contract to third parties was based upon the "infinity of actions" and the "most absurd and outrageous consequences" which might ensue, and this is still the chief obstacle to holding contractors liable to third persons. . . .

Capacity to Bear Loss. Another factor to which the courts have given weight in balancing the interests before them is the relative ability of the respective parties to bear the loss which must necessarily fall upon one or the other. This is not so much a matter of their respective wealth, although certainly juries, and sometimes judges, are not indisposed to favor the poor against the rich. Rather it is a matter of their capacity to absorb the loss or avoid it. The defendants in tort cases are to a large extent public utilities, industrial corporations, commercial enterprises, automobile owners, and others who by means of rates, prices, taxes or insurance are best able to distribute to the public at large the risks and losses which are inevitable in a complex civilization. Rather than leave the loss on the shoulders of the individual plaintiff, who may be ruined by it, the courts have tended to find reasons to shift it to the defendants. Probably no small part of the general extension of tort law to permit more frequent recovery in recent years has been due to this attitude. The development of the doctrine of strict liability "without fault" for dangerous conditions and activities has rested to some extent on this basis, as has that of vicarious liability for the torts of a servant; and the extension of the liability of a manufacturer to the ultimate consumer of his product has been favored by the feeling that he is best able to bear the loss. The same principle, of course, underlies such statutes as the workmen's compensation acts.

But there are obvious limitations upon the power of a defendant to shift the loss to the public, and the courts frequently have been reluctant to saddle an industry with the entire burden of the harm it may cause, for fear that it may prove ruinously heavy. This is particularly true where the liability may extend to an unlimited number of unknown persons, and is incapable of being estimated or insured against in advance. It is also likely to be true as to a new industry, which may be unduly hampered in its development, as is illustrated by the controversy over the liability of the aviation industry for damage to persons or property on the ground, which used to turn primarily on the policy of imposing such a burden upon a new enterprise.

Prevention and Punishment. The "prophylactic" factor of preventing future harm has been quite important in the field of torts. The courts are concerned not with only compensation of the victim, but with admonition of the wrongdoer. When the decisions of the courts become known, and defendants realize that they may be held liable, there is of course a strong incentive to prevent any occurrence of the harm. Not infrequently one reason for imposing liability is the deliberate purpose of providing that incentive. The rule of vicarious liability is intended, among other things, to result in greater care in the selection and instruction of servants than would otherwise be the case; the carrier which is held to the "highest practicable degree of care" toward its passengers will tend to observe it for their safety; the manufacturer who is made liable to the consumer for defects in his product will do what he can to see that there are no such defects. While the idea of prevention is seldom controlling, it very often has weight as a reason for holding the defendant responsible.

This idea of prevention shades into that of punishment of the offender for what he has already done, since one admitted purpose of punishment itself is to prevent repetition of the offense. There are those who believe that punishment or retaliation is an important and proper aim of the law in assessing damages, since what is paid to the plaintiff is taken away from the defendant. However this may be, it is not often mentioned in the award of compensatory damages, which usually are treated by the courts as a mere adjustment of the loss which has occurred in accordance with responsibility. To the extent that punitive damages are given, however, both prevention and retaliation become accepted objects of the administration of the law of torts.

NOTES

1. Dean William Prosser, who died in 1972, was the most influential American author in the field of torts in this century. For the discussion of his contribution to American tort law see White, *Tort Law in America* (1980).

2. As for the moral aspect of tort law, Professor Weinrib has argued that corrective justice, based on Aristotle's theories, is the proper foundation of tort law so that when one person harms another by substandard conduct, there is a moral and legal duty to reimburse that other person for the loss suffered. See Weinrib, *The Idea of Private Law* (1995). See also Coleman, "Moral Theories of Torts" (1982), 1 J. Law and Phil. 371 and (1983), 2 J. Law and Phil. 5.

FLEMING, THE LAW OF TORTS
9th ed. (1998)

The history of the law of torts has hinged on the tension between two basic interests of individuals — the interest in security and the interest in freedom of action. The first demands that one who has been hurt should be compensated by the injurer regardless of the latter's motivation and purpose; the second that the injurer should at best be held responsible only when his activity was intentionally wrongful or indicated an undue lack of consideration for others. The former is content with imposing liability for faultless causation; the latter insists on "fault" or "culpability".

Individual Responsibility and Deterrence

Primitive law, pre-occupied with preserving the peace and providing a substitute for private vengeance, looked to causation rather than fault: "not so much to the intent of the actor as the loss and the damage of the party suffering". Even so, notions of fault were not wholly excluded. For one thing, the apparent indifference of early law to the wrongdoer's state of mind may have been based on its inability or unwillingness to conceive the unintentional infliction of harm rather than a lack of concern with such intention. For another, the myth has long been exposed that early English law ever adhered to an unqualified principle that a man acted at his peril and became responsible for all resulting harm. Yet liability, if not "absolute", was nonetheless "strict" and scant regard was paid to the moral quality of the defendant's conduct. Gradually, however, the law began to pay greater heed to exculpatory considerations and, partially under the influence of the Church, tilted towards moral culpability as the proper basis for tort. This subjectivation of the test of civil liability necessarily tended to benefit the injurer and curtail the protection for the injured. During the nineteenth century, the "moral advance" of tort law vastly accelerated. With the blessings of the moral philosophy of individualism [Kant] and the economic postulate of *laissez faire*, the courts attached increasing importance to freedom of action and ultimately yielded to the general dogma of "no liability without fault". This movement coincided with, and was undoubtedly influenced by the demands of the Industrial Revolution. It was felt to be in the better interest of an advancing economy to subordinate the security of individuals, who happened to become casualties of the new machine age, rather than fetter enterprise with the cost of "inevitable" accidents. Liability for faultless causation was feared to impede progress because it gave the individual no opportunity for avoiding liability by being careful and thus confronted him with the dilemma of either giving up his projected activity or shouldering the cost of any resulting injury. Fault alone was deemed to justify a shifting of loss, because the function of tort remedies was seen as primarily admonitory or deterrent. An award against a tortfeasor served as a punishment for him and a warning to others; it was, in a sense, an adjunct to the criminal law designed to induce antisocial and inconsiderate persons to conform to the standards of reasonable conduct prescribed by law. The significance attached to the element of deterrence operated, of course, on the assumption that an adverse judgment would be paid out of the defendant's own pocket. Personal fortunes were regarded as the sole source of compensation, so that the deterrent lash would be both real and inescapable.

Today, we are in the process of revising this approach. Morality will, of course, continue to dominate intentional injuries, and tort law (whatever its prospects of survival elsewhere) appears to have an assured future in this regard. However, in the core area of tort — accidents — our viewpoint has been changing drastically. It is being increasingly realized that human failures in a machine age exact a large and fairly regular toll of life, limb and property, which is not significantly reducible by standards of conduct that can be prescribed and enforced through the operation of tort law. . . . Accident prevention is more effectively promoted through the pressure exerted by penal sanctions attached to safety regulations and such extra-legal measures as road safety campaigns, the practice of insurance companies to base the rate of premiums on the insured's accident rate, improvements in the quality of roads and motor vehicles and of production processes in industry. But despite all these controls, accidents and injuries remain. Some no doubt are attributable to negligence in the conventional sense, i.e. to unreasonable risks, but others to "unavoidable" accidents. Either may fairly be ascribed, not just to the immediate participants, but to the activity or enterprise itself with which they are connected. The progress of society is linked to the maintenance and continuance of industrial operations and fast methods of transport, and must therefore suffer the harms associated with them. The question is simply, who is to pay for them, the hapless victim who may be unable to pin conventional fault on any particular individual, or those who benefit from the accident-producing activity? If rules of law can be devised that will require each industry or those engaging a particular activity, like drivers of motor-cars, to bear collectively the burden of its own operating cost, public policy may be better served than under a legal system that is content to leave the compensation of casualties to a "forensic" lottery based on outdated and unrealistic and unreasonable notions of fault.

Loss Spreading

This approach suggests that a proper function of tort law should be not so much the shifting as the distribution of losses *typically* involved in modern living. Acceptance of this viewpoint must inevitably change evaluations of what is a fair allocation of risks. We have seen that no social value attaches to the mere shifting of loss so long as its effect is merely to impoverish one individual for the benefits of another. In order to warrant such a result, the law had to find a cogent reason for subordinating the defendant's interests to the plaintiff's, and inevitably focused attention on the moral quality of the conduct of the individual participants in the accident. On the other hand, if a certain type of loss is looked upon as a more or less inevitable by-product of a desirable but dangerous activity, it may well be just to distribute its costs among all who benefit from that activity, although it would be unfair to impose it upon each or any one of those individuals who happened to be the faultless instruments causing it. Such a basis for administering losses has been variously described as "collectivization of losses" or "loss distribution". It leads to the selection of defendants, not necessarily because they happen to be morally blameworthy, but because they represent a conduit for "internalising" the accident cost to the risk-creating activity and distributing it among its beneficiaries through higher prices and/or liability insurance.

Liability Insurance

A potent influence on the growing trend towards loss distribution is the modern prevalence of liability insurance. Insurance has the effect that an adverse judgment no longer merely shifts a loss from one individual to another, but tends to distribute it among all policy holders carrying insurance on this type of risk. The person cited as defendant is, in reality, only a nominal party to the litigation, a mere "conduit through whom this process of distribution starts to flow".

NOTES

1. See also Harper, James and Gray, *The Law of Torts*, 2nd ed. (1986), an excellent treatise expounding the loss distribution theory; Priest, "The Invention of Enterprise Liability" (1985), 14 J. Leg. Stud. 461; Atiyah, "American Tort Law in Crisis" (1987), 7 Oxford J. Leg. Stud. 279; Ehrenzweig, "Negligence Without Fault" (1951), reprinted (1966), 54 Calif. L. Rev. 1422; Friedman, "Social Insurance and the Principles of Tort Liability" (1950), 63 Harv. L. Rev. 241; Wright, "Adequacy of the Law of Torts", [1961] Cambridge L.J. 44. For some judicial support, see *Morgans v. Launchbury*, [1971] 2 Q.B. 245 (C.A.); revd, [1973] A.C. 127, [1972] 2 All E.R. 606; *Nettleship v. Weston*, [1971] 2 Q.B. 691, [1971] 3 All E.R. 581 (C.A.).

2. See generally, Winfield, "The Foundation of Liability in Tort" (1927), 27 Colum. L. Rev. 1; Goodhart, "The Foundation of Tortious Liability" (1938), 2 Mod. L. Rev. 1; Williams, "The Foundation of Tortious Liability" (1939), 7 Cambridge L.J. 111; Williams and Hepple, *Foundations of the Law of Tort*, 2nd ed. (1984); Stone, "Touchstones of Tort Liability" (1950), 2 Stan. L. Rev. 259; Malone, "Ruminations on the Role of Fault in the History of the Common Law of Torts" (1970), 31 La. L. Rev. 1.

CALABRESI, "FAULT, ACCIDENTS AND THE WONDERFUL WORLD OF BLUM AND KALVEN"
(1965), 75 Yale L.J. 216

There is no need to go to great length in reiterating what the "general deterrence" thesis is. Essentially it is the notion that in our society what is produced is by and large the result of market choices by individuals. These choices are influenced by the relative prices of competing goods. To the extent that these prices reflect the costs of producing the product involved, people get as near to what they want as is possible in a fallible world; but to the extent that these prices understate the actual cost to society of producing a product, more of that product gets made and bought (relative to other goods) than we in fact want, and unnecessary costs are undertaken. And finally, accident costs are as much costs to society and as worthy of being considered in deciding what goods we want as, say, the cost of the metal it takes to make a product. Specifically, the thesis holds that although, for instance, we may not want the *safest* possible product, we do want the manufacturer to choose a means of production which may be somewhat more expensive in terms of materials used if this expense is made up by savings in accident costs. Similarly, although we do not wish to abandon cars altogether (they give us more pleasures than they cost us — despite accident costs), we may, if we are made to pay for car-caused accidents, drive less, or less at night, or less when we are of accident- prone ages, or with more safety devices, than if we are not made to pay for accident costs when we decide to use a car. I call this thesis general deterrence, because it seeks to diminish accident costs not by directly attacking specific occasions of danger, but (like workmen's compensation) by making more expensive those activities which are accident prone and thereby making more attractive their safer substitutes.

NOTE

1. This "general deterrence" theory, perhaps better described as "market deterrence", was elaborated in several articles and finally in a book: Calabresi, *The Costs of Accidents: A Legal and Economic Analysis* (1970). See *infra* Chapter 18. See also Posner, *Economic Analysis of Law*, 3rd ed. (1986); Shavell, *Economic Analysis of Accident Law* (1987); Landes and Posner, *Economic Structure of Tort Law* (1987).

WEINRIB, "TWO CONCEPTIONS OF TORT LAW"

in Devlin (ed.), Canadian Perspectives on Legal Theory (1991)

In the common law world generally, tort law treats the two litigants as connected, one with the other, through an immediate personal interaction as doer and sufferer of the same harm. This interaction begins with the potential for harm in what the defendant does and is completed in the actualization of that harm in what the plaintiff suffers. Each instance of doing and suffering forms a discrete normative unit. Tort law is the juridical regime that reflects the implicit morality of interaction so understood.

This conception of tort law has the following features. First, the doing and the suffering of harm are correlative. Each is understood only through the other and, thus, through the relationship that they together constitute. Doing is significant inasmuch as someone suffers thereby, and suffering is significant inasmuch as someone has inflicted it. A doing that results in no suffering, and a suffering that is the consequence of no one's doing, fall beyond the concern of tort law.

Second, because doing and suffering are correlative, any justificatory consideration that pertains to the doing of harm also implicates the suffering of harm, and vice versa. The plaintiff and the defendant are locked in a reciprocal normative embrace. Factors whose justificatory force applies to only one of the parties have no place in this conception of tort law. For instance, consideration of the deterrent effect of liability is irrelevant, because deterrence can without any loss of its justificatory force focus on the doer even in the absence of any particular sufferer. Similarly, tort law does not have a goal of compensation, because compensation applies on one side to the sufferer and does not necessarily encompass the doer. The only pertinent justificatory considerations are those that capture and reflect the relational quality of doing and suffering.

Third, these justificatory considerations, whatever they are, themselves yield a normative structure that mirrors the correlativity of doing and suffering. The plaintiff has a right against the defendant that is correlative to the defendant's duty to the plaintiff. This normative correlativity fully reflects the correlativity of doing and suffering when the duty and the right are each intelligible through the other. For such a normative correlativity to obtain, the juridical position of both parties must be determinable by the same justificatory considerations.

Fourth, because the actor's duty is owed to the potential sufferer from the action and is correlative to the sufferer's right, an injurious breach of duty by the actor is also a violation of the sufferer's right. A tort is a wrong, not a permissible act that an award of damages retrospectively prices or licenses. Moreover, the defendant's wrongful act is a wrong not against the world at large, but against the injured plaintiff specifically. The defendant owes the plaintiff a duty, operative at the moment of action, to abstain from committing such an act.

Fifth, because the defendant has wronged the plaintiff, the plaintiff can sue to have the wrong set right. The plaintiff does not step forward as a private enforcer of a public interest. Nor is the defendant singled out as a convenient conduit to an accessible insurance pool. The plaintiff sues literally in his or her own right as victim of the defendant's wrongful act.

Sixth, the successful plaintiff is entitled to a remedy that the defendant is obligated to discharge. The damages represent a quantification of the wrong done by the defendant and suffered by the plaintiff. At the remedial stage too there is a correlativity, this time between the defendant's duty to pay and the plaintiff's right to receive the payment. The correlativity is expressed by the transfer of a single sum from the defendant to the plaintiff. The damage award is not the blending of various independent goals or incentives (the deterrence of carelessness and the compensation of injury, for instance), but the remedial embodiment of the correlativity of the doing and the suffering of harm.

Seventh, the morality implicit in the relationship of doer and sufferer assigns the court a properly adjudicative function. The court's task is to specify what the normative dimension of this relationship requires in the context of a particular dispute. Because tort adjudication involves justifications that pertain only to the relationship between the parties as doer and sufferer of the same harm, a court cannot impose on the relationship an independent policy of its own choosing. Rather, a court intervenes at the instance of the wronged party in order to undo or prevent the wrongful harm. Adjudication thus conceived makes explicit what is latent in the immediate interaction of the parties. It does not involve the legislative selection of a course of action that will promote the general welfare.

These aspects, and the relationship of doer and sufferer out of which they arise, account for all the fundamental doctrines of negligence law. The unit of analysis is the sequence from the unreasonable creation of risk by the defendant to the materialization of the risk in harm to the plaintiff. The transitivity of the doer's acting on the sufferer is reflected in the requirement of factual causation and, more broadly, in the law's insistence that liability presupposes misfeasance rather than nonfeasance. The rubrics of duty and proximate cause also link doing and suffering, by requiring the plaintiff's injury to be within the ambit of the unreasonable risk created by the defendant's negligence. The objective standard of care reflects the equal standing of the two parties to the interaction by preventing the terms of the relationship from being unilaterally determined by the subjective capacities of the doer. The correlativity of doing and suffering is further attested to by the damage award itself, which quantifies into a single sum both the defendant's wrongdoing and the plaintiff's injury. Finally, the entire moral relationship is implemented through the adjudication of the plaintiff's claim that the defendant's action has wronged him. Thus, the conceptual and institutional apparatus of tort law provides the signposts for judicially articulating the immediate interaction of the doer and the sufferer of a harm.

NOTES

1. Professor Weinrib rejects an "instrumental" or "legislative" concept of tort law, in favour of a concept which regards tort law as private law which serves only to order the interaction of self-determining actors. It seeks to represent a system of "corrective justice". As he puts it "the only function of the law of torts is to be the law of torts". Thus, the view that tort law seeks to compensate victims, deter wrongdoing, or that it is a vehicle through which to efficiently shift and redistribute the costs of accidents, is entirely rejected by Professor Weinrib.

2. In *Canadian Tort Law,* 6th ed. (1997), Linden has written of the psychological function of tort law in these terms:

> Tort law may perform certain psychological functions. For example, the tort action, like the criminal law, may provide some appeasement to those injured by wrongful conduct. Lord Diplock has contended that no one would suggest using tort law for the purpose of vengeance. Nevertheless, though it is distasteful to most of us, this has always been one of the unexpressed uses of tort law and criminal law. Too many human beings still seem to have need of such an outlet for their desire for revenge. The sad fact is that there is in many of us something primitive which tort law may satisfy.
>
> This questionable service that tort law performs can be put in a more positive and acceptable form. It can be said that tort law helps to keep the peace by providing a legal method of quenching the thirst for revenge. It will be recalled that this was the historical rationale for the creation of tort law. Money damages were paid to the victims of tortious conduct in the hope of curtailing blood feuds. If these legal avenues to revenge were closed today, some victims of wrongful conduct might once again take up clubs and tomahawks to "get even" with their aggressors. . . .
>
> There is some support for this view in the experience of the Soviet Union. Shortly after the revolution the tort action was abolished, but it soon had to be resurrected. Even Communists, purified as they were supposed to be from economic avarice, apparently obtained some psychological satisfaction from tort suits. It should also be pointed out that liability insurance was not permitted in the U.S.S.R. so that the tort sanction operated directly on the tortfeasors and their pocketbooks. Another clue to the personal revenge element in tort law is our insistence on defendants being sued personally, even though there is insurance against the loss. True, we say that we are playing this cat-and-mouse game in order to avoid distorting the deliberations of the jury, but in reality we

> may be doing it just to permit victims to obtain a semblance of personal retribution.
>
> Tort law may counteract the feeling of alienation and despair which pervades our society. Governments, corporations, unions, and universities have grown too large and impersonal. A feeling of helplessness and personal insignificance grips too many of our people. Many individuals feel that they have lost control over their lives. No one seems to care about them anymore. A protest march, a sit-in or some other dramatic act can change all this. For a time, people *do* seem to care about the protestors. The media takes notice of them. They seem to matter more. They become relevant. There seems to be a psychological need for personal recognition, which may contribute something to the popularity of this type of activity. A tort suit may likewise provide some psychological satisfaction. Instead of demonstrating with a picket sign, an aggrieved individual may begin a lawsuit. The tort trial is an institution which displays great concern for the individual, especially if there is a jury. The parties have the undivided attention of everyone in the court — judge, jury, counsel, witnesses, spectators and occasionally, the press and the public. The award of damages for pain and suffering clearly manifests fellow feelings. As much time as is necessary to conclude the case is allocated to it, whether it be a day, a week, a month or a year. With out doubt this is a lavish process, but each accident victim is entitled to demand such an exhaustive hearing.

Do you think that it is better for a tort victim, who is bent on revenge, to pursue a wrongdoer with a writ or a rifle? See also Ehrenzweig, "A Psychoanalysis of Negligence" (1953), 47 N.W.L. Rev. 815.

3. This psychological aspect of tort law has become significant in recent years in the context of tort suits for sexual abuse. Professor Feldthusen, in a recent article, (see "The Canadian Experiment with the Civil Action for Sexual Battery" in Mullany, *Torts in the Nineties*, LBC Information Services, Sydney (1977); see also "The Civil Action for Sexual Battery: Therapeutic Jurisprudence?" (1993), 25 Ottawa L. Rev. 203), has described tort action in these situations as a form of "therapeutic jurisprudence", as "part of the healing process" for assault victims. Even though many of these actions follow criminal convictions for the same events, are undefended and yield little in actual money recovered, they do "bring the problem into the open". They are a form of "symbolic public vindication" which seeks to meet the "unmet demand for public justice by sex abuse survivors".

4. This phenomenon is not limited to sexual abuse cases. After the O.J. Simpson acquittal in Los Angeles, Fred Goldman, the father of the young man murdered with Nicole Simpson, launched a civil suit against the defendant. He consistently stated that he did not care about the money, but merely wanted to prove through the civil suit what the criminal trial had failed to — that his son was murdered by O.J. Simpson. It was obvious to all that launching this action was in response to a psychological need; it was not a financially motivated lawsuit. This was clearly established when, after his victory in the civil case, Mr. Goldman offered to forego the collection of the multi-million dollar damage award if Simpson would publicly admit his guilt. The invitation was spurned, of course, but it was made and would have been honoured. Is this evidence of the psychological aspect of tort law? Is this a worthwhile function of tort law?

WILLIAMS, "THE AIMS OF THE LAW OF TORT"
(1951), Current Legal Problems 137

An intelligent approach to the study of law must take account of its purpose, and must be prepared to test the law critically in the light of its purpose. The question that I shall propound is the end or social function or *raison d'être* of the law of tort, and particularly of the action in tort for damages.

It is commonly said that the civil action for damages aims at compensation, as opposed to the criminal prosecution which aims at punishment. This, however, does not look below the surface of things. Granted that the immediate object of the tort action is to compensate the plaintiff at the expense of the tortfeasor, why do we wish to do this? Is it to restore the *status quo ante*? — but if so, why do we want to restore the *status quo ante*? And could not we restore this *status* in some other and better way, for instance by a system of national insurance? Or is it really that we want to deter people from committing torts? Or, again, is it that the payment of compensation is regarded as educational, or as a kind of expiation for a wrong?

An inquiry of this nature is familiar in criminal law. Every lawyer knows the various theories of criminal punishment: propitiation of the victim, expiation, deterrence, incapacitation, reform. The question is whether any of these interpretations fits the sanction in tort, and if not whether there is some other that does so. In asking this question we must be prepared to find that there is no simple answer. No one theory adequately explains the whole of the criminal law, and it may be that the law of tort, also, refuses to open to a single key. Then again, we must bear in mind that any inquiry into the social justification of the law of tort is really three inquiries: a doctrinal inquiry, what purpose the law of tort has been commonly thought to serve, a sociological inquiry, what purpose it does in fact serve, and a philosophical inquiry, what purpose we ourselves think it ought to serve. It is possible for a rule to be designed to do one thing and in fact to do another, and we may think it ought to do something different from both. It is also possible for different rules of the law of tort to have different justifications. Thus there may be a difference between torts to the person and torts to property, or between intentional and negligent torts.

THE FOUR POSSIBLE BASES OF THE ACTION FOR DAMAGES IN TORT

There are four possible bases of the action for damages in tort: appeasement, justice, deterrence and compensation.

Appeasement. — Crime and tort have common historical roots. The object of early law is to prevent the disruption of society by disputes arising from the infliction of injury. Primitive law looks not so much to preventing crime in general as to preventing the continuance of this squabble in particular. The victim's vengeance is bought off by compensation, which gives him satisfaction in two ways: he is comforted to receive the money himself, and he is pleased that the aggressor is discomfited by being made to pay. By this means the victim is induced to "let off steam" within the law rather than outside it.

In modern times the safety-valve function of the law of tort probably takes a subordinate place. We do not reckon on the recrudescence of family feuds as a serious possibility, or even that of duelling. However, it may be thought that unredressed torts would be a canker in society, and to that extent the law can still be regarded as having a pacificatory aim. . . .

Justice. — With the growth of moral ideas it came to be thought that the law of tort was the expression of a moral principle. One who by his fault has caused damage to another ought as a matter of justice to make compensation. Two variants of this theory may be perceived: (1) The first places emphasis upon the fact that the payment of compensation is an evil for the offender, and declares that justice requires that he should suffer this evil. This is the principal of ethical retribution, exemplified (in criminal law) by Kant's dictum about the moral necessity of executing even the last murderer. (2) The second variant looks at the same situation from the point of view of the victim; it emphasises the fact that the payment of compensation is a benefit to the victim of the wrong, and declares that justice requires that he should receive this compensation. We may call this ethical compensation. . . .

The existence within us of the sentiment of justice pre-supposed by this theory can easily be shown by an example. Suppose that you have borrowed a friend's book and lost it. As a conscientious person you will naturally wish to replace the book. It is not a question of intimidating yourself from losing books in future, but merely of doing the decent thing. (In fact, you will want to replace the book even though the loss occurred without your negligence, though the law says that you are liable only in the event of negligence.)

It is even held by some that the notion of rightness in this respect takes no account of the fact that money may have different values for the wrongdoer and the victim. In de Maupassant's story of the necklace, the poor Loisels replace for their rich friend her necklace that they have lost, though they have to drudge for ten years to make up the sum they think it is worth. Replacement is a point of honour with them, even though the burden of replacement is heavy beyond all comparison with the pleasure that it gives to the recipient. . . .

Deterrence. — Ranged against the theory of tort as part of the moral order are those who believe that it is merely a regime of prevention. The action in tort is a "judicial parable", designed to control the future conduct of the community in general. In England this view seems to have been first expounded by Bentham. Blackstone had expressed the opinion that civil injuries are "immaterial to the public", but Bentham thought that such a contrast with criminal law could not be maintained, and that the underlying object of civil and criminal law was the same. Both criminal punishment and tort damages were sanctions and therefore evils: the only difference was in the degree of evil. The purpose of threatening them was to secure obedience to rules. Austin followed Bentham in this. The proximate end of the civil sanction, said Austin, is redress to the injured party; but its remote and paramount end is the same as that of the criminal sanction: the prevention of offences generally. Salmond adopted the same opinion. "Pecuniary compensation", he wrote, "is not in itself the ultimate object or a sufficient justification of legal liability. It is simply the instrument by which the law fulfils its purpose of penal coercion.". . .

Whatever the imperfections of the moral interpretation of tort, the deterrent theory itself fails to provide a perfect rationale. For one thing, it offends against the principle that deterrent punishment must be kept to the effective minimum. According to utilitarian philosophy, of which the deterrent theory is an application, a punishment must not be greater than is necessary to repress the mischief in question. Damages in tort, however, may be far greater than are needful as a warning. If, in a moment of rage, I assault a film actor and unluckily spoil his looks, so that he is compelled thereafter to confine himself to broadcast drama, I am liable for damages based on his loss of earnings, which may be enormous; yet in a criminal court the same assault may be thought deserving only of a fine of £50. If a fine of £50 is sufficient to deter me and others from such assaults in future, the film actor's damages of say £50,000 cannot be justified from the point of view merely of deterrence. They can, however, be defended by reference to a principle of justice which says that since his loss of salary must be borne by him or me, in all the circumstances it is more just that I should bear it than he. This objection to the deterrent theory is not necessarily an out-and-out refutation of it, but at least shows that the theory, like the ethical one, does not explain the whole of the law.

Looked at as a deterrent system, tort can be regarded as lagging far behind the law of crime. In criminal law we have learnt the necessity of individualising punishment, and even, in many cases, of refraining from punishment altogether; but tort still imposes an arbitrary, mechanical forfeiture. Tort still seeks "the object all sublime — to make the punishment fit the crime" (or rather, the fortuitous result of the crime), when the criminal law is giving up the effort to do so. In general, tort does not even care about the degree of the offender's fault. For instance, in criminal law the punishment for an intentional crime is generally more severe than for a negligent crime, because a more severe sanction is thought to be necessary by way of example; yet in tort the measure of damages is almost the same whether the tort was intentional or negligent. All the objections to the criminal fine — that it is ineffective or harmful as applied to poor persons, that by impoverishing it may drive to further offences, and that it falls upon the offender's family as much as or more than it falls upon himself — apply with even greater force to tort damages, for (speaking generally) the amount of these damages is not under the control of the tribunal. Regarded merely as a deterrent system, the law of tort is nothing more than a crude rule of thumb, for the sanction will almost certainly be either too great or too little in any particular case.

Damages are particularly ineffective against poor persons, and for wrongs of acquisitiveness. A thief or cheat could do good business if he merely had to restore his gains on the occasions when he was found out. For torts of damage or destruction, however, the deterrent effect of damages may be considerable. Again, the civil indemnity is generally limited to cases where damage has been caused: it is inapplicable, for instance, to careless driving where no one is injured. On the other hand, the civil sanction is frequently more efficient than the criminal one in that there is a stronger inducement to sue than to prosecute. It also has the advantage that it may be settled without action; every criminal charge must go through the court. In some instances the admonitory effect of a money judgment is increased by the award of punitive damages. If we look from deterrence to prevention in general, it is arguable that compensation payable to the injured party is educationally superior to a fine: it teaches a moral lesson.

To say that the goal of the law of tort is deterrence (if that is true) is not the same as saying that it actually does deter. No one that I know of has investigated by mass observation or psycho-analysis or statistics whether it fulfils this function. On the face of things, for instance, it seems unlikely that the tort of enticement is responsible for the comparatively small number of "eternal triangles" in society; other causes could be named that are probably far more important. However, this absence of experimental proof has been almost as true for the criminal law as for the law of tort. The sanctions of the criminal law were imposed on the assumption that they would repress crime, long before scientific methods of sociological investigation were thought of. In the case of some of them there is grave doubt whether they do in fact deter, or whether a less severe punishment might not have the same salutary effect. This doubt does not detract from the fact that the aim of the criminal legislator, however clumsy the means he uses, is to prevent crime. Moreover, most lawyers would be ready to affirm (even though it is only a guess on their part) that both the law of crime and the law of tort do actually deter in a large number of cases. For instance, employers now take many precautions for the safety of their employees that they did not take before the Factory Acts and similar legislation created criminal and civil sanctions for lack of such precautions. It is true that the civil sanction can be insured against, but an employer with a high accident ratio is not likely to get favourable terms from his insurers. Again, it is probable that the publicity accorded to libel suits, and the high damages awarded, have had the result of making some people careful in making statements about others; in fact the cramping effect of the libel law upon freedom of discussion has been made, rightly or wrongly, the subject of complaint. There are probably many owners of dangerous structures who have spent money in putting them safe because of the fear of actions for damages, or because it was only upon those terms that they could get insurance against liability. There are probably many business men who have been restrained from passing off their goods as other people's because of fear of the law of tort. The law is particularly effective when it can be expounded in advance in a solicitor's letter, the prospective victim having had notice of the other's intentions, or the tort being a continuing one. Probably the law of tort is least successful in checking casual acts of inadvertent negligence.

Realisation of the preventive role of tort has led to various proposals for the extension of the law. Thus, it has been suggested that there would be an increase of road safety if highway authorities were made liable for accidents resulting from their omission to repair highways. Judges have created the tort of breach of statutory duty partly because they have thought the criminal sanction provided by the statute to be insufficient. When the question recently arose whether employers' liability in tort should be wholly replaced by State insurance, the argument was advanced that the common-law remedy tended to make employers more vigilant for the safety of their employees. The same idea is at the back of the legislative maxim that a mischief should not be made a crime if the civil sanction is sufficient.

If the deterrent theory of tort is right, and even if deterrence is a mere by-product of compensation, the current definition of crime as a wrong resulting in punishment fails to define. Tort also, on this supposition, is a wrong resulting in punishment, for damages are punishment. A more careful definition of crime then becomes necessary if it is to be kept separate from the law of tort.

Compensation. — Finally there is the compensatory or reparative theory, according to which one who has caused injury to another must make good the damage whether he was at fault or not. This is the same as the theory of ethical compensation except that it does not require culpability on the part of the defendant. If valid, it justifies strict liability, which the theory of ethical compensation does not. . . .

NOTES

1. Professor White has argued that the tort process is a "fundamentally important form of civic theatre", which is less important for what it does than for what it is. People in our society see in the tort system a "demonstration of how we value each other and of what the rules are by which we are held accountable. That is, it is a representation of one's responsibility to the community." See "The Function of Deterrence in Motor Vehicle Accident Compensation Schemes," *Osborne Report* (1987), Vol. 2, p. 436.

2. Mr. Justice Cory, like Glanville Williams and others, has recently ruminated about the multi-faceted essence and aims of tort law in *Hall v. Hebert,* [1993] 2 S.C.R. 159 at 199:

> It is difficult to define the nature of a tort. Indeed one of the greatest writers in the field, W. L. Prosser has expressed the opinion that it should not be defined. Perhaps it is easiest to begin by saying what it is not. A tort is not a

crime. Although criminal law and tort law grew from the same roots they are today quite distinct and different. Criminal law is designed to provide security for the citizens of the state. It attempts to define that conduct which society finds abhorrent and therefore necessary to control. Those who commit crimes are prosecuted by the state and are subject to punishment which reflects the state's or society's abhorrence for the particular crime.

Nor is the law of torts contractual in its nature. Contract law seeks to enforce the rights which arise out of an agreement whose parties have voluntarily agreed to be bound by its terms. The law of contract seeks to enforce the terms of the agreement specifically or provide compensation for its breach. Nor can torts fall under the title of quasi-contractual relief. That remedy seeks to prevent unjust enrichment that might, for example, arise out of payment of money under mistake.

The law of tort covers a much wider field than does contract or quasi-contract. It provides a means whereby compensation, usually in the form of damages, may be paid for injuries suffered by a party as a result of the wrongful conduct of others. It may encompass damages for personal injury suffered, for example, in a motor vehicle accident or as a result of falling in dangerous premises. It can cover damages occasioned to property. It may include compensation for injury caused to the reputation of a business or a product. It may provide damages for injury to honour in cases of defamation and libel. A primary object of the law of tort is to provide compensation to persons who are injured as a result of the actions of others. W. L. Prosser puts the aim of tort law in this way in *Handbook of the Law of Torts* (4th ed. 1971), at p. 6, quoting Cecil A. Wright, "Introduction to the Law of Torts" (1944), 8 Cambridge L.J. 238, in this way:

> . . . in short, doing all the things that constitute modern living — there must of necessity be losses, or injuries of many kinds sustained as a result of the activities of others. The purpose of this law of torts is to adjust these losses, and to afford compensation for injuries sustained by one person as the result of the conduct of another.

Allen M. Linden, *Canadian Tort Law* (4th) ed. (1988), describes it in this way at p. 3:

> First and foremost, tort law is a compensator. A successful action puts money into the pocket of the claimant. This payment is supposed to reimburse him for the economic and psychic damages he has suffered at the hands of the defendant.
>
> Although compensation may be the primary purpose of tort law, it must be noted that aggravated or exemplary damages which may sometimes be awarded are aimed at punishment and deterrence. Tort actions fulfil a role in appeasing the victim and may serve as a means of educating the public, as well as producers and manufactures, as to the dangers involved in the use of certain products or processes.

3. Mr. Justice Major in *Stewart v. Pettie*, recently articulated the deterrent role of negligence law as follows:

> One of the primary purposes of negligence law is to enforce reasonable standards of conduct so as to prevent the creation of reasonable foreseeable risks. In this way, tort law serves as a disincentive to risk-creating behaviour.

4. A contrary view was expressed by Mr. Justice Lederman in *Hudson's Bay Co. v. White* (1997), 32 C.C.L.T. (2d) 163, where the Bay sued an attempted shoplifter, from whom the stolen goods, ladies' gloves, had been recovered, for the cost of surveillance, investigation and apprehension as well as punitive damages. Only minimal damages were awarded, Lederman J. explaining at 174:

> ... it would also seem possible to say that, in reality, this action is not about nor is it truly motivated by the goal of compensation. It is about deterrence. And deterrence and the effort to reduce crime is in principle beyond the realm of tort law. They are objectives which ought properly to be pursued through the criminal justice system.
>
> If The Bay's goal is to really deal more effectively with shoplifters then perhaps it should seek to convince Parliament and the police to adopt a sterner stance rather than seek to invoke the aid of the already overburdened civil justice system.
>
> Criminal activity is an aspect of the human condition which affects all of society. The costs of combatting theft and crime generally are borne by everyone, on a collective basis through police services and on a private basis through security and alarm systems, fences, locks, etc. These are societal costs and cannot readily be recovered from offenders on an individual basis by way of civil process. It is primarily for this reason that I must deny The Bay's claim for surveillance, investigation and apprehension costs.

5. Professor Donald Harris, one of the world's leading torts scholars, has disparaged the deterrent impact of tort law. (see "Evaluating the Goals of Personal Injury law: Some Empirical Evidence" in *Essays for Atiyah* (1991). Relying on several studies including his own, and recognizing the difficulty of proving or disproving deterrence, he explains that only a small proportion of injured people recover tort damages, mainly in auto accident situations. This leads him to conclude that deterrence is ineffective and largely symbolic.

   Professor Harris, basing himself on the Harvard Study on malpractice explained that one percent of medical patients were victims of malpractice. Only one in eight of these victims sued and only one-half of them received any tort damages. Therefore, one in sixteen medical malpractice victims obtain tort recovery. He concludes that the "signal sent to the medical profession is that occasionally, in a symbolic way, there may be liability" — *i.e.*, in 6 per cent of actual negligence cases.

   The Harvard Study also showed that doctors overestimate the risk of their being sued — three times greater than the actual risk. Thus, strangely, the few successful cases against doctors have a magnified effect on their perceptions. Understandably, though, doctors felt "distress, worry, anger and frustration" and especially where media attention was directed at trials; in short, they felt they were unfairly punished. According to the Study, most doctors did not believe that "the tort system could play a role in preventing medical mishaps"; rather they felt education, peer pressure, better procedure guidelines and morbidity conferences would do the job better. Are these responses a natural reaction of a powerful economic group wanting to be left alone, reminiscent of complaints by the police, business, etc., who object to the unfairness of legal supervision of their conduct?

6. In "Up with Torts" (1987), 24 San Diego L. Rev. 861, Professor Little wrote that Judges view tort law as a "whip that makes industry safer and saner". See also Professor Gary Schwartz, "Mixed Theories of Tort Law: Affirming Both Deterrence and Corrective Justice", (1977) 75 Texas L. Rev. 1801, who concludes his excellent article as follows:

   > The discussions within criminal law scholarship of the goals of deterrence and retributive justice in many ways parallel the debate among tort scholars as to the goals of deterrence and corrective justice. Yet this parallel has gone largely unnoticed. In particular, the strong interest in mixed theories displayed by most criminal law analysts has largely been neglected by tort scholars, who generally align themselves with either the deterrence or the corrective justice camp.

Mixed theories of tort law hold promise. Admittedly, efforts to develop a mixed theory applicable to all of tort law do not immediately pay off. Possibly, as tort law has developed over time, it has drawn on deterrence and corrective justice in a rather haphazard and eclectic way. Still, several important tort doctrines seem firmly grounded in both corrective justice and deterrence. As tort objectives, then, corrective justice and deterrence can be recognized as collaborators rather than competitors. The collaboration makes it more likely that the tort system provides advantages that enable it to justify all its costs.

For that matter, the deterrence objective, while explainable in economic terms, can also appeal to those whose interests in tort law are humane and compassionate rather than narrowly utility-maximizing. Furthermore, the notion that a "justice" approach necessarily sees tort law in "non-instrumental" terms is simplistic. In light of the ethical basis for negligence liability, tort law, when it deters negligence, prevents the occurrence of injustice. To this extent the deterrence objective itself includes an important justice component.

LINDEN, "TORT LAW AS OMBUDSMAN"

(1973), 51 Can. Bar Rev. 155

Introduction

These are turbulent times. People everywhere are refusing to submit docilely to the rule of distant bureaucrats and managers. Because of a longing for more control over their own lives citizens are demanding that governmental institutions and private organizations be more responsive to their wishes. Undoubtedly this struggle will continue during the coming decades and may well intensify.

Many techniques are being employed to render institutions more considerate of human needs. One weapon Canadians have deployed effectively is the vote; in the last few years, eight provincial governments have been turned out of office and the federal government has been severely rebuked. Citizen groups have sprung up everywhere and, on occasion, as in the Spadina Expressway battle, have met with astonishing success. Protest marches, consumer boycotts, mass meetings and publicity campaigns are being used to pressure mass institutions into being more attuned to the aspirations of ordinary people.

To assuage this insatiable appetite for justice, some modern governments have turned to an old Swedish institution — the ombudsman. The five provinces of Nova Scotia, New Brunswick, Quebec, Manitoba and Alberta have already established such an office, and the federal government is considering following suit. The primary function of the ombudsman is to protect ordinary people from the abuse of governmental power. An individual who feels ill-treated by some government department may complain to the ombudsman, who may investigate his complaint and suggest a remedy, if that is warranted. This is a useful instrument for supervising governmental activity, one that deserves our support. One problem with it, however, is that, like all bureaucracies, it will eventually become overworked and insensitive. Another shortcoming of the ombudsman is its unavailability as a check on private power.

There is no need to despair, however, because tort law may serve society in much the same way as an ombudsman. In fact, tort law may sometimes be more effective in this watchdog role than the ombudsman. The resources available to tort law are almost limitless, for every court and lawyer in the land may be called upon to participate in this noble work. Moreover, tort law may be used against private as well as public institutions.

Despite this, some authors are singing a requiem for tort law. They allege that it is obsolescent. Social insurance, they claim, can provide swifter, more efficient and more universal coverage for those who are injured as a result of the inevitable accidents of the industrial world. They denigrate the deterrent force of tort law and suggest that the abuse of power should be curbed by criminal law and administrative regulations. They contend that, because insurance covers most of these activities, there is rarely any sting left in tort liability.

It is true that the compensation function of tort law is waning in importance. New social welfare schemes are gradually rendering superfluous the need for tort reparation, at least for economic losses. Criminal and administrative law *can* curb deviant conduct more effectively than civil sanctions. Widespread insurance *does* diminish the deterrent force of civil liability. However, this does not necessarily doom tort law to extinction.

The law of torts may still serve in the years ahead as an instrument of social pressure upon centres of governmental, financial and intellectual power. The financial damages awarded against transgressors are no longer the only deterrent. Bad publicity may be more important. When a tort suit is launched, the glare of publicity may be focused upon it. The officials of the defendant government or company are drawn into the litigation. They are publicly under attack and are required to justify their conduct and their methods of operation to the judge and the jury. This can have a salutary effect, even though the amount of damages they must actually pay is insignificant.

1. *The Tort Action and the Publicity Sanction*

By means of a tort suit, an injured individual may be able to direct unfavourable publicity against a tortfeasor. The use of this publicity sanction may have three effects. First, the adverse publicity can cost the defendant money. The amount involved may be far in excess of any possible damage award. For example, when Coca-cola is sued as a result of an exploding Coke bottle, this fact may be broadcast to millions of potential customers, some of whom may switch to Pepsi-cola or orange juice. Sales of Coke and other soft drinks will shrink and profits may shrink. Even if the impact of this unfavourable publicity is only temporary, the cost to the company can be substantial. When Air Canada is sued because of an air crash, some passengers may choose to travel on other airlines or go by train. When an action is launched against a particular doctor or hospital, some patients may turn to other doctors or hospitals for their medical care.

Another way in which negative publicity causes financial loss is through diminution in the value of corporate shares. For example, when Richardson-Merrell, the producer of thalidomide and Mer/29, was sued by hundreds of people injured by these products, the value of its stock, which had been selling at twenty-five to thirty-five times its earnings, plunged to fifteen to twenty times its earnings. In other words, the paper value of the shares fell to almost half. The shareholders suffered enormous financial losses, largely because investors feared that the numerous lawsuits against the company might bank rupt it. Actually, these lawsuits hardly impaired the financial security of the company. Indeed, some stockbrokers, at the height of the scare, were suggesting to their clients that they would be wise to buy Richardson-Merrell stocks at the abnormally low prices.

The second effect of the publicity sanction is that it brings about a loss of prestige. Of course, this may also result in monetary loss, but it is important for its own sake. Even the managers of modern corporations are anxious to be held high in public esteem. They want to be proud of their company. Businesses spend millions on public relations campaigns to shine their corporate images. A much-publicized civil suit may tarnish a company's reputation for quality goods and service. It is, therefore, to be avoided at all costs. The repair of a damaged corporate reputation may require a great deal of money, time and effort, that might be used more profitably elsewhere.

Third, harmful publicity may also induce governmental intervention. This is something that most businesses and enterprises would prefer to avoid, if they possibly could. Nevertheless, if an action is brought against an organization engaged in some dangerous activity, the attention of governmental officials may be attracted to it. This may trigger a criminal prosecution or an administrative sanction. If the government agency has no authority to do anything, public opinion may be stirred up to such an extent that the politicians may be forced to enact new legislation to control the perceived abuse. Thus, a tort may lead to the creation of new regulatory schemes.

It is difficult to measure the power of the publicity sanction. It depends for its impact upon the reaction of individuals to information, something that is difficult to fathom. This is both a weakness and a strength. It is a weakness because there is no way of insuring that a tort suit will receive any media attention at all. In fact, most ordinary lawsuits do not attract any publicity. More over, the public may not think that the challenged conduct is very reprehensible. If this is the case, no one's conduct will be affected and public officials will not be spurred to action. Furthermore, some defendants, like a monopoly or a governmental agency, may be able to withstand some bad publicity, with out being badly mauled. Other defendants may minimize the force of negative publicity by launching a counter-publicity campaign. Such a manoeuvre was employed by General Motors after the much-publicized United States Senate hearings about automobile safety in the mid-1960's. After it was shown how neglectful they were about auto safety, General Motors tried to convince the public, with their "Mark of Excellence" advertising, that their products were unimpeachable.

In some ways the indefinite nature of the publicity sanction may render it more powerful than a criminal prosecution or a civil suit. This is so because the amount of penal fines and damage awards are often easy to forecast, whereas the result of bad publicity is nearly impossible to prophesy. Some civil trials may drag on for weeks or even months under the glare of publicity. Newspapers, magazines, radio and television may give great coverage to the story. Politicians may be drawn into the fray. The defendant may be put out of business. It is no small wonder that corporate managers seem more concerned with the effect of negative publicity arising from lawsuits against them than they are about the actual penalties provided for by the law.

Perhaps the most advantageous aspect of the publicity sanction is that it is in the hands of ordinary citizens. It is both triggered by ordinary citizens and imposed by them. Thus anyone who feels injured by someone else may institute civil proceedings. He does not have to wait for some prosecutor or civil servant to take up his cause. Too often such public servants are reluctant to move. They may have only limited resources at their command. Politics may be involved. An aggrieved individual, however, labours under no such burden; he can unilaterally commence proceedings at any time, even if his case is by no means iron-clad.

Because of the ease with which civil litigation may be started, there is a danger of unfounded legal attacks upon innocent defendants. This hazard is minimized in several ways. First, totally unfounded actions may be struck out at the pleading stage. Moreover, an action properly pleaded may be dismissed at the trial before the defendant actually has to call evidence, if the plaintiff's evidence does not support the facts he has pleaded. Second, the technique of awarding costs against the losing side in litigation is a deterrent to spurious claims. Most claimants will not lightly undertake a lawsuit because, if they lose, it could cost them dearly. Third, the vexatious proceedings legislation may be used to deny access to the courts to some irresponsible persons. These measures do not remove the problem altogether, of course, but they do reduce it.

The application of the publicity sanction is also in the hands of ordinary citizens. Offenders are not jailed, nor do they lose their licences. If the people are repulsed by the conduct of the defendant they will change their purchasing habits and their attitudes. If they do not feel that anything seriously wrong has been done, they will not alter their conduct and the publicity sanction will be no sanction at all. . . .

Conclusion

Without doubt, this ombudsman role of tort law is a blunt and imperfect tool. Other weapons will also be needed to aid citizens in their struggle for more responsive institutions. But, however many governmental ombudsmen we appoint, however many criminal laws we pass, however many administrative regulations we enact, there will always remain grievances that are unresolved. The private tort suit is at the service of society as *one* way of rectifying some of these wrongs, or at least of exposing them to public view. Canadians would be wise to preserve the historic tort action as they may yet have need of it.

NOTES

1. See also Shapo, "Changing Frontiers in Torts: Vistas for the 70's" (1970), 22 Stan. L. Rev. 330; Rourke, "Law Enforcement Through Publicity" (1957), 24 U. Chi. L. Rev. 225; Fisse, "The Use of Publicity as a Criminal Sanction Against Business Corporations" (1971), 8 Melb. U.L. Rev. 107.

2. Professor Fridman in his book, *The Law of Torts in Canada* (1990), Vol. 2, p. 373, expresses misgivings about tort law playing any role as ombudsman:

> . . . it has been suggested that for cases of oppressive conduct by governmental or similar bodies or agents, the law of torts can be invoked, as a kind of "ombudsman", to ensure that improper behaviour or misuse of power does not occur or can be curtailed. An ombudsman is an official appointed to oversee certain, usually governmental activities. He or she has wide powers of investigation, and can deal with complaints that do not necessarily raise legal issues. The function of an ombudsman is to control the way in which power is exercised in order to ensure that it is used correctly and consistently with the legislative provisions or executive policies from which such power emanates. The role of an ombudsman and that of the law of torts are very different. Admittedly, the underlying threat or possibility of legal action and liability for misconduct may help to deter people from acting tortiously just as the existence of an ombudsman may act as a deterrent to maladministration or the abuse of power. In that sense, there is some similarity between an ombudsman and the law of torts. The similarity should not be carried too far. Control over administration may be a possible consequence or result of the constance of the law of torts: it is not a prime, or even secondary purpose of that law.

3. Professor Atiyah has also considered the potential of the role of tort law as an ombudsman in *Accidents, Compensation and the Law*, 5th ed. (1995):

> The tort system, based as it is on the notion of fault and on the public adversarial trial, does offer some scope for public vindication. This is clearly so when, for example, a court awards damages against a bully or thug who has beaten up the plaintiff. But even an ordinary finding of negligence may give satisfaction to an injured person. It has also been suggested that tort law can play a role as a public grievance mechanism similar to an Ombudsman, especially in cases against public authorities or large corporations (such as drug companies) whose actions have caused widespread damage or injury to many people (e.g. the thalidomide tragedy or the Bhopal chemical disaster). In such cases a tort action may serve as much to establish responsibility and to vindicate feelings of outrage and grief as to obtain compensation. It is true that statutory public inquiries are often held into major disasters such as aircraft or railway crashes; but the great attraction of tort law for the citizen is that he can set the system in motion himself and does not have to wait for the government to act. If the tort system of compensation for personal injuries were ever abolished entirely, it might be thought desirable to institute some procedure for citizen-initiated inquiries of this type.
>
> It must be noted, however, that the capacity of the tort system to provide vindication is limited by the fact that in most cases the real defendant is a liability insurer and the purpose of the action is chiefly to unlock the door to the insurance fund; and also by the fact that the vast majority of tort claims are settled out of court, in private, by administrative processes and without formal admission of liability. Furthermore, it is apparent that the law does not set a very high value on vindication: if the defendant offers sufficient compensation to the plaintiff by way of settlement of his claim but the plaintiff rejects the offer and insists on his day in court, not because he finds the offer insufficient but simply out of a desire for public vindication, he will, in the majority of cases, have to pay the costs of the hearing.

4. Professors Williams and Hepple have also dealt with this matter in *Foundations of the Law of Tort*, 2nd ed. (1984):

> It must be said, however, that an action in tort sometimes serves the valuable function of applying pressure on those in power to remedy a wrong. A recent example is the actions brought on behalf of the victims of the drug thalidomide. These actions dramatically brought to light the difficulties of proving negligence against the manufacturers of the drug and the disputed legal question whether a person can sue for damage done to him before his birth. The *Sunday Times* took a keen interest, and public pressure was aroused, so that the manufacturers — who had settled the claims of 65 victims for about £1m in 1968 — were eventually compelled to set up a £20m trust fund for 410 children. The legal difficulties raised led the Lord Chancellor to ask the Law Commission to consider the question of antenatal injuries, and contributed to the Government's decision to set up a Royal Commission to investigate civil liability and compensation for personal injury. Attention was focused on the plight of other children with congenital disabilities, and, in addition to substantial subventions of taxpayers' money, a Minister for the Disabled was appointed in 1974. It is by no means certain that the same results would have occurred without a tort action to highlight the legal problems. . . .

5. Professor James Henderson has attacked the notion that tort law could serve as a weapon of social betterment in his article, "Expanding the Negligence Concept: Retreat from the Rule of Law" (1976), 51 Ind. L.J. 467, as follows:

That recent years have witnessed revolutionary reforms and developments in the common law of torts, and particularly in negligence, comes as no surprise to anyone teaching, studying, or practising in this field. That these reforms and developments have been supported by a substantial majority of legal writers is equally obvious to anyone familiar with the literature on the subject. What may not be so obvious, and therefore what I have chosen to advance as the thesis of this article, is that these widely welcomed developments, taken together, seriously threaten the integrity and even the survival of the system of negligence- based liability toward the improvement of which they were originally advanced. Simply stated, we torts people, especially the torts teachers and scholars among us, are in serious trouble; and the sooner we wake up to what we are doing to ourselves and to our subject, the better.

The source of the difficulty, as I shall attempt to demonstrate in the following analysis, is the tendency in recent years to focus upon the substantive objectives of our liability system almost to the total exclusion of any shared concern for the realities and limitations of the processes by which those objectives are realized. The overlooked fact is that adjudication has limits which may be exceeded regularly only at great risk to the integrity of the judical process. The most basic limit of adjudication is that it requires substantive rules of sufficient specificity to support orderly and rational argument on the question of liability. The reforms and changes in the law of negligence in recent years have, purportedly to advance identifiable social objectives, eliminated much of the specificity with which negligence principles traditionally have been formulated. We are rapidly approaching the day when liability will be determined routinely on a case by case, "under all the circumstances" basis, with decision makers (often juries) guided only by the broadest of general principles. When that day arrives, the retreat from the rule of law will be complete, principled decision will have been replaced with decision by whim, and the common law of negligence will have degenerated into an unjustifiably inefficient, thinly disguised lottery. . . .

6. In Linden, "Reconsidering Tort Law as Ombudsman," in *Issues in Tort Law*, Steel and Rodgers-Magnet (eds.) (1983), p.1, the author had this observation to make:

When I first read Henderson's article, I was pretty badly shaken up. I honestly thought every living torts professor favoured a more influential role for tort law. I knew, of course, that many academic critics felt tort law should be abolished and be replaced by social insurance, but I was unaware that any responsible torts scholars thought that tort law was doing too much, and hence should be abolished, unless it kept within the old grooves that had been established for it in the past. I re-read my article on "Tort Law as Ombudsman". I re-read many of the articles and cases upon which I based my analysis. I talked to a number of torts scholars about it. I cogitated. I paid extra attention to the new torts cases dealing with what I consider ombudsman-type issues. I ruminated some more.

I then came to a conclusion. Henderson was wrong. We were and are right. Maybe our writings were too enthusiastic; maybe our language was a bit too colourful; but I remain convinced more than ever that there is a significant role for tort law to play in the Canada of the eighties and beyond. Clarity and stability in law are, of course, very important, but justice is more important. If the abolition of tort law is being risked by allowing it to accomplish too much for ordinary people, then it is worth it. If tort law is eliminated some day because it did too much to help ordinary people, that would be a noble way to exit. It would be preferable to an end in which tort law would gradually wither away because it is too timid to respond to the calls for its help. Rather than losing its credibility by doing too much, tort law would be in grave danger of losing its credibility by doing too little.

Is there a legitimate ombudsman role for tort law to play in the Canada of the next millennium? How effective are the alternative techniques for social control? Does it depend on the type of activity being regulated?

7. The advent of the class action suit has made tort law more potent, enabling individuals to launch tort suits heretofore impossible because they were not viable economically. By banding together in a class suit individuals with small but worthy tort claims can mount an action whereas before they were unable to do so. In the few years that these actions have been permitted in Canada, tort cases involving breast implants, heart pacemakers, hepatitis, toxic gas, tobacco injury, a subway accident and others have been certified. Several have been settled. One of them, involving the heart pacemakers, yielded $23 million, including $6 million for counsel. Figures such as these strengthen tort law, providing a major incentive for imaginative counsel to work very hard for their clients, and, hopefully, for defendants to use greater care in their activities.

8. Tort law has been vigorously attacked by scholars and special inquiries for years. It is said to be unjust, costly, slow and ineffective. Others feel that although tort law is far from perfect, it is worthy of survival because of the values it enshrines. Many reform proposals have been offered, some of which have been adopted. Others remain only dreams, at least for the time being. See *infra* Chapter 18 for a consideration of these issues of "tort law at a crossroads". See Dias and Markenisis, *Tort Law* (1984), p. 4. For a superb critique of modern tort law, see also Fleming, *The American Tort Process* (1988). See also Sugarman, "Doing Away with Tort Law" (1987), 73 Calif. L. Rev. 555. Professor Gary Schwartz believes that American tort law is also experiencing a retrenchment. See Schwartz, "The Beginning and the Possible End of the Rise of Modern American Tort Law" (1992), 26 Georgia L. Rev. 601.

9. Professor Klar has written that we may be witnessing a turning point in the evolution of negligence law, something that has been called a liability insurance crisis. The courts have been accused of having been excessively generous in damage assessments and of applying negligence law too liberally in order to assist claimants. This criticism, and what he calls the "attendant hysteria" have produced a judicial "backlash" or an overreaction, resulting in resistance to tort claims. He feels that after a readjustment, negligence law will emerge as a more principled and fault-based law which will be "less prone to compensation for compensation's own sake". "Comment" (1987), 66 Can. Bar. Rev. 159.

10. Linden has developed a new rationale for tort law in the next millennium, see "Empowering the Injured", in *Torts Tomorrow: A Tribute to Professor John G. Fleming*, (1998):

> Empowerment is a popular concept nowadays. Everyone favours empowering the disadvantaged — the poor, the minorities, the elderly, women, Natives, the socially excluded. It is an alluring idea, reminiscent of the 1960's, when "participatory democracy" and "power to the people" were the slogans of the day. There is a romantic flavour to this concept, a mystic, almost revolutionary tone to the idea. For empowerment is a recipe for healthy living, where individuals are able to control their own lives, to plan their own futures, and to thrive in harmony with their own choices.
>
> There are many ways in which the law has advanced the empowerment of individuals — human rights codes, constitutional Charters of Rights, legal aid, education, non-governmental organizations, and the social safety net. These and other devices have all sought to make a contribution toward empowering certain disadvantaged groups.
>
> There is one group of people, however, which is rarely mentioned in all this talk of empowerment — the injured. This is, however, a disadvantaged

> group which is also worthy of empowerment. Interestingly, there exists an ancient tool of empowerment which serves the injured rather well, but it is not usually described as such. I am referring, of course, to the law of torts, that historic common law civil action which enables injured individuals to empower themselves in many ways. Tort law has no monopoly in empowering the injured; it works along with other legal and non-legal mechanisms to achieve its goals. It is often used only as a last resort when all else fails. . . . .
>
> The mission of tort law in the next millennium should be empowering the injured, that is, those who are hurt in the multifarious activities of modern society. I believe that there will be a greater need for tort law than ever before in the next millennium. If social insurance continues to expand, there will be less need for tort compensation; but if, as is more likely, social insurance shrinks, there will be even more need for the compensation role of tort law. But, although the compensation function will remain important, it is the other, new empowerment role of tort law that will emerge as increasingly vital in the next millennium.
>
> There are several types of empowerment that may be supplied by tort law — (1) financial, (2) compliance, (3) didactic, (4) psychological, (5) economic and (6) political. It is hard to measure the exact impact or value of this empowerment, for much of it is ephemeral and spiritual, rather than being measurable or quantifiable. But that is also the case with other laws.
>
> Though tort law may be costly, complex and cumbersome, it possesses unique features which enable individuals to secure compensation, to foster compliance, to educate and to seek psychological satisfaction. With the aid of skilled counsel, powerful organizations can be forced to account for their harmful conduct. The lawsuit may come to the attention of politicians who may react. At the very least, tort actions force us to consider novel questions of morality, ethics and economics in a rational way in a dignified setting — not in the streets or in the legislatures, where the public interest so often is ignored or even rejected in favour of special interests. And the beauty of all of this is that it can be triggered by one injured individual, if he or she chooses to do so, as long as there is a factual and legal basis for the complaint. I realize that this is an idealized view of tort law, which does not always work as it should. Nevertheless, tort law is a wondrous instrument, because it enables injured individuals to confront their injurers in open Court to make them answer for their harmful conduct.

11. Professor Klar has a different view, which he expressed in "Downsizing Tort", *ibid:*

> Most common law jurisdictions utilize negligence law, which is predicated on the fault of a wrongdoer, as one vehicle for the compensation of victims suffering personal injury or property damage due to accident. As Professor Fleming's writings in this area developed over time, it became apparent that Professor Fleming was increasingly becoming disenchanted with fault-based compensation. Fleming regarded fault-based compensation for personal injury victims as an inadequate societal response, no-fault compensation, or alternatively enterprise liability, being preferable.
>
> Fleming articulated the persuasive argument that the courts themselves were increasingly recognizing this, and that as a result negligence law in its application even if not in its theory, was being converted into a vehicle for loss distribution. Thus the elements of the negligence action were being interpreted in a way largely to give effect to loss distribution goals, the moral fault of the actor becoming significantly less relevant to this inquiry.
>
> This author concurs with Fleming's view that loss distribution and not loss shifting has been negligence law's primary concern over the last several decades. This is not, however, a position which I endorse. It has been and remains my view that fault-based compensation, with a focus on wrongdoing and the full restoration of a victim, must remain an essential part of a system of civil

justice, and must not be replaced by no-fault or enterprise liability. In order for this to work, however, fault-based compensation must be based on fault. Judicial efforts to dilute fault in order to compensate accident victims fail in two ways. First, negligence law becomes an inefficient, expensive, and inequitable system for distributing losses. Second, issues of civil justice and the protection of an individual's security and dignity become marginalized and trivialized. Downsizing tort in the area of the compensation of personal injury victims caused by accidents means that tort law should return to the basic philosophy expressed by Lord Atkin in *Donoghue v. Stevenson*. Losses which have not been caused by the wrongful acts of others can then be addressed more sensibly by no-fault or other social insurance schemes.

Lord Atkin's decision in *Donoghue v. Stevenson* was based upon one simple but incredibly profound principle — "a general public sentiment of moral wrongdoing for which the offender must pay". It was not based on a loss distribution; manufacturers of ginger beer were not seen as efficient cost avoiders; the liability insurance of the manufacturer, if indeed there was any, was not seen as a welfare fund for the disabled, and the House of Lords did not wish to regulate the food and drug industry in Scotland. Through its fault the manufacturer of the drink harmed May Donoghue and, based upon a simple principle of morality which guides us all in our daily lives, the manufacturer was accordingly responsible for restoring her to the *status quo ante*.

In theory, the major elements of the negligence action — duty, breach, and cause — reflect the principle of moral wrongdoing which is the basis of negligence law. In theory, the elements are restrictive — their purpose is to restrict recovery to those injured as a result of the wrongdoing of others. In practice, they do not operate in this way. For the most part, the elements of the negligence action have become very short hurdles over which a plaintiff must step to reach a pool of insurance funds.

Professor John Fleming's contributions to the understanding and analysis of twentieth century tort law are enormous. Fleming understood the rules and principles of tort law, and the policies which underlay them. Fleming's view of the role of the twentieth century negligence law was to distribute losses in order to compensate victims in an economically sensible manner. Thus, for Fleming, the negligence aspect of fault-based compensation ultimately became an obstacle to the achievement of this goal. In pure economic loss disputes, Fleming did not view this as a significant problem, and was generally supportive of tort law's expansion.

This author, with much humility, has taken a different approach. I am a self-described tort law enthusiast. I very much believe in the importance of fault-based compensation to restore dignity to individuals, to fully compensate them for things which were wrongfully taken from them, and to hold wrongdoers accountable. Despite tort's defects and inefficiencies, no non-tort compensation scheme can accomplish tort law's goals. Correcting wrongs by requiring personal responsibility has a very strong attraction to victims.

It may appear ironic that a tort law supporter would advocate the downsizing of tort. This is advocated for both personal injury and property damage cases, as well as economic loss disputes. In the former area, it has been suggested that fault must be restored as a meaningful prerequisite to recovery and not merely as a gloss. This will ensure that the moral values which underlie the neighbour principle are taken seriously. It will also ensure that no-fault schemes can be developed to address serious gaps in compensation. In the second area, tort law must not be used as a mechanism to undermine the law as it has developed in other areas. The common law should continue to be seen as a seamless web. Changes to legal rules must be made consistently and intelligently. Tort law should operate within its boundaries and respect the need for other areas of the common law to do the same.

12. Do you favour an expansion or a reduction of tort law's role?

13. Remember always that the tort process is a very human one, involving human beings, their tragedies and their transgressions. Tort law strives for rationality, but there is much unavoidable irrationality and emotion involved in the tort process because people in pain and people under attack can react in strange ways. Everyone who participates in the system must be sensitive to these matters.

14. Keep the material in this chapter in mind, and return to it occasionally, as you study the rest of this casebook.

CHAPTER 2

TRESPASS AND INTENTIONAL INTERFERENCES WITH PERSONS, PROPERTY, AND CHATTELS

A. THE HISTORICAL CONTEXT

KLAR, TORT LAW

(Carswell, 2nd ed., 1996)

The tort actions dealing with direct interferences with persons, their chattels, and their land stem from the writs of trespass *vi et armis*, *de bonis asportatis*, and *quare clausum fregit*. Although these now commonly are referred to as the intentional torts, in Canada this reference is inaccurate. The writ of trespass was developed in the thirteenth century in order to assist those who were the victims of direct and forcible interferences. There was no requirement that the interference be intended by the defendant, nor that the conduct otherwise be wrongfully motivated. Fleming has suggested that direct and forcible interferences were actionable in order to preserve the peace and order in society, as this was the type of conduct "most likely to cause breach of peace by provoking retaliation." These torts were actionable without proof of damage, consistent with the theory that the defendant's conduct was wrongful not because actual physical damage had been caused, but because the plaintiff's security, and society's tranquility, had been disrupted.

The directness requirement of these torts was rigidly adhered to. This led to the creation of a new writ, the action on the case, to provide a remedy where a consequential injury had been caused by the defendant's wrongful conduct. Case differed from trespass in certain important respects. It was not actionable without proof of damage. In addition the defendant's conduct must have been wrongful. According to Fleming,

> Trespassory harm was prima facie wrongful and it was for the defendant to raise any justification or excuse ... In contrast, the action on the case from the beginning required proof by the plaintiff of either wrongful intent or negligence on the part of the defendant.

NOTES

1. It is generally assumed that the torts which will be discussed in this chapter, *i.e.*, assault, battery, false imprisonment, trespass to goods, and trespass to land, are "intentional" torts. As we shall see, these interferences are in fact usually committed intentionally. But can they be committed negligently? Does the concept, for example, of a "negligent battery", or a "negligent trespass" exist in Canadian tort law? What are the practical consequences of this possibility?

2. Professor Klar argues that the torts which stem from the Writs of Trespass can be committed either intentionally or negligently. The only criterion for these torts is that they are direct interferences with persons, property or chattels. Authority for this view derives from such cases as *Eisener v. Maxwell*, [1951] 1 D.L.R. 816 (N.S.); revd [1951] 3 D.L.R. 345, 28 M.P.R. 213 (C.A.), where after a lengthy review of the authorities, both judicial and textual, Ilsley C.J. concluded (at 827) that "[i]t will thus be seen that the view of Dr. Stallybrass that a battery does not necessarily involve intention is supported not only by *Covell v. Laming*, 1 Camp. 497, but by a long line of English and Canadian cases over a period of more than 300 years. There are no English or Canadian cases supporting the result of the American decisions ... or the views of Sir John Salmond and Dr. Winfield that a battery must be intentional."

3. A thorough analysis of this issue was written by Winfield and Goodhart, "Trespass and Negligence" (1933), 49 L.Q. Rev. 359. The authors point out that the action of trespass *vi et armis* gave rise to the torts of assault, battery and false imprisonment. They state:

> Nowadays, assault, battery, and false imprisonment are associated almost exclusively with direct and intentional force on the part of the offender, but until comparatively modern times it was not in the least necessary that the injury should have been intentional; the liability, except possibly for mitigation of damages, was just the same even if the injury had been inadvertent, nor do we know of any decision which makes it impossible even at the present day to commit a 'negligent' battery. However, that may be there are copious illustrations in the reports of defendants having been sued for 'negligent' assault and battery, and held just as much liable as if they had done the harm intentionally.

Similarly, the authors noted that "negligent injury to goods was just as culpable an act of trespass as intentional harm to them". The authors go on to explain why the action for negligence has overtaken the inadvertent forms of trespass in contemporary tort law.

4. Although statements frequently define battery as if it were exclusively an intentional tort, there have in fact been numerous examples of "negligent battery". See, for example, *Ellison v. Rogers*, [1968] 1 O.R. 501, 67 D.L.R. (2d) 21 (H.C.); *Goshen v. Larin* (1974), 10 N.S.R. (2d) 75, 46 D.L.R. (3d) 137; revd 10 N.S.R. (2d) 66, 56 D.L.R. (3d) 719 (C.A.); leave to appeal to S.C.C. refused Dec. 16, 1974; *Hatton v. Webb* (1977), 7 A.R. 303, 81 D.L.R. (3d) 377 (Dist. Ct.); and *Dahlberg v. Naydiuk* (1969), 10 D.L.R. (3d) 319, 72 W.W.R. 210 (Man. C.A.). Also see Sullivan, "Trespass to the Person in Canada: A Defence of the Traditional Approach" (1987), 19 Ott. L. Rev. 533.

5. The essential requirement of the torts which are based on trespass is that the interference is "direct". What does this mean? Professor Klar in *Tort Law*, 2nd ed. (1996), p. 27, defines directness in the following way:

> An injury can be described as being directly produced by the defendant's act when it flows naturally from it, without the necessity of an intervention by another independent factor. Where, however, the defendant's act merely creates the situation of danger, and requires an additional act to produce the ultimate injury, the injury can be described as only flowing indirectly from the initial act. A test of directness can be posed as follows: would the result have occurred had it not been for the intervention of another independent agency?

Does this definition and "test" adequately deal with problems of "directness"?

6. What is a "direct" application of force? Is there a battery if the defendant hits the plaintiff with a club? If the defendant throws a stone at the plaintiff? If the defendant

puts an overdose of pepper in the plaintiff's soup? What if a person with AIDS donates blood and someone then contracts the disease from that blood?

7. The defendant threw a lighted squib made of gunpowder into the stall belonging to Y, whereupon W instantly, to prevent injury to himself, picked up the lighted squib and threw it across the market-house into the stall belonging to R, who, instantly to save his goods, picked up the still lighted squib and threw it to another part of the market-house where it struck the plaintiff and the combustible matters, bursting, put out one of the plaintiff's eyes. Would this be considered a "direct" act? See Trindade, "Intentional Torts: Some Thoughts on Assault and Battery" (1982), Oxford J. Leg. Stud. 211, at 218, citing the case of *Scott v. Shepherd* (1773), 2 Wm. Bl. 892, 95 E.R. 1124.

8. The defendants sprayed a chemical into the air intake of a truck occupied by the plaintiff. The chemical resulted in a irritant which, when inhaled by the plaintiff, caused a reaction, including throat irritation, watering eyes and dizziness. Was this a battery? See *Swanson v. Mallow*, (1991), 94 Sask. R. 217, [1991] 5 W.W.R. 454; affd (1992), 97 Sask. R. 202, [1992] 2 W.W.R. 718 (Sask. C.A.).

GOSHEN v. LARIN

Nova Scotia Court of Appeal. (1974), 46 D.L.R. (3d) 137, 10 N.S.R. (2d) 75; revd (1975), 10 N.S.R. (2d) 66, 56 D.L.R. (3d) 719 (C.A.); leave to appeal to S.C.C. refused Dec. 17, 1974.

The defendant was a referee at a wrestling match who made an unpopular decision as far as the crowd was concerned. After leaving the ring he proceeded toward the dressing room escorted by the police amidst a mass of thrown objects. He was struck on the head by one of these objects and fell to his knees, a bit stunned. He got up and continued out of the arena with his right arm shielding his face. Although no one saw him strike anybody, the plaintiff alleged that the defendant pushed him down causing him to fracture his wrist. The defendant appeals from a decision for the plaintiff in the action for battery.

Macdonald J.A.: ... The action was originally framed in assault. The learned trial Judge permitted counsel for the respondent to amend the statement of claim to include an allegation that the injury complained of was caused by the appellant who "directly either intentionally or negligently caused physical contact with the person of the plaintiff without the plaintiff's consent". In other words, the action is one of battery, being a trespass to the person.

In *Fowler v. Lanning*, [1959] 1 All E.R. 290, Diplock, J., then of the Queen's Bench Division, held that the onus of proving negligence, where the trespass is *not* intentional, lies upon the plaintiff, whether the action be framed in trespass or negligence. Lord Denning in *Letang v. Cooper*, [1964] 2 All E.R. 929 (C.A.), said at p. 932:

> If he does not inflict injury intentionally, but only unintentionally, the plaintiff has no cause of action today in trespass. His only cause of action is in negligence, and then only on proof of want of reasonable care.

The English judicial view, as above expressed, appeals to me as being a fair and just one. I am, however, bound by the decision of the Supreme Court of Canada in *Cook v. Lewis*, [1952] 1 D.L.R. 1, [1951] S.C.R. 830, in which Cartwright, J., said (p. 15 D.L.R., p. 839 S.C.R.):

> In my view, the cases collected and discussed by Denman J. in *Stanley v. Powell*, [1891] 1 Q.B. 86, establish the rule … that where a plaintiff is injured by force applied directly to him by the defendant his case is made by proving this fact and the onus falls upon the defendant to prove 'that such trespass was utterly without his fault'. In my opinion *Stanley v. Powell* rightly decides that the defendant in such an action is entitled to judgment if he satisfies the onus of establishing the absence of both intention and negligence on his part.

Cook v. Lewis, supra, has been followed and applied in various jurisdictions: see *Walmsley et al. v. Humenick et al.*, [1954] 2 D.L.R. 232 (B.C.S.C.); *Tillander v. Gosselin* (1967), 60 D.L.R. (2d) 18, [1967] 1 O.R. 203 (Ont. H.C.) [affirmed 61 D.L.R. (2d) 192*n* (Ont. C.A.)]; *Dahlberg v. Naydiuk* (1970), 10 D.L.R. (3d) 319, 72 W.W.R. 210 (Man. C.A.).

The law in Canada at present is this: In an action for damages in trespass where the plaintiff proves that he has been injured by the direct act of the defendant, the onus falls upon the defendant to prove that his act was both *unintentional and without negligence* on his part, in order for him to be entitled to a dismissal of the action.

The learned trial Judge found that the appellant "actually did shove or push the defendant, Jacob Goshen, to the floor …" but that there was no malice and no intention on the part of the appellant to wilfully injure the respondent, but that the injuries occurred through his negligence [when he] blindly proceeded up the corridor. …

I accept, of course, the learned trial Judge's finding of facts. I respectfully disagree, however, as to the inference of negligence on the part of the appellant. This inference is a conclusion on the trial Judge's part from the facts by which, in my opinion, we are not bound.

I accept, of course, the finding of the learned trial Judge that the respondent received his injuries by being pushed unintentionally by the appellant. It is my opinion, however, that, due to the circumstances that existed at the time, the appellant was perfectly justified in proceeding up the corridor with his right arm in front of his face which, in all probability, is the reason he made contact with the respondent. Indeed, he was in protective police custody at the time and the police officers themselves had to push people away. Certainly, it could not be said that the police, in so doing, were guilty of assault or trespass to the person, unless, of course, they used excessive force. Although it is not necessary to decide this point, and I expressly refrain from doing so, it might well be argued that even if the appellant pushed the respondent intentionally, he was doing so in aid of and in consort with the peace officers, in achieving the common purpose of the police officers, namely, to get the appellant and the two wrestlers safely to their respective dressing rooms.

In the result, it is my opinion that the actions of the appellant did not amount to negligence under the circumstances, from which it follows that he has discharged the onus of showing that the respondent's injuries were not caused by his negligence.

The appeal should be allowed with costs, both here and in the Court below.

Appeal allowed;
action dismissed.

NOTES

1. The heavy hand of history plays an important role in modern law. Courts usually have difficulty shedding traditional methods of solving legal problems. *Fowler v. Lanning*, [1959] 1 Q.B. 426, [1959] 1 All E.R. 290 was a rare example of judicial boldness in discarding a time-worn concept. It was followed in another context in *Letang v. Cooper*, [1965] 1 Q.B. 232, [1964] 2 All E.R. 929 (C.A.), where Lord Justice Denning stated:

> The truth is that the distinction between trespass and case is obsolete. We have a different sub-division altogether. Instead of dividing actions for personal injuries into *trespass* (direct damage) or *case* (consequential damage), we divide the causes of action now according as the defendant did the injury intentionally or unintentionally. If one man intentionally applies force directly to another, the plaintiff has a cause of action in assault and battery, or, if you so please to describe it, in trespass to the person. "The least touching of another in anger is a battery." If he does not inflict injury intentionally, but only unintentionally, the plaintiff has no cause of action today in trespass. His only cause of action is in negligence, and then only on proof of want of reasonable care. If the plaintiff cannot prove want of reasonable care, he may have no cause of action at all. Thus, it is not enough nowadays for the plaintiff to plead that "the defendant shot the plaintiff" [see *Fowler v. Lanning*, [1959] 1 Q.B. 426]. He must also allege that he did it intentionally or negligently. If intentional, it is the tort of assault and battery. If negligent and causing damage, it is the tort of negligence.
>
> The modern law on this subject was well expounded by my brother Diplock J., in *Fowler v. Lanning* with which I fully agree. But I would go this one step further: when the injury is not inflicted intentionally, but negligently, I would say that the only cause of action is negligence and not trespass. If it were trespass, it would be actionable without proof of damage; and that is not the law today.

2. In *Ellison v. Rogers*, [1968] 1 O.R. 501, 67 D.L.R. (2d) 21 (S.C.), the plaintiff was struck by a golf ball driven by the defendant 100 yards away. The ball had "hooked" inexplicably. The plaintiff pleaded trespass, as well as negligence. Brooke J., in dismissing the action, explained that the "onus is on the defendant to disprove that the striking was either negligent or intentional if the plaintiff succeeds in proving that he was struck." The defendant satisfied the court by a preponderance of evidence, that he was not negligent in the circumstances, and the action was dismissed.

3. The vitality of this principle is evinced in *Dahlberg v. Naydiuk* (1970), 10 D.L.R. (3d) 319, 72 W.W.R. 210 (Man. C.A.). The action, framed in both negligence and trespass, arose when a farmer was accidentally shot by a hunter who had fired over the farmer's land. Mr. Justice Dickson (as he then was) referred to the onus shift as "one of those strange anomalies of the law" and quoted Dean Wright's critique of the rule as "irrational and unnecessary". Nevertheless, he held that "[i]f such a change is to be made in the law it must be made by a court higher than this". An insight into the policy rationale behind the stubborn longevity of this principle is provided by this statement of Mr. Justice Dickson:

> Hunters must recognize that firing over land without permission of the owner constitutes a trespass to land and if injury to person results, trespass to person. A hunter who fires in the direction in which he knows or ought to know farm buildings are located must accept full responsibility for resultant damage to person or property. It is no answer to say he thought the buildings were unoccupied.

> There are vast areas of western Canada in which deer abound and where no farming activities are carried on. Even in farming areas there are often hills from which one can fire at game in the valley below without risk of injury to others. If a hunter chooses to hunt in a farming area he must do so in full awareness of the paramount right of the farmer to carry on his lawful occupation without risk of injury from stray bullets.

4. In *Teece et al. v. Honeybourn et al.* (1975), 54 D.L.R. (3d) 549, [1974] 5 W.W.R. 592 (B.C.S.C.), the deceased was shot by the police as they pursued him on foot in connection with a stolen car problem. In an action by the family of the deceased, Rae J. found one of the defendant police officers 20 per cent at fault and the deceased 80 per cent to share. *Cook v. Lewis* and *Dahlberg v. Naydiuk* were relied upon because His Lordship felt bound to do so, but he indicated that he found the reasoning in *Fowler v. Lanning* and *Letang v. Cooper* "persuasive". See also *Tillander v. Gosselin*, [1967] 1 O.R. 203, 60 D.L.R. (2d) 18; affd 61 D.L.R. (2d) 192n (C.A.). *Bell Canada v. Bannermount Ltd.*, [1973] 2 O.R. 811, 35 D.L.R. (3d) 367 (C.A.), buried cable damaged during digging, onus on defendant not discharged; *Venning v. Chin* (1974), 10 S.A.S.R. 299 (Aust.); on appeal (1975), 49 A.L.J.R. (Aust. H.C.), trespass still available though of "dubious justice or utility". See generally Fridman, "Trespass or Negligence" (1971), 9 Alta. L. Rev. 250; Winfield and Goodhart, "Trespass and Negligence" (1933), 49 L.Q.Rev. 359; Trindade, "Comment" (1971), 49 Can. Bar Rev. 612.

5. Why have the Canadian courts taken this line? Are they more conservative than the English? Are they more cowardly? Or are they more progressive in that they are concerned with practical results rather than with theorizing?

   In *Bell Canada v. Cope (Sarnia) Ltd.* (1980), 11 C.C.L.T. 170 (H.C.); affd 31 O.R. (2d) 571, 119 D.L.R. (3d) 254 (C.A.), Mr. Justice Linden stated (in 11 C.C.L.T.):

   > Despite many attacks by judges and scholars, the trespass action has survived in Canada, even though it has long ago been eclipsed both in the United Kingdom and in the United States. The trespass action still performs several functions, one of its most important being a mechanism for shifting the onus of proof of whether there has been intentional or negligent wrongdoing to the defendant, rather than requiring the plaintiff to prove fault. The trespass action, though perhaps somewhat anomalous, may thus help to smoke out evidence possessed by defendants, who cause direct injuries to plaintiffs, which should assist courts to obtain a fuller picture of the facts, a most worthwhile objective.

   Does this make any sense? Is this a good methodology to adopt in achieving this goal? What is wrong with it? See Sullivan, "Trespass to the Person in Canada" (1987), 19 Ottawa L. Rev. 533.

B. ACCIDENTAL, NEGLIGENT, AND INTENTIONAL CONDUCT

KLAR, TORT LAW

(Carswell, 2nd ed., 1996)

All conduct can be seen as falling somewhere along a continuum, with accidental conduct falling at one end, and a deliberate attempt to injure falling at the other. When considering the defendant's conduct as an element of a cause of action in tort, and describing it as accidental, negligent, or intentional, one is having regard to the defendant's state of knowledge and appreciation of the *consequences* of the contemplated act, and the steps which ought to have been taken to avoid them.

Where a defendant acts and produces consequences which were either not reasonably foreseeable or not reasonably preventable, the conduct which produced the result may be seen as being accidental. Where, however, the defendant ought to have reasonably foreseen and avoided the result, the defendant's failure to have done so can be described as negligent. Finally, where a defendant acts either knowing with substantial certainty what the consequences of the act would be, or desiring them, the defendant can be said to have intended these consequences. These differences in knowledge and foreseeability of consequences, and the means which ought to have been taken to avoid them, explain the basic differences between torts of strict liability, negligence, and intention.

GARRATT v. DAILEY

Supreme Court of Washington. 46 Wash. 2d 197, 279 P. 2d 1091 (1955).

The plaintiff alleged that the defendant, aged 5 years, 9 months, pulled a lawn chair out from under her as she was about to sit down. The defendant denied the allegation, claiming that while the plaintiff was in the house he had moved the chair a few feet in order to sit in it, but that when the plaintiff returned to the back yard, she sat down not realizing that the chair had been moved. The trial judge dismissed the case, finding that while the defendant had moved the chair, he had not done so with the intention of injuring the plaintiff. The plaintiff appealed.

Hill J.: A battery would be established if it was proved that, when Brian moved the chair, he knew with substantial certainty that the plaintiff would attempt to sit down where the chair had been. ... The mere absence of any intent to injure the plaintiff or to play a prank on her or to embarrass her, or to commit an assault and battery on her would not absolve him from liability if in fact he had such knowledge.

Case remanded for clarification.

NOTES

1. On retrial, judgment was entered for the plaintiff, which decision was affirmed, 49 Wash. 2d 409, 304 P. 2d 681 (1956).

2. Do you find it odd that the court found that a child, less than six years old, was capable of forming the requisite intention to commit an intentional tort? For cases dealing with "capacity", see *infra*, at p. 40.

RESTATEMENT OF TORTS, SECOND

§8A. Intent

The word "intent" is used throughout the restatement of this Subject to denote that the actor desires to cause consequences of his act, or that he believes that the consequences are substantially certain to result from it.

Comment:

a. "Intent", as it is used through the *Restatement of Torts*, has reference to the consequences of an act rather than the act itself. When an actor fires a gun in the midst of the Mojave Desert, he intends to pull the trigger; but when the bullet hits a person who is present in the desert without the actor's knowledge, he does not intend that result. "Intent" is limited, wherever it is used, to the consequences of the act.

b. All consequences which the actor desires to bring about are intended, as the word is used in this *Restatement*. Intent is not, however, limited to consequences which are desired. If the actor knows that the consequences are certain, or substantially certain, to result from his act, and still goes ahead, he is treated by the law as if he had in fact desired to produce the result. As the probability that the consequences will follow decreases, and becomes less than substantial certainty, the actor's conduct loses the character of intent, and becomes mere recklessness. ... As the probability decreases further, and amounts only to a risk that the result will follow, it becomes ordinary negligence. ... All three have their important place in the law of torts, but the liability attached to them will differ.

NOTES

1. A throws a bomb into B's office for the purpose of killing B. A knows that C, B's stenographer, is in the office. A has no desire to injure C, but knows that his act is substantially certain to do so. C is injured by the explosion. Is A subject to liability to C for an intentional tort?

2. It is sometimes said that the intention here is "constructive" or that it has been "imputed" to the defendant.

CARNES v. THOMPSON

Supreme Court of Missouri. 48 S.W. 2d 903 (1932).

The defendant attempted to evict a former employee and his wife from a house on his farm. An argument developed, and the defendant struck at the employee with a pair of pliers. The employee dodged the blow, and the defendant unintentionally hit the wife, who was standing near her husband. The wife brought an action, in which the jury returned a verdict for the plaintiff, finding no actual damages but $100 punitive damages. Defendant appeals.

Hyde C.: ... Plaintiff's evidence, unquestionably, made a case for the jury. Defendant says that the evidence does not show that he at any time intended injury and harm to the plaintiff, and that he was never close enough to plaintiff's husband to strike him. However, plaintiff's evidence was sufficient to justify a finding that defendant struck at plaintiff's husband, in anger, with the pliers, and that, when he dodged the blow, plaintiff received it. If one person intentionally strikes at, throws at, or shoots at another, and unintentionally strikes a third person, he is not excused, on the ground that it was a mere accident, but it is an assault and battery of the third person. Defendant's intention, in such a case, is to strike an unlawful blow, to injure some person by his act, and it is not essential that the injury be to the one intended. ...

NOTES

1. The doctrine of "transferred intent", depicted in the principal case, came to tort law from the criminal law. It is utilized not only where a different *person* is the victim of a particular nominate tort, but also where a different *tort* results than the one intended, as long as both torts are descendants of the old action of trespass. Thus, if the defendant intends to commit battery, assault, false imprisonment, trespass to land or trespass to chattels, the defendant is liable for any of the others if they accidentally occur. See Prosser, "Transferred Intent" (1967), 45 Tex. L. Rev. 650; see also *Bunyan v. Jordan* (1937), 57 C.L.R. 1, 37 S.R.N.S.W. 119 (H.C. Aust.).

2. Donald shoots at Peter to frighten him. By accident, he hits Peter. What tort liability has arisen? What if Donald shoots at Peter to frighten him and he frightens a stranger, Paul? What if he shoots at Peter to frighten him and he hits the stranger, Paul?

BASELY v. CLARKSON

Common Pleas. (1681), 3 Levinz 37, 83 E.R. 565.

Trespass for breaking his clos called the *balk* and the *hade*, and cutting his grass, and carrying it away. The defendant disclaims any title in the lands of the plaintiff, but says that he hath a *balk* and *hade* adjoining to the *balk* and *hade* of the plaintiff, and in mowing his own land he involuntarily and by mistake mowed down some grass growing upon the *balk* and *hade* of the plaintiff, intending only to mow the grass upon his own *balk* and *hade*, and carried the grass, etc., *quae est eadem*, etc. *Et quod ante emanationem brevis* he tendered to the plaintiff 2s. in satisfaction, and that 2s. was a sufficient amends. Upon this the plaintiff demurred, and had judgment; for it appears the fact was voluntary, and his intention and knowledge are not traversable; they cannot be known.

NOTES

1. This is a case of mistake. Can you explain the result? Was the act voluntary? Was there an intention to intrude?

2. Why do you think the law was so strict in 1681? Should we preserve this rule? Is it as harsh in operation as it seems?

3. The City of Calgary expropriated the plaintiffs' land pursuant to an expropriation order. Many years later, the Supreme Court of Canada declared that the expropriation order was invalid. The plaintiffs sued for trespass. The city said that it did not intend to trespass. Picard J.A. in finding the city liable stated that "a trespass occurs, regardless of consciousness of wrongdoing, if the defendant intends to conduct itself in a certain manner and exercises its volition to do so." See *Costello v. Calgary (City)* (1997), 38 C.C.L.T. (2d) 101 at 112 (Alta. C.A.).

4. Defendant shoots the plaintiff's dog, believing it to be a wolf. Liability? Did the defendant "intend" to kill the dog? See *Ranson v. Kitner*, 31 Ill. App. 241 (1888).

5. An anaesthetized patient, Y, is wheeled into the operating room. Doctor Z performs an appendectomy without negligence, believing reasonably that Y is X, who has consented to such treatment. Y, who was supposed to have a hernia operation, sues Dr. Z. for battery. Result? What if a doctor erroneously operates on the wrong disc? Is this a

negligent battery or an intentional battery? See *Gerula v. Flores* (1995), 126 D.L.R. (4th) 506 (Ont.C.A.).

C. VOLITION AND CAPACITY

SMITH v. STONE

King's Bench. (1647), Styl. 65, 82 E.R. 533.

Smith brought an action of trespass against Stone, *pedibus ambulando*. The defendant pleads this special plea in justification, *viz.*, that he was carried upon the land of the plaintiff by force and violence of others, and was not there voluntarily, which is the same trespass for which the plaintiff brings his action. The plaintiff demurs to this plea. In this case, Rolle J. said that it is the trespass of the party that carried the defendant upon the land, and not the trespass of the defendant as he that drives my cattle into another man's land is the trespasser against him, and not I, who am owner of the cattle.

NOTES

1. What is the difference between voluntariness and intention? Is there such a thing as an intentional act that is not voluntary? Can voluntary conduct be unintentional?

2. Is it voluntary conduct if the defendant, while sleepwalking, enters another's property? See Fridman, "Mental Incompetency" (1964), 80 L.Q.Rev. 87.

3. The defendant, while asleep in the back of the plaintiff's car, pushed the driver's seat forward causing the plaintiff to lose control of the car. Liability? In *Stokes v. Carlson*, 240 S.W. 2d 132 (Mo. 1951), Commissioner Lozier stated:

   > A contraction of muscles which is purely a reaction to some outside force, convulsive movements of an epileptic, movements of the body during sleep, when will is in abeyance, and movements during periods of unconsciousness, are not 'acts' of the person, and the person will not be responsible for injuries inflicted thereby, since such movements are without volition.

4. What if a defendant is so drunk as to be unaware of his or her actions? See *D.P.P. v. Beard*, [1920] A.C. 479, [1920] All E.R. Rep. 21 (H.L.). Is drunkenness any different than sleepwalking? Does it matter whether the case is a civil one or a criminal one?

5. Twelve armed men, by threats, compel the defendant to enter the plaintiff's land to steal a horse. Is the defendant's conduct voluntary? Is it intentional? Should there be liability imposed? What are the conflicting policy goals? See *Gilbert v. Stone* (1648), Sty. 72, 82 E.R. 539.

6. Distinguish between motive and intention. Motive is the reason why an actor acts. Motive is seldom important in tort law. Does this shed any light on the above problem?

7. See Atrens, "Intentional Interference with the Person", in Linden (ed.), *Studies in Canadian Tort Law* (1968), at 378:

It is a general condition of tort liability that the act of the defendant must be voluntary in the sense that it was directed by his conscious mind. Where the defendant is forcibly carried onto the land of the plaintiff there is no voluntary act, and he is not liable for trespass. There is no liability for the results of movements made while asleep. Similarly, to borrow an example from negligence cases, there is no liability for an accident which occurs when the driver of an automobile is rendered unconscious by sudden illness, which he could not, as a reasonable man, have anticipated. Volition, in the above sense, may be present even though the act was performed under pressure from circumstances beyond the control of the actor under conditions which negative liability; for example, where he acted in self defence. Whether an act is voluntary when the mind directing it is incapable, due to mental illness, of exercising normal control is a matter of definition. As will be seen later, the authorities indicate that such incapacity is no defence.

TILLANDER v. GOSSELIN

Ontario High Court. [1967] 1 O.R. 203, 60 D.L.R. (2d) 18; affd 61 D.L.R. (2d) 192n (C.A.).

The infant defendant, one week less than three years old, removed the infant baby from her carriage and dragged her over 100 feet, fracturing her skull and causing some brain damage.

Grant J.: ... The infant defendant at the time of this mishap was about one week less than 3 years of age. If he was capable of forming an intent to do what he did his actions would amount to an assault. The question to be decided is, can an infant of that age be held responsible in damages in such circumstances?

The action is framed in trespass. It cannot be said to be in negligence because the defendant had no right whatever to touch or remove the infant.

It is clear that a child of such tender years could not be guilty of negligence. The reasons for such conclusion is that such an infant is considered to be lacking in sufficient judgment to exercise that reasonable care that is expected of one. His normal condition is one of recognized incompetency and he is devoid of ability to make effective use of such knowledge as he may have at that early age. ...

In recent years the weight of authority is to the effect that no action will lie in trespass if the act is not wrongful, either through wilfulness or as being the result of negligence. ...

The law applicable is fully discussed by Clyne J. of the British Columbia Supreme Court in a very learned judgment in *Walmsley et al. v. Humenick*, [1954] 2 D.L.R. 232, who reviewed the many cases touching on the point in question. In that case injury had been sustained by one of two five-year-old boys who were playing with bows and arrows. The learned trial judge held that the infant defendant could not be found guilty of negligence because of his tender years and as it was admitted that there was no intention on his part to injure, the plaintiff could not succeed.

Section 12 of the *Criminal Code* is as follows:

> 12. No person shall be convicted of an offence in respect of an act or omission on his part while he was under the age of seven years.

The reason for such provision is that a child under that age is considered incapable of knowing the nature and consequence of his conduct and to appreciate that it is wrong.

Although there has been considerable agitation in legal circles for the adoption of a theory of strict liability in the cases where one individual suffers physical or financial damage as the direct result of another's act, the present state of the law recognizes no such rule. The result of the decisions in *Holmes v. Mather*, *supra*; *Stanley v. Powell*, *supra*, and *Walmsley et al. v. Humenick*, *supra*, and the unequivocal words of Cartwright J., of the Supreme Court of Canada in *Cook v. Lewis*, *supra*, is this: in an action for damages in trespass where the plaintiff proves that he has been injured by the direct act of the defendant, the onus falls upon the defendant to prove that his act was both unintentional and without negligence on his part. If he fails to do so, the plaintiff must succeed: but if he succeeds, he is entitled to judgment dismissing the claim. In this action, the defendant's tender age at the time of the alleged assault satisfies me that he cannot be cloaked with the mental ability of the ordinary reasonable man and hence negligence cannot be imputed to him. That same condition satisfies me that he cannot be said to have acted deliberately and with intention when the injuries were inflicted upon the infant plaintiff.

I do not believe that one can describe the act of a normal three-year-old child in doing injury to the baby plaintiff in this case as a voluntary act on his part. There is no evidence as to what instrument, if any, was used to inflict the injury. The infant plaintiff may have been struck by some object or she might have been dropped on a stone, but as indicated, the plaintiff's rights must be considered on the basis of an action for assault. The defendant child, however, would not have the mental ability at the age of three to appreciate or know the real nature of the act he was performing. A child of that age emulates or imitates the actions of those about him rather than making his own decisions. In the present case there could be no genuine intent formulated in his mind to do harm to the child plaintiff or to perform whatever act he did that caused the injury.

For these reasons the action must be dismissed, but under the circumstances without costs.

Action dismissed.

NOTES

1. Is the basis of this decision the lack of intention or the absence of a voluntary act?

2. Is there a battery if a 6-year-old child pushes another child who falls and breaks a leg? In *Baldinger v. Banks*, 201 N.Y.S. 2d 629 (1960), Mr. Justice Baker imposed liability in such a case, saying:

   > ... the proof clearly indicates that the defendant, despite his tender years, had the capacity of mind to know and did, in fact, know, as would any normal 6 year old child, that his act, under the circumstances disclosed in the proof, was offensive; and it is equally clear that it was so intended.

   See also *Hawryluk v. Otruba* (1987), 62 O.R. (2d) 154, 42 C.C.L.T. 306 (H.C.), person pushed off hayride.

3. Should small children be held liable like adults for their conduct? Why would an injured person sue a young child in tort? What damages could a victim recover? Many American states have laws which make parents liable for the damage intentionally caused by their children to other persons or to their property. These laws were enacted

to encourage parents to control their children more effectively. Generally speaking, Canadian provinces do not have such provisions, although Manitoba has enacted the *Parental Responsibility Act*, S.M. 1996, c. 61 which makes parents liable, up to $5000, for damage to property deliberately caused by the child subject to the parent proving reasonable supervision and efforts to prevent the activity. Do you think that more provinces should adopt such legislation? What negative results might flow from laws which make parents liable for the damage caused by their children?

4. Zellers department store sent a letter to the plaintiff informing her that her 14-year-old son had been caught shoplifting. He had been apprehended as he was leaving the store with $46.96 of unpaid goods. The letter advised the plaintiff that she was legally responsible for this theft but that Zellers would settle their civil claim against her if she paid restitution of $225, to cover their damages and costs; otherwise Zellers would sue. The plaintiff paid. A while later, after receiving legal advice, the plaintiff sued Zellers for her money back. Was the plaintiff liable for the amount claimed, as Zellers had claimed? If not, should she get her money back? See *B.(D.C.) v. Arkin*, [1996] 8 W.W.R. 100, 138 D.L.R. (4th) 309 (Man. Q.B.); leave to appeal to C.A. refused [1996] 10 W.W.R. 689 (C.A.).

5. The current *Criminal Code* excuses persons under the age of 12 years from criminal liability. See R.S.C. 1985, c. C-46, s. 13. What effect, if any, should this have on tort liability?

6. See Alexander, "Tort Liability of Children and Their Parents" in *Studies in Canadian Family Law* (1972), at 845. See generally Wilson and Tomlinson, *Children and The Law*, 2nd ed. (1978).

LAWSON v. WELLESLEY HOSPITAL

Ontario Court of Appeal. (1975), 61 D.L.R. (3d) 445,
9 O.R. (2d) 677; affd on another ground, [1978] 1 S.C.R. 893,
76 D.L.R. (3d) 688.

The plaintiff, a non-psychiatric patient of the defendant hospital, sought damages for injuries sustained as the result of an attack by a psychiatric patient (Coxall) with a history of violent conduct. The action against the hospital was founded on an alleged breach of contract to provide care and protection to the plaintiff and, alternately, on the negligence of the hospital in permitting Coxall to be at large without adequate control or supervision.

The County Court Judge held that the action was barred by s. 59 of the *Mental Health Act*, R.S.O. 1970, c. 269, which reads:

> No action lies against any psychiatric facility or any officer, employee or servant thereof for a tort of any patient.

The Court of Appeal reversed this ruling and a further appeal to the Supreme Court of Canada was dismissed on the ground that the section could not relieve the hospital of liability for its own negligence. The Supreme Court refrained from considering the matter of the mental element required to commit a tort.

The majority in the Court of Appeal, however, held that s. 59 would be inapplicable if it were found that the patient was incapable of intending to commit a tort.

Dubin J.A.: ... I think it is now well established that if a mentally ill person is by reason of his illness incapable of the intent to assault a person, he is not liable in an action founded upon that assault.

I accept the principle that it is an essential element in the tort of assault that there be a voluntary act, the mind prompting and directing the act which is complained of. The authorities on that issue are fully canvassed in the judgment of McGregor, J., in *Beals v. Hayward*, [1960] N.Z.L.R. 131. However, in view of the observations in *Cook v. Lewis*, [1952] 1 D.L.R. 1, [1951] S.C.R. 830, the onus of showing that the act was involuntary appears to be on the person who makes that assertion.

In the instant case, if the plaintiff establishes the averments in the statement of claim, *i.e.*, that the patient Rupert suffered from such a profound mental disorder that he was incapable of appreciating the nature or quality of his act, no action would lie against him at the suit of the plaintiff. It is sometimes said that mental illness excuses one from liability for the tort committed by him. See 87 Hals. 3rd ed., p. 134, para. 236:

> Persons suffering from mental disorder are not liable for their tortious acts where, by reason of their mental infirmity, they are unable to understand the nature and consequences of their acts or, where intention is an element of the tort, they are unable to form the necessary intention.

However, with respect, I think it more accurate to state that where a person, by reason of mental illness, is incapable of appreciating the nature or quality of his acts, such person has committed no tort since the intention, which is an essential element of the cause of action, is missing. Prosser, *Handbook of the Law of Torts*, 4th ed. (1971), p. 1001, puts it this way:

> It has been recognized, however, that his insanity may be such that he is incapable of entertaining the specific intent necessary for a particular tort, such as deceit, malicious prosecution, defamation, or even battery, and so he should not be liable simply because he has not committed the tort.

In any event, unless the act complained of is one for which redress will be awarded by way of damages, it is not a tort. That being so, I am respectfully of the opinion that the learned County Court Judge erred in dismissing the action on the preliminary question of law. He ought to have let the action proceed to trial where the ultimate determination would have to be made as to whether the conduct of the psychiatric patient constituted a tort. ...

Appeal allowed;
Order directing that the action proceed to trial.

NOTES

1. What is the law concerning the mentally disabled and the requisite mental state required for the tort of battery? Did the court decide on the basis of lack of intention or lack of voluntariness? Do you agree with this decision?

2. In *Phillips v. Soloway* (1956), 6 D.L.R. (2d) 570, 19 W.W.R. 673 (Man. Q.B.), the defendant attacked the plaintiff with a knife, cutting an eye so badly that the eyeball had to be removed. To a defence of insanity, Williams C.J.Q.B. stated that the *M'Naghten* rules "are not applicable in a civil action of tort". He also found that defendant knew the nature and quality of his act but held "that it makes no difference

whether the defendant was or was not capable of knowing that his act was wrong." Plaintiff obtained judgment. Should there be a different test for tort and crime? Or should it be the same?

3. Mr. Justice Galligan employed this test in *Squittieri v. de Santis* (1976), 15 O.R. (2d) 416, 75 D.L.R. (3d) 629 (H.C.J.), where the defendant, who stabbed someone to death, was sued by the family in tort, even though he was found not guilty in the criminal trial by reason of insanity. His Lordship imposed liability and explained:

> ... it appears to be clear on the authorities that regardless of whether or not a person because of insanity did not know that his act was wrong, if he intended to kill and appreciated the nature and quality of his acts, the defence of insanity is not available to him.
>
> In this case, as I have indicated, he not only intended to kill but he appreciated that his conduct would result in the death and he knew and appreciated that at the time he was killing a man with a knife.

4. See also *Tindale v. Tindale*, [1950] 4 D.L.R. 363, [1950] 1 W.W.R. 941 (B.C.S.C.), where a mother, suffering under insane delusions, attacked her daughter with an axe. Macfarlane J. imposed liability on the mother. He assumed that the onus was on the defendant to establish that the insanity was "so extreme as to preclude any genuine intention to do the act complained of". The question of whether she "knew what she was doing was wrong for her to do or that her act was voluntary in the sense that she was capable of making a deliberate choice is much more difficult". He concluded by saying that the "child here is an innocent and unfortunate sufferer on whom no fault can possibly lie ... [and] ... the estate of the mother should be used, so far as it avails, to provide for the necessary medical expenses of the child ... in her crippled condition".

5. In two early Ontario cases, *Stanley v. Hayes* (1904), 8 O.L.R. 81 and *Taggard v. Innes* (1862), 12 U.C.C.P. 77, the defence of insanity was held to be unavailable to a lunatic who burned down a barn. Three policy reasons were advanced by the court: (1) when one of two innocent parties must bear a loss, the person must bear it whose act caused it; (2) if liability is imposed, relatives might be under inducement to restrain the lunatic; (3) the vexing problems of the criminal law with regard to simulation of insanity might be kept out of tort law. Eventually, the Ontario courts reversed themselves and allowed the insanity plea in tort cases. Were they wise to do so?

6. In *Gerigs v. Rose* (1979), 9 C.C.L.T. 222 (Ont. S.C.), the plaintiff, a police officer, was called to investigate a report that a man with a gun was threatening another person. The plaintiff went to the house, and when he entered he was shot by the defendant. The plaintiff instituted proceedings in assault. The defendant raised two defences — contributory negligence and mental incapacity.

Mr. Justice Eberle rejected both defences, after reviewing several recent authorities, including *Lawson v. Wellesley Hospital*, *supra*; *Squittieri v. de Santis*, *supra*; and *Phillips v. Soloway*, *supra*. His Lordship stated:

> When one comes to the area of civil cases, I am doubtful that the second of these tests (that is, whether an act or omission is wrong) has any real relevance. ... It is my view, on the basis of the authorities, that it is a sufficient defence in a civil case if the defendant establishes, on a balance of probabilities, that he did not, by reason of mental infirmity, appreciate the nature and quality of his acts; but if the defendant does not meet that onus of proof, then the defence is not made out.

It was Mr. Justice Eberle's view that the *moral* aspect of the defendant's act and the defendant's ability to appreciate this, is not a relevant consideration in civil cases.

However, in the course of his judgment Mr. Justice Eberle substituted the words "appreciate the nature and *consequence* of his acts" for the words "appreciate the nature and *quality* of his acts".

Are the words "consequence" and "quality" synonymous? What do the words "nature of one's acts", "quality of one's acts", and "consequences of one's acts" mean? As a layperson, as opposed to a psychiatrist, can you understand the subtle differences which these words suggest? Mr. Justice Eberle made the following comments on this aspect of the case:

> In the phrasing of the test, 'Was the defendant able to appreciate the nature and consequences of his act?' it appears to me that the word 'nature' focuses on the physical aspects of the act. 'Consequence' focuses on what may follow from it; in this sense, that is, what will a bullet do if it is fired from a gun and hits someone, what will it do to that person? In my view, the word "consequence" does not refer directly to the moral aspect of the act (*i.e.*, whether the acts are right or wrong), for that is the other branch of the test for criminal cases in s. 16 of the Code. I say we are not concerned, in civil cases with that branch of s. 16.
>
> The evidence of the psychiatrist, however, was based on his view of the meaning of the word 'consequence'; and it is clear from his evidence that he included as an element in the word 'consequence', the moral element of whether or not the acts were right or wrong. In my view, that is not the proper meaning in law of the word 'consequence'.
>
> Therefore, when, in the doctor's evidence, in answer to other questions, he suggested that in his view the defendant could not appreciate the consequence of the acts, he was clearly referring to the moral aspects of the acts, with which, in this case, we are not concerned.

7. See Bohlen, "Liability in Tort of Infants and Insane Persons" (1924), 23 Mich. L. Rev. 9; Robins, "Tort Liability of the Mentally Disabled," in Linden (ed.), *Studies in Canadian Tort Law* (1968), at 76, and in *Special Lectures of the Law Society of Upper Canada* (1963); Picher, "The Tortious Liability of the Insane in Canada" (1975), 13 Osgoode Hall L.J. 193; Fridman, "Mental Incompetency" Part II (1964), 80 L.Q. Rev. 84; Robertson, *Mental Disability and the Law in Canada* (1987), Ch. 9.

D. ASSAULT

I. DE S. & WIFE v. W. DE S.

(1348), Year-Book, Liber Assisarum, folio 99, p. 60.

I. *De S. & M. uxor ejus querunt de W. de S. de eo quod idem W. anno, &c., vi et armis, &c., apud S., in ipsam M. insultum fecit, et ipsam verberavit &c.* And W. pleaded not guilty. And it was found by verdict of the inquest that the said W. came in the night to the house of the said I., and would have bought some wine but the door of the tavern was closed; and he pounded on the door with a hatchet, which he had in his hand, and the female plaintiff put her head out at a window and told him to stop; and he saw her and struck at her with the hatchet, but did not hit her. Whereupon the inquest said that it seemed to them that there was no trespass, since there was no harm done.

Thorpe C.J.: There is harm done, and a trespass for which they shall recover damages, since he made an assault upon the woman as it is found, although he did no other harm. Wherefore tax his damages, &c. and they taxed the damages at half a mark. ... *Et sic. nota*, that for an assault one shall recover damages, &c.

STEPHENS v. MYERS

Nisi Prius. (1830), 4 C. & P. 349, 172 E.R. 735.

Assault. The declaration stated, that the defendant threatened and attempted to assault the plaintiff. Plea — not guilty.

It appeared, that the plaintiff was acting as chairman, at a parish meeting, and sat at the head of a table, at which table the defendant also sat, there being about six or seven persons between him and the plaintiff. The defendant having, in the course of some angry discussion which took place, been very vociferous, and interrupted the proceedings of the meeting, a motion was made, that he should be turned out, which was carried by a very large majority. Upon this, the defendant said, he would rather pull the chairman out of the chair than be turned out of the room; and immediately advanced with his fist clenched toward the chairman, but was stopped by the churchwarden, who sat next but one to the chairman, at a time when he was not near enough for any blow he might have meditated to have reached the chairman; but the witnesses said, that it seemed to them that he was advancing with intention to strike the chairman.

Spankie, Serit., for the defendant, upon this evidence, contended, that no assault had been committed, as there was no power in the defendant, from the situation of the parties, to execute his threat — there was not a present ability — he had not the means of executing his intention at the time he was stopped.

Tindal C.J., in his summing up, said: It is not every threat, when there is no actual personal violence, that constitutes an assault, there must, in all cases, be the means of carrying the threat into effect. The question I shall leave to you will be, whether the defendant was advancing at the time, in a threatening attitude, to strike the chairman, so that his blow would almost immediately have reached the chairman, if he had not been stopped; then, though he was not near enough at the time to have struck him, yet if he was advancing with that intent, I think it amounts to an assault in law. If he was so advancing, that, within a second or two of time, he would have reached the plaintiff, it seems to me it is an assault in law. If you think he was not advancing to strike the plaintiff, then only can you find your verdict for the defendant; otherwise you must find it for the plaintiff, and give him such damages as you think the nature of the case requires.

Verdict for the plaintiff, damages 1 s.

TUBERVILLE v. SAVAGE

King's Bench. (1699), 1 Mod. 3, 2 Keble 545, 86 E.R. 684.

Action of assault, battery and wounding. The defendant pleaded the plaintiff began first; and the stroke he received, whereby he lost his eye, was on his own assault, and in defence of the defendant. The evidence to prove a provocation was, that the plaintiff put his hand upon his sword and said, "If it were not assize-time, I would not take such language from you." The question was, if that were an assault.

The court agreed that it was not; for the declaration of the plaintiff was that he would not assault him, the judges being in town; and the intention as well as the act makes an assault. Therefore, if one strike another upon the hand or arm or breast, in discourse, it is no assault, there being no intention to assault; but if one, intending to assault, strike at another and miss him, this is an assault; so if he hold up his hand against another in a threatening manner and say nothing, it is an assault. In the principal case the plaintiff had judgment.

NOTES

1. Suppose the defendant said to the plaintiff, "Come one step closer, and I'll run you through." Assault? *Cf., Police v. Greaves*, [1964] N.Z.L.R. 295 (C.A.).

2. Suppose the defendant said, "I'll run you through, if you don't get out of here"? *Cf., Read v. Coker* (1853), 13 C.B. 850, 138 E.R. 1437.

3. What if he said, "Give me all your money, or I'll run you through"? *Cf., Restatement of Torts, Second* §30; *Holcombe v. Whittaker*, 318 So. 2d 289 (1975).

4. The defendant telephones the plaintiff and informs him that he is coming over to shoot him. The plaintiff, understandably, becomes apprehensive. Assault? The defendant arrives and knocks on the door. Assault now? The plaintiff answers the door and sees the defendant standing there with a gun pointed in his direction. Is there an assault now?

5. Does it make any difference if the gun is not loaded? Compare *Blake v. Barnard* (1840), 9 C. & P. 626, 173 E.R. 985; *R. v. St. George* (1840), 9 C. & P. 483, 173 E.R. 921; *Allen v. Hannaford*, 138 Wash. 423, 244 P. 700 (1926). See the *Criminal Code*, R.S.C. 1985, c. C-46, s. 87(1) which reads:

   > 87. (1) Every person commits an offence who, without lawful excuse, points a firearm at another person, whether the firearm is loaded or unloaded.

   What impact, if any, should this have on civil liability for assault?

6. Does it make any difference whether the plaintiff knew or did not know the gun was loaded? What interest is being protected here?

7. A points a gun at B, who is asleep, intending to shoot him. A changes his mind and goes away. B, upon awakening, hears about the incident and suffers a heart attack. What arguments would you advance on behalf of B? On behalf of A? What do you think a court would do with the case?

8. Does the plaintiff have to be "afraid" of the defendant? Suppose a little man shakes his fist in the nose of a heavyweight champion, who merely laughs at him. Assault? See *Brady v. Schatzel*, [1911] Q.S.R. 206.

9. It is sometimes said that words alone cannot amount to an assault. See *Read v. Coker* (1853), 13 C.B. 850, 138 E.R. 1437. Is it an assault if you telephone someone and say, "I have put dynamite in the telephone you are now holding and I am pushing the plunger that will cause it to blow up this instant"? See Handford, "Tort Liability for Threatening or Insulting Words" (1976), 54 Can. Bar Rev. 563, who argues for the adoption of §31, *Restatement of Torts Second*, which reads:

   > Words do not make an actor liable for assault, unless together with other acts or circumstances they put the other in reasonable apprehension of an imminent harmful or offensive contact with his person.

10. It is now a criminal offence to convey a threat of death or injury "in any manner". See the *Criminal Code*, R.S.C. 1985, c. C-46, s. 264.1. What effect, if any, on tort law? See Law Reform Commission of Canada, Working Paper No. 38, *Assault* (1984).

11. It is sometimes said that there must be some motion by the defendant before an assault is committed. Is it an assault if someone stands motionless, but pointing a gun at you?

12. Does tort law have any business trying to regulate this kind of conduct? Is the criminal law insufficient? Are we wasting our time on trivia? Or is this conduct more significant than it sometimes seems? Or should the criminal law stand aside, restrain itself, and let tort law regulate this type of conduct?

BRUCE v. DYER

[1970] 1 O.R. 482, 8 D.L.R. (3d) 592; affg [1966] 2 O.R. 705, 58 D.L.R. (2d) 211.

The plaintiff and defendant were driving in their respective cars in the same direction along a busy highway. When the defendant, attempting to pass a panel truck which was driving in front of the plaintiff's car, tried to re-enter the driving lane in front of the plaintiff, the plaintiff accelerated his car and prevented the defendant's re-entry. This forced the defendant to apply his brakes and to re-enter the driving lane behind the plaintiff's car. After the defendant followed the plaintiff for some distance, the plaintiff stopped his car in front of the defendant's and signalled for the defendant to stop. After both drivers got out of their cars, a fight ensued in which the defendant fractured the plaintiff's jaw. In an action brought by the plaintiff against the defendant, the defendant claimed self-defence on the basis that the plaintiff's conduct on the highway constituted an assault.

Ferguson J. (at trial): [After reviewing the facts] The law concerning assault goes back to earliest times. The striking of a person against his will has been, broadly speaking, always regarded as an assault. It has been defined in the 8th American Edition of *Russell on Crime* as "an attempt or offer with force and violence to do a corporal hurt to another". So an attempted assault is itself an assault; so an attempt to strike another is an assault even though no contact has been made.

Usually, when there is no actual intention to use violence there can be no assault. When there is no power to use violence to the knowledge of the plaintiff there can be no assault. There need not be in fact any actual intention or power to use violence, for it is enough if the plaintiff on reasonable grounds believes that he is in fact in danger of violence. So if a person shakes his fist at another the person so assaulted may strike back, if he, on reasonable grounds, believes that he is in danger.

When the plaintiff emerged from his vehicle waving his fist, I think the defendant had reasonable grounds for believing that he was about to be attacked and that it was necessary for him to take some action to ward it off.

In *Salmond on Torts*, 8th ed., p. 373, the following passage appears based on *R. v. St. George* (1840), 9 Car. & P. 483, 173 E.R. 921:

> There need be no actual intention or power to use violence, for it is enough if the plaintiff on reasonable grounds believes that he is in danger of it.

More modern cases point out that even if it later appears that no violence was intended, it is sufficient if the defendant or a reasonable man thinks that it is intended.

Bruce had not only emerged from his vehicle shaking his fist but in addition he blocked the defendant's passage on the road. In my opinion that blocking action on his part was an assault.

In *Innes v. Wylie* (1844), 1 Car. & K. 257, 174 E.R. 800, a plaintiff who had been expelled from a club attempted to enter the rooms of the club, but was prevented by a policeman who stood in the doorway and refused to move to let the plaintiff pass. Lord Denman C.J., instructing the jury, said [p. 263]:

> You will say, whether, on the evidence, you think the policeman committed an assault on the plaintiff, or was merely passive. If the policeman was entirely passive like a door or a wall put to prevent the plaintiff from entering the room, and simply obstructing the entrance of the plaintiff, no assault has been committed on the plaintiff, and your verdict will be for the defendant. The question is, did the policeman take any active measures to prevent the plaintiff from entering the room, or did he stand in the door-way passive, and not move at all.

The jury returned a verdict for the plaintiff so presumably they found that the policeman had taken active measures to block the plaintiff's way. So the police, I think, commit an assault when they bar the way of a householder from entering his own house by standing in the gateway with an arm projecting from his body or without lawful authority bar the way of one's motor vehicle.

If the plaintiff in the case at bar had left his auto in some place where subsequently it had blocked the defendant's way, I have no doubt that the proper remedy would be an action on the case, but when, as here, he drove his car to a position on the roadway to block the defendant's vehicle, he took active steps to block the defendant and so committed an assault upon him. The defendant was then justified in defending himself from the assault thus imposed upon him: *Re Lewis* (1874), 6 P.R. (Ont.) 236, where Gwynne J. illustrates when the action is one for assault or on the case. When a person is assaulted he may do more than ward off a blow, he may strike back: *R. v. Morse* (1910), 4 Ct. App. R. 50.

[The trial judge then applied the defence of self-defence to exonerate the defendant. This was upheld on appeal].

NOTES

1. Is the conclusion of Mr. Justice Ferguson that the blocking amounted to an assault consistent with the authorities? If not, is it in error or is it a bold new breakthrough? How did the Ontario Court of Appeal deal with this problem?

2. Did Mr. Bruce commit an assault when he closed the gap and kept Dr. Dyer from re-entering the driving lane from the passing lane?

3. Would an assault have been committed if Dr. Dyer had "tailgated" Mr. Bruce with his lights on high beam as alleged?

4. Would any tort liability have arisen if, as a result of the punch, Dr. Dyer had broken his own fist instead of Mr. Bruce's jaw?

5. The phenomenon called "road rage" is a serious social problem. Should tort law be employed more frequently to control the conduct of drivers who seem unable to exercise self-control while in their cars? See, for example, *Herman v. Graves*, [1998] 9 W.W.R. 542, 35 M.V.R. (3d) 197, 61 Alta. L.R. (3d) 17 (Alta. Q.B.).

6. If a driver attempts to scare someone by purposely swerving his or her car into that person without the intention to actually strike him or her, has an assault been committed? What happens if the driver does accidentally come into contact with the victim? See *Herbert v. Misuga* (1994), 111 D.L.R. (4th) 193 (Sask. C.A.).

RESTATEMENT OF TORTS, SECOND

§21. Assault.

(1) An actor is subject to liability to another for assault if

(a) he acts intending to cause a harmful or offensive contact with the person of the other or a third person, or an imminent apprehension of such a contact, and

(b) the other is thereby put in such imminent apprehension.

(2) An action which is not done with the intention stated in Sub-section (1)(a) does not make the actor liable to the other for an apprehension caused thereby although the act involves an unreasonable risk of causing it and, therefore, would be negligent or reckless if the risk threatened bodily harm.

CRIMINAL CODE OF CANADA

R.S.C. 1985, c. C-46, s. 265

265.(1) A person commits an assault when

(a) without the consent of another person, he applies force intentionally to that other person, directly or indirectly;

(b) he attempts or threatens, by an act or a gesture, to apply force to another person, if he has, or causes that other person to believe upon reasonable grounds that he has, present ability to effect his purpose …

E. BATTERY

COLE v. TURNER

Nisi Prius. (1705), 6 Mod. 149, 87 E.R. 907.

Holt C.J.: Upon evidence in trespass for assault and battery, declared:

First, that the least touching of another in anger is a battery.

Secondly, if two or more meet in a narrow passage, and without any violence or design of harm, the one touches the other gently, it will be no battery.

Thirdly, if either of them use violence against the other, to force his way in a rude inordinate manner, it will be a battery; or any struggle about the passage to that degree as may do hurt, will be a battery.

RESTATEMENT OF TORTS, SECOND

§13. Battery: Harmful Contact

An actor is subject to liability to another for battery if

(a) the acts intending to cause a harmful or offensive contact with the person of the other or a third person, or an imminent apprehension of such a contact, and

(b) a harmful contact with the person of the other directly or indirectly results.

NOTES

1. In *Stewart v. Stonehouse* (1926), 20 Sask. L.R. 459, [1926] 1 W.W.R. 929 (C.A.), McKay J.A. said:

> I find defendant did grab plaintiff by the nose and did commit an assault upon him. There is no evidence that plaintiff was physically injured on this occasion, but he is entitled to damages, nevertheless, for the assault. To touch a person without his consent or some lawful reason is actionable. … Judge Salmond in his *Law of Torts*, 6th ed., at pp. 419-420 says: "In respect of his personal dignity, therefore, a man may recover substantial damages for an assault which has done no physical harm whatever".

2. In *Collins v. Wilcock*, [1984] 3 All E.R. 374, at 378, [1984] 1 W.L.R. 1172, it was said:

> The fundamental principle, plain and incontestable, is that every persons's body is inviolate. It has long been established that any touching of another person, however slight, may amount to a battery.

3. Must there be an intention to cause injury? Is a "hostile" intent required? If so, what is meant by "hostile"? Is it ill will or malevolence? Is illegal conduct necessarily hostile? What about rough "horseplay" among young people? See *Wilson v. Pringle*, [1986] 2 All E.R. 440, at 447, [1986] 3 W.L.R. 1 (C.A.). In *Collins v. Wilcock*, L.J. Golf suggested that "physical contact generally acceptable in the ordinary conduct of life" was not actionable. Is this a useful test? Should it be a question of law or fact?

4. Is it a battery if X kicks Y in the rear end? See *Soon v. Jong et al.* (1968), 70 D.L.R. (2d) 160 (B.C.S.C.). What about an unsolicited hug? See *Spivey v. Battaglia*, 258 So. 2d 815 (S.C. Fla. 1972).

5. Jones, with the intention of attracting the attention of Smith, taps her on the shoulder. Is this a battery? What if Jones is excited and taps Smith with considerable force? Compare with *Coward v. Baddeley* (1859), 4 H. & N. 478, 157 E.R. 927 (Ex.).

6. In *Morgan v. Loyacomo*, 190 Miss. 656, 1 So. 2d 510 (1941), the defendants forcibly seized a package from under the plaintiff's arm. Mr. Justice Griffiths stated:

> The authorities are agreed that, to constitute an assault and battery, it is not necessary to touch the plaintiff's body or even his clothing; knocking or snatching anything from plaintiff's hand or touching anything connected with his person, when done in a rude or insolent manner, is sufficient.

See also *Fisher v. Carrousel Motor Hotel*, 424 S.W. 2d 627 (Tex. 1967).

7. Is it a battery if someone punches the horse you are riding on? What if someone kicks the tire of the car you are driving? What if someone intentionally bumps into the rear end of the car you are driving?

8. Can a kiss be a battery?

9. What if you are kissed while you are asleep and only find out about it later? What is the interest being protected here?

10. You are on a fast-moving bus and start to fall. You reach out and grab another passenger's leg. Battery? What if you grab the other bus passenger's leg not to steady yourself, but merely for enjoyment?

11. Is there a battery if the defendant spills water on someone? See *Soon v. Jong, supra*.

12. What if a defendant spits in a plaintiff's face? In *Alcorn v. Mitchell*, 63 Ill. 553 (1872), the defendant spat in the face of the plaintiff. Mr. Justice Sheldon, in upholding a trial verdict in favour of the plaintiff, said:

> The act in question was one of the greatest indignity, highly provocative of retaliation by force, and the law, as far as it may, should afford substantial protection against such outrages, in the way of liberal damages, that the public tranquility may be preserved by saving the necessity of resort to personal violence as the only means of redress.

13. Is there a battery if someone blows cigarette smoke in someone else's face?

14. Is there a battery if the plaintiff, in advance, forbids the defendant from making a contact that would ordinarily be considered inoffensive?

15. Is it a battery if a person, knowingly suffering from herpes, intentionally communicates the disease to another person through sexual activity? See *Kathleen K. v. Robert B.*, 198 Cal. Reptr. 273 (C.A. 1984).

BETTEL ET AL. v. YIM

Ontario County Court. (1978), 20 O.R. (2d) 617,
88 D.L.R. (3d) 543, 5 C.C.L.T. 66.

The plaintiff and his friends threw lighted matches into the defendant's store, one of which, thrown by the plaintiff, caused a bag of charcoal to ignite. The defendant grabbed hold of the plaintiff with both hands and while shaking him the defendant's head came in contact with the plaintiff's nose, severely injuring it. The defendant's purpose in grabbing and shaking the plaintiff was to force him to confess that he had set the fire. The defendant had no intention to injure the plaintiff in the manner which he did although he did intend to grasp him firmly by the collar and to shake him.

Borins (County Court Judge): The plaintiff has framed his action in assault. Properly speaking the action should have been framed in battery which is the intentional infliction upon the body of another of a harmful or offensive contact. However, in Canada it would appear that the distinction between assault and battery has been blurred and when one speaks of an assault, it may include a battery: *Gambriell v. Caparelli* (1974), 7 O.R. (2d) 205, 54 D.L.R. (3d) 661. It is on the basis that this is an action framed in battery that I approach the facts in this case.

It would appear to be well established in this country (although not necessarily warmly received), following the dictum of Cartwright, J. (as he then was), in *Cook v. Lewis*, [1951] S.C.R. 830 at p. 839, [1952] 1 D.L.R. 1 at p. 15, that once the plaintiff proves that he was injured by the direct act of the defendant, the defendant is entitled to judgment only "if he satisfies the onus of establishing the absence of both intention and negligence on his part": *Dahlberg v. Naydiuk* (1969), 10 D.L.R. (3d) 319, 72 W.W.R. 210 (Man. C.A.), *per* Dickson, J.A. (as he then was), at pp. 328-9. On the defendant's evidence, his act in grabbing the plaintiff with both his hands and shaking him constituted the intentional tort of battery. It is obvious that he desired to bring about an offensive or harmful contact with the plaintiff for the purpose of extracting a confession from him. Viewed as such, the defendant's own evidence proves, rather than disproves, the element of intent in so far as this aspect of his physical contact with the plaintiff is concerned. Indeed, the defendant's admitted purpose in grabbing and shaking the plaintiff does not fit into any of the accepted defences to the tort of battery — consent, self-defence, defence of property, necessity and legal authority: Fleming, *Law of Torts*, 5th ed. (1977), p. 74 *et seq.* Furthermore, assuming the onus created by *Cook v. Lewis* requires the defendant to establish absence of negligence in the sense that he must show that his trespass was not careless (which, I readily concede, can be seen to be a contradiction in terms), it is my opinion that he has failed to do so. In grabbing the plaintiff and shaking him firmly, it ought to have been apparent to the defendant that in doing so he created the risk of injury to the plaintiff resulting from some part of the plaintiff's body coming into contact with some part of the defendant's body while the plaintiff was being shaken. If Cartwright, J., meant that the defendant must disprove negligence such as would give rise to an action in negligence, the defendant would be put in a very unusual position because, with respect, the element of negligence is, by definition, absent from the intentional tort of battery.

That there is no liability for accidental harm is central to the submission of defence counsel who argues that the shaking of the plaintiff by the defendant and the striking of the plaintiff by the defendant's head must be regarded as separate and distinct incidents. While he concedes that the defendant intentionally grabbed and shook the plaintiff, he submits that the contact with the head was unintentional. I have, of course, accepted the defendant's evidence in this regard. This, in my view, gives rise to the important question: Can an intentional wrongdoer be held liable for consequences which he did not intend? Another way of stating the problem is to ask whether the doctrine of foreseeability as found in the law of negligence is applicable to the law of intentional torts? Should an intentional wrongdoer be liable only for the reasonably foreseeable consequences of his intentional application of force or should he bear responsibility for all the consequences which flow from his intentional act?

To approach this issue one must first examine what interests the law seeks to protect. A thorough discussion of the history of the old actions of trespass and case is found in Prosser, *Law of Torts*, 4th ed. (1971), p. 28 *et seq.* Terms such as battery, assault and false imprisonment, which were varieties of trespass, have come to be associated with intent. The old action on the case has emerged as the separate tort of negligence. Today it is recognized that there should be no liability for pure accident, and that for there to be liability the defendant must be found at fault, in the sense of being chargeable with a wrongful intent, or with negligence. Thus, "with rare exceptions, actions for injuries to the person, or to tangible property, now require proof of an intent to inflict them, or of failure to exercise proper care": Prosser, *supra*, p. 30. …

With respect to injuries caused by the negligence of a defendant, it is often necessary to determine whether, or to what extent, the defendant must answer for the consequences which his conduct actually helped to produce. It is well established that a person is not legally responsible for all the consequences of his negligent conduct, and so to limit liability certain rules or principles have been established.

...

The dominant limiting factor in modern negligence law is the "foreseeability" test as developed in *Overseas Tankship (U.K.) Ltd. v. Morts Dock & Engineering Co. Ltd.*, [1961] A.C. 388 (P.C.), and as explained in *Overseas Tankship (U.K.) Ltd. v. Miller Steamship Co. Pty. et al.*, [1967] 1 A.C. 617 (P.C.). For the purposes of this judgment, it is not necessary to explore the meaning and application of this test. It is only necessary to acknowledge it as a limiting factor to the ambit, or, indeed, the creation of liability arising from negligent conduct. The issue, here, is whether a similar limitation applies to intentional torts, such as battery.

This question has been the subject of discussion by legal academics who appear, on balance, to be of the view that the foreseeability test does not apply to intentional torts. Harper and James, after stating that by the fiction of "transferred intent" a defendant who intends to strike a third person is liable if his blow miscarries and he strikes the plaintiff, go on to say, *supra*, at pp. 218-9:

> As has been pointed out, it is not easy to explain on logical principles the liability of one who, having directed a blow at one person, injures another, if he had no reason to believe the other was present and thus likely to be hurt. There is no intention to harm the plaintiff and no negligence toward him. The rule has been likened to that imposing liability without fault. A similar situation is involved in the rule that where the defendant intended to inflict a harmful or offensive contact, he is liable for the results even though they are unintended and unforeseeable. But as a matter of sound social policy, it is clearly better that the risk of such unintended and unforeseeable consequences should fall on the intentional wrongdoer than on his victim. The former is a tortfeasor and the latter is innocent. The wrongdoer, thus, should bear the loss.

...

It is my respectful view that the weight of opinion is that the concept of foreseeability as defined by the law of negligence is a concept that ought not to be imported into the field of intentional torts. While strong policy reasons favour determining the other limits of liability where conduct falls below an acceptable standard, the same reasons do not apply to deliberate conduct, even though the ultimate result in terms of harm caused to the plaintiff is not what was intended by the defendant. In the law of intentional torts, it is the dignitary interest, the right of the plaintiff to insist that the defendant keep his hands to himself, that the law has for centuries sought to protect. In doing so, the morality of the defendant's conduct, characterized as "unlawful", has predominated the thinking of the Courts and is reflected in academic discussions. The logical test is whether the defendant was guilty of deliberate, intentional and unlawful violence or threats of violence. If he was, and a more serious harm befalls the plaintiff than was intended by the defendant, the defendant, and not the innocent plaintiff, must bear the responsibility for the unintended result. If physical contact was intended, the fact that its magnitude exceeded all reasonable or intended expectations should make no difference. To hold otherwise, in my opinion, would unduly narrow recovery where one deliberately invades the bodily interests of another with the result that the totally innocent plaintiff would be deprived of full recovery for the totality of the injuries suffered as a result of the deliberate invasion of his bodily interests. To import negligence concepts into the field of intentional torts would be to ignore the essential difference between the intentional infliction of harm and the unintentional infliction of harm resulting from a failure to adhere to a reasonable standard of care and would result in bonusing the deliberate wrongdoer who strikes the plaintiff more forcefully than intended. For example, in the case of a deliberate blow to the eye liability should cover not only the black eye and the bloody nose but also the resultant brain damage caused when the plaintiff falls to the ground and strikes his head, even though the latter was never intended. Thus, the intentional wrongdoer should bear the responsibility for the injuries caused by his conduct and the negligence test of "foreseeability" to limit, or eliminate, liability should not be imported into the field of intentional torts.

NOTES

1. Does Judge Borins' reasoning make sense to you? See also *Vosburg v. Putney*, 50 N.W. 403 (Wis. 1891). The extent of liability in negligence cases is dealt with in Chapter 8, Remoteness.

2. Would the defendant have been liable if the plaintiff had died? What if he had been treated negligently by a doctor and then died?

3. The limits of liability of an intentional tortfeasor were discussed in *Mayfair Ltd. v. Pears*, [1987] 1 N.Z.L.R. 459 (C.A.), where a defendant trespassed by leaving his car in the plaintiff's car park. When a fire was caused by the presence of the car, the defendant was held not liable. McMullin J. explained: "There are dangers in adopting an absolute rule that an intentional trespasser should be liable for all the consequences of his acts." What dangers did the judge have in mind? What would Judge Borins have done with this case? Which solution do you prefer and why?

4. When someone intentionally interferes with another person, it is a crime as well as a tort. Hence, the offender may be punished criminally for assault and sexual assault, as well as being held civilly responsible in damages to the victim. See R.S.C. 1985, c. C-46, ss. 266, 267, 268, 271.

5. Criminal proceedings are not a bar to a civil action, except in a few provinces where an old English statute remains in force (*Offences Against the Person Act*, 1828 (Imp.) c. 31) which may, in rare cases, bar civil proceedings. See R.S.C. 1985, c. C-46, s. 11. See also Klar and Elman in *Loedel v. Eckert* (1977), 3 C.C.L.T. 145 (B.C.S.C.). It is possible (but uncommon) to stay a civil action pending the outcome of a criminal case. *Stickney v. Trusz* (1973), 2 O.R. (2d) 469, 45 D.L.R. (3d) 275; affd (1974), 3 O.R. (2d) 538, 46 D.L.R. (3d) 80; leave to appeal to S.C.C. refused, 28 C.R.N.S. 127*n*; *Demeter v. Occidental Insurance Co. of California* (1975), 11 O.R. (2d) 369 (H.C.).

6. The recovery of tort damages for criminal conduct is nevertheless infrequent because offenders seldom have any money. See Linden, Osgoode Hall Study on Compensation for Victims of Crime (1968); Linden, "Victims of Crime and Tort Law" (1969), 12 Can. Bar J. 17, 1.8 per cent of victims collected.

7. Because the civil action is so rarely effective, the federal and provincial governments of Canada have co-operated to create in almost every province victims of crime compensation schemes. See Burns, *Criminal Injuries Compensation*, 2nd ed. (1992) and *infra*. This type of legislation was first enacted in 1964 in New Zealand, adopted in

the United Kingdom, and then throughout most of the Commonwealth and to a degree in the United States.

8. Restitution may also be ordered as part of the sentencing process in criminal cases. This remedy, too, has been seldom utilized in the past. See Linden, "Restitution" (1977), 19 Can. J. Crim. L. 49; Law Reform Commission of Canada, *Community Participation in Sentencing* (1976). In order to improve the chances of victims to receive restitution, Parliament has amended the *Criminal Code* to *require* courts to consider whether restitution is appropriate, as was recommended by the Law Reform Commission of Canada. If it is, an order may be made requiring the convicted person to pay the "replacement value" of the property or "pecuniary damages ... incurred as a result of ... bodily injury", where the amount is readily ascertainable. See R.S.C. 1985, c. C-46, s. 738(1)(*a*) and (*b*), am. 1995 c. 22, ss. 6, 11. See also *R. v. Zelensky*, [1978] 2 S.C.R. 940, 20 Crim. L.Q. 272.

9. The Ontario *Victims' Bill of Rights, 1995*, S.O. 1995, c. 6 provides damages for emotional distress and bodily harm to victims of prescribed crimes. In cases of sexual assaults, attempted sexual assaults, or assaults by present or former spouses, victims are presumed to have suffered emotional distress.

F. SEXUAL WRONGDOING

Unwanted sexual contact clearly constitutes a battery and may also constitute other torts such as assault and intentional infliction of emotional distress. In many instances, sexual wrongdoing amounts to a breach of trust. There has been a growing number of actions involving sexual wrongdoings which are being brought not only against parents, other relatives, teachers, priests, dates, but also against institutions and other employers. In most instances, the litigation involves not the issue of whether the wrongdoing occurred, but relates to limitation periods, assessment of damages, and the responsibility of employers or institutions. Commentators have written about the value of such actions to victims of sexual abuse, and the legal difficulties which they must surmount in achieving successful results. Dean Klar has written that:

> The renewed interest in the civil action for victims of egregious sexual misconduct, and the reasons why victims are seeking remedies through tort, reaffirms the principles of civil justice reflected in tort law. While one must hesitate before too quickly drawing analogies between this area of tort law and other areas, the lesson of what may be significant to victims of wrongdoing, other than purely monetary compensation, should not be lost on those contemplating tort law "reform".

See Klar, *Tort Law,* 2nd edition, at p. 46.

NOTES

1. In *Norberg v. Wynrib*, [1992] 2 S.C.R. 226, [1992] 4 W.W.R. 577, a female patient successfully sued her doctor for a sexual battery. The doctor had agreed to prescribe a drug to his addicted patient in exchange for sexual activities. The Supreme Court of Canada rejected the doctor's defence that his patient had consented to the relationship. The majority of the Court held that where two parties are in a position of inequality and where the dominant party exploits that position, consent is not a valid defence. Another approach, adopted by McLachlin J., was to find a breach of fiduciary duty. Also see *Taylor v. McGillivray* (1993), 110 D.L.R. (4th) 64 (N.B. Q.B.) where the

breach of fiduciary duty approach was used to invalidate the defence of consent in another doctor/patient relationship case. See discussion in Chapter 3, *infra.*

2. In *M. (K.) v. M. (H.)*, [1992] 3 S.C.R. 6, 96 D.L.R. (4th) 289, the Supreme Court upheld the claim of an incest victim against her father, both as a tort and a breach of a fiduciary duty. The action was allowed to succeed despite the fact that the incestuous activities occurred approximately 18 years before the action was brought. The Supreme Court dealt with the limitations issue by holding that the limitation period for a sexual battery based upon incest did not begin to run until the incest victim discovered the connection between the harm she has suffered and the incest, which in this case did not occur until the plaintiff began therapy. See also *C. (P.) v. C. (R.)* (1994), 114 D.L.R. (4th) 151 (Ont. Gen. Div.); *A. (D.A.) v. B. (D.K.)* (1995), 27 C.C.L.T. (2d) 256 (Ont. Gen. Div.) where this "reasonable discoverability" approach was used.

3. Some provinces have enacted special legislation to either extend or eliminate altogether the limitation period for bringing actions for sexual assault. The British Columbia *Limitation Act*, R.S.B.C. 1996, c. 266, s. 3(4)(k) and (l), for example, allows a victim of sexual misconduct to bring action without regard to any limitation period. This provision has resulted in a number of B.C. cases brought by adults for sexual misconduct which took place during their childhood. See, for example, *K. (W.) v. Pornbacher*, [1998] 3 W.W.R. 149, 34 C.C.L.T. (2d) 174 (B.C.S.C.); *T. (L.) v. T. (R.W.)* (1997), 36 C.C.L.T. (2d) 207 (B.C.S.C.); *M. (M.) v. F. (R.)*, [1996] 8 W.W.R. 704 (B.C.S.C.); revd in part (1997), 52 B.C.L.R. (3d) 127 (B.C.C.A.); and *S. v. M.* (1994), 113 D.L.R. (4th) 443 (B.C.S.C.). The Prince Edward Island statute illustrates a different approach. It expressly provides that in cases involving sexual abuse, the limitation period begins to run when the plaintiff understands the nature of the injuries and recognizes the effects of the abuse: see S.P.E.I. 1992, c. 63. s. 1(b).

4. A new development in this area is the litigation brought against institutions which were responsible for the care of persons victimized while in their custody. In *K. (W.) v. Pornbacher* (1997), 34 C.C.L.R. (2d) 174 (B.C.S.C.), for example, the bishop in whose church the abuse had occurred was found personally negligent and the Church vicariously liable for sexual assaults which a priest had inflicted upon the plaintiff. Also see *B. (P.A.) v. Curry* (1997), 34 C.C.L.T. (2d) 241, [1997] 4 W.W.R. 431, 146 D.L.R. (4th) 72 (B.C.C.A.); leave to appeal allowed (1997), 224 N.R. 318*n* (S.C.C.), where a foundation which operated group homes was held vicariously liable for the sexual abuse committed by one of its employees on the plaintiff. *Cf. T.J. (G.) v. Griffiths*, [1997] 5 W.W.R. 203 (B.C.C.A.).

5. Another tort action which a victim of sexual misbehaviour might be able to bring is "intentional infliction of mental suffering". In *Samms v. Eccles*, 11 Utah 2d 289, 358 P.2d 344 (1961), the plaintiff claimed damages from the defendant for injuries which she allegedly suffered as a result of his persistent indecent proposals. The plaintiff, a married woman, claimed that the defendant repeatedly and persistently called her by phone at various hours including late at night, solicited her to have sex with him, and even indecently exposed himself to her on one occasion. The court accepted her claim as being an intentional infliction of emotional distress even though the plaintiff did not incur an actual physical injury. See discussion of this tort, *infra.*

6. A new tort action which has emerged is that of "sexual harassment". In *Lajoie v. Kelly* (1997), 32 C.C.L.T. (2d) 115 (Man. Q.B.) the plaintiff, a waitress, complained that the defendant manager made lewd sexual advances and remarks to her in the presence of others. She left her employment due to this behaviour and brought action against the defendant. The court held that sexual harassment is a tort and awarded damages to the plaintiff. See also *Campbell-Fowler v. Royal Trust Co.*, [1994] 1 W.W.R. 193 (Alta. Q.B.).

7. The tort remedy for victims of sexual batteries has generally been seen as having a useful role. In West, "Rape in the Criminal Law and the Victim's Tort Alternative: A Feminist Analysis" (1992), 50 U. T. Fac. L. Rev. 96, the author states:

> The civil suit for rape, a rare but not untried strategy, may prove to be quite effective in achieving the goals sought by the proponents of extra-legal, empowerment-based rape prevention efforts. Its deterrent potential, based not only on practical but on ideological principles, may far outstrip that of the criminal process. The tort suit's applicability is not unproblematic: the more violent kinds of rape will not be its proper subject, rape victims may often lack both the emotional courage and the economic means to sue their attackers, and many rapists will be effectively judgment-proof. The number of situations, therefore, in which a civil suit for rape may be practically possible may be few and must be chosen with care; however, empowering women through the prosecution of their attackers may have an important impact on the acceptability of rape in society.
>
> When the tort suit for sexual assault is considered within the context of trying to eliminate rape from the realm of normal behaviour — by restructuring the sexist foundations that govern the interaction of men and women in society — the tort suit for sexual assault emerges as a largely unexploited possibility in the struggle to empower women against their aggressors. It may be a valuable step towards a world where real sexual equality makes rape meaningless and where women are free from sexual terrorism.

Also see Sutherland, "Measuring Pain: Quantifying Damages in Civil Suits for Sexual Assault" in Cooper-Stephenson and Gibson (eds.) *Tort Theory* (Captus Press, 1992); Kohler, "The Battered Woman and Tort Law: A New Approach To Fighting Domestic Violence" (1992), 25 L.A.L. Rev. 1025; Feldthusen, Bruce, "The Civil Action for Battery: Therapeutic Jurisprudence?" (1993), 25 Ottawa L. Rev. 203; Hughes, "Women, Sexual Abuse by Professionals and the Law: Changing Parameters" (1996), 21 Queen's L.J. 297.

8. The benefits of the tort suit as a remedy in rape cases are said to be several. First, unlike in a criminal prosecution, the victim will be able to control the proceedings and tell her own story. She can define her own issues. Second, due to the different burdens of proof, especially in relation to consent, the plaintiff may have a greater chance of success in the tort case. Third, the plaintiff, if she wins, can be compensated for her injuries and their consequences to her. Fourth, the tort suit can "reinforce the victim and her family in their courageous unwillingness to tolerate the abusive actions of a respected member of the community and help them to avoid the harmful self-blame that plagues so many victims": West, *supra*. West also discusses the empowering effect of tort law, as well as its deterrent effect, and its flexibility.

Do you think that these arguments about the benefits of tort are unique to the sexual assault context? Does this represent a growing realization of the benefits of a civil justice system or is that overstating the case somewhat?

G. INTENTIONAL INFLICTION OF MENTAL SUFFERING

WILKINSON v. DOWNTON

Queen's Bench, [1897] 2 Q.B. 57, 66 L.J.Q.B. 493, 13 T.L.R. 388, 76 L.T. 493.

Consideration by the trial judge of damages assessed by a jury. It was contended that as to damage caused by nervous shock the plaintiff had no cause of action.

Wright J.: In this case the defendant, in the execution of what he seems to have regarded as a practical joke, represented to the plaintiff that he was charged by her husband with a message to her to the effect that her husband was smashed up in an accident, and was lying at The Elms at Leytonstone with both legs broken, and that she was to go at once in a cab with two pillows to fetch him home. All this was false. The effect of the statement on the plaintiff was a violent shock to her nervous system, producing vomiting and other more serious and permanent physical consequences at one time threatening her reason, and entailing weeks of suffering and incapacity to her as well as expense to her husband for medical attendance. These consequences were not in any way the result of previous ill-health or weakness of constitution; nor was there any evidence of predisposition to nervous shock or any other idiosyncrasy.

In addition to these matters of substance there is a small claim for 1s. 10½d. for the cost of railway fares of persons sent by the plaintiff to Leytonstone in obedience to the pretended message. As to this 1s. 10 ½d. expended in railway fares on the faith of the defendant's statement, I think the case is clearly within the decision in *Pasley v. Freeman* (1789), 3 T.R. 51. The statement was a misrepresentation intended to be acted on to the damage of the plaintiff.

The real question is as to the £100, the greatest part of which is given as compensation for the female plaintiff's illness and suffering. It was argued for her that she is entitled to recover this as being damages caused by fraud, and therefore within the doctrine established by *Pasley v. Freeman* and *Langridge v. Levy* (1837), 2 M. & W. 519. I am not sure that this would not be an extension of that doctrine, the real ground of which appears to be that a person who makes a false statement intended to be acted on must make good the damage naturally resulting from its being acted on. Here there is no *injuria* of that kind. I think, however, that the verdict may be supported upon another ground. The defendant has, as I assume for the moment, wilfully done an act calculated to cause physical harm to the plaintiff — that is to say, to infringe her legal right to personal safety, and has in fact thereby caused physical harm to her. That proposition without more appears to me to state a good cause of action, there being no justification alleged for the act. This wilful *injuria* is in law malicious, although no malicious purpose to cause the harm which was caused nor any motive of spite is imputed to the defendant.

It remains to consider whether the assumptions involved in the proposition are made out. One question is whether the defendant's act was so plainly calculated to produce some effect of the kind which was produced that an intention to produce it ought to be imputed to the defendant, regard being had to the fact that the effect was produced on a person proved to be in an ordinary state of health and mind. I think that it was. It is difficult to imagine that such a statement, made suddenly and with apparent seriousness, could fail to produce grave effects under the circumstances upon any but an exceptionally indifferent person, and therefore an intention to produce such an effect must be imputed, and it is no answer in law to say that more harm was done than was anticipated, for that is commonly the case with all wrongs. The other question is whether the effect was, to use the ordinary phrase, too remote to be in law regarded as a consequence for which the defendant is answerable. Apart from authority, I should give the same answer and on the same ground as the last question, and say that it was not too remote. Whether, as the majority of the House of Lords thought in *Lynch v. Knight* (1861), 9 H.L.C. 577, at pp. 592, 596, the criterion is in asking what would be the natural effect on reasonable persons, or whether, as Lord Wensleydale thought, the possible infirmities of human nature ought to be recognized, it seems to me that the connection between the cause and the effect is sufficiently close and complete. It is, however, necessary to consider two authorities which are supposed to have laid down that illness through mental shock is a too remote or unnatural consequence of an *injuria* to entitle the plaintiff to recover in a case where damage is a necessary part of the cause of action.

[The decision of the Privy Council in *Victoria Ry. Comsrs. v. Coultas*, 13 App. Cas. 222, was considered and held not an authority in this case since it did not involve "any element of wilful wrong; nor perhaps was the illness so direct and natural a consequence of the defendant's conduct as in this case".]

A more serious difficulty is the decision in *Allsop v. Allsop*, 5 H. & N. 534, which was approved by the House of Lords in *Lynch v. Knight*. In that case it was held by Pollock C.B., Martin, Bramwell, and Wilde BB. that illness caused by a slanderous imputation of unchastity in the case of a married woman did not constitute such special damage as would sustain an action for such a slander. That case, however, appears to have been decided on the ground that in all the innumerable actions for slander there were no precedents for alleging illness to be sufficient special damage, and that it would be of evil consequence to treat it as sufficient, because such a rule might lead to an infinity of trumpery or groundless actions. Neither of these reasons is applicable to the present case. Nor could such a rule be adopted as of general application without results which it would be difficult or impossible to defend. Suppose that a person is in a precarious and dangerous condition, and another person tells him that his physician has said that he has but a day to live. In such a case, if death ensued from the shock caused by the false statement, I cannot doubt at this day the case might be one of criminal homicide, or that if a serious illness ensued damages might be recovered. I think, however, that it must be admitted that the present case is without precedent. ... In *Smith v. Johnson & Co.*, unreported, decided in January last, Bruce J. and I held that where a man was killed in the sight of the plaintiff by the defendant's negligence, and the plaintiff became ill, not from the shock from fear of harm to himself, but from the shock of seeing another person killed, this harm was too remote a consequence of the negligence. But that was a very different case from the present.

There must be judgment for the plaintiff for £100. 1s. 10½d.

Judgment for plaintiff.

NOTES

1. In *Janvier v. Sweeney*, [1919] 2 K.B. 316, 88 L.J.K.B. 1231 (C.A.), the defendant, a private detective, in order to obtain some letters from the plaintiff, made the following statement: "I am a detective from Scotland Yard and represent military authorities. You are the woman we want, as you have been corresponding with a German spy." The plaintiff, who was engaged to marry an interned German, sued for damages "for false statements wilfully and maliciously made by the defendant to the plaintiff, intended to cause and actually causing her physical injury". The plaintiff claimed to have sustained a severe shock and resulting neurasthenia. The plaintiff was held entitled to recover. See a criticism, from a medical point of view, in Smith and Solomon, "Traumatic Neuroses in Court" (1943), 30 Va. L. Rev. 87, at 124.

2. In *Bielitski v. Obadiak* (1922), 15 Sask. L.R. 153, 65 D.L.R. 627 (C.A.), speaking on the telephone, the defendant told a friend that Steve Bielitski had hanged himself.

After a number of repetitions, Steve's mother finally heard the statement and, believing the report to be true, "sustained a violent shock and mental anguish, which brought on physical illness and incapacitated her for some time". She brought an action against the defendant and was held entitled to recover, the court drawing the conclusion that the defendant made the statement with the intention that it should reach the plaintiff and that any reasonable man would know that it would "in all probability cause her not only mental anguish but physical pain". See notes in 35 Harv. L. Rev. 348; 22 Colum. L. Rev. 86. See also *Jinks v. Cardwell* (1987), 39 C.C.L.T. 168 (Ont. H.C.J.).

3. In *Purdy v. Woznesensky*, [1937] 2 W.W.R. 116 (Sask. C.A.), at a dance held at a rural school, the defendant twice struck the male plaintiff on the head, knocking him down and rendering him unconscious. This was done in the presence of the female plaintiff, his wife, who suffered a severe shock, requiring prolonged medical care. At the trial, both plaintiffs obtained judgments against the defendant which were upheld on appeal. Mackenzie J.A. said that as the defendant should have foreseen that such a violent assault might upset his victim's wife "an intention to produce such an effect must ... be imputed to him".

4. There is no liability for intentional infliction of mental suffering unless there is some "recognizable physical or psychopathological harm". See Wilson J. in *Frame v. Smith*, [1987] 2 S.C.R. 99, at 128, 23 O.A.C. 84. Another phrase that has been employed is "a visible and provable illness". See *Rahemtulla v. Vanfed Credit Union*, [1984] 3 W.W.R. 296, 29 C.C.L.T. 78 (B.C.S.C.). Is this a good idea or should liability be possible without this type of harm? What do we mean by these words?

5. In the United States such injury is not always required. In *State Rubbish Collectors Assoc. v. Silznoff*, 240 Pac. 2d 282 (1952), Mr. Justice Traynor of the Supreme Court of California stated:

> There are persuasive arguments and analogies that support the recognition of a right to be free from serious, intentional and unprivileged invasions of mental and emotional tranquility. If a cause of action is otherwise established, it is settled that damages may be given for mental suffering naturally ensuing from the acts complained of ... and in the case of many torts, such as assault, battery, false imprisonment and defamation, mental suffering will frequently constitute the principal element of damages. ... In cases where mental suffering constitutes a major element of damages it is anomalous to deny recovery because the defendant's intentional misconduct fell short of producing some physical injury.
>
> It may be contended that to allow recovery in the absence of physical injury will open the door to unfounded claims and a flood of litigation, and that the requirement that there be physical injury is necessary to insure that serious mental suffering actually occurred. The jury is ordinarily in a better position, however, to determine whether outrageous conduct results in mental distress than whether that distress in turn results in physical injury. From their own experience jurors are aware of the extent and character of the disagreeable emotions that may result from the defendant's conduct, but a difficult medical question is presented when it must be determined if emotional distress resulted in physical injury. (See Smith, *Relation of Emotions to Injury and Disease*, 30 Va. L. Rev. 193, at 303-306). Greater proof that mental suffering occurred is found in the defendant's conduct designed to bring it about than a physical injury that may or may not have resulted therefrom. ...

How does "physical injury" differ from "mental suffering"? Should liability be imposed if no damage is suffered at all? What kind of result is required for liability?

6. Suppose the custodial parent of a child engages in a nasty course of conduct, denying access to the other spouse in violation of a court order and causing mental distress and economic loss. Should liability be imposed in such a context or is it better to keep tort law out of this area? Do tort law's aims conflict with the best interests of children as set out in the legislative scheme? Can it be held that there is a breach of fiduciary duty? See *Frame v. Smith*, [1987] 2 S.C.R. 99, 23 O.A.C. 84; see Wilson J., dissenting, S.C.R. at 127. *Cf., Cant v. Cant* (1984), 49 O.R. (2d) 25, 43 R.F.L. (2d) 305 (Co. Ct.).

7. The tort of intentional infliction of emotional distress has proven to be a valuable remedy to victims of workplace harassment. In *Clark v. Canada* (1994), 20 C.C.L.T. (2d) 241 (Fed. Ct.), a female RCMP officer successfully sued the Crown for the persistent harassment which the plaintiff had suffered from male colleagues. This harassment ultimately resulted in stress and depression which forced the plaintiff to resign. Despite the fact that the harassment in this case took place over a period of time, involved several wrongdoers, and did not involve the classic single individual, single incident complaint, the elements of the cause of action were made out. The conduct was extreme, calculated to harm, and did result in illness. Also see *Boothman v. R.*, [1993] 3 F.C. 381, 49 C.C.E.L. 109.

RESTATEMENT OF TORTS, SECOND

§46. Outrageous Conduct Causing Severe Emotional Distress

(1) One who by extreme and outrageous conduct intentionally or recklessly causes severe emotional distress to another is subject to liability for such emotional distress, and if bodily harm to the other results from it, for such bodily harm.

(2) Where such conduct is directed at a third person, the actor is subject to liability if he intentionally or recklessly causes severe emotional distress

(a) to a member of such person's immediate family who is present at the time, whether or not such distress results in bodily harm, or

(b) to any other person who is present at the time, if such distress results in bodily harm.

Caveat:

The Institute expresses no opinion as to whether there may not be other circumstances under which the actor may be subject to liability for the intentional or reckless infliction of emotional distress.

NOTES

1. See generally Glasbeek, "Outraged Dignity: Do We Need a New Tort?" (1968), 6 Alta. L. Rev. 77; Prosser, "Insult and Outrage" (1956), 44 Calif. L. Rev. 40; Handford, "Tort Liability for Threatening or Insulting Words" (1976), 54 Can. Bar Rev. 563; Theis, "The Intentional Infliction of Emotional Distress: A Need for Limits on Liability" (1977-78), 27 De Paul L. Rev. 275; Handford, "Intentional Infliction of Mental Distress: Analysis of the Growth of a Tort" (1979), 8 Anglo-Am. L. Rev. 1.

H. FALSE IMPRISONMENT

BIRD v. JONES

Queen's Bench. (1845), 7 Q.B. 742, 115 E.R. 668.

At a trial of an action of assault and false imprisonment with a jury the trial judge, Lord Denman C.J., had instructed the jury that the facts disclosed at the trial constituted an imprisonment of the plaintiff. The plaintiff obtained a verdict, and after a rule *nisi* for a new trial had been obtained on the ground of misdirection, the arguments and judgments related to the sole question whether the following facts, taken from the judgment of Williams J., constituted an imprisonment of the plaintiff by the defendant:

> A part of Hammersmith Bridge, which is generally used as a public footway, was appropriated for seats to view a regatta on the river, and separated for that purpose from the carriage way by a temporary fence. The plaintiff insisted upon passing along the part so appropriated, and attempted to climb over the fence. The defendant (clerk of the Bridge Company) pulled him back; but the plaintiff succeeded in climbing over the fence. The defendant then stationed two policemen to prevent, and they did prevent, the plaintiff from proceeding forwards along the footway in the direction he wished to go. The plaintiff, however, was at the same time told that he might go back into the carriage way and proceed to the other side of the bridge, if he pleased. The plaintiff refused to do so, and remained where he was so obstructed, about half an hour.

Coleridge J.: The plaintiff, being in a public highway and desirous of passing along it, in a particular direction, is prevented from doing so by the orders of the defendant, and ... the defendant's agents for the purpose are policemen, from whom, indeed, no unnecessary violence was to be anticipated, or such as they believed unlawful, yet who might be expected to execute such commands as they deemed lawful with all necessary force, however resisted. But, although thus obstructed, the plaintiff was at liberty to move his person and go in any other direction, at his free will and pleasure; and no actual force or restraint on his person was used, unless the obstruction before mentioned amounts to so much.

I lay out of consideration the question of right or wrong between these parties. The acts will amount to imprisonment neither more nor less from their being wrongful or capable of justification.

And I am of opinion that there was no imprisonment. To call it so appears to me to confound partial obstruction and disturbance with total obstruction and detention. A prison may have its boundary large or narrow, visible and tangible, or, though real, still in the conception only; it may itself be moveable or fixed; but a boundary it must have; and that boundary the party imprisoned must be prevented from passing; he must be prevented from leaving that place, within the ambit of which the party imprisoning would confine him, except by prison-breach. Some confusion seems to me to arise from confounding imprisonment of the body with mere loss of freedom: it is one part of the definition of freedom to be able to go withersoever one pleases; but imprisonment is something more than the mere loss of this power; it includes the notion of restraint within some limits defined by a will or power exterior to our own. ...

On a case of this sort, which, if there be difficulty in it, is at least purely elementary, it is not easy nor necessary to enlarge; and I am unwilling to put any extreme case hypothetically; but I wish to meet one suggestion, which has been put as avoiding one of the difficulties which cases of this sort might seem to suggest. If it be said that to hold the present case to amount to an imprisonment would turn every obstruction of the exercise of a right of way into an imprisonment, the answer is, that there must be something like personal menace or force accompanying the act of obstruction, and that, with this, it will amount to imprisonment. I apprehend that is not so. If, in the course of a night, both ends of a street were walled up, and there was no egress from the house but into the street, I should have no difficulty in saying that the inhabitants were thereby imprisoned; but, if only one end were walled up, and an armed force stationed outside to prevent any scaling of the wall or passage that way, I should feel equally clear that there was no imprisonment. If there were, the street would obviously be the prison; and yet, as obviously, none would be confined to it. [**Williams J.** agreed with **Coleridge J.**]

Lord Denman C.J. (dissenting): … There is some difficulty perhaps in defining imprisonment in the abstract without reference to its illegality; nor is it necessary for me to do so, because I consider these acts as amounting to imprisonment. That word I understand to mean any restraint of the person by force. …

I had no idea that any person in these times supposed any particular boundary to be necessary to constitute imprisonment, or that the restraint of a man's person from doing what he desires ceases to be an imprisonment because he may find some means of escape.

It is said that the party here was at liberty to go in another direction. … But this liberty to do something else does not appear to me to affect the question of imprisonment. As long as I am prevented from doing what I have a right to do, of what importance is it that I am permitted to do something else? How does the imposition of an unlawful condition show that I am not restrained? If I am locked in a room, am I not imprisoned because I might effect my escape through a window, or because I might find an exit dangerous or inconvenient to myself, as by wading through water or by taking a route so circuitous that my necessary affairs would suffer by delay?

It appears to me that this is a total deprivation of liberty with reference to the purpose for which he lawfully wished to employ his liberty: and, being effected by force, it is not the mere obstruction of a way, but a restraint of the person. …

Rule absolute.

NOTES

1. Suppose the defendant locks the plaintiff in a room with an open window. The room is on the first floor of the house. Is this false imprisonment? Suppose the room is on the second floor and there is a ladder that reaches from the ground to the window? What if there is no ladder, but there is a rope, long enough to touch the ground?

2. The plaintiff, clothes hidden in some bushes, goes swimming in the nude. The defendant takes the plaintiff's clothes. The plaintiff cannot leave without being exposed to the public. Imprisonment?

3. Suppose the plaintiff's purse is held by the defendant but the plaintiff is free to go. Imprisonment? *Cf., Ashland Dry Goods Co. v. Wages*, 302 Ky. 577, 195 S.W. 2d 312 (1946).

4. Can a prisoner who is confined in segregated custody sue for false imprisonment on the ground that the confinement was illegal and that the prisoner should have been

allowed to remain within the general prison population? Should the fact that the prisoner has already lost his or her liberty by being in the prison in the first place be regarded as fatal to the prisoner's false imprisonment claim? See *Hill v. British Columbia* (1997), 148 D.L.R. (4th) 337, 38 C.C.L.T. (2d) 182 (B.C.C.A.), where the B.C. Court of Appeal reversed a trial decision and determined that a prisoner can succeed on a false imprisonment claim in such circumstances.

CHAYTOR ET AL. v. LONDON, NEW YORK AND PARIS ASSOCIATION OF FASHION LTD. AND PRICE

Supreme Court of Newfoundland. (1961), 30 D.L.R. (2d) 527, 46 M.P.R. 151.

The plaintiffs, Vera Chaytor and John Delgado, Jr., were employees of Bowring Brothers Ltd., a department store in St. John's, Newfoundland. On the day in question they went across the street from Bowring's and entered the department store of the defendant, a competitor, in order to do some "comparison shopping". In other words, they wished to look over their competitor's goods and prices. They were stopped by the manager of the defendant store, Mr. Price, who called them spies, asked his own store detectives to watch them and called the police to arrest them as "suspicious characters". The plaintiffs accompanied the police in order to avoid embarrassment and because they felt compelled to do so. They were detained about 15 minutes at the police station and were then released without any charge being laid. They sued Price and his employer for false imprisonment.

Dunfield J.: ... To treat generally, at this point of the question of what is called "comparison shopping", I think we must accept the situation that it is a normal practice among retailers. Reputable and competent witnesses have said that it is done here and in Great Britain and in Mainland Canada and in the United States; and apart from what they say, I think it is a matter of common knowledge. Retailing is a very competitive and catch-as-catch-can business, and a retailer who failed to keep a close watch on the goods and prices of his competitors would be likely to suffer for it. It has been sought to represent to me that it is a reprehensible practice, and amounts to stealing other people's ideas; but I do not accept this. Every branch of commerce must watch its competition. We all read, for example, of the many precautions taken by motor car manufacturers to conceal their tentative models, and by dressmakers to do the same, before they are ready for exhibition. I am strongly of the opinion that commercial enterprises spy on one another like nations; it is inevitable in acute competition and shares the general ethics of competition. And in any case, it is in practice impossible to prevent. A merchant admitted in evidence that his firm had private shoppers whose names were known to one person only in the firm. It would be the easiest possible thing for any of the large department stores here, where so many people pass through their service, to arrange for former employees, such as married women who had been in their service as girls, to tip them off regarding competitors' goods. Indeed, much could be done by keeping a careful watch on shop windows, and as Mrs. Chaytor humorously observed, she had once bought a hat for herself in The London Shop, which she had a perfect right to do; but obviously in the course of doing it she could have inspected and probably did inspect most of the hats in the shop. In my view, the close watching of competitors is a normal commercial practice and does not carry any opprobrium. Moreover, people like department managers and buyers are dependent for their own status within their own establishment upon being closely in touch with the competition, and even if they were not told to keep themselves in touch they would naturally do so.

Actually, I think that for a department head and a buyer, probably known to half the shop-hands on Water St., to go out and look round was an exceptionally open and aboveboard way of seeking information. Mrs. Chaytor said that she had occupied her present position for eight years and had often done this before and had never been challenged before. I gathered from another witness that it was an ordinary matter to recognise in the shop emissaries from another shop and, as it were, to tolerate them with a smile.

Now the proper course in my view for a shop manager who recognised such emissaries and did not want them in his shop would be to identify them and ask them politely to leave and, to wait a while and see whether they did so before taking any further measures; and further, in view of the well-recognised situation in the city, politeness would be in order and would be forthcoming from both sides. I think that any trouble there was brought on by the rather angry and hasty action of Mr. Price, which would, I feel, be not in accord with the common manners of the town. Whatever they may do in big cities among strangers, roughness and incivility are neither common nor necessary in this environment. …

I am quite satisfied that Mr. Delgado and Mrs. Chaytor were highly desirous of avoiding embarrassment to themselves, by being treated in a way which would make it look as if they were shoplifters or something of the kind, and also of avoiding embarrassment to their firm; and that they would have departed politely if they had been asked politely to do so; and that it was the rough behaviour of the store manager, together with the calling of the police, which brought about the whole trouble.

I consider therefore that there was what one might call a psychological type of imprisonment. In addition to this of course the plaintiffs were subjected to an objectionable form of public treatment. If they went to the Police Station voluntarily, I think it was because they felt they could hardly do otherwise; and by the mere operation of normal delays, they were psychologically compelled to remain there in the surroundings appropriate to suspected criminals for 15 or 20 minutes. …

A point was made by Mr. Dawe, Q.C., for the defence that there is another exit from the area where Mrs. Chaytor was, by a stair which leads to the street. But the plaintiffs may not have known that. It is not the regular main entrance known to everybody. And indeed, I do not think that anybody who had done something to detain a person can say that she could, if she had insisted or resisted, or been clear about her rights and position, have effected an escape … I hardly think we need argue the pretty obvious point that there can be restraint of freedom without touching of the person. …

I therefore award (a) to Mr. Delgado against the London, New York and Paris Association of Fashion Ltd. $100 and against Mr. Richard Price $100 and (b) to Mrs. Vera Chaytor against the London, New York and Paris Association of Fashion Ltd. $100 and against Mr. Richard Price $100. If I thought that the plaintiffs' reputations had been seriously affected I might have allowed much more; but the whole street knows now about the affair and knows also that the plaintiffs are respectable people.

NOTES

1. Is a suspect imprisoned when asked to accompany a police officer in order to avoid a "scene which would be embarrassing"? See *Campbell v. S.S. Kresge Co. Ltd.* (1976), 21 N.S.R. (2d) 236, 74 D.L.R. (3d) 717 (S.C.), *per* Hart J. See also *Kovacs v. Ontario Jockey Club* (1995), 126 D.L.R. (4th) 576 (Ont. Gen. Div.) where the plaintiff felt "moral pressure" to accompany security officers for questioning.

2. One study indicated that the action for false imprisonment is used most frequently against police officers (60 per cent of reported cases in Canada between 1950 and 1983) and store owners (30 per cent of cases). See Poirier, "Economic Analysis of False Imprisonment in Canada: A Statistical and Empirical Study" (1985), 34 U.N.B. L.J. 104. The litigation generally involves the issue of a defence, and not whether there has actually been an imprisonment. See the discussion of defences in Chapter 3, *infra*.

3. The question of what constitutes an "arrest" is an important issue when considering the actions of police officers. There have been numerous cases on this matter. Touching was once thought necessary for an arrest. See *Russen v. Lucas* (1824), 1 C. & P. 153, 171 E.R. 1141 (N.P.); *Genner v. Sparkes* (1704), 1 Salk. 79, 91 E.R. 74. This requirement seems to have been laid to rest. See *Warner v. Riddiford* (1858), 4 C.B.N.S. 180, 140 E.R. 1052.

4. The American cases are in accord. See, for example, *Martin v. Houck*, 141 N.C. 317, 54 S.E. 295 (1906), where the defendant told the plaintiff to consider himself under arrest and that he had to go with him. The plaintiff said that he would go. Mr. Justice Walker explained the principle as follows:

> In ordinary practice, words are sufficient to constitute an imprisonment, if they impose a restraint upon the person, and the party is accordingly restrained; for he is not obliged to incur the risk of personal violence and insult by resisting until actual violence be used. This principle is reasonable in itself, and is fully sustained by the authorities. Nor does it seem that there should be any very formal declaration of arrest. If the officer goes for the purpose of executing his warrant, and has the party in his presence and power, if the party so understands it, and in consequence thereof submits, and the officer, in the execution of the warrant, takes the party before a magistrate, or receives money or property in discharge of his person, it is in law an arrest, although he did not touch any part of the body. It is not necessary to constitute false imprisonment that the person restrained of his liberty should be touched or actually arrested. If he is ordered to do or not to do the thing, to move or not to move against his own free will, if it is not left to his option to go or stay where he pleases, and force is offered, or there is reasonable ground to apprehend that coercive measures will be used if he does not yield, the offense is complete upon his submission. A false imprisonment may be committed by words alone, or by acts alone, or by both, and by merely operating on the will of the individual, or by personal violence, or by both. It is not necessary that the individual be confined within a prison or within walls, or that he be assaulted, it may be committed by threats.

5. Relevant to this tort issue is the criminal case of *R. v. Whitfield*, [1970] S.C.R. 46, 7 D.L.R. (3d) 97. A police constable called Kerr spotted Whitfield at the wheel of an automobile which had stopped for a red light on St. Clair Avenue, Toronto. Kerr, being aware of an outstanding warrant for the arrest of Whitfield, approached the car and informed Whitfield that he had a warrant for his arrest. Whitfield accelerated in an attempt to get away, but was slowed down by the traffic. Kerr reached through the window of the car and grabbed Whitfield's shirt with both hands, saying, "You are

under arrest." Whitfield accelerated, causing Kerr to release his hold on the shirt and the car and fall to the ground.

Whitfield was apprehended shortly thereafter and charged with escaping from lawful custody. At trial he was convicted, but the Court of Appeal quashed the conviction, directing that a verdict of acquittal be entered. The Crown successfully appealed to the Supreme Court of Canada, the sole issue being whether the accused had been in lawful custody. Mr. Justice Judson (Fauteux, Martland, Ritchie and Pigeon JJ., concurring) relied on some of the older authorities to the effect that, if an officer is "near enough to touch him, and does touch him, and gives him notice of the writ, it is an arrest". These authorities were aimed at the preservation of the peace. Mr. Justice Judson concluded with these words:

> A police officer has the right to use such force as may be necessary to make an arrest. What kind of arrest are we to expect if it becomes a principle of law that a police officer, acting under a warrant of which he informs the accused, and who actually seizes the accused's person, is found not to have made an arrest because the accused is in the driver's seat of a motor car which enables him to shake off the arresting officer?

Mr. Justice Hall (Spence J., concurring) dissented and argued that the majority judgment was based on a principle "applicable to situations arising 100 years after the situations to which they applied became obsolete". Mr. Justice Hall concluded:

> The dead hand of the past cannot reach that far. These outdated procedures evolved before the organization of police forces as we now know them and had no relation to the arrest or taking into custody of a person charged with a criminal offence.
>
> Accordingly in my view this case does not fall to be decided upon the authority of cases applicable to the taking into custody under writs of *capeas ad satisfaciendum*, obsolete since 1869, civil in their nature, and not involving the criminal law doctrine of proof beyond a reasonable doubt but should be decided upon principles applicable to the circumstances obtaining in this century and particularly since Parliament has legislated in the very matter to cover both resisting lawful arrest and escaping from lawful custody as two distinct and separate offences.
>
> In the instant case the police officer, Kerr, had a lawful right and duty to arrest Whitfield. There is no question as to the fact that a warrant was outstanding and Kerr's attempt to arrest was lawful. Whitfield accordingly was under a legal obligation to submit to the lawful arrest. It is only by the recognition of these corresponding duties and obligations that we can avoid the notion that the person being arrested has to be restrained physically before he can be said to be 'arrested'. I do not see that it should be necessary to touch or hold the person being arrested. He must, of course, be informed that he is being arrested. If he does not submit or tries to flee, the arresting officer may use such force as may reasonably be necessary to detain his man having regard to the nature of the offence for which the person is wanted. If the man flees and is not in fact detained he cannot be said to have been in lawful custody, but that does not mean he has not committed an offence. Parliament has legislated specifically in this regard.

6. Is consciousness of confinement a requisite of false imprisonment? In *Meering v. Grahame-White Aviation Co.* (1919), 122 L.T. 44, (1918-19) All E.R. Rep. Ext. 1490 (C.A.), Lord Justice Atkin stated:

> ... It appears to me that a person could be imprisoned without his knowing it. I think a person can be imprisoned while he is asleep, while he is in a state of drunkenness, while he is unconscious, and while he is a lunatic. Those are cases where it seems to me that the person might properly complain if he were imprisoned, though the imprisonment began and ceased while he was in that state. Of course, the damages might be diminished and would be affected by the question whether he was conscious of it or not.
>
> So a man might in fact, to my mind, be imprisoned by having the key of a door turned against him so that he is imprisoned in a room in fact although he does not know that the key has been turned. It may be that he is being detained in that room by persons who are anxious to make him believe that he is not in fact being imprisoned, and at the same time his captors outside that room may be boasting to persons that he is imprisoned. ...

Compare with *Herring v. Boyle* (1834), 6 C. & P. 496, 149 E.R. 1126 (C. of Ex.), which seemed to require cognizance of restraint. The House of Lords has now adopted Lord Justice Atkin's view in *Murray v. Ministry of Defence*, [1988] 2 All E.R. 521, [1988] 1 W.L.R. 692 (H.L.), where Lord Griffiths stated, All E.R., at 529: "The law attaches supreme importance to the liberty of the individual and if he suffers a wrongful interference with that liberty it should remain actionable even without proof of special damage." See Prosser, "False Imprisonment — Consciousness of Confinement" (1955), 55 Colum. L. Rev. 847.

7. Is there such a thing as a "negligent" false imprisonment, or is the tort confined to intentional imprisonments? See Harding and Feng, "Negligent False Imprisonment — A Problem in the Law of Trespass" (1980), 22 Malaya L. Rev. 29.

8. What if a person consents to being confined and then has a change of mind? Is there an obligation to release immediately? Can conditions ever be imposed? If, for example, a person on an "express" bus, with no stops, wishes to get off the bus at a red light, or at some convenient time, but the bus driver refuses to open the door, is this a false imprisonment? See *Martin v. Berends*, February 2, 1989, Doc. No. 22997/87, Caswell J., [1989] O.J. No. 2644 (Ont. Prov. Ct.) — no false imprisonment because there was no urgent reason to let the passenger disembark.

9. In *Robinson v. Balmain New Ferry Co.*, [1910] A.C. 295, 79 L.J.P.C. 84, the plaintiff entered a turnstile at a wharf and paid the usual penny for a ride on a ferry. On discovering that he had missed the ferry, he sought to leave but was told he had to pay another penny before he would be permitted to leave. A notice board stated that "a fare of one penny must be paid on entering and leaving the wharf. No exception will be made to this rule, whether the passenger has travelled by ferry or not". After 20 minutes the plaintiff escaped. He sued, *inter alia*, for false imprisonment. Liability was denied. Lord Loreburn L.C. felt that the defendants were entitled to impose a "reasonable condition before allowing him to pass through their turnstile from a place to which he had gone of his own free will". See also *Herd v. Weardale Steel Coal & Coke Co. Ltd.*, [1915] A.C. 67, 84 L.J.K.B. 121 (H.L.).

10. At Honest Ed's, a discount department store in Toronto, there is a sign posted that reads "Everyone entering these premises agrees to be searched prior to exit." The plaintiff fails to read the sign upon entry. On trying to leave, the plaintiff is asked to submit to a search, but refuses. The plaintiff is detained for a time and is finally let go. Imprisonment?

11. The tort of false imprisonment stems from trespass and requires that the plaintiff's imprisonment be directly caused by the defendant. Where the plaintiff's arrest and imprisonment is the result of judicial intervention and discretion, the directness requirement fails and the defendant, even if he or she initiated the complaint, cannot be

held liable for false imprisonment. In this event a suit for malicious prosecution might be available. See discussion *infra*, note 13. See *Dendekker v. F.W. Woolworth Co.*, [1975] 3 W.W.R. 429 (Alta. S.C.); *Foth v. O'Hara* (1958), 24 W.W.R. 533, 120 C.C.C. 305 (Alta. S.C.); *Fasken v. Time/System International APS* (1986), 12 C.P.C. (2d) 1 (Ont. H.C.); and *Brady v. Bank of Nova Scotia*, [1992] O.J. 217.

12. It has been held that where the complainant directs the police to make an arrest, and the police act on this directive without exercising independent discretion, that an action for false imprisonment against the complainant can succeed. See *Valderhauq v. Libin* (1954), 13 W.W.R. 383 (Alta. C.A.) and *Otto v. J. Grant Wallace* (1988), 47 D.L.R. (4th) 439, [1988] 2 W.W.R. 728 (Alta. Q.B.).

13. The tort of malicious prosecution can be used by a person who has been wrongly prosecuted by someone else. In *Nelles v. Ontario*, [1989] 2 S.C.R. 170, 60 D.L.R. (4th) 609, Susan Nelles, a nurse at The Hospital for Sick Children in Toronto, brought an action for malicious prosecution against the Crown, the Attorney General, and several police officers. She had been charged with the murder of four infants who had died while under the hospital's care. The murder charges were dismissed at the preliminary hearing.

    The principle issue before the Supreme Court was whether the Attorney General was absolutely immune from suit for malicious prosecution. The Court decided that there was no immunity. It was clear, however, that a suit for malicious prosecution is very difficult to win. The following four elements must be satisfied:

    (i) The proceedings must be initiated by the defendant;
    (ii) The proceedings must terminate in the plaintiff's favour;
    (iii) The proceedings must have been instituted without reasonable cause;
    (iv) The defendant must have been malicious.

    It is the latter two elements which present the greatest difficulty. Not only must there have been no honest belief, based on reasonable grounds, that the accused was guilty, but there must also be proved to have been an ulterior motive, other than the pursuit of justice, on the defendant's part.

14. In one case, the defendant fabricated a rape charge against the plaintiff. The suit for malicious prosecution succeeded. See *Canada v. Lukasic* (1985), 37 Alta L.R. (2d) 170, 18 D.L.R. (4th) 245 (2d) 170 (Q.B.).

15. Do you think that this tort ought to be difficult to establish? What are the interests in issue here? See Sopinka, "Case Comment" (1995), 74 Can. Bar Rev. 366.

16. A related tort is that of "abuse of process". This arises where a person uses the process of the court for an improper purpose and where there is a definite act or threat, extraneous to the court action itself, in furtherance of that purpose. This latter requirement has been the stumbling block to most actions. See Klar, *Tort Law*, 2nd edition, at pp. 59-61.

I. TRESPASS TO LAND

ENTICK v. CARRINGTON

Common Pleas. (1765), 19 State Trials 1029,
[1558-1774] All E.R. Rep. 41.

Action of trespass for breaking and entering plaintiff's house and carrying away papers, against persons who claimed to act under a warrant from a Secretary of State.

Lord Camden L.C.J.: The great end, for which men entered into society, was to secure their property. That right is preserved sacred and incommunicable in all instances where it has not been taken away or abridged by some public law for the good of the whole. The cases where this right of property is set aside by positive law, are various. Distresses, executions, forfeitures, taxes, etc., are all of this description; wherein every man by common consent gives up that law for the sake of justice and the general good. By the laws of England every invasion of private property, be it ever so minute, is a trespass. No man can set his foot upon my ground without any licence but he is liable to an action, though the damage be nothing; which is proved by every declaration in trespass where the defendant is called upon to answer for bruising the grass or even treading upon the soil. If he admits the fact, he is bound to show by way of justification, that some positive law has empowered or excused him. ...

According to this reasoning, it is now incumbent upon the defendants to show the law by which this seizure is warranted. If that cannot be done, it is a trespass.

NOTES

1. In *Cooper v. Crabtree* (1882), 20 Ch. D. 589, 47 L.T.R. 5, 51 L.J. Ch. 544, the defendant had placed two small poles and a piece of board on land owned by the plaintiff but which, at the time, he had leased to a third person who was in occupation under the lease. The plaintiff brought an action to enjoin the defendant's conduct. The court held that the plaintiff's action failed. The plaintiff could not base his claim on trespass since possession of the land was in his tenant; a claim in nuisance failed since the plaintiff's use of the land was not interfered with. If the plaintiff could establish some damage of a permanent or substantial nature causing injury to the reversion he might have had a cause of action for such actual damage. The defendant had admitted that his object was the quite legitimate one of blocking the light of a window in a cottage on the land in order to prevent the acquisition of a right to light. The same result could have been achieved if the poles were on defendant's own land. See also *Townsview Properties Ltd. v. Sun Construction & Equipment Co.* (1974), 7 O.R. (2d) 666, 56 D.L.R. (3d) 330 (C.A.).

2. In *Epstein v. Cressey Development Corp.* (1992), 89 D.L.R. (4th) 32 (B.C.C.A.),the defendant developer sought but was refused permission to insert anchor rods into the plaintiff's property to provide shoring for its excavation. After attempting numerous other methods to provide support, all unsuccessful, the developer proceeded to insert the anchor rods, without permission. The developer did not tell the plaintiff that it was doing this. There was no disturbance to the surface of the plaintiff's land. The rods were later removed, although concrete and steel debris remained in the plaintiff's subsoil, which did not affect the future development of the plaintiff's property in any way. The plaintiff sued for trespass. The action was maintained and the plaintiff received both compensatory and exemplary damages. The compensatory damages were based on the diminished value of the plaintiff's land which resulted from the close proximity of the development, which could not have been accomplished without the trespass.

3. Ontario enacted the *Trespass to Property Act*, R.S.O. 1990, c. T.21, as a replacement to the earlier, and more limited *Petty Trespass Act*, R.S.O. 1970, c. 347. The Act now provides:

2. (1) Every person who is not acting under a right or authority conferred by law and who,

(a) without the express permission of the occupier, the proof of which rests on the defendant,

(i) enters on premises when entry is prohibited under this Act, or

(ii) engages in an activity on premises when the activity is prohibited under this Act; or

(b) does not leave the premises immediately after he or she is directed to do so by the occupier of the premises or a person authorized by the occupier,

is guilty of an offence and on conviction is liable to a fine of not more than $2,000.

The legislation provides that entry on premises may be prohibited by a notice to that effect, or in certain cases, even without notice. Generally speaking, enclosed areas or areas under cultivation do not require notices. Persons, who on reasonable and probable grounds, are believed to be on premises in contravention of the Act may be arrested by a police officer, or by the occupier, without warrant.

The legislation also provides for an award of damages to be made against the defendant in favour of the occupier:

12. (1) Where a person is convicted of an offence under section 2, and a person has suffered damage caused by the person convicted during the commission of the offence, the court shall, on the request of the prosecutor and with the consent of the person who suffered the damage, determine the damages and shall make a judgment for damages against the person convicted in favour of the person who suffered the damage, but no judgment shall be for an amount in excess of $1,000.

(2) Where a prosecution under section 2 is conducted by a private prosecutor, and the defendant is convicted, unless the court is of the opinion that the prosecution was not necessary for the protection of the occupier or the occupier's interests, the court shall determine the actual costs reasonably incurred in conducting the prosecution and, despite section 60 of the *Provincial Offences Act*, shall order those costs to be paid by the defendant to the prosecutor.

(3) A judgment for damages under subsection (1), or an award of costs under subsection (2), shall be in addition to any fine that is imposed under this Act.

(4) A judgment for damages under subsection (1) extinguishes the right of the person in whose favour the judgment is made to bring a civil action for damages against the person convicted arising out of the same facts.

(5) The failure to request or refusal to grant a judgment for damages under subsection (1) does not affect a right to bring a civil action for damages arising out of the same facts.

(6) The judgment for damages under subsection (1), and the award for costs under subsection (2), may be filed in the Small Claims Court and shall be deemed to be a judgment or order of that court for the purposes of enforcement.

Several other provinces have more limited *Petty Trespass Acts*. Do these Acts restrict or complement the common law action in trespass?

4. In *R. v. Burko*, [1969] 1 O.R. 598, 3 D.L.R. (3d) 330 (Mag. Ct.), six university students were found guilty under the Ontario *Petty Trespass Act*, R.S.O. 1970, c. 347, (now the *Trespass to Property Act*, R.S.O. 1990, c. T.21) when they entered a collegiate without permission and disseminated radical literature. Although the public has a right to use the corridors in an ordinary and reasonable manner, the magistrate felt that the distribution of newspapers was not such a use. This activity had nothing to do with furnishing of education, the prime purpose of the institution. Rather, the accused were motivated by hostility toward the system of education at the school. The magistrate suggested that it would be all right for a parent to enter the school without permission to locate a child if the parent proceeded directly to the classroom where the child was being taught. Would it make any difference if the students went to the school in question? Would it make any difference if the literature being distributed urged the students to attend church on Sunday? What if they distributed the literature in the school yard or on the street in front of the school? Magistrate Barton concluded (O.R., at 605) by warning that "our society will not progress through anarchy or deliberate flouting of its laws when there are democratic means by which our society can be changed". It may be "slow and cumbersome" but it will not "destroy those parts of society that are good. ... [N]o minority has the right to try to impose its will on the majority no matter how well-meaning or sincere their thinking may be".

5. See also *Harrison v. Carswell*, [1976] 2 S.C.R. 200, 62 D.L.R. (3d) 68, where picketers at a privately owned shopping centre were found guilty of violating the *Petty Trespass Act* of Manitoba. Dickson J. for the majority stated:

> The submission that this Court should weigh and determine the respective values to society of the right to property and the right to picket raises important and difficult political and socio-economic issues, the resolution of which must, by their very nature, be arbitrary and embody personal economic and social beliefs. It raises also fundamental questions as to the role of this Court under the Canadian Constitution. The duty of the Court, as I envisage it, is to proceed in the discharge of its adjudicative function in a reasoned way from principled decision and established concepts. I do not for a moment doubt the power of the Court to act creatively — it has done so on countless occasions, but manifestly one must ask — what are the limits of the judicial function? There are many and varied answers to this question. Holmes J., said in *Southern Pacific Co. v. Jenson* (1917), 244 U.S. 205, at p. 211: "I recognize without hesitation that judges do and must legislate, but they can do it only interstitially; they are confined from molar to molecular actions". ...
>
> Society has long since acknowledged that a public interest is served by permitting union members to bring economic pressure to bear upon their respective employers through peaceful picketing, but the right has been exercisable in some locations and not in others and to the extent that picketing has been permitted on private property the right hitherto has been accorded by statute. For example, s. 87 of the *Labour Code of British Columbia Act*, 1973 (B.C.) (2nd Sess.), c. 122, provides that no action lies in respect of picketing permitted under the Act for trespass to real property to which a member of the public ordinarily has access.
>
> Anglo-Canadian jurisprudence has transitionally recognized, as a fundamental freedom, the right of the individual to the enjoyment of property and the right not to be deprived thereof, or any interest therein, save by due process of law. The Legislature of Manitoba has declared in the *Petty Trespasses Act* that any person who trespasses upon land, the property of another, upon or through which he has been requested by the owner not to enter, is guilty of an offence. If there is to be any change in this statute law, if A is to be given the right to enter and remain on the land of B against the will of B, it would seem to me that such a change must be made by the enacting institution, the Legislature,

> which is representative of the people and designed to manifest the political will, and not by this Court.

Laskin J. dissented and declared:

> The considerations which underlie the protection of private residences cannot apply to the same degree to a shopping centre in respect of its parking areas, roads and sidewalks. Those amenities are closer in character to public roads and sidewalks than to a private dwelling. All that can be urged from a theoretical point of view to assimilate them to private dwellings is to urge that if property is privately owned, no matter the use to which it is put, trespass is as appropriate in the one case as in the other and it does not matter that possession, the invasion of which is basic to trespass, is recognizable in the one case but not in the other. There is here, on this assimilation, a legal injury albeit no actual injury. This is a use of theory which does not square with economic or social fact under the circumstances of the present case.
>
> What does a shopping centre owner protect, for what invaded interest of his does he seek vindication in ousting members of the public from sidewalks and roadways and parking areas in the shopping centre? There is no challenge to his title and none to his possession nor to his privacy when members of the public use those amenities. Should he be allowed to choose what members of the public come into those areas when they have been opened to all without discrimination? Human rights legislation would prevent him from discriminating on account of race, colour or creed or national origin, but counsel for the appellant would have it that members of the public can otherwise be excluded or ordered to leave by mere whim. It is contended that it is unnecessary that there be a reason that can stand rational assessment. Disapproval of the owner, in assertion of a remote control over the "public" areas of the shopping centre, whether it be disapproval of picketing or disapproval of the wearing of hats or anything equally innocent, may be converted (so it is argued) into a basis of ouster of members of the public. Can the common law be so devoid of reason as to tolerate this kind of whimsy where public areas of a shopping centre are concerned?
>
> If it was necessary to categorize the legal situation which, in my view, arises upon the opening of a shopping centre, with public areas of the kind I have mentioned (at least where the opening is not accompanied by an announced limitation on the classes of public entrants), I would say that the members of the public are privileged visitors whose privilege is revocable only upon misbehaviour (and I need not spell out here what this embraces) or by reason of unlawful activity. Such a view reconciles both the interests of the shopping centre owner and of the members of the public, doing violence to neither and recognizing the mutual or reciprocal commercial interests of shopping centre owner, business tenants and members of the public upon which the shopping centre is based.
>
> The respondent picketer in the present case is entitled to the privilege of entry and to remain in the public areas to carry on as she did (without obstruction of the sidewalk or incommoding of others) as being not only a member of the public but being as well, in relation to her peaceful picketing, an employee involved in a labour dispute with a tenant of the shopping centre, and hence having an interest, sanctioned by the law, in pursuing legitimate claims against her employer through the peaceful picketing in furtherance of a lawful strike.

6. In *Committee for the Commonwealth of Canada v. Canada*, [1991] 1 S.C.R. 139, 77 D.L.R. (4th) 385, the Supreme Court of Canada held that it was contrary to the *Canadian Charter of Rights and Freedoms* for the government to prohibit the respondent group from handing out leaflets and otherwise promoting their views at Montreal's

Dorval Airport. Regulations prohibiting this type of activity were stated to be inconsistent with freedom of expression rights guaranteed by the Charter. Although there were six separate judgments written in this case, a recurring theme was that the area in this case was government-owned and in the nature of a public forum. It was clear that this decision did not deal with the type of private ownership issue raised by *Harrison v. Carswell, supra.*

7. *Harrison v. Carswell, supra*, was distinguished in *Wildwood Mall Ltd. v. Stevens*, [1980] 2 W.W.R. 638 (Sask. Q.B.), where union members were picketing in a shopping mail. The plaintiff proprietor sought an injunction to restrain these activities. Mr. Justice Noble distinguished *Harrison v. Carswell* and *R. v. Peters* (1971), 17 D.L.R. (3d) 128n, 2 C.C.C. (2d) 339n (S.C.C.), on the ground that in those cases there were provincial statutes, such as the *Petty Trespass Act*, discussed above, which prohibited trespasses after the owner of premises has requested persons to leave. In Saskatchewan, there was no such legislation. His Lordship applied an earlier decision of the Saskatchewan Court of Appeal, *Grosvenor Park Shopping Centre Ltd. v. Waloshin* (1964), 46 D.L.R. (2d) 750, 49 W.W.R. 237 (Sask. C.A.), where Culliton C.J.S. said:

> The area upon which it is alleged the appellants have trespassed is part of what is well known as a shopping centre. While legal title to the area is in the respondent it admits in its pleadings that it has granted easements to the many tenants. The evidence also establishes that the respondent has extended an unrestricted invitation to the public to enter upon the premises. The very nature of the operation is one in which the respondent, both in its own interests and in the interests of its tenants, could not do otherwise. Under these circumstances, it cannot be said that the respondent is in actual possession. The most that can be said is that the respondent exercises control over the premises but does not exercise that control to the exclusion of other persons. For that reason, therefore, the respondent cannot maintain an action in trespass against the appellants.

The injunction was accordingly denied.

Do you agree that the existence of the legislation ought to make a difference? Has the legislation altered the substance of the common law relating to the law of trespass?

8. Contrast with *Russo v. Ontario Jockey Club* (1987), 62 O.R. (2d) 731, 43 C.C.L.T. 1 (H.C.J.), where racetrack owners successfully prevented a very successful bettor from entering their racetrack on the basis of a landowner's "absolute right to exclude persons" without regard to principles of natural justice. See also *Webb v. Attewell* (1993), 18 C.C.L.T. (2d) 299 at 322 (B.C.C.A.) where Southin J.A. stated that "a landowner's right to refuse entry upon his land to a neighbour is absolute and it is no part of a court's function to penalize a refusing landowner for what the court perceives to be unneighbourly behaviour."

9. Is it a trespass if the defendant's tree is allowed to grow so that its branches or trunk extend over the plaintiff's land, or its roots grow into the plaintiff's land? Will the plaintiff be liable for cutting off the offending branches or digging up the roots? Does the plaintiff have to use the best method of removing the offending growth so as to attempt to save the tree or can the plaintiff be merciless in his or her destruction? See *Anderson v. Skender* (1993), 17 C.C.L.T. (2d) 160 (B.C.C.A.).

10. Permanent overhanging parts of buildings or other artificial projections are held to constitute trespass. Thus, an advertising sign (*Kelsen v. Imperial Tobacco*, [1957] 2 Q.B. 334, [1957] 2 All E.R. 343 (Q.B.)); electric cables (*Didow v. Alberta Power Ltd.*, [1988] 5 W.W.R. 606, 45 C.C.L.T. 231 (C.A.); leave to appeal to S.C.C. denied Feb. 23, 1989, B.S.C.C. Feb. 24, 1989, p. 470; see Irvine, "Case Comment" (1986), 37

C.C.L.T. 99) and similar permanent structures are trespassory. (See *Woollerton v. Costain*, [1970] 1 All E.R. 483, [1970] 1 W.L.R. 411 (Ch. Div.), swinging crane.) Transitory intrusions, however, are generally held not to constitute trespass unless they strike the ground or damage some property of the owner, like a horse or a cat. See Fleming, *The Law of Torts*, 7th ed. (1987), p. 42. Encroaching branches and flying or shooting over another's land is best handled with nuisance principles. See *Didow* case, *supra*; *Big Point Club v. Lozon*, [1943] O.R. 491, [1943] 4 D.L.R. 136 (H.C.); *cf., Ellis v. Loftus Iron* (1874), L.R. 10 C.P. 10, [1874-80] All E.R. Rep. 232 (Common Pleas).

11. In *Turner v. Thorne*, [1960] O.W.N. 20, 21 D.L.R. (2d) 29 (H.C.), the defendant delivered a number of parcels at the wrong address. He placed them in the plaintiff's garage, believing that this was the garage of the consignee where he had formerly delivered parcels addressed as these were. The plaintiff entered the garage after dark, fell over the parcels and sustained damage. McRuer C.J.H.C. held defendant liable, adopting §§ 158 and 163 of the American *Restatement of Torts*. The continued presence of chattels on the land of another is a trespass, and a trespasser "is liable for any harm to the possessor ... irrespective of whether it was caused by conduct which, were the actor not a trespassor, would have subjected him to liability".

12. In *Mee v. Gardiner*, [1949] 3 D.L.R. 852, [1949] 1 W.W.R. 830 (B.C.C.A.); affg [1948] 4 D.L.R. 871, [1948] 2 W.W.R. 813, an employee of the owner of a tourist camp permitted a tramp to sleep in a cabin, the exclusive use of which had, by contract, been given to the plaintiff. As a result of the tramp's occupancy, the plaintiff contracted a skin disease. The defendant was held liable in damages to the plaintiff for "physical injuries inflicted on him without lawful excuse". The trial judge held that "the tramp was a trespasser, and, since defendant brought him onto the premises, ... is as responsible for the consequences of his trespass as he is".

13. In *Wyant v. Crouse*, 127 Mich. 158, 86 N.W. 527 (1901), the defendant entered the plaintiff's blacksmith shop as a trespasser and started a fire in the forge. He was not negligent in his supervision of the fire, but after he left, the building, in some way that could not be explained nor have been anticipated, caught fire and was destroyed. The defendant was held liable. "He was engaged in an unlawful act, and therefore was liable for all the consequences." See also *Wormald v. Cole*, [1954] 1 Q.B. 614, [1954] 1 All E.R. 683 (C.A.); *Sulisz v. Flin Flon*, [1979] 2 W.W.R. 728, 9 C.C.L.T. 89 (Man. Q.B.).

14. In *Johnson et al. v. B.C. Hydro and Power Authority* (1981), 27 B.C.L.R. 50, 123 D.L.R. (3d) 340, 16 C.C.L.T. 10 (S.C.), an Indian band recovered damages when the defendant authority, without permission, erected a power transmission line across the Indian Reserve. The Court considered that the presence of the lines constituted a "continuing trespass" and, in addition to general damages, awarded $15,000 in exemplary damages to the plaintiffs.

15. What interest must the plaintiff have in the land to support an action in trespass? In *Shea v. Noseworthy* (1975), 25 Nfld. & P.E.I.R. 20, 68 A.P.R. 20 (Nfld. T.D.), the Newfoundland Supreme Court held that the slightest amount of possession was enough to recover against a trespasser, if the land was vacant, unenclosed and incapable of cultivation.

16. See generally Magnet, "Intentional Interference with Land" in Klar (ed.), *Studies in Canadian Tort Law* (1977), at 287.

ATLANTIC AVIATION v. NOVA SCOTIA LIGHT & POWER CO. LTD.

Nova Scotia Supreme Court. (1965), 55 D.L.R. (2d) 554.

The plaintiff owned land on the shore of a lake in Nova Scotia and was licensed under the Aeronautics Act to give flying instructions there. The defendant, on land to which it had acquired either title or easements of a right-of-way had, in 1959, erected 14 steel transmission towers along the shore of the lake and about 1,500 feet from it. The towers ranged in height from 125-300 feet. The plaintiff claimed that the presence of the transmission towers had affected and will in future affect his operations to the extent that pilots or students in training might collide with the towers or wires. The plaintiff claimed an injunction to restrain the defendant from constructing or erecting towers or permitting him to maintain towers already erected in the position in which they were situated.

The defendant replied that the erection of the towers and wires was a lawful, reasonable and necessary use of the defendant's air space and that flying aircraft over the defendant's land is unlawful.

MacQuarrie J.: ... In my view of the law as it applies to the plaintiff's claim against the defendant in this case, the result is the same whether the plaintiff has succeeded or failed to show any loss sustained as a result of the erection of the defendant's transmission line.

Before the plaintiff can succeed, it must show that it as a member of the public had a right to use the air space blocked by the defendant's transmission line paramount to the right of the defendant to erect it. There are no English or Canadian authorities that I am aware of which deal with this type of problem, nor have any regulations been passed pursuant to the *Aeronautics Act*, which are relevant to this case. Section 4(1)(*j*) of that Act provides that the Minister of Air Transport has power to make Regulations with respect to the height used and location of structures on land adjoining airports. No such zoning regulations have been passed with respect to Lake William. ...

The question of the right of the landowner in relation to the rights, if any, in air space has been the subject of both legislation and judicial decision in the United States.

Fleming on Torts, 2nd ed., refers on pp. 47-48 to the four solutions set forth by the American Courts:

> There are no English or Australian decisions which have explored the transient and harmless use of air-space over private land, but the preceding case law is not opposed to the right of flight at reasonable height which does not impair the enjoyment of subjacent soil. Indeed, such *dicta* as have adverted to the question support this view. The use of aircraft has become of such social importance that it is idle to speculate whether the courts might not inhibit it by an extravagant application of the *ad coelum* maxim; the question is rather how to adjust, with the least friction, the conflict between the competing claims of aircraft operators to reasonable scope for their activities and of landowners to unimpaired enjoyment of their property.
>
> In the United States, four solutions have been put forward. First, that it is trespass only to fly within the zone of the landowner's 'effective possession' or such altitude up to which he might in the future make effective use of the airspace. Secondly, that there is no trespass unless the flight occurs within the zone of the landowner's *actual use*. This view, in effect, eliminates any concept of technical trespass justifying the recovery of nominal damages, and confers protection only against actual and substantial injury to the landowner in the enjoyment of the surface. Thirdly, that flight of aircraft is not trespass at all but that the proper remedy is in nuisance or negli-

gence. This approach is practically identical with the second, except that it might forestall recovery for an isolated act, since nuisance ordinarily involves continuity or recurrence. Fourthly, that flight at any altitude is trespass save for a privilege of reasonable flight, analogous to the public right of navigation on navigable rivers. On this basis, an aviator is protected if he traverses the air-space of another for a legitimate purpose, in a reasonable manner and at such height so as not to interfere unreasonably with the possessor's enjoyment of the surface and the air-space above it, but he cannot enjoin the surface owner from putting up a structure, like a transmission line, which has the effect of preventing the landing of aircraft at a near-by aerodrome.

The case cited in the footnote at the end of the closing words in the citation ... is *Guith et al. v. Consumers Power Co.* (1940), 36 F. Supp. 21. In *Guith* the common law on the relative rights of the landowner and the aviator is stated by Tuttle D.J. as follows:

> In the *Restatement of the Law of Torts* by The American Law Institute, the common law on the relative rights of the landowner and the aviator to the use of air-space above the surface of the earth is stated as follows:
>
> Section 159, Comment e:
>
> An unprivileged intrusion in the space above the surface of the earth, at whatever height above the surface, is a trespass.
>
> Section 194 — Travel Through Air Space.
>
> An entry above the surface of the earth, in the air space in the possession of another, by a person who is travelling in an aircraft, is privileged if the flight is conducted:
>
> (a) for the purpose of travel through the air space or for any other legitimate purpose,
>
> (b) in a reasonable manner,
>
> (c) at such a height as not to interfere unreasonably with the possessor's enjoyment of the surface of the earth and the air space above it, and
>
> (d) in conformity with such regulations of the State and federal aeronautical authorities as are in force in the particular State.

In my opinion, *Guith* is based on common law as well as on statute.

In Canada the common law position is unaffected by statute: Jack E. Richardson, "Private Property Rights in the Air Space at Common Law," 31 Can. Bar Rev. 117, at p. 119 (1953):

> It has been established in the United States that obstructions to aircraft may be a public nuisance, as in *Commonwealth of Pennsylvania v. von Bestecki*, [1937] U.S. & C. Av.R.1; 30 Pa. County R. 137, *Tucker v. United Airlines Inc. and the City of Iowa*, [1936] U.S. & C. Av. R. 10 and *United Airports Company of California Ltd. v. Hinman*, [1940] U.S. & C. Av. R.1. In each of these cases, however, the court found that the obstructions were deliberately raised by the defendant on his own land for the purpose of obstructing or embarrassing aircraft taking off from and landing on an adjoining airfield and not for any necessary or incidental use or enjoyment of the defendant's land. ...
>
> In *Guith v. Consumers Power Company* and *Strother v. Pacific Gas and Electric Company*, 211 P. 2d 624, the right of the landowner to erect structures on his land in the exercise of his use and enjoyment of his land, even if the obstructions interfered

with the free passage of aircraft taking off and landing on an adjoining airfield, was affirmed.

...

The point has been raised that the paramount right to navigate air space would depend on the actual use of the air space by aircraft prior to its use by the land-owner.

In my opinion, highways in the air cannot be so established.

...

The defendant's use of the land over which it acquired rights of way and was the lawful occupier was reasonable and necessary under the circumstances.

In my opinion, the only Canadian law which can prevent the defendant using its land (including land of which it is the lawful occupier) as it has would be zoning restrictions passed pursuant to the Aeronautics Act, with respect to land surrounding Lake William or land in the area of Lake William. No such zoning regulations have been passed.

The erection and use of the towers and wire by the defendant was a lawful, reasonable and necessary use of the defendant's air space.

In the result, the plaintiff's action will be dismissed with costs.

NOTES

1. In *Lacroix v. The Queen*, [1954] Ex C.R. 69, [1954] 4 D.L.R. 470, an owner of agricultural land on which there were no buildings, adjacent to the Dorval airport, claimed compensation from the Crown by reason of the latter's having established a "flight-way" over his land and, thus, having appropriated the air and space over his land. Fournier J. denied the claim:

> It seems to me that the owner of land has a limited right in the air space over his property; it is limited by what he can possess or occupy for the use and enjoyment of his land. By putting up buildings or other constructions the owner does not take possession of the air but unites or incorporates something to the surface of his land. This which is annexed or incorporated to his land becomes part and parcel of the property.
>
> The Crown could not expropriate that which is not susceptible of possession. It is contrary to fact to say that by the so-called establishment of a flightway and the flying of planes it had taken any property belonging to the suppliant or interfered with his rights of ownership.
>
> In this instance it did not appropriate any air or space over his land and did not interfere with his rights. I need go only so far as to say that the owner of land is not and cannot be the owner of the unlimited air space over his land, because air and space fall in the category of *res omnium communis*. For these reasons the suppliant's claim for damages by reason of the so-called establishment of a flightway over his land fails.

2. Problems similar to trespass to air space are raised by invasions below the surface. Such invasions have been held actionable: *Cox v. Glue* (1848), 5 C.B. 533. The limits of the protection given the interest of the surface owner have not been much debated. Suppose B places a sewer 150 feet below the surface of A's lot which is used for a

residence? *Cf., Boehringer v. Montalto*, 254 N.Y.S. 276 (1931). For a recent underground intrusion case, see *Lim v. Titov*, [1998] 5 W.W.R. 495 (Alta. Q.B.).

3. Is it a trespass if an airplane's engine fails and it falls onto the plaintiff's house? See *Rochester Gas & Electric Corp. v. Dunlop*, 266 N.Y.J. 469 (1933). See also Bohlen, "Aviation under Common Law" (1934), 48 Harv. L. Rev. 216; Hackley, "Trespassers in the Sky" (1937), 21 Minn. L. Rev. 733.

4. Is the proprietary right to one's air space so important that the courts ought to protect it at any costs? What if a person who owns a lot refuses to allow the building crane being used on a neighbour's multi-million dollar development to swing over the lot? Can this person continue to insist on the proprietary right and refuse to negotiate at any price? See *Lewvest Ltd. v. Scotia Towers Ltd.* (1981), 126 D.L.R. (3d) 239, 19 R.P.R. 192 (Nfld. S.C.).

J. INTERFERENCE WITH CHATTELS

There are several tort actions available to protect a person's property rights in chattels. The major ones are trespass, detinue and conversion, although there is also the special action on the case for permanent injury to reversionary interest, and replevin. As with the other intentional torts, these actions involve deliberate and direct interferences with the plaintiff's rights. Although a full discussion of these torts is outside the scope of this text, and is usually dealt with in a course dealing with personal property, the following cases and notes will highlight the major issues in this area.

1. Trespass to Goods

EVERITT v. MARTIN

Supreme Court of New Zealand. [1953] N.Z.L.R. 298.

The plaintiff, alighting from his car in a parking space, had his coat caught on a dilapidated fender of the defendant's adjoining car. In an action for damages the court found that the defendant was negligent in the sense that he, knowing of his car's condition, should have foreseen the likelihood of such an injury when parking his car in the heart of a big city. The defendant was held liable to the plaintiff. The following related only to one of the defendant's arguments.

F.B. Adams J.: ... As to the suggestion that plaintiff committed an act of trespass, the argument was that defendant could not be under a duty to foresee and guard against harm that could be incurred only by an act of trespass. This is an application to chattels of the familiar doctrine that an occupier of premises owes, in general, no duty to take care for the protection of trespassers on his premises. ... The first question is, of course, whether plaintiff was guilty of trespass in allowing his coat to come in contact with defendant's car. Counsel referred me to *Salmond on Torts*, 10th ed., 318, where it said that trespass to chattels, defined as consisting in any act of direct physical interference without lawful justification, is actionable *per se*. It may be that this is not to be read as including merely accidental contacts; but, even if it be limited to intentional touchings, it is, with respect, questionable law. *Pollock on Torts*, 15th ed., 264, speaks much more guardedly, as also do *Winfield on Torts* and *Clerk and Lindsell on Torts*, 10th ed., 412. It would appear that (1906) 1 *Street's Foundations of Legal Liability*, 16, is to the contrary, and in 1 *Restatement of the Law of Torts*, para. 218, there is a clear and emphatic statement negativing liability unless there is damage to the chattel, substantial deprivation of use, or bodily harm ensuing: see also 33 *Halsbury's Laws of England*, 2nd ed., 22, and the old case of *Slater v. Swann* (1731), 2 Stra. 782; 93 E.R. 906, which is direct authority for the proposition that trespass to another man's horse is not actionable without "a special damage".

The matter being in doubt at this late stage of our legal history, I would hesitate to be the first to hold that there is a right of action for the mere touching of another's goods without damage or asportation. But, however this may be in the case of intentional contacts, a consideration of the material discussed above leads me to the conclusion that there is no right of action in the case of merely accidental contacts where no damage is done. I cannot imagine that plaintiff is liable, even for nominal damages, on account of the casual and unintended contact of his coat with defendant's car.

This being my view, I hold that plaintiff is not disentitled to recover on the ground that he was a trespasser, and that, in such circumstances as existed here, there is a duty resting on users of the highway to take reasonable care to avoid injuries to other users which may arise from casual and unintended contacts of the kind in question. It is accordingly unnecessary to decide whether the doctrine as to the duties, or absence of duties, on the part of occupiers of land towards trespassers is applicable to chattels, or how far, if at all, a person who touches a chattel intentionally, but without moving or damaging it, is to be regarded as a trespasser.

NOTES

1. Is there any reason why damage should be necessary in a trespass to goods action and not in an assault action? See *Marentille v. Oliver*, 2 N.J.L. 358 (S.C.N.J. 1808).

2. The action in trespass remedies a wrongful interference with a person's *actual possession* of chattels. It does not matter whether the plaintiff acquired the possession lawfully or unlawfully. Even a thief can maintain a trespass action against a defendant who wrongfully interferes with the thief's possession. The law's interest is to prevent disorders which would result if persons were permitted to dispossess others who were holding goods solely on the ground that their possession was wrongful. Whether a person without actual possession but with an immediate right to possession can maintain an action in trespass against someone denying that right was in issue in *Penfold Wines Proprietary Ltd. v. Elliott* (1946), 74 C.L.R. 204 (H.C. Aust.). The court decided that a trespass action was not available unless there had been a wrongful interference with the plaintiff's actual possession or the actual possession of the plaintiff's servant, agent or bailee at will.

2. Detinue

A detinue is the wrongful detention of goods. A person who wishes to recover possession of goods wrongfully withheld must sue in detinue rather than in conversion. The essential elements of a successful detinue action are (i) that the plaintiff has a better right to possess the goods than the defendant, (ii) the plaintiff has requested the return of the goods, and (iii) the defendant has refused this request by not allowing the plaintiff to recover the goods. Case law has established that there is no obligation on a wrongful holder to actually return the goods to the plaintiff, unless previously agreeing to do so.

As long as the defendant refuses to allow the plaintiff to recover the goods, the detinue continues. Thus, when a plaintiff sues in detinue seeking damages instead of the return of the goods, the value of the goods are assessed from the time of the judgment and not from the time the first request was made. As shall be seen shortly this theoretically contrasts with the assessment of damages for conversion and can have important consequences for the parties depending upon whether the value of the goods has been increasing or decreasing.

3. Conversion

PROSSER, "THE NATURE OF CONVERSION"
(1957), 42 Cornell L.Rev. 168

Conversion has been confined, in effect, to those major interferences which are so important, or serious, as to justify the forced judicial sale of the chattel to the defendant which is the distinguishing feature of the action. There has been increasing recognition of the fact that the significance of conversion lies in the measure of damages, the recovery of the full value of the goods, and that the tort is therefore properly limited to those wrongs which justify imposing it.

Out of all this the laborers in the vineyard of the Restatement have brought forth the conclusion, be it mountain or mouse, that there is always, under any and all circumstances, a conversion; and that as to any particular type of act the existence of this tort is a matter of the seriousness of the interference with the plaintiff's rights, which in turn will depend upon the interplay of a number of different factors, each of which has its own importance, and may, in a proper case, be controlling.

This may be stated in the form of black letter propositions, and tested by a series of illustrations involving the various types of conduct which have been held to be sufficient for conversion.

Therefore:

(1) Conversion is an intentional exercise of dominion or control over a chattel, which so seriously interferes with the right of another to control it that the actor may justly be required to pay the other the full value of the chattel.

(2) In determining the seriousness of the interference and the justice of requiring the actor to pay the full value, the following factors are important:

(a) The extent and duration of the actor's exercise of dominion or control;
(b) The actor's intent to assert a right in fact inconsistent with the other's right of control;
(c) The actor's good faith;
(d) The extent and duration of the resulting interference with the other's right of control;
(e) The harm done to the chattel; and
(f) The expense and inconvenience caused to the other.

HOLLINS v. FOWLER
House of Lords. (1875), L.R. 7 H.L. 757, 44 L.J.Q.B. 169.

One Bayley, by fraudulently representing he was acting as purchasing agent for a third person with good credit, obtained possession of 13 bales of the plaintiff Fowler's cotton. Bayley offered it for sale to Hollins, a broker, who frequently purchased for prospective clients. Hollins sent a delivery note to Bayley stating that the cotton was bought by him for Micholls & Co. Hollins obtained the cotton from Bayley and delivered it to Micholls & Co. who spun the cotton into yarn at its plant. Bayley obtained the sale price from Hollins who was repaid by Micholls & Co. together with a brokerage commission. Learning of the fraud practised on him, and not having been paid, Fowler applied for the cotton to Hollins who informed him that Micholls & Co. had bought the cotton and used it. Fowler brought action against Hollins in trover.

At the trial before Willes J., he asked the jury whether (a) Hollins bought the cotton as agents, and (b) whether they dealt with the goods as agents for their principal. The jury answered both in the affirmative and Willes J. entered judgment for the defendant Hollins, reserving leave to the plaintiff to move for judgment. On a rule being granted, it was made absolute.

The defendant appealed to the Exchequer Chamber and, on equal division, the plaintiff's judgment was upheld. The defendant appealed to the House of Lords. The judges were summoned to give their opinions and the opinions so given were 4:2 in favour of the plaintiff. The House of Lords then dismissed the appeal. The following is the opinion of one of the four judges summoned to advise the House of Lords.

Blackburn J.: ... However hard it may be on those who deal innocently and in the ordinary course of business with a person in possession of goods, yet, as long as the law, as laid down in *Hardman v. Booth*, 1 H. & C. 803, is unimpeached, I think it is clear law, that if there has been what amounts in law to a conversion of the plaintiff's goods, by any one, however innocent, that person must pay the value of the goods to the real owners, the plaintiffs.

And, accordingly, I think it has not been disputed by any one, that if the plaintiffs had sued Micholls, who has worked this cotton up into yarn, Micholls must have had judgment against him for the value of the cotton, and would be liable to pay the price over again, though he honestly transmitted the price to the defendants, Hollins, who honestly handed it to Bayley.

And I take it that if the defendants have done what amounts in law to a conversion, they also must be liable to pay the plaintiffs.

It is hard on them, I agree, but I do not think that it is harder than it would have been on Micholls. ... When a loss has happened through the roguery of an insolvent, it must always fall on some innocent party; and that must be hardship. ... I own that it is not always easy to say what does and what does not amount to a conversion ... I think many cases which at first seem difficult are solved if the nature of the action is remembered.

It is generally laid down that any act which is an interference with the dominion and right or property of the plaintiff is a conversion, but this requires some qualification.

From the nature of the action, as explained by Lord Mansfield in *Cooper v. Chitty* (1756), 1 Burr. 20, it follows that it must be an interference with the property which would not, as against the true owner, be justified, or at least excused, in one who came lawfully into the possession of the goods. ...

NOTES

1. *Hollins v. Fowler, supra*, was applied in *Canadian Laboratory Supplies Ltd. v. Engelhard Industries of Canada Ltd.* (1975), 12 O.R. (2d) 113, 68 D.L.R. (3d) 65 (H.C.); revd 16 O.R. (2d) 202, 78 D.L.R. (3d) 232 (C.A,); affd in part, [1979] 2 S.C.R. 787, 97 D.L.R. (3d) 1. The plaintiff's employee was a "rogue" who devised the following fraudulent scheme. The employee, Cook, would, on behalf of his employer but unknown to the employer, order platinum from the defendant. Cook would arrange for the plaintiff to issue a cheque to the defendant for this purchase. Cook would then intercept this order and have it returned to the defendant as scrap, in the name of a fictitious customer. A cheque would then be issued to the customer, who was in truth Cook.

   The plaintiff sued the defendant in conversion, for having taken back platinum which belonged to the plaintiff. In effect Cook stole the plaintiff's platinum and sold it to the defendant.

   At trial, Mr. Justice O'Driscoll applied *Hollins v. Fowler*, and found that the defendant's conduct, though innocent, amounted to a conversion. The Ontario Court of Appeal reversed this decision on the basis that the plaintiff had given Cook the apparent authority to deal with the defendant and was estopped from denying this authority. The Supreme Court of Canada allowed the appeal in part, holding that the plaintiff was estopped from denying its employee's authority in relation to some, but not all, of the transactions. Also see *Nilsson Bros. Inc. v. McNamara Estate* (1992), 1 Alta. L.R. (3d) 252, [1992] 3 W.W.R. 761 (C.A.), for a case where an auctioneer of cattle was successfully sued in conversion.

2. In *Fouldes v. Willoughby* (1841), 8 M. & W. 540, 10 L.J. Ex. 364, the defendant was manager of a ferry on which the plaintiff embarked with two horses after paying the usual fare. The plaintiff, having misconducted himself after he came on board, was told by the defendant that he would not carry the horses over and that the plaintiff must take them on shore. The plaintiff refused to do so, and the defendant took the horses from the plaintiff, who was holding one of them by the bridle, put them on shore and turned them loose. Under a charge that the defendant's acts amounted to a conversion unless the plaintiff's conduct had justified his removal from the steamboat, the plaintiff had a verdict. Upon a rule *nisi*, a new trial was ordered on the ground that "a simple asportation of a chattel, without any intention of making further use of it, although it may be a sufficient foundation for an action of trespass, is not sufficient to establish a conversion". If defendant's act of removing plaintiff's horses from the boat was done simply to induce the plaintiff to go on shore himself, "it was not exercising over the horses any right inconsistent with, or adverse to, the rights which the plaintiff had in them. ..." Lord Abinger C.B. stated:

   > In order to constitute a conversion, it is necessary either that the party taking the goods should intend some use to be made of them, by himself or by those for whom he acts, or that, owing to his act, the goods are destroyed or consumed, to the prejudice of the lawful owner. As an instance of the latter branch of this definition, suppose, in the present case, the defendant had thrown the horses into the water, whereby they were drowned, that would have amounted to an actual conversion; or as in the case cited in the course of the argument, of a person throwing a piece of paper into the water; for, in these cases, the chattel is changed in quality, or destroyed altogether. But it has never yet been held that the single act of the removal of a chattel, independent of any claim over it, either in favour of the party himself or any one else, amounts to a conversion of the chattel.

   Was a trespass committed? See also *384238 Ontario Ltd. v. R. in Right of Canada* (1983), 8 D.L.R. (4th) 676, 84 D.T.C. 6101 (Fed. C.A.).

3. Is the use of wine bottles by filling them with wine a conversion of these bottles? See *Penfold Wines Proprietary Ltd. v. Elliott, supra.*

4. A landlord required that the tenant store her boxes and other goods in the storage area of the complex and not in her apartment. He had the goods moved for her. They were subsequently stolen from the storage area. Can the landlord be liable for conversion for having moved the goods, if there was no consent on the part of the tenant? See *Robertson v. Stang* (1997), 38 C.C.L.T. (2d) 62 (B.C.S.C.).

STEIMAN v. STEIMAN

Court of Appeal. (1982), 18 Man. R. (2d) 203, 23 C.C.L.T. 182; leave to appeal to S.C.C. granted (1983), 52 N.R. 236*n*.

A family quarrel developed over the ownership of a considerable amount of jewellery. The plaintiff claimed that jewellery taken from the house by her deceased husband's family was jewellery which she owned and she demanded the full market value. The defendant refused to grant her request and even refused to produce the jewellery so that it could be examined and appraised. The action was based in conversion and not detinue. The evidence indicated that, from the date of the conversion in 1976 to the date of the trial of the action in 1981, the jewellery had tripled in value. However, from the date of the trial to the date of the appeal the value of the jewellery had fallen dramatically. The trial judge assessed the jewellery as of the date of the trial and awarded the plaintiff judgment for $186,787.16. The defendant appealed.

O'Sullivan J.A.: Counsel for the appellants submits that the learned trial judge erred in valuing the missing jewellery at the date of the trial. He submits the value should be determined as of the date of the conversion (or more strictly the date at which the jewellery could reasonably have been replaced following the conversion). All parties agreed that the value of the jewellery at the date of conversion was one-third of the 1981 values. Plaintiff's appraiser, Stephen Powell, in his evaluation had said 1976 values would be between 30 and 35 per cent of the values shown as of the date of his appraisal, April 7, 1981. As I say, counsel agreed that we could take it that the 1976 values, the values at the time of conversion, were one-third of the 1981 values. So, if the learned trial judge erred in selecting the date of trial as the appropriate time for measuring damages, then the award as to item (c) should be reduced from $31,850.00 to $10,616.67 and the award as to item (d) should be reduced from $132,360.00 to $44,120.00. In both cases the reduced awards would carry 5% for sales tax and, if interest is payable, the interest rate would be 10% per year.

The learned trial judge said:

> ... surely it is reasonable and just to fix the date of valuation as of the time of judgment as opposed to conversion. The rationale is simply that had the goods not been converted from the plaintiff but left in her possession, or returned to her, then she would have had the benefit not only of the use of the jewellery but also of any increase in the value to date.

With respect, it seems to me this reasoning is flawed. A person who finds his goods taken may continue to regard the goods as his own and sue in detinue for their return but if he elects to claim damages for conversion his damages must be based on the supposition that he has replaced the missing goods at market prices.

The victim who replaces converted goods will not lose any appreciation in value by reason of a rising market. If the victim were permitted to recover damages as of the date of trial for goods which he has in fact replaced by purchase, he would gain twice from appreciation — once on the goods converted and once on the goods purchased.

Thousands of cases are settled every day on the basis that a wrongdoer who destroys a chattel is bound to pay only that amount which will cover the cost of replacing the chattel at the time of the tort (or a reasonable time thereafter) plus loss of use limited to the period of time required to find a replacement. In insurance law, motor vehicle law, many branches of the law, this principle is accepted as basic.

It is true that where there is a wrongful taking the victim may have the alternative of claiming in detinue, where the unsuccessful defendant must replace the goods or pay the value at the time of the trial. But the plaintiff then runs the risk of a failing market and of depreciation in value; the defendant's option to restore the goods continues to judgment and maybe even to execution.

In the case before us, the pleadings were drawn in such a way as to support a judgment in detinue as well as in conversion but the plaintiff has taken judgment in conversion. Perhaps the plaintiff preferred to have money damages rather than risk the restoration of the jewellery which has since the trial fallen dramatically in price. In any event, it seems clear that the plaintiff's judgment is one for conversion.

On the appeal, counsel for the plaintiff submitted that the measure of damages is the same in conversion as in detinue and the learned trial judge was of the same view. There have been some judicial pronouncements to the same effect ...

However, I think it is clear from an examination of the cases that the weight of authority is in favour of the proposition that in simple cases of conversion there is no right to be awarded as consequential damages the difference between the market value at the time when it would have been reasonable to replace the converted goods and either their value at the time of trial or their highest value at some intermediate point.

NOTES

1. What is wrong with the court's argument that a person whose goods are converted must be taken to have replaced the goods at market prices at the time of the conversion? Where will the person obtain the money at that time? Is it true to suggest that a person who decided to replace the goods will unfairly obtain a double appreciation if the court awards him the value of the converted goods at the date of the trial? For a similar decision see *Dominion Securities Ltd. v. Glazerman* (1984), 29 C.C.L.T. 194 (Man. C.A.).

2. Should a plaintiff be penalized by framing an action in conversion rather than in detinue? Are not the forms of action dead? Ought the solicitor to have realized that failing to claim in detinue would result in a much lower assessment?

K. INVASION OF PRIVACY

ROTH v. ROTH

Ontario Court of Justice. (1991), 9 C.C.L.T. (2d) 141, 4 O.R. (3d) 740.

The plaintiffs and defendants were involved in a heated dispute concerning an access road leading to their rural cottage properties. The plaintiffs alleged that the defendants engaged in a number of harassing activities and that one of the torts which they committed was an invasion of their right to privacy.

Mandel J.: [on the question of privacy]

Intimidation, Harassment and Invasion of Privacy

I have already dealt with the matter of intimidation and in my view the plaintiffs, for reasons hereinbefore given, have failed to establish such a cause of action in the case at bar. As for harassment and invasion of privacy, the two are interrelated. In the United States, harassment is an invasion of privacy. It is an intrusion into another's seclusion (see, for example, para. 64 of Am. Jr., 2d vol., 62A (Privacy)).

In England, it has been held that there is no general remedy for the infringement of privacy (*Re X*, [1975] 1 All E.R. 702 at 704, [1975] Fam. 54 (C.A.)). The report of the Younger Committee on Privacy, Cmnd. 5012 (1972) recommended that there should not be recognized any right of privacy. English law has given remedies under other long-established causes of action as nuisance, thus an owner of property has a right in nuisance from constant aerial surveillance and has tied harassment and invasion of privacy into such an action (*Lord Bernstein of Leigh v. Skyviews & General Ltd.*, [1978] Q.B. 479 at 489, [1977] 2 All E.R. 902, where it is stated:

> But if the circumstances were such that a plaintiff was subjected to the harassment of constant surveillance of his house from the air, accompanied by the photographing of his every activity, I am far from saying that the court would not regard such a monstrous invasion of his privacy as an actionable nuisance for which they would give relief.

However, as a plaintiff in nuisance must have a proprietary interest (see *Cunard v. Antifyre Ltd.*, [1933] 1 K.B. 551, [1932] All E.R. 588 (D.C.), at pp. 556-557 [K.B.]; *Southport Corp. v. Esso Petroleum Co.*, [1957] A.C. 218, [1955] 3 All E.R. 864, [1955] 2 Lloyd's Rep. 655 (H.L.), at p. 224 [A.C.]), a guest in the house as distinct from an occupier could not complain of such conduct. There appears however to be emerging a new cause of action where the complainant has not a proprietary interest. One of these appears to be harassment of the plaintiff in the exercise of a right. So Scott J. stated in *Thomas v. National Union of Mineworkers (South Wales) Area*, [1986] 1 Ch. 20, at p. 64:

> Unreasonable harassment of them in their exercise of that right (right to use the highway for the purpose of going to work) would, in my judgment, be tortious.

The words in parenthesis in the above quotation are mine.

What then is the position in Canada?

The first question to be answered is, is there a right to privacy? In *Canada (Director of Investigation & Research, Combines Investigation Branch) v. Southam*

Inc., [1984] 2 S.C.R. 145, 27 B.L.R. 297, 33 Alta. L.R. (2d) 193, 41 C.R. (3d) 97, [1984] 6 W.W.R. 577, (sub nom. *Hunter v. Southam Inc.*) 14 C.C.C. (3d) 97, 55 A.R. 291, 55 N.R. 241, 2 C.P.R. (3d) 1, 9 C.R.R. 355, 11 D.L.R. (4th) 641, 84 D.T.C. 6467, the Supreme Court of Canada acknowledged the existence of such a right, *i.e.*, " 'the right to be let alone by other people' " p. 113 [C.R.]; and that such a right is not dependent upon "the notion of trespass" but rather "'it is the right to be secure against encroachment upon the citizens' reasonable expectation of privacy in a free and democratic society'" [pp. 113-114]. It was there stated that such a right was a general right, one aspect of which is dealt with in s. 8 of the *Canadian Charter of Rights and Freedoms*, *viz.*, "everyone has the right to be secure against unreasonable search or seizure." Such a general right is then envisaged by s. 26 of the *Charter*, *viz.*, "the guarantee in this *Charter* of certain rights and freedoms shall not be construed as denying the existence of any other rights or freedoms that exist in Canada." There being such a general right not dependent on trespass to the person or property, nor in my view to proprietary interest as in nuisance, the next question to be answered is, is there an actionable cause for an invasion of such right in Canada?

In Ontario there is no remedy legislated as in some of the other provinces. If there is to be a remedy at present it must be forged by the courts. At the stage of pleadings the courts have refused to dismiss actions for invasion of privacy on the basis that it has not been shown that such a right does not exist (see *Capan v. Capan* (1980), 14 C.C.L.T. 191 (Ont. H.C.)). In my view such a right does exist (*Southam v. Hunter*, *supra*). Rather the question is, does the law give a remedy for the invasion of such a right?

It appears to me to make no sense where in certain circumstances as a result of an act of A both the privacy of B and C are invaded, that B would have cause of action because he has a proprietary interest whereas C who is a guest in his house would not, as in the case where A subjects B and C to aerial surveillance during the week that C is a guest at B's cottage (see *Lord Bernstein v. Skyviews Ltd.*, *supra*).

In my view the principle to follow is put thus by Fleming, *The Law of Torts*, 7th ed. (Sydney: Law Book, 1987) at p. 575:

> Clearly, no liability is warranted unless the intrusion is substantial and of a kind that a reasonable person of normal sensitivity would regard as offensive and intolerable. Merely knocking at another's door or telephoning on one or two occasions is not actionable, even when designed to cause annoyance; but if the calls are repeated with persistence, and in the midst of night, so as to interfere unreasonably with comfort or sleep, liability will ensue.

In my view as to whether the invasion of privacy of an individual will be actionable, will depend on the circumstances of the particular case and the conflicting rights involved. In such a manner the rights of the individual as well as society as a whole are served.

The matter was addressed in the case of *Motherwell v. Motherwell*, [1976] 6 W.W.R. 550, 1 A.R. 47, 73 D.L.R. (3d) 62 (C.A.), at p. 70 [D.L.R.] where it is stated that:

> Whether the approach is to review a principle, or to determine the need to broaden an existing category, or to determine whether the circumstances of the case warrant the recognition of a new category, the considerations are basically similar although the required urgencies may differ in degree.

The court there determined that the operation of the law is not confined to existing categories and that the spirit of the common law still exists and was to be applied. To hold otherwise and to deny any remedy where a right exists is to stultify the common law and its history.

In my view having regard to the numerous times that the defendants locked the gate on the road and interfered and blocked the use thereof by the plaintiffs in getting to and from their cottage even after the defendants Philip and Martin were convicted under the *Road Access Act*; the removal of the shed, pump and dock with the concomitant shutting off of electricity in the plaintiffs' cottage at a time when they were not there and without reasonable notice; and the verbal haranguing by Philip taken altogether constitute a harassment of the plaintiffs in the enjoyment of their property which is of a kind that a person of normal sensitivity would regard as offensive and intolerable and is an invasion of the plaintiffs' rights of privacy and I so find.

Even if it could be said that there is no remedy for the invasion of privacy such conduct by the defendants and the totality thereof in my view would give rise to a cause of action in harassment (see *Thomas v. National Union of Mineworkers*, supra) or to the female plaintiff who is the owner of the lands in nuisance (see *Motherwell v. Motherwell*, supra) being the undue interference with the comfort and enjoyment of her home.

NOTES

1. In addition to the above judgment, other decisions have begun to recognize a tort of invasion of privacy. See, for example, *Saconne v. Orr* (1981), 34 O.R. (2d) 317, 19 C.C.L.T. 37 (Co. Ct.), where the court upheld a plaintiff's action for invasion of privacy. The plaintiff complained that a tape of a telephone conversation which had been made without his permission was played at a city council meeting, causing him great embarassment. Also see *Lipiec v. Borsa* (1996), 31 C.C.L.T. (2d) 294 (Ont. Gen. Div.), which recognized the tort. Other judgments have refused to strike out statements of claim which alleged invasion of privacy as a cause of action. See *Krouse v. Chrysler Canada Ltd.*, [1970] 3 O.R. 135, 40 D.L.R. (3d) 15 (C.A.); *Burnett v. R.* (1979), 23 O.R. (2d) 109, 94 D.L.R. (3d) 281 (H.C.); *Capan v. Capan* (1980), 14 C.C.L.T. 191 (Ont. H.C.). *Cf.*, *Turton v. Buttler* (1988), 85 A.R. 195, 42 C.C.L.T. 74 (Alta. M.C.), no action for publishing private facts about someone. Do you think that there is a need for such a tort, or rather that the existing causes of action provide ample remedies for invasions of privacy?

2. Various aspects of the right to privacy have been protected in Canada and the Commonwealth under different legal theories, such as trespass, contract and defamation. (See for example *Green v. Minnes* (1891), 22 O.R. 177 (C.A.).) In Quebec, Art. 1053 of the *Civil Code* has been utilized to award damages to someone who was bothered by phone calls for three days. (See *Robbins v. C.B.C.* (1957), 12 D.L.R. (2d) 35, [1958] Que. S.C. 152). The theory of "passing off" has been used to protect what might be considered an aspect of privacy. See *Sim v. H.J. Heinz Co. Ltd.*, [1959] 1 W.L.R. 313, [1959] 1 All E.R. 547 (C.A.); Mathieson, "Comment" (1961), 39 Can. Bar Rev. 409; nuisance has also been relied on. See *Motherwell v. Motherwell* (1976), 73 D.L.R. (3d) 62, [1976] 6 W.W.R. 550 (Alta. C.A.).

3. In *Ontario (Attorney-General) v. Dieleman* (1994), 117 D.L.R. (4th) 449 (Ont. Gen. Div.); supp. reasons at (1995), 123 D.L.R. (4th) 757; supp. reasons at (1995), 123 D.L.R. (4th) 766, the Attorney General of Ontario sought an injunction to prevent

anti-abortion protesters from protesting within close proximity to the homes and offices of doctors, hospitals, and clinics. One of the arguments raised was that the conduct of the protesters, such as shouting at female patients, and drawing public attention to them, constituted an invasion of their privacy rights. Adams J. after an excellent review of the case law and literature, concluded that "invasion of privacy in Canadian common law continues to be an inceptive, if not ephemeral, legal concept, primarily operating to extend the margins of existing tort doctrine". In view of this, and "the need to accomodate broad counter privileges associated with free speech and the vast implications of living in a 'crowded society' ", Adams J. preferred to analyze the activities of the protestors with reference to more clearly defined and circumscribed torts, such as public and private nuisance.

4. One important development has been the recognition of the tort of "appropriation of one's personality". In *Krouse v. Chrysler Canada Ltd.* (1974), 1 O.R. (2d) 225, 40 D.L.R. (3d) 15 (C.A.); revg [1972] 2 O.R. 133, 25 D.L.R. (3d) 49, an action photograph of a football game was used in some advertising material. The plaintiff could be identified as one of the players depicted in the photo. Since he had not consented to this use of his photo, he claimed damages. Mr. Justice Estey recognized that there was a tort of appropriation of one's personality, but dismissed the claim because the usefulness of the player's name had not been diminished and therefore there had been no infringement of his legal right. In a similar type of case, where a photograph of the plaintiff waterskiing was used by the defendant to promote its business without his consent, damages of $500, the commercial value of the photo, was awarded. See *Athans v. Canadian Adventure Camps* (1977), 17 O.R. (2d) 425, 4 C.C.L.T. 20 (H.C.), *per* Henry J. Rather than being an invasion of privacy, it has been suggested that this is a form of "publicity piracy". See Gibson, Note on *Athans* case (1977), 4 C.C.L.T. 37, at 42. Also see Howell, "The Common Law Appropriation of Personality Tort" (1986), 2 Int. Prop. J. 149.

5. When Glenn Gould was a still unknown concert pianist a journalist interviewed and took numerous photos of him. Forty years later, after his death, the journalist published a book about Glenn Gould and used many of the original photos. The journalist owned the copyright in the photographs. Glenn Gould's estate had not authorized the publication of the book nor did it receive royalties. The estate sued for "approproiation of personality".

   In dismissing the claim, Lederman J. noted the 'sales vs. subject' distinction. Simply put, when a celebrity's image or *persona* is being used for commercial exploitation, *i.e.* for the sale of a product, the tort of appropriation of personality can be invoked. When, on the other hand, the celebrity is the subject matter of the work or enterprise, the tort cannot be invoked. In this case, Glenn Gould was the subject matter of the book; he was not being used to sell a product. See *Gould Estate v. Stoddart Publishing Co.* (1996), 31 C.C.L.T. (2d) 224 (Ont. Gen. Div.); affd for other reasons (1998), 39 O.R. (3rd) 545 (C.A.).

6. A potential catalyst for further movement in this area is the *Canadian Charter of Rights and Freedoms.* An early draft of the Charter had expressly recognized a "right to be secure against arbitrary invasion of privacy" along the lines of the International Declaration of Human Rights, but this was not included in the final draft of the Charter. There are two sections, however, that lend weight, albeit imperfectly, to a right of privacy. Section 7 guarantees the right to "life, liberty and security of the person". According to one scholar, these rights are "only meaningfully guaranteed if privacy is an implicit condition in the grant of such rights". (Cohen, "Invasion of Privacy: Police and Electronic Surveillance in Canada" (1982), 27 McGill L.J. 619, at 665.) In addition, s. 8, which guarantees the right to be secure against unreasonable search or seizure, may also indirectly promote the right to privacy, according to one writer. (Ehrcke, "Privacy and the Charter of Rights" (1985), 43 Adv. 53; *Hunter v. Southam Inc.*,

[1984] 2 S.C.R. 145, 11 D.L.R. (4th) 641). Additional encouragement to those advocating a right of privacy can be gleaned from s. 5 of the Quebec *Charter of Human Rights and Freedoms*, R.S.Q. 1977, c. C-12, s. 5, which provides that "every person has a right to respect for his private life."

7. Legislation has been enacted in some provinces, and by the federal government, in relation to privacy protection. See the *Privacy Act*, R.S.C. 1985, c. P-21, Sched. II, regarding the use of personal information; and Privacy Acts in B.C. (R.S.B.C. 1996, c. 373), Manitoba (R.S.M. 1987, c. P 125), Newfoundland (R.S.N. 1990, c. P-22), and Saskatchewan (R.S.S. 1978, c. P-24), which create a tort of violation of privacy. The provincial legislation deals with specific types of privacy protection, discusses the considerations which are relevant to determining whether there has been a violation, deals with the defences, and the available remedies. See Rainaldi (ed.), *Remedies In Tort*, Vol. 3, Chapter 24, for a good review of the various legislative provisions. For a discussion of the legislation see Deutscher, "The Protection of Privacy Act: Whose Privacy Is It Protecting?", and Osborne, "The Privacy Acts of B.C., Manitoba & Saskatchewan" in Gibson (ed.), *Aspects of Privacy Law* (1980), pp. 141 and 73; Vaver, "What's Mine is Not Yours: Commercial Appropriation of Personality under the Privacy Acts of British Columbia, Manitoba and Saskatchewan" (1981), 15 U.B.C. L. Rev. 241. A recently decided case under the Saskatchewan legislation is *Peters-Brown v. Regina District Health Board* (1995), 26 C.C.L.T. (2d) 316; affd (1996), 31 C.C.L.T. (2d) 302 (Sask. C.A.), and one under the B.C. legislation: *Hollinsworth v. BCTV* (1996), 34 C.C.L.T. (2d) 95 (B.C.S.C.); affd, unreported, October 6, 1998, Lambert, Esson and Braidwood JJ.A (B.C.C.A.).

NOTES ON DAMAGES FOR INTENTIONAL TORTS AND PUNITIVE DAMAGES

1. The ordinary principles for assessment of damages apply to intentional torts. Plaintiffs may recover any pecuniary losses, including medical expenses, loss of wages and increased living expenses. They may also recover non-pecuniary losses, such as pain and suffering and loss of enjoyment of life. See Atrens, "Intentional Interference with the Person" in Linden (ed.), *Studies in Canadian Tort Law* (1968), at 378.

2. Punitive damages or exemplary damages may also be permitted in appropriate cases in order to punish the defendant for high-handed, malicious or contemptuous conduct. Although this usual occurs in the field of the intentional torts, it can occur in other tort areas as well, such as in defamation cases. In a defamation case, *Hill v. Church of Scientology of Toronto*, [1995] 2 S.C.R. 1130, 126 D.L.R. (4th) 129, 25 C.C.L.T. (2d) 89, Cory J. clearly explained the rationale for such damages (at p. 1208 S.C.R.):

> Punitive damages may be awarded in situations where the defendant's misconduct is so malicious, oppressive and high-handed that it offends the court's sense of decency. Punitive damages bear no relation to what the plaintiff should receive by way of compensation. Their aim is not to compensate the plaintiff, but rather to punish the defendant. It is the means by which the jury or judge expresses its outrage at the egregious conduct of the defendant. They are in the nature of a fine which is meant to act as a deterrent to the defendant and to others from acting in this manner. It is important to emphasize that punitive damages should only be awarded in those circumstances where the combined award of general and aggravated damages would be insufficient to achieve the goal of punishment and deterrence.

3. The useful role that can be played by the award for punitive damages was amply demonstrated in the case of *Nantel v. Parisien* (1981), 18 C.C.L.T. 79, 22 R.P.R. 1 (Ont. S.C.). The plaintiff operated a small boutique on land purchased by the corporate

defendant. The corporate defendant had purchased the land in order to develop a shopping centre complex and wished the plaintiff out. Rather than negotiate with the plaintiff, the defendant chose the more expedient route of demolishing the plaintiff's boutique. In awarding the plaintiff $35,000 in punitive damages, Galligan J. (at 89-90) described the function of this award as follows:

> In this country we live by the rule of law; that woman, in my opinion, had the right to occupy those premises until August 31, 1980. Not only must the law not sanction the deliberate and callous disregard by the powerful of the weaker person's rights, the law must do what it can to ensure, by whatever means are at its disposal to ensure that the legal rights of a citizen are protected from the tyranny of another. Many cases have said that exemplary damages must not merely amount to a licence fee or to a reasonable cost or expense of doing business.
>
> It is my opinion that in proper cases damages should act as a deterrent to deter the powerful from subjugating the weaker to their business interests. It is difficult indeed to decide upon an amount which will be sufficient to demonstrate to these defendants and to those similarly inclined, that they may not illegally destroy the business of another so that their business interests may be served. It is difficult to decide on an amount which will demonstrate to the plaintiff and others who lack resources and apparent power, that if they wish to stand upon their rights, they will be protected by the law.

4. Punitive damages have been awarded in a variety of novel situations. In *Taylor v. Ginter* (1979), 19 B.C.L.R. 15, 108 D.L.R. (3d) 223 (S.C.), punitive damages were awarded against a corporate officer who tortiously removed the company files from its solicitor's office; in *Flame Bar-B-Q Ltd. v. Hoar* (1979), 27 N.B.R. (2d) 271, 106 D.L.R. (3d) 438 (C.A.), punitive damages were awarded against the estate of an accountant who had maliciously filed a petition in bankruptcy against a company, with the intention of wrecking the company unless it complied with certain demands; in *Barthropp v. Corp. of Dist. of West Vancouver* (1979), 17 B.C.L.R. 202 (S.C.), punitive damages were awarded against a municipality for its highhanded, insolent and arrogant behaviour in relation to the plaintiffs who were seriously obstructed in their attempts to obtain a building permit. In another example, two football players savagely beat some people in a hotel, and were required to pay exemplary damages because of their "outrageous and high-handed conduct". See *Delta Hotels Ltd. v. Magrum* (1975), 59 D.L.R. (3d) 126 (B.C.S.C.).

5. Punitive damages can be awarded in actions for negligence. In the United States this has long been permitted, but, until recently, not in Canada. This is changing. In *Robitaille v. Vancouver Hockey Club Ltd.* (1979), 19 B.C.L.R. 158; vard 30 B.C.L.R. 286, [1981] 3 W.W.R. 481 (C.A.), the plaintiff, a professional hockey player, sued his hockey club, alleging that due to its neglect in providing him with appropriate medical care, he suffered a permanent disability. The trial court held that the club had breached its duty of care owed to the plaintiff and that this breach was the cause of his disability.

   The court awarded the plaintiff $35,000 in exemplary damages, despite the fact that the case was essentially one of negligence. Mr. Justice Esson stated that this case was "an exception to the rule that exemplary damages may not be awarded for a negligent act". In most cases of personal injury caused by negligence, there is no deliberate action directed against the particular victim. However, in this case "the negligence consisted in the course of conduct, deliberately undertaken and persisted in, which was directed solely against the plaintiff". It was because of this that exemplary damages were awarded.

Following *Robitaille*, other courts have awarded punitive damages in a negligence context. In *Vlchek v. Koshel* (1988), 52 D.L.R. (4th) 371, 44 C.C.L.T. 314, the B.C. High Court awarded punitive damages in a products liability case because the reckless and indifferent conduct of the defendant in producing an all-terrain cycle "merited condemnation". In another British Columbia case *Coughlin v. Kuntz* (1987), 17 B.C.L.R. (2d) 265, 42 C.C.L.T. 142; affd (1987), 42 B.C.L.R. (2d) 108, [1990] 2 W.W.R. 737 (C.A.), punitive damages were awarded against an "arrogant" doctor for medical malpractice because the unorthodox operation he performed reflected a "callous" and "wanton disregard for the safety and health of the plaintiff".

In *C.N.R. Co. v. di Domenicantonia* (1988), 85 N.B.R. (2d) 404, 49 D.L.R. (4th) 342, the New Brunswick Court of Appeal held that exemplary damages should not be awarded in negligence cases except in the "most extreme circumstances, or when the act of the wrongdoer was consciously directed against the injured party."

6. In England, the availability of punitive damages has been severely limited. In *Rookes v. Barnard*, [1964] A.C. 1129, [1964] 1 All E.R. 367, the House of Lords expressed the view that tort law ought to be primarily aimed at compensation and not at punishment. It limited awards of exemplary damages (in addition to express statutory authorization, of course) to two situations: (1) where there was oppressive, arbitrary or unconstitutional action by servants of governments; (2) where the defendant's conduct was calculated by him to make a profit which may exceed the compensation payable to the plaintiff. "Aggravated" damages, however, as distinct from "exemplary" damages were said to remain available. *Rookes v. Barnard* was not received with enthusiasm. The courts in Canada, Australia and New Zealand refused to follow it, but the English courts submitted, that is, at least, until *Broome v. Cussell & Co. Ltd.*, [1971] 2 Q.B. 354, [1971] 2 All E.R. 187 (C.A.). In that case, although the facts of the case were actually within the second exception of *Rookes v. Barnard*, Lord Denning sought to overthrow the decision and urged that it no longer be followed. When the case was appealed, the House of Lords affirmed the result on the basis of the second exception, but used the occasion to reaffirm *Rookes v. Barnard* and to criticize the Court of Appeal "with studied moderation" for its course of conduct in defying them (see *Cussell & Co. Ltd. v. Broome*, [1972] A.C. 1027, [1972] 1 All E.R. 801). For a fine article on this topic, see Catzman, "Exemplary Damages: The Decline, Fall and Resurrection of *Rookes v. Barnard*", in *New Developments in the Law of Torts*, Special Lectures of the Law Society of Upper Canada (1973), p. 41.

7. More recently courts and scholars have been looking afresh at the idea of aggravated damages as a possible remedy in cases where punitive damages are too harsh but ordinary compensatory damages are insufficient. There is authority for awards of "aggravated" damages, as contrasted with "punitive" damages, the former being granted to compensate the plaintiff for the loss of dignity resulting from the defendant's malicious conduct, the latter being given to express the court's outrage and in order to deter such conduct in the future. *Rookes v. Barnard*, [1964] A.C. 1129, [1964] 1 All E.R. 367 (H.L.); *Brown v. Waterloo Regional Bd. of Com'rs of Police* (1982), 37 O.R. (2d) 277, 136 D.L.R. (3d) 49 (H.C.); revd in part 43 O.R. (2d) 113, 150 D.L.R. (3d) 729 (C.A.); Cooper-Stephenson, *Personal Injury Damages in Canada* (1981), p. 688; *Walker v. CFTO* (1987), 37 D.L.R. (4th) 224, 39 C.C.L.T. 121 (Ont. C.A.), *per* Robins J.A.; *Campbell v. Read*, [1988] 3 W.W.R 236, 43 C.L.L.T. 262 (B.C.C.A.). One reason for the use of aggravated damages is to avoid the narrow rules of *Rookes v. Barnard.* See *Banks v. Campbell* (1974), 14 N.S.R. (2d) 73, 45 D.L.R. (3d) 603 (S.C.T.D.). If *Rookes* is to be ignored, it is not as important to utilize aggravated damages, but if it is to be followed, the concept of aggravated damages may be more widely employed. The Supreme Court of Canada has recently clarified the law in *Vorvis v. I.C.B.C.*, [1989] 1 S.C.R. 1085, 58 D.L.R. (4th) 193.

8. Do you believe that punitive damages have a legitimate role in modern tort law? Is not criminal law the proper vehicle for punishing wrongdoers?

9. What if the defendant has been convicted of a criminal offence and sentenced? See *Loomis v. Rohan* (1974), 46 D.L.R. (3d) 423, [1974] 2 W.W.R. 599 (B.C.S.C.); *Amos v. Vawter* (1969), 6 D.L.R. (3d) 234, 69 W.W.R. 596 (B.C.S.C.); *Radovskis v. Tomm* (1957), 65 Man. R. 61, 21 W.W.R. 658 (Q.B.); *Natonson v. Lexier*, [1939] 3 W.W.R. 289 (Sask. K.B.). See *Fenwick v. Staples* (1977), 18 O.R. (2d) 128, 82 D.L.R. (2d) 145 (Co. Ct.). What if the defendant is convicted but given a conditional discharge? See *Loedel v. Eckert* (1977), 3 C.C.L.T. 145 (B.C.S.C.); *cf., Kenmuir v. Huetzelmann* (1977), 3 C.C.L.T. 153 (B.C. Co. Ct.), father suing. What if the defendant was charged but acquitted? Note that Ontario's *Victims' Bill of Rights*, S.O. 1995, c. 6, s. 4(4) requires that judges take into consideration the sentence of the convicted person before awarding punitive damages.

10. In *K. (W.) v. Pornbacher* (1997), 34 C.C.L.T. (2d) 174 (B.C.S.C.), the court awarded punitive damages even though the defendant had already been punished in criminal proceedings. The reason for the award related to the defendant's conduct, both in the criminal and civil proceedings. In the criminal proceedings, the accused entered a guilty plea only after the victim was forced to revisit the incidents through the Crown's case. In the civil case, the defendant again put the plaintiff through the ordeal of having to prove his case, even though there was no credible corroborative evidence for the defendant's denials. The court considered this to be "cruel, abusive and insolent".

11. Should punitive damages ever be awarded against the estate of a deceased? In *Breitkreutz v. Public Trustee* (1978), 89 D.L.R. (3d) 442, 6 C.C.L.T. 76 (Alta. S.C.), the deceased's estate was sued by the estate of a person who was killed by the deceased. The deceased killed himself after committing the murder. McLung J. refused the claim for punitive damages, doubting whether punitive damages would furnish any additional deterrent to others beyond criminal law. However, in *Flame Bar-B-Q Ltd. v. Hoar, supra*, punitive damages were awarded against the estate of a deceased accountant, who had maliciously filed a petition in bankruptcy against a company in order to force it to comply with his demands. Are these decisions reconcilable? Note that some statutes specifically prohibit any award of punitive or exemplary damages in favour of a deceased victim's estate. See, *e.g.*, *Survival of Actions Act*, R.S.A. 1980, c. S-30, s. 5.

12. Should a person be able to obtain liability insurance against the risk of having an award of punitive damages being made against him or her? There have been several United States cases, going both ways, on this issue. See Prosser, Wade and Schwartz, *Cases & Materials on Torts*, 8th ed. (1988), p. 536. If a person's liability insurer pays the punitive damages for the defendant, will the award have the desired punitive effect? Will it be a deterrent? Is this not a problem, not only in relation to the award of punitive damages but also in relation to the whole moral basis of a fault based tort law?

13. Will the doctrine of vicarious liability render an employer liable for the punitive damages awarded against its employee? What factors are involved here? This issue was reviewed by MacGuigan J. in *Peeters v. Canada* (1993), 18 C.C.L.T. (2d) 136 (Fed. C.A.). MacGuigan J.'s conclusion was that punitive damages must be based on deterrence and since there can be no possibility of deterrence if the employer is not complicit in the wrongdoing, punitive damages ought not to be awarded in the ordinary vicarious liability case.

ATRENS, "INTENTIONAL INTERFERENCE WITH THE PERSON"

in Linden (ed.), *Studies in Canadian Tort Law* (1968), p. 378.

The arguments for and against punitive damages cannot be considered in detail here. The main objection, and the one which found favour with Lord Devlin in *Rookes v. Barnard*, is that compensation, and not punishment, is the proper function of the law of torts. No one would suggest that punishment for its own sake is a justification for either a criminal sanction or punitive damages, but such justification may be found if it discourages antisocial behaviour. Theoretically, punitive damages may prevent antisocial behaviour in three ways: first, by deterring the defendant from repetition of the tortious behaviour; secondly, the example made of the defendant may dissuade others from similar conduct, and thirdly, the availability of punitive damages may encourage the injured party to seek a remedy in court, rather than resorting to private vengeance.

Assuming for the sake of argument that punitive damages can accomplish these deterrent objectives, is this a proper function of the law of torts? It has been argued that punitive damages may become an instrument of oppression because the law of torts denies the defendant certain safeguards which are available to him in the criminal law, for example, proof beyond a reasonable doubt and maximum penalties. Although this objection applies to any tort case, the absence of these safeguards is particularly objectionable where the purpose of the award of damages is not to compensate an innocent victim, but to use the defendant to promote a public policy of discouraging antisocial behaviour. Because an award of punitive damages is a windfall to the plaintiff, the danger is that, without effective controls, the plaintiff is unlikely to claim an award of punitive damages with a dispassionate concern for the public welfare.

Despite the persuasiveness of the above objections, it does not follow that punitive damages have no place in our legal system. The law of torts should, at least as a subsidiary aim, attempt to discourage certain forms of socially undesirable behaviour. To leave this function entirely to the criminal law would require a considerable extension of the existing law, bringing unnecessary restrictions on the freedom of the individual. If in borderline cases the choice is to be made between a criminal sanction and liability in tort, the latter should be chosen. An adverse civil judgment does not involve the possibility of imprisonment or the stigma of a criminal conviction. In most cases the admonitory function of the law of torts will be accomplished through an award of compensatory damages. As indicated above, such damages may be aggravated by the nature of the defendant's conduct. Where compensatory damages and the criminal law cannot perform an effective deterrent function, punitive damages may be considered.

REVIEW PROBLEM

Paul and Dick, both first year students at Osgoode Hall Law School, decided to spend a weekend camping together at Lake Muskoka. After arriving at the campsite on Friday evening, they pitched a tent, made a fire, had dinner, and drank a few beers. As darkness fell, Paul entered the tent to prepare for bed. Suddenly, a devilish gleam appeared in Dick's eye. Feigning a call of nature, he excused himself.

When Dick and Paul had first discussed this camping trip, Dick, an inveterate practical joker, had learned about Paul's irrational fear of snakes. Dick had assured

Paul that there were no longer any snakes to be found near the campsites in the Muskoka area. It was only then that Paul reluctantly agreed to accompany Dick on the trip.

The moon was bright, the stars twinkled, and silence reigned over the dark forest. "Now," Dick thought, "it is time to have some fun with Paul." He hid behind a bush some 50 feet away from the tent and imitated the sound of an angry rattlesnake. Paul, hearing the sound and believing it to be a rattlesnake, felt uneasy. Again Dick made the rattling sound, this time from behind a tree only 20 feet away. Trembling, Paul called out for Dick. Dick was now outside the tent door. Inside, he could hear Paul nervously pacing. Again, he imitated the fearsome sound of the "rattler". Paul, now frantic, picked up an axe and whirled around to defend himself but twisted his ankle and fell, breaking his left leg. Dick, laughing, burst into the tent to find his friend on the ground, writhing in pain and shaking uncontrollably.

Two months later, Paul retains you to sue his ex-friend, Dick. Paul is now fully recovered from the neurasthenia suffered as a result of his experience in the tent, but his left leg is still in a cast.

Do you think Paul will succeed in recovering damages from Dick and, if so, on what theory of tort liability?

CHAPTER 3

DEFENCES TO TRESPASS AND INTENTIONAL INTERFERENCES

Conduct which would ordinarily result in liability may not do so for a number of reasons. For example, plaintiffs who consent to invasions of their persons will not be allowed to claim the protection of the law. In these situations, no "wrongs" have been done. In addition to consent, there are other reasons that may excuse invasions of the plaintiffs' interests. These "privileges" may arise in cases of self-defence, defence of persons, of property, or of the public interest as a whole. In these cases, the courts must balance the interests being invaded and the interests being advanced by the defendants' conduct. Seemingly simple questions can become issues of serious social importance.

A. CONSENT

1. The Nature of Consent

O'BRIEN v. CUNARD S.S. CO.
Supreme Judicial Court of Massachusetts. 154 Mass. 272, 28 N.E. 266 (1891).

Tort, for an assault, and for negligently vaccinating the plaintiff, who was a steerage passenger on the defendant's steamship. The trial court directed a verdict for the defendant, and the plaintiff brings exceptions.

Knowlton J.: This case presents two questions: first, whether there was any evidence to warrant the jury in finding that the defendant, by any of its servants or agents, committed an assault on the plaintiff; secondly, whether there was evidence on which the jury could have found that the defendant was guilty of negligence towards the plaintiff. To sustain the first count, which was for an alleged assault, the plaintiff relied on the fact that the surgeon who was employed by the defendant vaccinated her on shipboard, while she was on her passage from Queenstown to Boston. On this branch of the case the question is whether there was any evidence that the surgeon used force upon the plaintiff against her will. In determining whether the act was lawful or unlawful, the surgeon's conduct must be considered in connection with the surrounding circumstances. If the plaintiff's behaviour was such as to indicate consent on her part, he was justified in his act, whatever her unexpressed feelings may have been. In determining whether she consented, he could be guided only by her overt acts and the manifestations of her feelings. [Citations omitted.] It is undisputed that at Boston there are strict quarantine regulations in regard to the examination of emigrants, to see that they are protected from smallpox by vaccination, and that only those persons who hold a certificate from the medical officer of the steamship, stating that they are so protected, are permitted to land without detention in quarantine, or vaccination by the port physician. It appears that the defendant is accustomed to have its surgeons vaccinate all emigrants who desire it, and who are not protected by previous vaccination, and give them a certificate which is accepted at quarantine as evidence of their protection. Notices of the regulations at quarantine, and of the willingness of the ship's medical officer to vaccinate such as needed vaccination, were posted about the ship in various languages, and on the day when the operation was performed the surgeon had a right to presume that she and other women who were vaccinated understood the importance and purpose of vaccination for those who bore no marks to show that they were protected. By the plaintiff's testimony, which, in this particular, is undisputed, it appears that about 200 women passengers were assembled below, and she understood from conversation with them that they were to be vaccinated; that she stood about 15 feet from the surgeon, and saw them form in a line, and pass in turn before him; that he "examined their arms, and, passing some of them by, proceeded to vaccinate those that had no mark"; that she did not hear him say anything to any of them; that upon being passed by they each received a card, and went on deck; that when her turn came she showed him her arm; he looked at it, and said there was no mark, and that she should be vaccinated; that she told him she had been vaccinated before, and it left no mark; "that he then said nothing; that he should vaccinate her again"; that she held up her arm to be vaccinated; that no one touched her; that she did not tell him she did not want to be vaccinated; and that she took the ticket which he gave her, certifying that he had vaccinated her, and used it at quarantine. She was one of a large number of women who were vaccinated on that occasion, without, so far as appears, a word of objection from any of them. They all indicated by their conduct that they desired to avail themselves of the provisions made for their benefit. There was nothing in the conduct of the plaintiff to indicate to the surgeon that she did not wish to obtain a card which would save her from detention at quarantine, and to be vaccinated, if necessary, for that purpose. Viewing his conduct in the light of the surrounding circumstances, it was lawful; and there was no evidence tending to show that it was not. The ruling of the court on this part of the case was correct. The plaintiff contends that, if it was lawful for the surgeon to vaccinate her, the vaccination was negligently performed, "There was no evidence of want of care or precaution by the defendant in the selection of the surgeon, or in the procuring of the virus or vaccine matter." Unless there was evidence that the surgeon was negligent in performing the operation, and unless the defendant is liable for this negligence, the plaintiff must fall on the second count. ...

Exceptions overruled.

NOTES

1. What was the test used by the court in determining whether or not the plaintiff consented? Is this an acceptable test?

2. It is now clear that a defendant, who relies on the defence of consent, bears the onus of proving it. *Kelly v. Hazlett* (1976), 75 D.L.R. (3d) 536, 1 C.C.L.T. 1 (Ont.), *per* Morden J.; *Hambley v. Shepley* (1967), 63 D.L.R. (2d) 94 at 95, [1967] 2 O.R. 217 (C.A.), *per* Laskin J.A.; *Schweitzer v. Central Hospital* (1974), 6 O.R. (2d) 606, 53 D.L.R. (3d) 494 (H.C.); *Allan v. New Mount Sinai Hospital et al.* (1980), 109 D.L.R. (3d) 634, 11 C.C.L.T. 299 (Ont. S.C.); revd on other grounds (1981), 125 D.L.R. (3d) 276, 19 C.C.L.T. 76*n* (C.A.).

NORBERG v. WYNRIB

Supreme Court of Canada. [1992] 4 W.W.R. 577,
[1992] 2 S.C.R. 226.

La Forest J. (**Gonthier** and **Cory JJ.** concurring): This case [appeal from [1990] 4 W.W.R. 193, 44 B.C.L.R. (2d) 47, 66 D.L.R. (4th) 553] concerns the civil liability of a doctor who gave drugs to a chemically dependent woman patient in exchange for sexual contact. The central issue is whether the defence of consent can be raised against the intentional tort of battery in such circumstances. The case also raises the issue whether the action is barred by reason of illegality or immorality.

FACTS

In 1978 the appellant, then a modestly educated young woman in her late teens, began to experience severe headaches and pains in her jaw. She went to doctors and dentists but none of them could diagnose the cause of her excruciating pain. They prescribed various types of painkillers. However, the medication provided no relief. The headaches became worse. More and more medication was prescribed in increasing amounts and dosages. In addition to this medication, her sister, a drug addict, gave her Fiorinal, a painkiller drug. Finally in December 1978, a dentist diagnosed her difficulty as being related to an abscessed tooth. It was extracted and at last her pain was relieved.

But now the appellant had a new problem. She had a craving for painkillers. Her sister gave her more Fiorinal. In 1981, when she broke her ankle, she found a doctor who was willing to prescribe Fiorinal for her. She continued to obtain prescriptions from him until he retired. However, his replacement refused to give her more pills. She discussed the situation with her sister and in March 1982 she commenced to see Dr. Wynrib, an elderly medical practitioner in his seventies. She told him she was experiencing pain in the ankle she had broken in 1981 and asked for Fiorinal. He gave her the prescription. She kept going back to him using the ankle injury and other illnesses as a pretext for obtaining prescriptions. Her dependence on Fiorinal continued to increase as did her dependence on Dr. Wynrib. But the pretext could not continue. Later in 1982, Dr. Wynrib confronted the appellant. The appellant described this confrontation as follows:

> I had gone into his office one day and I asked him — I asked him for a prescription of Fiorinal, and I remember that he sat back in his chair and he pulled out like the medical file and he looked at me and he asked me come on, Laura, why is the real reason you're taking the Fiorinal. I told him because it's for my back or my ankle, whatever it was that I had been asking him for, and he said — no he said. And he looked again over my file. He said you can't be taking them for this long and not be addicted to them. Why is the real reason. And I denied it again. I said it's for the pain. And he told me that if I didn't admit to him that I was addicted to the Fiorinal that he wouldn't give me any more prescriptions. And I remember that I had started crying and I had denied [*sic*] to him, and he had told me to leave the office. And I wouldn't leave the office and finally I admitted to him that I was addicted to the Fiorinal.

Dr. Wynrib responded by giving the appellant another prescription.

After the appellant admitted to Dr. Wynrib that she was addicted to Fiorinal, she testified that he told her that "if I was good to him he would be good to me" and he made suggestions by pointing upstairs where he lived above his office. The appellant recognized this for what it was and sought her drugs elsewhere. She managed to secure Fiorinal through other doctors and buying them off the street. Her tolerance and dependence grew. Eventually the other doctors reduced her supply. She was, as she put it, desperate. Near the end of 1983 she went back to Dr. Wynrib because she knew he would give her Fiorinal. She gave in to his demands.

Initially, the sexual encounters took place in the back examination room of his office. He kissed her and fondled her breasts. In time, he required her to meet him upstairs in his bedroom where he kept a bottle of Fiorinal in his dresser drawer beside the bed. She managed to stall him for awhile by asking for the Fiorinal first and then leaving after she obtained it. But this device did not work long. Dr. Wynrib told her that he would not give her the Fiorinal until she complied with his demands. The pattern was that he would tell her to undress and put the bottle of Fiorinal by his bed for her to see. Both parties would lie on the bed. Dr. Wynrib would kiss the appellant, touch her and then get on top of her. He would go through the motions of intercourse. There was no penetration, however, because he could not sustain an erection. On at least one occasion, however, he penetrated her with his fingers. He would give her pills each time she visited him in his apartment. She then would go back to his office the next day and he would write out a prescription. When the encounters began, the appellant did not want to believe what was happening. She thought he would do it once and then stop. However, the appellant testified that these incidences of simulated intercourse occurred 10 or 12 times, up to the early part of 1985.

During this period, the appellant was obtaining Fiorinal from a number of other sources: other doctors, off the street and from her sister. In February 1985, she left her job. She became depressed and no longer had the money to buy the drugs she needed off the street. She told Dr. Wynrib that she needed help. Her evidence at trial was:

> A. . . . I remember telling him that I needed help, and he told me to just quit. He said just quit. I said I can't. The pills were on my mind all the time.
>
> Q. Did he direct you anywhere else apart from telling you to quit, giving you advice?
>
> A. No, no.

At some point in 1985, the appellant became the subject of a criminal investigation leading the RCMP to visit Dr. Wynrib in April 1985. After this visit, Dr. Wynrib told the appellant that he could no longer give her prescriptions in the office. However, he still gave her pills from the bottle in his dresser drawer when she visited him upstairs. Eventually, she was charged with the summary conviction offence of "double doctoring" under s. 3.1(1) of the *Narcotic Control Act*, R.S.C. 1970, c. N-1, as am. by R.S.C. 1985, c. 19, s. 198, *i.e.*, obtaining narcotic prescription drugs from a doctor without disclosing particulars of prescriptions from other doctors. In July 1985, she went to a rehabilitation centre for drug addicts on her own initiative. She left the centre after one month and has not taken any drugs for non-medical reasons since. In September 1985, the appellant pleaded guilty to the offences for which she was charged and received an absolute discharge.

The appellant continues to attend Narcotics Anonymous and other similar programs. She has done volunteer work at the crisis and counselling centre in the area where she lives and has completed credits towards a social worker program. Her hope is to work in the area of drug rehabilitation. She daily thinks with shame and remorse about what happened with Dr. Wynrib. She returned to the rehabilitation centre for more treatment after her first child was born. She felt that she did not deserve to have a child because of what she had done with Dr. Wynrib. Her craving for drugs continues but she has learned to live without them.

JUDICIAL HISTORY

Supreme Court of British Columbia (1988), 27 B.C.L.R. (2d) 240

At trial, the appellant sought general and punitive damages against the respondent on the grounds of sexual assault, negligence and breach of fiduciary duty: see *Norberg v. Wynrib*, [1988] 6 W.W.R. 305, 27 B.C.L.R. (2d) 240, 50 D.L.R. (4th) 167, 44 C.C.L.T. 184.

The trial judge, Oppal J., rejected the appellant's claim of sexual assault holding that she had consented to it. At p. 244 [B.C.L.R.], he stated:

> By apparently voluntarily submitting to the doctor's advances on the various occasions, the plaintiff gave her implied consent to the sexual contact that constitutes the alleged battery. She obviously had deep misgivings about engaging in this conduct with the defendant. Clearly, she did not wish to do so. However, at no time did she express her feelings to the defendant that she did not wish to engage in sexual activities with him. In fact she went along with his demands.

Oppal J. recognized that for consent to be genuine, it must not be extorted by force or threats of force, or be obtained from an individual under the influence of drugs, but he held that these factors were not present in this case. The respondent did not exercise or threaten to use force, and there was no evidence that the appellant's addiction interfered with her capacity to consent to the sexual activity or with her ability to reason.

Court of Appeal (1990), 44 B.C.L.R. (2d) 47

The majority of the Court of Appeal, McEachern C.J.B.C. and Gibbs J.A., accepted the trial judge's finding that the appellant "gave her implied consent to the sexual contact that constitutes the alleged battery" and that there was no evidence that her addiction to Fiorinal interfered with her capacity to consent to the sexual activity. It further agreed that the appellant was not at any time deprived of her ability to reason. In the majority's view, Oppal J. was correct in dismissing the appellant's sexual assault claim on the basis of consent.

...

The Appeal to this Court

The appellant then appealed to this court. In addition to the parties, the Women's Legal Education and Action Fund appeared as intervenor. At trial and in the Court of Appeal, the appellant sought recovery on a number of grounds: sexual assault, negligence, breach of fiduciary duty and breach of contract. In this court, however, counsel particularly stressed the assault claim and I am content to dispose of the case on this basis. The other claims would appear to give rise to difficulties that would not arise in the ordinary doctor-client case. In particular, the appellant here did not come to the doctor for treatment. Rather she intended to use him to obtain drugs. Given the manner in which I propose to deal with the case, however, it is unnecessary for me to explore these matters.

ASSAULT — THE NATURE OF CONSENT

The alleged sexual assault in this case falls under the tort of battery. A battery is the intentional infliction of unlawful force on another person. Consent, express or implied, is a defence to battery. Failure to resist or protest is an indication of consent "if a reasonable person who is aware of the consequences and capable of protest or resistance would voice his objection"; see Fleming, *The Law of Torts* (7th ed., 1987), at pp. 72-73. However, the consent must be genuine; it must not be obtained by force or threat of force or be given under the influence of drugs. Consent may also be vitiated by fraud or deceit as to the nature of the defendant's conduct. The courts below considered these to be the only factors that would vitiate consent.

In my view, this approach to consent in this kind of case is too limited. As Heuston and Buckley, *Salmond and Heuston on the Law of Torts* (19th ed., 1987), at pp. 564-65, put it: "A man cannot be said to be 'willing' unless he is in a position to choose freely; and freedom of choice predicates the absence from his mind of any feeling of constraint interfering with the freedom of his will." A "feeling of constraint" so as to "interfere with the freedom of a person's will" can arise in a number of situations not involving force, threats of force, fraud or incapacity. The concept of consent as it operates in tort law is based on a presumption of individual autonomy and free will. It is presumed that the individual has freedom to consent or not to consent. This presumption, however, is untenable in certain circumstances. A position of relative weakness can, in some circumstances, interfere with the freedom of a person's will. Our notion of consent must, therefore, be modified to appreciate the power relationship between the parties.

An assumption of individual autonomy and free will is not confined to tort law. It is also the underlying premise of contract law. The supposition of contract law is that two parties agree or consent to a particular course of action. However, contract law has evolved in such a way that it recognizes that contracting parties do not always have equality in their bargaining strength. The doctrines of duress, undue influence, and unconscionability have arisen to protect the vulnerable when they are in a relationship of unequal power. For reasons of public policy, the law will not always hold weaker parties to the bargains they make. Professor Klippert in his book *Unjust Enrichment* (1983) refers to the doctrines of duress, undue influence, and unconscionability as "justice factors." He lumps these together under the general term "coercion" and states, at p. 156, that, "In essence the common thread is an illegitimate use of power or unlawful pressure which vitiates a person's freedom of choice." In a situation where a plaintiff is induced to enter into an unconscionable transaction because of an inequitable disparity in bargaining strength, it cannot be said that the plaintiff's act is voluntary: see Klippert, at p. 170.

If the "justice factor" of unconscionability is used to address the issue of voluntariness in the law of contract, it seems reasonable that it be examined to address the issue of voluntariness in the law of tort. This provides insight into the issue of consent: for consent to be genuine, it must be voluntary. The factual context of each case must, of course, be evaluated to determine if there has been genuine consent. However, the principles that have been developed in the area of unconscionable transactions to negate the legal effectiveness of certain contracts provide a useful framework for this evaluation.

. . .

It must be noted that in the law of contracts proof of an unconscionable transaction involves a two-step process: (1) proof of inequality in the position of the parties, and (2) proof of an improvident bargain. Similarly, a two-step process is involved in determining whether or not there has been legally effective consent to a sexual assault. The first step is undoubtedly proof of an inequality between the parties which, as already noted, will ordinarily occur within the context of a special "power dependency" relationship. The second step, I suggest, is proof of exploitation. A consideration of the type of relationship at issue may provide a strong indication of exploitation. Community standards of conduct may also be of some assistance. In *Harry v. Kreutziger* (1978), 9 B.C.L.R. 166, 95 D.L.R. (3d) 231 (C.A.), an unconscionable transaction case dealing with the sale of a commercial fishing boat for less than its value, Lambert J.A., at p. 177 [B.C.L.R.], approached the issue of unconscionability from a different angle:

> ... questions as to whether use of power was unconscionable, an advantage was unfair or very unfair, a consideration was grossly inadequate, or bargaining power was grievously impaired, to select words from both statements of principle, the *Morrison* case and the *Bundy* case, are really aspects of one single question. That single question is whether the transaction, seen as a whole, is sufficiently divergent from community standards of commercial morality that it should be rescinded.

If the type of sexual relationship at issue is one that is sufficiently divergent from community standards of conduct, this may alert the court to the possibility of exploitation.

APPLICATION TO THIS CASE

The trial judge held that the appellant's implied consent to the sexual activity was voluntary. Dr. Wynrib, he stated, exercised neither force nor threats of force and the appellant's capacity to consent was not impaired by her drug use. The Court of Appeal agreed that the appellant voluntarily engaged in the sexual encounters. However, it must be asked if the appellant was truly in a position to make a free choice. It seems clear to me that there was a marked inequality in the respective powers of the parties. The appellant was a young woman with limited education. More important, she was addicted to the heavy use of tranquilizers and painkillers. On this ground alone it can be said that there was an inequality in the position of the parties arising out of the appellant's need. The appellant's drug dependence diminished her ability to make a real choice. Although she did not wish to engage in sexual activity with Dr. Wynrib, her reluctance was overwhelmed by the driving force of her addiction and the unsettling prospect of a painful, unsupervised chemical withdrawal. That the appellant's need for drugs placed her in a vulnerable position is evident from the comments of the trial judge, at p. 243:

> [The appellant] stated that at first she ignored his suggestions and managed to stall him off. For a short period of time she stopped seeing him and managed to secure her drugs through other doctors. However, when the other doctors reduced her supply, she returned to Dr. Wynrib. She stated that she was desperate. She said that she complied with his demands.

And at p. 244, he added:

> She obviously had deep misgivings about engaging in this conduct with the defendant. Clearly, she did not wish to do so.
>
> ... her willingness to engage in sexual activity was obviously inspired by the prescriptions which the doctor would provide ...

The appellant's vulnerability on the basis of need is also evident from the following report of Dr. Fleming of the Department of Psychiatry, Faculty of Medicine, University of British Columbia, and entered as expert evidence:

> As she herself states, she wished to obtain a supply at any cost, and was willing to compromise her beliefs concerning appropriate behaviour in order to obtain supply. In the absence of dependence on and tolerance to Fiorinal it is my impression that Ms. Norberg would not have consented to have any social or sexual activity with Dr. Wynrib. On the basis of my clinical examination and the material provided it is my belief that she did so in order to obtain a supply of medication.

On the other side of the equation was an elderly, male professional — the appellant's doctor. An unequal distribution of power is frequently a part of the doctor-patient relationship. As it is stated in *The Final Report of the Task Force on Sexual Abuse of Patients*, An Independent Task Force Commissioned by the College of Physicians and Surgeons of Ontario (November 25, 1991) (Chair: Marilou McPhedran), at p. 11:

> Patients seek the help of doctors when they are in a vulnerable state — when they are sick, when they are needy, when they are uncertain about what needs to be done.
>
> The unequal distribution of power in the physician-patient relationship makes opportunities for sexual exploitation more possible than in other relationships. This vulnerability gives physicians the power to exact sexual compliance. Physical force or weapons are not necessary because the physician's power comes from having the knowledge and being trusted by patients.

In this case, Dr. Wynrib knew that the appellant was vulnerable and driven by her compulsion for drugs. It is likely that he knew or at least strongly suspected that she was dependent upon Fiorinal before she admitted her addiction to him. It was he who ferreted out that she was addicted to drugs. As a doctor, the respondent knew how to assist the appellant medically and he knew (or should have known) that she could not "just quit" taking drugs without treatment. Dr. Fleming stated:

> It is known that withdrawal from continuous use of short-acting barbiturates is an extremely unpleasant experience and it is natural that Ms. Norberg would attempt to maintain her supply in the absence of a comprehensive treatment program that would address her needs (pharmacological and psychological) during a withdrawal program.

The respondent's medical knowledge and knowledge of the appellant's addiction, combined with his authority to prescribe drugs, gave him power over her. It was he who suggested the sex-for-drugs arrangement.

However, it must still be asked if there was exploitation. In my opinion there was. Dr. Herbert of the Department of Family Practice, Faculty of Medicine, University of British Columbia, expressed the opinion that "a reasonable practitioner would have taken steps to attempt to help Ms. Norberg end her addiction by, for example, suggesting drug counselling, or, at the very least, by discontinuing her prescriptions of Fiorinal." However, Dr. Wynrib did not use his medical knowledge and expertise to address the appellant's addiction. Instead, he abused his power over her and exploited the information he obtained concerning her weakness to pursue his own personal interests. It seems to me that a sex-for-drugs arrangement initiated by a doctor with his drug addict patient is a relationship which is divergent from what the community would consider acceptable. The trial judge (at p. 246) stated that "Dr. Wynrib's conduct would in all likelihood be regarded by members of the medical profession and the community at large as disgraceful and unprofessional." McEachern C.J.B.C. (at p. 51) referred to the relationship as a "sordid arrangement."

There is also a body of opinion which regards sexual contact in any doctor-patient relationship as exploitative. In the opinion of the Task Force on Sexual Abuse of Patients, at p. 12:

> Due to the position of power the physician brings to the doctor-patient relationship, there are NO circumstances — NONE — in which sexual activity between a physician and patient is acceptable. Sexual activity between a patient and a doctor ALWAYS represents sexual abuse, regardless of what rationalization or belief system the doctor chooses to use to excuse it. Doctors need to recognize that they have power and status, and that there may be times when a patient will test the boundaries between them. It is ALWAYS the doctor's responsibility to know what is appropriate and never to cross the line into sexual activity.

Indeed, the Hippocratic Oath indicates that sexual contact between a doctor and his or her patient is fundamentally improper: see *Dorland's Illustrated Medical Dictionary*, 27th ed. (1988), at p. 768:

> In every house where I come I will enter only for the good of my patients, keeping myself far from all intentional ill-doing and all seduction, and especially from the pleasures of love with women or with men, be they free or slaves.

These observations were directed at the regulation of the doctor-patient relationship, rather than civil liability and I need not consider their precise implications in the latter context. For we are not here dealing with just a doctor-patient relationship but a doctor-drug addict relationship, and it was not just a sexual relationship but a sex-for-drugs relationship. These circumstances suggest that the appellant's consent was not genuine for the purposes of the law.

The respondent argues that the appellant exploited the weakness and loneliness of an elderly man to obtain drugs. While Dr. Wynrib, no doubt, had vulnerabilities of his own, it seems to me that the determining factor in this case is that he instigated the relationship — it was he, not the appellant, who used his power and knowledge to initiate the arrangement and to exploit her vulnerability. The respondent's argument might be more persuasive if it had been the appellant who had suggested that she would exchange sex for drugs. I am also not convinced by assertions that the respondent showed compassion and interest in the appellant's well-being. This does not square with his flagrant disregard for her need for treatment. If he was truly interested in her well-being, he would have helped her overcome her addiction.

The respondent argues that the position of the plaintiff is tantamount to an assertion that an addict cannot give consent. An addict, he continues, will thus not be held responsible for his or her actions. Although an addiction may indicate an inequality in power, this will not by itself render consent legally ineffective. Under the formulation I have suggested, there must also be exploitation. In *Black v.*

Wilcox (1976), 70 D.L.R. (3d) 192, 12 O.R. (2d) 759 (C.A.), at p. 197 [D.L.R.], Evans J.A., in discussing the principle of unconscionability, stated:

> ... the Court will invoke the equitable rule that a person who is not equal to protecting himself will be protected, *not against his own folly or carelessness, but against his being taken advantage of* by those in a position to do so by reason of their commanding and superior bargaining position. The combination of inequality of position and improvidence is the foundation upon which the doctrine is based. [emphasis added]

The aim is not to absolve an addict from all responsibility; rather it is to protect an addict from abuse from those in special positions of power.

To summarize, in my view, the defence of consent cannot succeed in the circumstances of this case. The appellant had a medical problem — an addiction to Fiorinal. Dr. Wynrib had knowledge of the problem. As a doctor, he had knowledge of the proper medical treatment, and knew she was motivated by her craving for drugs. Instead of fulfilling his professional responsibility to treat the appellant, he used his power and expertise to his own advantage and to her detriment. In my opinion, the unequal power between the parties and the exploitative nature of the relationship removed the possibility of the appellant's providing meaningful consent to the sexual contact.

Appeal allowed.

NOTES

1. Madam Justice McLachlin ([1992] 2 W.W.R., at 606) approached the issue not from the perspective of the tort of battery but from a breach of the fiduciary duty that a doctor owes to a patient. This allowed her to find the defendant liable despite the fact that the sexual relations in this case were, in Her Ladyship's opinion, consensual. Mr. Justice Sopinka (at 629) refused to follow the fiduciary route and did not agree with Mr. Justice La Forest's view that the sexual encounters in this case were not consensual. He held, therefore, that the battery claim failed. He did find, however, that the defendant doctor breached his duty to medically treat his patient with due competence. See *Taylor v. McGillivray* (1993), 110 D.L.R. (4th) 64 (N.B.Q.B.), where the court held that there was consent and therefore no battery, but that there was a breach of fiduciary duty between a doctor and his patient/foster daughter.

2. In an earlier case, *M. (M.) v. K. (K.)* (1989), 38 B.C.L.R. (2d) 273, 61 D.L.R. (4th) 392 (C.A.), a plaintiff sued her foster father for battery in relation to sexual acts that the parties had engaged in when the plaintiff was 15 years old. At trial, the defendant's defence of consent succeeded and the action for battery was dismissed. On appeal, however, the Court refused to allow the defence of consent to be put forward in this type of case as a matter of public policy. The Court stated that the defendant's conduct in this case was criminal, a breach of trust and a breach of his duty as a foster parent. Other cases of sexual battery, however, have allowed the defence of consent. In *Lyth v. Dagg* (1988), 46 C.C.L.T. 25 (B.C.S.C.), although initial sexual acts between a 16-year-old student and his male teacher were deemed to be unconsensual, their subsequent relationship was held to be consensual.

3. What is the best approach to this issue of sexual acts between those who are in positions of trust or authority and those who are under their influence? Should the courts create an irrebuttable presumption that consent in these cases can never be free, in-

formed and genuine? Or should each case be approached on its facts? Should the issue of consent simply be declared to be irrelevant?

4. Is there a danger in declaring that certain persons are irrebuttably presumed to be incapable of consent due to their age or vulnerability? What if a court, for example, declares that, as a matter of public policy, females who are under the age of majority cannot consent to abortions or other treatment? Professor Klar wrote in relation to this issue:

> I would suggest that the defence of consent should be based only on the reality of the consent and not on whether, for public policy or morality reasons, the courts wish to recognize it. It may very well be that consent in the case of adults and minors, teachers and pupils, or doctors and patients, should be disregarded but only if, due to the unequal relationship, the genuineness or freeness of the consent can be doubted. If an adult or a mature minor has freely and knowingly consented to conduct, that consent should be respected, at least insofar as tort actions involving that conduct are concerned. If a court's disapproval concerning an activity is allowed to override the reality of the consent of capable persons, the right of persons to make their own choices is thereby diminished.

See Klar, "Recent Developments in Canadian Law: Tort Law" (1991), 23 Ottawa L. Rev. 177, at 247.

5. Another issue in relation to the genuineness of consent concerns fraud or deceit regarding collateral risks or facts associated with the act. This is an important issue when a person engages in sexual acts with another person who conceals a sexually transmissible disease. Is this a battery based on the lack of an informed consent? See *Kathleen K. v. Robert B.*, 198 Cal. Rptr. 273 (1984). In *Bell-Ginsburg v. Ginsburg* (1993), 17 C.C.L.T. (2d) 167 (Ont. Gen. Div.), the plaintiff discovered that her husband was bisexual. She was concerned that she could have contracted the HIV virus from him, although she had tested negative for the virus and had no evidence that he was HIV positive. She sued for a host of actions including battery. Should she succeed?

6. The issue of whether fraud vitiates consent for the purpose of a charge of aggravated assault pursuant to s. 268 of the *Criminal Code*, R.S.C. 1985, c. C-46 was dealt with by the Supreme Court of Canada in *R. v. Cuerrier* (1998), 127 C.C.C. (3d) 1, 162 D.L.R. (4th) 513, 229 N.R. 279, 18 C.R. (5th) 1 (S.C.C.). The accused had unprotected sexual relations with two complainants without informing them that he was HIV-positive. The complainants testified that although they had consented to the unprotected sexual intercourse that they would not have had they known that the accused was HIV-positive. The accused was acquitted at trial and this was upheld by the Court of Appeal. The Supreme Court of Canada allowed an appeal and ordered a new trial. The majority of the Court held that where the accused's failure to disclose a condition results in the complainant being put at significant risk of suffering serious bodily harm, the fraud vitiates the consent for the purpose of aggravated assault. The fraud need not relate to the nature and quality of the act. The concurring opinion of L'Heureux-Dubé J. would go even further and find that any fraud which results in inducing another person to consent will vitiate the consent, whether or not the act in question was particularly risky or dangerous. The judgments of Gonthier J. and McLachlin J. were more restrictive. For fraud to vitiate consent the fraud must go to the nature and quality of the act, but in the case of unprotected sex with an HIV-positive partner, the HIV status does go to the very nature and quality of the act.

How do you think this case affects the issue of fraud with respect to the tort of battery? Do you think that the Supreme Court will be more or less forgiving of a defendant's deceit in a tort action?

2. Consent in the Sporting Context

Many sports involve physical contact which clearly would not be acceptable in ordinary daily life. The principle defence which can be used in a civil action for battery to justify this use of force in sports is the defence of consent. One must also keep in mind that the physical contact which occurs in sports may lead to criminal charges for assault. Here again the main issue involves consent. There are, of course, important differences between the civil action for battery and a criminal prosecution for assault. For example, the burden of proving consent in the civil action rests on the defendant, whereas the burden of proving that the accused did not have an honest belief that the victim expressly or impliedly consented to the sporting violence rests on the Crown in the assault prosecution. The onus of proof is different. The purposes of the actions differ, as does the process. Nevertheless, statements about the scope of a player's consent in the sporting context made in decisions dealing with criminal charges are similar to statements made about the scope of the defence of consent in the civil action stemming from the same type of sport violence.

NOTES

1. See Barnes, "Recent Developments in Canadian Sports Law" (1991), 23 Ottawa L. Rev. 623, at 680-89 for a discussion of important criminal cases dealing with consent as a defence to criminal charges stemming from sport violence. See *R. v. Cey* (1989), 75 Sask. R. 53, [1989] 5 W.W.R. 169; *R. v. Ciccarelli* (1988), 5 W.C.B. (2d) 310; affd (1989), 54 C.C.C. (3d) 121; *R. v. Leclerc* (1991), 4 O.R. (3d) 788, 67 C.C.C. (3d) 563 (C.A.).

2. In *Agar v. Canning* (1965), 54 W.W.R. 302 (Man. Q.B.); affd (1966), 55 W.W.R. 384 (Man. C.A.), the defendant hockey player hit the plaintiff with his stick after being hooked by him. Bastin J., in dealing with the question of consent, stated:

> Neither counsel has been able to find a reported case in which a claim was made by one player against another for injuries suffered during a hockey game. Since it is common knowledge that such injuries are not infrequent, this supports the conclusion that in the past those engaged in this sport have accepted the risk of injury as a condition of participating. Hockey necessarily involves violent bodily contact and blows from the puck and hockey sticks. A person who engages in this sport must be assumed to accept the risk of accidental harm and to waive any claim he would have apart from the game for trespass to his person in return for enjoying a corresponding immunity with respect to other players. It would be inconsistent with this implied consent to impose a duty on a player to take care for the safety of other players corresponding to the duty which, in a normal situation, gives rise to a claim for negligence. Similarly, the leave and licence will include an unintentional injury resulting from one of the frequent infractions of the rules of the game.
>
> The conduct of a player in the heat of the game is instinctive and unpremeditated and should not be judged by standards suited to polite social intercourse.
>
> But a little reflection will establish that some limit must be placed on a player's immunity from liability. Each case must be decided on its own facts

so it is difficult, if not impossible, to decide how the line is to be drawn in every circumstance. But injuries inflicted in circumstances which show a definite resolve to cause serious injury to another, even when there is provocation and in the heat of the game, should not fall within the scope of the implied consent. I have come to the conclusion that the act of the defendant in striking plaintiff in the face with a hockey stick, in retaliation for the blow he received, goes beyond the limit marking exemption from liability. See also *Pettis v. McNeil* (1979), 32 N.S.R. (2d) 146, 8 C.C.L.T. 299 (S.C.).

3. In *Wright v. McLean* (1956), 7 D.L.R. (2d) 253, 20 W.W.R. 305 (B.C.S.C.), the 12-year-old plaintiff was participating with some other boys in a game that involved throwing mud balls and lumps of clay at each other. He was injured when hit on the side of his head by a lump thrown by the 14-year-old defendant. In dismissing the action, Mr. Justice MacFarlane stated:

> This pleading raises the issue of consent. It is contended that there is no plea here of *volens*, but I think this pleading is sufficient to raise that issue.
>
> The subject is discussed in most text books and I might refer particularly to *Pollock on Torts*, 15th ed., pp. 112-116. The learned editor of Pollock there commences para. 10 on p. 112 with the words: "Harm suffered by consent is, within limits to be mentioned, not a cause of civil action." Very briefly, the purpose of that paragraph is that in sport where there is no malice, no anger and no mutual ill will, the combatants consent to take the ordinary risks of the sport in which they are engaged. In a note given at the foot of p. 114 in Pollock, there is a reference to an article in the Law Quarterly Review, vol. 6, pp. 111-112. In that article, the author uses this language: "The reasonable view is that the combatants consent to take the ordinary risk of the sport in which they engage, the risks of being struck, kicked, or cuffed, as the case may be, and the pain resulting therefrom; but only while the play is fair, and according to rules, and the blows are given in sport and not maliciously. ... If these tacit conditions of fair play and good temper are not kept the consent is at an end, and the parties are remitted to their rights."
>
> In all the circumstances where it is agreed that there was no ill will and where the evidence shows that the infant defendant was invited to join the game by the others, then I think that no liability arises apart from culpable carelessness. I think it is quite clear that there is no evidence of that in this case. ...

In his discussion of the subject, the learned editor of Pollock says (p. 115):

> Trials of strength and skill in such pastimes as those above-mentioned afford, when carried on within lawful bounds, the best illustrations of the principle by which the maxim *volenti non fit injuria* is enlarged beyond its literal meaning. A man cannot complain of harm (with the limits we have mentioned) to the chances of which he has exposed himself with knowledge and of his free will. Thus in the case of two men fencing, *volenti non fit injuria* would be assigned by most lawyers as the governing rule, yet the words must be forced. It is not the will of one player that the other should hit him; his object is to be hit as seldom as possible. But he is content that the other shall hit him as much as by fair play he can; and in that sense the striking is not against his will.
>
> I think the action must be dismissed with costs.

4. Merely because some type of physical contact is against the rules of the game and subjects the wrongdoer to a penalty, does this automatically mean that the defence of consent is inapplicable? In *Matheson v. Governors of Dalhousie University and College* (1983), 57 N.S.R (2d) 56, 25 C.C.L.T. 91 (S.C.), the defendant grabbed the plaintiff and tripped him. They were playing a fast-moving ballgame called "borden ball" which they had previously agreed would be played without contact and tackling.

In dismissing the plaintiff's action, the court found that a frequent or familiar infraction of the rules of a game can be within the ordinary risks of the game accepted by all the participants.

5. Contrast the above case with *Colby v. Schmidt* (1986), 37 C.C.L.T. 1 at 6, [1986] 6 W.W.R. 65 (B.C.S.C.), where the plaintiff was struck in the jaw during a game of rugby some time after he had parted with the ball. Mr. Justice Oppal awarded damages and explained that the plaintiff had not consented to the "type of conduct and actions exhibited by the defendant". The court stated:

> By playing a sport which involves physical contact, a player does not assume any and all risks. There must be a realistic limit as to that risk. Similarly, a person who engages in a sport in which violence and injuries prevail is not rendered immune from legal liability ... [This conduct] was clearly beyond the scope of any consent given ... either expressed or implied. It is agreed that a player's conduct in a game involving physical contact should not be judged by "standards suited to polite social intercourse". [These] acts were unusual and beyond the scope of the ordinary standards of the game.

See generally Barnes, *Sports and the Law in Canada*, 2nd ed. (1988).

6. Sport injury cases are sometimes framed in negligence. The issue, however, is the same: was the defendant's conduct consistent with how the game is ordinarily played? Thus, a flagrant abuse of the rules can be seen within the context of battery as vitiating the defence of consent, or within the context of negligence, as unreaonable behaviour. See, for example, *Unruh v. Webber* (1994), 112 D.L.R. (4th) 83 (B.C.C.A.), leave to appeal to S.C.C. refused (1994), 93 B.C.L.R. (2d) xxxviii*n* (S.C.C.), and *Zapf v. Muckalt,* [1997] 1 W.W.R. 617 (B.C.C.A.) where the negligence approach was used.

7. Should tort law condone fighting, even though the fight may be a criminal act, by refusing to award compensation to a person injured in the fight on the basis of the defence of "consent"? Should tort law and criminal law approach the problem of "mutual fights" differently? Tort law supports the view that consent is a good defence to an action brought for injuries resulting from a "mutual" fight, as long as the combatants adhered to the unwritten "rules" of the fight. See, for example, *Wade v. Martin*, [1955] 3 D.L.R. 635 (Nfld. S.C.); *Hartlen v. Chaddock* (1957), 11 D.L.R. (2d) 705 (N.S.S.C.); *Mazurkewich v. Ritchot* (1984), 30 Man. R. (2d) 245 (C.A.); leave to appeal to S.C.C. refused (1985), 32 Man. R. (2d) 160; and *Johnson v. Royal Can. Legion Grandview Branch No. 174*, [1986] B.C.W.L.D. 1128, 26 B.C.L.R. (2d) 124, [1988] 5 W.W.R. 267 (C.A.).

8. Participants in sporting events are often required to sign "liability release" forms, or waivers, before being permitted to engage in the activity. How do these forms differ from the normal common law rule that a participant consents to all the ordinary risks of the sport? See *infra*, Chapter 9.

9. What is the difference between the defence of consent *vis-à-vis* the intentional torts and the defence of *volenti non fit injuria* in the negligence action? See *infra*, Chapter 9.

10. See Mansfield, "Informed Choice in the Law of Torts" (1961), 22 La. L. Rev. 17, for this:

> the law will not compensate the plaintiff for those results of his choice that he finds undesirable. The plaintiff cannot see why such assistance would interfere with the benefits of a regime of individual choice; indeed, why would it not contribute to the fuller realization of his freedom by giving effect to a second

> choice to undo the unwanted consequences of the first? The answer is clear enough, at least in the situation we are now considering, where the defendant was induced to act by a belief in the plaintiff's willingness. Correlative to the plaintiff's freedom is the defendant's freedom. If the plaintiff is not compelled to observe an authoritatively prescribed course of conduct, no more is the defendant. In particular, the defendant is not required to respond to the plaintiff's wish that he should act in a certain manner. Our hopes for the realization of the common good are based not exclusively on the fulfillment of the plaintiff's choice, but also on cooperation between plaintiff and defendant in mutually acceptable action. Therefore, so long as the defendant is not required to act, and so long as the only source of compensation for the plaintiff is the wealth of the defendant (a limitation that should not be taken for granted), the plaintiff's freedom must be less than perfect in order to assure that the choice of those in his position will be, for the major part, effective. If defendants were bound to compensate whenever the results of choice turned out disadvantageously, they might well cease to act at all in response to the desires of willing plaintiffs. At least a plaintiff's chance of inducing action would be significantly reduced. Thus, it is to the interest of willing plaintiffs as a class that a defendant who has been induced to act by a willing plaintiff be shielded from liability.

11. The defence of consent may also be justified in terms of economic efficiency, because consent "transforms coercion into a mutually desired and, therefore, a value maximizing transaction: it transforms the brawl into the boxing match." See Landes and Posner, "An Economic Theory of Intentional Torts", 1 Int'l. Rev. L. and Econ. 127, at 143.

3. Consent in the Medical Context

MALETTE v. SHULMAN

Ontario Court of Appeal. (1990), 2 C.C.L.T. (2d) 1, 67 D.L.R. (4th) 321.

The plaintiff was a Jehovah's Witness who was injured in a motor vehicle accident. She was attended to at the local hospital by Dr. Shulman, the defendant. She was semi-conscious and in shock. Despite the fact that Dr. Shulman was made aware that the plaintiff carried a card in her purse which forbid any form of blood transfusion under any circumstances, Dr. Shulman determined that a blood transfusion was necessary and he administered one. The plaintiff eventually recovered from her injuries and sued the defendant doctor and others for negligence, assault and conspiracy. The trial judge held that Dr. Shulman was liable for a battery and awarded the plaintiff $20,000 in general damages. The defendant appealed.

Robins J.A.: Liability was imposed in this case on the basis that the doctor tortiously violated his patient's rights over her own body by acting contrary to the Jehovah's Witness card and administering blood transfusions that were not authorized. His honest and even justifiable belief that the treatment was medically essential did not serve to relieve him from liability for the battery resulting from his intentional and unpermitted conduct. As Donnelly J. put it at 268:

> The card itself presents a clear, concise statement, essentially stating, 'As a Jehovah's Witness, I refuse blood'. That message is unqualified. It does not exempt life threatening perils. On the face of the card, its message is seen to be rooted in religious conviction. Its obvious purpose as a card is as protection to speak in circumstances where the

card carrier cannot (presumably because of illness or injury). There is no basis in evidence to indicate that the card may not represent the current intention and instruction of the card holder.

I, therefore, find that the card is a written declaration of a valid position which the card carrier may legitimately take in imposing a written restriction on her contract with the doctor. Dr. Shulman's doubt about the validity of the card, although honest, was not rationally founded on the evidence before him. Accordingly, but for the issue of informed refusal, there was no rationally founded basis for the doctor to ignore that restriction.

On the issue of informed refusal, Donnelly J. said at 272-273:

The right to refuse treatment is an inherent component of the supremacy of the patient's right over his own body. That right to refuse treatment is not premised on an understanding of the risks of refusal.

However sacred life may be, fair social comment admits that certain aspects of life are properly held to be more important than life itself. Such proud and honourable motivations are long entrenched in society, whether it be for patriotism in war, duty by law enforcement officers, protection of the life of a spouse, son or daughter, death before dishonour, death before loss of liberty, or religious martyrdom. Refusal of medical treatment on religious grounds is such a value.

...

If objection to treatment is on a religious basis, this does not permit the scrutiny of 'reasonableness' which is a transitory standard dependent on the norms of the day. If the objection has its basis in religion, it is more apt to crystallize in life threatening situations.

The doctrine of informed consent does not extend to informed refusal. The written direction contained in the card was not properly disregarded on the basis that circumstances prohibited verification of that decision as an informed choice. The card constituted a valid restriction of Dr. Shulman's right to treat the patient and the administration of blood by Dr. Shulman did constitute battery.

III.

What then is the legal effect, if any, of the Jehovah's Witness card carried by Mrs. Malette? Was the doctor bound to honour the instructions of his unconscious patient or, given the emergency and his inability to obtain conscious instructions from his patient, was he entitled to disregard the card and act according to his best medical judgment?

To answer these questions and determine the effect to be given to the Jehovah's Witness card, it is first necessary to ascertain what rights a competent patient has to accept or reject medical treatment, and to appreciate the nature and extent of those rights.

The right of a person to control his or her own body is a concept that has long been recognized at common law. The tort of battery has traditionally protected the interest in bodily security from unwanted physical interference. Basically, any intentional nonconsensual touching which is harmful or offensive to a person's reasonable sense of dignity is actionable. Of course, a person may choose to waive this protection and consent to the intentional invasion of this interest, in which case an action for battery will not be maintainable. No special exceptions are made for medical care other than in emergency situations, and the general rules governing actions for battery are applicable to the doctor-patient relationship.

Thus, as a matter of common law, a medical intervention in which a doctor touches the body of a patient would constitute a battery if the patient did not consent to the intervention. Patients have the decisive role in the medical decision-making process. Their right of self-determination is recognized and protected by the law. As Justice Cardozo proclaimed in his classic statement:

> Every human being of adult years and sound mind has a right to determine what shall be done with his own body; and a surgeon who performs an operation without his patient's consent commits an assault, for which he is liable in damages.

The doctrine of informed consent has developed in the law as the primary means of protecting a patient's right to control his or her medical treatment. Under the doctrine, no medical procedure may be undertaken without the patient's consent, obtained after the patient has been provided with sufficient information to evaluate the risks and benefits of the proposed treatment and other available options. The doctrine presupposes the patient's capacity to make a subjective treatment decision, based on her understanding of the necessary medical facts provided by the doctor and on her assessment of her own personal circumstances. A doctor who performs a medical procedure without having first furnished the patient with the information needed to obtain an informed consent will have infringed the patient's right to control the course of her medical care and will be liable in battery, even though the procedure was performed with a high degree of skill and actually benefitted the patient.

The right of self-determination, which underlies the doctrine of informed consent, also obviously encompasses the right to refuse medical treatment. A competent adult is generally entitled to reject a specific treatment or all treatment, or to select an alternate form of treatment, even if the decision may entail risks as serious as death and may appear mistaken in the eyes of the medical profession or of the community. Regardless of the doctor's opinion, it is the patient who has the final say on whether to undergo the treatment. The patient is free to decide, for instance, not to be operated on or not to undergo therapy or, by the same token, not to have a blood transfusion. If a doctor were to proceed in the face of a decision to reject the treatment, he would be civilly liable for his unauthorized conduct, notwithstanding his justifiable belief that what he did was necessary to preserve the patient's life or health. The doctrine of informed consent is plainly intended to ensure the freedom of individuals to make choices concerning their medical care. For this freedom to be meaningful, people must have the right to make choices that accord with their own values, regardless of how unwise or foolish those choices may appear to others. …

IV.

The emergency situation is an exception to the general rule requiring a patient's prior consent. When immediate medical treatment is necessary to save the life or preserve the health of a person who, by reason of unconsciousness or extreme illness, is incapable of either giving or withholding consent, the doctor may proceed without the patient's consent. The delivery of medical services is rendered lawful in such circumstances either on the rationale that the doctor has implied consent from the patient to give emergency aid or, more accurately in my view, on the rationale that the doctor is privileged, by reason of necessity, in giving the aid and is not to be held liable for so doing. On either basis, in an emergency the law sets aside the requirement of consent, on the assumption that the patient, as a reasonable person, would want emergency aid to be rendered if she were capable of giving instructions. As Prosser & Keeton, op. cit., at 117-118 state:

> The touching of another that would ordinarily be a battery in the absence of the consent of either the person touched or his legal agent can sometimes be justified in an emergency. Thus, it has often been asserted that a physician or other provider of health care has implied consent to deliver medical services, including surgical procedures, to a patient in an emergency. But such lawful action is more satisfactorily explained as a privilege. There are several requirements: (a) the patient must be unconscious or without capacity to make a decision, while no one legally authorized to act as agent for the patient is available; (b) time must be of the essence, in the sense that it must reasonably appear that delay until such time as an effective consent could be obtained would subject the patient to a risk of a serious bodily injury or death which prompt action would avoid; and (3) under the circumstances, a reasonable person would consent, and the probabilities are that the patient would consent.

...

On the facts of the present case, Dr. Shulman was clearly faced with an emergency. He had an unconscious, critically-ill patient on his hands, who, in his opinion, needed blood transfusions to save her life or preserve her health. If there were no Jehovah's Witness card, he undoubtedly would have been entitled to administer blood transfusions as part of the emergency treatment and could not have been held liable for so doing. In those circumstances, he would have had no indication that the transfusions would have been refused had the patient then been able to make her wishes known and, accordingly, no reason to expect that, as a reasonable person, she would not consent to the transfusions.

However, to change the facts, if Mrs. Malette, before passing into unconsciousness, had expressly instructed Dr. Shulman in terms comparable to those set forth on the card that her religious convictions as a Jehovah's Witness were such that she was not to be given a blood transfusion under any circumstances and that she fully realized the implications of this position, the doctor would have been confronted with an obviously different situation. Here, the patient, anticipating an emergency in which she might be unable to make decisions about her health care contemporaneous with the emergency, has given explicit instructions that blood transfusions constitute an unacceptable medical intervention and are not to be administered to her. Once the emergency arises, is the doctor nonetheless entitled to administer transfusions on the basis of his honest belief that they are needed to save his patient's life?

The answer, in my opinion, is clearly no. A doctor is not free to disregard a patient's advance instructions any more than he would be free to disregard instructions given at the time of the emergency. The law does not prohibit a patient from withholding consent to emergency medical treatment nor does the law prohibit a doctor from following his patient's instructions. While the law may disregard the absence of consent in limited emergency circumstances, it otherwise supports the right of competent adults to make decisions concerning their own health care by imposing civil liability on those who perform medical treatment without consent.

The patient's decision to refuse blood, in the situation I have posed, was made prior to and in anticipation of the emergency. While the doctor would have had the opportunity to dissuade her on the basis of his medical advice, her refusal to accept his advice or her unwillingness to discuss or consider the subject would not relieve him of his obligation to follow her instructions. The principles of self-determination and individual autonomy compel the conclusion that the patient may reject blood transfusions even if harmful consequences may result and even if the decision is generally regarded as foolhardy. Her decision in this instance would be operative after she lapsed into unconsciousness, and the doctor's conduct would be unauthorized. To transfuse a Jehovah's Witness, in the face of her explicit instructions to the contrary, would, in my opinion, violate her right to control her own body and show disrespect for the religious values by which she has chosen to live her life. ...

NOTES

1. While upholding the plaintiff's claim, Robins J.A. specifically noted that this judgment was limited to the facts of this case, and did not address the following problems:

   (a) a patient who, with a "living will", rejects medical treatment by way of an advance directive;

   (b) a family which wishes to terminate the treatment of a relative patient who is in an irreversible vegetative state;

   (c) an otherwise healthy patient who asks that his or her life be terminated.

   Would the principles of *Malette v. Shulman* apply in these cases? What differences are there between the case of the patient in *Malette* and these other patients? See Silberfield, Madison & Dickens, "Liability Concerns about the Implementation of Advanced Directives" (1995), 14 Estates & Trust J. 241; Griener, "Stopping Futile Treatment and the Slide Toward Non-Voluntary Euthanasia" (1994), 2 Health L.J. 67.

2. *Malette v. Shulman* is a clear and dramatic example of the right of a competent person to refuse all medical treatment. It is unique because of the manner in which the treatment was refused, *i.e.*, a card, and because there was in this case no opportunity to ensure that the patient's refusal was "informed". Otherwise, there have been other earlier cases in which the right to refuse treatment has been recognized. See, for example, *Mulloy v. Hop Sang*, [1935] 1 W.W.R. 714 (Alta. C.A.).

3. The principle that a competent patient has the right to decide what can be done to him or her by a doctor was expressed in the following way by Linden J. in *Allan v. New Mount Sinai Hospital et al.* (1980), 109 D.L.R. (3d) 634, 11 C.C.L.T. 299; revd (1981), 33 O.R. (2d) 605, 19 C.C.L.T. 76 (C.A.):

   > While our courts rightly resist advising the medical profession about how to conduct their practice, our law is clear that the consent of a patient must be obtained before any surgical procedure can be conducted. Without consent, either written or oral, no surgery may be performed. This is not a mere formality, it is an important individual right to have control over one's own body, even where medical treatment is involved. It is the patient, not the doctor, who decides whether surgery will be performed, where it will be done, when it will be done and by whom it will be done.

4. Another dramatic case involving the right of a competent adult to refuse treatment occurred in the Quebec case of the patient Nancy B.

   The plaintiff, a 25-year-old woman, suffered from Guillain-Barre syndrome and could breathe only with the assistance of a respirator. She wanted to discontinue all treatment, including the use of the respirator. This would effectively end her life. She went to court to obtain an injunction ordering the hospital and her doctor to abide by her decision to discontinue treatment. The Court granted the injunction. The Court applied then s. 19.1 of the *Civil Code of Quebec* which states that "No person may be made to undergo care of any nature, whether for examination, specimen taking, removal of tissue, treatment or any other act, except with his consent." It was decided that this logically referred not only to the decision to undertake treatment but, as well, to the decision to terminate it. The Court considered that in this respect the technique of placing a person on a respirator qualified as medical treatment. The Court also held that the hospital or doctor would not be in violation of any criminal offences if the termination of treatment resulted in the patient's death. After the decision was rendered, the patient decided to terminate her treatment and she died. See *Nancy B. v. Hôtel-Dieu de Québec* (1992), 86 D.L.R. (4th) 385, 69 C.C.C. (3d) 450 (Que. S.C.).

5. Another extremely difficult issue concerning the right to die faced the Supreme Court of Canada in *Rodriguez v. B.C. (A.G.)* (1993), 82 B.C.L.R. (2d) 273, [1993] 7 W.W.R. 641 (S.C.C.). The plaintiff suffered from an incurable, terminal illness. She wanted the right to a doctor-assisted suicide in order to terminate her life, when she would be unable, due to her condition, to commit suicide on her own. This meant that s. 241(b) of the *Criminal Code*, R.S.C. 1985, c. C-46, which prohibits giving assistance to a person to commit suicide, would have to be declared invalid, based on the Charter. In a 5-4 decision, the Supreme Court dismissed the application and upheld the prohibition. The judgment entailed a consideration of s. 7 of the Charter, which grants the constitutional right to life, liberty and the security of the person, as well as to the s. 15 protection of the right to equality.

6. Doctors are not obligated to take heroic measures to maintain the life of a person and accordingly do not need the consent of anyone, or a court order, to decide not to treat. This is a matter for medical judgment and the principles of negligence law. A doctor can, for example, direct that rescuscitation measures be withheld from a patient without the consent of the patient, the family, or in lieu thereof a court order. See *Child and Family Services of Central Manitoba v. Lavallee* (1997), 154 D.L.R. (4th) 409 (Man. C.A.).

7. For a stimulating and perceptive article that deals, *inter alia*, with the problem of consent, see Castel, "Some Legal Aspects of Human Organ Transplantations in Canada" (1968), 46 Can. Bar Rev. 345, at 361. See also, McCoid, "A Reappraisal of Liability for Unauthorized Medical Treatment" (1957), 41 Minn. L. Rev. 381. As a result of the Supreme Court of Canada's judgments in *Lepp v. Hopp* (1979), 8 C.C.L.T. 260 (Alta. C.A.), and *Reibl v. Hughes*, [1980] 2 S.C.R. 880, 14 C.C.L.T. 1, the topic has been much discussed in the literature. See Scaletta, "Informed Consent and Medical Malpractice: Where Do We Go From Here?" (1980), 10 Man. L.J. 289; G. Sharpe, "Informed Consent: Some Consensus, More Confusion" (1979), 3 Can. Lawyer 10; Jazvac, "Informed Consent: Risk Disclosure and the Canadian Approach" (1978), 36 U. Toronto Fac. L. Rev. 191; Picard and Hertz, "Two Views on Consent in Trespass to the Person" (1979), 17 Alta. L.R. 318. The entire issue of (1981), 26 McGill L.J. 670 *et seq.*, is devoted to the topic "Issues in Medical Law in Canada". The question of "informed consent" is dealt with in Chapter 4, *infra*.

MARSHALL v. CURRY

Nova Scotia Supreme Court. [1933] 3 D.L.R. 260, 60 Can. C.C. 136.

Chisholm C.J.: The plaintiff, a master mariner residing at Clifton in the County of Colchester, brings this action in which he claims $10,000 damages against the defendant who is a surgeon of high standing, practising his profession in the City of Halifax.

The plaintiff in his statement of claim alleges:

(1) That after being employed to perform and while performing an operation on the plaintiff for the cure of a hernia and while plaintiff was under the influ-

ence of an anaesthetic, the defendant without the knowledge or consent of the plaintiff removed the plaintiff's left testicle;

(2) In the alternative, that the defendant was negligent in diagnosing the case and in not informing the plaintiff that it might be necessary in treating the hernia to remove the testicle; and

(3) In the further alternative, that in removing the testicle in the above-mentioned circumstances, the defendant committed an assault upon the plaintiff.

The defence, in addition to general denials, is, that the removal of the testicle was a necessary part of the operation for the cure of the hernia; that the necessity for removing the testicle could not have been reasonably ascertained by diagnosis before any operation was begun; and that consent to the further operation was implied by plaintiff's request to cure the hernia, and that the plaintiff's claim is barred by the Statute of Limitations. ...

The plaintiff says with respect to the hernia: — "I simply told him (the defendant) I wanted the hernia cured. He examined me. He said, 'all right'. That was his words."

The operation took place on July 19, 1929. A day or two later the plaintiff was informed by the defendant that the testicle had been removed because it might have caused trouble. He says he did not give consent to the removal and was never told that it might be necessary. After he became cognizant of what had been done, the plaintiff made no complaint until December, 1931.

The defendant states that plaintiff had asked him in July, 1929, what he thought of this hernia. The defendant replied that there was a reasonable chance of curing it; that he thought it was a case suitable for the ordinary hernia operation; the abdominal muscles were in a reasonably good condition. In the operation the defendant found the muscles very much weaker than he had anticipated. In opening the inguinal canal the testicle appeared and was found grossly diseased; it was enlarged, nodular and softened. In order to cure the hernia it was necessary in defendant's opinion to obliterate the canal completely so as not to leave any space. The defendant deemed it necessary to remove the testicle in order to cure the hernia, and also because it would be a menace to the health and life of the plaintiff to leave it. That he says was his best judgment in the circumstances. After the operation the defendant cut the testicle in two and found multiple abscesses in it. The defendant gave, as his opinion that if the testicle had not been removed, it might have become gangrenous, and the pus might be absorbed into the circulation, and condition of blood-poisoning have set up. ...

The defendant called as witnesses three eminent surgeons to support the propriety of his procedure. ... The defendant's professional skill was not challenged on the trial. ... Nor could it be contended on the evidence that the operations conducted by him were not skillfully performed. The evidence of the medical witnesses supports the opinion that the condition of the testicle revealed by the operation could not reasonably have been anticipated before the operation was begun. That removes from the case the allegation that there was negligence on defendant's part; and, as I conceive the matter, leaves only the question of the assault.

The following findings are supported by the evidence:

1. That there was no express consent by plaintiff to the removal complained of;
2. That there was no implied consent thereto in the conversations between plaintiff and defendant before the operation; the exigent situation which arose was not then in the mind of either of them;

3. That the extended operation was necessary for the health and in the opinion of the defendant reasonably necessary to preserve the life of the plaintiff.

On these findings it becomes necessary to consider the questions in law which arise with respect to the rights and liabilities of the patient and surgeon and on what principle the action of the defendant must be justified. It seems to me that that justification must be found either in an assent implied by the circumstances which arose or in some other principle — broader than and outside of any consent — founded on philanthropic or humanitarian considerations.

...

In the cases these propositions of law find support:

1. That in the ordinary case where there is opportunity to obtain the consent of the patient it must be had. A person's body must be held inviolate and immune from invasion by the surgeon's knife, if an operation is not consented to. The rule applies not only to an operation but also to the case of mere examination. ...
2. That such consent by the patient may be express or implied. If an operation is forbidden by the patient, consent is not to be implied; and ... "It must be constantly remembered that in this connection silence does not give consent, nor is compliance to be taken as consent."
3. That consent may be implied from the conversation preceding an operation or from the antecedent circumstances. It is said that if a soldier goes into battle with a knowledge beforehand that surgeons attached to the army are charged with the care of the wounded, the consent of the patient may be implied therefrom for such operations as the surgeon performs in good faith upon the soldier.

I am unable to see the force of the opinion, that in cases of emergency where the patient agrees to a particular operation, and in the prosecution of the operation, a condition is found calling in the patient's interest for a different operation, the patient is said to have made the surgeon his representative to give consent. There is unreality about that view. The idea of appointing such a representative, the necessity for it, the existence of a condition calling for a different operation, are entirely absent from the minds of both patient and surgeon. The will of the patient is not exercised on the point. There is, in reality, no such appointment. I think it is better, instead of resorting to a fiction, to put consent altogether out of the case, where a great emergency which could not be anticipated arises, and to rule that it is the surgeon's duty to act in order to save the life or preserve the health of the patient; and that in the honest execution of that duty he should not be exposed to legal liability. It is, I think, more in conformity with the facts and with reason, to put a surgeon's justification in such cases on the higher ground of duty, as was done in the Quebec cases. ...

The phrase "good surgery" has appeared in some of the cases. Its use is not helpful; it is general and vague and I think ambiguous. It may mean good execution by the surgeon, and in that meaning it does not touch the question of the surgeon's right to operate. In these emergency cases, it is not useful to strain the law by establishing consent by fictions — by basing consent on things that do not exist. Is it not better to decide boldly that apart from any consent the conditions discovered make it imperative on the part of the surgeon to operate, and if he performs the duty skillfully and with due prudence, that no action will lie against him for doing so; as I have stated, that is the jurisprudence established in the Province of Quebec, and I think it can well be adopted in other jurisdictions.

In the case at bar, I find that the defendant after making the incisions on plaintiff's body, discovered conditions which neither party had anticipated, and which the defendant could not reasonably have foreseen, and that in removing the testicle he acted in the interest of his patient and for the protection of his health and possibly his life. The removal I find was in that sense necessary, and it would be unreasonable to postpone the removal to a later date. I come to this conclusion despite the absence of expressed and possibly of implied assent on the part of the plaintiff. [The Court also decided that the case, being based on battery, was barred by the *Statute of Limitations*, R.S.N.S. 1923, c. 238, s. 2(1)(*a*)].

NOTES

1. Are *Malette v. Shulman* and *Marshall v. Curry* in conflict?

2. In *Murray v. McMurchy*, [1949] 2 D.L.R. 442, [1949] 1 W.W.R. 989 (B.C.S.C.), a surgeon, during a caesarian operation, discovered a number of fibroid tumors in the uterus wall. After consultation with another surgeon he tied off the Fallopian tubes to prevent the hazards of a second pregnancy. The plaintiff sued the surgeon and recovered $3,000 damages. Macfarlane J. distinguished the case where an operation was "necessary" as involving "urgency" and "immediate decision". In the present case the possibility of future hazard did not absolve the surgeon from obtaining consent no matter how "convenient or desirable" in order to prevent danger in a later contingency. That risk must be left to the decision of the plaintiff. See also *Tabor v. Scobee*, 254 S.W. 2d 474 (Ky. 1952).

3. In Alberta the *Dependent Adults Act*, R.S.A. 1980, c. D-32, s. 20.1 [re-en. 1980, c. 6 (Supp.), s. 16, originally the *Emergency Medical Aid Act*, s. 3(1), rep. R.S.A. 1980, c. 7 (Supp.), s. 1, eff. July 4, 1983] is as follows:

> **20.1**(1) Where an adult person
>
> (a) is, in the written opinion of 2 physicians, in need of an examination or medical, surgical or obstetrical treatment or is, in the written opinion of 2 dentists, in need of dental treatment,
>
> (b) is incapable by reason of mental or physical disability of understanding and consenting to the examination or medical, surgical, obstetrical or dental treatment needed, and
>
> (c) has not previously withheld consent to the examination or medical, surgical, obstetrical or dental treatment needed, to the knowledge of either of the physicians or the dentists referred to in clause (a),
>
> a physician or dentist may, without the consent of any person, examine the person, prescribe treatment for the person and provide the person with the medical, surgical or obstetrical treatment or with the dental treatment, as the case may be, in the manner and to the extent that is reasonably necessary and in the best interests of the person examined or treated, in the same way that the physician or dentist could have acted if the person had been an adult of full legal capacity who consented to the examination or treatment.

(2) Subsection (1) does not apply to a dependent adult who is the subject of an order under section 6 appointing a guardian with the power and authority to consent to health care for that dependent adult.

Do you think that legislation such as this complements or over-rides the common law position regarding emergency treatment stated in *Marshall v. Curry, supra*?

4. Upon admission for surgery to most hospitals, it is customary to sign a consent form similar to the following:

I HEREBY CONSENT TO A .... BEING
(Insert Name of Operation)

PERFORMED ON ME AND I FURTHER AUTHORIZE THE SURGEON TO CARRY OUT SUCH ADDITIONAL OR ALTERNATIVE OPERATIVE MEASURES AS IN HIS OPINION MAY BE FOUND ADVISABLE. THE NATURE OF THE SAID OPERATION AND THE MATTER OF ADDITIONAL OPERATIVE MEASURES HAVE BEEN EXPLAINED TO ME. I ALSO CONSENT TO THE ADMINISTRATION OF AN ANAESTHETIC AND A TRANSFUSION IF FOUND ADVISABLE.

Does this practice render cases like *Marshall v. Curry* irrelevant? Should the courts enforce such an agreement or should it be declared void as contrary to public policy?

5. Consent to the surgical treatment of children and young people poses some problems. In an emergency situation, at least where there is no express refusal to consent, a doctor can probably do what is necessary to save a young patient's life. However, in non-emergency situations, the situation is more complicated. If the patient has reached 18, the age of majority in Ontario, the doctor is able to deal with the patient as a mature adult. If a young person is under the age of majority, however, a valid consent may still be given by him. In *Johnston v. Wellesley Hospital*, [1971] 2 O.R. 103, 17 D.L.R. (3d) 139 (H.C.), a 20-year-old underwent an acne treatment by a dermatologist. The age of majority at that time was 21 years of age. The court held that the consent was valid, even though the young person was not yet 21. Addy J. expressed the law as follows:

... Although the common law imposes very strict limitations on the capacity of persons under 21 years of age to hold, or rather to divest themselves of, property or to enter into contracts concerning matters other than necessities, it would be ridiculous in this day and age, where the voting age is being reduced generally to 18 years, to state that a person of 20 years of age, who is obviously intelligent and as fully capable of understanding the possible consequences of a medical or surgical procedure as an adult, would, at law, be incapable of consenting thereto. But, regardless of modern trend, I can find nothing in any of the old reported cases, except where infants of tender age or young children were involved, where the Courts have found that a person under 21 years of age was legally incapable of consenting to medical treatment. If a person under 21 years were unable to consent to medical treatment, he would also be incapable of consenting to other types of bodily interference. A proposition purporting to establish that any bodily interference acquiesced in by a youth of 20 years would nevertheless constitute an assault would be absurd. If such were the case, sexual intercourse with a girl under 21 years would constitute rape. Until the minimum age of consent to sexual acts was fixed at 14 years by a statute, the Courts often held that infants were capable of consenting at a considerably earlier age than 14 years.

I feel that the law on this point is well expressed in the volume on *Medical Negligence* (1957), by Lord Nathan, p. 176:

> It is suggested that the most satisfactory solution of the problem is to rule that an infant who is capable of appreciating fully the nature and consequences of a particular operation or of particular treatment can give an effective consent thereto, and in such cases the consent of the guardian is unnecessary; but that where the infant is without that capacity, any apparent consent by him or her will be a nullity, the sole right to consent being vested in the guardian.

The plaintiff in the present case was, therefore, quite capable at law of consenting.

See also *Booth v. Toronto General Hospital* (1910), 17 O.W.R. 118.

6. In *Gillick v. West Norfolk & Wisbech Area Health Authority*, [1985] 3 W.L.R. 830, [1985] 3 All E.R. 403 (H.L.), Lord Scarman stated that a minor can consent to conduct which might otherwise be considered tortious as long as the child has "sufficient intelligence and understanding to make up his own mind". This was quoted with approval in *J.S.C. and C.H.C. v. Wren* (1987), 35 D.L.R. (4th) 419, [1987] 2 W.W.R. 669 (Alta. C.A.), where the court held that the parents of a 16-year-old girl were unable to prevent her from undergoing an abortion.

7. The problem of the consent of minors to health care was studied by the Alberta Institute of Law Research and Reform which issued a report in December, 1975. The report's major recommendations were:

   (1) That the general age for consent to health care be fixed at 16 years.

   (2) That a minor of any age may consent to health care in connection with any communicable disease, drug or alcohol abuse, prevention of pregnancy and its termination.

   As one might expect, these recommendations are very controversial. As of yet, legislation has not been enacted in Alberta implementing these proposals. Why not? What conflicting interests and policies are at stake in resolving this question?

   In Ontario, the Interministerial Committee on Medical Consent issued a series of recommendations and draft legislation in December, 1979 concerning the issues of medical consent. Among their recommendations, the Committee recommended that the age of consent be fixed at 16, subject to a rebuttable presumption that a child under 16 is incompetent to consent. As in Alberta, there has still been no legislative action.

8. In *Re "D" and the Council of the College of Physicians and Surgeons of B.C.* (1970), 11 D.L.R. (3d) 570, 73 W.W.R. 627 (B.C.S.C.), the court refused to set aside a determination made by the disciplinary committee of the College of Physicians and Surgeons that it was improper for a doctor to accept a 15-year-old girl as a patient and to insert an I.U.D. without her parents' consent. Even if the law is clear that a doctor is not liable in tort if he treats a consenting minor without her parents' knowledge, will this law be effective if the medical profession refuses to treat minors without parents' consent?

9. There is a growing body of literature in this area. See Gosse, "Consent to Medical Treatment: A Minor Digression" (1974), 9 U.B.C.L. Rev. 56; Wedlington, "Minors and Health Care: The Age of Consent" (1973), 11 Osgoode Hall L.J. 115; Skegg, "Consent to Medical Procedures on Minors" (1973), 36 Mod. L. Rev. 370; Bowker, "Minors and Mental Incompetents: Consent to Experimentation, Gifts of Tissue and Sterilization" (1981), 26 McGill L.J. 951; Picard and Robertson, *Legal Liability of Doctors and Hospitals in Canada*, 3rd ed. (1996).

10. Should a parent be able to prohibit emergency medical treatment that would save a child's life? Ought the answer to this question to depend upon the physical or mental state of the child prior to the proposed treatment? The case of Stephen Dawson has brought this issue squarely into legal and public debate. Stephen was a severely retarded six year old. He had no control over his faculties, limbs or bodily functions. According to Stephen's parents, he was legally blind, partly deaf, incontinent, could not communicate with his environment and was in constant pain. Stephen required an operation to clear a shunt which had been implanted in him at five months of age and which had become blocked. Stephen's parents refused to consent to this operation on the ground that their son should be allowed to die with dignity rather than to endure a life of suffering. The Superintendent of Family and Child Services took the position that Stephen was a child "in need of protection" under the *Family and Child Services Act*, 1980 (B.C.), c. 11 and asked for custody of the child, so that the operation could be performed. A Provincial Court judge ordered that Stephen be returned to his parents, holding that the right to refuse life sustaining treatment of an incompetent belongs to the family in consultation with doctors. The judge distinguished between treatment which would only prolong life as opposed to treatment which offered a cure or improvement of the condition in arriving at this decision. The former treatment was categorized as an "extraordinary surgical intervention" as opposed to the latter which was "necessary medical attention" and covered in the legislation. The British Columbia Supreme Court (in *Re Supt. of Fam. & Child Service and Dawson et al.; Re Russell et al. and Supt. of Fam. & Child Service et al.* (1983), 42 B.C.L.R. 173, 145 D.L.R. (3d) 610 (S.C.)) in its capacity as *parens patriae* reviewed and reversed the lower court's decision. After reviewing the experts' testimony concerning Stephen's condition and prognosis, Mr. Justice McKenzie stated:

> In considering the application of the *parens patriae* jurisdiction I recognize that the central concern is to discover what is in Stephen's best interest. This is not a "right to die" situation where the courts are concerned with people who are terminally ill from incurable conditions. Rather it is a question of whether Stephen has the right to receive appropriate medical and surgical care of a relatively simple kind which will assure to him the continuation of his life, such as it is.
>
> I am satisfied that the laws of our society are structured to preserve, protect and maintain human life and that in the exercise of its inherent jurisdiction this court could not sanction the termination of a life except for the most coercive reasons. The presumption must be in favour of life. Neither could this court sanction the wilful withholding of surgical therapy where such withholding could result not necessarily in death but in a prolongation of life for an indeterminate time but in a more impoverished and more agonizing form.
>
> I do not think that it lies within the prerogative of any parent or of this court to look down upon a disadvantaged person and judge the quality of that person's life to be so low as not to be deserving of continuance.
>
> The matter was well put in an American decision — *Re Weberlist* (1974), 360 N.Y.S. 2d 783 at p. 787, where Justice Asch said:
>
> > There is a strident cry in America to determinate the lives of *other* people — deemed physically or mentally defective ... Assuredly, one test of a civilization is its concern with the survival of the "unfittest", a reversal of Darwin's formulation. ...
> >
> > In this case, the court must decide what its ward would choose, if he were in a position to make a sound judgment.
>
> This last sentence puts it right. It is not appropriate for an external decision maker to apply his standards of what constitutes a liveable life and exercise the right to impose death if that standard is not met in his estimation. The de-

> cision can only be made in the context of the disabled person viewing the worthwhileness or otherwise of his life in its own context as a disabled person — and in that context he would not compare his life with that of a person enjoying normal advantages. He would know nothing of a normal person's life having never experienced it.

11. Cases involving Jehovah's Witnesses who refuse blood transfusions for their children pose similar problems. What happens if an adult mother who requires a blood transfusion to preserve the life of her unborn baby refuses such a transfusion? Can an adult's express rejection be ignored where a child, even an unborn child, depends for its health on the mother's health? See *Raleigh-Fitkin-Paul Morgan Mem. Hospital v. Anderson*, 201 A. 2d 537 (S.C.N.J. 1964).

12. The sterilization of mentally retarded patients poses special problems. In *Re F.*, [1989] 2 All E.R. 545, [1989] 2 W.L.R. 1025 (H.L.), the House of Lords held that a court could make a declaration that a proposed sterilization operation for a patient who was unable to consent due to mental disability was lawful. The test is whether the operation or treatment is in the best interests of the patient. Lord Brandon stated:

    > ... a doctor can lawfully operate on, or give other treatment to, adult patients who are incapable, for one reason or another, of consenting to his doing so, provided that the operation or other treatment concerned is in the best interests of such patients. The operation or other treatment will be in their best interests if, but only if, it is carried out in order to either save their lives or to ensure improvement or prevent deterioration on their physical or mental health.

    On this question, also see *Re D. (A Minor)*, [1976] 1 All E.R. 326, [1976] 2 W.L.R. 279 (Fam. D.); *Eve v. Mrs. E.*, [1986] 2 S.C.R. 388, 31 D.L.R. (4th) 1.

13. The eugenics movement resulted in the confinement and sterilization of hundreds of persons without their consent. Recently, these cases have been brought to light in Alberta and actions commenced on behalf of the victims. See *Muir v. The Queen in right of Alberta* (1996), 132 D.L.R. (4th) 695 (Alta. Q.B.). The plaintiff in that case received nearly $750,000 in damages for wrongful sterilization and wrongful confinement.

14. As indicated in the above material, a doctor who treats a patient without having received the patient's consent for that treatment is liable in an action for battery. A more difficult problem, however, concerns the situation where, although a patient has apparently consented to the basic treatment, it was done without the patient first having been informed of the risks of that treatment. These cases were once dealt with either as battery or negligence, depending upon the nature of the risks which were not disclosed (*Kelly v. Hazlett* (1976), 15 O.R. (2d) 290, 75 D.L.R. (3d) 536, 1 C.C.L.T. 1 (H.C.)). However, as a result of the Supreme Court of Canada's decision in *Reibl v. Hughes*, [1980] 2 S.C.R. 880, 14 C.C.L.T. 1, cases of "informed consent" will now be treated as claims in negligence, not in battery. For a complete discussion of this problem, see *infra*, Chapter 4.

B. SELF-DEFENCE

COCKCROFT v. SMITH

Queen's Bench. (1705), 11 Mod. 43, 88 E.R. 872.

Cockcroft, in a scuffle, ran her fingers towards Smith's eyes, who bit a joint off the plaintiff's finger. The question was, Whether this was a proper defence for the defendant to justify in an action of Mayhem?

Holt C.J.: If a man strike another, who does not immediately after resent it, but takes his opportunity, and then — sometime after — falls upon him and beats him, in this case *son assault* is no good plea. Neither ought a man, in case of a small assault, give a violent or unsuitable return. But, in such cases, plead what is necessary for a man's defence; and not who struck first, though this (he said), has been the common practice. But this, he wished, was altered; for hitting a man a little blow with a little stick on the shoulder, is not a reason for him to draw a sword and cut and hew the other.

NOTES

1. A case demonstrating the application of these principles is *MacDonald v. Hees* (1974), 46 D.L.R. (3d) 720 (N.S.T.D.). The defendant, a former cabinet minister in the Diefenbaker government, was in Nova Scotia campaigning on behalf of the local Progressive Conservative (P.C.) candidate in the federal election of 1972. The plaintiff, a P.C. worker and a friend who wished to meet the defendant, went to the motel where the defendant was staying at around midnight. They knocked, and, finding the door unlocked, they entered the room. To their surprise, they discovered the defendant, who was tired after a hard day of campaigning, already retired for the night. The defendant, who had an early morning appointment, got out of bed, grabbed the plaintiff and threw him towards the door. His head struck the glass and he was injured. In holding the defendant responsible, Chief Justice Cowan rejected the defence of self-defence and explained:

   > In my opinion, the defendant in this case was not required to use any force for the protection of himself. I find that, at no time did the plaintiff or his associate, Glen Boyd, do anything which could have led the defendant to believe that any force was to be used against the defendant. The defendant's evidence was to the effect that he saw that the plaintiff was smaller than he was; he agreed that the plaintiff did not pose a threat to him; that he was not afraid of the plaintiff or of his comrade and that he was not afraid of any physical violence to his person or property. I find that the defendant was not threatened in any way by the plaintiff or by Glen Boyd, and that the defendant was not under the impression that he was threatened in any way by the use of force. In addition, I find that the force which the defendant used in ejecting the plaintiff from his motel unit was not reasonable, and was far greater than could possibly be considered by any reasonable man to be requisite for the purpose of removing the plaintiff from the motel unit. I also find that the force used by the defendant in ejecting the plaintiff was entirely disproportionate to the evil to be prevented, *i.e.*, the continued presence of the plaintiff in the motel unit.
   >
   > I am, therefore, of the opinion that the defence of justification on the ground of self-defence fails.

   See also *McNeill v. Hill*, [1929] 2 D.L.R. 296 (Sask. C.A.), where Mr. Justice Martin stated:

   > While the law recognized the right of self-defence, the right to repel force with force, no right is to be abused, and the right of self-defence is one which may easily be abused. The force employed must not be out of proportion to the apparent urgency of the occasion.

2. The onus of proof rests upon the person invoking the defence of self-defence. The defendant must not only prove that the occasion was one which warranted defensive

action, but also that the force used was not excessive. In *Mann v. Balaban*, [1970] S.C.R. 74, 8 D.L.R. (3d) 548, Mr. Justice Spence (Hall, Pigeon JJ. concurring) summarized the law on this issue as follows:

> In an action for assault, it has been, in my view, established that it is for the plaintiff to prove that he was assaulted and that he sustained an injury thereby. The onus is upon the plaintiff to establish those facts before the jury. Then it is upon the defendant to establish the defences, first, that the assault was justified and, secondly, that the assault even if justified was not made with any unreasonable force and on those issues the onus is on the defence.

See also *Miska v. Sivec*, [1959] O.R. 144, 18 D.L.R. (2d) 363 (C.A.); *Veinot v. Veinot* (1977), 22 N.S.R. (2d) 630, 81 D.L.R. (3d) 549 (C.A.). *Cf. McClelland v. Symons*, [1951] V.L.R. 157.

3. It is permissible to kill in self-defence if it is necessary to preserve one's own life or to avoid serious bodily injury. See *R. v. Smith* (1837), 8 C. & P. 160, 173 E.R. 441.

4. For a discussion of the necessity of retreating before applying, in self-defence, force that may kill, see Beale, "Retreat From a Murderous Assault" (1903), 16 Harv. L. Rev. 567. Some American cases have recognized the right to stand one's ground but the author submits that "no killing can be justified upon any ground, which was not necessary to secure the desired and permitted result; and it is not necessary to kill in self-defence when the assailed can defend himself by the peaceful though often distasteful method of withdrawing to a place of safety".

5. In defence of one's own house, however, one need not retreat before the threat of grievous bodily harm. See *R. v. Hussey* (1924), 18 Cr. App. R. 160, 89 J.P. 28.

6. What if the defendant kills someone whom the defendant mistakenly, but reasonably, believes is about to kill the defendant? See *Keep v. Quailman*, 68 Wis. 451, 32 N.W. 233 (1887). *Cf. Ranson v. Kitner*, 31 Ill. App. 241 (1888).

7. What if the defendant, who is, in fact, in danger of being killed, shoots at the attacker but, without negligence, hits an innocent passerby? See *Morris v. Platt*, 32 Conn. 75 (1864); *Shaw v. Lord*, 41 Okl. 347, 137 P. 885 (1914). See generally, Forbes, "Mistake of Fact With Regard to Defences in Tort Law" (1970), 4 Ottawa L. Rev. 304.

8. Self-defence, which is a complete defence, should not be confused with provocation, which is not. The principle was correctly outlined by Mr. Justice Beck in *Evans v. Bradburn* (1915), 25 D.L.R. 611, 9 W.W.R 281 (Alta. C.A.) as follows:

> The instinct of human nature is to resent insult in many cases by physical force; and, according to the circumstances, this is more or less generally approved or even applauded, but the law, probably wisely, does not recognize any provocation, short of an assault or threats creating a case for self-defence, as a justification for an assault, but only takes it into account as a circumstance which may reduce culpable homicide from murder to manslaughter, and in all criminal cases involving an assault as a circumstance going in mitigation of punishment, and in civil cases in mitigation of damages.

9. Is it provocation to threaten someone? *Bruce v. Dyer*, [1966] 2 O.R. 705, 50 D.L.R. (2d) 211; affd [1970] 1 O.R. 482 (C.A.). To swear at someone? *Check v. Andrews Hotel Co. Ltd.* (1974), 56 D.L.R. (3d) 364, [1975] 4 W.W.R. 370 (Man. C.A.). To make love to someone's spouse? *White v. Conolly*, [1972] Q.S.R. 75. To collide with another person's vehicle? *Golnik v. Geissinger* (1967), 64 D.L.R. (2d) 754 (B.C.S.C.) To legally drive another person's cattle to the pound? *Fillipowich v. Nahachewsky* (1969), 3 D.L.R. (3d) 544 (Sask. Q.B.).

10. What is the effect of provocation on the awarding of damages? There are currently two lines of authority. The first is that the court can only reduce or eliminate the punitive damages, but not the plaintiff's compensatory damages, if provocation is found. The following cases support this approach: *Shaw v. Gorter* (1977), 77 D.L.R. (3d) 50, 2 C.C.L.T. 111 (Ont. C.A.); *Check v. Andrews Hotel Co. Ltd. et al.*, [1975] 4 W.W.R. 370, 56 D.L.R. (3d) 364 (Man. C.A.); *Lane v. Holloway*, [1968] 1 Q.B. 379, [1967] 3 All E.R. 129 (C.A.); *Landry v. Patterson* (1978), 22 O.R. (2d) 335, 93 D.L.R. (3d) 345 (C.A.). The second view is that provocation can reduce all of the plaintiff's damages. See *Mason v. Sears and Cruikshank* (1979), 31 N.S.R. (2d) 521, 52 A.P.R. 521 (Co. Ct.) and *Holt v. Verbruggen* (1981), 20 C.C.L.T. 29 (B.C.S.C.). See *Hurley v. Moore* (1993), 18 C.C.L.T. (2d) 78 (Nfld. C.A.), where the issue is thoroughly canvassed and the second view is adopted. Which view do you prefer? What are the policy implications underlying this issue? Can provocation be considered as a type of contributory negligence on the plaintiff's part which ought to reduce loss in the same way as contributory negligence? Should the courts allow a reduction in a victim's award when the victim's injury was the result of an intentional tort on the defendant's part? This question was raised, but not resolved, in *Long v. Gardner et al.* (1983), 144 D.L.R. (3d) 73 (Ont. H.C.).

11. In *Berntt v. Vancouver (City)* (1997), 33 C.C.L.T. 1, [1997] 4 W.W.R. 505 (B.C.S.C.), the plaintiff sued the police in assault and battery for the injuries which he received during a Stanley Cup riot in Vancouver. The court held that the plaintiff had been a ringleader in instigating the riot and found him 75 per cent contributorily negligent.

NOTES ON DEFENCE OF THIRD PERSONS

1. As well as defending themselves people are entitled to defend other people who are being attacked or threatened. The early English law seemed to limit this privilege to husbands protecting their wives, or to masters defending their servants and vice versa. Now it is clear that a mother may protect her son and a son his mother and that a police officer may protect a citizen and vice versa. See *Prior v. McNab* (1976), 54 D.L.R. (3d) 661, 1 C.C.L.T. 137 (H.C.), *per* Reid J.

2. If one defends another person in the reasonable belief that that person is in need of help, one may be excused from tort liability even if acting under a mistaken impression. In *Gambriell v. Caparelli* (1975), 7 O.R. (2d) 205, 54 D.L.R. (3d) 661 (Co. Ct.), a mother, believing her son was being choked by the plaintiff, shouted at the plaintiff to stop, picked up a three-pronged garden cultivator, struck the plaintiff three times on the shoulder with it, and finally hit the plaintiff on the head with considerable force. The mother was relieved of liability on the ground that she really had few options open to her, given her lack of knowledge of the English language and her size in relation to that of the plaintiff. His Honour Judge Carter, relying on the *Compensation for Victims of Crime Act*, 1971 (Vol. 2), c. 51, which he felt implied that the legislature "considered it meritorious to aid one's neighbour", explained:

> Where a person intervening to rescue another holds an honest (though mistaken) belief that the other person is in imminent danger of injury, he is justified in using force, provided that such force is reasonable.

   Would the result have been the same if the defendant had stabbed the plaintiff in the chest with the cultivator? What if, instead of beating up her son, the plaintiff was trying to kiss her daughter?

3. As in self-defence, the onus is on the person seeking to invoke this defence to prove the action was reasonable and excessive force was not used. See *Prior v. McNab*, *supra*, note 1.

4. The *Criminal Code*, R.S.C. 1985, c. C-46, s. 37(1) provides that "Every one is justified in using force to defend himself or any one under his protection from assault, if he uses no more force than is necessary to prevent the assault or the repetition of it."

Section 27 also provides that:

27. Every one is justified in using as much force as is reasonably necessary:
(a) to prevent the commission of an offence
(i) for which, if it were committed, the person who committed it might be arrested without warrant, and
(ii) that would be likely to cause immediate and serious injury to the person or property of anyone; or
(b) to prevent anything being done that, on reasonable grounds, he believes would, if it were done, be an offence mentioned in paragraph (a).

What relevance, if any, do these sections have to tort law?

C. DEFENCE OF PROPERTY

GREEN v. GODDARD

Queen's Bench. (1704), 2 Salk. 641, 91 E.R. 540.

Et per cur.: There is a force in law, as in every trespass *quare clausum fregit:* As if one enters into my ground, in that case the owner must request him to depart before he can lay hands on him to turn him out; for every *impositio manuum* is an assault and battery, which cannot be justified upon the account of breaking the close in law, without a request. The other is an actual force, as in burglary, as breaking open a door or gate; and in that case it is lawful to oppose force to force; and if one breaks down the gate, or comes into my close *vi et armis*, I need not request him to be gone, but may lay hands on him immediately, for it is but returning violence with violence: So if one comes forcibly and takes away my goods, I may oppose him without any more ado, for there is no time to make a request.

NOTES

1. In *Bigcharles v. Merkel et al.* (1973), 32 D.L.R. (3d) 511, [1973] 1 W.W.R. 324 (B.C.S.C.), a gang of burglars, discovered by the defendant while committing a burglary of his premises, tried to escape. In the darkness, the defendant fired one shot of his rifle at them and accidentally killed the plaintiff's husband who was one of the burglars. No intention to hit the deceased was attributed to the defendant but he was, nevertheless, held 25 per cent liable for his negligence, with the deceased bearing 75 per cent of the blame. Mr. Justice Seaton explained: "The act cannot be justified as preventing crime, preventing a continuance of a breach of the peace, a step in an arrest, protection of property, repelling a trespasser, protection of himself or those under his care, or preventing breaking in or breaking out of a dwelling." Under what circumstances would the killing have been justified?

2. In *MacDonald v. Hees* (1974), 46 D.L.R. (3d) 720 (N.S.T.D.), it was contended by the defendant that he was merely preventing an unlawful entry and an invasion of his privacy. Chief Justice Cowan rejected the defence, and stated:

> ... a trespasser cannot be forcibly repelled or ejected until he has been requested to leave the premises and a reasonable opportunity of doing so peaceably has been afforded him. It is otherwise in the case of a person who enters or seeks to enter by force. ... Even in such a case, however, the amount of force that may be used ... must amount to nothing more than forcible removal and must not include beating, wounding, or other physical injury. In the present case, I find that there was no forcible entry by the plaintiff. Even if there had been forcible entry, the defendant did not request the plaintiff and his companion to leave and give them any reasonable opportunity of doing so, peaceably.

3. For an economic analysis of this problem, see Posner, "Killing or Wounding to Protect a Property Interest" (1971), 14 J. Law & Econ. 201. See also *Katko v. Briney*, 183 N.W. 2d 657 (Iowa 1987); Palmer, "The Iowa Spring Gun Case: A Study in American Gothic" (1971), 56 Iowa L. Rev. 1219.

BIRD v. HOLBROOK

Common Pleas. (1828), 4 Bing. 628, 130 E.R. 911.

The defendant was the occupier of a walled garden in which he grew rare and expensive tulips. A short time before the accident in question someone had robbed his garden of flowers and roots of the value of £20. As a consequence the defendant placed a spring gun in the garden with wires crossing several paths at a height of about fifteen inches from the ground.

A witness to whom the defendant mentioned the fact of his having been robbed, and of having set a spring gun, proved that he had asked the defendant if he had put up a notice of such a gun being set, to which the defendant answered that "he did not conceive that there was any law to oblige him to do so", and the defendant desired such person not to mention to any one that the gun was set, "lest the villain should not be detected". No notice was given of the spring gun having been placed in the garden.

On the 21st of March, 1825, between the hours of six and seven in the afternoon, it being then light, a peahen belonging to the occupier of a house in the neighbourhood had escaped, and finally alighted in the defendant's garden. A female servant of the owner of the bird was in pursuit of it, and the plaintiff (a youth of the age of 19 years), seeing her in distress from fear of losing the bird, said he would go after it for her; he accordingly got upon the wall at the back of the garden, and having called out two or three times to ascertain whether any person was in the garden, and waiting a short space of time without receiving any answer jumped down into the garden. The boy's foot came in contact with one of the wires, close to the spot where the gun was set. It was thereby discharged, and a great part of its contents, consisting of large swan shot, was lodged in and about his knee-joint, and caused a severe wound.

The question for the opinion of the court was whether the plaintiff was entitled to recover.

Best C.J.: I am of opinion that this action is maintainable. ...

It has been argued that the law does not compel every line of conduct which humanity or religion may require; but there is no act which Christianity forbids, that the law will not reach: if it were otherwise, Christianity would not be, as it has always been held to be, part of the law of England. I am therefore, clearly of opinion that he who sets spring guns, without giving notice, is guilty of an inhuman act, and that, if injurious consequences ensue, he is liable to yield redress to the sufferer. But this case stands on grounds distinct from any that have preceded it. In general, spring guns have been set for the purpose of deterring; the defendant placed his for the express purpose of doing injury; for, when called on to give notice, he said, "If I give notice, I shall not catch him." He intended, therefore, that the gun should be discharged, and that the contents should be lodged in the body of his victim for he could not be caught in any other way. On these principles the action is clearly maintainable, and particularly on the latter ground.

Burrough J.: … The present case is of a worse complexion than those which have preceded it; for if the defendant had proposed merely to protect his property from thieves, he would have set the spring guns only by night. The plaintiff was only a trespasser: if the defendant had been present, he would not have been authorized even in taking him into custody, and no man can do indirectly that which he is forbidden to directly. …

[The concurring judgment of **Park J.**, is omitted.]

Judgment for the plaintiff.

NOTES

1. The *Criminal Code*, R.S.C. 1985, c. C-46, s. 247(1) enacts:

   > Every one who, with intent to cause death or bodily harm to persons, whether ascertained or not, sets or places or causes to be set or placed a trap, device or other thing whatever that is likely to cause death or bodily harm to persons is guilty of an indictable offence and is liable to imprisonment for a term not exceeding five years.

   What effect, if any, would a violation of this provision have on civil liability to someone injured thereby?

2. The defendant puts up a sign warning trespassers that they will be shot if they trespass. Is a defendant who does, in fact, shoot a trespasser who has read and ignored the sign liable?

3. Suppose that the defendant merely points a gun at a trespasser and says, "Get off or I'll shoot you?" The trespasser departs in haste and sues for assault. Liability?

4. The defendant fires a gun at the ground behind a trespasser, trying to frighten the trespasser. Assault? What if the bullet ricochets and hits the trespasser? Liability? Compare with *Harris v. Wong* (1971), 19 D.L.R. (3d) 589 (Sask. Q.B.), negligence liability.

5. The defendant keeps a large dog for protection from intruders. Peter intrudes and is chased off by the growling dog. Liability? What if the dog bites Peter? A landowner puts an electrically charged fence around the property. A trespasser, touching the fence, is given a shock. Liability? What if the electrical current is so strong that it kills the intruder? Can you articulate a rule that balances all the interests involved?

6. Suppose a visitor to your home becomes ill and wants to stay. Can you send that visitor out into the cold? See *Depue v. Flatau*, 100 Minn. 299, 111 N.W. 1 (S.C. Minn. 1907). Would it make any difference if the visitor had a dangerous, infectious disease?

7. See Hart, "Injuries to Trespassers" (1931), 47 L.Q. Rev. 92; Bohlen and Burns, "The Privilege to Protect Property by Dangerous Barriers and Mechanical Devices" (1926), 35 Yale L.J. 527; *Sycamore v. Ley* (1932), 147 L.T. 342, [1932] All E.R. Rep. 97; Williams, *Liability for Animals* (1939), p. 350.

8. With regard to the privilege to protect personal property, see *Cresswell v. Sirl*, [1948] 1 K.B. 241, [1947] 2 All E.R. 730 (C.A.).

9. The privilege of recapture of property is closely related to defence of property. It was first recognized where there was a momentary interruption of possession and an immediate repossession. It was then extended to dispossession by fraud or force and where the pursuit was fresh. There are many difficult and confusing decisions in this area. See *Devoe v. Long*, [1951] 1 D.L.R. 203, 26 M.P.R. 357 (N.B.C.A.); *Hemmings & Wife v. Stoke Pages Golf Club Ltd.*, [1920] 1 K.B. 720, 36 T.L.R. 77 (C.A.); *Napier v. Ferguson* (1878), 18 N.B.R. 415 (C.A.); *Phillips v. Murray*, [1929] 3 D.L.R. 770, [1929] 2 W.W.R. 314 (Sask. C.A.); *Wentzell v. Veinot*, [1940] 1 D.L.R. 536, 14 M.P.R. 323 (N.S.C.A.); see generally Branston, "The Forcible Recaption of Chattels" (1918), 28 L.Q. Rev. 262.

10. Another area of law which may be relevant here is that of occupier's liability. As will be seen, there is a common law duty not to wilfully or recklessly injure trespassers. Some provinces have adopted legislation which imposes a duty of care on occupiers even towards trespassers. How does the law reconcile the duty owed to trespassers with the right to defend one's property by using reasonable force? See Chapter 14.

D. NECESSITY

DWYER v. STAUNTON

Alberta District Court. [1947] 4 D.L.R. 393, [1947] 2 W.W.R. 21.

Sissons D.C.J.: The plaintiff sues for trespass and claims the sum of $500 as damages to his crop of special quality fall barley and $20 as damages to gates and fences, and also claims an injunction restraining the defendant from further trespass.

The plaintiff is a farmer and rancher residing near Lundbreck, Alberta. The defendant is a farmer and rancher living to the north of the plaintiff. The public highway running north and south past the farm of the plaintiff was on January 5, 1947, so blocked by snow drifts as to be impassable. On that day employees of an oil company operating in the area bulldozed a way to Lundbreck from a point some distance north of the plaintiff's farm, following the highway where possible and at other points going through the fields of the farmers and ranchers. The bulldozer was not able to follow the highway alongside the farm of the plaintiff and opened a way for about a quarter of a mile through the plaintiff's gates and fences and over his land. The bulldozer was followed by five trucks. The following morning, January 6th, taking advantage of the opened road, the defendant, in his car, with four or five other cars and trucks, started for Lundbreck. They were stopped by the plaintiff while following the way bulldozed across his farm. The plaintiff protested that his farm was not a road allowance and no one had any right to go over his land without his permission. There was some argument. The plaintiff says the defendant was the ringleader and was friendly, but insistent in his attitude. The plaintiff finally consented to the parties continuing their journey to town, but warned them that he would stop them if they attempted to return across his land. The defendant, and the others, while in town, interviewed the municipal authorities in regard to opening the highway, and were advised that the bulldozer of the municipality was broken and that the highway could not be ploughed out that day. The parties attempted to return home that evening by a different route, but could not get through, and then took the route across the plaintiff's land. They were stopped by the plaintiff at one of the gates. Following some argument, and the repeated refusal of the plaintiff to allow them to pass, the defendant drove his car through the two-strand barbed wire gate and was followed by the other cars and trucks. In reply to the plaintiff's protest, the defendant said he was able to pay for all the damage and took the position that he wished to see the case brought to court.

The real point in issue is whether the defendant, under the circumstances, had the right to leave the highway and proceed over the land of the plaintiff. A secondary point is whether the defendant, if he had such right, caused any unnecessary damage to the plaintiff in exercising that right.

My understanding of the law is that a traveller who is lawfully using a public road has the right to go upon private land at places where the public way is impassable.

> Where a public way is foundrous, as such ways frequently were in former times, the public have by the common law a right to travel over the adjoining lands, and to break through the fences for the purpose: *Williams on Real Property*, 24th ed., pp. 508-9.
>
> Where a highway becomes impassable, travellers are entitled to deviate from the established road on to adjacent land, taking care to do no unnecessary damage: 37 Cyc., p. 206.

Broom gives the principle upon which the right is based as that of *salus populi suprema lex* — "Regard for the public welfare is the highest law."

> The maxim is, that a private mischief shall be endured, rather than a public inconvenience; and, therefore, if a highway be out of repair and impassable, a passenger may lawfully go over the adjoining land, since it is for the public good that there should be, at all times, free passage along thoroughfares for subjects of the realm: *Broom's Legal Maxims*, 10th ed., p. 2.

Other authorities put the principle upon the doctrine of necessity.

> In such case, an interference with private property is obviously dictated and justified *summa necessitate*, by the immediate urgency of the occasion, and a due regard to the public safety or convenience: *Morey v. Fitzgerald* (1884), 56 Vt. 487, at p. 489. ...

One of the leading English cases is that of *Taylor v. Whitehead* (1781), 2 Doug. K.B. 745. In that case the facts had to do with a private way, and it was held that in respect of such ways the right to deviate was rather limited, but Lord Mansfield went on to say: "Highways are governed by a different principle. They are for the public service, and if the usual tract is impassable, it is for the general good that people should be entitled to pass in another line." ...

My conclusion is that the defendant was quite within his legal rights, under the circumstances, in leaving the highway and going through the gates and fences and over the land of the plaintiff. I find that the defendant did no unnecessary damage in so doing. ... In the result, the action of the plaintiff is dismissed, with costs. ... I have considerable sympathy with the plaintiff in his insistence on his private property rights. Those rights should be respected, but I must hold that there are higher rights — the rights of the public.

NOTES

1. Compare the resolutions of the justices concerning *The King's Prerogative in Saltpetre* (1606), 12 Co. Rep. 12, 77 E.R. 1294. As the "defence of the realm" was involved, it was resolved that the prerogative extended to digging for Saltpetre, even as "it is lawful to come upon my land ... to make trenches or bulwarks for the defence of the realm, for every subject hath benefit by it ... but after the danger is over, the trenches and bulwarks ought to be removed, so that the owner shall not have prejudice in his inheritance; and for the commonwealth, a man shall suffer damage; as, for saving of a city or town, a house shall be plucked down if the next be on fire; and the suburbs of a city in time of war for the common safety shall be plucked down; and a thing for the commonwealth every man may do without being liable to an action."

2. In *Burmah Oil Co. v. Lord Advocate*, [1965] A.C. 75, [1964] 2 All E.R. 348, the House of Lords held that when the Crown, in furtherance of its war aims, deprived a person of property for the benefit of the state — in the instant case the destruction of plaintiff's oil installations near Rangoon, in order to prevent their falling into the hands of the enemy, Japan — the loss must be compensated for at public expense. Such loss did not include damage done in the course of an actual battle, but "battle damage" did not include the taking of property for long-range strategic purposes. The United States Supreme Court in *United States v. Caltex (Philippines) Inc.*, 344 U.S. 149 (1952), reached a contrary conclusion, despite the Fifth Amendment which forbids taking "private property ... for public use, without just compensation". Speaking for the majority, Vinson C.J., said that "the common law has long recognized that in times of imminent peril — such as when fire threatened a whole community — the sovereign could, with immunity, destroy the property of a few that the property of many and the lives of many more could be saved". See (1966), 79 Harv. L. Rev. 614. The *Burmah Oil* case was nullified by the War Damage Act, 1965, c. 18.

3. There are other ways of dealing with this type of problem. When goods are jettisoned at sea to save the rest of the cargo, for example, the concept of "general average" is employed. Where property must be destroyed to prevent the spread of fire, there is legislation in Australia that defines this loss as "damage by fire" within the meaning of any insurance policy. See Fleming, *The Law of Torts*, 7th ed. (1987), p. 86; Williams, "The Defence of Necessity" (1953), 6 Current Legal Probs. 216.

VINCENT v. LAKE ERIE TRANSPORTATION CO.

Supreme Court of Minnesota. 109 Minn. 456, 124 N.W. 221 (1910).

Action to recover $1,200 for damage to the plaintiffs' wharf caused by the defendant negligently keeping its vessel tied to it. The defendant alleged that after the discharge of the cargo the wind had attained so great a velocity that the master and crew were powerless to move the vessel. At the trial the jury returned a verdict of $500 for the plaintiffs. Defendant appealed from an order denying a motion for judgment notwithstanding the verdict of the jury.

O'Brien J.: The steamship Reynolds, owned by the defendant, was for the purpose of discharging her cargo on November 27, 1950, moored to plaintiffs' dock in Duluth. While the unloading of the boat was taking place a storm from the northeast developed, which at about ten o'clock p.m., when the unloading was completed, had so grown in violence that the wind was then moving at 50 miles per hour and continued to increase during the night. There is some evidence that one, and perhaps two, boats were able to enter the harbour that night, but it is plain that navigation was practically suspended from the hour mentioned until the morning of the twenty-ninth, when the storm abated, and during that time no master would have been justified in attempting to navigate his vessel, if he could avoid doing so. After the discharge of the cargo the Reynolds signalled for a tug to tow her from the dock, but none could be obtained because of the severity of the storm. If the lines holding the ship to the dock had been cast off, she would doubtless have drifted away, but, instead, the lines were kept fast, and as soon as one parted or chafed it was replaced, sometimes with a larger one. The vessel lay upon the outside of the dock, her bow to the east, the wind and waves striking her starboard quarter with such force that she was constantly being lifted and thrown against the dock, resulting in its damage, as found by the jury, to the amount of $500.

We are satisfied that the character of the storm was such that it would have been highly imprudent for the master of the Reynolds to have attempted to leave the dock or to have permitted his vessel to drift away from it. One witness testified upon the trial that the vessel could have been warped into a slip, and that, if the attempt to bring the ship into the slip had failed, the worst that could have happened would be that the vessel would have been blown ashore upon a soft and muddy bank. The witness was not present in Duluth at the time of the storm, and, while he may have been right in his conclusions, those in charge of the dock and the vessel at the time of the storm were not required to resort to every possible experiment which could be suggested for the preservation of their property. Nothing more was demanded of them than ordinary prudence and care, and the record in this case fully sustains the contention of the appellant that, in holding the vessel fast to the dock, those in charge of her exercised good judgment and prudent seamanship.

It is claimed by the respondent that it was negligence to moor the boat at an exposed part of the wharf, and to continue in that position after it became apparent that the storm was to be more than usually severe. We do not agree with this position. The part of the wharf where the vessel was moored appears to have been commonly used for that purpose. It was situated within the harbour at Duluth, and must, we think, be considered a proper and safe place, and would undoubtedly have been such during what would be considered a very severe storm. The storm which made it unsafe was one which surpassed in violence any which might have reasonably been anticipated.

The appellant contends by ample assignments of error that, because its conduct during the storm was rendered necessary by prudence and good seamanship under conditions over which it had no control, it cannot be held liable for any injury resulting to the property of others, and claims that the jury should have been so instructed. An analysis of the charge given by the trial court is not necessary as in our opinion the only question for the jury was the amount of damages which the plaintiffs were entitled to recover, and no complaint is made upon that score.

The situation was one in which the ordinary rules regulating property rights were suspended by forces beyond human control, and if, without the direct intervention of some act by the one sought to be held liable, the property of another was injured, such injury must be attributed to the act of God, and not to the wrongful act of the person sought to be charged. If during the storm the Reynolds had entered the harbor, and while there had become disabled and been thrown against the plaintiffs' dock, the plaintiffs could not have recovered. Again, if while attempting to hold fast to the dock the lines had parted, without any negligence, and the vessel carried against some other boat or dock in the harbor, there would be no liability upon her owner. But here those in charge of the vessel deliberately and by their direct efforts held her in such a position that the damage to the dock resulted, and, having thus preserved the ship at the expense of the dock, it seems to us that her owners are responsible to the dock owners to the extent of the injury inflicted.

In *Depue v. Flatau*, 100 Minn. 299; 111 N.W. 1, this court held that where the plaintiff, while lawfully in the defendants' house, became so ill that he was incapable of travelling with safety, the defendants were responsible to him in damages for compelling him to leave the premises. If, however, the owner of the premises had furnished the traveller with proper accommodations and medical attendance, would he have been able to defeat an action brought against him for their reasonable worth?

In *Ploof v. Putnam* (Vt.), 71 Atl. 188, the Supreme Court of Vermont held that where, under stress of weather, a vessel was without permission moored to a private dock at an island in Lake Champlain owned by the defendant, the plaintiff was not guilty of trespass, and that the defendant was responsible in damages because his representative upon the island unmoored the vessel, permitting it to drift upon the shore, with resultant injuries to it. If, in that case, the vessel had been permitted to remain, and the dock had suffered an injury, we believe the shipowner would have been held liable for the injury done.

Theologians hold that a starving man may, without moral guilt, take what is necessary to sustain life; but it could hardly be said that the obligation would not be upon such person to pay the value of the property so taken when he became able to do so. And so public necessity, in times of war or peace, may require the taking of private property for public purposes; but under our system of jurisprudence compensation must be made.

Let us imagine in this case that for the better mooring of the vessel those in charge of her had appropriated a valuable cable lying on the dock. No matter how justifiable such appropriation might have been, it would not be claimed that, because of the overwhelming necessity of the situation, the owner of the cable could not recover its value.

This is not a case where life or property was menaced by any object or thing belonging to the plaintiffs, the destruction of which became necessary to prevent the threatened disaster. Nor is it a case where, because of an act of God, or unavoidable accident, the infliction of the injury was beyond the control of the defendant, but is one where the defendant prudently and advisedly availed itself of the plaintiffs' property for the purpose of preserving its own more valuable property, and the plaintiffs are entitled to compensation for the injury done.

Order affirmed.

Lewis J. (dissenting): I dissent. It was assumed on the trial before the lower court that appellant's liability depended on whether the master of the ship might, in the exercise of reasonable care, have sought a place of safety before the storm made it impossible to leave the dock. The majority opinion assumes that the evidence is conclusive that appellant moored its boats at respondents' dock pursuant to contract and that the vessel was lawfully in position at the time the additional cables were fastened to the dock, and the reasoning of the opinion is that, because appellant made use of the stronger cables to hold the boat in position, it became liable under the rule that it had voluntarily made use of the property of another for the purpose of saving its own.

In my judgment, if the boat was lawfully in position at the time the storm broke, the master could not, in the exercise of due care, have left that position without subjecting his vessel to the hazards of the storm, then the damage to the dock, caused by the pounding of the boat, was the result of an inevitable accident.

If the master was in the exercise of due care, he was not at fault. The reasoning of the opinion admits that if the ropes, or cables, first attached to the dock had not parted, or if, in the first instance, the master had used the stronger cables, there would be no liability. If the master could not, in the exercise of reasonable care, have anticipated the severity of the storm and sought a place of safety before it became impossible, why should he be required to anticipate the severity of the storm, and, in the first instance, use the stronger cables?

I am of the opinion that one who constructs a dock to the navigable line of waters, and enters into contractual relations with the owner of a vessel to moor the same, takes the risk of damage to his dock by a boat caught there by a storm, which event could not have been avoided in the exercise of due care, and further, that the legal status of the parties in such a case is not changed by renewal of cables to keep the boat from being cast adrift at the mercy of the tempest.

NOTES

1. How does this differ from *Dwyer v. Staunton*? See Bohlen, "Incomplete Privilege to Inflict Intentional Invasion of Property and Personality" (1926), 39 Harv. L. Rev. 307.

2. To protect your property against flood water, you erect an embankment to keep out the water. The water thus repelled damages your neighbour's lands. Liability? *Gerrard v. Crowe*, [1921] 1 A.C. 395, 37 T.L.R. 110 (P.C.), held there was no liability. In *Whalley v. Lancashire and Yorkshire Ry.* (1884), 13 Q.B.D. 131, 50 L.T. 472 (C.A.), a heavy rainfall accumulated on the defendant's land against an embankment. To protect the embankment the defendant cut timbers which carried the water off the defendant's land and on to the plaintiff's land. The defendant was held liable in damages to the plaintiff.

3. In *Romney Marsh v. Trinity House* (1870), L.R. 5 Exch. 204; affd (1872), L.R. 7 Exch. 247, 41 L.J. Ex. 106 (Ex. Ct.), the defendant's ship was, without negligence, thrown on the plaintiff's sea wall. The defendant did not break up the ship until all valuable property had been removed. During this period the ship could have been broken up, and because it was not removed it caused additional damage to the sea wall, for which damage the plaintiff brought action. *Held*, for the defendant. "There was no duty to sacrifice the vessel in the plaintiff's interests."

4. In *Manor & Co. Ltd. v. M. V. "Sir John Crosbie"* (1965), 52 D.L.R. (2d) 48 (Nfld.); affd [1967] 1 Ex. 94, on facts similar to those in the principal case, damages caused by the defendant's ship remaining moored to a wharf during a storm of hurricane force were claimed only in negligence. The court held that in light of the dangers involved in moving the ship, there had been no negligence and, therefore, the owner of the wharf could not recover. See Sussman, "The Defence of Private Necessity and the Problem of Compensation" (1967-68), 2 Ottawa L. Rev. 184.

5. Necessity is no defence, however, where in similar circumstances, the captain of a ship negligently contributes to the creation of the risk. See *Bell Canada v. The Ship "Mar-Tirenno"*, [1974] 1 F.C. 294, 52 D.L.R. (3d) 702 (T.D.), affd (1976), 71 D.L.R. (3d) 608 (F.C.A.).

6. Is the defence of necessity available to excuse the taking of life? In *R. v. Dudley* (1884), 15 Cox C.C. 624, 14 Q.B.D. 273, four survivors of a shipwreck were adrift in an open boat, a thousand miles from land, and dying of hunger. Two survivors killed

one of the other survivors and ate him. They were held criminally liable for his death, but the sentence was commuted to six months in prison.

7. In *United States v. Holmes* (1842), 1 Wall Jr. 1, a passenger ship had hit an iceberg and sank. Nine members of her crew and 32 passengers were adrift in a badly overloaded lifeboat. The wind freshened, the sea began to rise, and the boat was in imminent danger of being swamped. The crew then threw six of the passengers overboard to lighten the ship. The following morning the survivors were rescued by a passing ship. Holmes, who had taken a leading part in throwing the passengers over, was tried for manslaughter, convicted, and sentenced to hard labour for a long term, which the court subsequently reduced to six months. Considerable public sentiment arose in favour of Holmes, and there was much pressure upon President Tyler for a pardon. He refused to grant it because the court did not join in the request, but later changed his mind and remitted the sentence. See Fuller, "The Case of the Speluncean Explorers" (1949), 62 Harv. L. Rev. 616.

SOUTHWARK LONDON BOROUGH COUNCIL v. WILLIAMS AND ANDERSON

Court of Appeal. [1971] 2 W.L.R. 467, [1971] 2 All E.R. 175.

The defendants, who were in dire need of housing, made an orderly entry into two empty houses owned by the local authority. The authority owned hundreds of empty houses in areas that were awaiting redevelopment for public housing that would be supplied, on completion, to some of the thousands of people on the local authority's housing list. The authority secured an order for possession against the defendants who appealed to the Court of Appeal.

Lord Denning M.R.: ... I will next consider the defence of "necessity". There is authority for saying that in case of great and imminent danger, in order to preserve life, the law will permit of an encroachment on private property. That is shown by *Mouse's Case* (1609), 12 Co. Rep. 63, where the ferry-man at Gravesend took 47 passengers into his barge to carry them to London. A great tempest arose and all were in danger. Mouse was one of the passengers. The defendant threw a casket belonging to the plaintiff (Mouse) overboard so as to lighten the ship. Other passengers threw other things. It was proved that, if they had not done so, the passengers would have been drowned. It was held by the whole court "that in case of necessity, for the saving of the lives of the passengers it was lawful for the defendant, being a passenger to cast the casket of the plaintiff out of the barges ..." The court said it was like pulling down of a house, in time of fire, to stop it spreading, which has always been held justified *pro bono publico*.

The doctrine so enunciated must, however, be carefully circumscribed. Else necessity would open the door to many an excuse. It was for this reason that it was not admitted in *Reg. v. Dudley and Stephens* (1884), 14 Q.B.D. 273, where the three shipwrecked sailors, in extreme despair, killed the cabin boy and ate him to save their own lives. They were held guilty of murder. The killing was not justified by necessity. Similarly, when a man, who is starving, enters a house and takes food in order to keep himself alive. Our English law does not admit the defence of necessity. It holds him guilty of larceny. Lord Hale said that "if a person, being under necessity for want of victuals, or clothes, shall upon that account clandestinely, and *animo furandi*, steal another man's food, it is felony ..."; *Hale, Pleas of the Crown*, i. 54. The reason is because, if hunger were once allowed to be an excuse for stealing, it would open a way through which all kinds of disorder and lawlessness would pass. So here. If homelessness were once admitted as a defence to trespass, no one's house could be safe. Necessity would open a door which no man could shut. It would not only be those in extreme need who would enter. There would be others who would imagine that they were in need, or would invent a need, so as to gain entry. Each man would say his need was greater than the next man's. The plea would be an excuse for all sorts of wrongdoing. So the courts must, for the sake of law and order, take a firm stand. They must refuse to admit the plea of necessity to the hungry and the homeless; and trust that their distress will be relieved by the charitable and the good.

NOTES

1. What criticisms can you offer of the court's reasoning in this case? Of what relevance is the availability of social welfare services here? What if the temperature had been below zero? Just how much can the courts do to alleviate the problem dramatized in the principal case?

2. On November 8, 1972, there was an airplane crash in the Yukon. In order to keep from starving, the pilot, one Marten Hartwell, had to eat the flesh of one of his passengers who had died. Necessity?

3. The Supreme Court of Canada has redefined the defence of necessity in the criminal law context in such a way that it may affect the tort law principles. See *Perka v. The Queen*, [1984] 2 S.C.R. 232, 13 D.L.R. (4th) 1.

E. LEGAL AUTHORITY

KLAR, TORT LAW
(Carswell, 2nd ed., 1996)

The defence of legal authority is the broadest and probably the most frequently raised defence in terms of torts of trespass and other intentional interferences. The gist of the defence is the existence of legislative authority which entitles the defendant to engage in conduct which otherwise would be considered to be tortious and actionable. It usually is seen in cases alleging assault, battery, or false imprisonment, although it also has been raised in relation to trespass to land or chattels.

The defence of legal authority is not one defence with general principles capable of application to a variety of factual disputes, but an umbrella which covers a host of different statutory defences, each of which must be analyzed and interpreted in the context of the legislation in which it appears. In addition to the ordinary rules of statutory interpretation, constitutional and Charter issues also must be considered.

There are numerous statutes, both at the provincial and federal levels, which explicitly or implicitly provide defences to tort claims. Although relevant provisions of the *Criminal Code* are frequently raised, other statutes have been in the issue in recent cases. One may refer, for example, to cases dealing with the *Identification of Criminals Act*, the *Mental Health Act*, the *Mental Hygiene Act*, the *Liquor Control Act*, and the *Narcotic Control Act*, among numerous others.

There are several issues which must be considered when statutory provisions are raised as defences in civil actions. If the relevant statute contains an express immunity provision, is it constitutionally valid? ... the law of torts is a matter which falls within provincial jurisdiction. Several of the statutes which have been raised in tort cases, however, have been federally enacted. Even with regard to provincial statutes, one must now be concerned with their constitutional validity under the Canadian Charter of Rights and Freedoms. Even if constitutionally valid, the specific provision which allegedly, expressly or implicitly justifies tortious conduct must be interpreted according to the rules of statutory interpretation. *Prima facie*, courts ought to be cautious when deciding that statutory provisions deprive victims of compensation for their injuries or deprivation of their rights, especially when a statutory provision affording immunity can be restrictively interpreted.

CRIMINAL CODE OF CANADA

R.S.C. 1985, c. C-46, ss. 25, 494, 495

25. (1) Every one who is required or authorized by law to do anything in the administration or enforcement of the law

(a) as a private person,
(b) as a peace officer or public officer,
(c) in aid of a peace officer or public officer, or
(d) by virtue of his office,

is, if he acts on reasonable grounds, justified in doing what he is required or authorized to do and in using as much force as is necessary for that purpose.

(2) Where a person is required or authorized by law to execute a process or to carry out a sentence, that person or any person who assists him is, if that person acts in good faith, justified in executing the process or carrying out the sentence notwithstanding that the process or sentence is defective or that it was issued or imposed without jurisdiction or in excess of jurisdiction.

(3) Subject to subsections (4) and (5), a person is not justified for the purposes of subsection (1) in using force that is intended or is likely to cause death or grievous bodily harm unless the person believes on reasonable grounds that it is necessary for the self-preservation of the person or the preservation of any one under that person's protection from death or grievous bodily harm.

(4) A peace officer, and every person lawfully assisting a peace officer, is justified in using force that is intended or is likely to cause death or grievous bodily harm to a person to be arrested, if

(a) the peace officer is proceeding lawfully to arrest, with or without warrant, the person to be arrested;
(b) the offence for which the person is to be arrested is one for which that person may be arrested without warrant;
(c) the person to be arrested takes flight to avoid arrest;
(d) the peace officer or other person using the force believes on reasonable grounds that the force is necessary for the purpose of protecting the peace officer or any other person from imminent or future death or grievous bodily harm; and
(e) the flight cannot be prevented by reasonable means in a less violent manner.

(5) A peace officer is justified in using force that is intended or is likely to cause death or grievous bodily harm against an inmate who is escaping from a penitentiary within the meaning of subsection 2(1) of the *Corrections and Conditional Release Act*, if

(a) the peace officer believes on reasonable grounds that any of the inmates of the penitentiary poses a threat of death or grievous bodily harm to the peace officer or any other person; and
(b) the escape cannot be prevented by reasonable means in a less violent manner.

...

494. (1) Any one may arrest without warrant
(a) a person whom he finds committing an indictable offence; or
(b) a person who, on reasonable grounds, he believes
(i) has committed a criminal offence, and
(ii) is escaping from and freshly pursued by persons who have lawful authority to arrest that person.

(2) Any one who is
(a) the owner or a person in lawful possession of property, or
(b) a person authorized by the owner or by a person in lawful possession of property,

may arrest without warrant a person whom he finds committing a criminal offence on or in relation to that property.

(3) Any one other than a peace officer who arrests a person without warrant shall forthwith deliver the person to a peace officer.

495. (1) A peace officer may arrest without warrant
(a) a person who has committed an indictable offence or who, on reasonable grounds, he believes has committed or is about to commit an indictable offence;
(b) a person whom he finds committing a criminal offence; or
(c) a person in respect of whom he has reasonable grounds to believe that a warrant of arrest or committal, in any form set out in Part XXVIII in relation thereto, is in force within the territorial jurisdiction in which the person is found. ...

NOTES

1. The above provisions of the *Criminal Code* have been used frequently as defences in false arrest or false imprisonment actions. The right of a police officer to effect an arrest based upon "reasonable and probable grounds" is well established. It is not necessary that there has in fact been the commission of an indictable offence for the police to arrest someone, as long as the police have reasonable and probable grounds to believe that an offence has been committed. See, for example, *Lebrun v. High-Low Foods, Ltd.* (1968), 69 D.L.R. (2d) 433, 65 W.W.R. 353 (B.C.S.C.).

2. A case in which the defence of reasonable and probable grounds failed was *Koechlin v. Waugh*, [1957] O.W.N. 245, 11 D.L.R. (2d) 447 (C.A.). The 20-year-old plaintiff was stopped by the police late at night as he was walking home with a friend. The plaintiff refused to identify himself when asked by the police. A scuffle between the plaintiff and police eventually ensued and the plaintiff was arrested and taken to the police station. In an action against the police, the trial judge noted the plaintiff's dress, his conduct, and the fact that there had been a number of "break-ins" in the neighbourhood in his decision to dismiss the plaintiff's action. The decision was reversed on appeal, Laidlaw J.A. stating:

A police officer has not in law an unlimited power to arrest a law-abiding citizen. The power given expressly to him by the *Criminal Code* to arrest without warrant is contained in s. 435, but we direct careful attention of the public to the fact that the law empowers a police officer in many cases and under certain circumstances to require a person to account for his presence and to identify himself and to furnish other information, and any person who wrongfully fails to comply with such lawful requirements does so at the risk of arrest and imprisonment. None of these circumstance exist in this case. No unnecessary restriction on his power which results in increased difficulty to a police officer to perform his duties of office should be imposed by the court. At the same time, the rights and freedom under law from unlawful arrest and imprisonment of an innocent citizen must be fully guarded by the courts. In this case, the fact that the companion of the infant plaintiff was wearing rubber-soled shoes and a wind-breaker and that his dress attracted the attention of the police officers, falls far short of reasonable and probable grounds for believing that the infant plaintiff had committed an indictable offence or was about to commit such an offence. We do not criticize the police officers in any way for asking the infant plaintiff and his companion to identify themselves, but we are satisfied that when the infant plaintiff, who was entirely innocent of any wrongdoing, refused to do so, the police officer has no right to use force to compel him to identify himself. It would have been wise and, indeed, a duty as a good citizen, for the infant plaintiff to have identified himself when asked to do so by the police officers. It is altogether likely that if the infant plaintiff had been courteous and cooperative, the incident giving rise to this action would not have occurred, but that does not in law excuse the defendants for acting as they did in the particular circumstances.

We direct attention to an important fact. The infant plaintiff was not told by either of the police officers any reason for his arrest. The infant plaintiff was entitled to know on what charge or on suspicion of what crime he was seized. He was not required in law to submit to restraint on his freedom unless he knew the reason why that restraint should be imposed. …

Finally, we are not in accord with the view expressed by the learned trial judge that the actions of the infant plaintiff in resisting the efforts of the police officers can be regarded as justification for their belief that he "either had or was about to commit a crime". In the particular circumstances he was entitled in law to resist the efforts of the police officers, and they have failed in this case to justify their actions.

It was stated in the course of giving oral reasons for judgment that the courts would strive diligently to avoid putting any unnecessary obstacle in the way of the detection of crime or the lawful arrest of persons in the proper performance of the duties of a police officer. We repeat an expression of that policy of the courts. Nothing in these reasons for judgment should be taken as encouragement to any person to resist a police officer in the performance of his duties; on the contrary, it is not only highly desirable, but vitally important, that every person should co-operate to the utmost with police officers for the good of the public and to ensure the preservation of law and order in his community.

In this case the police officers exceeded their powers and infringed the rights of the infant plaintiff without justification. Therefore, the appeal will be allowed with costs.

3. The case of *Swansburg v. Smith* (1996), 141 D.L.R. (4th) 94 (B.C.C.A.) confirmed that s. 25(1) cannot be used by a police officer to justify the use of force in the case of an arrest which is unlawful and does not meet the requirements of s. 495.

4. The right of a person to be informed of the reasons for his or her arrest was confirmed by the House of Lords in *Christie and Another v. Leachinsky*, [1947] A.C. 573, [1947] All E.R. 567 (H.L.). The plaintiff was arrested and confined, purportedly under the provisions of the *Liverpool Corporation Act, 1921*, although, as the police later admitted, this was not the real basis for the arrest. The arrest was actually made because the police suspected the plaintiff of having committed a theft although this information was not told to the plaintiff. As to this matter, Lord Simonds stated:

> First, I would say that it is the right of every citizen to be free from arrest unless there is in some other citizen, whether a constable or not, the right to arrest him. I would say next that it is the corollary of the right of every citizen to be thus free from arrest that he should be entitled to resist arrest unless that arrest is lawful. How can these rights be reconciled with the proposition that he may be arrested without knowing why he is arrested? It is to be remembered that the right of the constable in or out of uniform is, except for a circumstance irrelevant to the present discussion, the same as that of every other citizen. Is citizen A bound to submit unresistingly to arrest by citizen B in ignorance of the charge made against him? I think, my Lords, that cannot be the law of England. Blind, unquestioning obedience is the law of tyrants and of slaves. It does not yet flourish on English soil. I would, therefore, submit the general proposition that it is a condition of lawful arrest that the man arrested should be entitled to know why he is arrested, and then, since the affairs of life seldom admit an absolute standard or an unqualified proposition, see whether any qualification is of necessity imposed on it. This approach to the question has, I think, a double support. In the first place, the law requires that, where arrest proceeds on a warrant, the warrant should state the charge on which the arrest is made. I can see no valid reason why this safeguard for the subject should not equally be his when the arrest is made without a warrant. The exigency of the situations, which justifies or demands arrest without a warrant, cannot, as it appears to me, justify or demand either a refusal to state the reason of arrest or a misstatement of the reason. Arrested with or without a warrant, the subject is entitled to know why he is deprived of his freedom, if only in order that he may without a moment's delay take such steps as will enable him to regain it. ...
>
> If, then, this is, as I think it is, the fundamental rule, what qualification, if any, must be imposed upon it? The cogent instances given by Lawrence L.J. are conclusive that an arrest does not become wrongful merely because the constable arrests a man for one felony, say, murder, and he is subsequently charged with another felony, say, manslaughter. It is not enough to say that in such a case the accused man could not recover any damages in an action for false imprisonment. It is more than that. It is clear that the constable has not been guilty of an illegal arrest, if he reasonably suspected that murder had been done. Again, I think it is clear that there is no need for the constable to explain the reason of arrest if the arrested man is caught redhanded and the crime is patent to high Heaven. Nor, obviously, is explanation a necessary prelude to arrest where it is important to secure a possibly violent criminal. Nor, again, can it be wrongful to arrest and detain a man on a charge of which he is reasonably suspected with a view to further investigation of a second charge on which information is incomplete. In all such matters a wide measure of discretion must be left to those whose duty it is to preserve the peace and bring criminals to justice.
>
> These and similar considerations lead me to the view that it is not an essential condition of lawful arrest that the constable should at the time of arrest formulate any charge at all, much less the charge which may ultimately be found in the indictment, but this, and this only, is the qualification which I would impose on the general proposition. It leaves untouched the principle, which

lies at the heart of the matter, that the arrested man is entitled to be told what is the act for which he is arrested. The "charge" ultimately made will depend on the view taken by the law of his act. In ninety-nine cases out of a hundred the same words may be used to define the charge or describe the act, nor is any technical precision necessary — for instance, if the act constituting the crime is the killing of another man, it will be immaterial that the arrest is for murder and at a later hour the charge of manslaughter is substituted. The arrested man is left in no doubt that the arrest is for that killing. This is, I think, the fundamental principle, that a man is entitled to know what, in the apt words of Lawrence L.J. are "the facts alleged to constitute crime on his part." If so, it is manifestly wrong that a constable arresting him for one crime should profess to arrest him for another. Of what avail is the prescribed caution if it is directed to an imaginary crime? And how can the accused take steps to explain away a charge of which he has no inkling? ...

It is clear then that, whatever may have been the secret thought of the constables at the time of the arrest and detention, they allowed the respondent to think that he was being arrested for being "in unlawful possession" of certain goods, an offence, if it be an offence, which was at the most a misdemeanour within the Liverpool Act and could not, except under conditions which did not here obtain, justify an arrest without a warrant, and was described in terms not calculated to bring home to him that he was suspected of stealing or receiving the goods. In these circumstances the initial arrest and detention were wrongful. He was not aware and was not made aware of the act alleged to constitute his crime, but was misled by a statement which was calculated to suggest to his uneasy conscience that he was guilty of a so-called black market offence. It is no answer that the constables had no sinister motive. They had from the administrative point of view a perfectly good motive. It will be found in an answer to a question, which, though it related to a later stage of the proceedings, is equally applicable to the earlier: "Why did you not then charge him with larceny?" To this the revealing answer was: "Because that larceny was committed at Leicester and it would then be a matter of withdrawing one charge and handing him over to Leicester. Unlawful possession was the most convenient charge at the time until he could be handed over to the Leicester City Police."

My Lords, the liberty of the subject and the convenience of the police or any other executive authority are not to be weighed in the scales against each other. This case will have served a useful purpose if it enables your Lordships once more to proclaim that a man is not to be deprived of his liberty except in due course and process of law.

5. Section 29(2) of the *Criminal Code* now provides that:

> It is the duty of every one who arrests a person, whether with or without a warrant, to give notice to that person, where it is feasible to do so, of
> (a) the process or warrant under which he makes the arrest, or
> (b) the reason for the arrest.

In addition, ss. 9 and 10 of the *Canadian Charter of Rights and Freedoms* provide that everyone has the right not to be arbitrarily detained and has the right on arrest to be informed promptly of the reasons for the arrest.

6. In *Sandison v. Rybiak* (1974), 1 O.R. (2d) 74, 39 D.L.R. (3d) 366 (H.C.), when the plaintiff asked the police why they were arresting his friend, they refused to inform him. They also refused to tell the friend why she was being arrested. A scuffle ensued and the plaintiff was charged with obstructing the police. After both the plaintiff and the friend were acquitted of the charges against them, the plaintiff brought an action

for assault, false imprisonment and malicious prosecution. He was successful on all theories before Mr. Justice Parker who explained:

> The prisoner or someone speaking for him or her is entitled to know the reasons for the arrest and make a statement in answer to it. The exercise of such a right cannot be converted into obstruction unless it is intemperate, unduly persistent, irrelevant or made in an unreasonable manner. ...
>
> The accused is not required to submit to a restraint of his freedom until he is told that he is under arrest and the reason for the restraint. ...
>
> If an arrest is unlawful then any restriction on the liberty of the subject is false imprisonment.

7. On the question of the speed with which an arrested person must be taken before a justice of the peace, see *Criminal Code*, R.S.C. 1985, c. C-46, s. 503, *John Lewis & Co. Ltd. v. Tims*, [1952] A.C. 676, [1952] 1 All E.R. 1203; *Dallison v. Caffery*, [1965] 1 Q.B. 348, [1964] 2 All E.R. 610 (C.A.). The right to be tried within a reasonable time is also guaranteed by s. 11 of the *Canadian Charter of Rights and Freedoms.*

8. For a superb analysis of this problem see Weiler, "The Control of Police Arrest Practices: Reflections of a Tort Lawyer", in Linden (ed.), *Studies in Canadian Tort Law* (1968), at 416. See also Wood, "Powers of Arrest in Canada Under Federal Law" (1970), 9 West. Ont. L. Rev. 55.

9. Section 25 of the *Criminal Code* has also been used by the courts to protect a police officer from civil liability if the wrong person is arrested under warrant, as long as the police had reasonable and probable grounds to make what was believed to be a lawful arrest. See, for example, *Fletcher v. Collins*, [1968] 2 O.R. 618, 70 D.L.R. (2d) 183 (H.C.), and *Crowe v. Noon*, [1971] 1 O.R. 530, 16 D.L.R. (3d) 22 (H.C.).

10. The powers of arrest of a private citizen are much narrower than those of the police. As s. 494 of the *Criminal Code* states, a private citizen can arrest "a person whom he finds committing an indictable offence". This has led numerous authorities to hold that unless the arresting person can actually prove that the person arrested was committing an indictable offence at the time of the arrest, there is no defence. Under this interpretation, even reasonable and probable grounds, under s. 25 of the Code, would not exonerate a private citizen. See, for example, *Hayward v. F. W. Woolworth Co. Ltd.* (1979), 98 D.L.R. (3d) 345, 8 C.C.L.T. 157 (Nfld. S.C.), where Goodridge J. stated:

    > [s. 25] does not justify the private arrest of a person not found to be committing an indictable offence, even though the apprehender may have had reasonable and probable ground for believing the person apprehended was committing an indictable offence.

    Other cases, however, have held that reasonable and probable grounds are sufficient to justify a private arrest. See, for example, *Dendekker v. F. W. Woolworth Co.*, [1975] 3 W.W.R. 429 (Alta. S.C.). Yet a third view is that as long as the defendant had reasonable grounds to arrest the plaintiff and can show that *someone* had committed an offence, the defendant has a valid defence: see *Briggs v. Laviolette* (1994), 21 C.C.L.T. (2d) 105 (B.C.S.C.). Which of the views do you think is best? Should a private citizen have the same powers of arrest as a police officer?

11. Courts agree that a security officer's powers of arrest are the same as those of a private citizen. See, for example, *Dendekker*, *supra*. Should security officers at stores have the same powers of arrest as the police? Do you think that store keepers should have the right to detain suspicious shoppers temporarily, in order to clear up any rea-

sonable questions? What are the conflicting values here? Is the problem really in the way in which we define the tort of false imprisonment in the first place?

12. In the United States such a privilege is beginning to emerge. See Prosser and Keeton, *Handbook of the Law of Torts*, 5th ed. (1984), p. 141. Can this be looked upon merely as an extension of the privilege of protection or recapture of property? There is a fine student note on this topic, "Shop-lifting and the Law of Arrest: The Merchant's Dilemma" (1953), 62 Yale L.J. 788.

13. Should private citizens be encouraged or discouraged to assist in law enforcement? What are the advantages and disadvantages of their participation? Who should bear the cost of these errors? The shops? The individuals suspected? The customers of the shops? The police departments? The taxpayers?

14. In *Bahher v. Marwest Hotel Co. Ltd. et al.* (1969), 6 D.L.R. (3d) 322, 69 W.W.R. 462; affd (1970), 12 D.L.R. (3d) 646, 75 W.W.R. 729 (B.C.C.A.), Mr. Bahner took two friends to dinner at Trader Vic's restaurant, operated by the defendant Marwest in the Bayshore Inn, Vancouver. At 11:30 p.m., the waiter asked if the party would care for another bottle of wine. A second bottle was brought, opened and left at the table, but, by 11:50, had not been touched. At this time the waiter informed the plaintiff that according to law the bottle of wine must be consumed by midnight. The plaintiff said this could not be done and refused to pay for the second bottle. When he said he would take it elsewhere to drink, he was told that this was against the law, which it was. The plaintiff attempted to leave the restaurant, after having offered to give his name and address, but was prevented from doing so by the restaurant's security officer, who blocked the exit and informed the plaintiff that he could not leave. After some discussion the police were called and the defendant constable ordered the plaintiff to pay for the wine or face arrest. The plaintiff still declined to pay and was arrested, taken to the police station and put in a cell. The police officer believed that the plaintiff had committed the offence of obtaining goods by false pretenses but when he discovered that this was an error, he then laid an unfounded charge of intoxication which was subsequently dismissed.

Wilson C.J.S.C. stated:

> I cannot take very seriously the argument of counsel for the hotel company that there were other exits from the cafe unbarred and that the plaintiff might have escaped through one of them. The plaintiff, commanded by a security officer to stay, and prevented by that officer from leaving by the ordinary exit, behaved with admirable restraint in making no forcible attempt to pass the security officer. After what the officer had said and done he could reasonably expect to be restrained by force if he tried to leave by any exit and he was not required to make any attempt to run away.

Mr. Justice Wilson continued as follows:

> It seems to me that there were here two false imprisonments. When Rocky, the Pinkerton man, barred the exit from the cafe and told the plaintiff he could not leave, there was false imprisonment by the defendant Marwest Hotel Co. Ltd. When Muir, without a warrant took into custody and gaoled the plaintiff, who was not committing an offence, and whom the constable had no reasonable cause to believe to be guilty of an offence, there was a second false imprisonment. There was no reasonable and probable cause for imprisonment in either case. As I have said, it must be assumed that the reason in Muir's mind justifying the arrest was the plaintiff's refusal to pay for the second bottle of wine, and the plaintiff also knew that his refusal to pay was almost certainly the reason for his arrest. But I find as a fact that Muir did not, at the moment of ar-

> rest, disclose to the plaintiff the reason for his arrest. I think that Muir had in his mind some confused notion that a failure to pay for a thing ordered was a crime, but did not know what crime it was. The attitude of the manager and house detective of this grand caravanserai, both of whom seemed to have thought that failure to pay was a crime, may have influenced Muir's thinking.
>
> But the fact that he was publicly humiliated by detention by the security officer in the hotel in the presence of the staff and a dozen guests, and by subsequent interrogation and arrest by a uniformed policeman was known to a considerable number of people, who have in all probability and very naturally, told other persons about it. It is hard to calculate how far news of this kind may spread and what harm it may have done. Few persons who witnessed his arrest are likely to be aware of his subsequent acquittal. The ripples from the boulder thrown in the water by the defendants may spread far. The degradation consequent upon the experiences suffered by the plaintiff is sore and not easily forgotten.

His Lordship then proceeded to award $3,500 in damages against Marwest, (including $1,000 punitive damages) and $2,500 against Muir (including punitive damages). In addition, the $75 legal fee that the plaintiff spent on his defence in police court was awarded against Muir.

On the appeal, Mr. Justice Tysoe affirmed the result. With regard to the defendant hotel, His Lordship indicated that he thought the purpose of the detention was "to frighten the respondent into paying for the wine he had ordered and into paying for it there and then". He just could not believe that the hotel could possibly have believed that the respondent had committed a criminal offence. After affirming against the police officer, Mr. Justice Tysoe stated that his conduct was "simply outrageous". He did not think that the courts should "hold their hands until it is seen what the police commission sees fit to do in the way of disciplining a member of the police force".

Is this a good way of supervising police behaviour?

For a surprisingly similar case, see *Perry v. Fried et al.* (1972), 9 N.S.R. (2d) 545, 32 D.L.R. (3d) 589 (S.C.), *per* Cowan C.J.

15. Police officers are wise to avoid interfering in what are essentially civil disputes between innkeepers and their guests or between landlords and their tenants. Where an innkeeper is charged by the police with breaking and entering and possession of stolen goods, when the innkeeper was only exercising legal rights under the *Innkeeper's Act* in relation to certain goods belonging to some guests, both false imprisonment and malicious prosecution are committed, since the officers should have realized that no crime had been perpetrated. See *Carpenter v. MacDonald* (1979), 21 O.R. (2d) 165, 91 D.L.R. (3d) 723 (Dist. Ct.); affd (1979), 108 D.L.R. (3d) 153 (Ont. C.A.).

16. The police power of arrest under s. 495(1)(*b*) of the *Criminal Code* has been held to have application to a situation in which a person is "apparently" committing a summary conviction offence, even though subsequently acquitted of the offence for which the arrest was made: *R. v. Biron*, [1976] 2 S.C.R. 56, 59 D.L.R. (3d) 409, Martland J., speaking for the majority, stated:

> If the words "committing a criminal offence" are to be construed in [a restrictive manner] para. (*b*) becomes impossible to apply. The power of arrest which that paragraph gives has to be exercised promptly, yet, strictly speaking, it is impossible to say that an offence is committed until the party arrested has been found guilty by the Courts. If this is the way in which this provision is to be construed, no peace officer can ever decide, when making an arrest without a warrant, that the person arrested is "committing a criminal offence".

> In my opinion the wording used in para. (*b*), which is over simplified, means that the power to arrest without a warrant is given where the peace officer himself finds a situation in which a person is apparently committing an offence.

Laskin C.J.C., in a strong dissent, refused to accept this construction and held that if the offence for which the accused was arrested had not in fact been committed, then the arrest was unlawful, and the accused was justified in resisting that arrest. He further remarked:

> ... a constable's lot is a heavy and even unenviable one when he has to make an on-the-spot decision as to an arrest. But he may be overzealous as well as mistaken, and it may be too that when a charge or charges come to be laid, the Crown attorney or other advising counsel may mistake the grounds and thus lay a charge which does not support the arrest. We cannot go on a guessing expedition out of regret for an innocent mistake or a wrong-headed assessment. Far more important, however, is the social and legal, and indeed political, principle upon which our criminal law is based, namely, the right of an individual to be left alone, to be free of private or public restraint, save as the law provides otherwise. Only to the extent to which it so provides can a person be detained or his freedom of movement arrested.

REYNEN v. ANTONENKO ET AL.

Alberta Supreme Court. (1975), 54 D.L.R. (3d) 124,
[1975] 5 W.W.R. 10, 20 C.C.C. (2d) 342, 30 C.R.N.S. 135.

The plaintiff was arrested by the defendant police officers on suspicion of possession of narcotics. They took him to a hospital in order to have a rectal search done. The plaintiff co-operated with the defendant physician in this examination, and, as a result, two condoms containing heroin were recovered. The plaintiff then brought suit for assault and battery against the physician and the police officers.

McDonald D.C.J.: The plaintiff's sole complaint is with the procedure that took place at the hospital. He contends that the examination of his anal canal constituted assault and battery, alleging it was done without consent, in the absence of any emergency and without legal justification. ...

The question in this case is whether or not the police officers were required or authorized by law to search for the drugs which were removed from the plaintiff, employing medical assistance to search through the anus into the rectum of the plaintiff.

A general power of search of a person under arrest is given by common law. ...

It seems clear ... that the police in this case had not only the right but also a duty to conduct a search of the plaintiff for drugs, and to seize any drugs found as evidence to be presented to the Court. In making this search and seizure the police are clearly authorized to use such force as is reasonable, proper and necessary to carry out their duty, providing that no wanton or unnecessary violence is imposed. It is also clear that what is reasonable and proper in any particular case will depend on all the circumstances of that particular case, it being impossible to lay down any hard and fast rule to be applied to all cases, except the test of reasonableness.

Under the *Narcotic Control Act*, R.S.C. 1970, c. N-1, it is not only the duty of the police to arrest persons whom they have good reason to believe are in breach of the Act but also to seize drugs that may be evidence of such breach as is specifically provided for in s. 10 (1)(*c*).

The decision in this case is therefore to be based on whether or not the actions of the police were reasonable under the circumstances.

The evidence showed that Constable Hudon told Dr. Antonenko that the plaintiff at the airport had consented to the search at the hospital. I find that although Constable Hudon may have misinterpreted the statement or response of the plaintiff, yet he had some reason to believe that the plaintiff had indicated consent, and that Constable Hudon acted in good faith. It is true that the plaintiff did not give his written consent or explicit verbal consent, for that matter, to the examination by the doctor, but neither was he asked for it.

In his evidence-in-chief, the plaintiff testified that in the examining room at the hospital he was asked by the doctor to position himself and that he did so believing "he had no choice".

...

It is clear from the plaintiff's own evidence and that of Dr. Antonenko that the plaintiff co-operated fully with the doctor in the conduct of the examination. Without the plaintiff's full co-operation the doctor made it clear that the examination would not have been made.

No doubt the plaintiff suffered some discomfort during the examination but he was not injured in any way by the examination. The total result of the examination was that the police obtained the heroin the plaintiff had secreted in his rectum. No doubt this induced the plaintiff to plead guilty to the charge later laid against him.

The examination being conducted in a hospital under conditions of high standard by an eminently qualified medical practitioner indicates that the police exercised every care to assure that the plaintiff was not subjected to any unreasonable force. The examination was only possible with his cooperation. ...

Under the circumstances of this case I find that the action of the police officers in obtaining the medical examination of the plaintiff's rectum was done in a reasonable and proper manner and without any unreasonable force or threat to the health and well-being of the plaintiff. I therefore dismiss the action of the plaintiff with costs. ...

Action dismissed.

NOTES

1. This case may be contrasted to *Laporte v. The Queen* (1972), 29 D.L.R. (3d) 651, 8 C.C.C. (2d) 343 (Que., Hugessen J.), in which a search warrant, authorizing a surgical search of the accused's body for police bullets months after his arrest, was quashed on the ground *inter alia* that the human body could not be said to be a "place" or "receptacle" within the meaning of s. 443 of the *Criminal Code* at the time.

2. The police, while arresting someone on a narcotics charge see the suspect put something in his mouth. They grab the suspect's throat to prevent the item from being swallowed. They find nothing. Liability? What if they get the suspect to spit out some heroin? See *Scott v. R.* (1975), 61 D.L.R. (3d) 130, 24 C.C.C. (2d) 261 (Fed. C.A.).

3. What if a police officer puts some fingers in the suspect's mouth to search it? What if the suspect bites him? See *R. v. Brezack*, [1949] O.R. 888, [1950] 23 D.L.R. 265, 96 C.C.C. 97 (C.A.).

4. At the time of arrest, the accused swallows something that the police believe is narcotics. They have the accused's stomach pumped at the hospital. Liability? Does it make any difference if the procedure turns up some narcotics or if it does not?

5. Can the police, aside from statutory authority, have a blood test made? What about an X-ray? See Law Reform Commission of Canada, Report 25, "Obtaining Forensic Evidence" (1985). See ss. 487.04-487.09 of the *Criminal Code*.

6. Although prison guards may use reasonable force in moving an inmate, they are not permitted to beat the inmate up while doing so. See *Dodge v. Bridger* (1977), 4 C.C.L.T. 83 (Ont. H.C.), *per* Keith J.; varied as to damages (1978), 6 C.C.L.T. 71 (Ont. C.A.).

7. The police seem to have some power to interfere with individual rights in order to prevent violence. In *Humphries v. Connor* (1864), 17 Ir. C.L.R. 1, the defendant police officer removed an orange lily from the clothes of the plaintiff for fear that it was provoking a crowd to possible violence against the plaintiff. Mr. Justice Hayes, on a demurrer by the plaintiff, explained:

   > ... When a constable is called upon to preserve the peace, I know no better mode of doing so than that of removing what he sees to be the provocation to the breach of the peace, and when a person deliberately refuses to acquiesce in such removal, after warning so to do, I think the constable is authorized to do everything necessary and proper to enforce it. It would seem absurd to hold that a constable may arrest a person whom he finds committing a breach of the peace, but that he must not interfere with the individual who has wantonly provoked him to do so. But whether the act which he did was or was not, under all the circumstances, necessary to preserve the peace, is for the jury to decide.

8. In *Thomas v. Sawkins*, [1935] 2 K.B. 249, 153 L.T. 419 (D.C.), the defendant, a constable, insisted on attending a meeting after having been refused admittance. The meeting had been advertised to the public to discuss a matter of public interest. The plaintiff, in occupation of the premises, having requested the defendant to withdraw, which the defendant refused to do, attempted to eject the defendant and the latter used reasonable force in resisting the ejection. In proceedings for assault and battery, it was held that the defendant was not liable since, as a police officer, he had reason to believe that if he and other police officers were not present a serious breach of the peace might have ensued. *Per* Lawrence J.: "If a constable in the execution of his duty to preserve the peace is entitled to commit an assault, it appears to me that he is equally entitled to commit a trespass." *Per* Avory J.: "No express statutory authority is necessary [to empower police to enter] where the police have reasonable grounds to apprehend a breach of the peace." On the general problem see Goodhart, "*Thomas v. Sawkins*: A Constitutional Innovation" (1936), 6 Camb. L.J. 22.

9. The police are privileged to enter private premises without a warrant to make an arrest (1) if they believe on reasonable and probable grounds that the person they are looking for is present, and (2) if they make a proper announcement to the occupier. Normally, the police should knock, identify themselves, and give the reason for their entry. Such an announcement may not be required in circumstances where it is impracticable to do so. See *Eccles v. Bourque et al.* (1974), 41 D.L.R. (3d) 392, [1973] 5 W.W.R. 434 (B.C.C.A.); affd 50 D.L.R. (3d) 735, 27 C.R.N.S. 325 (S.C.C.), *per* Dickson J. See also *Levitz v. Ryan*, [1972] 3 O.R. 783, 29 D.L.R. (3d) 519 (C.A.). Has tort law a valuable role to play in supervising police misconduct?

10. Although many of the cases involving the defence of legal authority relate to *Criminal Code* provisions, there are other statutes which provide legislative justification for arresting and imprisoning persons.

In *Barrett v. Lorette and Ross* (1979), 27 N.B.R. (2d) 621, 60 A.P.R. 621 (Q.B.), s. 5 of the *Intoxicated Persons Detention Act*, R.S.N.B. 1973, c. I-14, was successfully invoked by police officers who had arrested the plaintiff on reasonable and probable grounds that the plaintiff was drunk. In *Besse v. Thorn* (1979), 96 D.L.R. (3d) 657 (B.C. Co. Ct.); revd 107 D.L.R. (3d) 644 (C.A.), a similar defence under the *Liquor Control and Licensing Act, 1975* (B.C.), c. 38, failed. In that case, the interpretation of the legislation was that an arrest without warrant was justified if the person was *apparently* intoxicated in a public place. In *Tanner v. Norys*, [1980] 4 W.W.R. 33 (Alta. C.A.), the *Mental Health Act, 1972* (Alta.), c. 118, was in issue. The Act provided that a person may be "conveyed" to a facility and "detained" there for a period of time, upon the issuance of a conveyance and examination certificate in the prescribed form by a therapist or a physician. The trial judge found that there had been a gross abuse of the procedures and awarded judgment in favour of the plaintiff against the defendant psychiatrist. The Court of Appeal reversed the decision.

11. Is tort law a useful tool for controlling police arrest practices? What are its advantages and shortcomings? See Weiler, "The Control of Police Arrest Practices" in Linden (ed.), *Studies in Canadian Tort Law* (1968), at 416; Page, "Of Mace and Men; Tort Law as a Means of Controlling Domestic Chemical Warfare" (1969), 57 Georgetown L.J. 1238. Do you think that the *Canadian Charter of Rights and Freedoms* will have an effect on police behaviour? Why have there not been more cases brought for damages as a result of Charter violations?

REVIEW PROBLEMS

1. While on her way to the corner of Eglinton and Yonge Streets in Toronto, where she planned to spend the morning selling copies of *The Watchtower* and *Awake*, Penny, a devout Jehovah's Witness, negligently slipped and fell, cutting herself severely. Penny lay there bleeding, calling for someone to telephone the J.W. Ambulance Service, a service owned by Jehovah's Witnesses. An ambulance soon arrived but it had "AAA Ambulance" written on the side of it. Penny saw this sign as the men came for her with the stretcher and declared, "I will not go into your ambulance. I want J.W. and I want to go to the J.W. Hospital for Jehovah's Witnesses". Penny then fainted from loss of blood. The AAA attendants placed the unconscious Penny on the stretcher, put her in the ambulance and rushed her to the nearest hospital, the Toronto General Hospital.

   Penny came to in the emergency room as Donald, an intern, approached her with blood transfusion equipment. She looked around, realized that she was not in the J.W. Hospital and what was about to happen. She stated, "I am a Jehovah's Witness and would rather die than take a blood transfusion. Let me out of here and get me to the J.W.!" She fainted again from loss of blood. Donald, assessing rightly that this woman would die without an immediate transfusion, administered the required blood, sewed up the cut she had suffered, put her into a private room and called her husband, Paul.

   Paul arrived with a J.W. ambulance, went up to Penny's room and angrily demanded his wife's release.

   When Donald appeared, he stated that she could not be released unless the hospital bill of $35 was paid first. Paul refused to pay and insisted upon the immediate release of Penny, who was now awake and overheard everything. When Donald refused again, Paul picked up his wife and carried her out to the waiting J.W. ambulance. What tort liabilities have arisen?

2. Penelope was a photographer who loved to take pictures of Ontario. One Sunday she drove to the Scarborough Bluffs and began to take pictures. She noticed that a par-

ticularly fantastic view of the coastline might be seen from inside the confines of a private dwelling owned by Dimwit. Desperately wanting this photograph for a contest that she had entered, Penelope parked her car and sneaked up to the high fence that surrounded the property. She noticed two signs on the fence. One read: "Trespassers will be shot" and the other stated: "This fence is electrically charged — Beware."

Penelope was undeterred, mainly because she did not believe the signs. She reached over and touched the fence prior to climbing over and received a small jolt of electricity. Penelope put on a pair of rubber gloves and shoes and, thus insulated, climbed over the fence. On the other side, she hurried to the edge of the cliff and took some photographs.

Suddenly she heard a voice behind her say, "If you are not off my land in one minute, I shall blow your brains out." Penelope quickly turned around and saw Dimwit standing there with a large shotgun aimed at her. Realizing that Dimwit meant business, Penelope sprinted back to the fence, received another jolt of electricity because she forgot to put her rubber gloves and shoes back on, and climbed back over to safety.

What tort liabilities, if any, have arisen?

CHAPTER 4

INTRODUCTION TO NEGLIGENCE: DAMAGE AND CAUSATION

Negligence is by far the most important field of tort liability at present. Its principles regulate most of the activities of our society. Tort lawyers spend most of their time working on negligence actions. It is, therefore, understand able why the bulk of this book deals with problems of negligence law.

Negligence is not a state of mind but conduct which falls below the standard accepted in the community. There is not a single nominate tort of negligence; rather negligence is a basis of liability which protects some interests and not others.

The word negligence has two meanings, a restricted one and a broader one. In its narrow sense, it refers to certain *conduct* that falls below the standard required by society. In this context, negligence connotes more than a mere state of mind. The second and wider meaning of negligence makes reference to a *cause of action for negligence*. Negligence in the first sense is only one fragment of this expanded meaning of negligence.

To establish a cause of action for negligence several elements must be present. There is disagreement, however, over the number of these components. Perhaps the most commonly accepted formulation has been called the "A.B.C. rule". According to this rule, a plaintiff in a negligence action in order to succeed is required to establish three things to the satisfaction of the court: (A) a duty of care exists; (B) there has been a breach of that duty; and (C) damage has resulted from that breach. This is the traditional English approach to negligence liability, and it has been repeated countless times in the cases. The trouble with the A.B.C. rule is its beguiling simplicity. It blurs together issues that should not be treated under one rubric. Complexities that should be illuminated are disguised. Thus, when the English courts are forced to consider the problem of the extent of liability, none of the three elements seem to cover the issue satisfactorily. Duty, remoteness and proximate cause may be utilized interchangeably without any explanation.

Another division of the subject of negligence is that advocated by the American scholars. They suggest that there are four elements in a cause of action for negligence: (1) duty; (2) failure to conform to the standard required; (3) a reasonably close causal connection between the conduct and the resulting injury, sometimes termed "proximate cause"; (4) actual loss or damage resulting to the interest of another. This categorization also produces difficulties. A court sometimes handles the proximate cause question in terms of duty or remoteness, which leads to a blending of the first and third elements. Similarly, a court sometimes confuses the first and second components. Another deficiency is that this approach neglects the consideration of the conduct of the plaintiff, as an element to be assessed in the process. Professor Fleming, in his masterful text, *The Law of Torts*, 9th ed. (1998), overcomes this last criticism by adumbrating five elements of a cause of action for negligence. To the four listed in the paragraph above, he adds a fifth component, the absence of any conduct by the injured party which would preclude or limit recovery. Consequently, the defences of contributory negligence, voluntary assumption of risk and illegality are considered as one of the five elements

This work will use a six-part division of negligence in order to facilitate an examination of the subject from all possible angles. A cause of action for negligence arises if the following elements are present: (1) the defendant's conduct must be negligent, that is, in breach of the standard of care set by the law; (2) the claimant must suffer some damage; (3) the damage suffered must be caused by the negligent conduct of the defendant; (4) there must be a duty recognized by the law to avoid this damage; (5) the conduct of the defendant must be a proximate cause of the loss or, stated in another way, the damage should not be too remote a result of the defendant's conduct; and (6) the conduct of the plaintiff should not be such as to bar or limit recovery; that is, one must, in determining liability, examine the defences of contributory negligence, voluntary assumption of risk and illegality.

The number of elements in a cause of action for negligence does not really matter very much, because they are only artificial divisions scholars construct in order to clarify the different aspects of a negligence case. Sometimes components are substituted for one another. For example, a court may approach a "duty" problem with "proximate cause" language or, depending on your bias, a judge might attack a "proximate cause" question with "duty" vernacular. Judges have frequently intermixed the "causation" and "proximate cause" questions. Although it has been argued that cause-in-fact is purely a factual question and that proximate cause is a legal issue based on policy, not all courts have recognized this. Moreover, it may be well-nigh impossible to eliminate all matters of value from the issue of causation. The whole debate is probably a tempest in a teapot, but if our understanding is at all deepened, the discussion may be worthwhile.

This chapter will deal briefly with the second and third elements of a cause of action for negligence — damage and causation. In the next chapter, the standard of care will be examined. The following chapters will treat the other elements *seriatim*.

A. DAMAGE

There can be no liability for negligence unless some damage has been suffered by the plaintiff. Although damage is not required in tort actions which developed out of the writ of trespass, some loss is necessary in those tort actions which evolved out of the action on the case. Since negligence is such a cause of action, proof of damage is necessary in order to succeed.

Mr. Justice Laskin has stated that, "where a claim for personal injuries is made, proof of damage would be required to complete the cause of action". (*Schwebel v. Telekes*, [1967] 1 O.R. 541 (C.A.); overruled on another point in *Consumers Glass Co. v. Foundation Co. of Canada* (1985), 33 C.C.L.T. 104 (Ont. C.A.)).

The requirement of damage is not based on history alone, there are policy reasons supporting it. In *Pfiefer v. Morrison,* (1973), 42 D.L.R. (3d) 314 (B.C.S.C.), Wilson J., in dismissing an action, stated at 316:

> In this highly mobile age collisions between motor vehicles occur in great numbers every day. Many of them have grave consequences in injury to persons and damage to property. In other instances, more numerous, slight damage or no damage is caused to the vehicles and there is no injury to person. If, in the latter class of cases, a litigant claiming damages for personal injury is able to establish a cause of action and a right to at least nominal damages merely by proving negligence then, I say, needless lawsuits must proliferate, each one giving damages and costs to per-

sons who have suffered no injury. Such actions would proceed to trial, at no risk to the plaintiff of failure and penalty costs, and with the assurance that he would recover costs. The undesirability of such a state of affairs is self-evident.

What is meant by the word damage is some "head of loss for which compensation will be awarded"? See *Vile v. Von Wendt* (1979), 26 O.R. (2d) 513, at p. 517 (Div. Ct.) (*per* Linden J.). This is to be contrasted with the term "damages", which is "generally used to identify the amount of money that is paid by a tortfeasor for inflicting the various items of damage". Thus, the damage caused by negligent conduct may consist of several different items such as medical expenses, hospital bills, loss of income as well as the non-pecuniary heads of loss such as pain and suffering, loss of enjoyment of life, etc. Consequently, negligent conduct can cause several types of damage which may be incurred by various people in more than one place (at p. 518).

Negligence actions have been dismissed, on occasion, despite the clear presence of negligent conduct, on the basis that no loss has been established. For example, in earlier times suits launched by the parents of young children killed in accidents have been dismissed where no damages "either actual or prospective" were incurred. See *Barnett v. Cohen,* [1921] 2 K.B. 421, four-year old. See also *Pedlar v. Toronto Power Co.* (1913), 29 O.L.R. 527 (H.C.); affd (1914), 30 O.L.R. 581 (C.A.), two-year-old; *Cashin v. Mackenzie,* [1951] 3 D.L.R. 495 (N.S. T.D.), five-year-old; *Nickerson v. Forbes* (1956), 1 D.L.R. (2d) 463 (N.S.C.A.), child nearly six; *Alaffe v. Kennedy* (1973), 40 D.L.R. (3d) 429 (N.S. T.D.), four-month-old child. *Cf.*, *Schmidt, Re (sub nom. Thornborrow v. MacKinnon)* (1981), 16 C.C.L.T. 198 (Ont. H.C.) (*per* Linden J.).

1. Limitation Periods

Limitations statutes have created some difficulties in the past. Where statutes clearly specify the particular event from which the time is to run, little difficulty arises. However, most limitation periods stipulate that the time is to run from the date the "cause of action arose". (*Limitations Act*, R.S.O. 1990, c. L.15, s. 45.) In the past, this was interpreted to mean that the time ran from the date the damage was incurred, because, at that time, all the facts required for liability in negligence were present. (*Roberts v. Read* (1812), 16 East 214, 104 E.R. 1070). Pursuant to this rule, some harsh decisions were rendered, denying plaintiffs the right to sue, even though they had been unaware and unable to become aware of the damage they had suffered prior to the expiry of the limitation period. (*Archer v. Catton & Co. Ltd.*, [1954] 1 All E.R. 896).

All this has now changed, the law having been reshaped to the effect that the time does not run until the "date of discoverability of the damage". See *Wilson J.* in *Kamloops v. Nielsen,* [1984] 5 W.W.R. 1, at p. 46 (S.C.C.).

In the case of *Kamloops v. Nielsen,* (at p. 20) Madame Justice Wilson condemned the "injustice of a law which statute-bars a claim before the plaintiff is even aware of its existence" (at p. 49). She felt that to be required to investigate facts years later was the "lesser of two evils" than to deny compensation altogether.

The "discoverability rule" was explained in *Central Eastern Trust Co. v. Rafuse,* (1986), 37 C.C.L.T. 117 (S.C.C.), where Mr. Justice LeDain, expressed the new principle as follows (at p. 180):

> ... a cause of action arises for purposes of a limitation period when the material facts on which it is based have been discovered or ought to have been discovered by the plaintiff by the exercise of reasonable diligence...

There has also been legislative reform, as for example, the Ontario *Health Disciplines Act,* which expressly stipulates a similar principle for negligence in the medical area, that is, no lability unless the action is commenced within one year "from the date when the person commencing the action knew or ought to have known the fact or facts upon which the person alleges negligence or malpractice". (R.S.O. 1990, c. H.4, s.17, Act not retroactive, see *Martin v. Perrie* (1986), 36 C.C.L.T. 36 (S.C.C.)). The earlier language was much narrower, requiring action within one year of the date the "services terminated". In Manitoba this wording excludes the application of the discoverability rule; see *J. (A.) v. Cairnie Estate* (1993), 17 C.C.L.T. (2d) 1 (Man. C.A.); leave to appeal to S.C.C. refused (1994), 19 C.C.L.T. (2d) 306 (S.C.C.). See generally Linden, *Canadian Tort Law*, 6th ed., (1997) at p.103.

The Supreme Court of Canada has recently declared that the time period for suing in a motor vehicle case in Ontario, which limits tort actions to permanent serious impairment cases, cannot begin to run until the victim discovers the seriousness of the injury and whether it will meet the statutory threshold. (See *Peixeiro v. Haberman* (1997), 151 D.L.R. (4th) 429 (S.C.C.)).

In *M. (K.) v. M. (H.)*, [1992] 3 S.C.R. 6, 96 D.L.R. (4th) 289, the Supreme Court of Canada extended the limitation period for victims of incest. The plaintiff sued her father for incest 18 years after the first incestuous conduct occurred and ten years after she had reached the age of majority. Both the trial judge and the Ontario Court of Appeal dismissed the plaintiff's action due to the expiration of the two-year limitation period provided for in Ontario's limitations statute. The majority of the Supreme Court, while recognizing that incest is a tort of battery and is, therefore, subject to the legislation, held that due to the nature of this type of battery, that the running of the limitation period ought to be postponed until the victim becomes aware of the connection between the harm suffered and the incestuous conduct which is its cause. The majority further held that in incest cases there is a presumption that victims only discover this connection during therapy. The presumption can be rebutted by a defendant if there is evidence that the link was realized by the victim without the benefit of therapy.

Another approach suggested by the majority was to view incest as a breach of a parent's fiduciary duty which is not subject to any limitation period. Mr. Justice Sopinka and Madam Justice McLachlin, while agreeing with the majority as to the running of the limitation period, did not agree that there should be a presumption of non-discoverability and a shift in the legal burden of proof.

With whom do you agree? Do you think that a defendant can easily rebut the presumption? Should there be legislation eliminating any limitation period at all for certain heinous types of torts, such as sexual assault and incest?

B. CAUSATION

There can be no liability for negligent conduct unless some damage is caused by it. In other words, there must be some link or connection between the wrongful act and the loss being complained of. This issue is sometimes called the cause-in-fact issue, and should not be confused with the proximate cause, or remoteness issue which will be dealt with below.

For the most part the courts have, fortunately, adopted a common sense approach to this question, resisting the temptation to enter into an endless philosophical discourse on the concept of causation. Most commonly the "but for" text is employed to handle the issue. If the loss would not have occurred but for the conduct of the defendant, it is a cause of the loss. In other words, if the damage would have occurred in any event, with or without the act of the defendant, the conduct is not a cause of the damage. The defendant's act must make a difference; if it had nothing to do with the loss, then no liability can be imposed.

Although in most cases it is easy to tell if causation was present, some losses are very difficult to link to the defendant. In general, this issue must be proven on a balance of probabilities. To show that the defendant was a "possible" cause is not enough. The issues of proof of causation will be analyzed later.

The Supreme Court of Canada has employed a modern approach to causation. Mr. Justice Sopinka in *Snell v. Farrell* ((1990), 72 D.L.R. (4th) 289, at p. 298) declared that causation need not be proved with "scientific precision". He explained that "Causation is an expression of the relationship that must be found to exist between the tortious act of the wrongdoer and the injury to the victim in order to justify compensation of the latter out of the pocket of the former."

KAUFFMAN v. T.T.C.

Ontario Court of Appeal, [1959] O.R. 197, 18 D.L.R. (2d) 204; affd, [1960] S.C.R. 251, 80 C.R.T.C. 305, 22 D.L.R. (2d) 97.

While ascending an escalator in a Toronto subway station the plaintiff was injured when she fell after two scuffling youths ahead of her fell back on a man, who, in turn, fell back on her. The jury found for the plaintiff, but the Court of Appeal reversed the decision and this was affirmed by the Supreme Court of Canada. In addition to the negligence issues, there were two problems of causation raised in the case: (1) would the presence of a better hand rail have prevented the accident? (2) would the presence of an attendant have avoided the accident? Both of these questions were answered in the negative.

Morden J.A.: The theory advanced by the plaintiff's counsel to quote his own words was that "in the operation of an escalator, particularly in a public transit system where large crowds are to be expected, if a person near the top falls backward (for whatever reason) against the person behind him, each person will fall against the other knocking him down in much the same fashion as a row of dominoes". But there was a total absence of evidence that the man immediately ahead of the plaintiff or the two reckless and irresponsible youths ahead of him were grasping or attempted to grasp the hand rail before or in the course of the scuffle and consequent falling. Nor was there any evidence that in the circumstances the plaintiff would not have fallen if her hands had been grasping a rubber oval hand rail. In my opinion, there was no evidence to justify a finding that the type of hand rail in use at the St. Clair Ave. station was a contributing cause of the plaintiff's unfortunate and serious accident. It is a fundamental principle that the causal relation between the alleged negligence and the injury must be made out by the evidence and not left to the conjecture of the jury. ... The first finding of negligence in view of the evidence in this case does not justify a verdict against the defendant.

NOTES

1. Many negligence actions have failed for want of proof of causation. For example, in *Davidson v. Connaught Laboratories* (1980), 14 C.C.L.T. 251, 5 L. Med. Q. 131 (Ont. H.C.), a pharmaceutical company was said to have inadequately warned the medical profession about the possible side-effects of an anti-rabies serum, but they were relieved of liability in any event since there was no evidence that it would "have made any difference" to the medical practitioners, who would have recommended the use of the serum even if they had been fully informed of the risks. In other words, the negligent failure to warn the doctors was not a cause of the plaintiff's damage, and hence there could be no liability imposed.

2. In *Horsley v. MacLaren,* [1969] 2 O.R. 137 (*sub nom. Matthews v. MacLaren*), 4 D.L.R. (3d) 557 (H.C.); revd, [1970] 2 O.R. 487, 11 D.L.R. (3d) 277 (C.A.); affd, [1972] S.C.R. 441, 22 D.L.R. (3d) 545, someone fell overboard from a cabin cruiser into the frigid waters of Lake Ontario and suffered a fatal heart attack. An action against his negligent rescuer was dismissed on the ground, *inter alia,* that death would probably have resulted in any event. Mr. Justice Lacourciere, at trial stated:

> It is trite law that liability does not follow a finding of negligence, even where there exists a legally recognized duty, unless the defendant's conduct is the effective cause of the loss.

His Lordship indicated that "the burden is on the plaintiff to prove by a preponderance of evidence that the defendant's negligence was the effective cause" of death. He was, reluctantly, forced to the conclusion that "on the balance of probabilities, it has not been shown that Matthews' life could have been saved. The defendant's negligence therefore was not the cause of Matthews' death and there can be no liability."

3. Other cases that turned on the causation question were *Reed v. Ellis* (1916), 38 O.L.R. 123, 32 D.L.R. 592 (C.A.), where the court was not convinced that tuberculosis had been caused by dust and fumes inhaled on the job; *Pritchard v. Liggett & Myers Tobacco,* 295 F. 2d 292 (1961), where the court was not satisfied that lung cancer was caused by smoking; *cf., Cipollone,* 789 F. 2d 181 (3rd Circuit 1986); *Barnett v. Chelsea & Kensington Hospital Management Committee,* [1967] 1 Q.B. 428, [1968] 1 All E.R. 1068, where causation was not proved when a person sent home from the hospital died.

4. See Green, "The Causal Relation Issue in Negligence Law", (1962), 60 Mich. L. Rev. 547; Malone, "Ruminations on Cause-in-Fact", (1956), 9 Stan. L. Rev. 60; Hart and Honoré, "Causation in the Law", (1959).

I. Multiple Causes

There may be more than one cause of an accident. In other words, there may be several factors that contribute to a plaintiff's injury. Defendants who cause losses cannot be excused merely because other causal factors have helped produce the harm. It is sufficient if the defendant's negligence was a cause of the harm. As Mr. Justice Major has explained in *Athey v. Leonati* ([1996] 3 S.C.R. 458 at 467 and 469):

> It is not now necessary, nor has it ever been, for the plaintiff to establish that the defendant's negligence was the *sole cause* of the injury. There will frequently be a myriad of other background events which were necessary preconditions to the injury occurring. ... As long as a defendant is *part* of the cause of an injury, the defendant is liable, even though his [or her] act alone was not enough to create the injury. There

> is no basis for a reduction of liability because of the existence of other preconditions: defendants remain liable for all injuries caused or contributed to by their negligence. ... Apportionment between tortious causes is expressly permitted by provincial negligence statutes and is consistent with the general principles of tort law. The plaintiff is still fully compensated and is placed in the position he or she would have been in but for the negligence of the defendants. Each defendant remains fully liable to the plaintiff for the injury, since each was a cause of the injury. The legislation simply permits defendants to seek contribution and indemnity from one another, according to the degree of responsibility for the injury.

The "but for" test ran into stormy sailing where two or more defendants combined to cause loss. If the injury would have transpired if either cause alone had been operating, it might be said that neither party was a cause under the "but for" test. Suppose A and B negligently light fires at different places and the fires spread to engulf the plaintiff's house. A and B both might argue that the loss of the house would have resulted without their negligence. Consequently, a blinkered court might hold that neither of the defendants, although both negligent, was the cause of the loss, because it would have occurred in any event.

This just could be tolerated and, happily, the courts have handled this situation with common sense. They devised the substantial factor test, which holds that if the acts of two people are both substantial actors in bringing about the result, then liability is imposed on both on the theory that both "materially contributed to the occurrence". Consequently, in *Lambton v. Mellish*, [1894] 3 Ch. 163, at p. 166 (*per* Chitty J.), two merry-go-round operators were sued for nuisance as a result of the maddening noise made by their organs. Injunctions were granted against them individually because according to Mr. Justice Chitty:

> If the acts of two persons, each being aware of what the other is doing, amount in the aggregate to what is an actionable wrong, each is amenable to the remedy against the aggregate cause of complaint. The Defendants here are both responsible for the noise as a whole so far as it constitutes a nuisance affecting the Plaintiff and each must be restrained in respect of his own share in making the noise.

In another case, *Corey v. Havener*, (1920), 182 Mass. 250, the plaintiff, in a horse and wagon, was passed by two motorists driving at a high rate of speed, one on each side. The horse took fright and the plaintiff was injured. Although the defendants acted independently, judgment was given against both of them for the full amount of the plaintiff's damages because "if each contributed to the injury, that is enough to bind both". A similar case is *Arneil v. Paterson*, [1931] A.C. 560 (H.L.), where two dogs attacked some sheep, killing several of them. The owners of both dogs were held responsible for the entire damage "because each dog did in the eye of the law occasion the whole of the injury of which the pursuers complain". Thus, if the concurrent negligence of two people combined to kill someone, each would be equally responsible for the death. A group of polluters may be jointly liable though the harm caused by each cannot be determined. See also *Cowan v. Duke of Buccleuch* (1876), 2 App. Cas. 344 (H.L.), *Blair and Sumner v. Deakin* (1887), 57 L.T. 522, 3 T.L.R. 757.

If the loss is practically divisible, the court will hold each defendant liable only for the amount of damage that each personally inflicted. Thus, if the court could determine which sheep had been killed by each dog in *Arneil v. Paterson*, each owner would have been required to pay only for the loss caused by the dog each defendant owned. Moreover, if X injures P's leg and Y injures P's arm, each pays only for the damage each inflicted.

A similar division is made when the injuries are not concurrent, but follow one another in time. Thus, if one tortfeasor injures someone's leg, and a second tortfeasor later injured it further, necessitating amputation of the leg, the first defendant must pay the damages as they would have been assessed on the day before the second injury, and the second defendant would have to compensate only for the *additional* devaluation of the plaintiff caused by the second injury. A more complicated but consistent calculation is undertaken when there are three separate, successive, injuries.

If a non-culpable injury intrudes, a similar result ensues. Thus, where a victim of an accident is off work for 13 months, but three of these months would have been lost in any event because of an unrelated heart condition, recovery can be given only for ten months' lost income, for otherwise the victim would be "overcompensated". (*Berns v. Campbell* (1974), 8 O.R. 680 (H.C.)). So too, if a person is disabled by tortious conduct and it is discovered that a medical condition unconnected to the accident would have caused incapacitation in any event, the damages payable by the tortfeasor must be reduced to the extent that the medical condition caused the loss. (*Penner v. Mitchell* (1978), 6 C.C.L.T. 132, at 141 (Alta. C.A.)).

The rationale underlying these successive injury cases has been explained by Major J. in *Athey* as follows (at 472):

> ... the plaintiff is not to be placed in a position *better* than his or her original one. It is therefore necessary not only to determine the plaintiff's position after the tort but also to assess what the "original position" would have been. It is the difference between these positions, the "original position" and the "injured position", which is the plaintiff's loss. In the cases referred to above, the intervening event was unrelated to the tort and therefore not as great as it might have otherwise seemed, so damages were reduced to reflect this.

This is a complex area which is in need of rethinking. See, McLachlin, "Negligence Law – Proving the Connection" in Mullaney and Linden, *Torts Tomorrow: A Tribute to Professor John G. Fleming* (Sydney: The Law Book Co., 1998).

CHAPTER 5

THE STANDARD OF CARE

The standard of care issue is often the central aspect of a negligence action. While the damage and causation issues are often almost taken for granted, in no tort case can the court escape the obligation to assess the conduct of the defendant. Much of the time in most negligence lawsuits is devoted to this issue.

In some ways the issue is easy to understand. The question is whether this defendant departed from the standard of care that a reasonable person would have exercised in the circumstances. We usually employ the word "fault" to describe what must be proved, but it is not moral blameworthiness that is the standard; rather it is said that it is an objective standard. It will be seen, however, that often certain subjective aspects may intrude. There is no one standard for all actors. From some, like children and the mentally and physically disabled, we cannot expect compliance with the standard of the reasonable person. From others, like professional people, we expect more than the standard of reasonableness. We shall see that custom and legislation often play a role in all of this. As is so often said, what appears superficially to be a simple matter can become quite complicated.

A. UNREASONABLE RISK

BOLTON & OTHERS v. STONE

House of Lords. [1951] A.C. 850, [1951] 1 All E.R. 1078.

The defendants were the committee and members of a cricket club. During a match, a batter hit a ball which went over a fence seven feet high and 17 feet above the cricket patch, and hit the plaintiff who was standing on the adjoining highway. The distance to the fence from the batter was 78 yards and, to where the plaintiff was hit, 100 yards. The ground had been used for about 90 years and no one had been injured before in this way, although on about six occasions over a period of 30 years a ball had been hit into the highway. A witness, Mr. Brownson, said that five or six times during the last few years a ball had hit his house or come into his yard. His house was closer to the cricket grounds than the spot where the plaintiff was hit. The plaintiff brought action for damages for negligence and nuisance. At the trial her claim was dismissed on the ground that there was no evidence of negligence and nuisance was not established. On appeal to the Court of Appeal judgment was given the plaintiff on the basis of negligence, Somervell L.J. dissenting. The majority held ([1949] 2 All E.R. 851), there was a foreseeable risk of a ball being hit onto the road and the defendants had failed to take reasonable care to avoid injury to anyone on the road. The defendant appealed. In the House of Lords the plaintiff conceded that unless negligence was established, the claim in nuisance must fail.

Lord Reid: My Lords, it was readily foreseeable that an accident such as befell the respondent might possibly occur during one of the appellants' cricket matches. Balls had been driven into the public road from time to time, and it was obvious that if a person happened to be where a ball fell that person would receive injuries which might or might not be serious. On the other hand, it was plain that the chance of that happening was small. The exact number of times a ball has been driven into the road is not known, but it is not proved that this has happened more than about six times in about 30 years. If I assume that it has happened on the average once in three seasons I shall be doing no injustice to the respondent's case. Then there has to be considered the chance of a person being hit by a ball falling in the road. The road appears to be an ordinary side road giving access to a number of private houses, and there is no evidence to suggest that the traffic on this road is other than what one might expect on such a road. On the whole of the part of the road where a ball could fall there would often be nobody and seldom any great number of people. It follows that the chance of a person ever being struck even in a long period of years was very small.

This case, therefore, raises sharply the question what is the nature and extent of the duty of a person who promotes on his land operations which may cause damage to persons on an adjoining highway. Is it that he must not carry out or permit an operation which he knows or ought to know clearly can cause such damage, however improbable that result may be, or is it that he is only bound to take into account the possibility of such damage if such damage is a likely or probable consequence of what he does or permits, or if the risk of damage is such that a reasonable man, careful of the safety of his neighbour, would regard that risk as material? I do not know of any case where this question has had to be decided or even where it has been fully discussed. Of course there are many cases in which somewhat similar questions have arisen, but, generally speaking, if injury to another person from the defendant's acts is reasonably foreseeable the chance that injury will result is substantial and it does not matter in which way the duty is stated. …

I think that reasonable men do, in fact, take into account the degree of risk and do not act on a bare possibility as they would if the risk were more substantial. … For example, in *Fardon v. Harcourt-Rivington*, 146 L.T. 391, Lord Dunedin said: "This is such an extremely unlikely event that I do not think any reasonable man could be convicted of neglience if he did not take into account the possibility of such an occurrence and provide against it … people must guard against reasonable probabilities, but they are not bound to guard against fantastic possibilities."

I doubt whether Lord Dunedin meant the division into reasonable probabilities and fantastic possibilities to be exhaustive so that anything more than a fantastic possibility must be regarded as a reasonable probability. What happened in that case was that a dog left in a car broke the window and a splinter from the glass entered the plaintiff's eye. Before that had happened it might well have been described as a fantastic possibility and Lord Dunedin did not have to consider a case nearer the border-line. …

Counsel for the respondent in the present case had to put his case so high as to say that, at least as soon as one ball had been driven into the road in the ordinary course of a match, the appellants could and should have realized that that might happen again, and that, if it did, someone might be injured, and that that was enough to put on the appellants a duty to take steps to prevent such an occurrence. If the true test is foreseeability alone I think that must be so. Once a ball has been driven on to a road without there being anything extraordinary to account for the fact, there is clearly a risk that another will follow and if it does there is clearly a chance, small though it may be, that somebody may be injured. On the theory that it is foreseeability alone that matters it would be irrelevant to consider how often a ball might be expected to land on the road and it would not matter whether the road was the busiest street or the quietest country lane. The only difference between these cases is in the degree of risk. It would take a good deal to make me believe that the law has departed so far from the standards which guide ordinary careful people in ordinary life. In the crowded conditions of modern life even the most careful person cannot avoid creating some risks and accepting others. What a man must not do, and what I think a careful man tries not to do, is to create a risk which is substantial . ... In my judgment, the test to be applied here is whether the risk of damage to a person on the road was so small that a reasonable man in the position of the appellants, considering the matter from the point of view of safety, would have thought it right to refrain from taking steps to prevent the danger. In considering that matter I think that it would be right to take into account, not only how remote is the chance that a person might be struck, but also how serious the consequences are likely to be if a person is struck, but I do not think that it would be right to take into account the difficulty of remedial measures. If cricket cannot be played on a ground without creating a substantial risk, then it should not be played there at all. I think that this is in substance the test which Oliver J. applied in this case. He considered whether the appellants' ground was large enough to be safe for all practical purposes and held that it was. This is a question, not of law, but of fact and degree. It is not an easy question, and it is one on which opinions may well differ. I can only say that, having given the whole matter repeated and anxious consideration, I find myself unable to decide this question in favour of the respondent. I think, however, that this case is not far from the border-line. If this appeal is allowed, that does not, in my judgment, mean that in every case where cricket has been played on a ground for a number of years without accident or complaint those who organize matches there are safe to go on in reliance on past immunity. I would have reached a different conclusion if I had thought that the risk here had been other than extremely small because I do not think that a reasonable man, considering the matter from the point of view of safety, would or should disregard any risk unless it is extremely small. ... In my judgment, the appeal should be allowed.

NOTES

1. What are the factors that the court took into account in deciding that the risk created was not an unreasonable one?

2. Would the court have reached the same conclusion if the ball went over the fence six times a year? Six times a day? Six times an hour? Would it make any difference if the cricket pitch adjoined Picadilly Circus?

3. Would the court have reached the same conclusion if, instead of a cricket ball, the offending object was a bullet or a stick of dynamite?

4. Professor John Fleming has written that "not only the greater risk of injury, but also the risk of greater injury is a relative factor". See Fleming, *The Law of Torts,* 9th ed. (1998), p. 128.

5. Why did the court refuse to take into account the difficulty of remedial measures? Do you think this factor should be worthy of some weight? Did the court really fail to consider it? See *Botting v. B.C.* (1997), 33 C.C.L.T. (2d) at 294 (B.C.S.C.), where the

court imposed liability when a man fell off a poorly designed bridge saying, "Remedial measures would have been relatively inexpensive."

6. One need not weep for Mrs. Stone, the plaintiff, who was paid her damages and costs by the defendants following the decision in her favour by the Court of Appeal. After the House of Lords reversed the decision, the defendants, who were supported by the cricketers association in conducting the litigation because they felt an important principle was involved, decided not to pursue Mrs. Stone for repayment of the money they had paid to her. Mrs. Stone had to pay her own costs in the House of Lords, however. See Note (1952), 68 L.Q. Rev. 3. Do you believe that there was a matter of important principle involved here? See also a similar case brought in negligence and nuisance concerning the problem of whether there should be an injunction issued, *Miller and another v. Jackson and another,* [1977] 1 Q.B. 966, [1977] 3 All E.R. 338 (C.A.).

7. What does the court mean when it talks about a "reasonable probability"? Does it mean 51 per cent? Twenty-five per cent? Ten per cent? Can one chance in a thousand be considered a "reasonable probability"?

   Consider the statement by Lord Reid in *Southern Portland Cement Ltd. v. Cooper,* [1974] 2 W.L.R. 152, [1974] 1 All E.R. 87 (P.C.):

   > Chance probability or likelihood is always a matter of degree. It is rarely capable of precise assessment. Many different expressions are in common use. It can be said that the occurrence of a future event is very likely, rather likely, more probable than not, not unlikely, quite likely, not improbable, more than a mere possibility, etc.

8. In *Paris v. Stepney Borough Council,* [1951] A.C. 367, [1951] 1 All E. R. 32 (H.L.); revg, [1949] 2 All E.R. 843, [1950] 1 K.B. 320 (C.A.), the plaintiff was employed in the defendant's garage. To the defendant's knowledge he had the use of only one eye. While using a hammer to remove a bolt on the undercarriage of a truck, a chip of metal flew into his good eye resulting in total blindness. The plaintiff claimed damages alleging negligence in the failure of the defendant to supply him with goggles. The overwhelming evidence was that the usual practice in trades of this nature was not to supply goggles for men engaged in this work, at least if they were men with the use of two eyes. At trial the plaintiff recovered. The Court of Appeal reversed this judgment. Accepting the evidence of the trade as indicating that to normal employees the defendant owed no duty to supply goggles because the risk was not one against which a reasonable employer was bound to take precautions, the court held that the plaintiff's disability could be relevant only if it increased the risk. Asquith L.J. stated: "A one-eyed man is no more likely to get a splinter or a chip in his eye than is a two-eyed man. This risk is no greater, but the damage is greater to a man using his only good eye... *quantum* or damage is one thing... scope of duty is another. The greater risk of injury is not the same thing as the risk of greater injury, and the first thing seems to me relevant here." The House of Lords (3:2) reversed the judgment of the Court of Appeal holding that the gravity of the harm likely to be caused would influence a reasonable person and, therefore, even though no duty was owed to a person with two good eyes, the duty of care to a one-eyed employee should require the supply of goggles. In considering negligence, two factors must be considered: the magnitude of the risk and the likelihood of injury being caused. The dissenting law lords felt that loss of an eye to a man with two good eyes was so serious that there should be liability to all employees, two- or one-eyed, or to none at all. It was not a case of trivial as against grave injury.

9. The great American Justice Learned Hand attempted to explain the concept of unreasonable risk in terms of a mathematical equation in *United States v. Carroll Towing Co.*, 159 F. 2d 169 (2nd Cir. Ct. of Appeals 1947):

> [T]he owner's duty, as in other similar situations, to provide against resulting injuries, is a function of three variables: (l) The probability that she [a barge tied to a dock] will break away; (2) the gravity of the resulting injury, if she does; (3) the burden of adequate precautions. Possibly it serves to bring this notion into relief to state it in algebraic terms: if the probability be called P; the injury L; and the burden B; liability depends upon whether B is less than L multiplied by P; *i.e.*, whether B is less than PL.

Does this cast any additional light on the problem? Is the burden side of the equation sufficiently broken down? Would it be preferable to split up the burden element into two — object and cost (OC)? See Linden, *Canadian Tort Law,* 6th ed. (1997), p. 117.

10. See Posner, *Economic Analysis of Law,* 3rd ed. (1986), referring to Judge Learned Hand's formula:

> This is an economic test. The burden of precautions is the cost of avoiding the accident. The loss multiplied by the probability of the accident is the cost that the precautions would have averted. If a larger cost could have been avoided by incurring a smaller cost, efficiency requires that the smaller cost be incurred.

Should decisions such as these be made on the basis of an economic test?

11. The economic cost/benefit approach has been criticized by feminist scholar Professor Leslie Bender in her article "A Lawyer's Primer in Feminist Theory and Tort" (1989), 38 J. of Legal Educ. 3. Professor Bender argues that a feminist approach to tort law would produce a different way of thinking about tort than the male dominated approach. She writes (at 31):

> When the standard of care is equated with economic efficiency or levels of caution, decisions that assign dollar values to harms to human life and health and then balance those dollars against profit dollars and other evidences of benefit become commonplace. Such cost-benefit and risk-utility analyses turn losses, whether to property or to persons, into commodities in fungible dollar amounts. The standard of care is converted into a floor of unprofitability or inefficiency. People are abstracted from their suffering; they are dehumanized. The risk of their pain and loss becomes a potential debit to be weighed against the benefits or profits to others. The result has little to do with care or even with caution, if caution is understood as concern for safety.
>
> There is another possible understanding of "standard of care" that conforms more closely to Gilligan's "different voice," an alternative perspective rooted in notions of interconnectedness, responsibility, and caring. What would happen if we understood the "reasonableness" of the standard of care to mean "responsibility" and the "standard of care" to mean the "standard of caring" or "consideration of another's safety and interests"? What if, instead of measuring carefulness or caution, we measured concern and responsibility for the well- being of others and their protection from harm? Negligence law could begin with Gilligan's articulation of the feminine voice's ethic of care — a premise that no one should be hurt. We could convert the present standard of "care of a reason able person under the same or similar circumstances" to a standard of "conscious care and concern of a responsible neighbor or social acquaintance for another under the same or similar circumstances."
>
> The legal standard of care may serve as the minimally acceptable standard of behavior, failing which one becomes liable. But the standard need not be set at the minimum — we do not need to follow Justice Holmes' advice and write laws for the "bad man." Have we gained anything from legally condoning behavior that causes enormous physical and mental distress and yet is

economically efficient? The law can be a positive force in encouraging and improving our social relations, rather than reinforcing our divisions, disparities of power, and isolation.

The recognition that we are all interdependent and connected and that we are by nature social beings who must interact with one another should lead us to judge conduct as tortious when it does not evidence responsible care or concern for another's safety, welfare, or health. Tort law should begin with a premise of responsibility rather than rights, of interconnectedness rather than separation, and a priority of safety rather than profit or efficiency. The masculine voice of rights, autonomy, and abstraction has led to a standard that protects efficiency and profit; the feminine voice can design a tort system that encourages behavior that is caring about others' safety and responsive to others' needs or hurts, and that attends to human contexts and consequences.

PRIESTMAN v. COLANGELO AND SMYTHSON

Supreme Court of Canada. [1959] S.C.R. 615, 19 D.L.R. (2d) 1.

Cartwright J. (dissenting): On August 1, 1955, Smythson, then 17 years of age, stole a new Buick automobile. Priestman, the appellant, a police officer of the township, was in a police car driven by his senior, Constable Ainsworth. They were on patrol duty when, shortly before 8.30 p.m. while it was still broad daylight, they received a message on the radio telephone reporting the theft and giving the description and licence number of the stolen car. Almost immediately they saw a motor vehicle which they believed to be — and which later turned out to be — the stolen vehicle, driven by Smythson. The stolen vehicle was travelling west on Cosburn, turned south at the intersection with Donlands and continued southerly on Donlands Ave. at about 20 m.p.h. It came to a stop about 2 ft. from the west curb by reason of a red traffic light at the corner of Donlands and Mortimer Aves. The police car pulled up alongside the stolen car and Priestman ordered Smythson to stop. Both officers were in uniform and Smythson, no doubt, realized that they were police officers. Instead of stopping he pulled around the corner quickly and drove west on Mortimer Ave. at a high rate of speed. The police car followed and on three occasions attempted to pass the stolen car in order to cut it off, but each time Smythson pulled to the south side of the road and cut off the police car. On the third occasion the police car was forced over the south curb on to the boulevard and was compelled to slow up in order to avoid colliding with a hydro pole on the boulevard. Following this third attempt and as the police car went back on to the road, Priestman fired a warning shot from his .38 calibre revolver into the air. The stolen car increased its speed and when the police car was one and a half to two car lengths from the stolen car Priestman aimed at the left rear tire of the stolen car and fired. The bullet hit the bottom of the frame of the rear window, shattered the glass, ricocheted and struck Smythson in the back of the neck, causing him to lose consciousness immediately. The stolen car went over the curb on the south side of the road, grazed a hydro pole, crossed Woodycrest Ave. — an intersecting street — went over the curb on the southwest corner, through a low hedge about 2 ft. high, struck the verandah of the house, coming to a stop somewhere near the northwest corner of the house. On its course along the side of the house it struck and killed Columba Colangelo and Josephine Shynall, who were waiting for a bus.

On October 14, 1955, the administrator of Josephine Shynall commenced an action against Smythson and Priestman claiming damages under the *Fatal Accidents Act*, R.S.O. 1950, c. 132. On November 8, 1955, the administrator of Columba Colangelo commenced a similar action. On February 1, 1956, Smythson commenced an action against Priestman for damages for personal injuries. As mentioned above, these three actions were tried together.

The learned trial judge was of opinion that Smythson's action against Priestman failed on two grounds, (i) that the force used by Priestman was not more than was necessary to prevent Smythson's escape by flight and that Priestman was justified in firing as he did by the terms of s. 25(4) of the *Criminal Code*, and (ii) that the action, not having been commenced within 6 months of the act complained of, was barred by s. 11 of the *Public Authorities Protection Act*, R.S.O. 1950, c. 303.

Smythson's appeal in that action was dismissed. All members of the Court of Appeal agreed with the learned trial judge as to the second ground on which he proceeded. Laidlaw J.A. was also of opinion that Priestman was justified in using his revolver to prevent Smythson's escape and had acted without negligence. No appeal was taken by Smythson from the judgment of the Court of Appeal in that action.

In the Shynall and Colangelo actions the learned trial judge held (i) that the fatalities were caused by the negligence of Smythson, and (ii) that Priestman was justified in using the force he did use and that as against him the actions must be dismissed. In each action he assessed the damages at $1,250 and gave judgment accordingly against Smythson for the amount with costs, dismissed the action as against Priestman with costs and directed that the plaintiff should add to his judgment against Smythson the costs payable by him to Priestman.

From these judgments the plaintiffs and Smythson appealed to the Court of Appeal, the plaintiffs asking that Priestman also be found negligent and that the damages be increased, and Smythson asking that he be absolved from the finding of negligence made against him and that Priestman be found solely to blame for the fatalities.

The Court of Appeal were unanimous in upholding the finding that Smythson was guilty of negligence causing the fatalities and in refusing to increase the damages awarded. The majority held that Priestman also was guilty of negligence and that the blame should be apportioned equally between Smythson and Priestman. Laidlaw J.A., dissenting in part, would have dismissed the appeal. In the result, judgment was directed to be entered in each action against Smythson and Priestman jointly and severally for $1,250 damages.

It is clear that Priestman was a peace officer who was proceeding lawfully to arrest Smythson, without warrant, for an offence for which he might be arrested without warrant, and that Smythson had taken to flight to avoid arrest; Priestman was therefore justified in using as much force as was necessary to prevent the escape by flight unless the escape could be prevented by reasonable means in a less violent manner. … For the purposes of this branch of the matter, I will assume, without deciding, that Smythson's escape could not have been prevented by reasonable means in a less violent manner and that as between Priestman and Smythson the former was justified in using his revolver as he did. …

The question of difficulty is whether the justification afforded by the subsection is intended to operate only as between the peace officer and the offender who is in flight or to extend to injuries inflicted, by the force used for the purpose of apprehending the offender, upon innocent bystanders unconnected with the flight or pursuit otherwise than by the circumstances of their presence in the vicinity. The words of the subsection appear to me to be susceptible of either interpretation and that being so I think we ought to ascribe to them the more restricted meaning. In my opinion, if Parliament intended to enact that grievous bodily harm or death might be inflicted upon an entirely innocent person and that such person or his dependants should be deprived of all civil remedies to which they would otherwise have been entitled, in circumstances such as are present in this case, it would have used words declaring such intention without any possible ambiguity. ...

I conclude that the first main ground upon which Priestman's appeal is based fails and pass to the second, which raises the question whether the two fatalities were contributed to by negligence on the part of Priestman.

Under s. 45 of the *Police Act*, R.S.O. 1950, c. 279, Priestman was charged with the duty of apprehending Smythson. ... This duty to apprehend was not, in my opinion, an absolute one to the performance of which Priestman was bound regardless of the consequences to persons other than Smythson. Co-existent with the duty to apprend Smythson was the fundamental duty *alterum non laedere*, not to do an act which a reasonable man placed in Priestman's position should have foreseen was likely to cause injury to persons in the vicinity.

The identity of the persons likely to be injured or the precise manner in which the injuries would be caused, of course, could not be foreseen; but, in my opinion, that the car driven by Smythson would go out of control as a result of the shot fired by Priestman was not "a mere possibility which would never occur to the mind of a reasonable man" — to use the words of Lord Dunedin in *Fardon v. Harcourt-Rivington* (1932), 146 L.T. 391, at p. 392 — it was rather a reasonable probability; that causing a car travelling at a speed of over 60 m.p.h. on a street such as Mortimer Ave. to be suddenly thrown out of control would result in injury to persons who happened to be upon the street also seems to me to be a probability and not a mere possibility. To hold, as has been done by all the Judges who have dealt with this case, that Smythson should have foreseen the harm which was caused and at the same time to hold Priestman ought not to have foreseen it would, it seems to me, involve an inconsistency. In my opinion, Priestman's act in firing without due regard to the probabilities mentioned was an effective cause of the fatalities and amounted to actionable negligence unless it can be said that the existence of the duty to apprehend Smythson robbed his act of the neglient character it would otherwise have had.

The question which appears to me to be full of difficulty is how far, if at all, the duty which lay upon Priestman to apprehend Smythson required him to take, or justified him in taking, some risk of inflicting injury on innocent persons. Two principles are here in conflict, the one *alterum non laedere*, above referred to, the other *salus populi est suprema lex*. It is undoubtedly in the public interest that an escaping criminal be apprehended and the question is to what extent innocent citizens may be called upon to suffer, without redress, in order that that end may be achieved. In spite of the diligence of counsel, little helpful authority has been brought to our attention. I have already made it clear that for the purposes of this branch of the matter I am assuming that Priestman could not have prevented Smythson's escape otherwise than by firing his revolver, and, on this assumption, it appears to me that the question for the court is: "Should a reasonable man in Priestman's position have refrained from firing although that would result in Smythson escaping, or should he have fired although foreseeing the probability that grave injury would result therefrom to innocent persons?" I do not think an answer can be given which would fit all situations. The officer should, I think, consider the gravity of the offence of which the fugitive is believed to be guilty and the likelihood of danger to other citizens if he remains at liberty; the reasons in favour of firing would obviously be far greater in the case of an armed robber who has already killed to facilitate his flight than in the case of an unarmed youth who has stolen a suitcase which he has abandoned in the course of running away. In the former case it might well be the duty of the officer to fire if it seemed probable that this would bring down the murderer even though the firing were attended by risks to other persons on the street. In the latter case he ought not, in my opinion, to fire if to do so would be attended by any foreseeable risk of injury to innocent persons.

In the particular circumstances of the case at bar I have, although not without hesitation, reached the conclusion that Priestman ought not to have fired as he did and that he was guilty of negligence in so doing. …

I would dismiss the appeals with costs and the cross-appeals without costs.

Locke J.: The performance of the duty imposed upon police officers to arrest offenders who have committed a crime and are fleeing to avoid arrest may, at times and of necessity, involve risk of injury to other members of the community. Such risk, in the absence of a negligent or unreasonable exercise of such duty, is imposed by the statute and any resulting damage is in my opinion, *damnum sine injuria*. In the article in the last edition of *Broom's Legal Maxims*, p. 1, dealing with the maxim *salus populi est suprema lex* where the passage from the judgment of Buller J. in the *British Cast Plate* case is referred to, the learned author says: "This phrase is based on the implied agreement of every member of society that his own individual welfare shall, in cases of necessity, yield to that of the community; and that his property, liberty, and life shall, under certain circumstances, be placed in jeopardy or even sacrificed for the public good."

Assuming a case where a police officer sees a pickpocket stealing from a person in a crowd upon the street and the pickpocket flees through the crowd in the hope of escaping arrest, if the officer in pursuit unintentionally collides with some one, is it to be seriously suggested that an action for trespass to the person would lie at the instance of the person struck? Yet, if the test applied in the cases which are relied upon is adopted without restriction, it could be said with reason that the police officer would probably know that, if he ran through a crowd of people in an attempt to arrest a thief, he might well collide with some members of the crowd who did not see him coming. To take another hypothetical case, assume a police officer is pursuing a bank robber known to be armed and with the reputation of being one who will use a gun to avoid capture. The escaping criminal takes refuge in a private house. The officer, knowing that to enter the house through the front door would be to invite destruction, proceeds to the side of the house where through a window he sees the man and fires through the window intending to disable him. Would an action lie at the instance of the owner of the house against the officer for negligently damaging his property? If an escaping bank robber who has murdered a bank employee is fleeing down an uncrowded city street and fires a revolver at the police officers who are pursuing him, should one of the officers return the fire in an attempt to disable the criminal and, failing to hit the man, wound a pedestrian some distance down the street of whose presence he is unaware, is the officer to be found liable for damages or negligence?

The answer to a claim in any of these suppositious cases would be that the act was done in a reasonable attempt by the officer to perform the duty imposed upon him by the *Police Act* and the *Criminal Code*, which would be a complete defence, in my opinion. As contrasted with cases such as these, if an escaping criminal ran into a crowd of people and was obscured from the view of a pursuing police officer, it could not be suggested that it would be permissible for the latter to fire through the crowd in the hope of stopping the fleeing criminal.

The difficulty is not in determining the principle of law that is applicable but in applying it in circumstances such as these. … Police officers in this country are furnished with fire-arms and these may, in my opinion, be used when, in the circumstances of the particular case, it is reasonably necessary to do so to prevent the escape of a criminal whose actions, as in the present case, constitute a menace to other members of the public. I do not think that these officers having three times attempted to stop the fleeing car by endeavouring to place their car in front of it were under any obligation to again risk their lives by attempting this. No other reasonable or practical means of halting the car has been suggested than to slacken its speed by blowing out one of the tires. ...

The cause of action pleaded is in negligence which, in the case of an officer attempting to perform his duty in these difficult circumstances, is to be construcled, in my opinion, as meaning that what was done by him was not reasonably necessary and not a reasonable exercise of the constable's powers under s. 25 in the circumstances. As Laidlaw J.A. has pointed out, to find the constable guilty of negligence in the manner in which the revolver was fired, as distinct from firing at all, would necessitate finding that Priestman should have anticipated that his arm might be jolted at the instant he fired. That learned judge was not willing to make that finding nor am I.

I consider that the statement in Broom to which I have referred accurately states the law and that it is applicable in the present circumstances. ... In my opinion, the action of the appellant in the present matter was reasonably necessary in the circumstances and no more than was reasonably necessary, both to prevent the escape and to protect those persons whose safety might have been endangered if the escaping car reached the intersection with Pape Ave. So far as Priestman was concerned, the fact that the bullet struck Smythson was, in my opinion, simply an accident. As to the loss occasioned by this lamentable occurrence, I consider that no cause of action is disclosed as against the appellant.

For these reasons, I would allow these appeals and set aside the judgments entered in the Court of Appeal. In accordance with the provisions of the orders granting leave to appeal to this court, no costs should be awarded against the respondents Colangelo and Shynall. I would dismiss the cross-appeals without costs. The appeal of Smythson should be dismissed and without costs.

[**Taschereau J.** agreed with **Locke J., Fauteux J.** agreed with the result reached by **Locke J.**, and **Martland J.** concurred with **Cartwright J.**]

NOTES

1. What were the key factors relied on by the Supreme Court in dismissing the case? How does this treatment compare with the way that the difficulty of remedial measures was handled in *Bolton v. Stone, supra*?

2. In *Bittner v. Tait-Gibson Optometrists Ltd.*, [1964] 2 O.R. 52, 44 D.L.R. (2d) 113 (C.A.), a finding of contributory negligence on the part of the plaintiff, a police officer, who was injured by slipping on ice negligently permitted to accumulate in front of the defendant's store was set aside by the Ontario Court of Appeal. At the time of the fall, the plaintiff was moving quickly to the store in the belief that some unauthorized person was inside. His duty to detect crime and apprehend offenders outweighed any risk of speedy movement. "If there was a risk the end to be achieved outweighed that risk." Do you agree?

3. In *Watt v. Hertfordshire County Council*, [1954] 1 W.L.R. 835, [1945] 2 All E.R. 368 (C.A.), the defendant's fire station had a heavy jack to be used in case of need. It stood on wheels and only one vehicle was properly equipped to carry it safely. While that vehicle was out on other service an emergency call was received to rescue a

woman trapped under a heavy vehicle. The officer in charge ordered the jack loaded on a lorry on which there was no way of properly securing it. On the way to the scene of the accident the driver of the lorry had to stop suddenly and the jack rolled and injured the plaintiff, a foreman, who sued for damages caused by the defendant's negligence in failing to use reasonable care in supplying safe appliances and working conditions. The plaintiff's action failed. *Per* Denning L.J.: "It is well settled that in measuring due care one must balance the risk against the measures necessary to eliminate the risk. To that proposition there ought to be added this. One must balance the risk against the end to be achieved. If this accident had occurred in a commercial enterprise without any emergency, there could be no doubt that the servant would succeed. But the commercial end to make profit is very different from the human end to save life or limb. The saving of life or limb justifies taking considerable risk ... I quite agree that fire engines, ambulances and doctors' cars should not shoot past the traffic lights when they show a red light. That is because the risk is too great to warrant the incurring of the danger. It is always a question of balancing the risk against the end." Should the existence of an emergency situation be taken into account in determining whether a risk is unreasonable?

4. Are the hypothetical cases posed by Mr. Justice Locke involving the pickpocket and the two bank robbers analogous to the principal case? Would the dissenting judge have disagreed with Mr. Justice Locke's disposition of them? Do you?

5. Do you prefer the majority opinion of Mr. Justice Locke or the dissenting views of Mr. Justice Cartwright? Is the difference between them one of principle or merely the application of a principle?

6. In *Beim v. Goyer*, [1965] S.C.R. 638, 57 D.L.R. (2d) 253, liability was imposed when a police officer's gun accidentally fired and struck an unarmed car thief who was being chased on foot over rough ground in circumstances where there was no danger to the police officer.

   In *Woodward v. Begbie*, [1962] O.R. 60, 31 D.L.R. (2d) 22 (H.C.), liability was also imposed when the plaintiff, a prowler, was accidentally shot by one of two police officers who fired their pistols, intending to hit the ground near the fleeing suspect. Mr. Justice McLennan stated that, "more force was used than was necessary and the escape could have been prevented by the more reasonable means of overtaking the plaintiff...".

   Are these two cases consistent with the principal case? See Weiler, "Groping Towards a Canadian Tort Law: The Role of the Supreme Court" (1971), 21 U. Toronto L.J. 264.

7. What do you think of the way s. 25(4) of the *Criminal Code* was handled by the Supreme Court? It reads as follows:

   > (4) A peace officer who is proceeding lawfully to arrest, with or without warrant, any person for an offence for which that person may be arrested without warrant, and every one lawfully assisting the peace officer, is justified, if the person to be arrested takes flight to avoid arrest, in using as much force as is necessary to prevent the escape by flight, unless the escape can be prevented by reasonable means in a less violent manner.

   Should it be relevant at all in a civil case? See McDonald, "Use of Force by Police to Effect Lawful Arrest" (1966-67), 9 Crim. L.Q. 435. Geatros J. in *Arnault v. Prince Albert (City) Board of Police Commissioners* (1995), 28 C.C.L.T. (2d) 15, (Sask. Q.B.) at 17 indicated that subsection 25(4) applied only in the criminal, not the civil context; *cf. C. v. City of Vancouver* (1995), 28 C.C.L.T. (2d) 35 (B.C.S.C.), where it was held that s. 25 applied both in civil and criminal cases, but not where a person was not "fleeing". In British Columbia, the provincial *Police Act*, S.B.C. 1988, c.53, s. 21 excuses the police from civil liability, unless they are grossly negligent or dishonest. See *Doern v. Phillips Estate* (1994), 23 C.C.L.T. (2d) 283 (B.C.S.C.); affd (1997), 43 B.C.L.R. (3d) 53 (C.A.); *I.C.B.C. v. City of Vancouver* (1997), 38 C.C.L.T. (2d) 271 (B.C.S.C.).

8. In *Poupart v. Lafortune*, [1973] S.C.R. 175, 41 D.L.R. (3d) 720, the Supreme Court held that s. 25 applied to exempt a police officer from liability for a gunshot wound he accidentally inflicted on an innocent bystander, when some armed robbers opened fire on him after he tried to apprend them. Fauteux C.J.C. stated:

> First, I should say that if only because of the decision of this Court in the *Priestman* case, *supra*, there is no reason to doubt, in my view, that the justification created by the aforementioned provisions of s. 25 relieves the police officer of any civil or criminal liability, not only in respect of the fugitive but also in respect of any person who accidentally becomes an innocent victim of the force used by such an officer in the circumstances described in those provisions.... .
>
> ... in contrast with the driver of an automobile, Lafortune was not engaged merely in performing an act permitted by law, but, which is quite a different matter ... he was engaged in the hazardous performance of a grave duty imposed on him by law. In carrying out such a duty a peace officer must undoubtedly refrain from making any unjustifiable use of the powers relating to it. ...
>
> However, while a police officer is not relieved of a duty to take reasonable care, that is care the degree of which must be determined in relation to the particular circumstances of the case to be decided, the actions of Lafortune cannot, in a case like that before the Court, be evaluated as they would be if it were a case in which the precautions to be taken in accordance with the duty not to injure others were not conditioned by the requirements of a public duty. In short, the police officer incurs no liability for damage caused to another when without negligence he does precisely what the legislature requires him to do: see *Priestman* case, *supra*, interpreted otherwise the justification provided by s. 25(4) would be reduced to a nullity.

How does this case fit in with the above cases? If the court had found Lafortune negligent, would s. 25 have been of any help to him? What should be the effect of s. 25 in tort cases? See Linden, *Canadian Tort Law*, 6th ed. (1997), p. 123.

9. As Professor Fleming has explained: "there is a world of difference between throwing a burning object into the street below just for the fun of it or in order to save a house on fire,". See Fleming, *The Law of Torts*, 9th ed. (1998), at 130.

10. In *Hogan et al v. McEwan et al; Royal Ins. Co. et al., Third Parties* (1975), 10 O.R. (2d) 551, 64 D.L.R. (3d) 74 (H.C.J.), the defendant driver, suddenly confronted by a large German Shepherd dog on the road, swerved to the right and ended up in an accident, injuring the plaintiffs who were passengers. Mr. Justice Henry explained:

> On the evidence, he was presented with the three choices I have mentioned — to turn left, to hit the dog, or to turn right. All of these courses contained a risk. Any sudden swerve to avoid an impact, particularly on a wet roadway, would create an immediate hazard to the vehicle and its occupants. He rejected the first two choices and their attendant risks for the reasons already stated, and chose the third, which, as he saw it, presented the least danger of the three. I find that in so doing he acted reasonable in the emergency and that his conduct meets the standard of care required by the law in such a situation.

See also *Neufeld v. Landry* (1974), 55 D.L.R. (3d) 296, [1975] W.W.R. 19 (Man. C.A.); *Coderre v. Ethier; Gachot v. Ethier* (1978), 19 O.R. (2d) 503, 85 D.L.R. (3d) 621 (H.C.), vehicle must make way for ambulance; *Molson v. Squamish Transfer Ltd.* (1969), 7 D.L.R. (3d) 553 (B.C.S.C.).

11. The defendant is driving a truck loaded with heavy pipe along the road. A little child wanders out in front of the truck. On a sudden stop, the pipe will shift forward and crush the defendant. What should the defendant do? Would it make any difference to your answer if the defendant had a passenger in the truck? Compare with *Thurmond v. Pepper,* 119 S.W. 2d 900 (Tex. 1938).

12. The problem of shortage of medical resources and the need to save money arose in *Law Estate v. Simice* (1994), 21 C.C.L.T. (2d) 228 (B.C.S.C.), where it was alleged that the failure to take a CT scan in an emergency room caused the death of the plaintiff's husband. There was evidence that doctors felt constrained in using CT scans as diagnostic tools because they were costly to use. Spencer J. criticised this type of thinking, in imposing liability, saying:

> No doubt there are budgetary restraints on them. But this is a case where, in my opinion, those constraints worked against the patients' interest by inhibiting the doctors in their judgment of what should be done for him. That is to be deplored. I understand that there are budgetary problems confronting the health care system. I raise it in passing only to point out that there were a number of references to the effect of financial restraint to the treatment of this patient. I respectfully say it is something to be carefully considered by those who are responsible for financing it. I also say that if it comes to a choice between a physician's responsibility to his or her individual patient and his or her responsibility to the medicare system overall, the former must take the patient who is permitted to go undiagnosed is far greater than the financial harm that will occur to the medicare system if one more CT scan procedure only shows the patient is not suffering from a serious medical condition.

How should courts treat cases where the paucity of nursing resources or the unavailability of expensive equipment contribute to a medical mishap?

B. THE REASONABLE PERSON

VAUGHAN v. MENLOVE

Common Pleas. (1837), 3 Bing. N.C. 467, 132 E.R. 490.

The plaintiff was the owner of two cottages. The defendant owned land, with certain buildings and a hayrick thereon, near the said cottages. Owing to the spontaneous ignition of this hayrick, fire spread to the defendant's buildings. The fire spread to the plaintiff's cottages which were destroyed.

The rick in question had been made by the defendant near the boundary of his own premises. The hay was in such a state when put together, as to give rise to discussions on the probability of fire. Though there were conflicting opinions on the subject, during a period of five weeks the defendant was repeatedly warned of his peril. On one occasion, being advised to take the rick down to avoid all danger, he said, "he would chance it". He made an aperture or chimney through the rick, but in spite, or perhaps in consequence of this precaution, the rick at length burst into flames from the spontaneous heating of its materials. The flames communicated to the defendant's barn and stables and then to the plaintiff's cottages, which were entirely destroyed.

Patterson J.: before whom the case was tried, told the jury that the question for them to consider was, whether the fire had been occasioned by gross negligence on the part of the defendant, adding that he was bound to proceed with such reasonable caution as a prudent man would have exercised under such circumstances.

A verdict having been found for the plaintiff a rule *nisi* for a new trial was obtained, on the ground that the jury should have been directed to consider, not, whether the defendant had been guilty of gross negligence with reference to the standard of ordinary prudence, a standard too uncertain to afford any criterion; but whether he had acted bona fide to the best of his judgment; if he had, he ought not to be responsible for the misfortune of not possessing the highest order of intelligence. The action under such circumstances, was of the first impression. …

Tindal C.J.: It is contended, however, that the learned judge was wrong in leaving this to the jury as a case of gross negligence; and that the question of negligence was so mixed up with reference to what would be the conduct of a man of ordinary prudence that the jury might have thought the latter the rule by which they were to decide; that such a rule would be too uncertain to act upon; and that the question ought to have been whether the defendant had acted honestly and bona fide to the best of his own judgment. That, however, would leave so vague a line as to afford no rule at all, the degree of judgment belonging to each individual being infinitely various. And although it has been urged that the care which a prudent man would take is not an intelligible proposition as a rule of law, yet such has always been the rule adopted in cases of bailment, as laid down in *Coggs v. Bernard*, 1 Ld. Rym. 909. The care taken by a prudent man has always been the rule laid down; and as to the supposed difficulty of applying it, a jury has always been able to say, whether, taking that rule as their guide, there has been negligence on the occasion in question.

Instead, therefore, of saying that the liability for negligence should be coextensive with the judgment of each individual, which would be as variable as the length of the foot of each individual, we ought rather to adhere to the rule which requires in all cases a regard to caution such as a man of ordinary prudence would observe. That was in substance the criterion presented to the jury in this case, and therefore the present rule must be discharged.

[**Park Vaughan** and **Gaselee** JJ. concurred.]

Rule discharged.

NOTES

1. What was the standard employed by the court in evaluating the conduct of the defendant? Is it a subjective or objective standard? What reason did the court give for adopting this standard? What other policy reasons could be given in support of this approach?

2. Should any allowance be made in negligence law for stupid people? How can it be said that the defendant was "at fault" when he did his best?

3. How should tort law treat awkward individuals and those who are accident-prone? See James and Dickinson, "Accident Proneness and Accident Law" (1950), 63 Harv. L. Rev. 769.

4. In his book, *The Common Law* (1881), Oliver Wendell Holmes justified the principle in this way:

> The standards of the law are standards of general application. The law takes no account of the infinite varieties of temperament, intellect, and education which make the internal character of a given act so different in different men. It does not attempt to see men as God sees them, for more than one sufficient reason. In the first place, the impossibility of nicely measuring a man's powers and limitations is far clearer than that of ascertaining his knowledge of law, which has been thought to account for what is called the presumption that every man knows the law. But a more satisfactory explanation is, that, when men live in society, a certain average of conduct, a sacrifice of individual peculiarities going beyond a certain point, is necessary to the general welfare. If, for instance, a man is born hasty and awkward, is always having accidents and hurting himself or his neighbours, no doubt his congenital defects will be allowed for in the courts of Heaven, but his slips are no less troublesome to his neighbours than if they sprang from guilty neglect. His neighbours accordingly require him, at his proper peril, to come up to their standard, and the courts which they establish decline to take his personal equation into account.
>
> The rule that the law does, in general, determine liability by blameworthiness, is subject to the limitation that minute differences of character are not allowed for. The law considers, in other words, what would be blameworthy in the average man, the man of ordinary intelligence and prudence, and determines liability by that. If we fall below the level in those gifts, it is our misfortune; so much as that we must have at our peril, for the reasons just given. But he who is intelligent and prudent does not act at his peril, in theory of law. On the contrary, it is only when he fails to exercise the foresight of which he is capable, or exercises it with evil intent, that he is answerable for the consequences.

BLYTH v. BIRMINGHAM WATER WORKS CO.

Court of Exchequer. (1856), 11 Ex. 781, 156 E.R. 1047.

The defendants had installed a fire-plug made according to the best known system. Due, however, to an exceptionally severe frost in 1855, damage was caused to the plug resulting in the plaintiff's premises being flooded. The plug had worked satisfactorily for 25 years. The judge left it to the jury to consider whether the company had used proper care to prevent the accident. ...

Alderson B.: I am of opinion that there was no evidence to be left to the jury. The case turns upon the question, whether the facts proved show that the defendants were guilty of negligence. Negligence is the omission to do something which a reasonable man, guided upon those considerations which ordinarily regulate the conduct of human affairs, would do, or doing something which a prudent and reasonable man would not do. The defendants might have been liable for negligence, if unintentionally, they omitted to do that which a reasonable man would have done, or did that which a person taking reasonable precautions would not have done. A reasonable man would act with reference to the average circumstances of the temperature in ordinary years. The defendants had provided against such frosts as experience would have led men, acting prudently, to provide against; and they are not guilty of negligence, because their precautions proved insufficient against the effects of the extreme severity of the frost of 1855, which penetrated to a greater depth than any which ordinarily occurs south of the polar regions. Such a state of circumstances constitutes a contingency against which no reasonable man can provide. The result was an accident, for which the defendants cannot be held liable.

[Judgments to the same effect by **Martin B.** and **Bramwell B.** are omitted.]

NOTES

1. What was the standard employed by the court to measure the defendant's conduct? Does it differ from the test used in *Vaughan v. Menlove, supra*? Would the Court have come to the same conclusion if the frost had occurred in Saskatoon in January?

2. The reasonable person is a familiar figure in the law. A number of different adjectives have been used to express the same idea, for example, "prudent and reasonable", "reasonable and prudent", "reasonably careful", "reasonably prudent and careful", "typically prudent" and "average person of ordinary prudence".

3. One of the best judicial pronouncements about the reasonable person was issued by Mr. Justice Laidlaw in *Arland and Arland v. Taylor,* [1955] O.R. 131, at 142, [1955] 3 D.L.R. 358 (C.A.):

> [A reasonable person] is a mythical creature of the law whose conduct is the standard by which the Courts measure the conduct of all other persons and find it to be proper or improper in particular circumstances as they may exist from time to time. He is not an extraordinary or unusual creature; he is not superhuman; he is not required to display the highest skill of which anyone is capable; he is not a genius who can perform uncommon feats, nor is he possessed of unusual powers of foresight. He is a person of normal intelligence who makes prudence a guide to his conduct. He does nothing that a prudent man would not do and does not omit to do anything a prudent man would do. He acts in accord with general and approved practice. His conduct is guided by considerations which ordinarily regulate the conduct of human affairs. His conduct is the standard "adopted in the community by persons of ordinary intelligence and prudence".

4. Mr. Justice Major has declared:

> Tort law does not require the wisdom of Solomon. All it requires is that people act reasonably in the circumstances.

See *Stewart v. Pettie* [1995], 1 S.C.R. 131 at p.150.

5. See Green, *Judge and Jury* (1930), for this insight:

> The man of ordinary prudence can only serve his function as an abstraction. In this way he is a mere caution pointing the jury in as dramatic a way as possible in the direction their deliberations should take. The judge through him can indicate to the jury that they are dealing with society's power and not their own; therefore, they should act reasonable and not let their own desires run riot. The formula is as much for controlling the jury's deliberations as for measuring the party's conduct. Its beauty is that it can be used for both purposes without committing the judge to anything and without telling the jury anything that amounts to more than a sobering caution. It does exactly what any good ritual is designed to do; its function is psychological. It serves as a prophylaxis. Nothing more should be expected of it.

Professor Leon Green concludes that "we may have a process of passing judgment in negligence cases, but practically no "law of negligence" beyond the process itself"? Do you agree? If so, is this a good thing? What are the advantages and disadvantages?

6. A.P. Herbert, in his *Uncommon Law* (1935), humorously described the reasonable person, whose rule of life is "Safety First" and who has all the solid virtues "save only that peculiar quality by which the affection of other [people] is won". According to Herbert, a reasonable person never

   > ... swears, gambles or loses his temper ... uses nothing except in moderation, and even while he flogs his child is meditating only on the golden mean. Devoid, in short, of any human weakness, with not one single saving vice, sans prejudice, procrastination, ill-nature, avarice, and absence of mind, as careful for his own safety as he is for that of others, this excellent but odious creature stands like a monument in our Courts of Justice, vainly appealing to his fellow citizens to order their lives after his own example.

   Would it be proper to use this characterization when charging a Canadian jury? What if the phrase "ideal person" were used instead? (See *Prescott (Town) v. Connell* (1893), 22 S.C.R. 147, at 161, *per* Sedgewick J.)

7. Would it be proper to ask the jury to put themselves in the place of the defendant and to ask themselves what they would have done in the circumstances? See *Arland v. Taylor,* [1955] O.R. 131, [1955] 3 D.L.R. 358 (C.A.); *Eyers v. Gillis & Warren Ltd.* (1940), 48 Man. R. 164, [1940] 4 D.L.R. 747 (C.A.). Is it proper for the judge to use himself or herself as a measuring rod? See *Edwards v. Smith* (1941), 56 B.C.R. 53, [1941] 1 D.L.R. 736 (C.A.).

8. Does a reasonable person, who is ignorant of relevant facts, even have an obligation to make enquiries? Suppose you are visiting Africa and encounter a purple traffic signal. What should you do? What if someone immigrates to Canada and fails to wear a seat belt, being ignorant of the law requiring it? *Prasad v. Frandsen* (1985), 60 B.C.L.R. 343 (S.C.). Suppose you have a large elm tree with overhanging branches on your property. Can you rely on your own judgment about whether the tree needs lopping or must you consult an expert? Compare *Caminer v. Northern and London Investment Trust Ltd.,* [1951] A.C. 88, [1950] 2 All E.R. 486 (H.L.) with *Quinn v. Scott,* [1965] 1 W.L.R. 1004, [1965] 2 All E.R. 588 (Q.B.). A guest at a hunting lodge tries to start a fire in the fireplace with something the guest wrongly believes to be furnace oil. The something is gasoline and the cabin burns down. Liability? See *Cone v. Welock,* [1970] S.C.R. 494, 10 D.L.R. (3d) 257.

9. What level of competence should be expected of a beginner? Should a fledgling driver have to perform as well as an experienced one? See Denning M.R. in *Nettleship v. Weston,* [1971] 3 All E.R. 586, [1971] 2 Q.B. 691 (C.A.).

10. Should any allowance be made for the physically disabled? For example should a blind person be expected to live up to the same standard of care as a sighted individual? See *Carroll and Carroll v. Chicken Palace Ltd.,* [1955] O.R. 23, [1955] 2 D.L.R. 11 (H.C.); revd, [1955] O.R. 748, [1955] 3 D.L.R. 681 (C.A.). Should special precautions be taken to protect blind persons? See *Haley v. London Electricity Bd.,* [1965] A.C. 788, [1964] 3 All E.R. 185 (H.L.). A deaf and mute person? See *Dziwenka v. The Queen in Right of Alberta,* [1972] 2 S.C.R. 419, 25 D.L.R. (3d) 12. Other physically disabled people? See Lowrey, "The Blind and the Law of Tort: The Position of a Blind Person as Plaintiff in Negligence" (1972), 10 Chitty's L.J. 253.

11. Are you satisfied with the reasonable person test? Is it fair to minority groups? Can you think of a better yardstick with which to measure conduct? What about the "humane" person? See *Southern Portland Cement Ltd. v. Cooper,* [1974] A.C. 623, [1974] 2 W.L.R. 152 (P.C.), *per* Lord Reid. Is this standard any different than the reasonable person test? Can someone be reasonable and not humane?

12. Some feminist scholars have argued that the standard of care of the "reasonable person" fails to recognize the difference between the way men and women view the world. Professor Bender, referring to Carol Gilligan's *In a Different Voice: Psychological Theory and Women's Development* (1982), p. 28, explains the thesis as follows:

> The concept of an ethic based on care and responsibility informs a great deal of feminist scholarship. Carol Gilligan suggests that women's moral development reflects a focus on responsibility and contextuality, as opposed to men's, which relies more heavily on rights and abstract justice. After studying responses to interview questions in three studies (a college student study, an abortion-decision study, and a rights-and-responsibilities student), Gilligan recognized that there are two thematic approaches to problem solving that generally correlate with gender, although she makes no claims about the origin of the difference. Traditional psychological and moral-development theory recognizes and rewards one approach but undervalues or fails to define the other, the approach Gilligan calls "a different voice." When she asked what characterizes the different methods for resolving and analyzing moral dilemmas, Gilligan found that the "right" answers (according to the traditionally formulated stages of moral development) involve abstract, objective, rule-based decisions supported by notions of individual autonomy, individual rights, the separation of self from others, equality, and fairness. Often the answers provided by women focus on the particular contexts of the problems, relationships, caring (compassion and need), equity, and responsibility. For this different voice "responsibility" means "response to" rather than "obligation for". The first voice understands relationships in terms of hierarchies or "ladders," whereas the "feminine" voice communicates about relationships as "webs of interconnectedness."

Professor Bender suggests that we can "convert the present standard of 'care of a reasonable person under the same or similar circumstances' to a standard of 'conscious care and concern of a responsible neighbour or social acquaintance for another under the same or similar circumstances.' " See Bender, "A Lawyer's Primer on Feminist Theory and Tort" (1989), 38 J. of Legal Ed. 3. What do you think of this suggestion?

13. The idea that tort law ought to develop the "reasonable woman" standard as opposed to the "reasonable man" standard has not been favourably received by all feminist scholars. In Lucinda Finley's article "A Break in the Silence: Including Women's Issues in a Torts Course" (1989), 1 Yale J. of L. and Feminism 41, Professor Finley argues against replacing one "caricature" with another. "Many people do not fit their gender stereotype," writes Finley, and thus it may be better to "include consideration of the actual event and how someone with the individual's experiences would react" rather than merely assuming that all men or all women would react in one way. Professor Finley argues against all stereotypes and suggests that what tort law needs is a model of the reasonable person which is "expanded to include the perspectives of many people — or, more accurately, the majority of the population — who have been considered outside the mainstream in this society."

What do you think of this approach? Do you think that it will convert the standard of care test into a subjective test? What harm is there in that?

14. Negligence law imposes its standard of reasonable care on every type of activity under the sun. For example, a pedestrian can be held liable for bumping into and injuring another pedestrian. (See *Mills v. Moberg* (1997), 34 C.C.L.T. (2d) 103 (B.C.S.C.), plaintiff partially to blame). A door to an office swung open carelessly injuring someone can lead to liability. (See *O'Connor v. South Australia* (1976), 14 S.A.S.R. 187, plaintiff partially at fault). An airline can be liable for misdirecting passengers at a terminal causing them to miss their flight. (See *Duemler v. Air Canada* (1980), 109 D.L.R. (3d) 402 (Alta. Q.B.) passengers also negligent). Skiers can be liable for negligent skiing. (See *Reese v. Coleman (No. 1)*, [1979] 4 W.W.R. 58 (Sask. C.A.). Negligently made products and negligently designed products may yield liability as can a failure to warn about the dangers inherent in a product. (See generally Linden *Canadian Tort Law*, 6th ed. (1997); Waddams, *Products Liability*, 3rd ed. (1993).

15. See Seavey, "Negligence—Subjective or Objective" (1927), 41 Harv. L. Rev. 1; Green, "The Negligence Issue" (1928), 37 Yale L.J. 1029; James, "The Nature of Negligence" (1953), 3 Utah L. Rev. 275; Millner, *Negligence in Modern Law* (1967).

C. CUSTOM

WALDICK v. MALCOLM
[1991] 2 S.C.R. 456

Waldick fell on the icy parking area of the Malcolms' rented farmhouse. The parking area had not been salted or sanded. Apparently few people in that region did so. The main issue was whether the defendant met the standard of reasonable care imposed by the *Occupiers' Liability Act.* It was argued that there was a custom in the area not to put salt or sand on icy parking areas. On this matter, the Court explained:

Iacobucci J.: ... the Malcolms argued that the courts below should also have taken into account "the practices of persons in the same or similar situations as the person whose conduct is being judged", or in other words, local custom. This, it was argued, would inject an element of community standards into the negligence calculus, and would promote behaviour which better accords with the reasonable expectations of community members.

Professor Linden's (as he then was) article "Custom in Negligence Law" (1968), 11 Can. Bar J. 151, was cited in support of these propositions. At page 153, in the course of a discussion on the policy reasons for and against the relevance of custom Linden says that:

> ... customary practices can provide a fairly precise standard of care to facilitate the courts' task of deciding what is reasonable in the circumstances. Like penal statutes, customs can crystallize the ordinarily vague standard of reasonable care.

In the instant appeal, the relevant local custom which the courts below allegedly neglected to consider was "not sanding or salting driveways". I am unable to agree with the Malcolms' submissions for several reasons ...

Secondly, there are proof problems that complicate the Malcolms' argument in this regard. Acknowledging that custom can inform the court's assessment of what is reasonable in any given set of circumstances, it is nevertheless beyond dispute that, in any case where an alleged custom is raised, the "party who relies on either his own compliance with custom or the other person's departure from general practice bears the onus of proof that the custom is in effect." (Linden, *supra,* at p. 167). Only in the rarest and most patently obvious cases will the courts take judicial notice of a custom and even this, as Linden warns, is a "dangerous practice".

> It would be preferable for courts to demand evidence of the general practice or not to rely on custom at all. Counsel who wish to rely on custom would be most unwise to attempt to do so without adducing expert evidence of general practice. [at p.167.]

In the case at bar, there is nothing apart from the completely unsupported testimony of the appellant Mrs. Malcolm that tends to prove something that could qualify as custom ...

It was clearly open to the courts below to conclude that the evidence was, without more, insufficient to discharge the onus of proof that rests on the Malcolms. This is how I read the judgments below.

... even if there had been adequate evidence in the record of a general local custom of not salting or sanding driveways, I am not of the view that such a custom would necessarily be decisive against a determination of negligence in the case at bar. Shortly after the extract cited by the Malcolms, Linden (*supra,* at p.154) also points out that:

> ... tort courts have not abdicated their responsibility to evaluate customs, for negligent conduct cannot be countenanced, even when a large group is continually guilty of it.

In short, no amount of general community compliance will render negligent conduct "reasonable ... in all the circumstances". ... If, as the lower courts found, it is unreasonable to do absolutely nothing to one's driveway in the face of clearly treacherous conditions, it matters little that one's neighbours also act unreasonably. Presumably it is exactly this type of generalized negligence that the Act is meant to discourage.

As Linden points out, certain types of community practices will not be given weight by the courts. Commenting on *Drewry v. Towns* (1995), 2 W.W.R. (N.S.) 217, where Kelly J. found the habit of farmers who left their trucks on the snowbound roadside unlighted and unattended to be negligent, Linden says at p.162:

> ... the so-called parking "practice" of the farmers in the area *was not the type of general practice that earns the acceptance of the courts, that is, the customary way that a business or profession is conducted.* Such a custom is worthy of judicial protection as long as it is not shown to be negligent, but a mere "habit" of a few farmers does not deserve similar treatment. [emphasis added.]

In my view, it is far from self-evident that the "practice" of not salting the driveways in the area should earn the acceptance of the courts.

To conclude on this point, the existence of customary practices which are unreasonable in themselves, or which are not otherwise acceptable to courts, in no way ousts the duty of care owed by the occupiers under s. 3(l) of the Act. That duty is to take such care as is reasonable in the circumstances. ... I would accordingly agree that the Malcolms breached the statutory duty of care imposed by s. 3(l) of the Act.

NOTES

1. Why should the courts rely on custom or general practice at all? Does it have anything to do with the expectations of humankind? Is there an element of morals involved? Does it assure that the courts do not demand of citizens impossible or economically unfeasible standards? Does the use of custom facilitate judicial administration? See Linden, "Custom in Negligence Law" (1968), 11 Can. Bar. J. 151.

2. If compliance with custom were held to be dispositive of the negligence issue, would the development of safer techniques be hampered? Professor Paul Weiler has written that a plaintiff should be permitted to go to court as a "one-man lobby to demand recognition of the need for the safety device, and for a decision that the earlier failure to adopt it was indeed against contemporary mores, if not practice". See "Groping Towards a Canadian Tort Law: The Role of the Supreme Court of Canada" (1971), 21 U. Toronto L.J. 264, at 319.

3. Modern courts have refused to be ruled by custom. In *King v. Stolberg et al.* (1968), 70 D.O.R. (2d) 743, 65 W.W.R. 705; revd in part (1969), 8 D.L.R. (3d) 362, 70 W.W.R. 581 (B.C.C.A.), for example, Mr. Justice Rae stated, "... no amount of repetition of a careless practice will make it any less careless. The negligent driver is not any the less negligent by reason of being ubiquitous". See also *Drewry v. Towns* (1951), 59 Man. R. 119, 2 W.W.R. (N.S.) 217 (K.B.); *Kauffman v. T.T.C.*, [1960] S.C.R. 251, 22 D.L.R. (2d) 97; affg, [1959] O.R. 197, 18 D.L.R. (2d) 204, at 205; *Mercer v. Commrs for Road Transport & Tramways* (1937), 56 C.L.R. 580 (Aust. H.C.).

4. Compliance with custom, however, normally will be held to be reasonable. For example, in *Karderas v. Clow*, [1973] 1 O.R. 730, 32 D.L.R. (3d) 303 (H.C.), Cromarty J. relieved a defendant doctor of liability because he "followed standard, approved and widely accepted procedures..." See also *Savickas v. City of Edmonton*, [1940] 2 W.W.R. 675, 51 C.R.T.C. 333 (Alta. S.C.); *MacLeod v. Rowe*, [1947] S.C.R. 420, [1947] 3 D.L.R. 241.

5. In *Warren v. Camrose (City)* (1989), 64 Alta. L.R. (2d) 289, [1989] 3 W.W.R. 172; leave to appeal to S.C.C. refused, [1989] 6 W.W.R. lxviii, 102 N.R. 399*n*, the importance of custom in determining the standard of care was described by Mr. Justice J. Cote in the following way:

> The consensus of the recognized experts in a field on what is safe does not absolutely bind the courts. Neither does the uniform practice of a profession or industry. But they are very strong evidence: ... Indeed, leading authorities go much beyond questions of evidence and make such a consensus or uniform practice a substantive defence to a charge of want of care (subject to one exception); ... It is not enough for a plaintiff to show that other precautions were possible, if they were not commonly used by the profession or trade in question, unless their omission was clearly very unreasonable: ... Nor need a defendant warn that an unusual precaution is omitted, or recommend its use: ... The test is what was the generally accepted practice at the time of the accident; precaution which had been followed at an earlier age but have since been discarded by most of the people in the field are irrelevant: ... Nor does a plaintiff rebut the generally accepted practice by producing one respected expert or textbook which advocates a precaution not generally followed: ... The court can override expert evidence and brand a universal practice as negligent only in a strong case; the experts' thinking or the profession or trade's practice, properly understood, must offend logic or common sense, or flow from a gross error in weight, these cases say. ...

6. Just as compliance with custom is not conclusive of due care, so too deviation from custom is not conclusive of negligence. It does, however, provide a welcome guideline for the court.

The House of Lords in *Brown v. Rolls Royce Ltd.*, [1960] 1 W.L.R. 210, [1960] 1 All E.R. 577, had occasion to consider this matter. A workman, who contracted dermatitis from exposure to oil during his employment, sued the defendant, relying upon its omission to supply barrier cream to its employees, although this was alleged to be the common practice elsewhere. The trial decision for the plaintiff was reversed on two grounds: first, there was no proof that the barrier cream would have prevented dermatitis, that is, evidence of causation was lacking; second, since evidence of non-compliance with custom was not conclusive and since the defendant relied on competent medical evidence in not supplying this cream, he could be exonerated. Lord Denning stated that "if the defenders do not follow the usual precautions, it raises a *prima facie* case against them in this sense, that it is evidence from which negligence 'may' be inferred, but not in the sense that it 'must' be inferred unless the contrary is proved. At the end of the day, the court has to ask itself whether the defenders were negligent or not." Lord Keith of Avonholm contended that "a common practice in like circumstances not followed by an employer may no doubt be a weighty circumstance to be considered by judge or jury in deciding whether failure to comply with this practice, taken along with all the other material circumstances in the case, yields an inference of negligence on the part of the employers". In the last analysis, however, "the ultimate test is lack of reasonable care for the safety of the workman in all the circumstances of the case".

7. Are the words "prima facie" helpful to the court or jury in deciding the weight to be accorded evidence of custom? Is this formula giving sufficient weight to this evidence? Should the same weight be given to evidence of the violation of all customs? Compare with the problems on violation of statute, *infra.*

8. See generally Morris, "Custom and Negligence" (1942), 42 Colum. L. Rev. 1147; Fricke, "General Practice in Industry" (1960), 23 Mod. L. Rev. 653; Linden, "Custom in Negligence Law" (1968), 11 Can. Bar J. 151.

D. STATUTORY STANDARDS

R. IN RIGHT OF CANADA v. SASKATCHEWAN WHEAT POOL

Supreme Court of Canada. [1983] 1 S.C.R. 205, 143 D.L.R. (3d) 9.

Dickson J.: This case raises the difficult issue of the relation of a breach of a statutory duty to a civil cause of action. Where "A" has breached a statutory duty causing injury to "B", does "B" have a civil cause of action against "A"? If so, is "A's" liability absolute, in the sense that it exists independently of fault or is "A" free from liability if the failure to perform the duty is through no fault of his? In these proceedings the Canadian Wheat Board (the Board) is seeking to recover damages from the Saskatchewan Wheat Pool (the Pool) for delivery of infested grain out of a terminal elevator contrary to s. 86(c) of the *Canada Grain Act*, S.C. 1970-71-72, c. 7.

The Facts

The respondent Pool is a grain dealer and operates licensed primary country grain elevators in Saskatchewan. It also operates eight licensed terminal elevators at the port of Thunder Bay in Ontario where grain is received from Western Canada for export or shipment further east. …

The dispute in this case arises from an infestation of rusty grain beetle larvae. On September 19, 1975 the Board surrendered to the Pool terminal elevator receipts for a quantity of No. 3 Canada Utility Wheat at Thunder Bay and gave directions for the wheat to be loaded onto the vessel "Frankcliffe Hall". On September 22 and 23, No. 3 Canada Utility Wheat and other wheat was loaded from the Pool's terminal elevator No. 8 into the vessel which sailed on September 23, 1975. During the loading routine samples were taken from the wheat. This wheat was loaded under the scrutiny of the Canadian Grain Commission's inspectors as well as the scrutiny of the Pool's representatives. At the loading no one had any knowledge that the grain was infested with rusty beetle larvae. The exact cause of the infestation was not and could not be known. Visual inspection revealed no infestation. A berlase funnel test, however, conducted at the Grain Commission's headquarters after the ship had sailed disclosed an infestation of rusty grain beetle larvae in the 273,569 bushels of wheat loaded into holds No. 5 and 6. This was the first rusty beetle larvae infestation known to occur in a ship. The Canadian Grain Commission ordered the Board to fumigate the affected wheat. The Board directed the Frankcliffe Hall diverted to Kingston for fumigation and was obliged to pay the vessel owner and the elevator operator at Kingston $98,261.55 comprising detention claims, cost of unloading and reloading the grain and fumigation of the grain and holds. It is this amount which the Board is now claiming from Saskatchewan Wheat Pool.

The Board makes no claim in negligence. It relies entirely on what it alleges to be a statutory breach. It is common ground that the Board received grain of the kind, grade and quantity to which it was entitled. …

Statutory Breach Giving Rise to a Civil Cause of Action

(a) General

The uncertainty and confusion in the relation between breach of statute and a civil cause of action for damages arising from the breach is of long standing. The commentators have little but harsh words for the unhappy state of affairs, but arriving at a solution, from the disarray of cases, is extraordinarily difficult. It is doubtful that any general principle or rationale can be found in the authorities to resolve all of the issues or even those which are transcendant.

There does seem to be general agreement that the breach of a statutory provision which causes damage to an individual should in some way be pertinent to recovery of compensation for the damage. Two very different forces, however, have been acting in opposite directions. In the United States the civil consequences of breach of statute have been subsumed in the law of negligence. On the other hand, we have witnessed in England the painful emergence of a new nominate tort of statutory breach. This Court was given the opportunity to choose between the two positions in *Sterling Trusts Corporation v. Postma*, [1965] S.C.R. 324 but did not find it necessary for the determination of that case to attempt the difficult task:

> There have been differences of opinion as to whether an action for breach of a statutory duty which involves the notion of taking precautions to prevent injury is more accurately described as an action for negligence or in the manner suggested by Lord Wright in *Upson*'s case, p. 168, in the following words:

> A claim for damages for breach of a statutory duty intended to protect a person in the position of the particular plaintiff is a specific common law right which is not to be confused in essence with a claim for negligence. The statutory right has its origin in the statute, but the particular remedy of an action for damages is given by the common law in order to make effective, for the benefit of the injured plaintiff, his right to the performance by the defendant of the defendant's statutory duty. It is an effective sanction. It is not a claim in negligence in the strict or ordinary sense. ... I do not find it necessary in this case to attempt to choose between these two views as to how this cause of action should be described (at p. 329, per Cartwright J.).

It is now imperative for this Court to choose.

(b) The English Position

In 1948 in the case of *London Passenger Transport Board v. Upson*, [1949] 1 All E.R. 60 in the passage quoted above, cited by Cartwright J., the House of Lords affirmed the existence of a tort of statutory breach distinct from any issue of negligence. The statute prescribes the duty owed to the plaintiff who need only show (1) breach of the statute, and (ii) damage caused by the breach.

Legitimacy for this civil action for breach of statute has been sought in the *Statute of Westminster II* (1285), c. 50 which provided for a private remedy by action on the case to those affected by the breach of statutory duties. However, "old though it may be, the action upon the statute has rarely been the subject of careful scrutiny in English law, and its precise judicial character remains a thing of some obscurity" (Fricke, "The Juridical Nature of the Action upon the Statute" (1960), 76 L.Q.R. 240). As the gap widened between "public" and "private" law with the passing centuries this broad general right of action, enigmatic as it was, became hedged. Where a public law penalty was provided for in the statute a private civil cause of action would not automatically arise. The oft-quoted formulation of this principle was found in *Doe d. Rochester v. Bridges* (1831), 1 B & Ad. 847, 109 E.R. 1001:

> And where an Act creates an obligation, and enforces the performance in a specified manner, we take it to be a general rule that performance cannot be enforced in any other manner.

Although taken out of context, the dictum served the purpose of limiting the multiplication of suits of dubious value. "With the vast increase in legislative activity of modern times, if the old rule were still law it might lead to unjust, not to say absurd, results in creating liability wider than the legislature can possibly have intended" (Winfield & Jolowicz, *Tort*, 11th ed. (1979), at p. 154). By the end of the 19th century, however, the civil action on the statute began to revive as a response to industrial safety legislation. The statement of the doctrine propounded in *Doe d. Rochester v. Bridges* did not enjoy a long period of acceptance. *Couch v. Steel* (1854), 3 E & B 402, marked the beginning of a new era of construction. Lord Campbell C.J. relying on statements in Comyn's Digest concluded that the injured party has a common law right to maintain an action for special damage arising from the breach of a public duty. *Couch v. Steel* was questioned some twenty years later in *Atkinson v. Newcastle Waterworks Co.*, [1877] 2 Ex. D. 441. Lord Cairns L.C. dealing with the matter apart from authority concluded that the private remedy has been excluded. He expressed "grave doubts" whether the authorities cited by Lord Campbell in *Couch v. Steel* justified the broad general rule there laid down. Lord Cockburn, C.J. agreed that the correctness of *Couch v.*

Steel was "open to grave doubts", while Brett L.J. entertained the "strongest doubt" as to the correctness of the broad general rule enunciated in *Couch v. Steel.*

As Street puts it "The effect of the leading cases in the nineteenth century (which remain important authorities) however, was to make the cause of action rest on proof that the legislature intended that violation of the right or interest conferred by the statute was to be treated as tortious" (Street, *Law of Torts*, 2d, 273). Fricke pointed out (76 Law Quarterly Review, at p. 260) that that doctrine leads to many difficulties. In the first place it is not clear what the *prima facie* rule or presumption should be. Some of the cases suggest that *prima facie* an action is given by the statement of a statutory duty, and that it exists unless it can be said to be taken away by any provisions to be found in the Act. Other authorities suggest the *prima facie* rule is that the specific statement of a certain manner of enforcement excludes any other means of enforcement. Sometimes the courts jump one way, sometimes the other. Fricke concludes (pp. 263-64) that as a matter of pure statutory construction the law went wrong with the decision in 1854 in *Couch v. Steel:* "If one is concerned with the intrinsic question of interpreting the legislative will as reflected within the four corners of a document which made express provision of a fine, but makes no mention of a civil remedy, one is compelled to the conclusion that a civil remedy was not intended." Presence or absence of public law penalties was not determinative of the existence of a civil cause of action; all depended upon "the intention of the legislature" ...

Writing in 1960 Glanville Williams stated that:

> The present position of penal legislation in the civil law ... may be oversimplified into two generalisations. When it concerns industrial welfare, such legislation results in absolute liability in tort. In all other cases it is ignored. There are exceptions both ways, but, broadly speaking, that is how the law appears from the current decisions ("The Effect of Penal Legislation in the Law of Tort" (1960), 23 Modern L. Rev. 233).

This fragmentation of approach has given rise to some theoretical, and some not-so-theoretical, difficulties. The pretence of seeking what has been called a "will o' wisp", a non-existent intention of Parliament to create a civil cause of action, has been harshly criticized. It is capricious and arbitrary, "judical legislation" at its very worst.

> Not only does it involve an unnecessary fiction, but it may lead to decisions being made on the basis of insignificant details of phraseology instead of matters of substance. If the question whether a person injured by breach of a statutory obligation is to have a right of action for damages is in truth a question to be decided by the court, let it be acknowledged as such and some useful principles of law developed. (Winfield & Jolowicz, *supra*, at p. 159).

It is a "bare faced fiction" at odds with accepted canons of statutory interpretation: "the legislature's silence on the question of civil liability rather points to the conclusion that it either did not have it in mind or deliberately omitted to provide for it" (Fleming, *The Law of Torts*, 5th ed. (1977), at p. 123). Glanville Williams is now of the opinion that the "irresolute course" of the judicial decisions "reflects no credit on our jurisprudence" and, with respect, I agree. He writes:

> The failure of the judges to develop a governing attitude means that it is almost impossible to predict, outside the decided authorities, when the courts will regard a civil duty as impliedly created. In effect the judge can do what he likes, and then se-

lect one of the conflicting principles stated by his predecessors in order to justify his decision (*The Effect of Penal Legislation in the Law of Tort, supra*, at p. 246).

Prosser is of the same opinion:

> Much ingenuity has been expended in the effort to explain why criminal legislation should result in a rule for civil liability.
>
> ....
>
> ... Many courts have, however, purported to "find" in the statute a supposed "implied", "constructive", or "presumed" intent to provide for tort liability. In the ordinary case this is pure fiction concocted for the purpose. The obvious conclusion can only be that when the legislators said nothing about it, they either did not have the civil suit in mind at all, or deliberately omitted to provide for it.
>
> ...
>
> Perhaps the most satisfactory explanation is that the courts are seeking, by something in the nature of judicial legislation, to further the ultimate policy for the protection of individuals which they find underlying the statute, and which they believe the legislature must have had in mind. The statutory standard of conduct is simply adopted voluntarily, out of deference and respect for the legislature (Prosser, *Law of Torts*, 4th ed. (1971)).

The door to a civil cause of action arising from breach of statute had swung closed at the beginning of the 19th century with the proliferation of written legislation and swung open again, for reasons of policy and convenience, to accommodate the rising incidence of industrial accidents at the end of the 19th century. But the proposition that every statutory breach gave rise to a private right of action was still untenable, as it is today. The courts looked for a screening mechanism which would determine the cases to which an action should be limited.

Various presumptions or guidelines sprang up. "Thus, it has often been tediously repeated that the crucial test is whether the duty created by the statute is owed primarily to the State, and only incidentally to the individual, or vice versa" (Fleming, *supra*, at p. 125). A duty to all the public (ratepayers, for example) does not give rise to a private cause of action whereas a duty to an individual (an injured worker, for example) may. The purpose of the statute must be the protection of a certain "class" of individuals of whom the plaintiff is one and the injury suffered must be of a kind which it was the object of the legislation to prevent. Both requirements have, in the past, been fairly narrowly construed and fairly heavily criticized.

Although "[i]t is doubtful, indeed, if any general principle can be found to explain all the cases on the subject" (*Salmond on Torts*, (1977) 7th ed., at p. 243) several justifications are given for the tort of statutory breach. It provides fixed standards of negligence and replaces the judgment of amateurs (the jury) with that of professionals in highly technical areas. In effect, it provides for absolute liability in fields where this has been found desirable such as industrial safety. Laudable as these effects are, the state of the law remains extremely unsatisfactory. Professor Fleming has castigated the British courts:

> ... their inveterate practice of appealing to the oracle of a presumed legislative intent has served them well in hiding from public scrutiny not only their own unexpressed prejudices but also their startling lack of resourcefulness, compared with that of American courts, in so handling the doctrine that it may serve as a useful adjunct in negligence litigation without becoming tyrannical. At bottom, their failure to come to terms with it is primarily due to the fact that their frame of reference does not seem to admit of any *media via* between, on the one hand, the most literal application of the statutory mandate whose terms rarely make express allowance for

unavoidable inability to conform or some other equally compelling excuse and, on the other hand, refusing to ascribe any force to it at all other than, perhaps, as mere evidence of negligence (Fleming, *supra*, at p. 133).

(a) The American Position

Professor Fleming prefers the American approach which has assimilated civil responsibility for statutory breach into the general law of negligence:

> Intellectually more acceptable, because less arcane, is the prevailing American theory which frankly disclaims that the civil action is in any sure sense a creature of the statute, for the simple enough reason that the statute just does not contemplate, much less provide, a civil remedy. Any recovery of damages for injury due to its violation must, therefore, rest on common law principles. But though the penal statute does not create civil liability the court may think it proper to adopt the legislative formulation of a specific standard in place of the unformulated standard of reasonable conduct, in much the same manner as when it rules peremtorily (*sic*) that certain acts or omissions constitute negligence of the law (*The Law of Torts, supra*, at p. 124).

There are, however, differing views of the effect of this assimilation: at one end of the spectrum, breach of a statutory duty may constitute negligence *per se* or, at the other, it may merely be evidence of negligence. This distinction finds its roots in the seminal 1913 article by Professor Thayer:

> Unless the court were prepared to go to this length it would be bound to say that if the breach of the ordinance did in fact contribute to the injury as a cause the defendant is liable as a matter of law; but this is treating it as "negligence *per se*" to use the ordinary phraseology, and not merely "evidence of negligence".
>
> The doctrine that a breach of the law is "evidence of negligence" is in truth perplexing and difficult of comprehension. It stands as a sort of compromise midway between two extreme views: (1) that a breach of law cannot be treated as prudent conduct; (2) that the ordinance was passed *alio intuito* and does not touch civil relations (*Public Wrong and Private Action* (1913-14), 27 Harv. L.R. 317, at p. 323).

Professor Thayer's thesis was essentially that prudent men do not break the law. He thus applied the criminal standard of care, breach of which would give rise to penal consequences under the statute, to the civil action.

The majority view in the United States has been that statutory breach constitutes negligence *per se* — in certain circumstances:

> Once the statute is determined to be applicable — which is to say, once it is interpreted as designed to protect the class of persons in which the plaintiff is included, against the risk of the type of harm which had in fact occurred as a result of its violation — the great majority of the courts hold that an unexcused violation is conclusive on the issue of negligence, and that the court must so direct the jury. The standard of conduct is taken over by the court from that fixed by the legislature, and "jurors have no dispensing power by which to relax it", except in so far as the court may recognize the possibility of a valid excuse for disobedience of the law. This usually is expressed by saying that the unexcused violation is negligence "per se", or in itself. The effect of such a rule is to stamp the defendant's conduct as negligence, with all of the effects of common law negligence, but with no greater effect (Prosser, *Law of Torts*, 4th ed. (1971), at p. 200).

This approach has been adopted by the *Restatement, Torts, Second*, paragraph 288B:

> (1) The unexcused violation of a legislative enactment or an administrative regulation which is adopted by the court as defining the standard of conduct of a reasonable man, is negligence in itself.
> (2) The unexcused violation of an enactment or regulation which is not so adopted may be relevant evidence bearing on the issue of negligent conduct.

It is important to note two qualifications to the finding of negligence *per se*: (1) the violation must not be an "excused violation" and (2) the enactment must be one which is adopted by the court as defining the standard of conduct of a reasonable man. An excused violation is not negligence and occurs where:

> 288A(2)
> (a) The violation is reasonable because of the nature of the actor's incapacity;
> (b) he neither knows nor should know of the occasion for compliance;
> (c) he is unable after reasonable diligence or care to comply;
> (d) he is confronted by an emergency not due to his own misconduct;
> (e) compliance would involve a greater risk of harm to the actor or to others.

The American courts have not broken away from a consideration of the purpose or intent of the legislature; the *Restatement, Torts, Second* sets out the circumstances in which the court may adopt a legislative enactment as embodying the standard of care applicable in the circumstances;

> 286. When Standards of Conduct Defined by Legislation or Regulations Will be Adopted
> The court may adopt as the standard of conduct of a reasonable man the requirements of a legislative enactment or an administrative regulation whose purpose is found to be exclusively or in part
> (a) to protect a class of person which includes the one whose interest is invaded, and
> (b) to protect the particular interest which is invaded, and
> (c) to protect that interest against the kind of harm which has resulted, and
> (d) to protect that interest the particular hazard from which the harm results.

The so-called "minority view" in the United States considers breach of a statute to be merely evidence of negligence. There are, however, varying degrees of evidence. Statutory breach may be considered totally irrelevant, merely relevant, or *prima facie* evidence of negligence having the effect of reversing the onus of proof.

> California has arrived at what appears to be precisely the same result by holding that the violation creates a presumption of negligence which may be rebutted by a showing of an adequate excuse but calls for a binding instruction in the absence of such evidence. A considerable minority have held that a violation is only evidence of negligence, which the jury may accept or reject as it sees fit. Some of the courts which follow the majority rule as to statutes have held that the breach of ordinances, or traffic laws, or the regulations of administrative bodies, even though the latter are authorized by statute, is only evidence for the jury. Such cases seem to indicate a considerable distrust of the arbitrary character of the provision, and a desire to leave some leeway for cases where its violation may not be necessarily unreasonable. Even in such jurisdictions, however, it is recognized that there are cases in which, merely as a matter of evidence, reasonable men could not fail to agree that the violation is negligence (Prosser, *supra*, at p. 201).

The major criticism of the negligence *per se* approach has been the inflexible application of the legislature's criminal standard of conduct to a civil case. I agree with this criticism. The defendant in a civil case does not benefit from the technical defences or protection offered by the criminal law; the civil consequences may easily outweigh any penal consequences attaching to the breach of statute; and finally the purposes served by the imposition of criminal as opposed to civil liability are radically different. The compensatory aspect of tort liability has won out over the deterrent and punitive aspect; the perceptible evolution in the use of civil liability as a mechanism of loss shifting to that of loss distribution has only accentuated this change. And so "[t]he doctrine of negligence *per se* is, therefore, not fitted for relentless use, nor is it so used" (Morris, "The Relation of Criminal Statutes to Tort Liability," (1932-33), 46 Harv. L.R. 453, at p. 460). Thus the guidelines in the *Restatement, Torts, Second.*

(d) The Canadian Position

Professor Linden has said that the "Canadian courts appear to oscillate between the English and American positions without even recognizing this fact" (Comment *Sterling Trusts Corporation v. Postma* (1967), 45 Can. Bar Rev. 121, at p. 126). The most widely used approach, however, has been that stated in *Sterling Trusts Corporations v. Postma, supra:* The breach of a statutory provision is "*prima facie* evidence of negligence". There is some difficulty in the terminology used. "*Prima facie* evidence of negligence" in the *Sterling Trusts* case is used seemingly interchangeably with the expression "*prima facie* liable". In a later case in the Ontario Court of Appeal, *Queensway Tank Lines Ltd. v. Moise,* [1970] 1 O.R. 535, MacKay J.A. assumes *prima facie* evidence to be a presumption of negligence with concomitant shift in the onus of proof to the defendant.

The use of breach of statute as evidence of negligence as opposed to recognition of a nominate tort of statutory breach is, as Professor Fleming has put it, more intellectually acceptable. It avoids, to a certain extent, the fictitious hunt for legislative intent to create a civil cause of action which has been so criticized in England. It also avoids the inflexible application of the legislature's criminal standard of conduct to a civil case. Glanville Williams is of the opinion, with which I am in agreement, that where there is no duty of care at common law, breach of non-industrial penal legislation should not affect civil liability unless the statute provides for it. As I have indicated above, industrial legislation historically has enjoyed special consideration. Recognition of the doctrine of absolute liability under some industrial statutes does not justify extension of such doctrine to other fields, particularly when one considers the jejune reasoning supporting the juristic invention.

Regarding statutory breach as part of the law of negligence is also more consonant with other developments which have taken place in the law. More and more the legislator is heeding the admonition of Parcq L.J. given many years ago in *Cutler v. Wandsworth Stadium, Ltd., supra:*

> To a person unversed in the science, or art, of legislation it may well seem strange that Parliament has not by now made it a rule to state explicitly what its intention is in a matter which is often of no little importance, instead of leaving it to the courts to discover, by a careful examination and analysis of what is expressly said, what the intention may be supposed probably to be. There are no doubt, reasons which inhibit the legislature from revealing its intention to plain words. I do not know, and must not speculate, what those reasons may be. I trust, however, that it will not be thought impertinent, in any sense of that word, to suggest respectfully that those who are responsible for framing legislation might consider whether the traditional practice, which obscures, if it does not conceal, the intention which Parliament has, or must be presumed to have, might not safely be abandoned (at p. 549).

Statutes are increasingly speaking plainly to civil responsibility: consumer protection acts, rental acts, business corporations acts, securities acts. Individual compensation has become an active concern of the legislator.

In addition, the role of tort liability in compensation and allocation of loss is of less and less importance:

> [I]nstead of tort liability being the sole source of potential compensation (as it was throughout most of our history) it is now but one of several such sources, and (at that) carrying an ever diminishing share of the economic burden of compensating the injured (Fleming, *More Thoughts on Loss Distribution* (1966), 4 Osgoode H. L.J. 161).

Tort law itself has undergone a major transformation in this century with nominate torts being eclipsed by negligence, the closest the common law has come to a general theory of civil responsibility. The concept of duty of care, embodied in the neighbour principle has expanded into areas hitherto untouched by tort law.

One of the main reasons for shifting a loss to a defendant is that he has been at fault, that he has done some act which should be discouraged. There is then good reason for taking money from the defendant as well as a reason for giving it to the plaintiff who has suffered from the fault of the defendant. But there seems little in the way of defensible policy for holding a defendant who breached a statutory duty unwittingly to be negligent and obligated to pay even though not at fault. The legislature has imposed a penalty on a strictly admonitory basis and there seems little justification to add civil liability when such liability would tend to produce liability without fault. The legislature has determined the proper penalty for the defendant's wrong but if tort admonition of liability without fault is to be added, the financial consequences will be measured, not by the amount of the penalty, but by the amount of money which is required to compensate the plaintiff. Minimum fault may subject the defendant to heavy liability. Inconsequential violations should not subject the violator to any civil liability at all but should be left to the criminal courts for enforcement of a fine.

In this case the Board contends that the duty imposed by the Act is absolute, that is to say, the Pool is liable, even in absence of fault, and all that is requisite to prove a breach of duty is to show that the requirements of the statute have not, in fact, been complied with; it is not necessary to show how the failure to comply arose or that the Pool was guilty of any failure to take reasonable care to comply.

The tendency of the law of recent times is to ameliorate the rigors of absolute rules and absolute duty in the sense indicated, as contrary to natural justice. "Sound policy lets losses lie where they fall except where a special reason can be shown for interference": Holmes, *The Common Law*, 50. In the case at bar the evidence is that substantially all of the grain entering the terminal of the Pool at Thunder Bay came from agents of the Board. The imposition of heavy financial burden as in this case without fault on the part of the Pool does not incline one to interfere. It is better that the loss lies where it falls, upon the Board.

For all of the above reasons I would be adverse to the recognition in Canada of a nominate tort of statutory breach. Breach of statute, where it has an effect upon civil liability, should be considered in the context of the general law of negligence. Negligence and its common law duty of care have become pervasive enough to serve the purpose invoked for the existence of the action for statutory breach.

It must not be forgotten that the other elements of tortious responsibility equally apply to situations involving statutory breach, *i.e.* principles of causation and damages. To be relevant at all, the statutory breach must have caused the damage of which the plaintiff complains. Should this be so, the violation of the statute should be evidence of negligence on the part of the defendant.

IV

This Case

Assuming that Parliament is competent constitutionally to provide that anyone injured by a breach of the *Canada Grain Act* shall have a remedy by civil action, the fact is that Parliament has not done so. Parliament has said that an offender shall suffer certain specified penalties for his statutory breach. We must refrain from conjecture as to Parliament's unexpressed intent. The most we can do in determining whether the breach shall have any other legal consequences is to examine what is expressed. In professing to construe the Act in order to conclude whether Parliament intended a private right of action, we are likely to engage in a process which Glanville Williams aptly described as "looking for what is not there" (p. 244). The *Canada Grain Act* does not contain any express provision for damages for the holder of a terminal elevator receipt who receives infested grain out of an elevator.

The obligation of a terminal operator under s. 61(1) of the *Canada Grain Act* is to deliver to the holder of an elevator receipt for grain issued by the operator the identical grain or grain of the same kind, grade and quantity as the grain referred to in the surrendered receipt, as the receipt requires. That obligation was discharged.

Breach of s. 86(*c*) of the *Canada Grain Act* in discharging infested grain into the Frankcliffe Hall does not give rise, in and of itself, to an independent tortious action. The Board has proceeded as if it does. Statutory breach, and not negligence, is pleaded. The case has been presented exclusively on the basis of breach of statutory duty. The Board has not proved what Lord Atkin referred to as statutory negligence, *i.e.* an intentional or negligent failure to comply with a statutory duty. There is no evidence at trial of any negligence or failure to take care on the part of the Pool. The Pool has demonstrated that it operated its terminal up to the accepted standards of the trade; it made regular checks of its terminals for infested grain; it tested samples of wheat both upon admission to and upon discharge from its terminal elevator. Samples were taken on discharge of the wheat from the terminal elevator into the Frankcliffe Hall by both the Pool's employees and the Grain Commission inspectors. Visual inspection of the samples showed no defect. Berlase funnel tests conducted at the Grain Commission headquarters disclosed the infestation but the results could not be made available before the Frankcliffe Hall had sailed. The inspection procedures followed were those determined by the Canada Grain Commission (s. 12(1)(a), the *Canada Grain Act*) and the Pool and the Commission worked in cooperation. The Pool successfully demonstrated that the loss was not the result of any negligence on its part.

In sum I conclude that:

1. Civil consequences of breach of statute should be subsumed in the law of negligence.

2. The notion of a nominate tort of statutory breach giving a right to recovery merely on proof of breach and damages should be rejected, as should the view that unexcused breach constitutes negligence *per se* giving rise to absolute liability.
3. Proof of statutory breach, causative of damages, may be evidence of negligence.
4. The statutory formulation of the duty may afford a specific, and useful, standard of reasonable conduct.
5. In the case at bar negligence is neither pleaded nor proven. The action must fail.

I would dismiss the appeal with costs.

[**Ritchie, Beetz, Estey, McIntyre, Chouinard** and **Lamer** JJ. concurred.]

NOTES

1. Before *Saskatchewan Wheat Pool*, statutes could be relied on in at least five ways. First, they could be used as a basis for creating a statutory tort. This treatment has now been stopped by *Saskatchewan Wheat Pool*. Second, they could be relied on to establish a new tort duty where none existed before. This issue is dealt with below. Third, the fact that conduct was in violation of legislation, where a duty already existed, could be treated as negligence *per se*. Fourth, in crystallizing the standard of care, proof of statutory violation could be said to be *prima facie* evidence of negligence. This was the treatment developed in *Sterling Trusts v. Postma et al.*, [1965] S.C.R. 324, 48 D.L.R. (2d) 423 and explained in *Queensway Tank Lines v. Moise*, [1970] 1 O.R. 535, 9 D.L.R. (3d) 30 (C.A.), which was used for 18 years in Canada. Fifth, a breach of statute could be evidence of negligence, the approach adopted in *Saskatchewan Wheat Pool*, for all but a few situations. In one California case, each of these three latter approaches was favoured by at least one judge. See *Satterlee v. Orange Glenn School District*, 177 P. 2d 279 (1947). See also *Johnston v. A.G. of Canada* (1981), 34 O.R. (2d) 208, 18 C.C.L.T. 245 (S.C.), *per* Linden J., for an explanation of the various ways statutes can be used in tort cases. Is the new approach, evidence of negligence, the best way of dealing with statutes?

2. *Saskatchewan Wheat Pool* has been welcomed by Professor Brudner because it clarified the law and obviated the need to "search for a fictitious legislative intention". See "Comment" (1984), 62 Can. Bar Rev. 668, at 669. Professor Fridman wrote that the case of "utmost importance", was "convincing and justifiable" and exemplified the "independence of the Canadian judiciary", freeing it from the "disfiguring barnacles that have clung to the hull of English tort law". See "Civil Liability for Criminal Conduct" (1984), 16 Ottawa L. Rev. 34, at 61. See also Matthews (1984), 4 Oxford J.L.S. 429. The decision has also been criticized by Professor Brudner. He calls it "lamentable" because the court "disarmed itself of a means by which to extend common-law duties in the face of obsolete precedents without subjecting defendants to unfair surprise". He also complains that the court "surrendered the advantages of precise and uniform standards of care". Are these fears well founded? See Klar "Developments in Tort Law: The 1982-83 Term" (1984), 6 Supreme Court L. Rev. 309.

3. Following *Saskatchewan Wheat Pool*, the Canadian courts embraced the new approach with enthusiasm. See *Baird v. R. in Right of Canada* (1983), 148 D.L.R. (3d) 1, at 9, 48 N.R. 276 (Fed. C.A.); *James St. Hardware v. Spizziri* (1985), 51 O.R. (2d) 641 at 651, 33 C.C.L.T. 209 (H.C.J.); vard (1987), 240 O.A.C. 42, 43 C.C.L.T. 9

(C.A.); *Palmer v. N.S. Forest Industries* (1983), 2 D.L.R. (4th) 397, 26 C.C.L.T. 22 (N.S.S.C.); *Clark v. C.N.R.*, [1988] 2 S.C.R. 680, 54 D.L.R. (4th) 679. One court treated the breach of a municipal by-law requiring owners of taxicabs to keep them in good repair as evidence of negligence in a case where a passenger was injured when a door fell off a cab. See *Fraser v. U-Need A-Cab Ltd.* (1983), 1 D.L.R. (4th) 268 at 278, 43 O.R. (2d) 389 (alt. holding) *per* Henry J.; affd (1985), 50 O.R. (2d) 281, 17 D.L.R. (4th) 574 (C.A.). Evidence of violation of legislation has been used in cases other than negligence such as intentional torts (*Evans v. Canada* (1986), 4 F.T.R. 247, C.W.L.S. 8701 [58] (F.C.T.D.); affd (1988), 93 N.R. 252 (F.C.A.)), and other specific torts (*B.G. Ranches v. Manitoba Agricultural Lands Protection Bd.* (1983), 21 Man. R. (2d) 285, [1983] 4 W.W.R. 681 (Q.B.)), and contract actions (*Wild Rose Mills Ltd. v. Ellison Milling Co.* (1985), 32 B.L.R. 125 (B.C.S.C.)) The Supreme Court of Canada has itself employed *Saskatchewan Wheat Pool* in *Frame v. Smith*, [1987] 2 S.C.R. 99, 42 C.C.L.T. 1, holding that one cannot sue in tort for a breach of an order made under the then *Children's Law Reform Act*, R.S.O. 1980, c. 68 regarding custody and access.

4. Does a civil court have any business at all relying upon criminal statutes in deciding whether civil liability will be imposed? What policy arguments can be advanced in favour of the use of penal statutes in tort cases? What about the desirability of consistency between the criminal law and the civil law? Is the legislature better equipped with expertise than the judiciary to make decisions about the appropriate standards of conduct to be adhered to? Can the force of penal enactments be rendered more powerful by their adoption in tort cases? Does the reliance on criminal legislation simplify the administration of the reasonable care test by the judge and jury? Does the use of statutory standards move us closer to a regime of strict liability?

5. What policy reasons can be offered in opposition to the use of statutes in civil cases? Does this practice offend the principle of deference to the legislature by going beyond its expressed will? Can civil liability impose too onerous a burden upon the violator of a minor piece of legislation? What about the matter of double jeopardy? Can the expertise of the legislature be overestimated? Is it wise to control too closely the operation of the judge and jury in the daily administration of negligence law? Is it advisable to depart from "fault" liability in this area?

6. Suppose A's car crashes into B's car, injuring B. It is established that A's brakes were defective, in contravention of a *Highway Traffic Act* provision. Does A escape liability if it is shown (1) that he did not know that his brakes were defective? (2) that he checked his brakes bi-annually, as recommended in his car owner's manual? (3) that he had his brakes repaired the preceding day at a reliable garage? See Linden, "Automobile Equipment Legislation and Tort Liability" (1967), 5 Western L. Rev. 76. Is it up to the judge or jury to decide on the facts of each case?

7. Should evidence of a statutory violation *always* be treated in exactly the same way by a civil court? Would it be advisable to accord varying procedural effects to different statutes in different situations? What are the dangers of such an eclectic approach? In discussing the use of motor vehicle legislation in tort cases, Mr. Justice Rand in *Bruce v. McIntyre*, [1955] S.C.R. 251, at 254, [1955] 1 D.L.R. 785, stated:

> The appearance of automobiles upon our highways has obviously created crowding dangers and hazards undreamt of in 1840. The speed and the momentum of these vehicles and the complexity of their operations are such that it has become necessary to place every person concerned with or who may be affected by them under a greatly heightened exercise of care and imagination to stimulate awareness and anticipation. The elaborate and detailed requirements that are now set out in the statutes dealing with speed, lights, signals, positions, parking and other details of management and operation combine to

create more than a mere duty of abstention from affirmative action which may cause damage or injury to others; they may require action either by way of precautionary warning or by removing one's self or property from a range of danger which theoretically the prudent conduct of others would make unnecessary. They give rise to a responsibility for greater foresight than the mere first stage of minimum or formal measures of one's own proper conduct: they are intended to promote reciprocal, even overlapping, precautions. Always depending on the surrounding circumstances and subject to other demands of safety, they bind us to contemplate carelessness or oversight in others regardless of their duty under the rules of the road, and they require us to act within the limits of alerted reasonableness to ensure, in the interest of the public, the practicable maximum of generalized and mutual protection against injury to person and damage to property. The scandal of the ravages of our holidays from this cause is the more than sufficient justification for the insistence on the drastic measure to which our highway authorities have been aroused. ...

8. In the aftermath of the *Saskatchewan Wheat Pool* case, *supra*, are there any situations left, in addition to the industrial safety statutes, where violation of a statute can amount to negligence *per se*? In *Unsworth v. Mogk* (1979), 27 O.R. (2d) 645, 107 D.L.R. (3d) 454 (H.C.J.), Grange J. held an "employer" partially liable to a volunteer worker when the "employer" violated the regulations under the *Construction Safety Act* by failing to install guardrails on a scaffold. Grange J. explained: "When a statute is designed for the safety of certain persons and one of those persons is injured by reason of the failure to observe the provisions of the statute, an action will lie." Is this still good law? How will our courts now treat violation of legislation dealing with the safe handling of gas? (See *Ostash v. Sonnenberg; Ostash v. Aiello* (1968), 67 D.L.R. (2d) 311, 63 W.W.R. 257 (Alta. C.A.)).

9. What procedural effect will now be given to the breach of a pure food statute? See *Curll v. Robin Hood Multifoods* (1974), 14 N.S.R. (2d) 252, 56 D.L.R. (3d) 129 (S.C.T.D.). *Cf., Heimler v. Calvert Caterers Ltd.* (1974), 4 O.R. (2d) 667, 49 D.L.R. (3d) 36 (Co. Ct.); affd (1975), 8 O.R. (2d) 1, 56 D.L.R. (3d) 643 (C.A.).

10. In *Northern Helicopters Ltd. v. Vancouver Soaring Association et al.* (1972), 31 D.L.R. (3d) 321, [1972] 6 W.W.R. 342 (B.C.S.C.), a helicopter collided with a glider in mid-air, killing both pilots. Both pilots had violated the Air Regulations passed under the authority of the *Aeronautics Act*, R.S.C. 1952, c. 2. Mr. Justice Berger rationalized his use of these provisions as follows:

> We have the *Air Regulations*. They lay down a set of rules governing aircraft. They can be applied to the case at bar. They establish a reasonable standard of care. In my view, the court ought to apply those Regulations in a sensible way that takes into account the nature of flight and the special characteristics of the aircraft that collided here. ... To apply the law as developed in automobile cases or in collisions at sea, would involve the risk of introducing rules that might well be arbitrary and insensitive to the peculiarities of flight.
>
> Now, the *Air Regulations* are not a code governing civil liability on aircraft collisions. But they do represent a reasonable standard of care to be observed. A failure to observe that standard is negligence.

In this case, both pilots were in breach of their statutory duty and liability was split 66-2/3 against the plaintiff and 33-1/3 against the defendant. Which procedural effect has Mr. Justice Berger accorded these Air Regulations? What do you think of His Lordship's reasoning? Is this case still good law?

11. In *Maynes v. Galicz* (1976), 62 D.L.R. (3d) 385, [1976] 1 W.W.R. 557 (B.C.S.C.), a 7-year-old child was injured by a wolf at a zoo when she climbed over a barrier which

did not comply with certain regulations and put her fingers into the wire mesh cage housing the wolf. McKay J., in imposing liability, stated:

> In my view, the secondary barrier does not comply with the Regulations. It would not *prevent* an excited or inquisitive youngster from reaching the enclosure. It certainly did not in this case. I agree with counsel for the defendant that a breach of the Regulations does not *ipso facto* create liability. It is my view, however, that the Regulation in question sets a minimum standard of care that the public is entitled to expect from those who display wild and dangerous animals for financial gain.

Is this case still good law?

12. Do these last few cases have anything in common that might distinguish them from the situation in the *Saskatchewan Wheat Pool* case, *supra*?

13. What is the current status of *Cunningham v. Moore*, [1972] 3 O.R. 369, 28 D.L.R. (3d) 277 (Co. Ct.); affd, [1973] 1 O.R. 358, 31 D.L.R. (3d) 149 (H.C.), where it was held that a violation of the Ontario *Landlord and Tenant Act*, R.S.O. 1970, c. 236, s. 96(1) gave rise to a cause of action. The plaintiff-tenant sued the defendant-landlord in tort for damages resulting from a fire that, he alleged, occurred as a result of defective wiring in an electric stove. Although there was no cause of action at common law in these circumstances, he alleged that s. 96(1) created a new cause of action. Section 96(1) read:

> A landlord is responsible for providing and maintaining the rented premises in a good state of repair and fit for habitation during the tenancy and for complying with health and safety standards, including any housing standards required by law, and notwithstanding that any state of non-repair existed to the knowledge of the tenant before the tenancy agreement was entered into.

The defendant sought a determination of a question of law before trial on this issue. Scott Co. Ct. J. held that by introducing s. 96(1), "the intention of the legislation was to create a cause of action in favour of a particular class, to wit, tenants". His Honour explained that "the remedies provided are wholly inadequate and do not represent adequate compensation should damages be suffered". On appeal, Mr. Justice Holland agreed with Judge Scott and stated: "If a duty is imposed by statute then *prima facie*, the plaintiff is entitled to succeed upon showing a breach of that statutory duty resulting in injury or damage to the plaintiff." He concluded that "from a fair reading of s. 96 it was the intention of the Legislature to establish civil liability...".

See also *Fleischmann v. Grossman Holdings* (1976), 16 O.R. (2d) 746, 79 D.L.R. (3d) 142 (C.A.); *Dye v. McGregor* (1978), 20 O.R. (2d) 1, 86 D.L.R. (3d) 606 (C.A.); *Lindstrom v. Bassett Realty* (1978), 90 D.L.R. (3d) 238 (N.S.); *Re MacIssac and Beretanos* (1971), 25 D.L.R. (3d) 610 (B.C. Prov. Ct.); *Gaul v. King* (1979), 33 N.S.R. (2d) 61, 103 D.L.R. (3d) 233 (C.A.); *Bassett Realty v. Lindstrom* (1979), 34 N.S.R. (2d) 361, 103 D.L.R. (3d) 654 (C.A.).

14. Occasionally, a legislature will direct the civil courts to utilize evidence of a violation of one of its statutes in a particular way. Such aid, though welcome, is all too rare. One such provision is the United Kingdom *Road Traffic Act*, 1960, 8 & 9 Eliz. 2, c. 16, s. 74(5), which states:

> A failure on the part of a person to observe a provision of the Highway Code shall not of itself render that person liable to criminal proceedings of any kind, but any such failure may, in any proceedings (whether civil or criminal...), be relied upon by any party to the proceedings as tending to establish or to negative any liability which is in question in those proceedings.

In *Powell v. Phillips*, [1972] 3 All E.R. 864, 137 J.P. 31 (C.A.), the plaintiff, a pedestrian walking on a poorly-lit street, was struck by a speeding car and suffered severe injuries. Although it was proved that she was in breach of the Highway Code, by not wearing anything white or reflective and by not being on the proper side of the road, facing on-coming traffic, she received 100 per cent of her damages. Stephenson L.J. stated, at 868:

> In law a breach of the Highway Code has a limited effect. ... It is ... clear ... that a breach [by the plaintiff] creates no presumption of negligence calling for an explanation, still less a presumption of negligence making a real contribution to causing an accident or injury. The breach is just one of the circumstances on which one party is entitled to rely in establishing the negligence of the other and its contribution to causing the accident or injury. ... [I]t must be considered with all the other circumstances including the explanation. ... It must not be elevated into a breach of statutory duty which gives a right of action to anyone who can prove that his injury resulted from it.

Would the court have come to the same conclusion without s. 74(5) of the *Road Traffic Act*?

15. Legislatures may also use statutes in order to vary a standard of care required to find civil liability. This has occasionally been done by requiring that "gross negligence" be found against a defendant. For example, the *Municipal Act*, R.S.O. 1990, c. M.45, s. 284(4), imposes liability on municipalities for personal injuries caused by snow or ice upon a sidewalk only where there is "gross negligence". This also used to be a feature of "guest passenger" statutes, all of which have now been abolished.

16. What is "gross negligence"? In *Cowper v. Studer*, [1951] S.C.R. 450, [1951] 2 D.L.R. 81, it was defined as "very great negligence in the circumstances of a particular case". Is this a helpful phrase? What is the purpose in using degrees of negligence in defining a standard of care?

1. The Limitations on Statutory Use

GORRIS v. SCOTT

Exchequer Court. (1874), L.R. 9 Ex. 125, 43 L.J. Ex. 92, 30 L.J. 431.

Kelly C.B.: This is an action to recover damages for the loss of a number of sheep which the defendant, a shipowner, had contracted to carry, and which were washed overboard and lost by reason (as we take it to be truly alleged) of the neglect to comply with a certain order made by the Privy Council, in pursuance of the *Contagious Diseases (Animals) Act, 1869*. The Act was passed merely for sanitary purposes, in order to prevent animals in a state of infectious disease from communicating it to other animals with which they might come in contact. Under the authority of that Act, certain orders were made; amongst others, an order by which any ship bringing sheep or cattle from any foreign ports to ports in Great Britain is to have the place occupied by such animals divided into pens of certain dimensions, and the floor of such pens furnished with battens or foot-holds. The object of this order is to prevent animals from being overcrowded, and so brought into a condition in which the disease guarded against would be likely to be developed. This regulation has been neglected, and the question is, whether the loss, which we must assume to have been caused by that neglect, entitles the plaintiffs to maintain an action.

The argument of the defendant is, that the Act has imposed penalties to secure the observance of its provisions, and that, according to the general rule, the remedy prescribed by the statute must be pursued; that although, when penalties are imposed for the violation of a statutory duty, a person aggrieved by its violation may sometimes maintain an action for the damage so caused, that must be in cases where the object of the statute is to confer a benefit on individuals, and to protect them against the evil consequences which the statute was designed to prevent, and which have in fact ensued; but that if the object is not to protect individuals against the consequences which have in fact ensued, it is otherwise; that if, therefore, by reason of the precautions in question not having been taken, the plaintiffs had sustained that damage against which it was intended to secure them, an action would lie, but that when the damage is of such a nature as was not contemplated at all by the statute, and as to which it was not intended to confer any benefit on the plaintiffs they cannot maintain an action founded on the neglect. The principle may be well illustrated by the case put in argument of a breach of a railway company of its duty to erect a gate on a level crossing, and to keep the gate closed except when the crossing is being actually and properly used. The object of the precaution is to prevent injury from being sustained through animals or vehicles being upon the line at unseasonable times; and if by reason of such a breach of duty, either in not erecting the gate, or in not keeping it closed, a person attempts to cross with a carriage at an improper time, and injury ensues to a passenger, no doubt an action would lie against the railway company, because the intention of the legislature was that, by the erection of the gates and by their being kept closed individuals should be protected against accidents of this description. And if we could see that it was the object, or among the objects of this Act, that the owners of sheep and cattle coming from a foreign port should be protected by the means described against the danger of their property being washed overboard, or lost by the perils of the sea, the present action would be within the principle.

But, looking at the Act, it is perfectly clear that its provisions were all enacted with a totally different view; there was no purpose, direct or indirect, to protect against such damage; but, as is recited in the preamble, the Act is directed against the possibility of sheep or cattle being exposed to disease on their way to this country. The preamble recites that "it is expedient to confer on Her Majesty's most honourable Privy Council power to take such measures as may appear from time to time necessary to prevent the introduction into Great Britain of contagious or infectious diseases among cattle, sheep, or other animals, by prohibiting or regulating the importation of foreign animals," and also to provide against the "spreading" of such diseases in Great Britain. Then follow numerous sections directed entirely to this object. Then comes sec. 75, which enacts that "the Privy Council may from time to time make such orders as they think expedient for all or any of the following purposes." What, then, are these purposes? They are "for securing for animals brought by sea to ports in Great Britain a proper supply of food and water during the passage and on landing," "for protecting such animals from unnecessary suffering during the passage and on landing," and so forth; all the purposes enumerated being calculated and directed to the prevention of disease, and none of them having any relation whatever to the danger of loss by the perils of the sea. That being so, if by reason of the default in question the plaintiffs' sheep had been caused unnecessary suffering, and so had arrived in this country in a state of disease, I do not say that they might not have maintained this action. But the damage complained of here is something totally apart from the object of the Act of Parliament, and it is in accordance with all the authorities to say that the action is not maintainable.

NOTES

1. Is this a wise limitation for the civil courts to place upon their use of penal statutes? Why?

2. A boy runs into a pointed ornament on a stationary car and injures himself. The defendant contravened a statute that forbids the use of any ornament "which extends or protrudes to the front of the face of the radiator grill". Liability? See *Hatch v. Ford Motor Co.*, 163 Cal. App. 2d 293, 329 P. 2d 605 (1958).

3. The defendant violates a war-time speed limit of 35 m.p.h. and collides with the plaintiff on the highway. The purpose of the statute was found to be the conservation of gasoline, not safety. Liability? See *Cooper v. Hoeglund*, 221 Minn. 446, 22 N.W. 2d 450 (1946).

4. Penelope was blinded by a small particle of broken wire that was flung out of a machine she was operating. David, the defendant and owner of the factory, violated a statute that required unsafe machines to be securely fenced. If it were impossible to fence, it was permissible to provide a device which would "prevent the operator from coming into contact with that part". Would a civil court rely on the violation of this statute in a tort suit? Would it make any difference to your answer if the statute said nothing about the reason for the fencing requirement? Aside from the statutory breach, is David liable for negligence? Does it depend on how frequently this type of accident occurred in the past? Compare with *Kilgollan v. William Cooke & Co. Ltd.*, [1956] 1 W.L.R. 527, [1956] 2 All E.R. 294 (C.A.). See also *Keating v. Elvan Reinforced Concrete Co. Ltd. et al.*, [1968] 1 W.L.R. 722, [1968] 2 All E.R. 139 (C.A.); *Thordarson v. Zastre* (1968), 70 D.L.R. (2d) 91 (Alta. S.C.); *Beauchamp v. Ayotte et al.*, [1971] 3 O.R. 21, 19 D.L.R. (3d) 258, Lacourciere J.

5. Not only must the accident be of a type the statute was meant to prevent, but the claimant must be someone whom the statute was designed to protect. In *Kelly v. Henry Muhs Co.*, 71 N.J.L. 358, 59 A. 23 (1904), a statute aimed at protecting employees was violated when the defendant failed to place a guard rail or trapdoor on an elevator shaft. The plaintiff, a firefighter who came to put out a fire in the building, fell down the unguarded elevator shaft. He was denied recovery on the basis of the statutory breach. Police officers and other visitors have been treated in the same way. See *Davey v. Greenlaw*, 101 N.H. 134, 135 A. 2d 900 (1957). Is this a wise limitation?

6. In *Paulsen v. C.P.R.* (1963), 40 D.L.R. (2d) 761, 43 W.W.R. 513 (Man. C.A.), a section of the *Railway Act* required a railway to erect and maintain 4 ft., 6 in. fences on each side of the railway track. "Such fences shall be suitable and sufficient to prevent cattle and other animals from getting on the railway lands." A child of 27 months was struck by a train operated by the defendant railway. The Manitoba Court of Appeal held that the absence of a fence was a cause of the child's injuries and the defendant was, accordingly, liable in damages. The defendant's argument that the section was passed "for the safe passage of trains" was not adopted nor was the argument that infant trespassers were not intended to be protected by the statute. Is this decision consistent with *Kelly*? With *Gorris v. Scott*?

7. A tavernkeeper serves liquor to an intoxicated patron, in violation of a *Liquor Control Act*. As a result of this additional liquor, the drunken patron punches another patron in the nose. Is the fact of the violation of the statute relevant in an action against the tavernkeeper? (See *Stachniewicz v. Mar-Cam Corp.*, 259 Oregon 583, 488 P. 2d 436 (1971).) Would the result be any different if the drunken patron hit an employee of the tavern, rather than a fellow patron? Would the result vary if, instead of punching the other patron, the intoxicated person had tripped and fallen on the patron? What would

the result be if there was no statute? Should the courts be liberal or narrow in their assessment of the purpose of these statutes? What is the danger associated with a broad interpretation?

8. Someone leaves a car, engine running, outside a beer parlour. A thief takes the car and collides with the plaintiff. The plaintiff sues, relying on a statute making it an offence to leave a car standing or parked without having turned off the engine, locked the ignition, removed the key and braked the vehicle. Liability? See *Stavast v. Ludwar*, [1974] 5 W.W.R. 380 (B.C. Co. Ct.); *Ross v. Hartman*, 139 F. 2d 14, 78 App. D.C. 217 (1943). Would the result be any different without the statutory provision? See *Hewson v. City of Red Deer* (1975), 63 D.L.R. (3d) 168 (Alta.). Would the result vary if the collision took place a week after the theft of the car? Compare *Justus v. Wood*, 349 S.W. 2d 793 (Tenn. 1961).

9. The conduct in violation of the enactment must cause the injury. *Schofield v. Town of Oakville*, [1968] 2 O.R. 409, 69 D.L.R. (2d) 441 (C.A.), *per* McGillivray J.A. The Supreme Court of Canada in *Odlum and Sylvester v. Walsh*, [1939] 2 D.L.R. 545, stated that it was open to the jury to find that excess speed was "not in whole or in part a direct cause of the accident". See also *dictum* in *McKenzie v. Robar*, [1953] 1 D.L.R. 449 (S.C.C.), and *Service Fire Insurance v. Larouche*, [1956] Que. Q.B. 294, at 296, where Mr. Justice Martineau concluded, "Il n'y a aucun lien de causalité entre sa vitesse et la collision." A similar conclusion was reached in *Wright v. Ruckstull*, [1955] O.W.N. 728, at 729 (H.C.J.), where Mr. Justice Spence held that "no part of the accident is due to the plaintiff's speed". See Linden, "Speeding as Negligence" (1967), 10 Can. Bar. J. 94.

10. Would there be any liability if the defendant, who is in violation of a vehicle lighting statute, collides with another automobile in a brightly lit intersection? See *Collins v. General Service Transport* (1927), 38 B.C.R. 512, [1927] 2 D.L.R. 353 (C.A.); *Peacock v. Stephens*, [1927] 4 D.L.R. 1057, [1927] 3 W.W.R. 570 (Sask. C.A.). What if the defendant, driving a car with defective brakes, hits a pedestrian who darts out in front of the car before the defendant has a chance to apply the brakes? See *Johnson v. Sorochuk*, [1941] 1 W.W.R. 445 (Alta. S.C.); *Payne v. Lane*, [1949] O.W.N. 284 (H.C.).

11. What if the driver of a vehicle involved in a collision has no licence? Can he sue? Can this lack be used against him as a defendant? See *Godfrey v. Cooper* (1920), 46 O.L.R. 565, where Middleton J. answered both questions in this way:

> In my opinion, a mere failure to obtain a licence does not deprive the driver of any right of action he would otherwise have against any person who injures him by negligence. Nor can a defendant rely upon any breach of the provisions of the statute unless he can show that the breach of the statute was a proximate cause of the accident.

12. In *Field v. Supertest Petroleum Corp.*, [1943] O.W.N. 482, the statement of claim against a motorist alleged that "he was not a skilled or reasonably skilled operator [and did not hold an operator's licence as required by the *Highway Traffic Act*]". On a motion before the master the clause in brackets was struck out.

13. In *City of Vancouver v. Burchill*, [1952] S.C.R. 620, [1932] 4 D.L.R. 200, the plaintiff, a taxi driver, had failed to obtain a licence from the municipality in which he was operating, as provided by the British Columbia *Motor Vehicle Act*. He was injured because of the non-repair of the highway. The Supreme Court of Canada held that he was entitled to recover against the municipality notwithstanding his failure to hold a licence. *Per* Rinfret J.: "After all, we are concerned here with an action founded on negligence and, in actions of that kind, the guiding principle — we should say the inevitable principle — is the principle of cause and effect. The liability in such a case is

based — and can only be based — upon the causal connection between the tort and the resulting damage. Failure by the plaintiff to comply with a statute, in no way contributing to the accident, will not, in the absence of a specific provision to that effect, defeat the right of recovery of the plaintiff. ... The municipality, in respect of its streets, does not stand in the same position as a landowner with regard to his property." See also *Roy Swail Ltd. v. Reeves* (1956), 2 D.L.R. (2d) 326 (S.C.C.).

14. Would the courts take a different view if the alleged negligence was the defendant's poor driving ability? What if the defendant had actually tried to get a driver's licence and had failed the test? What if the defendant had failed ten times?

15. The defendant has a learner's licence which permits the defendant to drive only if accompanied by another fully-licenced driver. The defendant takes a car onto the road, alone, in violation of the legislation, and collides with someone. Is the evidence of the violation of the statute relevant to whether or not the defendant was negligent? What if one of the allegations of negligence was that the defendant had not noticed the plaintiff and would have if accompanied by someone else? *Cf., Feener v. McKenzie*, [1972] S.C.R. 525, 25 D.L.R. (3d) 283.

16. What if an unlicenced person, posing as a doctor, inflicts some injury on a patient during unauthorized treatment? *Cf., Brown v. Shyne*, 151 N.E. 197, 242 N.Y.S. 476 (1926), and *Whipple v. Grandchamp*, 158 N.E. 270 (1927).

2. Compliance with Statute

RYAN v. VICTORIA (CITY)

Supreme Court of Canada. Unreported, Doc. No. 25704, January 28, 1999.

The appellant was injured when he was thrown from his motorcycle while attempting to cross railway tracks running down the centre of a street in downtown Victoria. The front tire of his motorcycle became trapped in a "flangeway" gap running alongside the inner edge of the street-grade tracks. The motorcyclist sued the City and the railway companies which owned and operated the tracks. The Railways denied liability on the ground that the tracks were authorized by, and complied with, all applicable statutes, regulations and administrative orders.

The trial judge held the Railways and the City jointly and severally liable in negligence, the former for maintaining dangerously wide flangeways and the latter for failing to warn of the hazard. In addition, he held the Railways liable in public nuisance. The British Columbia Court of Appeal set aside the public nuisance finding and held all of the respondents liable only for failure to warn. The Court of Appeal also found the appellant to be contributorily negligent and liable for 50 per cent of his damages. The Supreme Court of Canada reversed and restored the decision of the trial judge.

Under a long-standing common law rule, the standard of care owed by railways to the public was normally limited to the discharge of statutory obligations. The main question before the Supreme Court was whether that rule should be discarded, and if so, how statutory compliance should affect the assessment of liability under ordinary negligence principles.

Major J. (for a unanimous court):

The respondents have not challenged the finding that they were liable for failing to warn the appellant of the hazard created by the flangeways on Store Street. That conclusion is not at issue in this appeal. The three issues are:

1. Did the Court of Appeal err in finding that the Railways were not negligent with regard to the width of the flangeways on Store Street?
2. Did the Court of Appeal err in finding that the flangeways on Store Street did not give rise to liability for public nuisance?
3. Did the Court of Appeal err in reversing the trial judge's findings with respect to contributory negligence?

This appeal focuses on the relationship between statutory authority and civil liability. The appellant submits that the Railways are liable under theories of negligence and nuisance for installing dangerous flangeways on Store Street. The Railways deny liability on the basis that the Store Street line is a "highway crossing" and its flangeways comply in all respects with the safety regulations governing such crossings. The questions are: (1) whether the regulations relied upon by the Railways are in fact applicable to the Store Street line, and (2) if so, whether the Railways are nevertheless liable for failing to exercise their discretion under those regulations so as to minimize the hazard created by the flangeways.

A. Were the Railways Negligent with Regard to the Width of the Flangeways on Store Street?

[The duty of care issue was analysed along the lines suggested by La Forest J. in *Hercules Management*]

...

Conduct is negligent if it creates an objectively unreasonable risk of harm. To avoid liability, a person must exercise the standard of care that would be expected of an ordinary, reasonable and prudent person in the same circumstances. The measure of what is reasonable depends on the facts of each case, including the likelihood of a known or foreseeable harm, the gravity of that harm, and the burden or cost which would be incurred to prevent the injury. In addition, one may look to external indicators of reasonable conduct, such as custom, industry practice, and statutory or regulatory standards.

Legislative standards are relevant to the common law standard of care, but the two are not necessarily co-extensive. The fact that a statute prescribes or prohibits certain activities may constitute evidence of reasonable conduct in a given situation, but it does not extinguish the underlying obligation of reasonableness. See *R. in right of Canada v. Saskatchewan Wheat Pool*, [1983] 1 S.C.R. 205. Thus, a statutory breach does not automatically give rise to civil liability; it is merely some evidence of negligence. See, *e.g.*, *Stewart v. Pettie*, [1995] 1 S.C.R. 131, at para. 36, and *Saskatchewan Wheat Pool*, at p. 225. By the same token, mere compliance with a statute does not, in and of itself, preclude a finding of civil liability. See Linden, *supra*, at p. 219. Statutory standards can, however, be highly relevant to the assessment of reasonable conduct in a particular case, and in fact may render reasonable an act or omission which would otherwise appear to be negligent. This allows courts to consider the legislative framework in which people and companies must operate, while at the same time recognizing that one cannot avoid the underlying obligation of reasonable care simply by discharging statutory duties.

The foregoing view, though generally accepted, has long been resisted in railway cases. For more than 90 years, railway companies have benefited from a "special rule" at common law which placed them in a privileged position within the law of negligence. As long as a railway complied with the requirements imposed upon it by applicable statutes, regulations and administrative orders, it was under no further obligation — absent extraordinary circumstances — to act in an objectively reasonable manner. This rule has usually been framed in terms of limiting the "duty of care" owed by railways to the public. It is more easily understood as limiting the *standard* of care which railways must meet under an existing legal duty. Either way, the effect of the rule was the same: it excused railway companies in most cases from the ordinary obligation of prudence which governs other members of society.

The roots of the special rule reach back to the turn of the century, when railways occupied a position of unparalleled economic and social importance in the development of Canada. In *Grand Trunk Railway Co. v. McKay* (1903), 34 S.C.R. 81, this Court held that the safety measures prescribed by the *Railway Act* and the Board of Railway Commissioners were exhaustive, and railways could not be held liable for failing to take precautions beyond those requirements. The harshness of that doctrine was tempered somewhat by a separate line of cases, beginning with *Lake Erie & Detroit River Railway Co. v. Barclay* (1900), 30 S.C.R. 360, which held that in the event of exceptional danger or extraordinary conditions, a railway would be required to take greater safety measures than those officially prescribed. The *McKay* and *Barclay* doctrines have been combined in subsequent judgments to yield the current rule, which was restated by Dickson J. (as he then was) in *Paskivski, supra*, at pp. 698-99:

> A long line of cases ... establishes that a railway company's duty of care to users of public crossings is limited to discharge of statutory obligations under the *Railway Act* ... and compliance with orders of the Canadian Transport Commission — unless there are special or exceptional circumstances, in which event a common law duty of care will require additional precautions or safeguards.

This Court upheld the special rule in *Paskivski*, but it did so with reluctance. Dickson J. questioned the ongoing relevance of the rule at p. 708:

> The past seventy years have wrought many changes within Canada and today one might perhaps be inclined to question the relevance and validity of a rule of law which limits the common law duty of care of a railway to the special case or the exceptional case, particularly if those words are to receive a strict or narrow construction. It may well be that the interests of a young and undeveloped nation are best served by a minimum of impediment to industrial growth and economic expansion but in a more developed and populous nation this attitude of *laissez faire* may have to yield to accommodate the legitimate concern of society for other vital interests such as the safety and welfare of children.

Laskin C.J., concurring in the result reached by Dickson J., was even more pointed in his criticism of the rule, at pp. 689-90:

> ... I am unable to appreciate why railway companies, in the conduct of their transportation operations, are today entitled to the benefit of a special rule, more favourable to them, by which their common law liability is to be gauged. When all allowances are made for the force and legal effect of the rules and regulations of the regulatory agency, the Canadian Transport Commission, to which railway companies are subject, and when the question of their liability turns on the common law of negligence, as is the case here, they cannot claim to be judged by any different standards than those that apply to other persons or entities charged with liability for negligence.

The calls for reform expressed 24 years ago in *Paskivski* are more compelling today. The special status enjoyed by railway companies under the law of negligence can no longer be justified in principle and the time has come for that rule to be set aside. Although a doctrine of such long standing should not lightly be discarded, there is little to be gained from maintaining for its own sake a line of jurisprudence which has lost is relevance.

The Railways contend that the *McKay/Barclay* rule should be preserved in deference to the expertise of the Board (now the Canadian Transportation Agency) on matters of railway safety. That argument is unpersuasive. The orders of an administrative board may be relevant to the determination of reasonable behaviour in specific circumstances. However, as noted, such orders do not oust the underlying standard of reasonableness imposed by common law. A railway, like any other company or individual, is subject to generally applicable principles of negligence, and should not enjoy special protection when its actions or omissions cause harm to other members of society. See *Harris v. Canadian Pacific Ltd.* (1989), 59 D.L.R. (4th) 151 (B.C.C.A.), at p. 154-55.

It is useful to note that even when applying the *McKay/Barclay* rule, courts have implicitly recognized that statutory compliance cannot replace the common law standard of care, and can be accepted as a substitute for that standard only in certain circumstances. Thus, in "ordinary" cases, compliance with the statute has been held to exhaust the requirement of reasonable conduct; in "exceptional" cases, however, the statutory standard has been deemed "insufficient" and the common law has been retrieved to fill the gap.

...

The problem with the *McKay/Barclay* rule was that instead of focusing the analysis on whether statutory compliance by the railway was reasonable in the circumstances, it assumed that step as a matter of law and forced the plaintiff to rebut the presumption. ... With the abolishment of the special rule, the correct principles can now be stated more clearly. Compliance with a statutory standard of care does not abrogate or supersede the obligation to comply with the common law standard of care. The requirements are concurrent, and each carries its own penalty for breach. However, in appropriate circumstances, compliance with statutory standards may entirely satisfy the common law standard of care and thus absolve a defendant of liability in negligence. See *Bux v. Slough Metals Ltd.*, [1974] 1 All E.R. 262 (C.A.).

...

Additional support for this view can be found in s. 367(4) of the *Railway Act* which provides:

> **367.** ...
>
> (4) No inspection under or by the authority of this Act ... and nothing in this Act ... and nothing done, ordered, directed, required or provided for, or omitted to be done ... under or by virtue of this Act ... shall, except in so far as a compliance with the Act in question or with the order, direction, requirement or provision, constitutes a justification for what would otherwise be wrongful, relieve ... any company of or from, or in any way diminish or affect, any liability or responsibility resting on it by law ... for anything done or omitted to be done by that company, or for any wrongful act, negligence, default, misfeasance, malfeasance or nonfeasance of that company.

Section 367(4) confirms that compliance with statutory standards does not normally exhaust a railway's obligations under principles of negligence. See *Vincent*, *supra*, at p. 373. A railway is presumptively bound by the common law, subject only to those situations where compliance with the statute or regulations provides "a justification for what would otherwise be wrongful". Like any exculpatory provision limiting common law rights, that passage should be narrowly construed. In the absence of a clear indication to the contrary, compliance with statutory standards should not be viewed as excusing a railway's obligation to take whatever precautions are reasonably required in the circumstances.

The weight to be accorded to statutory compliance in the overall assessment of reasonableness depends on the nature of the statute and the circumstances of the case. It should be determined whether the legislative standards are necessarily applicable to the facts of the case. Statutory compliance will have more relevance in "ordinary" cases — *i.e.*, cases clearly within the intended scope of the statute — than in cases involving special or unusual circumstances. See *Paskivski*, *supra*, and *Anderson*, *supra*. It should also be determined whether the legislative standards are specific or general, and whether they allow for discretion in the manner of performance. It is a well-established principle that an action will lie against any party, public or private, "for doing that which the legislature has authorized, if it be done negligently". See *Geddis v. Bann Reservoir (Proprietors of)* (1878), 3 App. Cas. 430 (H.L.), at pp. 455-56; see also *Kamloops*, *supra*, at p. 11, and *Just*, *supra*, at p. 1245. It follows that a party acting under statutory authority must still take such precautions as are reasonable within the range of that authority to minimize the risks which may result from its actions. See *Tock*, *supra* (applying similar principles in the nuisance context).

Where a statute authorizes certain activities and strictly defines the manner of performance and the precautions to be taken, it is more likely to be found that compliance with the statute constitutes reasonable care and that no additional measures are required. By contrast, where a statute is general or permits discretion as to the manner of performance, or where unusual circumstances exist which are not clearly within the scope of the statute, mere compliance is unlikely to exhaust the standard of care. This approach strikes an appropriate balance among several important policies, including deference to legislative determinations on matters of railway safety, security for railways which comply with prescribed standards, and protection for those who may be injured as a result of unreasonable choices made by railways in the exercise of official authority.

3. *Application to the Case at Bar*

The first question is whether the Railways owed the appellant a duty of care. The Store Street tracks ran down the centre of an urban street, in direct proximity to the public. It was plainly foreseeable that carelessness by the Railways with respect to those tracks could cause injury to users of the street. Accordingly, a *prima facie* duty of care arose under the first step of the *Anns/Kamloops* test. See *Harris*, *supra*, at p. 155. Turning to the second step of the test, the Railways have not identified any legislative or judicial policies which would negate that duty or limit it. As noted, the authorities relied upon by the Railways concern the manner of carrying out a specific activity, and do not purport to limit civil liability. Those regulations do not affect the existence of a duty of care.

The standard of care required of the Railways was that of a prudent and reasonable person in the circumstances, having regard to all relevant factors including applicable statutes and regulations. It is undisputed that the Railways complied with certain safety standards prescribed in regulations and Board orders. The question is whether such compliance satisfied the requirement of objective reasonableness in this case and absolved the Railways of liability for the appellant's injury. …

[The court held that it did not, and restored the decision of the trial judge].

E. MENTAL AND PHYSICAL DISABILITIES

WENDEN v. TRIKHA

Alberta Court of Queen's Bench. (1991), 8 C.C.L.T. (2d) 138, 116 A.R. 81; am. 118 A.R. 319; added reasons (1992), 1 Alta. L.R. (3d) 283, 6 C.P.C. (3d) 15; affd 14 C.C.L.T. (2d) 225.

The defendant suffered from a mental disorder. He escaped from the psychiatric ward of a local hospital, and acting under the influence of delusions, drove at a high speed through an intersection against a red light and hit the plaintiff's vehicle. The defendant apparently had been under the delusion that his soul was being taken away by a comet and that his car was a time machine. He had been speeding in order to escape. The plaintiff was seriously injured and sued the defendant, as well as the local hospital and the staff psychiatrist. The defendant was charged with criminal negligence with respect to this incident, but was acquitted on the grounds of insanity.

The trial judge dismissed the action against the hospital and the psychiatrist, but upheld the claim against the defendant motorist. On the matter of the defendant's liability the trial judge held:

Murray J: At trial, Trikha's recollection of events was very spotty, which in part may have been due to electroconvulsive therapy treatments administered during his first admission to Alberta Hospital. Immediately after the accident, he told Constable Pevan that he had no memory of what had happened. …

Both Drs. Pascoe and Tweddle, psychiatrists, testified that, in their opinion, at the time of the accident Trikha did not understand the nature and quality of his acts, nor did he understand that he owed a duty of care to others. If he did understand that he had a duty of care, they testified that he was incapable of discharging it. Dr. Yaltho testified to like effect. …

It was Dr. Pascoe's view that after the accident, Trikha was aware of what he was doing and indeed knew that his ability to operate a motor vehicle had been severely impaired. Dr. Tweddle expressed the opinion that it is quite possible for a person who had been lost in his psychotic thinking, when confronted with reality by another, to relate to that person, such as occurred after the accident with Hetherington and Pevan. We know that one and one-half hours after the accident, Trikha's delusions and psychotic thinking were not evident when he was seen by Dr. Yaltho. …

I am satisfied that during that period, Trikha was experiencing a delusion which manifested itself in an unpredictable manner. Though he knew that he was driving his motor vehicle, how he was doing so, why he was doing so, and where he was going, it was his overriding purpose to complete his mission which submerged his sense of reality and thus the appreciation of his duty of care to other users of the highway. Following the accident, his delusions were, in turn, submerged by reality, as evidenced by the testimony of Hetherington and Pevan.

Can Trikha be found to have been negligent given his state of mind? The law on this point befits the subject matter. I have been referred to a number of texts, articles, and cases dealing with the subject of whether or not a lunatic can be held liable in tort, both of an intentional and unintentional nature.

The majority of the cases involve intentional torts, an essential element of which is the particular state of mind, such as assault, battery, fraud or deceit, and, in the appropriate case, malice, where that is a necessary ingredient. Unintentional torts for the most part take the form of negligence actions. In a number of cases, the tendency seems to have been to determine liability by utilizing one or more of the subjective tests enunciated in the M'Naghten rules for establishing the defence of insanity in criminal actions. [authorities omitted] With respect, I do not agree with this position.

The law of negligence is not concerned with punishing the tortfeasor, nor is it concerned with his or her culpability. The concern is one of compensation for those who have suffered loss or damage by reason of the tortious acts of another. The standard used to determine whether or not the elements of the tort of negligence are present is the external standard of the reasonable person. There are exceptions to this, such as in the case of infants and possibly in some instances where people have disabilities, but these are matters of policy which the courts have formulated. However, except for the *Buckley* and *Connolly* cases, I am not aware of Canadian authorities which could be interpreted to say that mental incapacity has been found to be a defence as such.

...

Civil courts are not normally concerned with the punitive aspect of the law or one's moral culpability, particularly in this area of tort law. In certain unique circumstances, culpability may become a factor when the facts are such as to warrant punitive damages, but those instances are rare and normally only arise in cases involving an intentional tort, which is not this case.

Professor Fleming in his text, *The Law of Torts*, 7th ed. (London: Sweet & Maxwell, 1988), p. 104 said:

> The position of lunatics remains controversial. Some courts have been prepared to excuse defendants whose lunacy was so extreme as to preclude them from appreciating their duty to take care, on the ground that negligence presupposes an ability for rational choice. But the weight of authority supports the contrary view that it would be unfairly prejudicial to accident victims if any allowance were made for a defendant's mental abnormality. Although this conclusion may seem incompatible with the lingering practice to excluse loss of consciousness by 'normal' defendants, it is a welcome recognition of the fact that considerations of moral fault are out of place, especially in relation to traffic accidents where personal liability has been largely displaced by insurance.

I see no reason why a person whose mental state is such that he does not appreciate that he owes a duty of care to others while operating his motor vehicle, by reason of which he caused loss or damage to others, should not be subjected to the same criteria for establishing civil liability as anyone else, namely, the objective standard of the reasonable driver. In my opinion, Associate Professor Robertson is correct when he states at p. 202 of his text *Mental Disability and the Law in Canada*, (Toronto: Carswell, 1987), that: "the law of negligence does not and should not take account of the defendant's mental disability in determining the applicable standard of care." Or, as put by Mr. Justice Linden in the fourth edition of his text, *Canadian Tort Law*, 4th ed. (Toronto: Butterworths, 1988), at pp. 38-40 and pp. 132 & 133:

The puzzle of the liability of the mentally disabled in negligence law is not yet satisfactorily resolved. Perhaps the best solution, short of a complete overhaul of the law, would be to treat the insane in the same way as everyone else. Although this might be somewhat hard on them, it is harder still on their victims to excuse them. At least in the automobile cases, they should not be allowed to escape liability.

NOTES

1. On appeal, the Alberta Court of Appeal affirmed the trial judgment (1993), 14 C.C.L.T. (2d) 225. The Court held that in order to exonerate himself the plaintiff had to show both that he could not have foreseen the dangers when he decided to drive and that he was too insane at the time of the accident to be held negligent. The Court held that, based on the trial judge's findings of fact, neither was proved in this case.

2. Mr. Justice Murray conceded that although tort law does not take into account mental disability, it does take into account physical incapacity. Thus, if the defendant's acts were not conscious or voluntary acts, there can be no liability.

   Why should there be this difference between mental and physical disabilities? If the policy of the law is, as is suggested by Murray J., that an innocent victim be compensated by compulsory automobile insurance funds, why should people injured by involuntary acts not receive compensation, while those injured by the acts of the mentally disabled can be compensated? Do you agree with Murray J. that negligence law concerns itself with compensation and not moral culpability? If this is so, what is negligence law all about and why not just abolish it in favour of a more efficient system of no fault compensation?

3. In an earlier and somewhat similar case *Buckley and T.T.C. v. Smith Transport Ltd.*, [1946] O.R. 798, [1946] 4 D.L.R. 721 (C.A.), the defendant drove his truck past a stop sign and into an intersection where he collided with a streetcar. The defence was that the driver had become insane and was labouring under the delusion that his truck was under remote electrical control from the company's head office and, as a result, he could not control its speed or stop it. In his judgment, Roach J.A. concluded that the defendant's mind "was so ravaged by disease that it should be held, as a matter of reasonable inference, that he did not understand the duty which rested upon him to take care, and further that if it could be said that he did understand and appreciate that duty, the particular delusion prevented him from discharging it". Therefore, there was no liability.

   Is the *Wenden v. Trikha* judgment in conflict with *Buckley*? Which approach do you prefer? Also see *Hutchings v. Nevin* (1992), 90 O.R. (2d) 776, 12 C.C.L.T. (2d) 259 (Gen. Div.), where the Court followed *Buckley* and rejected *Wenden*. Harris J. held that a motorist who believed that he was one of the sons of God, and who drove his car at a high speed because he was "going to see God," could not be held liable for the accident which resulted. The defendant was freed from liability because he did not understand and appreciate the duty of care which he owed.

4. In criminal law the *M'Naghten* test excuses from criminal responsibility those who do not understand what they are doing or those who do not realize that what they are doing is wrong. Why does tort law not follow the criminal law test? Should the tests be the same? Should one be stricter than the other? Is the widespread existence of insurance relevant here?"

5. *The Restatement of Torts, Second,* §283B provides that "unless the actor is a child, his insanity or other mental deficiency does not relieve the actor from liability for conduct which does not conform to the standard of a reasonable man under like circumstances". See *Johnson v. Lambotte*, 363 P. 2d 165 (1961); *Sforza v. Green Bus Lines*, 268 N.Y.S. 446 (1934). What are the policies competing for recognition?

6. Should a person who suffers a sudden heart attack while driving a car be civilly responsible for an accident that follows? In *Slattery v. Haley* (1922), 52 O.L.R. 95, [1923] 3 D.L.R. 156; affd 52 C.L.R. 102 (C.A.), the defendant, the driver of a motor car, having had no previous symptoms, was suddenly taken ill and became unconscious. The car ran onto the sidewalk and killed a 15-year-old boy. The plaintiff brought an action under the Ontario *Fatal Accidents Act* (Lord Campbell's Act) to recover damages resulting from death. The court held that there was no liability. The only ground for liability resulting from a lawful use of the highway is negligence and a negligent act "must be shown to have been the conscious act of the defendant's volition". Do you agree with this? See also *Lawson v. Wellesley Hospital* (1975), 9 O.R. (2d) 677, 61 D.L.R. (3d) 445 (C.A.), *per* Dubin J.A.; affd on other grounds [1978] 1 S.C.R. 893, 6 D.L.R. (3d) 688. See Chapter 2, *supra*.

7. Does it matter if the defendant had a heart condition and knew it could cause a heart attack at any time? See *Gordon v. Wallace* (1974), 2 O.R. (2d) 202, 42 D.L.R. (3d) 342 (H.C.). Can an epileptic ever take a car onto the highway? What does it depend upon?

Van Camp v. McAfoos

8. In *Roberts v. Ramsbottom*, [1980] 1 W.L.R. 823, [1980] 1 All E.R. 7 (Q.B.D.), a defendant, without prior warning, suffered a minor stroke at home, 20 minutes before being involved in a car accident. He went out anyway and, along the way, had two other minor accidents, after which he felt queer. He was not rendered unconscious by the stroke, however, suffering only a "clouding or impairment of his consciousness". Neill J. imposed liability, saying:

> I am satisfied that in a civil action … [a] driver will be able to escape liability if his actions at the relevant time were wholly beyond his control. The most obvious case is sudden unconsciousness. But if he retained some control, albeit imperfect control, and his driving, judged objectively, was below the required standard, he remains liable. His position is the same as the driver who is old or infirm. In my judgment unless the facts establish what the law recognizes as automatism the driver cannot avoid liability on the basis that owing to some malfunction of the brain his consciousness was impaired … "One cannot accept as exculpation anything less than total loss of consciousness".

9. Suppose someone who is so drunk as to be unaware of his or her actions crashes into someone else. Is there liability? Why? What if that person is high on LSD? Are these people different from someone in a state of automatism? See *Michael v. Pennsylvania R. Co.,* 331 Pa. 584, 1 A. 2d 242 (1930); *Morriss v. Marsen* [1952] 1 T.L.R. 947, [1952] 1 All E.R. 925.

10. Does it make any difference if the person was drunk or under the influence of drugs involuntarily and without his or her knowledge? For example, suppose a person is given an injection at a dentist's office not knowing it will cause sleepiness. While driving home the person falls asleep at the wheel and injures somebody. Is that person liable?

11. Should the patient have asked the dentist about the possible effects of the drug? Should the dentist have allowed the patient to leave the office without a warning? Compare *R. v. King,* [1962] S.C.R. 746, 35 D.L.R. (2d) 386. See also *Boomer v. Penn,* [1965] 1 O.R. 119, 52 D.L.R. (2d) 673 (H.C.), insulin reaction.

12. For an extremely helpful article see Robins, "Tort Liability of the Mentally Disabled" in Linden (ed), *Studies in Canadian Tort Law* (1968), p. 76, as well as in the *Special Lectures of the Law Society of Upper Canada* (1963). See also Bohlen, "Liability in Tort of Infants and Insane Persons" (1921), 21 Colum. L. Rev. 333; Splane, "Tort Liability of Mentally Ill in Negligence Actions" (1983-84), 93 Yale L.J. 153.

13. The *Civil Code* of the Province of Quebec handles this problem in this way:

> **Art. 1457.** Every person has a duty to abide by the rules of conduct which lie upon him, according to the circumstances, usage or law, so as not to cause injury to another.
>
> Where he is endowed with reason and fails in this duty, he is responsible for any injury he causes to another person and is liable to reparation for the injury, whether it be bodily, moral or material in nature.
>
> He is also liable, in certain cases, to reparation for injury caused to another by the act or fault of another person or by the act of things in his custody.

14. As for the physical disabilities generally, Linden has written:

> Negligence law has departed from its objective standard in its treatment of physical disabilities; it has made the standard of care partially subjective in order to take them into account. A person with a hearing disability is not required to hear, a physically disabled person need not be nimble, nor is a person who is blind obliged to see, although they are expected to avoid getting themselves into positions of danger.

Can you think of any reason why physical disability should be treated differently than mental illness?

15. What is the best solution to this issue? Draft a legislative rule?

F. THE YOUNG

1. Liability of the Young

HEISLER v. MOKE

Ontario High Court of Justice. [1972] 2 O.R. 446, 25 D.L.R. (3d) 670.

Addy J. (orally): In this particular case I shall not bother reviewing the facts. They are rather simple and the issue is a very narrow one as to whether there was any negligence on the part of the infant child causing the second injury, and, if there was such negligence, what was the resulting degree of that negligence. ...

In the case of adults, when one is considering the question of whether the person was negligent, the test to be applied is purely an objective one. It is that of the proverbial reasonable man. One must not ask oneself whether the particular individual whose conduct is under investigation having regard to his education, his ability, and his general knowledge and his physical or mental attributes, acted reasonably under the circumstances, but whether a reasonable man acting reasonably under those circumstances would have acted in that particular fashion. Where an individual whose conduct is under investigation (unless he is not at all responsible for his action) has not the physical or mental attributes of a normal person, he cannot escape a finding of negligence on the basis that, although a reasonable man would be expected to act in a certain manner, he, because of his natural failings must not be expected to do so.

The test, I repeat, is therefore clearly an objective one.

In the case of children, however, other considerations enter into play. There are two separate questions to be determined. The first one is whether the child, having regard to his age, his intelligence, his experience, his general knowledge and his alertness is capable of being found negligent at law in the circumstances under investigation. In other words, we consider here the particular child. As has been stated frequently, there is no absolute rule as to age in order to determine this question. Age is merely one of the factors, although the age of seven is often regarded as the crucial or critical age where normally a child may be expected to assume responsibility for his actions.

The test in order to determine this preliminary question is therefore a very subjective one. All of the qualities and defects of the particular child and all of the opportunities or lack of them which he might have had to become aware of any particular peril or duty of care must be considered.

In the case at bar I have found the plaintiff child to be fully capable of being found negligent. He is a bright, alert child and was nine years of age at the time of the accident. His recollection of events which occurred over three years ago was very good and he gave his evidence most clearly — much better as a matter of fact than many adults would.

One must next consider the second question, namely, whether he was negligent at all and, if so, to what degree?

In the case of infants the law clearly does not assume that full knowledge and responsibility occurs all of a sudden and, that at a given time in a child's development, once that child has attained the age of reason or an age where some degree of negligence can be attributed to him, then the test to be applied is the test of the reasonable man. At the very least, one must ask oneself what a reasonable child of that particular age could reasonably be expected to do and to foresee under those particular circumstances.

This test, which is still a very objective one, in the sense that the child's conduct is analysed in the light of that of a reasonable child of that age, seems to have been applied in the English case of *Gough v. Thorne*, [1966] 3 All E.R. 398, at p. 400. I am reading at p. 400 from the judgment of Lord Justice Salmon:

> The question as to whether the plaintiff can be said to have been guilty of contributory negligence depends on whether any ordinary child of 13½ could be expected to have done any more than this child did. I say, 'any ordinary child'. I do not mean a paragon of prudence; nor do I mean a scatter-brained child; but the ordinary girl of 13½.

This fairly objective test was also applied in the Australian case of *McHale v. Watson* (1966), 39 A.L.J.R. 459, which was quoted in the text of Wright and Linden, *Law of Torts*, 5th ed. (1970), at p. 199, and I am reading from that text at p. 199 and also at p. 200. At p. 199 the judgment of Mr. Justice Kitto reads as follows:

> I take this to mean that the test to be applied in determining whether the appellant's injury resulted from a breach of duty owed to her by the respondent should be stated not in terms of the reasonable foresight and prudence of an ordinary [person, but in terms of the reasonable foresight and prudence of an ordinary boy of twelve; and that the respondent should succeed because an ordinary] boy of twelve would not have appreciated that any risk to the appellant was involved in what he did.

At p. 200 it clearly states as follows:

> The principle is of course applicable to a child. The standard of care being objective, it is no answer for him, any more than it is for an adult, to say that the harm he caused was due to his being abnormally slow-witted, quick-tempered, absent-minded or inexperienced. But it does not follow that he cannot rely in his defence upon a limitation upon the capacity for foresight or prudence, nor as being personal to himself, but as being characteristic of humanity at his stage of development and in that sense normal.

Now if I were not otherwise bound by authority I would think that is the proper test to be applied to negligence on the part of a child. It seems, however, that in Canada, the test is considerably more subjective in determining this question.

The question as to whether there was, in fact, negligence on the part of the child and the degree of that negligence was considered in the leading case of *McEllistrum v. Etches*, [1956] S.C.R. 787, 6 D.L.R. (2d) 1. That case seems to base the test on that of a child of like age, intelligence and experience. I will read from the report at p. 793 S.C.R., pp. 6-7 D.L.R.; this is a judgment, of course, of the Supreme Court of Canada; it was delivered by Chief Justice Kerwin who, at the time, was delivering judgment on behalf of the court. It reads as follows:

> The present view of the law is summarized by Glanville L. Williams in his work on Joint Torts and Contributory Negligence, 1951, s. 89, p. 355. It should now be laid down that where the age is not such as to make a discussion of contributory negligence absurd, it is a question for the jury in each case whether the infant exercised the care to be expected from a child of like age, intelligence and experience.

It ... therefore, seems to be quite clear, on the authority of the Supreme Court of Canada, in our province the test would be based not only on the age but on the intelligence of that particular child or a child of similar intelligence and also on the question of the experience of the child.

In the present case the child was warned against jumping. It is not clear on the evidence who warned him. It was not brought out in examination-in-chief or in cross-examination. The second injury occurred while he was pressing down with his leg on the clutch of a tractor while holding on to the steering wheel to brace himself. Although an adult might be expected to realize that this was a dangerous act having regard to the recent injury to the leg and that such action might exert as much force, if not more force, on the leg than jumping on it, it certainly cannot find applying either the objective test of a reasonable child of nine or the more subjective test of that particular child considering his intelligence and experience and what he had been told, that the plaintiff could possibly be guilty of negligence, for he could not be expected to realize or foresee the consequences of his act. Thus, I attribute no negligence to the infant defendant.

NOTES

1. Should there be any allowance made for children who cause accidents? Is a child any different than an ignorant person or a mentally disabled one? What are the policy considerations?

2. Is the Supreme Court's test, employed by Mr. Justice Addy, a workable one? In *McErlean v. Sarel* (1987), 61 O.R. (2d) 396, at 411, 42 D.L.R. (4th) 577; leave to appeal to S.C.C. dismissed Feb. 25, 1988, 28 O.A.C. 399*n*, the court employed the

McEllistrum v. Etches ([1956] S.C.R. 787) test and described it as "essentially a subjective test which recognizes that the capacities of children are infinitely various and accordingly treats them on an individual basis and, out of a public interest in their welfare and protection, in a more lenient manner than adults".

3. Do you prefer the test propounded by Mr. Justice Kitto in *McHale v. Watson* (1966), 39 A.L.J.R. 459, [1966] A.L.R. 513, that is referred to by Mr. Justice Addy? Mr. Justice Kitto explained his choice of the test in these words:

> In regard to the things which pertain to foresight and prudence — experience, understanding of causes and effects, balance of judgment, thoughtfulness — it is absurd, indeed it is a misuse of language, to speak of normality in relation to persons of all ages taken together. In those things normality is, for children, something different from what normality is for adults; the very concept of normality is a concept of rising levels until "years of discretion" are attained. The law does not arbitrarily fix upon any particular age for this purpose, and tribunals of fact may well give effect to different views as to the age at which normal adult foresight and prudence are reasonably to be expected in relation to particular sets of circumstances. But up to that stage the normal capacity to exercise those two qualities necessarily means the capacity which is normal for a child of the relevant age.

4. Are these tests subjective or objective or do they contain elements of subjectivity as well as objectivity? See *Strehlke v. Camenzind et al.* (1980), 111 D.L.R. (3d) 319, [1980] 4 W.W.R. 464 (Alta. Q.B.), three different tests outlined.

5. It is clear that children of "tender age", which probably includes children of up to five or six, are totally immune from liability and are also incapable of being contributorily negligent. The standard expressed in *Heisler v. Moke* comes into play only after children reach five or six years of age and is employed until they are well into their teens. At some point in their later teens, children begin to be judged by the ordinary adult standard. There have been no precise borderlines drawn between these two categories. The statutory age of majority that has been enacted in Ontario, for example, was not specifically made to apply for purposes of tort law, but anyone over 18 years of age should be expected to be treated as an adult. See Linden, *Canadian Tort Law,* 6th ed. (1997), p. 136.

6. Should we enact legislation to sort this out? Can you formulate an acceptable principle? The Ontario Law Reform Commission, in its *Report on Family Law, Part I, Torts* (1969) decided to make no recommendation on the matter on the ground that there was "no practical alternative to the existing law". It concluded that "the age of responsibility is best left to the courts to determine in each case owing to the great variety of circumstances that can exist". The *Criminal Code*, R.S.C. 1985, c. C-46, s. 13, on the other hand, excuses children under the age of 12 from all penal liability. Would a similar cutoff be acceptable for tort?

7. Should the same test be used whether the child is a plaintiff or a defendant? What can be said for a different rule in the two situations? In practice, would a jury be as strict with an infant plaintiff as with an infant defendant?

8. When young people are engaged in adult activity, they are now held to the objective standard as if they were adults. This idea was developed in the United States in *Dellwo v. Pearson* (1961), 107 N.W. 859, where Loevinger J. explained:

> While minors are entitled to be judged by standards commensurate with age, experience, and wisdom when engaged in activities appropriate to their age, experience, and wisdom, it would be unfair to the public to permit a minor in the operation of a motor vehicle to observe any other standards of care and

conduct than those expected of all others. A person observing children at play with toys, throwing balls, operating tricycles or velocipedes, or engaged in other childhood activities may anticipate conduct that does not reach an adult standard of care or prudence. However, one cannot know whether the operator of an approaching automobile, airplane, or powerboat is a minor or an adult, and usually cannot protect himself against youthful imprudence even if warned. Accordingly, we hold that in the operation of an automobile, airplane, or powerboat, a minor is to be held to the same standard of care as an adult.

9. This concept has been adopted by the *Restatement of Torts, Second,* 283A and Mr. Justice Goodman, in *Ryan v. Hickson* (1974), 7 O.R. (2d) 352, 55 D.L.R. (3d) 196 (H.C.J.), a case involving 12 and 14-year olds driving snowmobiles.

It was reaffirmed by the Ontario Court of Appeal in *McErlean v. Sarel* (1987), 61 O.R. (2d) 396, 42 D.L.R. (4th) 577 (C.A.); leave to appeal to S.C.C. dismissed Feb. 25, 1988, 28 O.A.C. 399*n*, at 412, a case in which there was a collision between two trail bikes driven by two teenagers (13 and 15) on different roadways in an abandoned gravel pit slated for park development. Both were held equally at fault, but the municipality escaped liability. The Court explained:

> Where a child engages in what may be classified as an "adult activity", he or she will not be accorded special treatment, and no allowance will be made for his or her immaturity. In those circumstances, the minor will be held to the same standard of care as an adult engaged in the same activity ... Just as the law does not permit a youth engaged in the operation of an automobile to be judged by standards other than those expected of other drivers, it cannot permit youths engaged in the operation of other motorized vehicles (whether there are any statutory restrictions with respect to age or not) to be judged by standards other than those expected of others engaged in the same or like activity. The critical factor requiring greater care is the motor-powered nature of the vehicle. Automobiles, snowmobiles, power boats, motorcycles, trail bikes, motorized mini-bikes and similar devices are, it is manifest, increasingly available to teenagers, and are equally as lethal in their hands as in the hands of an adult. Machines of this nature, capable as they are of high rates of speed, and demanding as they do the utmost caution and responsibility in conduct, present a grave danger to the teenage operator in particular, and to others in general if the care used in the course of the activity drops below the care which the reasonable and prudent adult would use. The potential risks of harm involved in such activities are apparent, and they must be recognized by parents who permit their teenagers the use of such powerful machines. While teenagers may in other instances be judged by standards commensurate with their age, intelligence and experience, it would be unfair and, indeed, dangerous to the public to permit them in the operation of these power-driven vehicles to observe any lesser standard than that required of all other drivers of such vehicles. The circumstances of contemporary life require a single standard of care with respect to such activities.

See Binchi "The Adult Activities Doctrine" (1985), 11 William Mitchell L. Rev. 733. What do you think of this principle?

10. If a 16-year-old drives an inebriated 14-year-old home and drops him off nearby, eventually resulting in an accident on the road causing his death and nervous shock to a third person, is the adult activity standard applicable or is it the *McEllistrum v. Etches* standard? Is the impugned activity here that of driving or is it the act of dropping off someone? See *Nespolon v. Alford et al* (1998), 40 O.R. (3d) 355 (C.A.), *per* Abella J.A. (Leave to appeal refused by S.C.C.).

11. There are problems involving parents' liability *for* the acts of their children. See, for example *Ryan v. Hickson* (1974), 7 O.R. (2d) 352, 55 D.L.R. (3d) 196 (H.C.J.). See *infra*, Chapter 7. Liability depends on whether in the circumstances the parents were negligent in the way they trained their children or in the way they supervised them.

12. There is also the problem of liability *to* children. In the case of *Teno v. Arnold* (1976), 11 O.R. (2d) 585, 67 D.L.R. (3d) 9 (C.A.); vard (1978), 3 C.C.L.T. 272 (S.C.C.). Zuber J.A. held a mother partially to blame for an accident in which her child was injured by an automobile while returning from purchasing ice cream from a street vendor. This decision was reversed by the Supreme Court on the facts. Zuber J.A. also held the ice cream vendor partially to blame, explaining "A pied piper cannot plead his inability to take care of his followers when it was he who played the flute." This aspect of the case was affirmed by the Supreme Court. See also *Gambino v. DiLeo*, [1971] 2 O.R. 131, 17 D.L.R. (3d) 167 (H.C,); *Harris v. T.T.C.*, [1967] S.C.R. 460, 63 D.L.R. (2d) 450. Must a parent secure a child in a seat belt? *Ducharme v. Davies* (1981), 12 Sask. R. 137; vard (1984), 29 Sask. R. 54, [1984] 1 W.W.R. 699 (C.A.). Must a non-parent driver strap a child in? See *Galaske v. O'Donnell* [1994] 1 S.C.R. 670.

13. Although the law is prepared to relax the standard of care demanded of children, it apparently is not prepared to be so lenient insofar as the elderly are concerned. According to one author, the unavoidable infirmities of old age, such as loss of memory or strength, impairment of hearing or vision, diminished perception, and loss of reflexes justify a relaxed standard of care for the elderly. See Barrett, "Negligence and the Elderly: A Proposal for a Relaxed Standard of Care" (1984), 17 John Marshall L. Rev. 873. Do you agree? Does this raise again the old issue of what negligence law's function is, especially in relation to activities which are covered by liability insurance, such as driving?

14. See Alexander, "Tort Responsibility of Parents and Teachers for Damage Caused by Children" (1965), 16 U. Toronto L.J. 165; Dunlop, "Torts Relating to Infants" (1966), 5 West L. Rev. 116; Shulman, "The Standard of Care Required for Children" (1927-28), 37 Yale L.J. 618; Bohlen, "Liability in Tort of Infants and Insane Persons" (1924), 23 Mich. L. Rev. 9; Hoyano, "The Prudent Parent" (1984), 18 U.B.C.L. Rev. 1.

G. PROFESSIONAL NEGLIGENCE

l. Doctors

CHALLAND v. BELL

Alberta Supreme Court. (1959), 18 D.L.R. (2d) 150, 27 W.W.R. 182.

Riley J.: On Sunday morning, August 16, 1953, about the hour of 9.30 a.m., the plaintiff fell while working in his cattle barn on his farm. He farms in the vicinity of Leeside in the Province of Alberta. In falling, he broke his left forearm, fracturing both the radial and ulnar bones at the mid-third of the forearm. Either the radius or the ulna punctured the flesh causing a compound or open fracture. The plaintiff was then taken to the defendant for medical treatment. The defendant is a general practitioner at the town of Rimbey in the Province of Alberta. He graduated with a medical degree in 1949 and commenced the practice of his profession at Rimbey in the year 1951.

The defendant looked at the plaintiff's fracture about the hour of 11.30 a.m. on the same day. The defendant looked at the wound which was oozing blood. The arm was x-rayed. The plaintiff was put under an anaesthetic. The defendant spread the wound with forceps but did not observe any foreign material in the wound. The tissue which he saw looked alive and with the blood oozing, the defendant's judgment was that the wound was a clean one. Very probably from the bone perforating from within out and the absence of any sign of foreign material, the defendant was led to the conclusion that the wound had not been contaminated. The defendant soaked gauze in merthiolate and applied it around the wound and the sharp edges of the wound. The defendant then proceeded to set the fracture and the arm was placed in a cast. The defendant made periodic checks of the plaintiff and instructed a dosage of 400,000 units of penicillin and one-half gram of streptomycin twice a day. On the same Sunday afternoon he noted some swelling of the arm which he concluded was not excessive and noted that when he, the defendant, touched the plaintiff's hand, the return of colour seemed to be adequate. The defendant personally checked the patient's condition on the Monday morning between 9 and 10 a.m., noted the circulation was probably not so good as it should be, noted excessive swelling, and made a saw cut in the upper and lower ends of the cast so as to loosen the same. On the same Monday afternoon, he made a further cut in the cast because the circulation still had not improved.

On Tuesday morning, the defendant became somewhat alarmed about the circulatory changes in the plaintiff's hand, concluded the plaintiff was running into considerable difficulty probably with spasms of blood vessels following the injury, concluded the plaintiff needed the services of a specialist, telephoned Dr. Gordon Wilson, a specialist in orthopaedic surgery, and arranged that the plaintiff be taken to the University Hospital, Edmonton, Alberta, for an examination by the said Dr. Wilson. The plaintiff arrived at the University Hospital on the same Tuesday afternoon, was seen by Dr. Wilson, who diagnosed acute fulminating gas gangrene and immediately amputated the plaintiff's arm at a point some three inches below the elbow.

The plaintiff alleges that the arm was lost as a result of negligent treatment by the defendant at the Rimbey Hospital. While many grounds of negligence are alleged in the statement of claim, at the trial the alleged negligence relied on was:

1. The defendant failed or neglected to properly clean out or debride the wound caused by the bone puncturing the plaintiff's skin. 2. The defendant failed to watch the circulation in the plaintiff's arm and failed to remove the cast and improve the circulation in the arm when he knew or ought to have known that the circulation of the arm was impaired.

The evidence shows that gas gangrene bacteria (bacillus welchii), are commonly found in soil contaminated by farm animals, and also upon the clothing and skin of farmers working around cattle. Farms are their natural habitat and where a fracture has been open to the air in a barn, it is particularly susceptible to gas gangrene infection. Gas gangrene bacteria flourish in dead and devitalized tissue as in such dead tissue there is a shortage of oxygen. Where such conditions exist, the bacteria if present thrive. The means commonly used to prevent such a condition from existing is debridement. Debridement or excision of the wound is the making of an incision and the removal of any dead and devitalized tissue to give all parts of the wound an adequate blood supply with sufficient oxygen.

As is not unusual in this type of case, the plaintiff, in support of his case, relief on the evidence of Dr. John E. Mitchell who is a specialist in the practice of surgery in the city of Red Deer, his evidence being supported by several authoritative text books; and the defendant called two learned and eminent specialists, Dr. E.P. Scarlett of the Calgary Associate Clinic, and Dr. Wilson to whom I previously made reference.

Before pinpointing the evidence of the experts, it might be useful to review briefly the law relating to the standard of care required of a general practitioner. In *Salmond on Torts*, 12th ed., pp. 420-1, it is stated:

> Doctors, surgeons, and dentists owe to their patients a duty in tort as well as in contract. It is expected of such a professional man that he should show a fair, reasonable and competent degree of skill, it is not required that he should use the highest degree of skill, for there may be persons who have higher education and greater advantages than he has, nor will he be held to have guaranteed a cure.

Fleming in his book, *The Law of Torts*, 1957, states at p. 128: "Thus a surgeon is expected to apply the degree of care which a normally skilled member of his profession may reasonably be expected to exercise."

And on p. 129: "The skill required of beginners presents an increasingly difficult problem in modern society. While it is necessary to encourage them, it is equally evident that they cause more than their proportionate share of accidents. The paramount social need for compensating accident victims, however, clearly outweighs all competing considerations, and the beginning is, therefore, held to the standard of those who are reasonably skilled and proficient in that particular occupation or calling." ...

The most authoritative Canadian decision is that of the Supreme Court of Canada in *Wilson v. Swanson*, 5 D.L.R. (2d) 113, [1956] S.C.R. 804. In that case a skilled surgeon operating at the Vancouver General Hospital embarked on radical surgery after receiving a pathologist's report during the course of the operation. His judgment was proved to have been wrong in that the lesion was not malignant and consequently there had been an unnecessary resection of a large portion of the stomach, pancreas and spleen. In the British Columbia Court of Appeal [(1956), 2 D.L.R. (2d) 193] the surgeon was held liable. In the Supreme Court of Canada the appeal was allowed and the trial judgment [[1955] 3 D.L.R. 171] was restored (*per* Rand, Abbott and Nolan, JJ., with Locke, J., and Kerwin, C.J.C., dissenting).

At pp. 119-20 Rand, J., (Nolan, J., concurring) said:

> In the presence of such a delicate balance of factors, the surgeon is placed in a situation of extreme difficulty; whatever is done runs many hazards from causes which may only be guessed at; what standard does the law require of him in meeting it? What the surgeon by his ordinary engagement undertakes with the patient is that he possesses the skill, knowledge and judgment of the generality or average of the special group or class of technicians to which he belongs and will faithfully exercise them. In a given situation some may differ from others in that exercise, depending on the significance they attribute to the factors in the light of their own experience. The dynamics of the human body of each individual are themselves individual and there are lines of doubt and uncertainty at which a clear course of action may be precluded.
>
> There is here only the question of judgment; what of that? The test can be no more than this: was the decision the result of the exercise of the surgical intelligence professed? or was what was done such that, disregarding it may be the exceptional case or individual, in all the circumstances, at least the preponderant opinion of the group would have been against it? If a substantial opinion confirms it, there is no breach or failure. ...
>
> An error in judgment has long been distinguished from an act of unskillfulness or carelessness or due to lack of knowledge. Although universally accepted procedure must be observed, they furnish little or no assistance in resolving such a predicament as faced the surgeon here. In such a situation a decision must be made without delay based on limited known and unknown factors; and the honest and in-

telligent exercise of judgment has long been recognized as satisfying the professional obligation.

The test laid down by the Supreme Court of Canada is a threefold one:

1. The surgeon undertakes that he possesses the skill, knowledge and judgment of the average. 2. In judging that average, regard must be had to the special group to which he belongs. From a general practitioner at a rural point, a different standard is exacted than from a specialist at an urban point. 3. If the decision was the result of exercising that average standard, there is no liability for an error in judgment.

[The expert evidence was reviewed.]

Where the experts disagree but some of them support the treatment given, then surely the treatment given by the general practitioner should not be criticized, and one must always keep in mind the importance of viewing the treatment and seeing matters through the eyes of the attending physician.

Dr. Wilson stated that as a specialist he had on many occasions treated similar injuries in the way the defendant treated this one. In other words, the defendant's treatment was not only correct for a general practitioner but in fact did not differ from that which a specialist would have given.

All of the medical witnesses agreed that following an injury such as this, the patient suffers from "tissue tension" and that complaints of a tight cast are common when in fact such is not the case. Thus the statements by the lay witnesses, relatives of the plaintiff, that the cast was too tight are of little significance. Further, another circulatory condition was present — Volkmann's ischemic paralysis — due to the trauma of the injury itself and not due to a tight cast.

It is impossible for this Court not to feel a profound sympathy for the plaintiff in his great misfortune, but "we must not condemn as negligence that which is only misadventure". No medical practitioner becomes an insurer that he will effect a cure, nor do the Courts condemn an honest exercise of judgment even though other practitioners may disagree with that judgment. It appears, too, that the text books quoted to this Court may generalize too much and that the need for debriding may depend on such things as the size of the wound and its nature. Was it a small puncture, one from within as in the case at bar, or a dirty, contused contaminated mess from without?

In the result the plaintiff's action must necessarily be dismissed.

NOTES

1. What standard of care must a doctor live up to? Is it objective or subjective? Does it provide sufficient protection for patients? Is it too demanding for medical practitioners? Do you agree with the result of *Challand v. Bell?*

2. In *ter Neuzen v. Korn* [1995], 3 S.C.R. 674 at 693, the plaintiff contracted HIV as a result of artificial insemination in 1985. The defendant doctor had acted in accordance with the usual medical practice at the time, when the risk of HIV was not widely known. He did not screen the semen donor. Mr. Justice Sopinka reiterated the standard of care expected of doctors:

> It is well settled that physicians have a duty to conduct their practice in accordance with the conduct of a prudent and diligent doctor in the same cir-

> cumstances. In the case of a specialist, such as a gynaecologist and obstetrician, the doctor's behaviour must be assessed in light of the conduct of other ordinary specialists, who possess a reasonable level of knowledge, competence and skill expected of professionals in Canada, in that field. A specialist, such as the respondent, who holds himself out as possessing a special degree of skill and knowledge, must exercise the degree of skill of an average specialist in his field.

As for the weight of the customary practice in the medical profession, Justice Sopinka stated:

> It is generally accepted that when a doctor acts in accordance with a recognized and respectable practice of the profession, he or she will not be found to be negligent. This is because courts do not ordinarily have the expertise to tell professionals that they are not behaving appropriately in their field. In a sense, the medical profession as a whole is assumed to have adopted procedures which are in the best interests of patients and are not inherently negligent.
>
> I conclude from the foregoing that, as a general rule, where a procedure involves difficult or uncertain questions of medical treatment or complex, scientific or highly technical matters that are beyond the ordinary experience and understanding of a judge or jury, it will not be open to find a standard medical practice negligent. On the other hand, as an exception to the general rule, if a standard practice fails to adopt obvious and reasonable precautions which are readily apparent to the ordinary finder of fact, then it is no excuse for a practitioner to claim that he or she was merely conforming to such a negligent common practice.

The doctor was relieved of liability concerning HIV since he acted in accordance with the general practice at that time in failing to screen the semen donor. The matter was sent back on the issue of screening with regard to other diseases.

3. The standard of care demanded of doctors and other professionals is the same both under Quebec civil law and English common law. In *Lapointe v. Hopital Le Gardeur*, [1992] 1 S.C.R. 382, 90 D.L.R. (4th) 7, Madame Justice L'Heureux-Dubé stated that the conduct of doctors "must be assessed against the conduct of a prudent and diligent doctor placed in the same circumstances".

4. In *Whitehouse v. Jordan*, [1981] 1 W.L.R. 246, [1981] 1 All E.R. 267 (H.L.), Lord Fraser explained what was meant by Lord Denning's statement that "an error of judgment is not negligent" in these words:

> ... Lord Denning M.R. must have meant to say that an error of judgment "is not *necessarily* negligent". But, in my respectful opinion, the statement as it stands is not an accurate statement of the law. Merely to describe something as an error of judgment tells us nothing about whether it is negligent or not. The true position is that an error of judgment may, or may not, be negligent; it depends on the nature of the error. If it is one that would not have been made by a reasonably competent professional man professing to have the standard and type of skill that the defendant held himself out as having, and acting with ordinary care, then it is negligent. If, on the other hand, it is an error that a man, acting with ordinary care, might have made, then it is not negligent.

In this case, an attempted forceps delivery failed and had to be stopped. A Caesarian was performed properly, but the baby suffered brain damage due to asphyxia during the aborted forceps delivery. The action was dismissed on the basis that there was no negligence proven against the doctor.

5. Courts recognize that doctors are human and cannot be expected to perform all of their work to perfection. Thus, it was said that "highly professional" and "honourable"

medical practitioners may, "like every human being does on occasion", make mistakes that are negligent. (See Galligan J. in *Moffat v. Witelson* (1980), 29 O.R. (2d) 7, at 12, 111 D.L.R. (3d) 712 (H.C.)). So too, it has been acknowledged that doctors may take a holiday occasionally and leave their patients to the care of others while they are away. As was stated, "Doctors are human, too, and they are entitled to attend conferences and take vacations, as long as appropriate steps are taken to see that a competent substitute is available to their patients during their absence." (See Linden J. in *White v. Turner* (1981), 31 O.R. (2d) 773, 120 D.L.R. (3d) 269, 15 C.C.L.T. 81, at 105; affd (1982), 47 O.R. (2d) 764*n*, 12 D.L.R. (3d) 319*n* (C.A.).)

6. What is the standard of care expected of a specialist? See *ter Neuzen v. Korn*, *supra.* A psychiatrist must live up to the standard of a reasonable psychiatrist. What about a psychologist? See *Haines v. Bellisimo* (1977), 18 O.R. (2d) 177 (H.C.). Must a general practitioner consult a specialist if the case requires one? See Dubin J.A. in *MacDonald v. York County Hospital* (1974), 10 O.R. (2d) 653; affd, [1976] 2 S.C.R. 825.

7. What standard of care is required of an inexperienced doctor? Mr. Justice Philp has recently declared that:

> The same degree of skill is expected of an inexperienced surgeon as of an experienced one.

See *Miles v. Judges* (1998), 37 C.C.L.T. (2d) 160 (Ont. H.C.), at p. 175; see also *Dale v. Munthali* (1977), 16 O.R. (2d) 532 (H.C.)

8. How should an intern be treated? What are the competing policies? See *Jones v. Manchester Corp.*, [1952] 2 Q.B. 852, [1952] 2 All E.R. 125; *McKeachie v. Alvarez* (1971), 17 D.L.R. (3d) 87 (B.C.S.C.), novice surgeon. In *Vancouver General Hospital v. Fraser,* [1952] 2 S.C.R. 36, at 46, [1952] 3 D.L.R. 785, Rand J. said that an intern "must use the undertaken degree of skill, and that cannot be less than the ordinary skill of a junior doctor in appreciation of the indications and symptoms of injury before him, as well as an appreciation of his own limitations and of the necessity for caution in anything he does". What does this mean? Does the post or office occupied by the doctor make a difference? See *Wilsher v. Essex Area Health Authority*, [1988] A.C. 1074, [1986] 3 All E.R. 801 (C.A.).

9. Should a higher standard of performance be required of a city doctor than a country doctor? In *McCormick v. Marcotte*, [1972] S.C.R. 18, 20 D.L.R. (3d) 345, in an *obiter dictum*, Abbott J. said that doctors must possess and use "that reasonable degree of learning and skill ordinarily possessed by practitioners *in similar communities* in similar cases" (emphasis added). Do you agree? Are not all the doctors in a province licensed by the same body? Would this disparity have been more justified in an earlier time when transportation and communications were less advanced? See *Town v. Archer* (1902), 4 O.L.R. 383, at 388 (H.C.); Waltz, "The Rise and Gradual Fall of the Locality Rule in Medical Malpractice Litigation" (1969), 18 de Paul L. Rev. 408. See Picard, *Legal Liability of Doctors and Hospitals in Canada*, 2nd ed. (1984).

10. Can a doctor rely on a patient to behave reasonably in following instructions with regard to medication? Does a doctor have to check up on whether the patient is taking or not taking medication as prescribed? Can a patient be contributorily negligent along with a doctor? See *Crossman v. Stewart* (1977), 82 D.L.R. (2d) 677, 5 C.C.L.T. 45 (B.C.S.C.), the plaintiff was two-thirds at fault for getting medication illegally and taking it beyond the period he should have, the doctor was one-third to blame.

11. Is a doctor liable for failing to report a case of child abuse? See *Brown v. University of Alberta Hospital* (1997), 33 C.C.L.T. (2d) 113 (Alta. Q.B.). Is a doctor liable for failing to warn an epileptic patient that there is a risk of an epileptic seizure while driving

by virtue of a change in the medication being prescribed? See *Joyal v. Starreveld*, [1996] 4 W.W.R. 707 (Alta. Q.B.).

12. What if a third person, not the patient, is injured as a result of a doctor's negligence, as for example, where an insane person, allowed to be at large, kills someone? See *Kines Estate v. Lychuk Estate* (1996), 10 W.W.R. 426 (Man. Q.B.); *cf. Tarasoff v. Regents of U.C.* (1976), 131 Cal. Rptr. 14. What if a doctor fails to perform an abortion and a child is born, causing financial loss to the biological father? Can he be liable to the father? See *Freeman v. Sutter* (1996), 29 C.C.L.T. (2d) 215 (Man. C.A.).

13. The problems of proof in a medical malpractice case are enormous, mainly because of the need for expert witnesses. According to some, the difficulties are compounded by a "conspiracy of silence" among doctors. Others deny that any such phenomenon exists. They explain that any hesitancy among doctors to testify stems from the uncertainty of medical science and the importance of judgmental factors in treatment.

    In 1971, a team from the Osgoode Law School circulated a medical-legal questionnaire to Ontario doctors. One of the questions asked concerned the physician's response if he or she were to witness some grossly negligent conduct by another doctor and if that other doctor was sued by his or her patient because of it. Of the 1,835 responses, 2.3 per cent said they would *volunteer* the information they had to the patient or to his or her lawyer; 22.2 per cent stated they would disclose the information if *asked* about it; 1.5 per cent claimed they would refuse to disclose the information or to co-operate even if asked; 72.1 per cent declared they would disclose the information in court if subpoenaed, but only if subpoenaed; while 2.0 per cent thought they would refuse to disclose the information in court even if subpoenaed. On the basis of this evidence, do you believe there is a "conspiracy" of silence? How willing would one lawyer be to testify in a malpractice suit against another lawyer? See generally *Report of the Attorney-General's Committee on Medical Evidence in Civil Cases* (1965); Sharpe, "The Conspiracy of Silence Dilemma" (1973), 40 Ont. Med. Rev. 25.

14. Some judges have expressed a reluctance to second-guess doctors: "The less the courts try to tell the doctors how to practise medicine the better", Gould J. in *McLean v. Weir*, [1977] 5 W.W.R. 609, 3 C.C.L.T. 801 (S.C.); affd 18 B.C.L.R. 325, [1980] 4 W.W.R. 330 (C.A.).

15. Expert evidence is usually required but not always. For example, in *Sylvester v. Crits*, [1956] S.C.R. 991, 5 D.L.R. (2d) 601, during an operation an explosion occurred by reason of a spark of electricity setting an ether-oxygen mixture aflame. The court indicated that, although steps in the procedure may be governed by "standard practice", the avoidance of danger from static electricity is not a question to be decided by such a criterion and, indeed, a practice may involve such an unnecessary risk as to be held improper. In *Taylor v. Gray* (1937), 11 M.P.R. 588, [1937] 4 D.L.R. 123, the Court of Appeal for New Brunswick dealt with a claim against a surgeon for negligence, based on the fact that forceps were discovered in the plaintiff's abdomen after an operation performed by the defendant. The court used the following language:

    > While men eminent in their profession have given evidence of their system of practice, yet every system put forward must stand the test of judicial examination and, possibly, of reprobation by a jury. There is no question here of skill displayed in the operation itself, nor of the technique employed in performing it. In such matters we have to be governed by the best professional opinion we can get. But in a case which involves none of these elements but simply whether or not the defendant has shown that he was not negligent in respect to the non-removal of the instrument from the abdominal cavity, the opinion of one man is about as good as that of another.

16. In a similar vein, in *Anderson v. Chasney,* [1950] 4 D.L.R. 223 (S.C.C.), the Chief Justice of Manitoba had this to say in the Court of Appeal:

> While the method in which the operation was performed may be purely a matter of technical evidence, the fact that a sponge was left in a position where it was or was not dangerous is one which the ordinary man is competent to consider in arriving at a decision as to whether or not there was negligence.

The Supreme Court merely concluded:

> Since the appellant had not used sponges with tapes attached, which were available, or had a count kept by the nurse in attendance of the number used and removed, it was his clear duty to make a thorough search following the operation to determine whether any sponges remained in the cavity. We agree ... that the proper inference to be drawn from the evidence is that the appellant failed in the discharge of this duty and that the death of the child was attributable to this failure.

17. See Picard and Robertson, *Legal Liability of Doctors and Hospitals in Canada,* 3rd ed. (1996); Linden, "The Negligent Doctor" (1973), 11 Osgoode Hall L.J. 31.

(a) Duty of Disclosure

Canadian doctors have a duty to disclose to their patients certain risks that may arise out of surgical and other procedures in order to facilitate an informed choice by them. In the past, this issue was dealt with as "informed consent", which, if absent, could yield liability for battery. Following the leading case of *Reibl v. Hughes*, [1980] 2 S.C.R. 880 (S.C.C.), however, negligence principles are to be employed in this area, battery law being limited only to those cases where there was no consent at all, where the treatment went beyond the consent or where there was fraud. As will be seen the cases have become rather complex. There are debates about what must be disclosed and disagreement about the causal connection required. See Picard and Roberts, *Legal Liability of Doctors and Hospitals in Canada*, 3rd ed. (1996), chapter 3; Linden, *Canadian Tort Law*, 6th ed. (1997) at p. 163; Klar, *Tort Law*, 2nd ed. (1996) at p. 306.

REIBL v. HUGHES

Supreme Court of Canada. [1980] 2 S.C.R. 880, 114 D.L.R. (3d) 1, 33 N.R. 361, 14 C.C.L.T. 1.

Laskin C.J.C.: The plaintiff-appellant, then 44 years of age, underwent serious surgery on March 18, 1970 for the removal of an occlusion in the left internal carotid artery, which had prevented more than a 15 per cent flow of blood through the vessel. The operation was competently performed by the defendant-respondent, a qualified neurosurgeon. However, during or immediately following the surgery the plaintiff suffered a massive stroke which left him paralyzed on the right side of his body and also impotent. The plaintiff had, of course, formally consented to the operation. Alleging, however, that his was not an "informed consent", he sued for damages and recovered on this ground in both battery and negligence. The trial Judge, Jaines J. [reported at 16 O.R. (2d) 306, 78 D.L.R. (3d) 35, 1 L. Med. Q. 50], awarded a global sum of $225,000.

A majority of the Ontario Court of Appeal ordered a new trial on both liability and damages [reported at 21 O.R. (2d) 14, 89 D.L.R. (3d) 112, 6 C.C.L.T. 227, 2 L. Med. Q. 153]. Speaking through Brooke J.A. (Blair J.A. concurring) the Court ruled out battery as a possible ground of liability on the facts of the case. Jessup

J.A., dissenting in part, would have ordered a new trial on damages alone, accepting the judgment at trial on liability.

It is now undoubted that the relationship between surgeon and patient gives rise to a duty of the surgeon to make disclosure to the patient of what I would call all material risks attending the surgery which is recommended. The scope of the duty of disclosure was considered in *Hopp v. Lepp*, a judgment of this Court, reported at (1980), 13 C.C.L.T. 66, [1980] 4 W.W.R. 645, where it was generalized as follows (C.C.L.T., p. 87):

> In summary, the decided cases appear to indicate that, in obtaining the consent of a patient for the performance upon him of a surgical operation, a surgeon, generally, should answer any specific questions posed by the patient as to the risks involved and should, without being questioned, disclose to him the nature of the proposed operation, its gravity, any material risks and any special or unusual risks attendant upon the performance of the operation. However, having said that, it should be added that the scope of the duty of disclosure and whether or not it has been breached are matters which must be decided in relation to the circumstances of each particular case.

The Court in *Hopp v. Lepp* also pointed out that even if a certain risk is a mere possibility which ordinarily need not be disclosed, yet if its occurrence carries serious consequences, as for example, paralysis or even death, it should be regarded as a material risk requiring disclosure.

In the present case, the risk attending the surgery or its immediate aftermath was the risk of a stroke, of paralysis and, indeed, of death. This was, without question, a material risk. At the same time, the evidence made it clear that there was also a risk of a stroke and of resulting death if surgery for the removal of the occlusion was refused by the patient. The delicacy of the surgery is beyond question, and its execution is no longer in any way faulted. (I would note here that in this Court no issue was raised as to the adequacy of post-operative care.) How specific, therefore, must the information to the patient be, in a case such as this, to enable him to make an "informed" choice between surgery and no surgery? One of the considerations weighing upon the plaintiff was the fact that he was about a year and a half away from earning a lifetime retirement pension as a Ford Motor Company employee. The trial Judge noted (to use his words) that "due to this tragedy befalling him at the time it did, he was not eligible for certain extended disability benefits available under the collective agreement between the Ford Motor Company of Canada, Limited and its hourly employees of ten years' standing". At the time of the operation, the plaintiff had 8.4 years' service with his employer. He stated in his evidence that if he had been properly informed of the magnitude of the risk involved in the surgery he would have elected to forego it, at least until his pension had vested and, further, he would have opted for a shorter normal life than a longer one as a cripple because of the surgery. Although elective surgery was indicated for the condition from which the plaintiff suffered, there was (as the trial Judge found) no emergency in the sense that immediate surgical treatment was imperative.

This brings me back to the question of the nature of the information provided by the respondent surgeon to the plaintiff and its adequacy in the circumstances. I will deal, in turn, with (1) the findings and conclusions of the trial Judge on this issue; (2) whether, even on his findings, there was a basis for imposing liability for battery; (3) the assessment made by the Court of Appeal in ordering a new trial; and (4) the evidence in the case, which consisted, in support of the plaintiff's case, mainly of the testimony of the plaintiff and of two neurosurgeons, Dr. Irving Schacter and Dr. Robert Elgie, and portions of the examination for discovery of the defendant and, in support of the defendant's case, the testimony of the defendant and a neurosurgeon, Dr. William Lougheed, who were the only two witnesses called for the defendant; (5) the duty of disclosure and review of the findings below; and (6) whether causation was established.

1. The Findings of the Trial Judge

[After reviewing the evidence, the trial Judge, Mr. Justice Edson L. Haines, held the defendant liable both in battery and in negligence.]

2. Liability for Battery

In my opinion, these findings do not justify the imposition of liability for battery. The popularization of the term "informed consent" for what is, in essence, a duty of disclosure of certain risks of surgery or therapy appears to have had some influence in the retention of battery as a ground of liability, even in cases where there was express consent to such treatment and the surgeon or therapist did not go beyond that to which consent was given. It would be better to abandon the term when it tends to confuse battery and negligence. Haines J., the trial Judge, adopted the distinction drawn by Morden J., as he then was, in *Kelly v. Hazlett* (1976), 15 O.R. (2d) 290, 1 C.C.L.T. 1, 75 D.L.R. (3d) 536 between situations where a failure in the duty of disclosure would support an action of battery and where such a failure is indicative of negligence alone. ...

I find the attempted distinction not only very difficult of application but also as incompatible with the elements of the cause of action in battery. The tort is an intentional one, consisting of an unprivileged and unconsented to invasion of one's bodily security. True enough, it has some advantages for a plaintiff over an action of negligence since it does not require proof of causation and it casts upon the defendant the burden of proving consent to what was done. Again, it does not require the adducing of medical evidence, although it seems to me that if battery is to be available for certain kinds of failure to meet the duty of disclosure there would necessarily have to be some such evidence brought before the Court as an element in determining whether there has been such a failure.

The well-known statement of Cardozo J. in *Schloendorff v. Society of New York Hospital* (1914), 211 N.Y. 125 at 129, 105 N.E. 92 at 93 that "every human being of adult years and sound mind has a right to determine what shall be done with his own body; and a surgeon who performs an operation without his patient's consent commits an assault, for which he is liable in damages", cannot be taken beyond the compass of its words to support an action of battery where there has been consent to the very surgical procedure carried out upon a patient but there has been a breach of the duty of disclosure of attendant risks. In my opinion, actions of battery in respect of surgical or other medical treatment should be confined to cases where surgery or treatment has been performed or given to which there has been no consent at all or where, emergency situations aside, surgery or treatment has been performed or given beyond that to which there was consent.

This standard would comprehend cases where there was misrepresentation of the surgery or treatment for which consent was elicited and a different surgical procedure or treatment was carried out. See, for example, *Marshall v. Curry*, 60 C.C.C. 136, [1933] 3 D.L.R. 260 (consent given to operation to cure hernia; doctor removes patient's testicle; action in battery); *Murray v. McMurchy*, [1949] 1 W.W.R. 989, [1949] 2 D.L.R. 442 (B.C.) (consent given to a caesarian operation; doctor goes on and sterilizes the patient; doctor liable for trespass to the person); *Mulloy v. Hop Sang*, [1953] 1 W.W.R. 714 (Alta. C.A.) (doctor told to repair hand

and not to amputate; performs amputation; held liable in trespass); *Winn v. Alexander*, [1940] O.W.N. 238 (consent given to caesarian; doctor goes further and sterilizes the patient); *Schweizer v. Central Hospital* (1974), 6 O.R. (2d) 606, 53 D.L.R. (3d) 494 (patient consented to operation on his toe; doctor operated on back instead (spinal fusion); doctor liable for trespass to the person).

In situations where the allegation is that attendant risks which should have been disclosed were not communicated to the patient and yet the surgery or other treatment carried out was that to which the plaintiff consented (there being no negligence basis of liability for the recommended surgery or treatment to deal with the patient's condition), I do not understand how it can be said that the consent was vitiated by the failure of disclosure so as to make the surgery or other treatment an unprivileged, unconsented to and intentional invasion of the patient's bodily integrity. I can appreciate the temptation to say that the genuineness of consent to medical treatment depends on proper disclosure of the risks which it entails, but in my view, unless there has been misrepresentation or fraud to secure consent to the treatment, a failure to disclose the attendant risks, however serious, should go to negligence rather than to battery. Although such a failure relates to an informed choice of submitting to or refusing recommended and appropriate treatment, it arises as the breach of an anterior duty of due care, comparable in legal obligation to the duty of due care in carrying out the particular treatment to which the patient has consented. It is not a test of the validity of the consent.

3. The Assessment of the Court of Appeal

[The Chief Justice considered the reasons of Brooke J.A., who applied the professional standard of disclosure test.]

To allow expert medical evidence to determine what risks are material and, hence, should be disclosed and, correlatively, what risks are not material is to hand over to the medical profession the entire question of the scope of the duty of disclosure, including the question whether there has been a breach of that duty. Expert medical evidence is, of course, relevant to findings as to the risks that reside in or are a result of recommended surgery or other treatment. It will also have a bearing on their materiality but this is not a question that is to be concluded on the basis of the expert medical evidence alone. The issue under consideration is a different issue from that involved where the question is whether the doctor carried out his professional activities by applicable professional standards. What is under consideration here is the patient's right to know what risks are involved in undergoing or foregoing certain surgery or other treatment.

The materiality of non-disclosure of certain risks to an informed decision is a matter for the trier of fact, a matter on which there would, in all likelihood, be medical evidence but also other evidence, including evidence from the patient or from members of his family. It is, of course, possible that a particular patient may waive aside any question of risks and be quite prepared to submit to the surgery or treatment, whatever they be. Such a situation presents no difficulty. Again, it may be the case that a particular patient may, because of emotional factors, be unable to cope with facts relevant to recommended surgery or treatment and the doctor may, in such a case, be justified in withholding or generalizing information as to which he would otherwise be required to be more specific.

A useful summary of issues on which medical evidence in non-disclosure cases remains significant is found in a Comment, *New Trends in Informed Consent* (1975), 54 Neb. L. Rev. 66, at p. 90, where, after noting that medical evidence should not control determination of the breach of the standard of care, it continued, as follows (referring to *Canterbury v. Spence* (1972), 464 F. 2d 772):

> ... Even *Canterbury* specifically notes that expert testimony will still be required, in all but the clearest instances, to establish (1) risks inherent in a given procedure or treatment, (2) the consequences of leaving the ailment untreated, (3) alternative means of treatment and their risks, and (4) the cause of the injury suffered by the plaintiff-patient. Finally, if the defendant-physician claims a privilege, expert testimony is needed to show the existence of (1) an emergency which would eliminate the need for obtaining consent, and (2) the impact upon the patient of risk disclosure where a full disclosure appears medically unwarranted.

[The Chief Justice quoted from the reason of Brooke J.A. on the issue of causation, adopting a subjective test, but which he thought should also be tested objectively.]

If Canadian case law has so far proceeded on a subjective test of causation, it is in Courts other than this one that such an approach has been taken ... The matter is *res integra* here. An alternative to the subjective test is an objective one, that is, what would a reasonable person in the patient's position have done if there had been proper disclosure of attendant risks. The case for the objective standard has been tersely put in the following passage from a comment in (1973), 48 N.Y.U.L. Rev. 548 at 550 entitled *Informed Consent — A Proposed Standard for Medical Disclosure:*

> Since proximate causation exists only if disclosure would have resulted in the patient's foregoing the proposed treatment, a standard must be developed to determine whether the patient would have decided against the treatment had he been informed of its risks. Two possible standards exist: whether, if informed, the particular patient would have foregone treatment (subjective view); or whether the average prudent person in plaintiff's position, informed of all material risks, would have foregone treatment (objective view). The objective standard is preferable since the subjective standard has a gross defect: it depends on the plaintiff's testimony as to his state of mind, thereby exposing the physician to the patient's hindsight and bitterness.

However, a vexing problem raised by the objective standard is whether causation could ever be established if the surgeon has recommended surgery which is warranted by the patient's condition. Can it be said that a reasonable person in the patient's position, to whom proper disclosure of attendant risks has been made, would decide against the surgery, that is, against the surgeon's recommendation that it be undergone? The objective standard of what a reasonable person in the patient's position would do [seems] to put a premium on the surgeon's assessment of the relative need for the surgery and on supporting medical evidence of that need. Could it be reasonably refused? Brooke J.A. appeared to be sensitive to this problem by suggesting a combined objective-subjective test.

I doubt that this will solve the problem. It could hardly be expected that the patient who is suing would admit that he would have agreed to have the surgery, even knowing all the accompanying risks. His suit would indicate that, having suffered serious disablement because of the surgery, he is convinced that he would not have permitted it if there had been proper disclosure of the risks, balanced by the risks of refusing the surgery. Yet, to apply a subjective test to causation would, correlatively, put a premium on hindsight, even more of a premium than would be put on medical evidence in assessing causation by an objective standard.

I think it is the safer course on the issue of causation to consider objectively how far the balance in the risks of surgery or no surgery is in favour of undergoing surgery. The failure of proper disclosure pro and con becomes therefore very material. And so too are any special considerations affecting the particular patient. For example, the patient may have asked specific questions which were either brushed aside or were not fully answered or were answered wrongly. In the present case, the anticipation of a full pension would be a special consideration, and, while it would have to be viewed objectively, it emerges from the patient's particular circumstances. So too, other aspects of the objective standard would have to be geared to what the average prudent person, the reasonable person in the patient's particular position, would agree to or not agree to, if all material and special risks of going ahead with the surgery or foregoing it were made known to him. Far from making the patient's own testimony irrelevant, it is essential to his case that he put his own position forward.

The adoption of an objective standard does not mean that the issue of causation is completely in the hands of the surgeon. Merely because medical evidence establishes the reasonableness of a recommended operation does not mean that a reasonable person in the patient's position would necessarily agree to it, if proper disclosure had been made of the risks attendant upon it, balanced by those against it. The patient's particular situation and the degree to which the risks of surgery or no surgery are balanced would reduce the force, on an objective appraisal, of the surgeon's recommendation. Admittedly, if the risk of foregoing the surgery would be considerably graver to a patient than the risks attendant upon it, the objective standard would favour exoneration of the surgeon who has not made the required disclosure. Since liability rests only in negligence, in a failure to disclose material risks, the issue of causation would be in the patient's hands on a subjective test, and would, if his evidence was accepted, result inevitably in liability unless, of course, there was a finding that there was no breach of the duty of disclosure. In my view, therefore, the objective standard is the preferable one on the issue of causation.

In saying that the test is based on the decision that a reasonable person in the patient's position would have made, I should make it clear that the patient's particular concerns must also be reasonably based; otherwise, there would be more subjectivity than would be warranted under an objective test. Thus, for example, fears which are not related to the material risks which should have been but were not disclosed would not be causative factors. However, economic considerations could reasonably go to causation where, for example, the loss of an eye as a result of non-disclosure of a material risk brings about the loss of a job for which good eyesight is required. In short, although account must be taken of a patient's particular position, a position which will vary with the patient, it must be objectively assessed in terms of reasonableness.

4. The Evidence

[There was a lengthy consideration of the evidence including many excerpts from the transcript.]

5. Breach of Duty of Disclosure: The Findings Below Reviewed

In my opinion, the record of evidence amply justifies the trial Judge's findings that the plaintiff was told no more or understood no more than that he would be better off to have the operation than not to have it. This was not an adequate, not a sufficient disclosure of the risk attendant upon the operation itself, a risk well appreciated by the defendant in view of his own experience that of the 60 to 70 such operations that he had previously performed, 8 to 10 resulted in the death of the patients. Although the mortality rate was falling by 1970, the morbidity (the sickness or disease) rate, according to Dr. Hughes, was still about 10 per cent. The trial Judge was also justified in finding that the plaintiff, who was concerned about his continuing headaches and who was found to be suffering from hypertension, had the impression that the surgery would alleviate his headaches and hypertension so that he could carry on with his job. Dr. Hughes made it plain in his evidence that the surgery would not cure the headaches but did not, as the trial Judge found, make this plain to the plaintiff. ...

...

In the light of the defendant's own evidence that there was a failure on his part to disclose the risk, even though the plaintiff himself raised the question of the risks he faced on the operating table, I do not see how there could be any doubt of a breach in this respect of the duty of disclosure.

6. Causation

Relevant in this case to the issue whether a reasonable person in the plaintiff's position would have declined surgery at the particular time is the fact that he was within about one and one-half years of earning pension benefits if he continued at his job; that there was no neurological deficit then apparent; that there was no immediate emergency making the surgery imperative; that there was a grave risk of a stroke or worse during or as a result of the operation, while the risk of a stroke without it was in the future, with no precise time fixed or which could be fixed except as a guess of three or more years ahead. Since, on the trial Judge's finding, the plaintiff was under the mistaken impression, as a result of the defendant's breach of the duty of disclosure, that the surgery would relieve his continuing headaches, this would in the opinion of a reasonable person in the plaintiff's position, also weigh against submitting to the surgery at the particular time.

In my opinion, a reasonable person in the plaintiff's position would, on a balance of probabilities, have opted against the surgery rather than undergoing it at the particular time.

Conclusion

I would, accordingly, allow the appeal, set aside the order of the Court of Appeal and restore the judgment at trial. The appellant is entitled to costs throughout.

Appeal allowed.

NOTES

1. How is the problem of "informed consent" to be handled in the future?

2. Can liability for battery still be imposed on a medical doctor? If so, in what circumstances?

3. What standard of disclosure is now demanded of medical practitioners?

4. How would you define a "material" risk? What definition would you give for a "special or unusual" risk? An attempt at definition was made in *White v. Turner* (1981), 31 O.R. (2d) 773 (H.C.) by Linden J. as follows:

> The meaning of "material risks" and "unusual or special risks" should be considered. In my view, material risks are significant risks that pose a real threat to the patient's life, health or comfort. In considering whether a risk is

> material or immaterial, one must balance the severity of the potential result and the likelihood of its occurring. Even if there is only a small chance of serious injury or death, the risk may be considered material. On the other hand, if there is a significant chance of slight injury this too may be held to be material. As always in negligence law, what is a material risk will have to depend on the specific facts of each case.
>
> As for "unusual or special risks", these are those that are not ordinary, common, everyday matters. These are risks that are somewhat extraordinary, uncommon and not encountered every day, but they are known to occur occasionally. Though rare occurrences, because of their unusual or special character, the Supreme Court has declared that they should be described to a reasonable patient, even though they may not be "material". There may, of course, be an overlap between "material risks" and "unusual or special risks". If a special or unusual risk is quite dangerous and fairly frequently encountered, it could be classified as a material risk. But even if it is not very dangerous or common, an unusual or special risk must be disclosed.

There are many cases seeking to apply this test to the multifarious procedures that occur daily. See, for a detailed listing, Picard and Robertson *Legal Liability of Doctors and Hospitals in Canada*, 3rd ed. (1996) at p.121 *et ff.*

5. What role, if any, will evidence of the customary disclosure given by doctors in the field play in this determination?

6. In commenting on the objective standard of disclosure and of causation adopted in *Reibl v. Hughes,* Professor Sanda Rodgers-Magnet has written that the approach had the advantage of "logical consistency". She explains as follows:

> The patient is expected, in law, to behave as would a reasonable person in his circumstances. He is to be given the information a reasonable person would expect to receive, and to take the decision a reasonable person would take. Neither physician nor patient may hide behind an amorphous unverifiable experience, whether professional or personal. Each party's behaviour may be measured by the Court against the Court's own experience. Finally, if an objective standard of disclosure increases the burden on the treating physician at the time of risk disclosure to the benefit of the patient, that increase is balanced by an increase of the burden placed on the patient who would allege that a causal element is present. The patient reaps both the benefits and the burdens of being measured by an objective standard.

Do you agree with this summary? See "Comment" (1980), 14 C.C.L.T. 61, at 76.

7. How accurate a summary of *Reibl v. Hughes* is the following discussion in *White v. Turner* (1981), 31 O.R. (2d) 773, 120 D.L.R. (3d) 269, 15 C.C.L.T. 81; affd 47 O.R. (2d) 764*n*, 12 D.L.R. (4th) 319*n* (C.A.), *per* Linden J.?

> It is clear that Canadian doctors are obligated to disclose to their patients "the nature of a proposed operation, its gravity, any material risks and any special or unusual risks attendant upon the performance of the operation". ... It is also clear that these problems are to be analyzed with negligence law theory, rather than with the law of battery. Further the language of "informed consent" should be avoided in these cases, since it spawns confusion between these two distinct theories of liability.
>
> The law of battery is to be used no longer in cases involving the adequacy of information about risks that is given to these patients, but it remains available where there is no consent to the operation, where the treatment given goes beyond the consent, or where the consent is obtained by fraud or misrepresentation. Thus, it would still be battery to amputate someone's hand

without his consent. ... to administer an anaesthetic in the left arm when this is objected to by the patient. ... to sterilize a patient when the consent was only for a Caesarian operation. ... and to operate on someone's back when his consent related to his toe. ...

The future use of battery is, therefore, to be limited to cases involving a real lack of consent. Where there has been a basic consent to the treatment, there is no place left for discussions of battery. The problems associated with inadequacy of information about risks are to be handled with negligence theory. ...

The matter of disclosure of risks by a doctor may be viewed as not entirely unlike the manufacturers' duty to warn consumers about the dangerous properties of their products. In relation to products, there is an obligation to inform consumers reasonably about the dangers inherent in the product they are about to purchase. Recently, the Supreme Court has required a high degree of explicitness in these warnings, especially when they deal with dangerous products (*Lambert v. Lastoplex*, [1972] S.C.R. 569, 25 D.L.R. (3d) 121). It is, therefore, consistent to expect full information about the dangers involved in a surgical operation to be communicated to patients. There are, of course, differences in the two situations, but the similarities should be kept in mind.

Further, in analyzing the quality and quantity of the information given to a patient under negligence principles, the test to be employed is no longer the professional medical standard, heretofore used by our Courts, but rather the reasonable patient standard. This is a major shift heralded by the Supreme Court of Canada in *Reibl v. Hughes, supra.* No longer does the medical profession alone collectively determine, by *its* own practices, the amount of information a patient should have in order to decide whether to undergo an operation. From now on, the Court also has a voice in deciding the appropriate level of information that must be conveyed to a patient in the circumstances as a question of fact. ...

In summary then, this exercise of defining the scope of the duty of disclosure is now a complex one for the Court, requiring much time, effort, thought and evidence. The cooperation and assistance of the medical profession will be vital to the task. The Courts will, as always, move very cautiously in this area. In most cases, the Courts will probably continue to accept as reasonable the customary practices of the profession as to disclosure, since they are, after all, based on experience, common sense and what doctors honestly perceive their patients wish to know. However, it is now open to the Courts, if invited, to participate in the process of evaluating the information that has been communicated and to find it wanting in appropriate cases, even if the medical profession disagrees.

The decision in *Reibl v. Hughes* has also declared that an objective test of causation is to be employed in assessing whether the patient would have consented to the operation if he had been properly warned. Unlike the situation in battery, where proof of actual damage is unnecessary, negligence law will only furnish compensation if the substandard conduct being assessed has caused some loss to the plaintiff.

If the patient would still have agreed to the operation, even if he had been supplied with full information about the risks, the failure to inform him fully cannot be described as a cause of the damage he may suffer. Hence, he could not succeed in negligence theory. In order to recover in negligence law, therefore, it must be established that the patient would have refused to undergo the surgery if he had been told about all the relevant risks.

There is a danger here, though, that every patient who becomes a plaintiff will insist that he would have foregone the operation if he had been properly warned. Hindsight is always wiser than foresight. The Courts have always mistrusted judgments made from hindsight and have sought to minimize the danger of such evidence. Hence, the Supreme Court of Canada has wisely adopted an objective test here, not a subjective one. It is not enough, therefore, for the Court to be convinced that the plaintiff would have refused the treatment if he had been fully informed; the Court must *also* be satisfied that a reasonable patient, in the same situation, would have done so. That is the meaning of the objective test adopted in *Reibl v. Hughes*, ...

This is a sensible stance which is quite consistent with tort principles in other contexts. For example, the requirement is not unlike the need for proof of reasonable reliance in actions for deceit and negligent misrepresentation. In those types of cases, our Courts have avoided assisting gullible fools, who rely on every bit of silly advice they receive. ... Consequently, a patient, who says he would have foregone life-saving treatment because it might have caused a rash or a headache, cannot recover on the basis of inadequate disclosure, even if he is believed, because a reasonable patient would have gone ahead.

8. The Ontario Court of Appeal has summarized these principles in *Videto v. Kennedy* (1981), 33 O.R. (2d) 497 at 502-503, 125 D.L.R. (3d) 127, 17 C.C.L.T. 307 (C.A.), as follows:

1. The question of whether a risk is material and whether there has been a breach of the duty of disclosure are not to be determined solely by the professional standards of the medical profession at the time. The professional standards are a factor to be considered.
2. The duty of disclosure also embraces what the surgeon knows or should know that the patient deems relevant to the patient's decision whether or not to undergo the operation. If the patient asks specific questions about the operation, then the patient is entitled to be given reasonable answers to such questions. In addition to expert medical evidence, other evidence, including evidence from the patient or from members of the patient's family is to be considered. In *Reibl v. Hughes, supra*, at p. 894 S.C.R., p. 12 D.L.R., Laskin C.J.C. stated:

   The patient may have expressed certain concerns to the doctor and the latter is obliged to meet them in a reasonable way. What the doctor knows or should know that the particular patient deems relevant to a decision whether to undergo prescribed treatment goes equally to his duty of disclosure as do the material risks recognized as a matter of required medical knowledge.

3. A risk which is a mere possibility ordinarily does not have to be disclosed, but if its occurrence may result in serious consequences, such as paralysis or even death, then it should be treated as a material risk and should be disclosed.
4. The patient is entitled to be given an explanation as to the nature of the operation and its gravity.
5. Subject to the above requirements, the dangers inherent in any operation such as the dangers of the anaesthetic, or the risks of infection, do not have to be disclosed.
6. The scope of the duty of disclosure and whether it has been breached must be decided in relation to the circumstances of each case.
7. The emotional condition of the patient and the patient's apprehension and reluctance to undergo the operation may in certain cases justify the surgeon in withholding or generalizing information as to which he would otherwise be required to be more specific.
8. The question of whether a particular risk is a material risk is a matter for the trier of fact. It is also for the trier of fact to determine whether there has been a breach of that duty of disclosure.

These principles were circulated to all the members of the medical profession by the Ontario College of Physicians and Surgeons in January 1982. (See College Notices, Issue No. 3.) Do they accurately reflect what the Supreme Court of Canada said in *Reibl v. Hughes*? What effect, if any, would this circular have on the doctors of Ontario?

9. The Supreme Court of Canada revisited the issue of the doctor's duty to disclose in *Ciarlariello v. Schacter*, [1993] 2 S.C.R. 119, 100 D.L.R. (4th) 609. The case concerned a patient who, during a testing procedure, became agitated and asked that the test be stopped. After a few minutes, the doctor sought and obtained her consent for the resumption of the test. The plaintiff suffered a rare injury as a result of the test and sued, alleging that her consent for the resumption of the test had not been an informed one.

   Cory J. reviewed the legal principles relevant to this type of situation. He stated that where there is a question as to whether a patient is attempting to withdraw a consent which was given earlier, a doctor must ascertain anew whether there is consent before continuing with treatment. Where consent has been withdrawn, a doctor must then inform the patient of any significant change in the risks of treatment or in the circumstances of the treatment, before continuing with it. Finally, a doctor has a duty to ensure that the information is understood by the patient and has the burden of proving this. Applied to the facts of this case, the Court found that there was consent to the resumption of the treatment, that the circumstances and risks of the treatment had not changed and therefore did not need to be explained again, and that the patient had understood the risks of the treatment.

10. Would the court's approach to the duty of disclosure be different if the operation was exclusively a "cosmetic" one? In *Hankins v. Papillon* (1980), 14 C.C.L.T. 198, at 203 (C.S. Que.), Mr. Justice Rothman stated:

    > In cases of plastic surgery, however, where the decision to be made by the patient is more subjective and personal than therapeutic, I believe the doctor has a duty to be especially careful to disclose completely all material risks and, certainly, any special risks, as well as the consequences for the patient should such risks materialize. … In matters of this kind, there is normally no urgency, the relevant problems can be explained to the patient, and the patient can weigh the medical risks against his own non-medical desires and priorities. Since there is no therapeutic need for the operation, the patient might well decide that he would prefer to live with a blemish rather than take the risk.

    See also Mr. Justice Grange's comment in *Videto v. Kennedy* (1980), 27 O.R. (2d) 747, at 758, 107 D.L.R. (3d) 612; revd (1981), 33 O.R. (2d) 497, 125 D.L.R. (3d) 127, 17 C.C.L.T. 307 (C.A.), to the effect that "the frequency of the risk becomes much less material when the operation is unnecessary for his medical welfare".

11. In *Halushka v. University of Sask.* (1965), 52 D.L.R. (2d) 436, 52 W.W.R. 608 (Sask. C.A.), for $50 a student allowed himself to be used during a medical experiment testing a new anesthetic at the university hospital. He was told, wrongly, that the test was "safe" and there was nothing to "worry" about. He was not fully informed about the nature of the test, that involved inserting a catheter into his vein and advancing it to his heart. During the procedure the plaintiff suffered a cardiac arrest, that he survived with serious injuries. The new anesthetic was later withdrawn from clinical use. The plaintiff, who was held not to have consented, recovered both in battery and negligence theory. Would this case be decided in the same way after *Reibl*? Could the decision still be based on battery theory?

12. The objective test of causation set out in *Reibl v. Hughes* has caused much confusion. It has been somewhat adjusted by the later cases, and is now being called the "modified objective test of causation". See Stratton C.J.N.B. in *Mason v. Forgie* (1984), 31 C.C.L.T. 66 (N.B.Q.B.) affd (1986), 38 C.C.L.T. 171 (N.B.C.A.) There is some slight disagreement over the meaning of the test even in the Supreme Court of Canada. In *Arndt v. Smith* (1997), 35 C.C.L.T. (2d) 233 (S.C.C.), the majority reaffirmed its commitment to the modified objective test but three judges indicated a desire to move to a more subjective test. In the case, a woman sued her doctor for costs incurred in

rearing her daughter, who was congenitally injured by chicken pox the woman had contracted during the pregnancy. The claim was based on the ground that the woman would have terminated the pregnancy if the doctor had properly warned her of the risk of injury to the foetus posed by the chicken pox. The action was ultimately dismissed.

For the majority, Cory J. explained:

> The [modified objective] test... relies on a combination of objective and subjective factors in order to determine whether the failure to disclose *actually* caused the harm of which the plaintiff complains. It requires that the court consider what the reasonable patient *in the circumstances of the plaintiff* would have done if faced with the same situation. The trier of fact must take into consideration any "particular concerns" of the patient and any "special considerations affecting the particular patient" in determining whether the patient would have refused treatment if given all the information about the possible risks... In my view this means that the "reasonable person" who sets the standard for the objective test must be taken to possess the patient's reasonable beliefs, fears, desires and expectations. Further, the patient's expectations and concerns will usually be revealed by the questions posed. Certainly, they will indicate the specific concerns of the particular patient at the time consent was given to a proposed course of treatment. The questions, by revealing the patient's concerns, will provide an indication of the patient's state of mind, which can be relevant in considering and applying the modified objective test.

Thus, it was felt that the modified objective test "serves to eliminate from consideration the honestly held but idiosyncratic and unreasonable or irrational beliefs of patients".

Three of the judges disagreed, preferring a more subjective test, explained by McLachlin J. as follows:

> The approach suggested by the fundamental principles of tort law is subjective, in that it requires consideration of what the plaintiff at bar would have done. However, it incorporates elements of objectivity; the plaintiff's subjective belief at trial that she would have followed a certain course stands to be tested by her circumstances and attitudes at the time the decision would have been made as well as the medical advice she would have received at the time.

Thus, McLachlin J. favoured a test that would ask "what the particular plaintiff would have done in all the circumstances, but accepts that the reasonableness of the one choice over another, as reflected in the medical advice the plaintiff would have received, is an important factor bearing on that decision".

13. Although there does not seem to be a vast difference between the two approaches, the dissenters' views are clearly more favourable to patients. A careful observer would note that Cory J.'s view is also somewhat more advantageous to patients than the original formulation by Laskin J., which seemed to lack many subjective elements. The subtle difference seems to be one of emphasis mainly and should not lead to different results in many cases. Note, for example, that both Cory J. and McLachlin JJ. agreed on the result in this case.

14. This modified objective standard governs not only doctors but also dental surgeons, and dentists. It may apply also to "non-surgical" as well as surgical treatment, so that chiropractors are subject to it. It does not, however, cover pharmaceutical manufacturers or producers of breast implant material.

15. What do you make of the following thoughts about the effect of *Reibl v. Hughes*?

> This does not mean that Canadian doctors must now give complicated seminars on medicine to all of their patients. It does mean, though, that more time may have to be spent explaining things to their patients than in the past. The law as espoused by the Supreme Court of Canada requires that patients should be treated as intelligent, mature and rational individuals. The ultimate effect of this new approach should be medical practitioners who are even more sensitive, concerned and humane than they now are. Moreover, the doctor-patient relationship should be improved greatly by the better communication between doctors and their patients. The high level of trust Canadians now have in their doctors should be even higher. Another beneficial consequence may be even fewer malpractice actions than are now instituted in this country. If these results flow from *Reibl v. Hughes*, it will have rendered our community a most valuable service.

See Linden J. in *White v. Turner* (1981), 31 O.R. (2d) 773, 120 D.L.R. (3d) 269, 15 C.C.L.T. 81, at 104; affd 47 O.R. (2d) 764*n*, 12 D.L.R. (4th) 319*n* (C.A.).

16. The effect of *Reibl v. Hughes* has been empirically studied in Robertson, "Informed Consent in Canada: An Empirical Study" (1984), 22 Osgoode Hall L.J. 139. The study showed that 74 per cent of the doctors who responded to the survey had not heard of *Reibl v. Hughes*. Of those who were aware of the case, 59 per cent stated that the decision had some effect on their practice with regard to informing patients. Taking into account those doctors who had not heard of *Reibl v. Hughes*, and those who had heard of it but whose practice was unaffected by it, Robertson was able to conclude that *Reibl v. Hughes* had no effect on the practice of approximately 85 per cent of surgeons in Canada. Does this result surprise you? Does it show that tort law's educational role has been overstated? Do you think that the fact that 15 per cent of doctors have changed their attitude towards informing their patients of medical risks as a result of one tort case is proof of tort law's positive role? Do more doctors know about *Reibl* now?

17. In his article "Informed Consent Ten Years Later: The Impact of *Reibl v. Hughes*" (1991), 70 Can. Bar Rev. 423, Professor Robertson analyzes 117 cases decided since *Reibl*. He finds that the plaintiffs in these cases were almost always unsuccessful because of the "causation" requirement. Nevertheless, Robertson now finds that *Reibl* may be having some effect on medical practice, and that doctors are now spending more time discussing treatment with their patients. He also suggests that the decision may have assisted in altering the nature of the doctor/patient relationship — shifting power away from the doctors to their patients.

18. There has been some concern about a so-called "medical malpractice crisis," raising insurance rates unduly, driving doctors out of the profession and forcing them to practice defensive medicine. It has been suggested that, while there is cause for concern, such a crisis, even if it has occurred in the United States, has not developed in Canada. In their book *Legal Liability of Doctors and Hospitals in Canada* 3rd ed. (1996), Picard and Robertson explain:

> Is there a medical malpractice "crisis" in Canada, or likely to be one in the near future? The first step in obtaining an answer is to make a commitment to a Canadian perspective on the question. For while the United States has apparently suffered from a "malpractice crisis" for years and there may be "no effective quarantine along the world's longest undefended border," let us be sure we have the disease before we take the medicine. Rozovsky has said about the fear in Canada:
>
> > The fear of such a crisis already exists in this country on the theory that what happens in the United States eventually takes place in Canada. This fear has led to irresponsible and uninformed public statements,

> unnecessary and sometimes foolish administrative actions and misguided legislative enactments.
>
> The factors which have been identified as contributing to the crisis in the United States can be roughly grouped as arising from the legal process, the insurance programs, the relationships between the professions, the changing nature of medical practice (including group practice, specialization and urbanization), and public attitudes and expectations. Within the legal process there are great differences between Canada and the United States, ranging from the style of advocacy and use of the jury to the size of damage awards and the type of contingency fee used. The absence of national health insurance in the U.S. and the practices of the private insurance companies who cover doctors there are a striking contrast to our scheme of medicare and the Canadian Medical Protective Association. The style of practice and inter-professional relations of doctors and lawyers are different in the United States. No doubt some of the antagonism is the consequence of the crisis, but the large numbers of professionals and the more businesslike approach have led to a more competitive atmosphere wherein, for example, professional services are advertised and fees are paid directly by the patient.
>
> These differences make it especially important to have a Canadian perspective on the issue, and not to be unduly influenced by what has happened in the United States.

See also Dickens, "The Effects of Legal Liability on Physicians' Services" (1991), 41 U.T.L.J. 168.

19. A major study *Liability and Compensation in Health Care* was conducted by the Prichard Commission for the Conference of Deputy Ministers of Health of the Federal, Provincial and Territorial governments. The Commission's four-volume report was published in 1990. Based on its commissioned research papers and studies, some of the Commission's findings were as follows:

> (1) There have not been any major doctrinal changes in Canadian law over the past 15 years which could explain the growth in the frequency of medical malpractice claims over that period.
>
> (2) There have been upward trends in both the frequency and severity of medical malpractice claims in Canada in the period 1971-1987. The average compound annual growth rate in claims filed per 100 CMPA member physicians was about 9 per cent, in claims paid was about 6.6 per cent, and in average amount paid over 9.5 per cent per year. The claim rate in Canada is about 1/5 of the U.S. rate. The data do not support the sometimes exaggerated sense that there is a "crisis" of claims, but the increases are large enough to justify the concerns of the medical profession.
>
> (3) Despite the increased frequency of claims, only a very small percentage of persons suffering avoidable health care injuries receive compensation. Rather than there being an excess of litigated claims, there is a "litigation gap".
>
> (4) Although precise costs are impossible to ascertain, it is a fair assessment that the costs of the present liability system are high, with the total costs likely equalling or exceeding the total compensation paid out.
>
> (5) The health care system has been influenced by its awareness of potential liability. Initiatives taken in response to liability concerns can be seen as having made a positive contribution to the quality of health care.

The Commission's "basic strategy of reform" was described as follows:

> the appropriate strategy for reform of the current liability and compensation regime for health care injuries should contain three principal elements: maintaining and reforming tort actions for negligence against physicians and health

care institutions; increasing the responsibility of health care institutions for higher quality health care; and developing a no-fault compensation system alternative for persons suffering significant avoidable injuries.

While recognizing the shortcomings of tort law, the Report was very supportive of tort law's continued rule, especially in regards to the incentives it creates for a higher quality health care system. Suggestions for reform, in addition to a voluntary no-fault scheme for "significant avoidable health care injuries" offering lesser amounts than tort law, were directed at limitation periods, and a variety of issues relating to damage assessments.

20. In the years following the Prichard Commission, the frequency and size of medical claims have moderated to a degree. Since 1985, the number of claims has "remained fairly stable" and the ratio per 100 members was "exactly the same in 1994 as it was in 1985 (2.13)." The average size of claim paid has varied slightly but in 1995 it was less than in 1991, $181,282 compared to $182,451. In any event, this is a costly and aggravating situation for doctors whose membership fees in the C.M.P.A. have risen sharply, especially for those in specialties more prone to being targets of law suits, like obstetricians, orthopaedic surgeons and anaesthetists, where doctors pay over $20,000 annually. Part of the increase in fees was attributable to concern about the need to build up substantial reserves for future claims. That reserve is now worth over one billion dollars. Another reason for the increasing cost of these fees is that counsel fees paid to defend claims are substantial. In 1996, for example, legal costs were approximately sixty-one million dollars, while awards and settlement were one-hundred and two million dollars. In other years, legal fees ate up almost as much of the membership fees as the payments to claimants. See Picard and Robertson, *supra,* at p.424.

21. In England, the Pearson Commission, after considering the various alterative reform possibilities, concluded that they would make no major recommendations for reforming the way in which medical malpractice claims are handled by the courts. The only change it suggested was that volunteers for research and clinical trials should be allowed to sue on a strict liability basis. The Commission also urged that developments elsewhere should be studied and assessed in the event that changing circumstances indicated that a no-fault plan should be instituted. See "Report of the Royal Commission on Civil Liability and Compensation for Person Injury" (1978). Are you disappointed about this? Many changes have taken place in the U.S. See Prosser, Wade & Schwartz, *Torts: Cases and Materials* (9th) ed. (1994) at p.195.

22. Should medical malpractice cases ever be tried by a jury? What are the policy considerations on both sides? See *Smith v. Rae* (1919), 46 O.L.R. 518, at 520, 51 D.L.R. 323 (C.A.); *Hodgins v. Banting* (1906), 12 O.L.R. 117 (H.C.); *Leadbetter v. Brand* (1980), 37 N.S.R. (2d) 581, 107 D.L.R. (3d) 252 (T.D.); *Soldwisch v. Toronto Western Hospital* (1983), 43 O.R. (2d) 449, 1 D.L.R. (4th) 446 (H.C.J.).

23. Should doctors be subject to malpractice suits at all? Mr. Justice Haines thought not. He preferred the use of no-fault insurance to cover all medical "accidents". See "The Medical Profession and the Adversary Process" (1973), 11 Osgoode Hall L.J. 41:

> Doctors do not take kindly to the adversary system. It is entirely foreign to their way of settling disputes. When they disagree on a diagnosis or a treatment technique, they attempt to resolve it by obtaining the assistance of more experienced scientists and each joins in an objective search for the truth. It would be unthinkable for them to refer the matter to an independent layman, whether he be a judge or jury. Even if they did, there are no specialist judges in malpractice matters and the majority have no training in basic anatomy and physiology. The courts seem to dislike calling an expert assistant to sit with the judge and assist him in understanding the evidence. Leaving aside those few cases of such obvious error that the law implies negligence from the event

(*res ipsa loquitur*), the great bulk of bad results from medical care arise in a terribly grey area where the law may see negligence but medicine sees merely an unexpected occurrence in a very inexact art. Here we must recognize the difference in thinking between lawyers and doctors. The lawyer is armed with the most accurate diagnostic instrument, the "retroscope". With twenty-twenty vision he seizes on the unfortunate result, second-guesses the doctor and charges him with fault, although at the time of treatment the symptoms and the various tests presented a very foggy picture and resulted in a complex, differential diagnosis.

However, the major objection of the doctor to a malpractice action is the confirmed belief of the medical profession that the suit is a reflection on his professional abilities and standing. The very name "malpractice" repels him, and in the minds of some denotes quasi-criminal or unethical conduct, a loss of standing with his colleagues in the medical profession, degradation in the eyes of his patients and the community in which he practices, or loss of possible promotion and staff privileges in local hospitals.

See also Ehrenzweig, "Hospital Accident Insurance: A Needed First Step Towards the Displacement of Liability for Medical Malpractice" (1964), 31 U. Chi. L. Rev. 279; O'Connell, "Expanding No-Fault Beyond Auto Insurance" (1973), 59 Va. L. Rev. 749; Keeton, "Compensation for Medical Accidents" (1973), 121 U. Pa. L. Rev. 590; Callaghan, A.C.J.H.C., in *Koerber v. Kitchener-Waterloo Hospital* (1987), 62 O.R. (2d) 613 (H.C.J.).

24. Do you think the medical malpractice action should be abolished? If it was, would there remain enough independent supervision of medical practice? Is professional self-regulation adequate? Are coroners' inquests sufficient? Is the role of the hospital important here? Should tort law seek to upgrade the quality of medical practice? See Kretzmer, "The Malpractice Suit: Is It Needed?" (1973), 11 Osgoode Hall L.J. 55.

25. What do you think of the following quote from Linden, "Tort Law as Ombudsman" (1973), 51 Can. Bar Rev. 155, at 160:

All professional groups come under the aegis of tort law. The expertise of doctors, lawyers, engineers and accountants may be impugned in a tort suit. Of course, negligence law normally adopts as its own the standards that the professions require of themselves. But this does not make negligence law redundant, because professional groups are less than zealous in policing themselves. Hardly ever does a doctor, for example, lose his licence to practice medicine because of his incompetence or professional misconduct. It is far more common for a physician to be sued by a patient injured by his malpractice. Consequently, it is the judges, not the College of Physicians and Surgeons, who by default become regulators of the quality of medical practice.

The courts can encourage the medical profession to develop safer procedures. In *Chasney v. Anderson* an action was brought because a child suffocated on a sponge left behind in its throat after a tonsillectomy. No sponge count had been done. Nor were strings attached to the sponges that were used. Still worse, the search that had been conducted did not discover anything. Liability was imposed. Following the decision, two articles were written in the *Canadian Medical Association Journal* warning doctors about the need for special precautions in relation to sponges. It is not unlikely that these articles, coupled with the publicity in the daily press at the time, had some impact on the habits of medical men.

There is reason to suspect that, when malpractice actions are successfully brought against doctors for negligently performing an operation, administering an anaesthetic or putting on a cast, other physicians are alerted to the dangers involved in those medical procedures and the need for utmost care. The impact of these decisions is amplified because reports of them are published in

> the annual report of the Canadian Medical Protective Association, something that is received by almost every doctor in Canada. Even if the law suit is not successful, it will still be reported and will serve to remind doctors of the wisdom of caution.
>
> Thus, medical malpractice actions serve a useful function, despite the fact that doctors do not pay the awards personally. It is the publicity that carries the sting. However, this sanction is not as severe on the individual doctor as might be expected. His practice generally survives the litigation. In fact, so small a threat is the civil action to the profession that the Ontario Committee on the Healing Arts dismissed it as almost useless in controlling the quality of medical practice. This body, however, failed to appreciate the educational value of malpractice litigation. No doubt malpractice actions are a costly and cumbersome way of dramatizing the risks of medical practice, but they should provide incentives to care. True, the medical profession could do a much better job of regulating the quality of medical practice if it would exert itself more in this area. True, a medical ombudsman would assist greatly in exposing some acts of wrong-doing. In their absence, however, the malpractice action stands as a temporary ombudsman, constantly reminding doctors of the risks involved in their acts. Other professional groups are in much the same position as doctors, and stand to learn in the same way.

See also Prichard, "Professional Civil Liability and Continuing Competence", in Klar (ed.), *Studies in Canadian Tort Law* (1977), at 377.

26. There has been a problem in Canada and around the world with regard to tainted blood being transfused into patients without proper testing. About 2,000 Canadians contracted HIV between 1980 and 1985 and as many as 60,000 contracted hepatitis C. The problem was the subject of a Royal Commission (Krever) and spawned many tort suits including class actions against doctors, hospitals, governments and the Red Cross. The federal and provincial governments, because of their likely tort liability, have offered compensation to some of the victims, but not all, depending on the date of the offending transfusion, because prior to 1986 it was not thought to be necessary to test blood for these diseases. In one case, *Pitman Estate v. Bain* (1994), 112 D.L.R. (4th) 257 (Ont. Gen. Div.), the Canadian Red Cross was held liable for failing to warn about the risk of HIV contamination after the defendant learned that some transfused blood had come from a person with HIV. See also *Walker Estate v. York-Finch Hospital* (1997), 39 C.C.L.T. (2d) 1 (Ont. Gen. Div.). This problem has triggered a debate about no-fault compensation for the victims of a major medical tragedy who are unable to prove anyone at fault. What, if anything, should be done for the victims? In addition to any potential tort remedy for those who can prove fault, it should be pointed out that the medical and hospital costs of all the victims are being covered in the same way as for all Canadians. Is there any reason why they should not be limited to the same remedies and social welfare support as any other victims of medical mishaps? Is there any logical basis for distinguishing between the two groups? Is there any moral basis for a distinction? If these victims are all to be compensated, how can we deny similar treatment to all victims of medical and indeed other mishaps? Perhaps this tragedy at long last will generate a sensible no-fault compensation scheme for all victims of accidents.

27. Another area of potential liability for doctors, as well as other professionals, that is getting a lot of attention from courts, stems from their fiduciary responsibilities to their clients. This was the focus of Madame Justice McLachlin's judgment in *Norberg v. Wynrib*, see Chapter 3, *supra*. Finding a doctor liable for trading drugs for sex with his patient, McLachlin J. stated:

> The relationship of physician and patient can be conceptualized in a variety of ways. It can be viewed as a creature of contract, with the physician's failure to fulfil his or her obligations giving rise to an action for breach of contract. It

> undoubtedly gives rise to a duty of care, the breach of which constitutes the tort of negligence. In common with all members of society, the doctor owes the patient a duty not to touch him or her without his or her consent; if the doctor breaches this duty, he or she will have committed the tort of battery. But perhaps the most fundamental characteristic of the doctor-patient relationship is its *fiduciary* nature. All the authorities agree that the relationship of physician to patient also falls into that special category of relationships which the law calls fiduciary.

McLachlin J. went on to discuss the fundamental elements of the fiduciary relationship, found that they existed in this case, and that the fiduciary obligations were breached. Mr. Justice Sopinka disagreed. He held that while some of the obligations which arise from the doctor and patient relationship may be fiduciary in nature, such as the obligation not to disclose confidential information, the obligation to treat the patient is not one of these fiduciary obligations.

Although this debate relating to the nature of the fiduciary relationship is outside the scope of our discussion, it is important nevertheless to recognize that the law of fiduciaries is having an increasingly more important role in the professional malpractice context.

See *Taylor v. McGillivray* (1993), 110 D.L.R. (4th) 64 (N.B.Q.B.); *Seney v. Crooks* (1996), 30 C.C.L.T. (2d) 66 (Alta. Q.B.).

2. Lawyers

BRENNER v. GREGORY

Ontario High Court. [1973] 1 O.R. 252, 30 D.L.R. (3d) 672.

The plaintiff agreed to purchase four town lots after several inspections thereof. The defendant, Gregory, a lawyer, was retained to search the title and to close the transaction, which he did. It turned out that a building on the land in question encroached on the street. The vendor had warned the plaintiff of this danger before closing, but only a survey could prove if this was correct, and none was done. The plaintiff sued his lawyer *inter alia*.

Grant J.: ... As against the defendant Gregory, the plaintiffs allege that he was negligent in not obtaining a survey or warning the plaintiffs of the danger of purchasing such a property without a survey. It is admitted by all parties that there was no discussion between the purchasers and Mr. Gregory at any time prior to the closing of the transaction in regard to the necessity of acquiring a survey. Mr. Gregory knew that the purchasers had seen the property on a number of occasions before purchasing. It was apparent to the purchasers that the building had stood on that location for many years. There is no doubt in my mind that the purchasers knew there was some question as to whether or not the store was out in the street because of the conversations with him about the closing and the conveyance of the one-half of the street. The fact that they said nothing to Mr. Gregory in these circumstances indicates that they were prepared to deal with the matter themselves and did not rely upon their solicitor therefor.

Mr. Robert E. Mountain Q.C., a solicitor who has practised extensively in Stratford since 1954 with considerable experience in the closing of real estate transactions, stated that in the circumstances of this case a reasonably competent and diligent solicitor in that area acting for a purchaser would not be expected either to secure a survey or to advise his client to do so and his failure to do so would not amount to negligence. In any event, I cannot see that the plaintiffs have lost anything by reason of the failure to advise them about a survey because prior to the commencement of this action it was abundantly clear to them that they could have all of the land on which the building is supposed to have encroached with more to the north thereof.

In an action against the solicitor for negligence it is not enough to say that he has made an error of judgment or shown ignorance of some particular part of the law, but he will be liable in damages if his error or ignorance was such that an ordinarily competent solicitor would not have made or shown it: *Aaroe and Aaroe v. Seymour et al.*, [1956] O.R. 736, 6 D.L.R. (2d) 100, [1956-60] I.L.R. 1010*n*.

The obligation of a solicitor to exercise due care in protecting the interests of a client who is a purchaser in a real estate transaction will have been discharged if he has acted in accordance with the general and approved practice followed by solicitors unless such practice is inconsistent with prudent precautions against a known risk, as where particular instructions are given which the solicitor fails to carry out: *Winrob and Winrob v. Street and Wollen* (1959), 19 D.L.R. (2d) 172, 28 W.W.R. 118. In a recent case of *Grima et al v. MacMillan*, [1972] 3 O.R. 214, 27 D.L.R. (3d) 666, Parker J. found that it was not the usual practice for solicitors to make a search to find out if a party was alive before issuing a writ of summons against him in a personal injury claim. Thus, where the defendant had died previous to the issue of the writ and the same was then a nullity and the limitation period had expired, the solicitor was not negligent. The responsibility of a solicitor is set out in *Charlesworth on Negligence*, 4th ed. (1962), pp. 1032-1035, para. 1034, as follows:

> The standard of care and skill which can be demanded from a solicitor is that of a reasonably competent and diligent solicitor. Lord Ellenborough has said: "An attorney is only liable for *crassa negligentia*." Again, Lord Campbell in discussing the essential elements to sustain an action for negligence has said: "What is necessary to maintain such an action? Most undoubtedly that the professional adviser should be guilty of some misconduct, some fraudulent proceeding, or should be chargeable with gross negligence or with gross ignorance. It is only upon one or other of those grounds that the client can maintain an action against the professional adviser." This, however, does not mean that the standard of care imposed upon a solicitor is below that imposed on other professional men; it only means that it is not enough to prove that the solicitor has made an error of judgment or shown ignorance of some particular part of the law, but that it must be shown that the error or ignorance was such that an ordinary competent solicitor would not have made or shown it.

I have therefore come to the conclusion that there was no negligence in this case on the part of Mr. Gregory.

The action therefore should be dismissed as against all the defendants, with costs.

Action dismissed.

NOTES

1. The duty of a lawyer was founded on contract for over a century, but now it is clear that lawyers may be concurrently liable to their clients, either in contract or tort. Hence, a plaintiff "has the right to assert the cause of action that appears to be most advantageous to him..." save, of course, for specific contractual limitations. See *Cen-*

tral Trust Co. v. Rafuse, [1986] 2 S.C.R. 147, 37 C.C.L.T. 117, at 167. Mr. Justice Le Dain described the standard of care as follows:

> A solicitor is required to bring reasonable care, skill and knowledge to the performance of the professional service which he has undertaken ... the requisite standard of care has been variously referred to as that of the reasonably competent solicitor, the ordinary competent solicitor and the ordinary prudent solicitor. ... A solicitor is not required to know all the law applicable to the performance of a particular legal service, in the sense that he must carry it around with him as part of his "working knowledge", without the need of further research, but he must have sufficient knowledge of the fundamental rules or principles of law applicable to the particular work he has undertaken to enable him to perceive the need to ascertain the law on relevant points.

2. Does the degree of care expected of a criminal lawyer or a tax lawyer differ from that of a lawyer in general practice? Should the court recognize the *de facto* specialization of lawyers by holding specialists to a higher standard just as their counterparts in medicine are so held? What are the problems of doing so? Should a Queen's Counsel be expected to have a greater degree of skill than the average lawyer? Should less be demanded of a country lawyer than a city lawyer? See *Elcano Acceptance Ltd. v. Richmond, Richmond, Stambler & Mills* (1985), 31 C.C.L.T. 201, 47 C.P.C. 256 (Ont. H.C.); revd 55 O.R. (2d) 56, 9 C.P.C. (2d) 260 (C.A.).

3. The British courts have granted advocates an immunity from tort liability during the conduct of litigation. See *Rondel v. Worsley*, [1969] A.C. 191, [1967] 3 All E.R. 993 (H.L.); Catzman, Comment (1968), 46 Can. Bar Rev. 505. This immunity, that relies on barristers acting "honourably in accordance with the recognized standards of their profession" (see Lord Reid), is not a blanket protection against all the errors that an advocate may make. It will not apply to errors while giving advice or while drafting documents, etc. Nor will it excuse a barrister from liability for failing to sue a particular defendant. See *Saif Ali v. Sydney Mitchell & Co.*, [1980] A.C. 198, [1978] 3 All E.R. 1033 (H.L.); Catzman, "Comment" (1979), 57 Can. Bar Rev. 339. The policy grounds upon which the House of Lords relied in supporting the immunity were:

> ... first, the proper administration of justice demands that lawyers carry out their duties fearlessly; second, justice would not be served if it were necessary to retry law suits in order to evaluate the conduct of the counsel; and third, it is unfair to make a barrister civilly responsible when he cannot refuse to accept a brief.

4. The British rule was resoundingly rejected by Krever J. in *Demarco v. Ungaro et al.* (1979), 21 O.R. (2d) 673, 95 D.L.R. (3d) 385 (H.C.). The defendants, who were lawyers, brought a motion to strike out a statement of claim alleging negligence against them for losing a case on the ground that they failed to call certain evidence that they should have called. In a learned judgment dismissing the motion, Mr. Justice Krever held that the immunity afforded a British lawyer has no place in Ontario. He explained:

> I have come to the conclusion that the public interest ... in Ontario does not require that our Courts recognize an immunity of a lawyer from action for negligence at the suit of his or her former client by reason of the conduct of a civil case in Court. It has not been, is not now, and should not be, public policy in Ontario to confer exclusively on lawyers engaged in Court work an immunity possessed by no other professional person. Public policy and the public interest do not exist in a vacuum. They must be examined against the background of a host of sociological facts of the society concerned. Nor are they lawyers' values as opposed to the values shared by the rest of the community. In the light of recent developments in the law of professional negligence and the rising

incidence of "malpractice" actions against physicians (and especially surgeons who may be thought to be to physicians what barristers are to solicitors), I do not believe that enlightened, non-legally trained members of the community would agree with me if I were to hold that the public interest requires that litigation lawyers be immune from actions for negligence. I emphasize again that I am not concerned with the question whether the conduct complained about amounts to negligence. Indeed, I find it difficult to believe that a decision made by a lawyer in the conduct of a case will be held to be negligence as opposed to a mere error of judgment. But there may be cases in which the error is so egregious that a court will conclude that it is negligence. The only issue I am addressing is whether the client is entitled to ask a Court to rule upon the matter.

Many of the sociological facts that are related to public policy and the public interest may be judicially noticed. The population of Ontario is approximately eight and a quarter million people. In 1978 there were approximately 12,300 lawyers licensed by the Law Society of Upper Canada to practise law in Ontario. All of them have a right of audience in any Court in Ontario as well as in the Federal Court of Canada and the Supreme Court of Canada. The vast majority of these lawyers are in private practice and, as such, are required to carry liability insurance in respect of negligence in the conduct of their clients' affairs. No distinction is made in this respect between those exclusively engaged in litigation and all other lawyers. The current rate of increase in the size of the profession is approximately 1,000 lawyers annually. It is widely recognized that a graduating class of that size places such an enormous strain on the resources of the profession that the articling experience of students-at-law is extremely variable. Only a small percentage of lawyers newly called to the Bar can be expected to have had the advantage of working with or observing experienced and competent counsel. Yet very many of those recently qualified lawyers will be appearing in Court on behalf of clients. To deprive these clients of recourse if their cases are negligently dealt with will not, to most residents of this Province, appear to be consistent with the public interest.

It is with a great sense of deference that I offer a few brief remarks on the grounds and consideration which formed the basis of the public policy as expressed by the House of Lords in *Rondel v. Worsley*. I am only concerned with the applicability of those considerations to Ontario conditions and have no hesitation in accepting them as entirely valid for England. With respect to the duty of counsel to the Court and the risk that, in the absence of immunity, counsel will be tempted to prefer the interest of the client to the duty to the Court and will thereby prolong trials, it is my respectful view that there is no empirical evidence that the risk is so serious that an aggrieved client should be rendered remediless. Between the dates of the decisions in *Leslie v. Ball*, 1863, and *Rondel v. Worsley*, 1967, immunity of counsel was not recognized in Ontario and negligence actions against lawyers respecting their conduct of Court cases did not attain serious proportions. Indeed, apart from the cases I have cited I know of no case in Court. A very similar argument is advanced in many discussions of the law of professional negligence as it applies to surgeons. Surgeons, it is claimed, are deterred from using their best judgment out of fear that the consequence will be an action by the patient in the event of an unfavourable result. This claim has not given rise to an immunity for surgeons. As to the second ground — the prospect of relitigating an issue already tried, it is my view that the undesirability of that event does not justify the recognition of lawyers' immunity in Ontario. It is not a contingency that does not already exist in our law and seems to me to be inherently involved in the concept of *res judicata* in the recognition that a party, in an action *in personam*, is only precluded from relitigating the same matter against a person who was a party to the earlier action. I can find no fault with the way in which Hagarty, C.J., dealt with this consideration in *Wade v. Bell et al.* (1870), 20 U.C.C.P. 302 at p. 304: "Practically, such a suit as the present may involve the trying over again of *Wade v. Hoyt.* This cannot be avoided." Better that than that the client should be without recourse.

The third consideration related to the obligation of a lawyer to accept any client. Whether that has ever been the universally accepted understanding of a lawyer's duty in Ontario is doubtful. In any event, I do not believe such a duty exists in the practice of civil litigation and that is the kind of litigation with which I am now concerned.

What do you think of this decision? Are you, as a future lawyer, afraid? Can anything be said in favour of the retention of the advocate's immunity? See Laskin, "The British Tradition in Canadian Law" (1969), p. 26; Hutchinson, "Comment" (1979), 57 Can. Bar Rev. 346.

5. Despite the fact that barristers are not immune from negligence suits in Canada, it is very difficult to prove negligence in the conduct of a trial. In *Wechsel v. Stutz* (1980), 15 C.C.L.T. 132 (Ont. Co. Ct.), the plaintiff alleged that his barrister has been negligent in the cross-examination of witnesses. The Court dismissed the action, noting that the manner in which witnesses are examined "must be left to the judgment of counsel".

6. A criminal defence counsel who handles a case and treats his client negligently however, can be held responsible for the mental suffering caused to the client, even though the result of the case would have been no different than the plea bargain arranged if he had performed reasonably. See *Boudreau v. Benaiah* (1998), 154 D.L.R. (4th) 650 (*per* Greer J.) (Ont. Gen. Div.).

7. Judges are immune from tort liability for their mistakes. This immunity extends apparently to judges of any court of record, including provincial court judges. See Steele J. in *Re Clendenning and Bd. of Police Commrs of City of Belleville* (1976), 15 O.R. (2d) 97, at 101, 75 D.L.R. (3d) 33 (Div. Ct.). See also *Unterreiner v. Wilson* (1983), 40 O.R. (2d) 197, 142 D.L.R. (3d) 588 (H.C.J.); affd 41 O.R. (2d) 472, 146 D.L.R. (3d) 322 (C.A.); *Sirros v. Moore*, [1975] Q.B. 118, [1974] 3 All E.R. 776 (C.A.); *Morier v. Rivard*, [1985] 2 S.C.R. 716, 23 D.L.R. (4th) 1; *McC v. Mullan*, [1985] A.C. 528, [1984] 3 All E.R. 908 (H.L.).

8. Can solicitors (or other professionals) owe duties not only to their own clients but to third persons as well? One can easily see how the potential liability of professionals would expand if third parties detrimentally affected by the negligent work of professionals were given a cause of action. See *Whittingham v. Crease & Co.* (1978), 88 D.L.R. (3d) 353, [1978] 5 W.W.R. 45, 6 C.C.L.T. 1 (B.C.S.C.); *Ross v. Caunters*, [1980] 1 Ch. 297, [1979] 3 All E.R. 580, where solicitors were held liable to third party beneficiaries of a will. Cf., *Seale v. Perry*, [1982] V.R. 193 (Full Ct.). See Litman and Robertson, "Solicitors' Liability for Failure to Substantiate Testamentary Capacity" (1984), 62 Can. Bar Rev. 457; Klar, "A Comment on Whittingham v. Crease" (1979), 6 C.C.L.T. 311; Rawlins, "Liability of a Lawyer for Negligence in the Drafting and Execution of a Will" (1983), 6 Estates & Trusts Q. 117; Luntz, "Solicitors' Liability to Third Parties" (1983), 3 Oxford J. Leg. Studies 284.

9. As with doctors, malpractice claims against lawyers and other professionals have increased in frequency over the past decade. The Prichard Commission which looked into the liability of physicians found that like Canadian doctors, Canadian lawyers and dentists have experienced "sharp increases" in the frequency of claims. Curiously, the size of the average claim paid was found to have increased for Ontario lawyers, but not for non-Ontario lawyers, chartered accountants, architects, engineers or dentists. See Liability and Compensation in Health Care, (1990), App. A, p. 54.

10. The field of professional liability is a vast one. There are many cases involving engineers, auditors and other professional groups. See Campion and Dimmer, *Professional Liability in Canada* (1994) (looseleaf service). See Klar, *supra,* chapter 10.

CHAPTER 6

PROOF

The trial of a negligence case is usually more concerned with facts and evidence than it is with substantive law. Historically, a negligence trial was usually conducted before a judge and a jury. This is still the case in some jurisdictions, notably Ontario, British Columbia and the United States, but in many places the use of the jury is diminishing. Where a jury is utilized, the judge does not become irrelevant. The judge still exercises a good deal of control over the jury by ruling on the evidence, instructing the jury about the law, commenting on the evidence and deciding whether there is sufficient evidence to be considered by a jury.

Many problems of proof may arise in a negligence action. While most of these issues will be dealt with in courses of Evidence and Procedure, it is necessary to consider some of these problems here.

As for proof of negligence, it will be seen that, except for statutory changes, the onus of proof is on the plaintiff. There was once a doctrine that played an important role here, called *res ipsa loquitur,* which puzzled judges, lawyers and students alike, but it is now "expired". When there are multiple defendants and uncertainty about whether either or both were negligent, it will be seen that the courts have developed some sensible approaches to the problems of proof.

As for proof of causation, the courts presently have departed from their strict adherence to rigid rules of proof and have adopted a more common sense approach. In cases of multiple causes, some unusual but wise approaches have also been developed.

Sometimes it is hard to tell whether we are dealing with proof of negligence or proof of causation or both. This is an area where the demands of science, logic and social justice may conflict, generating pressures on courts to adjust the way they have dealt with these questions in the past.

A. THE ONUS OF PROOF OF NEGLIGENCE

WAKELIN v. THE LONDON & S.W. RY. CO.

House of Lords. (1886), 2 App. Cas. 41, 56 L.J.Q.B. 229.

An action was brought by the administratrix of Henry Wakelin for damages arising from the death of Wakelin due to the alleged negligence of the defendant railway.

At the trial the evidence showed that the deceased left his house shortly after ten and was not seen until his body was found on the railway line near a crossing. There was no evidence as to the circumstances under which he got there. The defendant admitted Wakelin was struck by one of its trains. The plaintiff put in evidence the defendant's answers to interrogatories showing that pedestrians had a clear view of the track and that the company did not give any special signal at the crossing. The defendant called no evidence at the trial and submitted there was no case. The trial judge left the case to the jury who returned a verdict of £800 for the plaintiff. On appeal the Divisional Court set aside the verdict and entered judgment for defendant. The Court of Appeal affirmed this decision. The plaintiff appealed.

Lord Halsbury L.C.: My lords, it is incumbent upon the plaintiff in this case to establish by proof that her husband's death has been caused by some negligence of the defendants, some negligent act, or some negligent omission, to which the injury complained of in this case, the death of the husband, is attributable. That is the fact to be proved. If that fact is not proved the plaintiff fails, and if in the absence of direct proof the circumstances which are established are equally consistent with the allegation of the plaintiff as with the denial of the defendants, the plaintiff fails, for the very simple reason that the plaintiff is bound to establish the affirmative of the proposition. . . .

If the simple proposition with which I started is accurate, it is manifest that the plaintiff, who gives evidence of a state of facts which is equally consistent with the wrong of which she complains having been caused by — in this sense that it could not have occurred without — her husband's own negligence as by the negligence of the defendants, does not prove that it was caused by the defendants' negligence. She may indeed establish that the event has occurred through the joint negligence of both, but if that is the state of the evidence the plaintiff fails, because *in pari delicto potior est conditio defendentis*. It is true that the onus of proof may shift from time to time as matter of evidence, but still the question must ultimately arise whether the person who is bound to prove the affirmative of the issue, *i.e.*, in this case the negligent act done, has discharged herself of that burden. I am of opinion that the plaintiff does not do this unless she proves that the defendants have caused the injury in the sense which I have explained.

In this case I am unable to see any evidence of how this unfortunate calamity occurred. One may surmise, and it is but surmise and not evidence, that the unfortunate man was knocked down by a passing train while on the level crossing; but assuming in the plaintiff's favour that fact to be established, is there anything to shew that the train ran over the man rather than that the man ran against the train? I understand the admission in the answer to the sixth interrogatory to be simply an admission that the death of the plaintiff's husband was caused by contact with the train. If there are two moving bodies which come in contact, whether ships, or carriages, or even persons, it is not uncommon to hear the person complaining of the injury describe it as having been caused by his ship, or his carriage, or himself having been run into, or run down, or run upon; but if a man ran across an approaching train so close that he was struck by it, is it more true to say that the engine ran down the man, or that the man ran against the engine? Neither man nor engine were intended to come in contact, but each advanced to such a point that contact was accomplished. ... The peculiarity about this case is that no one knows what the circumstances were. The body of the deceased man was found in the neighbourhood of the level crossing on the down line, but neither by direct evidence nor by reasonable inference can any conclusion be arrived as to the circumstances causing his death.

It has been argued before your Lordships that we must take the facts as found by the jury. I do not know what facts the jury are supposed to have found, nor is it, perhaps, very material to inquire, because if they have found that the defendants' negligence caused the death of the plaintiff's husband, they have found it without a fragment of evidence to justify such a finding.

Under these circumstances, I move that the judgment appealed from be affirmed, and the appeal dismissed.

[The speeches of **Lord Watson** and **Lord Fitzgerald** to the same effect are omitted. **Lord Blackburn** concurred.]

NOTES

1. Do you think that it is wise to require the plaintiff to establish by proof that the defendant's negligence caused the loss? Why not place the onus of disproof upon the defendant?

2. How is it that the jury found for the plaintiff in this case? Is this an argument for the abolition of the civil jury? Is it an argument for greater judicial control over the jury?

3. If both plaintiff and defendant are at fault the plaintiff no longer loses. See, *infra*, Chapter 11.

4. On the function of judges and juries in negligence actions, Lord Cairns stated in *Metropolitan Railway Co. v. Jackson* (1877), 3 App. Cas. 193, 37 L.T. 679 (H.L.):

> The judge has a certain duty to discharge and the jurors have another and a different duty. The judge has to say whether any facts have been established by evidence from which negligence may be reasonably inferred; the jurors have to say whether, from those facts, when submitted to them, negligence ought to be inferred. It is, in my opinion, of the greatest importance in the administration of justice that these separate functions should be maintained, and should be maintained distinct. It would be a serious inroad on the province of the jury, if in a case where there are facts from which negligence may reasonably be inferred, the judge were to withdraw the case from the jury upon the ground that, in his opinion, negligence ought not to be inferred; and it would, on the other hand, place in the hands of the jurors a power which might be exercised in the most arbitrary manner, if they were at liberty to hold that negligence might be inferred from any state of facts whatever. To take the instance of actions against railway companies: a company might be unpopular, unpunctual, and irregular in its service; badly equipped as to its staff; unaccommodating to the public; notorious, perhaps for accidents occurring on the line; and when an action was brought for the consequences of an accident, jurors, if left to themselves, might, upon evidence of general carelessness, find a verdict against the company in a case where the company was really blameless.

B. INFERRING NEGLIGENCE

For over 100 years, the so-called doctrine of *res ipsa loquitur* — the thing speaks for itself — has plagued the courts. Although it was mentioned many times in cases, its true meaning remained mysterious. It was attacked by judges and scholars and, finally, has been laid to rest in Canada, but not elsewhere, by the Supreme Court. It turns out that when the thing spoke for itself it did not have very much to say after all. For historical purposes only, the case of *Byrne v. Boadle,* the source of the problem, is included here. It is the case of *Fontaine v. I.C.B.C.,* however, that will guide courts in the years to come. It will be seen that there are still some unanswered questions that remain.

BYRNE v. BOADLE

Exchequer. (1863), 2 H. & C. 722, 159 E.R. 299.

In an action for negligence, the evidence for the plaintiff was to the effect that as he was walking past the shop of the defendant, a dealer in flour, a barrel of flour fell from a window above the shop and seriously injured him. The defendant submitted that there was no evidence of negligence for the jury, and the Assessor being of that opinion non-suited the plaintiff, reserving leave to the latter to move the Court of Exchequer to enter a verdict for him for £50 damages, the amount assessed by the jury. The plaintiff obtained a rule *nisi*.

Charles Russell now shewed cause. ... There was no evidence that the defendant, or any person for whose acts he would be responsible, was engaged in lowering the barrel of flour. It is consistent with the evidence that the purchaser of the flour was superintending the lowering of it by his servant, or it may be that a stranger was engaged to do it without the knowledge and authority of the defendant. [Pollock C.B.: The presumption is that the defendant's servants were engaged in removing the defendant's flour; if they were not it was competent to the defendant to prove it.] Surmise ought not to be substituted for strict proof when it is sought to fix a defendant with serious liability. The plaintiff should establish his case by affirmative evidence.

Secondly, assuming the facts to be brought home to the defendant or his servants, these facts do not disclose any evidence for the jury of negligence. The plaintiff was bound to give affirmative proof of negligence. But there was not a scintilla of evidence, unless the occurrence is of itself evidence of negligence. ... [Pollock C.B.: There are certain cases of which it may be said *res ipsa loquitur*, and this seems one of them. ...] On examination of the authorities, that doctrine would seem to be confined to the case of a collision between two trains upon the same line, and both being the property and under the management of the same company. ...

Pollock C.B.: We are all of opinion that the rule must be absolute to enter the verdict for the plaintiff. The learned counsel was quite right in saying that there are many accidents from which no presumption of negligence can arise, but I think it would be wrong to lay down as a rule that in no case can presumption of negligence arise from the fact of an accident. Suppose in this case the barrel had rolled out of the warehouse and fallen on the plaintiff, how could he possibly ascertain from what cause it occurred? It is the duty of persons who keep barrels in a warehouse to take care that they do not roll out, and I think that such a case would, beyond all doubt, afford *prima facie* evidence of negligence. A barrel could not roll out of a warehouse without some negligence, and to say that a plaintiff who is injured by it must call witnesses from the warehouse to prove negligence seems to me preposterous. So in the building or repairing of a house, or putting pots on the chimneys, if a person passing along the road is injured by something falling upon him, I think the accident alone would be *prima facie* evidence of negligence. Or if an article calculated to cause damage is put in a wrong place and does mischief, I think that those whose duty it was to put it in the right place are *prima facie* responsible, and if there is any state of facts to rebut the presumption of negligence, they must prove them. The present case upon the evidence comes to this man, a man passing in front of the premises of a dealer in flour, and there falls down upon him a barrel of flour, I think it apparent that the barrel was in the custody of the defendant who occupied the premises, and who is responsible for the acts of his servants who had the control of it; and in my opinion the facts of its falling is *prima facie* evidence of negligence, and the plaintiff who was injured by it is not bound to show that it could not fall without negligence, but if there are any facts inconsistent with negligence, it is for the defendant to prove them.

[The judgments of **Bramwell**, **Channell** and **Pigott BB.**, to the same effect are omitted.]

FONTAINE v. INSURANCE CORPORATION OF BRITISH COLUMBIA

[1998] 1 S.C.R. 424

Appellant claimed damages with respect to the death of her husband, Edwin Fontaine, who was found several weeks after his expected return from a hunting trip. His body and that of his hunting companion, Larry Loewen, (which was still buckled in the driver's seat) were in the companion's badly damaged truck which had been washed along a flood swollen creek flowing along side a mountain highway. No one saw the accident and no one knew precisely when it occurred. A great deal of rain had fallen in the vicinity of the accident the weekend of their hunting trip and three highways in the area were closed because of weather-related road conditions. The trial judge found that negligence had not been proven against the driver and dismissed the appellant's case. An appeal to the Court of Appeal was dismissed. At issue here was when *res ipsa loquitur* applies and the effect of invoking it.

Major J.:

Analysis

A. When does *res ipsa loquitur* apply?

Res ipsa loquitur, or "the thing speaks for itself", has been referred to in negligence cases for more than a century. In *Scott v. London and St. Katherine Docks Co.* (1865), 3 H. & C. 596, 159 E.R. 665, at p. 596 and p. 665, respectively, Erle C.J. defined what has since become known as *res ipsa loquitur* in the following terms:

> There must be reasonable evidence of negligence.
>
> But where the thing is shown to be under the management of the defendant or his servants, and the accident is such as in the ordinary course of things does not happen if those who have the management use proper care, it affords reasonable evidence, in the absence of explanation by the defendants, that the accident arose from want of care.

These factual elements have since been recast (see *Clark and Lindsell on Torts* (13th ed. 1969), at para. 967 at p. 968, quoted with approval in *Jackson v. Millar,* [1976] 1 S.C.R. 225, at p. 235, and *Hellenius v. Lees,* [1972] S.C.R. 165 at p. 172):

> The doctrine applies (1) when the thing that inflicted the damage was under the sole management and control of the defendant, or of someone for whom he is responsible or whom he has a right to control; (2) the occurrence is such that it would not have happened without negligence. If these two conditions are satisfied it follows, on a balance of probability, that the defendant, or the person for whom he is responsible, must have been negligent. There is, however, a further negative condition; (3) there must be no evidence as to why or how the occurrence took place. If

there is, then appeal to *res ipsa loquitur* is inappropriate, for the question of the defendant's negligence must be determined on that evidence.

For *res ipsa loquitur* to arise, the circumstances of the occurrence must permit an inference of negligence attributable to the defendant. The strength or weakness of that inference will depend on the factual circumstances of the case. As described in *Canadian Tort Law* (5th ed. 1993), by Allen M. Linden, at p.233, "[t]here are situations where the facts merely whisper negligence, but there are other circumstances where they should it aloud."

As the application of *res ipsa loquitur* is highly dependent upon the circumstances proved in evidence, it is not possible to identify in advance the types of situations in which *res ipsa loquitur* will arise. The application of *res ipsa loquitur* in previous decisions may provide some guidance as to when an inference of negligence may be drawn, but it does not serve to establish definitive categories of when *res ipsa loquitur* will apply. It has been held on numerous occasions that evidence of a vehicle leaving the roadway gives rise to an inference of negligence. Whether that will be so in any given case, however, can only be determined after considering the relevant circumstances of the particular case.

Where there is direct evidence available as to how an accident occurred, the case must be decided on that evidence alone. K.M. Stanton in *The Modern Law of Tort* (1994), stated at p.76:

> *Res ipsa loquitur* only operates to provide evidence of negligence in the absence of an explanation of the cause of the accident. If the facts are known, the inference is impermissible and it is the task of the court to review the facts and to decide whether they amount to the plaintiff having satisfied the burden of proof which is upon him.

See also R.P. Balkin and J.L.R. David, *Law of Torts* (1966), at p. 289; Lewis Klar in *Tort Law* (2nd ed. 1996), at p. 421.

Finally, the phrase "in the ordinary course of things" in the passage quoted from *St. Katherine Docks, supra,* has been the source of some confusion. It has been suggested that the circumstances themselves must be ordinary in order for *res ipsa loquitur* to apply. That is not necessarily true. The question that must be asked is whether, in the particular circumstances established by the evidence, the accident would ordinarily occur in the absence of negligence. Granted, some circumstances may be so extraordinary or; unusual that it cannot be said with any degree of certainty what would ordinarily happen in those circumstances. In such cases, *res ipsa loquitur* will not apply. In other cases, expert evidence may be presented to assist the trier of fact in understanding what would ordinarily occur in a given set of circumstances.

B. Effect of the application of res ipsa loquitur

As in any negligence case, the plaintiff bears the burden of proving on a balance of probabilities that negligence on the part of the defendant caused the plaintiff's injuries. The invocation of *res ipsa loquitur* does not shift the burden of proof to the defendant. Rather, the effect of the application of *res ipsa loquitur* is as described in *The Law of Evidence in Canada* (1992), by John Sopinka, Sidney H. Lederman and Alan W. Bryant, at p. 81:

> *Res ipsa loquitur,* correctly understood, means that circumstantial evidence constitutes reasonable evidence of negligence. Accordingly, the plaintiff is able to overcome a motion for a non-suit and the trial judge is required to instruct the jury on the issue of negligence. The jury may, but need not, find negligence: a permissible fact

inference. If, at the conclusion of the case, it would be equally reasonable to infer negligence, the plaintiff will lose since he or she bears the legal burden on this issue. Under this construction, the maxim is superfluous. It can be treated simply as a case of circumstantial evidence.

Should the trier of fact choose to draw an inference of negligence from the circumstances, that will be a factor in the plaintiff's favour. Whether that will be sufficient for the plaintiff to succeed will depend on the strength of the inference drawn and any explanation offered by the defendant to negate that inference. If the defendant produces a reasonable explanation that is as consistent with no negligence as the *res ipsa loquitur* inference is with negligence, this will effectively neutralize the inference of negligence and the plaintiff's case must fail. Thus, the strength of the explanation that the defendant must provide will vary in accordance with the strength of the inference sought to be drawn by the plaintiff.

The procedural effect of *res ipsa loquitur* was lucidly described by Cecil A. Wright in "Res Ipsa Loquitur" (Special Lectures of the Law Society of Upper Canada (1955), *Evidence,* pp. 103-136), and more recently summarized by Klar in *Tort Law, supra,* at pp. 423-24:

> If the plaintiff has no direct or positive evidence which can explain the occurrence and prove that the defendant was negligent, appropriate circumstantial evidence, as defined by the maxim *res ipsa loquitur*, may be introduced. Should the defendant, at this stage of the proceeding, move for a nonsuit, on the basis that the plaintiff's evidence has not even made out a *prima facie* case for it to answer, the practical effect of the maxim will come into play. The court will be required to judge whether a reasonable trier of fact could, from the evidence introduced, find an inference of the defendant's negligence. That is, could a reasonable jury find that on these facts the maxim *res ipsa loquitur* applies? If it could so find, the motion for a nonsuit must be dismissed. If such an inference could not reasonably be made, the motion must be granted. In other words, the maxim, at least, will get the plaintiff past a nonsuit.
>
> This, however, does not end the matter. What, if anything, must the defendant do at this point? In theory, where the case is being tried by a judge and jury, the defendant still need not do anything. Although the judge has decided that as a matter of law it would not be an error for the trier of fact to find for the plaintiff on the basis of the circumstantial evidence which has been introduced, it is still up to the jury to decide whether it has been sufficiently persuaded by such evidence. In other words, the judge has decided that as a matter of law, the maxim can apply. Whether as a question of fact it does, is up to the jury. The jury may decide, therefore, that even despite the defendant's failure to call evidence, the circumstantial evidence ought not to be given sufficient weight to discharge the plaintiff's onus. Thus, even if a defendant has decided not to introduce evidence, a trial judge should not, in an action tried by judge and jury, either take the case from the jury and enter judgment for the plaintiff, or direct the jury to return a verdict in favour of the plaintiff. It is up to the trial judge to determine whether the maxim can apply, but up to the jury to decide whether it does apply.

Whatever value *res ipsa loquitur* may have once provided is gone. Various attempts to apply the so-called doctrine have been more confusing than helpful. Its use has been restricted to cases where the facts permitted an inference of negligence and there was no other reasonable explanation for the accident. Given its limited use it is somewhat meaningless to refer to that use as a doctrine of law.

It would appear that the law would be better served if the maxim was treated as expired and no longer used as a separate component in negligence actions. After all, it was nothing more than an attempt to deal with circumstantial evidence. That evidence is more sensibly dealt with by the trier of fact, who should weigh the circumstantial evidence with the direct evidence, if any, to determine whether the plaintiff has established on a balance of probabilities a *prima facie* case of negligence against the defendant. Once the plaintiff has done so, the defendant must present evidence negating that of the plaintiff or necessarily the plaintiff will succeed.

C. Application to this case

In this appeal, the trial judge had to consider whether there was direct evidence from which the cause of the accident could be determined, or, failing that, whether there was circumstantial evidence from which it could be inferred that the accident was caused by negligence attributable to Loewen.

The trial judge found that the only potential evidence of negligence on Loewen's part concerned the fact that the vehicle left the roadway and was travelling with sufficient momentum to break a path through some small trees. She concluded that, when taken together with other evidence concerning the road and weather conditions, this was no more than neutral evidence and did not point to any negligence on Loewen's part. That conclusion was not unreasonable in light of the evidence, which at most established that the vehicle was moving in a forward direction at the time of the accident, with no indication that it was travelling at an excessive rate of speed.

There was some evidence about "excessive wear" on the front tires of the vehicle. ... I agree with Gibbs J.A. that the trial judge did not err when she apparently treated this evidence as of negligible value.

There are a number of reasons why the circumstantial evidence in this case does not discharge the plaintiff's onus. Many of the circumstances of the accident, including the date, time and precise location, are not known. Although this case has proceeded on the basis that the accident likely occurred during the weekend of November 9, 1990, that is only an assumption. There are minimal if any evidentiary foundations from which any inference of negligence could be drawn.

As well, there was evidence before the trial judge that a severe wind and rainstorm was raging at the presumed time of the accident. While it is true that such weather conditions impose a higher standard of care on drivers to take increased precautions, human experience confirms that severe weather conditions are more likely to produce situations where accidents occur and vehicles leave the roadway regardless of the degree of care taken. In these circumstances, it should not be concluded that the accident would ordinarily not have occurred in the absence of negligence.

If an inference of negligence might be drawn in these circumstances, it would be modest. The trial judge found that the defence had succeeded in producing alternative explanations of how the accident may have occurred without negligence on Loewen's part. Most of the explanations offered by the defendants were grounded in the evidence and were adequate to neutralize whatever inference the circumstantial evidence could permit to be drawn. The trial judge's finding was not unreasonable and should not be interfered with on appeal.

The finding of facts and the drawing of evidentiary conclusions from those facts is the province of the trial judge, and an appellate court must not interfere with a trial judge's conclusions on matters of fact unless there is palpable or overriding error: see *Toneguzzo-Norvell (Guardian Ad Litem of) v. Burnaby Hospital*, [1994] 1 S.C.R. 114, at p. 121 *per* McLachlin J. There is no indication that the trial judge committed a palpable or overriding error here.

The appellant submitted that an inference of negligence should be drawn whenever a vehicle leaves the roadway in a single-vehicle accident. This bald proposition ignores the fact that whether an inference of negligence can be drawn is highly dependent upon the circumstances of each case: see *Gauthier & Co. v. The King*, *supra*, at p. 150. The position advanced by the appellant would virtually subject the defendant to strict liability in cases such as the present one.

D. Disposition

The trial judge did not err in concluding based on either the direct or circumstantial evidence or both that the plaintiff failed to establish on a balance of probabilities that the accident occurred as a result of negligence attributable to Loewen. The appeal is therefore dismissed with costs.

NOTES

1. This result was foreseen and advocated by many. In *Hellenius v. Lees*, [1971] 1 O.R. 273 at 288 (C.A.); affd, [1972] S.C.R. 165, Mr. Justice Laskin stated that *res ipsa* "means only that there is circumstantial evidence from which an inference of negligence is warranted". See also Wright, "*Res Ipsa Loquitur*" in Linden (ed). *Studies in Canadian Tort Law* (1968); Schiff, "A *Res Ipsa Loquitur* Nutshell" (1976, 26 U.T.L.J. 451.

2. Does *Fontaine* herald a major change that will lead to different outcomes in cases or does it merely forbid the use of a phrase and so-called doctrine that spawned confusion?

3. Explain the meaning and effect of establishing "a *prima facie* case of negligence against the defendant".

4. Explain the obligation of a defendant who "must present evidence negating that of the plaintiff or necessarily the plaintiff will succeed".

5. How do these principles differ from those developed under the former doctrine of *res ipsa loquitur*? Is this new approach any less confusing?

6. *Res ipsa loquitur* was used in many types of cases including medical malpractice cases (see *Mahon v. Osborne,* [1939] 1 All E.R. 535 (C.A.)) and products liability cases, where it actually shifted the burden of proof to the defendant to disprove negligence (see *Zeppa v. Coca Cola Ltd.,* [1955] O.R. 855 (C.A.)). Presumably, the doctrine is to be treated as expired in these cases as well. Do you think the outcome in cases such as these will be any different in the years ahead?

C. MULTIPLE DEFENDANTS

LEAMAN v. REA

New Brunswick Supreme Court, Appeal Division. [1954] 4 D.L.R. 423, 35 M.P.R. 125.

Appeals by the plaintiff and the defendant from a decision of the trial judge dismissing their claim and counterclaim, respectively, for damages sustained in a collision between their motor vehicles.

Harrison J.: This case arose out of a collision between two passenger cars, one owned and driven by the defendant, Rea, and the other owned by the plaintiff Leaman, and driven by one Crossman, with the plaintiff, Smith and Collier as passengers.

The plaintiff's car was proceeding northerly towards Moncton and the defendant's car was proceeding southerly on a gravel road, the travelled portion of which was 26 feet wide. The road had some ice and snow on it but was in good driving condition.

The collision occurred about 7.30 a.m. on the south edge of the crest of a blind knoll on a straight road. According to the evidence of plaintiff and others in the plaintiff's car, they were travelling between 35 and 40 m.p.h. and first saw the defendant at a distance of some 50 yards. They say he was approaching at about the same speed on the plaintiff's side of the road, that is to say the eastern side. They also testified that, when he was only 30 feet distant the defendant tried to go over to his own side. While proceeding crosswise to the road, the left front of the defendant's car collided with the left front of the plaintiff's car. This collision, they said, took place on the plaintiff's side of the road. After the collision the defendant's car was almost at right angles to the road with the rear wheels in the west ditch and the front wheels on the shoulder, pointing roughly south-east. The plaintiff's car was also at an angle across the road with its rear end some 3 feet from the east ditch.

The defendant gave evidence that he was travelling on his own side of the road in going over the knoll and that when he saw the plaintiff's car it was distant about 100 feet and was travelling on the defendant's side of the road. He said that the plaintiff's driver first went to his own side (the east) and "then as he got to me he cut her in again and hit the left front of my car". Some anti-freeze liquid which came from the plaintiff's radiator was found on the road after the collision some 6 or 8 feet from the west side of the highway, also some glass and mud, and the trial judge found that the impact occurred slightly west of the centre of the highway. The learned trial judge also said: "My guess is that both cars were proceeding over the knoll in the centre of the highway and neither driver saw the other in time to completely avoid a collision. But after considerable thought I am unable to reach to the necessary degree of certainty in conclusion as to how the accident happened or who was at fault. Accordingly I must hold that neither party has established his case and, therefore, the claim and the counterclaim are both dismissed."

In the case of *Bray v. Palmer*, [1953] 2 All E.R. 1449, a case of collision between a motorcycle and a motor car, the trial judge took the view that the accident must have been due to the exclusive negligence of one or the other side. He rejected the possibility of both sides being to blame and being unable to make up his mind which was the right story, dismissed both the claim and the counterclaim. In the Court of Appeal, it was held that the judge was not entitled to dismiss the claim and the counterclaim on the ground that he was unable to decide which party was in the right. It was his duty to come to some conclusion on the evidence and he should not have excluded the possibility of both parties being in some measure to blame, and therefore, there must be a new trial.

In the cases of *Baker v. Market Harborough, etc., Soc., Wallace v. Richards (Leicester) Ltd.*, [1953] 1 W.L.R. 1472, two motor vehicles travelling in opposite directions collided and both drivers were killed. The evidence disclosed that the two motor vehicles were proceeding in opposite directions, both coming down hill. At the trial of the *Wallace* case Sellers J. said that it was clearly established that "these vehicles came together with the off-side of one vehicle against the off-side of the other in the centre of the roadway," and added that the two vehicles overlapped by some 2 or 3 feet at least in what must have been practically a straight head-on collision. Sellers J. held that the facts gave rise to the inference that both drivers were negligent in failing to keep a proper lookout and that both were therefore equally to blame for the accident which resulted therefrom. Denning L.J. said at pp. 1476-7:

> It is pertinent to ask, what would have been the position if there had been a passenger in the back of one of the vehicles who was injured in the collision? He could have brought an action against both vehicles. On proof of the collision in the centre of the road, the natural inference would be that one or other or both were to blame. If there was no other evidence given in the case, because both drivers were killed, would the court, simply because it could not say whether it was only one vehicle that was to blame or both of them, refuse to give the passenger any compensation? The practice of the courts is to the contrary. Every day, proof of the collision is held to be sufficient to call on the two defendants for an answer. Never do they both escape liability. One or the other is held to blame, and sometimes both. If each of the drivers were alive and neither chose to give evidence, the court would unhesitatingly hold that both were to blame. They would not escape simply because the court had nothing by which to draw any distinction between them. So, also, if they are both dead and cannot give evidence, the result must be the same. In the absence of any evidence enabling the court to draw a distinction between them, they must be held both to blame, and equally to blame.
>
> Now take this case where there is no passenger, but both drivers are killed. The natural inference, again, is that one or other was, or both were, to blame. The court will not wash its hands of the case simply because it cannot say whether it was only one vehicle which was to blame or both. In the absence of any evidence enabling the court to draw a distinction between them, it should hold them both to blame, and equally to blame.
>
> It is very different from a case where one or other only is to blame but clearly not both. Then the judge ought to make up his mind between them, as this court said recently in *Bray v. Palmer*, [1953] 1 W.L.R. 1455. But when both may be to blame, the judge is under no such compulsion and can cast the blame equally on each.

The Court of Appeal in both cases apportioned the responsibility equally on both parties.

In the case before this court the same principles would apply and, in the absence of any evidence enabling the court to draw a distinction between the parties, they must be held both to blame and equally to blame. The damages assessed by the learned trial judge do not differ substantially in amount and the result of holding both parties to blame may not be greatly different from dismissing both claims, but in principle, where there is clearly fault, since we have a collision in broad daylight between two cars travelling in opposite directions on a road the travelled portion of which is 26 feet wide, both parties must be held liable and in equal degree.

The appeal should be allowed with full costs and judgment entered for the plaintiff for 50 per cent of his damages as assessed by the trial judge with 50 per cent of his costs. Judgment should also be entered for the defendant for 50 per cent of his damages as assessed, with 50 per cent of his costs of trial.

Bridges J.: I concur in the judgment of Harrison J. It is my opinion that where there has been a collision between two motor vehicles under such circumstances that there must have been negligence on the part of one or both drivers and the court is unable to distinguish between such drivers as to liability, both drivers should be found equally at fault.

In the last part of the All England Reports received by me, there is a case reported *France v. Parkinson*, [1954] 1 All E.R. 739, where a motor collision took place between two motor vehicles in the middle of crossroads of equal status. The trial judge dismissed the action on the ground that no negligence had been proven. His judgment was reversed on appeal, the court holding that in the absence of special circumstances the inference should be drawn that both drivers were equally negligent.

The appeal should be allowed with costs and judgments entered for the plaintiff and defendant as directed by Harrison J. with costs as allowed by him.

[**Richards C.J.** concurred **with Harrison J.**]

NOTES

1. How does this case differ from *Fontaine*?

2. See Prosser, "*Res Ipsa Loquitur* in California" (1949), 37 Calif. L. Rev. 183, at 207: "There is room for a conclusion of the jury that when two vehicles collide and injure a third person the great probability is that *both* drivers were at fault. Certainly that is the experience of liability insurance companies. ..." Do you agree?

3. It should be emphasized that there must be some evidence that *both* parties were negligent; if the proof indicates that *one or other* of the parties were to blame, but *not both*, the action must be dismissed.

   In *Wotta v. Haliburton Oil Well Cementing Co. Ltd.*, [1955] S.C.R. 377, [1955] 2 D.L.R. 785, two large motor vehicles, proceeding in opposite directions collided. The only witnesses of the accident were the two drivers and their evidence was conflicting. It appeared that the forward part of each vehicle passed the other and contact occurred between the rear parts of both trucks. There were no marks on the road to assist in determining the respective positions of the trucks. In an action and counterclaim for damages, the trial judge held he could not make any finding of negligence and dismissed the action and the counterclaim. This judgment was upheld by the Saskatchewan Court of Appeal and by the Supreme Court of Canada. Taschereau J. held that if *Leaman v. Rea* meant that where the evidence shows that *one* of two drivers was negligent and the court is unable to distinguish between them, then both should be found equally at fault, it should be overruled. There is no principle on which a person may be held liable unless negligence is proved. There was no evidence here, as there was in *France v. Parkinson* and *Baker v. Market Harborough* from which an inference could be drawn that *both* parties were negligent. Locke J. indicated that, in *Leaman v. Rea*, the evidence disclosed a collision in the centre of the road, from which it could be inferred that there was negligence on both drivers. Here, as the forward parts of both vehicles were on the proper side of the road, something occurred to produce a collision of the rear parts. There was no evidence to justify an inference that both drivers were negligent and liability cannot be imposed on the basis that one or other of the drivers was negligent. Does this case conflict with *Leaman v. Rea*?

4. One should not be deluded into thinking that all automobile collision claims will be successful. In *Haswell v. Enman* (1961), 28 D.L.R. (2d) 537 (B.C.C.A.), one party died, the other party had amnesia and other evidence was almost non-existent. The court dismissed both actions. Davey J.A. stated that "the cause of the collision is surrounded by so much speculation and conjecture that it is impossible to find that either party discharged the burden of proving negligence resting upon him". This was a case

of "absence of evidence" rather than one of "the probabilities being evenly divided". A similar result obtained in *Binda v. Waters Const. Co.* (1960), 24 D.L.R. (2d) 431 (Man. C.A.), where the plaintiff motorist, proceeding north, collided with a tractor that was travelling south. The accident occurred in a dense cloud of smoke or steam blown across the highway by a nearby railway locomotive. There being ample room for both vehicles to pass on the highway, the crucial fact issue at the trial was on which side of the highway the accident occurred. The trial judge, after stating that there was "no evidence", found that both parties were equally responsible, purportedly in accordance with the contributory negligence legislation. The Manitoba Court of Appeal said that this was improper and sent the case back for a new trial. Mr. Justice Freedman stated:

> The statutory provision is not a substitute for a judicial finding of negligence, nor does its existence obviate the need of the tribunal making such a judicial finding. Admittedly the learned trial judge faced a difficult problem. But the resolution of that problem called for a judicial decision on the issue of negligence. Only then could the statutory provision be called into play. Instead the learned trial judge resorted to the section and found equal responsibility on the basis thereof. His use of the section in these circumstances involved him — altogether innocently of course — in an abdication of the judicial task which he was required to perform.

Tritschler J.A. would have dismissed the action on the ground that the trial judge had really said he could not find on the evidence that the defendant was negligent. "To grant a new trial is to give the plaintiff a second chance to persuade another court to come to a different conclusion of fact."

5. In the United States *res ipsa loquitur* has been used in medical malpractice cases involving several potential wrongdoers.

In *Ybarra v. Spangard*, 154 P. 2d 687 (Cal. 1944), in the course of an operation for appendicitis, the patient suffered an injury to his shoulder which developed into paralysis of the muscles. He brought suit in one action against the diagnostician, the surgeon, the anaesthetist, the owner of the hospital, and two nurses. At the trial the plaintiff was non-suited. On appeal the non-suit was set aside and the case sent back for trial invoking the doctrine of *res ipsa loquitur*. "Without the aid of the doctrine a patient who received permanent injuries of a serious character, obviously the result of someone's negligence, would be entirely unable to recover unless the doctors and nurses in attendance voluntarily chose to disclose the identity of the negligent person and the facts establishing liability."

Is this a dangerous decision? Can it be justified because of the so-called "conspiracy of silence" among doctors? See Seavey, "*Res Ipsa Loquitur: Tabula in Naufragio*" (1950), 63 Harv. L. Rev. 643, and compare Prosser, "*Res Ipsa Loquitur* in California" (1949), 37 Calif. L. Rev. 183, at 223.

In the trial which was held later, the court found the defendants all liable, even though each of them testified that they "saw nothing occur which could have produced the injury". This was so, even though "all of them were not present at all times". (See 208 P. 2d 445 (2nd D.C.A. 1949), *per* Dooling J.)

6. *Ybarra v. Spangard* has been followed in *Anderson v. Somberg*, 338 A. 2d 1 (N.J. 1975), where a surgical instrument (forceps) broke during an operation, injuring the plaintiff. When the jury dismissed an action against the manufacturer, the hospital, the doctor and the distributor, the appeal court sent the case back for a new trial on the ground that at least one defendant should have been held responsible. The Court held that the burden of proof shifts to the defendants. It explained:

> All those in custody of that patient or who owed him a duty, as here, the manufacturer and the distributor, should be called forward and should be made to prove their freedom from liability.
>
> The rule would have no application except in those instances where the injury lay outside the ambit of the surgical procedure in question; for example, an injury to an organ, when that organ was itself the object of medical attention, would not by itself make out a *prima facie* case for malpractice or shift the burden of proof to the defendants.

There was a strong dissent contending that such a holding would "visit liability, in a wholly irrational way, upon parties that are more probably than not totally free of blame".

At the new trial, the jury found against the manufacturer and the distributor. (See 386 A. 2d 413 (1978)).

7. One court refused to extend the operation of *Ybarra* to a fire which was started by a cigarette in a hotel room occupied by four guests. (See *Firemen's Fund v. Knobbe*, 562 P. 2d 825 (Nev. 1977)). Why is this case different than *Ybarra*? Would you extend *Ybarra* to a situation such as this? See *Valleyview Hotel Ltd. v. Montreal Trust Co.* (1985), 39 Sask. R. 229, 33 C.C.L.T. 282 (C.A.); *Kilgannon v. Sharpe Bros.* (1986), 4 N.S.W.L.R. 600. See also *Roe v. Ministry of Health*, [1954] 2 All E.R. 131 (C.A.) *per* Denning L.J.

8. Will reasoning and results such as these be available in the post *res ipsa* era?

D. STATUTORY ONUS SHIFT IN PROVING NEGLIGENCE

HIGHWAY TRAFFIC ACT

R.S.O. 1990, c. H.8, s. 193

193. (1) When loss or damage is sustained by any person by reason of a motor vehicle on a highway, the onus of proof that the loss or damage did not arise through the negligence or improper conduct of the owner or driver of the motor vehicle is upon the owner or driver.

(2) This section does not apply in cases of a collision between motor vehicles or to an action brought by a passenger in a motor vehicle in respect of any injuries sustained while a passenger.

NOTES

1. The purpose of the "onus" section, as this provision has been called, has been well-explained by Matheson C.C.J. in *MacDonald v. Woodard* (1973), 2 O.R. (2d) 438, 43 D.L.R. (3d) 182 (Co. Ct.). At 440, O.R., he stated:

> This section was enacted in order to overcome difficulties experienced by plaintiffs in obtaining and presenting sufficient evidence of a motorist's negligence to avoid a non-suit at the close of their case. Knowledge of relevant acts and circumstances leading up to an accident might be in the possession only of the defendant and injustice might result if a plaintiff was unable to overcome the initial obstacle of a *prima facie* case and to avoid having his case determined before all the evidence was before the Court. Hence the introduction of

> a type of statutory *res ipsa loquitur* doctrine under which the owner or driver is *prima facie* liable for damage caused by his motor vehicle unless he satisfied the Court on a preponderance of evidence that he was not in fact negligent.
>
> A plaintiff must therefore show, in order that the section may apply, that his damages were occasioned by the presence of a motor vehicle on the highway.
>
> This does not mean that before the onus begins to operate, the plaintiff must first prove that the effective cause of the collision was the conduct of the driver; he need only show that the collision — not the conduct of the driver — was the cause of the damage: ...

With regard to the procedural effect of the section, do you agree that the section creates a type of statutory *res ipsa loquitur* doctrine which operates as suggested by Matheson C.C.J.?

2. What is the procedural effect of this section? See *Winnipeg Electric Co. v. Geel*, [1932] A.C. 690, [1932] 3 W.W.R. 49, where the Privy Council considered the application of such a section. Lord Wright, quoting Duff J., stated: "The statute creates, as against the owners and drivers of motor vehicles, in the conditions therein laid down, a rebuttable presumption of negligence. The onus of disproving negligence remains throughout the proceedings. If, at the conclusion of the evidence, it is too meagre or too evenly balanced to enable the tribunal to determine this issue as a question of fact, then, by force of the statute, the plaintiff is entitled to succeed." Lord Wright also noted: "The position of the defendants under the statute is thus analogous to the position of the defendant in a case to which the principle often called *res ipsa loquitur* applies." Do you agree? What is the difference between the effect of the statute and the way the rule of *res ipsa loquitur* usually operates.

3. This onus section has been used primarily by pedestrians who are run down. Do you think it is of any practical use? The *Osgoode Hall Study on Compensation for Victims of Automobile Accidents* (1965), found that 54 per cent of all those injured recovered. Is any of this due to the onus section?

4. The onus of proof of negligence is also shifted in cases of direct injury. This is a holdover from the days of trespass and case but, despite criticism, the rule is still invoked sometimes. For example, in *Dahlberg v. Naydiuk* (1969), 10 D.L.R. (3d) 319 (Man. C.A.), the plaintiff who was working on a farm was hit by a bullet from the defendant's gun. Mr. Justice Dickson, as he then was, explained:

> Mr. Dahlberg's action was framed both in negligence and in trespass. This give rise to one of those strange anomalies of the law. It is this. If Mr. Dahlberg relies on negligence the onus rests upon him to prove Mr. Naydiuk was negligent. This follows the normal evidentiary rule that he who asserts must prove. However, if Mr. Dahlberg relies upon trespass, (i) Mr. Naydiuk is entitled to judgment only "if he satisfies the onus of establishing the absence of both intention and negligence on his part" (*Cook v. Lewis, supra,* p. 15 [D.L.R.] that is to say the onus rests upon him to disprove negligence. ...
>
> The late Dean C.A. Wright has referred (Linden, *Studies in Canadian Tort Law,* at p. 44) to "this irrational and unnecessary exception of trespass", expressing the hope that some Canadian Court would "put an end to the possibility of a difference in burden of proof depending solely on the direct or indirect application of the force." If such a change is to be made in the law it must be made by a Court higher than this.

See also *Bell Canada v. Cope (Sarnia) Ltd.* (1980), 11 C.C.L.T. 170 affd (1980), 119 D.L.R. (3d) 254 (Ont. C.A.); Sullivan, "Trespass to the Person in Canada: A Defence of the Traditional Approach" (1987), 19 Ottawa L. Rev. 533.

E. INFERRING CAUSATION

In the past, our courts have insisted on strict proof of causation. Unless it could be shown that, on a balance of probabilities, *i.e.*, 51 per cent, the defendant caused the injury, no liability could be imposed. This strictness is being relaxed to some degree nowadays. (See McLachlin, "Negligence Law: Proving the Connection" in *Torts Tomorrow* (1998); Robertson, "Common Sense of Cause in Fact" (1997), 75 Texas L. Rev. 1765). For a time the English courts flirted with a principle set out by Lord Wilberforce in *McGee v. National Coal Board*, [1972] 3 All E.R. 1008 (H.L.) to the effect that the onus of proof of lack of causation shifted to the defendant if the plaintiff could show that the defendant materially increased the risk of injury to the plaintiff. This idea was jettisoned in England in *Wilsher v. Essex Area Health Authority,* [1988] 2 W.L.R. 557 at p. 569 (H.L), where Lord Bridge declared that, rather than shifting the onus of proof, it would be better to adopt a "robust and pragmatic" approach to proof of causation. Such an approach was also advocated by Mr. Justice MacGuigan who suggested a "more practical, common-sense approach" to proof of causation. (See *Letnik v. Metro Toronto* (1988), 49 D.L.R. (4th) 707, at p. 721 (Fed. C.A.)). This view is now enshrined in Canadian law.

SNELL v. FARRELL

Supreme Court of Canada. (1990), 72 D.L.R. (4th) 289, [1990] 2 S.C.R. 311.

The plaintiff became blind in one eye following a cataract operation performed by the defendant doctor. The doctor was found negligent by the trial judge for having continued the operation after noticing bleeding in the plaintiff's eye. The decision to continue with the operation despite the bleeding was determined to be a possible cause of the blindness, although there were other possible causes. The trial judge applied *McGhee* and shifted the onus of disproving cause to the defendant. This was affirmed by the Court of Appeal, and a final appeal was made to the Supreme Court of Canada.

Sopinka J.:

Causation — Principles

Both the trial judge and the Court of Appeal relied on *McGhee*, which (subject to its reinterpretation in the House of Lords in *Wilsher*) purports to depart from traditional principles in the law of torts that the plaintiff must prove on a balance of probabilities that, but for the tortious conduct of the defendant, the plaintiff would not have sustained the injury complained of. In view of the fact that *McGhee* has been applied by a number of courts in Canada to reverse the ordinary burden of proof with respect to causation, it is important to examine recent developments in the law relating to causation and to determine whether a departure from well-established principles is necessary for the resolution of this appeal.

The traditional approach to causation has come under attack in a number of cases in which there is concern that due to the complexities of proof, the probable victim of tortious conduct will be deprived of relief. This concern is strongest in circumstances in which, on the basis of some percentage of statistical probability, the plaintiff is the likely victim of the combined tortious conduct of a number of defendants, but cannot prove causation against a specific defendant or defendants on the basis of particularized evidence in accordance with traditional principles. The challenge to the traditional approach has manifested itself in cases dealing with non-traumatic injuries such as man-made diseases resulting from the widespread diffusion of chemical products, including product liability cases in which a product which can cause injury is widely manufactured and marketed by a large number of corporations. The developments in this area are admirably surveyed by Professor John G. Fleming in "Probabilistic Causation in Tort Law" (1989), 68 Can. Bar Rev. 661. Except for the United States, this challenge has had little impact in the common law jurisdictions. Even in the United States, its effect has been sporadic. In the area referred to above, courts in some states have experimented with a theory of probability which requires proof on the basis of probability at less than 51%, and apportionment of liability among defendant manufacturers of the product in question on the basis of market share: see Fleming, *op. cit.*; *Sindell v. Abbott Laboratories*, 607 P. 2d 924 (Cal. 1980).

Although, to date, these developments have had little impact in other common law countries, it has long been recognized that the allocation of the burden of proof is not immutable. The legal or ultimate burden of proof is determined by the substantive law "upon broad reasons of experience and fairness": J.H. Wigmore, *Evidence in Trials at Common Law*, 4th ed., vol. 9 (Boston: Little, Brown & Co., 1981), s. 2486, at p. 292. In a civil case, the two broad principles are:

1. that the onus is on the party who asserts a proposition, usually the plaintiff;
2. that where the subject-matter of the allegation lies particularly within the knowledge of one party, that party may be required to prove it.

...

Proof of causation in medical malpractice cases is often difficult for the patient. The physician is usually in a better position to know the cause of the injury than the patient. On the basis of the second basic principle referred to above, there is an argument that the burden of proof should be allocated to the defendant. In some jurisdictions, this has occurred to an extent by operation of the principle of *res ipsa loquitur*: . . .

In Canada, the rule has been generally regarded as a piece of circumstantial evidence which does not shift the burden of proof. As the rule was properly held not to be applicable in this case and no argument was directed to this issue, I will refrain from commenting further upon it.

...

[The discussion of *McGhee* and *Wilsher v. Essex* has been omitted.]

The question that this court must decide is whether the traditional approach to causation is no longer satisfactory in that plaintiffs in malpractice cases are being deprived of compensation because they cannot prove causation where it in fact exists.

Causation is an expression of the relationship that must be found to exist between the tortious act of the wrongdoer and the injury to the victim in order to justify compensation of the latter out of the pocket of the former. Is the requirement that the plaintiff prove that the defendant's tortious conduct caused or contributed to the plaintiff's injury too onerous? Is some lesser relationship sufficient to justify compensation? I have examined the alternatives arising out of the *McGhee* case. They were that the plaintiff simply prove that the defendant created a risk that the injury which occurred would occur. Or, what amounts to the same thing, that the defendant has the burden of disproving causation. If I were convinced that defendants who have a substantial connection to the injury were escaping liability because plaintiffs cannot prove causation under currently applied principles, I would not hesitate to adopt one of these alternatives. In my opinion, however, properly applied, the principles relating to causation are adequate to the task. Adoption of either of the proposed alternatives would have the effect of compensating plaintiffs where a substantial connection between the injury and the defendant's conduct is absent. Reversing the burden of proof may be justified where two defendants negligently fire in the direction of the plaintiff and then by their tortious conduct destroy the means of proof at his disposal. In such a case it is clear that the injury was not caused by neutral conduct. It is quite a different matter to compensate a plaintiff by reversing the burden of proof for an injury that may very well be due to factors unconnected to the defendant and not the fault of anyone.

The experience in the United States tells us that liberalization of rules for recovery in malpractice suits contributed to the medical malpractice crisis of the 1970s: see Glen O. Robinson, "The Medical Malpractice Crisis of the 1970's: A Retrospective", 49 Law & Contemp. Probs. (Spring, 1986) 5 at p. 18. Insurance premiums in some states increased up to 500%. Some major commercial insurers withdrew from the market entirely, creating serious problems of availability of insurance: see James R. Posner, "Trends in Medical Malpractice Insurance, 1970-85", 49 Law & Contemp. Probs. (Spring, 1986) 37 at p. 38.

In Britain, proposals to reverse the burden of proof in malpractice cases which gained momentum by virtue of the *McGhee* case were not adopted. In 1978, the Royal Commission on Civil Liability and Compensation for Personal Injury (Pearson Report, vol. I, London: H.M. Stationery Off., 1978), reported as follows (at p. 285):

> Some witnesses suggested that, if the burden of proof were reversed, the patient's difficulties in obtaining and presenting his evidence would be largely overcome. It was said that doctors were in a better position to prove absence of negligence that patients were to establish liability. At the Council of Europe colloquy, however, although it was agreed that the patient was at a disadvantage when he sought to establish a claim, serious doubts were expressed on the desirability of making a radical change in the burden of proof. We share these doubts. We think that there might well be a large increase in claims, and although many would be groundless, each one would have to be investigated and answered. The result would almost certainly be an increase in defensive medicine.

The *Wilsher* decision in the House of Lords which followed ensured that the common law did not undermine this recommendation.

I am of the opinion that the dissatisfaction with the traditional approach to causation stems to a large extent from its too rigid application by the courts in many cases. Causation need not be determined by scientific precision. It is, as stated by Lord Salmon in *Alphacell Ltd. v. Woodward*, [1972] 2 All E.R. 475 (H.L.), at p. 490, "... essentially a practical question of fact which can best be answered by ordinary common sense rather than abstract metaphysical theory." Furthermore, as I observed earlier, the allocation of the burden of proof is not immutable. Both the burden and the standard of proof are flexible concepts. In *Blatch v. Archer* (1774), 1 Cowp. 63 at p. 65, 98 E.R. 969 at p. 970, Lord Mansfield stated: "It is certainly a maxim that all evidence is to be weighed according to the proof which it was in the power of one side to have produced, and in the power of the other to have contradicted."

In many malpractice cases, the facts lie particularly within the knowledge of the defendant. In these circumstances, very little affirmative evidence on the part of the plaintiff will justify the drawing of an inference of causation in the absence of evidence to the contrary. This has been expressed in terms of shifting the burden of proof.

[Reference to *Cummings v. City of Vancouver* (1911), 1 W.W.R. 31 (B.C.C.A.); *Dunlop Holdings Ltd.*, [1979] R.P.C. 523 (C.A.)]

These references speak of the shifting of the secondary or evidential burden of proof or the burden of adducing evidence. I find it preferable to explain the process without using the term secondary or evidential burden. It is not strictly accurate to speak of the burden shifting to the defendant when what is meant is that evidence adduced by the plaintiff may result in an inference being drawn adverse to the defendant. Whether an inference is or is not drawn is a matter of weighing evidence. The defendant runs the risk of an adverse inference in the absence of evidence to the contrary. This is sometimes referred to as imposing on the defendant a provisional or tactical burden: see Cross, *op. cit.*, at p. 129. In my opinion, this is not a true burden of proof, and use of an additional label to describe what is an ordinary step in the fact-finding process is unwarranted.

The legal or ultimate burden remains with the plaintiff, but in the absence of evidence to the contrary adduced by the defendant, an inference of causation may be drawn, although positive or scientific proof of causation has not been adduced. If some evidence to the contrary is adduced by the defendant, the trial judge is entitled to take account of Lord Mansfield's famous precept. This is, I believe, what Lord Bridge had in mind in *Wilsher* when he referred to a "robust and pragmatic approach to the... facts" (p. 569).

[**Sopinka J.** held that the evidence supported the drawing of an inference of causation between the appellant's negligence and the respondent's injury and dismissed the appeal.]

NOTES

1. Professor Klar has written that although *McGhee* is no longer good law, the "spirit and intention" of *McGhee* are "still alive". Do you agree?

2. Did the plaintiff in *Snell v. Farrell* prove on the balance of probabilities that the defendant's negligence caused him his injury? Is this an example of the court using the so-called objective test of causation in order to produce the desired result and hence support certain values?

3. Another way to approach the issue raised by cases such as *McGhee, Wilsher,* and *Snell,* is to argue that materially increasing a risk of an injury is *an injury in itself.* Or, in other words, to negligently deprive a person of a chance to avoid an injury is to damage that person. The advantage of this approach is that it maintains the common law's position that a plaintiff must prove on a balance of probabilities that the defendant's negligence caused the plaintiff's injury. It, however, redefines the nature of the injury by describing it as a loss of a chance.

   This argument was used in the Quebec case of *Laferiere v. Lawson* (1991), 78 D.L.R. (4th) 609, 6 C.C.L.T. (2d) 119 (S.C.C.). The deceased had a tumour removed from her breast in 1971. Although the tumour was found to have been malignant, the deceased was not told of this and was not advised of the available forms of treatment for cancer. In 1975, the deceased discovered that she was suffering from generalized cancer. She died in 1978. Prior to her death, she commenced an action against her doctor claiming, among other things, that the doctor's failure to inform her of her cancer deprived her of the chance to obtain treatment. After she died, the suit was continued by her estate.

The facts indicated that even if the deceased had been informed of her earlier cancer and had received treatment that it was not certain, nor even probable, that her cancer would have been cured or she would have had a remission. Thus, one of the issues of this case was whether the failure to advise her of her cancer had, on the balance of probabilities, caused her any injury. The trial judge rejected the estate's claim on the basis of lack of causation. The Court of Appeal reversed and the case went to the Supreme Court of Canada.

Gonthier J. rejected the loss of chance approach as being inappropriate, particularly where the event which was initially contingent had already occurred. According to Gonthier J. "[i]n such cases, classical principles of causation suffice, and, further, are essential in order for individual responsibility to attach." After carefully reviewing the civil law writings on this issue, Gonthier J. concluded:

> In conclusion, then, and with all due deference to those who have expressed other opinions, I do not feel that the theory of loss of chance, at least as it is understood in France and Belgium, should be introduced into the civil law of Quebec in matters of medical responsibility. In the Court of Appeal, Jacques J.A. states without elaboration that loss of chance is recognized in the common law. I have taken note of the vigorous debate which is taking place in the United States and can find no dominant jurisprudential position favouring loss of chance in that country. In the United Kingdom, the House of Lords has expressed reservations about loss of chance analysis, but has not, as yet, reached a settled conclusion about its possible application: *Hoston v. East Berkshire Health Area Authority*, [1987] A.C. 750. I have also made note of this Court's recent decision in *Snell v. Farrell*, supra, which I take to endorse traditional principles of causation, properly applied.
>
> By way of summary, I would make the following brief, general observations:
>
> - The rules of civil responsibility require proof of fault, causation and damage.
> - Both acts and omissions may amount to fault and both may be analyzed similarly with regard to causation.
> - Causation in law is not identical to scientific causation.
> - Causation in law must be established on the balance of probabilities, taking into account all the evidence: factual, statistical and that which the judge is entitled to presume.
> - In some cases, where a fault presents a clear danger and where such a danger materializes, it may be reasonable to presume a causal link, unless there is a demonstration or indication to the contrary.
> - Statistical evidence may be helpful as indicative but is not determinative. In particular, where statistical evidence does not indicate causation on the balance of probabilities, causation in law may nonetheless exist where evidence in the case supports such a finding.
> - Even where statistical and factual evidence do not support a finding of causation on the balance of probabilities with respect to particular damage (*e.g.*, death or sickness), such evidence may still justify a finding of causation with respect to lesser damage (*e.g.*, slightly shorter life, greater pain).
> - The evidence must be carefully analyzed to determine the exact nature of the fault or breach of duty and its consequences as well as the particular character of the damage which has been suffered, as experienced by the victim.
> - If after consideration of these factors a judge is not satisfied that the fault has, on his or her assessment of the balance of probabilities, caused any real damage, then recovery should be denied.

Although the Supreme Court did not allow the estate to recover damages for the deceased's death, it was allowed to recover damages for the deceased's psychological anguish and frustration related to the defendant's failure to inform, and, as well, damages for a loss in the quality of the deceased's life due to her failure to receive treatment. For a critical comment on the judgment see Mirandola, "Lost Chances in Medical Negligence" (1992), 50 U. Toronto Fac. L. Rev. 258.

4. *Lawson* was a Quebec case, and civil law authorities were used to justify the result. Do you think that the result will be the same in the common law? Why is the law prepared to recognize future possibilities when assessing a plaintiff's damages but apparently not prepared to recognize past possibilities in determining whether or not a plaintiff has suffered injury as a result of the defendant's negligence?

5. The loss of a chance doctrine was rejected by the Manitoba Court of Appeal in *Cabral v. Gupta*, [1993] 1 W.W.R. 648, 13 C.C.L.T. (2d) 323. The trial judge's findings were that there was a 70 per cent probability that the defendant doctor's negligence caused the plaintiff to lose his vision, but a 30 per cent chance that the vision would have been lost anyway. In this case, should the plaintiff be entitled to full damages or 70 per cent of his damages? The trial judge reduced the damages by 30 per cent. The Court of Appeal said that this was wrong and that full damages were appropriate. With whom do you agree?

6. A recent case indicated that the loss of a chance was not compensable in tort but that damages for loss of a chance might be available in an action against a doctor for breach of contract. (See *de la Giroday v. Brough*, [1997] 6 W.W.R. 585 (B.C.C.A.).) Does this make any sense?

F. MULTIPLE CAUSES: TWO NEGLIGENT DEFENDANTS BUT ONLY ONE CAUSE OF ACCIDENT

COOK v. LEWIS

Supreme Court of Canada. [1951] S.C.R. 830, [1952] 1 D.L.R. 1

The defendants, Cook and Akenhead, together with a third person, were in one party hunting for grouse. The plaintiff, Lewis, with two others, was in another party in the same vicinity, also engaged in grouse hunting. Lewis was injured by gun shot when his party came close to that of the defendants. Lewis brought action against Cook and Akenhead claiming that they had negligently injured him by discharging their guns knowing he was in the vicinity and without making sure that he was out of their line of fire.

The evidence at the trial showed that shortly after the defendants had seen some of the plaintiff's party both Cook and Akenhead had fired but, according to the evidence, at different birds, and in different directions, and that the plaintiff was injured as a result. The jury answered questions in a confusing way leading the trial judge to dismiss the case. The Court of Appeal of British Columbia ordered a new trial and the Supreme Court of Canada agreed.

Cartwright J. (Estey, Fauteux, concurring): I think that the learned trial judge did not charge the jury correctly in regard to the onus of proof of negligence. While it is true that the plaintiff expressly pleaded negligence on the part of the defendants he also pleaded that he was shot by them and in my opinion the action under the old form of pleading would properly have been one of trespass and not of case. . . .

In my opinion *Stanley v. Powell* rightly decides that the defendant in such an action is entitled to judgment if he satisfies the onus of establishing the absence of both intention and negligence on his part. ...

This, however, is not enough to dispose of the appeal. It is necessary to consider the answer to the question in which the jury have indicated that they were unable to find which of the two defendants did fire the shot which did the damage.

The general rule is, I think, stated correctly in *Starkie on Evidence*, 4th ed. p. 860, quoted with approval by Patterson J.A., in *Moxley v. Can. Atlantic Ry.* (1887), 14 O.A.R. 309, at p. 315. " 'Thus in practice, when it is certain that one of two individuals committed the offence charged, but it is uncertain whether the one or the other was the guilty agent, neither of them can be convicted.' "

This rule, I think, is also applicable to civil actions so that if at the end of the case A has proved that he was negligently injured by either B or C but is unable to establish which of the two caused the injury, his action must fail against both unless there are special circumstances which render the rule inapplicable.

[There was no joint enterprise here and no relationship of agency.]

The judgment in *Summers v. Tice* (5 A.L.R. 2d 9) reads in part as follows (p. 96):

> When we consider the relative position of the parties and the results that would flow if plaintiff was required to pin the injury on one of the defendants only, a requirement that the burden of proof on that subject be shifted to defendants becomes manifest. They are both wrongdoers — both negligent towards plaintiff. They brought about a situation where the negligence of one of them injured the plaintiff, hence, it should rest with them each to absolve himself if he can. The injured party has been placed by defendants in the unfair position of pointing to which defendant caused the harm. If one can escape the other may also and plaintiff is remediless. Ordinarily defendants are in a far better position to offer evidence to determine which one caused the injury. This reasoning has recently found favour in this court.

I do not think it necessary to decide whether all that was said in *Summers v. Tice* should be accepted as stating the law of British Columbia, but I am of opinion, for the reasons given in that case, that if under the circumstances of the case at bar the jury, having decided that the plaintiff was shot by either Cook or Akenhead, found themselves unable to decide which of the two shot him because in their opinion both shot negligently in his direction, both defendants should have been found liable. I think that the learned trial judge should have sent the jury back to consider the matter further with a direction to the above effect. ...

It may be that at the new trial no question of the application of the rule laid down in *Summers v. Tice*, will arise. I respectfully agree with the Court of Appeal that the jury should have been able to decide which one of the defendants fired the shot which struck the plaintiff.

In my respectful opinion the perverse finding on the question of negligence following the insufficient direction on the question of onus, the failure of the jury to reach a finding as to who fired the shot which struck the plaintiff and the failure of the learned trial judge to send them back for reconsideration of this question with the added direction indicated above, made it proper for the Court of Appeal to direct a new trial.

Rand J. (concurring): There remains the answer that, although shots from one of the two guns struck the respondent, the jury could not determine from which they came. ... The essential obstacle to proof is the fact of multiple discharges so related as to confuse their individual effects: it is that fact that bars final proof. But if the victim, having brought guilt down to one or both of two persons before the court, can bring home to either of them a further wrong done him in relation to his remedial right of making that proof, then I should say that on accepted principles, the barrier to it can and should be removed. . . .

What, then, the culpable actor has done by his initial negligent act is, first, to have set in motion a dangerous force which embraces the injured person within the scope of its probable mischief; and next, in conjunction with circumstances which he must be held to contemplate, to have made more difficult if not impossible the means of proving the possible damaging results of his own act or the similar results of the act of another. He has violated not only the victim's substantive right to security, but he has also culpably impaired the latter's remedial right of establishing liability. By confusing his act with environmental conditions, he has, in effect, destroyed the victim's power of proof.

The legal consequence of that is, I should say, that the onus is then shifted to the wrongdoer to exculpate himself; it becomes in fact a question of proof between him and the other and innocent member of the alternatives, the burden of which he must bear. The onus attaches to culpability, and if both acts bear that taint, the onus or *prima facie* transmission of responsibility attaches to both, and the question of the sole responsibility of one is a matter between them. …

Assuming, then, that the jury have found one or both of the defendants here negligent, as on the evidence I think they must have, and at the same time have found that the consequences of the two shots, whether from a confusion in time or in area, cannot be segregated, the onus on the guilty person arises. This is a case where each hunter would know of or expect the shooting by the other and the negligent actor has culpably participated in the proof-destroying fact, the multiple shooting and its consequences. No liability will, in any event, attach to an innocent act of shooting, but the culpable actor, as against innocent, must bear the burden of exculpation.

Locke J. (dissenting): … On the argument before us, it was contended for the respondent that in the circumstances there was a presumption of fault against the defendant and that the onus was on them to prove by affirmative evidence that they had exercised due care, but clearly this contention cannot be supported. There were here no circumstances which could, in my opinion, raise any such presumption. …

The facts in the present matter do not, however, in my opinion, support a claim upon [the] basis [of joint design.] Cook and Akenhead were merely hunting in each other's company: there was no common design … they were rather each pursuing their own design of shooting grouse, as they were lawfully entitled to do. I am unable to understand how the fact that, like most hunters, they at the end of the day divided up the bag, the more fortunate sharing his luck with the other, can be a basis for any legal liability. …

In my opinion, this is decisive of the present appeal since, in the absence of a finding that the respondent was shot by Cook and since the latter is not liable if the damage was caused by the act of Akenhead, the action was properly dismissed. … A finding that one or other of the defendants was negligent would clearly not have furthered the matter. …

NOTES

1. Is this a proof of negligence or proof of causation problem? How does this case compare with *Leaman v. Rea, supra*? See also *Joseph Brant Memorial Hospital v. Koziol* (1977), 2 C.C.L.T. 170, at 180, 77 D.L.R. (3d) 161 (S.C.C.).

2. In *Beecham v. Henderson*, [1951] 1 D.L.R. 628 (B.C.S.C.), two men engaged in work adjoining a highway each threw a handful of sand at a bus carrying high school students. The sand passed through the open window of the bus and hit the plaintiff in the eye. It was impossible to say which of the defendants threw the sand that hit the plaintiff. Coady J., held both defendants liable as "joint tortfeasors and not independent tortfeasors" but he also added, "unless one or other of them can establish that his wrongful act did not cause the injury".

3. In *Woodward v. Begbie et al.*, [1962] O.R. 60, 31 D.L.R. (2d) 22 (H.C.), two police officers shot at an escaping suspect, but only one bullet hit him. Not being able to decide which officer's bullet did the damage, Mr. Justice MacLennan held both liable.

4. Although this principle has withstood the test of time, it will not be lightly extended. In *Lange v. Bennett*, [1964] 1 O.R. 233, 41 D.L.R. (2d) 691 (H.C.J.), the 18-year-old plaintiff was hunting with two 16-year-old friends. He knelt down in front of them to shoot and then suddenly stood up in the line of fire of the other two boys. He was hit by a bullet fired by one of them, but it could not be determined which defendant was responsible. Mr. Justice McRuer found that, since the plaintiff was himself contributorily negligent, *Cook v. Lewis* would not apply. He explained:

> Negligence must necessarily be relative to the circumstances in each case and to the ages of the parties in question. The plaintiff at the time of the accident was two years older than the defendants. He kneeled down to shoot and knew that he was in the approximate line of fire of two younger boys, shooting from behind him. He was unquestionably negligent in standing up without warning and putting himself into the line of fire. He must be taken to have known that he might have been struck by a shot fired by either of them and it would be difficult to say in such circumstances which boy fired the shot that struck him. He had himself participated as a "negligent actor" in "the proof destroying fact". To hold on these facts that the one who may have done him no harm should pay damages because he could not clear himself from blame would be grossly unjust. These are not special circumstances. ...

Do you agree with Mr. Justice McRuer's disposition of the case and his reasoning?

5. There is some indication that *Cook v. Lewis* might even be employed in strict liability and nuisance cases. See *dictum* of Dubinsky J. in *MacDonald v. Desourdy Construction Ltée* (1972), 27 D.L.R. (3d) 144, at 159 (N.S.S.C.).

G. MARKET SHARE LIABILITY

SINDELL v. ABBOTT LABORATORIES ET AL.

Supreme Court of California. 26 Cal. 3d 588, 607 P. 2d 924 (1980).

The plaintiff's mother ingested the drug DES during her pregnancy for the purpose of preventing miscarriage. As a result of this drug, the plaintiff developed a malignant bladder tumor. Although the plaintiff knew the type of drug which was taken by her mother, she could not identify the manufacturer of the precise product. The plaintiff, on behalf of herself and other women in a similar position, brought action against eleven drug companies, all of which had been in the business of manufacturing, promoting and marketing DES. In a landmark decision, the Court held that the plaintiff could hold the manufacturers of the drug which was produced from an identical formula liable for her injuries upon showing that the manufacturers produced a substantial percentage of the drug in question. Each manufacturer would be liable for the proportion of the judgment represented by its share of the drug market unless it demonstrated that it could not have made the product that caused the plaintiff's injuries.

Mosk J.: We begin with the proposition that, as a general rule, the imposition of liability depends upon a showing by the plaintiff that his or her injuries were caused by the act of the defendant or by an instrumentality under the defendant's control. The rule applies whether the injury resulted from an accidental event . … or from the use of a defective product.

[The learned Justice reviewed the plaintiff's arguments. The plaintiff argued that there were three theories which would support its case: the "alternative liability" theory of *Summers v. Tice, supra*, the "concert of action" theory, and "enterprise liability". These three were held inapplicable to the circumstances of this case. But the learned Justice continued:]

In our contemporary complex industrialized society, advances in science and technology create fungible goods which may harm consumers and which cannot be traced to any specific producer. The response of the courts can be either to adhere rigidly to prior doctrine, denying recovery to those injured by such products, or to fashion remedies to meet these changing needs. Just as Justice Traynor in his landmark concurring opinion in *Escola v. Coca Cola Bottling Company* (1944) 24 Cal. 2d 453, 467-468, 150 P. 2d 436, recognized that in an era of mass production and complex marketing methods the traditional standard of negligence was insufficient to govern the obligations of manufacturer to consumer, so should we acknowledge that some adaptation of the rules of causation and liability may be appropriate in these recurring circumstances. The Restatement comments that modification of the *Summers* rule may be necessary in a situation like that before us.

The most persuasive reason for finding plaintiff states a cause of action is that advanced in *Summers*: as between an innocent plaintiff and negligent defendants, the latter should bear the cost of the injury. Here, as in *Summers*, plaintiff is not at fault in failing to provide evidence of causation, and although the absence of such evidence is not attributable to the defendants either, their conduct in marketing a drug the effects of which are delayed for many years played a significant role in creating the unavailability of proof.

From a broader policy standpoint, defendants are better able to bear the cost of injury resulting from the manufacture of a defective product. As was said by Justice Traynor in *Escola*, "[t]he cost of an injury and the loss of time or health may be an overwhelming misfortune to the person injured, and a needless one, for the risk of injury can be insured by the manufacturer and distributed among the public as a cost of doing business." . … The manufacturer is in the best position to discover and guard against defects in its products and to warn of harmful effects; thus, holding it liable for defects and failure to warn of harmful effects will provide an incentive to product safety. … These considerations are particularly significant where medication is involved, for the consumer is virtually helpless to protect himself from serious, sometimes permanent, sometimes fatal, injuries caused by deleterious drugs.

Where, as here, all defendants produced a drug from an identical formula and the manufacturer of the DES which caused plaintiff's injuries cannot be identified through no fault of plaintiff, a modification of the rule of *Summers* is warranted. As we have seen, an undiluted *Summers* rationale is inappropriate to shift the burden of proof of causation to defendants because if we measure the chance that any particular manufacturer supplied the injury-causing product by the number of producers of DES, there is a possibility that none of the five defendants in this case produced the offending substance and that the responsible manufacturer, not named in the action, will escape liability.

But we approach the issue of causation from a different perspective: we hold it to be reasonable in the present context to measure the likelihood that any of the defendants supplied the product which allegedly injured plaintiff by the percentage which the DES sold by each of them for the purpose of preventing miscarriage bears to the entire production of the drug sold by all for that purpose. Plaintiff asserts in her briefs that Eli Lilly and Company and 5 or 6 other companies produced 90 per cent of the DES marketed. If at trial this is established to be the fact, then there is a corresponding likelihood that this comparative handful of producers manufactured the DES which caused plaintiff's injuries, and only a 10 per cent likelihood that the offending producer would escape liability.

If plaintiff joins in the action the manufacturers of a substantial share of the DES which her mother might have taken, the injustice of shifting the burden of proof to defendants to demonstrate that they could not have made the substance which injured plaintiff is significantly diminished. While 75 to 80 per cent of the market is suggested as the requirement by the Fordham Comment (at p. 996), we hold only that a substantial percentage is required.

The presence in the action of a substantial share of the appropriate market also provides a ready means to apportion damages among the defendants. Each defendant will be held liable for the proportion of the judgment represented by its share of that market unless it demonstrates that it could not have made the product which caused plaintiff's injuries. In the present case, as we have seen, one DES manufacturer was dismissed from the action upon filling a declaration that it had not manufactured DES until after plaintiff was born. Once plaintiff has met her burden of joining the required defendants, they in turn may cross-complaint against other DES manufacturers, not joined in the action, which they can allege might have supplied the injury-causing product.

Under this approach, each manufacturer's liability would approximate its responsibility for the injuries caused by its own products. Some minor discrepancy in the correlation between market share and liability is inevitable; therefore, a defendant may be held liable for a somewhat different percent age of the damage than its share of the appropriate market would justify. It is probably impossible, with the passage of time, to determine market share with mathematical exactitude. But just as a jury cannot be expected to determine the precise relationship between fault and liability in applying the doctrine of comparative fault . ... or partial indemnity ... . the difficulty of apportioning damages among the defendant producers in exact relation to their market share does not seriously militate against the rule we adopt. As we said in *Summers* with regard to the liability of independent tortfeasors, where a correct division of liability cannot be made "the trier of fact may make it the best it can." . ...

We are not unmindful of the practical problems involved in defining the market and determining market share, but these are largely matters of proof which properly cannot be determined at the pleading stage of these proceedings. Defendants urge that it would be both unfair and contrary to public policy to hold them liable for plaintiff's injuries in the absence of proof that one of them supplied the drug responsible for the damage. Most of their arguments, however, are based upon the assumption that one manufacturer would be held responsible for the products of another or for those of all other manufacturers if plaintiff ultimately prevails. But under the rule we adopt, each manufacturer's liability for an injury would be approximately equivalent to the damages caused by the DES it manufactured.

The judgments are reversed.

NOTES

1. There was a vigorous dissent by Richardson J. He held that the majority's approach was "directly contrary to long established tort principles". It was both "inequitable and improper". He stated:

> I believe that the scales of justice tip against imposition of this new liability because of the foregoing elements of unfairness to some defendants who may have had nothing whatever to do with causing any injury, the unwarranted preference created for this particular class of plaintiffs, the violence done to traditional tort principles by the drastic expansion of liability proposed, the injury threatened to the public interest in continued unrestricted basic medical research as stressed by the Restatement, and the other reasons heretofore expressed.
>
> The majority's decision effectively makes the entire drug industry (or at least its California members) an insurer of all injuries attributable to defective drugs of uncertain or unprovable origin, including those injuries manifesting themselves a generation later, and regardless of whether particular defendants had any part whatever in causing the claimed injury. Respectfully, I think this is unreasonable overreaction for the purpose of achieving what is perceived to be a socially satisfying result.
>
> Finally, I am disturbed by the broad and ominous ramifications of the majority's holding. The law review comment, which is the wellspring of the majority's new theory, conceding the widespread consequences of industry-wide liability, openly acknowledges that 'The DES cases are only the tip of an iceberg.' (Comment, DES and a Proposed Theory of Enterprise Liability (1978) 46 Fordham L. Rev. 963, 1007). Although the pharmaceutical drug industry may be the first target of this new sanction, the majority's reasoning has equally threatening application to many other areas of business and commercial activities.
>
> Given the grave and sweeping economic, social, and medical effects of 'market share' liability, the policy decision to introduce and define it should rest not with us, but with the Legislature which is currently considering not only major statutory reform of California product liability law in general, but the DES problem in particular. (See Sen. Bill No. 1392 (1979-1980 Reg. Sess.), which would establish and appropriate funds for the education, identification, and screening of persons exposed to DES, and would prohibit health care and hospital service plans from excluding or limiting coverage to persons exposed to DES.) An alternative proposal for administrative compensation, described as "a limited version of no-fault products liability" has been suggested by one commentator. (*Coggins*, … 13 Suffolk L. Rev. at pp. 1019-1021.) Compensation under such a plan would be awarded by an administrative tribunal from funds collected "via a tax paid by all manufacturers." (P. 1020, fn. omitted.) In any event, the problem invites a legislative rather than an attempted judicial solution.
>
> I would affirm the judgments of dismissal.

Do you prefer the approach of the majority or of the dissent? Does this case offer anything that Canadian courts should adopt?

2. Some courts have expressly rejected *Sindell* while others have followed and expanded upon it. The decision was based on a student law review contribution: "Comment, DES and a Proposed Theory of Enterprise Liability" (1978), 46 Ford L. Rev. 963. See Delgado, "Beyond *Sindell*: Relaxation of Cause-in-fact Rules for Indeterminate Plaintiffs" (1983), 70 Calif. L. Rev. 881; Rosenberg, "The Causal Connection in Mass Exposure Cases: A 'Public Law' Vision of the Tort System" (1984), 97 Harv. L. Rev. 851.

NEGLIGENCE ACT

R.S.O. 1990, c. N.1, s. 1

1. Where damages have been caused or contributed to by the fault or neglect of two or more persons, the court shall determine the degree in which each of such persons is at fault or negligent, and, where two or more persons are found at fault or negligent, they are jointly and severally liable to the person suffering loss or damage for such fault or negligence, but as between themselves, in the absence of any contract express or implied, each is liable to make contribution and indemnify each other in the degree in which they are respectively found to be at fault or negligent.

NOTES

1. This section first appeared in the 1930 revision of the original 1924 Ontario *Contributory Negligence Act* which dealt only with fault on the part of a plaintiff (see the 1924 Act in R.S.O. 1927, c. 103). When originally enacted in 1930 (Ont. Stat., c. 27) the present section provided for contribution "where two or more persons are found to be liable". A section similar to Ontario's appears in the *Contributory Negligence Acts* of Alberta, British Columbia, New Brunswick, Newfoundland, Nova Scotia, Prince Edward Island, and Saskatchewan.

2. When two defendants are both liable jointly or severally to the plaintiff, the plaintiff is entitled to collect the entire damages from either of the defendants, who are individually liable for all of the damages they caused. As Dickson J. stated in *County of Parkland v. Stetar*, [1975] 2 S.C.R. 884, [1975] 1 W.W.R. 441, "the plaintiff may elect to recover the full amount of his damage from a tortfeasor only partly to blame". Of course, the plaintiff cannot recover more than the total of the damages assessed.

3. The right of one tortfeasor to recover contribution from another tortfeasor has often raised difficult questions. This is due to inadequate legislation which merely creates the right without dealing with the many complexities involved. Questions concerning settlements, insolvency, limitation periods, the extent of the right are not addressed by the provincial apportionment statutes and raise thorny problems for lawyers and courts.

4. Can one tortfeasor seek contribution from a second tortfeasor who has never actually been found liable to the injured party? Often plaintiffs fail to sue all those responsible for their injuries, but select the more obvious or solvent defendants. When those defendants who are found liable to the plaintiff attempt to obtain contribution from others who they think ought to share in the responsibility, they are often met with limitation problems.

   In *Campbell et al. v. Bartlett (No. 2)* (1979), 107 D.L.R. (3d) 591, [1980] 1 W.W.R. 758 (Sask. C.A.), the Court of Appeal permitted third party proceedings to be commenced against a doctor despite the fact that the one-year limitation period provided by the *Medical Profession Act*, R.S.S. 1978, c. M-10, in which the patient might have sued the doctor, had already expired. A similar decision was arrived at by the Alberta Court of Appeal in *J.R. Paine & Associates Ltd. v. Strong, Lamb & Nelson Ltd.* (1979), 103 D.L.R. (3d) 579, [1979] 6 W.W.R. 353 (C.A.). In *Paquette et al. v. Batchelor* (1980), 28 O.R. (2d) 59, 13 C.C.L.T. 237 (*sub nom. Batchelor v. Brown*) (Ont. H.C.), third party proceedings were commenced against a police constable several years after the accident which caused the injuries. Despite a six-month limitation provided for in *The Public Authorities Protection Act*, R.S.O. 1970, c. 374, s. 11, as am. 1976, c. 19, in which the injured party might have brought action against the police officer, the Ontario High Court upheld the third party claim. For a comment on *J.R. Paine v. Strong* see Klar (1980), 18 Alta. L. Rev. 515, and on *Paquette v. Batchelor*, see Cheifetz (1980), 13 C.C.L.T. 239.

5. What is the result if the plaintiff has in fact sued all the tortfeasors, but the action has been dismissed against one due to a procedural defect in the plaintiff's case, *e.g.* failure to give a required notice of action? In *County of Parkland v. Stetar, supra*, the Supreme Court held that in this case contribution was not available.

6. Must the claim for contribution and the principal action be brought together? Can a claim for contribution be commenced before the principal action has been settled or decided by judgment?

In *Glass v. Avenue Dodge Chrysler* (1979), 26 O.R. (2d) 592, 10 C.C.L.T. 70 (Co. Ct.), it was held that a claim for contribution could be commenced, even prior to the settlement of the principal claim. See Cheifetz, "Annotation" (1979), 10 C.C.L.T. 70. Cheifetz was critical of the further finding in the *Glass* case that the claim for contribution arises when the tortious act occurs. According to Cheifetz, the settled view in Ontario is that the claim for contribution arises when the claimant's liability to the injured party is settled either by judgment or by settlement.

In *Inglis Ltd. v. South Shore Sales* (1979), 31 N.S.R. (2d) 541, 104 D.L.R. (3d) 507, the Appeal Division of the Nova Scotia Supreme Court held that an action for contribution need not be brought together with the main action. An earlier decision in Ontario, *Cohen v. S. McCord*, [1944] 3 D.L.R. 207; affd [1944] 4 D.L.R. 753 (C.A.), held that in certain cases all issues must be decided in the one action. The decision in *Cohen v. McCord* itself might now be in some doubt as a result of the Supreme Court of Canada's decision in *R. v. Foundation Co. of Canada*, [1980] 1 S.C.R. 695, 106 D.L.R. (3d) 193 (*sub nom. Foundation Co. of Canada Ltd. v. Canada*), 12 C.P.C. 248 (*sub nom. R. v. Thomas Fuller Const. Co. (1958) Ltd.*). For a discussion of this case see Klar, "Developments in Tort Law: The 1979-80 Term" (1981), 2 Supreme Court L. Rev., at 325.

In *Cristovao v. Doran's Beverages Inc.* (1983), 40 O.R. (2d) 737, 143 D.L.R. (3d) 641 (H.C.J.), the Court held that third party proceedings for contribution can be taken independently from the principal action. See also *Hannigan v. City of Edmonton* (1983), 1 D.L.R. (4th) 397, [1983] 6 W.W.R. 644 (Alta. Q.B.), the "innocent" party settled action and recovered 100 per cent from the "co-tortfeasor".

7. Does the right to claim contribution apply only when both wrongdoers are "tortfeasors"? There have been numerous claims made when a breach of contract was involved. Most, but not all, of these cases allowed contribution claims. For cases allowing contribution claims in the contractual setting, see *De Meza and Stuart v. Apple, Van Straten, Shena and Stone*, [1975] 1 Lloyd's Rep. 498 (C.A.); *Groves-Raffin Const. Ltd. v. Bank of Nova Scotia* (1975), 51 D.L.R. (3d) 380, [1975] 2 W.W.R. 97 (B.C.S.C.); varied, 64 D.L.R. (3d) 78, [1976] 2 W.W.R. 673 (*sub nom. Groves-Raffin Const. Ltd. v. Can. Imperial Bank of Commerce*) (B.C.C.A.); Jessup J.A. in *Dominion Chain v. Eastern Constr.* (1976), 12 O.R. (2d) 201, 68 D.L.R. (3d) 385; affd on other grounds, [1978] 2 S.C.R. 1346 (*sub nom. Giffels Associates Ltd. v. Eastern Const. Co.*), 84 D.L.R. (3d) 344, Pigeon J. dissenting; in *Smith v. McInnis* (1978), 91 D.L.R. (3d) 190, 4 C.C.L.T. 154 (S.C.C.); *Truman v. Sparling Real Estate Ltd.* (1977), 3 C.C.L.T. 205, [1977] I.L.R. 1-893 (B.C.C.A.). For cases denying the right to claim contribution in the contractual setting, see *Dabous v. Zuliani* (1976), 12 O.R. (2d) 230, 68 D.L.R. (3d) 414 (C.A.); *Allcock Laight & Westwood v. Patten*, [1967] 1 O.R. 18 (C.A.); *Ma Wai Kay*

et al. v. McGay Ltd. (1979), 101 D.L.R. (3d) 286, [1979] 5 W.W.R. 279 (Man. Q.B.). *Cosyns v. Smith* (1983), 41 O.R. (2d) 488, 146 D.L.R. (3d) 622 (C.A.).

For an excellent analysis of this problem, see Weinrib, "Contribution in a Contractual Setting" (1975), 54 Can. Bar Rev. 338.

8. One way to avoid the debate as to whether the legislation applies in a contractual setting is to find concurrent liability in tort and contract. This was done in *Corp. of District of Surrey v. Carroll-Hatch and Associates Ltd.*, 14 B.C.L.R. 156, [1979] 6 W.W.R. 289 (C.A.). The topic of the contract—tort borderland—is dealt with *infra*.

9. The potential complexities involved in deciding issues of contribution and apportionment reveal themselves in *Urquhart v. Hatt et al.* (1982), 132 D.L.R. (3d) 685, 27 C.P.C. 296 (Ont. Co. Ct.). A passenger, injured in a motor vehicle accident, sued the owner and driver of the car in which she had been riding, as well as the owner and driver of the second car involved. The owner of the first car settled with the plaintiff and a release was executed releasing all the defendants from further liability. Ultimately a notice of discontinuance of the original action was served and the action was accordingly dismissed. The party who had settled the passenger's action then commenced proceedings against the driver and owner of the second car, claiming contribution and indemnity from them for the settlement. These two defendants defended this claim for contribution by arguing that they had never been found liable for the injuries to the passenger and, furthermore, that they could not now be found liable since the two-year limitation period had expired before the institution of the action claiming contribution. The court rejected this contention. The court held that only where an action has been dismissed after trial on the merits is a defendant relieved from an obligation to contribute. Moreover, the court held that where there has been a settlement if there was potential liability of the person from whom contribution is claimed at any time before the settlement was made, this would be sufficient to support a contribution claim. Finally, the court held that the limitation period for claiming contribution begins to run only from the time of the settlement and not from the time the original damages were caused.

10. For an excellent treatment of this area see Cheifetz, *Apportionment of Fault in Tort* (1981).

CHAPTER 7

DUTY

Our law has never reached the stage where all losses caused by negligent conduct attract liability. Certain losses are felt to be beyond the sphere of protection that the law should afford, even though such harms result from negligent conduct. Various techniques such as "duty of care", "remoteness of damage", and "proximate cause" have been used to place limits on liability for negligent conduct. This chapter and the next are designed to bring into focus these concepts, which are among the most complex in the law of torts.

We shall first examine the concept of duty, an idea that is not known to the civil law. Courts use the duty concept as a limiting device to deny liability, even when the defendant's negligence may have caused a loss, where the loss suffered is not one that the law deems worthy of protection or where the person hurt is not thought to be someone who is entitled to the protection of the law. As Lord Esher once said, a person is "entitled to be as negligent as he pleases towards the whole world if he owes no duty to them". (See *Le Lievre v. Gould,* [1893] 1 Q.B. 491, at 497.)

Courts often use the idea of risk in this context, asking whether the plaintiff was within the scope of the risk created by the defendant. If so, a duty is owed to the plaintiff. When the issue is more a matter of the way that the risk has culminated, that is, the type of accident that has occurred, the courts may prefer to invoke the language of remoteness or proximate cause (see Chapter 8). In cases of nonfeasance, duty language is usually used to deny recovery. In cases of special activities that must remain immune from tort liability, duty analysis is also employed.

A. THE CONCEPT OF DUTY GENERALLY

M'ALISTER (OR DONOGHUE) v. STEVENSON

House of Lords. [1932] A.C. 562, 101 L.J.P.C. 119.

The appellant, a shop assistant, sought to recover from the respondent, an aerated water manufacturer, on the ground of his alleged negligence, £500 as damages for the injurious effects alleged to have been produced on her by the presence of a snail in a bottle of ginger beer manufactured by the respondent and ordered for the appellant by a friend in a shop in Paisley. In consequence having drunk part of the contaminated contents of the bottle the appellant alleged that she contracted a serious illness. The bottle was dark opaque glass so the condition of its contents could not be ascertained by inspection. The bottle was closed with a metal cap and on the side was a label bearing the name of the respondent.

The Lord Ordinary rejected the respondent's plea in law that the appellant's averments were irrelevant and insufficient to support the conclusions of the summons and allowed a proof. The Second Division, by a majority (the Lord

Justice-Clerk, Lord Ormidale, and Lord Anderson; Lord Hunter dissenting), recalled the interlocutor of the Lord Ordinary and dismissed the action.

Lord Atkin: The sole question for determination in this case is legal: Do the averments made by the pursuer in her pleading, if true, disclose a cause of action? I need not restate the particular facts. The question is whether the manufacturer of an article of drink sold by him to a distributor in circumstances which prevent the distributor or the ultimate purchaser or consumer from discovering by inspection any defect is under any legal duty to the ultimate purchaser or consumer to take reasonable care that the article is free from defect likely to cause injury to health. I do not think a more important problem has occupied your Lordships in your judicial capacity, important both because of its bearing on public health and because of the practical test which it applies to the system of law under which it arises. The case has to be determined in accordance with Scots law, but it has been a matter of agreement between the experienced counsel who argued this case, and it appears to be the basis of the judgments of the learned judges of the Court of Session, that for the purposes of determining this problem the law of Scotland and the law of England are the same. ... The law of both countries appears to be that in order to support an action for damages for negligence the complainant has to show that he has been injured by the breach of duty owed to him in the circumstances by the defendant to take reasonable care to avoid such injury. In the present case we are not concerned with the breach of the duty; if a duty exists, that would be a question of fact which is sufficiently averred and for the present purposes must be assumed. We are solely concerned with the question whether as a matter of law in the circumstances alleged the defender owed any duty to the pursuer to take care.

It is remarkable how difficult it is to find in the English authorities statements of general application defining the relations between parties that give rise to the duty. The Courts are concerned with the particular relations which come before them in actual litigation, and it is sufficient to say whether the duty exists in those circumstances. The result is that the Courts have been engaged upon an elaborate classification of duties as they exist in respect of property, whether real or personal, with further divisions as to ownership, occupation or control, and distinctions based on the particular relations of the one side or the other, whether manufacturer, salesman or landlord, customer, tenant, stranger, and so on.

In this way it can be ascertained at any time whether the law recognizes a duty, but only where the case can be referred to some particular species which has been examined and classified. And yet the duty which is common to all the cases where liability is established must logically be based upon some element common to the cases where it is found to exist. To seek a complete logical definition of the general principle is probably to go beyond the function of the judge, for the more general the definition the more likely it is to omit essentials or to introduce non-essentials. The attempt was made by Brett M.R. in *Heaven v. Pender*, in a definition to which I will later refer. As framed, it was demonstrably too wide, though it appears to me, if properly limited, to be capable of affording a valuable practical guide.

At present I content myself with pointing out that in English law there must be, and is, some general conception of relations giving rise to a duty of care, of which the particular cases found in the books are but instances. The liability for negligence, whether you style it such or treat it as in other systems as a species of "culpa", is no doubt based upon a general public sentiment of moral wrongdoing for which the offender must pay. But acts or omissions which any moral code would censure cannot in a practical world be treated so as to give a right to every person injured by them to demand relief. In this way rules of law arise which limit the range of complainants and the extent of their remedy. The rule that you are to love your neighbour becomes in law, you must not injure your neighbour, and the lawyer's question, Who is my neighbour? receives a restricted reply. You must take reasonable care to avoid acts or omissions which you can reasonably foresee would be likely to injure your neighbour. Who, then, in law, is my neighbour? The answer seems to be — persons who are so closely and directly affected by my act that I ought reasonably to have them in contemplation as being so affected when I am directing my mind to the acts or omissions which are called in question. ...

Lord Macmillan:... The law takes no cognizance of carelessness in the abstract. It concerns itself with carelessness only where there is a duty to take care and where failure in that duty has caused damage. In such circumstances carelessness assumes the legal quality of negligence and entails the consequences in law of negligence. What then are the circumstances which give rise to this duty to take care? In the daily contacts of social and business life human beings are thrown into or place themselves in an infinite variety of relationships with their fellows, and the law can refer only to the standards of the reasonable man in order to determine whether any particular relationship gives rise to a duty to take care as between those who stand in that relationship to each other. The grounds of action may be as various and manifold as human errancy, and the conception of legal responsibility may develop in adaptation to altering social conditions and standards. The criterion of judgment must adjust and adapt itself to the changing circumstances of life. The categories of negligence are never closed. The cardinal principle of liability is that the party complained of should owe to the party complaining a duty to take care and that the party complaining should be able to prove that he has suffered damage in consequence of a breach of that duty. Where there is room for diversity of view is in determining what circumstances will establish such a relationship between the parties as to give rise on the one side to a duty to take care and on the other side to a right to have care taken. ...

Lord Buckmaster (dissenting):

> ... the duty, if it exists, must extend to every person who, in lawful circumstances, uses the article made. There can be no special duty attaching to the manufacture of food apart from that implied by contract or imposed by statute. If such a duty exists it seems to me it must cover the construction of every article, and I cannot see any reason why it should not apply to the construction of a house. If one step, why not fifty? Yet if a house be, as it sometimes is, negligently built, and in consequence of that negligence the ceiling falls and injures the occupier or any one else, no action against the builder exists according to the English law, although I believe such a right did exist according to the laws of Babylon.

[**Lord Tomlin** agreed with **Lord Buckmaster**. The judgment of **Lord Thankerton**, agreeing in the result with **Lord Atkin** and **Lord MacMillan**, is omitted.]

NOTES

1. On the fiftieth anniversary of *Donoghue v. Stevenson*, Justice Linden waxed eloquent about its contribution to tort law in "The Good Neighbour on Trial: A Fountain of Sparkling Wisdom" (1983), 17 U.B.C.L. Rev. 59:

> In an article written on the 25th anniversary in 1957, Professor Heuston, then and still the editor of *Salmond on Torts*, suggested that on its 50th

anniversary in 1982, the decision might be of little more than antiquarian interest, a mere "repository of ancient learning", because he thought that tort law would likely be abolished and be replaced by a social insurance scheme by that time.

How wrong he was! As *Donoghue v. Stevenson* celebrates its 50th anniversary, it is not only alive and well, it is thriving, vigorous, lusty, youthful and energetic. For me, it is still and will remain like a seed of an oak tree, a source of inspiration, a beacon of hope, a fountain of sparkling wisdom, a skyrocket bursting in the midnight sky. ...

The ... most important contribution that *Donoghue v. Stevenson* has made is to serve as a testimonial to the creative power of tort law and indeed of the common law generally. By transforming one of the basic teachings of Christianity — that you should love your neighbour — into the central principle of negligence law — that you should use reasonable care not to injure your neighbour — a glorious idea was born and indelibly imprinted on our minds. In addition to this, the statement that "the categories of negligence are never closed" furnishes a continuing invitation to tort courts to innovate if they are so inclined.

In the last fifty years, there have been many examples of judicial lawmaking based on the neighbour principle, both directly and indirectly. There have also been examples where courts have sought to restrict the scope of the neighbour principle, but I believe that has been a losing battle. The dominant sweep of history in negligence law has been toward expanding the neighbour principle into every nook and cranny of negligence law.

The case of *Donoghue v. Stevenson* has attracted almost a cult following. Led by Mr. Justice Martin Taylor of B.C., a group of Canadian judges and lawyers did a "pilgrimage to Paisley" in 1990 to pay tribute to the descendants of the key players and the town where the famous events transpired. A video was prepared about the case and a book of essays was published, containing the papers delivered at the conference. See *Donoghue and Stevenson and the Modern Law of Negligence,* (1991). Justice Linden repeated and embellished his lavish praise for the case in his article "Viva *Donoghue v. Stevenson*". See for a contrary view, Smith and Burns, "The Good Neighbour on Trial: Good Neighbours Make Bad Law" (1983), 17 U.B.C. L. Rev. 93.

2. Although *Donoghue v. Stevenson* is generally regarded as the source of contemporary negligence law, tort actions for negligent conduct of various kinds existed long before this case was decided. As Professor Klar notes in *Tort Law,* (2nd. ed. 1996), pp. 126 *et seq.*, "negligence as a type of wrongful conduct leading to liability was part of the common law of torts hundreds of years before *Donoghue v. Stevenson.*" Professor Winfield details the development in his article "The History of Negligence in Torts" (1926), 42 L.Q. Rev. 184, which, as you can see, was written several years before *Donoghue v. Stevenson* was even decided.

3. *Donoghue v. Stevenson* contributed to the law of negligence in two major ways. First, it finally overruled the principle ostensibly created by *Winterbottom v. Wright* (1842), 10 M. & W. 109, 152 E.R. 402 (Exch.), that a person injured as a result of a negligent act of another could not sue that wrongdoer if the negligent act constituted a breach of contract between the wrongdoer and a co-contractant. As a result of this, the whole field of products liability developed, holding that a duty was owed by negligent manufacturers of all types of products to all foreseeable plaintiffs. Second, as Professor Klar states *op. cit. supra* at p.134, "it established the proposition that the duty of care owed in negligence actions is not confined to a closed list of specific relationships, but is based upon an open-ended and general concept of a relationship of proximity which is capable of extension to new situations". It gave negligence a formula, a universal principle, which not only wove together the previous threads, but was capable of being applied to new situations.

4. In *Home Office v. Dorset Yacht Co. Ltd.*, [1970] A.C. 1004, some borstal trainees escaped from the control of their "guards" during the night and damaged a yacht. Lord Reid elaborated on the principle laid down in *Donoghue v. Stevenson* as follows:

> About the beginning of this century most eminent lawyers thought that there were a number of separate torts involving negligence each with its own rules, and they were most unwilling to add more. They were of course aware from a number of leading cases that in the past the courts had from time to time recognized new duties and new grounds of action. But the heroic age was over, it was time to cultivate certainty and security in the law; the categories of negligence were virtually closed. The learned Attorney-General invited us to return to those halcyon days, but, attractive though it may be, I cannot accede to his invitation.
>
> In later years there has been a steady trend towards regarding the law of negligence as depending on principle so that, when a new point emerges, one should ask not whether it is covered by authority but whether recognised principles apply to it. *Donoghue v. Stevenson* may be regarded as a milestone, and the well-known passage in Lord Atkin's speech should I think be regarded as a statement of principle. It is not to be treated as if it were a statutory definition. It will require qualification in new circumstances. But I think that the time has come when we can and should say that it ought to apply unless there is some justification or valid explanation for its exclusion. For example, causing economic loss is a different matter; for one thing it is often caused by deliberate action. Competition involves traders being entitled to damage their rivals' interests by promoting their own, and there is a long chapter of the law determining in what circumstances owners of land can, and in what circumstances they may not, use their proprietary rights so as to injure their neighbours. But where negligence is involved the tendency has been to apply principles analogous to those stated by Lord Atkin (*cf.*, *Hedley Byrne & Co. Ltd. v. Heller & Partners Ltd.*). And when a person has done nothing to put himself in any relationship with another person in distress or with his property mere accidental propinquity does not require him to go the that person's assistance. There may be a moral duty to do so, but it is not practicable to make it a legal duty. And then there are cases, *e.g.*, with regard to landlord and tenant, where the law was settled long ago and neither Parliament nor this House sitting judicially has made any move to alter it. But I can see nothing to prevent our approaching the present case with Lord Atkin's principles in mind.

...

Viscount Dilhorne dissented, saying:

> If the foreseeability test is applied to determine to whom the duty is owed, I am at a loss to perceive any logical ground for excluding liability to persons who suffer injury or loss, no matter how far they or their property may be from the place of escape if the loss or injury was of a character reasonable foreseeable as the consequence of failure to take proper care to prevent the escape . ...
>
> I think that it is clear that the *Donoghue v. Stevenson* principle cannot be regarded as an infallible test of the existence of a duty of care; nor do I think that if that test is satisfied, there arises any presumption of the existence of such a duty. ...

5. The majority of the House of Lords in *Home Office* decided that, as a matter of law, the defendant owed the plaintiffs a duty of care. More importantly for our purposes, however, is the role that this judgment played in the development of the duty concept. *Donoghue v. Stevenson* certainly started the ball rolling in terms of the growth of negligence law. The next major step was taken by the House of Lords in *Hedley Byrne v.*

Heller, [1964] A.C. 465, [1963] 2 All E.R. 575 (H.L.), a case which is discussed later and which applied the duty principle to cases involving negligent statements causing economic losses. *Home Office* was the next big step. Not only was negligence law being applied to public authorities, but Lord Reid's statement that Lord Atkin's speech in *Donoghue v. Stevenson* "should apply unless there is some justification or valid explanation for its exclusion" is the forerunner to Lord Wilberforce's "*prima facie* duty of care doctrine" which appeared in *Anns v. Merton London Borough Council*, [1978] A.C. 728, [1977] 2 All E.R. 492 (H.L.), a controversial case to be studied later. In that case, Lord Wilberforce stated:

> Through the trilogy of cases in this House — *Donoghue v. Stevenson*, [1932] A.C. 562, *Hedley Byrne & Co. Ltd. v. Heller & Partners Ltd.*, [1964] A.C. 465, [1963] 2 All E.R. 575, and *Dorset Yacht Co. Ltd. v. Home Office*, [1970] A.C. 1004, [1970] 2 All E.R. 294, the position has now been reached that in order to establish that a duty of care arises in a particular situation, it is not necessary to bring the facts of that situation within those of previous situations in which a duty of care has been held to exist. Rather the question has to be approached in two stages. First one has to ask whether, as between the alleged wrongdoer and the person who has suffered damage there is a sufficient relationship of proximity or neighbourhood such that, in the reasonable contemplation of the former, carelessness on his part may be likely to cause damage to the latter — in which case a prima facie duty of care arises. Secondly, if the first question is answered affirmatively, it is necessary to consider whether there are any considerations which ought to negative, or to reduce or limit the scope of the duty or the class of person to whom it is owed or the damages to which a breach of it may give rise ...

6. The *Anns* "*prima facie* duty of care doctrine" soon proved to be too much for the House of Lords. In a series of important decisions in the 1980s, particularly with respect to cases involving pure economic losses or public authority defendants, the House retreated from and, ultimately, rejected Lord Wilberforce's approach. The House of Lords abandoned the idea of a general principle of duty, based upon foreseeability, in favour of a more cautious step-by-step approach, which defined duty in terms of "proximity". In this respect, "proximity" means foreseeability, policy, fairness, justice and so forth. See Feng, "Reassertion of the Old Approach to Duty in Negligence" (1987), 29 Mal. L. Rev. 308; Feng, "The Three-Part Test: Yet Another Test of Duty in Negligence" (1989), 31 Mal. L. Rev. 223; Klar, "Recent Developments in Canadian Law: Tort Law" (1991), 23 Ottawa L. Rev. 183, at 184.

7. This two-stage approach to the test of duty was adopted by the Supreme Court of Canada in *Kamloops v. Nielsen*, [1984] 2 S.C.R. 2, at p.10, where Madam Justice Wilson particularized it to a degree:

> (1) is there a sufficiently close relationship between the parties ... so that, in the reasonable contemplation of the [defendant], carelessness on its part might cause damage to that person? If so,
>
> (2) are there any considerations which ought to negative or limit (a) the cope of the duty and (b) the class of persons to whom it owed or (c) the damages to which a breach of it may give rise?

This test was consistently followed in other Supreme Court of Canada cases. (See *B.D.C. Ltd. v. Hofstrand Farms Ltd.*, [1986] 1 S.C.R. 228, at p. 243 (*per* Estey J.); *Just v. British Columbia* (1989), 64 D.L.R. (4th) 689 (S.C.C.); *Rothfield v. Manolakos* (1989), 63 D.L.R. (4th) 449 (S.C.C.) *per* Cory J.: "*Anns* is sound").

8. Following the retreat from *Anns* in the United Kingdom (see *Murphy v. Brentwood District Council*, [1990] 2 All E.R. 908 (H.L.)), the Supreme Court of Canada, in *Canadian National Railway Co. v. Norsk Pacific Steamship Co.*, (1992), 91 D.L.R. (4th)

289 (S.C.C.), unanimously and resoundingly refused to alter its course and reiterated its faith in *Anns*. Madam Justice McLachlin explained that the approach still required that two questions be asked: "(l) is there a duty relationship sufficient to support recovery? and, (2) is the extension desirable from a practical point of view, *i.e.* does it serve useful purposes or, on the other hand, open the floodgates to unlimited liability?"

The *Anns* case is, therefore alive and well in Canada even though it has been buried in the land of its birth. This is encouraging because it was merely a crystallization of the neighbour principle espoused in *Donoghue v. Stevenson* which is and should remain the bedrock principle of negligence law.

9. Foresight of risk remains important, therefore, but policy factors must also be taken into account in assessing whether or not to establish a duty of care. The fact is that some foreseeable risks are not within the scope of the duty owed, while some unforeseeable risks are considered within the duty. (See Green, "*The Wagon Mound (No. 2)* — Foreseeability Revised", [1967] Utah L. Rev. 197.) Nevertheless, Lord Atkin's neighbour principle, as revised by *Anns,* unleashed a force that can be used to expand the reach of negligence law, even though some courts will continue to resist its allure. For, after all, as was explained by President Robin Cooke of the New Zealand Court of Appeal, "the decision on a duty of care issue depends on a judgment, not a formula". (See *South Pacific Mfg. v. N.Z. Consultants* (1922), 2 N.Z.L.R. 282, at p. 295 (C.A.)).

10. The potency of Lord Atkin's neighbour principle for establishing a duty of care is underlined in the recent Supreme Court of Canada judgment in *London Drugs Ltd. v. Kuehne & Nagel International Ltd.* (1993), 73 B.C.L.R. (2d) 1, [1993] 1 W.W.R. 1. Two employees of the defendant storage company negligently dropped an expensive piece of machinery belonging to the plaintiff, a client of the storage company. The employees were moving the machinery as part of their jobs when they damaged it. The amount of the damage was over $33,000. The plaintiff sued both the storage company and its employees for the damage. There was, however, a $40 limitation of liability clause in the storage contract. The main issue in this case revolved around the applicability of this clause with respect to the employees' tort liability.

The Supreme Court of Canada ultimately decided that based on contract law, the limitation of liability clause would protect the employees. However, on the question of the existence of the employees' tort duty in the first place, the majority of the Court was clear. As Iacobucci J. stated:

> In my opinion, the respondents unquestionably owed a duty of care to the appellant when handling the transformer. I arrive at this conclusion with as little difficulty as the judges in the courts below. I do not base my conclusion on the terms of the contract of storage or on s. 2(4) of the *Warehouse Receipt Act* but on well established principles of tort law. In all the circumstances of this case, it was reasonably foreseeable to the respondent employees that negligence on their part in the handling of the transformer would result in damage to the appellant's property. In sum, there was such a close relationship between the parties as to give rise to a duty on the respondents to exercise reasonable care.

Mr. Justice La Forest dissented. Although His Lordship agreed with the two-stage test and did not dispute the fact that the first stage, *i.e.,* reasonable foreseeability of damage, was satisfied with respect to the employees, he argued that policy considerations operated in this case to deny the duty. The policy concerns in this case were about the "contractual allocation of risk in cases in which tort and contract claims co-exist… ". La Forest J. decided that in ordinary cases of employees' misconduct, that liability should rest only with the employer. This will be referred to later.

11. An early Canadian case grappling intelligently with the concept of duty was *Nova Mink v. Trans-Canada Airlines*, [1951] 2 D.L.R. 241 (N.S.S.C.), where, unbeknownst to the pilot, the noise of a landing airplane, while passing over a mink farm, frightened some female mink, which had just whelped, causing them to devour their young. Former law Professor, Vincent MacDonald J., reversed a decision for the plaintiff, explaining:

> In considering these questions it is material to keep in mind that the law of negligence has developed through the discharge by judges and juries of their respective functions. It is the function of the judge to determine whether there is any duty of care imposed by the law upon the defendant and if so, to define the measure of its proper performance; it is for the jury to determine, by reference to the criterion so declared, whether the defendant has failed in his legal duty. In every case, the judge must decide the question: Is there a duty of care in this case owing by the defendant to the plaintiff and, if so, how far does that duty extend? This question relates both to the existence of a duty and to its quantum; for the case can only go to the jury on the issue of breach of duty, if duty has been found to exist in law, and the jury can only determine that issue if it has been provided with a statement of the standard of care required by the law in performance of that duty. ...
>
> The common law yields the conclusion that there is such a duty only where the circumstances of time, place, and person would create in the mind of a reasonable man in those circumstances such a probability of harm resulting to other persons as to require him to take care to avert that probable result. This element of reasonable provision of expectable harm soon came to be associated with a fictional reasonable man whose apprehensions of harm became the touchstone of the existence of duty, in the same way as his conduct in the face of such apprehended harm became the standard of conformity to that duty. ...
>
> When upon analysis of the circumstances and application of the appropriate formula, a court holds that the defendant was under a duty of care, the court is stating as a conclusion of law what is really a conclusion of policy as to responsibility for conduct involving unreasonable risk. It is saying that such circumstances presented such an appreciable risk of harm to others as to entitle them to protection against unreasonable conduct by the actor. It is declaring also that a cause of action can exist in other situations of the same type, and *pro tanto* is moving in the direction of establishing further categories of human relationships entailing recognized duties of care. ...
>
> Accordingly there is always a large element of judicial policy and social expediency involved in the determination of the duty-problem, however it may be obscured by use of the traditional formulae. ...
>
> In short, I hold that the circumstances apparent to the defendant and its servants in this case did not suggest a probability of harm to the plaintiff's ranch as to give rise to a duty of care to avoid it by any greater distance than ordinary prudence would suggest in the case of an ordinary farm. ...
>
> It would be unthinkable for a court to hold a litigant bound to take care in respect of a condition of affairs of which the facts give no warning. ... It would be equally absurd to hold one bound to exercise a degree of care incapable of ascertainment; for in this case even the "hypothetical reasonable man" could not exercise reasonable care in respect of the mink without knowledge of their hearing powers and of the complex factors entering into the physical laws of sound.
>
> I hold, therefore, that in law the defendant owed no duty of care to the plaintiff in respect of the harm of which he complains and the case should have been withdrawn from the jury as matter or law.

SMITH, "THE MYSTERY OF DUTY"

in Klar (ed.), *Studies in Canadian Tort Law* (1977), p. 1
(also in Smith, *Liability in Negligence* (1984))

I Introduction

Lawyers, judges and academics generally take one of two approaches to the concept of duty of care in the law of negligence. There are those whom I would call "the true believers". They take the concept seriously. This is to say that they believe that the concept of duty of care is a meaningful doctrine of the law of negligence. It has three aspects: foreseeability, limitation in regard to the scope of the law of negligence, and limitation to the scope of recovery. Somehow these three are aspects of one unity — duty of care. Like the mystery of the Holy Trinity, three in one, yet not one but three. This is a confused position which leads to ambiguity in the law.

Then there are those whom I would term "the sceptics". For them, duty of care is so much jargon which can cover a variety of different policy issues and is resorted to by judges when they are unable to clearly articulate the policies at stake or the reasons for taking one alternative rather than another in decision-making. This approach leads to uncertainty in the law, and prediction of decisions becomes impossible. Some sceptics such as Lord Denning recommend banishing the term altogether from the language of negligence. In dealing with the difficult question of recovery for economic loss he writes:

> The more I think about these cases, the more difficult I find it to put each into its proper pigeon-hole. Sometimes I say: "There was no duty." In others I say: "The damage was too remote." So much so that I think the time has come to discard those tests which have proved so elusive. It seems to me better to consider the particular relationship in hand, and see whether or not, as a matter of policy, economic loss should be recoverable, or not.

As much as this might be desirable, I doubt that it will happen within the near future as the term and concept are too firmly entrenched in the jurisprudence of this subject. We may at least, however, be able to dispel the mystery with careful analysis.

There are certain ideas or notions which are basic to the concept of negligence, whether within or without the law. We say of a person that he is negligent when he acts without due care and attention in regard to harmful consequences of his actions. The concept of negligence thus assumes the notion of risk, and the notion of risk entails the idea of foreseeable harm. When we say that a person has been negligent we are passing a normative judgment on or about him. We are saying that he acted in a way that he ought not to have acted. This assumes that we know how he ought to have acted. The way in which we consider that he ought to have acted is the norm or standard which entitles us to condemn him for being negligent when he fails to comply with it. When a person complies with the norm or standard of care expected of him, he cannot be judged to be at fault or found to be negligent.

Where a person's actions do not comply with the standard of care expected of him and injury to others results, we say of the person at fault that he 'caused' the damage. When a person causes injury to someone else through the doing of an act which he ought not to have done, we consider him to blame or responsible for the damage. This responsibility is the basis or justification for the law requiring the person at fault to compensate the other party for his loss.

There are also certain steps which must be taken before we can reach the conclusion that a person has been negligent, and decide what legal consequences ought therefore to result. To begin with, a decision must be made as to whether the law of negligence ever covers or applies to a particular kind of situation. It must then be ascertained whether the defendant has created a risk of harm which would be recognized as negligence in the legal sense. Next, it must be determined whether or not the negligence was the cause of the loss. Finally, it must be decided whether the particular kind of loss suffered is recoverable under the law, and if so, how that loss is to be measured in monetary terms. Each of these steps raises particular kinds of legal problems, and most are closely interrelated with the basic ideas or notions which are a constitutive part of the concept of negligence.

I have identified above certain ideas or notions, such as 'risk', 'foreseeability', 'standard of care', 'causation' and 'responsibility', which are entailed in, are a constitutive part of, or are related to the concept of negligence. I have also enumerated a number of steps which must be followed before it can be decided that a particular person is liable in the law of negligence to pay another person a specified amount in damages. Is the concept of 'duty' equivalent to any of these ideas or notions? If not, is it an independent idea or concept in its own right which is entailed in or related to the concept of negligence? If so, how is it to be explained? Does it refer to a particular step in an action of negligence? If so, which one?

The fact that an answer to these questions is not obvious indicates that the concept of 'duty of care' is confusing and ambiguous. It is so because it is not entailed by or assumed in the concept of negligence, nor does it refer to a particular step in reaching a conclusion as to whether a person has been negligent and what his liability will be. Rather, it is often used as equivalent to a number of the notions or ideas related to the concept of negligence, and as well, is used to refer to several of the different steps in a negligence action.

If the confusion stemming from the use of the ambiguous concept 'duty of care' is to be clarified and not perpetuated, the problem must be tackled in terms of categories and concepts which are independent of duty language. ...

I am not necessarily advocating that lawyers argue cases without resort to duty language. If a judge wants to know whether or not the defendant owed the plaintiff a duty of care, then counsel must be prepared to argue the case in those terms; but at least we need not be prisoners of our own concepts. If we are able to pierce the mystery of duty of care and have our own analogies and understanding of the problems at issue, we can use the right cases and make the right policy arguments, dressing them in duty language if needs be. ...

III The Ambiguity of the Duty Concept

There are at least four different kinds of questions which can be isolated in terms of the analysis of an action in negligence set out in the previous section, each of which can be, and often is, phrased in terms of duty of care language. One kind of question raises issues of extension of the limits to the law of negligence. Another raises the issue of the presence of a foreseeable risk of harm. A third raises the issue of what standard of care ought to be taken in regard to the risk, and a fourth raises the issue of remoteness.

When issues in the law of negligence are framed in duty of care language, problems of extension, foreseeability of harm, standard of care, and remoteness become muddled. The failure to distinguish the basic kinds of problems leads to the use of tests and policy considerations which are not appropriate to the real issue before the court. Thus, considerations relevant only to problems of risk are used to solve remoteness issues, and problems of remoteness are dealt with in terms of policies and considerations relevant only to questions of extension. Much of the conceptual confusion in the law of negligence can be traced to this failure to distinguish between these various basic problems. Once these questions are separated, an examination of the relevant policies can then be made.

The reason that duty of care language has been used to refer to at least four different kinds of problems (with the result that we fail to distinguish between them) lies, I think, in the distinction which the common law historically made between questions of fact and questions of law. Under the traditional common law theory regarding the distinction between the role of the judge and that of the jury, questions of law were to be decided by the judge and questions of fact by the jury. If, however, the judge wished to take from or keep a case from being put to the jury, he could do so by framing the issue in terms of a question of law which was then conceived to be only appropriate for the judge to decide. This way of conceiving of legal problems has remained, although for all practical purposes the jury system has nearly ceased to exist as far as civil actions are concerned. This historical pattern, plus the fact that psychologically a question of law appears to be susceptible of a more decisive and certain answer than does a question of fact, has led the common law judge to express decisions wherever possible in terms of responses to issues of law rather than to issues of fact. The presence or absence of a duty of care has always been considered to be a matter of law, consequently, any issue which can be phrased as a matter of duty of care becomes a question of law.

(a) DUTY LANGUAGE USED TO DEAL WITH ISSUES OF EXTENSION

There are … certain areas of human activity with which the courts will not interfere on grounds of public policy. That is, they will not impose any standard of care on a person in regard to a particular kind of activity or a particular kind of loss. Where the judge feels that no standard of care ought to be imposed on a particular kind of activity, the court will rule that, as a matter of law (and this is a true question of law and not of fact) no duty of care is owed by the defendant. Thus, duty of care language is used to deal with problems of extension, or the limits of the law of negligence.

For example, public bodies such as municipalities and public officials or employees were generally not held liable for damages caused by a failure to act. The English Court of Appeal radically departed from the old line of precedents in *Dutton v. Bognor Regis Urban District Council* when they held a municipal body liable for damages resulting from the failure of a municipal building inspector to inspect properly the foundations of a house. When the members of the Court raised and dealt with the issue of whether the municipality and the inspector owed a duty of care to a subsequent purchaser of a house, the Court was grappling with a problem of extension, and its finding that a duty exists means no more than that the law of negligence now extends to such bodies and persons in the sense that the law will impose a standard of care upon them not only in regard to risks arising from their actions, but for risks which they did not create, but failed to remove. A similar issue of extension was raised in *Home Office v. Dorset Yacht Co. Ltd.*, where the House of Lords ruled that the Home Office was liable for damage to a yacht caused by inmates of a borstal institution when supervision became lax. Lord Diplock first stated the issue in terms of duty of care language, then interpreted the question as a problem as to the perimeters or limits of the law of negligence. …

(b) DUTY LANGUAGE USED TO DEAL WITH ISSUES OF RISK

Given that the case deals with conduct where the courts will impose a standard of care, the next question is whether or not a reasonable person would have foreseen a risk of harm. It the judge believes that he would not, he will often express this conclusion by saying that the defendant owes no duty of care to the plaintiff. This would be the case, not because the defendant's conduct was the kind where courts will not impose any standard of care, but because the court believes there was in fact no foreseeable risk of harm, he often expresses this by saying that the defendant owed the plaintiff a duty of care.

This use of duty language may be illustrated by the judgment of *Nova Mink Ltd. v. Trans-Canada Airlines* where the court held that a pilot was not negligent in causing female mink to eat their young as the result of the noise of the aircraft which he flew overhead, because he did not know and could not reasonably have foreseen that there were mink farms in the district. The issue of whether there was a foreseeable risk of harm was stated and answered in duty language. …

Lord Atkin's famous dictum in *Donoghue v. Stevenson* is the classic formulation of the risk issue in terms of duty language:

> At present I content myself with pointing out that in English law there must be, and is, some general conception of relations giving rise to a duty of care, of which particular cases found in the books are but instances. … You must take reasonable care to avoid acts or omissions which you can reasonably foresee would be likely to injure your neighbour.

(c) DUTY LANGUAGE USED TO DEAL WITH ISSUES OF STANDARD OF CARE

Even though there might be a reasonably foreseeable risk of harm, the judge may believe that on the facts the defendant did all that could reasonably be expected to prevent the harm. This conclusion is often expressed in the form of a ruling that the defendant did not have a duty to take the particular action which would have prevented the risk of harm from materializing. If, on the other hand, the court is of the opinion that it is reasonable to expect the defendant to guard against the risk the conclusion could be expressed as a finding that the defendant owed a duty of care.

Deyong v. Shenburn furnishes us with a paradigm case of this kind of usage. That case dealt with whether an employer was liable to an employee for the theft of some clothing due to the employer's failure to provide lockers. It is clear that theft of articles is a very foreseeable risk. It is equally clear that acts or failures to act which make theft possible can constitute negligence. The basic issue in these cases is whether a person can reasonably be expected to take whatever care is necessary to prevent the theft. …

(d) DUTY LANGUAGE USED TO DEAL WITH ISSUES OF REMOTENESS

We judge a person negligent when, as a result of failing to take due care in his actions, he creates a foreseeable risk of harm. But as it is so often pointed out, negligence and risk are terms of relation. The relation is between an act or failure to act and its foreseeable consequences in terms of a particular kind of harm happening to particular persons. Often, however, other things happen that those which are entailed within the ambit of the risk. A different kind of harm may result. Thus A, by his action, creates a risk of harm *x* to B, but B may suffer harm *y* as well as, or in place of harm *x*. Or harm may result to someone other than, or as well as, the person who is the subject of the risk; as well as, or instead of B, C may suffer either harm *x* or harm *y*. The courts will not always give full damages for all injuries or losses resulting from the acts of a negligent person as obvious policy reasons dictate that there must be some limits placed on a person's legal liability. Where a judge feels that a particular loss falls outside these limits he can express this conclusion by holding that the defendant did not owe a duty of care in regard to the particular kind of harm or to the particular person where he considers that either the harm or the person who suffers it, or both, fall outside the limits which must be placed on the defendant's legal liability. Duty language in such instances is thus used to deal with problems of remoteness.

The so-called foreseeability test of remoteness furnishes us with a classic example of the confusion which can arise from multiple uses of 'duty' language. The issue of whether a particular injury to a particular person is too remote is stated in terms of whether or not the defendant owed a duty of care to that person in regard to the particular loss. The judge or court then surreptitiously shifts to a usage of the term duty appropriate for the issue of the presence of a reasonably foreseeable risk of harm. The test of foreseeability of harm, appropriate for dealing with an issue of risk, is then introduced as a test of remoteness.

...

VII Conclusion

I doubt whether, in the foreseeable future, the legal profession will give up the use of duty language in negligence cases. Judges like to use it because with it they can turn a factual question or a difficult policy problem into the legal issue, "Did the defendant owe the plaintiff a duty of care?" Such a question can be answered with a decisive "Yes!" or "No!", and the conclusion, whatever it is, has the appearance of being reached by an inevitable pattern of legal logic. Even though a judge may realize that it is circular reasoning to conclude that there is no liability because the defendant did not owe the plaintiff a duty of care, or that there is because he does, it is easier for the judge to sneak in his conclusion in the disguise of a premise about the existence of a duty, than to attempt to articulate some of the policy premises which were the actual bases of his decision. Few judges dare be a Denning. In any case, the duty language is so ingrained in the jurisprudence of negligence that it is unlikely that a precedent-oriented conservative profession such as ours will make such a change lightly. And as long as the judge asks counsel, "Did the defendant owe the plaintiff a duty of care?", then the lawyer must be prepared to deal with the case in that manner. In consequence, those who teach torts to the budding lawyer must equip him to deal with a problem in duty language.

The issue, as I see it, is not whether or not we continue to use duty language, but whether we are to be masters of the language or be caught up in the morass.

The purpose of this analysis is to enable one to recognize the separate fundamental steps or problems in a negligence action and the basic policies which are at stake in each, and to deal with them clearly. Then it doesn't matter whether or not the conclusion is stated in terms of the existence of a duty of care. Presumably both judge and counsel can better serve justice and the ends of the law if they recognize the basic issues and can muster the right precedents and policies. Surely a lawyer will be more effective if he is able to distinguish among questions about the perimeters of the law of negligence, questions of risk or harm, questions of standard of care, and questions about remoteness. A judge has to be more competent or proficient if he focuses his attention on the policy which leads the law to favour recovery for rescuers than he does if he is trying to decide whether or not the rescuer is foreseeable.

Judges and practitioners who function within the law of negligence are continually going to be faced with shocked mothers, prenatally injured infants, explosions, cricket balls hitting heads, snails in bottles, toes in chewing tobacco, weird chains of events, and simple crushing, breaking, burning and cutting of the human body. A decision must be reached and given as to whether a loss will be shifted from the person suffering the loss to the actor who may have caused it. That decision must be justified in terms of 'the Law'. If that justification is to be meaningful and not mere empty words we must at least have a theory about "duty of care". The above is offered for that purpose.

Since it is unlikely that either judge of academic will exorcize the "spirit" or "ghost" of duty from the law, we must be satisfied with attempting to banish the mystery surrounding the concept and the way it functions in the law.

NOTE

1. See also Smith, "Clarification of Duty-Remoteness Problems Through a New Physiology of Negligence: Economic Loss, A Test Case" (1974), 9 U.B.C.L. Rev. 213; Smith, *Liability in Negligence* (1984).

B. THE UNFORESEEABLE PLAINTIFF

HAY (OR BOURHILL) v. YOUNG

House of Lords. [1943] A.C. 92, [1942] 2 All E.R. 396, 167 L.T. 261.

The plaintiff had alighted from a bus and was engaged in removing her fish-basket from the driver's platform, when a speeding motorcyclist passed on the other side of the bus and collided with a motor car at an intersection 45 to 50 feet ahead of the bus. The plaintiff heard a crash and said she "just got in a pack of nerves". She saw and heard nothing until the noise of the impact. Later, after the cyclist's dead body had been removed, the plaintiff saw the blood in the roadway. As a result of the shock, the plaintiff claimed to have sustained a wrenched back and about a month later her child was stillborn, which she attributed to shock and reaction to the event. The plaintiff sued the cyclist's executor. A judgment for the defendant was affirmed by the Second Division of the Court of Session. The plaintiff appealed to the House of Lords.

Lord Wright: ... [The] general concept of reasonable foresight as the criterion of negligence or breach of duty (strict or otherwise) may be criticized as too vague, but negligence is a fluid principle, which has to be applied to the most diverse conditions and problems of human life. It is a concrete, not an abstract, idea. It has to be fitted to the facts of the particular case. Willes J. defined it as absence of care according to the circumstances. . . . It is also always relative to the individual affected. This raises a serious additional difficulty in the cases where it has to be determined, not merely whether the act itself is negligent against someone, but whether it is negligent *vis-a-vis* the plaintiff. This is a crucial point in cases of nervous shock. Thus, in the present case John Young was certainly negligent in an issue between himself and the owner of the car which he ran into, but it is another question whether he was negligent *vis-a-vis* the appellant. In such cases terms like "derivative" and "original" and "primary" and "secondary" have been applied to define and distinguish the type of the negligence. If, however, the appellant has a cause of action it is because of a wrong to herself. She cannot build on a wrong to someone else. Her interest, which was in her own bodily security, was of a different order from the interest of the owner of the car. ...

I cannot accept that John Young could reasonably have foreseen, or, more correctly, the reasonable hypothetical observer could reasonably have foreseen, the likelihood that anyone placed as the appellant was, could be affected in the manner in which she was. In my opinion, John Young was guilty of no breach of duty to the appellant, and was not in law responsible for the hurt she sustained. I may add that the issue of duty or no duty is, indeed, a question for the court, but it depends on the view taken of the facts. In the present case both courts below have taken the view that the appellant has, on the facts of the case, no redress, and I agree with their view.

Lord Porter: In the case of a civil action there is no such thing as negligence in the abstract. There must be neglect of the use of care towards a person towards whom the defendant owes the duty of observing care. The duty is not to the world at large. It must be tested by asking with reference to each several complainant: was a duty owed to him or her? If no one of them was in such a position that physical injury could reasonably be anticipated to them or their relations or friends normally I think no duty would be owed. ...

[**Lords MacMillan, Thankerton** and **Russell** wrote concurring opinions.]

NOTES

1. See *Palsgraf v. Long Island Railroad Co.*, 162 N.E. 99, 248 N.Y. Supp. 339 (C.A. 1928). The defendant's guard, trying to assist a man who was rushing for a departing train, pushed him, knocking a package of fireworks from his arms. An explosion ensued, knocking over a scale, which in turn hit the woman plaintiff who was standing some distance away. She was denied recovery on the ground that she was beyond the range of foreseeable danger. Mr. Justice Cardozo rationalized the position as follows:

> The conduct of the defendant's guard, if a wrong in its relation to the holder of the package, was not a wrong in its relation to the plaintiff standing far away. Relatively to her it was not negligence at all. ... If no hazard was apparent to the eye of ordinary vigilance, an act innocent and harmless, at least to outward seeming, with reference toward her, did not take to itself the quality of a tort because it happened to be wrong, though apparently not one involving the risk of bodily insecurity, with reference to someone else. "In every instance before negligence can be predicated of a given act, back of the act must be sought and found a duty to the individual complaining". ... The plaintiff sues in her own right for a wrong personal to her, and not as the vicarious beneficiary of a breach of duty to another. ...

Mr. Justice Andrews, who spoke for the dissenting minority, rejected this view and argued:

> Every one owes to the world at large a duty of refraining from those acts which unreasonably threaten the safety of others. Such an act occurs. Not only is he wronged to whom harm might reasonably be expected to result, but he

> also who is in fact injured, even if he be outside ... the danger zone. There needs to be duty due the one complaining but this is not a duty to a particular individual because as to him harm might be expected.

See Prosser, "Palsgraf Revisited" (1952), 52 Mich. L. Rev. 1.

2. Why should negligence not be transferred like intent is transferred?

3. In *Farrugia v. Great Western Ry.*, [1947] 2 All E.R. 565 (C.A.), the defendant had loaded a lorry so high that in passing an overhead bridge a container was knocked off and fell onto the plaintiff. The plaintiff, shortly before the accident, had been on the lorry as a trespasser and at the time of the injury he was running slightly behind the lorry preparing to steal a second ride. It was argued that as the defendant's driver had no reason to foresee or expect that the plaintiff would be running behind the lorry attempting to get on it, he could owe no duty toward him. For this reliance was placed on *Bourhill v. Young*, [1943] A.C. 92, [1942] 2 All E.R. 396. The Court of Appeal, however, held that the duty was owed to anybody who happened to be in the neighbourhood at the crucial moment.

4. In *Law v. Visser*, [1961] Queensland R. 46, the defendant motorist, driving at night at a high rate of speed, saw in his headlights a large object which looked like an abandoned bundle or, possibly, an animal killed by a passing car. The defendant made no effort to avoid the object and ran over it. The object proved to be the plaintiff, lying on the road in a drunken stupor. The court held the defendant liable. It was no excuse that he did not know the nature of the object. He took a chance that it might be more valuable than he thought, or that it might even be a human being.

5. Is an unborn child an unforeseeable plaintiff? Much controversy existed over this issue until Mr. Justice Fraser, in an auto accident case where a child was born defective as a result of an injury while it was *en ventre sa mère,* resolved the matter in *Duval v. Séguin*, [1972] 2 O.R. 686, at 701, 26 D.L.R. (3d) 418 (H.C.J.); affd (1974), 1 O.R. (2d) 482 (*sub nom. Duval v. Blais*), 40 D.L.R. (3d) 666 (C.A.), as follows:

> [The] mother, was plainly one of a class within the area of foreseeable risk and one to whom the defendants therefore owed a duty. Was [the child] any the less so? I think not. Procreation is normal and necessary for the preservation of the race. If a driver drives on a highway without due care for other users it is foreseeable that some of the other users of the highway will be pregnant women and that a child *en ventre sa mère* may be injured. Such a child therefore falls well within the area of potential danger which the driver is required to foresee and take reasonable care to avoid.
>
> In my opinion it is not necessary in the present case to consider whether the unborn child was a person in law or at which stage she became a person. For negligence to be a tort there must be damages. While it was the foetus or child *en ventre sa mère* who was injured, the damages sued for are the damages suffered by the plaintiff [the child] since birth and which she will continue to suffer as a result of that injury. ...
>
> Some of the older cases suggest that there should be no recovery by a person who has suffered prenatal injuries because of the difficulties of proof and of the opening it gives for perjury and speculation. Since those cases were decided there have been many scientific advances and it would seem that chances of establishing whether or not there are causal relationships between the act alleged to be negligent and the damage alleged to have been suffered as a consequence are better now than formerly. In any event the courts now have to consider many similar problems and plaintiffs should not be denied relief in proper cases because of possible difficulties of proof.
>
> To refuse to recognize such a right would be manifestly unjust and unreasonable. In my opinion, and for the reasons I have tried to formulate, such a

refusal would not be consonant with relevant legal principles as they have developed and have been applied in the last 50 years. Under the doctrine of *M'Alister (or Donoghue) v. Stevenson, supra*, and the cases cited, an unborn child is within the foreseeable risk incurred by a negligent motorist. When the unborn child becomes a living person and suffers damages as a result of prenatal injuries caused by the fault of the negligent motorist the cause of action is completed. A tortfeasor is as liable to a child who has suffered prenatal injury as to the victim with a thin skull or other physical defect. In the instant case the plaintiff sues, as a living person, for damages suffered by her since her birth as a result of prenatal injury caused by the fault of the defendant. In my opinion she is entitled to recover such damages. I refrain from expressing any opinion as to what, if any, are the legal rights of a child *en ventre sa mère* or of a foetus. Many difficult problems in this area of the law remain to be resolved.

6. The holding in *Duval* has now been enshrined in Ontario legislation as follows:

> No person is disentitled from recovering damages in respect of injuries for the reason only that the injuries were incurred before his or her birth.

See *Family Law Act*, R.S.O. 1990, c. F.3, s. 66; see also U.K. *Congenital Disabilities (Civil Liability) Act, 1976*, c. 28.

7. In *Dobson (Litigation Guardian of) v. Dobson* (1997), 37 C.C.L.T. (2d) 103 (N.B.C.A.), it was held that an infant plaintiff could sue his mother for damages for pre-natal injuries he sustained as a result of her negligent driving. Chief Justice Hoyt explained:

> It is common ground that a child may sue a third party for pre-natal injuries. ... Likewise it is common ground that a child may sue its parents in tort. ...
>
> Before us, the appellant submitted that a foetus has no legal status to sue and that there are sound policy reasons for not permitting a child to sue its mother for prenatal injuries occasioned by the mother's actions.
>
> In my view, the first submission fails because of the very real distinction between an action brought by or on behalf of a foetus and one brought by or on behalf of a child. The law seems settled that a foetus has no right to sue or be the subject of an action. See, for example, *Tremblay v. Daigle, supra; Sullivan supra; F. (in utero), Re,* [1988] 2 All E.R. 193 (Eng. C.A.) and *Winnipeg Child & Family Services (Northwestern Area), supra* (which is under appeal to the Supreme Court of Canada). These cases, however, do not have application where, as here, it is not a foetus but a child who is bringing the action.
>
> Nor am I attracted to the appellant's submission that there are social policy reasons for rejecting this claim. Mrs. Dobson raises a spectre of mothers being sued by their children for various activities or lifestyle choices, such as smoking, drinking and the taking or refusal of medication, during pregnancy that injure the child, with the result that mothers will be unable to control their own bodies and make autonomous choices. Cases alleging negligent conduct of such a nature by a mother during pregnancy may well involve difficult policy decisions, but they do not arise here. As noted, the narrow issue here concerns pre-natal injuries received by a child as a result of a mother's negligent driving of her motor vehicle and not injuries occasioned as a result of a mother's lifestyle choices.
>
> The differing policy reasons unique to the facts in this case and those involving lifestyle choices were canvassed in *Bonte v. Bonte* 136 N.H. 286 (U.S. N.H. S.C. 1992) and in *Lynch v. Lynch* (1991), 25 N.S.W.L.R. 4ll (New South Wales C.A.). Clarke, J.A. in *Lynch* said at p. 415:

> There are, however, different policy considerations which arise in the context of a claim based on negligent driving and those which may arise, for instance, in a claim based on the mother's taking of unjustified risks of physical injury ...

Professor Fleming has made the same distinction. He said at p. 168:

> ... A distinction is in order between the general duty to avoid injury which the defendant owes to all others and those peculiar to parenthood. An instance of the former is the duty to drive carefully, which even the mother at the wheel owes to her foetus. On the other hand, there is strong aversion against inquisition into alleged parental indiscretions during pregnancy, like excessive smoking, drinking or taking drugs.

The duty on Mrs. Dobson in this situation arises from her general duty to drive carefully and cannot be characterized as one "peculiar to parenthood". The same distinction is made in the *Congenital Disabilities (Civil Liability) Act 1976* (U.S.), 1976, c. 28, which exempts a mother from actions in tort for pre-natal injury to her children who are born alive. By s. 2 of the Act, however, the exemption does not extend to prenatal injury that occurs when the mother is in breach of her general duty to others to drive with care.

To repeat, the issue is very narrow. A pregnant mother has a general duty to drive carefully, a duty she owes to her children as well as to the general public. If, as it is alleged here, the child suffers injury during his or her lifetime as a result of the mother's negligent driving during pregnancy, there is no reason that the child should not be able to enforce is or her rights. To hold otherwise would create a partial exclusion to a pregnant mother's general duty to drive carefully. The Supreme Court granted leave in this case.

8. Whether a cause of action lies for the negligent "lifestyle" choices of a pregnant mother is another, far more complicated matter. In *Winnipeg Child and Family Services v. G. (D.F.)*, [1997] 2 S.C.R. 925, the Supreme Court affirmed the Manitoba Court of Appeal in refusing to mandate treatment of a pregnant mother to protect her foetus from the harmful effects of her chemical dependency. Would the child, when born, be able to sue the mother in tort for any injury it suffered?

A NOTE ON WRONGFUL BIRTH, WRONGFUL LIFE AND WRONGFUL PREGNANCY

A cause of action now exists for negligence which results in "wrongful birth"; "wrongful life" or "wrongful pregnancy". According to Lax J., a "wrongful birth" action is usually brought by the parents of a child born with birth defects who allege that their entitlement to make an informed choice regarding whether or not to proceed with a pregnancy was denied by the negligent conduct of a doctor. In Canada, "wrongful birth" claims arising from the birth of an injured child have yielded damages for both pain and suffering by the parents and damages for the cost of raising the child, as in *Cherry (Guardian) v. Borsman*, where, following a failed abortion, the parents of a severely handicapped child and the child recovered. It is unlikely that an action by a biological father, who is not married to the mother, seeking the cost of raising the child would succeed.

"Wrongful life" actions arise from similar situations, but are usually brought on behalf of the child. Generally, courts have been reluctant to recognize such actions because of the difficulty in quantifying the difference between a healthy life, a life with birth defects and non-existence. It is also "repugnant to our cultural ethos to complain about the circumstances of one's conception". An independent "wrongful life" action by an injured child has yet to succeed in Canada, although the court in *Cherry* awarded damages to the injured child in conjunction with the "wrongful birth" claims of its parents. In *Arndt v. Smith*, the British Columbia Supreme Court stated that the abandonment of a wrongful life claim brought by an injured child following her mother's infection with chicken pox during pregnancy was a proper acceptance of "... the inevitable finding of the Court that no such action lies."

Finally, "wrongful pregnancy" is a third and related section which is brought by parents who allege that a particular act of negligence has resulted in an unplanned pregnancy which may produce a healthy or an injured child. It differs from "wrongful birth" to the extent that it deals with pre-conception rather than post-conception negligence. In such cases, where the child is born healthy, Canadian courts have been willing to award damages related to the pregnancy and birth itself, but not for the cost of raising the child. In *Cryderman v. Ringrose*, the Alberta Court of Appeal awarded $5,000 for pain and suffering as a result of an abortion necessitated by a failed sterilization. In *Doiron v. Orr*, although no negligence was found when a child was born following an unsuccessful sterilization procedure, Garett J. would have awarded $1,000 in pain and suffering. He refused to assess damages for the cost of raising the child, labelling the claim as "grotesque". In *Suite v. Cooke*, the Quebec Court of Appeal insisted on considering not simply the cost of maintaining the child, but also the emotional benefit and financial support which a healthy child would eventually bring to the family.

More recently, in *Kealey v. Berezowski*, Lax J. adopted a different approach to the assessment of damages for the unplanned birth of a healthy child following a negligently performed sterilization procedure. An award of $30,000 in general damages was given to the mother for having to undergo the pregnancy, labour, delivery and a second tubal litigation. The mother and the father were also awarded special damages for lost income. No damages were awarded, however, for the cost of rearing a child whom the plaintiffs loved and were able to provide for financially. Rather than basing this decision on public policy arguments or on a corresponding benefits and burdens analysis, Lax J. found that such damages did not "... fall within the scope of the wrongdoing", because the existence of the healthy child did not it itself constitute a harm. Referring to the court's reasons in *Doiron, supra*, Lax J. commented that "[t]he time has long passed when a court if free (if indeed there ever was such a time) to discuss a claim such as this as 'grotesque' ". (See Linden, *Canadian Tort Law*, 6th ed. (1997), *supra*, at 282.)

A NOTE ON PSYCHIATRIC DAMAGE

The law concerning liability for negligent infliction of "nervous shock", as it was called began to change after *Bourhill v. Young,* with damages for psychiatric losses being covered in specific situations, but there were and still remain many problems regarding the extent of liability. Concern about the floodgates and possible fake claims impeded development. The cases are legion and often conflicting, but several principles have emerged.

In Canada, the main test for establishing a duty is foreseeability of shock (*Marshall v. Lionel v. Lionel Enterprises Inc.* [1972] 2 O.R. 177). There must be a "recognizable psychiatric illness" suffered, not merely an emotional upset. (See *Duwyn v. Kaprielian* (1978), 7 C.C.L.T. 121 (Ont. C.A.), per Morden J.A.). By themselves, mere grief and sorrow are not compensable. (See *Schneider v. Eisovitch* [1960] 1 All E.R. 169). It is necessary for plaintiffs to have been endangered themselves or to have witnessed with their own unaided senses the accident or its immediate aftermath. (*Marshall, supra*). There is some question about whether seeing an accident on television would be sufficient. (See *Alcock v. Chief Constable of South Yorkshire Police*, [1991] 3 W.L.R. 1057 (H.L.), no liability).

The class of plaintiff who can recover includes close relatives and loved ones, but is not limited in this way. For example, rescuers are entitled to recover if they witness a horrible accident. (See *Bechard v. Haliburton Estate* (1991), 10 C.C.L.T. (2d) 156, at p. 171 (Ont. C.A.), *per* Griffiths J.A.). Mere bystanders are less likely to be able to recover, unless they are fellow workers of the people hurt in the accident or unless they were involved in some way.

Until recently, it was plain that suffering psychiatric damage on being told about an accident was insufficient to qualify for damages for psychiatric damage, unless that person was also injured in the accident. (See *Abramzik v. Brenner* (1967), 65 D.L.R. (2d) 651 (Sask. C.A.); *Rhodes v. C.N.R. Co.* (1990), 5 C.C.L.T. (2d) 118 (B.C.C.A.)).

In the case of *Lew v. Mount Saint Joseph Hospital Society* (1997), 36 C.C.L.T. (2d) 35 (B.C. S.C.), however, the possibility was left open for compensation for negligent communication of bad news. If false information is negligently communicated, causing psychiatric damages, that is compensable. See *Jinks v. Cardwell* (1987), 39 C.C.L.T. 168 (Ont. H.C.) revd on another point June 23, 1989, Ont. C.A. In addition, it is now possible that a hospital that did not forewarn the plaintiff, who was allowed to see the terrible effects of brain injury on his wife, may be liable. Henderson J., relying on Mullany and Handfield's book, explained:

> The plaintiff is alleging that the Hospital was negligent in permitting him to enter the Intensive Care Unit unaccompanied and without any forewarning or preparation as to what he could expect to find when he first saw his wife. The plaintiff is alleging that the hospital owed him a duty of care and that it fell below the standard of care required.
>
> The plaintiff says it would be unjust, in all the circumstances for the action to be disposed of summarily without examinations for discovery and production of documents. I agree.

This area of the law has been much debated in England, where the courts have created a confusing distinction between primary and secondary victims. For the former, foresight of physical injury suffices to create a duty, but, for the latter, foresight of psychiatric injury to a person of normal fortitude is required. (See *Page v. Smith*, [1995] 2 All E.R. 736).

See generally Fleming, *The Law of Torts*, 9th ed. (1998) at 173; Linden, 6th ed. (1997) at 385; see Klar, *Tort Law*, 2nd ed. (1996) at 341; Mullany & Handford, *Tort Liability for Psychiatric Damage* (London: Sweet & Maxwell, 1993).

C. FAILURE TO ACT

There has been much written and said about the problem of the Good Samaritan and, more particularly, the Bad Samaritan, who fails to come to the aid of someone in peril. Whether this is a worse problem today in the large urban areas than it was in years gone by is problematic. Some contend that the media are merely making us more aware of these shocking incidents and that their frequency has not increased. It is hard to know.

The law of torts is relevant to the problem of the Good Samaritan. By awarding or withholding damages it may encourage or discourage Good Samaritanism. Historically, the common law, in denying liability in Bad Samaritan cases, may well have served to discourage citizens from offering help to one another. In most countries of Europe, where it is an offence to withhold succour when it is needed, the law is in marked contrast. In Quebec, the *Charter of Human Rights and Freedoms*, R.S.Q. 1977, c. C-12, mandates Good Samaritanism. Whether common law should be altered to reflect more closely the European tradition is an issue that raises many questions about the inter-relation of law and morals. The answers are not as self-evident as they may seem.

Tort law treats this problem as one of "duty". Unless the court finds that there was a "duty" on the defendant to take positive action, there will be no liability imposed, even if harm to someone else is foreseeable and preventable by the defendant. Lawyers and judges use the terms "nonfeasance" and "misfeasance"; there is no liability for mere nonfeasance, but there is liability for misfeasance. There is "no duty" in the former case, but there is in the latter.

However, it is not as simple as that. The difference *in principle* between a failure to act to prevent or mitigate a threatened harm and positive conduct that creates a risk of harm is not hard to grasp. *In practice,* however, it is more difficult to distinguish between them because a failure to act can sometimes take on the attributes of positive conduct. Moreover, in certain circumstances there can be liability imposed for failure to act. In particular instances, legislatures have evinced a willingness to require someone to give aid and common law courts have not hesitated to follow their lead by imposing civil liability for breach of these statutes. This chapter provides background material indicating how the courts have handled these problems and poses the question of what legal steps, if any, should be taken to encourage altruism.

1. "Nonfeasance" and "Misfeasance"

THE HOLY BIBLE

Luke, 10:30-10:37

... A certain man went down from Jerusalem to Jericho, and fell among thieves, which stripped him of his raiment, and wounded him, and departed, leaving him half dead.

And by chance there came down a certain priest that way; and when he saw him, he passed by on the other side.

And likewise a Levite, when he was at the place, came and looked on him, and passed by on the other side.

But a certain Samaritan, as he journeyed, came where he was; and when he saw him he had compassion on him.

And went to him, and bound up his wounds, pouring in oil and wine, and set him on his own beast, and brought him to an inn, and took care of him.

And on the morrow, when he departed, he took out two pence, and gave them to the host, and said unto him, "Take care of him; and whatsoever thou spendest more, when I come again, I will repay thee."

Which now of these, thinkest thou, was neighbour unto him that fell among the thieves?

And he said, "He that shewed mercy of him." Then said Jesus unto him, "Go, and do thou likewise".

NOTE

1. Professor Honoré, in his article "Law, Morals and Rescue," in Ratcliffe, *The Good Samaritan and the Law* (1966), comments on this story as follows:

> This story in Luke, Chapter 10, is simple enough. Jesus is questioned by a lawyer who asks what is necessary to inherit eternal life. When Jesus asks him what the law on the matter is, it turns out the lawyer can recite the law perfectly, but — the nature of lawyers being apparently everywhere the same — he wants to argue the interpretation of one of the words in it.
>
> The law is this: "Love the Lord thy God with all thy heart and with all thy soul and with all thy strength; and thy neighbour as thyself." The lawyer wants to know: "Who *is* my neighbour?" Whereupon Jesus tells the story of the Samaritan. ...
>
> This story, like many traditional stories at the time, turns upon the differing responses of priest, Levite, and layman. But typically in such stories, the layman as well as the other two would be Jews. Jesus, however, substitutes a Samaritan, a geographical neighbour but one who was despised and hated by the Jews of the time as being uncouth, unclean, immoral, and heretical. Thus the story as told by Jesus was intended to teach most emphatically that love of neighbour is so universal, so unqualified a principle as to include even the meanest of men being neighbour to the most self-righteous of enemies. The Gospel source also emphasizes *acting* as a neighbour, *decision* rather than legalistic classification. Finally, and of highest importance, the story has to do with eternal life, personal salvation — not with problems of keeping the public order.
>
> When I say that his parable is concerned with the ultimate question of personal salvation through personal decision and unqualified commitment, I have in mind the other side of the coin: whether my soul is saved or not is none of the state's business. Let Caesar regulate his own affairs: keeping the public order and the public well-being. My soul is *my* affair. This was Jesus' teaching; it is also central to our own political tradition.

HORSLEY ET AL. v. MACLAREN ET AL.
"THE OGOPOGO"

[1969] 2 O.R. 137, 4 D.L.R. (3d) 557; revd, [1970] 2 O.R. 487, 11 D.L.R. (3d) 277 (C.A.); affd, [1972] S.C.R. 441, 22 D.L.R. (3d) 545. See *infra*, Chapter 8.

Lacourcière J. (at trial): ... It is still the modern law of negligence that, there is no general duty to come to the rescue of a person who finds himself in peril from a source completely unrelated to the defendant, even where little risk or effort would be involved in assisting; thus a person on a dock can with legal impunity ignore the call for help of a drowning person, even refusing to throw a life ring. The law leaves the remedy to a person's conscience.

Jessup J.A. (in the Court of Appeal): ... Conceived in the forms of action and nurtured by the individualistic philosophies of past centuries, no principle is more deeply rooted in the common law than that there is no duty to take positive action in aid of another no matter how helpless or perilous his position is. In this area the Civil law has shown more regard for morality. It is a principle which is not reached by the doctrine of *Donoghue v. Stevenson*, [1932] A.C. 562 since that case leaves open only the categories of neighbours to whom there is owed a duty not to cause harm; its ratio has not yet been extended to enlarge the class to whom there is owed a duty to confer a benefit. So, despite the moral outrage of the text writers, it appears presently the law that one can, with immunity, smoke a cigarette on the beach while one's neighbour drowns and, without a word of warning, watch a child or blind person walk into certain danger. ...

NOTES

1. In *Buch v. Amory Manufacturing Co.*, 69 N.H. 257, 44 A. 809 (1897), the court stated: "With purely moral obligations the law does not deal. For example, the priest and the Levite who passed by on the other side were not, it is supposed, liable at law for the continued suffering of the man who fell among thieves, which they might and morally ought to have prevented or relieved." He may be called a "moral monster" or a "ruthless savage", but he is not liable in damages.

2. Chief Justice Best once stated in another context — "there is no act which Christianity forbids, that the law will not reach: if it were otherwise, Christianity would not be, as it has always been held to be, part of the law of England". See *Bird v. Holbrook* (1828), 4 Bing. 628, 130 E.R. 911. Is not the Good Samaritan tale a part of Christianity?

3. See Ames, "Law and Morals" (1908), 22 Harv. L. Rev. 97, where the following appears:

   > ... however revolting the conduct of the man who declined to interfere, he was in no way responsible for the perilous situation, he did not increase the peril, he took away nothing from the person in jeopardy, he simply failed to confer a benefit upon a stranger. As the law stands today there would be no legal liability, either civilly or criminally, in any of these cases. The law does not compel active benevolence between man and man. It is left to one's conscience whether he shall be the good Samaritan or not.

4. Can you think of any reasons why such a rule is desirable? What about encouraging self-reliance?

5. Should the law try to enforce morality? Does this smack of excessive interference with individual freedom? Can the law make people altruistic and unselfish? How should law and morality interact?

6. What about the danger to the person who tries to help someone being attacked or someone drowning? Can we define the degree of danger one should encounter for another?

7. Are there any problems of administration? How does one select which person on the crowded beach will be held liable for failing to rescue a drowning child? Who in the city of Toronto is liable if someone starves to death on Bay St.? When does the duty to the rescued person terminate? If you feed a starving person, do you have to continue feeding that person forever?

8. Is there really a problem in Canada of citizens failing to help one another? How much of this is merely something the media has generated?

9. Are we wise to want people to help one another? Some police officers say that they would prefer it if untrained personnel did not interfere with their work. Do we want to develop a nation of intermeddlers and "stool pigeons"? What is so wrong with minding one's own business?

10. Why do people refrain from helping others when they are in danger? Dr. L.Z. Freedman, a professor of psychiatry, in an essay entitled "No Response to the Cry for Help", attempted to answer this question. See Ratcliffe, *The Good Samaritan and the Law* (1966), at 175:

> Let us speculate, rather more systematically, on what happens when someone does *not intercede* in the crisis of another human being in trouble.
>
> Let me say at the outset that in my view apathy and indifference are the least likely primary psychic vectors in response to such an event. The sequence as I see it is, first, the intense emotional shock — characterized predominantly, but not exclusively, by anxiety; second, the cognitive perception and awareness of what has happened; third, an inertial paralysis of reaction, which as a non-act becomes in fact an act, and fourth, the self-awareness of one's own shock anxiety, non-involvement which is followed by a sense of guilt and intra-psychic and social self-justification.
>
> I do not assume that these things happen in such neat sequence. For all practical purposes they seem to occur simultaneously. Not all the things I am to discuss happen to everyone; when they do occur, if they do occur, their relative strength and importance appear in the unique proportions of each idiosyncratic individual. I am talking about emotions as well as ideas, fantasies as well as accurate perceptions, subjective experiences which are unconscious as well as those that are conscious.

11. Should we impose a general civil duty to render aid? See Ames, "Law and Morals" (1908), 22 Harv. L. Rev. 97:

> But ought the law to remain in this condition? Of course any statutory duty to be benevolent would have to be exceptional. The practical difficulty in such legislation would be in drawing the line. But that difficulty has continually to be faced in the law. We should all be better satisfied if the man who refuses to throw a rope to a drowning man or to save a helpless child on the railroad track could be punished and be made to compensate the widow of the man drowned and the wounded child. We should not think it advisable to penalize the surgeon who refused to make the journey. These illustrations suggest a possible working rule. One who fails to interfere to save another from impending death or great bodily harm, when he might do so with little or no inconvenience to himself, and the death or great bodily harm follows as a consequence of his inaction, shall be punished criminally and shall make compensation to the party injured or to his widow and children in case of death.

What is the proper function of the law here? See Weinrib, "The Case for a Duty to Rescue" (1980), 90 Yale L.J. 247.

12. Should we brand the failure to assist a person in peril as criminal conduct? Some American states and numerous European countries have done so. See Rudzinski, "The Duty to Rescue: A Comparative Analysis", printed in Ratcliffe, *The Good Samaritan and the Law* (1966); Franklin, "Vermont Requires Rescue" (1972), 25 Stan. L. Rev. 51; Tunc, "The Volunteer and the Good Samaritan," in Ratcliffe, *The Good Samaritan and the Law* (1966). The Law Reform Commission of Canada has suggested that we enact a criminal duty of easy rescue. See *Omissions, Negligence and Endangering*, Working Paper 46 (1985).

13. Would the imposition of a criminal sanction be preferable to a tort liability? Should there be *both* criminal and civil liability imposed?

14. A survey done in the United States has indicated that 75 per cent of the respondents felt that assistance should remain only as a matter of conscience. In Germany it was 62 per cent and in Austria 42 per cent. Zeisel, "An International Experiment of the

Effects of a Good Samaritan Law," in Ratcliffe, *The Good Samaritan and the Law* (1966). Does this affect your answer?

2. Relationships Requiring Rescue

Although there is no general common law duty to rescue, the law does recognize a duty to rescue or to assist in a variety of circumstances. Professor Klar has attempted to find similar components in the different types of cases and has presented the following categories in which a duty to assist is imposed:

(a) relationships of economic benefit;
(b) relationships of control or supervision;
(c) creators of dangerous situations;
(d) reliance relationships; and
(e) statutory duties.

Professor Klar argues that although there occasionally may be some overlap between these categories, they adequately account for and explain why the common law imposes a duty to rescue. See Klar, *Tort Law*, 2nd ed. (1996), Chapter 6.

(a) Relationships of Economic Benefit

JORDAN HOUSE LTD. v. MENOW AND HONSBERGER
Supreme Court of Canada. (1973), 38 D.L.R. (3d) 105, [1974] S.C.R. 239.

Laskin J.: This is a case of first instance. The principal issue is whether the operator of a hotel may be charged with a duty of care to a patron of the hotel beverage room who becomes intoxicated there, a duty to take reasonable care to safeguard him from the likely risk of personal injury if he is turned out of the hotel to make his way alone. If such a duty may be imposed, it falls to determine the nature or scope of the duty to the intoxicated patron. This determination must then be related to the present case by inquiring whether, on its facts, there has been a breach of the duty by the appellant hotel so as to engage its liability to the respondent plaintiff for personal injuries. I shall refer later in these reasons to another issue raised on behalf of the respondent Honsberger.

There are concurrent findings of fact in this case by the trial judge Haines J. [7 D.L.R. (3d) 494, [1970] 1 O.R. 54], and by the Ontario Court of Appeal in favour of Menow [14 D.L.R. (3d) 545, [1971] 1 O.R. 129], on the basis of which he was awarded damages against the appellant hotel and against the respondent Honsberger under an equal apportionment of fault among all three parties. Honsberger was the driver of a car which struck Menow as he was walking east near the centre line of Highway No. 8, after having been ejected from the hotel. Neither the quantum of damages nor the apportionment of fault is in issue in this appeal.

The hotel premises front on Highway No. 8, a much-travelled two-lane highway running east and west between Hamilton and Niagara Falls, Ontario. The road is asphalt, 21 ft. wide, and, at the material time, January 18, 1968, the shoulders were icy, with snowbanks beyond them, and the pavement itself was wet, although not slippery. Menow was employed by a fruit farmer and lived alone on his employer's farm which was on a side road about two and one-half miles east of the hotel. The direct route to his abode was along the highway and then north along the side road.

Menow was a frequent patron of the hotel's beverage room, where beer was served, and was well-known to the owner-operator of the hotel, one Fernick. He was often there in the company of his employer and the latter's foreman, also well known to Fernick. Menow had a tendency to drink to excess and then act recklessly, although ordinarily he was courteous and mannerly. The hotel management and the beverage room employees knew of his propensities and indeed, about a year before the events out of which this case arose he had been barred from the hotel for a period of time because he annoyed other customers, and thereafter the hotel's employees were instructed not to serve him unless he was accompanied by a responsible person.

On January 18, 1968, Menow, his employer and the foreman arrived at the hotel at about 5:15 p.m. and drank beer. The employer and the foreman departed within a short time, leaving the plaintiff there alone. Fernick came on duty at about 7 p.m. and saw that the plaintiff was then sober. He was served with beer from time to time, and there is a finding that towards 10 p.m. Fernick was aware that Menow was drinking to excess and that he had become intoxicated, the hotel having sold beer to Menow past the point of visible or apparent intoxication. At about 10 p.m. or 10:15 p.m. Menow was seen wandering around the other tables in the beverage room and consequently was ejected from the hotel by employees thereof, Fernick then knowing that the plaintiff was unable to take care of himself by reason of intoxication and that he would have to go home, probably by foot, by way of a main highway.

No excessive force was used in turning Menow out of the hotel. The evidence shows that he was put out on a dark and rainy night and that he was wearing dark clothes not readily visible to motorists. It appears that Menow, when he was outside the hotel, was picked up by an unknown third person and taken part of the way home, being let out on Highway No. 8 at 13th St. The ride had not been arranged by the hotel. It was while continuing in an easterly direction and, indeed, while walking beyond 11th St., his turn-off point (because, according to his testimony, he was looking for a friend), that Menow was struck by the Honsberger vehicle. It is unnecessary to detail the circumstances attending the accident because Honsberger does not challenge in this court the finding of negligence and the apportionment of one-third fault against him. It is enough to say that the accident occurred within half an hour after Menow was ejected from the hotel, and that he was staggering near the centre of the highway when he was hit by the Honsberger vehicle which was travelling east. ...

The following are the statutory provisions referred to by the trial judge in the course of his reasons relating to the hotel's liability to Menow:

Liquor Licence Act, s. 53(3):

> 53(3) No liquor shall be sold or supplied on or at any licensed premises to or for any person who is apparently in an intoxicated condition.
>
> (4) No person holding a licence under this Act shall permit or suffer in the premises for which the licence is issued,
>
> (b) any gambling, drunkenness or any riotous, quarrelsome, violent or disorderly conduct to take place;
>
> (6) Any person holding a licence under this Act who has reasonable grounds to suspect from the conduct of any person who has come upon the premises in respect of which such licence is issued that such person, although not of notoriously bad character, is present for some improper purpose or is committing an offence against this Act or the regulations, may request such person to leave the licensed premises immediately and, unless the requestion is forthwith complied with, such person may be forcibly removed.

Section 67 [now s. 68]:

67. Where any person or his servant or agent sells liquor to or for a person whose condition is such that the consumption of liquor would apparently intoxicate him or increase his intoxication so that he would be in danger of causing injury to his person or injury or damage to the person or property of others, if the person to or for whom the liquor is sold while so intoxicated,

(a) commits suicide or meets death by accident, an action under *The Fatal Accidents Act* lies against the person who or whose servant or agent sold the liquor; or

(b) causes injury or damage to the person or property of another person, such other person is entitled to recover an amount to compensate him for his injury or damage from the person who or whose servant or agent sold the liquor.

Liquor Control Act, s. 81:

81. No person shall sell or supply liquor or permit liquor to be sold or supplied to any person under or apparently under the influence of liquor.

Section 67 of the *Liquor Licence Act* has no direct application to the facts of the present case, and the trial judge did not attempt to apply it even indirectly as pointing to a standard of care resting upon the hotel. Counsel for the appellant hotel urged, however, that the express provision for civil liability upon a breach of s. 67 reflected a legislative policy precluding the founding of a cause of action upon breach of the other terms of the *Liquor Licence Act* (or of the *Liquor Control Act*) invoked by the trial judge. In my opinion, this is to mistake the use to which the trial judge put s. 53(3) of the *Liquor Licence Act* and s. 81 of the *Liquor Control Act*. I do not read his reasons as holding that the mere breach of those enactments and the fact that Menow suffered personal injury were enough to attach civil liability to the hotel. He regarded them rather as crystallizing a relevant fact situation which because of its authoritative source, the court was entitled to consider in determining, on common law principles, whether a duty of care should be raised in favour of Menow against the hotel. ...

The common law assesses liability for negligence on the basis of breach of a duty of care arising from a foreseeable and unreasonable risk of harm to one person created by the act or omission of another. This is the generality which exhibits the flexibility of the common law; but since liability is predicated upon fault, the guiding principle assumes a nexus or relationship between the injured person and the injuring person which makes it reasonable to conclude that the latter owes a duty to the former not to expose him to an unreasonable risk or harm. Moreover, in considering whether the risk or injury to which a person may be exposed is one that he should not reasonably have to run, it is relevant to relate the probability and the gravity of injury to the burden that would be imposed upon the prospective defendant in taking avoiding measures. ...

In the present case, it may be said from one point of view that Menow created a risk of injury to himself by excessive drinking on the night in question. If the hotel's only involvement was the supplying of the beer consumed by Menow, it would be difficult to support the imposition of common law liability upon it for injuries suffered by Menow after being shown the door of the hotel and after leaving the hotel. Other persons on the highway, seeing Menow in an intoxicated condition, would not, by reason of that fact alone, come under any legal duty to steer him to safety, although it might be expected that good Samaritan impulses would move them to offer help. They would, however, be under a legal duty, as motorists for example, to take reasonable care to avoid hitting him, a duty in which Honsberger failed in this case. The hotel, however, was not in the position of persons in general who see an intoxicated person who appears to be unable to control his steps. It was in an invitor-invitee relationship with Menow as one of its patrons, and it was aware, through its employees, of his intoxicated condition, a condition which, on the findings of the trial judge, it fed in violation of applicable liquor licence and liquor control legislation. There was a probable risk of personal injury to Menow if he was turned out of the hotel to proceed on foot on a much-travelled highway passing in front of the hotel.

There is, in my opinion, nothing unreasonable in calling upon the hotel in such circumstances to take care to see that Menow is not exposed to injury because of his intoxication. No inordinate burden would be placed upon it in obliging it to respond to Menow's need for protection. A call to the police or a call to his employer immediately come to mind as easily available preventive measures; or a taxi-cab could be summoned to take him home, or arrangements made to this end with another patron able and willing to do so. The evidence shows that the hotel has experience with or was sensitive to the occasional need to take care of intoxicated patrons. The operator had, in other like instances, provided rides. He also had spare rooms at the time into one of which Menow could have been put.

Given the relationship between Menow and the hotel, the hotel operator's knowledge of Menow's propensity to drink and his instruction to his employees not to serve him unless he was accompanied by a responsible person, the fact that Menow was served, not only in breach of this instruction, but as well in breach of statutory injunctions against serving a patron who was apparently in an intoxicated condition, and the fact that the hotel operator was aware that Menow was intoxicated, the proper conclusion is that the hotel came under a duty to Menow to see that he got home safely by taking him under its charge or putting him under the charge of a responsible person, or to see that he was not turned out alone until he was in a reasonably fit condition to look after himself. There was, in this case, a breach of this duty for which the hotel must respond according to the degree of fault found against it. The harm that ensued was that which was reasonably foreseeable by reason of what the hotel did (in turning Menow out), and failed to do (in not taking preventive measures).

The imposition of liability upon the hotel in the circumstances that I have recounted has roots in an earlier decision of this court when related to the evolutionary principles stemming from *Donoghue v. Stevenson*, [1932] A.C. 562, which have become part of this court's course of decision. The affinity of *Dunn v. Dominion Atlantic Ry. Co.* (1920), 52 D.L.R. 149, 60 S.C.R. 310, with the present case, is sufficiently shown by the following three sentences from the reasons of Anglin J. who was one of the plurality of this court which allowed the appeal of the administrator of the estate of a deceased passenger, killed by a passing train when put off at a closed and unlighted station in a drunken condition [at 154]:

> The right of removal of a disorderly passenger which is conferred on the conductor [under a railway by-law] is not absolute. It must be exercised reasonably. He cannot under it justify putting a passenger off the train under such circumstances that, as a direct consequence, he is exposed to danger of losing his life or of serious personal injury.

I do not regard the *Dunn* case as turning on the fact that the defendant was a common carrier, any more than I regard it as relevant here whether or not the defendant hotel was under innkeeper's liability in respect of the operation of its beverage room.

The risk of harm to which Menow was exposed by the hotel was not abated to its exoneration by reason of the fortuitous circumstance that Menow obtained a ride part of the way home. The short period of time that elapsed between the time that he was removed from the hotel and the time of the accident is telling in this respect, as is the fact that the risk was not increased or changed in kind when he was dropped off at 13th St. Counsel for the appellant did not argue on causation, but did contend that any duty that the hotel might have had evaporated because of voluntary assumption of risk. The argument is untenable, whether put on the basis of Menow's self-intoxication or on the basis of the situation that faced him when he was put out of the hotel. In his condition, as found by the trial judge, it is impossible to say that he both appreciated the risk of injury and impliedly agreed to bear the legal consequences. However, the trial judge did find Menow contributorily negligent in becoming intoxicated, adverting in this connection to s. 80(2) of the *Liquor Control Act*, which enjoins any person against being in an intoxicated condition in a public place. This finding has not been attacked.

The result to which I would come here does not mean (to use the words of the trial judge [at 503]), that I would impose "a duty on every tavern-owner to act as a watch dog for all patrons who enter his place of business and drink to excess". A great deal turns on the knowledge of the operator (or his employees) of the patron and his condition where the issue is liability in negligence for injuries suffered by the patron.

I would dismiss the appeal with costs.

[**Martland** and **Spence JJ**. concur with **Laskin J**.]

Ritchie J.: I agree with my brother Laskin that this appeal should be dismissed.

For my part, however, the circumstances giving rise to the appellant's liability were that the innkeeper and his staff, who were well aware of the respondent's propensity for irresponsible behaviour under the influence of drink, assisted or at least permitted him to consume a quantity of beer which they should have known might well result in his being incapable of taking care of himself when exposed to the hazards of traffic. Their knowledge of the respondent's somewhat limited capacity for consuming alcoholic stimulants without becoming befuddled and sometimes obstreperous, seized them with a duty to be careful not to serve him with repeated drinks after the effects of what he had already consumed should have been obvious.

In my view, it was a breach of this duty which gave rise to liability in the present case.

[**Judson J.** concurs with **Ritchie J**.]

NOTES

1. What was the basis of Mr. Justice Laskin's decision? How did Mr. Justice Ritchie's reasons differ?

2. A, a passenger on the B railway, is intoxicated when the station is reached. The conductor leads A off the train and part way up a flight of stairs leading to the street level, and leaves A halfway up. A falls and is seriously injured. Is the B railway liable? See *Black v. New York, New Haven & Hartford Ry. Co.*, 79 N.E. 797 (Mass. 1907); *Fagan v. Atlantic Coast Line Ry. Co.*, 115 N.E. 704 (N.Y. 1917). Compare *Dunn v. Dominion Atlantic Ry. Co.* (1920), 60 S.C.R. 310, 52 D.L.R. 149, [1920] 2 W.W.R. 705;

Howe v. Niagara St. Catharines and Toronto Ry. Co. (1925), 56 O.L.R. 202, [1925] 2 D.L.R. 115 (C.A.).

3. Do you think that the hotel would have been liable if Menow had wandered out of the hotel rather than being ejected?

4. Would the hotel have been liable if Menow had entered the hotel in an intoxicated state and had been ejected immediately before he could buy another drink? What if he had come to the door, drunk, and had been turned away before he could enter?

5. If he could be found, would the unidentified driver who had picked Menow up and later dropped him off be partially liable?

6. Would Menow's friend, the foreman, have been partially to blame if he had not left earlier but had remained in his seat until, and after, Menow was ejected?

7. If the same thing that occurred in the hotel had transpired in a private home, would the same result have followed? See *Kelly v. Gwinnell*, 476 A. 2d 1219 (N.J.S.C. 1984). Note dissent by Garibaldi J., at 1230. Also see (1984), 60 Notre Dame L. Rev. 191. What if the social host behaved reasonably and tried to stop the drinking? See *Baumeister v. Drake* (1986), 5 B.C.L.R. (2d) 382, 38 C.C.L.T. 1 (S.C.).

8. What effect, if any, would the *Menow* case have on the conduct of tavernkeepers across Canada? Several reports of this case appeared in the journal of the Ontario Hotels Association which helped to finance the defendant's legal costs. A report of the decision in this case was written up in *Time* magazine and on the front page of the *Toronto Daily Star.* In the next few days, several students at the Osgoode Hall Law School did a survey of 28 tavernkeepers in the Toronto area. Over 70 per cent of them had read a media story about the decision. In one bar, the story from the newspaper had been clipped out and posted on the employees' notice board. When asked if they had altered their conduct as a result of this case, they said "no", insisting that they never served drunk patrons and that, if an intoxicated person came into their bar, they would send that person home in a taxi. Do you believe them? Is this an area where tort law may be a more powerful force for social control than the criminal law?

9. Would a hotel be liable for serving an underaged drinker who is later involved in an accident? See *Schmidt v. Sharpe et al.* (1983), 27 C.C.L.T. 1 (Ont. H.C.). See Kligman, "Comment" (1984), 27 C.C.L.T. 49. What if one patron in a bar harms another? See *McGeogh v. Don Enterprises Ltd.* (1984), 28 Sask. R. 126, [1984] 1 W.W.R. 256 (Q.B.).

10. The Supreme Court of Canada reaffirmed its support for the *Jordan House* principle in *Crocker and Sundance Northwest Resorts Ltd.*, [1988] 1 S.C.R. 1186, 44 C.C.L.T. 225. The defendant company was a ski resort which ran a "tubing race" for the enjoyment of its customers. Contestants raced down mogulled ski hills in oversized tire inner tubes. The plaintiff competitor was inebriated, but was still permitted to compete. He seriously injured himself. In finding for the plaintiff, Wilson J. noted the commercial advantages which the defendant resort hoped to gain from the race, and stated:... "when a ski resort establishes a competition in a highly dangerous sport and runs the competition for profit, it owes a duty of care towards visibly intoxicated patrons".

11. The Supreme Court of Canada has again expressed its fidelity to *Jordan House* in *Stewart v. Pettie,* [1995] 1 S.C.R. 131, where Mr. Justice Major stated:

> [There was] no question that commercial vendors of alcohol owe a general duty of care to persons who can be expected to use the highways.

On the facts, however, the court found that there was no negligence and that no causation had been established. Are *Jordan House, Crocker* and *Stewart v. Pettie* really based on a theory of economic benefit or can they be explained as cases of control or creation of danger?

12. The issue of liability of a host at a social gathering who serves alcohol to a guest, who later injures himself, herself or a third person, is more controversial. Does it make any difference if the host personally served alcohol to someone he or she knew or should have known to be drunk? What if the defendant merely threw a party at which someone got drunk on his or her own liquor? Compare *Baumeister v. Drake* (1986), 5 B.C.L.R. (2d) 382 (S.C.) and *Wince v. Ball* (1996), 136 D.L.R. (4th) 104 (Alta. Q.B.).

(b) Relationships of Control or Supervision

KLAR, TORT LAW
2nd. ed. (1996)

There are several relationships of control or supervision which require dominant parties to take affirmative steps to either prevent injury to or assist others in vulnerable positions. The hallmark of these relationships is that those who enter into them do so willingly, knowing that situations may develop which will require them to act in order to assist others. Thus the imposition of duties of affirmative action in these cases is not inconsistent with the common law's desire not to interfere unduly with one's freedom of action. As well, concomitant with the duty to assist those who are in one's control is the duty to protect others from being injured by them.

NOTES

1. Some relationships of control or supervision are governed by contract, while others are not. It is Professor Klar's submission, however, that even in the absence of contract, there is inherent in these relationships the tort obligation to assist. The argument is made that it is only fair that if a person's freedom of action is limited by another person, that the latter has a duty to protect or assist the former. Do you agree?

2. The most obvious relationship of control which requires a duty to assist is that of parent and child. Can children sue their parents in tort for their negligence in failing to protect them, for example, for failing to ensure that they are safely buckled up in a car? Would you expect children to sue their parents, even if they could? When might they? See *Ducharme v. Davies* (1984), 29 Sask. R. 54, [1984] 1 W.W.R. 699 (C.A.).

3. Even if a child does not wish to sue a parent, a third party involved in the accident is entitled to bring the negligent parent into the action and seek contribution. See *Teno v. Arnold* (1975), 7 O.R. (2d) 276, 55 D.L.R. (3d) 57; affd (1976), 11 O.R. (2d) 585, 67 D.L.R. (3d) 9 (C.A.); varied (1978), 3 C.C.L.T. 272 (S.C.C.).

4. Other relationships of control or supervision include teacher and pupil, employer and employee, carrier and passenger, prisons and inmates, and hospitals and patients. In all of these relationships the freedom of action of the subservient party is limited by the dominant party. A clear explanation of why teachers must assist pupils was given by Winnecke C.J. in *Richards v. State of Victoria*, [1969] V.R. 136, at 138-39:

> The reason underlying the imposition of the duty would appear to be the need of a child of immature age for protection against the conduct of others, or indeed of himself, which may cause him injury coupled with the fact that, during school hours the child is beyond the control and protection of his parent and is placed under the control of the schoolmaster who is in a position to exercise authority over him and afford him, in the exercise of reasonable care, protection from injury. ...

5. A doctor owes a civil duty as well as a statutory one to report when he or she observes instances of child abuse (See *Brown v. University of Alberta Hospital* (1997), 33 C.C.L.T. (2d) 113 (Alta. Q.B.)). Is this a control case, an economic benefit case, or a statutory duty case?

(c) Creation of Danger

OKE v. WEIDE TRANSPORT LTD. AND CARRA

Manitoba Court of Appeal. (1963), 41 D.L.R. (2d) 53, 43 W.W.R. 203.

The defendant driver, without negligence, knocked down a traffic sign located in the middle of a gravel strip dividing the eastbound and westbound lanes of a highway. The defendant stopped his vehicle and removed the debris except for a metal post which was too securely imbedded. This post was left bent over and projecting at right angles towards the near side of the eastbound lane. The defendant subsequently mentioned the accident to a garage attendant and evidenced an intention to report it to the authorities but was dissuaded from doing so by the attendant. The next day, while using the gravel strip to pass a vehicle in the eastbound lane, which was forbidden, a driver passed over the metal post and was fatally injured when he was "speared" by the post which deflected upwards, through the floor boards and pierced his chest. At trial, the defendant and his employer were held liable for the death on grounds of negligence in failing to notify the police of the hazardous condition created by the projecting metal post so that action could be taken to remove the hazard. The majority of the Court of Appeal dismissed the action on grounds of lack of foresight.

Freedman J.A. (dissenting): ... Counsel for the defendant advanced another argument that I must now consider. Starting from the premise that the defendant's collision with the sign-post was not the result of his negligence, he urged that thereafter the defendant was under no duty whatever with respect to the broken sign. Without such a duty towards other motorists, including the plaintiff, no negligence could be ascribed to him. His position, it was argued, was no different from that of any other motorist who, driving by and observing the broken sign, did nothing about it.

Concerning this argument I have two observations to make. In the first place, no such other motorist is before the court as a defendant in this case and it is therefore unnecessary to consider what his position might have been. In the second place, even if we assume that such other motorist would not be liable, it is wrong to think that the defendant's position is on all fours with his. Indeed it is decidedly different. Our other motorist did not collide with the sign; the defendant did, even if it was without negligence. The former, if observing the broken sign-post at all, could do so only fleetingly, while in the act of driving by; the latter stood at the very spot, where he could see the precise results of the collision and the hazard they created. The former, having had no part in the destruction of the sign, was never anything more than an innocent passer-by who might not be under a legal duty to take active steps to control the situation; the defendant on the other hand participated in the creation of the hazard, recognized his obligation to do something by way of rectification, and in fact took some steps in that direction — the removal of debris, the resolve to inform the police — but then failed to go far enough. It is entirely unrealistic, in my view, to try to assimilate his position to that of some passing motorist.

NOTES

1. If the defendant was not negligent in creating the danger, why should he have tort responsibilities differing from those of other innocent parties? Do you think that this goes too far in turning tort law into a system of distributive, rather than corrective, justice?

2. The current Ontario *Highway Traffic Act*, R.S.O. 1990, c. H.8, s. 200 states:

> **200.** (1) Where an accident occurs on a highway, every person in charge of a vehicle or street car that is directly or indirectly involved in the accident shall,
> (a) remain at or immediately return to the scene of the accident;
> (b) render all possible assistance; and
> (c) upon request, give in writing to anyone sustaining loss or injury, or to any police officer or to any witness his or her name, address, driver's licence number and jurisdiction of issuance, motor vehicle liability insurance policy insurer and policy number, name and address of the registered owner of the vehicle and the vehicle permit number.
> (2) Every person who contravenes this section is guilty of an offence and on conviction is liable to a fine of not less that $200 and not more that $1,000 or to imprisonment for a term of not more than six months, or to both, and in addition the person's licence or permit may be suspended for a period of not more than two years.

See also *Criminal Code*, R.S.C. 1985, c. C-46, s. 252 for a similar provision. Would a violation of the *Highway Traffic Act*, or of the *Criminal Code* give rise to tort liability? What are the problems? What would be the benefits? See Linden, "Tort Liability for Criminal Nonfeasance" (1966) 44 C.B.R. 25.

3. In *Stermer v. Lawson* (1977), 79 D.L.R. (3d) 366, [1977] 5 W.W.R. 628 (B.C.) percentage varied (1979), 107 D.L.R. (3d) 36, 11 C.C.L.T. 76 (B.C.C.A.), someone lent his motorcycle to an unlicensed driver. This was in violation of the British Columbia *Motor-vehicle Act*, R.S.B.C. 1960, c. 253. Do you think that, in addition to the legislative penalty, the common law ought to impose a duty on the owner of the motorcycle to properly instruct the borrower on how to drive the motorcycle? Would this be an example of the common law requiring those who create potential dangers to take steps to prevent accidents from occurring?

4. X lends a car to Y, who is intoxicated. Y collides with a tree. Is X liable? Compare with *Hempler v. Todd* (1970), 14 D.L.R. (3d) 637, 74 W.W.R. 758 (Q.B.). What if X instructs an incompetent driver, who has failed the driving test several times, to drive an automobile which is involved in a one-car collision? See *Ontario Hospital Services Commn. v. Borsoski* (1973), 7 O.R. (2d) 83, 54 D.L.R. (3d) 339 (H.C.) (Lerner J.).

5. A and B are both intoxicated. A, the owner of the car, allows B, a friend, to drive. B drives off the road and is injured. B sues A for allowing B to drive. Liability? See *Hall v. Hebert, infra*, Chapter 11.

(d) Reliance Relationships

ZELENKO v. GIMBEL BROS.

Supreme Court of New York. 287 N.Y.S. 134 (1935); affd 287 N.Y.S. 136 (1936).

Motion to dismiss amended complaint on the ground that it does not state facts sufficient to constitute a cause of action.

Lauer J.: The general proposition of law is that if a defendant owes a plaintiff no duty, then refusal to act is not negligence. ...But there are many ways that a defendant's duty to act may arise. Plaintiff's intestate was taken ill in defendant's store. We will assume that defendant owed her no duty at all — that defendant could have let her be and die. But if a defendant undertakes a task, even if under no duty to undertake it, the defendant must not omit to do what an ordinary man would do in performing the task.

Here the defendant undertook to render medical aid to the plaintiff's intestate. Plaintiff says that defendant kept his intestate for six hours in an infirmary without any medical care. If defendant had left plaintiff's intestate alone, beyond doubt some bystander, who would be influenced more by charity than by legislative duty, would have summoned an ambulance. Defendant segregated this plaintiff's intestate where such aid could not be given and then left her alone.

The plaintiff was wrong in thinking that the duty of a common carrier of passengers is the same as the duty of this defendant. The common carrier assumes its duty by its contract of carriage. This defendant assumed its duty by meddling in matters with which legalistically it had no concern. The plaintiff is right in arguing that when the duty arose, the same type of neglect is actionable in both cases. The motion is denied.

NOTES

1. In *Mercer v. S.E. & C. Ry. Co.*, [1922] 2 K.B. 549, 92 L.J.K.B. 25, 127 L.T. 723, the defendants had made a practice of keeping a wicket gate locked to pedestrians when a train was passing. This practice was known to the plaintiff who was injured by a passing train when, owing to the carelessness of the defendants' servant, the gate was left unlocked. The defendants were held liable. *Per* Lush J.: "To those who knew of the practice this was a tacit invitation to cross the line. ... It may seem a hardship on a railway company to hold them responsible for the omission to do something which they were under no legal obligation to do, and which they only did for the protection of the public. They ought, however, to have contemplated that if a self-imposed duty is ordinarily performed, those who knew of it will draw an inference if on a given occasion it is not performed. It they wish to protect themselves against the inference being drawn they should do so by giving notice, and they did not do so in this case." *Cf., Soulsby v. City of Toronto* (1907), 15 O.L.R. 13.

2. In *Barnett v. Chelsea and Kensington Hospital Management Committee*, [1967] 1 Q.B. 428, [1968] 1 All E.R. 1068 (Q.B.D.), a watchman, after drinking some "tea" which made him vomit, went to the casualty department of the defendant's hospital. The watchman "entered the ... hospital without hindrance. ... made complaints to the nurse who received them and she in turn passed [them] on to the medical casualty officer and he sent a message through the nurse purporting to advise the [watchman]" to go home and see his own doctor. He died some hours later from arsenical poisoning. Although Mr. Justice Nield found that the negligence of the defendant's employees

did not cause the death, he said in a *dictum* that because there was a "close and direct relationship between the hospital and the [plaintiff] ... there was imposed on the hospital a duty of care. ..." Mr. Justice Nield distinguished this case from a case of a casualty department that closes its doors and says that no patients can be received.

3. The Supreme Court of Canada has indicated that an undertaking and reliance thereon may lead to the establishment of a legal duty to take care, at least in the case of government safety activity. In *R. v. Nord-Deutsche et al.*, [1971] S.C.R. 849, 20 D.L.R. (3d) 444, employees of the Crown negligently permitted a set of range lights, upon which pilots relied, to become displaced, and thereby contributed to a collision between two ships. At trial, Mr. Justice Noel based liability on the ground that the Crown had "engendered reliance on the guidance afforded by [the lights]", and was therefore required to keep them in good working order or, failing that, to warn about the danger. In the Supreme Court of Canada, Mr. Justice Ritchie divided liability among the Crown and the two shipowners and explained that there was a "breach of duty on the part of the servants of the Crown responsible for the care and maintenance of the range lights ... upon which lights mariners were entitled to place reliance". See also *Hendricks v. R.*, [1970] S.C.R. 237, 9 D.L.R. (3d) 454; *Grossman v. R.*, [1952] 1 S.C.R. 571, [1952] 2 D.L.R. 241.

4. A husband makes an agreement with a doctor to look after his wife during her confinement. Although called, the doctor is not present when the baby is born. The baby dies and the wife suffers physical injury, pain, etc. Can the wife recover if the doctor's absence is found to be due to carelessly overlooking the call? Is a contract with the wife a necessary prerequisite for liability? Compare with *Smith v. Rae* (1919), 46 O.L.R. 518, 51 D.L.R. 323 (C.A.).

5. What if someone starts to assist, even though under no duty to do so? The leading American case on this issue is *H. R. Moch Co. v. Rensselaer Water Co.*, 159 N.E. 896 (1928), where Mr. Justice Cardozo of the New York Court of Appeals stated:

> It is ancient learning that one who assumes to act, even though gratuitously, may thereby become subject to the duty of acting carefully, if he acts at all. ... The plaintiff would bring its case within the orbit of that principle. The hand once set to a task may not be withdrawn with impunity though liability would fail if it had never been applied at all. A time-honoured formula often phrases the distinction as one between misfeasance and nonfeasance. Incomplete the formula is, and so at times misleading. Given a relation involving in its existence a duty of care irrespective of a contract, a tort may result, as well from acts of omission as of commission in the fulfilment of the duty thus recognized by law. ... What we need to know is not so much the conduct to be avoided when the relation and its attendant duty are established as existing. What we need to know is the conduct that engenders the relation. It is here that the formula, however incomplete, has its value and significance.
>
> If conduct has gone foreward to such a stage that inaction would commonly result, not negatively merely in withholding a benefit, but positively or actively in working an injury, there exists a relation out of which arises a duty to go foreward. Bohlen, *Studies in the Law of Torts*, p. 87. So the surgeon who operates without pay is liable, though his negligence is the omission to sterilize his instruments... ; the engineer, though his fault is in the failure to shut off steam... ; the maker of automobiles, at the suit of some one other than the buyer, though his negligence is merely in inadequate inspection. ... The query always is whether the putative wrongdoer has advanced to such a point as to have launched a force or instrument of harm, or has stopped where inaction is at most a refusal to become an instrument for good. ..."

6. This problem surfaced, but was not resolved, in *Horsley v. MacLaren*, [1970] 2 O.R. 487, 11 D.L.R. (3d) 277 (C.A.); affd [1972] S.C.R. 441, 22 D.L.R. (3d) 545. See

Chapter 8, *infra*. A passenger on a private yacht, Matthews, fell overboard and the owner of the boat began a rescue attempt by backing up towards him. Expert evidence was adduced to the effect that this was the wrong procedure. A would-be rescuer died while attempting to rescue the person who fell overboard and his widow sued. At trial, Mr. Justice Lacourcière asked, "What could the reasonable boat operator do in the circumstances... ?" Because the defendant used the "wrong procedure" in backing the boat up and because of his "excessive consumption of alcohol", Mr. Justice Lacourcière held that he was negligent and, therefore, liable to the plaintiff. The Court of Appeal, however, reversed the trial judge and decided that the defendant was guilty only of an error in judgment, which did not amount to negligence. Mr. Justice Jessup explained that "where a person gratuitously and without any duty to do so undertakes to confer a benefit upon or go to the aid of another, he incurs no liability unless what he does worsens the condition of the others". Mr. Justice Jessup argued: "I think it is an unfortunate development in the law which leaves the Good Samaritan liable to be mulcted in damages, and apparently in the United States, it is one that has produced marked reluctance of doctors to aid victims." Mr. Justice Schroeder echoed this view and argued that "if a person embarks upon a rescue, and does not carry it through, he is not under any liability to the person to whose aid he has come so long as discontinuance of his efforts did not leave the other in a worse condition than when he took charge".

In the Supreme Court of Canada, the majority did not deal with this point, and Mr. Justice Laskin, dissenting, left it to be decided on another occasion. Mr. Justice Laskin (referring to *Moch* and *Kent*) said:

> Whether a case involving the exercise of statutory powers (but not duties) by a public authority should govern the issue of liability or non-liability to an injured rescuer is a question that need not be answered here.

For a thorough analysis of *Horsley v. MacLaren* see Alexander, "One Rescuer's Obligation to Another: The Ogopogo Lands in the Supreme Court of Canada" (1972), 22 U. Toronto L.J. 98.

7. Doctors sometimes say that they are afraid to stop at the scene of an accident because they fear being sued by the person they treat if something goes wrong. Do they have much to worry about in the light of these cases?

8. When is there an "undertaking" by affirmative action? A would-be rescuer sees a victim drowning and shouts "Don't worry! I'll save you!" The rescuer gets the life jacket and throws it in. It misses. The rescuer throws it in again, pulls the victim five feet closer to shore and then decides to abandon the rescue attempt. The victim sinks and is seen no more. Is the rescuer liable? What if there were dozens of other potential rescuers around? What if there was no one else in sight?

9. Two other categories of reliance cases involve (a) the liability of statutory authorities for failing to exercise their statutory duties or powers, and (b) the liability of those who undertake to perform services for others, who fail to do so, and as a result, cause them economic losses. Since these categories involve special and complicated concerns they are discussed separately, *infra*.

THE EMERGENCY MEDICAL AID ACT

R.S.A. 1980, c. E-9, s. 2.

2. If, in respect of a person who is ill, injured or unconscious as the result of an accident or other emergency, (*a*) a physician, registered health discipline member, or registered nurse voluntarily and without expectation of compensation or reward renders emergency medical services or first aid assistance and the services or assistance are not rendered at a hospital or other place having adequate medical facilities and equipment, or

(*b*) a person other than a person mentioned in clause (a) voluntarily renders emergency first aid assistance and that assistance is rendered at the immediate scene of the accident or emergency,

the physician, registered health discipline member, registered nurse or other person is not liable for damages for injuries to or the death of that person alleged to have been caused by an act or omission on his part in rendering the medical services or first aid assistance, unless it is established that the injuries or death were caused by gross negligence on his part.

NOTES

1. Do you think that the above statute encourages more people to become Good Samaritans? Do you think that fear of liability is a factor in discouraging altruistic behaviour? Five other provinces and the two territories have similar provisions. See McInnes, "Good Samaritan Statutes: A Summary and Analysis" (1992), 26 U.B.C.L. Rev. 239, for an excellent discussion of these statutes.

2. Should the state compensate rescuers who offer assistance and are injured in the attempt? If the person being rescued was placed in peril by a negligent person or by self-negligence, the rescuer is entitled to recover in tort. If there is no negligence, however, or insolvency, there is no compensation available. Some jurisdictions grant compensation to those injured by criminal acts. Consequently, if the rescuer is injured by criminal conduct, the rescuer may claim compensation from one of these funds, but not if there was no crime committed.

3. The Canadian Bankers Association gives rewards to those injured while trying to prevent bank robberies. Recently, in Toronto, a dentist, shot while chasing a bank robber, was granted $5,000 by the C.B.A. Sometimes a municipality will make a gratuitous award to a person injured while doing some heroic act. On occasion, the publicity generated by such acts prompts citizens to send small gifts of money to the hero or the hero's family. Is this a better way of dealing with this problem?

4. Certain institutions and authorities have been held not to owe a civil duty of care. As has been seen, Judges are immune from suit as are other quasi-judicial officers. A Law Society, for example, owes no duty to supervise solicitors, unless there is malice, for it acts in a quasi-judicial capacity. (See *Voratovic v. L.S.U.C.* (1978), 20 O.R. (2d) 214). A professional association of accountants was also cleared of liability for theft by one of its members, when they failed to notify clients that he had been disciplined. (See *Schilling v. C.G.A. Ass'n. of B.C.* (1996), 29 C.C.L.T. (2d) 44).

5. The English courts have been most protective of their government agencies. There is no tort duty in England on a soldier or the military to protect another soldier under battle conditions. (See *Mulcahy v. Ministry of Defence*, [1996] 2 All E.R. 758, no liability to soldier knocked down by Howitzer fire in the Gulf War). There is a reluctance to create civil duties on the police to prevent crime, (*Hill v. Chief Constable of West Yorkshire*, [1988] 2 All E.R. 258 (H.L.) *cf. Swinney v. Chief*

Constable of Northumbria Police Force, [1996] 3 All E. R. 449 (C.A.) or on fire departments to put out fires unless they make things worse. (See *Capital and Counties p.l.c. v. Hampshire City Council,* [1997] 2 All E.R. 365 (C.A.). The coastguard is under no civil duty to rescue children in canoes who are in danger, unless they worsen their situation. (See *Oll Ltd. v. Sect. of State for Transport,* [1997] 3 All E. R. 897). A municipality is not required to move a building which blocks the view of motorists on the road. (*Stovin v. Wise,* [1996] 3 All E. R. 801 (H.L.); see also *Barrett v. Enfield London Borough Council,* [1997] 3 All E. R. 171 (C.A.), local authority owes no duty for decisions re child care.)

(e) Statutory Duties

As we have seen, the Supreme Court of Canada's decision in *R. v. Saskatchewan Wheat Pool, supra,* Chapter 4, held that there is no tort of breach of statutory duty in Canadian law, and that a statute which was silent as to the imposition of civil liability, could not automatically give rise to a tort duty. Nevertheless, the existence of a statutory duty can be used to convince courts to create a concomitant common law duty. In the public tort liability area especially, statutory duties have given rise to private law duties of care.

O'ROURKE v. SCHACHT

Supreme Court of Canada. [1973] 1 O.R. 221; affd (1975), 55 D.L.R. (3d) 96.

A well-lighted barrier that marked a detour around some highway construction was knocked over by a car, at night, so that it was no longer visible to other motorists on the highway. The Ontario Provincial Police (O.P.P.) investigated the accident, but failed to warn traffic about the danger on the road. The plaintiff was injured when he drove his automobile into the unmarked excavation. The *Police Act* of Ontario, R.S.O. 1970, c. 351, required that the O.P.P., *inter alia* "shall maintain a traffic patrol … ". The *Highway Traffic Act,* R.S.O. 1970, c. 202, empowered the police officers to "direct traffic" in order "to ensure orderly movement" and "to prevent injury or damage to persons or property". The court allowed the plaintiff to recover 50 per cent of his damages against the police administration:

Schroeder J.A.:

…

Police forces exist in municipal, provincial, and federal jurisdictions to exercise powers designed to promote the order, safety, health, morals, and general welfare of society. It is not only impossible but inadvisable to attempt to frame a definition which will set definite limits to the powers and duties of police officers appointed to carry out the powers of the state in relation to individuals who come within its jurisdiction and protection. The duties imposed on them by statute are by no means exhaustive. It is infinitely better that the courts should decide as each case arises whether, having regard to the necessities of the case and the safeguards required in the public interest, the police are under a legal duty in the particular circumstances. …

Section 55 of the *Police Act* which sets out the duties of members of a municipal police force declares that they "have generally all the powers and privileges and they are liable to all the duties and responsibilities that belong to constables".

This is a legislative recognition of the fact that while constables have certain duties imposed upon them by statute, they are, in addition, subject to the traditional duties of police officers of which cognizance is taken under the common law.

The respondent police officers were under a statutory duty to maintain a traffic patrol of the highway in question. The word 'patrol' is used in reference to police passing along or over highways or streets in the performance of their duties. The word is sometimes used to refer to duties assigned to soldiers in reference to a camp, or to the duties of a caretaker of large buildings to protect the property against fire and burglary. There is a definite purpose in requiring the police to patrol the highways under their jurisdiction, namely, to ensure that traffic laws will be obeyed, to investigate road accidents, and to assist injured persons. All this is directed to the prevention of accidents and the preservation of the safety of road users. If an unlighted truck or other large obstruction presenting a danger to traffic were on a highway after nightfall any traffic officer, sensible of his duty, would feel obligated to adopt reasonable means of ensuring that adequate warning was given of their presence on the highway. A cavity such as existed here would be even less visible to a road user, and clearly presented a much greater hazard than an obstruction located above the road surface.

Negligence as commonly defined includes both acts and omissions which involve an unreasonable risk of injury. In earlier times the common law furnished redress only for injury resulting from affirmative misconduct, and inaction was regarded as too remote to furnish a ground for the imposition of legal liability. Much as the humanitarian spirit which motivated the conduct of the Good Samaritan has been lauded, it was rooted in a moral philosophy, hence from the legal standpoint the *laissez-faire* attitude of the priest and the Levite was condoned. A member of a traffic detachment of the Ontario Provincial Police in the situation of Constable Boyd and Corporal Johnston is in an entirely different position from the ordinary citizen or the priest and the Levite. These officers were under a positive duty by virtue of their office to take appropriate measures in the face of a hazardous condition such as they encountered here to warn approaching traffic of its presence.

It is undoubtedly true that the nuisance was created in the first instance by the northbound motorist, Blancke, but the removal of the important large signs brought about by Blancke's act imperatively required officers patrolling the highway to deal with the dangerous situation so caused in an effective manner. The means of guarding against the danger of motorists driving into the excavation before the Department of Highways workmen could replace the large illuminated signs were readily available, since each of the defendant police officers was driving a police cruiser equipped with a revolving flashing light on the roof and nothing more was necessary than to place a cruiser across the highway at the southerly edge of the depression or to place a cruiser at both the south and north limits thereof.

Looked upon superficially the passivity of these two officers in the face of the manifest dangers inherent in the inadequately guarded depression across the highway may appear to be nothing more than non-feasance, but in the case of public servants subject not to a mere social obligation, but to what I feel bound to regard as a legal obligation, it was non-feasance amounting to misfeasance. Traffic officers are subject to all the duties and responsibilities belonging to constables. The duties which I would lay upon them stem not only from the relevant statutes to which reference has been made, but from the common law, which recognizes the existence of a broad conventional or customary duty in the established constabulary as an arm of the State to protect the life, limb and property of the subject. ...

... Each case must, in the final analysis, depend upon its own peculiar circumstances, but to hold that the proven neglect attributed by the learned judge to both defendant police officers in the most emphatic terms was not an actionable wrong which attracted liability to the plaintiff in the degrees apportioned by the learned judge would be to make the phrase 'police protection' hollow and meaningless.

[The Supreme Court of Canada affirmed, although it excused one of the several police officers involved. Mr. Justice Spence quoted at length from Mr. Justice Schroeder's opinion, which he described as "forthright and enlightened" and concluded:

I have the same view as to the duty of a police officer under the provisions of the said s. 3(3) of the *Police Act* in carrying out police traffic patrol. In my opinion, it is of the essence of that patrol that the officer attempt to make the road safe for traffic. Certainly, therefore, there should be included in that duty the proper notification of possible road users of a danger arising from a previous accident and creating an unreasonable risk of harm.

In a dissenting opinion, **Martland J. (Judson** and **Pigeon JJ.**, concurring), stated that he found nothing in the legislation that would "indicate an intention on the part of the Legislature to impose a liability upon a member of that Force who fails to carry out a duty assigned to him under the statute".]

NOTES

1. In *Jane Doe v. Toronto (Metropolitan) Commissioners of Police* (1998), 39 O.R. (3d) 486 (Ont. Gen. Div.), a rape victim succeeded in an action against the police for failing to live up to its statutory duty under the *Police Act* of Ontario to, *inter alia*, prevent crime. See, *infra,* Chapter 10 for a fuller discussion of this case.

   Compare with *Hill v. Chief Constable of West Yorkshire*, [1988] 2 All E.R. 238 (H.L.), where the Court struck out the plaintiffs' statement of claim seeking damages against the police for negligently failing to arrest a serial killer before he killed their daughter. It was said that there was no duty owed to victims of crime, unless the killer committed the crime while in custody or after escaping from custody. Can this case be distinguished from Jane Doe's?

   See also *Millette v. Coté et al.*, [1971] 2 O.R. 155, 17 D.L.R. (3d) 247; affd [1972] 3 O.R. 224, 27 D.L.R. (3d) 676 (C.A.); vard on other grounds [1976] 1 S.C.R. 595 (*sub nom. R. v. Coté; Millette v. Kalogeropoulos*), 51 D.L.R. (3d) 244.

2. In *Colonial Coach Lines v. Bennett and C.P.R.*, [1968] 1 O.R. 333, 66 D.L.R. (2d) 396 (C.A.), the plaintiff's bus was damaged when it collided with a cow that had escaped from a farmer's land onto the highway through a defective fence along the railway's right of way. Mr. Justice Laskin held that the railway was partially responsible to the plaintiff. He relied on ss. 277 and 392 of the *Railway Act*, R.S.C. 1952, c. 234. Section 277 created an obligation to erect fences "suitable to prevent cattle ... from getting on the railway lands". Section 392 imposed civil liability for failing to do so. Although s. 392 could not be applied in this case because the loss did not occur on "railway lands", Mr. Justice Laskin reasoned as follows:

> I am of opinion that having regard to the statutory duty to fence resting upon the railway under s. 277, there was a foreseeable risk of harm from escaping cattle to persons or property on the adjoining highway so as to impose a duty upon the railway for the breach of which it was liable at common law for the damage that occurred in this case. …
>
> This liability for negligence is not founded merely on breach of a statutory duty to fence, but proceeds on the footing of a state of facts comprehending maintenance of a fence to prevent the escape, from the adjoining land, of cattle which, if not contained, might stray on to a highway open from the right of way and expose oncoming traffic to the risk of injury. The triggering elements of liability are the railway's awareness of the defective condition of the fence and failure to take remedial measures to avert injury which could be reasonably foreseen. Existence of a statutory obligation to fence and actual assumption thereof by the railway were simply factors in the raising of a duty of care to the plaintiff by the railway when it knew that the obligation had not been met.

In what way did Mr. Justice Laskin use the statute in this case? Was it really relevant? What about *Gorris v. Scott*?

3. In *Bhadauria v. Bd of Governors of the Seneca College of Applied Arts and Technology* (1979), 27 O.R. (2d) 142, 11 C.C.L.T. 121 (C.A.), the plaintiff, a highly educated East Indian woman, qualified to teach in Ontario, alleged that she had applied for ten openings on the teaching staff of the defendant college but was not interviewed for any of them. She alleged that this was because of her ethnic origin. Rather than filing a complaint under the Ontario *Human Rights Code*, R.S.O. 1970, c. 318, she sued the defendant, which moved to strike out her Statement of Claim as disclosing no cause of action. Although the action was initially struck out, the Ontario Court of Appeal reversed that decision and sent the matter on to trial.

   Madam Justice Bertha Wilson (Houlden, Morden concurring) cited the principle of *Ashby v. White* (1703), 2 Ld. Raym. 938, 1 E.R. 417; revd 1 Bro. Parl. Cas. 62 (H.L.) to the effect that, "[i]f the plaintiff has a right, he must of necessity have a means to vindicate and maintain it, and a remedy if he is injured in the execution or enjoyment of it; and indeed it is a vain thing to imagine a right without a remedy; for want of right and want of remedy are reciprocal." The court held that the facts alleged gave rise to a cause of action at common law and explained:

> While no authority cited to us has recognized a tort of discrimination, none has repudiated such a tort. The matter is accordingly *res integra* before us. …
>
> I think there can be no doubt that the interests of persons of different ethnic origins are entitled to the protection of the law. The preamble to *The Ontario Human Rights Code* reads as follows:
>
> Whereas recognition of the inherent dignity and the equal and inalienable rights of all members of the human family is the foundation of freedom, justice and peace in the world and is in accord with the Universal Declaration of Human Rights as proclaimed by the United Nations;
>
> And Whereas it is public policy in Ontario that every person is free and equal in dignity and rights without regard to race, creed, colour, sex, marital status, nationality, ancestry or place of origin;
>
> And Whereas these principles have been confirmed in Ontario by a number of enactments of the Legislature;
>
> And Whereas it is desirable to enact a measure to codify and extend such enactments and to simplify their administration;
>
> *Therefore, Her Majesty, by and with the advice and consent of the Legislative Assembly of the Province of Ontario, enacts as follows:*
>
> I regard the preamble to the Code as evidencing what is now, and probably has been for some considerable time, the public policy of this Province

respecting fundamental rights. If we accept that "every person is free and equal in dignity and rights without regard to race, creed, colour, sex, marital status, nationality, ancestry or place of origin", as we do, then it is appropriate that these rights receive the full protection of the common law.

The plaintiff has a right not to be discriminated against because of her ethnic origin and alleges that she has been injured in the exercise or enjoyment of it. If she can establish that, then the common law must, on the principle of *Ashby v. White et al., supra*, afford her a remedy.

I do not regard the *Code* as in any way impeding the appropriate development of the common law in this important area. While the fundamental human right we are concerned with is recognized by the *Code*, it was not created by it. Nor does the *Code*, in my view, contain any expression of legislative intention to exclude the common law remedy. Rather the reverse since s. 14(1) appears to make the appointment of a board of inquiry to look into a complaint made under the *Code* a matter of ministerial discretion.

It is unnecessary, in view of the finding that a cause of action exists at common law, to determine whether or not the *Code* gives rise to a civil action.

What is the legal basis for this action?

4. Shortly after the *Seneca College* case, another came down, *Aziz v. Adamson* (1979), 11 C.C.L.T. 134 (Ont. H.C.), in which the plaintiff, a "Green Hornet" (a parking control officer) sued the Chief of Police of Metropolitan Toronto, alleging that he was discriminated against, in being rejected on five different occasions when he applied to become a police constable. Following *Seneca College*, which he described as an "eminently sensible decision", Linden J. said:

   By enacting these principles in the preamble of the Code, the Legislature of Ontario has chosen to underscore its commitment to equal rights for all of our citizens and its opposition to all forms of discrimination. The Court of Appeal made it clear, however, that this new tort action for discrimination did not depend for its life on *The Ontario Human Rights Code*, but rather was based on the common law. The public policy against racial and other discrimination existed in Ontario before the enactment of the Human Rights Code and was not created by the *Code*. The *Code* merely recognizes that pre-existing policy in its preamble and then establishes an agency and procedures that seek to eliminate or reduce the number of incidents of discrimination in this province. The courts of Ontario should cooperate with the Legislature, where possible, in promoting the public policy enshrined in *The Ontario Human Rights Code*. I, therefore, find that the plaintiff's statement of claim does allege facts which, if proved, could support a cause of action in tort for discrimination.

5. Professor Dale Gibson described this development as a "blessed event" and hoped that the "infant tort of discrimination can grow to productive adulthood" (see "The New Tort of Discrimination: A Blessed Event for the Great-Grandmother of Torts", (1980), 11 C.C.L.T. 141).

6. Alas, that was not meant to be. After 18 months of existence, the Supreme Court of Canada ended the life of the new tort of discrimination: *Bd of Governors of Seneca College of Applied Arts and Technology v. Bhadauria*, [1981] 2 S.C.R. 181, 124 D.L.R. (3d) 193. Chief Justice Laskin, speaking for a unanimous court, praised Madam Justice Wilson's view as a "bold one" which "may be commended as an attempt to advance the common law", but held that the Code foreclosed a "civil action based directly on the breach thereof" as well as any "common law action based on an invocation of the public policy expressed in the Code". The Chief Justice stated that the Code "laid out the procedures for vindication of that public policy". The civil courts are not an alternative route to recovery, he decided, but are a "part of the

enforcement machinery under the Code" to be involved only through the appeal procedure (s. 14(d)4) or perhaps through judicial review.

The Supreme Court, thus, has held that a cause of action in tort for discrimination was not available either under the common law nor for breach of the provisions of the statute. It was thought that the Legislature meant to grant *exclusive* jurisdiction to the Commission in the field of human rights, the court's role being limited to a supervisory one and not as an additional path to tort compensation. The fact that the Commission has the power to award damages undoubtedly influenced that view. (Section 14c.).

7. Are you happy about this decision? Should the Human Rights Commission have a monopoly on these problems? What are the pros and cons? See also, to the same effect, *Tenning v. Govt. of Manitoba* (1984), 25 Man. R. (2d) 179, 4 D.L.R. (4th) 418 (C.A.).

8. The apparent gap here is now being filled by civil actions on the basis of a violation of the Charter pursuant to s. 24(l). See, *infra,* Chapter 10, *Jane Doe.*

REVIEW PROBLEM

Diana, Princess of Wales, was killed along with Dodi Fayed in a car accident in Paris on August 31, 1997. There was much study of the causes of the tragedy. The primary culprit, the drunk driver, Henri Paul, also died in the accident, so that criminal charges against him were impossible. The French have investigated the possibility of bringing criminal charges against the so-called paparazzi and others.

Assume that the accident had occurred in Canada and you were being consulted by the sons of the Princess about bringing a tort action. What possible defendants, in addition to the driver, can you identify who else might owe a duty and share some of the blame for this accident?

1. What about the employer of the driver and the person who assigned him to do the driving in his drunken state, and lacking the appropriate limousine chauffeur's licence? Each of these possible defendants may turn out to be the same individual, *i.e.*, the Ritz Hotel, owned by the senior Mr. Fayed, or one of his different corporate entities.

2. What about the company that leased the Mercedes S280 to the Ritz, Étoile Limousines, knowing it had brake problems and a tendency to "slew at the back end", so that it should not have been driven by a person unfamiliar with this problem? In addition, the airbags may not have worked properly. What about the manufacturer of the car? What about the repairer of the car, which had been earlier involved in an accident?

3. What about the many paparazzi who followed the car, endangering the occupants? Further, following the accident, did they stop and render assistance, as they were required to do both under French law and our law?

4. Is there any chance of holding partly liable the employers of the paparazzi not only vicariously, but also for their direct negligence in encouraging dangerous conduct such as this to obtain photos at any cost, to the endangerment of the public.

5. Can the Fayed organization be held partly responsible if it can be shown, as has been now being alleged, that they incited the paparazzi by leaking information to them about where the couple could be found, thus contributing in part to a potential chase?

6. The bodyguard, Trevor Rees-Jones, who survived the accident, was hired to protect the Princess from harm. In allowing Paul to drive, then sitting in the car going around 100 m.p.h. with a drunk driver and unbuckled passengers, can it be said that he owed a tort duty and was partly to blame for the accident?

7. Are the City of Paris, its engineers and roadbuilders potential defendants on the basis of the design of the tunnel, which was often traversed at high speed, because of the unprotected concrete pillars, the 13th of which the Mercedes crashed into?

8. Should you consider the Paris police as potential defendants? Were they doing their duty controlling traffic reasonably in allowing this Mercedes with the paparazzi in pursuit to roar through the streets of Paris at high speeds without detection?

9. Is there any chance of holding partly liable the driver of the suspicious Fiat Uno, which was clipped and which has disappeared?

10. Can it be said that the ambulance operators were liable, having taken over an hour to get the Princess to the nearby hospital? If they had transported her to the hospital more quickly, instead of administering on-site attention and driving slowly, might the Princess's life have been saved?

11. Did any of the doctors and other staff at the hospital act unreasonably in their emergency treatment of their patient?

12. Is it possible that a civil action might be launched against the Estate of Dodi Fayed? Depending on the evidence of the bodyguard, when and if it surfaces, can it be that Mr. Fayed, who had been in a high speed chase before in the 1980s with Koo Stark, Prince Andrew's former friend, was not only allowing but possibly encouraging the driver to speed in order to evade the pursuers.

13. Rather indelicately, must one consider the possibility of negligence by the Princess herself? Did she ask her host to outrun the pursuers? Should she have urged him to slow down? *Volenti* would no longer bar a claim such as this, but contributory negligence might be a partial defence. By the way, would the failure to wear seat belts by the Princess amount to contributory negligence?

14. Can you think of any other potential defendants and theories of liability?

CHAPTER 8

REMOTENESS

Another method of limiting liability for negligent conduct is the concept of remoteness which we treat as a fifth element. If a consequence of an accident is thought to be too remote, there will be no liability for it. Other language has been used to express the same idea, such as proximate cause or proximity. The issue here is the extent to which an actor will be held liable for his or her substandard conduct. The type of questions being considered in this chapter are: Will someone, negligently dropping a lighted match into a waste basket, be held liable for damages for the building if it burns down, for the entire block if it goes, for the whole city if it is destroyed? Must that person compensate someone who is burned in the neighbouring building? What if the victim receives only a slight burn, but later develops cancer? What if the victim becomes mentally deranged because of disfigurement? What if a rescuer is hurt trying to extricate the victim? What if the doctor treating the victim bungles the operation? What if the victim commits suicide?

This has become one of the most complex and controversial areas of negligence law. Sometimes these problems are dealt with using the language of duty, even though that is an idea better reserved for the broader questions of policy which lead courts to deny the protection of negligence law altogether. The remoteness analysis is more appropriate to the drawing of lines in cases where unusual or strange results flow from negligent conduct. Various ideas have been used over the years to help courts. One such idea was that there should be liability for all the direct consequences of the act. This was the teaching of *Re Polemis and Furness, Withy & Co. Ltd.*, [1921] 3 K.B. 560, which was much criticized for bringing to the discussion of tort liability complex and unhelpful ideas from physics and philosophy.

All that was swept away in the 1960s with the decision of *The Wagon Mound (No. 1)*, [1961] A.C. 388 (P.C.). It will be seen that, despite the new language, the complex exercise of deciding which unusual consequences will yield liability and which will not has not been rendered much easier, although the recurring situations are being dealt with more satisfactorily.

A. THE GENERAL PRINCIPLE

THE WAGON MOUND (NO. 1)
OVERSEAS TANKSHIP (U.K.) LTD. v. MORTS DOCK & ENGINEERING CO. LTD.

Privy Council. [1961] A.C. 388, [1961] 1 All E.R. 404.

Appeal from an order of the Full Court of the Supreme Court of New South Wales (Owen, Maguire and Manning JJ.) dismissing an appeal by the appellants, Overseas Tankship (U.K.) Ltd., from a judgment of Kinsella J. exercising the Admiralty Jurisdiction of that court in an action in which the appellants were defendants and the respondents, Morts Dock & Engineering Co., Ltd. were plaintiffs.

The following facts are taken from the judgment of the Judicial Committee: In the action the respondents sought to recover from the appellants compensation for the damage which its property known as the Sheerlegs Wharf, in Sydney Harbour, and the equipment thereon had suffered by reason of fire which broke out on November 1, 1951. For that damage they claimed that the appellants were in law responsible.

The relevant facts can be comparatively shortly stated inasmuch as not one of the findings of fact in the exhaustive judgment of the trial judge had been challenged.

The respondents at the relevant time carried on the business of ship-building, ship-repairing and general engineering at Morts Bay, Balmain, in the Port of Sydney. They owned and used for their business the Sheerlegs Wharf, a timber wharf about 400 feet in length and 40 feet wide, where there was a quantity of tools and equipment. In October and November, 1951, a vessel known as the *Corrimal* was moored alongside the wharf and was being refitted by the respondents. Her mast was lying on the wharf and a number of the respondents' employees were working both upon it and upon the vessel itself, using for that purpose electric and oxy-acetylene welding equipment.

At the same time the appellants were charterers by demise of the *S.S. Wagon Mound*, an oil-burning vessel, which was moored at the Caltex Wharf on the northern shore of the harbour at a distance of about 600 feet from the Sheerlegs Wharf. She was there from about 9 a.m. on October 29 until 11 a.m. on October 30, 1951, for the purpose of discharging gasolene products and taking in bunkering oil.

During the early hours of October 30, 1951, a large quantity of bunkering oil was, through the carelessness of the appellants' servants, allowed to spill into the bay, and by 10.30 on the morning of that day it had spread over a considerable part of the bay, being thickly concentrated in some places and particularly along the foreshore near the respondents' property. The appellants made no attempt to disperse the oil. The *Wagon Mound* unberthed and set sail very shortly after.

When the respondents' works manager became aware of the condition of things in the vicinity of the wharf he instructed their workmen that no welding or burning was to be carried on until further orders. He inquired of the manager of the Caltex Oil Company, at whose wharf the *Wagon Mound* was then still berthed, whether they could safely continue their operations on the wharf or upon the *Corrimal*. The results of the inquiry coupled with his own belief as to the inflammability of furnace oil in the open led him to think that the respondents could safely carry on their operations. He gave instructions accordingly, but directed that all safety precautions should be taken to prevent inflammable material falling off the wharf into the oil.

For the remainder of October 30 and until about 2 p.m. on November 1 work was carried on as usual, the condition and congestion of the oil remaining substantially unaltered. But at about that time the oil under or near the wharf was ignited and a fire, fed initially by the oil, spread rapidly and burned with great intensity. The wharf and the *Corrimal* caught fire and considerable damage was done to the wharf and the equipment upon it.

The outbreak of fire was due, as the judge found, to the fact that there was floating in the oil underneath the wharf a piece of debris on which lay some mouldering cotton waste or rag which had been set on fire by molten metal falling from the wharf; that the cotton waste or rag burst into flames: that the flames from the cotton waste set the floating oil afire either directly or by first setting fire to a wooden pile coated with oil, and that after the floating oil became ignited the flames spread rapidly over the surface of the oil and quickly developed into a conflagration which severely damaged the wharf.

The judgment of their Lordships was delivered by

Viscount Simonds: The trial judge also made the all-important finding which must be set out in his own words: "The *raison d'être* of furnace oil is, of course, that it shall burn, but I find that the defendant did not know and could not reasonably be expected to have known that it was capable of being set afire when spread on water." This finding was reached after a wealth of evidence, which included that of a distinguished scientist, Professor Hunter. It receives strong confirmation from the fact that at the trial the respondents strenuously maintained that the appellants had discharged petrol into the bay on no other ground than that, as the spillage was set alight, it could not be furnace oil. An attempt was made before their Lordships' Board to limit in some way the finding of fact, but it is clear that it was intended to cover precisely the event that happened.

One other finding must be mentioned. The judge held that apart from damage by fire the respondents had suffered some damage from the spillage of oil in that it had got upon their slipways and congealed upon them and interfered with their use of the slips. He said: "The evidence of this damage is slight and no claim for compensation is made in respect of it. Nevertheless it does establish some damage, which may be insignificant in comparison with the magnitude of the damage by fire, but which nevertheless is damage which, beyond question, was a direct result of the escape of the oil." It is upon this footing that their Lordships will consider the question whether the appellants are liable for the fire damage. …

It is inevitable that first consideration should be given to the case of *In re Polemis and Furness, Withy & Co. Ltd.*, [1921 [3 K.B. 560; 37 T.L.R. 940, which will henceforward be referred to as *Polemis.* For it was avowedly in deference to that decision and to decisions of the Court of Appeal that followed it that the Full Court was constrained to decide the present case in favour of the respondents. In doing so Manning J., after a full examination of that case, said: "To say that the problems, doubts and difficulties which I have expressed above render it difficult for me to apply the decision in *In re Polemis* with any degree of confidence to a particular set of facts would be a grave understatement. I can only express the hope that, if not in this case, then in some other case in the near future, the subject will be pronounced upon by the House of Lords or the Privy Council in terms which, even if beyond my capacity fully to understand, will facilitate, for those placed as I am, its everyday application to current problems." This *cri de coeur* would in any case be irresistible, but in the years that have passed since its decision *Polemis* has been so much discussed and qualified that it cannot claim, as counsel for the respondents urged for it, the status of a decision of such long standing that it should not be reviewed. …

If the line of relevant authority had stopped with *Polemis*, their Lordships might, whatever their own views as to its unreason, have felt some hesitation about overruling it. But it is far otherwise. It is true that both in England and in many parts of the Commonwealth that decision has from time to time been followed; but in Scotland it has been rejected with determination. It has never been subject to the express scrutiny of either the House of Lords or the Privy Council, though there have been comments upon it in those Supreme Tribunals. Even in the inferior courts judges have, sometimes perhaps unwittingly, declared themselves in a sense adverse to its principle.

[Several examples were given.]

...

Enough has been said to show that the authority of *Polemis* has been severely shaken though lip-service has from time to time been paid to it. In their Lordships' opinion it should no longer be regarded as good law. It is not probable that many cases will for that reason have a different result, though it is hoped that the law will be thereby simplified, and that in some cases, at least, palpable injustice will be avoided. For it does not seem consonant with current ideas of justice or morality that for an act of negligence, however slight or venial, which results in some trivial foreseeable damage the actor should be liable for all consequences however unforeseeable and however grave, so long as they can be said to be "direct". It is a principle of civil liability, subject only to qualifications which have no present relevance, that a man must be considered to be responsible for the probable consequences of his act. To demand more of him is too harsh a rule, to demand less is to ignore that civilized order requires the observance of a minimum standard of behaviour.

This concept applied to the slowly developing law of negligence has led to a great variety of expressions which can, as it appears to their Lordships, be harmonized with little difficulty with the single exception of the so-called rule in *Polemis*. For, if it is asked why a man should be responsible for the natural or necessary or probable consequences of his act (or any other similar description of them) the answer is that it is not because they are natural or necessary or probable, but because, since they have this quality, it is judged by the standard of the reasonable man that he ought to have foreseen them. Thus it is that over and over again it has happened that in different judgments in the same case, and sometimes in a single judgment, liability for a consequence has been imposed on the ground that it was reasonably foreseeable or, alternatively, on the ground that it was natural or necessary or probable. The two grounds have been treated as coterminous, and so they largely are. But, where they are not, the question arises to which the wrong answer was given in *Polemis*. For, if some limitation must be imposed upon the consequences for which the negligent actor is to be held responsible — and all are agreed that some limitation there must be — why should that test (reasonable foreseeability) be rejected which, since he is judged by what the reasonable man ought to foresee, corresponds with the common conscience of mankind, and a test (the "direct" consequence) be substituted which leads to nowhere but the never-ending and insoluble problems of causation. "The lawyer," said Sir Frederick Pollock, "cannot afford to adventure himself with philosophers in the logical and metaphysical controversies that beset the idea of cause." Yet this is just what he has most unfortunately done and must continue to do if the rule in *Polemis* is to prevail. A conspicuous example occurs when the actor seeks to escape liability on the ground that the "chain of causation" is broken by a "*nova causa*" or "*novus actus interveniens*". ...

In the same connection may be mentioned the conclusion to which the Full Court finally came in the present case. Applying the rule in *Polemis* and holding therefore that the unforeseeability of the damage by fire afforded no defence, they went on to consider the remaining question. Was it a "direct" consequence? Upon this Manning J., said: "Notwithstanding that, if regard is had separately to each individual occurrence in the chain of events that led to this fire, each occurrence was improbable and, in one sense, improbability was heaped upon improbability. I cannot escape from the conclusion that if the ordinary man in the street had been asked, as a matter of common sense, without any detailed analysis of the circumstances, to state the cause of the fire at Mort's Dock, he would unhesitatingly have assigned such cause to spillage of oil by the appellant's employees." Perhaps he would, and probably he would have added, "I never should have thought it possible." But with great respect to the Full Court this is surely irrelevant, or, if it is relevant, only serves to show that the *Polemis* rule works in a very strange way. After the event even a fool is wise. But it is not the hindsight of a fool; it is the foresight of the reasonable man which alone can determine responsibility. The *Polemis* rule by substituting "direct" for "reasonably foreseeable" consequence leads to a conclusion equally illogical and unjust.

At an early stage in this judgment their Lordships intimated that they would deal with the proposition which can best be stated by reference to the well-known *dictum* of Lord Sumner: "This however goes to culpability not to compensation." It is with the greatest respect to that very learned judge and to those who have echoed his words, that their Lordships find themselves bound to state their view that this proposition is fundamentally false.

It is, no doubt, proper when considering tortious liability for negligence to analyse its elements and to say that the plaintiff must prove a duty owed to him by the defendant, a breach of that duty by the defendant, and consequent damage. But there can be no liability until the damage has been done. It is not the act but the consequences on which tortious liability is founded. Just as (as it has been said) there is no such thing as negligence in the air, so there is no such thing as liability in the air. Suppose an action brought by A for damage caused by the carelessness (a neutral word) of B, for example, a fire caused by the careless spillage of oil. It may, of course, become relevant to know what duty B owed A, but the only liability that is in question is the liability for damage by fire. It is vain to isolate the liability from its context and to say that B is or is not liable, and then to ask for what damage he is liable. For his liability is in respect of that damage and no other. If, as admittedly it is, B's liability (culpability) depends on the reasonable foreseeability of the consequent damage, how is that to be determined except by the foreseeability of the damage which in fact happened — the damage in suit? And, if that damage is unforeseeable so as to displace liability at large, how can the liability be restored so as to make compensation payable?

But, it is said, a different position arises if B's careless act has been shown to be negligent and had caused some foreseeable damage to A. Their Lordships have already observed that to hold B liable for consequences however unforeseeable of a careless act, if, but only if, he is at the same time liable for some other damage however trivial, appears to be neither logical nor just. This becomes more clear if it is supposed that similar unforeseeable damage is suffered by A and C but other foreseeable damage, for which B is liable, by A only. A system of law which would hold B liable to A but not to C for the similar damage suffered by each of them could not easily be defended. Fortunately, the attempt is not necessary. For the same fallacy is at the root of the proposition. It is irrelevant to the question whether B is liable for unforeseeable damage that he is liable for foreseeable damage, as irrelevant as would the fact that he had trespassed on Whiteacre be to the question whether he has trespassed on Blackacre. Again, suppose a claim by A for damage by fire by the careless act of B. Of what relevance is it to that claim that he has another claim arising out of the same careless act? It would surely not prejudice his claim if that other claim failed; it cannot assist it if it succeeds. Each of them rests on its own bottom, and will fail if it can be established that the damage could not reasonably be foreseen. We have come back to the plain common sense stated by Lord Russell of Killowen in *Bourhill v. Young*. As Denning L.J., said in *King v. Phillips*, [1953] 1 Q.B. 429, 441: "there can be no doubt since *Bourhill v. Young* that the test of *liability for shock* is foreseeability of *injury by shock*". Their Lordships substitute the word "fire" for "shock" and endorse this statement of the law.

Their Lordships conclude this part of the case with some general observations. They have been concerned primarily to displace the proposition that unforeseeability is irrelevant if damage is "direct". In doing so they have inevitably insisted that the essential factor in determining liability is whether the damage is of such a kind as the reasonable man should have foreseen. This accords with the general view thus stated by Lord Atkin in *Donoghue v. Stevenson:* "The liability for negligence, whether you style it such or treat it as in other systems as a species of 'culpa', is no doubt based upon a general public sentiment of moral wrongdoing for which the offender must pay." It is a departure from this sovereign principle if liability is made to depend solely on the damage being the "direct" or "natural" consequence of the precedent act. Who knows or can be assumed to know all the processes of nature? But if it would be wrong that a man should be held liable for damage unpredictable by a reasonable man because it was "direct" or "natural", equally it would be wrong that he should escape liability, however "indirect" the damage, if he foresaw or could reasonably foresee the intervening events which led to its being done: *cf. Woods v. Duncan*, [1946] A.C. 401, 442. Thus foreseeability becomes the effective test. In reasserting this principle their Lordships conceive that they do not depart from, but follow and develop, the law of negligence as laid down by Baron Alderson in *Blyth v. Birmingham Waterworks Co.* (1856), 11 Exch. 781, 784.

It is proper to add that their Lordships have not found it necessary to consider the so-called rule of "strict liability" exemplified in *Rylands v. Fletcher* (1868), L.R. 3 H.L. 330, and the cases that have followed or distinguished it. Nothing that they have said is intended to reflect on that rule.

One aspect of this case remains to be dealt with. The respondents claim, in the alternative, that the appellants are liable in nuisance if not in negligence. Upon this issue their Lordships are of opinion that it would not be proper for them to come to any conclusion upon the material before them and without the benefit of the considered view of the Supreme Court. On the other hand, having regard to the course which the case has taken, they do not think that the respondents should be finally shut out from the opportunity of advancing this plea, if they think fit. They therefore propose that on the issue of nuisance alone the case should be remitted to the Full Court to be dealt with as may be thought proper.

Their Lordships will humbly advise Her Majesty that this appeal should be allowed, and the respondents' action so far as it related to damage caused by the negligence of the appellants be dismissed with costs, but that the action so far as it related to damage caused by nuisance should be remitted to the Full Court to be dealt with as that court may think fit. The respondents must pay the costs of the appellants of this appeal and in the courts below.

NOTES

1. Professor Fleming in his excellent article "The Passing of Polemis" (1961), 39 Can. Bar Rev. 489, was not enthusiastic about the *Wagon Mound (No. 1)* decision. He wrote:

> ... the Privy Council's opinion in the *Wagon Mound* may seem a retrograde step, ill-attuned to general trends in the law of torts. For, if it is to have any

practical effect on the future course of adjudication at all, it will be by setting somewhat narrower limits to the range of recovery than heretofore, and to that extent impairing the process of shifting and distributing losses. It is therefore at least open to argument whether Viscount Simonds correctly gauged the tenor of "current ideas of justice or morality" in expressing the belief that it would be "out of consonance" and "too harsh" to countenance liability beyond the ambit of foreseeable risks. On the fact of it, at any rate, it is a trifle paradoxical that the apotheosis of foresight had to await a moment of decision when the very notion of fault liability was already under the lengthening shadow of decline and, as happens not infrequently, the acceptance of a rule is so long deferred that its destined role is merely to impede the next stage of legal process. However that may be, the Board's opinion does not seem to have been uninfluenced by the noticeable trend towards stricter liability, and its sympathetic reference to the predicament of defendants who are held responsible for an "act of negligence, however slight or venial", involving the risk of but "trivial foreseeable damage", rather suggests an inclination to temper a little the wind to the shorn lamb. But previous experience in the judicial handling of the foresight test, both in relation to the issue of initial culpability (breach of duty) and remoteness of damage in cases involving "indirect" consequences, lends scant support to sanguine expectations of any appreciable change in the future direction of the law. This impression is reinforced by the fact that, as already noted, very few cases indeed ever fell to be decided on the basis of the defunct *Polemis* rule — a telling index of the very limited practical effect to be anticipated from the decision [of *The Wagon Mound (No. 1)*].

2. *The Wagon Mound* case has been the subject of much academic discussion. See Williams, "The Risk Principle" (1961), 77 L.Q. Rev. 179, Smith, "Requiem for *Polemis*" (1965), 2 U.B.C.L. Rev. 159 and "The Limits of Tort Liability in Canada: Remoteness, Foreseeability and Proximate Cause" printed in Linden (ed.), *Studies in Canadian Tort Law*" (1968), at 88; Gibson, "*The Wagon Mound* in Canadian Courts" (1963), 2 Osgoode Hall L.J. 416; McLaren, "Negligence and Remoteness — The Aftermath of *Wagon Mound*" (1967), 1 Sask. L.J. 45; Honoré, "Comment" (1961), 39 Can. Bar Rev. 267; Green, "Foreseeability in Negligence Law" (1961), 61 Colum. L. Rev. 1401.

B. RETREAT FROM THE WAGON MOUND (NO. 1)

1. The Thin-Skull Problem

SMITH v. LEECH BRAIN & CO.

Queen's Bench Division. [1962] 2 Q.B. 405, [1961] 3 All E.R. 1159.

The defendant's negligence resulted in a piece of molten metal striking and burning the lip of the plaintiff's husband. At the time, the burn was treated as a normal burn. Ultimately the place where the burn had been began to ulcerate and cancer was diagnosed. After radium treatments and several operations the plaintiff's husband died. In an action for damages it was proved that the burn was a cause of the cancer and death.

Lord Parker C.J.: The third question is damages. Here I am confronted with the recent decision of the Privy Council in *Overseas Tankship (U.K.) Limited v. Morts Dock and Engineering Co. Ltd. (The Wagon Mound)*. But for that case, it seems to me perfectly clear that, assuming negligence proved, and assuming that the burn caused in whole or in part the cancer and the death, the plaintiff would be entitled to recover. It is said on the one side by Mr. May that although I am not strictly bound by the *Wagon Mound* since it is a decision of the Privy Council, I should treat myself as free, using the arguments to be derived from that case, to say that other cases in these courts — other cases in the Court of Appeal — have been wrongly decided, and particularly that *In re Polemis* and *Furness Withy & Co.* was wrongly decided, and that a further ground for taking that course is to be found in the various criticisms that have from time to time in the past been made by members of the House of Lords in regard to the *Polemis* case.

It is said, on the other hand, by Mr. Martin Jukes, that I should hold that the *Polemis* case was rightly decided and, secondly, that even if that is not so I must treat myself as completely bound by it. Thirdly, he said that in any event, whatever the true view is in regard to the *Polemis* case, *The Wagon Mound* has no relevance at all to this case.

For my part, I am quite satisfied that the Judicial Committee in *The Wagon Mound* case did not have what I may call, loosely, the thin skull cases in mind. It has always been the law of this country that a tortfeasor takes his victim as he finds him. It is unnecessary to do more than refer to the short passage in the decision of Kennedy J. in *Dulieu v. White & Sons*, where he said: "If a man is negligently run over or otherwise negligently injured in his body, it is no answer to the sufferer's claim for damages that he would have suffered less injury, or no injury at all, if he had not had an unusually thin skull or an unusually weak heart."

To the same effect is a passage in the judgment of Scrutton L.J., in *The Arpad*. But quite apart from those two references, as is well known, the work of the courts for years and years has gone on on that basis. There is not a day that goes by where some trial judge does not adopt that principle, that the tortfeasor takes his victim as he finds him. If the Judicial Committee had any intention of making an inroad into that doctrine, I am quite satisfied that they would have said so.

It is true that if the wording in the advice given by Lord Simonds in *The Wagon Mound* case is applied strictly to such a case as this, it could be said that they were dealing with this point. But, as I have said, it is to my mind quite impossible to conceive that they were and, indeed, it has been pointed out that they disclose the distinction between such a case as this and the one they were considering when they comment on *Smith v. London & South Western Railway Company.* Lord Simonds, in dealing with that case said: "Three things may be noted about this case: the first, that for the sweeping proposition laid down no authority was cited; the second, that the point to which the court directed its mind was not unforeseeable damage of a different kind from that which was foreseen, but more extensive damage of the same kind." In other words, Lord Simonds is clearly there drawing a distinction between the question whether a man could reasonably anticipate a type of injury, and the question whether a man could reasonably anticipate the extent of injury of the type which could be foreseen.

The Judicial Committee were, I think, disagreeing with the decision in the *Polemis* case that a man is no longer liable for the type of damage which he could not reasonably anticipate. The Judicial Committee were not, I think, saying that a man is only liable for the extent of damage which he could anticipate, always assuming the type of injury could have been anticipated. I think that view is really supported by the way in which cases of this sort have been dealt with in Scotland. Scotland has never, so far as I know, adopted the principle laid down in *Polemis*, and yet I am quite satisfied that they have throughout proceeded on the basis that the tortfeasor takes the victim as he finds him.

In those circumstances, it seems to me that this is plainly a case which comes within the old principle. The test is not whether these employers could reasonably have foreseen that a burn would cause cancer and that he would die. The question is whether these employers could reasonably foresee the type of injury he suffered, namely, the burn. What, in the particular case, is the amount of damage which he suffers as a result of that burn, depends upon the characteristics and constitution of the victim.

Accordingly, I find that the damages which the widow claims are damages for which the defendants are liable.

NOTES

1. The thin-skull rule has clearly survived *The Wagon Mound (No. 1)*. It applies equally if there is a pre-existing susceptibility or if the injury renders someone vulnerable to additional loss. See Linden, *Canadian Tort Law*, 6th ed. (1997), p. 345.

2. Is the thin-skull rule an exception to *The Wagon Mound (No. 1)* or is it consistent with the foresight principle? See the case of *Negretto v. Sayers*, [1963] S.A.S.R. 313, where a woman whose pelvis was fractured had a post-concussional psychosis as a result of "pre-existing tendency to mental disorder". In applying the thin-skull rule, the court tried to explain that the principle is not inconsistent with foresight for the "consequences of even the simplest accident are unpredictable". One must foresee any consequence "between a negligible abrasion and permanent incapacity or death". Mr. Justice Chamberlain admitted that the defendant did not expect to run down anyone, let alone someone with a personality defect, yet one should foresee that a pedestrian might be hit "with quite possible disastrous consequences of one sort or another".

3. What policy reasons can be advanced in support of the thin-skull rule? Does it foster the compensatory aim of tort law? Does it deter? Does it obviate the administrative problems associated with distinguishing between foreseeable injuries and unforeseeable ones? See *Toronto Railway v. Toms* (1911), 44 S.C.R. 268, at 276, 12 C.R.C. 250 (*per* Davies C.J.). What can be said against the thin-skull rule?

4. Mental suffering flowing from physical injury is compensable under the thin-skull rule. In *Malcolm v. Broadhurst*, [1970] 3 All E.R. 508 (Q.B.), a husband and wife were both injured, physically and mentally, in a car accident caused by the defendant's negligence. The husband's serious head injuries led to his intellectual deterioration and the diminution of his learning powers. His personality changed so that he became bad-tempered and violent. Her husband's changed behaviour caused additional nervous symptoms in the wife by aggravating a pre-existing nervous condition. In awarding the wife damages for these aggravated nervous symptoms, Geoffrey Lane J. stated:

> The defendant must take the wife as he finds her and there is no difference in principle between an egg-shell skull and an egg-shell personality, *Love v. Port of London Authority*, [1959] 2 Ll. R. 541. Exacerbation of her nervous depression was a readily foreseeable consequence of injuring her. Does the fact that it was caused, or caused to continue, by reaction to the husband's pathological bad-temper (itself the result of the defendant's negligence) put a stop the defendant's liability? I think not. Once damage of a particular kind, in this case psychological, can be foreseen, as here it could, the fact that it arises or is continued by reason of an unusual complex of events does not avail the defendant, *Hughes v. Lord Advocate*, [1963] A.C. 837. Moreover, it is not beyond the range of reasonable anticipation to foresee that if one does severe injury to husband and wife, when the wife is temperamentally unstable, her instability may be adversely affected by the injury done to her husband.

5. In *Duwyn v. Kaprelian* (1978), 22 O.R. (2d) 736, 7 C.C.L.T. 121 (C.A.), a child injured in an accident was treated in such a way by a parent, who suffered guilt feelings about the accident, that it caused the child additional mental suffering. Morden J.A. permitted compensation for this additional suffering on the basis that ineffective parental care was similar to improper medical treatment and, hence, "within the limits of foreseeability".

6. If an injured person suffers traumatic neurosis, compensation is payable. Depression as a result of a physical injury is reasonably foreseeable, but not if it flows from worry over financial losses. See Linden, *Canadian Tort Law*, 6th ed., *supra*.

7. Changes in personality, a common problem, are compensable under the thin-skull rule. In *Marconato et al. v. Franklin*, [1974] 6 W.W.R. 676 (B.C.S.C.), a woman, injured slightly in a car accident, developed symptoms of depression, hostility, anxiety, tension, hysteria and some characteristics of paranoia. She underwent a personality change, from a happy and contented woman to a very unhappy woman. She was allowed recovery for these damages by Aikens J. who explained:

> One would not ordinarily anticipate, using reasonable foresight, that a moderate cervical strain with soft tissue damage would give rise to the consequences which followed for Mrs. Marconato. These arose, however, because of her pre-existing personality traits. She had a peculiar susceptibility or vulnerability to suffer much greater consequences from a moderate physical injury than the average person. The consequences for Mrs. Marconato could no more be foreseen than it could be foreseen by a tortfeasor that his victim was thin-skulled and that a minor blow to the head would cause very serious injury. It is plain enough that the defendant could foresee the probability of physical injury. It is implicit, however, in the principle that a wrongdoer takes his victim as he finds him, that he takes his victim with all the victim's peculiar susceptibilities and vulnerabilities. The consequences of Mrs. Marconato's injuries were unusual but arose involuntarily. Granted her type of personality they arose as night follows day because of the injury and the circumstances in which she found herself because of the injury.

8. The thin-skull rule must be contrasted with the crumbling skull problem which has been concisely explained by Mr. Justice Major in *Athey v. Leonati,* [1996] 3 S.C.R. 458 at 473-74, as follows:

> The respondent argued that the plaintiff was pre-disposed to disc herniation and that this is therefore a case where the "crumbling skull" rule applies. The "crumbling skull" doctrine is an awkward label for a fairly simple idea. It is named after the well-known "thin-skull" rule, which makes the tortfeasor liable for the plaintiff's injuries even if the injuries are unexpectedly severe owing to a pre-existing condition. The tortfeasor must take his or her victim as the tortfeasor finds the victim, and is therefore liable even though the plaintiff's losses are more dramatic than they would be for the average person.
>
> The so-called "crumbling skull" rule simply recognizes that the pre-existing condition was inherent in the plaintiff's "original position". The defendant need not put the plaintiff in a position *better* than his or her original position. The defendant is liable for the injuries caused, even if they are extreme, but need not compensate the plaintiff for any debilitating effects of the pre-existing condition which the plaintiff would have experienced anyway. The defendant is liable for the additional damage but not the pre-existing damage. ... Likewise, if there is a measurable risk that the pre-existing condition would have detrimentally affected the plaintiff in the future, regardless of the defendant's negligence, then this can be taken into account in reducing the overall award. ... This is consistent with the general rule that the plaintiff must

be returned to the position he would have been in, with all of its attendant risks and shortcomings, and not a better position.

9. Consequently, it is clear that compensation must be made for thin-skull injuries, but the defendant need not pay full damages as if there were no thin skull, for a thin skull is less valuable than a normal one. In *Smith v. Maximovitch* (1968), 68 D.L.R. (2d) 244 (Sask. Q.B.), the plaintiff lost eight teeth in a collision. Because his remaining teeth were in poor condition, as a result of pyorrhoea, they were unsuitable to anchor bridgework and, therefore, all the teeth had to be extracted and dentures put in. The claimant received damages for all the teeth, except that they were evaluated in accordance with their worth at the time of loss.

10. Should a person with a thin skull ever be considered contributorily negligent for taking risks which endanger a thin-skull person but would not endanger an ordinary person? See *Murphy v. McCarthy* (1974), 9 S.A.S.R. 424, where Zelling J. declined to so hold, but commented as follows:

> Where a plaintiff such as this one, with the disabilities which she had, goes as pillion passenger on a scooter, perhaps the real answer is that it ought to be treated as contributory negligence rather than as a problem in causation in damages. Contributory negligence was not pleaded in this case and the matter is only before me for assessment, but it may be that in some subsequent case the emphasis in argument may have to shift from the question of the impact of *The Wagon Mound* upon the "eggshell skull" cases to the question of whether or not the plaintiff exhibited due care for his or her own safety when, knowing of his or her pre-existing disability, he or she exposed themselves to the risk of accident, with predictable consequences much graver to themselves than to a plaintiff without the pre-existing disabilities.

11. If extra loss is caused to plaintiffs because of their impecuniosity, this was, until recently, not compensable, for a thin pocket book was thought to be less deserving of protection than a thin skull. (See *Dredger Liesbosch v. S.S. Edison (Owners)*, [1933] A.C. 449). This principle was criticized, and has been described as "unCanadian". (See *Rollinson v. R.* (1994), 20 C.C.L.R. (2d) 92 (Fed. T.D.) (Muldoon J.)). It now appears that, if extra loss because of impecuniosity is reasonably foreseeable, there can be compensation for that loss (See *Amar Cloth House v. La Van Co.* (1997), 35 C.C.L.T. (2d) 99 at 110 (B.C.S.C.), *per* Huddart J.A.).

12. See generally Linden, "Down With Foreseeability: Of Thin Skulls and Rescuers" (1969), 47 Can. Bar Rev. 545; Linden, "Foreseeability in Negligence Law" in Law Society of Upper Canada, *Special Lectures on New Developments in the Law of Torts* (1973), at 69; Linden, *Canadian Tort Law,* 6th ed. (1997), p. 345.

2. Type of Damage

HUGHES v. LORD ADVOCATE

House of Lords. [1963] A.C. 837, [1963] 1 All E.R. 705.

This was an appeal from a decision of the First Division of the Court of Session (The Lord President (Lord Clyde), Lord Sorn and Lord Guthrie; Lord Carmont dissenting, reported [1961] S.C. 310). The court affirmed an interlocutor of the Lord Ordinary (Lord Wheatley), who had held that the respondent was not liable for injuries suffered by a boy of eight years of age on the ground that, although danger to children was reasonably foreseeable in the circumstances, the particular accident that happened was not reasonably foreseeable.

The following statement of facts is taken from the speech of Lord Guest:

In November, 1958, some Post Office employees had opened a manhole in Russell Road, Edinburgh, for the purpose of obtaining access to a telephone cable. The manhole from which the cover had been removed was near the edge of the roadway. A shelter tent had been erected over the open manhole. The manhole was some nine feet deep, and a ladder had been placed inside the manhole to give access to the cable. Around the area of the site had been placed four red warning paraffin lamps. The lamps were lit at 3.30 p.m. About 5 p.m. or 5.30 p.m. the Post Office employees left the site for a tea break for which purpose they went to an adjoining Post Office building. Before leaving they removed the ladder from the manhole and placed it on the ground beside the shelter and pulled a tarpaulin cover over the entrance to the shelter, leaving a space of two feet to two feet six inches between the lower edge of the tarpaulin and the ground. The lamps were left burning. After they left, the appellant, aged eight, and his uncle, aged ten, came along Russell Road and decided to explore the shelter. According to the findings of the Lord Ordinary (Lord Wheatley), the boys picked up one of the red lamps, raised up the tarpaulin sheet and entered the shelter. They brought the ladder into the shelter with a view to descending into the manhole. They also brought a piece of rope which was not the Post Office equipment, tied the rope to the lamp and, with the lamp, lowered themselves into the manhole. They both came out carrying the lamp. Thereafter, according to the evidence, the appellant tripped over the lamp, which fell into the hole. There followed an explosion from the hole with flames reaching a height of 30 feet. With the explosion the appellant fell into the hole and sustained very severe burning injuries.

In an action by the pursuer directed against the Lord Advocate, as representing the Postmaster-General, on the ground that the accident was due to the fault of the Post Office employees in failing to close the manhole before they left or to post a watchman while they were away, the Lord Ordinary assoilized the respondent. His judgment was affirmed by a majority of the First Division, Lord Carmont dissenting. Before the Lord Ordinary and the First Division a preliminary point was taken by the respondent that the appellant was a trespasser in the shelter and that the Post Office employees therefore owed no duty to take precautions for his safety. This point was not persisted in before this House and it is therefore unnecessary to say anything about it.

The Lord Ordinary, after a very careful analysis of the evidence, has found that the cause of the explosion was as a result of the lamp which the appellant knocked into the hole being so disturbed that paraffin escaped from the tank, formed vapour and was ignited by the flame. The lamp was recovered from the manhole after the accident; the tank of the lamp was half out and the wickholder was completely out of the lamp. This explanation of the accident was rated by the experts as a low order of probability. But as there was no other feasible explanation it was accepted by the Lord Ordinary and this House must take it as the established cause.

Lord Reid: ... It was argued that the appellant cannot recover because the damage which he suffered was of a kind which was not foreseeable. That was not the ground of judgment of the First Division or of the Lord Ordinary and the facts proved do not, in my judgment, support that argument. The appellant's injuries were mainly caused by burns and it cannot be said that injuries from burns were unforeseeable. As a warning to traffic the workmen had set lighted red lamps round the tent which covered the manhole, and if boys did enter the dark tent it was very likely that they would take one of these lamps with them. If the lamp fell and broke it was not at all unlikely that the boy would be burned and the burns might well be serious. No doubt it was not to be expected that the injuries would be as serious as those which the appellant in fact sustained. But a defender is liable, although the damage may be a good deal greater in extent than was foreseeable. He can only escape liability if the damage can be regarded as differing in kind from what was foreseeable.

So we have (first) a duty owed by the workmen, (secondly) the fact that if they had done as they ought to have done there would have been no accident, and (thirdly) the fact that the injuries suffered by the appellant, though perhaps different in degree, did not differ in kind from injuries which might have resulted from an accident of a foreseeable nature. The ground on which this case has been decided against the appellant is that the accident was of unforeseeable type. Of course the pursuer has to prove that the defender's fault caused the accident and there could be a case where the intrusion of a new and unexpected factor could be regarded as the cause of the accident rather than the fault of the defender. But that is not this case. The cause of this accident was a known source of danger, the lamp, but it behaved in an unpredictable way. The explanation of the accident which has been accepted, and which I would not seek to question, is that, when the lamp fell down the manhole and was broken, some paraffin escaped, and enough was vaporized to create an explosive mixture which was detonated by the naked light of the lamp. The experts agreed that no one would have expected that to happen: it was so unlikely as to be unforeseeable. The explosion caused the boy to fall into the manhole: whether his injuries were directly caused by the explosion or aggravated by fire which started in the manhole is not at all clear. The essential step in the respondent's argument is that the explosion was the real cause of the injuries and that the explosion was unforeseeable. ... This accident was caused by a known source of danger, but caused in a way which could not have been foreseen, and in my judgment that affords no defence. I would therefore allow the appeal.

Lord Morris of Borth-y-Gest: ... The fact that the features or developments of an accident may not reasonably have been foreseen does not mean that the accident itself was not foreseeable. The pursuer was in my view injured as a result of the type or kind of accident or occurrence that could reasonably have been foreseen. In agreement with Lord Carmont I consider that the defenders do not avoid liability because they could not have foretold the exact way in which the pursuer would play with the alluring objects that had been left to attract him or the exact way in which in so doing he might get hurt. ...

My Lords, in my view there was a duty owed by the defenders to safeguard the pursuer against the type or kind of occurrence which in fact happened and which resulted in his injuries, and the defenders are not absolved from liability because they did not envisage "the precise concatenation of circumstances which led up to the accident". For these reasons, I differ with respect from the majority of the First Division and I would allow the appeal.

[**Lord Jenkins, Lord Guest** and **Lord Pearce** concurred.]

NOTES

1. What is the effect of this case on *The Wagon Mound (No. 1)*?

2. In *Doughty v. Turner Manufacturing Co. Ltd.*, [1964] 1 Q.B. 518, [1964] 1 All E.R. 98 (C.A.), one of the defendant's servants either knocked an asbestos and cement compound cover of a heating bath (containing molten liquid of a heat of 800° centigrade), into the liquid, or allowed it to slide in. In a short time there was an eruption of the liquid which seriously injured the plaintiff, a bystander. It was later discovered that the asbestos cement compound would at the high temperature undergo a chemical

change releasing water which would produce an explosion. The defendants did not appreciate that the immersion of the lid would produce an explosion and, indeed, similar covers had been used in England and the United States for some 20 years, and there was no blame in failing to appreciate that the immersion of the cover would produce an explosion. It was argued that knocking a cover into the liquid gave rise to a foreseeable risk of burning the plaintiff since there was a foreseeable risk of splashing. As the plaintiff was burned, the actual damage was of the same kind as could be foreseen by knocking in the lid; hence it was argued that even though the risk of explosion was unforeseeable, the defendant should be liable. Reliance was placed on *Hughes v. Lord Advocate*. The Court of Appeal held, however, that the only duty owed to the plaintiff was in relation to the foreseeable risk of splashing. Merely knocking in the lid, or putting it in intentionally was no breach of duty to the plaintiff since in the state of existing knowledge mere immersion of the cover could not be foreseen as likely to injure anyone. The plaintiff's argument was supported by *Re Polemis*, but that case was no longer law. In the *Hughes* case the defendants created a risk of burning by failure to guard an allurement. That risk materialised although the combination of the circumstances by which the burns were more serious than they might have been expected to be could not reasonably have been foreseen. The burns were, however, a consequence of "defendants' breach of duty". In the present case the only duty related to splashing and there was no evidence of any splash and hence no breach of duty.

Is this an acceptable distinction in your opinion? Is the result just? Is it logical? Is it simple?

3. In *Lauritzen v. Barstead* (1965), 53 D.L.R. 267, 53 W.W.R. 207 (Alta. S.C.), the plaintiff asked the defendant for a ride in his car to a nearby town. While in the town the defendant did considerable drinking and eventually became intoxicated. He asked the plaintiff to drive the car back. On the way back the defendant decided he wanted more beer and ordered the plaintiff to take a turn-off into the first town. The plaintiff refused and continued on the highway. The defendant grabbed at the steering wheel putting the car out of control and off the road. While the plaintiff was out of the car investigating the situation the defendant made an attempt to drive back on the road but this merely resulted in the car becoming more precariously situated on the bank of a ditch some 30 ft. in depth. The plaintiff tried to walk to town for help but was forced to turn back because of the cold. The plaintiff and the defendant agreed to stay in the car overnight. While the plaintiff slept, the defendant drove the car across the prairie towards a river intending to drive to town on the frozen surface but the car went into a hole and became stuck. The plaintiff made several other efforts to go for help but was turned back by wind and cold. About 36 hours after they left the road the plaintiff walked several miles down river where he was found by a farmer. Frost-bite necessitated the amputation of parts of both feet. In an action by the plaintiff for damages it was argued that *The Wagon Mound (No. 1)* prevented recovery for the plaintiff's injuries. Kirby J., held the defendant liable. He ought to have foreseen "the dangerous consequences likely to flow from his negligent act in grabbing the steering-wheel. It does not seem to me that ... the *Wagon Mound* case implies that recovery of damages should be conditional upon foreseeability of the particular harm and the precise manner or sequence of events in which it occurred."

   Is this consistent with *The Wagon Mound (No. 1)*? Is it just? Is it logical? Is it simple?

4. In *Oke v. Weide Transport Ltd.* (1963), 41 D.L.R. (2d) 53, 43 W.W.R. 203 (*sub nom. Oke v. Gov't. of Man.*) (Man. C.A.), the defendant motorist, who had knocked over a metal post on a strip of gravel between two highway lanes, left the scene leaving the post bent over. The deceased, improperly using the strip for the purpose of passing another car, was killed when the post broke through the floor boards of his car and impaled him. The majority of the Manitoba Court of Appeal held the defendant not li-

able, purporting to follow *The Wagon Mound (No. 1)*. The defendant could not have anticipated that someone would endeavour to pass a car at a point where it was wrong to do so, or that the damaged post would break through the floor of the car and cause a fatal accident. It was a "freak accident" and the defendant could not reasonably have foreseen such an unusual occurrence. Freedman J.A., dissenting, said it was not necessary to foresee "either the precise manner in which the accident would occur or that its consequences would be so tragic. ... It is enough that he ought to have foreseen that [the post] left in the state it was, could be a source of danger to a motorist ... and become the cause of ... an automobile accident of some kind."

Is this consistent with *The Wagon Mound (No. 1)*? Is the result a just one? Is it logical? Is it simple?

5. In *Weiner v. Zoratti* (1970), 11 D.L.R. (3d) 598, 72 W.W.R. 299 (Man. Q.B.), the defendant driver negligently collided with a fire hydrant and sheared it off, with the result that the basement of the plaintiff's pharmacy was flooded, damaging his stock-in-trade and personal effects. Matas J. held that damages were recoverable and explained:

> ... it is not necessary to engage in speculation about the specific foreseeability of each specific event from the moment of impact to the damage to the [plaintiff's] property; nor is it necessary to embark on an exercise in metaphysical subtleties. The plaintiff's loss was a direct, probable and foreseeable result of the negligent breaking of the hydrant just as much as if a piece of the broken hydrant had been propelled by the impact through the window of the [plaintiff's] shop or had struck a passing pedestrian causing physical injury.

Can you formulate a distinction between injury to a passing pedestrian and water dam age to a pharmacist's stock? Would liability be imposed if someone had been sleeping in the basement and had been drowned in the flood? See also *Kennedy v. Hughes Drug (1969) Inc.* (1974), 5 Nfld. & P.E.I.R. 435, 47 D.L.R. (3d) 277 (P.E.I.).

Do you agree with this analysis?

6. In *Tremain v. Pike*, [1969] 1 W.L.R. 1556, [1969] 3 All E.R. 1303 (Exeter Assizes), the plaintiff, a farm hand, contracted Weil's disease while working on the defendant's farm. This rare disease was spread by contact with the urine of rats. The more usual diseases caused by rats came from rat bites or from food contaminated by rats. Lord Justice Payne held that there was no negligence in the control of the rats. In an *obiter dictum*, His Lordship stated:

> The kind of damage suffered here was a disease contracted by contact with rats' urine. This, in my view, was entirely different in kind from the effect of a rat-bite, or food poisoning by the consumption of food or drink contaminated by rats. I do not accept that all illness or infection arising from an infestation of rats should be regarded as the same kind. [His Lordship then referred to *Smith v. Leech Brain* and *Bradford v. Robinson Rentals*]. The distinction between those two cases and the present case is crystal clear. There the risk of injury from a burn in the first case and from extreme cold in the second was foreseeable, and it was only the degree of injury or the development of the *sequelae* which was not foreseeable. In this case, the risk or the initial infection of the plaintiff, was, in my view, not reasonably foreseeable.

Is the distinction "crystal clear" to you?

7. In *School Division of Assiniboine South, No. 3 v. Hoffer and Greater Winnipeg Gas Co. Ltd.* (1970), 16 D.L.R. (3d) 703, [1971] 1 W.W.R. 1; affd 21 D.L.R. (3d) 608; [1971] 4 W.W.R. 746; affd 40 D.L.R. (3d) 480, [1973] 6 W.W.R. 765 (S.C.C.), a

14-year-old boy started his father's snowmobile in a negligent manner, causing it to escape from his control. It collided with a defective and unprotected gas-riser pipe. This caused some gas to escape and enter a nearby school building through a window where the gas exploded. The school sued the young operator of the snowmobile, his father and the Gas Company that had improperly installed the gas-riser pipe. All three defendants were found liable for the damage, and as between themselves, 50 per cent Gas Company, 25 per cent son, 25 per cent father.

In discussing the liability of the boy, Dickson J.A. (as he then was) stated:

> It is enough to fix liability if one could foresee in a general way the sort of thing that happened. The extent of the damage and its manner of incidence need not be foreseeable if physical damage of the kind which in fact ensues is foreseeable. In the case at bar, I would hold that the damage was of the *type* or *kind* which any reasonable person might foresee. Gas-riser pipes on the outside of … buildings are common. Damage to such a pipe is not of a kind that no one could anticipate. When one permits a power tobaggan to run at large, and when one fires a rifle blindly down a city street, one must not define narrowly the outer limits of reasonable provision. The ambit of foreseeable damage is indeed broad.

8. The test of *The Wagon Mound (No. 1)* as expanded in *Hughes v. Lord Advocate* has been well-articulated by Mr. Justice Dickson of the Supreme Court of Canada in *R. v. Coté* (1974), 51 D.L.R. (3d) 244, at 252, 3 N.R. 341:

> It is not necessary that one foresee the "precise concatenation of events"; it is enough to fix liability if one can foresee in a general way the class or character of injury which occurred. …

9. In *Falkenham v. Zwicker* (1978), 32 N.S.R. (2d) 199, 93 D.L.R. (3d) 289 (S.C.), the defendant motorist negligently crashed into a wire fence while trying to avoid hitting a cat. As a result some metal fence staples were catapulted into an empty field. In the spring, when the plaintiff farmer was fixing his fences, he noticed some missing staples. He spent some time looking for them and found a few, but not all of them. Later, when the cows were pastured in the field, several of them fell ill with "hardware disease" from having ingested metal staples. Mr. Justice MacIntosh held the defendant liable, stating that the "damage was of the type or kind which a reasonable person might foresee. Damage to the plaintiff's wire fence under the circumstances is what a reasonable person could anticipate. It is common knowledge that wire on pasture fences is usually held by means of staples. Breaking the fence, as was done in this instance, indicates a reasonable foreseeability of staples being ejected and eventually damaging the cattle that use this pasture".

The court went on to reduce the plaintiff's damage because he failed to "mitigate his loss" rather than because of contributory negligence. Since the defendant only took 15 minutes to search for staples this was not "reasonable steps to take in mitigation of damages". The plaintiff was awarded 60 per cent of his loss.

Do you agree with the court that these consequences were reasonably foreseeable? Why did the court choose to deal with the conduct of the plaintiff in terms of mitigation rather than contributory negligence? Could the same result have been achieved using contributory negligence?

3. Possibility of Damage

THE WAGON MOUND (NO. 2)
OVERSEAS TANKSHIP (U.K.) LTD. v. THE MILLER S.S. CO. PTY. LTD.

Privy Council. [1966] 2 All E.R. 709, [1967] 1 A.C. 617.

Appeal by Overseas Tankship (U.K.) Ltd. and a cross-appeal by The Miller Steamship Co. Pty. Ltd., and R.W. Miller & Co. Pty. Ltd., by leave of the Supreme Court of New South Wales, from the judgment of Walsh J. wherein judgment was entered against the appellant in favour of the respondents for £80,000 and £1,000 respectively. The circumstances which gave rise to the actions were the same as those which came before the Judicial Committee in *The Wagon Mound (No. 1)*. The plaintiffs in *The Wagon Mound (No. 1)* were the owners of a wooden wharf known as Sheerlegs Wharf which was damaged by the fire. Each of the plaintiffs in the present action was the owner of a ship which at the material time was lying at Sheerlegs Wharf and was damaged by the fire.

Lord Reid: ... In the present case the respondents sue alternatively in nuisance and in negligence. Walsh J., had found in their favour in nuisance but against them in negligence. Before their Lordships the appellant appeals against his decision on nuisance and the respondents appeal against his decision on negligence.

...

It is now necessary to turn to the respondents' submission that the trial judge was wrong in holding that damage from fire was not reasonably foreseeable. In *Wagon Mound (No. 1)* the finding on which the Board proceeded was that of the trial judge: "... [the appellants] did not know and could not reasonably be expected to have known that [the oil] was capable of being set afire when spread on water". In the present case the evidence led was substantially different from the evidence led in *Wagon Mound (No. 1)* and the findings of Walsh J. are significantly different. That is not due to there having been any failure by the plaintiffs in *Wagon Mound (No. 1)* in preparing and presenting their case. The plaintiffs there were no doubt embarrassed by a difficulty which does not affect the present plaintiffs. The outbreak of the fire was consequent on the act of the manager of the plaintiffs in *Wagon Mound (No. 1)* in resuming oxy-acetylene welding and cutting while the wharf was surrounded by this oil. So if the plaintiffs in the former case had set out to prove that it was foreseeable by the engineers of the Wagon Mound that this oil could be set alight they might have had difficulty in parrying the reply that then this must also have been foreseeable by their manager. Then there would have been contributory negligence and at that time contributory negligence was a complete defence in New South Wales.

The crucial finding of Walsh J., in this case is in finding (v): that the damage was "not reasonably foreseeable by those for whose acts the defendant would be responsible". That is not a primary finding of fact but an inference from the other findings, and it is clear from the learned judge's judgment that in drawing this inference he was to a large extent influenced by his view of the law. The vital parts of the findings of fact which have already been set out in full are (i) that the officers of the Wagon Mound "would regard furnace oil as very difficult to ignite on water" — not that they would regard this as impossible, (ii) that their experience would probably have been "that this had very rarely happened" — not that they would never have heard of a case where it had happened, and (iii) that they would have regarded it as a "possibility, but one which could become an actuality only in very exceptional circumstances" — not as in *Wagon Mound (No. 1)* that they could not reasonably be expected to have known that this oil was capable of being set afire when spread on water. The question which must now be determined is whether these differences between the findings in the two cases do or do not lead to a different result in law.

In *Wagon Mound (No. 1)* the Board were not concerned with degrees of foreseeability because the finding was that the fire was not foreseeable at all. So Viscount Simonds has no cause to amplify the statement that the "essential factor in determining liability is whether the damage is of such a kind as the reasonable man should have foreseen". Here the findings show, however, that some risk of fire would have been present to the mind of a reasonable man in the shoes of the ship's chief engineer. So that first question must be what is the precise meaning to be attached in this context to the word "foreseeable" and "reasonably foreseeable".

Before *Bolton v. Stone*, [1951] A.C. 850, the cases had fallen into two classes: (i) those where, before the event, the risk of its happening would have been regarded as unreal either because the event would have been thought to be physically impossible or because the possibility of its happening would have been regarded as so fantastic or far-fetched that no reasonable man would have paid any attention to it — "a mere possibility which would never occur to the mind of a reasonable man" (*per* Lord Dunedin in *Fardon v. Harcourt-Rivington*, [1932] All E.R. 81) — or (ii) those where there was a real and substantial risk or chance that something like the event which happens might occur and then the reasonable man would have taken the steps necessary to eliminate the risk.

Bolton v. Stone posed a new problem. There a member of a visiting team drove a cricket ball out of the ground on to an unfrequented adjacent public road and it struck and severely injured a lady who happened to be standing in the road. That it might happen that a ball would be driven on to this road could not have been said to be a fantastic or far-fetched possibility: according to the evidence it had happened about six times in twenty-eight years. Moreover it could not have been said to be a far-fetched or fantastic possibility that such a ball would strike someone in the road: people did pass along the road from time to time. So it could not have been said that, on any ordinary meaning of the words, the fact that a ball might strike a person in the road was not foreseeable or reasonably foreseeable. It was plainly foreseeable; but the chance of its happening in the foreseeable future was infinitesimal. A mathematician given the data could have worked out that it was only likely to happen once in so many thousand years. The House of Lords held that the risk was so small that in the circumstances a reasonable man would have been justified in disregarding it and taking no steps to eliminate it.

It does not follow that, no matter what the circumstances may be, it is justifiable to neglect a risk of such a small magnitude. A reasonable man would only neglect such a risk if he had some valid reason for doing so: e.g., that it would involve considerable expense to eliminate the risk. He would weigh the risk against the difficulty of eliminating it. If the activity which caused the injury to Miss Stone had been an unlawful activity there can be little doubt but that *Bolton v. Stone* would have been decided differently. In their Lordships' judgment *Bolton v. Stone* did not alter the general principle that a person must be regarded as negligent if he does not take steps to eliminate a risk which he knows or ought to know is a real risk and not a mere possibility which would never influence the mind of a reasonable man. What that decision did was to recognise and give effect to the qualification that it is justifiable not to take steps to eliminate a real risk if it is small and if the circumstances are such that a reasonable man, careful of the safety of his neighbour, would think it right to neglect it.

In the present case there was no justification whatever for discharging the oil into Sydney Harbour. Not only was it an offence to do so, but also it involved considerable loss financially. If the ship's engineer had thought about the matter there could have been no question of balancing the advantages and disadvantages. From every point of view it was both his duty and his interest to stop the discharge immediately.

It follows that in their Lordships' view the only question is whether a reasonable man having the knowledge and experience to be expected of the chief engineer of the Wagon Mound would have known that there was a real risk of the oil on the water catching fire in some way: if it did, serious damage to ships or other property was not only foreseeable but very likely. Their Lordships do not dissent from the view of the trial judge that the possibilities of damage "must be significant enough in a practical sense to require a reasonable man to guard against them", but they think that he may have misdirected himself in saying "there does seem to be a real practical difficulty, assuming that some risk of fire damage was foreseeable, but not a high one, in making a factual judgment as to whether this risk was sufficient to attract liability if damage should occur". In this difficult chapter of the law decisions are not infrequently taken to apply to circumstances far removed from the facts which give rise to them, and it would seem that here too much reliance has been placed on some observations in *Bolton v. Stone* and similar observations in other cases.

In their Lordships' view a properly qualified and alert chief engineer would have realised there was a real risk here, and they do not understand Walsh J., to deny that; but he appears to have held that, if a real risk can properly be described as remote, it must then be held to be not reasonably foreseeable. That is a possible interpretation of some of the authorities; but this is still an open question and on principle their Lordships cannot accept this view. If a real risk is one which would occur to the mind of a reasonable man in the position of the defendant's servant and which he would not brush aside as far-fetched, and if the criterion is to be what the reasonable man would have done in the circumstances, then surely he would not neglect such a risk if action to eliminate it presented no difficulty, involved no disadvantage and required no expense.

In the present case the evidence shows that the discharge of so much oil on to the water must have taken a considerable time, and a vigilant ship's engineer would have noticed the discharge at an early stage. The findings show that he ought to have known that it is possible to ignite this kind of oil on water, and that the ship's engineer probably ought to have known that this had in fact happened before. The most that can be said to justify inaction is that he would have known that this could only happen in very exceptional circumstances; but that does not mean that a reasonable man would dismiss such risk from his mind and do nothing when it was so easy to prevent it. If it is clear that the reasonable man would have realised or foreseen and prevented the risk, then it must follow that the appellants are liable in damages. The learned judge found this a difficult case: he said that this matter is "one on which different minds would come to different conclusions". Taking a rather different view of the law from that of the learned judge, their Lordships must hold that the respondents are entitled to succeed on this issue.

The judgment appealed from is in the form of a verdict in favour of the respondents on the claim based on nuisance, a verdict in favour of the appellant on the claim based on negligence, and a direction that judgment be entered for the respondents in the sums of £80,000 and £1,000 respectively. The result of their Lordships' findings is that the direction that judgment be entered for the respondents must stand, but that the appeal against the verdict in favour of the respondents and the cross-appeal against the verdict in favour of the appellant must both be allowed.

Accordingly their Lordships will humbly advise Her Majesty that the appeal and the cross-appeal should be allowed and that the judgment for the respondents in the sums of £80,000 and £1,000 should be affirmed. The appellant must pay two-thirds of the respondents' costs in the appeal and cross-appeal.

[The Judicial Committee of the Privy Council that decided *The Wagon Mound (No. 1), supra*, was composed of **Viscount Simonds, Lord Reid, Lord Radcliffe, Lord Tucker** and **Lord Morris of Borth-y-Gest.**]

[The Judicial Committee of the Privy Council that decided *The Wagon Mound (No. 2), supra*, was composed of **Lord Reid, Lord Morris of Borth-y-Gest, Lord Pearce, Lord Wilberforce** and **Lord Pearson.**]

NOTES

1. What, if anything, does *The Wagon Mound (No. 2)* do to *The Wagon Mound (No. 1)*? Did it strike a "mortal blow"? See Smith, "The Passing of *The Wagon Mound*" (1967), 45 Can. Bar Rev. 336; Glasbeek, "*Wagon Mound II — Re Polemis* Revived; Nuisance Revived" (1967), 6 West. L. Rev. 192. Or is its impact more limited? How important were the different findings of fact? To what type of activity is *The Wagon Mound (No. 2)* confined? Is *The Wagon Mound (No. 2)* a remoteness case or is it a standard of care problem? See Green, "*The Wagon Mound No. 2* — Foreseeability Revised" (1967), Utah L. Rev. 197. Compare with *Bolton v. Stone, supra.*

2. This test for determining the limits of liability for negligent conduct — that of foresight of a *possibility* of damage, rather than its "reasonable probability" — as enunciated in *The Wagon Mound (No. 2)*, has lain largely dormant for years, while *The Wagon Mound (No. 1)* occupied centre stage. Hailed by some scholars, it has been viewed rather skeptically by others. Some have argued that *The Wagon Mound (No. 2)* test is little different than the *Re Polemis* test, since all "direct" consequences must be considered foreseeable as "possible". Others have suggested that the place of *The Wagon Mound (No. 2)* is limited only to conduct that is "unlawful", "unjustifiable" and totally devoid of any social utility, such as the act of illegally spilling oil into the water in Sydney harbour, as occurred in *The Wagon Mound (No. 2)* case.

3. There have been several instances where courts have used the language of "possibility" based on *The Wagon Mound (No. 2)*. It is too early to tell whether a significant shift is coming, but it is worth noting these instances. For example, Mr. Justice Dickson has explained *The Wagon Mound (No. 2)* as follows:

   > These words would suggest that recovery may be had, provided the event giving rise to the damage is not regarded as "impossible", and even though it "very rarely happened", "only in very exceptional circumstances". The test of foreseeability of damage becomes a question of what is possible rather than what is probable.

   See *Hoffer v. School District of Assiniboine South* (1971), 21 D.L.R. (3d) 608, at 613, [1971] 4 W.W.R. 746; affd (1973), 40 D.L.R. (3d) 408, [1973] 6 W.W.R. 765 (S.C.C.). See also *McKenzie v. Hyde* (1967), 64 D.L.R. (2d) 362, at 376, 61 W.W.R. 1 (Man. Q.B.):

The injury complained of was of a class or character foreseeable as a possible result of the negligence.

See also *Malat et al. v. Bjornson*, [1978] 5 W.W.R. 429, 6 C.C.L.T. 142, at 152 (B.C.S.C.); affd, [1981] 2 W.W.R. 67, 14 C.C.L.T. 206 (B.C.C.A.); *Leonard v. Knott et al.*, [1978] 5 W.W.R. 511 (B.C.S.C.); affd in part, [1980] 1 W.W.R. 673 (B.C.C.A.), rare medical reaction found "possible" and not "far-fetched".

4. Another instance of reliance on this possibility test was that of Arnup J.A. in *Price v. Milawski* (1977), 18 O.R. (2d) 113, 82 D.L.R. (3d) 130 (C.A.), where he stated:

> [A] person doing a negligent act may, in circumstances lending themselves to that conclusion, be held liable for future damages arising in part from the subsequent negligent act of another, and in part from his own negligence, where such subsequent negligence and consequent damage were reasonably foreseeable as a *possible* result of his own negligence. [Emphasis added.]

5. In *Shirt v. Wyong Shire Council*, [1978] 1 N.S.W.L.R. 631, the court, relying on *The Wagon Mound (No. 2)*, concluded:

> It could not be said that the kind of injury the plaintiff suffered is remote according to the accepted tests. There was evidence which would have entitled the jury to hold that, if a skier is induced by negligent conduct to ski in water the depth of which varies from 3 feet 6 inches to 4 feet, there is a foreseeable possibility that, if he is thrown off his skis and precipitated headfirst into the water, he may suffer injury of the kind which occurred.

6. The possibility test was adopted by Linden J. in *Gallant v. Beitz; Nissan Automobile Co. (Canada) Ltd.* (1983), 42 O.R. (2d) 86, 25 C.C.L.T. 81, at 88 (H.C.J.): "The test of determining remoteness now is foreseeability of the possibility of the type of harm that transpires. If a defendant can reasonably foresee the risk that certain consequences may result, he can be liable for them. If he cannot reasonably foresee the possibility of such matters occurring, then he is excused from liability for those items".

   Is this a correct statement of the Canadian law today?

7. Should this development be encouraged or discouraged? What are the advantages and disadvantages? Does it more accurately reflect the position the courts have *actually* taken in most of these remoteness cases? Is it any more "honest" than *The Wagon Mound (No. 1)* test? Would the "possibility" test lead to more or fewer remoteness cases being decided in favour of plaintiffs? Would it stimulate more or less safety effort by those engaged in risky activities?

8. In *McKenzie et al. v. Hyde et al.* (1967), 64 D.L.R. (2d) 362, 61 W.W.R. 1 (Man. Q.B.), liability was imposed on someone who, during digging operations, broke a gas line permitting gas to seep into a nearby basement window, ignite and explode. Mr. Justice Dickson held that these consequences were "reasonably foreseeable". His Lordship confessed that he could not say that the damage and the explosion were "freakish" or "one in a million". In *Abbott et al. v. Kasza*, [1975] 3 W.W.R. 163, at 170; vard (1974), 71 D.L.R. (3d) 581, [1976] 4 W.W.R. 20 (Alta. C.A.). McDonald J. used the words "fantastic or improbable" to convey the idea. *The Restatement of Torts, Second*, §435 uses the words "Highly Extraordinary" to limit liability. What do you think of these words as aids in determining for which results a defendant should pay?

9. See Green, "*The Wagon Mound (No. 2)* — Foreseeability Revised" (1967), Utah L. Rev. 197:

> The chief criticism that can be levelled at Lord Reid's formula is his overloading of the foreseeability concept. Foreseeability is a delightful and useful fiction with no restrictions in itself, and when linked with the fictitious reasonable man as a jury formula to determine whether a defendant failed to exercise reasonable care to avoid the risk to his victim, it serves in every case to call forth a fresh judgment. As a judge's formula it is perhaps too glaringly fictitious unless given substantive additives so as to convert it into a meaningful concept for the assessment of policy factors. That a court, exercising the function of a jury in the determination of the issue of negligence, should take into account the risks a defendant should have taken into account when engaged in conduct hurtful to the plaintiff is sensible, but it is hardly an adequate formula for determining the "measure of damages" or extent of duty after the victim has suffered injury. Many foreseeable risks do not fall within the scope of any duty owed a plaintiff while many unforeseeable risks do fall within the duty owed him. After the event hindsight takes over and becomes the basis of judgment in measuring the adjustment that should be made; foreseeability becomes what should have been foreseen, not what was foreseen; what should have been foreseen becomes what the defendant should be liable for, and this brings into consideration the policy factors that give rationality to the law. This progression in meaning can scarcely be labelled foreseeability. There must be some more serviceable term available for describing the process of judgment in the practical affairs of everyday life.

10. This skepticism about the foresight doctrine has been echoed by Haines J. in *Attorney-General for Ontario v. Crompton* (1976), 14 O.R. (2d) 659, 74 D.L.R. (3d) 345, at 349 (H.C.J.), where an action was brought to recover the expense incurred to fight a fire caused by a car accident. Haines J. wrote:

> It has been a frequent criticism of writers and jurists alike that the foreseeability concept is a strained mode of analysis, a fiction at best justifiable as a jury formula, but one too transparent for meaningful use by Judges.

11. Professor Joseph C. Smith concludes his article "The Limits of Tort Liability in Canada: Remoteness, Foreseeability and Proximate Cause" in Linden (ed.), *Studies in Canadian Tort Law* (1968), p. 88, as follows:

> The majority of negligence cases do not present problems of remoteness. Such problems only arise where there is a risk of harm which materializes and which results, as well, in damage that, because of its extent, kind, other factors bearing a cause-effect relationship, or because of its unforeseeable nature, presents a problem of proportion in relation to the degree of fault.
>
> The underlying principle in remoteness cases appears to be that, as between a person without fault who has suffered a loss and one who has fault and his departure from the norm bears a cause-effect relationship between the damage and the departure, the one with the fault should bear the loss, except where the fault is insignificant or the damage is so extensive that it is out of all proportion in comparison with the fault. There can be no objective test for deciding when these two factors are so out of proportion that liability ought not to be imposed. This decision will be a value judgment largely dependent upon the unique facts of each particular case. The decision of the Privy Council in *The Wagon Mound (No. 2)*, for this reason, is far more significant for the law of remoteness than its decision in *The Wagon Mound (No. 1)*, since in the second *Wagon Mound* case the court articulated some of the factors relevant to its decision rather than attempting to apply a rule of thumb test. This is probably what Canadian courts do in fact, though not in word, in dealing with remoteness problems. The unique nature of each particular case would become more evident, however, if the courts would articulate the factors upon which their

decision is based rather than attempting to justify their decisions in traditional terms of proximate cause or foreseeability.

PALSGRAF v. LONG ISLAND RAILROAD CO.

New York Court of Appeals. 248 N.Y. 339, 162 N.E. 99 (1928).

Action by Helen Palsgraf against the Long Island Railroad Company. Judgment entered on the verdict of a jury in favour of the plaintiff was affirmed by the Appellate Division by a divided court (222 App. Div. 166, 225 N.Y.S. 412), and the defendant appeals.

Cardozo C.J.: Plaintiff was standing on a platform of defendant's railroad after buying a ticket to go to Rockaway Beach. A train stopped at the station, bound for another place. Two men ran forward to catch it. One of the men reached the platform of the car without mishap, though the train was already moving. The other man, carrying a package, jumped aboard the car, but seemed unsteady as if about to fall. A guard on the car, who had held the door open, reached forward to help him in, and another guard on the platform pushed him from behind. In this act, the package was dislodged, and fell upon the rails. It was a package of small size, about 15 inches long, and was covered by a newspaper. In fact it contained fireworks, but there was nothing in its appearance to give notice of its contents. The fireworks when they fell exploded. The shock of the explosion threw down some scales at the other end of the platform, many feet away. The scales struck the plaintiff, causing injuries for which she sues.

The conduct of the defendant's guard, if a wrong in its relation to the holder of the package, was not a wrong in its relation to the plaintiff, standing far away. Relatively to her it was not negligence at all. Nothing in the situation gave notice that the falling package had in it the potency of peril to persons thus removed. Negligence is not actionable unless it involves the invasion of a legally protected interest, the violation of a right. "Proof of negligence in the air, so to speak, will not do". ... The plaintiff as she stood upon the platform of the station might claim to be protected against intentional invasion of her bodily security. Such invasion is not charged. She might claim to be protected against unintentional invasion by conduct involving in the thought of reasonable men an unreasonable hazard that such invasion would ensue. These, from the point of view of the law, were the bounds of her immunity, with perhaps some rare exceptions, survivals for the most part of ancient forms of liability, where conduct is held to be at the peril of the actor. If no hazard was apparent to the eye of ordinary vigilance, an act innocent and harmless, at least to outward seeming, with reference to her, did not take to itself the quality of a tort because it happened to be wrong, though apparently not one involving the risk of bodily insecurity, with reference to some one else. "In every instance before negligence can be predicated of a given act, back of the act must be sought and found a duty to the individual complaining, the observance of which would have averted or avoided the injury." ... "The ideas of negligence and duty are strictly correlative" (Bowen L.J. in *Thomas v. Quartermaine*, 18 Q.B.D. 685, 694). The plaintiff sues in her own right for a wrong personal to her, and not as the vicarious beneficiary of a breach of duty to another.

A different conclusion will involve us, and swiftly too, in a maze of contradictions. A guard stumbles over a package which has been left upon a platform. It seems to be a bundle of newspapers. It turns out to be a can of dynamite. To the eye of ordinary vigilance, the bundle is abandoned waste, which may be kicked or trod on with impunity. Is a passenger at the other end of the platform protected by the law against the unsuspected hazard concealed beneath the waste? If not, is the result to be any different, so far as the distant passenger is concerned, when the guard stumbles over a valise which a truckman or a porter has left upon the walk? The passenger far away, if the victim of a wrong at all, has a cause of action, not derivative, but original and primary. His claim to be protected against invasion of his bodily security is neither greater nor less because the act resulting in the invasion is a wrong to another far removed. In this case, the rights that are said to have been invaded, are not even of the same order. The man was not injured in his person nor even put in danger. The purpose of the act, as well as its effect, was to make his person safe. If there was a wrong to him at all, which may very well be doubted, it was a wrong to a property interest only, the safety of his package. Out of this wrong to property, which threatened injury to nothing else, there has passed, we are told, to the plaintiff by derivation or succession a right of action for the invasion of an interest of another order, the right to bodily security. The diversity of interests emphasizes the futility of the effort to build the plaintiff's right upon the basis of a wrong to some one else. The gain is one of emphasis, for a like result would follow if the interests were the same. Even then, the orbit of the danger as disclosed to the eye of reasonable vigilance would be the orbit of the duty. One who jostles one's neighbour in a crowd does not invade the rights of others standing at the outer fringe when the unintended contact casts a bomb upon the ground. The wrongdoer as to them is the man who carries the bomb, not the one who explodes it with out suspicion of the danger. Life will have to be made over, and human nature transformed, before prevision so extravagant can be accepted as the form of conduct, the customary standard to which behaviour must conform. …

Negligence, like risk, is thus a term of relation. Negligence in the abstract, apart from things related, is surely not a tort, if indeed it is understandable at all. …

The law of causation, remote or proximate, is thus foreign to the case before us. The question of liability is always anterior to the question of the measure of the consequences that go with liability. If there is no tort to be redressed, there is no occasion to consider what damage might be recovered if there were a finding of a tort. We may assume, without deciding, that negligence, not at large or in the abstract, but in relation to the plaintiff, would entail liability for any and all consequences, however novel or extraordinary. [Citations omitted.]

There is room for argument that a distinction is to be drawn according to the diversity of interests invaded by the act, as where conduct negligent in that it threatens an insignificant invasion of an interest in property results in an unforeseeable invasion of an interest of another order, as,*e.g.*, one of bodily security. Perhaps other distinctions may be necessary. We do not go into the question now. The consequences to be followed must first be rooted in a wrong.

The judgment of the Appellate Division and that of the Trial Term should be reversed, and the complaint dismissed, with costs in all courts.

Andrews J. (dissenting): … Negligence may be defined roughly as an act or omission which unreasonably does or may affect the rights of others, or which unreasonably fails to protect one's self from the dangers resulting from such acts. Here I confine myself to the first branch of the definition. Nor do I comment on the word "unreasonable". For present purposes it sufficiently describes that average of conduct that society requires of its members. …

But we are told that "there is no negligence unless there is in the particular case a legal duty to take care, and this duty must be one which is owed to the plaintiff himself and not merely to others". (Salmond, *Torts* (6th ed.), 24.) This, I think too narrow a conception. Where there is the unreasonable act, and some right that may be affected there is negligence whether damage does or does not result. That is immaterial. Should we drive down Broadway at a reckless speed, we are negligent whether we strike an approaching car or miss it by an inch. The act itself is wrongful not only to those who happen to be within the radius of danger but to all who might have been there — a wrong to the public at large. Such is the language of the street. Such the language of the courts when speaking of contributory negligence. Such again and again their language in speaking of the duty of some defendant and discussing proximate cause in cases where such a discussion is wholly irrelevant on any other theory. ... As was said by Mr. Justice Holmes many years ago, "the measure of the defendant's duty in determining whether a wrong has been committed is one thing, the measure of liability when a wrong has been committed is another". ... Due care is a duty imposed on each one of us to protect society from unnecessary danger, not to protect A, B or C alone.

It may well be that there is no such thing as negligence in the abstract. "Proof of negligence in the air, so to speak, will not do." In an empty world negligence would not exist. It does involve a relationship between man and his fellows. But not merely a relationship between man and those whom he might reasonably expect his act would injure. Rather, a relationship between him and those whom he does in fact injure. If his act has a tendency to harm some one, it harms him a mile away as it does those on the scene. ...

In the well-known *Polemis* case, [1921] 3 K.B. 560, Scrutton L.J. said that the dropping of a plank was negligent for it might injure "workman or cargo or ship". Because of either possibility the owner of the vessel was to be made good for his loss. The act being wrongful the doer was liable for its proximate results. Criticized and explained as this statement may have been, I think it states the law as it should be and as it is.

The proposition is this. Every one owes to the world at large the duty of refraining from those acts that may unreasonably threaten the safety of others. Such an act occurs. Not only is he wronged to whom harm might reasonably be expected to result, but he also who is in fact injured, even if he be outside what would generally be thought the danger zone. There needs be duty due the one complaining but this is not a duty to a particular individual because as to him harm might be expected. Harm to some one being the natural result of the act, not only that one alone, but all those in fact injured may complain. We have never, I think, held otherwise. ...

What is a cause in a legal sense, still more what is a proximate cause, depends in each case upon many considerations, as does the existence of negligence itself. Any philosophical doctrine of causation does not help us. A boy throws a stone into a pond. The ripples spread. The water level rises. The history of that pond is altered to all eternity. It will be altered by other causes also. Yet it will be forever the resultant of all causes combined. Each one will have an influence. How great only omniscience can say. You may speak of a chain, or, if you please, a net. An analogy is of little aid. Each cause brings about future events. Without each the future would not be the same. Each is proximate in the sense it is essential. But that is not what we mean by the word. Nor on the other hand do we mean sole clause. There is no such thing.

Should analogy be thought helpful, however, I prefer that of a stream. The spring, starting on its journey, is joined by tributary after tributary. The river, reaching the ocean, comes from a hundred sources. No man may say whence any drop of water is derived. Yet for a time distinction may be possible. Into the clear creek, brown swamp water flows from the left. Later, from the right comes water stained by its clay bed. The three may remain for a space, sharply divided. But at last inevitably no trace of separation remains. They are so commingled that all distinction is lost.

As we have said, we cannot trace the effect of an act to the end, if end there is. Again, however, we may trace it part of the way. A murder at Sarajevo may be the necessary antecedent to an assassination in London 20 years hence. An overturned lantern may burn all Chicago. We may follow the fire from the shed to the last building. We rightly say that fire started by the lantern caused its destruction.

A cause, but not the proximate cause. What we do mean by the word "proximate" is that, because of convenience, of public policy, of a rough sense of justice, the law arbitrarily declines to trace a series of events beyond a certain point. This is not logic. It is practical politics. Take our rule as to fires. Sparks from my burning haystack set on fire my house and my neighbour's. I may recover from a negligent railroad. He may not. Yet the wrongful act as directly harmed the one as the other. We may regret that the line was drawn just where it was, but drawn somewhere it had to be. We said the act of the railroad was not the proximate cause of the neighbour's fire. Cause it surely was. The words we used were simply indicative of our notions of public policy. Other courts think differently. But somewhere they reach the point where they cannot say the stream comes from any one source.

Take the illustration given in an unpublished manuscript by a distinguished and helpful writer on the law of torts. A chauffeur negligently collides with another car which is filled with dynamite, although he could not know it. An explosion follows. A, walking on the sidewalk nearby, is killed. B, sitting in a window of a building opposite is cut by flying glass. C, likewise sitting in a window a block away, is similarly injured. And a further illustration: A nursemaid ten blocks away, startled by the noise, involuntarily drops a baby from her arms to the walk. We are told that C may not recover but A may. As to B it is a question for court or jury. We will all agree that the baby might not. Because, we are again told, the chauffeur had no reason to believe his conduct involved any risk of injuring either C or the baby. As to them he was not negligent.

But the chauffeur, being negligent in risking the collision, his belief that the scope of the harm he might do would be limited is immaterial. His act unreasonably jeopardized the safety of any one who might be affected by it. C's injury and that of the baby were directly traceable to the collision. Without that, the injury would not have happened. C had the right to sit in his office, secure from such dangers. The baby was entitled to use the sidewalk with reasonable safety.

The true theory is, it seems to me, that the injury to C, if in truth he is to be denied recovery, and the injury to the baby, is that their several injuries were not the proximate result of the negligence. And here not what the chauffeur had reason to believe would be the result of his conduct, but what the prudent would foresee, may have a bearing — may have some bearing, for the problem of proximate cause is not to be solved by any one consideration. It is all a question of expediency. There are no fixed rules to govern our judgment. There are simply matters of which we may take account. We have in a somewhat different connection spoken of "the stream of events". We have asked whether that stream was deflected — whether it was forced into new and unexpected channels: . ... This is rather rhetoric than law. There is in truth little to guide us other than common sense.

There are some hints that may help us. The proximate cause, involved as it may be with many other causes, must be, at the least, something without which the event would not happen. The court must ask itself whether there was a natural and continuous sequence between cause and effect. Was the one a substantial factor in producing the other? Was there a direct connection between them, without too many intervening causes? Is the effect of cause on result not too attenuated? Is the cause likely, in the usual judgment of man kind, to produce the result. Or, by the exercise of prudent foresight, could the result be foreseen? Is the result too remote from the cause, and here we consider remoteness in time and space: . ... where we passed upon the construction of a contract — but something was also said on this subject. Clearly we must so consider, for the greater the distance either in time or space, the more surely do other causes intervene to affect the result. When a lantern is overturned, the firing of a shed is a fairly direct consequence. Many things contribute to the spread of the conflagration — the force of the wind, the direction and width of streets, the character of intervening structures, other factors. We draw an uncertain and wavering line, but draw it we must as best we can.

Once again, it is all a question of fair judgment, always keeping in mind the fact that we endeavour to make a rule in each case that will be practical and in keeping with the general understanding of mankind.

Here another question must be answered. In the case supposed, it is said, and said correctly, that the chauffeur is liable for the direct effect of the explosion although he had no reason to suppose it would follow a collision. "The fact that the injury occurred in a different manner than that which might have been expected does not prevent the chauffeur's negligence from being in law the cause of the injury." But the natural results of a negligent act — the results which a prudent man would or should foresee — do have a bearing upon the decision as to proximate cause. We have said so repeatedly. What should be foreseen? No human foresight would suggest that a collision itself might injure one a block away. On the contrary, given an explosion, such a possibility might be reasonably expected. I think the direct connection, the foresight of which the courts speak, assumes prevision of the explosion, for the immediate results of which, at least, the chauffeur is responsible.

It may be said this is unjust. Why? In fairness he should make good every injury flowing from his negligence. Not because of tenderness toward him we say he need not answer for all that follows his wrong. We look back to the catastrophe, the fire kindled by the spark, or the explosion. We trace the consequences, not indefinitely, but to a certain point. And to aid us in fixing that point we ask what might ordinarily be expected to follow the fire or the explosion.

This last suggestion is the factor which must determine the case before us. The act upon which defendant's liability rests is knocking an apparently harmless package onto the platform. The act was negligent. For its proximate consequences the defendant is liable. If its contents were broken, to the owner; if it fell upon and crushed a passenger's foot, then to him; if it exploded and injured one in the immediate vicinity, to him also as to A in the illustration. Mrs. Palsgraf was standing some distance away. How far cannot be told from the record — apparently 25 to 30 feet, perhaps less. Except for the explosion, she would not have been injured. We are told by the appellant in his brief, "It cannot be denied that the explosion was the direct cause of the plaintiff's injuries." So it was a substantial factor in producing the result — there was here a natural and continuous sequence — direct connection. The only intervening cause was that, instead of blowing her to the ground, the concussion smashed the weighing machine which in turn fell upon her. There was no remoteness in time, little in space. And surely, given such an explosion as here, it needed no great foresight to predict that the natural result would be to injure one on the platform at no greater distance from its scene than was the plaintiff. Just how no one might be able to predict. Whether by flying fragments, by broken glass, by wreckage of machines or structures no one could say. But injury in some form was most probable.

Under these circumstances I cannot say as a matter of law that the plaintiff's injuries were not the proximate result of the negligence. That is all we have before us. The court refused to so charge. No request was made to submit the matter to the jury as a question of fact, even would that have been proper upon the record before us.

The judgment appealed from should be affirmed, with costs.

[**Pound, Lehman** and **Kellogg JJ.**, concurred with **Cardozo C.J., Crane** and **O'Brien JJ.**, concurred with **Andrews J.**]

NOTES

1. See Goodhart, "The Unforeseeable Consequences of a Negligent Act" (1930), 39 Yale L.J. 449, reprinted in Goodhart, *Essays in Jurisprudence and the Common Law* (1936), Ch. VII; Green, "The Palsgraf Case" (1930), 30 Colum. L. Rev. 789; Gregory, "Proximate Cause in Negligence — a Retreat from Rationalization" (1938), 6 U. Chi. L. Rev. 36; Wright, "The Law of Torts: 1923-1947" (1948), 26 Can. Bar. Rev. 46; Prosser, "Palsgraf Revisited" (1953), 52 Mich. L. Rev. 1; Fleming, "Remoteness and Duty: The Control Devices in Liability for Negligence" (1953), 31 Can. Bar Rev. 471.

2. The late Professor Seavey, in his influential article "Mr. Justice Cardozo and the Law of Torts" (1939), 52 Harv. L. Rev. 372, 48 Yale L.J. 390, 39 Colum. L. Rev. 20, asks three questions about the approach of Chief Justice Cardozo as compared to that of Justice Andrews: (1) Is it more consistent with our sense of justice? (2) Is it more consistent with the underlying theory of negligence law?, and (3) Is it more easily applied? Do you think that the Cardozo treatment is more just, more logical and simpler?

3. Lord Justice Denning, in *Roe v. Ministry of Health*, [1954] 2 Q.B. 66, at 85, [1954] 2 All E.R. 131, at 138, said:

   > The three questions, duty, causation, and remoteness, run continually into one another. It seems to me that they are simply three different ways of looking at one and the same question which is this: Is the consequence fairly to be regarded as within the risk created by the negligence? If so, the negligent person is liable for it: but otherwise not. ... Instead of asking three questions, I should have thought in many cases it would be simple and better to ask the one question: Is the consequence within the risk? and to answer it by applying ordinary plain common sense.

   Does this make sense?

4. A similar view has been expressed by Clement J.A. of the Alberta Court of Appeal in *Abbott et al. v. Kasza* (1976), 71 D.L.R. (3d) 581, [1976] 4 W.W.R. 20, at 29, where he said:

   > The question raised is whether in cases such as the present there is an appreciable difference in law in the projection of the reasonably foreseeable between remoteness of damage and duty and causation. For myself, I think that the law does not compel any distinction to be drawn and that the interests of a workable jurisprudence militate against it. As Denning L.J. points out, each component of liability is only a facet of the whole, and judgment must be on the entirety, not piecemeal on refractions from each facet.

   Do you agree?

LINDEN, "FORESEEABILITY IN NEGLIGENCE LAW"

from *Special Lectures of the Law Society of Upper Canada on New Developments in the Law of Torts* (1973).

A NEW APPROACH TO REMOTENESS

It must now be apparent to everyone that there are no easy answers to the remoteness and proximate cause issues. *Polemis* has been discarded. *The Wagon Mound (No. 1)* has been largely undermined. Similarly, all future attempts to resolve these cases with an automatic formula are doomed. There is no magic phrase that can furnish automatic answers to all of the freakish and bizarre situations that arise in negligence cases. These "flukes", by their very nature, cannot be tamed by legal rules.

Not every accident, however, is unique. Certain events tend to recur from time to time. For such recurring situations, we should develop stable legal rules. It should be easy to forecast the outcome of a thin-skull case, for example, because these cases recur and the rules are settled. ...

Understandably, the courts have encountered the most difficulty in handling the results that are uncommon. On occasion, courts have been bewitched by the word foresight and, as a result, have arrived at unsatisfactory decisions. They must resist the allure of foreseeability, because its power is largely an illusion. It can be as broad or as narrow as the beholder wishes to make it. It can disguise value choices as much as causation did. If we must use the term foreseeability, we must not allow it to blind us. Foresight does not excuse courts from the onerous responsibility of making difficult decisions.

Simply stated, the remoteness problem is concerned with whether the defendant, whose conduct has fallen below the accepted standard of the community, should be relieved from paying for damage that his conduct helped to bring about. By formulating the question in this way, we spotlight the value choices that are present in the case. We should not disguise the fact that some intuition and feeling are and should be involved in this determination.

We must admit that these freakish accidents do not lend themselves to effortless resolution by the application of ready-made rules. In the memorable words of Mr. Justice Andrews in *Palsgraf v. Long Island Railway Co.,* what is involved here "is not logic. It is practical politics". The "policy factors that give rationality to the law" are more important considerations than foresee ability. This does not mean that foresight should be an irrelevant consideration. It suggests only that other matters, in addition to foreseeability, deserve attention. The courts, according to Mr. Justice Andrews, consider a variety of matters, like was there a "natural and continuous sequence between the cause and effect", was the conduct a "substantial factor" in producing the result, was there a "direct connection" and was the result "too remote ... in time and space". He concluded by explaining:

> [We] draw an uncertain and wavering line, but draw it we must as best we can. ... It is all a question of fair judgment, always keeping in mind the fact that we endeavour to make a rule in each case that will be practical and in keeping with the general understanding of mankind.

Consequently, the courts must assess certain policy factors in the process of decision-making. If the case deals with a personal injury rather than a property loss, this should be considered. If the defendant is an industrial undertaking rather than some private citizen, this should be evaluated. The probability of insurance coverage cannot be ignored. The potential for deterrence must be examined. If there remains any prophylatic power in tort law, it would be strengthened by forcing enterprisers to pay for all the costs of their negligent activities, including the unforeseeable results, so that they will be stimulated to exercise greater care. In addition, perhaps the occasional huge award for some bizarre event will dramatize publicly the importance of safety measures. Lastly, some market deterrence may be accomplished by transferring the entire cost of mishaps to the activity which produces them. It is only after full consideration of all of these policy matters and after the deployment of each of the available tests that the courts should try to decide the case. Even then it might be wise to put the matter to the jury to solve.

In sum, it is hard to escape the conclusion that the best we can ever do is to rely on the common sense of the judge and jury. It is not an admission of defeat to admit that these judgments lie "in the realm of values and what you choose depends on what you want". It is merely being realistic.

NOTES

1. A similar view has been expressed by Morden J.A. in *Duwyn v. Kaprielian* (1978), 7 C.C.L.T. 121 as follows:

   > Obviously there is a significant element of experience and value judgment in the ultimate application of the foresight requirement.

2. This idea, using the language of causation, however, has also been given support by Clement J.A. of the Alberta Court of Appeal when he said, in *Abbott et al. v. Kasza* (1976), 71 D.L.R. (3d) 581, [1976] 4 W.W.R. 20, at 28:

   > The common law has always recognized that causation is a concept that in the end result must be limited in its reach by a pragmatic consideration of consequences: the chain of cause and effect can be followed only to the point where the consequences of an act will be fairly accepted as attributable to that act in the context of the social and economic conditions then prevailing and the reasonable expectations of members of the society in the conduct of each other. ...
   >
   > The precise point at which an original cause ceases to have a consequential legal effect cannot be determined by didactic structures. ...
   >
   > ... [T]he reach of causation is limited by what the court determines is reasonably foreseeable.

3. Should questions such as these be left to a Canadian jury to decide? Can this be done if the issue is classified as one of duty or of remoteness, rather than one of proximate cause?

   Support for this approach was furnished by Linden J. in *Gallant v. Beitz; Nissan Automobile Co. (Canada) Ltd.* (1983), 42 O.R. (2d) 86, 25 C.C.L.T. 81 (H.C.J.), where it was alleged that the plaintiff was injured during a collision by a tire-changing iron situated behind his own driver's seat. When he sued the other motorist, the latter added Nissan, alleging their negligent design contributed to the injury. Nissan moved unsuccessfully to strike out the third party notice on two grounds. During the course of his reasons, Linden J. explained:

What must be decided, then is whether a negligent motorist can be liable for any additional injury suffered by his victim as a result of a defect in design of the victim's vehicle. This is a pure remoteness issue since, clearly, the defendant motorist owes the plaintiff a duty to drive carefully so as to avoid injuring him. The issue here is simply to determine the *extent* of the defendant's liability for his negligent driving. That is the function of the concept of remoteness — to draw the appropriate line between the *additional* consequences for which an admittedly negligent defendant will be liable, and those for which he will escape liability. Unlike the duty issue, which is a pure question of law, remoteness is a mixed question of law and fact. Whether a particular consequence is too remote or whether it is proximate enough to attract liability always depends on the individual circumstances of the case. Hence, the issue cannot remain the exclusive territory of the Judge; the jury may be asked to participate in the exercise in appropriate cases. [See *Cotic v. Gray* (1981), 33 O.R. (2d) 356, 17 C.C.L.T. 138, 124 D.L.R. (3d) 641 (C.A.); affd (1983), 2 O.A.C. 187, 26 C.C.L.T. 163 (S.C.C.).] Needless to say, the courts have been reluctant to relieve negligent defendants from liability for any of the consequences of their conduct, doing so only in cases where it is thought to be too harsh to hold them responsible.

4. Recently there has emerged in England a new "test" to assist courts in deciding what is too remote — "instinctive feeling". In *Lamb v. Camden London Borough Council*, [1981] 1 Q.B. 625, [1981] 2 All E.R. 408 (C.A.), Watkins L.J. held that damage done to a home by squatters was too remote because he had an "instinctive feeling that the event or act being weighed in the balance is too remote to sound in damages". This case was followed by *Crossley v. Rawlinson*, [1982] 1 W.L.R. 369, [1981] 3 All E.R. 674 (Q.B.), where Richard H. Tucker Q.C. held that his "instinctive feeling" was that it was too remote and unforeseeable to award compensation to someone who fell while running to put out a fire. What do you think of this "test?"

C. INTERVENING FORCES

HARRIS v. T.T.C. AND MILLER

Supreme Court of Canada. [1967] S.C.R. 460, 63 D.L.R. (2d) 450.

The infant appellant sustained injuries when he was a passenger in a bus owned by the respondent Transit Commission and operated by its servant, the second respondent Miller. As the bus in question pulled away from a bus stop, it brushed against a steel pole which was set in the sidewalk some 5½ inches from the curb with the result that the infant appellant's arm, which he had extended through a window in order to point out some object to his companion, was crushed and broken. In an action for damages brought on behalf of the infant appellant, the trial judge found that the negligence of the bus operator was a proximate cause of the collision but that the appellant was also guilty of negligence in putting his arm out of the window of the bus, having regard to the fact that a by-law of the respondent Commission, of which the appellant was aware, prohibited passengers from doing this and was posted in the bus together with a sign below the window reading: "Keep arm in". The trial judge divided the fault equally between the parties. On appeal, the Court of Appeal found that on the facts of the case there could be no recovery. With leave, an appeal was brought to the Supreme Court of Canada.

Ritchie J. (Cartwright, Martland, Spence JJ., concurring): ... The decision of the Court of Appeal was rendered orally by Laskin J.A. at the conclusion of the argument. The learned judge did not refer to any authorities but reached his conclusion on the following grounds:

We are of the opinion that there was no negligence in this case attributable to the defendants which, as a matter of law, operated in favour of the infant plaintiff. On the facts, he was the author of his own misfortune. We do not think that the bus operator could reasonably be expected to foresee that the infant plaintiff would have his arm in the position in which it was outside the window when he pulled away from the curb. The evidence is clear that the infant plaintiff knew of the warning which was posted on the window ledge to keep his arm in, and it was his carelessness for his own safety and not any carelessness that may have existed in the way in which the driver pulled away from the curb that was the operative cause of the accident. ...

[The court felt there was no voluntary assumption of risk.]

It will also be observed that Mr. Justice Laskin did not consider that the bus driver could reasonably be expected to foresee that the little boy's arm would have been out of the window.

In my opinion we are relieved from the task of speculating on whether the bus driver could reasonably have foreseen such a thing by reason of the fact that he indicates in his own evidence that he was aware of the propensity of children on his own bus to put their arms and indeed their heads out of the window, notwithstanding the warning which the Commission had posted. ...

I have no difficulty in drawing the conclusion from [the] evidence that the bus driver knew that children had a tendency to put their arms out of the windows and that he could therefore reasonably be expected to foresee that such a thing would happen in the case of the infant plaintiff. ...

The relevant by-law of the respondent Commission, which was approved by the Ontario Municipal Board and therefore has the force of law by virtue of s. 167 of *The Railway Act*, R.S.O. 1950, c. 331, provided as follows:

> No person shall ride or stand on any extreme portion of any car or bus operated by the Commission nor lean out of or project any portion of his body through any window of such car or bus nor enter any such bus at other than the designated entries.

It was contended on behalf of the respondent that by passing this by-law and otherwise giving notice to its passengers of the danger of projecting any portion of their body through any window of the bus, the respondent Commission had fully discharged its duty of care in relation to the dangers involved in such conduct and that it owed no further duty to them in this regard. There may be circumstances in which a public carrier can discharge its duty to its passengers in relation to a specific danger by passing such a by-law and giving such notice, but when, as in this case, the respondent's negligence was an effective cause of the accident and its driver should have foreseen the likelihood of children passengers extending their arms through the window notwithstanding the warning, different considerations apply and in my opinion it becomes a case where the damages should be apportioned in proportion to the degree of fault found against the parties respectively.

...

[**Judson J.** dissented.]

NOTES

1. *Harris v. T.T.C.* illustrates that merely because the plaintiff's injury was caused or contributed to by the plaintiff's own negligent act, or the wrongful act of a third person, does not necessarily mean that the defendant is freed from liability. Where a defendant has a duty to take reasonable care to protect the plaintiff from injury caused either by the plaintiff's own act or the act of a third person, these acts cannot be considered to be intervening forces which shield the defendant from liability.

2. Numerous relationships involve a duty to protect the plaintiff from injury caused either by himself or herself or by others. Parents have a duty to protect their children, schools and teachers must take care to protect their students, prisons, hospitals and other institutions must take reasonable steps to ensure the safety of their patients and inmates. See the discussion in Chapter 5.

3. Those who are in charge or in possession of dangerous products must take reasonable care to prevent these instruments from falling into the hands of those who are unable to competently use them. This rule can apply to things like guns, vehicles, and the like. See, for example, *Stermer v. Lawson* (1977), 79 D.L.R. (3d) 366, [1977] 5 W.W.R. 628; percentage vard (1980), 107 D.L.R. (3d) 36, 11 C.C.L.T. 76 (B.C.C.A.) — a motorcycle; *Hatfield v. Pearson* (1956), 6 D.L.R. (2d) 593, 20 W.W.R. 580 (B.C.C.A.) — a rifle; *Hewson v. City of Red Deer* (1976), 63 D.L.R. (3d) 168, [1976] W.W.D. 6 (Alta. S.C.T.D.) — a tractor.

4. In *Spagnolo v. Margesson's Sports Ltd.* (1981), 127 D.L.R. (3d) 339 (Ont. Co. Ct.), a car was left on a parking lot with the keys in the ignition. A thief stole the car and, six days later, collided with the plaintiff's vehicle. Judge Rapson imposed liability on the parking lot operator, relying on statistical evidence, *inter alia*, that 44 per cent of those arrested for car theft were juveniles, that 71 per cent of stolen cars were recovered in large urban centres, that 45 per cent of stolen vehicles were used for transportation and that there was a "high incidence of thefts of unsecured vehicles from fee-paid parking lots". His Honour reasoned that a parking lot operator "with better knowledge of thefts than the general public, should be able to foresee that a thief being an irresponsible person, possibly a juvenile, is likely to drive negligently and become involved in an accident". He explained that it is "good public policy to prevent the theft of motor vehicles and the damage which can result therefrom".

   On appeal (1983), 41 O.R. (2d) 65, 145 D.L.R. (3d) 381 (C.A.), the action was dismissed. Mr. Justice Zuber explained that he might have agreed if the accident had occurred "in the course of the theft or even in the course of the immediate flight therefrom" because in these circumstances it would be "reasonably foreseeable as an ordinary consequence of the nervousness and panic which may accompany the theft". But here, the court could not "conclude that the likelihood of damage to third parties six days after the theft is any greater with a thief at the wheel of the vehicle than with a driver lawfully in possession". Do you agree?

5. A U.S. study has shown that 18 per cent of cars stolen were involved in accidents, a rate of "approximately 200 times the normal accident rate". Further, 42 per cent of cars stolen had been left with keys in the ignition. See Peck (1969), Wis. L. Rev. 909. Would Canadian figures like this make any difference?

6. In *Bradford v. Kanellos*, [1971] 2 O.R. 393, 18 D.L.R. (3d) 60 (C.A.); affd, [1974] S.C.R. 409, 40 D.L.R. (3d) 578, a flash fire in a restaurant was caused by negligence. An employee activated an extinguisher system which released some gas and created a hissing sound. On hearing this, a patron shouted that gas was escaping and that there was danger of an explosion. Patrons stampeded to the exits. During this rush the

plaintiff was injured. Although held liable initially, the original wrongdoer was ultimately relieved of liability.

In the Supreme Court of Canada, Mr. Justice Martland (Judson and Ritchie JJ. concurring) declared that the injuries "resulted from the hysterical conduct of a customer which occurred when the safety appliance properly fulfilled its function. Was that consequence fairly to be regarded as within the risk created by the respondent's negligence in permitting an undue quantity of grease to accumulate on the grill? The Court of Appeal has found that it was not and I agree with that finding."

Mr. Justice Spence (Laskin J., concurring), dissented and observed:

> I am not of the opinion that the persons who shouted the warning of what they were certain was an impending explosion were negligent. I am, on the other hand, of the opinion that they acted in a very human and usual way and that their actions ... were utterly foreseeable and were a part of the natural consequence of events leading inevitably to the plaintiff's injury. ... Even if the actions of those who called out "gas" and "it is going to explode" were negligent ... then I am of the opinion that the plaintiffs would still have a right of action against the defendants. ...

Which of these opinions do you prefer? What if no one had shouted but the plaintiff had seen the fire, attempted to escape and had fallen, injuring herself? Compare with *Mauney v. Gulf Refining Co.*, 9 So. 2d 780 (Miss. S.C. 1942) and *Zervobeakos v. Zervobeakos* (1970), 8 D.L.R. (3d) 377 (N.S.C.A.).

7. In *Canphoto Ltd. et al. v. Aetna Roofing (1965) Ltd. et al.*, [1965] 3 W.W.R. 116 (Man. Q.B.), the employees of the defendant company left three propane gas tanks in a public laneway over a weekend. In so doing, they breached a provincial regulation concerning the storage of such tanks with respect to the required distances they should be kept from buildings and fences. They were also found to be negligent in failing to chain the tanks closed and in an upright position. During the night someone apparently meddled with the tanks, causing a serious fire that damaged the plaintiff's premises.

   Wilson J. gave judgment for the plaintiff, rejecting the contention of the defendants that the meddling with the tanks constituted an intervening act which broke the chain of causation, explaining: "If what is relied upon as *novus actus interveniens* is the very kind of thing which is likely to happen if the want of care which is alleged takes place, the principle embodied in the maxim is no defence. ..." Mr. Justice Wilson found that the intervention was not a "fresh, independent cause" of the damage and that "... the person guilty of the original negligence will still be the effective cause if he ought reasonably to have anticipated such interventions...".

8. In *Stansbie v. Troman*, [1948] 2 K.B. 48, [1948] 1 All E.R. 599 (C.A.), a decorator, hired by a householder, left the house unlocked when he went out to purchase some material. While he was gone, a thief entered the house and stole some goods. The decorator sued the householder for the cost of his services, and the householder counterclaimed for the value of the stolen articles.

   In considering whether or not the decorator's negligence was the cause of the theft, Tucker L.J. stated:

   > [Here the] act of negligence itself consisted in the failure to take reasonable care to guard against the very thing that in fact happened. The reason why the decorator owed a duty to the householder to leave the premises in a reasonably secure state was because otherwise thieves or dishonest persons might gain access to them; and it seems to me that if the decorator was, as I think he was,

negligent in leaving the house in this condition, it was as a direct result of his negligence that the thief entered by the front door, which was left unlocked, and stole these valuable goods. Except that I would have phrased the nature of the duty somewhat differently from the way in which the county court judge put it, I am in entire agreement with his judgment, and in my view the appeal fails.

9. In *Allison v. Rank City Wall Canada* (1984), 45 O.R. (2d) 141, 6 D.L.R. (4th) 144 (H.C.J.), a woman was brutally assaulted in the underground garage of her apartment building. Relying in part on certain "assurances" made as to safety, and on the new *Occupiers' Liability Act*, R.S.O. 1980, c. 322, Mr. Justice Smith imposed liability, explaining that the assault was "a reasonably foreseeable one and ought to have been guarded against in this case." What if she had been raped? See *Q v. Minto Mgt.* (1985), 15 D.L.R. (4th) 581, 31 C.C.L.T. 158 (Ont. H.C.), *per* Gray J.; affd 57 O.R. (2d) 781*n*, 34 D.L.R. (4th) 767*n* (C.A.); see also *Jane Doe, infra*.

D. RECURRING SITUATIONS

1. Rescue

HORSLEY ET AL. v. MACLAREN ET AL. "THE OGOPOGO"

Supreme Court of Canada. (1972), 22 D.L.R. (3d) 545, [1972] S.C.R. 441; affg [1970] 2 O.R. 487, 11 D.L.R. (3d) 277 (C.A.); revg [1969] 2 O.R. 137, 4 D.L.R. (3d) 557.

The defendant, MacLaren, owned a cabin cruiser named The Ogopogo. On May 7, 1961, a cool spring day, he invited some friends to accompany him on a cruise on Lake Ontario. After visiting the Port Credit Yacht Club, they headed out into the harbour to return to Oakville, from where the cruise began. Brisk winds came up and made the water choppy, driving most of the passengers below. Matthews remained on the deck for a while, but he soon got up and proceeded toward the stern of the boat. For no apparent reason, he lost his footing and fell off the boat into the 44°F. water of the lake. This mishap was not caused by the negligence of anyone. Another passenger, Jones, exclaimed, "Roly's overboard." The craft had reached a point 40 to 50 feet beyond Matthews, and the appellant put the motor into reverse and backed the cruiser at once toward the man in the water. When it was within 4 or 5 feet of Matthews the engine was put into neutral position, but the wind caused the boat to drift away towards the port side. When Matthews was 10 feet from the vessel the appellant again put the engine into reverse and reached a point within 3 or 4 feet of him and he was drifting down towards the boat. At this juncture the passenger Marck was attempting to retrieve Matthew's body with a pikepole, but his efforts were unsuccessful.

Matthews had been in the water for a period estimated at approximately 3 to 4 minutes and at all times he was motionless, his head was well above the surface of the water and his arms were extended in front of him in a slightly elevated position, but his eyes were glassy. A life ring or life jacket thrown to him went unobserved and he was not making the slightest effort to assist himself. Marck came within 1 or 2 feet of him with the pikepole but Matthews did not react in any way and presented every appearance of having lost consciousness.

The appellant had no knowledge of Horsley's experience with watercraft and in the early stages of the journey had therefore warned him to remain in the cockpit or cabin and not to go on deck. When Horsley observed the difficulty which was being experienced in the effort to rescue Matthews, he removed his trousers and dived into the water, emerging from his dive approximately 10 feet away from Matthews who, at this time, was 3 or 4 feet from the vessel. A few seconds after Horsley's act of diving into the water Matthew's body sank below the surface and under the bottom of the boat on its starboard side near the stern. It disappeared from view and has never been recovered.

On observing what had happened to Matthews, Mrs. Jones, an experienced cold-water swimmer, plunged into the water in an effort to keep Matthews's head above water but she never had an opportunity to afford him this aid. Fearing for his wife's safety Jones, who was himself an experienced boatman, took the controls and caused the boat to describe a circle, moved it forward and brought it starboard side alongside his wife. She was thrashing about in the water and extended her arms towards MacLaren and Marck who succeeded in grasping her. Jones, responding to a call from MacLaren and Marck, came to their assistance and the trio succeeded in bringing her aboard.

MacLaren then resumed control of the vessel and drove it in a forward direction towards Horsley whose body was also retrieved from the water. From the moment that he re-appeared after his dive into the water, although he was known to have some ability as a swimmer, Horsley made no effort to help himself; his feet were down, he was floating with his head well above the surface of the water and his arms were extended forward, but when the rescuers reached him his head went under the water at that precise moment. The water of Lake Ontario is very cold in the hottest season of the year, but on the day in question it was bitterly cold.

A pathologist found that Horsley's death was caused by shock resulting from sudden immersion in the cold water.

Since the body of Matthews was never recovered, the exact cause of death remained unknown, but it was believed that he also died of a heart attack.

There had been some consumption of beer and champagne but there was no finding that any one was intoxicated as a result.

At the trial, Matthew's family was denied recovery on the ground that there was no evidence of causal relation between his death and MacLaren's conduct. Horsley's family, however, was successful. On appeal, the Ontario Court of Appeal reversed and dismissed the Horsley action. [The Matthews did not appeal.] The Supreme Court of Canada affirmed this disposition in a three-two decision.

Appeal allowed.

Ritchie J. (**Spence** and **Judson JJ.** concurring, in the Supreme Court of Canada): ... If, upon Matthews falling overboard, Horsley had immediately dived to his rescue and lost his life, as he ultimately did upon contact with the icy water, then I can see no conceivable basis on which the respondent could have been held responsible for his death.

There is, however, no suggestion that there was any negligence in the rescue of Horsley and if the respondent is to be held liable to the appellants, such liability must in my view stem from a finding that the situation of peril brought about by Matthews falling into the water was thereafter, within the next three or four minutes, so aggravated by the negligence of MacLaren in attempting his rescue as to induce Horsley to risk his life by diving in after him.

I think that the best description of the circumstances giving rise to the liability to a second rescuer such as Horsley is contained in the reasons for judgment of Lord Denning M.R., in *Videan v. British Transport Commission*, [1963] 2 Q.B. 650, where he said, at p. 669:

> It seems to me that, if a person *by his fault* creates a situation of peril, he must answer for it to any person who attempts to rescue the person who is in danger. He owes a duty to such a person above all others. The rescuer may act instinctively out of humanity or deliberately out of courage. But whichever it is, so long as it is not wanton interference, if the rescuer is killed or injured in the attempt, he can recover damages *from the one whose fault has been the cause of it*.

The italics are my own.

In the present case a situation of peril was created when Matthews fell overboard, but it was not created by any fault on the part of MacLaren, and before MacLaren can be found to have been in any way responsible for Horsley's death, it must be found that there was such negligence in his method of rescue as to place Matthews in an apparent position of increased danger subsequent to and distinct from the danger to which he had been initially exposed by his accidental fall. In other words, any duty owing to Horsley must stem from the fact that a new situation of peril was created by MacLaren's negligence which induced Horsley to act as he did. …

The finding of the learned trial judge that MacLaren was negligent in the rescue of Matthews is really twofold. On the one hand he finds that there was a failure to comply with the "man overboard" rescue procedure recommended by two experts called for the plaintiff, and on the other hand he concludes that MacLaren "was unable to exercise proper judgment in the emergency created because of his excessive consumption of alcohol". In the course of his reasons for judgment in the Court of Appeal, Mr. Justice Shroeder expressly found that there was nothing in the evidence to support the view that MacLaren was incapable of proper management and control owing to the consumption of liquor, the question was not seriously argued in this Court, and like my brother Laskin, I do not think there is any ground for saying that intoxicants had anything to do with the fatal occurrences. …

I share the view expressed by my brother Laskin when he says, in the course of his reasons for judgment, that:

> Encouragement by the common law of the rescue of persons in danger would, in my opinion, go beyond reasonable bounds if it involved liability of one rescuer to a succeeding one where the former has not been guilty of any fault which could be said to have induced a second rescue attempt.

In the present case, however, although the procedure followed by MacLaren was not the most highly recommended one, I do not think that the evidence justifies the finding that any fault of his induced Horsley to risk his life by diving as he did. In this regard I adopt the conclusion reached by Mr. Justice Schroeder in the penultimate paragraph of his reasons for judgment where he says [at p. 287]:

> … if the appellant erred in backing instead of turning the cruiser and proceeding towards Matthews "bow on", the error was one of judgment and not negligence, and in the existing circumstances of emergency ought fairly to be excused.

I think it should be made clear that, in my opinion, the duty to rescue a man who has fallen accidentally overboard is a common law duty, the existence of which is in no way dependent upon the provisions of s. 526(1) of the *Canada Shipping Act*, R.S.C. 1952, c. 29.

I should also say that, unlike Jessup J.A., the failure of Horsley to heed MacLaren's warning to remain in the cockpit or cabin plays no part in my reasoning.

For all these reasons I would dismiss this appeal with costs.

Laskin J. (dissenting, **Hall J.** concurring): In this court, counsel for the appellants relied on three alternative bases of liability. There was, first, the submission that in going to the aid of Matthews, as he did, MacLaren came under a duty to carry out the rescue with due care in the circumstances, and his failure to employ standard rescue procedures foreseeably brought Horsley into the picture with the ensuing fatal result. The second basis of liability was doubly founded as resting (a) on a common law duty of care of a private carrier to his passengers, involving a duty to come to the aid of a passenger who has accidentally fallen overboard, or (b) on a statutory duty under s. 526(1) of the *Canada Shipping Act*, R.S.C. 1952, c. 29, to come to the aid of a passenger who has fallen overboard. There was failure, so the allegation was, to act reasonably in carrying out these duties or either of them, with the foreseeable consequence of Horsley's encounter of danger. The third contention was the broadest, to the effect that where a situation of peril, albeit not brought about originally by the defendant's negligence, arises by reason of the defendant's attempt at rescue, he is liable to a second rescuer for ensuing damage on the ground that the latter's intervention is reasonably foreseeable.

None of the bases of liability advanced by the appellants is strictly within the original principle on which the "rescue" cases were founded. That was the recognition of a duty by a negligent defendant to a rescuer coming to the aid of the person imperilled by the defendant's negligence. The evolution of the law on this subject, originating in the moral approbation of assistance to a person in peril, involved a break with the "mind your own business" philosophy. Legal protection is now afforded to one who risks injury to himself in going to the rescue of another who has been foreseeably exposed to danger by the unreasonable conduct of a third person. The latter is now subject to liability at the suit of the rescuer as well as at the suit of the imperilled person, provided, in the case of the rescuer, that his intervention was not so utterly foolhardy as to be outside of any accountable risk and thus beyond even contributory negligence.

Moreover, the liability to the rescuer, although founded on the concept of duty, is now seen as stemming from an independent and not a derivative duty of the negligent person. As *Fleming on Torts*, 3rd ed. (1965), has put it (at p. 166), the cause of action of the rescuer in arising out of the defendant's negligence, is based "not in its tendency to imperil the person rescued, but in its tendency to induce the rescuer to encounter the danger. Thus viewed, the duty to the rescuer is clearly independent. ..." This explanation of principle was put forward as early as 1924 by Professor Bohlen (see his *Studies in the Law of Torts*, at p. 569) in recognition of the difficulty of straining the notion of foreseeability to embrace a rescuer of a person imperilled by another's negligence. Under this explanation of the basis of liability, it is immaterial that the imperilled person does not in fact suffer any injury or that, as it turns out, the negligent person was under no liability to him either because the injury was not caused by the negligence or the damage was outside the foreseeable risk of harm to him: *cf.*, *Videan v. British Transport Commission*, [1963] 2 Q.B. 650. It is a further consequence of the recognition of an independent duty that a person who imperils himself by his carelessness may be as fully liable to a rescuer as a third person would be who imperils another. In my opinion, therefore, *Dupuis v. New Regina Trading Co. Ltd.*, [1943] 4 D.L.R. 275, [1943] 2 W.W.R. 593, ought no longer to be taken as a statement of the common law in Canada in so far as it denies recovery because the rescuer was injured in going to the aid of a person who imperilled himself. The doctrinal issues are sufficiently canvassed by the late Dean Wright in 21 Can. Bar Rev. 758 (1943); and see also *Ward v. T.E. Hopkins & Son, Ltd.; Baker v. T.E. Hopkins & Son Ltd.*, [1959] 3 All E.R. 225.

I realize that this statement of the law invites the conclusion that Horsley's estate might succeed against that of Matthews if it was proved that Matthews acted without proper care for his own safety so that Horsley was prompted to come to his rescue. This issue does not, however, have to be canvassed in these proceedings since the estate of Matthews was not joined as a co-defendant.

The thinking behind the rescue cases, in so far as they have translated a moral impulse into a legally protectible interest, suggests that liability to a rescuer should not depend on whether there was original negligence which created the peril and which, therefore, prompted the rescue effort. It would appear that the principle should be equally applicable if, at any stage of the perilous situation, there was negligence on the defendant's part which induced the rescuer to attempt the rescue or which operated against him after he had made the attempt. If this be so, it indicates the possibility of an action by a second rescuer against a first. On one view of the present case, this is what we have here. It is not, however, a view upon which, under the facts herein, the present case falls to be decided.

The reason is obvious. MacLaren was not a random rescuer. As owner and operator of a boat on which he was carrying invited guests, he was under a legal duty to take reasonable care for their safety. This was a duty which did not depend on the existence of a contract of carriage, nor on whether he was a common carrier or a private carrier of passengers. Having brought his guests into a relationship with him as passengers on his boat, albeit as social or gratuitous passengers, he was obliged to exercise reasonable care for their safety. That obligation extends, in my opinion, to rescue from perils of the sea where this is consistent with his duty to see to the safety of his other passengers and with concern for his own safety. The duty exists whether the passenger falls overboard accidentally or by reason of his own carelessness.

I would hold that *Vanvalkenburg v. Northern Navigation Co.* (1913), 19 D.L.R. 649, 30 O.L.R. 142, should no longer be considered as good law in so far as it declared that operators of a ship were not under any legal duty to a seaman in their employ to go to his rescue when he fell overboard through his own carelessness. The Ontario Appellate Division in that case saw the facts through the classifications of non-feasance and misfeasance, and was not prepared to read the contract of hiring as imposing an affirmative obligation to protect the drowning seaman from the consequences of his own carelessness. Since the ship operators did not create any unreasonable risk of harm, the Appellate Division could not find any ground for holding them liable.

I do not accept this reasoning, based as it was on the state of the law of torts that did not yet know even *M'Alister (or Donoghue) v. Stevenson*, [1932] A.C. 562. Affirmative duties of care arise out of the relationship of employer and employee and out of the relationship of carrier and passenger, to take two examples. Where these relationships occur on board a ship at sea, the employee or passenger, who falls overboard from whatever cause, should be entitled to look for succour to the operators of the ship because of necessary dependency on them for return to shore. Such a duty of rescue was recognized in *Harris v. Pennsylvania Railroad Co.* (1931), 50 F. 2d 866, and in *The "Cappy", Hutchinson v. Dickie* (1947), 162 F. 2d 103; *cert.* denied, 332 U.S. 830, a case to which I will return because it is so strikingly similar on its facts to the present case.

I do not rest the duty to which I would hold MacLaren in this case on s. 526(1) of the *Canada Shipping Act*, even assuming that its terms are broad enough to embrace the facts herein. That provision, a penal one, is as follows:

> 526(1) The master or person in charge of a vessel shall, so far as he can do so without serious danger to his own vessel, her crew and passengers, if any, render assistance to every person, even if that person be a subject of a foreign state at war with Her Majesty, who is found at sea and in danger of being lost, and if he fails to do so he is liable to a fine not exceeding one thousand dollars.

I do not find it necessary in this case to consider whether s. 526(1), taken alone, entails civil consequences for failure to perform a statutory duty; or, even, whether it fixes a standard of conduct upon which the common law may operate to found liability. There is an independent basis for a common law duty of care in the relationship of carrier to passenger, but the legislative declaration of policy s. 526(1) is a fortifying element in the recognition of that duty, being in harmony with it in a comparable situation.

It follows from this assessment that MacLaren cannot be regarded as simply a good Samaritan. Rather it is Horsley who was in that role, exposing himself to danger upon the alleged failure of MacLaren properly to carry out his duty to effect Matthews' rescue. The present case is, therefore, not one to which the principles propounded in *East Suffolk Rivers Catchment Board v. Kent*, [1941] A.C. 74, are applicable. In the Court of Appeal, both Schroeder J.A., and Jessup J.A., referred to this case with approval. The former relied on it to support his rejection of the trial judge's holding that MacLaren was liable when, having undertaken to rescue Matthews, he failed to use reasonable care in the rescue operation. In the opinion of Schroeder J.A., as noted earlier in these reasons, there was no basis for holding that MacLaren's rescue efforts, even if improperly carried out, worsened Matthews' condition and thus induced Horsley to come to his rescue. Jessup J.A. would have applied this test of liability if the case, for him, had turned on the voluntary undertaking by MacLaren of rescue operations. Since, on the view taken by Jessup J.A. MacLaren had an antecedent or original duty to render assistance, the *East Suffolk Rivers Catchment Board* case did not apply.

Whether a case involving the exercise of statutory powers (but not duties) by a public authority should govern the issue of liability or non-liability to an injured rescuer is a question that need not be answered here. It has been widely noted that there is some incongruity in imposing liability upon a good Samaritan when he who passes by does not attract it. Legislation has been called in aid in some jurisdictions: see Note, 64 Col. L. Rev. 1301 (1964). However, the problem raised by the rescue cases with respect to the *East Suffolk Rivers Catchment Board* principles is the more ramified if the issue thereunder is one of liability to a rescuer as well as to a rescuee, and if it turns on an independent rather than on a derivative duty to the rescuer by the volunteer defendant. There is, hence, all the more reason to leave the problem to be considered on facts which raise it squarely.

On the view that I take of the issues in this case and, having regard to the facts, the appellants cannot succeed on the first of their alternative submissions on liability if they cannot succeed on the second ground of an existing common law duty of care. Their third contention was not clearly anchored in any original or supervening duty of care and breach of that duty; and, if that be so, I do not see how their counsel's submission on the foreseeability of a second rescuer, even if accepted, can saddle a non-negligent first rescuer with liability either to the rescuee or to a second rescuer. Encouragement by the common law of the rescue of persons in danger would, in my opinion, go beyond reasonable bounds if it involved liability of one rescuer to a succeeding one where the former has not been guilty of any fault which could be said to have induced a second rescue attempt.

If the appellant's third contention was based on any element of fault, it could only be fault in carrying out the attempt at rescue; and, moreover, it would have to be founded on a wide view of Lord Denning's statement in the *Videan* case, *supra,* at p. 669 where he said that "if a person by his fault creates a situation of peril, he must answer for it to any person who attempts to rescue the person who is in danger". There is no factual basis upon which to consider the extension of Lord Denning's proposition which underlies the appellants' third submission in the alternative view of it that I have taken. In so far as it rests on an allegation that fault arose only in the bungling of the rescue attempt (there being no anterior duty), no such finding is warranted. Beyond this, it invites a return to the principles of the *East Suffolk Rivers Catchment Board* case, and I do not wish to repeat what I have already said with respect to them.

The present case is thus reduced to the question of liability on the basis of (1) an alleged breach of a duty of care originating in the relationship of carrier and passenger; (2) whether the breach, if there was one, could be said to have prompted Horsley to go to Matthews' rescue; and (3) whether Horsley's conduct, if not so rash in the circumstances as to be unforeseeable, none the less exhibited want of care so as to make him guilty of contributory negligence.

Whether MacLaren was in breach of his duty of care to Matthews was a question of fact on which the trial judge's affirmative finding is entitled to considerable weight. That finding was, of course, essential to the further question of a consequential duty to Horsley. Lacourciere J., came to his conclusion of fact on the evidence, after putting to himself the following question: "What would the reasonable boat operator do in the circumstances, attributing to such person the reasonable skill and experience required of the master of a cabin cruiser who is responsible for the safety and rescue of his passengers?" (see 4 D.L.R. (3d) 557 at p. 564, [1969] 2 O.R. 137). It was the trial judge's finding that MacLaren, as he himself admitted, had adopted the wrong procedure of rescuing a passenger who had fallen overboard. He knew the proper procedure, and had practised it. Coming bow on to effect a rescue was the standard procedure and was taught as such.

MacLaren's answer to the allegation of a breach of duty was that he had been guilty merely of an error of judgment. This was the view taken by the majority in the Ontario Court of Appeal who were moved by the element of emergency. What makes this view vulnerable is that this was not a case where MacLaren had failed to execute the required manoeuvre properly, but rather one where he had not followed the method of rescue which, on the uncontradicted evidence, was the proper one to employ in an emergency. There was no external reason for his failure to do so. Jones demonstrated that in the rescue of his wife. Further, after MacLaren's first abortive attempt at rescue, over a period of time which the evidence indicated would have been sufficient to effect a bow-on rescue, he made a second attempt with the wrong procedure. It was only then, with the lapse of three or four minutes after Matthews had fallen overboard, that Horsley went to his rescue. I note also that after MacLaren resumed control of his boat from Jones he went bow on to rescue Horsley.

I do not see how it can be said that the trial judge's finding against MacLaren on the issue of breach of duty is untenable. In relation to Horsley's intervention, the finding stands unembarrassed by any question of causation in relation to Matthews. This, at least, distinguishes the present case from *Hutchinson v. Dickie, supra.*

There, as here, an invited guest on a cabin cruiser fell overboard and drowned during a lake cruise. The owner and operator of the boat was blameless in respect of the fall overboard, but the trial judge found liability for wrongful death on breach of duty to act reasonably to effect a rescue. There, as here, the owner-operator, on hearing the cry "man overboard", reversed and backed astern towards the drowning man. He was then about 75 ft. away from the boat. Two life rings were thrown to Dickie, the drowning man, one falling within 20 ft. and the other within six feet of him, but he paid no attention to them. A boat hook was then made ready for use, but Dickie disappeared when the boat was 20 to 25 ft. away. The trial judge found negligence, *inter alia*, in the failure to turn the boat and come bow on. On appeal the action was dismissed on several grounds. The appellate Court held that there was "an entire lack of evidence that anything appellant did or left undone caused his efforts at rescue to fail". This was enough to dispose of the case, as it was enough to dispose of the Matthews' action. On a question more germane to the present case, the court agreed that there was a duty of rescue owed to Dickie, but held that a breach was not established by the backing-up procedure that was employed; and, if there was an error, it was one of judgment only in dealing with an emergency. The court noted that there was a conflict of evidence on the issue of coming bow on or backing up, and this too distinguishes *Hutchinson v. Dickie* (which, moreover, was not an action by a rescuer's estate) from the present case which was decided more than 20 years later.

I turn to the question whether the breach of duty to Matthews could properly be regarded in this case as prompting Horsley to attempt a rescue. Like the trial judge, I am content to adopt and apply analogically on this point the reasoning of Cardozo J., as he then was, in *Wagner v. International R. Co.* (1921), 133 N.E. 437, and of Lord Denning M.R., in *Videan v. British Transport Commission, supra*. To use Judge Cardozo's phrase, Horsley's conduct in the circumstances was "within the range of the natural and probable". The fact, moreover, that Horsley's sacrifice was futile is no more a disabling ground here than it was in the *Wagner* case, where the passenger thrown off the train was dead when the plaintiff went to help him, unless it be the case that the rescuer acted wantonly.

In the Ontario Court of Appeal, Schroeder J.A., as previously noted, took the view that Horsley was not justified in going to the rescue of Matthews unless MacLaren worsened Matthews' situation through want of reasonable care. I need say no more on this view than that it proceeds on the basis of the *East Suffolk Rivers Catchment Board* principles which are not applicable to the facts of the present case.

Of more concern here is the position taken by Jessup J.A., which, to put it again briefly, was that whoever MacLaren should have foreseen as a rescuer, it could not be Horsley. I cannot agree with this ground of exoneration of MacLaren when it is founded merely on his having told Horsley to confine himself to the cabin and cockpit. MacLaren's evidence on this matter was that he had not previously met Horsley, he did not know his experience with boating and water, and hence he did not want him on deck. In my opinion, this evidence is no more telling against Horsley as a rescuer than it would be against Horsley as a rescuee if he had come on deck and had then fallen overboard. Moreover, the considerations which underlie a duty to a rescuer do not justify ruling out a particular rescuer if it be not wanton of him to intervene. The implication of Jessup J.A.'s position is that Horsley required MacLaren's consent to go to Matthews' rescue. This is not, in my view, a sufficient answer in the circumstances which existed by reason of MacLaren's breach of duty. To quote again Judge Cardozo in the *Wagner* case, "The law does not discriminate between the rescuer oblivious of peril and the one who counts the cost. It is enough that the act whether impulsive or deliberate is the child of the occasion." (133 N.E. 437 at p. 438).

In responding as he did, and in circumstances where only hindsight made it doubtful that Matthews could be saved, Horsley was not wanton or foolhardy. Like the trial judge, I do not think that his action passed the point of brave acceptance of a serious risk and became a futile exhibition of recklessness for which there can be no recourse. There is, however, the question whether Horsley was guilty of contributory negligence. This was an alternative plea of the respondent based, *inter alia*, on Horsley's failure to put on a life-jacket or secure himself to the boat by a rope or call on the other passengers to stand by, especially in the light of the difficulties of Matthews in the cold water. The trial judge rejected the contentions of contributory negligence, holding that although "Wearing a life-jacket or securing himself to a lifeline would have been more prudent. ... Horsley's impulsive act without such precautions was the result of the excitement, haste and confusion of the moment, and cannot be said to constitute contributory negligence" (see 4 D.L.R. (3d) at p. 569). In view of its conclusions on the main issue of MacLaren's liability, the Ontario Court of Appeal did not canvass the question of contributory negligence.

The matter is not free from difficulty. About two minutes passed after Matthews had fallen overboard and MacLaren made his first abortive attempt at rescue by proceeding astern. Two life-jackets had been successively thrown towards Matthews without any visible effort on his part to seize them. Then came the second attempt at rescue by backing the boat, and it was in progress when Horsley dived in. Horsley had come on deck at the shout of "Roly's overboard" and was at the stern during MacLaren's first attempt at rescue, and must have been there when the life-jackets were thrown towards Matthews. However, in the concern of the occasion, and having regard to MacLaren's breach of duty, I do not think that Horsley can be charged with contributory negligence in diving to the rescue of Matthews as he did. I point out as well that the evidence does not indicate that the failure to put on a life-jacket or secure himself to a lifeline played any part in Horsley's death.

NOTES

1. The leading American case on this issue is considered to be *Wagner v. International Railway Co.*, 133 N.E. 437 (N.Y.C.A. 1921), in which Mr. Justice Benjamin Cardozo wrote these memorable words:

> Danger invites rescue. The cry of distress is the summons to relief. The law does not ignore these reactions of the mind in tracing conduct to its consequences. It recognizes them as normal. It places their effects within the range of the natural and probable. The wrong that imperils life is a wrong to the imperilled victim; it is a wrong also to his rescuer. The state that leaves an opening in a bridge is liable to the child that falls into the stream, but liable also to the parent who plunges to its aid. ... The railroad company whose train approaches without a signal is a wrongdoer toward the traveler surprised between the rails, but a wrongdoer also to the bystander who drags him from the path. ... The risk of rescue, if only it be not wanton, is born of the occasion. The emergency begets the man. The wrongdoer may not have foreseen the coming of a deliverer. He is accountable as if he had.

The leading English case is considered to be *Haynes v. Harwood*, [1953] 1 K.B. 146, [1934] All E.R. Rep. 103 (C.A.).

2. Apparently unnoticed by most scholars, the Canadian courts had much earlier recognized a duty to the rescuer. In *Seymour v. Winnipeg Electric Ry.* (1910), 19 Man. R. 412, 13 W.L.R. 566 (C.A.), the court on a demurrer declared that a rescuer could recover. Mr. Justice Richards recognized that "the promptings of humanity towards the saving of life are amongst the noblest instincts of mankind..." and concluded that "The trend of modern legal thought is toward holding that those who risk their safety in attempting to rescue others who are put in peril by the negligence of third parties are entitled to claim such compensation from such third parties for injuries they may receive in such attempts. ..." This is particularly the case if "those whom it is sought to rescue are infirm or helpless". As an afterthought, Mr. Justice Richards added that the company had "notice" that "some brave man is likely to risk his own life to save the helpless", which indicates that the idea of notice or knowledge (or foresight if you will) was a relevant consideration.

3. Does a rescued person owe the rescuer a duty to avoid getting into a position of peril? See *Baker v. Hopkins*, [1958] 3 All E.R. 147; affd, [1959] 1 W.L.R. 966, [1959] 3 All E.R. 225 (C.A.), where, at trial, Mr. Justice Barry stated:

> Although no one owes a duty to anyone else to preserve his own safety, yet if, by his own carelessness a man puts himself into a position of peril of a kind that invites rescue, he would in law be liable for any injury caused to someone whom he ought to have foreseen would attempt to come to his aid.

See also *C.N.R. v. Bakty* (1977), 18 O.R. (2d) 481 (Co. Ct.); *Chapman v. Hearse* (1961), 106 C.L.R. 112 (H.C. Aust.), rescued person held 25 per cent liable to rescuer who was hit by negligently driven vehicle. The case of *Dupuis v. New Regina Trading Post,* [1943] 4 D.L.R. 275, [1943] 2 W.W.R. 593 (Sask. C.A.), which indicated that there was no such duty, was discredited by Mr. Justice Laskin in *Horsley v. MacLaren*. The English courts have also adopted this view; see *Harrison v. British Railways Bd.*, [1981] 3 All E.R. 679 (Q.B.). Could Mrs. Horsley have recovered from Matthews? What would it depend upon? Why do you think she refrained from suing?

4. Does one rescuer owe a duty to another potential rescuer to use care? Should a rescuer of a rescuer be able to recover from the negligent person who created the initial danger?

5. Should a rescuer of property be entitled to recover for personal injury? See *Connell v. Prescott* (1892), 20 O.A.R. 49; affd 22 S.C.R. 147; *Hutterly v. Imperial Oil*, [1956] O.W.N. 681, [1956] 3 D.L.R. (2d) 719 (H.C.); *Hyett v. Great Western Ry.*, [1948] 1 K.B. 345, [1947] 2 All E.R. 264 (C.A.); *Toy v. Argenti* (1980), 17 B.C.L.R. 365, [1980] 3 W.W.R. 276 (S.C.). What if the damage suffered during the attempt is to property only? See *Thorn v. James* (1903), 14 Man. R. 373.

6. What about a futile rescue attempt? For example, what if the person being rescued is already dead? Does it make any difference if the plaintiff reasonably believes the person being rescued is not dead? What if the person being rescued is not really in any danger? Does it make any difference if the rescuer reasonably believes the person being rescued is in danger?

7. In *Moddejonge et al. v. Huron County (Bd. of Education) et al.*, [1972] 2 O.R. 437, 25 D.L.R. (3d) 661 (H.C.), an employee of the defendant school board took some young people for a swim. Two girls were carried out into deep water by a surface current caused by a fresh breeze that suddenly developed. Geraldine Moddejonge immediately swam to their assistance, rescued one of them [Sandra Thompson] but drowned while trying to save the other girl. The parents of both deceased girls successfully

sued the board for negligence. In discussing the liability to the rescuer, Mr. Justice Pennell stated:

> There is no general duty to assist anyone in peril. It is a great reproach to our legal institutions that rescuers for many years were denied recovery by a train of reasoning based on the concept of voluntary assumption of the risk. Eventually justice comes to live with men rather than with books. It fell to Justice Cardozo to allow the claim of humanity. I borrow, with respectful gratitude, a passage from his judgment in *Wagner v. Int'l R. Co.* [His Lordship quoted the famous passage beginning "Danger invites rescue."]
>
> The principle thus established has been followed since. It was delicately argued that the efforts of Geraldine Moddejonge constituted a rash and futile gesture; that reasonableness did not attach to her response. Upon this, the rescue of Sandra Thompson is sufficient answer. One must not approach the problem with the wisdom that comes after the event. Justice is not to be measured in such scales. To Geraldine Moddejonge duty did not hug the shore of safety. Duty did not give her a choice. She accepted it. She discharged it. More need not be said. The law will give her actions a sanctuary.

8. What if the conduct of the rescuer is not foolhardy but merely negligent? What about the contributory negligence technique? In *Sayers v. Harlow Urban District Council*, [1958] 1 W.L.R. 623, [1958] 2 All E.R. 342 (C.A.), the plaintiff was negligently locked into a public lavatory. In attempting to extricate herself from her predicament by climbing out of the stall, she was injured. Lord Justice Morris stated:

> The conduct being examined has to be tested and considered in the light of the circumstances. The question in the present case is whether the injury sustained by the plaintiff resulted either entirely or partly from the defendants' breach of duty. The defendants assert that, as the plaintiff was in no danger and was in no serious inconvenience, she acted unreasonably in doing what she did, so that she and she alone was the authoress of the injury that befell her.
>
> I do not think that the plaintiff should be adjudged in all the circumstances to have acted unreasonably or rashly or stupidly. As to nearly everything that she did, in my judgment she acted carefully and prudently. Indeed, she showed a very considerable measure of self-control. My Lord has fully recited the facts, and there is no need for me to refer to them again. The learned Judge has found them carefully, and the only advantage that he has over us is that he actually saw the plaintiff herself. Subject to that advantage which in the present is comparatively slight, we are in as good a position as the Judge to determine this matter. What did the plaintiff do? First, she did her best to operate the lock. She tried with her finger to see whether there was any way of making it work. There was not. She then tried to get her hand through the window. She was unable to do that. She then banged on the door. Nobody came. She shouted. There was no response. Ten or fifteen minutes went by. The situation could not have been an agreeable one. What did she then do? It appears to me on the evidence that what she did was to explore the possibility of climbing over the door. That I cannot think was unwise or imprudent, or rash or stupid. I have therefore come to the same conclusion as that expressed by my Lord. Like my Lord, I feel that the plaintiff cannot entirely be absolved from some measure of fault — the fault described by my Lord — and I am in agreement that that measure should be marked by depriving her of one-quarter of that to which she would otherwise be entitled. I consider that the appeal should be allowed to the extent that my Lord has indicated.

If the plaintiff did not act "unreasonably" but "carefully and prudently", why deprive her of one-quarter of her damages?

9. In *Cleary v. Hansen* (1981), 18 C.C.L.T. 147, at 156, 13 M.V.R. 161 (Ont. S.C.), Linden J. held a rescuer contributorily negligent and reduced his damages by 10 per cent explaining that:

> ... even during an attempt to assist someone in an emergency, the law expects reasonable care to be exercised, even though the standard is relaxed to a certain extent. The court does not expect perfection, but rescuers must be sensible. They, like anyone else, must weigh the advantages and risks of their conduct. Their conduct too, however laudable, must measure up to the standard of the reasonable person in similar circumstances.

10. Should a father who donates a kidney to his daughter, who lost her kidney through the negligence of a doctor, recover damages from that doctor? Is he like a rescuer? Is this foreseeable? See *Urbanski v. Patel* (1978), 84 D.L.R. (3d) 650, at 671, 2 L.M.Q. 54 (Man. Q.B.), *per* Wilson J.

11. In *Corothers et al. v. Slobodian et al.* (1973), 36 D.L.R. (3d) 597 (Sask. C.A.); revd in part (1975), 51 D.L.R. (3d) 1, [1975] 3 W.W.R. 142 (S.C.C.), the plaintiff, Bonnie Corothers, was driving along the highway when the vehicle in front of her, driven by Anton Hammerschmid, collided with a vehicle being driven negligently by one Neil Poupard, who was killed in the accident. The plaintiff stopped her car and went over to assist. Seeing several severely injured people, she decided that she should try to get help. She ran along the highway intending to get aid. At this point, about 50 feet down the road, a semi-trailer truck, driven by Slobodian, approached. Slobodian, on seeing the plaintiff, Bonnie Corothers, put on his brakes, but the truck jack-knifed, went into the ditch and injured her.

The plaintiff's actions against both Slobodian and the estate of the late Neil Poupard were dismissed at trial. The Saskatchewan Court of Appeal affirmed.

With regard to the action against Poupard, Woods J.A. observed:

> ... the female plaintiff had completed all that she was going to do at the scene of the collision before the arrival of the truck driven by Slobodian. She had left the scene of the accident and her activities had reached a new stage. The situation of peril created by Poupard had ended. The plaintiff was not then acting in danger nor anticipating any danger created by the acts of Poupard. The injury suffered arose from a new act or circumstance, which was not one that ought reasonably to have been foreseeable by Poupard. ...

As to the defendant Slobodian, Woods J.A. explained that he came upon an "unusual situation not of his own creation. The standards to be applied are not those of perfection. If he made a mistake of judgment, it is excusable in the circumstances."

The Supreme Court of Canada unanimously reversed the decision as against Poupard but the majority affirmed as against Slobodian. With regard to Poupard, Mr. Justice Ritchie explained that Mrs. Corothers' acts "in attempting to flag down the approaching traffic were, in my view, perfectly normal reactions to the cry of distress...". It was a "reasonably foreseeable consequence of Poupard's negligence which in my view was a cause, if not the only cause, of Mrs. Corothers' injury". In relation to Slobodian, Mr. Justice Ritchie stated that "faced with a gesticulating woman on the side of the highway ... he was acting in a moment of imminent emergency" so that "his error of judgment" was not actionable negligence.

Mr. Justice Pigeon, for the minority, felt that both Poupard and Slobodian should be liable. On the issue of Poupard's liability, His Lordship stated:

> I just cannot accept that this can be said not to be foreseeable by the author of the first collision. Multiple collisions are such frequent occurrences that dangerous emergency manoeuvres to avoid them are to be expected.
>
> ... To say that [Mrs. Corothers] was not acting in danger nor anticipating any danger created by the acts of Poupard is to ignore the realities of the situation. What she was doing was nothing but the proper reaction to those acts and an attempt to avoid or to mitigate some of their dreadful consequences.

See Binchi, "Comment" (1974), 52 Can. Bar Rev. 292.

12. Should a professional rescuer (a firefighter or police officer) be able to sue for injuries sustained during the course of duties? See *Ogwo v. Taylor*, [1987] 3 All E.R. 961 (H.L.).

13. See Linden, "Down With Foreseeability! Of Thin Skulls and Rescuers" (1969), 47 Can. Bar Rev. 545:

> In these rescue cases the same decisions have been reached whatever formula was used. This is because the courts have decided to use tort law to encourage rescuers by rewarding them if they are injured. In addition, the courts are hopeful that they will deter, both specifically and generally, enterprisers who cause accidents. If someone knows that he will be liable not only to those he injures but to their rescuers, he may be more careful. It is also better for an activity to pay its way by being required to reimburse not only those injured by the activity directly but also the rescuers of those injured. Furthermore, the loss distribution and social welfare goals of tort law are served by spreading liability. Foreseeability disguises this analysis and, therefore, I say down with foreseeability!

Do you agree?

2. Second Accident

WIELAND v. CYRIL LORD CARPETS, LTD.

Queen's Bench Division. [1969] 3 All E.R. 1066.

On October 4, 1965, the plaintiff was injured in a bus accident due to the negligence of the defendant. She was X-rayed in the hospital and told to return two days later. She did and was fitted with a collar for her neck. On leaving the hospital, she felt "rather muzzy", as though her head was useless. She was also in a nervous condition, both because of the accident and the visit to the doctor. The plaintiff wore bifocal glasses and had done so for ten years. The collar on her neck deprived her of the ability to adjust herself to the use of the bifocals. The combination of these factors produced some unsteadiness.

She called on her son at his office to ask him to take her home. He saw her as she reached the first floor of his office building. He told her to stay where she was and he would come down to her. This he did, and together they descended the stairs and on reaching the last step or about the last step, the plaintiff fell, because she did not show her habitual skill in descending the stairs when wearing bifocal glasses.

Eveleigh J.: In those circumstances, I have to value this claim. On behalf of the defence it has been argued that this plaintiff's fall and the injury to the ankles resulting therefrom was not caused by the defendant's negligence. Alternatively it is said, if that injury was so caused then it was not foreseeable and reliance is placed on *Overseas Tankship (U.K.) Ltd. v. Morts Dock & Engineering Co. Ltd., The Wagon Mound (No. 1)*. As to the first contention, I find that the fall and the resulting injury was caused by the defendant's negligence. I find that it was the result of the injury inflicted in that accident. The plaintiff's ability to negotiate stairs was impaired and this resulted in a fall, which was a fall, in my view, in one of the ordinary activities of life for which she had been rendered less capable than she previously was. ...

I think it is also important in the present case to bear in mind that her fall occurred very soon after she was fitted with the collar. The position might have been different if a person were to persist in wearing bifocal glasses for a long time after an injury such as this and then sustain another injury. The effect of the original accident might be more difficult to demonstrate.

It has long been recognised that injury sustained in one accident may be the cause of a subsequent injury. The injury sustained by accident victims on the operating table is an example of that situation. So too are cases of suicide resulting from a mental condition produced by an accident. ... It is always a question of course for the court in each case to determine whether or not on the facts of that case the accident did cause the second injury or death as the case might be. ...

So now I turn to the second part of the defendants' argument, namely that the fall and the resulting injury was something that was not foreseeable and therefore does not attract damages...

I do not read *The Wagon Mound (No. 1)* as dealing with the extent of the original injury or the degree to which it has affected the plaintiff. Still less do I regard it as requiring foreseeability of the manner in which that original injury has caused harm to the plaintiff. Indeed the precise mechanics of the way in which the negligent act results in the original injury does not have to be foreseen....

Once actionable injury is established, compensation is rarely if ever a valuation of the injury simpliciter. It is a valuation of harm suffered as a result of that injury. The valuation which the law adopts is the valuation of that injury with its attendant consequences to the victim. Consequences of a kind which human experience indicates may result from an injury are weighed in the scale of valuation to a greater or lesser extent depending on the probability of their materialising. When they have materialised they attract full value. When they are only a risk they attract less value. But in determining liability for those possible consequences it is not necessary to show that each was within the foreseeable extent or foreseeable scope of the original injury in the same way that the possibility of injury must be foreseen when determining whether or not the defendant's conduct gives a claim in negligence. ...

I think that it is perfectly permissible in the present case to say that it is no answer to the claim for damages, that she would not have suffered had she not had eyesight that required her to wear bifocal lenses. ...

In the present case I am concerned with the extent of the harm suffered by the plaintiff as a result of actionable injury. In my view the injury and damage suffered because of the second fall are attributable to the original negligence of the defendants so as to attract compensation. If necessary I think the plaintiff's case can also be put against the defendant in another way. It can be said that it is foreseeable that one injury may affect a person's ability to cope with the vicissitudes of life and thereby be a cause of another injury and if foreseeability is required, that is to say, if foreseeability is the right word in this context, foreseeability of this general nature will, in my view, suffice. ...

Judgment for the plaintiff.

McKEW v. HOLLAND ET AL.

House of Lords. [1969] 3 All E.R. 1621, 170 S.L.T. 68.

The plaintiff's leg had been weakened in an accident for which the defendants were liable. As a result, his leg would give way beneath him occasionally. One day, as he commenced to descend some steep stairs, unassisted and without holding on, his leg collapsed and he began to fall downstairs. He pushed his daughter, who was with him, out of the way and tried to jump so as to land in a standing position, rather than falling down the stairs. On landing, he broke his ankle, a much more serious injury than the original one.

Lord Reid: ... The appellant's case is that this second accident was caused by the weakness of his left leg which in turn had been caused by the first accident. The main argument for the respondents is that the second accident was not the direct or natural and probable or foreseeable result of their fault in causing the first accident.

In my view the law is clear. If a man is injured in such a way that his leg may give way any moment he must act reasonably and carefully. It is quite possible that in spite of all reasonable care his leg may give way in circumstances such that as a result he sustains further injury. Then that second injury was caused by his disability which in turn was caused by the defender's fault. But if the injured man acts unreasonably he cannot hold the defender liable for injury caused by his own unreasonable conduct. His unreasonable conduct is *novus actus interveniens*. The chain of causation has been broken and what follows must be regarded as caused by his own conduct and not by the defender's fault or the disability caused by it. Or one may say that unreasonable conduct of the pursuer and what follows from it is not the natural and probable result of the original fault of the defender or of the ensuing disability. I do not think that foreseeability comes into this. A defender is not liable for a consequence of a kind which is not foreseeable. But it does not follow that he is liable for every consequence which a reasonable man could foresee. What can be foreseen depends almost entirely on the facts of the case, and it is often easy to foresee unreasonable conduct or some other *novus actus interveniens* as being quite likely. But that does not mean that the defender must pay for damage caused by the *novus actus*. It only leads to trouble if one tries to graft on to the concept of foreseeability some rule of law to the effect that a wrongdoer is not bound to foresee something which in fact he could readily foresee as quite likely to happen. For it is not at all unlikely or unforeseeable that an active man who has suffered such a disability will take some quite unreasonable risk. But if he does he cannot hold the defender liable for the consequences.

So in my view the question is whether the second accident was caused by the appellant doing something unreasonable. It was argued that the wrongdoer must take his victim as he finds him and that that applies not only to a thin skull but also to his intelligence. But I shall not deal with that argument because there is nothing in the evidence to suggest that the appellant is abnormally stupid. This case can be dealt with equally well by asking whether the appellant did something which a moment's reflection would have shown him was an unreasonable thing to do.

He knew that his leg was liable to give way suddenly and without warning. He knew that this stair was steep and that there was no handrail. He must have realised, if he had given the matter a moment's thought, that he could only safely descend the stair if he either went extremely slow and carefully so that he could sit down if his leg gave way, or waited for the assistance of his wife and brother-in-law. But he chose to descend in such a way that when his leg gave way he could not stop himself. I agree with what the Lord Justice-Clerk says at the end of his opinion and I think that this is sufficient to require this appeal to be dismissed.

But I think it right to say a word about the argument that the fact that the appellant made to jump when he felt himself falling is conclusive against him. When his leg gave way the appellant was in a very difficult situation. He had to decide what to do in a fraction of a second. He may have come to a wrong decision; he probably did. But if the chain of causation had not been broken before this by putting himself in a position where he might be confronted with an emergency, I do not think that he would put himself out of court by acting wrongly in the emergency unless his action was so utterly unreasonable that even on the spur of the moment no ordinary man would have been so foolish as to do what he did. In an emergency it is natural to try to do something to save oneself and I do not think that his trying to jump in this emergency was so wrong that it could be said to be no more than an error of judgment. But for the reasons already given I would dismiss this appeal.

Appeal dismissed.

NOTES

1. Are *Wieland v. Cyril Lord Carpets Ltd.* and *McKew v. Holland et al.* in conflict? How can they be rationalized? Why not contributory negligence and a reduced recovery?

2. In *Priestley v. Gilbert*, [1972] 3 O.R. 502, 28 D.L.R. (3d) 553; affd (1973), 1 O.R. (2d) 365, 40 D.L.R. (3d) 349 (C.A.), the plaintiff's leg was seriously injured as a result of an accident in which the defendant driver was found to be grossly negligent. At a Christmas party, the plaintiff, after becoming quite intoxicated, began dancing, and, as his leg was still weak from the injury, he fell and broke it again. In refusing the claim for damages arising from this second break, Osler J. stated:

   > ... there is an onus upon a person who knows or should know of a physical weakness to act reasonably and carefully and to protect himself from harm. ... [T]o get up and dance on this occasion was not a reasonable action in his condition ... and the principle of *novus actus interveniens* protects the defendant from responsibility for that injury.

   What if he had been dancing while sober and fell? What if he was drunk, but not dancing? What about contributory negligence here?

3. In *Lucas v. Juneau*, 127 F. Supp. 730 (Alaska 1955), the defendant negligently injured the plaintiff. After a stay in an Alaska hospital, it was decided that he should be taken to Seattle for treatment. While he was being transported in an ambulance the driver had an epileptic fit, the ambulance went off the road, and plaintiff was injured. The court declared: "I conclude, therefore, that the risk which must be borne by the original wrongdoer includes not only negligent medical treatment but also negligent transportation of the plaintiff to a place where treatment of the kind indicated by the nature of the injury may be obtained. A corollary of this conclusion is that the first tortfeasor is in no position to avoid liability for an aggravation sustained by the plaintiff in taking one of the steps necessary to obtain further treatment." In accord is *State ex. rel.*

Smith v. Weinstein, 398 S.W. 2d 41 (Mo. 1965), where the ambulance had a collision. Do you agree? What if the ambulance had been hit by lightning?

4. Is a negligent defendant liable if the second "accident" is the theft of the injured person's property?

In *Patten v. Silberschein* (1936), 51 B.C.R. 133, [1936] 3 W.W.R. 169 (S.C.), the defendant motorist negligently struck the plaintiff rendering him unconscious. While unconscious the plaintiff lost $80 which was in his pocket. McDonald J., held the defendant liable. In *Duce v. Rourke* (1951), 1 W.W.R. (N.S.) 305 (Alta. S.C.), Egbert J., disapproved of *Patten v. Silberschein*, and held a defendant, who had negligently injured the plaintiff, not liable for tools stolen from the plaintiff's car while the car was left on the highway after the plaintiff's removal to a hospital. The theft "was the consequence of some conscious intervening independent act, for which the defendant was in no wise responsible".

Which result do you prefer? What is the difference between these cases and *Stansbie v. Troman*, [1948] 2 K.B. 48, [1948] 1 All E.R. 599 (C.A.)? Is it more important for the defendant to get the victim to a hospital or to stay and guard the property at the scene of the accident?

A NOTE ON INTERVENING MEDICAL ERROR

Errors in medical treatment pose some fascinating problems. *Mercer v. Gray*, [1941] O.R. 127 (C.A.) has been the leading Canadian case for years. A child's broken leg became worse when her doctor mistakenly failed to cut her cast soon enough after a cyanosed condition became evident. At the trial, the damages suffered as a result of the lack of skill in treatment were not taken into account. The Ontario Court of Appeal sent the case back for a new trial on the ground that, "if reasonable care is used to employ a competent physician or surgeon to treat personal injuries wrongfully inflicted, the results of the treatment, even though by an error of treatment the treatment is unsuccessful, will be a proper head of damages". Mr. Justice McTague indicated, however, that, if the treatment "is so negligent as to be actionable", it would be "*novus actus interveniens* and the plaintiff would have his remedy against the physician or surgeon". Such a principle distinguishes between innocent errors of judgment and actionable mistakes.

It has been made clear that the onus rests on defendants to prove that the intervening medical error was a negligent one, if they are to escape liability for it. In *Papp v. Leclerc* (1977), 77 D.L.R. (3d) 536 (Ont. C.A.), Lacourciere J.A. stated:

> Every tortfeasor causing injury to a person placing him in the position of seeking medical or hospital help, must assume the inherent risks of complications, *bona fide* medical error or misadventure, and they are reasonable and not too remote. ... It is for the defendant to prove that some new act rendering another person liable has broken the chain of causation.

Later cases have adopted this dichotomy, often without mentioning it specifically. (See *Thompson v. Toorenburgh* (1972), 29 D.L.R. (3d) 608 (B.C.S.C.), affd (1973), 50 D.L.R. (3d) 717 (B.C.C.A.)).

This position created tactical difficulties for plaintiffs who suffered additional injuries at the hands of doctors, for they must conduct two different actions to recover fully, one against the original wrongdoer and another against the doctor. It seems rather harsh to require this, when the original defendant set the whole thing in motion. It would be preferable, except in the extreme cases perhaps, to hold liable for the losses the initial defendant who could then sue the negligent physicians for contribution. The wrongdoer instead of the innocent injured person would thus bear the procedural burdens.

Such is the law in the United States. In *Thompson v. Fox* (1973), 192 Atl. 107, at 108 (Pa.) it was put as follows:

> Doctors, being human, are apt occasionally to lapse from prescribed standards, and the likelihood of carelessness, lack of judgment or of skill, on the part of one; employed to effect a cure for a condition caused by another's act, is therefore considered in law as an incident of the original injury, and, if the injured party has used ordinary care in the selection of a physician or surgeon, any additional harm resulting from the latter's mistake or negligence is considered as one of the elements of the damages for which the original wrongdoer is liable.

The Canadian law has moved in the same sensible direction. In *Kolesar v. Jeffries* (1974), 9 O.R. (2d) 41 (H.C.); vard (1976), 12 O.R. (2d) 142 (C.A.); affd on other grounds without mentioning this point (1977), 77 D.L.R. (3d) 161 (*sub nom. Joseph Brant Memorial Hospital et al. v. Koziol et al.*) (S.C.C.), Mr. Justice Haines indicated that an original defendant may be responsible for the later negligence of a doctor or hospital which aggravates a plaintiff's injuries "unless it is completely outside the range of normal experience". This test implies that certain acts of medical malpractice might well be within the realm of reasonable foresight and, therefore, compensable, whereas other, presumably gross and shocking acts of malpractice, would be beyond the scope of foresight and not compensable.

A more far-reaching decision is *Price v. Milawski* (1977), 82 D.L.R. (3d) 130 (Ont. C.A.), where Arnup J.A. held that one negligent doctor could be liable for the additional loss caused by another doctor's negligence. He explained:

> ... a person doing a negligent act may, in circumstances lending themselves to that conclusion, be held liable for future damages arising in part from the subsequent negligent act of another, and in part from his own negligence, where such subsequent negligence and consequent damage were reasonably foreseeable as a possible result of his own negligence.
>
> It was reasonably foreseeable by Dr. Murray that once the information generated by his negligent error got into the hospital records, other doctors subsequently treating the plaintiff might well rely on the accuracy of that information, *i.e.*, that the X-ray showed no fracture of the ankle. It was also foreseeable that some doctor might do so without checking, even though to do so in the circumstances might itself be a negligent act. The history is always one factor in a subsequent diagnosis and the consequent treatment. Such a possibility was not a risk which a reasonable man (in the position of Dr. Murray) would brush aside as far-fetched — see "*Wagon Mound" (No. 2)*. ...
>
> The later negligence of Dr. Carbin compounded the effects of the earlier negligence of Dr. Murray. It did not put a halt to the consequences of the first act and attract liability for all damage from that point forward. In my view the trial Judge was correct in holding that each of the appellants was liable to the plain- tiff and that it was not possible to try to apportion the extent to which each was responsible for the plaintiff's subsequent operation and his permanent disability.

This case appears to be in conflict with *Mercer v. Gray,* but Mr. Justice Arnup referred to it without adverse comment and purported to follow it. There is a real likelihood, however, that future courts will consider *Mercer v. Gray* to have been overruled and, consequently, will permit full recovery in all of these cases. Such a solution would be more in accord with the general principles of remoteness as well as with the American rule. It would still allow contribution in appropriate cases, but would ensure that plaintiffs are initially covered, whether doctors are negligent or not. Following that, steps could be taken by wrongdoers to get reimbursement from doctors.

NOTES

1. If someone commits suicide because of depression after being negligently injured, should the original tortfeasor be liable for the death? In *Pigney v. Pointers Transport Services Ltd.*, [1957] 1 W.L.R. 1121, [1957] 2 All E.R. 807 (Norwich Assizes), an accident victim, suffering from anxiety neurosis hanged himself. He was not legally insane in that he knew what he was doing and that it was wrong. Relying on *Polemis*, the court imposed liability because the death was "directly traceable" to the physical injury. In its reasons, however, the court found that it was "clearly a matter which could not reasonably have been foreseen". How would a court treat this problem in *The Wagon Mound (No. 1)* era?

2. Canadian courts deal with the suicide issue by imposing liability on the defendant if the victim committed suicide while insane, and if this insanity could be traced directly to the injuries received in the accident. However, if the suicide was the deliberate decision of a sane individual, it will be treated as a *novus actus interveniens*. See, for example, *Swami v. Lo (No. 3)* (1979), 105 D.L.R. (3d) 451, 11 C.C.L.T. 210 (B.C.S.C.); and *Wright Estate v. Davidson* (1992), 88 D.L.R. (4th) 698, [1992] 3 W.W.R. 611 (B.C.C.A.). Why should sanity or lack of it make a difference? Is suicide by an insane person more foreseeable? Should the thin-skull rule be applied in this situation?

3. In *Costello v. Blakeson*, [1993] 2 W.W.R. 562 (B.C.S.C.), the thin-skull rule was used by Spencer J. to hold the negligent defendant 25 per cent to blame for injuries caused to the plaintiff accident victim as a result of her suicide attempt by jumping out of a window, even though she had also attempted suicide before the accident. What do you think of this resolution of this problem?

4. What are the policy concerns raised by the suicide cases? In *Robson v. Ashworth* (1985), 33 C.C.L.T. 229 (H.C.); affd 40 C.C.L.T. 164 (Ont. C.A.), Mr. Justice Galligan stated that it is a "well-recognized rule of public policy that survivors of a person who commits suicide are not entitled to benefit from the suicide". Why does the common law so willingly embrace the notion that rescue is a reasonably foreseeable event following an accident, but that suicide is not?

E. INTERMEDIATE INSPECTION

In the products liability area, the fact that different parties at different stages can become involved with a product complicates the question as to who should be liable when something to do with the product goes wrong. A product may be manufactured by one party, assembled by a second party, distributed by a third party, sold by a fourth party, and repaired by a fifth party, before it is finally used by a consumer. Which, if any, of these intermediate acts should be treated as intervening forces?

IVES v. CLARE BROTHERS LTD. ET AL.

High Court of Ontario. [1971] 1 O.R. 417, 15 D.L.R. (3d) 519.

Wright J. (orally): ... The basic facts are simple enough. The plaintiff was bound to take gas service from Twin City Gas. In January, 1967, he bought a Clare Hecla Gas Furnace Model G.101 from the supplier and installer. This was manufactured by the defendant Clare Brothers Limited and shipped assembled. It was installed by the supplier. Its installation was inspected by the defendant Twin City Gas on its own behalf and, as I understand it, on behalf of the Minister charged with the administration of the *Energy Act*, 1964 (Ont.), c. 27.

I find as a fact that there were three service calls answered by Twin City Gas with respect to the Clare Hecla Gas Furnace thus installed. …

At no time was the plaintiff given any warning of danger.

On Wednesday morning, April 3, 1968, the plaintiff testified that he felt unwell and called his employer to be excused from work. From then on he was in distress and helpless in his home. A paper-boy heard moaning on Thursday and again on Friday. He then entered and found Mr. Ives on his back in the living-room, having suffered the injuries giving rise to his damages. …

I find that the defendant Twin City Gas was negligent in that it and its service men on three occasions failed to appreciate, as was their duty, the serious and cumulative effect of the reasons which gave rise to their three service calls, failed to remedy the defects indicated by the customer's complaints, and failed to warn the plaintiff of the danger which they should have detected. These were duties owed to the customer who might have been saved from injury by their performance.

I find that the defendant Clare Bros. Ltd. was negligent in that it manufactured and supplied a defective furnace which was, in design and in particular, a peril by reason of the fact that the screws used did not, in some furnaces known to it and in the plaintiff's furnace, ensure that there would not be a gap leading to the production and emission in the home of carbon monoxide, in that it failed to warn customers, suppliers and service men of this danger of which it had been made aware, and in that it failed to provide other means to hold the gaps closed. These were duties owed to the consumer who might have been saved from injury by their performance.

It was strongly urged by Mr. Outerbridge that even if his client, the defendant Clare Bros. Ltd., had been negligent, there had in fact been inspection which broke the chain of causation from that negligence to the damage and thus completely exonerated the negligent manufacturer — a doctrine of foregiveness of sin by inspection. I must say I marvel at the redemptive effect of intermediate inspection. Despite the many cases which have been paid heed to this doctrine, and its affinity to Lord Dunedin's "conscious act of another volition", I find it hard to relate it in this case to the sensible proportionate rule of the *Negligence Act*, R.S.O. 1960, c. 261. In *Shields v. E.V. Larson Co. Ltd. et al.*, [1962] O.R. 355, at p. 357, 32 D.L.R. (2d) 273 at p. 275; affirmed [1962] S.C.R. 716, 34 D.L.R. (2d) 307, Porter C.J.O. discusses the questions of the opportunity to inspect and the *Negligence Act* and says: "If there were no duty, there would be no negligence. *The Negligence Act*, R.S.O. 1960, c. 261, adds nothing to the duty. It merely eliminates contributory negligence as a complete defence, and provides for apportionment of the damages."

Here I find that both the remaining defendants had duties and were negligent and that their acts of negligence led to the damage. They caused or contributed to the cause. *The Negligence Act* applies.

Mr. Outerbridge also put his argument in the form that the proximate cause or the *causa causans* was the negligence of the defendant Twin City Gas. It is true that liability under most insurance policies only arises if the risk insured against is the proximate cause of the loss, and that there can only be one proximate cause for that purpose. … I venture the view that where there are duties on two or more parties and negligence by each causing or contributing to the cause of damage, it is the *Negligence Act* and not the doctrine of proximate cause which is applied. If this is so, then inspection may cease to be the gospel of redemption it sometimes appears to be, but will continue to be, as it should be, a significant element of fact in considering liability.

I find each of the defendants, Clare Bros. Ltd. and [Twin City] Gas Corp. Ltd., equally negligent and give judgment for the plaintiff against them for $22,000.

NOTES

1. There were some early cases which absolved negligent manufacturers completely because of negligent inspection or negligent failure to inspect by intermediaries. See *Buckner v. Ashby and Horner Ltd.*, [1941] 1 K.B. 321; affd [1941] 1 K.B. 337 (C.A.), government inspector failed to discover defect; see also *Saccardo v. City of Hamilton*, [1971] 2 O.R. 479, at 489, 18 D.L.R. (3d) 27 (H.C.J.), when Christmas decorations fell off a hydro pole during a strong wind, injuring the plaintiff, the manufacturer of the decorations was relieved of liability on the ground that "the intervening actions of the installer in erecting and placing [them] effectively insulate the supplier from responsibility".

2. A preferable group of cases was more lenient. See, for example, *Dutton v. Bognor Regis U.D.C.*, [1972] 1 Q.B. 373, [1972] 2 W.L.R. 299 (C.A.), in which Denning M.R. would have held both the builder and the inspector liable for negligence in the construction of a house. The inspector failed to make a proper inspection and, therefore, did not discover a defect in the foundations that subsequently led to damage to the house. See also *Ostash v. Sonnenberg et al.* (1968), 67 D.L.R. (2d) 311, 63 W.W.R. 257 (Alta. C.A.); *Kubach v. Hollands*, [1937] 3 All E.R. 907, 53 T.L.R. 1024 (K.B.).

3. In *Taylor v. Rover Co., Ltd.*, [1966] 2 All E.R. 181, [1966] 1 W.L.R. 1491, in the course of his employment by the first defendant, the plaintiff was injured when a splinter of steel flew from a chisel he was using. The chisel had been manufactured by the second defendant. Some three or four weeks earlier the first defendant's lead hand had been injured when a small piece had flown off the chisel and cut his cheek. Assuming the second defendant manufacturer to have been responsible for the improper heat-hardening of the chisel, Baker J. held the second defendant not liable to the plaintiff since the first defendant, through their lead hand, had actual knowledge of the defect in the chisel. His Lordship stated:

> This was not carelessness which failed to reveal the defect, the defect was known. This was a dangerous chisel. A piece had flown and cut Mr. Jones's cheek. Secondly, the guilty chisel ought then to have been taken out of circulation; it was the keeping of the chisel in circulation with the knowledge that it was dangerous that caused the accident. It seems to me, therefore, that, in this case, the second defendant cannot be liable to the plaintiff. ...

How does *Taylor v. Rover Co. Ltd.* differ from *Dutton*? Is this a sensible basis upon which to distinguish when a manufacturer will be insulated and when it will not? What if such intervening activity is foreseeable?

4. In *Smith v. Inglis Ltd.* (1978), 25 N.S.R. (2d) 38, 6 C.C.L.T. 41 (C.A.), when the plaintiff touched the oven with one hand at the same time the other hand was touching the refrigerator, he received an electric shock from the refrigerator, which had been manufactured by the defendant. The shock resulted from two things: (1) an electrical defect in the fridge caused by the negligence of the manufacturer, and (2) the absence of a third prong on the plug of the fridge. The third prong had been cut off by a third

person sometime earlier. The key issue was whether the removal of the third prong was a *novus actus interveniens* isolating the manufacturer from liability for its prior negligence. MacKeigan C.J.N.S. refused to grant "absolution" to the defendant explaining:

> Many persons involved, ... did not realize the serious danger involved in removing a third or grounding plug or in nullifying its purpose by using an easily obtained adaptor which can receive a three-prong plug and then be plugged into a usual two-prong household wall-plug. The evidence shows that everyone in the business knew or should have known that prongs are often cut off and adaptors used. The respondent should thus have foreseen that this might happen.
>
> I must express the hope that the public may be instructed on this issue by advertising or otherwise, and that [the] legislature may, as in some other jurisdictions, by statute prohibit the sale of adaptors and the removal of third prongs, require manufacturers to provide three-prong plugs, where appropriate, as the respondent did, and to affix notices to appliances notifying users of the risk in nullifying this safety feature.

The plaintiff was held contributorily negligent by the court. MacKeigan C.J.N.S. observed as follows:

> With his knowledge of building and of electrical hazards, the appellant should in my opinion have checked the plug when he bought the refrigerator and had it installed. He must have been aware of the danger of using a two-prong plug in a three-hole outlet and did not reasonably guard against the danger.
>
> The appellant must thus share responsibility for the damage he suffered. It is not possible to establish the degree of fault, which should thus be apportioned equally between him and the respondent — *Contributory Negligence Act*, R.S.N.S. 1967, c. 54, s. 1(1).

5. Following this decision, Inglis sued the repairer, who had cut off the third prong, and the retailer, who had sold the refrigerator with the two prongs to the plaintiff, for contribution and indemnity. This action was dismissed because the negligence of these two parties related to the removal of the third prong which was "in effect imputed to Smith ... in finding him contributorily negligent. In other words, responsibility for the portion of his damage that related to the ground prong removal was assigned to him." Consequently, stated the court, "it cannot be said that their respective faults contributed to the damage". See *Inglis Ltd. v. South Shore Sales & Service Ltd.* (1979), 31 N.S.R. (2d) 541, 104 D.L.R. (3d) 507 (C.A.); vard as to costs 104 D.L.R. (3d) 507, at 522.

   Does this make sense? What would have been the result if Smith in the original case, instead of suing only the manufacturer, had also sued the repairer who removed the third prong and the store which sold him the refrigerator with only two prongs?

   There are other cases where plaintiffs in products cases have been held contributorily negligent. See *Shields v. Hobbs Mfg.*, [1962] S.C.R. 716, 34 D.L.R. (2d) 307; *Tompkins Hardware Ltd. v. North Western Flying Services Ltd.* (1982), 139 D.L.R. (3d) 329, 22 C.C.L.T. 1 (Ont. C.A.), *per* Saunders J.; *St. Amand v. St. John Propane Gas Co.* (1978), 22 N.B.R. (2d) 539 (C.A.).

6. In *Good-Wear Treaders Ltd. v. D. & B. Holdings Ltd.* (1979), 98 D.L.R. (3d) 59, 8 C.C.L.T. 87 (N.S.C.A.), someone was sold a retreaded tire with a warning that the tire should not be used on the front end of a gravel truck. The seller, however, knew that its warning would be disregarded by the buyer. The tire was mounted on a loaded gravel truck by the buyer, ignoring the warning. The tire later failed and caused a fatal

accident. The seller was held 20 per cent liable for the accident, the trucker 80 per cent liable.

Chief Justice MacKeigan stated that "a warning that will be disregarded ... does not absolve from all liability". MacKeigan C.J. continued:

> The defendant owed a duty to other users of the highway who would likely be adversely affected by [the] intended use of the tires. That duty was not to sell the tires to the [buyer] when [it] made clear its intention to use them on the ... truck on the highway. That duty was breached by selling the tires with knowledge of the intended use. ... The kind of damage done ... ought to have been anticipated as being a probable result of the sale of the tires and their use by the customer in that particular way.
>
> This is merely an application of established negligence law to an unusual and rare fact situation — rarely would a seller know that a prospective buyer firmly intended to use a normal and safe product in an unsafe way dangerous to persons other than the buyer, persons who cannot be warned or otherwise protected...

MacKeigan C.J. concluded:

> The tires themselves were not defective and were not dangerous per se. ... The danger arose from the improper use to which [the buyer] put them. Perfectly good tires became "defective" and dangerous when so used, and the truck became dangerous when equipped with the tires and loaded with gravel. Supplying the tires ... and knowing the danger [the buyer] proposed to create, Good-Wear became a participant in so creating and letting loose the danger, to the same degree as if, instead of [the buyer], had placed the tires on the truck. This is thus not a case of an intermediate buyer who having acquired dangerous goods with notice of the danger resells them without warning, and whose responsibility may be said to have superseded that of his supplier.
>
> ... This is not really a product liability case at all, where duty and liability follow a defective product through several hands. It is rather a case of a dangerous product being supplied to a person whom the supplier knew or should have known would use it dangerously. ...

Is this a dangerous development in the law? How is it limited?

7. All automobile manufacturers require their dealers to conduct detailed pre-delivery inspections on all new vehicles. By so instructing their dealers, are the car producers relieved of all liability for negligently-included defects that are not discovered on this inspection? Should they be? Is it reasonably foreseeable that a dealer will fail to discover a defect? Or that the dealer will discover it, but fail to notify the purchaser? Compare with the problems raised in *Ford Motor Co. v. Wagoner*, 183 Tenn. 392, 192 S.W. 2d 840 (1946); and *Comstock v. General Motors Corp.*, 358 Mich. 163, 99 N.W. 2d 627 (1959).

8. Can manufacturers of guns be held liable to someone who is shot with one of their weapons? What if the gun is not of sufficient quality for police or sportspeople to use but, to the knowledge of the maker, it is employed almost exclusively for purposes of robberies and is, therefore, called a "Saturday Night Special"? Compare with *Kelley v. R.G. Industries*, 497 A. 2d 1143 (Md. 1985).

9. What policies are served by relieving the first defendant of responsibility in these cases? What policies are served by holding everyone jointly liable? Which solution do you prefer?

10. How is the goal of deterrence of careless conduct best served? Will we be able to encourage the dominant party in the transaction to supervise the operations of the others? Is this good? What are the dangers of such a policy?

11. How is the goal of loss distribution best served? Is the plaintiff in any better position under joint liability? Does the plaintiff not usually sue everyone in any event?

12. Do we need the special language of intermediate inspection in products cases? Are these problems the same ones as those dealt with under proximate cause, remoteness and duty?

13. Can you articulate a verbal test that will solve the questions raised in these cases? What about the terms "risk" and "foresight"?

F. WARNINGS AND THE LEARNED INTERMEDIARY

There is a clear duty owed by manufacturers, not only to make and design their products reasonably, but to warn about any dangerous aspects of their products. These warnings must be explicit and reasonably communicated. (see *Lambert v. Lastoplex Chemicals Co. Ltd.,* [1972] S.C.R. 569; see also *Buchan v. Ortho Pharmaceuticals (Canada) Ltd.* (1986), 35 C.C.L.T. 1 (Ont. C.A.)). Mr. Justice La Forest summarized the content and the rationale for the warning principles in *Hollis v. Dow Corning,* [1995] 4 S.C.R. 634, at 653 as follows:

> The rationale for the manufacturer's duty to warn can be traced to the "neighbour principle", which lies at the heart of the law of negligence, and was set down in its classic form by Lord Atkin in *Donoghue v. Stevenson*, [1932] A.C. 562 (H.L.). When manufacturers place products into the flow of commerce, they create a relationship of reliance with consumers, who have far less knowledge than the manufacturers concerning the dangers inherent in the use of the products, and are therefore put at risk if the product is not safe. The duty to warn serves to correct the knowledge imbalance between manufacturers and consumers by alerting consumers to any dangers and allowing them to make informed decisions concerning the safe use of the product.
>
> The nature and scope of the manufacturer's duty to warn varies with the level of danger entailed by the ordinary use of the product. Where significant dangers are entailed by the ordinary use of the product, it will rarely be sufficient for manufacturers to give general warnings concerning those dangers; the warnings must be sufficiently detailed to give the consumer a full indication of each of the specific dangers arising from the use of product.

Superfluous warnings are not required. "A manufacturer of a butcher knife is not under a legal duty to warn consumers that a butcher knife may cut flesh". (See Galligan J.A. in *Deshane v. Deere & Co.* (1993), 17 C.C.L.T. (2d) 130 at 147 (Ont. C.A.), plaintiff fell into unguarded harvester machine, no duty to warn; leave to appeal refused (1994), 20 C.C.L.T. (2d) 318*n* (S.C.C.)).

This duty to warn is a continuing duty, requiring manufacturers to warn not only of dangers known at the time of sale but also of dangers discovered after the product has been sold and delivered. (See La Forest J. in *Hollis v. Dow Corning, supra,* at 653; see also *Rivtow Marine Ltd. v. Washington Iron Works* (1973), 40 D.L.R. (3d) 530 (S.C.C.)). Where products are not sold directly to consumers but to doctors or other experts who prescribe them or use them on consumers, the problem arises as to the effect of a warning to a so-called "learned intermediary", as these people are called.

HOLLIS v. DOW CORNING CORP.

Supreme Court of Canada. [1995], 4 S.C.R. 634

In 1983, Ms. Hollis, on the advice of her surgeon (Dr. Birch), underwent breast implant surgery to correct a congenital deformity. She was not warned by him of the risks of post-surgical complications or of the possibility that the implants might rupture inside her body. In 1984, after further surgery and an examination by Dr. Birch, who gave the opinion that there was no problem with her breasts, Ms. Hollis began a baker's course which required vigorous upper body movement. In 1985, Ms. Hollis noticed a lump in her right breast and began to feel pain there as well as in her right side. She attended another surgeon, Dr. Quayle, who operated to remove the implant. He discovered that the left implant was intact but that the right implant had ruptured. Dr. Quayle removed the gel from the right implant but could not find the envelope. After the removal of the breast implants, Ms. Hollis' physical condition worsened. A visit to a third surgeon in 1987 resulted in Ms. Hollis' undergoing a successful subcutaneous mastectomy on both breasts and opting for a new, different model of breast implants.

Dr. Birch received little warning from the implant manufacturer as to the possibility of the implants' rupturing. Even as early as 1979, Dow was aware that implant ruptures could cause adverse reactions in the body arising from loose gel. While the 1985 warning referred to the dangers of "enlarged lymph nodes, scar formation, inflammation" and the potential, after a rupture, for "distant migration of the gel", the 1976 and 1979 warnings made no reference to any such potential consequences. Nor did these earlier warnings make reference to ruptures occurring from anything less than "abnormal squeezing or trauma".

Ms. Hollis brought action in 1989 against Dow, Dow's Canadian agent, Dr. Birch and Dr. Quayle. At trial, she successfully claimed against Dow for the negligent manufacture of the breast implant and was awarded damages and costs; her other claims were dismissed. A majority of the Court of Appeal overturned the finding that Dow had negligently manufactured the implant, but dismissed the appeal on the ground that Dow had failed to warn Ms. Hollis adequately concerning the risks of rupture. A majority of the B.C. Court of Appeal allowed Ms. Hollis' appeal from the dismissal of her action against Dr. Birch and ordered a new trial in respect of that claim. The sole issue here is whether the Court of Appeal erred in finding Dow liable to Ms. Hollis for failing to warn Dr. Birch adequately of the risk of a post-surgical implant rupture.

La Forest J. (for the majority) stated:

> As a general rule, the duty to warn is owed directly by the manufacturer to the ultimate consumer. However, in exceptional circumstances, a manufacturer may satisfy its informational duty to the consumer by providing a warning to what the American courts have, in recent years, termed a "learned intermediary". The "learned intermediary" rule was first elaborated in *Sterling Drug Inc. v. Cornish*, 370 F. 2d 82 (8th Cir., 1966), a suit brought by a patient blinded after taking the drug chloroquine phosphate. The rationale for the rule was outlined by Wisdom J. in *Reyes v. Wyeth Laboratories,* 498 F. 2d 1264 (5th Cir., 1974), at p. 1276, certiorari denied 419 U.S. 1096 (1974), a suit against a manufacturer of oral polio vaccine, in the following terms:
>
>> Prescription drugs are likely to be complex medicines, esoteric in formula and varied in effect. As a medical expert, the prescribing physician can take into account the propensities of the drug, as well as the susceptibilities of his patient. His is the task of weighing the benefits of any medication against its potential dangers. The choice he makes is an informed one, an individualized

> medical judgment bottomed on a knowledge of both patient and palliative. Pharmaceutical companies then, who must warn ultimate purchasers of dangers inherent in patent drugs sold over the counter, in selling prescription drugs are required to warn only the prescribing physician, who acts as a "learned intermediary" between manufacturer and consumer.

The rule was later reaffirmed and developed in a series of American cases during the 1970s and 1980s involving the liability of manufacturers of prescription drugs. ... In Canada, the rule was first considered in an *obiter* passage by Linden J. in *Davidson v. Connaught Laboratories* (1980), 14 C.C.L.T. 251 (Ont. H.C.), at p. 273, and later applied by a five-member panel of the Ontario Court of Appeal in *Buchan, supra.*

While the "learned intermediary" rule was originally intended to reflect, through an equitable distribution of tort duties, the tripartite informational relationship between drug manufacturers, physicians and patients, the rationale for the rule is clearly applicable in other contexts. Indeed, the "learned intermediary" rule is less a "rule" than a specific application of the long-established common law principles of intermediate examination and intervening cause developed in *Donoghue v. Stevenson, supra*, and subsequent cases; see, for example, *Holmes v. Ashford*, [1950] 2 All E.R. 76 (C.A.) at p. 80. Generally, the rule is applicable either where a product is highly technical in nature and is intended to be used only under the supervision of experts, or where the nature of the product is such that the consumer will not realistically receive a direct warning from the manufacturer before using the product. In such cases, where an intermediate inspection of the product is anticipated or where a consumer is placing primary reliance on the judgment of a "learned intermediary" and not the manufacturer, a warning to the ultimate consumer may not be necessary and the manufacturer may satisfy its duty to warn the ultimate consumer by warning the learned intermediary of the risks inherent in the use of the product.

However, it is important to keep in mind that the "learned intermediary" rule is merely an exception to the general manufacturer's duty to warn the consumer. The rule operates to discharge the manufacturer's duty not to the learned intermediary, but to the ultimate consumer, who has a right to full and current information about any risks inherent in the ordinary use of the product. Thus, the rule presumes that the intermediary is "learned", that is to say, fully apprised of the risks associated with the use of the product. Accordingly, the manufacturer can only be said to have discharged its duty to the consumer when the intermediary's knowledge approximates that of the manufacturer. To allow manufacturers to claim the benefit of the rule where they have not fully warned the physician would undermine the policy rationale for the duty to warn, which is to ensure that the consumer is fully informed of all risks. Since the manufacturer is in the best position to know the risks attendant upon the use of its product and is also in the best position to ensure that the product is safe for normal use, the primary duty to give a clear, complete, and current warning must fall on its shoulders.

(b) *Application of the General Principles to the Case at Bar*

The first question to be answered in this appeal is whether Dow owed Ms. Hollis a duty to warn her that the Silastic implant could rupture post-surgically inside her body and, if so, whether Dow satisfied that duty. In light of the foregoing jurisprudence, it is clear that the answer to this question depends on the answers to two subsidiary questions. First, did Dow have a duty to warn Ms. Hollis directly, or could it satisfy its duty to warn her by warning a "learned intermediary", namely Dr. Birch? Second, assuming that Dow could properly discharge its duty to Ms. Hollis by warning Dr. Birch, did Dow adequately warn Dr. Birch of the risk of post-surgical rupture in light of its state of knowledge at that time?

Turning to the first of these questions, it is my view that the "learned intermediary" rule is applicable in this context, and that Dow was entitled to warn Dr. Birch concerning the risk of rupture without warning Ms. Hollis directly. A breast implant is distinct from most manufactured goods in that neither the implant nor its packaging are placed directly into the hands of the ultimate consumer. It is the surgeon, not the consumer, who obtains the implant from the manufacturer and who is therefore in the best position to read any warnings contained in the product packaging. In this respect, breast implants are, in my view, analogous to prescription drugs, where the patient places primary reliance for information on the judgment of the surgeon, who is a "learned intermediary", and not on the manufacturer; see *Buchanan*, supra, at p. 368. They are not analogous to oral contraceptives, with respect to which many American courts have recently imposed a direct duty to warn, because direct warnings from manufacturers of breast implants are simply not feasible given the need for intervention by a physician. …

Further, His Lordship concluded that the Court of Appeal made no error in ruling that Dow did not discharge its duty to Ms. Hollis by properly warning Dr. Birch concerning the risk of post-surgical implant rupture. In addition, Mr. Justice La Forest felt that it was not necessary for the consumer to prove that the learned intermediary would have imparted the warning in order to comply with the proof of causation element, for that would require proof of a hypothetical. In a sense, proof of causation was presumed from the situation.

Simply put, I do not think a manufacturer should be able to escape liability for failing to give a warning it was under a duty to give, by simply presenting evidence tending to establish that even if the doctor had been given the warning, he or she would not have passed it on to the patient, let alone putting an onus on the plaintiff to do so. Adopting such a rule would, in some cases, run the risk of leaving the plaintiff with no compensation for her injuries. She would not be able to recover against a doctor who had not been negligent with respect to the information that he or she did have; yet she also would not be able to recover against a manufacturer who, despite having failed in its duty to warn, could escape liability on the basis that, had the doctor been appropriately warned, he or she still would not have passed the information on to the plaintiff. Our tort law should not be held to contemplate such an anomalous result.

As I see it, the plaintiff's claim against the manufacturer should be dealt with in accordance with the following rationale. The ultimate duty of the manufacturer is to warn the plaintiff adequately. For practical reasons, the law permits it to acquit itself of that duty by warning an informed intermediary. Having failed to warn the intermediary, the manufacturer has failed in its duty to warn the plaintiff who ultimately suffered injury by using the product. The fact that the manufacturer would have been absolved had it followed the route of informing the plaintiff through the learned intermediary should not absolve it of its duty to the plaintiff because of the possibility, even the probability, that the learned intermediary would not have advised her had the manufacturer issued it. The learned intermediary rule provides a means by which the manufacturer can discharge its duty to give adequate information of the risks to the plaintiff by informing the intermediary, but if it fails to do so it cannot raise a defence that the intermediary could have ignored this information.

[Furthermore, **La Forest J.** applied the subjective test of causation here, not the modified objective test used in *Reibl* and *Arndt, supra*, so that the plaintiff could succeed if she could show that, given the full information, she would not have gone ahead with the procedure, whether she was reasonable or not.]

CONCLUSION

On the basis of the foregoing, it is my view that Dow breached its duty to warn Dr. Birch concerning the risks of post-surgical rupture in the Silastic implant and because of this failure to warn is liable to Ms. Hollis for her injuries. Accordingly, I would dismiss the appeal.

NOTES

1. In *Buchan v. Ortho Pharmaceutical (Canada) Ltd.*, the trial court determined that the learned intermediary rule does not apply in the case of oral contraceptives. The Ontario Court of Appeal upheld the decision of the court below but relied on the narrower point of the manufacturer's failure to adequately warn the prescribing doctor. However, Justice Lacourcière, writing for the Court of Appeal, stressed that, unlike other prescription drugs, there should also be a duty to warn women directly of the risks involved in the use of prescription contraceptives.

2. What if *Dow Corning* had fully warned the doctor, but he failed to impart that warning to the plaintiff?

3. There are federal regulations requiring a certain warning to be printed on packages of cigarettes. If a company complies with that regulation, can it be held liable for inadequate warning? See *Buchan, supra,* and *Lambert v. Lastoplex, supra.*

CHAPTER 9

DEFENCES TO THE NEGLIGENCE ACTION

Despite the presence of a duty, a breach of duty and proximate damage, an action in negligence may still be defeated because of the plaintiff's own conduct, because of an agreement between the parties, or because the court is of the opinion that it would be contrary to the dignity of the judicial process to uphold the plaintiff's claim. This chapter examines the defences of contributory negligence, voluntary assumption of risk, and illegality.

A. CONTRIBUTORY NEGLIGENCE

BUTTERFIELD v. FORRESTER

King's Bench. (1809), 103 E.R. 926, 11 East. 60.

This was an action on the case for obstructing a highway, by means of which obstruction the plaintiff, who was riding along the road, was thrown down with his horse and injured, &c. At the trial before Bayley J., at Derby, it appeared that the defendant, for the purpose of making some repairs to his house, which was close by the roadside at one end of the town, had put up a pole across this part of the road, a free passage being left by another branch or street in the same direction. That the plaintiff left a public house not far distant from the place in question at 8 o'clock in the evening in August, when they were just beginning to light candles, but while there was light enough left to discern the obstruction at 100 yards distance: and the witness, who proved this, said that if the plaintiff had not been riding very hard he might have observed and avoided it; the plaintiff, however, who was riding violently, did not observe it, but rode against it, and fell with his horse and was much hurt in consequence of the accident; and there was no evidence of his being intoxicated at the time. On this evidence Bayley J. directed the jury, that if a person riding with reasonable and ordinary care could have seen and avoided the obstruction; and if they were satisfied that the plaintiff was riding along the street extremely hard, and without ordinary care, they should find a verdict for the defendant, which they accordingly did. The plaintiff moved for a new trial.

Bayley J.: The plaintiff was proved to be riding as fast as his horse could go, and this was through the streets of Derby. If he had used ordinary care he must have seen the obstruction, so that the accident appeared to happen entirely from his own fault.

Lord Ellenborough C.J.: A party is not to cast himself upon an obstruction which has been made by the fault of another, and avail himself to it, if he do not himself use common and ordinary caution to be in the right. In cases of persons riding upon what is considered to be the wrong side of the road, that would not authorize another person purposely to ride up against them. One person being in fault will not dispense with another's using ordinary care for himself. Two things must concur to support this action, an obstruction in the road by the fault of the defendant, and no want of ordinary care to avoid it on the part of the plaintiff.

Rule refused.

NOTES

1. What was the reason advanced for denying compensation to the plaintiff? Did causation play a role?

2. Does the defence have a penal basis in that the plaintiff was being punished for his own wrongdoing?

3. Is the defence a deterrent to negligent conduct by potential plaintiffs? Does the defence have the opposite effect on potential defendants who will be relieved from responsibility for otherwise negligent conduct?

4. For an historical account of contributory negligence, see Malone, "The Formative Era of Contributory Negligence" (1946), 41 Ill. L. Rev. 151. See also James, "Contributory Negligence" (1953), 62 Yale L.J. 691; Bohlen, "Contributory Negligence" (1908), 21 Harv. L. Rev. 151.

DAVIES v. MANN

Exchequer Court. (1842), 10 M. & W. 566, 12 L.J. Ex. 10, 152 E.R. 588.

Case for negligence. The declaration stated that the plaintiff theretofore and at the time of the committing of the grievance therein mentioned, to wit, on, &c., was lawfully possessed of a certain donkey, which said donkey of the plaintiff was then lawfully in a certain highway, and the defendant was then possessed of a certain wagon and of certain horses drawing the same, which said wagon and horses of the defendant were then under the care, government, and direction of a certain then servant of the defendant, in and along the said highway; nevertheless the defendant, by his said servant, so carelessly, negligently, unskilfully, and improperly governed and directed his said wagon and horses, that by and through the carelessness, negligence, unskilfulness, and improper conduct of the defendant, by his said servant, the said wagon and horses of the defendant then ran and struck with great violence against the said donkey of the plaintiff, and thereby then wounded, crushed, and killed the same, &c.

The defendant pleaded not guilty.

At the trial, before Erskine J., at the last Summer Assizes for the county of Worcester, it appeared that the plaintiff, having lettered the fore-feet of an ass belonging to him, turned it into a public highway, and at the time in question the ass was grazing on the off side of a road about eight yards wide, when the defendant's wagon, with a team of three horses, coming down a slight descent, at what the witness termed a smartish pace, ran against the ass, knocked it down, and the wheels passing over it, it died soon after. The ass was fettered at the time, and it was proved that the driver of the wagon was some little distance behind the horses. The learned judge told the jury, that though the act of the plaintiff, in leaving the donkey on the highway so fettered as to prevent his getting out of the way of carriages travelling along it might be illegal, still, if the proximate cause of the injury was attributable to the want of proper conduct on the part of the driver of the wagon, the action was maintainable against the defendant; and his Lordship directed them, if they thought that the accident might have been avoided by the exercise of ordinary care on the part of the driver, to find for the plaintiff. The jury found their verdict for the plaintiff, damages 40s.

Godson now moved for a new trial on the ground of misdirection.

Lord Abinger C.B.: I am of opinion that there ought to be no rule in this case. The defendant has not denied that the ass was lawfully in the highway, and therefore we must assume it to have been lawfully there; but even were it otherwise, it would have made no difference, for the defendant might, by proper care, have avoided injuring the animal, and did not he is liable for the consequences of his negligence, though the animal may have been improperly there.

Parke B.: This subject was fully considered by this court in the case of *Bridge v. The Grand Junction Railway Company*, 3 M. & W. 246 where, as appears to me, the correct rule is laid down concerning negligence, namely, that the negligence which is to preclude a plaintiff from recovering in an action of this nature, must be such as that he could, by ordinary care, have avoided the consequences of the defendant's negligence. I am reported to have said in that case, and I believed quite correctly, that "the rule of law is laid down with perfect correctness in the case of *Butterfield v. Forrester*, that, although there may have been negligence on the part of the plaintiff, yet unless he might, by the exercise of ordinary care, have avoided the consequences of the defendant's negligence, he is entitled to recover; if by ordinary care he might have avoided them, he is the author of his own wrong". In that case of *Bridge v. Grand Junction Railway Co.*, there was a plea imputing negligence on both sides; here it is otherwise; and the judge simply told the jury, that the mere fact of negligence on the part of the plaintiff in leaving his donkey on the public highway, was no answer to the action, unless the donkey's being there was the immediate cause of the injury; and that, if they were of opinion that it was caused by the fault of the defendant's servant in driving too fast or, which is the same thing, at a smartish pace, the mere fact of putting the ass upon the road would not bar the plaintiff of his action. All that is perfectly correct; for, although the ass may have been wrongfully there, still the defendant was bound to go along the road at such a pace as would be likely to prevent mischief. Were this not so, a man might justify the driving over goods left on a public highway, or even over a man lying asleep there, or the purposely running against a carriage going on the wrong side of the road.

[**Gurney B.** and **Rolfe B.** concurred.]

Rule refused.

NOTES

1. What explanation for the doctrine of "last clear chance" was offered by the court? Was the court influenced by the causation theory?

2. Was the defendant the more culpable of the two parties?

3. Was the doctrine a reaction to the harshness of the contributory negligence doctrine? See MacIntyre, "The Rationale of Last Clear Chance" (1940), 18 Can. Bar Rev. 665; also in Linden (ed.), *Studies in Canadian Tort Law* (1968), p. 160, and in (1940), 53 Harv. L. Rev. 1225, where the author outlines the development of the doctrine.

4. For a fuller study of the complex theories that were spun by courts about "last clear chance", see *Long v. Toronto Railway Company* (1914), 50 S.C.R. 224, 20 D.L.R. 369; *B.C. Electric Ry. Co. Ltd. v. Loach*, [1916] 1 A.C. 719, 23 D.L.R. 4, 8 W.W.R. 1263 (P.C.); *Gives v. C.N.R.*, [1941] O.R. 341, [1941] 4 D.L.R. 625 (C.A.); *Davies v. Swan Motor Co. (Swansea) Ltd.*, [1949] 2 K.B. 291, [1949] 1 All E.R. 620. See also Goodhart, "The Last Opportunity Rule" (1949), 65 L.Q. Rev. 237.

5. There was much criticism of the "stalemate rule", which denied all recovery to negligent plaintiffs. The "last clear chance" doctrine helped in some cases, but it lacked both flexibility and candour. Reform of this "monstrously unjust" situation was overdue. See Schroeder, "Courts and Comparative Negligence", [1950] Ins. L.J. 791, at 794. Agitation began in the law reviews. See McMurchy, "Contributory Negligence — Should the Rule in Admiralty and Civil Law Be Adopted?" (1923), 1 Can. Bar Rev. 844; Anglin, "Law of Quebec and Other Provinces" (1923), 1 Can. Bar Rev. 33, at 49. Even the Supreme Court of Canada expressed its displeasure with the "stalemate rule" and praised the more equitable principle of "common fault" that was used in Quebec. See *Grand Trunk Pacific Railway v. Earl*, [1923] S.C.R. 397, at 398, *per* Duff J., at 406, *per* Anglin J., and at 408, *per* Mignault J. The next year, 1924, the Legislature of Ontario responded and enacted the first Canadian comparative negligence statute (Stat. Ont. 1924, c. 32), most of which is reproduced below as amended.

NEGLIGENCE ACT

R.S.O. 1990, c. N.1, ss. 1 to 8

1. Where damages have been caused or contributed to by the fault or neglect of two or more persons, the court shall determine the degree in which each of such persons is at fault or negligent, and, where two or more persons are found at fault or negligent, they are jointly and severally liable to the person suffering loss or damage for such fault or negligence, but as between themselves, in the absence of any contract express or implied, each is liable to make contribution and indemnify each other in the degree in which they are respectively found to be at fault or negligent.

2. A tortfeasor may recover contribution or indemnity from any other tortfeasor who is, or would if sued have been, liable in respect of the damage to any person suffering damage as a result of a tort by settling with the person suffering such damage, and thereafter commencing or continuing action against such other tortfeasor, in which event the tortfeasor settling the damage shall satisfy the court that the amount of the settlement was reasonable, and in the event that the court finds the amount of the settlement was excessive it may fix the amount at which the claim should have been settled.

3. In any action for damages that is founded upon the fault or negligence of the defendant if fault or negligence is found on the part of the plaintiff that contributed to the damages, the court shall apportion the damages in proportion to the degree or fault or negligence found against the parties respectively.

4. If it is not practicable to determine the respective degree or fault or negligence as between any parties to an action, such parties shall be deemed to be equally at fault or negligent.

5. Whenever it appears that a person not already a party to an action is or may be wholly or partly responsible for the damages claimed, such person may be added as a party defendant to the action upon such terms as are considered just or may be made a third party to the action in the manner prescribed by the rules of court for adding third parties.

6. In any action tried with a jury, the degree of fault or negligence of the respective parties is a question of fact for the jury.

7. Where the damages are occasioned by the fault or negligence of more than one party, the court has power to direct that the plaintiff shall bear some portion of the costs if the circumstances render this just.

8. Where an action is commenced against a tortfeasor or where a tortfeasor settles with a person who has suffered damage as a result of a tort, within the period of limitation prescribed for the commencement of actions by any relevant statute, no proceedings for contribution or indemnity against another tortfeasor are defeated by the operation of any statute limiting the time for the commencement of action against such other tortfeasor provided,

(a) such proceedings are commenced within one year of the date of the judgment in the action or the settlement, as the case may be; and

(b) here has been compliance with any statute requiring notice of claim against such tortfeasor.

NOTES

1. All the other common law provinces and most of the other Commonwealth jurisdictions have enacted similar legislation. In 1945, England adopted *The Law Reform (Contributory Negligence) Act*, 8 & 9 Geo. VI, c. 28. In the United States, comparative negligence legislation was enacted only in a handful of states until recently. Most states have now enacted legislation. In Florida, comparative negligence has been adopted by judicial legislation. See *Hoffman v. Jones*, 280 So. 2d 431 (Fla. S.C. 1973). See generally, Schwartz, *Comparative Negligence* (1974). Concerning the operation of what was then s. 5, see Dickson J. dissenting in *Taylor v. Asody* (1975), 49 D.L.R. (3d) 724 (S.C.C.).

2. Why was the common law changed? In *Bow Valley Husky (Bermuda) Ltd. v. Saint John Shipbuilding Ltd.* (1997), 153 D.L.R. (4th) 385 (S.C.C.), the Supreme Court held that although the *Contributory Negligence Act,* R.S.N. 1990, c. C-33 did not apply to maritime law that the common law contributory negligence bar should be abolished. In arriving at this decision, McLachlin J. stated at 421:

> The considerations on which the contributory negligence bar was based no longer comport with the modern view of fairness and justice. Tort law no longer accepts the traditional theory underpinning the contributory negligence bar that the injured party cannot prove that the tortfeasor "caused" the damage. The contributory negligence bar results in manifold unfairness, particularly where the negligence of the injured party is slight in comparison with the negligence of others. Nor does the contributory negligence bar further the goal of modern tort law of encouraging care and vigilance. So long as an injured party can be shown to be marginally at fault, a tortfeasor's conduct, no matter how egregious, goes unpunished.

McLachlin J. decided thus to eliminate the common law bar, and apply a regime of joint and several liability to maritime law cases, subject to a right of contribution between the defendants.

3. The standard of care demanded of plaintiffs is no different than that expected from defendants — they must exercise such care for their own safety, as a reasonable person would in like circumstances. The contributory negligence issue, like the negligence question, goes to the jury, if there is one in the case. In practice, juries and courts might be a little less demanding of plaintiffs, but there is no differentiation in theory between plaintiffs and defendants. Should there be? See James, "Contributory Negligence" (1953), 62 Yale L.J. 691; James and Dickinson, "Accident Proneness and Accident Law" (1950), 63 Harv. L. Rev. 769. For a critique challenging the assumptions underlying contributory negligence, see Kenneth Simons, "The Puzzling Doctrine of Contributory Negligence" (1995), 16 Cardozo L.R. 1693.

4. To whom does the plaintiff owe a duty to be careful — to himself or herself or to the defendant? In *Potter v. The Mercantile Bank of Canada*, [1980] 2 S.C.R. 343, 112 D.L.R. (3d) 88, Mr. Justice Ritchie rejected the defendant trustee's argument that the plaintiff, who was the trust's beneficiary, ought to be held partly to blame for his losses due to his own carelessness. Ritchie J. stated that there was no authority for the proposition that a beneficiary of a trust owed a duty to its trustee to ensure that the terms of the trust were observed and that accordingly the plaintiff could not be held to have been contributorily negligent. Compare this approach with that of Linden J. in *Bell Canada v. Cope (Sarnia) Ltd.* (1980), 11 C.C.L.T. 170 (Ont.); affd (1981), 31 O.R. (2d) 571, 15 C.C.L.T. 190 (C.A.). In rejecting the plaintiff's argument that it was not contributorily negligent since it owed no duty to the defendant, Linden J. stated:

> ... this question of duty is not relevant here, since this is a situation of contributory negligence by the plaintiff only. There is no need to establish any duty owed to anyone by the person who is contributing to his own damages by his fault or negligence. Duty is only relevant where another person is damaged by the actor's conduct.

Which view best explains the contributory negligence issue? For a critical comment on *Potter*, see Klar, "Developments in Tort Law: 1979-80 Term" (1981), 2 Supreme Court L.R. 325.

5. There are three ways in which plaintiffs can contribute to their own injuries by their own negligence. They can (1) contribute to the accident which caused the injuries, (2) expose themselves to a risk of being involved in an accident, or (3) fail to take reasonable precautions to minimize injuries should an accident occur. All three are examples of contributory negligence. Can you illustrate these three scenarios with examples? See Gravells, "Three Heads of Contributory Negligence" (1977), 93 L.Q. Rev. 581.

6. Even with apportionment legislation, the rule of "last clear chance" has not disappeared. In some provinces — Alberta, P.E.I., Saskatchewan, and Newfoundland — a modified version of the rule is expressly provided for in the legislation. In Alberta, for example, the *Contributory Negligence Act*, R.S.A. 1980, c. C-23, s. 6, directs the judge or jury not to consider the question of last clear chance unless the evidence indicates that the act or omission of one party "was so clearly subsequent to and severable from the act or omission" of another so as not to be "substantially contemporaneous therewith". The statutes of Nova Scotia, New Brunswick, Manitoba and Ontario contain no reference to the rule; however, even here the rule has occasionally been applied. See, for example, *Keough v. Royal Canadian Legion, Henderson Highway Branch*, [1978] 6 W.W.R. 335, 7 C.C.L.T. 146 (Man. C.A.).

In British Columbia, the rule has expressly been abolished.

7. The issue of the fate of "last clear chance" was extensively reviewed by the Alberta Court of Appeal in *Wickberg v. Patterson* (1997), 33 C.C.L.T. (2d) 231, [1997] 4 W.W.R. 591, 145 D.L.R. (4th) 263. The plaintiff motorcyclist collided into the back of the defendant's stationary truck. The trial judge found that the plaintiff had the last clear chance to avoid the accident, and dismissed the action. The Court of Appeal reversed. Madam Justice Ellen Picard at 235 C.C.L.T. wrote:

> *(2) Last Clear Chance*
>
> Last clear chance is the dandelion of causation analysis. It continues to survive in spite of the efforts to choke it out by courts, law reform bodies, and respected academics: M.M. MacIntyre, "Last Clear Chance after Thirty Years Under the Apportionment Status" (1995) 33 Can. Bar. Rev. 257; M.M. MacIntyre, "The Rationale of Last Clear Chance" (1940) 18 Can. Bar. Rev. 655; W.F. Bowker, "Ten More Years Under the Contributory Negligence Acts" [1964-1966] U.B.C.L. Rev. 198; D. Caswell, "Avoiding Last Clear Chance" (1990) 69 Can. Bar. Rev. 129; L.N. Klar, *Tort Law, supra.*
>
> Its origins were noble. In a time when even the slightest act of negligence would bar a plaintiff from any recovery, it allowed courts to compensate when it could be found that, in spite of the plaintiff's negligence, the defendant had the *last clear chance* to avoid the accident: *Butterfield v. Forrester* (1809), 103 E.R. 926 (K.B.); *Davies v. Mann* (1842), 152 E.R. 588 (Ex.).
>
> However, causation analysis became more flexible and sophisticated and legislation was enacted allowing for and, indeed, requiring the determination of degrees of negligence including the situation where it was a plaintiff who was negligent. The absence of the need and role for last clear chance resulted in law reform bodies such as the Uniform Law Conference of Canada (1978), the Ontario Law Reform Commission (1988) and the Alberta Law Reform Institute (1979) recommending that the doctrine of last clear chance be abolished. British Columbia and Prince Edward Island did enact legislation doing so: the *Negligence Act*, S.B.C. 1979, c. 298, s. 8; the *Contributory Negligence Act*, R.S.P.E.I. 1974, c. C-19, s. 4, as am. by S.P.E.I. 1980, c. 17, s. 1.
>
> The decisions of the Supreme Court of Canada have not given clear guidance. There are cases in which the court said that the last clear chance doctrine survived the enactment of apportionment legislation and yet there is an *obiter* comment in the 1976 case, *Hartman v. Fisette*, [1977] 1. S.C.R. 248 that it did not.
>
> The picture is made more complicated in Alberta (as well as Newfoundland, Saskatchewan, the Northwest Territories and the Yukon) where legislation retains the concept of last clear chance. (Although in the opinion of one respected academic, the legislation was an attempt to abolish it. See Bowker, *supra.*)
>
> The legislation says:
>
>> 6. If the trial is before a judge with a jury, the judge shall not submit to the jury any question as to whether, notwithstanding the fault of one party, the other could have avoided the consequences thereof, unless in his opinion there is evidence upon which the jury could reasonably find that the act or omission of the latter was so clearly subsequent to and severable from the act or omission of the former as not to be substantially contemporaneous with it.
>>
>> 7. If the trial is before a judge without a jury the judge shall not take into consideration any question as to whether, notwithstanding the fault of one party, the other could have avoided the consequences thereof, unless he is satisfied by the evidence that the act or omission of the latter was so clearly subsequent to and severable from the act or omission of the former as not to be substantially contemporaneous therewith.

It is significant that this court has never applied these sections of the *Contributory Negligence Act*, even where it has been faced by what Caswell, *supra*, terms the "classic" last clear chance fact situations. Nor has this court upheld a trial level decision applying the last clear chance doctrine. Rather, in *Lengauer v. Bate* (1974), 2 N.R. 586 (Alta. C.A.), aff'd (1974), 2 N.R. 585 (S.C.C.) and in *Abbott v. Kasza* (1976), 71 D.L.R. (3d) 581, this court overturned trial level decisions that applied the last clear chance rule. In *Abbott,* for example, Clement J.A., at p. 589, held that the proper approach was to recognize that "each component of liability is only a facet of the whole, and judgment must be on the entirety, not piecemeal on refractions from each facet."

With the exception of Newfoundland, the Courts of Appeal of other provinces have all expressed concern and doubt as to the applicability of the last clear chance doctrine in light of the passage of contributory negligence statutes. In Ontario and New Brunswick, the courts have given particularly strong pronouncements against the use of the doctrine. For example, Laskin J.A., as he then was, held that apportionment legislation "dispens[ed] with any need to look hard over one's shoulder for the doctrine of ultimate negligence or the 'last opportunity rule'." (*F.W. Argue Ltd. v. Howe* (1966), 57 D.L.R. (2d) 691 (Ont. C.A.)). In New Brunswick, Hoyt C.J.N.B. in *Fillier v. Whittom* (1995), 171 N.B.R. (2d) 92 (C.A.), held:

> In my view, if our decision in *Valais* and *Stamper* did not do so in sufficiently clear terms, it is time to clearly say that the doctrine of last chance or ultimate negligence or last opportunity has no application in New Brunswick. There is no justification, with apportionment legislation, for retaining a rule that was designed to ameliorate the harshness of the common law that defeated a plaintiff's claim if he or she was partly at fault.

It is interesting to note that despite these strong pronouncements, the applicability of the last clear chance doctrine continues to be raised and sometimes applied in the lower courts of those provinces. Consequently, the status of the last clear chance doctrine remains in confusion. This is particularly true in those provinces, like Manitoba and Saskatchewan, where the Courts of Appeal have expressed doubt as to the doctrine's applicability, but have not ruled specifically on that issue.

The confusion created by this out-dated doctrine of tort law is most poignantly revealed through an examination of the jurisprudence addressing this issue in British Columbia. It is to be recalled that the *Negligence Act, supra*, specifically abrogated the doctrine of last clear chance from the law of British Columbia. Despite the statutory abrogation, the Court of Appeal has been called upon no less than five times since 1990 to reverse trial decisions that continue to apply last clear chance. Thus, the jurisprudence in British Columbia highlights the tremendous tenacity and inherent confusion surrounding the doctrine of last clear chance.

Against this background of many challenges to the necessity for last clear chance, but without clear direction from the Supreme Court of Canada or this court, it is necessary to look at the rationale for it.

One possibility is that it has a role to play in determining causation which is, after all, the reason it was created. But as Professor Klar says at p. 371 of his text, *Tort Law, supra*:

> Whether a party's negligent conduct should be described as proximate or remote in view of the intervening act of negligence of a subsequent party cannot be resolved on the basis of who had the last clear chance to avoid the injury.

If a party's conduct has not been the factual and proximate cause of the injuries, that party is not negligent. If the party's conduct meets the two tests, the party is negligent and the degree of fault must be determined. Unfortunately last clear chance has become confused with the analysis for remoteness referred to earlier. But it has nothing to add to modern causation analysis.

The second possibility is that it is useful in determining causation because it is a technique by which comparative fault can be ascertained. But as Professor Klar says, *supra*, at p. 372:

> If last clear chance is looked at as a rule of comparative fault, it is clearly inconsistent with apportionment legislation. It is no longer necessary to use the rule to avoid the stalemate solution of the earlier common law. Notions of comparative fault leading to an all or nothing approach are inconsistent with apportionment laws.

In conclusion, it is clear that last clear chance is an anachronism. It is no longer helpful or necessary in the causation analysis. Unfortunately, its continued existence in ss. 6 and 7 of the *Contributory Negligence Act* is a trap. Professor Caswell, *supra*, has summarized it this way, at p. 131:

> ... the rule lingers on as a potential pitfall for the unwary in any fact situation involving successive acts of negligence of the plaintiff and defendant and ... it may still subvert the purpose served by apportionment legislation, namely fixing liability according to degrees of fault.

I cannot read ss. 6 or 7 as attempts by the Legislature to undermine the purpose of the statute, which manifestly is to divide fault among all tort-feasors. The sections should only be invoked in those cases where the distance between accident and alleged fault is so great in time and circumstance that it could be said that the fault is too remote from the injury for liability. But that is a test to be applied in all cases of negligence, so the sections add nothing to the general law. Meanwhile, the duty of a judge is, in every case where the tort-feasor's negligence is not too remote but where another tort-feasor has contributed to the injury, to divide liability.

I urge the government to act on the recommendations of the Alberta Law Reform Institute and repeal s. 6 and s. 7 of the *Contributory Negligence Act*.

(3) The Resolution of Cause By The Trial Judge

The trial judge found that the appellant had 12 to 18 seconds to respond and this, apparently, was the basis for his decision that there was a "clear line" between the negligence of the parties and that the appellant had the last clear chance to avoid the collision. These facts do not meet the temporal test required by the Act. This was an attempt to apply s. 7 of the *Contributory Negligence Act* and the last clear chance analysis. In the result the trial judge was persuaded that in reconciling the successive acts of negligence of the appellant and respondent he had to apply last clear chance: draw a line and determine ultimate negligence. This was an error in law. Having found the respondent negligent, he was required to set degrees of negligence.

(4) Determining Degrees of Negligence

Having accepted the fact finding of the trial judge and having been asked by the appellant and respondent to consider the issue of degrees of negligence, it falls to this Court to set the degrees of negligence. Certain conduct of the respondent is relevant in determining his degree of negligence. The respondent backed up to assist at the scene of an accident but chose to stop in the travel lane for his own convenience. There is no evidence that he had flashers on and, since he had parked, there were no brake lights on. His vehicle, seconds before the collision, blocking the driving line, unmarked and on a highway, created a real hazard. The risk it presented was heightened by the fact of the overturned vehicle in the ditch. It is common knowledge that an accident itself, may create a risk situation. The only reason given by the respondent for parking in the driving lane rather than on the shoulder was that the latter was soft. Presented with the two possibilities of getting stuck on the shoulder or parking in the driving lane of a highway, it is clear which choice the reasonable driver would have taken. In conclusion, the respondent's actions were not only a cause in fact and proximate cause of the appellant's injuries, but were a significant cause of them.

The negligence of the appellant flows from his inattention and his failure to take effective evasive actions as described by the expert: stopping, changing lanes or swerving. His actions were negligent and a significant cause of his injuries. As plaintiff he is accountable for his contributory negligence.

Based on the negligence of both parties, and pursuant to s. 2(1) of the *Contributory Negligence Act*, the parties are equally responsible and the degree of negligence of each is 50%.

In the result, the appeal on liability is allowed and the respondent is liable for 50% of the appellant's damages. The appeal of the damage assessment by the trial judge is dismissed.

8. Should the defence of contributory negligence be available to a defendant who is in violation of a penal statute?

   Usually, the defence is available where the defendant violates a statute. In *Graham v. R.* (1978), 90 D.L.R. (3d) 223, [1978] 6 W.W.R. 48 (Sask. Q.B.), the contributory negligence defence was employed, even though the defendant was in breach of a statute regarding the maintenance of a highway.

   In the United States, however, there is authority that, in certain situations, the defence may be unavailable to a defendant who violates a statute. See *Dart v. Pure Oil Co.*, 223 Minn. 326, 27 N.W. 2d 555 (1947), outlining some of the exceptional statutes, the violation of which may forbid a defendant in the United States from relying on the defence.

9. Is this defence available in actions for intentional torts? For actions based on trespass? What is meant by the words "fault or negligence" as used in s. 1 of the *Ontario Act*?

   In *Hollebone v. Barnard*, [1954] O.R. 236, [1954] 2 D.L.R. 278 (H.C.), the plaintiff was struck by a golf ball driven by the defendant. In an action for damages, presented as an action of "trespass", the jury found: (1) that the defendant had not satisfied them that the plaintiff's injuries were suffered without negligence on the part of the defendant, (2) that there was contributory negligence on the part of the plaintiff which caused or contributed to his injuries, and (3) that the plaintiff's and the defendant's negligence contributed equally to the plaintiff's injuries. The trial judge held that the Ontario *Contributory Negligence Act*, directing apportionment of damages in proportion to the degree of fault or negligence found against the parties in an action "founded upon the fault or negligence of the defendant", did not apply to an action based on trespass. In his view a plea of contributory negligence had never been a defence to an action of trespass and the Act was confined "to cases arising in negligence". "[This] is not an action which was founded upon the fault or negligence of the defendant. It is in fact an action which is founded on the alleged trespass of the defendant to the person of the plaintiff. That is something entirely different."

   The plaintiff, therefore, recovered the full amount of the damages sustained by him.

10. Compare with *Bell Canada v. Cope (Sarnia) Ltd.* (1980), 11 C.C.L.T. 170 (S.C.); affd (1980), 31 O.R. (2d) 571, 15 C.C.L.T. 190 (C.A.), where Bell was suing the defendant in both negligence and trespass for cutting one of its live service wires. The defendant was unable to show that it did not damage the wire as a result of its negligence or intentional conduct. The defendant, however, did prove that the plaintiff was negligent

in the way it staked the underground wires, among other things. Mr. Justice Linden apportioned liability, two-thirds against Bell and one-third against Cope. Linden J. explained as follows:

> Fault and negligence, as these words are used in the Statute, are not the same thing. Fault certainly includes negligence, but it is much broader than that. Fault incorporates all intentional wrongdoing, as well as other types of sub-standard conduct. In this case, both intentional and negligent wrongdoing were satisfactorily proved.
>
> Our courts today should, where possible, refrain from deciding important substantive questions, such as whether *The Negligence Act* applies here, on the basis of whether the pleading alleges trespass, or negligence, or both. ...
>
> The gist of the trespass action today is fault; if it can be established by the defendant that there was no negligence and no intentional interference then the action will fail because no fault exists. Consequently, trespass is based on fault and is no longer a strict liability cause of action. (See *Weaver v. Ward* (1616), 80 E.R. 284). I find, therefore, that a trespass action comes within the opening words of section 4 of *The Negligence Act.*

Mr. Justice Linden distinguished *Hollebone v. Barnard* as a case based *solely* on trespass. He also declared that, since *Hollebone v. Barnard* was a decision of a trial judge, he was "not strictly bound by it". In any event, he felt that it was "based on an erroneous reliance upon certain early authorities dealing with the scope of the *Negligence Act* ..." which had "no relevance at all in the interpretation of the meaning of the words 'fault or negligence' in this context." See also *Verbrugge v. Bush*, [1976] W.W.D. 79 (B.C.S.C.); *Teece v. Honeybourne* (1974), 54 D.L.R. (3d) 549, [1974] 5 W.W.R. 592 (B.C.S.C.); *Anderson v. Stevens* (1981), 125 D.L.R. (3d) 736, [1981] 5 W.W.R. 550 (B.C.S.C.); *Gillen v. Noel* (1984), 50 N.B.R. (2d) 379, 131 A.P.R. 379 (Q.B.); and *Berntt v. Vancouver (City)* (1997), 33 C.C.L.T. (2d) 1 (B.C.S.C.).

11. Does the defence of contributory negligence apply to actions for breach of contract?

In *Speed and Speed Ltd. v. Finance America Realty Ltd.* (1979), 38 N.S.R. (2d) 374, 12 C.C.L.T. 4 (C.A.), MacKeigan C.J.N.S. said "yes". The Chief Justice stated:

> I have little doubt that the Nova Scotia *Act* applies where loss is caused by any "fault"; the word "tort" does not appear. I agree with Pigeon J., who (dissenting on other issues with the majority) in *Smith v. McInnis*, [1978] 2 S.C.R. 1357 at pp. 1379-81 ... held that "fault" in s. 1(1) of the Act means fault in the civil law sense and includes common law liability in contract.

Also see *Caners v. Eli Lilly Canada Inc.*, [1996] 5 W.W.R. 381 (Man. C.A.).

In *Tompkins Hardware Ltd. v. North Western Flying Services Ltd.* (1982), 139 D.L.R. (3d) 329, 22 C.C.L.T. 1 (Ont. H.C.), the Court held that, although the *Negligence Act*, R.S.O. 1980, c. 315, did not permit contributory negligence in actions for breach of contract, at common law apportionment of liability is possible in cases of breach of contract and that the measure of apportionment would be the same in tort or contract. Saunders J., in reducing the damage by 20 per cent, explained (at 16 C.C.L.T.) as follows:

> The principle that, where a man is part author of his own injury he cannot call upon the other party to compensate him in full, has long been recognized as applying in cases of tort. ... I see no reason why it should not equally be applicable in cases of contract. I have been unable to find any authority that says otherwise and, in my opinion, it makes sense. The plaintiff is under an

> obligation to mitigate his damages. ... In such circumstances, there should, in my opinion, be apportionment whether the action be brought in contract or in tort.

12. In *Canadian Western Natural Gas Co. Ltd. v. Pathfinder Surveys Ltd.* (1980), 12 Alta. L.R. (2d) 135, 12 C.C.L.T. 211 (C.A.), Mr. Justice Prowse held that a plaintiff cannot avoid the possibility of being found contributorily negligent by framing a negligence action in contract rather than in tort, if both are suitable. Prowse J.A. had this further observation:

> One further comment I would make is that if I had concluded that the negligence set out above does not fall within s. 2 of *The Contributory Negligence Act*, I would not have considered it beyond the scope of the common law to hold that when contributory negligence is set up as a shield against the obligation to satisfy the whole of a plaintiff's claim it should be given effect to on the principle that, where a man is part author of his own injury, he cannot call on the other party to compensate him in full. ... The fact that contributory negligence is often pleaded in answer to claims in contract, as it was here, and the fact that it is regularly applied by the business community in such circumstances should be considered as support for the Court extending the application of such principle to claims such as this. In doing so it would merely be applying generally a principle adopted in particular circumstances by the Legislature in *The Contributory Negligence Act*.

13. There are some extremely difficult procedural and mathematical problems arising out of the apportionment legislation. Some of the more important problems are:

    (a) How is the apportionment between the parties to be done? Are we comparing the relative "blameworthiness" of the parties, the degrees to which each party's fault caused or contributed to the injuries, or a combination of both? For a good discussion of this issue see *Clyke v. Blenkhorn* (1958), 13 D.L.R. (2d) 293, 41 M.P.R. 1 (N.S.C.A.); *Ottosen v. Kasper* (1986), 37 C.C.L.T. 270 (B.C.C.A.).

    (b) When you have one plaintiff and more than one defendant, do you compare the fault of the plaintiff on one hand and the *combined* fault of all the defendants jointly, or do you compare the plaintiff with each defendant separately? This issue was discussed in great detail by the House of Lords in *Fitzgerald v. Lane*, [1988] W.L.R. 356, [1988] 2 All E.R. 961, where it was decided that the correct approach is to consider the fault of the plaintiff on one hand and that of the defendants jointly on the other. Another excellent discussion of these issues is found in the Australian case of *Barisic v. Devenport*, [1978] 2 N.S.W.L.R. 111 (C.A.). For a much earlier Canadian case see *Colonial Coach Lines Ltd. v. Bennett and C.P.R. Co.*, [1968] 1 O.R. 333, 66 D.L.R. (2d) 396 (C.A.).

    (c) When you have a contributorily negligent plaintiff and more than one defendant do you use a "joint and several" approach or is the plaintiff entitled only to several judgments against each defendant? Most provinces use the joint and several judgment approach, whereas in British Columbia the several judgments approach has prevailed. See the Alberta case, *Campbell Estate v. Calgary Power Ltd.*, [1989] 1 W.W.R. 36, 46 C.C.L.T. 229 (Alta. C.A.), for an example of the former, and the B.C. case, *Leischner v. West Kootenay Power* (1986), 24 D.L.R. (4th) 641, [1986] 3 W.W.R. 97 (B.C.C.A.), for an example of the latter.

    (d) Most agree that a set-off should not be ordered between the contributorily negligent plaintiff and the negligent defendant where insurance is involved. Why? See, for example, *Wells v. Russell*, [1952] O.W.N. 521 (C.A.).

14. See generally Williams, *Joint Torts and Contributory Negligence* (1951); Cheifetz, *Apportionment of Fault in Tort* (1981); Klar, "Contributory Negligence and Contribution between Tortfeasors," in Klar (ed.), *Studies in Canadian Tort Law* (1977), p. 145.

LINDEN AND SOMMERS, "THE CIVIL JURY IN THE COURTS OF ONTARIO: A POSTSCRIPT TO THE OSGOODE HALL STUDY"

(1968), 6 Osgoode Hall L.J. 252, at 254.

THE RESULT OF TRIALS

Critics of the civil jury charge that it is biased in favour of the plaintiff and, consequently, the defendants do not get a fair hearing. This allegation is not borne out by the facts. Table I shows that, although the jury decided wholly in favour of the plaintiff in 48.6 percent of the cases studied, the trial judges alone found completely in the plaintiff's favour 71.7 percent of the time, indicating a more marked inclination on the part of judges to favour the plaintiff, contrary to what has been charged. When one studies the dismissals, however, this trend is modified, for judges alone tended to dismiss law suits more readily than juries did; judges exonerated the defendant in 18.8 percent of the cases, while juries did so only in 2.7 percent of the cases they decided.

Table I

THE RESULT OF JURY TRIALS COMPARED WITH NON-JURY TRIALS

Type of Case	For Plaintiff Wholly		Apportionment Plaintiff 1-50% At Fault		Apportionment Plaintiff 51-99% At Fault		Case Dismissed		Total	
	No.	%	No.	%	No.	%	No.	%	No.	%
Jury	18	48.6	11	29.7	7	18.9	1	2.7	37	99.9
Non-jury	38	71.1	3	5.6	2	3.7	10	18.8	53	99.8

It is in the treatment of contributory negligence that one of the main distinctions between judge and jury trial is demonstrated; judges rarely apportion negligence, whereas juries do so frequently. Liability was split in 48.6 per cent of the jury trials, but only in 9.3 per cent of the judge trials. This indicates that judges have hardly taken notice of the comparative negligence legislation which permits liability to be divided, feeling themselves able to decide completely one way or the other on the facts. The jury is less confident of its own powers and chooses rather to divide responsibility between the two parties, a practice that may well accord better with the true position with regard to blameworthiness. This willingness on the part of juries to reduce the awards of plaintiffs shows a lack of bias on their part. As another consequence, however, plaintiffs before juries receive some reparation in 97.2 per cent of the decisions, while those before judges do in 81 per cent of the cases. This indicates that the jury system does in fact assist to broaden the incidence of tort recovery, but these payments are often reduced in amount because of comparative negligence. Indeed, if the jury trial were jettisoned, the laudable objective of the *Negligence Act* would be severely undermined, since judges seem so reluctant to avail themselves of it.

NOTES

1. Overall satisfaction with our comparative negligence legislation has been expressed by Mr. Justice Schroeder in these words:

> ... the change effected by our statute was more consonant with the modern needs and concepts of society in a changing world, and better adapted to the requirements and habits of the age in which we live: ... the doctrines established long before the days of the steam engine, the incandescent lamp, the modern automobile and the jet-propelled airplane, no longer served to promote the welfare of the members of our modern society and needed to be replaced by a law which was better adjusted to the increasing complexities of the daily routine and the greater tempo of life in our day and generation.

He concluded that there is not "a progressive and socially conscious member of the judiciary or of the bar of our province who would wish to repeal the legislation ... and return to the discarded common-law doctrine of contributory negligence". See "Courts and Comparative Negligence", [1950] Ins. L.J. 791. *Cf.*, Davie, *Common Law and Statutory Amendment in Relation to Contributory Negligence in Canada* (1936), reviewed by MacDonald (1936), 14 Can. Bar Rev. 368.

2. Information concerning the operation of juries has been provided by the Osborne *Report of Inquiry into Motor Vehicle Accident Compensation in Ontario*, 1988. In relation to motor vehicle accident litigation the study found that there has been a significant increase in the number of jury actions, that most jury notices are served by defendants, and that pre-trial settlements are as likely in jury and non-jury trials. Why do you think that defendants, who are insurers in motor vehicle cases, prefer juries?

B. THE SEAT BELT DEFENCE

GALASKE v. O'DONNELL

Supreme Court of Canada (1994), 112 D.L.R. (4th) 109

The plaintiff, aged eight, and his father, were passengers in the defendant's truck. The plaintiff was not wearing a seat-belt. An accident occurred, through no fault of the defendant, and the plaintiff was injured, due to the fact that he was not wearing a seat-belt. The plaintiff sued the defendant driver alleging negligence in not ensuring that the plaintiff was wearing a seat-belt. The trial judge and the Court of Appeal dismissed the action. The plaintiff appealed to the Supreme Court of Canada.

Cory J.:

The general duty resting on all occupants of a car to wear seat-belts

It has long been recognized that all occupants of a motor vehicle have a duty to wear their seat-belts. In his excellent text, *Canadian Tort Law*, 5th ed. (Toronto: Butterworths, 1993), Justice Linden carefully reviewed the cases involving the use of seat-belts. He observed that Canadian courts have recognized that passengers and drivers have a duty to ensure their own safety in a car by wearing seat-belts. A failure to do so will result in an assessment of contributory negligence against that person. The author notes that where the seat-belt defence was rejected, there was no evidence that the failure to wear the seat-belt caused or aggravated the injury. That is certainly not at issue in this case.

The reasoning of Lord Denning in *Froom v. Butcher*, [1975] 3 All E.R. 520 (C.A.) at pp. 525-7, has often been cited in support of the need to wear seat-belts. There he stated:

> *The sensible practice*
>
> It is compulsory for every motor car to be fitted with seat belts for the front seats. The regulations so provide. They apply to every motor car registered since 1st 1965. In the regulations seat belts are called, in cumbrous language, "body-restraining seat belts". A "seat belt" is defined as "a belt intended to be worn by a person in a vehicle and designed to prevent or lessen injury to its wearer in the event of an accident to the vehicle..."
>
> Seeing that it is compulsory [*sic*] to fit seat belts, Parliament must have thought it sensible to wear them. But it did not make it compulsory for anyone to wear a seat-belt. Everyone is free to wear it, or not, as he pleases. Free in this sense, that if he does not wear it, he is free from any penalty by the magistrates. Free in the sense that everyone is free to run his head against a brick wall, if he pleases. He can do it if he likes without being punished by the law. But it is not a sensible thing to do. If he does it, it is his own fault; and he has only himself to thank for the consequences.
>
> Much material has been put before us about the value of wearing a seat belt. It shows quite plainly that everyone in the front seats of a car should wear a seat belt. Not only on long trips, but also on short ones. Not only in the town, but also in the country. Not only when there is fog, but also when it is clear. Not only by fast drivers, but also by slow ones. Not only on motorways, but also on side roads.
>
> ...
>
> Quite a lot of people, however, think differently about seat belts. Some are like Mr. Froom here. They think that they would be less likely to be injured if they were thrown clear than if they were strapped in. They would be wrong.... In determining responsibility, the law eliminates the personal equation. It takes no notice of the views of the particular individual; or of others like him. It requires everyone to exercise all such precautions as a man of ordinary prudence would observe.
>
> ...
>
> Other people take the view that the risk of an accident is so remote that it is not necessary to wear a seat belt on all occasions; but only when there are circumstances which carry a high risk.... I cannot accept this view either. You never know when a risk may arise. It often happens suddenly and when least anticipated, when there is no time to fasten the seat belt. Besides, it is easy to forget when only done occasionally. But, done regularly, it becomes automatic. Every time that a car goes out on the road there is the risk of an accident. Not that you yourself will be negligent. But that someone else will be. That is a possibility which a prudent man should, and will, guard against. He should always, if he is wise, wear a seat belt.
>
> ...
>
> Lastly, there are many people who do not wear their seat belts, simply through forgetfulness or inadvertence or thoughtlessness.... The case for wearing seat belts is so strong that I do not think the law can admit forgetfulness as an excuse.

These reasons are as sensible and compelling in 1994, as they were in 1975, and should have been in 1985.

The courts in this country have consistently deducted from 5% to 25% from claims for damages for personal injury on the grounds that the victims were contributorily negligent for not wearing their seat-belts. This has been done whenever it has been demonstrated that the injuries would have been reduced if the belts had in fact been worn. [Citations to cases omitted.]

The same principle has been applied in British Columbia, as the following cases demonstrate: *Yuan v. Farstad* (1967), 66 D.L.R. (2d) 295, 62 W.W.R. 645 (B.C.S.C.)....

The decision of Munroe J. in *Yuan* appears to be one of the first Canadian decisions to hold that occupants of a car have a duty to wear a seat-belt. That is to say, there is a duty of care resting upon the occupants of a motor vehicle to wear a seat-belt. The accident in that case occurred in 1966 in a residential area of the City of Vancouver. The following prescient statements made by Munroe J. at pp. 300-2, in my view, are a correct expression of the principles applicable to the wearing of seat-belts.

> It is the submission of the defendants that the deceased, by his failure to use his seat belt, failed to use reasonable care or to take proper precautions for his own safety and thereby contributed to his own injuries. If that is so, the defence of contributory negligence must succeed: See *Nance v. British Columbia Electric R. Co.*, [1951] 3 D.L.R. 705, [1951] A.C. 601, 67 C.R.T.C. 340, 2 W.W.R. (N.S.) 665; *Car & General Insurance Corp. Ltd. v Seymour and Maloney*, 2 D.L.R. (2d) 369, [1956] S.C.R. 322; *Prior et al. v. Kyle* (1965), 52 D.L.R. (2d) 272, 52 W.W.R. 1 (B.C.C.A.).
>
> In support of such submission the defendants called as witnesses Capt. E.T. Corning, retired captain of the Seattle Police Force, and Dr. Peter Fisher, a Seattle physician and surgeon and specialist in internal medicine. Each of these men had made a study of the effectiveness of seat belts in safeguarding motorists from injuries. Their qualifications and experience entitle them to give opinion evidence. Capt. Corning has investigated hundreds of automobile accidents. Based upon his experience and studies, he is firmly of opinion that lap seat belts, when worn, do tend to lessen the severity of injuries in most automobile accidents. Based upon personal observations made at race tracks as well as other studies done by him, Dr. Fisher is of opinion that a lap seat belt will prevent ejection from a vehicle and will lessen the severity of any steering wheel injury because it prevents body displacement.... Based upon the evidence of these two experts, which was uncontraverted, and based upon the general knowledge of mankind, it is clear, and I find, that lap seat belts are effective in reducing fatalities and minimizing injuries resulting from automobile accidents. I adopt the view of Mr. Justice Frankfurter who once said, "there comes a point where this court should not be ignorant as judges of what we know as men."... In the face of such knowledge, and despite the apparent absence of any Canadian precedents upon the matter, I am of opinion that a reasonable and prudent driver of a motor vehicle in a city would and should make use of a seat belt provided for his use. I am not unmindful of the fact that in driving without having his seat belt done up, the deceased was committing neither a crime nor any breach of statute. He was lawfully entitled to drive without using his seat belt, but that is not determinative of the issue as to whether or not in so doing he failed to take proper precautions for his safety and thus contributed to his injuries. If he did so fail the defendants are entitled to be relieved of some degree of responsibility for the resulting injuries, as is provided by the *Contributory Negligence Act.*

Munroe J. further supported his decision on the basis of American cases which found that a duty to wear a seat-belt could be based upon common law standards of care. He referred to *Bentzler v. Braun*, 149 N.W. 2d 626 (Wis., 1967), and to the California District Court of Appeal in *Mortensen v. Southern Pacific Co.*, 53 Cal. Rptr. 851 (1966)].

These cases demonstrate that since 1968 courts in Canada have properly recognized that the exercise of reasonable care requires occupants of a motor vehicle to wear seat-belts. This is true whether a vehicle is being driven on a highway or in the city, over a long or short distance. The cases correctly reflect the dictates of common sense. Long before 1985, when this accident occurred, it was a reasonable requirement that seat-belts be worn.

The duty owed by a driver to ensure that passengers under 16 wear seat belts

There is therefore a duty of care owed by an occupant of a car to wear a seat-belt. This duty is based upon the sensible recognition of the safety provided by seat-belts and the forseeability of harm resulting from the failure to wear them. What then of children in a car? Children under 16, although they may contest it, do require guidance and direction from parents and older persons. This has always been recognized by society. That guidance and protection must extend to ensuring that those under 16 properly wear their seat-belts. To the question of who should assume that duty, the answer must be that there may be two or more people who bear that responsibility. However, one of those responsible must always be the driver of the car.

A driver taking children as passengers must accept some responsibility for the safety of these children. The driving of a motor vehicle is neither a God-given nor a constitutional right. It is a licensed activity that is subject to a number of conditions, including the demonstration of a minimum standard of skill and knowledge pertaining to driving. Obligations and responsibilities flow from the right to drive. Those responsibilities must include some regard for the safety of young passengers. Children, as a result of their immaturity, may be unable to properly consider and provide for their own safety. The driver must take reasonable steps to see that young passengers wear their seat-belts. This is so since it is forseeable that harm can result from the failure to wear a seat-belt, and since frequently, a child will, for any number of reasons, fail to secure the seat-belt.

The driver of a car is in a position of control. The control may not be quite as great as that of a master of a vessel or the pilot of an aircraft. Nevertheless, it exists. Coexistent with the right to drive and control a car is the responsibility of the driver to take reasonable steps to provide for the safety of passengers. Those reasonable steps must include not only the duty to drive carefully but also to see that seat-belts are worn by young passengers who may not be responsible for ensuring their own safety.

In my view, quite apart from any statutory provisions, drivers must accept the responsibility of taking all reasonable steps to ensure that passengers under 16 years of age are in fact wearing their seat-belts. The general public knowledge of the vital importance of seat-belts as a safety factor requires a driver to ensure that young people make use of them. I would observe that this same conclusion was reached by Paris J. in *Da Costa (Guardian ad litem of) v. Da Costa* (1993), 41 A.C.W.S. (3d) 456, [1993] B.C.J. No. 1485 (S.C.). He too concluded that there is a duty owed by a driver to ensure that children are wearing their seat-belts. The statutory provisions pertaining to seat-belts must now be considered.

The effect of the Motor Vehicle Act

Section 217(6) of the *Motor Vehicle Act* reads as follows:

> 217(6) A person shall not drive on a highway a motor vehicle in which there is a passenger who has attained age 6 but is under age 16 and who occupies a seating position for which a seat belt assembly is provided unless that passenger is wearing the complete seat belt assembly in a properly adjusted and securely fastened manner.

In *Canada v. Saskatchewan Wheat Pool, supra*, the issue was whether a breach of the *Candian Grain Act*, S.C. 1970-71-72, c. 7, by delivery of infested grain out of a grain elevator, conferred upon the Canadian Wheat Board a civil right of action against the Saskatchewan Wheat Pool for damages. No allegation of negligence at common law was put forward. The notion of a nominate tort of statutory breach giving rise to recovery simply on proof of breach of the statute was rejected. So, too, was the argument that an unexcused breach of statute constituted negligence *per se* which would lead to an automatic finding of liability. The court, in the clear and convincing reasons delivered by Dickson J. (as he then was), took the position that proof of a statutory breach which causes damages *may* be evidence of negligence. Further, it was held that the statutory formulation of the duty *may*, but not necessarily will, afford a specific or useful standard of reasonable conduct.

It follows that the statutory requirement pertaining to seat-belts is subsumed in the general law of negligence. However, the statute can, I think, be taken as a public indication that the failure of a driver to ensure that children in the vehicle are wearing seat-belts constitutes unreasonable conduct. Further, it may be taken as indicating that such a failure on the part of the driver demonstrates conduct which falls below the standard required by the community and is thus negligent. In this case, the legislation is simply another factor which can be taken into account by the court in the course of determining whether the failure to ensure children in the car are wearing seat-belts constituted negligent behaviour on the part of the driver.

It is clear that the breach of a statutory provision is not conclusive of liability. Yet the existence of the section does provide further support for finding that a duty of care rests on the driver to take all reasonable steps to see that seat-belts are worn by children. The statute reflects the public importance placed on safety measures and a societal concern for promoting the safety of children. It is, as well, a public recognition that children often require the help and supervision of adults, particularly in ensuring that when they are passengers in a vehicle, they are made reasonably safe.

Is the driver's duty of care negated by the presence of a parent?

The duty of a driver to ensure that young passengers wear their seat-belts is well-established. It then must be asked whether the presence of a parent in the car negates this duty of care owed by the driver. The trial judge and the Court of Appeal took the position that the presence of the parent in the car removed or terminated the duty of care owed by the driver. In support of that position, the respondent relies on the decisions of this court in *Arnold v. Teno* (1978), 83 D.L.R. (3d) 609 at pp. 623-4, [1978] 2 S.C.R. 287, 3 C.C.L.T. 272, and of the New Zealand Court of Appeal in *McCallion v. Dodd,* [1969] N.Z.L.R., 710 at p. 721. In my view, these decisions simply indicate that there may be a joint responsibility or duty of care resting upon both a parent and a third party. The presence of a parent in the car may mean that the responsibility is shared, but it cannot negate the duty owed by the driver to the passengers under the age of 16.

The driver of a car owes a duty of care to a child who is a passenger. For example, the driver must obey the rules of the road and drive carefully whether a parent is present or not. That duty of care is owed and continues to be owed by a driver to all child passengers, irrespective of their parents' presence. The relationship between driver and passenger is such that the driver's negligent actions or negligent failure to act can lead to injuries to the passengers. Further, it is well-established and clearly forseeable that harm may result from the failure to wear a seat-belt just as much as it may result from negligent driving.

Again, as I have said, the driver of a car is in a position of control. The driver's control remains even in the presence of a child passenger's parent. The responsibility of the driver to take reasonable steps to provide for the safety of passengers flows, in part, from this control, and it includes not only a duty to drive carefully, but also to take reasonable steps to ensure that seat-belts are worn by young passengers who may not be able to ensure their own safety.

In my view, there is a duty of care resting upon a driver of a motor vehicle to ensure that the seat-belts of young passengers are in place. That duty exists whether or not a parent of the child is in the car. The presence of the parent does no more than indicate that the duty of care or responsibility towards the child may be shared by both the parent and the driver.

It is true that the conclusion I have reached is one of public policy which imposes a positive duty. That in itself is not novel. The need to impose a positive duty on a party was recognized by this court in *Jordan House Ltd. v. Menow* (1974), 38 D.L.R. (3d) 105, [1974] S.C.R. 239, and in *Crocker v. Sundance Northwest Resorts Ltd.* (1988), 51 D.L.R. (4th) 321, [1988] 1 S.C.R. 1186, 44 C.C.L.T. 225. This decision is no more than an attempt to provide reasonable care for the safety of children.

There will undoubtedly be those who will decry the decision on the ground that it may lead to an increase in vehicle insurance premiums. The cold fiscal response to that criticism is to observe that this same decision will result in a far greater saving in health care premiums by reducing the cost of health care required for seriously injured children who are victims of injuries which result from the failure to wear a seat-belt. Yet far more important than any financial benefits which may flow from the decision is the fostering of the safety of children. In this case, if seat-belts had been worn, there can be no doubt that the appellant could have led a fulfilling and useful life. If the fixing of responsibility on a driver to ensure that young passengers wear seat-belts saves one child from death or devastating injury, then all society will have benefited

The trial judge and the Court of Appeal were in error in failing to recognize that the duty of care owed by the driver of the motor vehicle to young passengers continued to exist despite the presence of a parent in the vehicle. This is an error of law that can and should be corrected by an appellate court.

Standard of care or the extent of the duty owed by the driver

The definition of the standard of care is a mixed question of law and fact. It will usually be for the trial judge to determine, in light of the circumstances of the case, what would constitute reasonable conduct on the part of the legendary reasonable man placed in the same circumstances. In some situations a simple reminder may suffice, while in others, for example when a very young child is the passenger, the driver may have to put the seat-belt on the child himself. In this case, however, the driver took no steps whatsoever to ensure that the child passenger wore a seat-belt. It follows that the trial judge's decision on the issue amounted to a finding that there was no duty at all resting upon the driver. This was an error of law.

The extent of the duty owed by the driver of a vehicle to a child passenger when a parent is present will undoubtedly vary with the circumstances. Although the duty will always exist, the extent of it will vary infinitely. For example, a 17-year-old driving a car with an eight-year-old and his father, who is an old friend of the family, may well owe a much smaller duty of care to the child than the father. On the other hand, the driver of a motor vehicle who is driving home a mother who is an employee, and her child, may have a significantly higher degree of responsibility for the child. The difference in degree of responsibility will vary widely, depending on the circumstances of each case. The degree of responsibility will have to be determined in this case.

Disposition

In the result, the appeal is allowed. The question of the degree of contributing negligence of Stauffer should be remitted to the trial judge for determination at the same time as the determination is made as to whether there was any negligence on the part of the infant Karl Thomas Galaske or the late Peter Helmut Galaske, or both. The appellant should have his costs in this court and throughout.

NOTES

1. Major J. dissented. Although Major J. agreed that the driver did owe a duty of care to his passenger, he held that that the trial judge had found that there had been no breach of the duty. Breach of duty being a question of fact not lightly interfered with by an appellate court, Major J. concluded that there was no palpable and overriding error which would justify a reversal. The case points out the importance in distinguishing between duty and breach and the difficulty in doing so.

2. Not everyone is enamoured with the seat belt defence. See, for example, Kleist, "Seat Belt Defence — An Exercise in Sophistry" (1967), 18 Hastings L.J. 613:

> There is a basic legal fallacy to the seat belt "defence". It fails to take into account the established rule that a motorist has a right to assume that others upon the highway will obey the traffic laws; he need not take protective measures against the mere possibility of some future negligent act by another.
> The logic of the seat belt reasoning can be extended indefinitely, and various ridiculous conclusions envisioned. Would not a motorist be guilty of contributory negligence for failing to wear a shoulder harness? for failing to wear a crash helmet? for failing to drive in an armored car? for falling to utilize all of these protective devices simultaneously? If not, why not? They follow the reasoning advanced in the seat belt "defence". As protective measures, they are certainly as valuable as the use of seat belt.

Are you frightened by the parade of horribles mooted by the author? What would be so terrible about being expected to wear a helmet, for example, if it can be shown that many lives could be saved thereby? See also Roethe, "Seat Belt Negligence in Automobile Accidents," [1967] Wis. L. Rev. 288; Linden, "Seat Belts and Contributory Negligence" (1971), 49 Can. Bar Rev. 475; Hicks, "Seat Belts and Crash Helmets" (1974), 37 Mod. L. Rev. 308; Williams, "Seat Belts — Contributory Negligence — Position of English Courts" (1975), 53 Can. Bar Rev. 113.

3. In *Philip v. Hironaka*, [1998] 3 W.W.R. 703 (Alta. Q.B.), Girgulis J. agreed that it is unreasonable not to wear a seat belt and that generally seat belts reduce the severity of injuries. Nevertheless, he questioned whether the *Contributory Negligence Act* should apply to plaintiffs who fail to wear seat belts. According to his reasoning, a failure to wear a seat belt does not "cause" any damage or loss, which is a requirement under the legislation. Rather, a seat belt may only serve to reduce or lessen an injury which is caused by the defendant's negligence. Not wearing a seat belt may prevent this reduction in injuries from occurring. Nevertheless, Girgulis J. agreed that a failure to wear a seat belt is within "the spirit and intention" of the legislation. He would impose, however, a maximum 25 percent reduction of damages, save for the very exceptional case. This view clearly does not however represent Alberta law. See, for example, *Palek v. Hansen*, [1998] 1 W.W.R. 475, where the Alberta Court of Appeal approved of a 50 per cent reduction for failure to wear a seat belt.

4. There is really no dispute among the experts on the value of seat belts in reducing the number and severity of injuries and death. Virtually all agree that seat belts help in most cases.

   Dr. Hodson-Walker, "The Value of Safety Belts: A Review" (1970), 102 Can. Med. Ass. J. 391, surveyed the medical literature and prepared the following table.

Table II

REDUCTION IN MAJOR AND FATAL
INJURIES BY THE
USE OF SEAT-BELTS

Authors	No. of injuries studied	Percentage reduction
Tourin and Garrett	9717	35
Backstrom	712	50
Moreland	121	55
Lister and Milsom	893	67
Lindgren and Warg	382	69
Herbert	not stated	80
Gikas and Huelke	79	45
Kihlberg and Robinson	1302	59

   He concluded that safety belts reduce the risk of major or fatal injuries by nearly 60 per cent. An incidence of abdominal trauma of the order of .5 per cent is ascribed to seat belts. However, "they have never been shown to worsen injury and, while themselves producing injuries, they have prevented more serious ones". A study on the effectiveness of seat belt legislation in Manitoba, published in 1987 by the University of Manitoba, showed a decrease in head, facial and neck injuries after the seat belt law went into force. There was, however, an increase in chest and abdominal injuries. See, "The Impact of Bill 60 …", University of Manitoba, 1987. Also see the National Highway Traffic Safety Administration 1986 study which stated that seat belts reduce fatal injuries by 40-50 per cent.

5. There has been considerable case law on the seat belt defence. Most cases acknowledge that the failure to wear a seat belt is conduct which can amount to contributory negligence, while some authorities are still resistant to this development.

An admirable summary of the predominant view on this issue has been given by Fulton J. in *Gagnon v. Beaulieu*, [1977] 1 W.W.R. 702 (B.C.S.C.), as follows:

> (a) Failure, while travelling in a motor vehicle on a street or highway, to wear a seat belt or any part thereof as provided in a vehicle in accordance with the safety standards from time to time applicable is failure to take a step which a person knows or ought to know to be reasonably necessary for his own safety.
>
> (b) If in such circumstances he suffers injury as the result of the vehicle being involved in an accident, and if it appears from the evidence that if the seat belt had been worn the injuries would have been prevented or the severity thereof lessened, then the failure to wear a seat belt is negligence which has contributed to the nature and extent of those injuries.
>
> (c) In the case of this particular form of contributory negligence, the onus is on the defendant to satisfy the court, in accordance with the usual standard of proof, not only that the seat belt was not worn but also that the injuries would have been prevented or lessened if the seat belt had been worn. The court should not find the second of these facts merely by inference from the first, even if that has been established.

His Lordship reduced the damages by 25 per cent in a case where the plaintiff was thrown out of the vehicle.

6. Is it always unreasonable not to wear a seat belt? What do you think of the following views expressed by Huband J. in *Genik v. Ewanylo* (1980), 3 Man. R. (2d) 317, 12 C.C.L.T. 121 (C.A.)?

> The circumstances make an enormous difference. Take two extreme examples. On the one hand, suppose that a person is invited to be a passenger in the front seat of a motor vehicle. The intended trip will be lengthy, at night, over icy roads which are heavily travelled and with no division between lanes of traffic going in opposite directions. The intended driver has been awake for a protracted period of time, has had a few drinks, and is known to drive habitually at or in excess of the speed limit. Under those circumstances, the prudent man would probably not go on the trip, but having done so, only a fool would fail to utilize all available protective devices.
>
> On the other extreme, a person walking down the street is picked up by a neighbour on a quiet summer afternoon, and is offered a ride to the store two blocks away. Weather conditions are good, there is no visible traffic, the trip will be of short duration. The driver's past record is impeccable, and he is known for his prudent and careful driving. A suggestion that a failure to utilize a seat belt and a shoulder harness under those circumstances constitutes a departure from the standards of reasonable care, is utterly divorced from reality.

Huband J.A. concluded:

> In the instant case I do not think that a finding of contributory negligence should be made against the plaintiff. The circumstances pointed to no impending risk. It was a fine day for driving. The road was straight and in good condition for driving. Traffic was not heavy. The driver was cautious to ensure that he did not exceed the speed limit on his journey through the countryside. While the trip was a fairly lengthy one, the defendant says that he was feeling fine and was not fatigued. He had consumed no alcohol. No suggestion had been made by the driver to the passenger that she should use the seat belt. Accordingly, I would conclude that the plaintiff has been guilty of no departure from the standard by which a reasonable and prudent person will govern himself in relationship to his own safety.

7. How does tort law determine whether something is reasonable or not? If you were to apply the formula expressed in *United States v. Carroll Towing Co.*, 159 F.2d 69 (2nd Cir. Ct. of App. 1947), to the seat belt issue, what would your conclusion be? Professor Philip Osborne in a case comment at (1980), 12 C.C.L,T. 123, wrote:

> The decision in *Yuan v. Furstad* reflects a traditional and outdated view of the law of torts as it operates in automobile accidents. It is based on the view that the tort of negligence is a loss-shifting device based on concepts of personal responsibility where the purpose of tort law is not only to compensate, but equally to punish and deter individuals from careless conduct, and to educate the public in acceptable standards of conduct. This quaint old-fashioned view still has an insidious appeal but it is out of touch with modern trends in tort law particularly in relation to automobile accidents.

Do you agree that it is a "quaint, old-fashioned view" that tort law punishes, deters and educates? Would the public "buckle up" more willingly if they knew that a failure to use seat belts might reduce their damages in case of injury? Would you? Why does Professor Osborne regard this approach to tort law as being "insidious"?

8. What if the unbelted passenger is unaware of the presence of a seat belt in the vehicle? What if the passenger should reasonably be aware that a seat belt is there to be used? See *Haley v. Richardson* (1975), 10 N.B.R. (2d) 653, at 667 (*sub nom. McRae v. Richardson*), 60 D.L.R. (3d) 480 (C.A.), *per* Hughes C.J. Is there an obligation on the driver to advise a passenger to wear the seat belt? See *Beaver v. Crowe* (1975), 18 N.S.R. (2d) 562, 49 D.L.R. (3d) 114 (T.D.). What if there is no seat belt in the car? Is it unreasonable for the passenger to accept the ride anyway? See *Watson v. Kang* (1994), 4 B.C.L.R. (3d) 60 (C.A.); *Strandon v. Le*, unreported, April 29, 1994, Doc. No. 9010-00873, Tressler J., [1994] A.J. No. 428 (Q.B.); *cf. Fennellow v. Falez*, unreported, November 26, 1993, Doc. Nos. C900781, C90364, Coultras J., [1993] B.C.J. No. 2445 (S.C.); *Woodgate v. Watson et al.* (1995), 59 B.C.A.C. 226 (C.A.).

9. All provinces have enacted legislation requiring the use of seat belts. Does the existence of legislation affect the contributory negligence issue?

10. Do mandatory seat belt laws work? Studies have shown a much greater use of seat belts in provinces with mandatory laws. See the 1987 *Road Safety Annual Report*, Transport Canada, stating that use of seat belts in provinces with seat belt laws was 67.8 per cent, while use in non-mandatory provinces was only 27.2 per cent. Also see the 1987, University of Manitoba study, *supra.* The use of seat belts also depends upon other factors; for example, night-time driving shows a decrease in seat belt use, longer trips show an increase; drivers who are inebriated do not wear seat belts very frequently. See "The Characteristics of Night-time Drivers in British Columbia", 1982.

11. Is it wise to use the criminal law to force people to protect themselves against injury? If people want to take the risk of being injured more severely in a crash, why not respect their judgment?

12. Is the use of the contributory negligence principle of tort law a better way of encouraging seat belt use? What are the limitations of tort law in this area? Do people generally have any knowledge of tort law? What is the proper role of the courts in this area? See Weiler, "Legal Values and Judicial Decision-Making" (1970), 48 Can. Bar Rev. 1.

13. There are many proof problems presented by the seat belt defence. There are also some thorny mathematical issues. In *Yuan v. Furstad*, should the widow receive 75 per cent of her total loss; or 75 per cent of the difference between the loss she would have suffered had her husband strapped in and the loss she in fact suffered? Is the 75

per cent figure an estimate by the court of the difference between the damages actually suffered and those that would have been suffered if the seat belt had been worn? Should there be a "rough upper limit," say 25 per cent, beyond which a court should not go when reducing damages for the failure to wear a seat belt? See *Chamerland v. Fleming* (1984), 12 D.L.R. (4th) 688, 29 C.C.L.T. 213 (Alta. Q.B.), (failure to wear a life jacket).

14. Is an injured child "identified" with the parents, so that their negligence in failing to supervise the child will reduce the child's damages in an action against a tortfeasor? The answer to this is "no"; however, if the child's injury was in part contributed to by the parents' failure to supervise, the tortfeasor can seek contribution for the damages from the parents. See *Sgro et al. v. Verbeek* (1980), 28 O.R. (2d) 712, 111 D.L.R. (3d) 479 (H.C.), and *Peter v. Anchor Transit Ltd.* (1979), 100 D.L.R. (3d) 37, [1979] 4 W.W.R. 150 (B.C.C.A.). In *Galaske v. O'Donnell, supra,* Cory J. suggested that the parent has a joint responsibility with the driver to ensure that the child is properly secured in a seat belt. What is the real effect of allowing a tortfeasor to recover from the injured child's parents some of the damages the tortfeasor had to pay to the injured child? Would a parent's liability insurance cover this?

C. VOLUNTARY ASSUMPTION OF RISK

HAMBLEY v. SHEPLEY

Ontario Court of Appeal. (1967), 63 D.L.R. (2d) 94, [1967] 2 O.R. 217.

Laskin J.A.: ... This case, which appears to be a novel one on its facts, concerns the claim of a policeman to recover damages for personal injuries. On radio instructions, he used his police cruiser as a roadblock against the defendant, a motorist, who was escaping arrest. The defendant's car, then being driven at high speed and in the wrong lane, proceeded into an intersection against the traffic lights and struck the police cruiser, which was athwart the intersection, before the plaintiff could get out. The trial judge dismissed the action on the ground that the policeman was barred under the principle of *volenti non fit injuria*.

The neat question for determination is whether that principle applies against a person whose injuries occur in the discharge by him of a public duty (see s. 47 [am. 1966, c. 118, s. 15] of the *Police Act*, R.S.O. 1960, c. 298) so as to absolve an otherwise negligent defendant whose conduct caused those injuries. In my opinion, the *volenti* doctrine — in negligence cases, perhaps more properly referred to as the doctrine of voluntary assumption of risk — is inapplicable to such a case.

The trial judge reached his conclusion by analogizing the case of a policeman using a gun (instead of a motor vehicle) to stop and arrest an escaping armed prisoner. No doubt, consent, on the principle of *volenti*, may be a defence to an intentional tort, but I do not think it follows from the illustration used by the trial judge that a policeman is necessarily without civil remedy against a person who assaults him, albeit this occurs in the course of affecting an arrest. However, I need not pursue such a question here.

The doctrine of *volenti* or voluntary assumption of risk as a defence in negligence actions has two correlative effects; it means that the plaintiff is agreeable to bearing the injurious consequences of the defendant's negligent conduct, and that the defendant is relieved of any duty of care to the plaintiff in respect of the particular risk of harm: see Fleming, *Law of Torts*, 3rd ed., p. 256. Clearly, the plaintiff in the present case knew of the risk of harm to which he might be exposing himself, but it would be a reversion of the rigid mid-19th century conception of *volenti* to hold that he thereby accepted that risk so as to absolve the defendant of any duty of care towards him. It seems to me that just as the doctrine of *volenti* no longer immunizes an employer from common law liability to an employee who in carrying out his duties of employment is injured because of an unsafe working system of which he is aware, so the doctrine should have no application to a policeman who is aware of a risk of injury which in fact befalls him in the discharge of the duties of his office... .

There is not, of course, the relationship between a policeman and member of the public that exists between employee and employer, and I do not press any perfect analogy; but neither the policeman nor the employee can reasonably be charged with sufferance of injury resulting from negligence simply because each persists in his employment in full awareness of the risk: see *Merrington v. Ironbridge Metal Works Ltd.*, [1952] 2 All E.R. 1101. I agree with the view of Fleming, *op. cit.*, at p. 59 that "the defence [of *volenti*] cannot succeed unless the evidence permits a genuine inference that the plaintiff consented not merely to the risk of injury, but to the lack of reasonable care which may produce that risk". I do not see in the present case any such consent as is last referred to, and I so hold aside entirely from the contention made in some textbooks and cases that the doctrine only applies where the parties have first come into some association, such as that of driver and passenger, or occupier and visitor: see Fleming, *op. cit.*, at p. 263; and *cf. Car & Gen'l Ins. Corp. Ltd. v. Seymour and Maloney*, [1956] S.C.R. 322, 2 D.L.R. (2d) 369. [The court considered whether the plaintiff was contributorily negligent, and concluded that he was not.]

I would allow the appeal, set aside the judgment below, and in its place direct judgment for the plaintiff for the general and special damages assessed by the trial judge. The plaintiff is entitled to his costs here and below.

Appeal allowed.

NOTES

1. An agreement to accept the risks of unreasonable conduct can be made expressly or implicitly. There have been numerous cases dealing with contractual exemptions or waivers of liability. See, for example, *Dyck v. Manitoba Snowmobile Assn.*, [1985] 4 W.W.R. 319, 32 C.C.L.T. 153 (S.C.C.), where such a clause was upheld by the courts, and *Crocker v. Sundance Northwest Resorts Ltd.*, [1988] 1 S.C.R. 1186, 44 C.C.L.T. 225, where the court refused to uphold a contractual exemption clause.

2. The traditional requirements for a defendant to establish the non-contractual defence of voluntary assumption of risk were "(1) that the plaintiff clearly knew and appreciated the nature and character of the risk he ran and (2) that he voluntarily incurred it". See Lamont J. in *Kelliher (Village) v. Smith*, [1931] S.C.R. 672, at 679, [1931] 4 D.L.R. 102, quoting from *C.P.R. v. Frechette*, [1915] A.C. 871, at 880. However, more recently, judicial hostility towards the defence, and its absolute bar to the plaintiff's cause of action, have made the requirements more stringent. The ambit of the defence of *volenti* has been narrowed considerably to require evidence of an express or an implied agreement to exempt the defendant of any liability for injury suffered.

3. One case that is demonstrative of the judicial attitude to *volenti* is *Lagasse et al. v. Rural Municipality of Ritchot et al.* (1973), 37 D.L.R. (3d) 392, [1973] 4 W.W.R. 181 (Man. Q.B.). The plaintiff's husband was a tractor-operator who agreed to plow some

snow on a lake, at the request of the defendant municipality. While plowing the snow, the ice gave way and the tractor sank into the lake, drowning the plaintiff's husband. In deciding if *volenti non fit injuria* applied, Matas J. quoted the statement of Denning M.R. in *Nettleship v. Weston*:

> This brings me to the defence of *volenti non fit injuria*. ... In former times this defence was used almost as an alternative defence to contributory negligence. Either defence defeated the action. Now that contributory negligence is not a complete defence, but only a ground for reducing the damages, the defence of *volenti non fit injuria* has been closely considered, and, in consequence, it has been severely limited. Knowledge of the risk of injury is not enough. Nor is a willingness to take the risk of injury. Nothing will suffice short of an agreement to waive any claim for negligence. The plaintiff must agree, expressly or impliedly, to waive any claim for that injury that may befall him due to the lack of reasonable care by the defendant: or more accurately, due to the failure of the defendant to measure up to the standard of care that the law requires of him. ...

Matas J. concluded:

> Nothing in [the deceased's] words or conduct, either express or by necessary implication, showed that he gave a real consent to the assumption of risk without compensation or that he absolved the defendants from the duty to take care.

His Lordship went on, however, to reduce the widow's recovery by 25 per cent because of her husband's contributory negligence.

4. The development in the law requiring an expressed or implied agreement to waive one's legal rights as the basis of the *volenti* defence emanated from the so-called "willing passenger" cases. These cases dealt with passengers who rode with drivers who they knew had been drinking. In a series of willing passenger cases in the 1950s and 1960s, the Supreme Court of Canada adopted the view that the conduct of the parties must amount to a tantamount agreement between them that the plaintiff exempted the defendant from liability for damages resulting from the defendant's negligence in order for the defence of *volenti* to succeed. See *Car & General Insurance Corp. Ltd. v. Seymour & Maloney*, [1956] S.C.R. 322; *Miller v. Decker*, [1957] S.C.R. 624; and *Lehnert v. Stein*, [1963] S.C.R. 38 where this approach was adopted. In view of the difficulty in ever finding such a waiver of liability, the *volenti* defence has virtually disappeared from negligence law.

5. *Volenti* still has a role to play in the sport cases. The general principle is that the person who participates in a sporting activity accepts the "normal", "ordinary" and "obvious" risks of that sport. This was discussed in Chapter 3, A. Consent, 1. The Nature of Consent, in relation to intentional torts, but applies equally to negligence actions.

One of the classic cases on the point is *Murphy v. Steeplechase Amusement Co.*, 250 N.Y. 479, 166 N.E. 173 (1929), where the plaintiff was injured when he was thrown on the floor on an amusement ride called the "flopper". He testified that he "took a chance" in going on the ride. Cardozo C.J. denied liability and said:

> *Volenti non fit injuria*. One who takes part in such a sport accepts the dangers that inhere in it so far as they are obvious and necessary, just as a fencer accepts the risk of a thrust by his antagonist or a spectator at a ball game the chance of contact with the ball. ... The antics of the clown are not the paces of the cloistered cleric. The rough and boisterous joke, the horseplay of the crowd, evokes its own guffaws, but they are not the pleasures of tranquility. The plaintiff was not seeking a retreat for mediation. Visitors were tumbling

> about the belt to the merriment of onlookers when he made his choice to join them. He took the chance of a like fate, with whatever damage to his body might ensue from such a fall. The timorous may stay at home.

See *Fink v. Greeniaus* (1974), 2 O.R. (2d) 541, 43 D.L.R. (3d) 485 (H.C.J.); *Elliot v. Amphitheatre Ltd.*, [1934] 3 W.W.R. 225 (Man. K.B.); *Payne v. Maple Leaf Gardens*, [1949] O.R. 26, [1949] 1 D.L.R. 369 (C.A.); *Zapf v. Muckalt*, [1997] 1 W.W.R. 617 (B.C.C.A.); among others. See Barnes, *Sports and the Law*, 2nd ed. (Toronto: Butterworths, 1988).

6. There are two theoretical approaches to the consent issue. The first is to concede that the defendant owed the plaintiff a duty to take care and that this duty was breached, but to deny the plaintiff's claim on the ground of voluntary assumption of risk. The second is to deny the plaintiff's claim on the basis that no duty of care was owed due to the express or implied agreement to hold the defendant to a lower standard than normal. The case law demonstrates both approaches. An example of the "no duty" approach is *Hagerman v. City of Niagara Falls* (1980), 29 O.R. (2d) 609, 114 D.L.R. (3d) 184 (S.C.). The plaintiff spectator was hit in the eye by a puck, during a hockey game played in the defendant's arena. The plaintiff brought action against the defendant.

Mr. Justice Labrosse stated:

> In order to succeed on the basis of negligence, the plaintiff has to establish that the defendant was in breach of a duty of care owed to her as a spectator of a hockey game held in the arena. In determining whether or not a duty of care exists and, if so, its extent, the nature of the risk or danger from which the injuries resulted has to be considered. Furthermore, the duty owed in respect of reasonably foreseeable risks may be limited where the person, to whom the duty might otherwise be owed, appreciates those risks and it is reasonable to expect him to assume them. No duty of care arises with respect to those risks appreciated and assumed. I use the word "assumed" reluctantly because this situation is not the same as that in which the defence of *volenti non fit injuria* or voluntary assumption of risk arises only after a finding of negligence has been made. It applies where a person, to whom a duty is owed, agrees to assume the risk of that duty being breached.

The High Courts of Ontario held that the plaintiff failed to establish a breach of a duty of care owed to her.

The same approach was used in *Dolby v. McWhirter* (1979), 24 O.R. (2d) 71, 99 D.L.R. (3d) 727 (H.C.), and *King v. Redlich*, [1984] 6 W.W.R. 705, 30 C.C.L.T. 247 (B.C.S.C.); affd (1986), 24 D.L.R. (4th) 634, [1986] 4 W.W.R. 567 (B.C.C.A.). What is the practical difference between the two approaches?

7. See generally James, "Assumption of Risk" (1952), 61 Yale L.J. 141; Bohlen, "Voluntary Assumption of Risk" (1906), 20 Harv. L. Rev. 14; Green, "Assumed Risk as a Defense" (1961), 22 La. L. Rev. 77; Wade, "The Place of Assumption of Risk in the Law of Negligence" (1961), 22 La. L. Rev. 5; Payne, "Assumption of Risk and Negligence" (1957), 37 Can. Bar Rev. 950; Hertz, "*Volenti Non Fit Injuria*: A Guide" in Klar (ed.), *Studies in Canadian Tort Law* (1977), p. 101 ; Jaffey, "*Volenti Non Fit Injuria*", [1985] Cambridge L.J. 87; Ingman, "A History of the Defence of *Volenti Non Fit Injuria*" (1981), 26 Jur. Rev. 1.

D. ILLEGALITY

HALL v. HEBERT

Supreme Court of Canada. [1993] 2 S.C.R. 159, 101 D.L.R. (4th) 129.

The plaintiff and the defendant, who had both been drinking, were in the defendant's car when it stalled on a dark, gravel road at night. They decided to try a "rolling start", with the plaintiff at the steering wheel. The plaintiff lost control of the car, which went off the road into a ditch, and turned upside down. Although the parties were able to walk away from the accident, it was later discovered that the plaintiff had suffered significant head injuries.

The plaintiff's action against the defendant was based on the defendant's negligence in allowing the plaintiff to drive the defendant's car despite the fact that the defendant knew that the plaintiff was impaired. The trial judge allowed the action and apportioned liability 75 per cent to the defendant and 25 per cent to the plaintiff. The Court of Appeal allowed the defendant's appeal and dismissed the action. The majority of the Court held that there was no duty of care owed by the defendant to the plaintiff and further that the action should be dismissed based on the doctrine of illegality, otherwise known as *ex turpi causa non oritur actio*. The plaintiff appealed to the Supreme Court of Canada.

McLachlin J. (La Forest, L'Heureux-Dubé, Iacobucci JJ. concurring): This case is one of great importance. The Court is asked to rule on the question of whether and, if so, in what circumstances and under what doctrinal rubric courts may prevent a plaintiff from recovering compensation in tort for loss suffered by the fault of another on the ground that the plaintiff's conduct violated legal or moral rules.

...

My own view is that courts should be allowed to bar recovery in tort on the ground of the plaintiff's immoral or illegal conduct only in very limited circumstances. The basis of this power, as I see it, lies in the duty of the courts to preserve the integrity of the legal system, and is exercisable only where this concern is in issue. This concern is in issue where a damage award in a civil suit would, in effect, allow a person to profit from illegal or wrongful conduct, or would permit an evasion or rebate or a penalty prescribed by the criminal law. The idea common to these instances is that the law refuses to give by its right hand what it takes away by its left hand. It follows from this that, as a general rule, the *ex turpi causa* principle will not operate in tort to deny damages for personal injury, since tort suits will generally be based on a claim for compensation, and will not seek damages as profit for illegal or immoral acts. As to the form the power should take, I see little utility and considerable difficulty in saying that the issue must be dealt with as part of the duty of care. Finally, I see no harm in using the traditional label of *ex turpi causa non oritur actio*, so long as the conditions that govern its use are made clear.

...

One situation in which there seems to be a clear role for the doctrine is the case where to allow the plaintiff's tort claim would be to permit the plaintiff to profit from his or her wrong. It is important at the outset to define what is meant by profit. As the cases illustrate, what is meant is profit in the narrow sense of a direct pecuniary reward for an act of wrongdoing. Compensation for something other than wrongdoing, such as for personal injury, would not amount to profit in this sense. ...

...

Another example of a case in which the courts would not permit a wrongdoer to use a tort action to profit from the wrongdoing is where one bank robber sues another for fraud or negligent misrepresentation. If the action were brought in contract, it would clearly be defeated on the basis of *ex turpi causa non oritur actio*. The fact that the disgruntled robber chooses to frame his action in tort should make no difference.

In some cases the courts may disallow a particular head of damages on the basis that to award that head of damages would be to permit the plaintiff to indirectly profit from his or her crime, in the sense of obtaining remuneration for it. A claim for damages for personal injuries under the head of loss of future earnings, where the claimed earnings are based on an illegal occupation, will not be allowed because it would amount to the court's rewarding the plaintiff for an illegal activity, permitting the plaintiff to profit from his or her wrong. Courts in other jurisdictions have refused to make such awards in cases of claims by a burglar, a bookies' clerk, a vendor of illegal patent medicines, a fisherman using an unlawful net, and an operator of an illegal gambling den.

...

Another example of a case where a particular type of damage may violate the rule against profiting from wrongdoing, this time a little further removed from the contractual situation, is the case of exemplary damages awarded to a wrongdoer. Because such damages are, by definition, not compensatory, their function (apart from punishing the defendant) would be to reward the wrongdoer for his or her crime. As such, they would arguably constitute a case of enabling a wrongdoer to profit from crime. ...

The narrow principle illustrated by the foregoing examples of accepted application of the maxim of *ex turpi causa non oritur actio in tort*, is that a plaintiff will not be allowed to profit from his or her wrongdoing. This explanation, while accurate as far as it goes, may not, however, explain fully why courts have rejected claims in these cases. Indeed, it may have the undesirable effect of tempting judges to focus on the issue of whether the plaintiff is "getting something" out of the tort, thus carrying the maxim into the area of compensatory damages where its use has proved so controversial, and has defeated just claims for compensation. A more satisfactory explanation for these cases, I would venture, is that to allow recovery in these cases would be to allow recovery for what is illegal. It would put the courts in the position of saying that the same conduct is both legal, in the sense of being capable of rectification by the court, and illegal. It would, in short, introduce an inconsistency in the law. It is particularly important in this context that we bear in mind that the law must aspire to be a unified institution, the parts of which — contract, tort, the criminal law — must be in essential harmony. For the courts to punish conduct with the one hand while rewarding it with the other, would be to "create an intolerable fissure in the law's conceptually seamless web": Weinrib, *supra*, at p. 42. We thus see that the concern, put at its most fundamental, is with the integrity of the legal system.

At this point it may be useful to consider in more depth the distinction between compensatory damages and damages which amount to profit from an illegal act. The foregoing comments indicate that compensatory damages are not properly awarded as compensation for an illegal act, but only as compensation for personal injury. Such damages accomplish nothing more than to put the plaintiff in the position he or she would have been in had the tort not occurred. No part of the award which compensates injury can be said to be the profit of, or the windfall from, an illegal act. It may be that had the plaintiff not committed an illegal act, like driving while impaired as in this case, he or she would never have suffered injury. But the same point could be made in the context of every tort: had the injured party not first done X or Y, he or she would not have been subject to the negligence of the tortfeasor. The question that the law asks is whether an injured party suffered a recognized sort of injury, at the hands of someone who owed this party a duty of care, and who caused reasonably foreseeable damage by falling below the standard of care that the law imposes. The plaintiff's behaviour will be relevant to the extent to which it can be shown, according to the established principles just referred to, that the plaintiff contributed to, or voluntarily accepted, the injury he or she suffered; his or her behaviour will be otherwise irrelevant, unless the plaintiff's claim falls into that narrow group of excluded claims referred to above. None of the foregoing propositions changes the fact that such compensation as a plaintiff properly recovers arises not from the character of his or her conduct, illegal or otherwise, but from the damage caused to him or her by the negligent act of the defendant. He or she gets only the value of, or a substitute for, the injuries he or she has suffered by the fault of another. He or she gets nothing for or by reason of the fact he or she was engaged in illegal conduct.

...

I conclude that there is a need in the law of tort for a principle which permits judges to deny recovery to a plaintiff on the ground that to do so would undermine the integrity of the justice system. The power is a limited one. Its use is justified where allowing the plaintiff's claim would introduce inconsistency into the fabric of the law, either by permitting the plaintiff to profit from an illegal or wrongful act, or to evade a penalty prescribed by criminal law. Its use is not justified where the plaintiff's claim is merely for compensation for personal injuries sustained as a consequence of the negligence of the defendant. ...

[McLachlin J. concluded that the issue of the plaintiff's illegal or immoral conduct is best seen as a defence rather than as a factor going to the existence of a duty of care, and applied the defence to the facts of this case as follows:]

The doctrine of *ex turpi causa non oritur actio* properly applies in tort where it will be necessary to invoke the doctrine in order to maintain the internal consistency of the law. Most commonly, this concern will arise where a given plaintiff genuinely seeks to profit from his or her illegal conduct, or where the claimed compensation would amount to an evasion of a criminal sanction. This appellant need not be denied recovery since these grounds are not relevant to his claim. The compensation sought by this appellant is for injuries received. This compensation can be reduced to the extent of the appellant's contributory negligence, but cannot be wholly denied by reason of his disreputable or criminal conduct.

Appeal allowed with costs.

NOTES

1. Cory J. also extensively considered the application of the illegality defence to tort claims. He rejected three standard justifications frequently put forward to support the

defence's application to tort: (1) that the plaintiff should not be entitled to profit from the plaintiff's own wrong, (2) that the use of the doctrine would allow tort law to reinforce criminal law, and (3) that the defence is necessary for the integrity of the justice system. Rather, he concluded that the legitimate concerns underlying these justifications could better be accomplished in other ways, for example, by using apportionment legislation, by applying the defence of voluntary assumption of risk, or by denying the existence of a duty based on public policy. He likened the defence to a "noxious weed" which has been "difficult to eradicate". Thus, according to Cory J. the defence of *ex turpi causa* should not be applied to tort cases. There were in this case no reasons to deny the plaintiff's claim. Public policy could not be used to deny the duty of care in this type of accident. Cory J. would have altered the apportionment to make the liability equal.

2. Sopinka J. dissented, and would have dismissed the plaintiff's action. His Lordship felt that cases such as *Jordan House Ltd. v. Menow*, [1974] S.C.R. 239, 38 D.L.R. (3d) 105, or *Crocker v. Sundance Northwest Resorts Ltd.*, [1988] 1 S.C.R. 1186, 64 O.R. (2d) 64*n*, could not be applied to the facts of this case so as to impose a duty of care upon the defendant for the plaintiff's protection. There was no commercial relationship, or invitor-invitee relationship between the parties to support such a duty of affirmative protection. A second reason for denying a duty of care was based on the policy that where a plaintiff does not reasonably expect that the defendant owed him a duty of care, a duty should not be imposed on the defendant. According to Sopinka J., this was clearly the case here.

3. Has the Supreme Court of Canada now effectively put an end to the use of the illegality defence in negligence actions? If so, do you think that is a good thing? Why couldn't the defence of voluntary assumption of risk have applied to *Hall v. Hebert*?

4. There had been a few cases prior to *Hall v. Hebert* where the defence of illegality succeeded in negligence actions brought by plaintiffs seeking compensation for their personal injuries. See, for example, *Mack v. Enns* (1981), 30 B.C.L.R. 337, 17 C.C.L.T. 291; varied in part 44 B.C.L.R. 145, 25 C.C.L.T. 134 (C.A.); leave to appeal to S.C.C. refused 52 N.R. 235. Have these cases now been effectively overruled?

5. As with voluntary assumption of risk, a plaintiff's illegal or antisocial behaviour is now likely to be treated as contributory negligence. See, for example, *C. (T.L.) v. Vancouver (City)* (1995), 28 C.C.L.T. (2d) 35 (B.C.); and *Berntt v. Vancouver (City)* (1996), 33 C.C.L.T. (2d) 1 (B.C.S.C.). This is a welcomed development by Justice Linden, who wrote in *Canadian Tort Law* (6th ed.), at 497:

> It makes more sense to treat a plaintiff's illegal conduct as contributory negligence and reduce the recovery accordingly rather than to deny recovery altogether. This technique makes tort law a much more humane and flexible instrument, something that is to be encouraged.

CHAPTER 10

ECONOMIC LOSSES

The recovery of purely economic losses poses one of the greatest challenges to contemporary negligence law. These claims arise when persons who have suffered neither personal injury nor property damage seek compensation for their financial losses which they claim resulted from the defendant's negligence.

There is a great diversity between the different types of economic loss cases. Some arise in the context of business or commercial relationships, others in the more typical accident cases, and still others in the products liability context. Most jurists now recognize that one cannot formulate one general principle or criterion for recovery which can apply to the different categories of cases, and that each category must be examined individually.

In Professor Feldthusen's text, *Economic Negligence*, 3rd ed, (1994), five categories of cases are discussed: negligent statement, negligent performance of services, defective products, relational losses, and public authority liability. Since the Supreme Court of Canada has now adopted that structure (see *Winnipeg Condominium, infra*), this casebook will follow that organization as well. In this chapter, the issue of the recovery of pure economic losses will be examined by breaking the cases down into four separate categories. The liability of public authorities will be discussed separately in the next chapter.

A. LIABILITY FOR NEGLIGENT STATEMENTS

Until the 1960s, there was no liability for negligent statements, unless a contractual or a fiduciary relation was involved. Those who relied on negligent representations to their detriment had no recourse in tort. The main reason for this was the fear of "liability in an indeterminate amount for an indeterminate time to an indeterminate class". (See *Ultramares v. Touche Niven & Co.* (1931), 255 N.Y. Supp. 170, at 179, *per* Cardozo J.). There were also concerns about restricting freedom of speech; people often prone to loose talk might find themselves being sued. Despite these concerns, the power of *Donoghue v. Stevenson* could not be resisted. In 1951, the dissent of Lord Justice Denning, assailing the majority in *Candler v. Crane, Christmas & Co.*, [1951] 1 All E.R. 426, for being "timorous souls who were fearful of allowing a new cause of action" for negligent statement and inhibiting the "bold spirits" from doing so, led the way. For the majority, holding no liability, Asquith L.J. admitted that the law was not "strictly logical", but felt unable to change things. He concluded "If this relegates me to the company of 'timorous souls', I must face that consequence with such fortitude as I can muster."

The "bold spirits" finally conquered and the "timorous souls" were vanquished in *Hedley Byrne & Co. Ltd. v. Heller & Partners Ltd.*, [1963] 2 All E.R. 575, [1964] A.C. 465, at p. 534 (H.L.). The plaintiffs, a firm of advertising agents, placed several orders for television time and advertising space in newspapers on behalf of a client, Easipower Ltd., on terms under which the plaintiffs became personally liable. The plaintiffs caused their bank, the National Provincial Bank Ltd., to make inquiries concerning the financial position of Easipower. The National Bank telephoned the defendants, who were bankers for Easipower, and asked in confidence and without responsibility on behalf of the defendants about the respectability and standing of Easipower, and whether the latter would be good for an advertising contract. Some months later, the National Bank wrote to the defendants again asking them, in confidence, whether they would consider Easipower trustworthy to the extent of £100,000 per annum in advertising contracts. The defendants replied to both inquiries that Easipower was a respectably constituted company and considered good for its normal business requirements. The defendants' letter in reply to the second inquiry read: "For your private use and without responsibility on the part of the bank or its officials." The defendants' replies to the National Provincial Bank's inquiries were communicated to the plaintiff who, relying on these replies, placed orders for advertising time and space on behalf of Easipower Ltd. Soon after, the latter went into liquidation and the plaintiff lost of £17,000 on the advertising contracts.

The House of Lords dismissed the case on the basis of the disclaimer clause, but it went out of its way, in a lengthy and confusing *dictum*, to overthrow *Candler v. Crane, Christmas & Co.*, and to establish a new liability for negligent statements that cause economic loss. All five Law Lords agreed that a duty could be imposed in certain circumstances for negligent words in the absence of contract and without fiduciary relations. Some criticism was voiced of the distinction between financial and physical damage. Lord Devlin, for example, remarked that he could find "neither logic or common sense" in the distinction and felt bound to call it "nonsense". Nonetheless, the court refused to go all the way and adopt the neighbour principle of *Donoghue v. Stevenson* to govern negligent statements. Instead, certain confusing and conflicting parameters within which the new liability would operate were outlined. We are still struggling to clarify these parameters.

Simple foreseeability of harm, the cornerstone of Lord Atkin's neighbour principle, suggested the daunting prospect of a virtually limitless range of actionable injury resulting from negligent words, and, therefore, required some modification. In Canada, this modification has developed as the concept of "special relationship".

The germ of this concept may be traced to the speeches of the various Law Lords in *Hedley Byrne*, who sought to intelligibly limit the new liability. Several of the Lords borrowed from the language of business and contract. Lord Pearce, for example, observed that to impart a duty, the representation must normally concern "a business or professional transaction". Lord Devlin declared that a duty to take care in word includes relationships "equivalent to contract" where there is an "assumption of responsibility", or an "implied" undertaking. Others, however, offered a more liberal foundation for the limit. Lord Reid, for example, emphasized reasonable reliance. Similarly, Lord Morris of Borth-y-Gest opined that, where a defendant "quite irrespective of contract" knows that another will reasonably rely on the defendant's judgment or skill, a duty will arise.

Most Canadian cases subsequent to *Hedley Byrne* favoured the broader views of Lords Reid and Morris and did not insist upon an "undertaking" or "something equivalent to contract" as proposed by Lord Devlin.

The scores of articles and hundreds of cases dealing with *Hedley Byrne* are no longer very helpful since two significant cases, decided by the Supreme Court of Canada, have clarified the Canadian law:

QUEEN v. COGNOS INC.

Supreme Court of Canada. [1993] 1 S.C.R. 87, 99 D.L.R. (4th) 626.

The plaintiff, a chartered accountant, applied for a position with the defendant company. During the job interview, it was represented to him that the project for which he was being recruited was a major one, would be developed over a period of two years and had a bright and long future, with good prospects for the successful candidate. In fact, unknown to the plaintiff, the company did not yet possess guaranteed funding for the project nor had budgetary approval been received for the proposed position. The plaintiff was offered the job, he accepted it, gave up his position with another company in Calgary, and moved to Ottawa. In the next few months, the company decided to substantially scale down the funding proposal for the project, and within five months of his taking the job, the plaintiff was informed that he would be reassigned within the company, or possibly laid off. The plaintiff's position was ultimately terminated. He sued in tort for negligent statement.

Iacobucci J.: This appeal involves an action in tort to recover damages caused by alleged negligent misrepresentations made in the course of a hiring interview by an employer (the respondent), through its representative, to a prospective employee (the appellant) with respect to the employer and the nature and existence of the employment opportunity. Though a relatively recent feature of the common law, the tort of negligent misrepresentation relied on by the appellant and first recognized by the House of Lords in *Hedley Byrne, supra* is now an established principle of Canadian tort law. This Court has confirmed on many occasions, sometimes tacitly, that an action in tort may lie, in appropriate circumstances, for damages caused by a misrepresentation made in a negligent manner: [Case authorities omitted] .

While the doctrine of *Hedley Byrne, supra*, is well established in Canada, the exact breadth of its applicability is, like any common law principle, subject to debate and to continuous development. At the time this appeal was heard, there have only been a handful of cases where the tort of negligent misrepresentation was used in a pre-employment context such as the one involved here: [Case authorities omitted].

Without question, the present factual situation is a novel one for this Court.

Some have suggested that it is inappropriate to extend the application of *Hedley Byrne, supra*, to representations made by an employer to a prospective employee in the course of an interview because it places a heavy burden on employers. As will be apparent from my reasons herein, I disagree in principle with this view. However, I find it unnecessary for the purposes of this appeal to engage in a general and abstract discussion on the applicability of the tort of negligent misrepresentation to pre-employment representations. The thrust of the respondent's argument before this Court is not that the appellant's action is unfounded in law. Rather, the respondent argues that the appellant has not made out a case for compensation based on negligent misrepresentation. Accordingly, this appeal may be disposed of simply by considering whether or not the required elements under the *Hedley Byrne* doctrine are established in the facts of this case. In my view, they are.

The required elements for a successful *Hedley Byrne* claim have been stated in many authorities, sometimes in varying forms. The decisions of this Court cited above suggest five general requirements: (1) there must be a duty of care based on a "special relationship" between the representor and the representee; (2) the representation in question must be untrue, inaccurate, or misleading; (3) the representor must have acted negligently in making said misrepresentation; (4) the representee must have relied, in a reasonable manner, on said negligent misrepresentation; and (5) the reliance must have been detrimental to the representee in the sense that damages resulted. In the case at bar, the trial judge found that all elements were present and allowed the appellant's claim.

In particular, White J. found, as a fact, that the respondent's representative, Mr. Johnston, had misrepresented the nature and existence of the employment opportunity for which the appellant had applied, and that the appellant had relied to his detriment on those misrepresentations. These findings of fact were undisturbed by the Court of Appeal and, except for a few passing remarks, the respondent does not challenge them before this Court. Thus, the second, fourth, and fifth requirements are not in question here.

The only issues before this Court deal with the duty of care owed to the appellant in the circumstances of this case and the alleged breach of this duty (i.e., the alleged negligence). The respondent concedes that a "special relationship" existed between itself (through its representative) and the appellant so as to give rise to a duty of care. However, it argues that this duty is negated by a disclaimer contained in the employment contract signed by the appellant more than two weeks after the interview. Furthermore, the respondent argues that any misrepresentations made during the hiring interview were not made in a negligent manner. For reasons that follow, it is my view that both submissions fail.

[Discussion of contractual context omitted.]

C. The Duty of Care Owed to the Appellant

The respondent concedes that it itself and its representative, Mr. Johnston, owed a duty of care towards the six job applicants being interviewed, including the appellant, not to make negligent misrepresentations as to Cognos and the nature and permanence of the job being offered. In so doing, it accepts as correct the findings of both the trial judge and the Court of Appeal that there existed between the parties a "special relationship" within the meaning of *Hedley Byrne, supra*.

In my view, this concession is a sensible one. Without a doubt, when all the circumstances of this case are taken into account, the respondent and Mr. Johnston were under an obligation to exercise due diligence throughout the hiring interview with respect to the representations made to the appellant about Cognos and the nature and existence of the employment opportunity.

There is some debate in academic circles, fuelled by various judicial pronouncements, about the proper test that should be applied to determine when a "special relationship" exists between the representor and the representee which will give rise to a duty of care. Some have suggested that "foreseeable and reasonable reliance" on the representations is the key element to the analysis, while others speak of "voluntary assumption of responsibility" on the part of the representor. Recently, in *Caparo Industries plc v. Dickman*, [1990] 1 All E.R. 568 (H.L.), a case unlike the present one in that there the whole issue revolved around the existence of a duty of care, the House of Lords suggested that three criteria determine the imposition of a duty of care: foreseeability of damage, proximity of relationship, and the reasonableness or otherwise of imposing a duty.

For my part, I find it unnecessary — and unwise in view of the respondent's concession — to take part in this debate. Regardless of the test applied, the result which the circumstances of this case dictate would be the same. It was foreseeable that the appellant would be relying on the information given during the hiring interview in order to make his career decision. It was reasonable for the appellant to rely on said representations. There is nothing before this Court that suggests that the respondent was not, at the time of the interview or shortly thereafter, assuming responsibility for what was being represented to the appellant by Mr. Johnston. As noted by the trial judge, Mr. Johnston discussed the Multiview project in an unqualified manner, without making any relevant *caveats*. The alleged disclaimers of responsibility are provisions of a contract signed more than two weeks after the interview. For reasons that I give in the last part of this analysis, these provisions are not valid disclaimers. They do not negate the duty of care owed to the appellant or prevent it from arising as in *Hedley Byrne* and *Carman Construction, supra*. It was foreseeable to the respondent and its representative that the appellant would sustain damages should the representations relied on prove to be false and negligently made. There was, undoubtedly, a relationship of proximity between the parties at all material times. Finally, it is not unreasonable to impose a duty of care in all the circumstances of this case; quite the contrary, it would be unreasonable *not* to impose such a duty. In short, therefore, there existed between the parties a "special relationship" at the time of the interview. The respondent and its representative Mr. Johnston were under a duty of care during the pre-employment interview to exercise reasonable care and diligence in making representations as to the employer and the employment opportunity being offered.

Although it was not argued before this Court, I wish to add what is implicit in my acceptance of the respondent's concession, namely, that I reject the so-called restrictive approach as to who can owe a *Hedley Byrne* duty of care, often associated with the majority judgment in *Mutual Life and Citizens' Assurance Co. Ltd. v. Evatt*, [1971] A.C. 793 (P.C.). In my opinion, confining this duty of care to "professionals" who are in the business of providing information and advice, such as doctors, lawyers, bankers, architects, and engineers, reflects an overly simplistic view of the analysis required in cases such as the present one. The question of whether a duty of care with respect to representations exists depends on a number of considerations including, but not limited to, the representor's profession. While this factor may provide a good indication as to whether a "special relationship" exists between the parties, it should not be treated in all cases as a threshold requirement. There may be situations where the surrounding circumstances provide sufficient indicia of a duty of care, notwithstanding the representor's profession. Indeed, the case at bar is a good example. I find support for a more flexible approach on this question in a number of authorities: [Case authorities omitted].

D. The Breach of the Duty of Care

(1) Introduction

The next issue deals with whether the above duty of care was breached during the course of the pre-employment interview of February 14, 1983. The main question to be addressed here is whether the misrepresentations of Mr. Johnston during the interview were negligently made, as found by the trial judge.

The applicable standard of care should be the one used in every negligence case, namely the universally accepted, albeit hypothetical, "reasonable person". The standard of care required by a person making representations is an objective one. It is a duty to exercise such reasonable care as the circumstances require to ensure that representations made are accurate and not misleading: [Case authorities omitted]. Professor Klar provides some useful insight on this issue (at p. 160):

> An advisor does not guarantee the accuracy of the statement made, but is only required to exercise reasonable care with respect to it. As with the issue of standard of care in negligence in general, this is a question of fact which must be determined

according to the circumstances of the case. Taking into account the nature of the occasion, the purpose for which the statement was made, the foreseeable use of the statement, the probable damage which will result from an inaccurate statement, the status of the advisor and the level of competence generally observed by others similarly placed, the trier of fact will determine whether the advisor was negligent.

In my opinion, the trial judge did not depart from the applicable standard of care in rendering his decision. He found that, "in all the circumstances", the misrepresentations made by the respondent's representative were negligently made. Unlike the Court of Appeal, I find no reason to interfere with his careful and considered finding on this point.

Appeal allowed.

NOTES

1. One of the important issues in *Queen v. Cognos* was how the employment contract entered between the parties affected the tort duty. This will be discussed further, *infra.*

2. Defining the "special relationship" of proximity or neighbourhood which gives rise to a duty of care has been the major task of the courts since *Hedley Byrne.* See *Hercules Management, infra*, for a detailed analysis of this issue.

3. One of the points dealt with in *Queen v. Cognos* was whether the *Hedley Byrne* duty of care was owed only by professionals or those who are in the business of giving advice. The issue arose due to the majority judgment of the Privy Council in a much earlier case *Mutual Life & Citizens Assur. Co. v. Evatt,* [1971] A.C. 793, [1971] 2 W.L.R. 23, which seemed to restrict the special relationship to professional defendants. This restriction has been rejected by numerous Canadian courts, (see, for example, *Nelson Lumber Co. Ltd. v. Koch* (1980), 111 D.L.R. (3d) 140, 13 C.C.L.T. 201 (Sask. C.A.)) and now clearly by the Supreme Court.

4. In order for a duty of care to exist, the advisor must foresee that the advisee will rely on the advice, and the reliance must be reasonable. What factors ought the courts to consider in determining when reliance is both foreseeable and reasonable? In Klar, *Tort Law* (1991), the following factors are suggested: the skill of the advisor, the skill of the advisee, the nature of the occasion, whether the advice was solicited, and what the nature of the advice was, *i.e.*, was it a statement of fact?, or opinion?, was it speculative? and so forth. Can you think of any other factors?

5. Can there be a duty if the reliance was not reasonable? Some cases have dismissed the action where the reliance was not reasonable — see, for example, *Kingu et al. v. Walmar Ventures Ltd.* (1986), 10 B.C.L.R. (2d) 15, 38 C.C.L.T. 51 (C.A.): not reasonable for purchasers to rely on vendors' statements; *John Bosworth Ltd. v. Professional Syndicated Developments Ltd.* (1979), 24 O.R. (2d) 97, 97 D.L.R. (3d) 112 (H.C.): not reasonable for developer to rely on informal statements about zoning made by a mayor, who was not responsible for zoning matters, during an unsolicited telephone conversation and at a social luncheon. Other cases have applied the duty but found the plaintiff contributorily negligent where the reliance was not reasonable; see, for example, *Grand Restaurants of Canada Ltd. v. City of Toronto* (1981), 32 O.R. (2d) 757, 123 D.L.R. (3d) 349 (H.C.); affd (1982), 39 O.R. (2d) 752, 140 D.L.R. (3d) 191 (C.A.), where Mr. Justice Trainor stated:

> In the case of fault that contributes to the damage suffered, reliance that is "unreasonable" simply goes to reducing damages otherwise recoverable by the plaintiff; it does not go to cancelling the prima facie liability of the defendant.

See also *H.B. Nickerson v. Wooldrige & Sons Ltd.* (1980), 115 D.L.R. (3d) 97, at 138 (N.S.C.A.) Can these two viewpoints be reconciled?

6. Mr. Justice Linden argues that it makes "good sense" to allow contributory negligence in appropriate cases, "where the loss occurred because of the combined negligence of both the advisor and the advisee". Professor Klar counters by arguing that "it is a contradiction to hold that a plaintiff can be considered to have been reasonable in relying on advice for the purposes of the establishment of a duty, but unreasonable for having relied upon it for the purposes of contributory negligence". Who is right? See Linden, *Canadian Tort Law*, 6th ed. (1997), p. 423, and Klar, *Tort Law*, 2nd ed., (1996) at 111.

7. In order for there to be liability, reliance on the advice must be proved. This is akin to the need to prove causation in other negligence cases. In *Town of the Pas v. Porky Packers Ltd.* (1976), 65 D.L.R. (3d) 1, [1976] 3 W.W.R. 138 (S.C.C.), a plaintiff, who knew as much about the municipal by-laws as the employees of the municipality, could not recover because he did not rely on their advice when spending money to build an abattoir in violation of those by-laws. Mr. Justice Spence explained that the representations must be made "to a person who has no expert knowledge himself by a person whom the representee believes has a particular skill or judgment in the matter, and that the representations were relied upon to the detriment of the representee".

8. An omission to disclose something may give rise to actionable negligence. In *Spinks v. Canada,* [1996] 2 F.C.R. 563 (C.A.), the Federal Court of Appeal held a defendant liable for not fully disclosing information pertinent to the plaintiff's pension rights. The plaintiff was an employee of the Australian public service who emigrated to Canada to work for the Atomic Energy Commission Limited. Upon his sign-up, the employer failed to inform the plaintiff that his Australian pension rights could be "bought back" and thereby rolled into a Canadian public service pension. The court stated simply that "a person may be 'misled' by a failure to divulge as much as by advice that is inaccurate or untrue. Missing information can be just as harmful as mistaken information." Similarly, the failure to inform on insurance matters may also give rise to liability. In *Fletcher v. Manitoba Public Insurance Co., Re* (1990), 5 C.C.L.T. (2d) 1 (S.C.C.), the failure of the agent for the government insurer to inform the plaintiff properly about the availability of underinsured motorist coverage led to economic losses. Liability was imposed.

HERCULES MANAGEMENTS LTD. v. ERNST & YOUNG

Supreme Court of Canada. [1997] 2 S.C.R. 165, 146 D.L.R. (4th) 577.

The plaintiffs were shareholders in two corporations. They both had relied on the defendants' audits of their corporations' financial statements to make investment decisions. The plaintiffs claimed that, as a result of relying on these audits, they incurred investment losses and losses in the value of their shareholdings. They brought an action for negligence against the defendants. The defendants brought a motion for summary dismissal of the action and succeeded on the grounds that they owed no duty of care to the shareholders in tort and any action should have been brought in the names of the corporations. The Manitoba Court of Appeal dismissed the appeal. The Supreme Court of Canada also dismissed the appeal.

La Forest J.: — This appeal arises by way of motion for summary judgment. It concerns the issue of whether and when accountants who perform an audit of a corporation's financial statements owe a duty of care in tort to shareholders of the corporation who claim to have suffered losses in reliance on the audited statements. It also raises the question of whether certain types of claims against auditors may properly be brought by shareholders as individuals or whether they must be brought by the corporation in the form of a derivative action.....

Issues

The issues in this case may be stated as follows:

(1) Do the respondents owe the appellants a duty of care with respect to
  (a) the investment losses they incurred allegedly as a result of reliance on the 1980-82 audit reports; and
  (b) the losses in the value of their existing shareholdings they incurred allegedly as a result of reliance on the 1980-82 audit reports?
(2) Does the rule in *Foss v. Harbottle* affect the appellants' action?

[The court dealt with some preliminary matters before dealing with the duty of care analysis. The only one of interest for our purposes is the court's finding, pursuant to *Queen v. Cognos,* that "actual reliance is a necessary element of an action in negligent misrepresentation and its absence will mean that the plaintiff cannot succeed in holding the defendant liable for his or her losses".]

Issue 1: Whether the Respondents owe the Appellants a Duty of Care

(i) Introduction

[19] It is now well established in Canadian law that the existence of a duty of care in tort is to be determined through an application of the two-part test first enunciated by Lord Wilberforce in *Anns v. Merton London Borough Council,* [1978] A.C. 728 (H.L.), at pp. 751-52:

> First one has to ask whether, as between the alleged wrongdoer and the person who has suffered damage there is a sufficient relationship of proximity or neighbourhood such that, in the reasonable contemplation of the former, carelessness on his part may be likely to cause damage to the latter — in which case a prima facie duty of care arises. Secondly, if the first question is answered affirmatively, it is necessary to consider whether there are any considerations which ought to negative, or to reduce or limit the scope of the duty or the class of person to whom it is owed or the damages to which a breach of it may give rise....

While the House of Lords rejected the *Anns* test in *Murphy v. Brentwood District Council*, [1991] 1 A.C. 398, and in *Caparo, supra,...*(citing Brennan J. in *Sutherland Shire Council v. Heyman)...,* the basic approach that test embodies has repeatedly been accepted and endorsed by this Court. (See, *e.g.*: *Kamloops (City) v. Nielsen,...; B.D.C. Ltd. v. Hofstrand Farms Ltd.,...; Canadian National Railway Co. v. Norsk Pacific Steamship Co.,...; London Drugs Ltd. v. Kuehne & Nagel International Ltd.,...; Winnipeg Condominium Corp. No. 36 v. Bird Construction Co.,...)*

[20] In *Kamloops, supra*, at p. 10, Wilson J. restated Lord Wilberforce's test in the following terms:

> (1) is there a sufficiently close relationship between the parties (the [defendant] and the person who has suffered the damage) so that, in the reasonable contemplation of the [defendant], carelessness on its part might cause damage to that person? If so,
>
> (2) are there any considerations which ought to negative or limit (a) the scope of the duty and (b) the class of persons to whom it is owed or (c) the damages to which a breach of it may give rise?

As will be clear from the cases earlier cited, this two-stage approach has been applied by this Court in the context of various types of negligence actions, including actions involving claims for different forms of economic loss. Indeed, it was implicitly endorsed in the context of an action in negligent misrepresentation in *Edgeworth Construction Ltd. v. N.D. Lea & Associates Ltd.*, [1993] 3 S.C.R. 206, at pp. 218-19, 107 D.L.R. (4th) 169. The same approach to defining duties of care in negligent misrepresentation cases has also been taken in other Commonwealth courts. In *Scott Group Ltd. v. McFarlane*, [1978] 1 N.Z.L.R. 553, for example, a case that dealt specifically with auditors' liability for negligently prepared audit reports, the *Anns* test was adopted and applied by a majority of the New England Court of Appeal.

[21] I see no reason in principle why the same approach should not be taken in the present case. Indeed, to create a "pocket" of negligent misrepresentation cases (to use Professor Stapleton's term) in which the existence of a duty of care is determined differently from other negligence cases would, in my view, be incorrect; see: Jane Stapleton, "Duty of Care and Economic Loss: A Wider Agenda" (1991), 107 L.Q.R. 249. This is not to say, of course, that negligent misrepresentation cases do not involve special considerations stemming from the fact that recovery is allowed for pure economic loss as opposed to physical damage. Rather, it is simply to posit that the same general framework ought to be used in approaching the duty of care question in both types of case. Whether the respondents owe the appellants a duty of care for their allegedly negligent preparation for the 1980-82 audit reports, then, will depend on (a) whether a *prima facie* duty of care is owed, and (b) whether that duty, if it exists, is negatived or limited by policy considerations. Before analysing the merits of this case, it will be useful to set out in greater detail the principles governing this appeal.

(ii) The Prima Facie Duty of Care

[22] The first branch of the *Anns/Kamloops* test demands an inquiry into whether there is a sufficiently close relationship between the plaintiff and the defendant that in the reasonable contemplation of the latter, carelessness on its part may cause damage to the former. The existence of such a relationship — which has come to be known as a relationship of "neighbourhood" or "proximity" — distinguishes those circumstances in which the defendant owes a *prima facie* duty of care to the plaintiff from those where no such duty exists. In the context of a negligent misrepresentation action, then, deciding whether or not a *prima facie* duty of care exists necessitates an investigation into whether the defendant-representor and the plaintiff-representee can be said to be in a relationship of proximity or neighbourhood.

[23] What constitutes a "relationship of proximity" in the context of negligent misrepresentation actions? In approaching this question, I would begin by reiterating the position I took in *Norsk, supra*, at pp. 1114-15, that the term "proximity" itself is nothing more than a label expressing a result, judgment or conclusion; it does not, in and of itself, provide a principled basis on which to make a legal determination. This view was also explicitly adopted by Stevenson J. in *Norsk,*

supra, at p. 1178, and McLachlin J. also appears to have accepted it when she wrote, at p. 1151, of that case that "[p]roximity may usefully be viewed, not so much as a test in itself, but as a broad concept which is capable of subsuming different categories of cases involving different factors"; see also: M.H. McHugh, "Neighbourhood, Proximity and Reliance", in P.D. Finn, *Essays on Torts* (Sydney: Law Book Co., 1989), 5, at pp. 36-37; and John G. Fleming, "The Negligent Auditor and Shareholders" (1990), 106 L.Q.R. 349, at p. 351, where the author refers to proximity as a "vacuous test". While *Norsk, supra*, was concerned specifically with whether or not a defendant could be held liable for "contractual relational economic loss" (as I called it, at p. 1037), I am of the view that the same observations with respect to the term "proximity" are applicable in the context of negligent misrepresentation. In order to render "proximity" a useful tool in defining when a duty of care exists in negligent misrepresentation cases, therefore, it is necessary to infuse that term with some meaning. In other words, it is necessary to set out the basis upon which one may properly reach the conclusion that proximity inheres between a representor and a representee.

[24] This can be done most clearly as follows. The label "proximity", as it was used by Lord Wilberforce in *Anns, supra*, was clearly intended to connote that the circumstances of the relationship inhering between the plaintiff and the defendant are of such a nature that the defendant may be said to be under an obligation to be mindful of the plaintiff's legitimate interests in conducting his or her affairs. Indeed, this idea lies at the very heart of the concept of a "duty of care", as articulated most memorably by Lord Atkin in *Donoghue v. Stevenson*, [1932] A.C. 562, at pp. 580-81. In cases of negligent misrepresentation, the relationship between the plaintiff and the defendant arises through reliance by the plaintiff on the defendant's words. Thus, if "proximity" is meant to distinguish the cases where the defendant has a responsibility to take reasonable care of the plaintiff from those where he or she has no such responsibility, then in negligent misrepresentation cases, it must pertain to some aspect of the relationship of reliance. To my mind, proximity can be seen to inhere between a defendant-representor and a plaintiff-representee when two criteria relating to reliance may be said to exist on the facts: (a) the defendant ought reasonably to foresee that the plaintiff will rely on his or her representation; and (b) reliance by the plaintiff would, in the particular circumstances of the case, be reasonable. To use the term employed by my colleague, Iacobucci J., in *Cognos, supra*, at p. 110, the plaintiff and the defendant can be said to be in a "special relationship" whenever these two factors inhere.

[25] I should pause here to explain that, in my view, to look to whether or not reliance by the plaintiff on the defendant's representation would be reasonable in determining whether or not a *prima facie* duty of care exists in negligent misrepresentation cases as opposed to looking at reasonable foreseeability alone is not, as might first appear, to abandon the basic tenets underlying the first branch of the *Anns/Kamloops* formula. The purpose behind the *Anns/Kamloops* test is simply to ensure that enquiries into the existence of a duty of care in negligence cases is conducted in two parts: The first involves discerning whether, in a given situation, a duty of care would be imposed by law; the second demands an investigation into whether the legal duty, if found, ought to be negatived or ousted by policy considerations. In the context of actions based on negligence causing physical damage, determining whether harm to the plaintiff was reasonably foreseeable to the defendant is alone a sufficient criterion for deciding proximity or neighbourhood under the first branch of the *Anns/Kamloops* test because the law has come to recognise (even if only implicitly) that, absent a voluntary assumption of risk by him or her, it is always reasonable for a plaintiff to expect that a defendant will take

reasonable care of the plaintiff's person and property. The duty of care inquiry in such cases, therefore, will always be conducted under the assumption that the plaintiff's expectations of the defendant are reasonable.

[26] In negligent misrepresentation actions, however, the plaintiff's claim stems from his or her detrimental reliance on the defendant's (negligent) statement, and it is abundantly clear that reliance on the statement or representation of another will not, in all circumstances, be reasonable. The assumption that always inheres in physical damage cases concerning the reasonableness of the plaintiff's expectations cannot, therefore, be said to inhere in reliance cases. In order to ensure that the same factors are taken into account in determining the existence of a duty of care in both instances, then, the reasonableness of the plaintiff's reliance must be considered in negligent misrepresentation actions. Only by doing so will the first branch of the *Kamloops* test be applied consistently in both contexts.

[27] As should be evident from its very terms, the reasonable foreseeability/reasonable reliance test for determining a *prima facie* duty of care is somewhat broader than the tests used both in the cases decided before *Anns*, *supra*, and in those that have rejected the *Anns* approach. Rather than stipulating simply that a duty of care will be found in any case where reasonable foreseeability and reasonable reliance inhere, those cases typically require (a) that the defendant know the identity of either the plaintiff or the class of plaintiffs who will rely on the statement, and (b) that the reliance losses claimed by the plaintiff stem from the particular transaction in respect of which the statement at issue was made. This narrower approach to defining the duty can be seen in a number of the more prominent English decisions dealing either with auditors' liability specifically or with liability for negligent misstatements generally. (See, *e.g.*, *Candler v. Crane, Christmas & Co.*, *per* Denning L.J. (dissenting); *Hedley Byrne & Co. v. Heller & Partners Ltd.,...; Caparo, supra,...* It is also evident in the approach taken by this Court in *Haig v. Bamford,...*)

[28] While I would not question the conclusions reached in any of these judgments, I am of the view that inquiring into such matters as whether the defendant had knowledge of the plaintiff (or class of plaintiffs) and whether the plaintiff used the statements at issue for the particular transaction for which they were provided is, in reality, nothing more than a means by which to circumscribe — for reasons of policy — the scope of a representor's potentially infinite liability. As I have already tried to explain, determining whether "proximity" exists on a given set of facts consists in an attempt to discern whether, as a matter of simple justice, the defendant may be said to have had an obligation to be mindful of the plaintiff's interests in going about his or her business. Requiring, in addition to proximity, that the defendant know the identity of the plaintiff (or class of plaintiffs) and that the plaintiff use the statements in question for the specific purpose for which they were prepared amounts, in my opinion, to a tacit recognition that considerations of basic fairness may sometimes give way to other pressing concerns. Plainly stated, adding further requirements to the duty of care test provides a means by which policy concerns that are extrinsic to simple justice — but that are, nevertheless, fundamentally important — may be taken into account in assessing whether the defendant should be compelled to compensate the plaintiff for losses suffered. In other words, these further requirements serve a policy-based limiting function with respect to the ambit of the duty of care in negligent misrepresentation actions....

[30] In light of this Court's endorsement of the *Anns/Kamloops* test, however, enquiries concerning (a) the defendant's knowledge of the identity of the plaintiff (or of the class of plaintiffs) and (b) the use to which the statements at issue are

put may now quite properly be conducted in the second branch of that test when deciding whether or not policy considerations ought to negative or limit a *prima facie* duty that has already been found to exist. In other words, criteria that in other cases have been used to define the legal test for the duty of care can now be recognised for what they really are — policy-based means by which to curtail liability — and they can appropriately be considered under the policy branch of the *Anns/Kamloops* test. To understand exactly how this may be done and how these criteria are pertinent to the case at bar, it will first be useful to set out the prevailing policy concerns in some detail.

(iii) Policy Considerations

[31] As Cardozo C.J. explained in *Ultramares Corp. v. Touche*, 174 N.E. 441 (N.Y.C.A. 1931), at p. 444, the fundamental policy consideration that must be addressed in negligent misrepresentation actions centres around the possibility that the defendant might be exposed to "liability in an indeterminate amount for an indeterminate time to an indeterminate class". This potential problem can be seen quite vividly within the framework of the *Anns/Kamloops* test. Indeed, while the criteria of reasonable foreseeability and reasonable reliance serve to distinguish cases where a *prima facie* duty is owed from those where it is not, it is nevertheless true that in certain types of situations these criteria can, quite easily, be satisfied and absent some means by which to circumscribe the ambit of the duty, the prospect of limitless liability will loom.

[32] The general area of auditors' liability is a case in point. In modern commercial society, the fact that audit reports will be relied on by many different people (*e.g.*, shareholders, creditors, potential takeover bidders, investors, etc.) for a wide variety of purposes will almost always be reasonably foreseeable to auditors themselves. Similarly, the very nature of audited financial statements — produced, as they are, by professionals whose reputations (and, thereby, whose livelihoods) are at stake — will very often mean that any of those people would act wholly reasonably in placing their reliance on such statements in conducting their affairs. These observations are consistent with the following remarks of Dickson J. in *Haig, supra*, at pp. 475-76, with respect to the accounting profession generally:

> The increasing growth and changing role of corporations in modern society has been attended by a new perception of the societal role of the profession of accounting. The day when the accountant served only the owner-manager of a company and was answerable to him alone has passed. The complexities of modern industry combined with the effects of specialization, the impact of taxation, urbanization, the separation of ownership from management, the rise of professional corporate managers, and a host of other factors, have led to marked changes in the role and responsibilities of the accountant, and in the reliance which the public must place upon his work. The financial statements of the corporations upon which he reports can affect the economic interests of the general public as well as of shareholders and potential shareholders....

[33] Certain authors have argued that imposing broad duties of care on auditors would give rise to significant economic and social benefits in so far as the spectre of tort liability would act as an incentive to auditors to produce accurate (*i.e.*, non-negligent) reports. (See, *e.g.*: Howard B. Wiener, "Common Law Liability of the Certified Public Accountant for Negligent Misrepresentation" (1983), 20 San Diego L. Rev. 233.) I would agree that deterrence of negligent conduct is an important policy consideration with respect to auditors' liability. Nevertheless, I am of

the view that, in the final analysis, it is outweighed by the socially undesirable consequences to which the imposition of indeterminate liability on auditors might lead. Indeed, while indeterminate liability is problematic in and of itself inasmuch as it would mean that successful negligence actions against auditors could, at least potentially, be limitless, it is also problematic in light of certain related problems to which it might give rise....

[35] I should, at this point, explain that I am aware of the arguments put forth by certain scholars and judges to the effect that concerns over indeterminate liability have sometimes been overstated. (See, *e.g.*: J. Edgar Sexton and John W. Stevens, "Accountants' Legal Responsibilities and Liabilities", in *Professional Responsibility in Civil Law and Common Law* (Meredith Memorial Lectures, McGill University, 1983-84))...Arguments to this effect rest essentially on the premise that actual *liability* will be limited in so far as a plaintiff will not be successful unless both negligence and reliance are established in addition to a duty of care. While it is true that damages will not be owing by the defendant unless these other elements of the cause of action are proved, neither the difficulty of proving negligence nor that of proving reliance will preclude a disgruntled plaintiff from bringing an action against an auditor and such actions would, we may assume, be all the more common were the establishment of a duty of care in any given case to amount to nothing more than a mere matter of course. This eventually could pose serious problems both for auditors, whose legal costs would inevitably swell, and for courts, which, no doubt, would feel the pressure of increased litigation. Thus, the prospect of burgeoning negligence suits raises serious concerns, even if we assume that the arguments positing proof of negligence and reliance as a barrier to liability are correct. In my view, therefore, it makes more sense to circumscribe the ambit of the duty of care than to assume that difficulties in proving negligence and reliance will afford sufficient protection to auditors, since this approach avoids both "indeterminate liability" and "indeterminate litigation".

[36] As I have thus far attempted to demonstrate, the possible repercussions of exposing auditors to indeterminate liability are significant. In applying the two-stage *Anns/Kamloops* test to negligent misrepresentation actions against auditors, therefore, policy considerations reflecting those repercussions should be taken into account. In the general run of auditors' cases, concerns over indeterminate liability will serve to negate a *prima facie* duty of care. But while such concerns may exist in most such cases, there may be particular situations where they do not. In other words, the specific factual matrix of a given case may render it an "exception" to the general class of cases in that while (as in most auditors' liability cases) considerations of proximity under the first branch of the *Anns/Kamloops* test might militate in favour of finding that a duty of care inheres, the typical concerns surrounding indeterminate liability do *not* arise. This needs to be explained.

[37] As discussed earlier, looking to factors such as "knowledge of the plaintiff (or an identifiable class of plaintiffs) on the part of the defendant" and "use of the statements at issue for the precise purpose or transaction for which they were prepared" really amounts to an attempt to limit or constrain the scope of the duty of care owed by the defendants. If the purpose of the *Anns/Kamloops* test is to determine (a) whether or not a *prima facie* duty of care exists and then (b) whether or not that duty ought to be negated or limited, then factors such as these ought properly to be considered in the second branch of the test once the first branch concerning "proximity" has been found to be satisfied. To my mind the presence of such factors in a given situation will mean that worries stemming from indeterminacy should not arise, since the scope of potential liability is sufficiently delimited. In other words, in cases where the defendant knows the identity of the

plaintiff (or of a class of plaintiffs) and where the defendant's statements are used for the specific purpose or transaction for which they were made, policy considerations surrounding indeterminate liability will not be of any concern since the scope of liability can readily be circumscribed. Consequently, such considerations will not override a positive finding on the first branch of the *Anns/Kamloops* test and a duty of care may quite properly be found to exist....

[41] The foregoing analysis should render the following points clear. A *prima facie* duty of care will arise on the part of a defendant in a negligent misrepresentation action when it can be said (a) that the defendant ought reasonably to have foreseen that the plaintiff would rely on his representation and (b) that reliance by the plaintiff, in the circumstances, would be reasonable. Even though, in the context of auditors' liability cases, such a duty will often (even if not always) be found to exist, the problem of indeterminate liability will frequently result in the duty being negated by the kinds of policy considerations already discussed. Where, however, indeterminate liability can be shown not to be a concern on the facts of a particular case, a duty of care will be found to exist. Having set out the law governing the appellants' claims, I now propose to apply it to the facts of the appeal.

(iv) Application to the Facts

[42] In my view, there can be no question that a *prima facie* duty of care was owed to the appellants by the respondents on the facts of this case. As regards the criterion of reasonable foreseeability, the possibility that the appellants would rely on the audited financial statements in conducting their affairs and that they may suffer harm if the reports were negligently prepared must have been reasonably foreseeable to the respondents. This is confirmed simply by the fact that shareholders generally will often choose to rely on audited financial statements for a wide variety of purposes. It is further confirmed by the fact that under ss. 149(1) and 163(1) of the Manitoba *Corporations Act*, it is patently clear that audited financial statements are to be placed before the shareholders at the annual general meeting....

In my view, it would be untenable to argue in the face of these provisions that some form of reliance by shareholders on the audited reports would be unforeseeable.

[43] Similarly, I would find that reliance on the audited statements by the appellant shareholders would, on the facts of this case, be reasonable. Professor Feldthusen (at pp. 62-63) sets out five general *indicia* of reasonable reliance; namely:

(1) The defendant had a direct or indirect financial interest in the transaction in respect of which the representation was made.
(2) The defendant was a professional or someone who possessed special skill, judgment or knowledge.
(3) The advice or information was provided in the course of the defendant's business.
(4) The information or advice was given deliberately, and not on a social occasion.
(5) The information or advice was given in response to a specific enquiry or request.

While these *indicia* should not be understood to be a strict "test" of reasonableness, they do help to distinguish those situations where reliance on a statement is reasonable from those where it is not. On the facts here, the first four of these *in-*

dicia clearly inhere. To my mind, then, this aspect of the *prima facie* duty is unquestionably satisfied on the facts.

[44] Having found a *prima facie* duty to exist, then, the second branch of the *Anns/Kamloops* test remains to be considered. It should be clear from my comments above that were auditors such as the respondents held to owe a duty of care to plaintiffs in *all* cases where the first branch of the *Anns/Kamloops* test was satisfied, the problem of indeterminate liability would normally arise. It should be equally clear, however, that in certain cases, this problem does not arise because the scope of potential liability can adequately be circumscribed on the facts. An investigation of whether or not indeterminate liability is truly a concern in the present case is, therefore, required.

[45] At first blush, it may seem that no problems of indeterminate liability are implicated here and that this case can easily be likened to *Glanzer, Hedley Byrne*, and *Haig*, *supra*. After all, the respondents knew the very identity of all the appellant shareholders who claim to have relied on the audited financial statements through having acted as NGA's and NGH's auditors for nearly 10 years by the time the first of the audit reports at issue in this appeal was prepared. It would seem plausible to argue on this basis that because the identity of the plaintiffs was known to the respondents at the time of preparing the 1980-82 reports, no concerns over indeterminate liability arise.

[46] To arrive at this conclusion without further analysis, however, would be to move too quickly. While knowledge of the plaintiff (or of a limited class of plaintiffs) is undoubtedly a significant factor serving to obviate concerns over indeterminate liability, it is not, alone, sufficient to do so. In my discussion of *Glanzer, Hedley Byrne*, and *Haig*, *supra*, I explained that indeterminate liability did not inhere on the specific facts of those cases not only because the defendant knew the identity of the plaintiff (or the class of plaintiffs) who would rely on the statement at issue, but also because the statement itself was used by the plaintiff *for precisely the purpose or transaction for which it was prepared.* The crucial importance of this additional criterion can clearly be seen when one considers that even if the specific identity or class of potential plaintiffs is known to a defendant, use of the defendant's statement for a purpose or transaction other than that for which it was prepared could still lead to indeterminate liability.

[47] For example, if an audit report which was prepared for a corporate client for the express purpose of attracting a $10,000 investment in the corporation from a known class of third parties was instead used as the basis for attracting a $1,000,000 investment or as the basis for inducing one of the members of the class to become a director or officer of the corporation or, again, as the basis for encouraging him or her to enter into some business venture with the corporation itself, it would appear that the auditors would be exposed to a form of indeterminate liability, even if they knew precisely the identity or class of potential plaintiffs to whom their report would be given. With respect to the present case, then, the central question is whether or not the appellants can be said to have used the 1980-82 audit reports for the specific purpose for which they were prepared. The answer to this question will determine whether or not policy considerations surrounding indeterminate liability ought to negate the *prima facie* duty of care owed by the respondents.

[48] What, then, is the purpose for which the respondents' audit statements were prepared?...

[49]...The directors of a corporation are required to place the auditors' report before the shareholders at the annual meeting in order to permit the shareholders, as a body, to make decisions as to the manner in which they want the corporation

to be managed, to assess the performance of the directors and officers, and to decide whether or not they wish to retain the existing management or to have them replaced. On this basis, it may be said that the respondent auditors' purpose in preparing the reports at issue in this case was, precisely, to assist the collectivity of shareholders of the audited companies in their task of overseeing management.

[50] The appellants, however, submit that, in addition to this statutorily mandated purpose, the respondents further agreed to perform their audits for the purpose of providing the appellants with information on the basis of which they could make personal investment decisions....

... Despite the appellants' submissions, the respondents did not, in fact, prepare the audit reports in order to assist the appellants in making personal investment decisions or, indeed, for any purpose other than the standard statutory one. This finding accords with that of Helper J.A. in the Court of Appeal, and nothing in the record before this Court suggests the contrary.

[51] It follows from the foregoing discussion that the only purpose for which the 1980-82 reports could have been used in such a manner as to give rise to a duty of care on the part of the respondents is as a guide for the shareholders, as a group, in supervising or overseeing management. In assessing whether this was, in fact, the purpose to which the appellants purport to have put the audited reports, it will be useful to take each of the appellants' claims in turn. First, the appellant Hercules seeks compensation for its $600,000 injection of capital into NGA over January and February of 1983 and the appellant Freed seeks damages commensurate with the amount of money he contributed in 1982 to his investment account in NGH. Secondly, all the appellants seek damages for the losses they suffered in the value of their existing shareholdings.

[52] The claims of Hercules and Mr. Freed with respect to their 1982-83 investments can be addressed quickly. The essence of these claims must be that these two appellants relied on the respondents' reports in deciding whether or not to make further investments in the audited corporations. In other words, Hercules and Mr. Freed are claiming to have relied on the audited reports for the purpose of making personal investment decisions. As I have already discussed, this is not a purpose for which the respondents in this case can be said to have prepared their reports. In light of the dissonance between the purpose for which the reports were actually prepared and the purpose for which the appellants assert they were used, then, the claims of Hercules and Mr. Freed with respect to their investment losses are not such that the concerns over indeterminate liability discussed above are obviated; *viz.*, if a duty of care were owed with respect to these investment transactions, there would seem to be no logical reason to preclude a duty of care from arising in circumstances where the statements were used for any other purpose of which the auditors were equally unaware when they prepared and submitted their report. On this basis, therefore, I would find that the *prima facie* duty that arises respecting this claim is negated by policy considerations and, therefore, that no duty of care is owed by the respondents in this regard.

[53] With respect to the claim concerning the loss in value of their existing shareholdings, the appellants make two submissions. First, they claim that they relied on the 1980-82 reports in monitoring the value of their equity and that, owing to the (allegedly) negligent preparations of those reports, they failed to extract it before the financial demise of NGA and NGH. Secondly, and somewhat more subtly, the appellants submit that they each relied on the auditors' reports in overseeing the management of NGA and NGH and that had those reports been accurate, the collapse of the corporations and the consequential loss in the value of their shareholdings could have been avoided.

[54] To my mind, the first of these submissions suffers from the same difficulties as those regarding the injection of fresh capital by Hercules and Mr. Freed. Whether the reports were relied upon in assessing the prospect of further investments or in evaluating existing investments, the fact remains that the purpose to which the respondents' reports were put, on this claim, concerned individual or personal investment decisions. Given that the reports were not prepared for that purpose, I find for the same reasons as those earlier set out that policy considerations regarding indeterminate liability inhere here and, consequently, that no duty of care is owed in respect of this claim.

[55] As regards the second aspect of the appellants' claim concerning the losses they suffered in the diminution in value of their equity, the analysis becomes somewhat more intricate. The essence of the appellants' submission here is that the shareholders would have supervised management differently had they known of the (alleged) inaccuracies in the 1980-82 reports, and that this difference in management would have averted the demise of the audited corporations and the consequent losses in existing equity suffered by the shareholders. At first glance, it might appear that the appellants' claim implicates a use of the audit reports which is commensurate with the purpose for which the reports were prepared, *i.e.*, overseeing or supervising management. One might argue on this basis that a duty of care should be found to inhere because, in view of this compatibility between actual use and intended purpose, no indeterminacy arises. In my view, however, this line of reasoning suffers from a subtle but fundamental flaw.

[56] As I have already explained, the purpose for which the audit reports were prepared in this case was the standard statutory one of allowing shareholders *as a group*, to supervise management and to take decisions with respect to matters concerning the proper overall administration *of the corporations*.

In other words, it was,...to permit the shareholders to exercise their role, *as a class,* of overseeing the *corporations*' affairs at their annual general meetings. The purpose of providing the auditors' reports to the appellants, then, may ultimately be said to have been a "collective" one; that is, it was aimed not at protecting the interests of individual shareholders but rather at enabling the shareholders, acting as a group, to safeguard the interests of the corporations themselves. On the appellants' argument, however, the purpose to which the 1980-82 reports were ostensibly put was not that of allowing the shareholders as a class to take decisions in respect of the overall running of the corporation, but rather to allow them, as *individuals*, to monitor management so as to oversee and protect their own personal investments. Indeed, the nature of the appellants' claims (*i.e.* personal tort claims) *requires* that they assert reliance on the auditors' reports *qua* individual shareholders if they are to recover any personal damages. In so far as it must concern the interests of each individual shareholder, then, the appellants' claim in this regard can really be no different from the other "investment purposes" discussed above, in respect of which the respondents owe no duty of care.

[La Forest J. then went on to consider the effect of the rule in *Foss v. Harbottle* on the appellants' claim. He found that the effect of that rule is that individual shareholders cannot raise individual claims in respect of a wrong done to the corporation. However, he further held that the rule does not preclude a separate and distinct claim from being raised with respect to a wrong done to a shareholder *qua* individual. On the facts of this case, no such claim could be established.]

Conclusion

[64] In light of the foregoing, I would find that even though the respondents owed the appellants (*qua* individual claimants) a *prima facie* duty of care both

with respect to the 1982-83 investments made in NGA and NGH by Hercules and Mr. Freed and with respect to the losses they incurred through the devaluation of their existing shareholdings, such *prima facie* duties are negated by policy considerations which are not obviated by the facts of the case. Indeed, to come to the opposite conclusion on these facts would be to expose auditors to the possibility of indeterminate liability, since such a finding would imply that auditors owe a duty of care of any known class of potential plaintiffs regardless of the purpose to which they put the auditors' reports. This would amount to an unacceptably broad expansion of the bounds of liability drawn by this Court in *Haig*, *supra*.

[65] I would dismiss the appeal with costs.

Appeal dismissed.

NOTES

1. The judgment of La Forest J. narrows the category of cases where recovery for economic loss resulting from a negligent statement will be allowed to those in a known class who use the information for a known purpose. This is consistent with the English authorities. Is this a positive development? Linden, in his book, states that this development "will undoubtedly narrow the range of plaintiffs allowed to succeed, but it should also clarify the law and prevent cases of indeterminate liability".

2. The decision in *Hercules* is also important because it clarifies the purpose of the *Anns* test and explains the court's use of the test in this context. That is, we see in this case a very straightforward admission that the court is concerned with policy and that, in order to succeed in a claim for pure economic loss, a plaintiff will have to convince the court that policy concerns about indeterminate liability should not be a bar.

3. On balance, are you happy about this decision? Is it too restrictive? It has been recently followed by Major J. in an unanimous Supreme Court decision in *Ryan v. Victoria (City)*, unreported, January 28, 1999, Doc. No. 25704 (S.C.C.), *supra*, Chapter 5.

1. Contract and Tort

An interesting subcategory of cases arising in the negligent statement context are those dealing with the issue of whether there can exist concurrent liability in tort and contract. It will be recalled that in *Hedley Byrne* the defendant was not found liable due to the existence of a contractual waiver of responsibility (the defendant had sent its reply prefaced by the remarks "For your private use and without responsibility on the part of the bank or its officials.") As the bank had limited its liability, it was found to be not liable for its statements. In *Central Trust Co. v. Rafuse* (1986), 37 C.C.L.T. 117 (S.C.C.) (rehearing, [1988] 1 S.C.R. 1026) Mr. Justice LeDain (adopting the dissenting viewpoint of Mr. Justice Spence in *Nunes Diamonds Ltd. v. Dominion Electric Protection Co.*, [1972] S.C.R. 769, 26 D.L.R. (3d) 699) held that the existence of a contract did not preclude concurrent or alternative liability in tort. However, he noted that "concurrent liability in tort will not be admitted if its effect would be to permit the plaintiff to circumvent or escape a contractual exclusion or limitation of liability". There are other issues as well, which will be considered.

BG CHECO INTERNATIONAL LTD. v. B.C. HYDRO & POWER AUTHORITY

Supreme Court of Canada. [1993] 1 S.C.R. 12, 99 D.L.R. (4th) 577.

B.C. Hydro called for tenders to erect transmission towers and string transmission lines. BG Checo was the successful bidder and entered into a contract with B.C. Hydro. The tender documents, upon which the plaintiff relied, and the contract both stated that clearing of the right-of-way would be done by others and would not form part of the contract.

The clearing of the right-of-way was inadequate. This caused the plaintiff difficulties and additional expenses in completing its work. The plaintiff sued for fraud, negligent misrepresentation, and breach of contract. The Court of Appeal, reversing the trial judge, rejected the claim for fraud ((1990), 44 B.C.L.R. (2d) 145, [1990] 3 W.W.R. 69), but upheld the claim for negligent misrepresentation. On appeal to the Supreme Court, the following issues were raised. First, whether a pre-contractual representation which becomes a contractual term can found liability in negligent misrepresentation. Second, whether the terms of the contract in this case operated to exclude Hydro's potential tort liability.

La Forest and **McLachlin JJ.**:

The Claim in Tort

The Theory of Concurrency

The first question is whether the contract precludes Checo from suing in tort.

Iacobucci J. concludes that a contract between the parties may preclude the possibility of suing in tort for a given wrong where there is an express term in the contract dealing with the matter. We would phrase the applicable principle somewhat more narrowly. As we see it, the right to sue in tort is not taken away by the contract in such a case, although the contract, by limiting the scope of the tort duty or waiving the right to sue in tort, may limit or negate tort liability.

In our view, the general rule emerging from this Court's decision in *Central Trust Co. v. Rafuse*, [1986] 2 S.C.R. 147, is that where a given wrong *prima facie* supports an action in contract and in tort, the party may sue in either or both, except where the contract indicates that the parties intended to limit or negative the right to sue in tort. This limitation on the general rule of concurrency arises because it is always open to parties to limit or waive the duties which the common law would impose on them for negligence. This principle is of great importance in preserving a sphere of individual liberty and commercial flexibility. Thus if a person wishes to engage in a dangerous sport, the person may stipulate in advance that he or she waives any right of action against the person who operates the sport facility: *Dyck v. Manitoba Snowmobile Association Inc.*, [1985] 1 S.C.R. 589. Similarly, if two business firms agree that a particular risk should lie on a party who would not ordinarily bear that risk at common law, they may do so. So a plaintiff may sue either in contract or in tort, subject to any limit the parties themselves have placed on that right by their contract. The mere fact that the parties have dealt with a matter expressly in their contract does not mean that they intended to exclude the right to sue in tort. It all depends on *how* they have dealt with it.

Viewed thus, the only limit on the right to choose one's action is the principle of primacy of private ordering — the right of individuals to arrange their affairs and assume risks in a different way than would be done by the law of tort. It is only to the extent that this private ordering contradicts the tort duty that the tort duty is diminished. The rule is not that one cannot sue concurrently in contract and tort where the contract limits or contradicts the tort duty. It is rather that the tort duty, a general duty imputed by the law in all the relevant circumstances, must yield to the parties' superior right to arrange their rights and duties in a different way. In so far as the tort duty is not contradicted by the contract, it remains intact and may be sued upon. For example, where the contractual limitation on the tort duty is partial, a tort action founded on the modified duty might lie. The tort duty as modified by the contractual agreement between the parties might be raised in a case where the limitation period for an action for breach of contract has expired but the limitation period for a tort action has not. If one says categorically, as we understand Iacobucci J. to say, that where the contract deals with a matter expressly, the right to sue in tort vanishes altogether, then the latter two possibilities vanish.

This is illustrated by consideration of the three situations that may arise when contract and tort are applied to the same wrong. The first class of case arises where the contract stipulates a more stringent obligation than the general law of tort would impose. In that case, the parties are hardly likely to sue in tort, since they could not recover in tort for the higher contractual duty. The vast majority of commercial transactions fall into this class. The right to sue in tort is not extinguished, however, and may remain important, as where suit in contract is barred by expiry of a limitation period.

The second class of case arises where the contract stipulates a lower duty than that which would be presumed by the law of tort in similar circumstances. This occurs when the parties by their contract indicate their intention that the usual liability imposed by the law of tort is not to bind them. The most common means by which such as intention is indicated is the inclusion of a clause of exemption or exclusion of liability in the contract. Generally, the duty imposed by the law of tort can be nullified only by clear terms. We do not rule out, however, the possibility that cases may arise in which merely inconsistent contract terms could negative or limit a duty in tort, an issue that may be left to a case in which it arises. The issue raises difficult policy considerations, viz. an assessment of the circumstances in which contracting parties should be permitted to agree to contractual duties that would subtract from their general obligations under the law of tort. These important questions are best left to a case in which the proper factual foundation is available, so as to provide an appropriate context for the decision. In the second class of case, as in the first, there is usually little point in suing in tort since the duty in tort and consequently any tort liability is limited by the specific limitation to which the parties have agreed. An exception might arise where the contract does not entirely negate tort liability (*e.g.*, the exemption clause applies only above a certain amount) and the plaintiff wishes to sue in tort to avail itself of a more generous limitation period or some other procedural advantage offered by tort.

The third class of case arises where the duty in contract and the common law duty in tort are co-extensive. In this class of case, like the others, the plaintiff may seek to sue concurrently or alternatively in tort to secure some advantage peculiar to the law of tort, such as a more generous limitation period. The contract may expressly provide for a duty that is the same as that imposed by the common law. Or the contractual duty may be implied. The common calling cases, which have long permitted concurrent actions in contract and tort, generally fall into this class. There is a contract. But the obligation under that contract is typically defined by implied terms, *i.e.*, by the courts. Thus there is no issue of private ordering as opposed to publicly imposed liability. Whether the action is styled in contract or tort, its source is an objective expectation, defined by the courts, of the appropriate obligation and the correlative right.

The case at bar, as we see it, falls into this third category of case. The contract, read as we have proposed, did not negate Hydro's common law duty not to negligently misrepresent that it would have the right-of-way cleared by others. Had Checo known the truth, it would have bid for a higher amount. That duty is not excluded by the contract, which confirmed Hydro's obligation to clear the right-of-way. Accordingly, Checo may sue in tort.

We conclude that actions in contract and tort may be concurrently pursued unless the parties by a valid contractual provision indicate that they intended otherwise. This excludes, of course, cases where the contractual limitation is invalid, as by fraud, mistake or unconscionability. Similarly, a contractual limitation may not apply where the tort is independent of the contract in the sense of falling outside the scope of the contract, as the example given in *Elder, Dempster & Co. v. Paterson, Zochonis & Co.*, [1924] A.C. 522 (H.L.), of the captain of a vessel falling asleep and starting a fire in relation to a claim for cargo damage.

Iacobucci J. (dissenting): As a general rule, the existence of a contract between two parties does not preclude the existence of a common law duty of care. Subject to the substantive and procedural differences that exist between an action in contract and an action in tort, both the duty of care and the liability may be concurrent in contract and tort. In such circumstances, it is for the plaintiff to select the cause of action most advantageous to him or her. That was the position adopted by Le Dain J. in *Central Trust v. Rafuse, supra.*

In my opinion, the compromise struck by Le Dain J. is an appropriate one. If the parties to a contract choose to define a specific duty as an express term of the contract, then the consequences of a breach of that duty ought to be determined by the law of contract, not by tort law. Whether or not an implied term of a contract can define a duty of care in such a way that a plaintiff is confined to a remedy in contract is not at issue in this case. I leave that determination to another day. While the rule articulated by Le Dain J. is a rule of law which does not depend on the presumed or actual intention of the parties, the intention which can be inferred from the fact that the parties have made the duty an express term of the contract provides policy support for the rule. If a duty is an express term of the contract, it can be inferred that the parties wish the law of the contract to govern with respect to that duty.

...

A further policy rationale for the rule advanced by Le Dain J. is that contracts have become, particularly in commercial contexts, increasingly complex. Commercial contracts allocate risks and fix the mutual duties and obligations of the parties. Where there is an express term creating a contractual duty, it is appropriate that the parties be held to the bargain which they have made. Tort duties are of "uncertain definition and scope": H. Johnson, "Contract and Tort: Orthodoxy Reasserted!" (1990), 9 *Int'l Banking L.* 306. Commercial parties ought to be able to fix their respective rights and obligations in a particular transaction with certainty. Contractual certainty is a *sine qua non* without which reliance and the execution of obligations are seriously impaired. Moreover, without certainty, the transaction costs associated with a given commercial arrangement would most likely increase, perhaps drastically. In *V.K. Mason Construction Ltd. v. Bank of Nova Scotia*, [1985] 1 S.C.R. 271, Wilson J. alluded to these considerations stating, at p. 282, that "much of the value of commercial contracts lies in their ability to produce certainty. Parties are enabled to regulate their relationship by means of words rather than by means of their understanding of what each other's actions are intended to imply."

However, I do not believe that the rule advanced by Le Dain J. that forecloses a claim in tort is absolute in all circumstances. In this respect, I would favour a contextual approach which takes into account the context in which the contract is made, and the position of the parties with respect to one another, in assessing whether a claim in tort is foreclosed by the terms of a contract. The policy reasons in favour of the rule advanced by Le Dain J. are strongest where the contractual context is commercial and the parties are of equal bargaining power. There was no question of unconscionability or inequality of bargaining power in *Central Trust v. Rafuse, supra*, as there is no such question in this case. If such issues, or others analogous to them, were to arise, however, a court should be wary not to exclude too rapidly a duty of care in tort on the basis of an express term of the contract, especially if the end result for the plaintiff would be a wrong without a remedy.

Appeal dismissed and cross-appeal allowed in part.

NOTES

1. While the majority allowed both the tort and contract claim, and the minority only the claim in contract, both sides agreed that there was nothing in the contract to limit or exclude the defendant's liability. The case was remitted to the trial judge for the assessment of damages.

2. With whom do you agree in the above case? Do you think that it is sound policy to restrict to an action for breach of contract only those who have made a representation an express term of a contract? What if the representation becomes an "implied" term of the contract?

3. Why did the plaintiff, who had a breach of contract remedy, want to pursue its action in tort? One of the reasons for choosing tort is possibly to receive a higher damage award. The argument is as follows. In tort, damages are based on what the plaintiff lost as a result of the misrepresentation. The test is this: had the misrepresentation not occurred, what would the plaintiff's financial situation be? If the plaintiff, for example, would not have entered into the contract, all of the plaintiff's losses flowing from the fact that it did contract would be recoverable, even if some of these losses had nothing to do with the misrepresentation. Thus, in tort, the plaintiff could get out of its bad contract. In contract, the damages are assessed on the basis of "expectation"; that is, if the representation made had been correct, what would the plaintiff's situation have been? The plaintiff could recover only these losses; it could not recover other losses unrelated to this misrepresentation. Not all agree, however, that there is this difference in the assessment of contract and tort awards. For a full discussion of the damage issue, see *Rainbow Industrial Caterers Ltd. v. C.N.R.*, [1991] 3 S.C.R. 3, 84 D.L.R. (4th) 291.

4. The precontractual negligent representation issue was also an important question in *Queen v. Cognos, supra*. The plaintiff was told in the employment interview that the project for which he was being hired had a bright future for him. However, the employment contract that the plaintiff entered into expressly stated that the employer could terminate the plaintiff's position at any time, without cause upon one month's notice, and that the plaintiff could be reassigned within the company. In view of this, could the plaintiff use a tort action when his position was terminated? The Supreme Court stated that the plaintiff could sue in tort since his action was based on a misrep-

resentation concerning the nature and existence of the job being offered and not on the plaintiff's security of employment. In other words, the contract did not deal with the misrepresentation which was at the heart of the plaintiff's complaint. Do you think this is an overly subtle distinction?

5. The Supreme Court of Canada recently decided yet another negligent representation case in the contract/tort context. In *Edgeworth Const. Ltd. v. N.D. Lea & Associates Ltd.*, [1993] 3 S.C.R. 206, [1993] 8 W.W.R. 129, contractors who successfully bid on a contract with the Province of British Columbia sued the engineering firm and the individual engineers who had prepared the specifications and construction drawings. The plaintiffs had relied on these documents when they prepared their bid, and they alleged that due to errors in the documents, they suffered economic losses.

There were several different issues in this case. The contract entered into between the province and the plaintiffs contained a clause exonerating the province for any liability arising from errors in the bidding documents. While this contract was sufficient to exclude the provinces's liability, it was held to be inapplicable insofar as the engineers were concerned. This case was thus distinguished from the Supreme Court's earlier decision in *London Drugs*, [1992] 3 S.C.R. 299, 97 D.L.R. (4th) 261. The Court also held the engineering firm liable, but exonerated the individual engineers from personal liability. This was because the Court found no representation made between the individual engineers and the plaintiffs, even though the engineers had affixed their seals to the documents. There was therefore no duty. La Forest J. could not but help pointing out the apparent inconsistency between the Supreme Court's judgment in *London Drugs* and the present judgment. Recall that the individual employees in *London Drugs* did owe a duty of care to their employer's customers.

Can you explain why the individual engineers in this case owed no duty of care? Is it because the losses were purely economic as opposed to physical? Is it because the nature of the *Hedley Byrne* duty differs from the nature of the *Donoghue v. Stevenson* duty? Do you see a problem here in need of some further thought from the Court?

6. The question as to whether a negligence action can be brought by one contracting party against a co-contractant remained unsettled until the issue was definitively put to rest by Mr. Justice Le Dain in *Central Trust Co. v. Rafuse* (1986), 37 C.C.L.T. 117, at 165, 31 D.L.R. (4th) 481 (S.C.C.). The case involved a negligence action brought by a client against its solicitor. After a scholarly and exhaustive review of the Canadian, Commonwealth and American authorities, Le Dain J. arrived at the following conclusions:

1. The common law duty of care that is created by a relationship of sufficient proximity, in accordance with the general principle affirmed by Lord Wilberforce in *Anns v. Merton London Borough Council, supra*, is not confined to relationships that arise apart from contract. Although the relationships in *Donoghue v. Stevenson, Hedley Byrne* and *Anns* were all of a non-contractual nature and there was necessarily reference in the judgments to a duty of care that exists apart from or independently of contract, I find nothing in the statements of general principle in those cases to suggest that the principle was intended to be confined to relationships that arise apart from contract....
2. What is undertaken by the contract will indicate the nature of the relationship that gives rise to the common law duty of care, but the nature and scope of the duty of care that is asserted as the foundation of the tortious liability must not depend on specific obligations or duties created by the express terms of the contract. It is in that sense that the common law duty of care must be independent of the contract. The distinction, insofar as the terms of the contract are concerned, is, broadly speaking, between what is to be done and how it is to be done. A claim cannot be said to be in tort if it depends for the nature and scope of the asserted duty of care on the manner in which an obligation or duty has

been expressly and specifically defined by a contract. Where the common law duty of care is co-extensive with that which arises as an implied term of the contract it obviously does not depend on the terms of the contract, and there is nothing flowing from contractual intention which should preclude reliance on a concurrent or alternative liability in tort. The same is also true of reliance on a common law duty of care that falls short of a specific obligation or duty imposed by the express terms of a contract.

3. A concurrent or alternative liability in tort will not be admitted if its effect would be to permit the plaintiff to circumvent or escape a contractual exclusion or limitation of liability for the act or omission that would constitute the tort. Subject to this qualification, where concurrent liability in tort and contract exists the plaintiff has the right to assert the cause of action that appears to be most advantageous to him in respect of any particular legal consequence.

7. A related issue involves the liability of an employee for negligence in the performance of employee duties. In *Sealand of the Pacific Ltd. v. Robert C. McHaffie Ltd. and Robert McHaffie* (1975), 51 D.L.R. (3d) 702 [1974] 6 W.W.R. 224 (B.C.C.A.), the plaintiff hired a firm of naval architects to repair its underwater aquarium in Victoria, B.C. When the work was not done to the plaintiff's satisfaction, it sued the architect firm, which was a limited company, and its principle architect, an employee of the firm, personally. The action was based on negligent statement. The Court of Appeal dismissed the action against the architect holding that he was undertaking his skill not for the benefit of the plaintiff, but for his firm's benefit. It was the firm's skill and not the architect's skill upon which the plaintiff was relying.

8. The decision in *Sealand v. McHaffie* pre-dated *Central Trust* and has been frequently criticized. The issue of an employee's personal tort liability was carefully looked at by the Supreme Court of Canada in the case of *London Drugs Ltd. v. Kuehne & Nagel International Ltd.* (1993), 73 B.C.L.R. (2d) 1, [1993] 1 W.W.R. 1. In this case, two employees of the defendant storage company dropped an expensive piece of equipment belonging to a client of their employer, the storage company. The majority of the Supreme Court reaffirmed the principle that as long as a relationship of proximity existed between the employees and the client, a duty of care was owed. It did not matter that the employees were performing the very essence of the contract between their employer and its client at the time of their careless act. The Court then went on to consider whether a limitation clause in the contract between the employer and the client could be interpreted widely enough to protect the employees as well, and it decided that the doctrine of privity could be relaxed sufficiently in order to achieve this result.

What does this decision do to *Sealand*?

See generally Fleming, "Tort in a Contractual Matrix" (1995), 33 Osgoode Hall L.J. 661.

B. NEGLIGENT PERFORMANCE OF SERVICES

Another category of economic loss case arises from reliance on the negligent performance of a service for the plaintiff's benefit. These cases are very similar to the negligent representation cases, the difference being that, instead of dealing with negligent words, they deal with negligent actions. As such, whether they should be categorized as a separate category is open to debate (see Linden, p. 451). Many of them can be dealt with as negligent advice cases, but, to do so, it may be necessary to construct or imply the statement. Nevertheless, the Supreme Court of Canada has stated that this line of cases is a separate category of economic loss case, and, therefore, it will be dealt with as such here.

B.D.C. LTD. v. HOFSTRAND FARMS LTD.

Supreme Court of Canada. [1986] 1 S.C.R. 228.

The appellant, a courier company, entered into a contract with the province of British Columbia to deliver an envelope. The appellant was not aware of the contents of the envelope — a Crown grant in favour of the respondent which the respondent wanted registered before the close of business on December 31, 1976. The respondent had entered into a contract that provided that failure to register the grant in time entitled the purchaser to treat the contract as at an end. The courier did not deliver the envelope on time which delayed the registration of the land and led the purchaser to treat its contract with the respondent as at an end. The respondent brought an action against the Crown and the courier company. The Supreme Court ultimately dismissed the action against the courier.

Estey J. (**Chouinard** and **Lamer JJ.** concurring):

Here we are dealing with the careless performance of an undertaking by contract to provide services in a timely way....

On the facts as revealed by the evidence before the Court in this appeal, the appellant courier had no knowledge of the existence of the respondent, nor, because of the Crown practice of not disclosing the nature of the documents being forwarded, could it reasonably have known of the existence of a class of persons whose interests depended upon timely transmission of the envelope. There was, therefore, no actual or constructive knowledge in the courier that the rights of a third party could in any way be affected by the transmission or lack of transmission of the envelope in question. If a person in the position of the respondent is included in a class considered to be reasonably within the contemplation of the appellant, there is no logical point of breaking off so as to put a reasonable practical limitation on the courier's range of liability. It is a stretching of concept to conclude that anyone who might conceivably be affected by a failure by the Province of British Columbia to register a Crown grant within the calendar year, constitutes a "limited class" the existence of which is known to a courier employed to deliver the Crown grant to a registry office. In the words of Lord Reid in *Hedley Byrne*, *supra*, "... it would be going very far to say that (the defendant) owes a duty to every ultimate 'consumer'...."

Another aspect of proximity which was stressed by *Hedley Byrne, supra,* and by Lord Roskill in *Junior Books, supra,* at p. 214, is reliance by the plaintiff upon the undertaking or representation made by the defendant....

What was the reliance here by the respondent? There was none. The respondent was, by the time of the appellant's engagement by the Crown, in a position of risk through no act of its own. The situation of risk, in which a delay would be fatal to the respondent's interests, was created by the terms of the respondent's contract with the third party, in conjunction with the Crown's refusal to allow a representative of the respondent to carry the documents to Prince George himself. There was no assumption of risk in reliance upon the appellant's undertaking to deliver the documents. The respondent did not rely on the appellant in any way prior to the creation of this risk. The respondent did not permit the engagement of the appellant or reject the idea of engaging another courier by reason of any representation made by the appellant. Nor was the decision not to use the facilities of the Post Office motivated by any act or statement by the appellant.

In sum, the requirements of proximity contained in the principles, enunciated by *Hedley Byrne*, *supra*, and confirmed in *Anns, supra*, are not met on the facts of this appeal. As I have concluded that the respondent did not come within a limited class in the reasonable contemplation of a person in the position of the appellant, it is unnecessary to proceed to the second stage or test set out by Lord Wilberforce in *Anns, supra*.

...the realities of modern life must be reflected by the enunciation of a defined limit on liability capable of practical application, so that social and commercial life can go on unimpeded by a burden outweighing the benefit to the community of the neighbourhood historic principle....

Wilson J. (concurring): I agree with my colleague, Estey J., that no duty of care was owed by the appellant courier to the respondent Hofstrand on the facts of this case. The principle established by the House of Lords in *Anns v. Merton London Borough Council,* [1978] A.C. 728, and applied by the majority of this Court in *City of Kamloops v. Nielsen,* [1984] 2 S.C.R. 2, has accordingly no application in this situation.

I would respectfully adopt the following excerpt from the dissenting reasons of Carrothers J. in the British Columbia Court of Appeal:

> I consider that, as between the courier and Hofstrand, there is not any relationship of proximity or neighbourhood such that in the reasonable contemplation of the courier carelessness on the part of the courier may likely cause Hofstrand to suffer economic loss.

NOTES

1. See Blom, "Slow Courier in the Supreme Court" (1986-87), 12 Can. Bus. L.J. 43.

2. In *Whittingham v. Crease & Co.* (1977), 88 D.L.R. (3d) 353, 6 C.C.L.T. 1 (B.C. S.C.), the defendant law firm prepared a will for a testator. The testator had sought to leave his house and the residue of the estate to his son, the plaintiff. The solicitor, in the plaintiff's presence, mistakenly had the wife of the plaintiff sign the will as a witness, which had the legal effect of rendering the bequest to the plaintiff, her husband, void. The residue, therefore, went as on an intestacy and the plaintiff received only a part, instead of all of it. He sued the solicitor for the difference and recovered.

Mr. Justice Aikins explained his decision as follows:

> While I am not free to make pronouncements on such a broad basis without authority, I am of the opinion that the factual situation in the present case falls fairly within the principles enunciated in *Hedley Byrne* as expounded in *Haig v. Bamford*. I hold that in all the circumstances Mr. Cowan was subject to an implied duty to the plaintiff to use reasonable care, skill and diligence in attending to the witnessing of the testator's will.
>
> The facts in the present case differ in one particular and troublesome aspect from those in the general run of cases in which *Hedley Byrne* has been successfully invoked. I have not been referred to a case, nor have I been able to find one, in which the principle of *Hedley Byrne* has been applied where the plaintiff had not acted on the strength of the representation made by the defendant and it was the plaintiff's own act which was the *immediate* cause of the loss.
>
> In this case the plaintiff has suffered a loss but without his having done anything in reliance on the implied representation made by Mr. Cowan. In my opinion there are two reasons, linked to each other, which enable the plaintiff to succeed in this case, notwithstanding that he remained passive and did nothing, relying on Mr. Cowan's implied representation. First, it was unneces-

sary for the plaintiff to act at all on the implied representation in order to attract the loss which he has suffered; second, Mr. Cowan could reasonably foresee that if he, in the performance of his duty, failed to see to it that the will was properly witnessed, then that neglect would cause the very loss the plaintiff has suffered, without the plaintiff doing anything at all. Granted that there was an implied duty on the part of Mr. Cowan to the plaintiff and that the plaintiff relied on Mr. Cowan fulfilling that duty, it seems to me on principle that it is immaterial that the plaintiff himself did nothing, in reliance on the implied representation made by Mr. Cowan, which brought about his loss. This is so because the negligence of the solicitor caused the loss without there having to be any intervening act by the plaintiff to perfect the chain of causation.

For these reasons I hold on the line of authorities headed by *Hedley Byrne* and on the particular facts in this case that the defendant is liable to the plaintiff in negligence. I wish to make it clear my conclusion rests on the particular facts of this case and that I make no pronouncement on the more general issue of the liability of a solicitor to a third party beneficiary on the ground of negligence in the preparation of a will....

3. In *Ross v. Caunters*, [1980] Ch. 297, [1979] 3 W.L.R. 605, Megarry L.C. followed this decision, though not its reasoning, even though the beneficiary knew nothing about the will and did not rely on it. He summarized his conclusions as follows:

(1) There is no longer any rule that a solicitor who is negligent in his professional work can be liable only to his client in contract; he may be liable both to his client and to others for the tort of negligence.
(2) The basis of the solicitor's liability to others is either an extension of the *Hedley Byrne* principle, [1964] A.C. 465 or, more probably, a direct application of the principle of *Donoghue v. Stevenson*, [1932] A.C. 562.
(3) A solicitor who is instructed by his client to carry out a transaction that will confer a benefit on an identified third party owes a duty of care towards that third party in carrying out that transaction, in that the third party is a person within his direct contemplation as someone who is likely to be so closely and directly affected by his acts or omissions that he can reasonably foresee that the third party is likely to be injured by those acts or omissions.
(4) The mere fact that the loss to such a third party caused by the negligence is purely financial, and is in no way a physical injury to person or property, is no bar to the claim against the solicitor.
(5) In such circumstances there are no considerations which suffice to negative or limit the scope of the solicitor's duty to the beneficiary.

See also to the same effect *White v. Jones,* [1995] 1 All E.R. 691 (H.L.). Professor Klar is critical of these cases; see "Downsizing Tort Law" in Mullany and Linden, *Torts Tomorrow*, Sydney: The Law Book Company (1998).

4. Insurance and real estate agents have frequently been found liable in tort for their negligence in the performance of services upon which others rely. See, for example, *Fletcher v. Man. Public Ins. Corp.*, [1990] 3 S.C.R. 191, 74 D.L.R. (4th) 636, where the Manitoba Public Insurance Corporation was found liable in tort for neglecting to inform a customer of the availability of underinsured motorist protection.

See also *Miller v. Guardian Insurance Co. of Canada* (1995), 127 D.L.R. (4th) 717 (Alta. Q.B.) vard (1997), 149 D.L.R. (4th) 375 (Alta. C.A.).

5. What is the main issue in these cases involving a defendant's failure to perform services for the plaintiff's benefit? In the absence of consideration, the plaintiff has no contractual right to receive the service. Should tort law take over and give the plaintiff the protection that contract law refused to offer? Is tort law being used to provide protection that the plaintiff might have purchased but did not?

C. ECONOMIC LOSSES CAUSED BY DEFECTIVE PRODUCTS AND STRUCTURES

The problem of liability for economic loss caused by shoddy products is a controversial one, but it has recently been largely resolved by the Supreme Court of Canada, at least where there is a danger to safety. The early case of *Rivtow Marine Ltd. v. Washington Iron Works* (1973), 40 D.L.R. (3d) 530 (S.C.C.), allowed damages for the economic loss that resulted when a faulty crane could not be used during a busy period because it had to be repaired in order to prevent its collapse. There was a negligent failure to warn by the supplier upon learning of the defect. As for the cost of repair, the Court divided — the majority denied it, but Laskin J. in a powerful dissent would have allowed it.

> The case is not one where a manufactured product proves to be merely defective (in short, where it has not met promised expectations) but rather one where by reason of the defect there is a foreseeable risk of physical harm from its use and where the alert avoidance of such harm gives rise to economic loss. Prevention of threatened harm resulting directly in economic loss should not be treated differently from post-injury cure.

This dissent has now become law.

WINNIPEG CONDOMINIUM CORP. NO. 36 v. BIRD CONSTRUCTION CO.

Supreme Court of Canada. [1995] 1 S.C.R. 85.

A subsequent owner of an apartment building sued the original contractor (and others) alleging that the building had structural defects that were dangerous, as well as other defects. The pleadings were challenged and the case reached the Supreme Court of Canada on the narrow issue of whether a general contractor can be liable in tort to a subsequent purchaser for negligent construction. The Supreme Court of Canada answered this question affirmatively, at least where there is potential danger.

La Forest J.: May a general contractor responsible for the construction of a building be held tortiously liable for negligence to a subsequent purchaser of the building, who is not in contractual privity with the contractor, for the cost of repairing defects in the building arising out of negligence in its construction? That is the issue that was posed by a motion for summary judgment and a motion to strike out a claim as disclosing no reasonable cause of action....

[His Lordship referred to his reasons in *Norsk* and the adoption of Professor Feldthusen's five category approach.]

The present case, which involves the alleged negligent construction of a building, falls partially within the fourth category [of Feldthusen, *Negligent Supply of Shoddy Goods or Structures*], although subject to an important *caveat.* The negligently supplied structure in this case was not merely shoddy; it was dangerous. In my view, this is important because the degree of danger to persons and other property created by the negligent construction of a building is a cornerstone of the policy analysis that must take place in determining whether the cost of repair of the building is recoverable in tort. As I will attempt to show, a distinction can be drawn on a policy level between "dangerous" defects in buildings and merely "shoddy" construction in buildings and that, at least with respect to dangerous defects, compelling policy reasons exist for the imposition upon contractors of tortious liability for the cost of repair of these defects.

Traditionally, the courts have characterized the costs incurred by a plaintiff in repairing a defective chattel or building as "economic loss" on the grounds that costs of those repairs do not arise from injury to persons or damage to property apart from the defective chattel or building itself; see *Rivtow Marine Ltd. v. Washington Iron Works*, [1974] S.C.R. 1189, at p. 1207. For my part, I would find it more congenial to deal directly with the policy considerations underlying that classification....

However, I am content to deal with the issues in the terms in which the arguments were formulated. Adopting this traditional characterization as a convenient starting point for my analysis, I observe that the losses claimed by the Condominium Corporation in the present case fall quite clearly under the category of economic loss. In their statement of claim, the Condominium Corporation claim damages in excess of $1.5 million from the respondent Bird, the subcontractor Kornovski & Keller and the architects Smith Carter, representing the cost of repairing the building subsequent to the collapse of the exterior cladding on May 8, 1989. The Condominium Corporation is not claiming that anyone was injured by the collapsing exterior cladding or that the collapsing cladding damaged any of its other property. Rather, its claim is simply for the cost of repairing the allegedly defective masonry and putting the exterior of the building back into safe working condition....

In my view, where a contractor (or any other person) is negligent in planning or constructing a building, and where that building is found to contain defects resulting from that negligence which pose a real and substantial danger to the occupants of the building, the reasonable cost of repairing the defects and putting the building back into a non-dangerous state are recoverable in tort by the occupants. The underlying rationale for this conclusion is that a person who participates in the construction of a large and permanent structure which, if negligently constructed, has the capacity to cause serious damage to other persons and property in the community, should be held to a reasonable standard of care. Sir Robin Cooke expressed the rationale for this conclusion as follows "An Impossible Distinction" (1991), 107 L.Q. Rev. 46 at p. 70:

> The point is simply that, prima facie, he who puts into the community an apparently sound and durable structure, intended for use in all probability by a succession of persons, should be expected to take reasonable care that it is reasonably fit for that use and does not mislead. He is not merely exercising his freedom as a citizen to pursue his own ends. He is constructing, exploiting or sanctioning something for the use of others. Unless compelling grounds to the contrary can be made out, and subject to reasonable limitations as to time or otherwise, the natural consequences of failure to take due care should be accepted.

My conclusion that the type of economic loss claimed by the Condominium Corporation is recoverable in tort is therefore based in large part upon what seem to me to be compelling policy considerations....

Was There a Sufficiently Close Relationship Between the Parties so that, in the Reasonable Contemplation of Bird, Carelessness on its Part Might Cause Damage to a Subsequent Purchaser of the Building such as the Condominium Corporation?

In my view, it is reasonably foreseeable to contractors that, if they design or construct a building negligently and if that building contains latent defects as a result of that negligence, subsequent purchasers of the building may suffer personal injury or damage to other property when those defects manifest themselves. A lack of contractual privity between the contractor and the inhabitants at the time the defect becomes manifest does not make the potential for injury any less foreseeable. Buildings are permanent structures that are commonly inhabited by many different persons over their useful life. By constructing the building negligently, contractors (or any other person responsible for the design and construction of a building) create a foreseeable danger that will threaten not only the original owner, but every inhabitant during the useful life of the building....

In my view, the reasonable likelihood that a defect in a building will cause injury to its inhabitants is also sufficient to ground a contractor's duty in tort to subsequent purchasers of the building for the cost of repairing the defect if that defect is discovered prior to any injury and if it poses a real and substantial danger to the inhabitants of the building. In coming to this conclusion, I adopt the reasoning of Laskin J. in *Rivtow*, which I find highly persuasive. If a contractor can be held liable in tort where he or she constructs a building negligently and, as a result of that negligence, the building causes damage to persons or property, it follows that the contractor should also be held liable in cases where the dangerous defect is discovered and the owner of the building wishes to mitigate the danger by fixing the defect and putting the building back into a non-dangerous state. In both cases, the duty in tort serves to protect the bodily integrity and property interests of the inhabitants of the building....

Allowing recovery against contractors in tort for the cost of repair of dangerous defects thus serves an important preventative function by encouraging socially responsible behaviour.

This conclusion is borne out by the facts of the present case, which fall squarely within the category of what I would define as a "real and substantial danger". It is clear from the available facts that the masonry work on the Condominium Corporation's building was in a sufficiently poor state to constitute a real and substantial danger to inhabitants of the building and to passers-by. The piece of cladding that fell from the building was a story high, was made of 4" thick Tyndall stone, and dropped nine storeys. Had this cladding landed on a person or on other property, it would unquestionably have caused serious injury or damage. Indeed, it was only by chance that the cladding fell in the middle of the night and caused no harm. In this light, I believe that the Condominium Corporation behaved responsibly, and as a reasonable home owner should, in having the building inspected and repaired immediately. Bird should not be insulated from liability simply because the current owner of the building acted quickly to alleviate the danger that Bird itself may well have helped to create.

Given the clear presence of a real and substantial danger in this case, I do not find it necessary to consider whether contractors should also in principle be held to owe a duty to subsequent purchasers for the cost of repairing non-dangerous defects in buildings. It was not raised by the parties. I note that appellate courts in New Zealand (in *Bowen, supra*), Australia (*Bryan v. Moloney*),...and in numerous American states have all recognized some form of general duty of builders and contractors to subsequent purchasers with regard to the reasonable fitness and habitability of a building. In Quebec, it is also now well-established that contractors, subcontractors, engineers and architects owe a duty to successors in title in immovable property for economic loss suffered as a result of faulty construction, design and workmanship... However, it is right to note that from the tone of Dickson J.'s reasons in *Fraser-Reid v. Droumtsekas*, [1980] 1 S.C.R. 720, at pp. 729-31, he would appear to be cool to the idea, though he found it unnecessary to canvass the point. For my part, I would require argument more squarely focused on the issue before entertaining this possibility.

Without entering into this question, I note that the present case is distinguishable on a policy level from cases where the workmanship is merely shoddy or substandard but not dangerously defective. In the latter class of cases, tort law serves to encourage the repair of dangerous defects and thereby to protect the bodily integrity of inhabitants of buildings. By contrast, the former class of cases bring into play the questions of quality of workmanship and fitness for purpose. These questions do not arise here. Accordingly, it is sufficient for present purposes to say that, if Bird is found negligent at trial, the Condominium Corporation would be entitled on this reasoning to recover the reasonable cost of putting the building into a non-dangerous state, but not the cost of any repairs that would serve merely to improve the quality, and not the safety, of the building.

I conclude that the law in Canada has now progressed to the point where it can be said that contractors (as well as subcontractors, architects and engineers) who take part in the design and construction of a building will owe a duty in tort to subsequent purchasers of the building if it can be shown that it was foreseeable that a failure to take reasonable care in constructing the building would create defects that pose a substantial danger to the health and safety of the occupants. Where negligence is established and such defects manifest themselves before any damage to persons or property occurs, they should, in my view, be liable for the reasonable cost of repairing the defects and putting the building back into a non-dangerous state.

Are There Any Considerations that Ought to Negate (a) the Scope of the Duty and (b) the Class of Persons to Whom it is Owed or (c) the Damages to which a Breach of it May Give Rise?

There are two primary and interrelated concerns raised by the recognition of a contractor's duty in tort to subsequent purchasers of buildings for the cost of repairing dangerous defects. The first is that warranties respecting quality of construction are primarily contractual in nature and cannot be easily defined or limited in tort....

The second concern is that the recognition of such a duty interferes with the doctrine of *caveat emptor* which, as this Court affirmed in *Fraser-Reid*, *supra*, at p. 723, "has lost little of its pristine force in the sale of land". The doctrine of *caveat emptor* indicates that, in the absence of an express warranty, there is no implied warranty of fitness for human habitation upon the purchase of a house already completed at the time of sale....

In my view, these concerns are both merely versions of the more general and traditional concern that allowing recovery for economic loss in tort will subject a defendant to what Cardozo C.J. in *Ultramares Corp. v. Touche*, 174 N.E. 441 (N.Y.C.A. 1931), at p. 444, called "liability in an indeterminate amount for an indeterminate time to an indeterminate class". In light of the fact that most buildings have a relatively long useful life, the concern is that a contractor will be subject potentially to an indeterminate amount of liability to an indeterminate number of successive owners over an indeterminate time period. The doctrines of privity of contract and *caveat emptor* provide courts with a useful mechanism for limiting liability in tort. But the problem, as I will now attempt to demonstrate, is that it is difficult to justify the employment of these doctrines in the tort context in any principled manner apart from their utility as mechanisms for limiting liability.

The Concern with Overlap Between Tort and Contract Duties

Turning to the first concern, a duty on the part of contractors to take reasonable care in the construction of buildings can, in my view, be conceptualized in the absence of contract and will not result in indeterminate liability to the contractor. As I mentioned earlier, this Court has recognized that a tort duty can arise concurrently with a contractual duty, so long as that tort duty arises independently of the contractual duty; see *Rafuse, supra*; *Edgeworth, supra*. As I see it, the duty to construct a building according to reasonable standards and without dangerous defects arises independently of the contractual stipulations between the original owner and the contractor because it arises from a duty to create the building safely and not merely according to contractual standards of quality. It must be remembered that we are speaking here of a duty to construct the building according to reasonable standards of safety in such a manner that it does not contain *dangerous* defects. As this duty arises independently of any contract, there is no logical reason for allowing the contractor to rely upon a contract made with the original owner to shield him or her from liability to subsequent purchasers arising from a dangerously constructed building....

The tort duty to construct a building safely is thus a circumscribed duty that is not parasitic upon any contractual duties between the contractor and the original owner. Seen in this way, no serious risk of indeterminate liability arises with respect to this tort duty. In the first place, there is no risk of liability to an indeterminate class because the potential class of claimants is limited to the very persons for whom the building is constructed: the inhabitants of the building. The fact that the class of claimants may include successors in title who have no contractual relationship with the contractor does not, in my view, render the class of potential claimants indeterminate....

Secondly, there is no risk of liability in an indeterminate amount because the amount of liability will always be limited by the reasonable cost of repairing the dangerous defect in the building and restoring that building to a non-dangerous state. Counsel for Bird advanced the argument that the cost of repairs claimed for averting a danger caused by a defect in construction could, in some cases, be disproportionate to the actual damage to persons or property that might be caused if that defect were not repaired. For example, he expressed concern that a given plaintiff could claim thousands of dollars in damage for a defect which, if left unrepaired, would cause only a few dollars damage to that plaintiff's other property. However, in my view, any danger of indeterminacy in damages is averted by the requirement that the defect for which the costs of repair are claimed must constitute a real and substantial danger to the inhabitants of the building, and the fact that the inhabitants of the building can only claim the reasonable cost of repairing the defect and mitigating the danger. The burden of proof will always fall on the plaintiff to demonstrate that there is a serious risk to safety, that the risk was caused by the contractor's negligence, and that the repairs are required to alleviate the risk.

Finally, there is little risk of liability for an indeterminate time because the contractor will only be liable for the cost of repair of dangerous defects during the useful life of the building. Practically speaking, I believe that the period in which the contractor may be exposed to liability for negligence will be much shorter than the full useful life of the building. With the passage of time, it will become increasingly difficult for owners of a building to prove at trial that any deterioration in the building is attributable to the initial negligence of the contractor and not simply to the inevitable wear and tear suffered by every building;...

The Caveat Emptor Concern

Turning to the second concern, *caveat emptor* cannot, in my view, serve as a complete shield to tort liability for the contractors of a building. In *Fraser-Reid, supra*, this Court relied on the doctrine of *caveat emptor* in rejecting a claim by a buyer of a house for the recognition of an implied warranty of fitness for human habitation. However, the Court explicitly declined to address the question of whether *caveat emptor* serves to negate a duty in tort (pp. 726-27). Accordingly, the question remains at large in Canadian law and must be resolved on the level of principle.

In *Fraser-Reid*, Dickson J. (as he then was) observed that the doctrine of *caveat emptor* stems from the *laissez-faire* attitudes of the eighteenth and nineteenth centuries and the notion that purchasers must fend for themselves in seeking protection by express warranty or by independent examination of the premises (at p. 723). The assumption underlying the doctrine is that the purchaser of a building is better placed than the seller or builder to inspect the building and to bear the risk that latent defects will emerge necessitating repair costs. However, in my view, this is an assumption which (if ever valid) is simply not responsive to the realities of the modern housing market....

Philip H. Osborne makes the further point in "A Review of Tort Decisions in Manitoba 1990-1993", [1993] Man. L.J. 191, at p. 196, that contractors and builders, because of their knowledge, skill and expertise, are in the best position to ensure the reasonable structural integrity of buildings and their freedom from latent defect. In this respect, the imposition of liability on builders provides an important incentive for care in the construction of buildings and a deterrent against poor workmanship.

My conclusion that a subsequent purchaser is not the best placed to bear the risk of the emergence of latent defects is borne out by the facts of this case. It is significant that, when cracking first appeared in the mortar of the building in 1982, the Condominium Corporation actually hired Smith Carter, the original architect of the building, along with a firm of structural engineers, to assess the condition of the mortar work and exterior cladding. These experts failed to detect the latent defects that appear to have caused the cladding to fall in 1989. Thus, although it is clear that the Condominium Corporation acted with diligence in seeking to detect hidden defects in the building, they were nonetheless unable to detect the defects or to foresee the collapse of the cladding in 1989. This, in my view, illustrates the unreality of the assumption that the purchaser is better placed to detect and bear the risk of hidden defects. For this Court to apply the doctrine of *caveat emptor* to negate Bird's duty in tort would be to apply a rule that has become completely divorced, in this context at least, from its underlying rationale.

Conclusion

I conclude, then, that no adequate policy considerations exist to negate a contractor's duty in tort to subsequent purchasers of a building to take reasonable care in constructing the building, and to ensure that the building does not contain defects that pose foreseeable and substantial danger to the health and safety of the occupants.... The Manitoba Court of Appeal erred in deciding that Bird could not, in principle, be held liable in tort to the Condominium Corporation for the reasonable cost of repairing the defects and putting the building back into a non-dangerous state. These costs are recoverable economic loss under the law of tort in Canada.

NOTES

1. Should there be recovery in tort for negligently inflicted economic loss to a product or structure where there is no danger? See *Privest Properties Ltd. v. Foundation Co. of Canada Ltd.* (1997), 143 D.L.R. (4th) 635 (B.C.C.A.), no liability for cost of replacing non-dangerous fireproofing material.

One case, now overruled in England, thought so. In *Junior Books Ltd. v. The Veitchi Co. Ltd.*, [1982] 3 W.L.R. 477, [1982] 3 All E.R. 201, the defendants were subcontracted through a general contractor to do the flooring for a factory constructed for the plaintiff. There was no contractual relationship between the plaintiff and defendants. The floor was defectively manufactured and the plaintiff sued the defendants in tort for its economic losses. In upholding the plaintiff's claim, Lord Roskill stated:

> As my noble and learned friend, Lord Russell of Killowen, said during the argument, the question which your Lordships' House now has to decide is whether the relevant Scots and English law today extends the duty of care beyond a duty to prevent harm being done by faulty work to a duty to avoid such faults being present in the work itself. It was powerfully urged on behalf of the appellants that were your Lordships so to extend the law, a pursuer in the position of the pursuer in *Donoghue v. Stevenson* [1932] A.C. 562 could, in addition to recovering for any personal injury suffered, have also recovered for the diminished value of the offending bottle of ginger beer. Any remedy of that kind, it was argued, must lie in contract and not in delict or tort. My Lords, I seem to detect in that able argument reflections of the previous judicial approach to comparable problems before *Donoghue v. Stevenson* was decided. That approach usually resulted in the conclusion that in principle the proper remedy lay in contract and not outside it. But that approach and its concomitant philosophy ended in 1932 and for my part I should be reluctant to countenance its re-emergence some 50 years later in the instant case. I think today the proper control lies not in asking whether the proper remedy should lie in contract or instead in delict or tort, not in somewhat capricious judicial determination whether a particular case falls on one side of the line or the other, not in somewhat artificial distinctions between physical and economic or financial loss when the two sometimes go together and sometimes do not — it is sometimes overlooked that virtually all damage including physical damage is in one sense financial or economic for it is compensated by an award of damages — but in the first instance in establishing the relevant principles and then in deciding whether the particular case falls within or without those principles. To state this is to do no more than to restate what Lord Reid said in *Dorset Yacht Co. Ltd. v. Home Office* [1970] A.C. 1004 and Lord Wilberforce in *Anns v. Merton London Borough Council* [1978] A.C. 728. Lord Wilberforce, at p. 751, in the passage I have already quoted enunciated the two tests which have to be satisfied. The first is "sufficient relationship of proximity," the second any considerations negativing, reducing or limiting the scope of the duty or the class of person to whom it is owed or the damages to

which a breach of the duty may give rise. My Lords, it is I think in the application of those two principles that the ability to control the extent of liability in delict or in negligence lies. The history of the development of the law in the last 50 years shows that fears aroused by the floodgates argument have been unfounded. Cooke J. in *Bowen v. Paramount Builders (Hamilton) Ltd.* [1977] 1 N.Z.L.R. 394, 422 described the floodgates argument as "specious" and the argument against allowing a cause of action such as was allowed in *Dutton v. Bognor Regis Urban District Council* [1972] 1 Q.B. 373, *Anns v. Merton London Borough Council* [1978] A.C. 728 and *Bowen v. Paramount Builders (Hamilton) Ltd.* [1977] 1 N.Z.L.R. 394 as "in terrorem or doctrinaire."

Turning back to the present appeal I therefore ask first whether there was the requisite degree of proximity so as to give rise to the relevant duty of care relied on by the respondents. I regard the following facts as of crucial importance in requiring an affirmative answer to that question. (1) The appellants were nominated sub-contractors. (2) The appellants were specialists in flooring. (3) The appellants knew what products were required by the respondents and their main contractors and specialised in the production of those products. (4) The appellants alone were responsible for the composition and construction of the flooring. (5) The respondents relied upon the appellants' skill and experience. (6) The appellants as nominated sub-contractors must have known that the respondents relied upon their skill and experience. (7) The relationship between the parties was as close as it could be short of actual privity of contract. (8) The appellants must be taken to have known that if they did the work negligently (as it must be assumed that they did) the resulting defects would at some time require remedying by the respondents expending money upon the remedial measures as a consequence of which the respondents would suffer financial or economic loss.

Lord Brandon dissented. In addition to the objection that there was no authority for imposing a duty in a case such as this, Lord Brandon suggested that to impose such a duty of care between two parties not in a contractual relationship could create the following problems:

It is, I think, just worth while to consider the difficulties which would arise if the wider scope of the duty of care put forward by the respondents were accepted. In any case where complaint was made by an ultimate consumer that a product made by some persons with whom he himself had no contract was defective, by what standard or standards of quality would the question of defectiveness fall to be decided? In the case of goods bought from a retailer, it could hardly be the standard prescribed by the contract between the retailer and the wholesaler, or between the wholesaler and the distributor, or between the distributor and the manufacturer, for the terms of such contracts would not even be known to the ultimate buyer. In the case of subcontractors such as the appellants in the present case, it could hardly be the standard prescribed by the contract between the subcontractors and the main contractors, for, although the building owner would probably be aware of those terms, he could not, since he was not a party to such contract, rely on any standard or standards prescribed in it. It follows that the question by what standard or standards alleged defects in a product complained of by its ultimate user or consumer are to be judged remains entirely at large and cannot be given any just or satisfactory answer.

If, contrary to the views expressed above, the relevant contract or contracts can be regarded in order to establish the standard or standards of quality by which the question of defectiveness falls to be judged, and if such contract or contracts happen to include provisions excluding or limiting liability for defective products or defective work, or for negligence generally, it seems that the party sued in delict should in justice be entitled to rely on such provisions. This illustrates with especial force the inherent difficulty of seeking to impose what are really contractual obligations by unprecedented and, as I think, wholly undesirable extensions of the existing law of delict.

2. *Junior Books* has not fared well in England in the last few years. Its authority has been significantly weakened by two House of Lords's judgments. In *D & F Estates Ltd. v. Church Commrs for England*, [1988] 2 All E.R. 992 (H.L.), a tenant was denied recovery against the builder for the cost of repairing plaster in a flat. It was stated that *Junior Books* was limited to its unique facts and did not lay down any principle of general application in the law of torts. In fact it was Lord Brandon's dissent in *Junior Books* which was commended for having laid down with "cogency and clarity principles of fundamental importance which are clearly applicable to determine the scope of the duty of care owed by one party to another in the absence...of either any contractual relationship or any such uniquely proximate relationship as that on which the decision of the majority in *Junior Books* was founded".

   Economic losses were also denied to a purchaser of a defective building in *Murphy v. Brentwood Dist. Council*, [1991] A.C. 398, [1990] 2 All E.R. 908 (H.L.). Although the suit was brought against the public authority responsible for inspection of the construction, the House of Lords made it clear that a builder cannot be liable in tort for the economic losses flowing from defective buildings. In this respect, it does not matter where the defect poses an imminent danger to persons or to property. Only personal injuries and property damages caused by the builder's negligence can give rise to a tort claim in England. See also *Dept. of The Environment v. Thomas Bates & Son (New Towns Commn.)*, [1940] 2 All E.R. 943, [1990] 3 W.L.R. 457 (H.L.).

3. Canadian courts have not been as hard on *Junior Books*. While some courts have rejected it, *e.g.*, *Buthmann v. Balzer* (1983), 26 Alta. L.R. (2d) 122, 25 C.C.L.T. 273 (Q.B.); leave to appeal to S.C.C. refused January 31, 1985, others have allowed non-privity consumers to sue for their economic losses, *e.g.*, *SEDCO v. William Kelly Hldg. Ltd.* (1988), 68 Sask. R. 244, [1988] 4 W.W.R. 221; vard in part 83 Sask. R. 33, [1990] 4 W.W.R. 134 (C.A.); *Strike v. Ciro Roofing Products U.S.A. Inc.* (1988), 46 C.C.L.T. 209 (B.C.S.C.). More significantly, in actions against public authorities for their negligence in inspecting building construction, the fact that the plaintiffs' claims were for economic losses has not been an impediment to their actions. In *City of Kamloops v. Nielsen*, *infra*, Madam Justice Wilson spoke approvingly of *Junior Books*, commenting that it "carried the law a significant step forward".

4. Professor Joseph Smith has written that "if *Hedley Byrne v. Heller* announced the engagement of contract and tort, *Junior Books v. Veitchi* has solemnized the union". See "Economic Loss and the Marriage of Contracts and Torts" (1984), 18 U.B.C. L. Rev. 95, at 101. Is this a good or a bad thing? Later, he states that the risk principle of *Donoghue v. Stevenson* has been used to "reform not only the law of negligence but the law of contract as well". (See at 108.) Is this a good or a bad thing?

5. Professor David Cohen has argued that *Junior Books* "represents an unwarranted development in the law of tort and contract, unless its rationale and limitations are fully appreciated". In a powerful critique, he contends that loss-shifting in these circumstances is unnecessary in many cases, may "provide buyers with double recovery, will reduce incentives both for contractual risk allocation and for alternate buyer accident reduction measures, may exacerbate subsidization of high-risk buyers by low-risk buyers and...may not in the end reduce the costs of accidents to any significant degree." See "Bleeding Hearts and Peeling Floors: Recovery of Economic Loss at the House of Lords" (1984), 18 U.B.C.L. Rev. 289.

6. See generally Rafferty "Comment on *Winnipeg Condominium*" (1996), 34 Alta. L. Rev. 472, who describes the court's reasoning as "persuasive" and "defensible".

D. RELATIONAL ECONOMIC LOSSES

Economic losses that are relational are the most problematic. Until recently, there was virtually no recovery allowed for economic losses to one person suffered as a result of a physical loss to another person with whom he or she had a contractual relationship. When physical loss was caused to one person, another person could not claim for economic losses incurred as a result of a contractual or other relationship with that other person.

Gradually, under the onslaught of *Donoghue v. Stevenson* and *Hedley Byrne,* exceptions were developed to this rule. When personal or physical injury accompanied an economic loss, recovery was permitted. (See *Seaway Hotels Ltd. v. Consumers Gas Co.,* [1959] O.R. 581 (C.A.)). Certain positive outlays made as a result of economic loss were covered (See *Dominion Tape of Canada v. L.R. McDonald & Sons Ltd.*, [1971] 3 O.R. 627 (Co. Ct.)). There were other particular exceptions. Various tests were developed to determine which economic losses would be recoverable and which would not. They included "knowledge of the risk", "direct and foreseeable" and others. It was a confusing situation. (See Linden, *Canadian Tort Law, supra,* at p. 410).

Finally, the Supreme Court of Canada tackled the problem in *C.N.R. Co. v. Norsk Pacific Steamship Co. Ltd.* (1992), 91 D.L.R. (4th) 289.

Unfortunately the issue was not resolved because the court split — three judges, led by Madam Justice McLachlin, disagreed with three judges led by Mr. Justice La Forest, and the seventh judge, Mr. Justice Stevenson, disagreed with the reasons of both groups, while concurring in the result with Madam Justice McLachlin.

The facts involved severe damage to a railway bridge caused by a barge being negligently towed, in heavy fog, by a tugboat owned by Norsk. The bridge had to close for several weeks, resulting in economic loss to C.N. and others, who used it under an agreement with its owner, Public Works Canada. C.N. was the main user of the bridge (86 per cent) which connected land owned by C.N. on both sides of the bridge. C.N. had used the bridge since 1915, sending 32 trains with 1,530 cars across the bridge on an average day. As requested, C.N. provided maintenance and other services on a contractual basis with Public Works, along with certain voluntary services. The agreement provided for no indemnification for disruption of use. The repairs to the bridge were done and paid for by Public Works, which recovered the cost in an action against Norsk. C.N., having no claim for their economic losses against Public Works, sued Norsk and others for their actual costs incurred because of the bridge closure. C.N. was successful at trial in the Federal Court of Canada. An appeal was dismissed by the Federal Court of Appeal. The Supreme Court of Canada affirmed the decision in favour of C.N. (4-3).

Madam Justice McLachlin (L'Heureux-Dubé, Cory JJ. concurring), in a powerfully reasoned judgment, followed the course charted in *Kamloops* and rejected the narrow approach of the House of Lords in *Murphy*, as accepting "injustice merely for the sake of the doctrinal tidiness". Her Ladyship chose to adopt an incremental approach, voicing a "sturdy refusal to be confined by arbitrary forms and rules where justice indicates otherwise". The search, she declared "should not be for a universal rule but for the elaboration of categories where recovery of economic loss is justifiable on a case-by-case basis". All economic losses could not be reimbursed, she recognized, because that "may cripple [defendants'] ability to do business", but the "traditional exclusionary rule" was too confining. She sought a rule that "permits relief to be granted in new situations where it is merited...[but also] is sensitive to danger of unlimited liability". Recognizing that this approach would mean that a "small area of negligence may be uncertain", she felt this was the "price the common law pays for flexibility, for the ability to adapt to a changing world". Hence, she concluded:

> The matter may be put thus: before the law will impose liability there must be a connection between the defendant's conduct and the plaintiff's loss which makes it just for the defendant to indemnify the plaintiff. In contract, the contractual relationship provides this link. In trust, it is the fiduciary obligation which establishes the necessary connection. In tort, the equivalent notion is proximity. Proximity may consist of various forms of closeness — physical, circumstantial, causal or assumed — which serve to identify the categories of cases in which liability lies.
>
> Viewed thus, the concept of proximity may be seen as an umbrella, covering a number if disparate circumstances in which the relationship between the parties is so close that it is just and reasonable to permit recovery in tort. The complexity and diversity of the circumstances in which tort liability may arise defy indemnification of a single criterion capable of serving as the universal hallmark of liability. The meaning of "proximity" is to be found rather in viewing the circumstances in which it has been found to exist and determining whether the case at issue is similar enough to justify a similar finding.
>
> In summary, it is my view that the authorities suggest that pure economic loss is *prima facie* recoverable where, in addition to negligence and foreseeable loss, there is sufficient proximity between the negligent act and the loss. Proximity is the controlling concept which avoids the spectre of unlimited liability. Proximity may be established by a variety of factors, depending on the nature of the case. To date, sufficient proximity has been found in the case of negligent misstatements where there is an undertaking and correlative reliance (*Hedley Byrne*); where there is a duty to warn (*Rivtow*); and where a statute imposes a responsibility on a municipality toward the owners and occupiers of land (*Kamloops*). But the categories are not closed. As more cases are decided, we can expect further definition on what factors give rise to liability for pure economic loss in particular categories of cases. In determining whether liability should be extended to a new situation, courts will have regard to the factors traditionally relevant to proximity such as the relationship between the parties, physical propinquity, assumed or imposed obligations and close causal connection. And they will insist on sufficient special factors to avoid the imposition of indeterminate and unreasonable liability. The result will be a principled, yet flexible, approach to tort liability for pure economic loss. It will allow recovery where recovery is justified, while excluding indeterminate and inappropriate liability, and it will permit the coherent development of the law in accordance with the approach initiated in England by *Hedley Byrne* and followed in Canada in *Rivtow, Kamloops* and *Hofstrand*.

In this way, Her Ladyship indicated that proximity would parallel the civil law requirement of direct causation, positing a "close link" between the negligence and the loss, and excluding "[d]istant losses which arise from collateral relationships".

On the facts, the situation of the plaintiff was "closely allied" to the owner, creating a relationship akin to a "joint venture", placing it in the same position as if it owned the property. No floodgates would be opened by allowing recovery here.

Mr. Justice La Forest (Sopinka, Iacobucci JJ. concurring), in an equally brilliant excursus, chose to rely on a limited exclusionary rule that would apply to "contractual relational economic loss", unless there were good policy reasons to depart from it. Three exceptions were recognized: (1) possessory or proprietary interest; (2) general average cases; and (3) joint venture. Consequently, when plaintiffs contract for the use of another's property, they cannot recover from a defendant who negligently damages that property, causing the plaintiff economic loss because of their inability to use it. Mr. Justice La Forest engaged in a profound economic analysis of the law in order to determine the best way to allocate losses in a reasonable and efficient manner. He was not convinced that moral fault, deterrence (which was already in play here) nor common venture analysis, were of great value here. The proximity test has no allure for him, as it has little predictive value. He contended that only the exclusionary rule promises any predictability and supports it thus:

> [T]he reasons supporting the exclusionary rule...are, of course, essentially pragmatic, as has been recognized in cases of this type from the very beginning. First, denial of recovery places incentives on all parties to act in a way that will minimize overall losses, a legitimate and desirable goal for tort law in this area. Second, denial of recovery allows for only one party carrying insurance rather than both parties. Third, it will result in a great saving of judicial resources for cases in which more pressing concerns are put forward. The difficult job of drawing the line is at least done quickly without a great deal of factual investigation into the various factors that found proximity. The right to recover can be most often determined from the face of the contract. Fourth, it also eliminates difficult problems of sharing an impecunious defendant's limited resources between relational claims and direct claims. Fifth, the traditional rule is certain, and although like any pragmatic solution, borderline cases may cause problems, the exceptions to the rule in cases of joint ventures, general average contributions, and possessory and proprietorial interests are reasonably well defined and circumscribed. This case, in my view, does not even constitute a borderline case in this respect, since C.N. has no property interest of any kind. The consequence of that certainty is that contracting parties can be certain of where the loss with respect to the unavailability of property will lie in the absence of any contractual agreement.

Mr. Justice La Forest recognized the limitations of the exclusionary rule:

> The exclusionary rule is not itself attractive. It excludes recovery by people who have undeniably suffered losses as a result of an accident. It also leads to some arbitrary but generally predictable results in cases at the margin. The results with respect to time charters may be "capricious", but time charterers know their rights and obligations from the start and can act accordingly. The rule only becomes defensible when it is realized that full recovery is impossible, that recovery is, in fact, going to be refused in the vast majority of such claims regardless of the rule we adopt, and when the exclusionary rule is compared to the alternative. In my view, it should not be disturbed on the facts of this case.

In conclusion, Mr. Justice La Forest disagreed with Madam Justice McLachlin's characterization of his approach as "rigid", describing it instead as one incorporating a "principled flexibility, which adheres to a general rule in the absence of policy reasons for excluding its application". In response, he suggested that her proximity approach, as pointed out by Mr. Justice Stevenson, "expresses a conclusion, a judgment, a result, rather than a principle". It is subject to "arbitrariness", said Mr. Justice La Forest, that "allows judges to resolve cases as they see fit", something he thought unacceptable.

Stevenson J. held that, since the defendant had actual knowledge of the plaintiff, the problem of indeterminacy did not arise and recovery should be allowed.

In the recent case of *D'Amato v. Badger* (1996), 31 C.C.L.T. (2d) 1, Mr. Justice Major, for a unanimous Supreme Court, denied compensation to a company for loss of profits caused by an automobile accident injury to one of its key employees. Employing the five-categories approach, His Lordship identified this as a relational economic loss. The Court refused to choose between the two main tests set out in *Norsk,* saying that a "choice...will have to await the appropriate case".

Mr. Justice Major then proceeded to analyze the case according to both tests, which he suggested "will usually achieve the same result". Under the La Forest J. test of a general exclusionary rule, subject to specific exceptions on policy grounds, he found no such grounds to justify a departure from the exclusionary rule. Pursuant to the "somewhat broader" two-stage approach of McLachlin J., which requires "proximity", he stated that the loss was neither "foreseeable nor sufficiently proximate to the act of negligence to warrant recovery".

Finally, the Supreme Court seems, in the following case, to have reached a compromise position, expressed by Madame Justice McLachlin, which blends together her reasoning and that of La Forest J. in *Norsk* and other cases:

BOW VALLEY HUSKY (BERMUDA) LTD. ET AL v. SAINT JOHN SHIPBUILDING LTD.

Supreme Court of Canada. [1997] 3 S.C.R. 1210.

The plaintiffs in this action, Husky Oil Operations (HOOL) and Bow Valley Industries (BVI), made arrangements to have an oil drilling rig constructed by the defendant, Saint John Shipbuilding (SJSL). This contract was transferred to an offshore company established by the two plaintiffs, Bow Valley Husky (Bermuda) Ltd. (BVHB). HOOL and BVI entered into contracts with BVHB for the hire of the rig which provided they would continue to pay day rates to BVHB in the event that the rig was out of service. BVHB had a Raychem heat trade system installed on the rig. This system used Thermaclad wrap to keep moisture from the insulation and heat trade wire. A ground fault circuit breaker was not installed at the time the Raychem system was installed. A fire broke out which caused damages to a tray of electrical and communications cables. As a result of the damages, the rig had to be towed to port for repairs and was out of service for several months. BVHB, HOOL and BVI commenced an action against SJSL alleging breach of contract and negligence, and an action against Raychem for negligence. BVHB sought damages for the cost of repairs to the rig and for the revenue lost as a result of the rig being out of service for several months. HOOL and BVI sought to recover the day rates that they were contractually required to pay BVHB during the period the rig was out of service, as well as expenses they incurred for supplies to the rig, including food, drilling mud and additional equipment.

The trial judge held the defendant SJSL liable in contract and tort for failing to provide certificates of approval for the thermclad and in tort for breach of duty to warn of the inflammability of Raychem. Raychem was also held liable in tort for breach of its duty to warn. The Trial Judge also found that the major fault lay with BVHB and its operation of the heat trace system without a functioning circuit breaker system. Fault was apportioned to BVHB at 60 per cent and 40 per cent to SJSL and Raychem. No damages were awarded for breach of contract. The entire claim, however, was dismissed on the ground that the case arose out of negligence at sea and was governed by Canadian Maritime Law under which a finding of contributory negligence was a complete bar to recovery.

The Court of Appeal found that the Newfoundland *Contributory Negligence Act* could apply but dismissed the claims of HOOL and BVI on the ground that the loss suffered was economic in nature and therefore not recoverable. BVHB was allowed to recover 40 per cent of its loss from SJSL and Raychem.

The Supreme Court allowed the owner of the rig (BVHB) to recover 40 per cent of its loss in negligence from Raychem, the manufacturer of the Thermclad system, for failing to properly warn the owner about its inflammability. The shipbuilding, (SJSL), which had installed the Thermclad system was absolved of liability (4-2 , McLachlin J., La Forest J. dissenting on this issue) on the basis of its exclusion of liability in its contract with the owner. The claims of the two users of the rig (HOOL and BVI), who were bound by contract to pay for its use even if out of service, were unanimously dismissed.

McLachlin J. (dissenting in part, **La Forest J.** concurring):

IV. Issues

[17]

(1) Are the defendants liable to the plaintiffs in tort?
   - (a) Did the circumstances impose on SJSL and Raychem a duty to warn BVHB of the risks associated with using Thermaclad?
   - (b) Was SJSL's duty to warn excluded by its contract with BVHB?
   - (c) Is Raychem entitled to rely on the "learned intermediary" defence?
   - (d) Is causation established?
   - (e) How should fault be allocated between SJSL and Raychem?
   - (f) Did SJSL and Raychem owe BVI and HOOL a duty to warn? (Recovery of contractual relational economic loss)
   - (g) Was BVHB contributorily negligent?
   - (h) Does BVHB's contributory negligence bar its claims?

(2) Is SJSL liable to BVHB in contract?

V. Are the Defendants Liable to the Plaintiffs in Tort?

A. Did the Circumstances Impose on SJSL and Raychem a Duty to Warn BVHB of the Risks Associated With Using Thermaclad?

...

[19] The law may be simply stated. Manufacturers and suppliers are required to warn all those who may reasonably be affected by potentially dangerous products; *Lambert v. Lastoplex Chemicals Co.*, [1972] S.C.R. 569, 25 D.L.R. (3d) 121, and *Hollis v. Dow Corning Corp.*, [1995] 4 S.C.R. 634, 129 D.L.R. (4th) 609. This duty extends even to those persons who are not party to the contract of sale: *Rivtow Marine Ltd. v. Washington Iron Works*, [1974] S.C.R. 1189, 40 D.L.R. (3d) 530. The potential user must be reasonably foreseeable to the manufacturer or supplier manufacturers and suppliers (including a builder-supplier like SJSL) do not have the duty to warn the entire world about every danger that can result from improper use of their product.

[20] The plaintiff BVHB was clearly within the class of persons that SJSL and Raychem ought to have known might reasonably be affected by the use of Thermaclad. SJSL was in a contractual relationship with BVHB, and Raychem had directly approached BVHB's predecessor (a subsidiary of BVI) to encourage the use of its products in the construction of the rig.

...

[23] The evidence establishes that the plaintiff BVHB knew that Thermaclad would burn under some circumstances. The defendants SJSL and Raychem, however, had much more detailed knowledge of the specific inflammability characteristics of the Thermaclad. Raychem gained this knowledge through its own testing as manufacturer. SJSL gained it through its request to Raychem for information on Thermaclad's infallibility. BVHB did not have the degree of knowledge necessary to negate reliance on SJSL and Raychem. SJSL and Raychem did not demonstrate that BVHB accepted the risk of using Thermaclad. It follows that

both SJSL and Raychem owed BVHB a duty to warn, subject to the special defences raised by SJSL and Raychem, to which I now turn.

B. Was SJSL's Duty to Warn Excluded by Its Contract With BVHB?

[24] SJSL argues that any duty to warn BVHB which might otherwise arise from the circumstances is negatived by the contract between them. The trial judge rejected this submission, as did the Court of Appeal, on the ground that the contract provisions did not deal with or impact on SJSL's duty to warn. I agree....

[27] To borrow the language of La Forest J. in *London Drugs Ltd. v. Kuehne & Nagel International Ltd.*, [1992] 3 S.C.R. 299, at p. 327, 97 D.L.R. (4th) 261, tort liability in a case such as this falls to be assessed in a contractual matrix. The parties' planned obligations must be given appropriate pre-eminence. Where those planned obligations negate tort liability, contract "trumps" tort: see J. Fleming, "Tort in a Contractual Matrix" (1993), 5 Canterbury L. Rev. 269, at p. 270, citing P. Cane, *Tort Law and Economic Interests* (Oxford: Clarendon Press, 1991), at p. 293. It follows that a tort claim cannot be used to escape an otherwise applicable contractual exclusion or limitation clause: *Central Trust Co. v. Rafuse*, [1986] 2 S.C.R. 147, 31 D.L.R. (4th) 481....

[34] I conclude that the contractual matrix in which the duty to warn of the inflammability of Thermaclad arose does not negate or "contradict", to use the language of *BG Checo, supra*, that duty. It follows that BVHB was entitled to claim against SJSL based on the duty to warn. [The majority disagreed on this point, see *infra*.]

C. Is Raychem Entitled to Rely on the "Learned Intermediary" Defence?

...

[36] In my view, the facts of this case do not fall within the learned intermediary defence. This Court has left open the possibility that a manufacturer might discharge its duty to warn by warning an intermediary: *Hollis, supra*, at p. 659. However, La Forest J., for the majority, made it clear that the rule was an exception to the general rule requiring manufacturers to provide a warning to the ultimate consumers of their product. The exception will generally only apply either where the product is highly technical and is to be used with expert supervision, or where the nature of the product is such that is unrealistic for the consumer to receive a warning directly from the manufacturer. La Forest J. stated that since the rule operates to discharge the manufacturer's duty to the ultimate consumer, the intermediary must be "learned" in the sense that its knowledge of the product and its risks is essentially the same as that of the manufacturer.

[37] Thermaclad was not a highly technical product, nor did its use and application require expert supervision. Nor was it unrealistic to expect Raychem to have warned BVHB, the ultimate consumer, directly. There was direct contact between BVHB and Raychem, independent of SJSL. Raychem actively sought the business of BVHB, and the trial judge found that the Thermaclad was owner-directed supply. In these circumstances Raychem had both the opportunity and the duty to warn BVHB directly. I conclude that Raychem's duty to warn the plaintiffs was not discharged through its communications with SJSL....

D. Is Causation Established?

[39] I am satisfied that causation is established, on either a subjective or an objective standard. There is evidence that had BVHB been aware of Thermaclad's

specific inflammability characteristics, it would not have been used, or alternatively, that BVHB would have taken additional steps to compensate for its inflammability. BVHB, in accordance with applicable standards, would not have permitted inflammable materials to be used without careful consideration and investigation into the availability of nonflammable alternatives. I conclude that a reasonable plaintiff or BVHB itself would have either declined to use Thermaclad or taken steps to deal with its inflammability had it been warned. This suffices to meet the argument that the loss was not caused by the defendants' breach of their duty to warn....

E. How Should Fault Be Allocated Between SJSL and Raychem?

The next question is how fault should be allocated between SJSL and Raychem....

[41] There was ample evidence before the trial judge to support his conclusion that the relative fault of Raychem and SJSL was equivalent. Both defendants had a greater degree of knowledge of the risks inherent in the use of Thermaclad than did BVHB. Neither of the defendants communicated or attempted to communicate their knowledge to BVHB. Although SJSL might have had less knowledge of the specific characteristics of Thermaclad, its knowledge of the general regulatory requirements was arguably greater, and it had greater contact with BVHB. I would not interfere with the equal apportionment of fault.

F. Did SJSL and Raychem Owe BVI and HOOL a Duty to Warn? (Recovery of Contractual Relational Economic Loss)

(1) The Law

[42] The plaintiffs HOOL and BVI had contracts with BVHB for the use of the rig owned by BVHB. They seek damages for economic loss incurred as a result of the shutdown of the drilling rig during the period it was being repaired. In other words, the plaintiffs HOOL and BVI seek to recover the economic loss they suffered as a result of damage to the property of a third party. This sort of loss is often called "contractual relational economic loss". The issue is whether the loss suffered by HOOL and BVI is recoverable.

[43] The issue arises because common law courts have traditionally regarded many types of contractual relational economic loss as irrecoverable. The reasons for this were summarized by this Court, *per* Major J., in *D'Amato v. Badger*, [1996] 2 S.C.R. 1071, 137 D.L.R. (4th) 129. First, economic interests have customarily been seen by the common law courts as less worthy of protection than either bodily security or property. Second, relational economic loss presents the spectre of "liability in an indeterminate class": *Ultramares Corp. v. Touche*, 174 N.E. 441 (N.Y. 1931), at p. 444, *per* Cardozo C.J. Third, it may be more efficient to place the burden of economic loss on the victim, who may be better placed to anticipate and insure its risk. Fourth, confining economic claims to contract discourages a multiplicity of lawsuits.

[44] In England the situation is clear — no relational economic loss can ever be recovered: *Murphy v. Brentwood District Council*, [1991] 1 A.C. 398 (H.L.). Although *Murphy* concerned the liability of a public authority for approval of a negligently constructed building, not relational economic loss, the House of Lords stipulated that pure economic loss is recoverable only where there is actual physical damage to property of the plaintiff, thus excluding recovery for relational economic loss. In the civil law jurisdictions of Quebec and France, by contrast, the

law does not distinguish between loss arising from damage of one's own property and loss arising from damage to the property of another. If civil law judges restrict recovery, it is not as a matter of law, but on the basis of the facts and causal connection. The law in the common law provinces of Canada falls somewhere between these two extremes. While treating recovery in tort of contractual relational economic loss as exceptional, it is accepted in Canadian jurisprudence that there may be cases where it may be recovered.

[45] The foregoing suggests the need for a rule to distinguish between cases where contractual relational economic loss can be recovered and cases where it cannot be recovered. Such a rule, as I wrote in *Canadian National Railway Co. v. Norsk Pacific Steamship Co.*, [1992] 1 S.C.R. 1021, 91 D.L.R. (4th) 289, should be morally and economically defensible and provide a logical basis upon which individuals can predicate their conduct and courts can decide future cases (p. 1147). Although this Court attempted to formulate such a rule in *Norsk*, a split decision prevented the emergence of a clear rule. Given the commercial importance of the issue, it is important that the rule be settled. It is therefore necessary for this Court to revisit the issue.

[46] The differences between the reasons of La Forest J. and myself in *Norsk* are of two orders: difference in result and difference in methodology. The difference in the definition of what constitutes a "joint venture" for the purposes of determining whether recovery for contractual relational economic loss should be allowed. We both agreed that if the plaintiff is in a joint venture with the person whose property is damaged, the plaintiff may claim consequential economic loss related to that property. We parted company because La Forest J. took a stricter view of what constituted a joint venture than I did.

[47] The difference in methodology is not, on close analysis, as great as might be supposed. Broadly put, La Forest J. started from a general exclusionary rule and proceeded to articulate exceptions to that rule where recovery would be permitted. I, by contrast, stressed the two-step test for when recovery would be available, based on the general principles of recovery in tort as set out in *Anns v. Merton London Borough Council*, [1978] A.C. 728, and *Kamloops (City of) v. Nielsen*, [1984] 2 S.C.R. 2, 10 D.L.R. (4th) 641: (1) whether the relationship between the plaintiff and defendant was sufficiently proximate to give rise to a *prima facie* duty of care; and (2) whether, if such a *prima facie* duty existed, it was negated for policy reasons and recovery should be denied.

[48] Despite this difference in approach, La Forest J. and I agreed on several important propositions: (1) relational economic loss is recoverable only in special circumstances where the appropriate conditions are met; (2) these circumstances can be defined by reference to categories, which will make the law generally predictable; (3) the categories are not closed. La Forest J. identified the categories of recovery of relational economic loss defined to date as: (1) cases where the claimant has a possessory or proprietary interest in the damaged property; (2) general average cases; and (3) cases where the relationship between the claimant and property owner constitutes a joint venture.

[49] The case at bar does not fall into any of the above three categories. The plaintiffs here had no possessory or proprietary interest in the rig and the case is not one of general averaging. While related contractually, the Court of Appeal correctly held that the plaintiff and the property owner cannot, on any view of the term, be viewed as joint ventures.

[50] However, that is not the end of the matter. The categories of recoverable contractual relational economic loss in tort are not closed. Where a case does not fall within a recognized category the court may go on to consider whether the

situation is one where the right to recover contractual relational economic loss should nevertheless be recognized. This is in accordance with *Norsk*, per La Forest J., at p. 1134:

> Thus I do not say that the rights to recovery in all cases of contractual relational economic loss depends exclusively on the terms of the contract. Rather, I note that such is the tenor of the exclusionary rule and that *departures from that rule should be justified on defensible policy grounds*. [Emphasis added.]

More particularly, La Forest J. suggested that the general rule against recovery for policy-based reasons might be relaxed where the deterrent effect of potential liability to the property owner is low, or, despite a degree of indeterminate liability, where the claimant's opportunity to allocate the risk by contract is slight, either because of the type of transaction or an inequality of bargaining power. I agreed with La Forest J. that policy considerations relating to increased costs of processing claims and contractual allocation of the risk are important (p. 1164). I concluded that the test for recovery "should be flexible enough to meet the complexities of commercial reality and to permit the recognition of new situations in which liability ought, in justice, to lie as such situations arise" (p. 1166). It thus appears that new categories of recoverable contractual relational economic loss may be recognized where justified by policy considerations and required by justice. At the same time, courts should not assiduously seek new categories; what is required is a clear rule predicting when recovery is available.

[51] More recently, in *Hercules Managements Ltd. v. Ernst & Young*, [1997] 2 S.C.R. 165, 146 D.L.R. (4th) 577, this Court described the general approach that should be followed in determining when tort recovery for economic loss is appropriate....

[52] La Forest J. set out the methodology that courts should follow in determining whether a tort action lies for relational economic loss. He held that the two-part methodology of *Anns, supra*, adopted by this Court in *Kamloops, supra*, should be followed: (1) whether a *prima facie* duty of care is owed; and (2) whether that duty, if it exists, is negated or limited by policy considerations. In applying the second step, La Forest J. wrote that while policy considerations will sometimes result in the *prima facie* duty being negated, in certain categories of cases such considerations may give way to other overriding policy considerations.

[53] La Forest J. held that the existence of a relationship of "neighbourhood" or "proximity" distinguishes those circumstances in which the defendant owes a *prima facie* duty of care to the plaintiff from those where no such duty exists. The term "proximity" is a label expressing the fact of a relationship of neighbourhood sufficient to attract a *prima facie* legal duty. Whether the duty arises depends on the nature of the case and its facts. Policy concerns are best dealt with under the second branch of the test. Criteria that in other cases have been used to define the legal test for the duty of care can now be recognised as policy-based ways by which to curtail indeterminate or inappropriate recovery.

[54] Following this analysis, La Forest J. concluded that the first branch of the *Anns* test was satisfied and the defendant auditors owed a *prima facie* duty of care to the plaintiffs. First, the possibility that the plaintiffs would rely on the audited statements prepared for the company was reasonably foreseeable. Second, the relationship between the parties and nature of the statements themselves made the plaintiffs' reliance reasonable.

[55] Policy considerations under the second branch of the test, however, negatived a duty of care.... The policy considerations surrounding indeterminate liability accordingly inhered, negating the *prima facie* duty of care.

[56] The same approach may be applied to the contractual relational economic loss at stake in the case at bar. The first step is to inquire whether the relationship of neighbourhood or proximity necessary to found a *prima facie* duty of care is present. If so, one moves to the second step of inquiring whether the policy concerns that usually preclude recovery of contractual relational economic loss, such as indeterminacy, are overridden.

(2) Application of the Law

[59] I return to the question of whether, on the approach articulated in *Hercules, supra*, the plaintiffs' claim for contractual relational economic loss is actionable....

[60] As in *Hercules, supra*, the decision as to whether a *prima facie* duty of care exists requires an investigation into whether the defendant and the plaintiff can be said to be in a relationship of proximity or neighbourhood. Proximity exists on a given set of facts if the defendant may be said to be under an obligation to be mindful of the plaintiff's legitimate interests in conducting his or her affairs: *Hercules, supra*, at p. 190. On the facts of this case, I agree with the Court of Appeal that a *prima facie* duty of care arises. Indeed, the duty to warn raised against the defendants is the correlative of the duty to disclose financial facts raised against the auditors in *Hercules*.

[61] Where a duty to warn is alleged, the issue is not reliance (there being nothing to rely upon), but whether the defendants ought reasonably to have foreseen that the plaintiffs might suffer loss as a result of use of the product about which the warning should have been made. I have already found that the duty to warn extended to BVHB. The question is, however, whether it extended as far as HOOL and BVI. The facts establish that this was the case. The defendants knew of the existence of the plaintiffs and others like them and knew or ought to have known that they stood to lose money if the drilling rig was shut down.

[62] The next question is whether this *prima facie* duty of care is negatived by policy considerations. In my view, it is. The most serious problem is that seized on by the Court of Appeal — the problem of indeterminate liability. If the defendants owed a duty to warn the plaintiffs, it is difficult to see why they would not owe a similar duty to a host of other persons who would foreseeably lose money if the rig was shut down as a result of being damaged. Other investors in the project are the most obvious persons who would also be owed a duty, although the list could arguably be extended to additional classes of persons. What has been referred to as the ripple effect is present in this case. A number of investment companies which contracted with HOOL are making claims against it, as has BVI.

[63] No sound reason to permit the plaintiffs to recover while denying recovery to these other persons emerges. To hold otherwise would pose problems for defendants, who would face liability in an indeterminate amount for an indeterminate time to an indeterminate class. It also would pose problems for potential plaintiffs. Which of all the potential plaintiffs can expect and anticipate they will succeed? Why should one type of contractual relationship, that of HOOL, be treated as more worthy than another, *e.g.*, that of the employees on the rig? In this state, what contractual and insurance arrangements should potential plaintiffs make against future loss?

[64] The plaintiffs propose a number of solutions to the problem of indeterminacy. None of them succeeds, in my respectful view. The first proposal is to confine liability to persons whose *identity* was known to the defendants. This is a reversion to the "known plaintiff" test, rejected by a majority of this Court in *Norsk, supra*. As commentators have pointed out, the fact that the defendant knew the

identity of the plaintiff should not in logic or justice determine recovery. On such a test, the notorious would recover, the private would lose: *Norsk*, *supra*. The problem of indeterminate liability cannot be avoided by arbitrary distinctions for which there is no legal or social justification: *Norsk*, *supra*, at p. 1112. There must be something which, for policy reasons, permits the court to say this category of person can recover and that category cannot, something which justifies the line being drawn at one point rather than another.

[65] Second, and in a similar vein, the plaintiffs argue that determinacy can be achieved by restricting recovery to the users of the rig, a class which they say is analogous in time and extent to the owners and occupiers of the building in *Winnipeg Condominium Corporation No. 36 v. Bird Construction Co.*, [1995] 1 S.C.R. 85, 121 D.L.R. (4th) 193. This argument fails for the same reasons as the known plaintiff test. There is no logical reason for drawing the line at users rather than somewhere else.

[66] Third, the plaintiffs attempt to distinguish themselves from other potential claimants through the concept of reliance. The defendants correctly answer this argument by pointing out that any person who is contractually dependent on a product or a structure owned by another "relies" on the manufacturer or builder to supply a safe product.

[67] Finally, the plaintiffs argue that a finding of a duty to warn negates the spectre of indeterminate liability as the duty to warn does not extend to everyone in any way connected to the manufactured product. This argument begs the question. The duty to warn found to this point is only a *prima facie* duty to warn in accordance with the first requirement of *Anns*, *supra*, that there be sufficient proximity or neighbourhood to found a duty of care. It is not circumscribed and imports no limits on liability. Considerations of indeterminate liability arise in the second step of the *Anns* analysis. Hence the *prima facie* duty of care, by itself, cannot resolve the problem of indeterminate liability.

[68] The problem of indeterminate liability constitutes a policy consideration tending to negative a duty of care for contractual relational economic loss. However, the courts have recognized positive policy considerations tending to support the imposition of such a duty of care. One of these, discussed by La Forest J. in *Norsk*, is the need to provide additional deterrence against negligence. The potential liability to the owner of the damaged property usually satisfies the goal of encouraging persons to exercise due care not to damage the property. However, situations may arise where this is not the case. In such a case, the additional deterrent of liability to others might be justified. The facts in the case at bar do not support the liability to the plaintiffs on this basis. BVHB, the owner of the drilling rig, suffered property damage in excess of five million dollars. This is a significant sum. It is not apparent that increasing the defendants' potential liability would have led to different behaviour and avoidance of the loss.

[69] Another situation which may support imposition of liability for contractual relational economic loss, recognized by La Forest J. in *Norsk*, is the case where the plaintiff's ability to allocate the risk to the property owner by contract is slight, either because of the type of the transaction or inequality of bargaining power. Again, this does not assist the plaintiffs in this case. BVI and HOOL not only had the ability to allocate their risks; they did just that. It cannot be said that BVI and HOOL suffered from inequality of bargaining power with BVHB, the very company they created. Moreover, the record shows they exercised that power. The risk of loss caused by down-time of the rig was specifically allocated under the Drilling Contracts between BVI, HOOL and BVHB. The contracts provided for day rate payments to BVHB and/or termination rights in the event of lost or diminished

use of the rig. The parties also set out in the contracts their liability to each other and made provision for third party claims arising out of rig operations. Finally, the contracts contained provisions related to the purchase and maintenance of insurance.

[70] I conclude that the policy considerations relevant to the case at bar negative the *prima facie* duty of care to BVI and HOOL.

G. Was BVHB Contributorily Negligent?

[On the issue of contributory negligence McLachlin J. agreed with the courts below that BVHB was contributorily negligent and held that the Trial Judge made no error in apportioning liability. She further found that BVHB's right to recover was not banned by its contributory negligence. She also found that the contractual issues had been settled by the parties and were no longer litigatable.]

[112] **Iacobucci J. (Gonthier, Cory** and **Major JJ.** concurring): I have had the advantage of reading the lucid reasons of my colleague, Justice McLachlin. At the outset, I wish to commend my colleague for her treatment of the approaches taken by her and La Forest J. in *Canadian National Railway Co. v. Norsk Pacific Steamship Co.*, [1992] 1 S.C.R. 1021, 91 D.L.R. (4th) 289. In that respect, I simply wish to add one comment regarding the issue of contractual relational economic loss.

[113] I understand my colleague's discussion of this matter to mean that she has adopted the general exclusionary rule and categorical exceptions approach set forth by La Forest J. in *Norsk*. My colleague has found that the circumstances of the present case do not fall within any of the three exceptions identified in that case. She points out that both her reasons and those of La Forest J. in *Norsk* recognize that the categories of recoverable contractual relational economic loss are not closed and that whether or not a new category ought to be created is determined on a case-by-case basis. In that connection, I approve of her analysis of the facts of this case and applaud the approach she has taken to meld her reasoning in *Norsk* with that of La Forest J. in this very difficult area of the law.

[114] While I agree with most of her analysis in this case, I cannot, with respect, concur with her interpretation of…the contract between SJSL and BVHB. I agree with my colleague when she points out that limitation and exclusion clauses are to be strictly construed against the party seeking to invoke the clause. I also agree that, where the planned contractual obligations of two parties negate tort liability, contract will "trump" tort. But, I disagree with her conclusion that the clauses in question do not negate SJSL's duty to warn.…

[123] Accordingly, I must respectfully disagree with McLachlin J.'s conclusion that BVHB was entitled to claim against SJSL based on the tort duty to warn. I note that it is not open to Raychem to seek contribution from SJSL, as a contractor which has protected itself against liability cannot be said to have contributed to any actionable loss suffered by the plaintiff: *Giffels Associates Ltd. v. Eastern Construction Co.*, [1978] 2 S.C.R. 1346, 84 D.L.R. (3d) 344. Consequently, Raychem is liable for the entire 40 per cent quantum found by the trial judge.

[124] I would therefore dismiss the appeal brought by HOOL and BVI. Further, I would dismiss all of the cross-appeals save for that of SJSL with regard to the duty to warn, which I would allow with costs throughout. As to costs on the main appeal and all other cross-appeals, I would assess these in the same manner as McLachlin J.

NOTES

1. Iacobucci J. in his judgment states that he reads McLachlin J.'s judgment as adopting the general exclusionary rule and categorical exceptions approach set forth by La Forest J. in *Norsk.* Is this a correct interpretation or is it merely wishful thinking? See Feldthusen, "Comment on *Bow Valley*" (1998), 6 Tort Law Rev. 164.

2. If Iacobucci J. is correct that McLachlin J. has adopted the general exclusionary rule and categorical exceptions approach, what are the implications of this decision?

3. Is the concern of McLachlin J. with indeterminate liability in this case justified?

4. It will be noted that McLachlin J. mentions the Supreme Court's rejection of the known plaintiff test proposed by Stevenson J. in *Norsk.* What do you think of that test? Indeed, can it be said that the Supreme Court of Canada in *Hercules* essentially adopted a formulation of the known plaintiff test in the negligent misrepresentation context? Given that McLachlin J. indicates that *Hercules* was treated as a relational economic loss case, why was this approach rejected both here and in *Norsk?*

5. Has *D'Amato v. Badger* unwittingly abolished the action *per quod servitium amisit,* which allows compensation to an employer for losses incurred as a result of the injury or death of an employee? See *R. v. Buchinsky* (1983), 145 D.L.R. (3d) 1, where the Supreme Court upheld the right of the Canadian Armed Forces to sue *per quod.* See also Irvine, "The Action Per Quod Amisit? in Canada" (1980), 11 C.C.L.T. 241. There was also an action for the loss of consortium when a spouse was injured, but legislation has now largely replaced this. See, *infra*, Chapter 17, Damages.

6. A truck crashes into a hydro pole owned by a power company and 15,000 people lose power for 90 minutes. An insurance company loses valuable computer data as a result and sues. Recovery? Is the data property so that Seaway Hotels can apply? Or is it pure economic loss? See *Seaboard Life Insurance Co. v. Babich,* [1995] 10 W.R.R. 756 (B.C.S.C.).

7. The challenge to contemporary tort law will be to determine what exceptions will be allowed to the exclusionary rule and why. Would any of the old cases falling under this category be decided differently in light of *Bow Valley?* With the *Bow Valley* decision in mind, read the following factual problem and consider whether any of the relational economic loss claims would be allowed:

REVIEW PROBLEM

In Mississauga, Ontario, on November 10, 1979, a 106-car Canadian Pacific Railway train was derailed, causing one railway car, carrying propane gas, to explode and catch fire and another railway car carrying chlorine gas, to start leaking, endangering the entire neighbourhood. As a result some 240,000 people had to be evacuated from a 50-square-mile area for a period of one week, the largest such event in North American history.

Miraculously, no lives were lost as a result of this disaster. No one was even seriously injured. The losses that occurred were almost exclusively economic. The total has been estimated at between $100 million and $150 million dollars.

A host of fascinating legal questions is raised by this incident, but only the questions of extent of liability are to be considered here.

Assuming an admission of liability in negligence, which of the following items of economic loss would be compensable, applying the present Canadian law?

1. A homeowner, with children, living quite near the railway line, heard the explosion and saw the railway cars burning a few hundred feet away. In fear, and for safety, a few necessities were packed and the family moved into a motel. The dog was boarded in a kennel at $100 a week.

   They ended up staying in a motel for a week, eating all of their meals there and buying items, such as clothing and personal hygiene products, that had been left behind. The homeowner missed work and lost one week's pay, because the children were very frightened by the experience and needed the parents with them. On return home, the exterior of the house was covered in soot and its interior was a mess from the water the firefighters had used to extinguish the fire. Valuable goldfish were dead. In addition, there was some looting and $10,000 worth of jewellery was taken.

   Which, if any, of these individual expenses could the homeowner recover? Which, if any, are not recoverable?

2. Helping during this disaster were hundreds of police officers and firefighters from the local community, as well as from neighbouring counties. For example, some 600 Peel County Police, some 300 members of the Metropolitan Toronto Police, some members of the Ontario Provincial Police and some officers of the R.C.M.P. participated in the enormous task of protecting the people and property in the area. Are the costs of supplying any of these forces recoverable by the various municipalities and governments?

3. A grocery store in Mississauga had to be closed for a week as a result of the disaster. Most of the milk and produce to a value of $500 was spoiled and had to be thrown out after the owner returned. The owners felt duty bound to pay a week's wages of $200 to the one employee. An estimated $1,000 in profits was lost — the week's earnings had the owner been able to conduct the business as usual.

   Which, if any, of these losses are compensable?

4. As a result of the closure of a tavern, the owner's stock of liquor was not damaged, nor did the owner have to pay any of the employees any wages, but $5,000 in profits was lost. Recovery?

5. Can the bartender, who lived in Toronto and received no pay for the week the tavern was closed, recover lost wages in the amount of $300? See *Abromovic v. C.P. Ltd.* (1991), 85 D.L.R. (4th) 587 (Ont. C.A.), case allowed to continue.

   The Toronto Star suffered loss because it could not deliver its newspapers to Mississauga residents. Recovery?

6. The Max Motor Company has a plant in the area and was closed down for the week. Its losses included:

   (a) The full wages required by the collective agreement to be paid to all of its hourly employees, in the amount of $100,000;
   (b) The proportion of the annual salaries of its executives, accountants, engineers, etc., totalling $20,000;
   (c) The expenses, such as interest and taxes on the real property, the heating and electricity costs, advertising costs, etc., in the amount of $30,000;
   (d) The loss of profits from the cars that would have been produced during the week, an amount of $100,000.

7. Would there be recovery for loss of profits suffered by dealers of the Max Motor Company, who could not deliver on time the cars they had promised to their customers?

8. What about compensation to the dealers' employees who lost commission on these aborted sales?

9. What about any loss suffered by a buyer of a Max car, who had to wait an extra week to get it? What if the buyer is a taxi-driver who lost profits? What if his business went bankrupt because of this?

10. Would any of your answers to the above change if it turned out that the authorities had overreacted and that danger had existed only to a very few people in the immediate area of the derailment?

CHAPTER 11

TORT LIABILITY OF PUBLIC AUTHORITIES

Tort claims against governments have spawned special problems. While many have urged that governments should be liable in tort the same way as anyone else, others have contended that government business is different from ordinary business and therefore must, in many cases, be judged differently. It will be seen that, as usual, a compromise has been reached: some types of activities, policy functions, have been rendered immune from negligence law whereas others, operational functions, have been subjected to it. It is hard to understand why, in view of the Charter, Ombudsmen, Human Rights Commissions and broad administrative law oversight of governmental functions, there is still strong opposition to negligence law entering the area

Much of the reason for this reticence must derive from the history of this area dominated by the maxim, "the King can do no wrong". In earlier times, the only way a citizen could challenge government in court was by a petition of right. Even after the complicated procedures were reformed, it was obvious that the Crown had to be bought under the rule of law, including tort law. In 1947, the British *Crown Proceedings Act* was enacted, making the Crown liable in tort, "as if it were a person ... for torts committed by its servants". In the same year, the Canadian federal *Crown Liability Act*, was passed (now the *Crown Liability and Proceedings Act*, R.S.C. 1985, c. C-50, s. 3(a) [title am. S.C. 1990, c. 8, s. 20]) holding the Crown "liable in tort for damage for which if it were a private person of full age and capacity it would be liable in respect of a tort committed by a servant of the Crown". In the years 1951 to 1974, all of the provinces enacted similar laws, except for Quebec which accomplished the same purpose differently.

What is the proper role of tort law in this area? Can courts review the conduct of elected officials and public servants? Can a court of law by means of a tort action question decisions taken by the legislative branches of government? Does a court, through negligence law, have the capacity to review the exercise of discretion by policy makers? These are difficult issues which are dealt with in this chapter. It will become evident that this is a developing area of negligence law, where the resolution of these problems continues to perplex the courts.

A. PROCEEDINGS AGAINST THE CROWN

PROCEEDINGS AGAINST THE CROWN ACT

R.S.O. 1990, c. P.27, s. 5

5. (1) Except as otherwise provided in this Act, and despite section 11 of the *Interpretation Act*, the Crown is subject to all liabilities in tort to which, if it were a person of full age and capacity, it would be subject,

(*a*) in respect of a tort committed by any of its servants or agents;
(*b*) in respect of a breach of the duties that one owes to one's servants or agents by reason of being their employer;
(*c*) in respect of any breach of the duties attaching to the ownership, occupation, possession or control of property; and
(*d*) under any statute, or under any regulation or by-law made or passed under the authority of any statute.

(2) No proceeding shall be brought against the Crown under clause (1)(*a*) in respect of an act or omission of a servant or agent of the Crown unless proceedings in tort in respect of such act or omission may be brought against that servant or agent or the personal representative of the servant or agent.

(3) Where a function is conferred or imposed upon a servant of the Crown as such, either by a rule of the common law or by or under a statute, and that servant commits a tort in the course of performing or purporting to perform that function, the liability of the Crown in respect of the tort shall be such as it would have been if that function had been conferred or imposed by instructions lawfully given by the Crown.

(4) In a proceeding against the Crown under this section, an enactment that negatives or limits the liability of a servant of the Crown in respect of a tort committed by that servant applies in relation to the Crown as it would have applied in relation to that servant if the proceeding against the Crown had been a proceeding against that servant.

(5) Where property vests in the Crown independent of the acts or the intentions of the Crown, the Crown is not, by virtue of this Act, subject to liability in tort by reason only of the property being so vested; but this subsection does not affect the liability of the Crown under this Act in respect of any period after the Crown, or any servant of the Crown, has in fact taken possession or control of the property.

(6) No proceeding lies against the Crown under this section in respect of anything done or omitted to be done by a person while discharging or purporting to discharge responsibilities of a judicial nature vested in the person or responsibilities that the person has in connection with the execution of judicial process.

NOTES

1. For an excellent discussion of Crown liability see Hogg, *Liability of the Crown,* 2nd ed. (Toronto: Carswell, 1989), Lordon (ed.), *Crown Law,* (Markham: Butterworths, 1991). For an earlier account see Goldenberg, "Tort Actions Against the Crown in Ontario", Special Lectures of the Law Society of Upper Canada, 1973, p. 341; Sgayias, "Remedies Against Governments" (1995), Special Lectures L.S.U.C. on Remedies at 427. In the United States, governments can be sued under the *Federal Tort Claims Act*, 28 U.S.C. 1346(b), 2671-2680 (1994), as well as under 42 U.S.C. 1983 (1994); for an excellent article outlining the current law, see "Government Tort Liability" (1998), 111 Harv. L. Rev. 2008. See also Hogg, "Government Liability: Assimilating Crown and Subject" (1994), 16 Adv. Q. 366; see Symposium, (1995), 6 N.J.C.L. 1.

2. Actions against municipal corporations, boards, commissions or agencies are not dealt with by Crown proceedings legislation. Whether these parties are suable or not raises different considerations. See *B.G. Ranches v. Manitoba Agricultural Lands Protection Board* (1983), 21 Man. R. (2d) 285, [1983] 4 W.W.R. 681 (Q.B.); *Westlake v. R.,*

[1971] 3 O.R. 533, 21 D.L.R. (3d) 129; affd, [1972] 2 O.R. 605, 26 D.L.R. (3d) 273 (C.A.); affd, [1973] S.C.R. vii, 33 D.L.R. (3d) 256*n*.

3. As Goldenberg has noted, even with Crown proceedings legislation, "the intrepid plaintiff who brings a tort action against the Crown embarks on a precarious journey through what often appears to be an interlocking maze of statutory anomalies". In addition to special notice requirements and limitation periods, the rules differ depending upon whether the suit is being brought against the Crown directly or vicariously, and whether the alleged tort has been committed by a servant or agent of the Crown who is a natural person or a corporation or statutory agent. See Goldenberg for a good discussion of these provisions.

B. WHAT IS THE DUTY OWED?

JUST v. BRITISH COLUMBIA

Supreme Court of Canada. [1989] 2 S.C.R. 1228.

On January 16, 1982, the appellant and his daughter set out for a day of skiing at Whistler Mountain. While stopped in traffic on Highway 99, a great boulder weighing more than a ton worked itself loose from the wooded slopes above the highway and came crashing down on the appellant's car, killing his daughter and injuring him. The appellant sued the provincial Crown, but lost at trial and on appeal on the basis that this was a planning or policy matter out of which no tort duty could arise. The Supreme Court reversed the decision and sent the matter back for a new trial.

Cory J.: The functions of government and government agencies have multiplied enormously in this century. Often government agencies were and continue to be the best suited entities and indeed the only organizations which could protect the public in the diverse and difficult situations arising in so many fields. They may encompass such matters as the manufacture and distribution of food and drug products, energy production, environmental protection, transportation and tourism, fire prevention and building developments. The increasing complexities of life involve agencies of government in almost every aspect of daily living. Over the passage of time the increased government activities gave rise to incidents that would have led to tortious liability if they had occurred between private citizens. The early government immunity from tortious liability became intolerable. This led to the enactment of legislation which in general imposed liability on the Crown for its acts as though it were a person. However, the Crown is not a person and must be free to govern and make true policy decisions without becoming subject to tort liability as a result of those decisions. On the other hand, complete Crown immunity should not be restored by having every government decision designated as one of "policy". Thus the dilemma giving rise to the continuing judicial struggle to differentiate between "policy" and "operation". Particularly difficult decisions will arise in situations where governmental inspections may be expected.

The dividing line between "policy" and "operation" is difficult to fix, yet it is essential that it be done. ...

The duty of care should apply to a public authority unless there is a valid basis for its exclusion. A true policy decision undertaken by a government agency constitutes such a valid basis for exclusion. What constitutes a policy decision may vary infinitely and may be made at different levels although usually at a high level.

The decisions in *Anns v. Merton London Borough Council* and *City of Kamloops v. Nielsen, supra*, indicate that a government agency in reaching a decision pertaining to inspection must act in a reasonable manner which constitutes a *bona fide* exercise of discretion. To do so they must specifically consider whether to inspect and if so, the system of inspection must be a reasonable one in all the circumstances.

For example, at a high level there may be a policy decision made concerning the inspection of lighthouses. If the policy decision is made that there is such a pressing need to maintain air safety by the construction of additional airport facilities with the result that no funds can be made available for lighthouse inspection, then this would constitute a *bona fide* exercise of discretion that would be unassailable. Should then a lighthouse beacon be extinguished as a result of the lack of inspection and a shipwreck ensue no liability can be placed upon the government agency. The result would be the same if a policy decision were made to increase the funds for job retraining and reduce the funds for lighthouse inspection so that a beacon could only be inspected every second year and as a result the light was extinguished. Once again this would constitute the *bona fide* exercise of discretion. Thus a decision either not to inspect at all or to reduce the number of inspections may be an unassailable policy decision. This is so provided it constitutes a reasonable exercise of *bona fide* discretion based, for example, upon the availability of funds.

On the other hand, if a decision is made to inspect lighthouse facilities the system of inspections must be reasonable and they must be made properly. See *Indian Towing Co.*, 350 U.S. 61 (1955). Thus once the policy decision to inspect has been made, the Court may review the scheme of inspection to ensure it is reasonable and has been reasonably carried out in light of all the circumstances, including the availability of funds, to determine whether the government agency has met the requisite standard of care.

At a lower level, government aircraft inspectors checking on the quality of manufactured aircraft parts at a factory may make a policy decision to make a spot check of manufactured items throughout the day as opposed to checking every item manufactured in the course of one hour of the day. Such a choice as to how the inspection was to be undertaken could well be necessitated by the lack of both trained personnel and funds to provide such inspection personnel. In those circumstances the policy decisions that a spot check inspection would be made could not be attacked. (See *United States v. S.A. Empresa De Viacao Aerea Rio Grandense (Varig Airlines)*, 467 U.S. 797 (1984)).

Thus a true policy decision may be made at a lower level provided that the government agency establishes that it was a reasonable decision in light of the surrounding circumstances.

The consideration of the duty of care that may be owed must be kept separate and distinct from the consideration of the standard of care that should be maintained by the government agency involved.

Let us assume a case where a duty of care is clearly owed by a governmental agency to an individual that is not exempted either by a statutory provision or because it was a true policy decision. In those circumstances the duty of care owed by the government agency would be the same as that owed by one person to another. Nevertheless the standard of care imposed upon the Crown may not be the same as that owed by an individual. An individual is expected to maintain his or her sidewalk or driveway reasonably, while a government agency such as the respondent may be responsible for the maintenance of hundreds of miles of highway. The frequency and the nature of inspection required of the individual may well be different from that required of the Crown. In each case the frequency and method must be reasonable in light of all the surrounding circumstances. The governmental agency should be entitled to demonstrate that balanced against the nature and quantity of the risk involved, its system of inspection was reasonable in light of all the circumstances including budgetary limits, the personnel and equipment available to it and that it had met the standard duty of care imposed upon it.

It may be convenient at this stage to summarize what I consider to be the principles applicable and the manner of proceeding in cases of this kind. As a general rule, the traditional tort law duty of care will apply to a government agency in the same way that it will apply to an individual. In determining whether a duty of care exists the first question to be resolved is whether the parties are in a relationship of sufficient proximity to warrant the imposition of such a duty. In the case of a government agency, exemption from this imposition of duty may occur as a result of an explicit statutory exemption. Alternatively, the exemption may arise as a result of the nature of the decision made by the government agency. That is, a government agency will be exempt from the imposition of a duty of care in situations which arise from its pure policy decisions.

In determining what constitutes such a policy decision, it should be borne in mind that such decisions are generally made by persons of a high level of authority in the agency, but may also properly be made by persons of a lower level of authority. The characterization of such a decision rests on the nature of the decision and not on the identity of the actors. As a general rule, decisions concerning budgetary allotments for departments or government agencies will be classified as policy decisions. Further, it must be recalled that a policy decision is open to challenge on the basis that it is not made in the *bona fide* exercise of discretion. If after due consideration it is found that a duty of care is owed by the government agency and no exemption by way of statute or policy decision-making is found to exist, a traditional torts analysis ensues and the issue of standard of care required of the government agency must next be considered.

The manner and quality of an inspection system is clearly part of the operational aspect of a governmental activity and falls to be assessed in the consideration of the standard of care issue. At this stage, the requisite standard of care to be applied to the particular operation must be assessed in light of all the surrounding circumstances including, for example, budgetary restraints and the availability of qualified personnel and equipment.

Turning to the case at bar, it is now appropriate to apply the principles set forth by Mason J. in *Sutherland Shire Council v. Heyman, supra*, to determine whether the decision or decisions of the government agency were policy decisions exempting the province from liability. Here what was challenged was the manner in which the inspections were carried out, their frequency or infrequency and how and when trees above the rock cut should have been inspected, and the manner in which the cutting and scaling operations should have been carried out. In short, the public authority had settled on a plan which called upon it to inspect all slopes visually and then conduct further inspections of those slopes where the taking of additional safety measures was warranted. Those matters are all part and parcel of what Mason J. described as "the product of administrative direction, expert or professional opinion, technical standards or general standards of care". They were not decisions that could be designated as policy decisions. Rather they were manifestations of the implementation of the policy decision to inspect and were operational in nature. As such, they were subject to review by the Court to determine whether the respondent had been negligent or had satisfied the appropriate standard of care.

At trial the conclusion was reached that the number and frequency of inspections, of scaling and other remedial measures were matters of policy; as a result no findings of fact were made on the issues bearing on the standard of care. Since the matter was one of operation the respondent was not immune from suit and the negligence issue had to be canvassed in its entirety. The appellant was therefore entitled to a finding of fact on these questions and a new trial should be directed to accomplish this.

...

Sopinka J. (dissenting): My colleague's reasons are based essentially on an attack on the policy of the respondent with respect to the extent and manner of the inspection program. In my opinion, absent evidence that a policy was adopted for some ulterior motive and not for a municipal purpose, it is *not* open to a litigant to attack it, nor is it appropriate for a court to pass upon it. ...

If, as here, the statute creates no duty to inspect at all, but simply confers a power to do so, it follows logically that a decision to inspect and the extent and manner thereof are all discretionary powers of authority. ...

In this case, the extent of the inspection program was delegated to the Rockwork Section. The respondent acted with its statutory discretion in making that decision. It was a decision that inspections should be done and the manner in which they should be done. In order for a private duty to arise, it would have to be shown that the Rockwork Section acted outside its delegated discretion to determine whether to inspect and the manner in which the inspection is to be made.

NOTES

1. At the new trial, liability was imposed by Mr. Justice Donald for over $1,000,000 and this decision was not appealed. (See (1992), 60 B.C.L.R. (2d) 209 (B.C.S.C.); see *Lewis (Guardian ad Litem of) v. B.C.* (1997), 153 D.L.R. (4th) 594 (S.C.C.), rock falling case, non-delegable duty on the Crown; see also *Mochinski v. Trendline Industries Ltd.* (1997), 154 D.L.R. (4th) 212 (S.C.C.), block of ice falling onto road, liability on government, non-delegable duty).

2. It should be noted that, even if the government conduct is immune from negligence liability because it is a matter of policy, it is still possible for liability to be imposed, but on another much narrower and more complicated basis. A claimant can still recover if it can be shown that a policy decision was made in bad faith or that it was so irrational that it was not a proper exercise of discretion. Further, if these hurdles cannot be jumped, it is also possible to hold liable a government agency that fails to follow properly the policy it has adopted. See *Kamloops (City) v. Nielsen*, [1984] 2 S.C.R. 2.

3. One explanation of *Just* is given by Linden, *Canadian Tort Law* (6th ed. 1997), at 623:

> Another way of looking at this issue is to say that a government must be entitled to govern free from the restraints of tortious liability. It cannot be a tort for a government to govern. However, when a government is supplying services, that is, doing things for its people other than governing, it should be

> subject to ordinary negligence principles. Since, in the words of Mr. Justice Cory "the Crown ... must be free to govern", an immunity is necessary, but it must be limited only to those functions of government that properly can be considered to be "governing" and not extended to the other tasks of government that might be styled "servicing". In other words, governing is normally concerned with large issues, macro decisions, if you will, not routine items, that is, micro decisions. For example, an unemployed person or a business that goes bankrupt cannot be allowed to sue the Crown for the cabinet's negligent management of the economy. Courts are not institutionally suited for such a task; only the ballot box can control this type of conduct.

Does this distinction between governing and servicing advance the quest for a rational solution to these questions? Will cases such as these influence government officials to act with greater care? See Cohen, "Regulating the Regulators" (1990), 40 U.T.L.J. 1213, "Suing the State" *ibid.* at 630, doubting this.

4. In *Swanson & Peever v. Canada* (1991), 124 N.R. 218 (Fed. C.A.) an airplane owned by Wapiti Aviation crashed, killing six of the nine passengers. The pilot had been flying in contravention of safety regulations, something that was a common occurrence at Wapiti. Transport Canada knew of Wapiti's past safety violations but took insufficient measures to make them correct their system. A report by one of Transport Canada's inspectors had warned his superiors about Wapiti's "total disregard for regulations, rights of others and safety of passengers" and concluded that if it continued "we are virtually certain to be faced with a fatality". The families of some of the victims sued the Government of Canada, Wapiti having become insolvent. The trial judge found that there was a duty owed to the families and that it had been breached. The Federal Court of Appeal affirmed the decision. Following *Just*, the court reasoned:

> In this case, the trial judge correctly decided that the Crown's response to the complaints and reports was an operational decision, not a policy matter. ... He later concluded that it was "more than a matter of policy but one of operation". The official making the enforcement decisions was not a high elected official like a Minister or even a Deputy Minister; he was only a regional director. His work involved not policy, planning or governing, but only administering, operations or servicing. The decision had no "polycentric" aspects, nor was there evidence of any lack of resources to permit more rigorous enforcement of the regulations. There were available numerous specific guidelines upon which the court could rely in evaluating the conduct of the decision-maker. This was not a budgetary, macro exercise.
>
> These people were essentially inspectors of airlines, aircraft and pilots, who did not make policy, but rather implemented it; although they certainly had to exercise some discretion and judgment during the course of their work, much like other professional people. ...
>
> These officials were not involved in any decisions involving "social, political or economic factors". Indeed it was another emanation of the Department of Transport altogether, the Canadian Transport Commission, a quasi-judicial body whose function it was to take into account such grounds, which granted the initial licence to Wapiti and other airlines; whereas this branch concerned itself with operating certificates that focused mainly on the matter of safety. These officials were not concerned with the health of the airline industry, with supplying service to remote areas or with employment for young pilots and, if such matters were considered by them in making their decisions, they probably should not have been. Nor was it their job to worry about airlines "going political". Their task was to enforce the regulations and the ANO's as far as safety was concerned to the best of their ability with the resources at their disposal. This function was clearly operational. Hence, a civil

duty of care was owed to the plaintiffs to exercise reasonable care in the circumstances.

But *cf. Gosselin v. Moose Jaw (City)* (1997), 155 D.L.R. (4th) 374 (Sask. C.A.), crack in sidewalk causing injury, no liability since policy decision to inspect 1/3 of sidewalks annually.

5. Another case which relied on *Just* was *Brewer Brothers v. Canada (A.G.)*, where several grain producers sued the Government of Canada because the Canadian Grain Commission had negligently allowed a "producer elevator" to operate without having posted adequate bond security, as required by the *Canada Grain Act*. The plaintiffs, who delivered grain to the "producer elevator", suffered financial losses when the elevator operator's licence was cancelled and it was placed in receivership before paying the plaintiffs. The trial judge held the Government of Canada liable and the Federal Court of Appeal affirmed.

This being a case of economic loss, the analysis was more complex. Mr. Justice Stone explained, however, that the Act was "enacted with a view to protecting those grain producers ... and cast upon the commission an obligation to be satisfied as to the sufficiency of that security". The evidence, said Mr. Justice Stone, was that the "commission's role in duly administering the licensing and bonding provisions ... was a cardinal component of the Canadian grain trade. ... I am satisfied that a relationship of proximity, such as gave rise to a private law duty of care, came into existence".

Mr. Justice Stone, relying on *Just*, explained further that there is "no basis for exempting the [government] from the imposition of liability on the ground that the decisions made were 'policy' decisions. ... ". Nor was Justice Stone prepared to say that there was an exemption "from private law liability because its functions were quasi-judicial or analogous to police functions. While it is arguable that certain of the commission's powers might be so characterized, the acts and omissions of which the [plaintiffs] complain are not among them." His Lordship then went on to consider whether the expected standard of care had been met in implementing their policy and concluded that it had not.

(See also *M-Jay Farms Enterprises Ltd. v. Canadian Wheat Board* (1997), 32 C.C.L.T. (2d) 199, Wright J. (Man. Q.B.) following *Brewer*, [1998] 2 W.W.R. 48 (Man. C.A.); leave to appeal to S.C.C. refused (1998), 126 Man. R. (2d) 154*n* (S.C.C.), *per* Huband J.A.; see also *Riske v. Canadian Wheat Board* (1976), 71 D.L.R. (3d) 686 (F.C.T.D.)).

6. There have been two recent decisions of the Supreme Court of Canada in which governments have been relieved of liability on the basis of the principles espoused in *Just*. In *Brown v. British Columbia (Minister of Transportation and Highways)*, the plaintiff motorist skidded on an icy road on Vancouver Island. While the court felt that there was a duty owed generally to maintain the road, in this case, the government was exempt from ordinary negligence principles because its decision to adopt a summer schedule of reduced service was one of policy. This decision, said Mr. Justice Cory, involved the "classic policy considerations of financial resources, personnel and, as well, significant negotiations with government unions. It was truly a governmental decision involving social, political and economic factors." Consequently, as there was neither proof of irrationality or bad faith nor proof of negligence in the operational aspect of the policy decision, no liability was imposed. While the court was unanimous in the result, Mr. Justice Sopinka, in concurring, indicated that he was not happy with "the 'policy/operational' test as the touchstone of liability", hinting that he would like the court to reconsider its continued usefulness at some future time.

7. In *Swinamer v. Nova Scotia (Attorney General)*, the second case, the plaintiff was injured by a tree that fell on his truck on a highway maintained in the province. There

had been a survey made of trees near the highway that might be a hazard and 200 dead trees — not including the one that hit the plaintiff — were marked. Money was requested to remove these trees over a three-year period. Whereas the court recognized again the duty to maintain the highway, it concluded that the decision to inspect and identify dangerous trees was a preliminary step in the policy-making process. It was, according to Mr. Justice Cory, a "classic example of a policy decision" — that is, one of "setting priorities for the allocation of available funds". "Policy decisions of government must be immune from the application of private law standards of tort liability" he concluded. Since there was no proof of irrationality or bad faith, nor of negligence in relation to the operational aspects of the policy decision, no liability could be found.

8. Are these last two decisions evidence of "backsliding"? Mr. Justice Cory, the author of *Just,* was the author of both these decisions as well. Could they have been decided as standard of care cases, that is, there was no negligence in the circumstances?

9. In Cohen, "The Public and Private Law Dimensions of the UFFI Problem" (1984), 8 Can. Bus. L.J. 410, the author states "that we do not have policy and operational decisions in government. We have decisions, some of which are appropriate for judicial review, and some of which are not. What we need are the tools to assist us in making the distinction." The author identifies several variables which he considers to be relevant to this determination. The variables include such things as:

(1) was there a standard of conduct against which the bureaucrat's behaviour can be judged?;
(2) was the decision a routine one?;
(3) was there a great degree of discretion involved in the decision?;
(4) what type of interest was involved?;
(5) was the injury deliberate or unintentional?;
(6) what was the nature of the government activity which was alleged to have been negligent?;
(7) what was the status of the decision maker?;
(8) can the wrong be pinpointed to one party?;
(9) was there only one victim?;
(10) did the decision involve resource allocation?

Professor Cohen explains how these factors affect the court's willingness to judicially review the decision in the determination of civil liability.

10. Mr. Justice Sopinka has written that the Canadian approach was "more adaptable to claims against public bodies than initially thought". (See "The Liability of Public Authorities: Drawing the Line" (1994) Tort Law Rev. 123 at 139; Linden "Tort Liability of Governments for Negligence" (1995), 53 The Advocate 535.) There remains, however, much discontent with the law as it stands. (See Klar, "The Supreme Court of Canada: Extending the Tort Liability of Public Authorities" (1990), 28 Alta. L. Rev. 648; Klar, "Falling Boulders, Falling Trees and Icy Highways" (1994), 33 Alta. L. Rev. 167; Feldthusen, "*Economic Negligence*," 3rd ed. (1994), ch. 6.)

11. The English courts have grappled unsuccessfully for over a century with the problems of tort liability of public authorities. Even after their Crown liability legislation was enacted, English judges have evinced considerable reluctance to impose liability on governments. Many phrases have been utilized in decisions over the years including power, duty, discretion, policy, operational, but none have proven satisfactory. For a time, under *Anns v. Merton*, [1978] A.C. 728, there was hope for some stability in the area, but the decision was criticised in many cases and by some scholars, which led to its being overruled in *Murphy v. Brentwood District Council*, [1991] A.C. 398, a "retreat" that has become a "rout", according to one House of Lords member. Most of the cases dealt with economic losses, a field that has been most unsettled and most unset-

tling for judges. In our view, a thorough analysis of these old English cases is not worthwhile here, given the fact that the Supreme Court of Canada has disavowed them, refusing to retreat along with their British counterparts. The fact is that the Canadian law is now in much better condition than the English, given *Just, Winnipeg Condominium, Hercules Management* and *Husky Oil, supra.*

12. Some Canadian cases decided in the interlude between *Anns* and *Murphy* are still of significance in Canada, even though legislative steps have been taken in some provinces to overrule them. One of these cases in the heyday of *Anns* is *City of Kamloops v. Nielsen,* [1984] 2 S.C.R. 2, where a municipality, whose inspectors failed to enforce its by-laws, was found liable to subsequent purchases for their economic loss. Madam Justice Wilson, for the majority, explained:

> It seems to me that Lambert J.A. was correct in concluding that the courses of conduct open to the Building Inspector called for "operational" decisions. The essential question was what steps to take to enforce the provisions of the by-law in the circumstances that had arisen. He had a duty to enforce its provisions. He did not have a discretion whether to enforce them or not. He did, however, have a discretion as to how to go about it. This may, therefore, be the kind of situation envisaged by Lord Wilberforce when, after discussing the distinction between policy decisions and operational decisions, he added the rider ... :
>
> > Although this distinction between the policy area and the operational area is convenient, and illuminating, it is probably a distinction of degree; many "operational" powers or duties have in them some element of "discretion." It can safely be said that the more "operational" a power or duty may be, the easier it is to superimpose upon it a common law duty of care. [[1978] A.C. at p. 754]
>
> It may be, for example, that although the Building Inspector had a duty to enforce the by-law, the lengths to which he should go in doing so involved policy considerations. The making of inspections, the issuance of stop orders and the withholding of occupancy permits may be one thing; resort to litigation, if this became necessary, may be quite another. Must the city enforce infractions by legal proceedings or does there come a point at which economic considerations, for example, enter in? And if so, how do you measure that "operational" against the "policy" content of the decision in order to decide whether it is more "operational" than "policy" or vice versa? Clearly this is a matter of very fine distinctions.
>
> Lambert J.A. resolves this problem, as I apprehend the passage already quoted from his reasons, by concluding that the city could have made a policy decision either to prosecute or to seek an injunction. If it had taken either of those steps, it could not be faulted. Moreover, if it had considered taking either of those steps and decided against them, it could likewise not be faulted. But not to consider taking them at all was not open to it. In other words, as I read his reasons, his view was that the city at the very least had to give serious consideration to taking the steps toward enforcement that were open to it. If it decided against taking them, say on economic grounds, then that would be a legitimate policy decision within the operational context and the courts should not interfere with it. It would be a decision made, as Lord Wilberforce put it, within the limits of a discretion *bona fide* exercised.
>
> There is no evidence to support the proposition that the city gave serious consideration to legal proceedings and decided against them on policy grounds. Rather the evidence gives rise to a strong inference that the city, with full knowledge that the work was progressing in violation of the by-law and that the house was being occupied without a permit, dropped the matter because one of its aldermen was involved. Having regard to the fact that we are

here concerned with a statutory duty and that the plaintiff was clearly a person who should have been in the contemplation of the city as someone who might be injured by any breach of that duty, I think this is an appropriate case for the application of the principle in *Anns*. I do not think the appellant can take any comfort from the distinction between non-feasance and misfeasance where there is a duty to act or, at the very least, to make a conscious decision not to act on policy grounds. In my view, inaction for no reason or inaction for an improper reason cannot be a policy decision taken in the *bona fide* exercise of discretion. Where the question whether the requisite action should be taken has not even been considered by the public authority, or at least has not been considered in good faith, it seems clear that for that very reason the authority has not acted with reasonable care. I conclude therefore that the conditions for liability of the city to the plaintiff have been met.

It is of interest to note in this connection that other courses were open to the city. It could have posted warning notices on the building and it could have condemned it. In fact, it did neither even although it knew that work was continuing despite the stop work order and that the house was being occupied without an occupancy permit. Indeed, it issued a plumbing permit in August 1974 before the Hughes moved in.

Responding to the floodgates argument, Wilson J. stated:

> I should like to say a word or two about what has come to be known as the "floodgates" argument. The floodgates argument would discourage a finding of private law duties owed by public officials on the ground that such a finding would open the floodgates and create an open season on municipalities. No doubt a similar type of concern was expressed about the vulnerability of manufacturers following the decision in *Donoghue v. Stevenson* [[1932] A.C. 562]. While I think this is an argument which cannot be dismissed lightly, I believe that the decision in *Anns* contains its own built-in barriers against the flood. For example, the applicable legislation or the subordinate legislation enacted pursuant to it must impose a private law duty on the municipality or public official before the principle in *Anns* applies. Further, the principle will not apply to purely policy decisions made in the *bona fide* exercise of discretion. This is, in my view, an extremely important feature of the *Anns* principle because it prevents the courts from usurping the proper authority of elected representatives and their officials. At the same time, however, the principle ensures that in the operational area, *i.e.*, in implementing their policy decisions, public officials will be exposed to the same liability as other people if they fail in discharging their duty to take reasonable care to avoid injury to their neighbours. The only area, in my view, which leaves scope for honest concern is that difficult area identified by Lord Wilberforce where the operational subsumes what might be called secondary policy considerations, *i.e.*, policy considerations at the secondary level. This, I believe, is the area into which this case falls. This case, however, is more easily disposed of by virtue of the complete failure of the municipality to deal with the policy considerations. On the assumption that, by and large, municipalities and their officials discharge their responsibilities in a conscientious fashion, I believe that such a failure will be the exception rather than the rule and that the scope for application of the principle in *Anns* will be relatively narrow. I do not see it, as do some commentators, as potentially ruinous financially to municipalities. I do see it as a useful protection to the citizen whose ever-increasing reliance on public officials seems to be a feature of our age: see Linden "Tort Law's Role in the Regulation and Control of the Abuse of Power" Special Lectures of the Law Society of Upper Canada (1979), p. 67.

McIntyre J. (Estey J. concurring), dissented:

Liability for negligence of a public authority, as dealt with in *Anns* and the other cases considered with it, would arise out of the activities of the public authority in the conduct of its business. Public authorities, in addition to their administrative and regulatory functions, must perform many tasks. They enter into a wide variety of contracts covering business, commercial and industrial enterprises, and public works. They enter the market place and operate as do private corporations and private individuals. In these circumstances there would seem to be no reason why a public authority should not be liable for its own acts of negligence and vicariously liable for the negligence of its servants in the performance of their duties of employment. The public authority, as has been noted in *Anns*, from the private citizen in that, while it must undertake much in accordance with its mandate, it has as a rule limited resources and frequently limited credit and relatively fixed revenues. The employment of those resources, frequently not sufficient to cover completely all responsibilities, will involve policy choices as to their application. The policy choice protective provision developed in *Anns* meets this problem. It will be observed, however, that in *Anns* and in the various other cases which preceded it (*Dutton v. Bognor Regis* and *Dorset Yacht Co. Ltd. v. Home Office*) and in many later cases which have applied it, the policy choice required of the public authority was one which would protect it against negligence in carrying out the corporate functions and such negligence is ordinarily found in the conduct of its employees for which the authority may be vicariously liable.

No such negligence occurred in the case at bar. …

The exercise of the discretion by the city regarding enforcement proceedings in court differs fundamentally from the "policy choice" contemplated by *Anns*. In my opinion, it does not involve considerations of negligence because it is not properly subject to restriction by a private law duty of care. It involves, in my view, such considerations as those discussed by Laskin J. (as he then was) in *Welbridge Holdings Ltd. v. Metropolitan Corp. of Greater Winnipeg*, [1971] S.C.R. 957, [1972] 3 W.W.R. 433, 22 D.L.R. (3d) 470. …

In the case at bar the record discloses little as to what, if any, steps were taken by the council towards the enforcement of its by-law. It is clear that the defective foundations rendered the house unsafe. It is equally clear that the building inspectors, having found the defective work, reported the matter to the council and took such steps as were open to them to correct matters including the refusal to lift the stop work order or give an occupancy permit. It is also evident that the council was aware of the infraction of the by-law and that the respondents Hughes were living in the house. There is no evidence of any positive step taken in the matter by the council, save that at one time it consulted its city solicitor who shortly after returned the file with a covering letter which is not before us. From all this, the only conclusion that can be reached is that the council took no further step towards enforcement and there is no evidence which would justify any inference of bad faith or impropriety.

I would conclude as follows:

1. This is not a case of underlying negligence by employees of a public authority which could visit liability upon the appellant city.

2. At common law, a municipality has no duty to enforce its by-laws by court proceedings. The matter is discretionary. Failure to exercise enforcement powers in court does not give rise to a private cause of action in negligence to those suffering harm from non-enforcement.

3. The concept of negligence as developed in *Anns* and its predecessors may apply to render a public authority liable for its own negligent acts or omissions or vicariously liable for the negligence of its employees, but municipal prosecutorial or enforcement powers by court proceedings, like mu-

nicipal legislative functions, are different in kind and are not amenable to judicial constraint by the imposition of a private law duty of care.

4. The discretion regarding enforcement proceedings in court is not, however, unfettered and may be subject to judicial constraint in cases of corruption, bad faith, or in cases where extraneous or irrelevant considerations affect the exercise of the discretion. In the case at bar there was, however, no evidence of bad faith or reliance on irrelevant considerations arising from the mere failure to take legal proceedings, and no private cause of action can therefore arise.

See also *Barratt v. The Corporation of the District of North Vancouver,* [1980] 2 S.C.R. 418, the authority of which is now doubtful.

13. The Supreme Court of Canada reaffirmed its support for *Anns* with respect to the liability of public authorities for negligence in building supervision in *Rothfield v. Manolakos*, [1989] 2 S.C.R. 1259, 63 D.L.R. (4th) 449.

The respondent owners hired a contractor, who engaged a subcontractor, to build a backyard retaining wall. A building permit was applied for and obtained, on the basis of a rough sketch of the project. Although at a certain stage of the project the owners and builders were required to advise the city so that the project could be inspected, this was not done. A crack in the wall appeared at a later date. The city building inspector was called and advised a delay in the backfilling to monitor the wall. This was done, and the wall eventually was completed. Several months later it collapsed.

Lawsuits were initiated by the owners against the contractors, the city inspectors, and the city; and by neighbours against the owners, who third partied the others. The trial judge found the contractors and the city liable. The owners were found liable to the neighbours, but they were entitled to indemnity from the contractors and city. The Court of Appeal dismissed the appeal, brought by the city. On appeal to the Supreme Court of Canada, the seven justices split three ways. Dickson C.J., La Forest and Gonthier JJ. held that having made the policy decision to inspect plans and construction, the city owed a duty to all who it is reasonable to conclude might be injured by the negligent exercise of these powers. The city was negligent in not having examined the specifications and sketches for the wall, before it issued the permit. The inspector was negligent in not having ordered that the work be stopped and that corrective measures be taken. The owners were negligent in not having complied with the requirements of the by-law. Two of the justices, Lamer and Cory JJ., held that the owners' own negligence in not having complied with the by-law superseded any act of negligence by the city and absolved the latter from any liability to the owners. The other two justices, Wilson and L'Heureux-Dubé JJ., would have allowed the owners to recover the whole of their damages against the city.

Despite the various complexities of the case, and the diverse findings, what is noteworthy is that none of the judges would refuse to impose liability upon the municipal authority for negligence in the exercise of its powers. It was unanimously agreed that the city owed a duty to take reasonable care in exercising its functions, and the "policy/operational" dichotomy posed no difficulty for the Court. The negligence of the city and its inspector was at the operational level.

The law of Quebec is to the same effect, see *Laurentide Motels Ltd. v. Beauport (City)*, [1989] 1 S.C.R. 705, liability for negligent firefighting.

14. In *Mortimer v. Cameron* (1994), 111 D.L.R. (4th) 428 (Ont. C.A.), a complicated case involving an injury caused by a fall through a defectively built wall around an exterior stairway, which had been built pursuant to a permit issued by a city, the city was held partially at fault, along with the landowner. Robins J.A., following *Kamloops* and *Rothfield* explained:

This tragic accident was within the ambit of the risk created by the City's negligent performance of the inspection duties it had assumed under its by-law. In my opinion there are no policy considerations here which can properly be invoked to limit or negative the scope of the duty imposed on the city. ... This structure, on the city's own evidence, should never have been approved.

See also *Oosthoek v. Thunder Bay (City)* (1996), 139 D.L.R. (4th) 6ll (Ont. C.A.), failure to enforce by-law caused flooding and liability; *Tarjan v. Rockyview No. 44* (1992), 3 Alta. L.R. (2d) 216, liability for wrongly issuing residential building permit erroneously believing set-back provision did not apply.

15. In British Columbia, legislation was enacted to overturn the effect of *Kamloops* and exempt in the future municipalities from similar liability. See *Municipal Act,* S.B.C. 1987, c. 14, section 755.2:

> A municipality, regional district or a member of its council, or a member of its board, or any officer or employee of the municipality or district is not liable for any damages or other loss, including economic loss, sustained by any person, or to the property of any person, as a result of neglect or failure, for any reason, to enforce, by the institution of a civil proceeding or a prosecution, a bylaw made under Division (5) of Part 21 or a regulation made under section 740(l).

See also section 755.4, re reliance on engineer or architect of applicant. Far more extensive amendments were enacted in Alberta relieving municipalities of liability in many other situations; see *Municipal Government Act,* S.A. 1994, c. M-26.1, Part 13.

16. There was earlier authority, prior to *Just,* exempting from liability legislative and *quasi*-judicial action by governments. In the leading Canadian case, *Welbridge Holdings Ltd. v. Metropolitan Corp. of Greater Winnipeg* (1970), [1971] S.C.R. 957, 22 D.L.R. (3d) 470, the Supreme Court of Canada held that a municipal corporation could not be sued in tort for its negligence in passing an invalid by-law zoning plan. A developer who relied on the initial by-law and had already started construction lost money when the by-law was declared invalid, forcing him to terminate his development. In rejecting the developer's action, Laskin J. stated:

> The defendant is a municipal corporation with a variety of functions, some legislative, some with also a *quasi*-judicial component (as the *Wiswell* case determined) and some administrative or ministerial, or perhaps better categorized as business powers. In exercising the latter, the defendant may undoubtedly (subject to statutory qualification) incur liabilities in contract and in tort, including liability in negligence. There may, therefore, be an individualization of responsibility for negligence in the exercise of business powers which does not exist when the defendant acts in a legislative capacity or performs a *quasi*-judicial duty.
>
> Its public character, involving its political and social responsibility to all those who live and work within its territorial limits, distinguishes it, even as respects its exercise of any *quasi*-judicial function, from the position of a voluntary or statutory body such as a trade union or trade association which may have *quasi*-judicial and contractual obligations in dealing with its members: *cf. Abbott v. Sullivan*, [1952] 1 All E.R. 226; *Orchard et al. v. Tunney*, 8 D.L.R. (2d) 273, [1957] S.C.R. 436. A municipality at what may be called the operating level is different in kind from the same municipality at the legislative or *quasi*-judicial level where it is exercising discretionary statutory authority. In exercising such authority, a municipality (no less than a provincial Legislature or the Parliament of Canada) may act beyond its powers in the ultimate view of a Court, albeit it acted on the advice of counsel. It would be incredible to say in such circumstances that it owed a duty of care giving rise to liability in damages for its breach. "Invalidity is not the test of fault and it

should not be the test of liability": see Davis, 3 *Administrative Law Treatise* (1958), at p. 487.

A narrower basis of liability is, however, proposed in the present case, one founded only on the failure to carry out the anterior procedural requirements for the enactment of By-law 177. Although those requirements were held in the *Wiswell* case to be expressions of a *quasi*-judicial function, this did not mean that the hearing to which they were relevant was a step unrelated to the legislative exercise in which the defendant was engaged. In approving what Freedman, J.A., said in the *Wiswell* case in the Manitoba Court of Appeal, Hall, J., agreed that the enactment of the by-law was "[not] simply a legislative act": see 51 D.L.R. (2d) 754 at p. 763. But that did not import that there was no legislative function involved in the enactment. There clearly was.

Moreover, even if the *quasi*-judicial function be taken in isolation, I cannot agree that the defendant in holding a public hearing as required by statute comes under a private tort duty, in bringing it on and in carrying it to a conclusion, to use due care to see that the dictates of natural justice are observed. Its failure in this respect may make its ultimate decision vulnerable, but no right to damages for negligence flows to any adversely affected person, albeit private property values are diminished or expense is incurred without recoverable benefit. If, instead of rezoning the land involved herein to enhance its development value, the defendant had rezoned so as to reduce its value and the owners had sold it thereafter, could it be successfully contended, when the rezoning by-law was declared invalid on the same ground as By-law 177, that the owners were entitled to recoup their losses from the municipality? I think not, because the risk of loss from the exercise of legislative or adjudicative authority is a general public risk and not one for which compensation can be supported on the basis of a private duty of care. The situation is different where a claim for damages for negligence is based on acts done in pursuance or in implementation of legislation or of adjudicative decrees.

17. Before *Welbridge,* a municipality was held liable in *Windsor Motors Ltd. v. District of Power River* (1969), 4 D.L.R. (3d) 155, 68 W.W.R. 173 (B.C.C.A.), when an inspector had negligently advised the plaintiff that a certain location was zoned for a used car business and issued a licence to him to operate such a business. The land was not zoned as such and the plaintiff had to relocate. What is the difference between this case and the above case? Could you argue that passing a by-law zoning land for certain uses is akin to advising persons that it is legitimate for them to operate such businesses? What about issuing a building permit wrongly thinking set-back provisions did not apply? See *Tarjan, supra.*

18. Another area of tort liability for public officials involves the tort of "misfeasance in a public office" or "abuse of power". The leading case is *Roncarelli v. Duplessis,* [1959] S.C.R. 121, 16 D.L.R. (2d) 689. The proprietor of a restaurant sued the Prime Minister/Attorney-General of the Province of Quebec when the proprietor's liquor licence was permanently cancelled. The licence had been cancelled by the Quebec Liquor Commission at the order of the defendant. The plaintiff was a Jehovah's Witness and had been active in the community, supplying bail for numerous members of his faith who had been arrested for their religious activities. In upholding the plaintiff's action, Rand J. stated:

> The field of licensed occupations and businesses of this nature is steadily becoming of greater concern to citizens generally. It is a matter of vital importance that a public administration that can refuse to allow a person to enter or continue a calling which, in the absence of regulation, would be free and legitimate, should be conducted with complete impartiality and integrity; and that the grounds for refusing or cancelling a permit should unquestionably be such and such only as are incompatible with the purposes envisaged by the statute: the duty of a Commission is to serve those purposes and those only. A

decision to deny or cancel such a privilege lies within the "discretion" of the Commission; but that means that decision is to be based upon a weighing of considerations pertinent to the object of the administration.

In public regulation of this sort there is no such thing as absolute and untrammelled "discretion", that is that action can be taken on any ground or for any reason that can be suggested to the mind of the administrator; no legislative Act can, without express language, be taken to contemplate an unlimited arbitrary power, exercisable for any purpose, however capricious or irrelevant, regardless of the nature or purpose of the statute. Fraud and corruption in the Commission may not be mentioned in such statutes but they are always implied as exceptions. "Discretion" necessarily implies good faith in discharging public duty; there is always a perspective within which a statute is intended to operate; and any clear departure from its lines or objects is just as objectionable as fraud or corruption. Could an applicant be refused a permit because he had been born in another Province, or because of the colour of his hair? The ordinary language of the Legislature cannot be so distorted.

To deny or revoke a permit because a citizen exercises an unchallengable right totally irrelevant to the sale of liquor in a restaurant is equally beyond the scope of the discretion conferred. There was here not only revocation of the existing permit but a declaration of a future, definitive disqualification of the appellant to obtain one: it was to be "forever". This purports to divest his citizenship status of its incident of membership in the class of those of the public to whom such a privilege could be extended. Under the statutory language here, that is not competent to the Commission and *a fortiori* to the Government or the respondent: *McGillivray v. Kimber* (1915), 26 D.L.R. 164, 52 S.C.R. 146. There is here an administrative tribunal which, in certain respects, is to act in a judicial manner; and even on the view of the dissenting Justices in *McGillivray*, there is liability: what could be more malicious than to punish this licensee for having done what he had an absolute right to do in a matter utterly irrelevant to the *Alcoholic Liquor Act?* Malice in the proper sense is simply acting for a reason and purpose knowingly foreign to the administration, to which was added here the element of intentional punishment by what was virtually vocation outlawry. ...

The act of the respondent through the instrumentality of the Commission brought about a breach of an implied public statutory duty toward the appellant; it was a gross abuse of legal power expressly intended to punish him for an act wholly irrelevant to the statute, a punishment which inflicted on him, as it was intended to do, the destruction of his economic life as a restaurant keeper within the Province. Whatever may be the immunity of the Commission or its members from an action for damages, there is none in the respondent. He was under no duty in relation to the appellant and his act was an intrusion upon the functions of a statutory body. The injury done by him was a fault engaging liability within the principles of the underlying public law of Quebec: *Mostyn v. Fabrigas* (1774), 1 Cowp. 161, 98 E.R. 1021, and under art. 1053 of the *Civil Code*. That, in the presence of expanding administrative regulation of economic activities, such a step and its consequences are to be suffered by the victim without recourse or remedy, that an administration according to law is to be superseded by action dictated by and according to the arbitrary likes, dislikes and irrelevant purposes of public officers acting beyond their duty, would signalize the beginning of disintegration of the rule of law as a fundamental postulate of our constitutional structure. An administration of licences on the highest level of fair and impartial treatment to all may be forced to follow the practice of "first come, first served", which makes the strictest observance of equal responsibility to all of even greater importance; at this stage of developing government it would be a danger of high consequence to tolerate such a departure from good faith in executing the legislative purpose. ...

> "Good faith" in this context, applicable both to the respondent and the General Manager, means carrying out the statute according to its intent and for its purpose; it means good faith in acting with a rational appreciation of that intent and purpose and not with an improper intent and for an alien purpose; it does not mean for the purposes of punishing a person for exercising an unchallengeable right; it does not mean arbitrarily and illegally attempting to divest a citizen of an incident of his civil status. ...

19. In *Farrington v. Thompson*, [1959] V.R. 286, some police officers, purporting to exercise their power under the *Licensing Act* which provided that conviction of a third offence would render a licence forfeited, required the plaintiff to close down his hotel. There was no third conviction, according to the judge, and the jury found that the defendants failed to exercise due care in ascertaining whether a third conviction had been obtained. The court found, nevertheless, that the defendants were liable for "misfeasance in a public office". Mr. Justice Smith said that "if some other public officer does an act, which, to his knowledge, amounts to an abuse of his office, and thereby causes damage to another person, then an action in tort for misfeasance in a public office will lie" (*ibid.*: see also Molot, "Tort Remedies Against Administrative Tribunals for Economic Loss", Law Society of Upper Canada Special Lectures, *New Developments in the Law of Torts* (1973), p. 425). There was apparently sufficient knowledge of lack of jurisdiction to satisfy the court that liability was called for.

20. There is authority to the effect that an unintentional error in the exercise of discretion is not actionable. See *Harris v. Law Society of Alberta*, [1936] S.C.R. 88, [1936] 1 D.L.R. 401. More recent authority, however, seems to be relaxing the requirement of intention. In *McGillivray v. Kimber* (1950), 52 S.C.R. 146, 26 D.L.R. 164, a pilot, licensed at Sydney, Nova Scotia, under the *Shipping Act*, was dismissed from the service by the Sydney Pilotage Authority before his licence expired. Although the minority of the court felt that malice had to be proven for liability for a quasi-judicial act, the majority decided that the Authority was responsible. It had failed to abide by the statutorily required procedures of giving the plaintiff notice and an opportunity to be heard. Mr. Justice Anglin stated: "They committed an unwarranted and illegal act which subjected them to liability to the plaintiff for such damages as he sustained as a natural and direct consequence thereof." Mr. Justice Idington observed that "the respondents were acting entirely without jurisdiction and so acting must be held liable".

21. What if a Minister of the Crown announces that he or she will grant fishing licences to certain fishermen, who, in anticipation, expend funds to refurbish their boats, and the Minister then changes his or her mind? See *Comeau's Sea Foods Ltd. v. Canada (Minister of Fisheries and Oceans)* (1995), 24 C.C.L.T. (2d) 1, at 47 (F.C.A.) affd on ground that no statutory violation occurred, [1997] 1 S.C.R. 12. See DaRe, "Comment", (1997) 76 Can. Bar Rev. 253.

22. The courts of Quebec have been most diligent in this area. In *Lapointe v. Le Roi* (1924), 87 B.R. 170, the petitioner was the holder of a fishing licence revoked by the Minister who lacked the statutory power to do so. The court ordered the Minister to compensate the petitioner for his loss. In another case, *Leroux v. City of Lachine*, [1942] C.S. 352, a licence permitted the plaintiff to operate a dance hall. The city revoked the licence, without permitting him an opportunity to be heard. The court awarded damages on the ground that this was an "unwarranted and negligent action" on the defendant's part, amounting to an abuse of rights.

23. In *Chartier v. Attorney-General of Quebec*, [1979] 2 S.C.R. 475, 48 C.C.C. (2d) 34, the Supreme Court of Canada described as "an abuse of power" the unjustifiable issuance of a coroner's warrant which was purportedly issued under the *Coroners' Act*, R.S.Q. 1964, c. 29. The Supreme Court awarded the plaintiff $50,000 for moral damage.

24. Is this a valuable role for Canadian tort law to play in the new millennium? Do you think that the *Canadian Charter of Rights and Freedoms* should take over this role, and remove tort law from this area?

C. CONSTITUTIONAL TORTS

JANE DOE v. BOARD OF POLICE COMMISSIONERS FOR THE MUNICIPALITY OF METROPOLITAN TORONTO

Ontario Court of Justice, General Division (1998), 39 O.R. (3d) 487.

Jane Doe was raped at knife point in her own bed in 1986 by a stranger. She was the fifth known victim of someone called the "balcony rapist", who climbed into the apartments of his victims from their apartment balconies. The police failed to warn her about the danger they were aware of in her neighbourhood because they feared that women, if warned, might become hysterical and cause the rapist to flee and thwart their efforts to apprehend him. The victim felt she had been used as "bait".

Macfarland J.: Section 57 of the *Police Act*, R.S.O. 1980, c. 381 (the governing statute at the time these events occurred) provides:

> 57. ... members of police forces ... are charged with the duty of preserving the peace, preventing robberies and other crimes ...

The police are statutorily obligated to prevent crime and at common law they owe a duty to protect life and property. As Schroeder J.A. stated in *Schacht v. The Queen in right of the Province of Ontario et al* (1973), 1 O.R. 221 at 231:

> The duties which I lay upon them stem not only from the relevant statutes to which reference has been made, but from the common law, which recognizes the existence of a broad conventional or customary duty in the established constabulary as an arm of the state to protect the life, limb and property of the subject.

[Her Ladyship cited the reasons of Moldaver J. given in the Divisional Court when the adequacy of the pleadings was approved:]

> The law is clear that in certain circumstances, the police have a duty to warn citizens of foreseeable harm. ... The obvious purpose of the warning is to protect the citizens.
>
> I would add to this by saying that in some circumstances where foreseeable harm and a special relationship of proximity exist, the police might reasonably conclude that a warning ought not to be given. For example, it might be decided that a warning would cause general and unnecessary panic on the part of the public which could lead to greater harm.
>
> It would, however, be improper to suggest that a legitimate decision not to warn would excuse a failure to protect. The duty to protect would still remain. It would simply have to be accomplished by other means.
>
> In this case the plaintiff claims, *inter alia*, that the duty owed to her by the defendants required (1) that she be warned of the impending danger; or (2) in the absence of such a warning, that she be adequately protected. It is alleged that the police did neither.
>
> Instead she claims they made a conscious decision to sacrifice her in order to apprehend the suspect. They decided to use her as "bait". They chose not to warn her due to a stereotypical belief that because she was a woman, she and others like her

would become hysterical. This would have "scared off" the attacker, making his capture more difficult.

The evidence establishes that Det. Sgt. Cameron clearly had linked the four rapes which preceded Jane Doe by the early days of August in 1986 and he and Det. Sgt. Derry knew that the rapist would continue to attack women until he was stopped. The knew the rapist was attacking single white women living alone in second and third floor apartments with balconies in the Church/Wellesley area of the City of Toronto.

On the evidence, I find the plaintiff has established a private law duty of care. …

In my view, the police failed utterly in their duty to protect these women and the plaintiff in particular from the serial rapist the police knew to be in their midst by failing to warn them so that they may have had the opportunity to take steps to protect themselves.

It is no answer for the police to say women are always at risk and as an urban adult living in downtown Toronto they have an obligation to lookout for themselves. Women generally do, every day of their lives, conduct themselves and their lives in such a way as to avoid the general pervasive threat of male violence which exists in our society. Here police were aware of a specific threat or risk to a specific group of women and they did nothing to warn those women of the danger they were in, nor did they take any measures to protect them. … In this respect, they are liable to her in damages.

Discrimination

The plaintiff's argument is not simply that she has been discriminated against, because she is a woman, by individual officers in the investigation of her specific complaint — but that systemic discrimination existed within the MTPF in 1986 which impacted adversely on all women and, specifically, those who were survivors of sexual assault who came into contact with the MTPF — a class of persons of which the plaintiff was one. She says in effect, the sexist stereotypical views held by the MTPF informed the investigation of this serial rapist and caused that investigation to be conducted incompetently and in such a way that the plaintiff has been denied the equal protection and equal benefit of law guaranteed to her by s. 15(1) of the Charter. …

Charter Law

In my view the decision of the Divisional Court in this matter has already determined that the Charter can apply, in the circumstances of this case to the police conduct. The s. 15(1) violation alleged relates to discriminatory conduct by state officials in the carrying out and enforcing of the law. In the view of Moldaver J. (as he then was) the pleadings supported a violation of the plaintiff's rights under s. 15(1). At that time the plaintiff's pleadings were mere allegations. It is implicit in the court's decision — if the allegations were proved it would constitute a violation of rights.

For reasons given above I am satisfied on the evidence and the plaintiff has established that the defendants had a legal duty to warn her of the danger she faced; that they adopted a policy not to warn her because of a stereotypical discriminatory belief that as a woman she and others like her would become hysterical and panic and scare off an attacker, among others.

A man in similar circumstances, implicit from Det. Sgt. Cameron's comment, would have been warned and therefor had the opportunity to choose whether to expose himself to danger in order to help catch the attacker.

It is not necessary that their decision not to warn be based solely on discriminatory grounds. It is enough that one of the basis for it was as the plaintiff has submitted:

> It need not have been the only factor, nor even the major or primary factor, in order for discrimination to be found.

Counsel in this respect goes on to quote from the decision of Chief Justice Dickson in *Janzen v. Platy Enterprises Ltd.*, [1989] 1 S.C.R. 1252 at 1288.

In the result the plaintiff has established a breach of her s. 15(1) right to equal benefit and protection of the law.

As for the breach of s. 7 the decision of the Divisional Court in respect of the pleadings is:

Section 7 reads as follows:

> 7. Everyone has the right to life, liberty and security of the person and the right not to be deprived thereof except in accordance with the principles of fundamental justice.

[As the Divisional Court has stated:]

> The plaintiff claims that she was deprived of her right to security of the person. The defendants chose, or at least adopted a policy which favoured the apprehension of the criminal over her protection as a targeted rape victim. By using Ms. Doe as "bait" without her knowledge or consent, the police knowingly placed her security interest at risk. This stemmed from the same stereotypical and therefore discriminatory belief already referred to.
>
> According to the plaintiff, she was deprived of her right to security of the person in a manner which did not accord with the principles of fundamental justice. These principles, while entitled to broad and general interpretation, especially in the area of law enforcement, could not be said to embrace a discretion exercised arbitrarily or for improper motives. ...
>
> As a result, the plaintiff claims that her rights under s. 7 of the *Charter* were violated. Again, in my opinion, these pleadings do support such a violation.

As I have found in relation to s. 15, the plaintiff has established on the evidence, the factual foundation pleaded for reasons set out herein. In the result, I am of the view that the decision of the Divisional Court was that in that event a violation of s. 7 is established. I agree with that determination but even if I did not, I would consider myself bound.

Section 1

As indicated earlier the defendants called no evidence *per se* in support of "demonstrating" a s. 1 defence. They point out in written argument that their conduct can be examined in all the circumstances to see if a s. 1 defence is made out. The argument shortly put is that policing is a complicated business and the courts should stay out of it.

In this respect their conduct was determined to have fallen short in part, because of their discriminatory treatment of women. Women were treated differently because some members of the force adhered to sexist notions that if warned, women would panic and scare off the attacker. The defendants do not suggest, even in argument, why such conduct in the circumstances of this case may be "justifiable". I suggest the answer is a simple one — because it cannot.

Section 24

I am satisfied on the facts of this case that the plaintiff's damages are the same in respect of the two basis upon which her action is founded *i.e.* negligence and breach of Charter rights.

The result of the breaches which she has established are the personal repercussion to her having been raped at knife point by a stranger. They are profound.

It is the same conduct by the police which I have found supports and establishes both causes of action.

In such circumstances the plaintiff is entitled to one award of damages to compensate her for the damage she has suffered. She is not, in my view, in these circumstances, entitled to any additional or "extra" damages because the police conduct has breached her charter rights. In this respect assuming she is otherwise fully compensated, a declaration will suffice.

[The Trial Judge fixed $175,000 general damages plus special damages.]

NOTES

1. In *S. et al v. Clement et al* (1995), 122 D.L.R. (4th) 449 (Ont. Gen. Div.), the government of Canada was held liable to the plaintiff who was sexually assaulted by an escaped prisoner, who had been serving time in a federal prison for sexual assault and murder. Madame Justice Lang reviewed all the authorities and said: "It was reasonably foreseeable that a known violent sex offender, in the course of his escape, posed a significant risk of violence to any woman he met in the vicinity of the institution. ... [The government] owed a duty of care ... " The decisions not to look for the offender right away and not to notify the O.P.P. were "operational" and negligently made. See also *B. (D.) v. C.A.S. of Durham Region* (1996), 30 C.C.L.T. (2d) 310 (Ont. C.A.), father wrongly accused of child abuse by social worker recovered in negligence against C.A.S.

2. As the *Jane Doe* case indicates, not only do breaches of statute affect tort liability, but Charter violations may also lead to damage awards. Subsection 24(l) reads as follows:

> Anyone whose rights or freedoms, as guaranteed by this Charter, have been infringed or denied may apply to a court of competent jurisdiction to obtain such remedy as the court considers appropriate and jus in the circumstances.

Damage awards for what are called "constitutional torts" have become increasingly common. (See Ryan J.A. in *R. v. McGillivary* (1990), 56 C.C.C. (3d) 304 at 309 (N.B.C.A.)). They have been awarded for the "cruel and unusual treatment" of the plaintiff by customs officers (*Rollinson v. R.* (1994), 20 C.C.L.T. (2d) 92 (F.C.T.D.)), for the conduct of police officers who refused to allow a lawyer access to his client contrary to para. 10(b) (see *Crossman v. R.,* [1984] l F.C. 681 (T.D.), and other similar violations. See Linden, *supra*, at p. 312. See also Pilkington "Damages as a Remedy for Infringement of the Canadian Charter of Rights and Freedoms" (1984), 62 Can. Bar. Rev. 5l7; Cooper-Stephenson, *Charter Damage Claims* (1990); Mullan, "Damages for Violation of Constitutional Rights — A False Spring?" (1995), 6 N.J.C.L. 105.

3. The Supreme Court of Canada has recognized that "damage may be awarded for breach of Charter rights", but it has indicated that "no body of jurisprudence has yet developed in respect of the principles which might govern the award of damages under subsection 24(l) of the Charter." See Beetz J. in *RJR-Macdonald Inc. v. Canada (Attorney General)*, [1994] 1 S.C.R. 3ll.

4. In *Hill v. British Columbia* (1997), 38 C.C.L.T. (2d) 182 (B.C.C.A.), a prisoner was segregated because he was suspected of being involved in a riot. The required review of his decision, which was made in error, was delayed past the required time period for 11 extra days during which he remained segregated. The officials were held to be negligent, the conduct not quasi-judicial, and damages of $500 were awarded to the prisoner. The tort action was said to supply the "fundamental justice" right mandated by s. 7 of the Charter. Compare with *Olutu v. Home Office,* [1997] 1 All E.R. 655 (C.A.) where a person kept in custody longer than he should have been was denied tort recovery.

5. In *Chrispen v. Kalinowski* (1997), 35 C.C.L.T. (2d) 214 (Sask. Q.B.), the plaintiff's s. 8 rights were violated when six police officers unlawfully entered and searched his home before sunrise. All charges that were laid were later dismissed, the illegally seized evidence having been excluded. The plaintiff sued the six officers claiming damages. Zarzeczny J. found for the plaintiff, explaining:

> In my view, [*Persaud v. Donaldson* (1997), 21 O.R. (3d) 349] is support for the proposition that so long as good faith is demonstrated and the evidence does not support a finding that the police acted recklessly or that their behaviour was intimidating, the subsequent finding that the process (search warrant or search as conducted) was unlawful will not properly support a finding of damages. ...
>
> In the circumstances of the case before me I have concluded that the defendant officers were reckless in their behaviour both with respect to their investigation of this complaint and person (Chrispen) who was the object of it and in the way the search was conducted, the intrusive and threatening way it was conducted, the intimidating nature of it and the potential dangers which it created to all concerned. Is all the circumstances the action taken was unreasonable. Compensation in damages is appropriate.

Should recklessness be required for all Charter damage claims? Is good faith always a full defence to a case such as this? Is this concept of a constitutional tort a second development?

6. Would *Seneca College* be decided differently today using the Charter?

7. In the United States, constitutional tort actions are expressly allowed under 42 U.S.C. 1983 (1994) for violation of constitutional rights. See *Memphis School District v. Stachura* (1986), 477 U.S. 299; Whitman, "Government Responsibility for Constitutional Torts" (1986), 85 Mich. L. Rev. 225; see Linden, Canadian Tort Law (6th ed. 1997) at 312.

8. Cases such as these are sometimes brought, not only for compensation and deterrence, but for psychological and even political purposes. During the trial, Jane Doe was quoted as saying that she had to "seek the justice that I need to heal myself". (*The Globe & Mail*, September 17, 1997). Following the trial, she was quoted as follows: "It was a political action for me, and that was accomplished. I won the day the trial started". (*The Globe and Mail*, July 4, 1998). In the days after the decision, the Chief of Police and the Chairman of the Board of Police Commissioners at a public meeting apologized to Ms. Doe who was present along with many members of the public, the press and the T.V. cameras. Can it be said that this case is an example of tort law empowering an individual psychologically and politically? Is this a good thing?

CHAPTER 12

STRICT LIABILITY

As must have become apparent in preceding chapters, negligence frequently involves no moral fault and consists merely in a failure to conform to certain standards of conduct. Only a slight shifting of emphasis is required to impose liability where not only is there no moral wrongdoing, but no failure to observe a standard of care, however highly pitched. There are certain types of conduct which, although they cannot be styled wrongful, are either so fraught with danger, or so unusual in a given community, that it is felt that the risk of loss should be shifted from the person injured to the person who, merely by engaging in such conduct, created the risk which resulted in harm. The extent to which the growth of such liability is due to a feeling that certain inevitable risks of harm can better be distributed than to leave it on the shoulders of the injured person is shown by modern *Workers' Compensation Acts*. The haphazard advance of judicial decisions in the same direction must have become evident in earlier chapters in connection with the part played by "*res ipsa loquitur*" and other devices which, while preserving the language of "fault", frequently produce results far removed from that concept. This chapter is devoted to the cases which have consciously admitted the principle of liability for non-negligent and unintended harms.

A. ORIGIN AND SCOPE

RYLANDS v. FLETCHER

House of Lords. (1868), L.R. 3 H.L. 330, 37 L.J. Ex. 161;
affg (1866), L.R. 1 Ex. 265.

Fletcher brought an action against Rylands and Horrocks to recover damages for injury to his mines caused by water flowing into them from a reservoir built on the defendants' land. The declaration alleged negligence on the part of defendants. When the case came on for trial, it was referred to an arbitrator who was later asked to state a special case for the consideration of the Court of Exchequer.

The special case stated the material facts as follows: Fletcher was, with the permission of the landowners and the lessee, Lord Wilton, working coal mines and had worked the mines up to a place where old passages of disused mines and a vertical shaft filled with rubbish were encountered. Rylands and Horrocks owned a mill near the land under which Fletcher's mines were being worked. With Lord Wilton's permission they constructed a reservoir on Lord Wilton's land in order to supply water to their mill. They employed competent engineers and contractors to construct the reservoir and Rylands and Horrocks did not know that coal had ever been worked under or near the site of the reservoir. The site chosen, however, was over old coal mines which communicated with the workings of Fletcher. While there was no negligence on the part of the defendants, the contractors did encounter old shafts while building the reservoir and it was found that they did not use reasonable care to provide sufficient supports for the reservoir when filled with water.

The reservoir was completed early in December, 1860, and was partially filled with water. On the 11th of December one of the old shafts gave way and the water in the reservoir flowed into the old mine workings and large quantities of the water found their way into Fletcher's workings and flooded them.

The question for the court was whether the plaintiff was, on these facts, entitled to recover damages from the defendants.

The Court of Exchequer (Pollock C.B. and Martin B., Bramwell B. dissenting) gave judgment for the defendants: (1865), 2 H. & C. 774. The plaintiff brought error in the Exchequer chamber.

Blackburn J.: ... The plaintiff, though free from all blame on his part, must bear the loss unless he can establish that it was the consequence of some default for which the defendants are responsible. The question of law therefore arises. What is the obligation which the law casts on the person who, like the defendants, lawfully brings on his land something which, though harmless whilst it remains there, will naturally do mischief if it escape out of his land? It is agreed on all hands that he must take care to keep in that which he has brought on the land and keeps there, in order that it may not escape and damage his neighbours, but the question arises whether the duty which the law casts upon him, under such circumstances, is an absolute duty to keep it in at his peril, or is, as the majority of the Court of Exchequer have thought, merely a duty to take all reasonable and prudent precautions, in order to keep it in, but no more. If the first be the law, the person who has brought on his land and kept there something dangerous, and failed to keep it in, is responsible for all the natural consequences of its escape. If the second be the limit of his duty, he would not be answerable except on proof of negligence, and consequently would not be answerable for escape arising from any latent defect which ordinary prudence and skill could not detect.

Supposing the second to be the correct view of the law, a further question arises subsidiary to the first, *viz*, whether the defendants are not so far identified with the contractors whom they employed, as to be responsible for the consequences of their want of care and skill in making the reservoir in fact insufficient with reference to the old shafts of the existence of which they were aware, though they had not ascertained where the shaft went to.

We think that the true rule of law is, that the person who for his own purposes brings on his lands and collects and keeps there anything likely to do mischief if it escapes, must keep it in at his peril, and, if he does not do so, is *prima facie* answerable for all the damage which is the natural consequence of its escape. He can excuse himself by shewing that the escape was owing to the plaintiff's default; or perhaps that the escape was the consequence of *vis major*, or the act of God; but as nothing of this sort exists here, it is unnecessary to inquire what excuse would be sufficient, The general rule, as above stated, seems on principle just. The person whose grass or corn is eaten down by the escaping cattle of his neighbour, or whose mine is flooded by the water from his neighbour's reservoir, or whose cellar is invaded by the filth of his neighbour's privy, or his habitation is made unhealthy by the fumes and noisome vapours of his neighbour's alkali works, is damnified without fault of his own; and it seems but reasonable and just that the neighbour, who has brought something on his own property which was not naturally there, harmless to others so long as it was confined to his own property, but which he knows to be mischievous if it gets on his neighbour's, should be obliged to make good the damage which ensues if he does not succeed in confining it to his own property. But for his act in bringing it there no mischief could have accrued, and it seems but just that he should at his peril keep it there so that no mischief may accrue, or answer for the natural and anticipated consequences. And upon authority, this we think is established to be the law whether the things so brought be beasts, or water, or filth, or stenches.

The case that has most commonly occurred, and which is most frequently to be found in the books, is as to the obligation of the owner of cattle which he has brought on his land, to prevent them escaping and doing mischief. The law as to them seems to be perfectly settled from early times; the owner must keep them in at his peril, or he will be answerable for the natural consequences of their escape; that is with regard to tame beasts, for the grass they eat and trample upon, though not for any injury to the person of others, for our ancestors have settled that it is not the general nature of horses to kick, or bulls to gore, but if the owner knows that the beast has a vicious propensity to attack men, he will be answerable for that too. ... These authorities, and the absence of any authority to the contrary, justify Williams J., in saying as he does in *Cox v. Burbidge*, that the law is clear that in actions for damage occasioned by animals that have not been kept in by their owners, it is quite immaterial whether the escape is by negligence or not.

As has been already said, there does not appear to be any difference in principle between the extent of the duty cast on him who brings cattle on his land to keep them in, and the extent of the duty imposed on him who brings on his land, water, filth, or stenches, or any other thing which will, if it escape, naturally do damage to prevent their escaping and injuring his neighbour, and the case of *Tenant v. Goldwin*, 1 Salk. 21, 360, is an express authority that the duty is the same, and is to keep them in at his peril. [Blackburn J. discussed this case, in which a defendant was held liable for the seepage of filth from a privy on his premises to the plaintiff's premises.] As Lord Raymond in his report, 2 Ld. Raym, at p. 1092, said: "The reason of this case is upon this account, that every one must so use his own as not to do damage to another; and as every man is bound so to look to his cattle as to keep them out of his neighbour's ground, that so he may receive no damage; so he must keep in the filth of his house or office that it may not allow in upon and damnify his neighbour. ..."

No case has been found in which the question as to the liability for noxious vapours escaping from a man's works by inevitable accident has been discussed, but the following case will illustrate it. Some years ago several actions were brought against the occupiers of some alkali works at Liverpool for the damage alleged to be caused by the chlorine fumes of their works. The defendants proved that they at great expense erected contrivances by which the fumes of chlorine were condensed and sold as muriatic acid, and they called a great body of scientific evidence to prove that this apparatus was so perfect that no fumes possibly could escape from the defendants' chimneys. On this evidence it was pressed upon the jury that the plaintiff's damage must have been due to some of the numerous other chimneys in the neighbourhood; the jury, however, being satisfied that the mischief was occasioned by chlorine, drew the conclusion that it had escaped from the defendants' works somehow, and in each case found for the plaintiff. No attempt was made to disturb these verdicts on the ground that the defendants had taken every precaution which prudence or skill could suggest to keep those fumes in, and that they could not be responsible unless negligence were shown. ... The uniform course of pleading in actions on such nuisances is to say that the defendant caused the noisome vapours to arise on his premises, and suffered them to come on the plaintiff's, without stating that there was any want of care or skill in the defendant, and that the case of *Tenant v. Goldwin*, *supra*, showed that this was founded on the general rule of law, that he whose stuff it is must keep it that it may not trespass. ...

But it was further said by Martin B. that when damage is done to personal property, or even to the person, by collision, either upon land or at sea, there must be negligence in the party doing the damage to render him legally responsible; and this is no doubt true, and as was pointed out by Mr. Mellish during his argument before us, this is not confined to cases of collision, for there are many cases in which proof of negligence is essential, as, for instance, where an unruly horse gets on the footpath of a public street and kills a passenger: *Hammack v. White*, 11 C.B.N.S. 588; or where a person in a dock is struck by the falling of a bale of cotton which the defendant's servants are lowering: *Scott v. London Dock Company*, 3 H. & C. 596: and many other similar cases may be found. But we think these cases distinguishable from the present. Traffic on the highways, whether by land or sea, cannot be conducted without exposing those whose persons or property are near it to some inevitable risk; and that being so, those who go on the highway, or have their property adjacent to it, may well be held to do so subject to their taking upon themselves the risk of injury from that inevitable danger; and persons who by the licence of the owner pass near to warehouses where goods are being raised or lowered, certainly do so subject to the inevitable risk of accident. In neither case, therefore, can they recover without proof of want of care or skill occasioning the accident: and it is believed that all the cases in which inevitable accident has been held an excuse for what *prima facie* was a trespass, can be explained on the same principle, *viz.*, that the circumstances were such as to show that the plaintiff had taken that risk upon himself. But there is no ground for saying that the plaintiff here took upon himself any risk arising from the uses to which the defendants should choose to apply their land. He neither knew what these might be, nor could he in any way control the defendants, or hinder their building what reservoirs they liked, and storing up in them what water they pleased, so long as the defendants succeeded in preventing the water which they there brought from interfering with the plaintiff's property.

The view which we take of the first point renders it unnecessary to consider whether the defendants would or would not be responsible for the want of care and skill in the persons employed by them, under the circumstances stated in the case.

We are of opinion that the plaintiff is entitled to recover, but as we have not heard any argument as to the amount, we are not able to give judgment for what damages. The parties probably will empower their counsel to agree on the amount of damages; should they differ on the principle the case may be mentioned again.

[Rylands and Horrocks appealed to the House of Lords.]

The Lord Chancellor (Lord Cairns): ... My Lords, the principles on which this case must be determined appear to me to be extremely simple. The defendants, treating them as the owners or occupiers of the close on which the reservoir was constructed, might lawfully have used that close for any purpose for which it might in the ordinary course of the enjoyment of land be used; and if, in what I may term the natural user of that land, there had been any accumulation of water, either on the surface or under ground, and if, by the operation of the laws of nature, that accumulation of water had passed off into the close occupied by the plaintiff, the plaintiff could not have complained that that result had taken place. If he had desired to guard himself against it, it would have lain upon him to have done so by leaving, or by interposing, some barrier between his close and the close of the defendants in order to have prevented that operation of the laws of nature. ...

On the other hand, if the defendants, not stopping at the natural use of their close, had desired to use it for any purpose which I may term a non-natural use for the purpose of introducing into the close that which in its natural condition was not in or upon it, for the purpose of introducing water either above or below ground in quantities and in a manner not the result of any work or operation on or under the land; and if in consequence of their doing so, or in consequence of any imperfection in the mode of their doing so, the water came to escape and to pass off into the close of the plaintiff, then it appears to me that that which the defendants were doing they were doing at their own peril; and if in the course of their doing it the evil arose to which I have referred, the evil, namely, of the escape of the water and its passing away to the close of the plaintiff and injuring the plaintiff, then for the consequence of that, in my opinion, the defendants would be liable ...

My Lords, these simple principles, if they are well founded, as it appears to me they are, really dispose of this case.

[Lord Cairns then quoted from Blackburn J.'s opinion in the Exchequer Chamber.] My Lords, in that opinion I must say I entirely concur. Therefore, I have to move your Lordships that the judgment of the Court of Exchequer Chamber be affirmed, and that the present appeal be dismissed with costs.

Lord Cranworth: My Lords, I concur with my noble and learned friend in thinking that the rule of law was correctly stated by Mr. Justice Blackburn in delivering the opinion of the Exchequer Chamber. If a person brings, or accumulates, on his land anything which, if it should escape, may cause damage to his neighbour, he does so at his peril. If it does escape and cause damage, he is responsible, however careful he may have been, and whatever precautions he may have taken to prevent the damage.

In considering whether a defendant is liable to a plaintiff for damage which the plaintiff may have sustained, the question in general is not whether the defendant has acted with due care and caution, but whether his acts have occasioned the damage. This is all well explained in the old case of *Lambert v. Bessey*, reported by Sir Thomas Raymond: Sir T. Raym. 421. And the doctrine is founded on good sense. For when one person, in managing his own affairs, causes, however innocently, damage to another, it is obviously only just that he should be the party to suffer. He is bound *sic uti suo ut non laedat alienum.* This is the principle of law applicable to cases like the present, and I do not discover in the authorities which were cited anything conflicting with it. ...

The defendants, in order to effect an object of their own, brought on to their land, or on to land which for this purpose may be treated as being theirs, a large accumulated mass of water, and stored it up in a reservoir. The consequence of this was damage to the plaintiff, and for that damage, however skilfully and carefully the accumulation was made, the defendants, according to the principles and authorities to which I have adverted, were certainly responsible.

I concur, therefore, with my noble and learned friend in thinking that the judgment below must be affirmed, and that there must be judgment for the defendant in error.

NOTES

1. Why was the defendant not held liable for the negligence of the contractor? Why was there no trespass? Why was there no liability for nuisance?

2. Are the opinions of Mr. Justice Blackburn and Lord Cairns in accord? What is the difference between them? What is the rule in *Rylands v. Fletcher*?

3. In addition to the term strict liability, the phrases "absolute liability" and "liability without fault" have been used to describe this doctrine. Which is the best phrase? See Bohlen, "The Rule in *Rylands v. Fletcher*" (1911), 59 U. Pa. L. Rev. 298, 373, 423; Stallybrass, "Dangerous Things and the Non-Natural User of Land" (1929), 3 Camb. L.J. 376; Thayer, "Liability Without Fault" (1916), 29 Harv. L. Rev. 801; Prosser, "The Principle of *Rylands v. Fletcher*" printed in *Selected Topics on the Law of Torts* (1953), p. 135; Gregory, "Trespass to Negligence to Absolute Liability" (1951), 37 Va. L. Rev. 359; Fridman, "The Rise and Fall of *Rylands v. Fletcher*" (1956), 34 Can. Bar Rev. 810; MacDonald, "*Rylands v. Fletcher* and Its Limitations" (1923), 1 Can. Bar Rev. 140; Goodhart, "The Rule in *Rylands v. Fletcher*" (1947), 63 L.Q. Rev. 160; Morris, "Absolute Liability for Dangerous Things" (1948), 61 Harv. L. Rev. 515; Winfield, "The Myth of Absolute Liability" (1926), 41 L. Q. Rev. 37; Linden, "Whatever Happened to *Rylands v. Fletcher*?" in Klar (ed.), *Studies in Canadian Tort Law* (1977), p. 325. For two stimulating historical accounts, see Heuston, "Judges and Judgements In Torts" (1986), 20 U.B.C.L. Rev. 33; and Simpson, "Legal Liability for Bursting Reservoirs" (1984), 13 J. of Leg. Stud. 209.

1. Non-natural User

RICKARDS v. LOTHIAN

Privy Council. [1913] A.C. 263, 82 L.J.P.C. 42.

The defendant was the occupier of a business building and leased part of the second floor to the plaintiff. On the fourth floor was a men's lavatory containing a basin. The lavatory was provided for the use of the tenants and persons in their employ. One morning the plaintiff's stock in trade was found seriously damaged one morning by water. Such water came from the basin on the fourth floor and examination showed that the waste pipe had been plugged with various articles such as nails, pen holders, string and soap and that the water tap had been turned full on. The defendant's caretaker had found the lavatory in proper order at 10.20 p.m. the previous evening.

The plaintiff brought action against the defendant alleging carelessness in construction and management, and also for allowing large quantities of water to escape and to flow into the plaintiff's premises. At the trial the jury found the defendant negligent in not providing further equipment against flooding. They also found that "this was the malicious act of some person". The trial judge entered judgment for the plaintiff, which judgment was set aside by the Supreme Court of Victoria and judgment entered for the defendant. By a majority, this judgment, in turn, was reversed by the High Court of Australia. The defendant, by leave of the High Court appealed to the Judicial Committee of the Privy Council.

Lord Moulton: … The arguments on behalf of the plaintiff in the Courts of Appeal were mainly directed to bring the case under one of two well-known types of action, namely: (1) it was contended that the defendant ought to have foreseen the probability of such a malicious act and to have taken precaution against it, and that he was liable in damages for not having done so. (2) It was contended that the defendant was liable apart from negligence on the principles which are usually associated with the well-known case of *Fletcher v. Rylands*. [Lord Moulton then found there was no evidence of negligence on which to find liability.]

The principal contention, however, on behalf of the plaintiff was based on the doctrine customarily associated with the case of *Fletcher v. Rylands*. It was contended that it was the defendant's duty to prevent an overflow from the lavatory basin, however caused, and that he was liable in damages for not having so done, whether the overflow was due to any negligent act on his part or to the malicious act of a third person.

The legal principle that underlies the decision in *Fletcher v. Rylands* was well known in English law from a very early period, but it was explained and formulated in a strikingly clear and authoritative manner in that case and therefore is usually referred to by that name. It is nothing other than an application of the old maxim "*Sic utere tuo ut alienum non laedas.*"

It will be seen that Blackburn J., with characteristic carefulness, indicates that exceptions to the general rule may arise where the escape is in consequence of *vis major*, or the act of God, but declines to deal further with the question because it was unnecessary for the decision of the case then before him. A few years later the question of law thus left undecided in *Fletcher v. Rylands* came up for decision in a case arising out of somewhat similar circumstances.

[His Lordship dealt with the case of *Nichols v. Marsland* (1876-77), 2 Ex. D. 1 and quoted from the opinion of Mellish L.J. to this effect:]

> A defendant cannot, in our opinion, be properly said to have caused or allowed the water to escape, if the act of God or the Queen's enemies was the real cause of its escaping without any fault on the part of the defendant. If a reservoir was destroyed by an earthquake, or the Queen's enemies destroyed it in conducting some warlike operation, it would be contrary to all reason and justice to hold the owner of the reservoir liable for any damage that might be done by the escape of the water. We are of opinion therefore that the defendant was entitled to excuse herself by proving that the water escaped through the act of God.

Their Lordships are of opinion that all that is there laid down as to a case where the escape is due to "*vis major* or the King's enemies" applies equally to a case where it is due to the malicious act of a third person, if indeed that case is not actually included in the above phrase. To follow the language of the judgment just recited — a defendant cannot in their Lordships' opinion be properly said to have caused or allowed the water to escape if the malicious act of a third person was the real cause of its escaping without any fault on the part of the defendant. ...

But there is another ground upon which their Lordships are of opinion that the present case does not come within the principle laid down in *Fletcher v. Rylands*. It is not every use to which land is put that brings into play that principle. It must be some special use bringing with it increased danger to others, and must not merely be the ordinary use of the land or such a use as is proper for the general benefit of the community. ... This is more fully expressed by Wright J., in his judgment in *Blake v. Woolf*, [1898] 2 Q.B. 426. In that case the plaintiff was the occupier of the lower floors of the defendant's house, the upper floors being occupied by the defendant himself. A leak occurred in the cistern at the top of the house which without any negligence on the part of the defendant caused the plaintiffs premises to be flooded. In giving judgment for the defendant Wright J. says: "The general rule as laid down in *Rylands v. Fletcher* is that *prima facie* a person occupying land has an absolute right not to have his premises invaded by injurious matter, such as large quantities of water which his neighbours keep upon his land. That general rule is, however, qualified by some exceptions, one of which is that, where a person is using his land in the ordinary way and damage happens to the adjoining property without any default or negligence on his part, no liability attaches to him. The bringing of water on to such premises as these and the maintaining of a cistern in the usual way seems to me to be an ordinary and reasonable user of such premises as these were; and, therefore, if the water escapes without any negligence or default on the part of the person bringing the water in and owning the cistern, I do not think that he is liable for any damage that may ensue."

The provision of a proper supply of water to the various parts of a house is not only reasonable, but has become, in accordance with modern sanitary views, an almost necessary feature of town life. It is recognized as being so desirable in the interests of the community that in some form or other it is usually made obligatory in civilized countries. Such a supply cannot be installed without causing some concurrent danger of leakage or overflow. It would be unreasonable for the law to regard those who install or maintain such a system of supply as doing so at their own peril, with an absolute liability for any damage resulting from its presence even when there has been no negligence. It would be still more unreasonable if, as the respondent contends, such liability were to be held to extend to the consequences of malicious acts on the part of third persons. In such matters as the domestic supply of water or gas it is essential that the mode of supply should be such as to permit ready access for the purpose of use, and hence it is impossible to guard against wilful mischief. Taps may be turned on, ball-cocks fastened open, supply pipes cut, and waste-pipes blocked. Against such acts no precaution can prevail. It would be wholly unreasonable to hold an occupier responsible for the consequences of such acts which he is powerless to prevent, when the provision of the supply is not only a reasonable act on his part but probably a duty. Such a doctrine would, for example, make a householder liable for the consequences of an explosion caused by a burglar breaking into his house during the night and leaving a gas tap open. There is, in their Lordships' opinion, no support either in reason or authority for any such view of the liability of a landlord or occupier. In having on his premises such means of supply he is only using those premises in an ordinary and proper manner, and, although he is bound to exercise all reasonable care, he is not responsible for damage not due to his own default, whether that damage be caused by inevitable accident or the wrongful acts of third persons. ...

The appeal must therefore be allowed and judgment entered for the defendant in the action with costs in all the courts, and the plaintiff must pay the costs of this appeal, and their Lordships will humbly advise His Majesty accordingly.

NOTES

1. In *Tock v. St. John's Metro. Area Bd.*, [1989] 2 S.C.R. 1181, 1 C.C.L.T. (2d) 113, a storm sewer maintained by the defendant Board became obstructed during a heavy rainstorm. It overflowed and the basement of the plaintiff's house was flooded. One of the causes of action on which the plaintiff's claim was based was *Rylands v. Fletcher*. In rejecting this aspect of the plaintiff's action, La Forest J. stated, at 1189:

> The definitive statement of the meaning to be ascribed to Lord Cairn's qualification in *Rylands v. Fletcher*, at pp. 338-339 [L.R. 3 H.L.], that strict liability would only attach in respect of "non-natural user" of land is generally agreed

to be that of Moulton L.J. in *Rickards v. Lothian*, [1913] A.C. 263, at p. 280 [[1911-13] All E.R. Rep. 71]. Moulton L.J. thus expressed himself:

> It is not every use to which land is put that brings into play that principle. It must be some special use bringing with it increased danger to others, and must not merely be the ordinary use of the land or such a use as is proper for the general benefit of the community.

The courts, as noted by Fleming, *The Law of Torts*, 6th ed., [(Sydney, Aust.: Law Book, 1983)] at p. 308, have, on the basis of this qualification, interpreted the notion of non-natural user as a flexible concept that is capable of adjustment to the changing patterns of social existence.

In the evolution of the patterns of social existence since the formulation of the rule in *Rylands v. Fletcher*, one of the most salient developments has been the ever-increasing degree of involvement by all levels of government in land planning. The point is nicely put by Williams in his article, "Non-natural Use of Land" (1973) 32 Cambridge L.J. 310, at p. 319, when he argues that the existence of planning authorities which ensure that virtually all development of land occurs pursuant to planning decisions "puts the question of land use into a completely different context to that in which Messrs. Rylands and Horrocks built their little reservoir".

Public sewerage and drainage systems are an indispensable part of the infrastructure necessary to support urban life, and it is clear in my mind that the storm sewer in question here was constructed pursuant to planning decisions of the very sort alluded to in Williams' comments. As such, it would be difficult to conceive of a user of land falling more squarely within those that may be said to be ordinary and proper for the general benefit of the community; see the *obiter* remarks of Lord Denning to the same effect in *Pride of Derby and Derbyshire Angling Association Ltd. v. British Celanese Ld.*, [1953] Ch. 149, at p. 189 [[1953] 1 All E.R. 179 (C.A.)].

In summary, if, as argued by Prosser at p. 147 of his essay, "The Principle of *Rylands v. Fletcher*" in *Selected Topics on the Law of Torts* [(Buffalo: Hein & Co., 1982)], the touchstone for the application of the rule in *Rylands v. Fletcher* is to be damage occurring from a user inappropriate to the place where it is maintained (Prosser cites the example of the pig in the parlour), I would hold that the rule cannot be invoked where a municipality or regional authority, acting under the warrant of statute and pursuant to a planning decision taken in good faith, constructs and operates a sewer and storm drain system in a given locality.

What does this do to the utility of *Rylands v. Fletcher* as a principle of strict liability for dangerous or ultra-hazardous uses? If something is ordinary and proper for the general benefit of the community, but yet is dangerous, who should pay for the inevitable accident costs—the hapless individual victim or the community which benefits from the facility? Note that in *Cambridge Water Co. Ltd. v. Eastern Counties Leather plc*, [1994] 1 All E.R. 53, Lord Goff in *obiter* held that the storage of chemicals in substantial quantities and their use in an industrial process was not a natural use of land, even though the factory employed many persons in the community.

2. What if the sewage system is not a public one, but privately owned? Would *Tock* apply? See *Danku v. Town of Fort Frances* (1976), 14 O.R. (2d) 285, 73 D.L.R. (3d) 377 (Dist. Ct.), where a municipality was relieved of liability but not a trailer park whose private sewer system broke.

3. There are two possible ways of defining the non-natural use requirement. The first is to see any use which involves higher than normal risks of injury as non-natural. The

second is to require that a use be out of the ordinary, or unusual, to be non-natural. What approach was taken by the Supreme Court in *Tock*?

4. In *Mihalchuk v. Ratke* (1966), 57 D.L.R. (2d) 269, 55 W.W.R. 555 (Sask. Q.B.), the plaintiffs sued the defendants for damages to their crops caused by reason of the drift of herbicide. The defendants had been aerial spraying their land. In finding for the plaintiffs on the basis of *Rylands v. Fletcher*, the court emphasized that this type of aerial spraying was "an unusual operation. The neighbours gathered to watch." Evidently the usual method was boom-spraying behind a tractor. If aerial spraying was not unusual, would *Rylands v. Fletcher* have applied? See *Cruise v. Niessen*, [1977] 2 W.W.R. 481; revd [1978] 1 W.W.R. 688 (Man. C.A.); *cf.*, Solomon J. at 483, in [1977] 2 W.W.R., with Matas J.A. (dissenting) at 694 in [1978] 1 W.W.R.

5. There have been many cases which have adopted a strict liability approach due to the heightened danger presented by the activity in question. Cases involving damage caused by explosives, leaking gas, and fires are good examples of this approach. Even "innocent" objects, such as a flag-pole (*Shiffman v. Order of St. John*, [1936] 1 All E.R. 557, 80 Sol. Jo. 346 (K.B.)), Christmas decorations (*Saccardo v. Hamilton*, [1971] 2 O.R. 479, 18 D.L.R. (3d) 271 (Ont. H.C.J.)), and an advertising balloon (*Calgary (City) v. Yellow Submarine Deli Inc.* (1994), 158 A.R. 239 (Prov. Ct.)) have been held to be dangerous and, therefore, non-natural uses of land.

6. Some courts have rejected strict liability, even for dangerous activities, because the use was a normal, everyday use generally accepted by the community. See, for example, *St. Anne's Well Brewery Co. v. Roberts* (1928), 140 L.T. 1, 44 T.L.R. 703 (C.A.), where a falling brick wall did not give rise to strict liability since "One of the most normal uses of land … is to put buildings on it." Ordinary fires are also not subject to the principle of *Rylands v. Fletcher*.

7. In *Gertsen v. Municipality of Metropolitan Toronto et al.* (1974), 2 O.R. (2d) 1, 41 D.L.R. (3d) 646 (H.C.J.), the defendants used organic matter as land fill in a residential area. As it decomposed, it generated methane gas which escaped onto adjoining lands and into the plaintiff's garage. One day, when the plaintiff turned on the ignition of his car, an explosion occurred destroying the garage, damaging the car and injuring the plaintiff. Mr. Justice Lerner imposed liability on negligence, nuisance and strict liability theories. He explained that the gas was a "dangerous substance" which "escaped onto the plaintiff's land and caused them damage". Therefore, *prima facie*, liability should follow without proof of negligence. He went on to explain that if the

> potential source of mischief is an accepted incident of some ordinary purpose to which the land is reasonably applied by the occupier, the *prima facie* rule of absolute responsibility for the consequences of its escape must give way. In applying this qualification, the courts have looked not only to the thing or activity in isolation, but also to the place and manner in which it is maintained and its relation to the surroundings. Time, place and circumstance, not excluding purpose, are most material. The distinction between natural and non-natural use is both relative and capable of adjustment to the changing patterns of social existence.

In deciding whether the garbage fill was natural or non-natural use of land, Mr. Justice Lerner stressed that the purpose was "selfish and self-serving" and not justifiable on any "overriding public welfare theory" which was to the "general benefit of the community". In the light of the "time, place and circumstances and not excluding purpose", he held that the activity was a "non-natural use of the land". A similar approach was taken by Medhurst J. in *Wei's Western Wear Ltd. v. Yui Holdings Ltd.* (1984), 5 D.L.R. (4th) 681, 27 C.C.L.T. 292 (Alta. Q.B.), where he held that water being used for "commercial" purposes in a restaurant, that is a "profit-making undertaking", was a "special use ... with increased danger to others" and, hence, within *Rylands v. Fletcher.* See also *Danku v. Fort Frances* (1976), 14 O.R. (2d) 285, 73 D.L.R. (3d) 377 (Dist. Ct.); *Lyon v. Village of Shelburne; Triton Engineering Services Ltd. et al. (Third Parties)* (1981), 130 D.L.R. (3d) 307 (Ont. Co. Ct.) (sewage pipes are non-natural use of land).

8. The American Law Institute in its *Restatement of Torts, Second,* §519 provides:

> one who carries on an abnormally dangerous activity is subject to liability for harm to the person, land or chattels of another resulting from the activity, although he has exercised the utmost care to prevent the harm.

Section 520 lists the following six factors to be considered in determining whether the activity is "abnormally dangerous":

> In determining whether an activity is abnormally dangerous, the following factors are to be considered:
> (a) whether the activity involves a high degree of risk of some harm to the person, land or chattels of others;
> (b) whether the gravity of the harm which may result from it is likely to be great;
> (c) whether the risk cannot be eliminated by the exercise of reasonable care;
> (d) whether the activity is not a matter of common usage;
> (e) whether the activity is inappropriate to the place where it is carried on; and
> (f) the value of the activity to the community.

This is a change from the first *Restatement* which talked about "ultrahazardous activities" and not "abnormally dangerous" activities. Is this change significant? For a good discussion, see Nolan and Ursin, "The Revitalization of Hazardous Activity Strict Liability" (1986-87), 65 N.C.L. Rev. 257. For commentary on the first *Restatement,* see Ehrenzweig, "Negligence Without Fault" (1951), reprinted at (1966), 54 Calif. L. Rev. 1422.

9. The Pearson Commission suggested that strict liability should be imposed on the controllers of things and operations that are:

   (1) unusually hazardous things, like explosives and flammable liquids, or
   (2) things that pose a risk of serious and extensive casualties, like dams, bridges and stadiums.

The Commission proposed that a detailed list of the things and operations subject to strict liability be enacted in a statutory instrument so as to provide certainty as well as some flexibility. See *Report of the Royal Commission on Civil Liability and Compensation for Personal Injury* (1978).

LINDEN, "WHATEVER HAPPENED TO RYLANDS v. FLETCHER?"

in Klar (ed.), *Studies in Canadian Tort Law* (1977), p. 325.

Enough has been said to demonstrate that Canadian courts, in these strict liability cases, are concerned with more than non-natural use, mischief and escape as outlined in *Rylands v. Fletcher.* Although these phrases are still frequently employed in the cases, there are also references to increased danger or extra-hazardous activities, concepts that resemble the notions of abnormal danger and ultra-hazardous activities, embedded in the American jurisprudence. The latter concepts are a more appropriate foundation for strict liability today than the archaic language of *Rylands v. Fletcher*. They provide a better reason for adopting a different standard of care to regulate a particular group of activities.

Those who create extraordinary peril to society should be treated in an extraordinary way. Rather than being subject to negligence law, which applies to the ordinary risks of society, they should be subject to strict liability, which applies to dangers out of the ordinary. When it also appears that the activity is pursued for profit or for the purposes of the actor, it is hard to avoid the conclusion that liability should be strict. Further, when one realizes that such activities are usually, though not always, conducted by business enterprises or by governments who can well afford to furnish compensation for the victims of their actions, either directly or through insurance, the case for strict liability becomes unanswerable.

This philosophy of strict liability is consistent with the main purpose of tort law. Compensation, which remains the prime aim of tort law, is awarded to more victims under strict liability theory than under negligence theory. Deterrence is achieved because the enterpriser should exercise "super-care" in order to avoid being held strictly liable, rather than the ordinary care he would be required to exercise under the negligence standard. The educational aims of tort law are promoted by teaching society that certain types of activities, which are more perilous than others, labour under special responsibilities. Moreover, the psychological needs of the victims of these enterprises (and of society generally) are provided for by individual court actions that dramatize the "rights" and "wrongs" of this group of human encounters. Market deterrence, *a la* Calabresi, is achieved by forcing these enterprisers to pay all the costs of the accidents generated by their activities, whether or not they are negligently caused. Lastly, the ombudsman role of tort law is served by focussing attention on the kinds of things that may go wrong with these unique activities, fostering public re-assessment of the value of these pursuits and the way they are regulated.

Mr. Justice Windeyer of Australia has recognized what has become of *Rylands v. Fletcher*, and has suggested that, although strict liability was not "called into existence in 1866 for the purpose of ensuring that industrial enterprises make good the harm they do" that is the "socially beneficial result" of the doctrine today. His Lordship explained further:

> Actions for negligence dominate the work of common law courts today, mainly because railway trains, motor-cars and industrial machinery, have so large a place in men's lives. But to regard negligence as the normal requirement of responsibility in tort, and to look upon strict liability as anomalous and unjust, seems to me to mistake present values as well as past history. In an age when insurance against all forms of liability is commonplace, it is surely not surprising or unjust if law makes persons who carry on some kinds of hazardous undertakings liable for the harm they do, unless they can excuse or justify it on some recognized ground. That is, I think, the position today in the countries of the common law. In England, and in those countries which have the common law as it is in England, this comes about through the principle of *Rylands v. Fletcher*.

Such a view of *Rylands v. Fletcher* is full of potential for the future. It furnishes a solid basis for tort liability — that of strict liability — which can regulate certain types of abnormally hazardous activities, for which negligence law provides insufficient protection. The concept lies hidden in the cases, waiting to be discovered. It has survived for more than a century, and one could forecast that it will be alive, hopefully, in an altered form, a century from now. If it is reoriented in the way suggested, one could forecast that the future of *Rylands v. Fletcher* will be one of steady growth and continuing service to society, not one of decay and ultimate eclipse.

And that is what has happened to *Rylands v. Fletcher*.

---

2. Escape

READ v. J. LYONS & CO. LTD.

House of Lords. [1947] A.C. 156, [1946] 2 All E.R. 471.

The defendants operated, on behalf of the Ministry of Supply, a factory for the manufacture of high explosive shells. The plaintiff, under the National Service Acts, was directed by the Ministry, in whose employ she was considered to be, to work at the defendants' plant as an inspector in the filling of shells. In the course of her work an explosion took place seriously injuring the plaintiff. The latter sued, alleging no negligence, and based her claim on the ground that the defendants carried on the manufacture of shells which to their knowledge were dangerous things.

At the trial, [1944] 2 All E.R. 98, Cassels J. gave judgment for the plaintiff, holding that "defendants were under a strict liability to the plaintiff … and it was unnecessary to aver negligence because they were dealing with dangerous things which got out of control and did damage to the plaintiff". He held that liability for damage arising from dangerous animals was merely an instance of strict liability of *Rylands v. Fletcher* and that escape from defendants' premises was unnecessary to the general principle. The defendants appealed.

In the Court of Appeal, [1945] K.B. 216, [1945] 1 All E.R. 106, the judgment was reversed and the action dismissed. Scott L.J. delivered an elaborate judgment in which he refuted the argument that the American Law Institute's *Restatement of Tort*, ss. 519-20 (defining "ultrahazardous activities" and recognizing a liability for harm caused to "person, land or chattels" by such "activity") represented English law. He held that the principle of *Rylands v. Fletcher*, in common with cattle-trespass and nuisance, involved "interference with an existing proprietary right of the plaintiff". "The vital feature in *Rylands v. Fletcher* … was the defendant's interference with the plaintiff's right to enjoy his land without interference by the defendant." Du Parq L.J. said that the "mediaeval principle" of *Rylands v. Fletcher* was not to be extended; that in the dangerous animal cases it was "more accurate to speak of presumed negligence", and the present case was one which depended on the rules governing an occupier's liability to persons coming on the premises. The plaintiff appealed to the House of Lords.

Viscount Simon L.C.: … The classic judgment of Blackburn J., besides deciding the issue before the court and laying down the principle of duty between neighbouring occupiers of land on which the decision was based, sought to group under a single and wider proposition other instances in which liability is independent of negligence, such, for example, as liability for the bite of a defendant's monkey. See also the case of a bear on a chain on the defendant's premises. There are instances, no doubt, in our law in which liability for damage may be established apart from proof of negligence, but it appears to me logically unnecessary and historically incorrect to refer to all these instances as deduced from one common principle. …

Now, the strict liability recognized by this House to exist in *Rylands v. Fletcher* is conditioned by two elements which I may call the condition of "escape" from the land of something likely to do mischief if it escapes, and the condition of "non-natural use" of the land. This second condition has in some later cases, which did not reach this House, been otherwise expressed, *e.g.*, as "exceptional" user, when such user is not regarded as "natural" and at the same time is likely to produce mischief if there is an "escape". Dr. Stallybrass, in a learned article in 3 Cambridge Law Review, p. 376, has collected the large variety of epithets that have been judicially employed in this connection. The American *Restatement of the Law of Torts, III*, s. 519, speaks of "ultrahazardous activity", but attaches qualifications which would appear in the present instance to exonerate the respondents. It is not necessary to analyse this second condition on the present occasion, for in the case now before us the first essential condition of "escape" does not seem to me to be present at all. "Escape", for the purpose of applying the proposition in *Rylands v. Fletcher*, means escape from a place which the defendant has occupation of, or control over, to a place which is outside his occupation or control. ...

In these circumstances it becomes unnecessary to consider other objections that have been raised, such as the question of whether the doctrine of *Rylands v. Fletcher* applies where the claim is for damages for personal injury as distinguished from damages to property. ... On the much litigated question of what amounts to "non-natural" use of land, the discussion of which is also unnecessary in the present appeal, I content myself with two further observations. The first is that when it becomes essential for the House to examine this question it will, I think, be found that Lord Moulton's analysis in delivering the judgment of the Privy Council in *Rickards v. Lothian* is of the first importance. The other observation is as to the decision of this House in *Rainham Chemical Works, Ltd. v. Belvedere Fish Guano Co.*, [1921] 2 A.C. 465, to which the appellant's counsel in the present case made considerable reference in support of the proposition that manufacturing explosives was a "non-natural" use of land.

I think it not improper to put on record, with all due regard to the admission and *dicta* in that case, that if the question had hereafter to be decided whether the making of munitions in a factory at the government's request in time of war for the purpose of helping to defeat the enemy is a "non-natural" use of land, adopted by the occupier "for his own purposes", it would not seem to me that the House would be bound by this authority to say that it was. In this appeal the question is immaterial, as I hold that the appellant fails for the reason that there was no "escape" from the respondents' factory. I move that the appeal be dismissed with costs.

Lord Macmillan: ... In my opinion, the appellant's statement of claim discloses no ground of action against the respondents. The action is one of damages for personal injuries. Whatever may have been the law of England in early times I am of opinion that, as the law now stands, an allegation of negligence is in general essential to the relevancy of an action of reparation for personal injuries.

The process of evolution has been from the principle that every man acts at his peril and is liable for all the consequences of his acts to the principle that a man's freedom of action is subject only to the obligation not to infringe any duty of care which he owes to others. The emphasis formerly was on the injury sustained and the question was whether the case fell within one of the accepted classes of common law actions; the emphasis now is on the conduct of the person whose act has occasioned the injury and the question is whether it can be characterized as negligent. I do not overlook the fact that there is at least one instance in the present law in which the primitive rule survives, namely in the case of animals *ferae naturae* or animals *mansuetae naturae* which have shown dangerous proclivities. The owner or keeper of such an animal has an absolute duty to confine or control it so that it shall not do injury to others and no proof of care on his part will absolve him from responsibility, but this is probably not so much a vestigial relic of otherwise discarded doctrine as a special rule of practical good sense. At any rate, it is too well established to be challenged. But such an exceptional case as this affords no justification for its extension by analogy. ...

The doctrine of *Rylands v. Fletcher*, as I understand it, derives from a conception of the mutual duties of adjoining or neighbouring landowners and its congeners are trespass and nuisance. If its foundation is to be found in the injunction *sic utere tuo ut alienum non laedas*, then it is manifest that it has nothing to do with personal injuries. The duty is to refrain from injuring not *alium* but *alienum*. The two prerequisites of the doctrine are that there must be the escape of something from one man's close to another man's close and that which escapes must have been brought on the land from which it escapes in consequences of some non-natural use of that land, whatever precisely that may mean. Neither of these features exists in the present case. I have already pointed out that nothing escaped from the defendants' premises, and, were it necessary to decide the point, I should hesitate to hold that in these days and in an industrial community it was a non-natural use of land to build a factory on it and conduct there the manufacture of explosives. I could conceive it being said that to carry on the manufacture of explosives in a crowded urban area was evidence of negligence, but there is no such case here and I offer no opinion on the point.

Your Lordships' task in this House is to decide particular cases between litigants and your Lordships are not called on to rationalize the law of England. That attractive, if perilous, field may well be left to other hands to cultivate. In has been necessary in the present instance to examine certain general principles advanced on behalf of the appellant because it was said that consistency required that these principles should be applied to the case in hand. Arguments based on legal consistency are apt to mislead, for the common law is a practical code adapted to deal with the manifold diversities of human life and as a great American judge has reminded us "the life of the law has not been logic: it has been experience". For myself, I am content to say that, in my opinion, no authority has been quoted from case or text-book which would justify your Lordships, logically or otherwise, in giving effect to the appellant's plea. I should, accordingly, dismiss the appeal.

Lord Porter: ... Normally at the present time in an action of tort for personal injuries if there is no negligence there is no liability. To this rule, however, the appellant contends that there are certain exceptions, one of the best known of which is to be found under the principle laid down in *Rylands v. Fletcher*. ... To make the rule applicable, it is at least necessary for the person whom it is sought to hold liable to have brought on to his premises, or, at any rate, to some place over which he has a measure of control, something which is dangerous in the sense that, if it escapes, it will do damage. Possibly a further requisite is that to bring the thing to the position in which it is found is to make a non-natural use of that place. Such at any rate, appears to have been the opinion of Lord Cairns, and this limitation has more than once been repeated and approved. ...

In all cases which have been decided, it has been held necessary, to establish liability, that there should have been some form of escape from the place in which the dangerous object has been retained by the defendant to some other place not subject to his control. ... It was urged on your Lordships that it would be a strange result to hold the respondents liable if the injured person was just outside their premises but not liable if she was just within them. There is force in the objection, but the liability is itself an extension of the general rule, and, in my view, it is undesirable to extend it further. …

I would add that, in considering the matter now in issue before your Lordships, it is not, in my view, necessary to determine whether injury to the person is one of those matters in respect of which damages can be recovered under the rule. Atkinson J. thought it was: *Shiffman v. Order of St. John*, [1936] 1 All E.R. 557, and the language of Fletcher Moulton L.J. in *Wing v. L.G.O. Co.*, [1909] 2 K.B. 652. … is to the same effect, and … in *Miles v. Forest Rock Granite Co. Ltd.*, 34 T.L.R. 500, the Court of Appeal applied the rule in *Rylands v. Fletcher* in support of a judgment in favour of the plaintiff in respect of personal injuries. Undoubtedly, the opinions expressed in these cases extend the application of the rule and may some day require examination. For the moment it is sufficient to say that there must be escape from a place over which a defendant has some measure of control to a place where he has not. In the present case there was no such escape and I would dismiss the appeal.

[Concurring opinions were also given by **Lord Simonds** and **Lord Uthwatt**.]

NOTES

1. What did the House of Lords actually decide in *Read v. Lyons*?

2. Does the requirement of escape make any sense? Can you think of any policy reasons in support of it? What can be said against the requirement? See *Musgrove v. Pandelis*, [1919] 2 K.B. 43, 88 L.J.K.B. 915 (C.A.); *Attorney-General for Canada v. Diamond Waterproofing Ltd.* (1974), 4 O.R. (2d) 489 (C.A.), *per* Schroeder J.A. See also Linden, "Whatever Happened to *Rylands v. Fletcher*?" in Klar (ed.), *Studies in Canadian Tort Law* (1977), where at 334, this appears:

   > This requirement of escape makes little sense. Where two people are injured by the same type of conduct, their tort recovery should not depend on whether they were on the land or off the land upon which the activity was conducted. Such distinctions are ludicrous. Indeed, it might be argued that a preferable differentiation, if one were required, would allow the person on the land to recover but deny compensation to the person off the land. A more rational treatment, however, would be to ignore the escape limitation, as the Americans have done.

3. Did the House of Lords actually decide that there could never be any liability for personal injuries under *Rylands v. Fletcher*? Are the statements to this effect binding on the English courts? Are they binding on the Canadian courts? In *Perry v. Kendricks Transport Ltd.*, [1956] 1 All E.R. 154, [1956] 1 W.L.R. 85, at 92, Lord Justice Parker stated:

   > I feel bound to approach the matter upon the basis that the facts here bring the case within the rule in *Rylands v. Fletcher*: nor do I think it is open to this court to hold that the rule only applies to damage to adjoining land or to a proprietary interest in land and not to personal injury. It is true that in *Read v. Lyons & Co. Ltd.*, Lord MacMillan, Lord Porter and Lord Simonds all doubted whether the rule extended to cover personal injuries, but the final decision in the matter was expressly left over, and as the matter stands at present, I think we are bound to hold that the defendants are liable in this case, quite apart

> from negligence, unless they can bring themselves within one of the well-known exceptions to the rule.

See also *Benning v. Wong* (1969), 122 C.L.R. 249, where Barwick C.J. said:

> Personal injuries sustained by reason of the escape to the plaintiff's land of a dangerous thing or substance brought to land by a defendant are, in my opinion, to be included in the damages caused by such escape.

4. If one sees the principle of *Rylands v. Fletcher* to be historically nothing more than a simple case of nuisance, as has been suggested by some authors and judges, then the escape requirement makes perfectly good sense. As will be seen, nuisance regulates the conflicting uses of land and has little to do with personal injuries caused by accidents. If, however, we see in *Rylands v. Fletcher* a principle of strict liability for ultrahazardous activities, then the requirement of escape is meaningless. Which view of *Rylands v. Fletcher* seems to prevail in Canadian tort law? Is the problem that Canadian tort law has not yet made up its mind what it wants to do with *Rylands v. Fletcher*? See, for example, *Deyo v. Kingston Speedway Ltd.*, [1954] O.R. 223, [1954] 2 D.L.R. 419; affd [1955] 1 D.L.R. 718 (S.C.C.), where a *Rylands v. Fletcher* action for personal injuries was dismissed, partly because there was no escape from the lands occupied by and under the control of the respondent corporation.

5. The House of Lords revisited the rule in *Rylands v. Fletcher* in their recent decision in *Cambridge Water Co. Ltd. v. Eastern Counties Leather plc.*, [1994] 1 All E.R. 53. The action concerned the leakage of a solvent from the defendant's tannery operations. The solvent contaminated the plaintiff's water supply, over a mile away. Lord Goff held that in order for their to be liability under *Rylands v. Fletcher* the damage which occurred must have been foreseeable. This requirement of foreseeability derives from the law of nuisance, which has a close historical connection to the rule in *Rylands*. Lord Goff favoured the view of Newark, in his article "The Boundaries of Nuisance" (1949), 65 L.Q. Rev. 480, that "the rule in *Rylands v. Fletcher* was essentially concerned with an extension of the law of nuisance to cases of isolated escape". Lord Goff rejected the view that the rule in *Rylands* should be seen as developing a principle of strict liability from which can be derived a general rule of strict liability for damage caused by ultra-hazardous operations. This development was, for one thing, precluded by the escape requirement of the rule in *Rylands*. In respect to the non-natural use requirement, while Lord Goff conceded that the concept of what is a non-natural use of land has retracted in the years to exclude "ordinary" uses, he held that the storage of substantial quantities of chemicals in industrial premises should be regarded as an almost "classic case" of non-natural use. However, since the damage caused in this case was not foreseeable, the action was dismissed.

   Has this decision now firmly closed the door to the development of a principle of strict liability for ultra-hazardous activities in English tort law?

6. The Australian High Court carefully reviewed the rule in *Rylands v. Fletcher* in *Burnie v. Port Authority* (1994), 68 A.L.J.R. 331. The case concerned the destruction of the respondent's property which had been stored in a building owned by the appellant. The building was itself destroyed by fire. The Court noted the uncertainty concerning the requirements for the rule's application and the growth of negligence law in the century and a quarter since the rule was first enunciated. This led the Court to conclude, subject only to the qualification that there still may be scope for the rule as an action for nuisance, that "the rule in *Rylands v. Fletcher*, with all its difficulties, uncertainties, qualifications and exceptions, should now be seen, for the purposes of the common law of this country, as absorbed by the principles of ordinary negligence. Under those principles, a person who takes advantage of his or her control of premises to introduce a dangerous substance, to carry on a dangerous activity, or to allow another one to do one of these things, owes a duty of reasonable care to avoid a reasonably

foreseeable risk of injury or damage to the person or property of another. In a case where the person or property of the other person is lawfully in a place outside the premises that duty of care both varies in degree according to the magnitude of the risk involved and extends to ensuring that such care is taken." (At p. 349).

Now that the rule in *Rylands v. Fletcher* has been weakened in England, and virtually eliminated in Australia, being seen as not having any function not otherwise provided by negligence or nuisance law, do you think that the Canadian Supreme Court should adopt the same approach?

7. In *Aldridge v. Van Patter, Martin, and Western Fair Assoc.*, [1952] O.R. 595, [1952] 4 D.L.R. 93, the defendant, Western Fair, was in occupation of a park on which there was a grandstand and race-track. For a fee, it licensed the defendant, Wilmer, to conduct stock-car racing on the race-track. A car driven by the defendant, Van Patter, while engaged in racing, crashed through a rail fence and injured the two plaintiffs who were in the park and proceeding to a wicket to buy a ticket to see the races. In an action against the three defendants for damages, Spence J. held: (1) Wilmer and Western Fair liable under the principle of *Rylands v. Fletcher*. Despite Lord Macmillan's dictum, in *Read v. Lyons*, this doctrine extended to personal damages sustained "by anyone to whom the probability of such damage would naturally be foreseen"; (2) Wilmer and Western Fair liable in nuisance; and (3) all three defendants liable for negligence. See also *Hale v. Jennings Brothers, infra*.

8. In *Charing Cross Electricity Supply Co. v. Hydraulic Power Co.*, [1914] 3 K.B. 772, [1914-15] All E.R. Rep 85 (C.A.), the defendant's hydraulic mains, laid under a public street, burst and damaged the plaintiff's cables, also laid under the street. The defendant was held liable. See Lord Sumner at 779:

> I think that this present case is also indistinguishable from *Rylands v. Fletcher*. Two grounds of distinction have been suggested. It is said that the doctrine of *Rylands v. Fletcher* is applicable between the owners of adjacent closes, which are adjacent whether there be any intermediate property or not; and that it is a doctrine depending upon the ownership of land and the rights attaching to the ownership of land, under which violations of that species of right can be prevented or punished. In the present case, instead of having two adjacent owners of real property, you have only two neighbouring owners, not strictly adjacent, of chattels, whose chattels are there under a permission which might have been obtained by the private licence of the owners of the soil, though in fact obtained under Parliamentary powers; hence the two companies are in the position of co-users of a highway or at any rate of co-users of different rooms in one house, and *Rylands v. Fletcher* does not apply. The case depends on doctrines applicable to the highways, or houses let out in tenements. I am unable to agree with any of these distinctions, though they have been pressed upon us by both learned counsel with great resource and command of the authorities. *Midwood v. Manchester Corporation*, [1905] K.B. 597, is not decided as a case of a dispute arising between the owners of two adjacent closes. The case is treated as one between a corporation, whose business under the roadway is exactly similar to that of the defendant corporation here, and injured occupiers of the premises. If the distinction drawn between the present case and that of adjacent landowners in *Rylands v. Fletcher* be a good one, it either was not taken in *Midwood v. Manchester Corporation*, or was taken and treated as of no importance. Further I am satisfied that *Rylands v. Fletcher* is not limited to the case of adjacent free-holders, I shall not attempt to shew how far it extends. It extends as far as this case, and that is enough for the present purposes.

9. In *Dokuchia v. Domansch*, [1945] O.R. 141, [1945] 1 D.L.R. 757 (C.A.), the plaintiff was riding in a truck with the defendant. The truck stalled and the defendant had the

plaintiff lie on the fender and pour gasoline into the carburettor. After the truck was driven a short distance an explosion occurred. The plaintiff was thrown off the truck and the truck ran over him. In an action for damages the plaintiff obtained a judgment based on an assessment of comparative fault, 20 per cent to the plaintiff, 80 per cent to the defendant. On appeal this judgment was upheld. Laidlaw J.A. affirmed the judgment on the ground that the handling of gasoline involved the principle of *Rylands v. Fletcher*. The rule was not confined to landowners but made the owner of a dangerous thing liable for "any mischief thereby occasioned; and it was immaterial whether damage be caused on or off the defendant's premises."

10. In *Ekstrom v. Deagon and Montgomery*, [1946] 1 D.L.R. 208, [1945] 2 W.W.R. 385 (Alta. S.C.), the defendant had his stalled truck towed to the front of the plaintiff's garage where he began to look for the trouble. He obtained the plaintiff's permission to use an electric light on the end of an extension cord. While draining his fuel tank the fumes took fire and the plaintiff's garage was burned. Parke J. held the defendant liable without proof of negligence. This was not a natural use of the garage premises by the defendant even though the plaintiff might conceivably have done exactly the same thing on his own premises. "If a person brings on his own land a dangerous substance which escapes and injury results to another and for which he thus becomes liable, how much more so would a person who takes a dangerous article on another person's property and causes damage to the latter be liable?" See also *Crown Diamond Paint Co. Ltd. v. Acadia Holding Realty Ltd.*, [1952] 2 S.C.R. 161, [1952] 2 D.L.R. 541; *Jackson v. Drury Construction* (1974), 4 O.R. (2d) 735 (C.A.).

11. Does *Rylands v. Fletcher* apply if the offensive substance did not escape accidentally but was intentionally discharged? In *North York (Municipality) v. Kert Chemical Industries Inc.* (1985), 33 C.C.L.T. 184 (Ont. S.C.), a case which involved the deliberate discharge of acidic wastes into a sewer system, Mr. Justice Krever suggested that *Rylands v. Fletcher* "may not be entirely appropriate for a case in which the discharges of the offending substances were intentional". In an English case, *Rigby v. Chief Constable of Northamptonshire*, [1985] 2 All E.R. 985, [1985] 1 W.L.R. 1242 (Q.B.), a fire was started when a police officer deliberately fired a gas cannister into a shop in order to flush out a person who was hiding there. In considering whether *Rylands v. Fletcher* applied, the court had to consider two issues. First, was it necessary that the substance escaped from the defendant's land onto the plaintiff's land? In answer to this, Taylor J. stated:

> I can see no difference in principle between allowing a man-eating tiger to escape from your land onto that of another and allowing it to escape from the back of your wagon parked on the highway.

In terms of the issue of intentional as opposed to accidental discharge, the court was inclined to agree with the defendant's argument that an accidental escape was required. Do you agree? Should a defendant be able to avoid strict liability by arguing that he or she intentionally discharged the offensive substance? What tort would apply to the deliberate discharge of an offensive object?

B. DEFENCES

PETERS v. PRINCE OF WALES THEATRE (BIRMINGHAM) LTD.

Court of Appeal. [1943] K.B. 73, [1942] 2 All E.R. 533.

The defendants leased to the plaintiff a shop in a building which contained a theatre and, over the plaintiff's shop, a rehearsal room. In the latter, at the time the lease was granted, there was, to the plaintiff's knowledge, a sprinkler system installed as a precaution against fire. The system extended to the plaintiff's shop. During a thaw, following a severe frost, water from the sprinklers in the defendant's rehearsal room damaged the plaintiff's stock. The plaintiff brought action claiming (a) negligence and (b) liability under *Rylands v. Fletcher*. At the trial negligence was negatived but the plaintiff obtained judgment on the latter ground. The defendants appealed.

The judgment of the court (**Scott, MacKinnon** and **Goddard L.JJ.**) was read by **Goddard L.J.** [The court agreed with the finding that the defendant had not been negligent.]

... This is not a case of the escape of water brought on the premises merely for domestic purposes, and the sprinkler system cannot be treated as analogous to ordinary water-closets, lavatories and baths. It is a system in which there is potential danger of the escape of an enormous quantity of water. Accordingly [the trial judge] held that the case was not within the exception to the rule which has been established by a series of cases of which ... *Rickards v. Lothian* [is] perhaps the leading example. ...

Carstairs v. Tallor (1871), L.R. 6 Exch. 217, established the first exception to *Rylands v. Fletcher*. The plaintiff occupied the ground floor of a warehouse and the defendant, from whom he hired it, occupied the upper floor. Rain water percolated into the plaintiff's floor owing to the guttering being rendered defective by rats, but no negligence was found. It was held that the plaintiff had no cause of action. Kelly C.B. put his judgment on the ground of *vis major*. Bramwell B. with whom Pigott B. concurred, relied on the roof being for the common protection of both plaintiff and defendant and the collection of water running from it was for their joint benefit. The decision of Martin B. was that one who takes a floor in a house must be held to take the premises as they are and cannot complain that the house was not constructed differently. ...

We agree with the criticism of Hallet J. of the passage in Charlesworth's *Law of Negligence*, p. 552, where it is stated that "Water brought on the premises for business purposes, as opposed to domestic purposes gives rise to the liability in *Rylands v. Fletcher*, whether or not there is negligence." That is too wide a statement. It is not the purpose to which the water is being put which is decisive. It is that the plaintiff takes the premises as they are, and, accordingly, consents to the presence there of the installed water system with all its advantages and disadvantages.

Applying the principles which we have endeavoured to deduce from the authorities to the present case, the plaintiff took a lease from theatre proprietors of part of the building in which they carried on their theatre. When he took it the sprinkler system was installed and he knew of it. It is not to be supposed that the defendants would have consented to have let to him had he stipulated for the removal of that system. He took the place as he found it for better or worse. Indeed, if common benefit be the material consideration, although, in our opinion, it is not, considering that theatres are generally regarded as buildings exposed to more than ordinary risk of fire, it may well be for the benefit of tenants in the building that the most effective apparatus should exist for dealing with this danger. It is, however, on the implied consent of the plaintiff to the presence of this installation that we base our decision that the doctrine of *Rylands v. Fletcher* does not apply. The appeal must be allowed, and judgment entered for the defendants.

NOTES

1. In *Holinaty v. Hawkins*, [1966] 1 O.R. 9, 52 D.L.R. (2d) 289 (C.A.), the plaintiff, owner of a garage, entered into a contract with the defendant company to remove existing underground tanks and to replace them with larger tanks. The defendant company entered into a subcontract with Hawkins to do the excavation work which all parties knew would involve the use of dynamite. As a result of blasting, the plaintiff's building was damaged. In an action for damages against the company and Hawkins, the trial judge held that *Rylands v. Fletcher* was inapplicable since the plaintiff had consented to the use of dynamite. On appeal this was reversed, "While … the plaintiff consented … to the use of dynamite … [he did not] consent to its improper or excessive use, [nor did he] knowingly and willingly assume the risk of loss or damage which would flow from such use." The court also found Hawkins negligent and the company liable for the negligence of its independent contractor in the use of a "dangerous thing". Compare with *Gilson v. Kerrier R.D.C.*, [1976] 1 W.L.R. 904, [1976] 3 All E.R. 343 (C.A.).

2. In *Federic v. Perpetual Investments Ltd. et al.*, [1969] 1 O.R. 186, 2 D.L.R. (3d) 50 (H.C.), carbon monoxide gas escaped from the landlord's garage up into the apartment of his tenant, causing her to suffer chronic carbon monoxide poisoning. The landlord relied mainly on the defence of "caveat lessee". Stark J. pointed out that the problem here was not with the demised premises that were defective but the penetration of the gas from outside, and explained:

> In the particular facts of this case, however, in my view liability does rest upon the landlord for two very different reasons, both of which properly emerge from the plaintiff's pleading. In the first place, it must be borne in mind that there was nothing inherently defective in the premises occupied by this tenant. The injuries arose because the landlord in conducting his garage undertaking on his own premises directly below the tenant, failed to keep within the bounds of this neighbouring property the dangerous gaseous fumes. Thus, it appears to me that the rule in *Fletcher v. Rylands* (1866), L.R. 1 Ex. 265, is applicable. In *Salmond on Torts*, 14th ed., p. 441, the rule formulated thus:
>
>> The occupier of land who brings and keeps upon it anything likely to do damage if it escapes is bound at his peril to prevent its escape, and is liable for all the direct consequences of its escape, even if he has been guilty of no negligence.
>
> *A fortiori*, it would seem that he should be liable if his negligence in failing to close and seal openings to the plaintiff's apartment directly above his garage undertaking permitted easy ingress for the gaseous fumes. …

The landlord was also held liable in negligence and for breach of the covenant of quiet enjoyment.

3. In *Pattison v. Prince Edward Region Conservation Authority* (1988), 27 O.A.C. 174, 45 C.C.L.T. 162 (C.A.), the plaintiffs, along with other cottage owners, were asked to sign an agreement with the defendant authority prior to the construction of a dam to stabilize the water level of the lake. The agreement noted that the plaintiffs' property was "affected by the flooding rights which go with the dam". When the plaintiffs' land was flooded 12 years after the dam's construction, the courts interpreted the agreement as a "consent" to the flooding and dismissed the plaintiffs' action which was based both on strict liability and nuisance.

HALE v. JENNINGS BROTHERS

Court of Appeal. [1938] 1 All E.R. 579, 82 Sol. Jo. 193.

The plaintiff was the owner of a shooting-gallery on ground leased from the defendants for that purpose. The defendants occupied the adjoining ground on which they erected, as amusement proprietors, a chair-o-plane — a contrivance that whirled customers around in attached chairs at a considerable rate of speed. While a patron, Crampton, was riding in a chair and fooling about in it, the chair came loose and struck and injured the plaintiff. In an action for damages, evidence showed that the chairs and equipment were properly made and maintained and that the defendants had done everything possible to stop this particular patron from fooling with the mechanism. The trial judge found the defendants were not negligent and dismissed the action on the ground that *Rylands v. Fletcher* did not apply, since although "the chair-o-plane was something of an unusual danger" it "was not essentially dangerous in itself. It is dangerous ... only if it is not in a proper state of repair, or if passengers on it behave recklessly." The plaintiff appealed.

Scott L.J.: ... The behaviour of Crampton in causing the chair to become detached, was in my view just the kind of behaviour which ought to have been anticipated as being a likely act with a per centage of users of the apparatus. People go there in a spirit of fun. Many of them are ignorant, and many of them are wholly unaware of the dangers incidental to playing with the chairs in that sort of way, and they cause a danger that they do not in the least realize. That kind of accident does not come within the exceptions to the rule at all. The apparatus is dangerous within the meaning of the rule because it is intended to be used by that sort of person; and is likely to produce this very danger. I consider that the rule in *Rylands v. Fletcher* applies to the facts of this case because the apparatus was set up by the defendants for the purpose of profit. It was a non-natural user of the land. It was inherently dangerous, and the defendants have to take the risk of any damage which may result from it. For these reasons, I think that the judgment of the county court judge should be reversed.

[The judgments of **Slesser** and **Clauson L.JJ.** to the same effect are omitted.]

NOTES

1. Why did the court not dismiss the case on the basis of the conduct of the third person, as in *Rickards v. Lothian*? Is the reasoning of the court on this point familiar?

2. In *Perry v. Kendricks Transport Ltd.*, [1956] 1 W.L.R. 85, [1956] 1 All E.R. 154 (C.A.), the defendants had parked on their parking area a disused coach from which the petrol had been drained and a cap screwed over the entrance pipe. The plaintiff, a boy of ten, was injured by an explosion of petrol fumes from this coach as he approached the parking area. In an action for damages, the trial judge found that the cap had been removed by some unknown person and that a lighted match had been thrown into the tank by one of two boys who hurried away as the plaintiff approached. He dismissed the action. On appeal, the court held that the case was within *Rylands v. Fletcher*, but the defendants were not liable since the escape was caused by the act of a stranger. It was argued that the act of a young child could not be a *novus actus interveniens*. The court held that if the act causing the escape was one which could not rea-

sonably have been anticipated and was one over which the defendants had no control, then the real cause of the escape was not due to the defendants' action in having the dangerous thing on its premises, nor of any failure on its part to keep the thing, nor to any latent or patent defect in protective measures. "The real cause is the act of the stranger, for whose acts the occupier of the land is in no sense responsible, because he cannot control them."

3. What is an "act of God"? In *Seneka v. Leduc* (1985), 59 A.R. 284 (Q.B.), an act of God was said to contain three elements:

   (1) it must be due to natural causes exclusively;
   (2) it must be of an extraordinary nature;
   (3) it cannot be anticipated or provided against.

   Is a heavy rainstorm an "act of God"? Compare *Seneka v. Leduc*, *supra*, with *Metson v. R. W. De Wolfe Ltd* (1980), 117 D.L.R. (3d) 278, 14 C.C.L.T. 216 (N.S.S.C.).

NORTH WESTERN UTILITIES, LTD. v. LONDON GUARANTEE & ACCIDENT CO. LTD.

Privy Council. [1936] A.C. 108, 105 L.J.P.C. 18.

The defendant maintained, pursuant to statute, a 12-inch gas main some 3½ feet below the surface of the street in Edmonton. The municipality in constructing a storm sewer immediately beneath the defendant's main had weakened the latter so that it sagged and finally sprung a leak. A year later gas from this main percolated through the soil and entered the plaintiff's building, where it caught fire and destroyed the building. An action for damages against the defendant was dismissed at the trial, but on appeal to the Supreme Court of Alberta judgment, for damages to be assessed, was entered for the plaintiff. The defendant appealed to the Judicial Committee of the Privy Council.

Lord Wright M.R.: ... That gas is a dangerous thing within the rules applicable to things dangerous in themselves is beyond question. Thus the appellants who are carrying in their mains the inflammable and explosive gas are *prima facie* within the principle of *Rylands v. Fletcher*: that is to say, that though they are doing nothing wrongful in carrying the dangerous thing so long as they keep it in their pipes, they come *prima facie* within the rules of strict liability if the gas escapes; the gas constitutes an extraordinary danger created by the appellants for their own purposes, and the rule established by *Rylands v. Fletcher* requires that they act at their peril and must pay for damage caused by the gas if it escapes, even without any negligence on their part. The rule is not limited to cases where the defendant has been carrying or accumulating the dangerous thing on his own land; it applies equally in a case like the present where the appellants were carrying the gas in mains laid in the property of the City (that is in the sub-soil) in exercise of a franchise to do so: *Charing Cross Electricity Supply v. Hydraulic Power Co.*, [1914] 3 K.B. 772.

This form of liability is in many ways analogous to a liability for nuisance, though nuisance is not only different in its historical origin but in its legal character and many of its incidents and applications. But the two causes of action often overlap, and in respect of each of these causes of action the rule of strict liability has been modified by admitting as a defence that what was being done was properly done in pursuance of statutory powers, and the mischief that has happened has not been brought about by any negligence on the part of the undertakers. As an illustration of this well known doctrine, reference may be made to *Green v. Chelsea Waterworks Co.*, 70 L.T. 547, 549, where Lindley L.J. said of *Rylands v.*

Fletcher: "That case is not to be extended beyond the legitimate principle on which the House of Lords decided it. If it were extended as far as strict logic might require, it would be a very oppressive decision." By the same reasoning the rule has been held inapplicable where the casualty is due to an act of God; or to the independent or conscious volition of a third party, as in *Box v. Jubb*, 4 Ex. D. 76, which was approved by the Judicial Committee in *Rickards v. Lothian*; and not to any negligence of the defendants. In *Box v. Jubb* the act which caused the escape of the water was a malicious (which their Lordships think means no more than conscious or deliberate) act of a third person. It was said by Kelly C.B.: "I think the defendants could not possibly have been expected to anticipate that which happened here, and the law does not require them to construct their reservoir and the sluices and gates leading to it to meet any amount of pressure which the wrongful act of a third person may impose." ...

It is not here intended to enumerate all the defences which might be available to a defendant in this class of action: but the two defences mentioned are both material in this case. ...

Where undertakers are acting under statutory powers it is a question of construction, depending on the language of the statute, whether they are only liable for negligence or whether they remain subject to the strict and unqualified rule of *Ryland v. Fletcher*. Thus in *Charing Cross Electricity Supply Co. v. Hydraulic Power Co.*, it was held (following the previous decision in *Midwood & Co. v. Manchester Corporation*, [1905] 2 K.B. 597) that the defence of statutory authority was limited by a clause in the statutory Order providing that nothing therein should exonerate the Corporation from liability for nuisance. In *Hammond v. St. Pancras Vestry*, L.R. 9 C.P. 316, where the Act imposed on the Vestry the duty of properly cleansing their sewers, it held that as these words were susceptible of meaning either that an absolute duty was imposed or that the duty was only to exercise due and reasonable care, the latter meaning was to be preferred, since the absolute duty could not be held to be imposed save by clear words. That case was followed in Stretton's *Derby Brewery Co. v. Mayor of Derby*, [1894] 1 Ch. 431.

It accordingly now becomes necessary to consider the meaning of ss. 11 and 13 of the Alberta Water, Gas, Electric and Telephone Company Act, cited above. ... [It was found that the Act did not impose an absolute duty to maintain.] But in any event, the question is not eventually material in this case, for, even if the section applies to maintenance, and is absolute in its terms, the duty it imposes is still no more than the duty under the rule in *Rylands v. Fletcher*, according to which the appellants would not be liable for damage caused, without default on their part, by the independent act of a third party. Then, whether or not s. 13 applies to maintenance, and whether or not it imposes, where it does apply, a liability unqualified in terms, the position is the same for purposes of this case: the appellants' real defence was that the damage was caused by the act of the city, for which they were not responsible and could not control, and that they were guilty of no negligence in the matter. That defence could be equally good on any view of the effect of s. 13; and the same reasoning applies to s. 11, if indeed that section is open at all to the respondents in this case.

It accordingly becomes necessary to consider the issues of fact which have occupied the greater part of the hearing of this appeal, as they seem to have done in the courts below. The respondents have contended that the original construction of the pipeline was improper, and that the damage was solely caused thereby; the appellants have contended that not only was their original construction proper but the breaking of the pipe was solely due to the ground beneath it being let down by the new sewerage works constructed by the city in 1931. [The defendant was found not to have been negligent in the original construction.]

There remains the further point, which is, that assuming that the city in fact let down the ground and caused the pipe to break, still the appellants should have foreseen and guarded against the risk of their pipes being affected. ...

The authorities already cited herein show that, though the act of a third party may be relied on by way of defence in cases of this type, the defendant may still be held liable in negligence if he failed in foreseeing and guarding against the consequences to his work of that third party's act. ...

In truth, the gravamen of the charge against the appellants in this matter is that though they had the tremendous responsibility of carrying this highly inflammable gas under the streets of a city, they did nothing at all in all the facts of this case. If they did not know of the city works, their system of inspection must have been very deficient. If they did know they should have been on their guard; they might have ascertained what work was being done and carefully investigated the position, or they might have examined the pipes likely to be affected so as to satisfy themselves that the bed on which they lay was not being disturbed. Their duty to the respondents was at the lowest to be on the watch and to be vigilant: they do not even pretend to have done as much as that. In fact, so far as it appears, they gave no thought to the matter. They left it all to chance. It is, in their Lordships' judgment, impossible for them now to protest that they could have done nothing effective to prevent the accident: and in any case their Lordships cannot accept that as the true view.

In the result their Lordships agree with the decision on this point of the Appellate Division, and are of opinion that the appeal should be dismissed.

NOTES

1. What is the holding of this case? A similar case is *Fenn v. Corporation of the City of Peterborough; Peterborough Utilities Commission et al. (Third Parties)* (1979), 25 O.R. (2d) 399, 9 C.C.L.T. 1 (C.A.); affd, [1981] 2 S.C.R. 613, 18 C.C.L.T. 258 (*sub nom. Consumers' Gas Co. v. Fenn*).

2. With regard to the effect of statutory authorization, see Lord Russell C.J. in *Price v. South Metropolitan Gas Co.* (1895), 65 L.J.Q.B. 126, 12 T.L.R. 31 (D.C.):

   > It is clear that where a gas company such as this, having statutory authority to lay pipes, does so in the exercise of its statutory powers, the "wild beast" theory referred to in the well-known case of *Fletcher v. Rylands* is inapplicable.

   And see Lord Blackburn in *Geddis v. Proprietors of Bann Reservoir* (1878), 3 App. Cas. 430, at 455 (H.L.):

   > It is now thoroughly well established that no action will lie for doing that which the Legislature has authorized, if it be done without negligence, although it does occasion damage to anyone; but an action does lie for doing that which the Legislature has authorized, if it be done negligently.

   Most of these statutory authorization cases are nuisance cases, but they are equally applied in *Rylands v. Fletcher* situations. See dictum in *Charles R. Bell Ltd. v. City of St. John's* (1965), 54 D.L.R. (2d) 528, at 555 (Nfld. S.C.).

3. As has been seen, the Supreme Court of Canada in *Tock v. St. John's Metro Area Bd.*, [1989] 2 S.C.R. 1181, 64 D.L.R. (4th) 620, held that *Rylands v. Fletcher* cannot be applied to statutorily authorized sewer and storm drain systems maintained for the general benefit of the community. Does this decision effectively put an end to the use of *Rylands v. Fletcher* in all cases of statutorily authorized activities? See as well *Dunne et al. v. North Western Gas Board et al.*, [1964] 2 Q.B. 806, [1963] 3 All E.R. 916 (C.A.), where the court, for the same reason, held that the strict liability rule was inapplicable in the case of a burst water main which caused a break in a gas main and a subsequent explosion. Also see *Benning v. Wong* (1969), 43 A.L.J.R. 467, [1970] A.L.R. 585, for a similar Australian decision.

4. The onus of proving absence of negligence lies on the defendant. See *Manchester Corp. v. Farnworth*, [1930] A.C. 171, 99 L.J.K.B. 83; *Lawrysyn v. Town of Kipling* (1966), 55 D.L.R. (2d) 471, 55 W.W.R. 108 (Sask. C.A.). But *cf.*, *Benning v. Wong*, *supra*, where the majority felt onus was on the plaintiff, not the defendant.

5. The word negligence is not used in the ordinary sense here; the courts have narrowed its meaning. "If the damages could be prevented it is, within the meaning of this rule, negligence not to make such reasonable exercise of powers," See *Geddis v. Proprietors of Bann Reservoir* (1978), 3 App. Cas. 430, at 455 (H.L.). Similarly, it has been suggested that "it is negligence to carry out work in a manner which results in damage, unless it can be shown that that, and that only, was the way in which the duty could be performed". See *Provender Millers Ltd. v. Southampton County Council*, [1940] 1 Ch. 131, at p. 140, [1939] 4 All E.R. 157.

6. Other techniques of minimizing the importance of this defence are described in Linden, "Strict Liability, Nuisance and Legislative Authorization" (1966), 4 Osgoode Hall L.J. 196:

> The importance of the defence of legislative authority is on the wane. Only rarely does the legislation authorizing activity expressly deal with the question of tort liability. This has left the judiciary in a position to fabricate legislative intention where none really exists, which path has created considerable confusion. Part of this confusion results from a changed attitude toward activities authorized by legislation and the need to compensate the victims of progress. Because the historical and policy reasons which prompted the creation of the immunity have ceased to be influential, the courts have commenced to circumscribe its operation. However, rather than leading a direct frontal attack on the immunity, the courts have used subterfuge and have created several judicial techniques whereby invocation of the immunity can he avoided. At the same time lip service is paid to the received doctrine. ...
>
> [T]here were certain factors that courts weigh in deciding whether to rely on the immunity or one of the techniques for its avoidance. The immunity will tend to be invoked and recovery denied where a plaintiff is seeking to gain increased compensation by avoiding a statutory compensation scheme, where the defendant is a non-profit making operation, where the authority is by statute rather than by an inferior legislative enactment, where an injunction is sought, and where a particularly important industry is involved. On the other hand, courts will tend to avoid the immunity and impose nuisance or strict liability where the defendant is a profit-making organization, where the legislative authority is a by-law or governmental contract, where the defendant's conduct was reprehensible and where loss could be easily avoided. Although the best solution to this problem is for legislatures to consider this aspect of tort liability when legislation is drafted, experience dictates that this will not be done. The judiciary, as always, is left to do its best to reconcile the conflicting interests. It would be helpful if in so doing they would refuse to rely

on fictions and disclose the true basis of their decisions. If this is done one can prophesy that the future of the immunity will be shortlived.

NOTES ON LIABILITY FOR FIRES

1. Damage caused by fires, both in rural and urban environments, poses a serious problem today as it always has in the past. The law concerning liability for fires is complex, combining principles of strict liability and negligence law with statutory intervention. It is also a law that as Fleming notes "has undergone many changes during its long history". See Fleming, *The Law of Torts*, 9th ed. (1998), Chapter 17; Ogus, "Vagaries in Liability for the Escape of Fire", [1969] Cam. L.J. 104.

2. Even before the judgments in *Rylands v. Fletcher*, the common law recognized a special action of trespass on the case against occupiers for their "negligent" use of fire, resulting in its escape. As Fleming notes, however, despite the use of the word "negligence", liability for fire was strict. It was presumed that fire was started by the occupier or by someone for whom the occupier was responsible, and the only defences which were permitted were act of stranger or act of God. See Fleming, *supra*. See *Burnie Port Authority v. General Jones Pty. Ltd.* (1994), 68 A.L.J.R. 331 for a discussion of the early case law.

3. Legislation was introduced in the eighteenth century with the enactment of the *Fires Prevention (Metropolis) Act, 1774*, (U.K. 14 Geo. III). This statute which, as Professor Irvine has stated, "is as loquacious as it is obscure", seemed on its face to provide to occupiers an immunity from liability for fires "accidentally" begun in their premises. But, as Professor Irvine has also pointed out, "the Courts have long since discarded any such obvious interpretation, and have construed it very narrowly indeed". See Irvine, "Annotation to *Franks v. Sanderson*" (1986), 35 C.C.L.T. 307.

   According to Professor Irvine, the statute has been interpreted in a way that makes it applicable only to those fires which have arisen spontaneously without any human agency, or started "by the uncontrollable agency of third-party intermeddlers". In other words, the statute's immunity does not apparently apply to fires deliberately started for a legitimate purpose, *e.g.*, for cooking, light or heat, and then accidentally spread. The statute seems to be still in force in several Canadian provinces, for example, B.C., Alta., Sask., and Man., and in Ontario has been re-enacted as the *Accidental Fires Act*, R.S.O. 1990, c. A.4. The case law includes *Hallick v. Doroschuk* (1985), 41 Sask. R. 151, 35 C.C.L.T. 81 (Q.B.); *Franks v. Sanderson* (1986), 35 C.C.L.T. 307 (B.C.S,C.); affd (1988), 25 B.C.L.R. (2d) 248, 44 C.C.L.T. 208 (C.A.); *Dudek v. Brown* (1980), 33 O.R. (2d) 460, 124 D.L.R. (3d) 629 (H.C.). However, since the statute seems only to apply to provide an immunity for fires started by an act of God or an act of a stranger, which were, according to the common law, legitimate defences anyway, it has aptly been described by Professor Irvine as a "superfluous and idle encumbrance".

4. Even an "accidentally" and spontaneously ignited fire might not be protected by the statute if the fire is not properly controlled and hence spreads. The "new" fire is not then considered to be an accidental one. See *Musgrove v. Pandelis*, [1919] 2 K.B. 43, 35 T.L.R. 299 (C.A.); *Goldman v. Hargrave*, [1967] 1 A.C. 645, [1966] 2 All E.R. 989 (P.C.).

5. There is then the question of the burden of proof. According to the common law action, once the plaintiff has proved that the fire originated from the defendant's property, the defendant has to establish the defence of act of God or act of stranger. Has the statute at least altered that? Does the plaintiff now have to prove that the fire was not "accidentally" begun and is not covered by the statute? Irvine, *supra*, notes that

the authorities are divided, although the weight of the authorities seems to favour the view that the burden of proof is now on the plaintiff. The importance of this matter is seen in the case of *Franks v. Sanderson, supra*. Here a fire started in the defendant's garage and spread to the plaintiff's cafe and grocery store. There was very little evidence as to the cause of the fire. The Court of Appeal affirmed the trial court's dismissal of the action, holding that the plaintiff failed to prove that the fire had been started by the defendant or someone for whom he was responsible, as opposed to a "stranger". Esson J.A. held that although liability for fires is "strict", in the sense that the occupier will be liable for not only his or her own negligence, but that of his or her servants, independent contractors, guests, other licensees, *i.e.*, anyone but a "stranger", it is up to the plaintiff to prove that the fire was not caused by a stranger to succeed in the action.

6. Apart from this, the principle of *Rylands v. Fletcher* applies to some fires. However, the qualifications of the *Rylands v. Fletcher* principle apply. Thus, the fire must be a "non-natural" use of land. In *Maron et al. v. Baert & Siguaw Devs. Ltd.* (1981), 31 A.R. 216, 126 D.L.R. (3d) 9 (Q.B.), the principle was not applied to a fire which started in a garage, since the use of the garage for welding was not a non-natural use, and there was no escape. The court did impose "a very high degree of care", however. See also *Dudek v. Brown, supra*, where the court held that *Rylands v. Fletcher* applies only to "unreasonable" fires. Isn't this the same as negligence?

7. Grass fires present special problems. It has been held that fires set by farmers to burn off scrub is a natural use of land. See *Smith v. Widdicombe* (1987), 45 Man. R. (2d) 53, 39 C.C.L.T. 98 (Q.B.); affd 49 Man. R. (2d) 52, [1987] 6 W.W.R. 687 (C.A.). For a contrary case see *Hudson v. Riverdale Colony* (1980), 5 Man. R. (2d) 304, 114 D.L.R. (3d) 352 (C.A.), where a "slough grass" fire which was started to prevent the spread of an initial fire was held to be a "non-natural" use of land.

NOTES ON LIABILITY FOR ANIMALS

1. Damage done by animals has long been a subject of concern to tort law. Certain concepts of strict liability have been utilized for years to resolve cases where dangerous animals caused injury. There are two types of dangerous animals. First, there are *ferae naturae*, animals that are dangerous as a group. Included in their number are lions, elephants, zebras, bears and the like. If damage is done by any of these creatures, strict liability is automatically imposed. Second, there are animals that may be dangerous as individuals, even though they are members of a species considered harmless. They are called *mansuetae naturae*; these include dogs, cats, horses and the like. Where an individual animal of this *mansuetae naturae* group is known to be dangerous, and harms someone, strict liability will be imposed. This action has been called the *scienter* action. It is from this notion that the mythical legal principle that "every dog is entitled to one bite" emerged. It is not necessarily so, because *scienter* may exist even where a dog has not yet bitten anyone, for example, where a dog is constantly barking at, chasing and trying to bite passersbys.

2. Liability for injuries caused by wild animals is strict, even where there has been no escape. Some cases have held, however, that for strict liability to apply, there must have been an escape from "control". See *Lewis v. Oeming* (1983), 42 A.R. 58, 24 C.C.L.T. 81 (Q.B.); and *Maynes v. Galicz* (1976), 62 D.L.R. (3d) 385, [1976] 1 W.W.R. 557 (B.C.S.C.). For a useful commentary on this question, see Irvine, "Annotation" (1983), 24 C.C.L.T. 82.

3. Most provinces have enacted legislation altering the *scienter* requirement of the common law. In Ontario, for example, the *Dog Owners' Liability Act*, R.S.O. 1990, c. D.16, provides strict liability for dog bites. See *Wong v. Arnold* (1987), 59 O.R. (2d)

299, 38 D.L.R. (4th) 319 (C.A.); *Morsillo v. Migliano* (1985), 52 O.R. (2d) 319, 13 C.C.L.I. 1 (Dist. Ct.); and *Purcell v. Taylor* (1994), 120 D.L.R. (4th) 161 (Ont. Gen. Div.). In Nova Scotia, see the *Stray Animals Act*, R.S.N.S. 1989, c. 448, and the case of *Brewer v. Saunders* (1986), 28 D.L.R. (4th) 45, 37 C.C.L.T. 237 (N.S.C.A.). In P.E.I. see the *Dog Act*, R.S.P.E.I. 1988, c. D.13, and the case of *Phillips v. Robinson* (1982), 35 Nfld. & P.E.I.R. 509, 133 D.L.R. (3d) 189 (P.E.I.C.A.). In Saskatchewan see the *Rural Municipality Act*, 1989, S.S. 1989-90, c. R-26.1, and the case of *Karras v. Richter*, [1995] 7 W.W.R. 406 (Sask. Q.B.).

4. Strict liability is also imposed for cattle that trespass on neighbouring land. See Fleming, *The Law of Torts*, 8th ed. (1992), p. 354. See *Stray Animals Act*, R.S.A. 1980, c. S–23, s. 5. See *Block v. Cole*, [1995] 7 W.W.R. 57 (Sask. Q.B.) for a case dealing with the *Stray Animals Act*, R.S.S. 1978, c. S-60. For the effect of legislation prohibiting animals from running at large, see *Wolfe v. Dayton* (1974), 55 D.L.R. (3d) 552, [1975] 1 W.W.R. 665 (B.C.S.C.).

5. In addition to these strict liability doctrines, animals may render their owners liable on a negligence theory. If a dog bites a child the owner will be held responsible if the owner could reasonably have foreseen such an event occurring and failed to take reasonable steps to prevent it. See *Draper v. Hotter*, [1972] 2 Q.B. 556, [1972] 2 All E.R. 210 (C.A.). In *Bacon v. Ryan* (1995), 27 C.C.L.T. (2d) 308 (Sask. Q.B.), the court stated that it is not the ownership of the dog which creates the responsibility, but the possession and control of it.

6. In *Sgro v. Verbeek* (1980), 28 O.R. (2d) 712, 111 D.L.R. (3d) 479 (H.C.), the seven-year-old plaintiff was bitten by a German shepherd dog, while the child was petting it. An action was brought both in negligence and strict liability. It was clear that the dog was not used to having children around. It had never bitten anyone, but it had a propensity for running towards strangers and barking at them. The court felt this evidence supported liability for negligence but not on the basis of strict liability. Mr. Justice Craig explained:

> To establish liability based on the common law doctrine of *scienter*, it is essential to prove that [the dog] (an animal *mansuetae naturae*) had vicious or mischievous propensities. It was not established that [it] had shown vicious propensities prior to this occasion or that any vicious propensity was known to the defendant. However, in the application of the *scienter* doctrine it is not accurate to say that "every dog is allowed one bite". Liability in *scienter* may result from known mischievous propensities: *Morris v. Baily*, [1970] 3 O.R. 386, 13 D.L.R. (3d) 150 (C.A.). In the instant case Dino had a propensity for running towards and barking at strangers coming on to the property. If that is a mischievous propensity, it can be said that this boy was not injured as a result of that propensity. For these reasons I find that the defendant is not liable in *scienter*.

What if the boy had been knocked over by the dog, instead of being bitten? (See *Kirk v. Trerise* (1979), 14 B.C.L.R. 310, 103 D.L.R. (3d) 78 (S.C.); revd (1981), 28 B.C.L.R. 165, 122 D.L.R. (3d) 642 (C.A.), dealing with a similar case under the legislation in British Columbia.). What if a motorcyclist is thrown off his bike as a result of a jumping dog? See *Ruckheim v. Robinson*, [1995] 4 W.W.R. 284 (B.C.C.A.).

7. In *Acheson v. Dory* (1993), 8 Alta. L.R. (3d) 128 (Q.B.), affd (1994), 24 Alta. L.R. (3d) 187 (C.A.), the defendant's stallion, in an attempt to lunge at and bite the gelding upon which the plaintiff was riding, bit the plaintiffs leg instead. Picard J. decided to apply negligence law principles, rather than the strict liability of *scienter*. Although Picard J. was of the view that ordinary negligence law principles applied, she referred to two English judgments, *Ellis v. Johnstone*, [1963] 2 Q.B. 8, [1963] 1 All E.R. 286 (C.A.), and *Searle v. Wallbank*, [1947] A.C. 341, [1947] 1 All E.R. 12 (H.L.), which

seemed to require that there be "special circumstances" or some "special propensity" on the tame animal's part before there could be liability, even for negligence. Although doubting the correctness of this view, Picard J. found that these requirements were met in any event, and decided in the plaintiff's favour. Why should the law require anything in addition to the defendant's lack of reasonable care to find that person liable in negligence for injuries caused by tame animals? Does this not just muddy the already cloudy waters of negligence law?

8. Damage done by cattle straying on Canadian roads is now regulated by negligence law, although, in England, under *Searle v. Wallbank*, [1947] A.C. 341, [1947] 1 All E.R. 12, no duty of care is owed for such conduct. The old English rule was decisively rejected in Canada by *Fleming v. Atkinson*, [1959] S.C.R. 513, 18 D.L.R. (2d) 81. In the Court of Appeal, Mr. Justice Roach declared:

> It is now over 200 years since Thomas Gray wrote his famous lines descriptive of rural England at eventide, "The lowing herd winds slowly o'er the lea". The lea no doubt included such highways as then traversed the landscape. As I read the modern English cases the herd may still wander along those same highways without the owner being subject to civil liability for the injuries they may cause.
>
> No longer in this Province does "the ploughman homeward plod his weary way". He goes now in his tractor, oft-times along the highway. The farmer whose land adjoins the King's Highway can in this modern era scarcely know the meaning of "the solemn stillness" of which Gray wrote. No longer can he be conscious of the beetle wheeling his droning flight. What he hears, instead, is the whir of motor cars wheeling their way at legalized speed along the adjoining highway. The common law of England may have been adequate in Gray's day. The Courts in England have held that it is still adequate, but surely it must be apparent that today in this Province it is not.

Collisions on the highways between animals and cars have provoked considerable litigation. Cars have collided with pigs (*Rozon v. Patenaude* (1982), 35 O.R. (2d) 619 (Co. Ct.)), horses (*Reynoldson v. Simmons* (1982), 14 Sask. R. 257 (Q.B.)), and cows (*Pellizzari v. Miller* (1981), 35 O.R. (2d) 700 (H.C.)).

9. See the recommendation in the *Report of the Committee on the Law of Civil Liability for Damage Done by Animals* (1953), Cmd. 8746. On this topic generally, see Williams, *Liability for Animals* (1939); and North, *Modern Law of Animals* (1972).

10. *Diversified Holdings Ltd. v. R. in Right of British Columbia* (1982), 133 D.L.R. (3d) 712, [1982] 3 W.W.R. 516, 20 C.C.L.T. 202 (S.C.); affd 41 B.C.L.R. 29, [1983] 2 W.W.R. 289 (C.A.), presented issues of a much more difficult nature. The Crown is given the power, by virtue of the *Wildlife Act* S.B.C. 1982, c. 57, s. 2, to manage all wildlife in the Province of British Columbia. To accomplish this objective, the statute provides that the property in all wildlife in the province is vested in the Crown. The Act also gives the Crown an immunity from suit for any property damage caused by the wildlife under the Crown's control. The Fish and Wildlife Branch of the provincial Ministry of the Environment embarked upon a program of feeding elk in the vicinity of the plaintiff's ranch. As a result of the success of the program the elk flourished and multiplied. When the program was terminated, the elk, accustomed as they had become to their enriched diet, invaded the plaintiff's ranch and began to feed on his crops. The numbers of elk which fed on the plaintiff's crops grew considerably and did considerable damage to the plaintiff's crops and property. The plaintiff sued the Crown alleging that the acts of the Ministry employees, in commencing and terminating their ambitious feeding program, were negligent and actionable. The Court held that the legislative immunity applied to damage done by animals in the Crown's control, but did not apply to the negligence of the Crown itself in administering its

programs. Having said that, however, the Court held that the feeding program was within the *bona fide* exercise of the Crown's statutory discretion, and thus could not form the basis of an action in negligence, and that there were no negligent acts committed in the operation of the program. Expressing sympathy for the plaintiff's plight, the Court dismissed its action.

NOTES ON VICARIOUS LIABILITY

1. One form of strict liability arises when a "servant" is guilty of tortious conduct in the course of employment. In such a situation, the servant's "master" is called upon to make good the loss, even though not personally at fault. The employer is said to be vicariously liable. The theory of vicarious liability was developed through the use of various fictions attempting to implicate the employer. In reality, however, it was probably the desire to spread the losses that inevitably occur in industry among a larger group than the victims that fostered its growth. It is strange, however, that the fault principle seems to have worked its way back into this area. For example, an employer may be reimbursed at the expense of the employee, whose negligence gave rise to the master's vicarious responsibility. See *Lister v. Romford Ice & Cold Storage Co. Ltd.*, [1957] A.C. 555, [1957] 1 All E.R. 125 (H.L.).

2. There are limits upon employers' liability for the acts of employees. The master must be in a position to exercise "detailed control" over the "manner in which [the servant] shall do his work". See *Performing Right Society Ltd. v. Mitchell & Booker (Palais de Danse) Ltd.*, [1924] 1 K.B. 762, [1924] All E.R. Rep. Ext. 860; *cf., T.G. Bright Co. Ltd v. Kerr*, [1939] S.C.R. 63, [1939] 1 D.L.R. 193; *Egginton v. Reader* (1936), 52 T.L.R. 212, [1936] 1 All E.R. 7; *Wilson v. Vancouver Hockey Club* (1983), 5 D.L.R. (4th) 282 (B.C.S.C.); affd (1985), 22 D.L.R. (4th) 516 (C.A.); leave to appeal to S.C.C. refused, 22 D.L.R. (4th) 516*n*. More recently this test has been enlarged and is being displaced by "something like an 'organization test'". See *Co-operators Insurance Association v. Kearney*, [1965] S.C.R. 106, 48 D.L.R. (2d) 1, *per* Spence J.; *Armstrong v. Mac's Milk* (1975), 7 O.R. (2d) 478, 55 D.L.R. (3d) 510 (H.C.J.) (Lerner J.); *Kennedy v. C.N.A. Assur. Co.* (1978), 20 O.R. (2d) 674, 88 D.L.R. (3d) 592; affd (1979), 26 O.R. (2d) 352*n* (C.A.) (Linden J.); Magnet, "Vicarious Liability and the Professional Employee" (1978-9), 6 C.C.L.T. 208. For a good discussion of this issue see *Lake v. Callison Outfitters Ltd.* (1991), 7 C.C.L.T. (2d) 274 (B.C.S.C.).

3. For the master to be held vicariously liable, the servant must have been in the course of employment. See *Battistoni v. Thomas*, [1932] S.C.R. 144, [1932] 1 D.L.R. 577; *Hoar v. Wallace*, [1938] O.R. 666, [1938] 4 D.L.R. 774 (Ont. C.A.); *C.P.R. v. Lockhart*, [1942] A.C. 591, [1942] 3 D.L.R. 529 (P.C.).

4. Vicarious liability can even extend to intentional torts perpetrated by employees while on the job. See *Griggs v. Southside Hotel Ltd. & Berman*, [1947] O.R. 674, [1947] 4 D.L.R. 49 (C.A.); *Pettersson v. Royal Oak Hotel Ltd.*, [1948] N.Z.L.R. 136; *Jennings v. C.N.R.*, [1925] 2 D.L.R. 630, [1925] 1 W.W.R. 918 (B.C.C.A); *B.C. Ferry Corp. v. Invicta Security Services Corp.* (1997), 35 C.C.L.T. (2d) 182 (B.C.S.C.). It also may be used in cases of fraud. See *Lloyd v. Grace, Smith & Co.*, [1912] A.C. 716, [1911-13] All E.R. Rep. 51 (H.L.).

5. The vicarious liability of employers for the sexual misconduct of employees has been dealt with in several recent cases. In *B. (P.A.) v. Curry* (1997), 34 C.C.L.T. (2d) 241 (B.C.C.A.), leave to appeal to S.C.C. granted (1997), 224 N.R. 318*n* (S.C.C.), a non-profit foundation which operated residential care facilities for emotionally troubled children was sued by the plaintiff, a former resident, who had been sexually abused by an employee. The Court of Appeal agreed that the traditional course of employment test is inappropriate in cases of intentional torts, especially where the impugned acts

are not done in furtherance of the employer's objectives and involve morally offensive behaviour. In a lengthy discussion of this issue, Huddart J.A. reviewed the vicarious liability jurisprudence and literature dealing with actions for fraud and conversion, and discussed the policies justififying the imposition of vicarious liability. A critical feature identified by Huddart J.A. in the sexual assault cases which justified vicarious liability was that the employer created the situation of trust between the employee and the victim. Huddart J.A. concluded that "when the conferral of authority provides not mere opportunity, but the power over another that makes more probable a wrong, that employer should be vicariously liable for any such wrong that results from the abuse of that power". (At p. 263, C.C.L.T.). In her judgment, Huddart J.A. referred to numerous authorities and authors, including Sykes, "The Boundaries of Vicarious Liability: An Economic Analysis of the Scope of the Employment Rule and Related Legal Doctrienes" (1988), 101 Harv.L.R. 563; and Weber, "Scope of Employment Redefined: Holding Employers Vicariously Liable for Sexual Assaults Committed by Their Employees" (1992), 76 Minn.L.R. 1513. Other recent sexual assault cases imposing vicarious liability include *A.(C.) v. C.(J.W.)* (1997) 36 C.C.L.T. (2d) 224 (B.C.S.C.); and *K. (W.) v. Pornbacher* (1997), 34 C.C.L.T. (2d) 174 (B.C.S.C.).

6. Some recent judgments have rejected vicarious liability for sexual assaults. These include *M. (F.W.) v. Mombourquette* (1996), 152 N.S.R. (2d) 109 (C.A.), and *T. (G.) v. Griffiths*, [1997] 5 W.W.R. 203 (B.C.C.A.). The appeal of the latter case was heard at the same time as that of *B. (P.A.) v. Curry, supra.* The *Griffiths* case involved sexual assaults committed by the program director of the Vernon Boys and Girls Club on two children. One assault took place on a bus, while the group was going to an activity, and the others in the employee's home, but not during the club's program. In rejecting vicarious liability, Huddart J.A. distinguished the two B.C. cases. She stressed that it is not merely the fact that an employer provides the employee with an opportunity to develop a trust relationship with the child that creates the employer's responsibility. The employer must confer on the employee "the very authority that the employee abuses". Thus, the fact that the Vernon Boys and Girls Club, unlike the residential school, had no power or authority over the children, and did not stand *in loco parentis* with the children, but only organized and supervised day time activities for children, was a decisive difference. The club did not through its activities or mandate increase the probability of sexual assaults occurring beyond the risk ordinarily present when adults and children participate together in common activities. Is this distinction sufficiently clear to you?

7. There are some difficult problems concerning the transfer of a servant. In other words, who bears the responsibility for the act of a servant temporarily loaned to another person? Here, too, control has been the key notion. See *Century Insurance Co. v. Northern Ireland Road Transport Bd.*, [1942] A.C. 509, [1942] 1 All E.R. 491 (H.L.); *Mersey Docks Harbour Bd. v. Coggins*, [1947] A.C. 1, [1946] 2 All E.R. 345 (H.L). This perplexing issue often arises in cases of operating room accidents. See *Aynsley et al. v. Toronto General Hospital*, [1969] 2 O.R. 829, 7 D.L.R. (3d) 193 (C.A.); affd [1972] S.C.R. 435, 25 D.L.R. (3d) 241 (*sub nom. Toronto General Hospital v. Matthews*), for a consideration of whether an anaesthetist or a hospital should bear the vicarious responsibility for the act of a senior resident. See Linden, "Changing Patterns of Hospital Liability in Canada" (1967), 5 Alta. L. Rev. 212. See generally Atiyah, *Vicarious Liability in the Law of Torts* (1967). A fascinating case, dealing with some of these issues, is *Morgans v. Launchbury et al.*, [1973] A.C. 127, [1972] 2 All E.R. 606 (H.L.).

8. There is disagreement about whether a hospital has a non-delegable duty to treat its patients and, consequently, whether it would be liable for the torts of its specialist staff members, even though they are not employees of the hospital. See *Yepremian v. Scarborough General Hospital et al.* (1978), 20 O.R. (2d) 510, at 534, 88 D.L.R. (3d) 161, 6 C.C.L.T. 81 (S.C.) (R.E. Holland J.); revd (1980), 28 O.R. (2d) 494, 110

D.L.R. (3d) 513, 13 C.C.L.T 105 (C.A.); later settled (1981), 15 C.C.L.T. 73 (Ont. S.C.); *cf. Osburn v. Mohindra and St. John Hospital* (1980), 29 N.B.R. (2d) 340, 66 A.P.R. 340 (Q.B.).

9. One way around vicarious liability is to deal with this issue on the basis of the "non-delegable" duty concept. In two recent Supreme Court of Canada judgments, *Lewis (Guardian ad Litem of) v. British Columbia* (1997), 153 D.L.R. (4th) 594 and *Mochinski v. Trendline Industries* (1997), 154 D.L.R. (4th) 212, the Court held that "a party upon whom the law has imposed a strict statutory duty to do a positive act cannot escape liability simply by delegating the work to an independent contractor. Rather a defendant subject to such a duty will always remain personally liable for the acts or omissions of the contractor to whom it assigned the work"; at 153 D.L.R. (4th) 603. In addition, carrying out a statutorily authorized function, such as the maintenance of highways, imposes upon the defendant a duty to take reasonable care and, in some circumstances, may also impose liability for the negligence of independent contractors who are engaged to do the work. Whether such liability exists depends upon whether the legislature intended that the duty be non-delegable. Based upon the legislation, the jurisprudence, and policy, the Supreme Court of Canada concluded that the duties to maintain roads imposed upon the Ministry of Transportation were non-delegable. The Court conceded that there is no categorical rule delineating which statutory duties are non-delegable and which are delegable, holding that it depended upon the legislative provisions and the circumstances of each case. In the case of highway maintenance, for example, Cory J. considered that the reasonable expectations of highway users, the control exercised over the work by the Ministry, and the need for fair and consistent treatment of all highway users dictated that the Ministry's duty should be categorized as a non-delegable duty. For a case comment, see Irvine (1996), 29 C.C.L.T. (2d) 2.

10. In *Lachambre v. Nair* (1989), 74 Sask. R. 87, [1989] 2 W.W.R. 748 (Q.B.), it was held that although a hospital cannot be vicariously liable for the torts of independent doctors, it can be held personally liable for its own failures; for example, for failing to inform a patient of risks. In another recent medical case, *Rothwell v. Raes* (1988), 66 O.R. (2d) 449, 54 D.L.R. (4th) 193 (H.C.J.); affd (1990), 2 O.R. (2d) 332, 76 D.L.R. (4th) 280 (C.A.), it was held that one doctor cannot be liable for the negligence of a locum.

11. In *London Drugs Ltd. v. Kuehne & Nagel (Int.) Ltd.*, [1992] 3 S.C.R. 299, 97 D.L.R. (4th) 261, employees of a storage company were held personally liable to a customer when they negligently damaged a piece of its equipment. Mr. Justice La Forest, in dissent, forcefully argued, however, that employees should be immune from liability when they are negligent in the course of their employment duties. In coming to this decision, La Forest J. reviewed the policy concerns expressed by the vicarious liability rule. The first is that it allows plaintiffs to obtain financial compensation from someone who can afford to pay it. Secondly, it places the liability for losses on the party who stands to benefit most from the enterprise. Third, it promotes a wider distribution of losses. Fourth, it encourages the deterrence of unsafe practices. In his view, adopting a policy of "vicarious immunity" for employees would not impact negatively on these policies, but rather would impact positively on most of them. La Forest J. stated that in the normal personal injury or property damage cases, not involving "contractual overtones", the negligent employee should continue to be held liable to the victim, but even here there should be a full indemnity of the employee by the employer. What do you think of these views which, if accepted would radically change Canadian law with respect to vicarious liability and vicarious immunity?

12. In *Edgeworth Construction Ltd. v. N.D. Lea & Associates*, [1993] 3 S.C.R. 206, [1993] 8 W.W.R. 129, the issue of an employee's liability was revisited by the Supreme Court. In this case, professional engineers working for an engineering firm

were held not to owe a duty of care to third parties which had relied on the firm's engineering services. The Court held that the plaintiff's reliance was on the firm, and not on individuals working for that firm. Although La Forest J. agreed, he noted the inconsistency between this finding and the one in *London Drugs*. How do you explain it?

NOTES ON PRODUCTS LIABILITY

GREENMAN v. YUBA POWER PRODUCTS INC.

Supreme Court of California. 53 Cal. 2d 57, 377 P. 2d 897 (1963).

A wife bought for her husband a Shopsmith combination power tool that could be used as a saw, drill and wood lathe. While the husband was using the Shopsmith, the piece of wood he was working on flew out of it, hitting him on the forehead. In an action against the retailer and manufacturer, the jury found for the plaintiff against the manufacturer but dismissed the action against the retailer. Both the manufacturer and the plaintiff appealed.

Traynor J.: A manufacturer is strictly liable in tort when an article he places on the market, knowing that it is to be used without inspection of defects, proves to have a defect that causes injury to a human being. Recognized first in the case of unwholesome food products, such liability has now been extended to a variety of other products that create as great or greater hazards if defective. [Citations omitted.]

Although in these cases strict liability has usually been based on the theory of an express or implied warranty running from the manufacturer to the plaintiff, the abandonment of the requirement of a contract between them, the recognition that the liability is not assumed by agreement but imposed by law ... and the refusal to permit the manufacturer to define the scope of its own responsibility for defective products ... make clear that the liability is not one governed by the law of contract warranties, but by the law of "strict liability in tort". Accordingly, rules defining and governing warranties that were developed to meet the needs of commercial transactions cannot properly be invoked to govern the manufacturer's liability to those injured by its defective products unless those rules also serve the purposes for which such liability is imposed.

We need not recanvass the reasons for imposing strict liability on the manufacturer. They have been fully articulated in the cases cited above. (See also 2 Harper and James, *Torts*, §§28.15-28.16, pp. 1569-1574: Prosser, "Strict Liability to the Consumer", 69 Yale L.J. 1099; *Escola v. Coca Cola Bottling Co.*, 24 Cal. 2d 453, 461 [150 P. 2d 436], concurring opinion.) The purpose of such liability is to insure that the costs of injuries resulting from defective products are borne by the manufacturers that put such products on the market rather than by the injured persons who are powerless to protect themselves. Sales warranties serve this purpose fitfully at best. (See Prosser, "Strict Liability to the Consumer", 69 Yale L.J. 1099, 1124-1134.) In the present case, for example, plaintiff was able to plead and prove an express warranty only because he read and relied on the representations of the Shopsmith's ruggedness contained in the manufacturer's brochure. Implicit in the machine's presence on the market, however, was a representation that it would safely do the jobs for which it was built. Under these circumstances, it should not be controlling whether plaintiff selected the machine because of the statements in the brochure, or because of the machine's own appearance of excellence that belied the defect lurking beneath the surface, or because he merely assumed that it would safely do the jobs it was built to do. It should not be controlling whether the details of the sales from manufacturer to retailer and from retailer to plaintiff's wife were such that one or more of the implied warranties of the sales act arose. (Civ. Code, §1735.) "The remedies of injured consumers ought not to be made to depend upon the intricacies of the law of sales." [Citations omitted.] To establish the manufacturer's liability it was sufficient that the plaintiff proved that he was injured while using the Shopsmith in a way it was intended to be used as a result of a defect in design and manufacture of which plaintiff was not aware that made the Shopsmith unsafe for its intended use.

The judgment is affirmed.

NOTES

1. The development of strict liability in the United States has been described by the late Dean Prosser as the "most rapid and spectacular overthrow of an established rule in the entire history of the law of torts". See Prosser "The Fall of the Citadel" (1966), 50 Minn. L. Rev. 791. See also Wade "Strict Tort Liability of Manufacturers" (1965), 19 Sw. L.J. 5; Dickerson, "The ABC's of Products Liability" (1969), 36 Tenn. L. Rev. 439.

2. Nearly two decades before *Greenman*, Mr. Justice Traynor had articulated this heresy, in a concurring opinion in *Escola v. Coca Cola Bottling Co. of Fresno*, 150 P. 2d 436 (1944). The majority of the court had held that *res ipsa loquitur* applied and permitted the plaintiff who was injured when a Coca Cola bottle exploded in her hand, to recover in negligence. Mr. Justice Traynor wrote:

> ... I concur in the judgment, but I believe the manufacturer's negligence should no longer be singled out as the basis of a plaintiff's right to recover in cases like the present one. In my opinion it should now be recognized that a manufacturer incurs an absolute liability when an article that he has placed on the market, knowing that it is to be used without inspection, proves to have a defect that causes injury to human beings. *MacPherson v. Buick Motor Co.*, 217 N.Y. 382; 111 N.E. 1050, established the principle recognized by this court, that irrespective of privity of contract, the manufacturer is responsible for an injury caused by such an article to any person who comes in lawful contact with it. ... In these cases the source of the manufacturer's liability was his negligence in the manufacturing process or in the inspection of component parts supplied by others. Even if there is no negligence, however, public policy demands that responsibility be fixed wherever it will most effectively reduce the hazards to life and health inherent in defective products that reach the market. It is evident that the manufacturer can anticipate some hazards and guard against the recurrence of others, as the public cannot. Those who suffer injury from defective products are unprepared to meet its consequences. The cost of an injury and the loss of time or health may be an overwhelming misfortune to the person injured, and a needless one, for the risk of injury can be insured by the manufacturer and distributed among the public as a cost of doing business. It is to the public interest to discourage the marketing of products having defects that are a menace to the public. If such products nevertheless find their way into the market it is to the public interest to place the responsibility for whatever injury they may cause upon the manufacturer who, even if he is not negligent in the manufacture of the product, is responsible for its reaching the market. However intermittently such injuries may occur and however haphazardly they may strike, the risk of their occurrence is a constant

risk and a general one. Against such a risk there should be general and constant protection and the manufacturer is best situated to afford such protection. …

3. In 1965 the American Law Institute in the *Restatement of the Law of Torts, Second*, felt able to include the following section as a statement of existing law in the United States:

> 402A. (1) One who sells any product in a defective condition unreasonably dangerous to the user or consumer or to his property is subject to liability for physical harm thereby caused to the ultimate user or consumer, or to his property if (a) the seller is engaged in the business of selling such a product, and (b) it is expected to and does reach the user or consumer without substantial change in the condition in which it is sold. (2) The rule stated in subsection (1) applies although (a) the seller has exercised all possible care in the preparation and sale of his product, and (b) the user consumer has not bought the product from or entered into any contractual relation with the seller.

The Institute expressed no opinion whether this rule might apply to persons other than users or consumers; to the seller of a product expected to be processed or otherwise substantially changed before it reaches the user or consumer; or to the seller of a component part of a product to be assembled. In Boivin, "Strict Products Liability Revisited" (1995), 33 Osgoode Hall L.J. 485, the author notes that the American Law Institute plans to overhaul this section in the *Restatement (Third)* in order to clarify the relationship between product defects, negligence and strict liability.

4. Some American courts utilized the concept of warranty to move into a regime of strict liability for defective products. In *Henningsen v. Bloomfield Motors Inc. et al.*, 32 N.J. 358, 161 A. 2d 69 (1960), the plaintiff was injured when something went wrong with the steering gear of the 1955 Plymouth her husband had bought for her at Christmas. Although the actions against the dealer and the manufacturer in negligence were dismissed, the jury found that there had been a breach of the implied warranty of merchantability. Francis J. affirmed and stated:

> There is no doubt that under early common-law concepts of contractual liability only those persons who were parties to the bargain could sue for a breach of it. In more recent times a noticeable disposition has appeared in a number of jurisdictions to break through the narrow barrier of privity when dealing with sales of goods in order to give realistic recognition to a universally accepted fact. The fact is that the dealer and the ordinary buyer do not, and are not expected to, buy goods, whether they be foodstuffs or automobiles, exclusively for their own consumption or use. Makers and manufacturers know this and advertise and market their products on that assumption; witness, the "family" car, the baby foods, etc. The limitations of privity in contracts for the sale of goods developed their place in the law when marketing conditions were simple, when maker and buyer frequently met face to face on an equal bargaining plane and when many of the products were relatively uncomplicated and conducive to inspection by a buyer competent to evaluate their quality. [Citation omitted.] With the advent of mass marketing, the manufacturer became remote from the purchaser, sales were accomplished through intermediaries, and the demand for the product was created by advertising media. In such an economy it became obvious that the consumer was the person being cultivated. Manifestly, the connotation of "consumer" was broader than that of "buyer". He signified such a person who, in the reasonable contemplation of the parties to the sale, might be expected to use the product. Thus, where the commodities sold are such that if defectively manufactured they will be dangerous to life or limb, then society's interests can only be protected by eliminating the requirement of privity between the maker and his dealers and the reasonably expected ultimate consumer. In that way the burden of

losses consequent upon use of defective articles is borne by those who are in a position to either control the danger or make an equitable distribution of the losses when they do occur. …

Under modern conditions the ordinary layman, on responding to the importuning of colourful advertising, has neither the opportunity nor the capacity to inspect or to determine the fitness of an automobile for use; he must rely on the manufacturer who has control of its construction, and to some degree on the dealer who, to the limited extent called for by the manufacturer's instructions, inspects and services it before delivery. In such a marketing milieu his remedies and those of persons who properly claim through him should not depend "upon the intricacies of the law of sales". The obligation of the manufacturer should not be based alone on privity of contract. It should rest, as was once said, upon the "demands of social justice". …

Accordingly, we hold that under modern marketing conditions, when a manufacturer puts a new automobile in the stream of trade and promotes its purchase by the public, an implied warranty that it is reasonably suitable for use as such accompanies it into the hands of the ultimate purchaser. Absence of agency between the manufacturer and the dealer who makes the ultimate sale is immaterial.

5. The American *Uniform Commercial Code*, ss. 2-318, expanded the protection of the implied conditions of sales law to other members of the family or household of the buyer and buyer's guests. A few states have gone further and extended the operation of the implied warranties to a person who may "reasonably be expected to use, consume or be affected by the goods and who is injured". There has been much controversy about the conflicting merits of the warranty approach as contrasted to the strict liability in tort theory. See Franklin, "When Worlds Collide: Liability Theories and Disclaimers in Defective Products Cases" (1966), 18 Stan. L. Rev. 974; Speidel, "The Virginia Antiprivity Statute: Strict Liability Under the U.C.C." (1965), 51 Va. L. Rev. 804; Titus, "Restatement (Second) Torts, Section 402A and the U.C.C." (1970), 22 Stan. L. Rev. 713.

NOTE ON THE CANADIAN POSITION

Despite the revolution that is proceeding apace in the United States, the Canadian courts have so far clung to negligence liability. To be sure, *res ipsa loquitur*, statutory negligence and other devices have been utilized to widen liability. Nevertheless, the big jump to strict liability has not been taken. The reasons for this are hard to determine. Perhaps Canadian industry, being less developed than American, needed more protection. Perhaps our judges are less willing to intrude on what they believe is a legislative responsibility. Perhaps our bar has not been as bold in advancing new theories of liability. In any event, the time is drawing near when our courts will have to choose which path they will follow.

The Canadian courts have so far largely ignored the issue. There are two little-known *dicta* of Mr. Justice Riddell indicating that he favoured a form of liability for defective products, but these have not been adopted by the courts. Whether this will continue to be the case remains to be seen. In the case *Shandloff v. City Dairy Ltd. et al.*, [1936] O.R. 579, [1936] 4 D.L.R. 712 (C.A.), the plaintiff purchased a bottle of chocolate milk from a retail merchant, to whom the milk had been supplied by City Dairy Ltd. The bottle contained particles of glass which caused injury to the plaintiff. Without citing any authorities and without the support of his brethren, Mr. Justice Riddell declared:

It is good sense and should be good law, that anyone manufacturing for public consumption an article of food should be held to warrant to the consumer that it is free

> from hidden defects, which are or may be dangerous: and it is no hardship to hold the vendor of food as warranting to the purchaser and consumer in the same way.

But Mr. Justice Riddell was only a voice crying in the wilderness. Five years later in the case of *Arendale et al. v. Canada Bread Company Ltd.*, [1941] O.W.N. 69, [1941] 2 D.L.R. 49 (C.A.), the plaintiff was injured by particles of glass in a loaf of bread made and supplied by Canada Bread Company Ltd. There was in that case evidence called by the defendant to show the process of manufacture, that its machinery and equipment were the best and most modern available, designed to safeguard the ingredients entering into the finished loaf, and that a high degree of care was used to prevent glass or other foreign substances from getting into the bread. The learned trial judge found that the plaintiff had failed to prove that the glass was in the bread at the time it was delivered by Canada Bread Company Ltd. to the plaintiff, and accordingly dismissed the action. The Court of Appeal reversed the finding of fact as to the glass being in the bread at the time of delivery and reversed the judgment.

Riddell J.A., at p. 70, expressed the opinion that:

> ... when one manufactures for human consumption any article, fluid or solid, he putting it on the market gives an implied warranty that it contains no deleterious substance; and felt that if the ultimate consumer is injured by the presence of such deleterious substance he is entitled to damages unless the manufacturer proves that it was there introduced by some agency other than his own — in other words he must prove that this deleterious article did not obtain entrance through his act or negligence but that of some other. The onus is on the manufacturer so to prove.

His fellow judges decided the case on other grounds.

Although the pure doctrine of strict liability in tort has not been adopted in Canada, there survives a concept that resembles this theory in some ways — inherently dangerous things or thing dangerous in themselves. Under this doctrine, which applies to such things as guns, poison and explosives, a higher standard of care is required than is ordinarily demanded. There are some who contend that this notion should be jettisoned, but somehow it clings to life. Mr. Justice Patterson of the Nova Scotia Supreme Court expressed the Canadian law in *Rae v. T. Eaton Co. Maritimes Ltd.* (1961), 28 D.L.R. (2d) 522, at 528, thus:

> ... The test of liability is not whether the product sold was or was not a "dangerous thing", but considering its nature and all relevant circumstances whether there has been a breach of duty by the manufacturer which he owed to the injured person. The duty is to use that due care that a reasonable person should use under all circumstances. And one of the most important circumstances — and often the controlling circumstance — is the character of the article sold and its capacity to do harm.

Mr. Justice Middleton explained the notion in *Shandloff v. City Dairy*, [1936] O.R. 579, at 590:

> The lack of care essential to the establishment of such a claim increases according to the danger to the ultimate consumer, and where the thing is in itself dangerous, the care necessary approximates to, and almost becomes, an absolute liability.

This theory was given a boost, at least in food cases, by Evans J.A. in *Heimler v. Calvert Caterers Ltd.* (1975), 8 O.R. (2d) 1, 56 D.L.R. (3d) 643 (C.A.), a case in which a supplier of contaminated food was held liable to someone who contracted typhoid. His Lordship stated:

> The standard of care demanded from those engaged in the food-handling business, is an extremely high standard and as Middleton, J.A., observed in *Shandloff v. City Dairy Ltd. and Moscoe*, ... the lack of care essential to the establishment of such a claim increases according to the danger to the ultimate consumer, and where the thing is in itself dangerous, the care necessary approximates to and almost becomes an absolute liability. While the facts in the *Shandloff case* are considerably different to the present situation, the same principle is applicable. The degree of care is extremely high.

In relation to dangerous products such as herbicide, it has been suggested by Mr. Justice Nicholson of Prince Edward Island that a manufacturer will be held liable in negligence to those suffering damage therefrom unless it establishes that it took "all reasonable and possible care to ensure that the product was safe and reasonably fit for the purpose of controlling weeds ...". Mr. Justice Nicholson felt that the manufacturer should have known about the "possibility of the damage to the turnip crop". See *Willis v. F.M.C. Machinery & Chemicals Ltd.* (1976), 68 D.L.R. (3d) 127 (P.E.I. S.C.).

Another remnant of the inherently dangerous article theory is that the onus of proof is shifted to the manufacturer and the other defendants. For example, in *Ives v. Clare Bros. Ltd.*, [1971] 1 O.R. 417, 15 D.L.R. (3d) 519, responsibility was attached for a defective gas furnace that leaked gas and caused injury to a home-owner. Mr. Justice Peter Wright of the Ontario High Court stated:

> Once it is established that injury or damages have been caused by the usage of natural gas through an installation made, installed or serviced by others, the onus of proving that there is no negligence is on each defendant who made, installed or serviced the installation. In other words, the position of an innocent gas user harmed by the use of gas is analogous to that of a pedestrian under s. 106(1) of the *Highway Traffic Act.*

His Lordship indicated that he was prepared to extend this theory even to ordinary products:

> Although I find this a sure ground for determination of legal problems in the use of natural gas, which our legislation and regulations establish to be hazardous. I would not find it unjust or illogical in the modern world of faceless plants and suppliers to apply it to the case of manufacturers and distant powers generally distributing their products in our society. It seems to be a recognition of the position of the lonely hurt citizen in the face of power so great and so remote that the common injured consumer cannot reasonably be expected to discover the secrets and complexities which may have caused him harm. I do not assert that that is the law of products' liability generally, but I shall not be shocked or surprised when higher authority free to do so avers it to be the law.

Both the producers and the service people were unable to "discharge the burden" and consequently both were held liable.

It is difficult to tell whether this special category of dangerous articles will eventually disappear or whether it will be expanded to include other products. The concept is not dissimilar to the rule of *Rylands v. Fletcher* and it does improve the legal position of the consumer. It would undoubtedly be neater to promote product safety without reliance on such an artificial distinction. Nevertheless, as long as the tradition of bolder judicial approaches is lacking, perhaps this device, which permits an indirect response to a felt social need, is preferable to the *status quo*.

See Stallybrass, "Dangerous Things and Non-Natural User" (1929), 3 Camb. L.J. 376.

NOTES

1. Should the Canadian courts adopt the American theory of strict liability in tort for defective products? See Calabresi, *The Costs of Accidents* (1970); Ison, *The Forensic Lottery* (1967); Weiler, "Defamation, Enterprise Liability and Freedom of Speech" (1967), 17 U. Toronto L.J. 278. See also Stradiotto, "Products Liability in Tort", Law Society of Upper Canada, *Special Lectures On New Developments in the Law of Torts* (1973), at 174; Thompson, "Manufacturers Liability" (1970), 7 Alta. L. Rev. 305, at 314; compare with Linden, *Canadian Tort Law*, 6th ed. (1997).

2. A discussion of the Canadian and American position is found in Boivin, "Strict Products Liability Revisited" (1995), 33 Osgoode Hall L.J. 487. The author points out that the standard of care required for liability cannot be separated from the type of liability in issue; *i.e,* design defect, manufacturing defect, or failure to warn. He notes that in design defect and failure to warn cases, there is not strict liability, even in the U.S., since in defining whether there has been a defect or a default, fault plays a role. The author does argue, however, that there is strict liability in the U.S. for manufacturing defects, and that this ought to be adopted by Canadian law.

3. There has been legislative reform in New Brunswick and Saskatchewan in 1978, in Europe in 1985, in Australia in 1992 and in the new Civil Code of Quebec in 1992 (#1468). In the United States, there has been some "retreat", according to Professor Waddams:

> State legislatures have enacted a wide variety of provisions that tend to favour defendants in civil litigation; federal legislation on products liability has been several times proposed, though not yet enacted; the *Restatement of Torts, Third* while maintaining the general principle of strict liability for manufacturing defects, has proposed what is in effect a negligence standard for design and labelling defects.
>
> There is a curious irony in these developments. It was the American jurisdictions that developed the concept of strict liability in the 1960s. The principal reason for this development, guided by the influential commentary of Dean William Prosser, was the need to avoid anomalies of privity of contract....
>
> The concern in the United States has, it may be suggested, more to do with the fear of excessive jury awards than with the substantive law. Several interrelated features of the American civil litigation system are relevant here, including the widespread use of the civil jury, the entrepreneurial attitude of the legal profession, the reluctance of judges to control jury awards, the ability of juries to award punitive damages and the use of contingent fees. Even more significant is the American rule that a losing plaintiff need not pay the costs of the successful defendant, permitting litigation at no risk to the plaintiff. The generally low levels of social security compared to other Western countries also tends to encourage litigation.
>
> It is clear that many of the recent and proposed reforms in American law are driven by the need to control the jury. The distinction proposed by the *Restatement of Torts, Third,* for example, between manufacturing defects and design defects, is principally designed to enable the judge to withdraw the case from the jury where there is no evidence that a safer design was feasible. It is doubtful that there would be much objection to strict liability, even from defendants' interests, if there were assurance that compensation would only be made where a defect has been clearly and reliably established, and compensation would be at moderate levels, with no possibility of punitive damages. This suggestion is borne out by experience in England and Australia, where the adoption of strict liability has caused no discernible increase in rates of litigation or in the costs borne by defendants or their insurers.

. . .

> The case for reform of the Canadian common law therefore is a strong one. Adoption of a non-contractual principle of strict liability would remove the anomalies of privity of contract and of withholding compensation in those comparatively rare cases where the manufacturer of a defective product can be shown not to have been negligent. It would bring the law into conformity with the law in Quebec, and with that in Europe, Australia and with the law generally prevailing in American jurisdictions. The increased burden on defendants of such a change in the law would be small, but the advance in justice would be large, both in terms of avoiding anomalous distinctions and in terms of affording compensation to injured persons who at present receive none.

See "New Directions in Products Liability" in Mullany and Linden (eds.) *Torts Tomorrow* (1998), at p. 128-29.

4. The [U.K. Pearson Commission] (*Report of the Royal Commission on Civil Liability and Compensation for Personal Injury* (1978)) has suggested the adoption of a regime of strict liability for the producers of defective products. A product would be considered defective "when it does not provide the safety which a person is entitled to expect, having regard to all the circumstances including the presentation of the product". The Commission did not recommend any maximum amount for liability, nor was it willing to exclude liability for developmental risks. See Fleming, "The Pearson Report: Its Strategy" (1979), 42 Mod. L. Rev. 249.

5. What about a no-fault solution? See O'Connell, *Ending Insult to Injury: No-Fault Insurance for Products and Services* (1975).

6. An emerging area of importance deals with the manufacturer's duty to warn of defects or dangers. This has been dealt with by the Supreme Court of Canada in two recent cases: *Bow Valley Husky (Bermuda) Ltd. v. Saint John Shipbuilding Ltd.* (1997), 153 D.L.R. (4th) 385; and *Hollis v. Dow Corning Corp.* (1993), 103 D.L.R. (4th) 520. Once the court determines that the conditions for the duty to warn have been met, *i.e.* that there are dangers associated with the product, that the users were reasonably foreseeable, and that there was a reliance relationship between the manufacturer or supplier and consumer, liability for failure to warn seems to be strict.

CHAPTER 13

NUISANCE

McLAREN, "NUISANCE IN CANADA"
in Linden (ed.), *Studies in Canadian Tort Law* (1968), p. 320

Canadian courts have readily accepted the distinction in the modern law between private and public nuisance. At its simplest, private nuisance is definable as an interference of an indirect or consequential nature with the use and enjoyment of land by the occupier thereof. When a wrong of this nature becomes the object of litigation, the fundamental issue before the court is whether the degree of interference complained of is such that it should not be tolerated by the "ordinary occupier" in the position of the plaintiff. If the court accepts that the degree of interference is unwarranted, then liability follows as a matter of course. There is no concern with a comparison of the plaintiff's position with that of any other members of society. It is of no consequence to the question of liability that other members of the community have or have not suffered interference emanating from the same source. In short, private nuisance is exclusively a civil wrong.

Public nuisance, on the other hand, has a schizophrenic character. Basically it refers to a rather motley group of criminal or quasi-criminal offences which involve actual or potential interference with the public convenience or welfare. In substance, they range from the placing of obstructions on a public highway or a navigable river to the running of an odious institution such as a brothel. Since a public nuisance may be committed and its effects may be felt almost anywhere, it has no obvious connection with interference with interests in land. Further, as this type of nuisance is by definition detrimental to the public interest, the initiative in proceeding against the perpetrator lies with an official representative of that interest. If a criminal action is considered appropriate the offender will be charged under the *Criminal Code* with committing an indictable offence and if found guilty subjected to the prescribed penalty. In the case of civil proceedings the provincial attorney-general is responsible for starting an action to enjoin the continuance of the public nuisance. As long as suffering or inconvenience is general and uniformly injurious, there is no place for independent intervention by private citizens, whether it be an individual or group effort. Certainly they have the right to complain to the appropriate authorities in an attempt to stir the latter to positive action, but they cannot take upon themselves the role of champions of the public interest. In this sense a public nuisance is solely within the ambit of administrative discretion.

Public nuisance, however, has another face. It sometimes transpires that an act or omission which may be characterized as a public nuisance in the criminal sense causes substantial damage to a particular private individual. For instance, he may experience an aggravated degree of inconvenience and financial expenditure in circumventing an obstruction on the highway, or he may suffer a significant diminution in profits because of the proximity of his business to a bawdy house. The knowledge that the offending structure is a public nuisance, and thus ripe for official action may be of little consolation to him. Even if proceedings are initiated by the appropriate authorities, a successful outcome will only benefit him insofar as it excises the source of future damage. He is still left with the sober reality of the loss incurred as a result of the defendant's conduct prior to trial. It is for this reason that a private individual has traditionally been allowed a civil action in certain circumstances. If he is a land occupier and the damage he incurs relates to his use and enjoyment of land, then his course of action is clear. He simply frames his action in private nuisance. The fact that the *casus delicti* is a public nuisance is in most cases irrelevant. Where, however, his complaint is not directly related to an interest in land, he is compelled to initiate a civil action for public nuisance. In order to succeed in this venture he has to persuade the court that the injury or damage he has suffered places him in an adverse position as compared with other members of the public. In short he has to prove damage that is special to him.

Given this basic dichotomy in both substance and procedure, it is quite evident that the use of the term "nuisance" to describe both areas of liability has no inherent rational quality. Indeed the connection can only be explained in terms of a quirk of legal history. It so happened that judges sympathetic to the idea of a limited form of civil recovery for the injurious effects of a group of heterogeneous misdemeanours found a springboard for creativity in a tenuous analogy between certain of the offences in question and situations already covered by private nuisance. Since the association of the two is historical rather than functional, an explanation of the peculiar nuances of both is desirable.

A. PUBLIC NUISANCE

HICKEY v. ELECTRIC REDUCTION CO. OF CANADA

Supreme Court of Newfoundland. (1970), 21 D.L.R. (3d) 368, 2 Nfld. & P.E.I.R. 246.

Furlong C.J.: We are dealing with a preliminary objection in law which has been pleaded by the defendants in para. 6 of their defence:

> 6. The defendant will object that the Statement of Claim is bad in law and discloses no cause of action against the defendant on the grounds that the damages claimed by the plaintiffs are too remote in law.

In his argument counsel for the defendant, F.J. Ryan, Q.C., says in effect that an action in nuisance does not lie on the part of the plaintiffs because the facts as pleaded disclose nothing on which to ground an action for private nuisance, but merely give grounds for argument that the actions of the defendant resulted in the creation of a public nuisance the remedy for which is not at the disposal of the plaintiffs. He further takes the position that even if the plaintiffs had a right of action their damages are too remote to sustain the action.

On the pleadings it is apparent that the plaintiffs' attack was a two-pronged one, in negligence, and in nuisance, but counsel for them, Mr. Robert Wells, accepted the position that there was no case in negligence and confined his argument to his claim in nuisance.

In dealing with an objection in point of law we have to proceed on the assumption that the facts as pleaded by the plaintiffs are established. If the objection is not sustained and the trial of the issues takes place, then, of course, the pleaded facts require proof.

For our present purposes then, I am assuming that the plaintiffs' assertion is true in substance, and that is, that the defendant discharged poisonous material into the waters of Placentia Bay, from its plant at Long Harbour, Placentia Bay, polluting the waters of the bay, poisoning fish "and rendering them of no commercial value".

So at the outset, we are put on inquiry to consider whether the facts disclose the creation of a tortious act, that is to say, the creation of a private nuisance, or the commission of a criminal act, which is to say, a public nuisance. The former is a civil wrong, actionable at the suit of an affected person.

The latter has been defined by Sir James Stephen in his *Digest of the Criminal Law*, 9th ed. (1950) (using the term "common nuisance"), in these words at p. 179:

> A common nuisance is an act not warranted by law or an omission to discharge a legal duty, which act or omission obstructs or causes inconvenience or damage to the public in the exercise of rights common to all His Majesty's subjects.

Salmond, *The Law of Torts*, 15th ed. (1969), expresses it more succinctly at p. 64:

> A public or a common nuisance is a criminal offence. It is an act or omission which materially affects the reasonable comfort or convenience of life of a class of Her Majesty's subjects ...

and he adds:

> A public nuisance falls within the law of torts only in so far as it may in the particular case constitute some form of tort also. Thus the obstruction of a highway is a public nuisance; but if it causes any special and peculiar damage to an individual, it is also a tort actionable at his suit.

What has happened here? The defendants by the discharge of poisonous waste from its phosphorous plant at Long Harbour, Placentia Bay, destroyed the fish life of the adjacent waters, and the plaintiffs, as all other fishermen in the area suffered in their livelihood. I have said "all other fishermen", but the resulting pollution created a nuisance to all persons — "all Her Majesty's subjects" — to use Stephen's phrase. It was not a nuisance peculiar to the plaintiffs, nor confined to their use of the waters of Placentia Bay. It was a nuisance committed against the public.

A somewhat similar occurrence happened at a fishing settlement in Labrador, at Little Grady Island, in 1927, when a whaling company erected a factory at Watering Cove on Big Grady Island and polluted the waters adjacent to the premises of a fishing establishment on the former island. In the event an action was taken by the fishery owners against the whaling company. The case was heard in this Court in 1929 by Kent J., and his judgment has remained unchallenged. He found that amongst other things, that there was serious pollution of the fishing waters from the waste materials of the whale factory. The case is *McRae v. British Norwegian Whaling Co., Ltd.*, [1927-31] Nfld. L.R. 274. After declaring at p. 282 that:

> It is an established principle that the right to fish in the sea and public navigable waters is free and open to all. It is a public right that may be exercised by any of the King's subjects, and for any interference with it the usual remedies to vindicate a public right must be employed.

he proceeded to apply the principle to the facts before him at pp. 283-4:

> The plaintiffs in the present action must, therefore, in order to succeed on this cause of complaint, show that the injury inflicted upon them by the acts of the defendants, insofar as they affect the right of fishing in the public navigable waters in the vicinity of Little Grady Island, is, in regard to them, particular direct and substantial, over and above the injury thereby inflicted upon the public in general. It is not enough for the plaintiffs to show that their business is interrupted or interfered with, by the public nuisance, to enable them to maintain a private action against the defendants in respect thereof, for such interruption or interference is not a direct but merely a consequential damage resulting to them from the nuisance. Neither is it an injury peculiar to the plaintiffs themselves, but is suffered by them in common with everyone else whose right to fish in these public waters is affected by the nuisance. The plaintiffs' right, as one of the public, to fish may be affected to a greater extent than that of others, but they have no ground of complaint different from anyone else who fishes or intends to fish in these waters. If the nuisance took the form of obstructing the right of the plaintiffs as adjacent land owners, of access from their land to the public navigable waters, the injury would be peculiar to themselves, not because it interrupted their right to fish in common with others in the public waters, but because it interrupted their right of access to these waters, which is an incident to the occupation of property adjacent to the sea and would therefore be an interference with a right peculiar to themselves and distinct from their right as one of the public to fish in the public waters. For these reasons I have come to the conclusion that the plaintiffs have failed to establish their right to maintain a private action in respect of the pollution by the defendants of these public navigable waters.

A somewhat similar situation arose in New Brunswick in 1934 in *Fillion v. New Brunswick International Paper Co.*, [1934] 3 D.L.R. 22, 8 M.P.R. 89. The waste from a paper-mill into the Restigouche River in that Province polluted the waters of a bay where the plaintiff, with others, carried on smelt fishing. An action was taken in nuisance against the owners of the paper-mill and that part of the case was dismissed, Baxter, J., saying at p. 26:

> Assuming then, that the defendant's act constituted a public nuisance, and if it is wrongful I do not see how it can be anything else, the plaintiff has suffered differently from the rest of the public only in degree. That is not enough to entitle him to recover. Nearly all of the cases in which this principle has been invoked concern the obstruction of a highway, but *Ashby v. White*, 2 Ld. Raym. 938, at p. 955, 92 E.R. 126, *per* Holt, C.J., and the case of *Williams* in 5 Co. Rep. 72(b), 77 E.R. 163, show that the *ratio decidendi* is that it is inexpedient that there should be multiplicity of actions and that where a nuisance or injury is common to the whole public the remedy is by indictment but that no private right of action exists unless there is a special or particular injury to the plaintiff. *Iveson v. Moore*, 1 Ld. Raym. 486, 91 E.R. 1224, is perhaps the leading case. It is unnecessary to trace its application through a long series of cases under *Expropriation Acts* which often turn upon the language of a particular statute. In the present case the plaintiff's rights were only those which he possessed as one of the public and he suffered exactly the same interference as any other who assumed to exercise the public right of fishing. The jury have so found. Lord Haldane in *A.G.B.C. v. A.G. Can.*, 15 D.L.R. at p. 315, assimilates the right of public fishing to that of navigation or "the right to use a navigable river as a highway." He also held in *A.G. Can. v. A.G. Que., Re Quebec Fisheries* (1920), 56 D.L.R. 358, at p. 361, that the right of fishing in tidal waters is "a public and not a proprietary right." It follows that on this branch of the case the plaintiff can not succeed.

I think it is clear that the facts, as we have them, can only support the view that there has been pollution of the waters of this area of Placentia Bay which amounts to a public nuisance. If I am right in this view then the law is clear that a private action by the plaintiffs is not sustainable.

Counsel for the plaintiffs, Mr. Robert Wells, argued that when a public nuisance has been created anyone who suffers special damage, that is direct damage has a right of action. I am unable to agree to this rather wide application of Salmond's view that a public nuisance may become a tortious act. I think the right view is that any person who suffers peculiar damage has a right of action, but where the damage is common to all persons of the same class, then a personal right of action is not maintainable. Mr. Wells suggests that the plaintiffs' right to outfit for the fishery and their right to fish is a particular right and this right having been interfered with they have a cause of action. This right which they enjoy is a right in common with all Her Majesty's subjects, an interference with which is the whole test of a public nuisance; a right which can only be vindicated by the appropriate means, which is an action by the Attorney-General, either with or without a relator, in the common interest of the public.

Rose et al. v. Miles, [1814-23] All E.R. Rep. 580, which has been cited is not in point, as the judgment of Lord Ellenborough, C.J., clearly shows [at p. 581], "This is something substantially more injurious to this person, than to the public at large," and Dampier, J., said "The present case admits of this distinction from most other cases, that here the plaintiff was interrupted in the actual enjoyment of the highway." With great respect I hold that view that that judgment was applicable only to the particular facts of that case, and can only support the general proposition that a peculiar and particular damage, distinct from that of the general public, is necessary to sustain an action.

I think the law as stated by Kent, J., in the *McRae* case remains unchallenged. In this case the facts are indistinguishable and what Mr. Justice Kent said is fully applicable.

In the light of what I have said it becomes unnecessary to deal at length with the further point raised by the defendant, that the remoteness of damage must bar the plaintiffs' action. Mr. Wells suggests that this is a point applicable only to an action in negligence and plays no part in an action in nuisance. He fails to convince me that this is so. I would only say that to sustain an action the damages asserted must be direct and not consequential. There have been several recent judgments dealing with this point: *SCM (U.K.) Ltd. v. W.J. Whittall & Son Ltd.*, [1970] 3 All E.R. 245, was decided in the Court of Appeal, and though the action here was in negligence, I would be prepared to adopt the view of Lord Denning, M.R., that economic loss without direct damage is not usually recoverable at law. Similar considerations apply in this case; I think it would be a matter of extreme difficulty to say what direct damages the plaintiffs could pin-point as deriving from the defendant's operations. In negligence the damages would not likely be recoverable, and I think that this is equally so in an action in nuisance.

It is clear then, that the objection raised by the defendant's pleading should be upheld; this disposes of the sufficiency of the plaintiffs' cause of action, and their claims must be dismissed, so that the judgment goes for the defendant, with costs.

Action dismissed.

NOTES

1. Do you agree that the fishermen of Placentia Bay suffered no special damage and thus should be denied recompense for public nuisance? Why do Attorneys-General not take a more active role in cases such as these on behalf of the public?

2. Compare with *Burgess v. M/V Tamano*, 370 F. Supp. 247 (U.S.D.C. Maine 1973), where oil was discharged into a bay affecting commercial fishers, clam diggers and other local businesspeople. The court found that the fishers suffered particular damage, but that the businesspeople did not. Gignoux D.J. said:

> The commercial fishermen and clam diggers in the present case clearly have a special interest, quite apart from that of the public generally, to take fish and harvest clams from the coastal waters of the State of Maine. The injury of which they complain has resulted from defendants' alleged interference with *their* direct exercise of the public right to fish and to dig clams. It would be an incongruous result for the Court to say that a man engaged in commercial fishing or clamming, and dependent thereon for his livelihood, who may have had his business destroyed by the tortious act of another, should be denied any right to recover for his pecuniary loss on the ground that his injury is no different in kind from that sustained by the general public. Indeed, in substantially all of those cases in which commercial fishermen using public waters have sought damages for the pollution or other tortious invasion of those waters, they have been permitted to recover.... These cases are no more than applications of the more general principle that pecuniary loss to the plaintiff will be regarded as different in kind "where the plaintiff has an established business making a commercial use of the public right with which the defendant interferes. ..."

As to the businesspeople, Judge Gignoux stated:

> Unlike the commercial fishermen and clam diggers, the Old Orchard Beach businessmen do not assert any interference with *their* direct exercise of a public right. They complain only of loss of customers indirectly resulting from alleged pollution of the coastal waters and beaches in which they do not have a property interest. Although in some instances their damage may be greater in degree, the injury of which they complain, which is derivative from that of the public at large, is common to all businesses and residents of the Old Orchard Beach area. In such circumstances, the line is drawn and the courts have consistently denied recovery.

3. In *Esso Petroleum v. Southport Corp.*, [1954] 2 Q.B. 182, [1954] 2 All E.R. 561 (C.A.); revd [1956] A.C. 212, [1955] 3 All E.R. 864 (H.L.), some oil was discharged by a ship into the water and washed up on the plaintiff's shore, causing considerable damage. Many issues were discussed in the case, but on the issue of public nuisance Denning M.R. had this to say:

> ... [I]t is, in my opinion, a public nuisance to discharge oil into the sea in such circumstances that it is likely to be carried on to the shores and beaches of our land to the prejudice and discomfort of Her Majesty's subjects. It is an offence punishable by the common law. Furthermore, if any person should suffer greater damage or inconvenience from the oil than the generality of the public, he can have an action to recover damages on that account, provided, of course, that he can discover the offender who discharged the oil. This action would have been described in the old days as an action on the case, but it is now simply an action for a nuisance. I realize that by a statute passed in 1922 the discharge of oil in navigable waters has been made an offence punishable sum-

> marily; but that does not mean that it is not also a public nuisance by the common law,

Lord Radcliffe agreed with this view that the discharged oil "may possibly have constituted a public nuisance from which the respondent suffered special damage ...".

See also *National Harbours Board v. Hildon Hotel (1963) Ltd.* (1967), 61 W.W.R. 75 (B.C.S.C.), public nuisance to discharge oil into bay.

4. In *Manitoba (Attorney General) v. Adventure Flight Centres Ltd.* (1983), 22 Man. R. (2d) 142, 25 C.C.L.T. 295 (Q.B.), the defendant leased a field which it used as a training school and airfield for "ultra-light" aircraft. The local residents complained about the noise generated by these aircraft, as well as the dangers posed by them in residential areas, The Attorney-General sought an injunction and a resident sought damages. The court decided that the defendant's activity constituted a public nuisance and granted the injunction. Damages were denied, however, on the basis that the individual plaintiff resident had not proved "particular, direct and substantial and special damage above that sustained by the public at large". Can you think of any other actions which might have been available to the plaintiff which would have awarded him damages without such proof? See Irvine, "Annotation" (1983), 25 C.C.L.T. 296.

5. In *R. v. The Ship "Sun Diamond" et al.*, [1984] 1 F.C. 3, 25 C.C.L.T. 19 (T.D.), the Crown brought an action as a result of the following facts. Two ships collided at sea outside of the limits of the Port of Vancouver. Two hundred and eleven tons of oil were discharged into the water fouling the port, parts of the foreshore, and ships belonging to fishermen. The Crown through the National Harbours Board commenced clean-up operations extending not only to their own property but to private property as well and paid compensation to individuals on a voluntary basis. The Crown wanted to be completely reimbursed for these expenditures. The court decided that in addition to its right to abate the nuisance for the protection of its own property the Crown had at least a moral duty to see that a clean-up was undertaken for the public welfare. The court stated:

   > While the Crown has no authority to act on behalf of private individuals who might have had claims, nor would it most probably have any legal responsibility towards them had it failed to do so since their action would be against the defendants, what was done was reasonable and appears to be a good example of the *parens patriae* principle with the Crown, through its agents, acting as what is referred to in civil law as "bon pere de famille" or "prudent administrator" as this phrase is usually translated.

   The court acknowledged, however, that it was a serious matter to allow someone to abate a nuisance caused to the property of someone else and then to allow them to claim compensation. The court allowed the Crown's claim for reimbursement of the total water clean-up, the voluntary payments made to fishers, the clean-up of its own beach and foreshore, but not the clean-up of private property.

6. In *Cormier et al. v. Blanchard* (1980), 112 D.L.R. (3d) 667, 70 A.P.R. 198 (N.B.C.A.), the plaintiff complained that her waterfront land, used for recreational purposes, was seriously interfered with by the defendant's fish processing plant. The effluent from the plant discoloured the water, left slime on the rocks, attracted seagulls who left excrement on the property, and rendered the property unsuitable for sunbathing, swimming, and scuba diving. Was this a public or a private nuisance? The New Brunswick Court of Appeal held that it was both a public and a private nuisance, and awarded judgment in the plaintiff's favour.

7. Attorneys-General have attempted to use public nuisance to stop street prostitution. In *British Columbia (Attorney General) v. Couillard* (1984), 11 D.L.R. (4th) 567, 31

C.C.L.T. 26 (B.C.S.C.), the Attorney-General of British Columbia was successful in obtaining a wide-sweeping injunction to stop street prostitution in Vancouver's west end. The prostitutes then moved downtown. As a result, businesses in the area sought an injunction to stop street prostitution there, but they failed since they could not prove special or particular damage; see *Stein and Tessler v. Gonzales* (1984), 14 D.L.R. (4th) 263, [1984] 6 W.W.R. 428 (B.C.S.C.). The Attorney-General of Nova Scotia also attempted to control street prostitution by using public nuisance, but failed; see *Nova Scotia (Attorney General) v. Beaver* (1984), 31 C.C.L.T. 54 (N.S.S.C.); affd (1985), 18 D.L.R. (4th) 287, 32 C.C.L.T. 170 (N.S.C.A.). What does all of this tell us? Do you think that it is appropriate to avoid the criminal laws and the constitution which regulates them by using civil actions and resurrecting the tort of public nuisance? Is law effective in stopping prostitution or does it merely change the venue of the problem? See Cassels J., "Prostitution and Public Nuisance: Desperate Measures and the Limits of Civil Adjudication" (1985), 63 Can. Bar Rev. 764.

8. In *Ontario (Attorney-General) v. Dieleman* (1994), 117 D.L.R. (4th) 449 (Ont. Gen. Div.), the Attorney General sought to enjoin anti-abortion protesters who had been picketing at the homes and offices of doctors, at hospitals, and at clinics. In granting an injunction enjoining some of the picketing, the court relied on the torts of private and public nuisance, among others. The court held that the picketing at the homes and private clinics was unreasonable in view of the nature of these premises and the type of disruption and disturbance it was causing, while the picketing at the public hospitals was acceptable.

9. In her book on *The Canadian Law of Nuisance* (Toronto: Butterworths, 1991), p. 64, Professor Beth Bilson makes the following observation regarding the future usefulness of the tort of public nuisance:

> At the outset of this chapter, reference was made to the work of some commentators who have lamented the shortcomings of the action in public nuisance as an instrument for forwarding the interests of injured parties in many circumstances.
>
> This kind of view is reinforced when one considers some of the tensions and paradoxes we have mentioned here. The identification of a public nuisance depends on widespread harm, yet the group who are affected are reliant on the Attorney-General to pursue an action, through which they can hope only for the cessation or removal of the impugned condition or activity. Afflicted individuals may only bring an action for redress for the harm they have suffered if they can show that their harm is of a different order than that affecting others; yet if the general harm is sufficiently bad, it would seem less feasible to demonstrate such special harm.
>
> If the public nuisance action is to have more than the limited and specialized role which has been suggested above, it would be necessary to alter many of the restrictive principles and technical categorizations which currently apply.
>
> Much of the ground which might be occupied by a liberalized law of public nuisance has been given over to statutory regulation. It may be argued that this is a more effective means of securing important social goals, and protecting the public from the evils of pollution or other harmful conditions. It will continue to be the case, however, that groups of people will be affected by particular conditions, not all of which may be addressed by statutory provisions. It is in these circumstances that a law of public nuisance more generously conceived might play a role in the protection of members of society.

10. See generally Prosser, "Private Action for Public Nuisance" (1966), 52 Va. L. Rev. 997; Estey, "Public Nuisance and Standing to Sue" (1972), 10 Osgoode Hall L.J. 563; Rothstein, "Private Action for Public Nuisance: The Standing Problem" (1974), 76 W. Va. L. Rev. 453; Morrison, "The Nuisance Action: A Useful Tool for the Environmental Lawyer" (1974), 23 U.N.B.L.J. 21; McLaren, "The Law of Torts and Pollution" in Special Lectures of the Law Society of Upper Canada, *New Developments in the Law of Torts* (1973); Sax, *Defending the Environment — A Strategy for Citizen Action* (1970); McLaren, "Common Law Nuisance and the Environmental Battle" (1972), 10 Osgoode Hall L.J. 505; Buckley, *The Law of Nuisance* (1981); Kodilnye, "Public Nuisance and Particular Damage in Modern Law" (1986), 6 Legal Stud. 182.

MINT v. GOOD

Court of Appeal. [1951] 1 K.B. 517, [1950] 2 All E.R. 1159, 94 Sol. Jo. 882.

The plaintiff, a boy, was injured by the collapse of a wall adjoining the highway. The wall was owned by the defendant who had leased the premises to a tenant. The trial judge found that, although the wall was a nuisance, the landlord was not liable for it. The appeal was allowed.

Denning L.J.: The law of England has always taken particular care to protect those who use a highway. It puts on the occupier of adjoining premises a special responsibility for the structures which he keeps beside the highway. So long as those structures are safe, all well and good; but if they fall into disrepair, so as to be a potential danger to passers-by, then they are a nuisance, and, what is more, a public nuisance; and the occupier is liable to anyone using the highway who is injured by reason of the disrepair. It is no answer for him to say that he and his servants took reasonable care; for, even if he has employed a competent independent contractor to repair the structure, and has every reason for supposing it to be safe, the occupier is still liable if the independent contractor did the work badly: see *Tarry v. Ashton*.

The occupier's duty to passers-by is to see that the structure is as safe as reasonable care can make it; a duty which is as high as the duty which an occupier owes to people to pay to come on to his premises. He is not liable for latent defects, which could not be discovered by reasonable care on the part of anyone, nor for acts of trespassers of which he neither knew, nor ought to have known: see *Barker v. Herbert*; but he is liable when structures fall into dangerous disrepair, because there must be some fault on the part of someone or other for that to happen; and he is responsible for it to persons using the highway, even though he was not actually at fault himself. That principle was laid down in this court in *Wringe v. Cohen*, when it is to be noted that the principle is confined to "premises on a highway", and is, I think, clearly correct in regard to the responsibility of an occupier to passers-by.

The question in this case is whether the owner, as well as the occupier, is under a like duty to passers-by. I think that in many cases he is. The law has shown a remarkable development on this point during the last sixteen years. The three cases of *Wilchick v. Marks and Silverstone, Wringe v. Cohen*, and *Heap v. Ind, Coope & Allsopp Ld.*, show that the courts are now taking a realistic view of these matters. They recognize that the occupying tenant of a small dwelling-house does not in practice do the structural repairs, but the owner does; and that if a passer-by is injured by the structure being in dangerous repair, the occupier has not the means to pay damages, but the owner has, or, at any rate, he can insure against it. If a passer-by is injured by its falling on him, he should be entitled to damages from someone, and the person who ought to pay is the owner, because he is in practice responsible for the repairs. This practical responsibility means that he has de facto control of the structure for the purpose of repairs and is therefore answerable in law for its condition. Parliament has long made owners responsible under the Public Health Acts for nuisances arising from defects of a structural character: see s. 94 of the *Public Health Act, 1875*, and s. 93(*b*) of the *Public Health Act, 1936*; and the common law now also in many cases makes them responsible for public nuisances due to the disrepair of the structure.

This seems to me to be a logical consequence of the cases to which we have been referred. In *Wilchick v. Marks and Silverstone* the landlord had covenanted to repair; in *Heap v. Ind, Coope & Allsopp Ltd.*, he had not covenanted to repair, but had reserved a right to enter. In the present case he has not reserved a right to enter, but he has in practice always done the structural repairs. I cannot think that the liability of the owner to passers-by depends on the precise terms of the tenancy agreement between the owner and the tenant, that is to say, on whether he has expressly reserved a right to enter or not. It depends on the degree of control exercised by the owner, in law or in fact, for the purpose of repairs. If a landlord is liable when he reserves an express right to enter, he is also liable when he has an implied right; and even if he has no strict right, but has been given permission to enter whenever he asked, it should make no difference. The landlord has in practice taken the structural repairs on himself and should be responsible for any disrepair.

That is sufficient for the decision of this case, but I venture to doubt whether in these days a landlord can in all cases exempt himself from liability to passers-by by taking a covenant from a tenant to repair the structure adjoining the highway. I know that in *Pretty v. Bickmore* a landlord managed to escape liability for a coalplate which was, at the beginning of the lease, in dangerous disrepair because he took from the tenant a covenant to repair. I doubt whether he would escape liability today. Again, suppose that a landlord of small houses took from weekly tenants a covenant to repair the structure, and then did not trouble to enforce the covenant or to repair himself? Could he escape liability by so doing? I doubt it. It may be that in such cases the landlord owes a duty to the public which he cannot get rid of by delegating it to another. These questions do not however arise here because there was no such covenant. In this case the judge found that the condition of the wall was a nuisance, and that a reasonable examination of the wall by a competent person would have detected the condition in which it was. That means that the duty of the landlord was not fulfilled. His duty was to see that the structure was as safe as reasonable care could make it. It was not so safe.

I agree, therefore, that the appeal should be allowed, and judgment entered accordingly.

NOTES

1. This principle has even been extended to people who are on private land near the highway. See *Harrold v. Watney*, [1898] 2 Q.B. 320, 67 L.J.Q.B. 771 (C.A.). It will not be invoked, however, if the person hurt is a long way from the road. See *Hardcastle v. South Yorkshire Ry.* (1859), 157 E.R. 761, [1843-60] All E.R. Rep. 405.

2. There are cases such as this, where there is a public nuisance, which demand proof of negligence before recovery will be allowed. See *Cowan v. Harrington*, [1938] 3

D.L.R. 271, 13 M.P.R. 5 (N.B.C.A.). See also *Hagen v. Goldfarb* (1961), 28 D.L.R. (2d) 746 (N.S.T.D.). If this is nuisance, why should proof of negligence be necessary?

3. In *Ware v. Garston Haulage Co.*, [1944] 1 K.B. 30, 113 L.J.K.B. 45 (C.A.), the plaintiff motorcyclist collided, at night, with a truck which had been left unlighted and unattended on a highway. He later died as a result of injuries sustained and an action was brought on behalf of his family, based on negligence and nuisance. Scott L.J. held that there was a nuisance and explained: "If anything is placed on a highway which is likely to cause an accident through being an obstruction to those who are using the highway on their lawful occasions ... and an accident results, there is an actionable nuisance." This case was criticized by Laskin in "Comment" (1944), 22 Can Bar Rev. 468.

4. *Ware v. Garston Haulage* was explained in *Maitland v. Raisbeck and Hewitt*, [1944] 1 K.B. 689, [1944] 2 All E.R. 272 (C.A.), where a bus collided with the back of a slow-moving truck, whose rear light had gone out. Greene M.R. observed:

> We must approach this question of nuisance on the footing of the county court judge's finding that there was no negligence on the part of the second defendants in respect of the extinction of this rear light. In other words, we assume that the rear light went out for some reason not referable to any negligence on the part of the second defendants. It was, therefore, a misfortune which occurred to the lorry without any fault by them. It is argued that, apart from the driver's knowledge or lack of knowledge that the light was out, and apart from any suggestion of negligence, the mere fact that the light was out at the time, of necessity turned the lorry into a nuisance on the highway. That is a proposition which the county court judge refused to accept, and in my opinion, he was right in doing so. Every person who uses the highway must exercise due care, but he has a right to use the highway, and, if something happens to him which, in fact, causes an obstruction to the highway, but is in no way referable to his fault, it is wrong to suppose that ipso facto and immediately a nuisance is created. A nuisance will obviously be created if he allows the obstruction to continue for an unreasonable time or in unreasonable circumstances, but the mere fact that an obstruction has come into existence cannot turn it into a nuisance. It must depend on the facts of each case whether or not a nuisance is created. If that were not so, it would seem that every driver of a vehicle on the road would be turned into an insurer in respect of latent defects in his machine.

How does this case affect *Ware v. Garston Haulage*? See also *Arm River Enterprises v. McIvor* (1978), 85 D.L.R. (3d) 758 (Sask. Q.B.) (slow-moving vehicle not public nuisance).

5. In *Ryan v. Victoria (City)*, unreported, January 28, 1999, Doc. No. 25704, Major J. (S.C.C.), the plaintiff was injured when one of his motorcycle tires lodged in a gap of a railway track which ran down the street. He sued the railway companies which owned and leased the tracks, and the city. At trial, the companies were found liable in negligence and public nuisance and the city was found liable in negligence. The Court of Appeal reversed the finding of nuisance. The Court of Appeal held that the tracks were an unreasonable interference but that the railway was protected by the defence of statutory authority.

On appeal to the Supreme Court of Canada, Major J. affirmed that the tracks constituted a public nuisance but reversed the Court of Appeal with reference to the defence of statutory authority. On the question of what constitutes a public nuisance, Major wrote:

> The doctrine of public nuisance appears as a poorly understood area of the law. "A public nuisance has been defined as any activity which unreasonably interferes with the public's interest in questions of health, safety, morality, comfort or convenience", see Klar, *supra*, at p. 525. Essentially, "[t]he conduct complained of must amount to ... an attack upon the rights of the public generally to live their lives unaffected by inconvenience, discomfort and other forms of interference": see G.H.L. Fridman, *The Law of Torts in Canada*, Vol. 1 (1989), at p. 168. An individual may bring a private action in public nuisance by pleading and proving special damage. See, *e.g.*, *Chessie v. J.D. Irving Ltd.* (1982), 22 C.C.L.T. 89 (N.B.C.A.). Such actions commonly involve allegations of unreasonable interference with a public right of way, such as street or highway.
>
> Whether or not a particular activity constitutes a public nuisance is a question of fact. Many factors must be considered, including the inconvenience caused by the activity, the difficulty involved in lessening or avoiding the risk, the utility of the activity, the general practice of others, and the character of the neighbourhood.

Having found that the tracks constituted a public nuisance, Major J. considered and rejected the railway companies' defence of statutory authority. See discussion of this defence, below.

6. In *Newell v. Smith* (1971), 20 D.L.R. (3d) 598 (N.S.T.D.), the defendants blocked a roadway preventing the plaintiffs from having access to their property. Whenever the blockage was removed, it would be replaced by the defendants. Liability was found by Justice Dubinsky on the ground that the plaintiffs suffered "particular damage and substantial inconvenience ..." and their damage was found to be "quite distinct from the general inconvenience endured by them in common with the public at large".

7. Particularly complex issues are raised with respect to injuries which persons suffer as a result of hazards occurring on highways, over highways, or next to highways. *Mint v. Good*, *supra*, was an example of a plaintiff being injured by the collapse of a wall adjoining a highway. The court required the defendant to make the structure "as safe as reasonable care can make it".

   Ross et al. v. Wall et al. (1980), 114 D.L.R. (3d) 758, 14 C.C.L.T. 243 (B.C.C.A.), also concerned defective premises adjoining a public sidewalk. A store awning fell onto the plaintiff. The Court of Appeal rejected the more stringent test of *Mint v. Good* and required that the defendant either knew or ought to have known of the danger before he could be found liable.

   For an instructive comment on these cases see: McLaren, "Annotation" (1977), 2 C.C.L.T. 256, and Irvine, "Annotation" (1980), 14 C.C.L.T. 243.

8. Can a wharf which extends 30 feet into a river amount to a public nuisance? In *Chessie v. J.D. Irving Ltd.* (1982), 140 D.L.R. (3d) 501, 22 C.C.L.T. 89 (N.B.C.A.), the plaintiff was seriously injured when his snowmobile collided with a wharf operated by the defendant company. The court compared the public's right to passage over the ice with the utility of the wharf, its dangers, and its purposes, and also took into consideration the conduct of the parties in deciding that the wharf did not amount to a public nuisance. Do you think the fact that the river was three-quarters of a mile wide at the point at which the wharf was located was an important factor in this case? One can hardly see why the plaintiff considered that his passage was unreasonably interfered with in view of this fact.

B. PRIVATE NUISANCE

PUGLIESE ET AL. v. NATIONAL CAPITAL COMMN.

Ontario Court of Appeal. (1977), 3 C.C.L.T. 18; affd but answer varied (1979), 25 N.R. 498, 8 C.C.L.T. 69 (S.C.C.).

The plaintiffs sued because their ground water table below their properties was substantially lowered by the construction of a collector sewer on nearby lands owned by the N.C.C. As a result, they claimed, their properties were damaged because of subsidence. They also contended that there was damage caused as a result of drilling and blasting. An application under Rule 124 was referred to the Court of Appeal, in accordance with s. 35 of the *Judicature Act*. The court agreed, *inter alia*, to answer the following question: "Does an owner of land have a right to the support of water beneath his land, not flowing in a defined channel, and does the owner have a right of action in negligence or nuisance ... for any damage resulting from the abstraction of such water?" The court found that both negligence and nuisance were available to the plaintiffs.

As to nuisance **Howland J.A.** wrote: Nuisance is a separate field of tortious liability and not merely an offshoot of the law of negligence. A nuisance may be caused by an intentional or by a negligent act. Negligence is not a prerequisite to an action for nuisance. A negligent act may, however, be a constituent element of a nuisance or may itself constitute a nuisance.

In *Salmond on The Law of Torts*, 16th ed. (1973), p. 51, the following is stated as a definition of "private nuisance" which has received judicial approval:

> Private nuisances, at least in the vast majority of cases, are interferences for a substantial length of time by owners or occupiers of property with the use or enjoyment of neighbouring property: *Cunard v. Antifyre Ltd.*, [1933] 1 K.B. 551 at 557.

At the outset a question arose whether the alleged facts in the present actions could give rise to a right of action in nuisance because the interference with the plaintiffs' use and enjoyment of their lands resulted from the removal of water rather than from an invasion of their property by some substance, as is usually the case in actions for nuisance. I am satisfied, however, from a consideration of the authorities that there is a sound basis for allowing recovery for nuisance in these circumstances: ...

In determining whether a nuisance exists, it is not sufficient to ask whether an occupier has made a reasonable use of his own property. One must ask whether his conduct is reasonable considering the fact that he has a neighbour. As Lord Wright pointed out in *Sedleigh-Denfield v. O'Callaghan*, [1940] A.C. 880 at 903, [1940] 3 All E.R. 349:

> A balance has to be maintained between the right of the occupier to do what he likes with his own, and the right of his neighbour not to be interfered with. It is impossible to give any precise or universal formula, but it may broadly be said that a useful test is perhaps what is reasonable according to the ordinary usages of mankind living in society, or more correctly in a particular society.

The matter is also well summarized in Fleming, *The Law of Torts*, 4th ed. (1971), p. 346, as follows:

> 'Liability is imposed only in those cases where the harm or risk to one is greater than he ought to be required to bear under the circumstances.' [Restatement of the Law of Torts, 1934, para. 822, comment *j*.]

> The paramount problem in the law of nuisance is, therefore, to strike a tolerable balance between conflicting claims of landowners, each invoking the privilege to exploit the resources and enjoy the amenities of his property without undue subordination to the reciprocal interests of the other. Reconciliation has to be achieved by compromise, and the basis for adjustment is reasonable user. Legal intervention is warranted only when an excessive use of property causes inconvenience beyond what other occupiers in the vicinity can be expected to bear, having regard to the prevailing standard of comfort of the time and place. Reasonableness in this context is a two-sided affair. It is viewed not only from the standpoint of the defendant's convenience, but must also take into account the interest of the surrounding occupiers. It is not enough to ask: Is the defendant using his property in what would be a reasonable manner if he had no neighbour? The question is, is he using it reasonably, having regard to the fact that he has a neighbour?
>
> Both the utility of his own conduct and the gravity of the harm to which he exposes others are important factors in this evaluating process.

Nuisances of a minor character arising from the ordinary use and occupation of residential property, such as the burning of weeds and the making of repairs, if performed reasonably and not to an excessive degree, are not actionable. As Bramwell B. said in *Bamford v. Turnley* (1862), 3 B. & S. 66, 122 E.R. 27 at 33:

> It is as much for the advantage of one owner as of another; for the very nuisance the one complains of, as the result of the ordinary use of his neighbour's land, he himself will create in the ordinary use of his own, and the reciprocal nuisances are of a comparatively trifling character. The convenience of such a rule may be indicated by calling it a rule to give and take, live and let live.

Beyond this point it is necessary to ask if the conduct of an occupier of land has been reasonable vis-à-vis his neighbour. The taking of all reasonable care is not a defence to an action for nuisance. If an operation cannot by the exercise of reasonable care and skill be prevented from causing a nuisance, then it cannot lawfully be undertaken unless there is either a statutory authorization or the consent of those injured: . ...

In *Storms v. M.G. Henninger Ltd.; Gonu v. M.G. Henniger Ltd.*, *supra*, this court held that the excavation of sand and gravel was a natural user of the land, and there was no right of action in damages with reference to the resulting flow of subterranean water. There remains open the question whether there might be a right of action in nuisance in the present actions if there was unreasonable user of the lands of the NCC.

The test for determining whether a nuisance was created is not whether the drainage of a very large quantity of water for the construction of the LCS was a reasonable user of the NCC lands when looked at from the point of view of the NCC. Rather it is a question whether it was reasonable so far as the plaintiffs were concerned.

Counsel for the plaintiffs contended that the pumping of the excessive amount of water by the defendants was unlawful, not in the sense that it was a statutory violation of s. 37 of *The Ontario Water Resources Act*, but as an unnatural, and therefore an unlawful, user of the lands of the NCC. In my opinion, it would be for the trial judge to determine whether the abstraction of a very large quantity of water causing damage to the plaintiffs' properties through subsidence, more particularly if it were abstracted in a negligent manner, constituted a nuisance. Did it subject the plaintiff's lands to damage beyond that which they could reasonably be expected to tolerate? In my opinion, the alleged conduct on the part of the defendants, if established at the trial, could constitute an excessive user of the lands of the NCC. I am of the opinion that interference with a right to the support of underground water can give rise to a cause of action in nuisance as well as in negligence.

[The Court, therefore, answered the question as follows:]

1. An owner of land does not have an absolute right to the support of water beneath his land not flowing in a defined channel, but he does have a right not to be subjected to interference with the support of such water amounting to negligence or nuisance.
2. Such an owner does have a right of action:
   (a) in negligence for damages resulting from the abstraction of such water; or
   (b) in nuisance for damages for unreasonable user of the lands in the abstraction of such water.

TOCK v. ST. JOHN'S METROPOLITAN AREA BD.
Supreme Court of Canada. (1989), 64 D.L.R. (4th) 620,
[1989] 2 S.C.R. 1181.

The basement of the plaintiffs' house was flooded by water which came from the defendant Board's obstructed storm sewer system after an exceptionally heavy rainfall. The plaintiffs brought action against the Board in nuisance, as well as in negligence, and for strict liability. The nuisance action succeeded and the major issue for the courts involved the defence of statutory authority, discussed *infra*. On the nature of the nuisance action, La Forest J. stated the following:

La Forest J.
Nuisance

Generically, as *Salmond on Torts*, 17th ed. (1977), by R.F.V. Heuston, at p. 50, notes, "nuisances are caused by an act or omission, whereby a person is unlawfully annoyed, prejudiced or disturbed in the enjoyment of land". The same passage makes it clear that a nuisance may take a variety of forms, ranging from actual physical damage to land to interference with the health, comfort or convenience of the owner or occupier of land.

The assessment whether a given interference should be characterized as a nuisance turns on the question, simple to state but difficult to resolve, whether in the circumstances it is reasonable to deny compensation to the aggrieved party. The courts have traditionally approached this problem of reconciling conflicting uses of land with an eye to a standard based, in large part, on the formulations of Knight Bruce V.-C. in *Walter v. Selfe* (1851), 4 De G. & Sm. 315, 64 E.R. 849, and Bramwell B. in *Bamford v. Turnley* (1862), 3 B. & S. 66, 122 E.R. 27, at pp. 83-4 and at pp. 32-3 respectively. There it was observed that the very existence of organized society depended on a generous application of the principle of "give and take, live and let live". It was therefore appropriate to interpret as actionable nuisances only those inconveniences that materially interfere with ordinary comfort as defined according to the standards held by those of plain and sober tastes. In effect, the law would only intervene to shield persons from interferences to their enjoyment of property that were unreasonable in the light of all the circumstances.

The courts are thus called upon to select among the claims for interference with property and exclude those based on the prompting of excessive "delicacy and fastidiousness", to employ the terms of Knight Bruce V.-C. The courts attempt to circumscribe the ambit of nuisance by looking to the nature of the locality in question and asking whether the ordinary and reasonable resident of that locality would view the disturbance as a substantial interference with the enjoyment of land. Among the criteria employed by the courts in delimiting the ambit of the tort of nuisance are considerations based on the severity of the harm, the character of the neighbourhood, the utility of the defendant's conduct, and the question whether the plaintiff displayed abnormal sensitivity.

It is important to bear in mind, however, that these criteria find their greatest application in cases where the interference complained of does not consist of material damage to property but rather interference with tranquility and amenity, *i.e.*, what Westbury L.C. in *St. Helen's Smelting Co. v. Tipping* (1865), 11 H.L.C. 642 at p. 650, 11 E.R. 1483, classified as "nuisance … productive of sensible personal discomfort … anything that discomposes or injuriously affects the senses or the nerves". Where "material damage" is concerned, it is clear that the criteria adverted to above are to be applied with great circumspection: see *Russell Transport Ltd. v. Ontario Malleable Iron Co. Ltd.* [1952] 4 D.L.R. 719 at pp. 729-30, [1952] O.R. 621 (H.C.J.), *per* McRuer C.J.H.C. In the presence of actual physical damage to property, the courts have been quick to conclude that the interference does indeed constitute a substantial and unreasonable interference with the enjoyment of property. As put by Westbury L.C. in *St. Helen's Smelting Co. v. Tipping*, *supra*, at pp. 650-1.

> … the submission which is required from persons living in society to that amount of discomfort which may be necessary for the legitimate and free exercise of the trade of their neighbours, would not apply to circumstances the immediate result of which is sensible injury to the value of the property.

On the basis of the foregoing considerations, I conclude that the escape of water at issue here would clearly constitute a compensable nuisance were this a case opposing two private individuals. The same view was taken by McIntyre J.A., later of this court, in the very similar case of *Royal Anne Hotel Co. v. Ashcroft (Village)* (1979), 95 D.L.R. (3d) 756, [1979] 2 W.W.R. 462, 8 C.C.L.T. 179 (B.C.C.A.).

Appeal allowed.

RUSSELL TRANSPORT LTD. v. ONTARIO MALLEABLE IRON CO. LTD.

Ontario High Court. [1952] O.R. 621, [1952] 4 D.L.R. 719.

The defendant had been carrying on the business of a foundry at its present site in the City of Oshawa, Ontario, since 1907. The plaintiffs bought land in the vicinity, in 1949, which it used, in connection with its business of transporting new motor vehicles by truck, as a marshalling yard for vehicles to be transported. In 1951 complaints were received that the finish on motor cars transported by them was contaminated and damaged, and that the cause was traced to particles of iron, manganese sulphide and other materials incident to foundry operation. Faced with a demand by its customers that motor vehicles must be removed from its marshalling yard, the plaintiffs brought action for nuisance to recover damages and for an injunction.

McRuer C.J.H.C. [After a lengthy examination of the scientific evidence dealing with the nature and effect of tests made to establish the source of the damage to the vehicles on plaintiffs' land.]: The irresistible conclusion on the evidence is, and I so find, that the defendant emits from its plant particles of iron and iron oxide together with other matters which settle on the plaintiffs' lands, rendering the plaintiffs' property unfit for the purpose for which it was purchased and developed. The plaintiffs have therefore suffered and will continue to suffer material and substantial damage to their property unless the emission of injurious substances is abated. …

Salmond on *Torts*, 10th ed., pp. 228-31, summarizes in a comprehensive manner "Ineffectual Defences" as follows:

1. It is no defence that the plaintiffs themselves came to the nuisance.
2. It is no defence that the nuisance, although injurious to the plaintiffs, is beneficial to the public at large.
3. It is no defence that the place from which the nuisance proceeds is a suitable one for carrying on the operation complained of, and that no other place is available in which less mischief would result.
4. It is no defence that all possible care and skill are being used to prevent the operation complained of from amounting to a nuisance. Nuisance is not a branch of the law of negligence.
5. It is no defence that the act of the defendant would not amount to a nuisance unless other persons acting independently of him did the same thing at the same time.
6. He who causes a nuisance cannot avail himself of the defence that he is merely making a reasonable use of his own property. No use of property is reasonable which causes substantial discomfort to others or is a source of damage to their property.

In opening his argument Mr. Sedgwick stated that the principal defences relied on by the defendant were a reasonable use of its land, and prescriptive right.

It is argued that the plaintiffs established their marshalling yard in an industrial area unsuitable for a business of that character. In the first place, the facts do not support this contention even if there were a sound basis of law for it. … It was not until the business had been carried on for nearly 2 years that either the plaintiffs or the defendant became aware of the nuisance. …

Any arguments based on the fact that the nuisance may have existed before the plaintiffs purchased their property is completely answered by the statement of Lord Halsbury in *Fleming v. Hislop* (1886), 11 App. Cas. 686 at pp. 696-7, where he said: "If the Lord Justice Clerk means to convey that there was anything in the law which diminished the right of a man to complain of a nuisance because the nuisance existed before he went to it, I venture to think that neither in the law of England nor in that of Scotland is there any foundation for any such contention. It is clear that whether the man went to the nuisance or the nuisance came to the man, the rights are the same, and I think that the law of England has been settled, certainly for more than 200 years, by a judgment of Lord Chief Justice Hide."

The last proposition that I have quoted from *Salmond* requires some qualification, but only a very limited one. Counsel bases his whole argument on the defence of reasonable use of the defendant's lands on a passage from the judgment of Thesinger, L.J., in *Sturges v. Bridgman* (1879), 11 Ch.D. 852 at p. 865, where the learned Lord Justice in dealing with two hypothetical cases said: "As regards the first, it may be answered that whether anything is a nuisance or not is a question to be determined, not merely by an abstract consideration of the thing itself, but in reference to its circumstances; what would be a nuisance in Belgrave Square would not necessarily be so in Bermondsey; and where a locality is devoted to a particular trade or manufacture carried on by the traders or manufacturers in a particular and established manner not constituting a public nuisance, judges and juries would be justified in finding, and may be trusted to find, that the trade or manufacture so carried on in that locality is not a private or actionable wrong."

This statement of the law has been applied with caution in some cases arising out of an alleged nuisance producing sensible personal discomfort, but it is not to be broadly applied nor is it to be isolated from the general body of law on the subject. It was an expression used in a case arising out of noise and vibration.

The judgment of the Lord Chancellor in *St. Helen's Smelting Co. v. Tipping* (1865), 11 H.L.C. 642 at p. 650; 11 E.R. 1483, is the classic authority in all cases similar to the one before me: "My Lords, in matters of this description it appears to me that it is a very desirable thing to mark the difference between an action brought for a nuisance upon the ground that the alleged nuisance produces material injury to the property, and an action brought for a nuisance on the ground that the thing alleged to be a nuisance is productive of sensible personal discomfort. With regard to the latter, namely, the personal inconvenience and interference with one's enjoyment, one's quiet, one's personal freedom, anything that discomposes or injuriously affects the senses or the nerves, whether that may or may not be denominated a nuisance, must undoubtedly depend greatly on the circumstances of the place where the thing complained of actually occurs. If a man lives in a town, it is necessary that he should subject himself to the consequences of those operations of trade which may be carried on in his immediate locality, which are actually necessary for trade and commerce, and also for the enjoyment of property, and for the benefit of the inhabitants of the town and of the public at large. If a man lives in a street where there are numerous shops, and a shop is opened next door to him, which is carried on in a fair and reasonable way, he has no ground for complaint, because to himself individually there may arise some discomfort from the trade carried on in that shop. But when an occupation is carried on by one person in the neighbourhood of another, and the result of that trade, or occupation, or business, *is a material injury to property*, then there unquestionably arises a very different consideration. I think, my Lords, that in a case of that description, the submission which is required from persons living in society to that amount of discomfort which may be necessary for the legitimate and free exercise of the trade of their neighbours, would not apply to circumstances *the immediate result of which is sensible injury to the value of the property*." (The italics are mine.)

Even if on any argument a doctrine of reasonable use of the defendant's lands could be expanded to cover a case where there is substantial and material injury to the plaintiffs' property I do not think it could be applied to this case. "Reasonable" as used in the law of nuisance must be distinguished from its use elsewhere in the law of tort and especially as it is used in negligence actions. In negligence, assuming that the duty to take care has been established, the vital question is, 'Did the defendant take reasonable care?' But in nuisance the defendant is not necessarily quit of liability even if he has taken reasonable care. It is true that the result of a long chain of decisions is that unreasonableness is a main ingredient of liability for nuisance. But here 'reasonable' means something more than merely 'taking proper care'. It signifies what is legally right between the parties, taking into account all the circumstances of the case, and some of these circumstances are often such as a man on the Clapham omnibus could not fully appreciate"; Winfield on *Torts*, 5th ed., p. 448. "At common law, if I am sued for a nuisance, and the nuisance is proved, it is no defence on my part to say, and to prove, that I have taken all reasonable care to prevent it": *per* Lindley, L.J., in *Rapier v. London Tramways Co.*, [1893] 2 Ch. 588, at pp. 599-600. This is not to be interpreted to mean that taking care is never relevant to liability for nuisance. In some cases if the defendant has conducted his trade or business as a reasonable man would have done he has gone some way toward making out a defence, but only some of the way: *Stockport Waterworks Co. v. Potter* (1861), 7 H. & N. 160; 158 E.R. 433.

On the other hand, if the defendant has taken no reasonable precautions to protect his neighbour from injury by reason of operations of his own property the defence of reasonable user is of little avail.

The evidence shows that in so far as the emissions from the cupola are responsible for the injury to the plaintiffs, and I think they are in large measure responsible for the injury complained of, the defendant has adopted no method of modern smoke or fume control. ... The defendant has considered the installation of a fume control system in the cupola but has refrained from doing anything pending the outcome of this action. ...

To give effect to the defence of reasonable user of the defendant's lands in this case would be to expand the doctrine of law involved in this defence far beyond any authority in British jurisprudence.

Although in this case there is no admission that the defendant has violated the plaintiffs' legal right by damaging the motor vehicles stored on their property, I find as a fact that it has done so, and I cannot find that the storing of automobiles in the open air on the lots in question is a particularly delicate trade or operation. The finish of an automobile is designed to resist reasonable atmospheric contamination and it would be manifestly unjust to hold that property owners in the vicinity of the defendant's plant have no legal right to have their automobiles protected from the emissions from the defendant's foundry simply because they do not keep them under cover.

NOTES

1. Applying different criteria to those activities which result in material damage to a neighbour's property, as opposed to those which only interfere with tranquility and amenity, to determine the reasonableness of the use, has a solid basis in Canadian nuisance law. There are difficulties, however, with this approach. First is the difficulty in drawing the line between the two types of interferences. Second is the question whether the mere fact of material damage always ought to make the offending activity a nuisance, no matter what the countervailing arguments may be. It is probably best to agree that the nature of the damage is a very important factor in deciding the nuisance issue, although it should never be determinative in and of itself.

2. In her book *The Canadian Law of Nuisance* (Toronto: Butterworths, 1991), Professor Bilson describes the criteria for assessing nuisance, at p. 32:

> Though an owner or occupier of property is entitled to protection from interference with enjoyment of that property through the tort of nuisance, such protection has never been unqualified. The ambition of nuisance law has never extended to providing every plaintiff with a serene hermitage, but has been limited to providing restrictions on the most intolerable or obnoxious of the unpleasant consequences of living in proximity to other members of society.

In this respect, the sanctity of any person's proprietary interests must be weighted against the competing interests put forward by others. As Fleming points out, quoting *Bamford v. Turnley*, the principle of "give and take, live and let live" must be part of the armoury of criteria for any system of tort law which hopes to deal with real, as opposed to ideal, society.

It is the recognition of competing property interests and of the need for accommodation which introduces into the law of private nuisance one of its most central characteristics, for, above all, private nuisance is a means by which owners or occupiers of property can obtain an evaluation or vindication of their proprietary interests in comparison with those of their neighbours. The court in a nuisance case must decide which neighbour's use of the occupied property should be allowed to prevail, and what restrictions, if any, should be placed on such use. This mediatory enterprise must be carried on in the face of a municipality of factual situations, kinds of harm and degrees of interference; like other areas of tort law, the tort of nuisance has developed a set of criteria in response to this which are aimed at generalizing the impact of decisions arrived at in specific cases.

The three major factors which have been looked to in order to restrict the ability of the plaintiff to insist on a degree of protection which is unrealistic have been the reasonableness of the use to which property is being put by the defendant, the character of the locality in which the property is situated, and any special sensitivities of the plaintiff or of the enterprises he or she wishes to protect.

NOR-VIDEO SERVICES LTD. v. ONTARIO HYDRO

Ontario Supreme Court. (1978), 4 C.C.L.T. 244, 19 O.R. (2d) 107.

The plaintiff cable television company sued Ontario Hydro for locating one of its electrical power installations where it would interfere with the transmission and reception of TV broadcast signals. The plaintiff was the only supplier of TV to a small northern community in Ontario named Atikokan. The defendant needed a new transformer and power transmission line and, after considering several sites, chose one next to the plaintiff's receiving tower because it was the most economical and convenient location available. The defendant had been made aware of the possible difficulties but assured the plaintiff that there would be no problem. They built the system and it interfered with the TV reception. Remedial efforts were made by Hydro, but in vain. Robins J. found the defendants liable in nuisance, but awarded only minimal damages because there was no proof of any large losses.

Robins J.: The interest which Nor-Video complains has been interfered with or invaded, and allegedly unreasonably so, is, in nuisance terms, its interest in the use and enjoyment of its land. The harm suffered is not, as in most nuisance cases, of a physical nature to land or tangible property nor is it personal discomfort, annoyance or inconvenience. The gravamen of the complaint is the inability to use and enjoy property to the same extent and with the same result as before Hydro's intervention; or, put another way, the plaintiff's complaint is that the interference with TV broadcast reception prevents it from freely enjoying its property and putting it to its full business use. Nor-Video, in short, contends that television reception is an integral part of the beneficial enjoyment of its property and it is entitled to nuisance to protection against the unreasonable and substantial interference with or invasion of such an interest.

Hydro's response to this contention is twofold. It says firstly that the reception of television does not constitute an interest in the use and enjoyment of land recognized in the law of nuisance and accordingly legal protection is not afforded against its interference. And secondly, it says, that, in any event, the plaintiff has applied its property to so abnormally sensitive a use that interference with it cannot amount to nuisance.

On the first submission Hydro finds support in dictum in a case arising out of a somewhat similar factual situation: *Bridlington Relay Ltd. v. Yorkshire Electricity Bd.*, [1965] Ch. 436, [1965] 1 All E.R. 264. There Buckley J. (p. 270) took "judicial notice of the widespread reception of television in domestic circles ... on the footing that in those circles television is enjoyed almost entirely for what I think must be regarded as recreational purposes ..." and proceeded to observe (p. 271) that:

> There are, of course, many reported cases in which something adversely affecting the beneficial enjoyment of property has been held to constitute a legal nuisance; but I have been referred to no case in which interference with a purely recreational facility has been held to do so. Considerations of health and physical comfort and well being appear to me to be on a somewhat different level from recreation considerations. I do not wish to be taken as laying down that in no circumstances can something which interferes merely with recreational facilities or activities amount to an actionable nuisance. It may be that in some other case the court may be satisfied that some such interference should be regarded, according to such "plain and sober and simple notions" as Sir J.L. Knight Bruce, V.-C., referred to in a well-known passage in his judgment in *Walter v. Selfe* (1851), 4 De G. & Sm. 315 at p. 322, as detracting from the beneficial use and enjoyment by neighbouring owners of their properties to such an extent as to warrant their protection by the law. For myself, however, I do not think that it can at present be said that the ability to receive television free from occasional, even if recurrent and severe, electrical interference is so important a part of an ordinary householder's enjoyment of his property that such interference should be regarded as a legal nuisance particularly, perhaps if such interference affects only one of the available alternative programmes.

From this it is argued that since the interference in this case is to a "recreational facility" it cannot constitute a sufficient interference with ordinary beneficial enjoyment as to amount to a legal nuisance. With deference I cannot agree. Whatever may have been the situation in England at the time of *Bridlington*, in my opinion it is manifest that in Canada today television viewing is an important incident of ordinary enjoyment of property and should be protected as such. It is clearly a principal source of information, education and entertainment for a large part of the country's population; an inability to receive it or an unreasonable interference with its reception would to my mind undoubtedly detract from the beneficial use and ownership of property even applying the test of "plain, sober and simple notions" referred to in the above passage. See note 81 L.Q.R. 181.

"A balance has to be maintained between the right of the occupier to do what he likes with his own and the right of his neighbour not to be interfered with. It is impossible to give any precise or universal formula, but it may broadly be said that a useful test is perhaps what is reasonable according to the ordinary usages of mankind living in society, or, more correctly, in a particular society. The forms which nuisance may take are protean": *Sedleigh-Denfield v. O'Callagan*, [1940] A.C. 880, [1940] 3 All E.R. 349 at 364 (H.L.) per Lord Wright.

The notion of nuisance is a broad and comprehensive one which has been held to encompass a wide variety of interferences considered harmful and actionable because of their infringement upon or diminution of an occupier's interest in the undisturbed enjoyment of his property. I can see no warrant for refinements in approach which would preclude from protection the interest in TV reception even assuming it to be a recreational amenity. In this day and age it is simply one of the benefits and pleasures commonly derived from domestic occupancy of property; its social value and utility to a community, perhaps even more so to a remote community such as the one in this case, cannot be doubted. The category of interests covered by the tort of nuisance ought not to be and need not be closed, in my opinion, to new or changing developments associated from time to time with normal usage and enjoyment of land. Accordingly I would reject the defendant's submission and hold that television reception is an interest worthy of protection and entitled to vindication in law.

This brings me to Hydro's next contention which is that Nor-Video has devoted its property to an unusually sensitive use and cannot by so doing make a nuisance out of conduct or activity which would otherwise be harmless. As a matter of general legal principle it is undisputed that an interference with something of abnormal sensitiveness or delicacy does not of itself constitute a nuisance. The law does not extend protection through nuisance to hyper-sensitive individuals or industries; it is against interferences to what objectively can be considered ordinary uses of property or enjoyments of life that protection is afforded.

"A man cannot increase the liabilities of his neighbour by applying his own property to special uses, whether for business or pleasure": ...

...

The question here is whether, as a matter of fact, the plaintiff's use of its property is of so "delicate" or "sensitive" a nature or constitutes so "special" or "abnormal" a use that injury to it is not actionable in nuisance. It is my opinion that the use to which Nor-Video put its property cannot and ought not to be so characterized. As I view this matter its position, in substance, is comparable to that of owners of domestic antennas who, but for the prohibitive cost involved, could, if they wished, receive the programmes of distant stations by erecting an antenna of similar height. A community antenna system, over-simply stated, provides TV viewers of the community with the advantage of more channels at an affordable cost. But the nature of the apparatus involved is not significantly different or more susceptible to TV than the installations of the ordinary homeowner and in my view should be treated as being in the same category.

In *Bridlington*, it was said that the cable operator "could not succeed in a claim for damages for nuisance if what I may call an ordinary receiver of television by means of an aerial mounted on his own house could not do so." Accepting that, and with the greatest respect for the contrary view indicated there, I do not appreciate why a domestic owner could not succeed in a nuisance claim or, more particularly, why his claim should be defeated on the ground of extra-sensitive use of property. If, to take an example, Hydro should install in a residential district (zoning bylaws aside) a new device to improve electrical services which resulted in the obliteration of TV in the area, I would not think that claims brought against it in nuisance should fail solely on the ground that the TV antennas of the residents amounted to an abnormally sensitive use of their land. To the contrary, as I see the matter, the residents were simply maintaining a commonplace domestic facility and using their property, in terms of modern society, in a normal, and by no means exceptional, manner.

Interference with a CATV system has the same net result and, in my view, should be treated in the same fashion. I do not believe it can be concluded at the present time that a cable operation, federally licensed and regulated, creates so exceptionally sensitive or vulnerable a condition or should be regarded as so special or abnormal an enterprise that it cannot seek the protection of the law of nuisance, particularly, I might add, against a defendant who by the exercise of reasonable care and foresight and without significant sacrifice to its project could have avoided the harm complained of. It provides, especially in the context of this case, the facility needed for an important aspect of a householder's ordinary enjoyment of his property and should be entitled to protection against unreasonable interference.

V

I move now to consider whether the conduct which caused the interference with Nor-Video's interest in the beneficial use of its land was of a type that should subject Hydro to liability.

Just as all interferences with use and enjoyment of land are not actionable, so all types of conduct causing such interferences do not constitute actionable wrongs. The complaint in this case is not that Hydro acted intentionally in invading the plaintiff's interest or that it engaged in the type of malevolent or unreasonable conduct devoid of or containing comparatively little social or economic utility such as is found in the line of cases of which *Hollywood Silver Fox Farm, Ltd. v. Emmett*, [1936] 2 K.B. 468, [1936] 1 All E.R. 825 is a classic example. Nor is it argued that the invasion was the consequence of an abnormally dangerous activity to which the rule in *Rylands v. Fletcher* [(1868), L.R. 3 H.L. 330] should apply and for which Hydro should be held strictly liable.

The complaint on which Nor-Video's case rests is that proprietary interests entitled to protection were invaded by Hydro's action in constructing high power electrical installations in locations where it knew or should have known that to do so would adversely affect the cable system. (The further contention that the installations were improperly designed or maintained is not, as I indicated, supported by the evidence).

It is manifest that Hydro is an important public utility which has been granted wide statutory powers to enable it to perform its highly essential undertakings: The Power Commission Act, R.S.O. 1970, c. 354 (renamed The Power Corporation Act, 1973 (Ont.), c. 57) [now R.S.O. 1990, c. P.18]. But it has not been granted immunity from tort liability and, in my opinion, such immunity cannot be implied from a reading of s. 24 of the Act. It was neither inevitable, nor necessary, that the plaintiff be detrimentally affected by Hydro's fulfilment of its legislative mandate. This occurred because Hydro failed to recognize, as it should in my opinion, that by its site selection it created an unreasonable risk to the activity conducted by the cable company on neighbouring lands. The locations in question were discretionary and not prescribed by statute; they did not constitute the only feasible places for Hydro's works. The fact that the acquisition and use of these sites was later retroactively authorized by Order in Council pursuant to s. 24 does not, in my view, render them mandatory locations so as to authorize a nuisance or afford Hydro any greater immunity from action than that extended by s. 24(5) which operates only to prevent it from being "restrained by injunction or other process or proceeding".

Without repeating the findings I set forth earlier, it can, in short, be stated that in planning and embarking on its project in the locations in question Hydro failed properly to apprehend or calculate a perceptible risk to the plaintiff's legitimate interests. It was bound in the circumstances prevailing in the instant case to do so. In planning its own undertaking it was required to act carefully and take into account the likelihood of unreasonably detrimental consequences to the plaintiff. Legislative authority cannot in my opinion be involved as a defence in this case:

see, *Hammersmith & City Ry. Co. v. Brand* (1869), L.R. 4 H.L. 171; *Manchester Corpn. v. Farnsworth*, [1930] A.C. 171 (H.L.); *Metropolitan Asylum Dist. Managers v. Hill* (1881), 6 App. Cas. 193 (H.L.); *Geddis v. Bann Reservoir Proprietors* (1878), 3 App. Cas. 430 (H.L.); *Guelph Worsted Spinning Co. v. Guelph; Guelph Carpet Mills Co. v. Guelph* (1914), 30 O.L.R. 466, 18 D.L.R. 73; and generally, for a comprehensive collection and analysis of the authorities, Linden "Strict Liability, Nuisance and Legislative Authorization" (1966), 4 Osgoode Hall L.J. 196.

The defendant's conduct in my view constitutes negligence in the usual sense of failing to take due care to avoid a foreseeable risk. But even if not, it amounts to conduct unreasonable enough to complete the tort of nuisance — there are elements of "fault" and "foreseeability" present sufficient to satisfy the tort: *The Wagon Mound (No. 2), supra, per* Lord Reid at p. 716. The defendant by the placement of its electrical installation commandeered, at least partially, the plaintiff's beneficial use of its property and thereby imposed a burden on it which it ought not to be required to bear without compensation for those damages it may establish. It is not without significance that Hydro obtained a substantial saving in cost by utilizing the locations it did and, in the circumstances, its submission that it should bear no liability even if it put the plaintiff out of business entirely seems to me patently unfair. In the balancing of interests appropriate to this department of the law the social utility of Hydro's undertaking does not provide, as argued, justification for the infringement in this case of private interests; nor can it be said here that the cost of compensation will impair a public utility's ability to achieve its statutory duty or impose undue hardship on it.

To sum up, it is my conclusion that an interest entitled to protection has been unreasonably invaded by conduct which forms the basis for liability and the tort of nuisance has been accordingly established.

NOTES

1. What role did negligence play in the reasoning of the court? Was a finding of negligence necessary before liability could be imposed?

2. Do you agree with the court's reasoning on the issue of "unusually sensitive use"? Is the cable TV station's user no different than that of an ordinary person who watches TV at home? What if this action had been brought by one TV viewer?

3. In *Hunter v. Canary Wharf Ltd.*, [1997] A.C. 655 (H.L.(E.)), the plaintiffs, neighbouring residents, sued the owners of a high-rise building in negligence and nuisance because the height of the building interfered with the reception of television broadcasts to their homes. A second claim was brought on account of dust caused by the construction of a link road. In an important decision defining the nature and scope of the tort of nuisance, the House of Lords was asked to determine two preliminary issues. First, did the owner of the building commit a nuisance by constructing a building which interfered with television reception? Second, which affected residents have the status to sue for a nuisance?

   On the first issue, the House of Lords was unanimous — the building did not constitute a nuisance. The fact that the presence of a building interfered with a neighbour's enjoyment of land by, for example, spoiling a neighbour's view, restricting the flow of air, or taking away light, did not in itself create a nuisance. Something more is required. According to Lord Goff, nuisances generally arise from something emanating from the offending land or from an activity conducted on the land and not from the mere presence of a building on the land. All of the Law Lords agreed with Lord Goff that the general rule that a "man's right to build on his land is not restricted by the fact that the presence of the building may of itself interfere with his neighbour's enjoyment of land" should not, either based on principle or policy, be departed from in this case. This was a matter for planning controls and in the absence of an easement or an agreement not a matter for the law of nuisance.

4. Do you agree with the decision in *Nor-Video* or with *Canary Wharf*? Are the two cases distinguishable? Is there a difference between an ordinary building and electrical power installations? Did the House of Lords decide that interference with televsion reception can under no circumstances constitute a nuisance or that a nuisance cannot be created by the mere presence of a building on land, notwithstanding what amenities enjoyed by the residents are interfered with? Lord Goff stated that "no action lay in private nuisance for the interference with television caused by the mere presence of a building. That a building may have such an effect has to be accepted" (at 686). Lord Hoffman stated quite clearly that he did not see why interference with television reception could not, "in the appropriate case", constitute an actionable nuisance, and left this question open. It was the erection of a building which could not constitute the nuisance. Lord Lloyd of Berwick stated, however, that "interference with television reception is not capable of constituting an actionable private nuisance" (at 699). It appears that the majority of the Lords were concerned not with the issue of television reception, but with whether the presence of a building blocking television reception could constitute a nuisance.

5. In addition to deciding that the building did not create a nuisance, the majority of the House of Lords decided that only those persons with a proprietary interest in the affected land could sue for nuisance, even if they were personally affected or injured by the nuisance. For Lord Goff this included the person in actual possession of the land, either as a freeholder, tenant, a licensee with exclusive possession, and even a person who cannot prove title but who has exclusive possession. It does not include those who are merely occupying the land, even if they are the spouses or children of the person with the interest. Lord Goff stressed that the essence of nuisance is that it is a tort directed against a person's enjoyment of *rights* over land and not at the person himself. Lord Goff was critical of the Alberta case of *Motherwell v. Motherwell* (1976), 73 D.L.R. (3d) 62 (Alta. C.A.), and the New Brunswick case of *Devon Lumber Co. Ltd. v. MacNeill* (1987), 45 D.L.R. (4th) 300 (N.B.C.A.) which allowed a spouse to sue for nuisance and of the other authorities and scholarly commentaries which argued that this property interest restriction was no longer appropriate to modern times. Of the five Law Lords, only Lord Cooke was in favour of extending the tort of nuisance to spouses, children, and others, who have been exercising a continuing right to enjoyment of the premises.

6. The issue raised in *Canary Wharf* goes to the very heart of the nuisance action. The narrow majority view is that nuisance is an action designed to protect interests in land, where the value of the interest has been diminshed as a result of unreasonable activities of the neighbour. The more expansive and modern view is that nuisance not only protects interests in land, but also the property and health of persons who occupy land. With which view do you agree? If the expansive view is adopted, how does nuisance law differ in its goals from negligence law? Is it sensible to have different standards of care for essentially the same types of injuries, merely because the activity occurs off or on land? For an earlier discussion of this issue, see Girard, "An Expedition to the Frontiers of Nuisance" (1980), 25 McGill L.J. 565.

7. In *O'Regan v. Bresson* (1977), 23 N.S.R. (2d) 507, 3 C.C.L.T. 214 (Co. Ct.), a plaintiff with an asthmatic condition was denied recovery against a stable operator on the

basis of his "abnormal sensitiveness", but the owner of the property was permitted to recover. See also *Devon Lumber v. MacNeill* (1987), 45 D.L.R. (4th) 300, 42 C.C.L.T. 192 (N.B.C.A.). Note that in the latter case, the majority of the Court of Appeal, allowed the claim of the children, rejecting the narrower interpretation of the law of nuisance.

8. In *Lewis v. Town of St. Stephen* (1980), 29 N.B.R. (2d) 167, 66 A.P.R. 167 (Q.B.); revd (1981), 34 N.B.R. (2d) 508, 85 A.P.R. 508 (C.A.), a 15-year-old girl developed an extreme "aircraft phobia" as a result of the defendant's activities. The defendant operated spray aircraft which flew low over the plaintiff's house, striking the house's radio antenna on one occasion, and generally causing a loud noise. Although the trial judge supported the plaintiff's claim, the Court of Appeal held that due to the plaintiff's unusual susceptability to "aircraft phobia" her claim should be rejected. With which judgment do you agree?

9. In *St. Pierre v. Ontario*, [1987] 1 S.C.R. 906, 40 C.C.L.T. 200, the plaintiffs complained when a highway was built on land adjacent to their retirement home. They relied upon *Nor-Video*, among other cases, as establishing that the concept of nuisance has been extended outside of the traditional categories. In rejecting their claim, McIntyre J. stated that the highway in this case did not alter the nature of their property or interfere to a significant extent with the actual use of it. It interfered with their loss of view, something which the courts have refused to protect from the very earliest times. McIntyre J. stated:

   > Highways are necessary: they cause a disruption. In the balancing process inherent in the law of nuisance, their utility for the public good far outweighs the disruption and injury which is visited upon some adjoining lands.

   Do you agree? Who should pay for the "public good" — an individual or the public?

10. Is foreseeability of damage a necessary requirement of a successful action for nuisance? In *Cambridge Water Co. Ltd. v. Eastern Counties Leather plc.*, [1994] 1 All E.R. 53 (H.L.), the House of Lords held that it was. Despite this, foreseeability does not seem to be an issue in most nuisance claims. Why do you think that this is so?

APPLEBY v. ERIE TOBACCO CO.

Divisional Court of the Supreme Court of Ontario.
(1910), 22 O.L.R. 533.

The plaintiff, a merchant in Windsor, complained of noxious odours coming from the defendants' tobacco factory and interfering with the plaintiff's enjoyment of his premises in the vicinity of the factory. The plaintiff claimed an injunction in respect of these odours and other matters. At the trial the claim for an injunction was dismissed but a reference granted to assess damages. The plaintiff appealed.

Middleton J.: The odour from the tobacco arises chiefly from the processes of steaming, steeping, and stewing which it undergoes, and the boiling of sugar, licorice, and other ingredients with which it is mixed before it is reduced to "plug tobacco" ready for the market. These odours cannot be prevented if the manufacture is to go on, and, upon the evidence, the defendants appear to be doing their best to prevent injury to their neighbours.

Many witnesses were called for the plaintiff who describe the odour as a "most sickening smell", a "very bad smell", "very, very offensive", and "very nauseating". Some say that it produces vertigo and dizziness, others nausea and headache. Some do not find any evil result beyond that incident to the disagreeable nature of the odour. The defendants produce a number of witnesses, many of whom say that the odour is "not unhealthy"; others say that it "does not affect" them; and one enthusiastic lover of the weed describes it as "just splendid".

Upon the whole evidence, there can be no doubt that there is a strong odour that to many, if not most, is extremely disagreeable ...

Now, it is to be borne in mind that an arbitrary standard cannot be set up which is applicable to all localities. There is a local standard applicable in each particular district, but, though the local standard may be higher in some districts than in others, yet the question in each case ultimately reduces itself to the fact of nuisance or no nuisance, having regard to all the surrounding circumstances. This is shown by the often quoted passage in Lord Halsbury's judgment in *Colls v. Home and Colonial Stores, Limited*, [1904] A.C. 179, at p. 185; "A dweller in towns cannot expect to have as pure air, as free from smoke, smell and noise as if he lived in the country, and distant from other dwellings, and yet an excess of smoke, smell and noise may give a cause of action, but in each of such cases it becomes a question of degree, and the question is in each case whether it is a nuisance which will give a right of action."

In *Rushmer v. Polsue and Alfiere Limited*, [1906] 1 Ch. 234; [1907] A.C. 121, this principle is applied to the case of a printing office established in a neighbourhood devoted to printing, next door to the plaintiff's residence, and which rendered sleep impossible. Cozens Hardy, L.J., [1906] 1 Ch. at p. 250, sums up the situation in a way that commended itself to the Lords. It was, he says, contended "that a person living in a district specially devoted to a particular trade cannot complain of any nuisance by noise caused by the carrying on of any branch of that trade without carelessness and in a reasonable manner. I cannot assent to this argument. A resident in such a neighbourhood must put up with a certain amount of noise. The standard of comfort differs according to the situation of the property and the class of people who inhabit it ... But whatever the standard of comfort in a particular district may be, I think the addition of a fresh noise caused by the defendant's works may be so substantial as to cause a legal nuisance. It does not follow that because I live, say, in the manufacturing part of Sheffield, I cannot complain if a steam-hammer is introduced next door, and so worked as to render sleep at night almost impossible, although previous to its introduction my house was a reasonably comfortable abode, having regard to the local standard; and it would be no answer to say that the steam-hammer is of the most modern approved pattern and is reasonably worked. In short ... it is no answer to say that the neighbourhood is noisy, and that the defendant's machinery is of first-class character."

It is plain, in this case, that the defendants' manufactory does constitute a nuisance. The odours do cause material discomfort and annoyance and render the plaintiff's premises less fit for the ordinary purpose of life, even making all possible allowances for the local standard of the neighbourhood.

The remaining question is: must an injunction follow? ... The working rule, stated by A.L. Smith, L.J., in *Shelfer v. City of London Electric Lighting Co.*, [1895] 1 Ch. 287, at p. 322, as defining the cases in which damages may be given in lieu of an injunction, shows that here an injunction is the proper remedy. No one should be called upon to submit to the inconvenience and annoyance arising from a noxious and sickening odour for a "small money payment", and the inconvenience and annoyance cannot be adequately "estimated in money." The cases in which damages can be substituted for an injunction sought to abate a nuisance of the first class must be exceedingly rare.

The injunction should, therefore, go, restraining the defendants from so operating their works as to cause a nuisance to the plaintiff by reason of the offensive odours arising from the manufacture of tobacco: the operation of this injunction to be stayed for six months to allow the defendants to abate the nuisance if they can do so, or to make arrangements for the removal of that part of the business causing the odour.

NOTES

1. In *Oakley v. Webb* (1916), 38 O.L.R. 151, 33 D.L.R. 35 (C.A.), the character of a neighbourhood prevented noise from a stone-cutting establishment from being held an actionable nuisance. There was a railway yard behind the plaintiff's property. There was also a yard 150 feet away where horses and vans were kept. What if the stone-cutting establishment was situated in a "good" neighbourhood? Does this make sense or does it discriminate against those who cannot afford to live in a "good" neighbourhood? See Lloyd, "Noise as a Nuisance" (1974), 82 U. Penn. L. Rev. 567.

2. In *Thompson-Schwab v. Costaki*, [1956] 1 W.L.R. 335, [1956] 1 All E.R. 652 (C.A.), the plaintiffs, who occupied homes on a "good" residential street in London, obtained an injunction against the defendant's use of an adjoining house for prostitution. The practise of soliciting men in nearby streets and bringing them to the house constituted a substantial interference with the comfortable enjoyment of the plaintiffs' homes. What if the defendant opened a "sex shop"? See *Laws v. Florinplace Ltd.*, [1981] 1 All E.R. 659 (Ch.D.).

3. In *Shuttleworth v. Vancouver General Hospital*, [1927] 2 D.L.R. 537, [1927] 1 W.W.R. 476 (B.C.S.C.), the defendant opened a hospital for communicable diseases across the street from the plaintiff's house, 110 feet away. The court refused to interfere. It felt that seeing human suffering would not unduly hamper the plaintiff's enjoyment and comfort. It was merely a matter of "sentiment". Moreover, the fear of possible infection, because it was unfounded in fact, could not be a basis for liability. The depreciation in the value of the land flowed not from a "legal wrong" but from an unfounded "sentiment of danger". Compare with *Everett v. Paschall*, 61 Wash. 47, 111 P. 879 (1910), where plaintiff obtained an injunction against the operation of a tuberculosis sanitarium in a residential district. The evidence showed that although there was no actual danger to those in the vicinity, there was a depreciation in sale value due to the dread of tuberculosis.

   > The question is, not whether the fear is rounded in science, but whether it exists, nor whether it is imaginary, but whether it is real, in that it affects the movements and conduct of men. Such fears are actual, and must be recognized by the courts as other emotions of the human mind.

4. Is a funeral home on a quiet residential street a nuisance? See Noel, "Unaesthetic Sights as Nuisance" (1939), 25 Cornell L.Q. 1.

5. Can the dust and noise from a gravel quarry amount to a nuisance? See *Muirhead v. Timber Bros. Sand & Gravel Ltd.* (1977), 3 C.C.L.T. 1 (Ont. H.C.).

6. What about the noise and dust of a building being demolished or built next door? See *Andreae v. Selfridge & Co. Ltd.*, [1938] Ch. 1, [1937] 3 All E.R. 255 (C.A.).

7. The plaintiff's house is next to a golf course. In the summer golf balls are constantly landing on the plaintiff's property (53 in one year). Nuisance? Trespass? See *Segal v. Derrick Golf & Winter Club* (1977), 76 D.L.R. (3d) 746, 2 C.C.L.T. 222 (Alta. T.D.); and *Schneider v. Royal Wayne Motel Ltd.*, [1995] 4 W.W.R. 760 (Alta. Prov. Ct.).

8. If a blasting operation causes cracks in rock, permitting water to be polluted from a nearby piggery, does an action for nuisance lie? What about *Rylands v. Fletcher* here? See *Jackson v. Drury Construction Co.* (1974), 4 O.R. (2d) 735 (C.A.), *per* Dubin J.A.

9. In balancing competing uses, what weight ought the court to give to the utility of the defendant's activity? Ought one person have to suffer some inconvenience for the greater good? In *Miller v. Jackson*, [1977] Q.B. 966, [1977] 3 All E.R. 338 (C.A.), the plaintiffs, whose houses lay adjacent to the village cricket field, complained because cricket balls occasionally landed in their gardens and damaged their homes. The cricket club offered to pay damages to the plaintiffs, but the plaintiffs wanted the court to prevent the future playing of cricket on that field. The trial judge granted the plaintiffs their injunction. On appeal, two of the three justices agreed that the defendant's activity constituted a nuisance, Lord Denning denying that it did. One of the majority justices, Cumming-Bruce L.J., while conceding the nuisance, denied the injunction. The other, Geoffrey Lane L.J. granted the injunction but suspended its operation for one year. Lord Denning dismissed the action. Thus, although the Court of Appeal found that the activity was a nuisance, the injunction was denied, 2-1. On the matter of the utility of the defendant's activity, Lord Denning had the following remarks:

> This case is new. It should be approached on principles applicable to modern conditions. There is a contest here between the interest of the public at large and the interest of a private individual. The *public* interest lies in protecting the environment by preserving our playing fields in the face of mounting development, and by enabling our youth to enjoy all the benefits of outdoor games, such as cricket and football. The *private* interest lies in securing the privacy of his home and garden without intrusion or interference by anyone. In deciding between these two conflicting interests, it must be remembered that it is not a question of damages. If by a million-to-one chance a cricket ball does go out of the ground and cause damage, the cricket club will pay. There is no difficulty on that score. No, it is a question of an injunction. And in our law you will find it repeatedly affirmed that an injunction is a discretionary remedy. In a new situation like this, we have to think afresh as to how discretion should be exercised. On the one hand, Mrs. Miller is a very sensitive lady who has worked herself up into such a state that she exclaimed to the judge: "I just want to be allowed to live in peace. Have we got to wait until someone is killed before anything can be done?" If she feels like that about it, it is quite plain that, for peace in the future, one or other has to move. Either the cricket club have to move, but goodness knows where. I do not suppose for a moment there is any field in Lintz to which they could move. Or Mrs. Miller must move elsewhere. As between their conflicting interests, I am of opinion that the public interest should prevail over the private interest. The cricket club should not be driven out. In my opinion the right exercise of discretion is to refuse an injunction; and, of course, to refuse damages in lieu of an injunction. Likewise as to the claim for past damages. The club were entitled to use this ground for cricket in the accustomed way. It was not a nuisance, nor was it negligent of them so to run it. Nor was the batsman negligent when he hit the ball for six. All were doing simply what they were entitled to do. So if the club had put it to the test, I would have dismissed the claim for damages also. But as the club very fairly say that they are willing to pay for any damage, I am content that there should be an award of £400 to cover any part or future damage.

Do you agree with this view? Is it fair that one person subsidize the cost of an activity designed for the whole community's benefit?

10. How about the argument that the defendant was there first and the plaintiff moved to the nuisance? In *Miller v. Jackson*, *supra*, Geoffrey Lane L.J. granted the injunction because he felt bound by previous authority to the following effect:

> ... it is no answer to a claim in nuisance for the defendant to show that the plaintiff brought the trouble on his own head by building or coming to live in a house so close to the defendant's premises that he would inevitably be affected by the defendant's activities, where no one had been affected previously. ... It may be that this rule works injustice, it may be that one would decide the matter differently in the absence of authority ... it is not for this court as I see it to alter a rule which has stood for so long.

Cumming-Bruce L.J. and Lord Denning did not feel so constrained and denied the injunction. With whom do you agree?

11. The fact that the Court of Appeal in *Miller v. Jackson* denied an injunction seemed to herald a new approach. This, however, turned out not to be so. See *Kennaway v. Thompson*, [1981] Q.B. 88, [1980] 3 All E.R. 329 (C.A.). Also see Tromans, "Nuisance-Prevention or Payment?", [1982] Camb. L.J. 87.

12. In *Ward v. Magna International Inc.* (1994), 21 C.C.L.T. (2d) 178 (Ont. Gen. Div.) the plaintiffs bought a home which was next to a recreational park. During the summer months, the plaintiffs were bothered by the loud noises from the park. In determining whether the park constituted a nuisance, the court considered the severity of the interference, the character of the location, the utility of the park, and the sensitivity of the plaintiffs. The court concluded that the park was a nuisance and asked that the parties attempt to agree on a remedy. The parties failed to agree and the court fashioned its own order requiring the defendant to modify its use of the park in some respects.

13. The important issue in many nuisance cases is not whether the defendant's activity constituted a nuisance, but what the remedy ought to be. The obvious choices have been to either award damages or grant an injunction. Recently, however, U.S. courts have been more innovative. In *Boomer v. Atlantic Cement Co.*, 26 N.Y. 2d 219, 309 N.Y. Supp. 2d 312, 257 N.E. 2d 870 (1970), landowners complained that the dirt, smoke and vibrations caused by a large cement plant constituted a nuisance and they sought an injunction. Due to the damaging consequences to the community which would result from the closure of a large plant employing numerous people the court refused the injunction. Instead the court ordered that the company pay "permanent damages" to the plaintiffs. This award would prevent the plaintiffs or even future owners of their properties from suing again. An even more interesting approach was adopted by the court in *Spur Industries Inc. v. Del E. Webb Development Co.*, 108 Ariz. 179, 494 P. 2d 700 (1972). The court granted the plaintiff an injunction only on the condition that the plaintiff compensate the defendant for the defendant's costs in preventing the nuisance.

14. On the question of whether an injunction will be granted, see *Black v. Canadian Copper Co.* (1917), 12 O.W.N. 243; affd 17 O.W.N. 349 (*sub nom. Taillifer v. Canadian Nickel Co.*) (C.A.); *McKie v. The K.V.P. Co. Ltd.*, [1948] O.R. 398, [1948] 3 D.L.R. 201 (H.C.); affd by the S.C.C. with variation [1949] S.C.R. 698; Read, "Equity and Public Wrongs" (1973), 11 Can. Bar Rev. 73.

15. Is the defendant's "motive" ever a relevant factor in determining the nuisance issue? In one important case, *The Mayor, Aldermen and Burgesses of the Borough of Bradford v. Pickles*, [1895] A.C. 587, [1895-9] All E.R. Rep. 984 (H.L.), the plaintiffs sought an injunction to restrain the defendant from sinking a shaft into his land. The defendant's activity would have had the result of diverting water from the plaintiffs' waterworks project which they conducted on their land. The defendant claimed that

the shaft was for the purpose of a mine, but the defendant's real motive was to obtain compensation or an outright purchase of its land by the plaintiffs. In disallowing the plaintiffs' claim for an injunction, the House of Lords held that the right to abstract subterranean water percolating through one's soil was an absolute right, and thus it could be done no matter what the object or purpose of the exercise was. Lord Halsbury phrased the issue in this way, at 594, A.C.:

> This is not a case in which the state of mind of the person doing the act can affect the right to do it. If it was a lawful act, however ill the motive might be, he had a right to do it. If it was an unlawful act, however good his motive might be, he would have no right to do it. Motives and intentions in such a question as is now before your Lordships seem to me to be absolutely irrelevant.

16. There are very few "absolute" rights. Thus, the motive or intention of the defendant is usually a factor in nuisance cases. In *Hollywood Silver Fox Farm Limited v. Emmett*, [1936] 2 K.B. 468, [1936] 1 All E.R. 825, a land developer was unhappy with his neighbour's notice-board, which publicized his "Silver Fox Farm" operation. When the plaintiff refused to take down the notice-board, the defendant retaliated by having his son fire a gun near the plaintiff's property line. This was done for the purpose of upsetting the plaintiff's vixens during their breeding season, and seriously reducing the number of offspring. The defendant claimed that he had a right to shoot as he pleased on his own land, and later tried to justify the firing as an attempt to control the rabbit population. The plaintiff sued in nuisance, and it was found that the defendant's motive for producing the noise was to frighten the plaintiff's vixens. The Court upheld the plaintiff's claim. It distinguished this case from *Bradford v. Pickles*, holding that there was no absolute right to make noise on one's land and, therefore, that the intention of the party was a relevant factor.

17. Do you agree that the motive behind the conduct should be a relevant consideration in deciding whether there has been a nuisance? If the defendant's son was really shooting rabbits, would the result have been different? What if he shot rabbits day and night without ever stopping?

18. The defendant keeps telephoning the plaintiff and bothering the plaintiff in the middle of the night and first thing in the morning. During one particular hour 30 calls were made. Nuisance? In *Motherwell v. Motherwell* (1976), 73 D.L.R. (3d) 62, [1976] 6 W.W.R. 550 (Alta. C.A.), Clement J.A. stated:

> It is clear to me that the protracted and persistent harassment of the brother and the father in their homes, and in the case of the brother as well in his office, by abuse of the telephone system is within the principle of private nuisance as it has been recognized in the authorities I have referred to. The question is whether the calls amounted to undue interference with the comfortable and convenient enjoyment by the plaintiffs of their respective premises. I can conceive that persistent and unwanted telephone calls could become a harassment even if the subject matter is essentially agreeable. The deliberate and persistent ringing of the telephone cannot but affect the senses in time and operate on the nervous system as the evidence discloses. No special damage is required to support an injunction: it is the loss of the amenities of the premises in substantial degree that is involved.

Would this be actionable as an invasion of privacy? Would it be actionable as an intentional infliction of mental suffering?

19. In *A.-G. of Manitoba et al. v. Campbell* (1983), 24 Man. R. (2d) 70, 26 C.C.L.T. 168; varied 34 Man. R. (2d) 20, 32 C.C.L.T. 57 (C.A.), the defendant owned a farm adjacent

to an airport. The airport authority announced that it was planning to extend the runway, bringing it closer to the defendant's property. The defendant was very annoyed, especially because low-flying aircraft had in the past disturbed his livestock. The defendant refused to grant an easement for flight over his land, and the authority refused to buy the defendant's land. Before a plan to control the height and location of structures in the area of the airport became effective, the defendant erected a steel tower in the corner of his farm. This tower effectively blocked night flights at the airport. The Attorney-General sought, and was granted, an interim injunction to force the defendant to dismantle his tower. Do you think this was fair? If you were the judge who heard the case at trial what would you do? Would you declare the airport's activity a nuisance? The tower a nuisance? Would you order that the airport pay damages to the defendant so as to enable it to continue to operate? Would you order that the airport purchase the defendant's farm? How would you go about this? See McLaren "Case Comment" (1983), 26 C.C.L.T. 326.

TOCK v. ST. JOHN'S METROPOLITAN AREA BD.

Supreme Court of Canada. [1989] 2 S.C.R. 1181,
64 D.L.R. (4th) 620.

The basement of the plaintiff's house was flooded by water which came from the defendant Board's obstructed storm sewer system after an exceptionally heavy rainfall. The Supreme Court Justices agreed that the defendant's activity constituted a nuisance, and considered the defendant's primary defence, that of statutory authority.

Wilson J. (Lamer and **L'Heureux-Dubé JJ.** concurring):

I agree that the flooding of the appellants' basement constituted an unreasonable interference with the appellants' use and enjoyment of the property and that, had the parties been two private individuals, it clearly would have been an actionable nuisance. However, since the respondent is a municipality, the law dictates that different considerations apply. The crucial question is whether or not the respondent is able to rely on the defence of statutory authority in the circumstances of this case.

Since the availability of the defence of statutory authority depends on the language of the statute, I set out the relevant provisions of the *Municipalities Act*, S.N. 1979, c. 33, on which the respondent must rely:

> 154.(1) The council may, subject to the provisions of *The Department of Environment Act* and regulations made thereunder, construct, acquire, establish, own and operate
>
> (*a*) a public water supply system for the distribution of water within or, with the approval of the Minister, outside of the town,
>
> (*b*) a public sewerage system, either independently of or in conjunction with a public water supply system, for the collection and disposal of sewerage within or, with the approval of the Minister, outside of the town, and
>
> (*c*) a storm drainage system within or, with the approval of the Minister, outside of the town.
>
> (2) For the purposes of subsection (1) the council may
>
> (*a*) acquire any waters required for the purpose of providing a sufficient supply of water for the town, and
>
> (*b*) acquire by purchase or expropriation any lands adjacent to such waters to prevent pollution of those waters.
>
> (3) For the purpose of exercising its powers under subsection (1) the council may lay out, excavate, dig, make, build, maintain, repair, and improve all such drains, sewers, and water supply pipes as the council deems necessary.

There is no doubt that these provisions authorize the respondent to construct and continue to operate and maintain the sewage system in question. They are, however, permissive as opposed to mandatory. They confer a power; they do not impose a duty. Is this distinction relevant to the question of the respondent's liability in nuisance? To answer this it is necessary to review some of the leading authorities on the subject.

[Discussion of authorities omitted.]

...

The principles to be derived from the foregoing authorities would seem to be as follows:

(a) if the legislation imposes a duty and the nuisance is the inevitable consequence of discharging that duty, then the nuisance is itself authorized and there is no recovery in the absence of negligence;

(b) if the legislation, although it merely confers an authority, is specific as to the manner or location of doing the thing authorized and the nuisance is the inevitable consequence of doing the thing authorized in that way or in that location, then likewise the nuisance is itself authorized and there is no recovery absent negligence.

However:

(c) if the legislation confers an authority and also gives the public body a discretion, not only whether to do the thing authorized or not, but how to do it and in what location, then if it does decide to do the thing authorized, it must do it in a manner and at a location which will avoid the creation of a nuisance. If it does it in a way or at a location which gives rise to a nuisance, it will be liable therefore, whether there is negligence or not.

In other words, in the situations described in (a) and (b) above the inevitability doctrine is a good defence to the public body absent negligence. In situation (c) it is no defence at all and it is unnecessary for the plaintiff to prove negligence in order to recover.

In my view, these principles make a great deal of sense. The inevitability doctrine represents a happy judicial compromise between letting no one who has suffered damage as a consequence of the statutorily authorized activities of public bodies recover and letting everyone so suffering damage recover. Recovery will be allowed unless it is shown that the interference with the plaintiff's rights was permitted by either:

(1) express language in the statute such as a provision specifying that no action for nuisance may be brought for any damage caused: see, for example, the decision of this court in *North Vancouver (District) v. McKenzie Barge & Marine Ways Ltd.* (1965), 49 D.L.R. (2d) 710, [1965] S.C.R. 377, 51 W.W.R. 193, or

(2) necessary implication from the language of the statute coupled with a factual finding that the damage was the inevitable consequence of what the statute ordered or authorized the public body to do.

...

The legislation in this case was purely permissive within the meaning of these cases. It authorized a sewer system to be constructed but did not specify how or where it was to be done. The respondent was accordingly obliged to construct and operate the system in strict conformity with private rights. It did not do so. The defence of statutory authority is not available to it and the appellants are entitled to recover. The case calls for a straightforward application of *Metropolitan Asylum District v. Hill.*

For these reasons I would allow the appeal, set aside the judgment of the Court of Appeal, and restore the judgment of the trial judge. The appellants are entitled to their costs both here and in the courts below.

La Forest J. (Dickson C.J.C. concurring):

Statutory authority

Briefly put, the test applied by the courts when faced with the decision whether a nuisance may be defended on the ground that it was created pursuant to the exercise of statutory authority takes the form of inquiring whether the statute expressly or impliedly authorizes the damage complained of, and whether the public or other body concerned has established that the damage was inevitable. This was the test applied by this court in *Portage La Prairie (City) v. B.C. Pea Growers Ltd.* (1965), 54 D.L.R. (2d) 503, [1966] S.C.R. 150, 54 W.W.R. 477.

The approach to this defence, though considerably refined, is a legacy of the Victorian age. The gist of the doctrine as it then emerged was to the effect that in the absence of negligence no action would lie for damage occasioned by a body acting within the confines of its statutory authority. Negligence, it may be noted, was understood in a special sense as the failure on the part of the body to observe all precautions consistent with the carrying out of the activity in question: see *Vaughan v. Tuff Valley R. Co.* (1860), 29 L.J. Ex. 247, *passim.* ...

The problem with this approach is that it directs the focus of the inquiry solely on the conduct of the defendant. Yet the fundamental issue before the court in a claim for nuisance is not whether the defendant has acted prudently. Rather, the issue for determination is whether, on a consideration of all the circumstances, it is reasonable or unreasonable to award compensation for the damage suffered. ...

...

The truth is that there is an air of unreality and contrivedness to the defence of statutory authority in this context, however one may seek to rationalize it. Where the statute in question does not expressly exempt a body for damages in nuisance, or, in the alternative, does not provide for a compensation scheme of its own or contain other clear legislative indications, I doubt that divination of an unexpressed intent of the legislature can shed much light on the question whether the person who has suffered damage should be denied compensation. At this remove from the 19th century, therefore, it would seem appropriate to reformulate the law in more functional terms. To give one instance, I would reject the notion that the distinction as to whether a statute is permissive or mandatory is, without more, determinative. ...

Turning to the question of inevitability, it seems to me that, in strict logic, most nuisances stemming from activities authorized by statute are in fact inevitable. Certainly, if one is to judge from the frequency with which storm drain and sewer cases occur in the reports, it would seem a safe conclusion that blockage of such systems is inevitable if one accepts this to mean that it is demonstrably impossible to operate these systems without such occurrences. But what escapes me is why any particular importance should be accorded this fact when weighing a nuisance claim against a statutory authority. The fact that the operation of a given system will inevitably visit random damage on certain unfortunate individuals among the pool of users of the system does not tell us why those individuals should be responsible for paying for that damage.

...

Constraints of time and money will always militate against the building of absolutely failsafe systems (on the assumption that such systems are possible) and the maintaining of the best conceivable inspection system. Accordingly, a public authority charged with operating any service will inevitably have to strike a balance between the need to give due consideration to factors bearing on efficiency and thrift, and the need to protect persons and property from damage that the system in question is likely to cause. In a word, it will be necessary to make compromises and I have no reason to doubt that these compromises, will take into account the possibility of a certain amount of inevitable damage. This, it seems to me, is bound to occur where the costs of preventing predictable damage far outweigh the actual costs of that damage. ...

In short, I question the applicability to the facts of the instant case of the defence of statutory authority as it is conventionally formulated. Where, as here, the authorizing statute does not specifically provide that a right of action in nuisance is taken away (see *Arif v. Fredericton (City)* (1986), 77 N.B.R. (2d) 34 (Q.B.), for an example of a statute that does take away such a right), I see no point in donning the cloak of a soothsayer to plumb the intent of the legislature. After all, if the legislature wishes to shift the risk from a public authority to the individual, it can do so in express terms. I see no reason why it should be presumed to be authorizing a serious nuisance. Nor do I accept that any weight should be accorded a showing by the public body that damage was inevitable. The determination that damage was inevitable, in the sense in which that term was defined earlier, does not provide a rationale for concluding that it is reasonable to demand of the person whom misfortune has singled out that he or she pay for the damage concerned. The costs of damage that is an inevitable consequence of the provision of services that benefit the public at large should be borne equally by all those who profit from the service.

Rather than approaching the matter in this way, I think the best way to resolve the problem is to proceed rather as one does when facing a claim in nuisance between two private individuals, and ask whether, given all the circumstances, it is reasonable to refuse to compensate the aggrieved party for the damage he has suffered. When the problem is stated in this fashion, I fail to see any reason that would compel this result on the facts of this case.

This does not denude the defence of statutory authority of all rigour. If, as Lord Dunedin explained, the legislature has authorized the construction of a work at a particular place, the owner of neighbouring land cannot complain if that work is built there. Similarly, if the legislature authorizes the construction of a work, such as a sewerage system, the adjacent landowners cannot complain of ordinary disturbances or loss of amenity that necessarily results to them from its construction or operation if it is built and operated with all reasonable care and skill. To permit action by a landowner in such circumstances (assuming this can be regarded as a nuisance) would, in effect, be to deny the statutory mandate. Again, if a municipality is given statutory authority to construct a garbage dump, landowners in the vicinity where it is built will not suffer an actionable wrong from unavoidable smells emitted from the dump or increased traffic from trucks. But if toxic waste escapes into their basements or wells, this would pose a completely different issue.

The damage in the present case is attributable to a single calamitous event which, in turn, finds its origin in the operation by the respondent of a service of undoubted public utility. This circumstance in itself provides no rationale for denying compensation. As McIntyre J.A. put it in *Royal Anne Hotel Co. v. Ashcroft*, *supra*, at p. 761, this would have the effect of visiting a disproportionate share of the cost of the beneficial service on the hapless individual who suffered the damage. As I earlier observed, damage attributable to a calamitous event such as the flooding that occurred here should rather be viewed as what it in fact is, a part of the overall cost of providing a beneficial service to the community. As such it is appropriate, in my view, that the obligation of meeting such costs be placed on the body that undertakes it. That body, unlike its hapless victim, is in a position to defray the cost by spreading it among all subscribers to the system. In the alternative, if the authority is to bear the costs of accidents of this nature, it may realize that it is more cost-effective to forestall their occurrence by increasing the frequency of inspections.

I do not share the qualms of the Court of Appeal that to hold the respondent liable in this instance, in the absence of a showing that it was negligent, will make of it an "absolute insurer in respect of all its works". To evoke this spectre of indeterminate liability is, with respect, to lose sight of the fact that a plaintiff does not, as a matter of course, win an action in nuisance on a mere showing that he has suffered damage as a result of interference with the use or enjoyment of his land; see the *Royal Anne* case, *supra*, at p. 760; see also *Street on Torts*, at p. 225. There is always the question whether the injury is one for which it is reasonable or unreasonable to award compensation, and this holds true whether the defendant is a private individual or a statutory body. I see no reason to doubt that in many cases the courts, when called upon to strike a balance between the interests of the private citizen and a statutory body, will conclude that it is appropriate that the interests of the private citizen yield to those of the public at large.

Without purporting to formulate a hard-and-fast rule, it seems to me that a useful distinction exists between isolated and infrequent occurrences which inflict heavy material damage on a single victim, such as we are concerned with in this case, and those ordinary disturbances diffuse in their effect and having a broad and general impact on the comfort, convenience and material well-being of the public at large. We all have to put up with a certain degree of inconvenience, and indeed some material harm as a price of living in organized society. We accept, for example, that we can look to no one for redress because salt on the roads causes our cars to rust out in five years, but as *Schenck v. Ontario*, *supra*, has shown, it is unreasonable that an individual's land be subjected to random and severe damage from that activity without compensation. The test for recovery in nuisance, after all, is whether the effect of the activity on a landowner's enjoyment of property is unreasonable or not. I, therefore, see no ground for viewing a finding of liability on the part of the board as in any way a floodgates decision that stands, in the long term, to compromise the ability of statutory authorities duly to carry out their legislative mandates.

Sopinka J.: I have had the privilege of reading the reasons for judgment of my colleagues Justice La Forest and Justice Wilson. Regrettably I am unable to agree with the reasons of either. I agree with Wilson J.'s comment that the approach proposed by La Forest J. would virtually abrogate the defence of statutory authority and would do "nothing to assist public bodies to make a realistic assessment of their exposure in carrying out their statutory mandate".

On the other hand, I am concerned that her approach would have the same consequences for the defence of statutory authority. She would eliminate it in respect of legislation that is permissive. Modern legislation authorizing the provision of the type of works which frequently give rise to nuisances is almost invariably permissive. This would expose public authorities to the same liability for nuisance as private enterprise. While this might assist them in estimating their exposure, that exposure would open the floodgates to the same extent as the approach proposed by La Forest J.

Both of my colleagues propose changes in the law as it is being applied at present. Change should not be made for its own sake or to solve a particular case unless the change constitutes an improvement in the law as generally applied. In my opinion, the changes proposed are not an improvement on the present law of nuisance, imperfect though it may be. ...

...

The rationale of the defence is that if the legislature expressly or implicitly says that a work can be carried out which can only be done by causing a nuisance, then the legislation has authorized an infringement of private rights. If no compensation provision is included in the statute, all redress is barred: see Fleming, *The Law of Torts*, 6th ed. (1983), at p. 407, and *Campbellton v. Gray's Velvet Ice Cream Ltd.*, *supra*, at p. 439. There is no question that legislation may expressly authorize an interference with private rights by so providing in explicit language. Where the only reasonable inference from the legislation is that such interference is authorized, then the same result obtains by implication. Hence, the language in the cases that the defence is made out if the nuisance is authorized expressly or by implication.

A work is authorized by statute whether the statute is mandatory or permissive, if the work is carried out in accordance with the statute. The distinction between mandatory and permissive, which Wilson J. makes to eliminate, in the latter case, the defence of statutory authority, has not been accepted in Canada or, apparently, in England: see *Allen v. Gulf Oil Refining Ltd.*, [1981] 1 All E.R. 353 (H.L.), and *Tate & Lyle Industries Ltd. v. Greater London Council*, [1983] 1 All E.R. 1159 (H.L.).

The criticism of the present state of the law which is the springboard for the desire to change it is largely based on the fact that the term "inevitable consequences" is too vague and uncertain. That term is the expression of the factual conclusion that the necessary causal connection exists between the work authorized and the nuisance. If the necessary connection exists, then it follows that the legislature authorized that which is the inevitable consequence of the work described in the statute.

The burden of proof with respect to the defence of statutory authority is on the party advancing the defence. It is not an easy one. The courts strain against a conclusion that private rights are intended to be sacrificed for the common good. The defendant must negative that there are alternate methods of carrying out the work. The mere fact that one is considerably less expensive will not avail. If only one method is practically feasible, it must be established that it was practically impossible to avoid the nuisance. It is insufficient for the defendant to negative negligence. The standard is a higher one. While the defence gives rise to some factual difficulties, in view of the allocation of the burden of proof they will be resolved against the defendant.

If we are to depart from this state of the law, so recently confirmed by two decisions of this court, there should be very strong ground for so doing. Moreover, there should be substantial unanimity. It is apparent from the reasons in this appeal that there is little unanimity as to whether we should retrench, advance or stay the same.

The change proposed by La Forest J. subsumes the defence of statutory authority within the test as to when it is reasonable to compensate the plaintiff. Trial judges will still have to grapple with the elements of the defence of statutory authority but in the context of a test of reasonableness. This will simply add uncertainty to any uncertainty which is said to exist.

Nor do I agree that it is logical or practical to distinguish between public works that are required and those that are permitted. While it was fashionable to require such works in the railway building age, mandatory public works are a feature of a bygone era.

The disagreement with the result reached in the Court of Appeal is not because the law is defective but because it was incorrectly applied. As La Forest J. points out, the Court of Appeal exonerated the respondent from liability in nuisance on the basis that there was an absence of negligence. In my opinion, the heavier onus which must be discharged was not met in this case. The trial judge so found. I, therefore, would dispose of the appeal as proposed by my colleagues.

Appeal allowed.

NOTES

1. The Supreme Court of Canada revisited the issue of the defence of statutory authority in *Ryan v. Victoria (City)*, the public nuisance case discussed earlier. As you will recall, the railway companies' defence to the claim was that it had statutory authority to operate trains and construct tracks. Major J. dealt with the defence in the following way:

> Statutory authority provides, at best, a narrow defence to nuisance. The traditional rule is that liability will not be imposed if an activity is authorized by statute and the defendant proves that the nuisance is the "inevitable result" or consequence of exercising that authority.... An unsuccessful attempt was made in *Tock, supra,* to depart from the traditional rule. Wilson J. writing for herself and two others, sought to limit the defence to cases involving either mandatory duties or statutes which specify the manner of performance. La Forest J. (Dickson C.J. concurring) took the more extreme view that the defence should be abolished entirely unless there is an express statutory exemption from liability. Neither of these positions carried a majority.

In the absence of a new rule it would be appropriate to restate the traditional view, which remains the most predictable approach to the issue and the simplest to apply. That aproach was expressed by Sopinka J. in *Tock*:

> The defendant must negative that there are alternate methods of carrying out the work. The mere fact that one is considerably less expensive will not avail. If only one method is practically feasible, it must be established that it was practically impossible to avoid the nuisance. It is insufficient for the defendant to negative negligence. The standard is a higher one. While the defence gives rise to some factual difficulties, in view of the allocation of the burden of proof they will be resolved against the defendant.

Turning to the facts of this case, the question raised by the traditional test is whether the hazards created on Store Street were an "inevitable result" of exercising statutory authority, that is, whether it was "practically impossible" for the railways to avoid the nuisance which arose from the flangeways. As noted previously in the context of negligence, the regulations relied upon by the railways prescribed a minimum width of 2.5 inches for flangeways. The railways' decision to exceed that minimum by more than one inch was a matter of discretion and was not an "inevitable result" or "inseparable consequence" of complying with the regulations. The same may be said of the railways' decision not to install flange fillers when such products became available after 1982. The flangeways created a considerably greater risk than was absolutely necessary. Accordingly, the Court of Appeal erred in permitting the railways to assert the defence of statutory authority against the claim for nuisance.

2. Where does Major J.'s decision now leave the defence of statutory authority in Canada? When can defendants rely on it? What do they have to prove?

3. Why should a person who is injured by an obstruction or danger on the highway be treated any differently than a person who is run over by a car on the highway? It seems that the former victim need not prove negligence and that there is a very high burden on the defendant. Does all of this make any sense? Has the law of public nuisance taken a wrong turn somewhere?

4. In *Mandrake Management Consultants Ltd. v. T.T.C.* (1993), 102 D.L.R. (4th) 12, 15 M.P.L.R. (2d) 131 (Ont. C.A.), the plaintiff s, owners and occupiers of an office building, complained of noise and vibrations coming from the defendant's subway. Based on a consideration of the nature of the locality, the severity of the harm, the sensitivity of the plaintiff, and the utility of the defendant's activity, the Court of Appeal, reversing the trial judge's finding, held that the defendant's conduct did not constitute a nuisance. Moreover, the Court of Appeal held that even if the activity did constitute a nuisance, the defence of statutory authority was available to deny the plaintiff's action. Galligan J.A. held that Wilson J.'s restrictive principles on the defence of statutory authority laid out in the *Tock* case did not apply to railways. According to Galligan J.A., the fact that Wilson J. reviewed the railway cases and described them as "authoritative", meant that these cases were still to be regarded as good law. Galligan J.A. also interpreted La Forest and Sopinka JJ.'s judgment as supporting the defence of statutory authority in this type of case.

   Do you agree with this? Do you think that Wilson J.'s restrictive principles were not intended to be applicable to a nuisance from a railway? Why treat railways differently than other statutorily authorized activities? Note that in *Ryan v. Victoria (City), supra,* the railways' defence of statutory authority was rejected on the basis that the railway had been negligent, and that the nuisance created was not an inevitable consequence of the activity.

5. In *Allen v. Gulf Oil Refining Ltd.*, [1981] A.C. 101, [1981] 1 All E.R. 353 (H.L.), the plaintiff claimed that the defendant's refinery was a nuisance. The defendant had statutory authorization to construct certain works in connection with an oil refinery they intended to establish. In the Court of Appeal, Lord Denning, following the traditional approach, strictly construed the statute and found in the plaintiff's favour. However, Lord Denning went even further and declared that:

   > modern statutes should be construed on a new principle. Wherever private undertakers seek statutory authority to construct and operate an installation which may cause damage to people living in the neighbourhood, it should not be assumed that Parliament intended that damage should be done to innocent people without redress. Just as in principle property should not be taken compulsorily except on proper compensation being paid for it, so also in principle property should not be damaged compulsorily except on proper compensation being made for the damage done.

The effect of Lord Denning's view would be to eliminate the defence of statutory authorization unless the statute explicitly exonerated a defendant. Do you agree with this? The House of Lords did not. The majority construed the statute as providing a defence to the plaintiff's action.

6. In *Schenck et al. v. R. in Right of Ontario* (1981), 34 O.R. (2d) 595, 131 D.L.R. (3d) 310, 20 C.C.L.T. 128 (H.C.); affd, re limitation issue, [1987] 2 S.C.R. 289, 50 D.L.R. (4th) 384, fruit farmers were compensated for damage done to their crops by salt used to de-ice the highways. The court upheld the principle that the absence of negligence is no defence to an action for nuisance and that the defence of legislative authority cannot prevail. Why allow recovery here for a policy decision taken by a governmental authority when the normal rule is that you cannot sue governmental authorities for discretionary decisions taken in good faith? Does the action in nuisance differ from other actions so as to permit this? See *Torino Motors Ltd. v. City of Kamloops* (1987), 37 D.L.R. (4th) 392, 40 C.C.L.T. 80 (B.C. Co. Ct.); affd, [1988] 6 W.W.R. 762, 44 C.C.L.T. 278 (B.C.C.A.).

7. See generally on this question Linden, "Strict Liability, Nuisance and Legislative Authorization" (1966), 4 Osgoode Hall L.J. 196.

C. AN ECONOMIC ANALYSIS OF NUISANCE

Since the early 1960s a major development in the study of law has been the emergence of what has been called "the new economics and the law". Due to the work of a few notable scholars, people like Coase, Calabresi, Melamed, Demsetz, Cheung and Posner, interest in the economic approach to the study of law has heightened and the field has grown. Entire legal journals and academic programs are now devoted to the topic. To many law students, professors, lawyers and judges, trained in the old jargon of legal analysis, the work of these "economist-lawyers" seems complex and intimidating. The work has also attracted considerable criticism from those equally expert in the field. It is undisputed, however, that the research has been significant and should not be ignored.

NOTES

In these brief notes, an effort is made to introduce the law student to some of the basic principles and purposes of this type of legal analysis. It has been thought appropriate to include this material in the chapter on "nuisance". While it is true that the economic approach to legal problems has not been confined to the law of nuisance, nor even to the law of torts, it was in the area of nuisance law that Coase, Calabresi and Melamed initially introduced this new type of legal analysis.

1. What is the "economic approach" to law? The following extract from Posner, "The Economic Approach to Law" (1975), 53 Tex. L. Rev. 757, helps answer this basic question:

> The hallmark of the "new" law and economics is the application of the theories and empirical methods of economics to the central institutions of the legal system, including the common law doctrines of negligence, contract, and property; the theory and practice of punishment; civil, criminal, and administrative procedure; the theory of legislation and of rulemaking; and law enforcement and judicial administration. Whereas the "old" law and economics confined its attention to laws governing explicit economic relationships, and indeed to a quite limited subset of such laws (the law of contracts, for exam-

ple, was omitted), the "new" law and economics recognizes no such limitation on the domain of economic analysis of law.

The new law and economics dates from the early 1960's, when Guido Calabresi's first article on torts and Ronald Coase's article on social cost were published. These were the first attempts to apply economic analysis in a *systematic* way to areas of law that did not purport to regulate economic relationships. To be sure, as appears to be generally true in the history of scientific thought, one can find earlier glimmerings of an economic approach to the problems of accident and nuisance law that Calabresi and Coase discussed, but these scattered insights had no impact on the development of scholarship.

Coase's article was the more significant for the long-run development of the new law and economics field. The article established a framework for analyzing the assignment of property rights and liability in economic terms, thereby opening a vast field of legal doctrine to fruitful economic analysis, a field that Demsetz, Cheung, and others have cultivated. A very important, although for a time neglected, feature of Coase's article was its implications for the positive analysis of legal doctrine. Coase suggested that the English law of nuisance had an implicit economic logic. Later writers have generalized this insight and argued that many of the doctrines and institutions of the legal system are best understood and explained as efforts to promote the efficient allocation of resources.

The basis of an economic approach to law is the assumption that the people involved with the legal system act as rational maximizers of their satisfactions. Suppose the question is asked, when will parties to a legal dispute settle rather than litigate? Since this choice involves uncertainty — the outcome of the litigation is not known for sure in advance — the relevant body of economic theory is that which analyzes decision-making by rational maximizers under conditions of uncertainty. If we are willing to assume, at least provisionally, that litigants behave rationally, then this well-developed branch of economic theory can be applied in straightforward fashion to the litigation context to yield predictions with respect to the decision to litigate or settle; we discover, for example, that litigation should be more frequent the greater the stakes in the dispute or the uncertainty of the outcome. These predictions can be, and have been, compared with the actual behavior of litigants in the real world. The comparisons indicate that the economic model is indeed a fruitful one as applied to litigation behavior, *i.e.*, it enables us to explain the actual behavior we observe.

It may be argued that if economic theory only involves exploring the implications of assuming that people behave rationally, then lawyers can apply the theory perfectly well without the help of specialists. In this view, the economic approach to law just supplies a novel and confusing vocabulary in which to describe the familiar analytical activities of the lawyer. There is indeed a good deal of implicit economic analysis in legal thought — a point to which I shall return — and a good deal of economic theory does consist of elegantly formalizing the obvious and the trivial. But it is not true that all of the useful parts of economic theory are intuitively obvious to the intelligent lawyer. The logic of rational maximization is subtle, frequently complex, and very often counterintuitive. That is why the level of public discussion of economic policy is so low, and why the application of economics to law is more than the translation of the conventional wisdom of academic lawyers into a different jargon.

2. In order to approach legal problems from an economic perspective, one has to accept certain basic economic assumptions. The economic approach assumes that individuals act rationally, maximize utility, and thus can be counted on to make wise choices from

the alternatives available. It notes that every choice involves a certain cost. For example, the decision to use your land in order to grow corn means that it cannot be used in other productive ways. The rational person will know what these "opportunity costs" are and will make the wisest choice. Burrows and Veljanovski, *The Economic Approach to Law* (1981), succinctly summarize this central point as follows:

> The economic approach places at the forefront of discussion the need to choose and the costs and benefits of alternative choices, which must always be a relevant consideration where resources are limited. All too often lawyers discuss the law in language that implies that costs are irrelevant or that a goal can be achieved at no cost and with no sacrifice of other goals. Economics tells us that nothing is free from society's viewpoint. Increasing access to the courts, for example, consumers resources that will then be unavailable for other uses, and the economic approach can assist in determining whether in allocating resources for this purpose rather than another society is "getting value for money". As Leff has succinctly put it, "the central tenet and most important operative principle of economic analysis is to ask of every move (1) how much will it cost; (2) who pays; and (3) who ought to decide both questions" (Leff, 1974, p. 460).

3. Not everyone is enamoured with the basic assumptions used by the economist to explain human behaviour. To these critics there must be more to law than mere economic efficiency. One of the most stinging indictments of the economic approach was written by Leff in a commentary on Posner, *Economic Analysis of Law* (1973) found at (1974), 60 Va. L. Rev. 451. Leff's concluding remarks were as follows:

> We all know that all value is not a sole function of willingness to pay, and that it's a grievous mistake to use a tone which implies (while the words deny) that it is. Man may be the measure of all things, but he is not beyond measurement himself. I don't know how one talks about it, but napalming babies *is* bad, and so is letting them or even their culpable parents starve, freeze, or merely suffer plain miserable discomfort while other people, more "valuable" than they are or not, freely choose snowmobiles and whipped cream. Whatever is wrong with all that, it is only partly statistical. People are neither above reproach, nor are they ever just "sunk costs." *And "the law" has always known it; that is the source of its tension and complexity.* If economic efficiency is part of the common law (and it is), so is *fait justitia, ruat coelum.*
>
> Thus, though one *can* graph (non-interpersonally comparable) marginal utilities for money which are the very picture of geometric nymphomania, we still preserve our right to say to those whose personalities generate such curves, "You swine," or "When did you first notice this anal compulsion overwhelming you?" or even "Beware the masses." And indeed "the law," even "the common law," has on impulses like those often said, even against efficiency — "Sorry buddy, you lose."
>
> I admit that it is not easy these days to be a moralist *manqué*, when what it is that one lacks is any rational and coherent way to express one's intuitions. That's why it is, today, so very hard to be a thinking lawyer. But I will tell you this: substituting definitions for both facts and values is not notably likely to fill the echoing void. Much as I admire the many genuine insights of American Legal Nominalism, I think we shall have to continue wrestling with a universe filled with too many things about which we understand too little and then evaluate them against standards we don't even have. That doesn't mean that any of us — especially bright, talented and sensitive people like Richard Posner — should stop what they are doing and gaze silently into the buzz. What he is doing and has done (including this book) enriches us all. But (to get back to where we started) he (and all of us) should keep in mind what I

think is the most lively moment in *Don Quixote*. When asked by a mocking Duke if he actually believes in the real existence of his lady Dulcinea, the Don replies:

> This is not one of those cases where you can prove a thing conclusively. I have not begotten or given birth to my lady, although I contemplate her as she needs must be. ...

One can understand the impulse, and be touched by the attempt, but the world is never as it needs must be. If it ever so seems, it is not the thing illuminated one is seeing, but the light.

4. When applied to nuisance law, the economic approach works roughly in the following way. Every nuisance dispute is seen as involving a conflict in land uses. "A" and "B", two neighbours, both want to use their land in a way which detrimentally affects the other's use. By looking at the "opportunity costs" involved, each will assess how much each is prepared to pay to be allowed to use the land without interference from the neighbour. This will ensure that the lands are used in the most economically efficient way. Assuming that the two land uses are completely incompatible, the neighbour who values the use more highly, in the sense of being prepared to pay the most for continuing with it, will be the one who continues the activity. If the court resolving the dispute happens to decide that the less valued use will prevail, the parties will negotiate with each other and will arrive at the economically efficient result nevertheless. See Ogus and Richardson, "Economics and the Environment: A Study of Private Nuisance", [1977] Camb. L.J. 284, for a full description of how this will work.

5. This approach to nuisance law was first developed by Coase, "The Problem of Social Cost" (1960), 3 J. of Law & Econ. 1. Coase gives the following example of his "theorem" using the case of *Sturges v. Bridgman* (1879), 11 Ch.D. 852, 48 L.J. Ch. 785 (C.A.). In that case a doctor built offices adjacent to premises occupied by a confectioner. The confectioner's machinery created noise and vibrations which made the doctor's work difficult. The doctor brought legal action to force the confectioner to stop using the machinery. The court granted the injunction. Coases's explanation of what now would happen is as follows:

> The court's decision established that the doctor had the right to prevent the confectioner from using his machinery. But, of course, it would have been possible to modify the arrangements envisaged in the legal ruling by means of a bargain between the parties. The doctor would have been willing to waive his right and allow the machinery to continue in operation if the confectioner would have paid him a sum of money which was greater than the loss of income which he would suffer from having to move to a more costly or less convenient location or from having to curtail his activities at this location or, as was suggested as a possibility, from having to build a separate wall which would deaden the noise and vibration. The confectioner would have been willing to do this if the amount he would have to pay the doctor was less than the fall in income he would suffer if he had to change his mode of operation at this location, abandon his operation or move his confectionery business to some other location. The solution of the problem depends essentially on whether the continued use of the machinery adds more to the confectioner's income than it subtracts from the doctor's. But now consider the situation if the confectioner had won the case. The confectioner would then have had the right to continue operating his noise and vibration-generating machinery without having to pay anything to the doctor. The boot would have been on the other foot: the doctor would have had to pay the confectioner to induce him to stop using the machinery. If the doctor's income would have fallen more through continuance of the use of this machinery than it added to the income of the confectioner, there would clearly be room for a bargain whereby the

doctor paid the confectioner to stop using the machinery. That is to say, the circumstances in which it would not pay the confectioner to continue to use the machinery and to compensate the doctor for the losses that this would bring (if the doctor had the right to prevent the confectioner's using his machinery) would be those in which it would be in the interest of the doctor to make a payment to the confectioner which would induce him to discontinue the use of the machinery (if the confectioner had the right to operate the machinery). The basic conditions are exactly the same in this case as they were in the example of the cattle which destroyed crops. With costless market transactions, the decision of the courts concerning liability for damage would be without effect on the allocation of resources. It was of course the view of the judges that they were affecting the work of the economic system — and in a desirable direction. Any other decision would have had "a prejudicial effect upon the development of land for residential purposes," an argument which was elaborated by examining the example of a forge operating on a barren moor, which was later developed for residential purposes. The judges' view that they were settling how the land was to be used would be true only in the case in which the costs of carrying out the necessary market transactions exceeded the gain which might be achieved by any rearrangement of rights. And it would be desirable to preserve the areas (Wimpole Street or the moor) for residential or professional use (by giving non-industrial users the right to stop the noise, vibration, smoke, etc., by injunction) only if the value of the additional residential facilities obtained was greater than the value of cakes or iron lost. But of this the judges seem to have been unaware.

6. One of the problems Coase recognized was the problem of "transaction costs". That is, the negotiations which might have to take place after the court's decision also cost money. If they cost too much, the parties will not negotiate and the economically efficient result will not be reached. Thus, what the court does in its determination is important to economic efficiency where there are high transaction costs.

7. Calabresi and Melamed in "Property Rules, Liability Rules, and Inalienability: One View of The Cathedral" (1972), 85 Harv. L. Rev. 1089, carried the economic approach to nuisance disputes further. They examined the four options which courts have to solve nuisance disputes and suggested which option was best from an economic efficiency perspective depending upon the circumstances. They stated that a court can do one of four things to resolve the dispute:

   (1) find for the plaintiff and grant an injunction;
   (2) find for the plaintiff and only award damages;
   (3) find for the defendant;
   (4) find for the plaintiff on the condition that the plaintiff compensate the defendant for the defendant's costs in avoiding the nuisance.

   Where there are no transaction costs, notwithstanding what the court decides the efficient result will follow. Where there are transaction costs, the authors suggest that the party who is in the best position to negotiate the efficient result, should be required to do so. See also Prichard, "An Economic Analysis of *Miller v. Jackson*", *The Cambridge Lectures, 1985*, p. 71.

8. For a critical comment concerning the use of economic considerations by courts to solve nuisance disputes, see Hawkins "'In and of Itself': Some Thoughts on the Assignment of Property Rights in Nuisance Cases" (1978), 36 U. Toronto Fac. L. Rev. 209.

CHAPTER 14

OCCUPIERS' LIABILITY

The Canadian law of occupiers' liability, which is concerned with the tort responsibility of those who control land to those who enter onto their land, until recently, was a mess. In this area, perhaps more than in any other part of tort law, rigid rules and formal categories spawned confusion and injustice. It is understandable in part because "the history of this subject is one of conflict between the general principles of the law of negligence and the traditional immunity of landowners".

From this clash, Canadian landowners emerged victoriously more often than not. The trend toward rationalization and generalization in the rest of negligence law made little headway in this area, except for one or two heroic attempts at reform. The courts were unwilling to alter the course of a century of jurisprudence despite its obvious inadequacy for the task. In response to this judicial paralysis, several legislatures have undertaken major legislative overhauls of the law. The new legislation, however, has not solved all the problems.

This chapter outlines briefly the main contours of the common law, which is still in force in several provinces (Saskatchewan, New Brunswick, Nova Scotia and Newfoundland), and then considers several of the legislative schemes that have been enacted in Canada.

A. THE COMMON LAW

LINDEN, CANADIAN TORT LAW

6th ed. (1997), pp. 637-638.

A. The Common Law

In the last century, the English courts developed three immutable categories of entrants to land: (1) trespassers, (2) licensees, and (3) invitees. To each of these three groups a different standard of care applied. This rigid scheme was embraced without question by Canadian courts and has been adhered to ever since, despite a flood of academic criticism. There were suggestions both to increase and to decrease the number of categories. Despite this, the three main categories survived, but with minor variations.

1. WHO IS AN OCCUPIER?

The status of "occupier" is not dependent on ownership of the premises, but rather is based on control over the premises. A person who has the immediate supervision and control of the premises and the power to admit and exclude the entry of others is without doubt an occupier. Thus a tenant in possession is an occupier. However, complete or exclusive control is not necessary. An auctioneer hired to conduct a sale on the vendor's premises may be considered an occupier of those premises. An independent contractor carrying out building or repair work may qualify as an occupier. Moreover, it has become apparent that in many circumstances there may be more than one occupier of premises.

The law of occupiers' liability applies to land, structures on land and moveable structures. Accordingly, it governs the liability of occupiers of elevators, scaffolding, ships, trains, streetcars and other similar things.

NOTES

1. Recent common law cases on the definition of occupier illustrate that the "control" requirement can be problematic. See, for example, *Lavoie v. Lavoie* (1983), 44 N.B.R. (2d) 573, 145 D.L.R. (3d) 158 (C.A.), the owner of property on which it conducted an agricultural fair was not in control of the area upon which the concessionaires operated rides. Contrast this case with *Kohler v. City of Calgary* (1980), 28 A.R. 190 (Q.B.).

2. What about the sidewalk which accesses a person's business? Even if this sidewalk belongs to someone else, is the store owner responsible for it? See *Snitzer v. Becker Milk Co. Ltd.* (1976), 15 O.R. (2d) 345, 75 D.L.R. (3d) 649 (H.C.J.); *Shwemer v. Odeon Morton Theatres Ltd.* (1985), 33 Man. R. (2d) 109 (Q.B.); affd (1985), 37 Man. R. (2d) 176 (C.A.).

LINDEN, CANADIAN TORT LAW

continued, pp. 639-641

2. TRESPASSERS

Trespassers are those who enter premises without the permission of the occupier. Licensees or invitees may subsequently become trespassers by exceeding the scope of their invitations or by overstaying their welcome. The category of trespasser is heterogenous, and would include both a burglar and a wandering child.

Historically, occupiers have been found liable to trespassers only if they wilfully injured them or acted in reckless disregard of their presence. Some attempts have been made to circumvent this rule in cases where its application causes unfairness or hardship. A court may, by some device or other, find that a trespasser, particularly if a child, has an implied licence to be on the premises and, therefore, is owed a duty of protection. In other cases, a generous meaning may be given to the phrase "reckless disregard" or a tenuous distinction drawn between the static condition of premises and current activities conducted upon the premises. In still other cases, a court may find that a particular defendant is not an occupier and, therefore, is not insulated from the higher standard of care which attaches as a result of ordinary negligence principles.

Recently, however, a new line of cases has developed which reject the use of fictions, and suggest instead a new test which requires the occupier to treat the trespasser with "common humanity". The Supreme Court of Canada adopted this test in the case of *Veinot v. Kerr-Addison Mines Ltd.*, [1975] 2 S.C.R. 311. In his judgment, Mr. Justice Dickson, speaking for three members of the court, quoted with approval from Denning M.R.'s reasons for judgment in *Pannett v. McGuiness & Co. Ltd.* in which Lord Denning suggested four factors for a judge to consider in determining whether the occupier is in breach of the duty of common humanity. These are:

(1) the gravity and likelihood of the probable injury;
(2) the character of the intrusion;
(3) the nature of the place where the trespass occurs; and
(4) the knowledge which the defendant has or ought to have of the likelihood of the trespasser being present.

A fifth factor which the courts also consider is the cost to the occupier, relative to financial and other resources, of guarding against the danger. These factors take into account, *inter alia*, the diverse character of the entrants who fall within the category of trespasser. In other words, "a wandering child or a straying adult stands in a different position from a poacher or a burglar. You may expect a child when you may not expect a burglar." Likewise, an open window which may not present a danger to an adult may present a grave peril to a small child.

The occupier's duty of common humanity arises only if the occupier has actual knowledge either of the presence of the trespasser on the premises or of facts which make it likely that the trespasser will come onto the land, and also actual knowledge of facts concerning the condition of the land or of activities carried out on it which are likely to cause injury to a trespasser who is unaware of the danger. The occupier is not under any duty to the trespasser to make inquiries or inspections to ascertain whether or not such facts exist. Furthermore, the duty, when it arises, is limited to taking reasonable steps to enable the trespasser to avoid the danger... Where the likely trespasser is a child, too young to understand or heed a warning, discharging the duty may involve providing reasonable physical obstacles to keep the child away from the danger. An occupier who has created the danger may be expected to take greater measures to safeguard trespassers.

It remains to be seen whether the "common humanity" test will allow the courts to reach an equitable compromise "between the demands of humanity and the necessity to avoid placing undue burdens on occupiers". The case law to date is encouraging in its liberal application of the test, even though it is still hard to tell how the duty of common humanity differs from the more onerous duty of reasonable care.

Child trespassers have for a long time presented the courts with a particularly difficult problem. It has recently been stated that child trespassers need no longer be classified but should be dealt with by the ordinary law of negligence. It is too early to forecast whether this view will ultimately prevail, although it is a consequence devoutly to be wished by most commentators.

NOTES

1. Can a plaintiff be both a "trespasser" and a "neighbour" at the same time? For an excellent discussion of this way of avoiding the harshness of the common law approach to trespassers see *Hackshaw v. Shaw* (1985), 59 A.L.J.R. 156 (H. Ct.).

2. The duty of "common humanity" has generally been accepted by Canadian courts. See, for example, *Laviolette v. C.N.R.* (1986), 69 N.B.R. (2d) 58, 36 C.C.L.T. 203 (Q.B.); affd (1987), 79 N.B.R. (2d) 110, 40 C.C.L.T. 138; leave to appeal to S.C.C. refused, 84 N.B.R. (2d) 272*n*; *Smith v. Hudzik Estate* (1986), 38 Man. R. (2d) 115

(C.A.); leave to appeal to S.C.C. refused (1986), 40 Man. R. (2d) 240*n*, 67 N.R. 156*n*. Not all are happy with this development. One trial court judge suggested that the standards applied by Lord Wilberforce in the *Herrington* case can only lead to "confusion if not chaos". See *Eastwick v. New Brunswick* (1987), 83 N.B.R. (2d) 77, 45 C.C.L.T. 191 (Q.B.).

3. A well-known case which illustrates the difficulties of categorization is *McErlean v. Sarel* (1987), 42 D.L.R. (4th) 577, 42 C.C.L.T. 78 (Ont. C.A.). A 14-year-old trail bike rider, injured while riding on vacant land owned by the City of Brampton, was classified as a licensee and not as a trespasser. The courts construed the city's "failure to object" to the presence of trail bike riders as "tacit permission" to come onto the land.

LINDEN, CANADIAN TORT LAW

continued, pp. 641-649.

3. LICENSEE OR INVITEE?

Lawful visitors who enter the premises, in circumstances where there is no contractual term relating to their safety, are divided into two categories, "invitees" and "licensees". The distinction between the licensee and the invitee is not always easy to fathom. Generally, a licensee is a person, such as a social guest, who enters the occupier's land with permission but who is not there for any business purpose. The invitee, on the other hand, is a "lawful visitor from whose visit the occupier stands to derive an economic advantage".

Thus, a customer who comes into a store with a view to making a purchase qualifies as an invitee. The exact nature and scope of the economic relationship necessary to qualify a visitor as an invitee, however, is somewhat nebulous. An employee's wife attending a social gathering involving only employees and their spouses, at the home of the employer, was considered an invitee of the employer. A friend helping another to clear underbrush from residential property was also held to be an invitee.

On occasion the courts have classified as invitees students at a free public school, visitors to a public library, visitors of patients in hospitals and a person meeting or seeing off a friend at a railroad station, who did not necessarily bring any economic advantage to the occupier. In contrast, visitors in public parks and public washrooms have been characterized as licensees on the ground that no benefit flows from them to the municipality. Likewise a person attending at a public dump has been classified as a licensee. Many of the cases on this issue are difficult to reconcile and are best understood as contortions of the applicable legal principles for the purpose of achieving what the courts perceive to be an equitable and just result in factual situations that do not easily fit the rigid category system.

The relationship between a landlord and persons visiting tenants, with respect to common facilities (*e.g.*, stairs, elevators, and entrances) over which the landlord retains control, has been a matter of some controversy and uncertainty. English courts held that such visitors were licensees, regardless of whether they were social or business guests of the tenant. In Canada, however, with few exceptions, social guests and relatives of residential tenants have been held to be licensees of the landlord, whereas business visitors of tenants in commercial premises have been held to be invitees of the landlord. It has not yet been determined whether business visitors of tenants in residential premises are invitees or licensees of the landlord. Likewise, the status of social guests of commercial tenants *vis à vis* the landlord is an open question.

4. LICENSEES

The occupier's duty to a licensee was traditionally expressed as a duty to prevent damage from concealed dangers or traps of which the occupier has actual knowledge. Traps and concealed dangers are hidden dangers which are not obvious or to be expected under the circumstances. Whether a dangerous condition is a trap or a concealed danger is not always self-evident. For example, what is an obvious danger in daylight may be transformed into a concealed danger after dark.

Knowledge of the concealed danger or trap is a condition precedent to the licensor's liability. However the courts have placed a gloss on the requirement of actual knowledge. In *White v. Imperial Optical Co.*, (1957) 7 D.L.R. (2d) 471 (Ont. C.A.) it was held that an occupier must actually know of the physical condition involved, but that once such knowledge is shown, the question is not whether the occupier knew that the condition constituted a concealed danger, but whether the occupier, as a reasonable person, ought to have realized that it constituted a concealed danger. Subsequent cases have modified even the requirement that the occupier must have actual knowledge of the physical condition. It is sufficient if the occupier has actual knowledge that such a condition has existed in the past and may exist again in the future if appropriate preventative steps are not taken. Thus, actual knowledge of the danger will be imputed if the licensor had reason to know of its existence. This has diluted the "actual knowledge" requirement significantly.

More recently there has been a further blurring of the distinction between the standard of care owning to licensees and that owing to invitees. Under the traditional formulation of the obligation, a licensee had no claim if the danger was known to the licensee or obvious. In *Mitchell v. C.N.R.* the Supreme Court of Canada openly abandoned the requirement that the danger be concealed, holding that a licensee's mere knowledge of the danger, falling short of voluntary assumption of risk, does not exonerate the licensor. Such knowledge is, however, still relevant to the issue of contributory negligence.

In a subsequent decision, the Ontario Court of Appeal basing itself on *Mitchell*, reformulated the licensor's responsibility — the licensor must "take reasonable care to avoid foreseeable risk of harm from any unusual danger on the occupier's premises of which the occupier actually has knowledge or of which he ought to have knowledge because he was aware of the circumstances. The licensee's knowledge of the danger goes only to the questions of contributory negligence or *volenti*." Not only was the knowledge required reduced, but the concept of unusual danger was incorporated into the new test as a replacement for the notion of a concealed danger or trap.

As a result of all this, all that remains of the distinction between the duty owed to an invitee and that owed to a licensee is that, while the invitor is under a duty of reasonable diligence to ascertain the existence of the unusual danger, the licensor is only liable if having knowledge of facts from which a reasonable person would either infer the existence of the unusual danger or would regard its existence as so highly probable that that person's conduct would be predicated on the assumption that it did in fact exist. Thus the distinction lies in the difference between unusual dangers of which the occupier "ought to know" and those which the occupier merely has "reason to know". The latter does not imply a duty to know.

The occupier's duty to a licensee can usually be discharged by warning the licensee of the danger. However, the warning will not exonerate the occupier if the licensee is not given reasonable time to act on it, or if it is given by means of a sign which is not readily visible. In the case of child licensees, who are usually impervious to warning, the circumstances may require positive physical precautions.

5. INVITEES

The duty that an occupier owes to an invitee was expressed by Willes J. in *Indermaur v. Dames* [(1866 1 C.P. 274, affd L.R. 2 C.P. 311 (Ex.Ch.)] as follows:

> ... we consider it settled law, that he, using reasonable care on his part for his own safety, is entitled to expect that the occupier shall on his part use reasonable care to prevent damage from unusual danger, which he knows or ought to know; ...

In *Smith v. Provincial Motors Ltd.* it was suggested that, once it is decided that the entrant is an invitee, four additional questions should be asked: First, was there an unusual danger? Second, did the defendant know or have reason to know about it? Third, did the defendant act reasonably? Fourth, did the plaintiff use reasonable care for safety or did the plaintiff voluntarily incur the risk?

The question of what is an unusual danger has been the subject of controversy. Madam Justice Reed has observed that "[W]hen the jurisprudence is reviewed, one finds an inordinate amount of ink spilled, respecting the rules applicable in occupiers' liability cases and, in particular, considerable confusion as to exactly what is meant by the test set out in *Indermaur v. Dames*". Indeed, it has been demonstrated that the concept of unusual danger was introduced into our law by mistake — a misreading of the authorities by Willes J. Nevertheless, the courts have clung to the concept to the present day.

The term unusual danger has been held to be a "relative" one, depending upon the kind of premises involved and the class of persons to which the invitee belongs. A danger is unusual if it "is not usually found in carrying out the task or fulfilling the function which the invitee has in hand". This is an objective notion rather than a subjective one, so that it is the perspective of the class which the particular invitee is a member of rather than the actual knowledge and experience of the particular invitee which controls. The plaintiff's knowledge is not relevant to the question of whether a danger is an unusual one; it is relevant only to the questions of contributory negligence and voluntary assumption of risk.

Dangers such as icy patches, unmarked clear glass panels and doors, wet floors and objects on store floors may be considered "unusual" in some situations but not in others. Also, a running lawnmower, a falling piece of an elevator, and soapy floors in a shower room have been held to be unusual dangers. Held not to be unusual dangers, however, have been an irregularity on a private walkway, a snow-covered concrete base at a skating rink, and the shallow end of a swimming pool, bleachers in a hockey arena, and ice in parking lots in New Brunswick during the winter. This concept is one of the most troublesome in the area and should be abandoned.

An invitor's duty extends both to unusual dangers known to the invitor and those of which the invitor ought to be aware; the invitor must stay acquainted with the state of the property. The invitor's duty is not to prevent unusual dangers but rather to use reasonable care to prevent damages to the invitee from such dangers. What acts will constitute reasonable care on the part of the invitor is a question of fact, depending on the particular circumstances of each case. An adequate warning of the danger will in many circumstances suffice, but some situations may indicate more extensive precautionary measures.

6. CONTRACTUAL ENTRANTS

In addition to the three traditional categories of entrants, the courts have developed a fourth category, that of contractual entrant, who is someone like a patron of a hotel, a theatre, a hockey arena or a health club, who has contracted and paid for the right to enter the premises. If the contract expressly prescribes the obligations of the occupier in relation to safety, the contractual standard prevails. If, however, the contract is silent on the matter, the law implies a term that the premises are as safe for the purpose as reasonable care and skill on the part of anyone can make them or at least that the premises are reasonably fit for the purpose intended. …

The duty owed to contractual entrants is higher than that owed to invitees. Responsibility is not limited to "unusual dangers". Furthermore, liability under the "higher" contractual standard applicable where the use of the premises is the main purpose of the contract, as, for example, in a contract for accommodation, attaches not only for personal negligence on the part of the occupier or occupier's servants but also in respect of dangers created by independent contractors employed in connection with the construction, alteration or repair of the premises and even for defects negligently created before the defendant commenced occupation.

The duty owed to a contractual entrant also requires the exercise of reasonable care by the occupier to supervise and control the conduct of persons whose activities on the premises are likely to endanger the entrant.

…

7. ACTIVITY DUTY

The field of occupier's liability has been complicated further by an overriding distinction between an "activity duty" and an "occupancy duty", which derives from the misfeasance-nonfeasance dichotomy. If an entrant is injured by "current operations" being carried out by the occupier on the land, as opposed to a defect or danger in the condition of the land, the courts will impose the general duty to use reasonable care. This general duty is owed to all persons lawfully on the premises, but it is unclear whether it is also applicable to trespassers whose presence is known or probable.

NOTES

1. For a fuller treatment of the common law position see North, *Occupiers' Liability* (1971); Di Castri, *Occupiers' Liability* (1981).

2. It appears that in at least one jurisdiction, Australia, the common law has been able to reform the law relating to occupiers' liability, without statutory intervention. In a series of cases the courts have held that ordinary principles of negligence law apply to the occupiers' liability situation, rather than the special duties traditionally imposed. See *Hackshaw v. Shaw* (1984), 155 C.L.R. 614; *Papantonakis v. Australian Telecommunications Commn.* (1985), 156 C.L.R. 7, 57 A.L.R. 1 (H.C.); and *Aust. Safeway Stores v. Zaluzna* (1986), 69 A.L.R. 615. Even some Canadian courts have begun to suggest the same thing. See *Austin v. Gendis Inc.* (1985), 68 N.B.R. (2d) 57, 175 A.P.R. 57 (Q.B.), and *Stuart v. Canada*, [1989] 2 F.C. 3, 45 C.C.L.T. 290 (T.D.); application for reconsideration dismissed, 67 Alta. L.R. (2d) 64, [1989] 5 W.W.R. 163. Is this preferable to statutory intervention?

3. Several Canadian provinces still rely on the common law principles relating to occupier's liability. Three recent judgments interpreting the common law are *Hale v. Westfair Foods Ltd.*, [1995] 3 W.W.R. 293 (Sask. Q.B.); *Kinsella v. St. John*

Commercial Developers Ltd. (1995), 167 N.B.R. (2d) 121 (C.A.); and *Ackerman v. Wascana Centre Authority*, [1998] 2 W.W.R. 678 (Sask. Q.B.).

B. STATUTORY REFORM

The pressure for reform of this area of the law led the English Parliament to enact, in 1957, the Occupiers' Liability Act, which was also enacted in identical form in Northern Ireland in the same year. This legislation abolished the distinction between licensees and invitees, holding occupiers to a "common duty of care" to all lawful entrants requiring them to take "such care as in all the circumstances of the case is reasonable to see that the visitor will be reasonably safe in using the premises for the purposes for which he is invited or permitted by the occupier to be there".

Three years later, Scotland enacted legislation which went further than the English legislation, containing provisions that governed all entrants, including trespassers, who had been excluded from the English statute.

In 1962, New Zealand also enacted legislation, modelled on the English statute. Reform has been recommended in other jurisdictions as well. (See N.S.W. Law Reform Commission, Working Paper on Occupiers' Liability (1969).)

It was not until the 1970s that the Canadian provinces began to move in this area, Alberta being first in 1973, British Columbia second in 1974, and Ontario third in 1980. In 1983 Manitoba passed an *Occupiers' Liability Act*, S.M. 1983, c. 29 (C.C.S.M., c. O8); in 1984 Prince Edward Island passed an *Occupiers' Liability Act*, S.P.E.I. 1984, c. 28; and in 1996 Nova Scotia passed an *Occupiers' Liability Act*, S.N.S. 1996, c. 27. There are also proposals in other provinces. See Linden, Canadian Tort Law, 6th edition, 1997 at pp. 650-673 for a description of the legislation.

WALDICK v. MALCOLM

Supreme Court of Canada. (1991), 8 C.C.L.T. (2d) 1,
[1991] 2 S.C.R. 456.

Iacobucci J.: The defendants, Marvin and Roberta Malcolm (the "Malcolms"), appeal from a judgment of the Ontario Court of Appeal dismissing their appeal from the judgment at trial finding the Malcolms liable for personal injuries suffered by the plaintiff, Norman Waldick ("Waldick").

The appeal involves the interpretation of the nature and extent of the duty of care under the Ontario *Occupiers' Liability Act*, R.S.O. 1980, c. 322 (the "Act") [now R.S.O. 1990, c. O.2]. In general terms, the Act sets out the duty of care owed by occupiers of premises to persons who come onto those premises and specifies certain exceptions to the prescribed duty of care. As this appeal is the first involving the Act to reach this Court, and as several provinces have similar statutory regimes, it is important to clarify the scope of the duties owed by occupiers to their visitors.

Briefly stated, Waldick was seriously injured in a fall on the premises occupied by the Malcolms. It was in this context that the questions arose as to whether the Malcolms had failed to fulfil their statutory duties under the Act, and whether Waldick had willingly assumed the risks of the injury. Also involved is an issue of contributory negligence of Waldick. But before going further, a further elaboration of the facts giving rise to this appeal is warranted.

Facts

On February 7, 1984, Waldick suffered a fractured skull when he fell on the icy parking area of the rural residential premises near Simcoe, Ontario, which were occupied by the Malcolms. Waldick is Mrs. Malcolm's brother. Mrs. Malcolm worked as a hairdresser, but she often cut hair at her home for friends and relatives without receiving any remuneration. The property, which consisted of a farmhouse and barn on approximately 3 acres of land, was owned by the other appellants, Betty Stainback and Harry Hill. The Malcolms rented the premises from them. Since they were not the occupiers of the farmhouse, the action and cross-claim against Stainback and Hill were dismissed on consent in June, 1986.

On the premises was a gravel laneway that ran for about 200 to 300 feet from the road, past the house, and to the barn. Opposite the house, the laneway widened to form a parking area which could accommodate three or four vehicles at any one time. The house had a small wooden porch with two steps. Leading from the steps toward the laneway was a walk made of cement slabs which was about 6 feet long, but which did not reach the laneway. The rest of the distance between the walk and the laneway was grass-covered. The trial Judge noted that there was "a perceptible grade downwards from the house to the parking area."

At the time of the injury, the porch and steps of the house had been shovelled and, while the walk and grassy area had also been shovelled, these were still snow-covered. The laneway had not been salted or sanded. The appellant, Roberta Malcolm, testified that she did not consider it necessary or reasonable to do so. She also testified that, to her knowledge, few of the residents in that rural region, including Waldick, salted or sanded their laneways in winter. Four days before the accident, the region had experienced an ice storm. Waldick was aware that the laneway was "slippery, very icy with a dusting of snow on it," and acknowledged that its condition could be seen without difficulty. Because of the ice, he took exceptional caution in driving up the laneway. He parked about 20 feet from where the gravel laneway met the grassy stretch, and entered the house, walking very carefully because of the ice. Some time later, he went out to his car to get a carton of U.S. cigarettes which he had purchased for his sister. He put on his winter boots, turned on the porch light, and got the cigarettes. As he was walking back to the house, he slipped on the ice, fell backwards in the parking area, and fractured his skull.

Waldick commenced an action in the Supreme Court of Ontario under the Act, alleging negligence on the part of the Malcolms and the owners of the premises; as noted above, the action against the owners was dismissed on consent. The trial Judge found the Malcolms liable for the injuries sustained by Waldick and, by agreement of the parties, deferred the determination of damages.

The Malcolms' appeal was dismissed by the Ontario Court of Appeal.

Relevant Statutory Provisions

Occupiers' Liability Act

2. Subject to section 9, the provisions of this Act apply in place of the rules of the common law that determine the care that the occupier of premises at common law is required to show for the purpose of determining his liability in law in respect of dangers to persons entering on the premises or the property brought on the premises by those persons.

3. — (1) An occupier of premises owes a duty to take such care as in all the circumstances of the case is reasonable to see that persons entering on the premises, and the

property brought on the premises by those persons are reasonably safe while on the premises.

[…]

4. — (1) The duty of care provided for in subsection 3(1) does not apply in respect of risks willingly assumed by the person who enters on the premises, but in that case the occupier owes a duty to the person to not create a danger with the deliberate intent of doing harm or damage to the person or his property and to not act with reckless disregard of the presence of the person or his property.

9. …

(3) The provisions of the *Negligence Act* apply with respect to the causes of action to which this Act applies….

Points in Issue

1. Whether the Court of Appeal of Ontario erred in holding that the Malcolms breached the duty of care imposed by s. 3(1) of the *Occupiers' Liability Act*;

2. Whether, in the event that the Court of Appeal of Ontario was correct that the Malcolms did not meet the duty of care, Waldick willingly assumed the risks of walking over the icy parking area, thus relieving them from liability, pursuant to s. 4(1) of the Act;

3. Whether the trial Judge made a "palpable and overriding error" when he found that Waldick was not contributorily negligent.

Analysis

1. *Did the Court of Appeal of Ontario Err in Holding that the Malcolms Breached the Duty of Care Imposed by s. 3(1) of the Occupiers' Liability Act?*

The Courts below concluded that, in light of all the circumstances, the Malcolms breached the duty of care owed under s. 3(1) of the Act by doing nothing to render the parking area entrance to their house less slippery. While the Act in no way obliged them to salt or sand "every square inch of their parking area," Austin J. was of the view [p. 631 O.R.] that doing nothing fell short of the reasonable care requirement. Blair J.A. agreed, noting the duty was limited only to salting or sanding that part of the parking area next to the entrance, and adding that it was undeniable that the Malcolms knew this part would be used by visitors like Waldick.

Both Austin J. and Blair J.A. also stressed that sand and salt are not expensive and are readily available.

Counsel for the Malcolms submitted that the lower Courts had reduced the statutory words "in all the circumstances of the case" to a consideration of only two factors: *foreseeability* of an accident, and the *costs* of its avoidance. In counsel's view, this was an oversimplified "calculus of negligence" which constituted a reviewable error of law. More specifically, the Malcolms argued that the Courts below should also have taken into account "the practices of persons in the same or similar situations as the person whose conduct is being judged," or, in other words, local custom. This, it was argued, would inject an element of community standards into the negligence calculus, and would promote behaviour which better accords with the reasonable expectations of community members.

Professor A. Linden's (as he then was) article, "Custom in Negligence Law" (1968) 11 Can. Bar J. 151, was cited in support of these propositions. At p. 153, in the course of a discussion of the policy reasons for and against the relevance of custom, Linden says that:

> customary practices can provide a fairly precise standard of care to facilitate the courts' task of deciding what is reasonable in the circumstances. Like penal statutes, customs can crystallize the ordinarily vague standard of reasonable care.

In the instant appeal, the relevant local custom which the Courts below allegedly neglected to consider was "not sanding or salting driveways."

I am unable to agree with the Malcolms' submissions for several reasons. First of all, I do not agree with the premise of their argument, viz., that the lower Courts failed to consider local custom. ...

The mere fact that the alleged custom was not decisive of the negligence issue does not in any way support the conclusion that it was not considered. After all, the statutory duty on occupiers is framed quite generally, as indeed it must be. That duty is to take reasonable care in the circumstances to make the premises safe. That duty does not change, but the factors which are relevant to an assessment of what constitutes reasonable care will necessarily be very specific to each fact situation — thus the proviso, "such care as *in all circumstances of the case* is reasonable." One such circumstance is whether the nature of the premises is rural or urban. Another is local custom, which Blair J.A. explicitly mentions, and I view his reasons as considering and rejecting the alleged customs.

...

To conclude on this point, the existence of customary practices which are unreasonable in themselves, or which are not otherwise acceptable to courts, in no way ousts the duty of care owed by occupiers under s. 3(1) of the Act. That duty is to take such care as is reasonable in the circumstances, and, in my view, both Austin J. and Blair J.A. correctly stated and applied the law in this regard. They both considered "all the circumstances of the case." I would accordingly agree that the Malcolms breached the statutory duty of care imposed by s. 3(1) of the Act.

2. *In the event that the Court of Appeal of Ontario was Correct that the Malcolms did not Meet the Duty of Care, did Waldick Willingly Assume the Risks of Walking over the Parking Area, thus Relieving them from Liability, Pursuant to s. 4(1) of the Act?*

At issue under this ground of appeal is the scope of the defence which s. 4(1) offers to occupiers. They will be absolved of liability in those cases where the losses suffered by visitors on their premises come as a result of "risks willingly assumed" by those visitors. As Austin J. and Blair J.A. noted, there are two quite distinct and conflicting trends in the jurisprudence as to the proper interpretation of this term. In essence, they reflect two standards of what assuming a risk means: the first involves merely knowing of the risk that one is running, whereas the second involves not only knowledge of the risk, but also a consent to the legal risk, or, in other words, a waiver of legal rights that may arise from the harm or loss that is being risked. The latter standard is captured by the maxim volenti non fit injuria (the volenti doctrine), whereas the former is sometimes referred to as "sciens", or, in other words, mere "knowing" as opposed to actually "willing."

Counsel for the Malcolms argued that s. 4(1) should be interpreted as meaning something between mere knowledge and the strict volenti approach. He suggested that s. 4(1) would be met where it could be shown that the visitor had a knowledge *and* appreciation of the danger on the premises.

In my view, the reasons of Blair J.A. on this issue are also an admirably correct statement of the law. I have no doubt that s. 4(1) of the Act was intended to embody and preserve the volenti doctrine. This can be seen by looking at the statutory scheme that is imposed by the Act as a whole. It is clear the intention of the Act was to replace, refine and harmonize the common law *duty of care* owed by occupiers of premises to visitors on those premises. That much seems evident from the wording of s. 2 of the Act:

> 2. Subject to section 9, the provisions of this Act apply in place of the rules of the common law that determine the care that the occupier of premises at common law is required to show for the purpose of determining his liability in law in respect of dangers to persons entering on the premises or the property brought on the premises by those persons.

I am of the view that the Act was *not* intended to effect a wholesale displacement of the common law defences to liability, and it is significant that no mention is made of common law defences in s. 2. Reinforcement of this view is found when one asks why this area of law should entail a defence other than volenti which is applicable to negligence actions generally. There does not appear to be anything special about occupiers' liability that warrants a departure from the widely accepted volenti doctrine.

...

The goals of the Act are to promote, and indeed, require where circumstances warrant, positive action on the part of occupiers to make their premises reasonably safe. The occupier may, however, wish to put part of his property "off limits" rather than to make it safe, and in certain circumstances that might be considered reasonable. Where no such effort has been made, as in the case at Bar, the exceptions to the statutory duty of care will be few and narrow. ...

...

In my view, the Legislature's intention in enacting s. 4(1) of the Act was to carve out a very narrow exception to the class of visitors to whom the occupier's statutory duty of care is owed. This exception shares the same logical basis as the premise that underlies volenti, *i.e.*, "that no wrong is done to one who consents. By agreeing to assume the risk the plaintiff absolves the defendant of all responsibility for it": per Wilson J. in *Crocker*, supra, at p. 1201. Rare may be the case where a visitor who enters on premises will fully know of and accept the risks resulting from the occupier's non-compliance with the statute. To my mind, such an interpretation of s. 4(1) accords best with general principles of statutory interpretation, is more fully consonant with the legislative aims of the Act, and is consistent with tort theory generally.

Both Austin J. and Blair J.A. were of the view that Waldick did not consent to the legal risk, or waive any legal rights that might arise from the negligence of the Malcolms. I agree with their disposition of this ground of appeal, and conclude that Waldick is not barred from recovery by the operation of s. 4(1) of the Act.

3. *Did the Trial Judge make a "Palpable and Overriding Error" when he Found that Waldick was not Contributorily Negligent?*

Blair J.A. refused, rightly in my view, to revisit the findings of Austin J. as to the issue of contributory negligence. The Malcolms, before this Court, simply reargued a point that was explicitly rejected by Blair J.A. They contest the failure of the trial Judge to draw an inference of carelessness from the proof that Waldick was not wearing a winter coat. In my view, there have been no new arguments presented before this Court that could in any way lead to the conclusion that Austin J. made a "palpable and overriding" error in his appreciation of the evidence or in his finding on the contributory negligence issue.

Conclusion

For the foregoing reasons, I would dismiss the appeal with costs.

Appeal dismissed.

NOTES

1. Based on the above decision, do you see any major difference now between the general principles of negligence law and the statutory reforms of occupier's liability? Would it be fair to say that courts should approach occupier's liability cases as they do ordinary negligence actions?

2. The provincial statutes are similar in most respects. There are some differences, however, the most important of which is Alberta's provision for trespassers. In Alberta, occupiers owe very little duty to trespassers; that is, not to injure them by wilful or reckless conduct. More duty is owed to child trespassers if the occupier knew or ought to have known of their presence. Other statutes have less protection for trespassers in certain circumstances. For example, Ontario and Prince Edward Island provide that certain types of trespassers (those who enter premises intending to commit criminal acts) shall be deemed to willingly have assumed all risks. Because of these and other differences between the statutes, it is important to pay close attention to the legislation when dealing with occupier's liability in these provinces.

3. As time passes, the jurisprudence interpreting the statutes is growing. Cases which have dealt with such matters as the definition of "occupier": (see, *e.g. Silva v. Winnipeg (City)*, [1993] 1 W.W.R. 691 (Man. Q.B.); *Moody v. Toronto (City)* (1996), 31 O.R. (3d) 53 (Gen. Div.); *Murray v. Bitango*, [1996] 7 W.W.R. 163 (Alta. C.A.); *Wiley v. Tymar Mgmt.*, [1995] 3 W.W.R. 684 (B.C.S.C.)); and the standard of care required under the legislation (see, *e.g. Portree v. Woodsmill,* [1994] 6 W.W.R. 597 (Man. C.A.); *Ling v. Calgary Co-op,* [1995] 6 W.W.R. 49 (Alta. C.A.); *Mortimer v. Cameron* (1994), 111 D.L.R. (4th) 428 (Ont. C.A.); and *Galts v. Ultra Care Inc.*, [1995] 4 W.W.R. 690 (Man. C.A.)). The cases under the legislation are generally easier to resolve than those under the more complicated common law regime.

CHAPTER 15

BUSINESS TORTS

There is a whole range of business activity that is regulated by tort law. Business interests, like personal and property interests, have cried out for the protection of tort law, and it has responded. Much of the early law in this area has now been taken over by legislation, such as the *Combines Investigation Act*, now the *Competition Act*, the labour relations acts, the *Copyright Act* and others. There remains, however, a broad area of activity that has been relatively untouched by legislation, where tort law still plays a role in preventing undesirable business practices.

These problems are being exacerbated nowadays by the fierce competition in the Canadian business community, by the aggressiveness of many modern entrepreneurs and by the increasing sophistication of consumers and others who are eager to call on the courts to assist them in combatting the improper tactics used in the marketplace. It is a field that is growing in importance for tort lawyers and Canadians generally.

The material in this section is meant to serve only as an introduction to a vast and complex field. Law school curricula normally deal with many of these problems in courses on labour law, copyrights, patents and trade marks, competition law and others. See generally Heydon, *Economic Torts*, 2nd ed. (1978).

A. DECEIT

DERRY v. PEEK

House of Lords. (1889), 14 A.C. 337, 58 L.J.Ch. 864, 61 L.T. 265.

The directors of a tramway company issued a prospectus which asserted that they were empowered to use steam-powered cars. They did not actually have this authority, but the directors honestly believed they would get it as a matter of course. The governmental consent was never obtained, however, and, as a result, the company went into liquidation. The plaintiff had invested in company shares on the strength of the assertion in the prospectus and sued the directors for deceit. The House of Lords dismissed his claim.

Lord Herschell: My Lords, in the statement of claim in this action the respondent, who is the plaintiff, alleges that the appellants made in a prospectus issued by them certain statements which were untrue, that they well knew that the facts were not as stated in the prospectus, and made the representations fraudulently, and with the view to induce the plaintiff to take shares in the company.

"This action is one which is commonly called an action of deceit, a mere common law action." This is the description of it given by Cotton, L.J., in delivering judgment. I think it important that it should be borne in mind that such an action differs essentially from one brought to obtain rescision of a contract on the ground of misrepresentation of a material fact. The principles which govern the two actions differ widely. Where rescission is claimed it is only necessary to prove that there was misrepresentation; then, however honestly it may have been made, however free from blame the person who made it, the contract, having been obtained by misrepresentation, cannot stand. In an action of deceit, on the contrary, it is not enough to establish misrepresentation alone, it is conceded on all hands that something more must be proved to cast liability upon the defendant, though it has been a matter of controversy what elements are requisite. I lay stress upon this because observations made by learned judges in actions for rescission have been cited and much relied upon at the bar by counsel for the respondent. Care must obviously be observed in applying the language used in relation to such actions to an action of deceit. Even if the scope of the language used extend beyond the particular action, which was being dealt with, it must be remembered that the learned judges were not engaged in determining what is necessary to support an action of deceit, or in discriminating with nicety the elements which enter into it. …

…

I think the authorities establish the following propositions: First, in order to sustain an action of deceit, there must be proof of fraud, and nothing short of that will suffice. Secondly, fraud is proved when it is shewn that a false representation has been made (1) knowingly, or (2) without belief in its truth, (3) recklessly, careless whether it be true or false. Although I have treated the second and third as distinct cases, I think the third is but an instance of the second, for one who makes a statement under such circumstances can have no real belief in the truth of what he states. To prevent a false statement being fraudulent, there must, I think, always be an honest belief in its truth. And this probably covers the whole ground, for one who knowingly alleges that which is false, has obviously no such honest belief. Thirdly, if fraud be proved, the motive of the person guilty of it is immaterial. It matters not that there was no intention to cheat or injure the person to whom the statement was made. …

[His Lordship analyzed the evidence.]

I quite admit that the statements of witnesses as to their belief are by no means to be accepted blindfold. The probabilities must be considered. Whenever it is necessary to arrive at a conclusion as to the state of mind of another person, and to determine whether his belief under given circumstances was such as he alleges, we can only do so by applying the standard of conduct which our own experience of the ways of men has enabled us to form; by asking ourselves whether a reasonable man would be likely under the circumstances so to believe. I have applied this test, with the result that I have a strong conviction that a reasonable man situated as the defendants were, with their knowledge and means of knowledge, might well believe what they state they did believe, and consider that the representation made was substantially true.

Adopting the language of Jessel, M.R., in *Smith v. Chadwick*, 20 Ch. D. at p. 67,

> I conclude by saying that on the whole I have come to the conclusion that the statement, "though in some respects inaccurate and not altogether free from imputation of carelessness, was a fair, honest and bona fide statement on the part of the defendants, and by no means exposes them to an action for deceit."

I think the judgment of the Court of Appeal should be reversed.

NOTES

1. Following this decision legislation was enacted in England imposing a stricter responsibility on those who issue prospectuses. See now *Companies Act*, 1948, c. 38. In Canada, detailed legislative provisions now govern the area of corporate fund raising. See *Securities Act*, R.S.O. 1990, c. S.5. The common law principles, however, survive in other contexts.

2. In another prospectus case, *Peek v. Gurney* (1873), L.R. 6 H.L. 377, the plaintiff did not acquire his shares in the company immediately but waited several months before deciding to purchase shares which were being openly traded on the exchange. The original allotment of shares which the prospectus had invited investors to purchase had in fact been fully subscribed several months earlier. In rejecting the plaintiff's action against the defendants for their allegedly false representations made in the prospectus, the House of Lords held that although a person can be held responsible to a third person for statements which were made to another, there must have been the intent that the third person would act upon the representation in the manner that occasioned the loss. Is this principle similar to the one later articulated by the Supreme Court of Canada in the negligent statement case of *Haig v. Bamford, supra.*? See Keeton, "Ambit of A Fraudulent Representor's Responsibility" (1938), 17 Tex. L. Rev.

3. The importance of this action has diminished since *Hedley Byrne v. Heller*, [1964] A.C. 465, [1963] 2 All E.R. 575 (H.L.) has been decided, because it is far more difficult to prove fraud than it is to establish negligence. Would the plaintiff in *Derry v. Peek* be successful today? See *supra*, Chapter 9. For a commentary on the elements of *Derry v. Peek* see Perell, "The Fraud Elements of Deceit and Fraudulent Misrepresentation" (1996), 18 Advocates Quarterly 23; and Perell, "False Statements" (1996), 18 Advocates Quarterly 232.

YOUNG v. McMILLAN ET AL.

Supreme Court of Nova Scotia. (1894), 40 N.S.R. 52.

Meagher J.: The plaintiffs bought from the defendant one-half of a fishing boat and her gear for $105. They now seek to recover back that sum and damages, on the ground of a false representation alleged to have been made to them by the defendant, with the intention that they should act upon it, and that they did act upon it. The representation relied on was that he had paid $210 for her, while the fact was that he only paid $150 for her. …

I am quite convinced that even if the defendant made the alleged statement in the terms claimed … it had not the remotest effect in inducing the purchase, nor in determining the price paid. I say this quite apart from what I may say as to the burden of proof.

It was incumbent upon the plaintiffs to show how the representation in question affected them and that they acted on the faith of it, and but for it, would not have purchased at the price paid, or at all; or, at all events, to show a state of facts from which those inferences could fairly be drawn. In other words, that if the truth had been stated they would not have purchased.

Caveat emptor applies to such a sale, and therefore the purchaser had no right to rely upon the vendor's representations as to what he had paid for the boat, etc. They were apparently strangers to each other; at all events, they were not intimately acquainted, and it ought to have been apparent to the plaintiffs that no reason existed why the defendant should sell to them on the same terms as he bought, and therefore there was greater ground for caution on their part. …

A misrepresentation, to support an action, must in its nature be material and be determining ground of the transaction; or, at least, a material inducement to it....

I am afraid a very substantial proportion of the sales made in the stores from day to day would be liable to be set aside if untrue statements as to what the vendors paid for the articles sold constituted a ground for their rescission. ...

Statements by a vendor concerning the value of the thing sold, former offers for it, etc. have everywhere been regarded as statements to be distrusted by the intending purchaser. ...

The real inducement to the purchase from the plaintiffs' standpoint was their belief that they could make more money fishing than in bricklaying. They were then earning $9.00 a day bricklaying, and, therefore, they must have had exaggerated notions of the profits to be made fishing.

The plaintiffs have failed to substantiate their case, both on the facts and the law. The defendant will have judgment with costs.

NOTES

1. Compare the following statement of Learned Hand J., in *Vulcan Metals Co. v. Simmons Manufacturing Co.*, 248 F. 853 (1918):

    > There are some kinds of talk which no sensible man takes seriously, and if he does he suffers from his credulity. If we were all scrupulously honest, it would not be so; but, as it is, neither party usually believes what the seller says about his own opinions and each knows it. Such statements, like the claims of campaign managers before election, are rather designed to allay the suspicion which would attend their absence than to be understood as having any relation to objective truth. It is quite true that they induce a compliant temper in the buyer, but it is by a much more subtle process than through the acceptance of his claims for his wares.

2. Do you agree with the principle embodied in these decisions? Does anyone really rely on this type of statement? If they do, should they be protected? Just how big a lie like this can a seller tell a buyer and still get away with it? Compare with *Clarke v. Dickson* (1859), 6 C.B.N.S. 453, 28 L.J.C.P. 225.

3. Although untruths as to the price paid for or the value of an item have been dealt with leniently by the courts because they are considered to be mere puffing, false representations as to the condition of articles may be actionable. See *Abel v. McDonald*, [1964] 2 O.R. 256, 45 D.L.R. (2d) 198 (C.A.).

4. A passive failure to disclose the truth is usually not considered to be a misrepresentation, unless there is some fiduciary obligation on the representor to do so, but active concealment or statements that are only half true may be actionable. See Fleming, *The Law of Torts*, 9th ed. (1998), p. 695. In *Canson Enterprises Ltd. v. Boughton & Co.*, [1991] 3 S.C.R. 534, 85 D.L.R. (4th) 129; affg 61 D.L.R. (4th) 732, [1990] 1 W.W.R. 375 (C.A.); affg (1988), 52 D.L.R. (4th) 323, 45 C.C.L.T. 209 (B.C.S.C.), it was held that although "simple reticence or silence does not amount to fraud", fraud in law must be distinguished from "equitable fraud". Where there is a fiduciary obligation, non-disclosure, even if it is innocent, may amount to equitable fraud.

5. Consider the facts of *Sidhu Estate v. Bains*, [1996] 10 W.W.R. 590 (B.C.C.A.). Mr. Bhandar telephoned his sister, Ms. Sidhu, and induced her to invest a large sum of

money in a venture. He represented to her that not only had he invested his own money in the venture, but so had Mr. Bains and another director. Mr. Bains was present in the room during this telephone conversation, but said nothing. In fact, Mr. Bains had lied to Mr. Bhandar and he had not invested any of his money in the venture. The investments of both Mr. Bhandar and his sister were ultimately lost. After Ms. Sidhu passed away, her estate sued Mr. Bains for fraud. Under these circumstances, could Mr. Bains' silence during the telephone conversation amount to a misrepresentation even in the absence of a fiduciary or other relationship between he and Ms. Sidhu? The Court of Appeal said "yes". Is this an exceptional case, or is it inconsistent with the proposition that a passive failure to tell the truth cannot amount to a misrepresentation?

6. Is it tortious for a vendor to sell property without disclosing serious defects (in addition to whatever contractual remedies might be available)?

In *Sorenson and Sorenson v. Kaye Holdings* (1974), 14 B.C.L.R. 204, [1979] 6 W.W.R. 193 (C.A.), the vendors sold a seaside resort to the purchasers without disclosing that the operation of the swimming pool was contrary to existing health regulations. The vendors had in fact been convicted of having violated these regulations. The B.C. Court of Appeal reversed a trial judgment in favour of the plaintiff.

Mr. Justice McFarlane found that on the evidence it was not proved that the purchasers were induced to purchase the resort by fraudulent and false representations made by the vendors with the intent to deceive, but that the purchasers were well aware of the true state of affairs before the deal was closed. His Lordship also held that the measure of damages for an action in fraud, inducing a sale, is the difference between the actual value and the price paid, and that on this test the purchasers had failed to prove damage.

C.R.F. Holdings Ltd. et al. v. Fundy Chemical Intl. Ltd. et al. (1980), 21 B.C.L.R. 345, 14 C.C.L.T. 87 (S.C.); affd as to liability, [1982] 2 W.W.R. 385, 19 C.C.L.T. 263 (C.A.); damages varied, 39 B.C.L.R. 43, [1982] 5 W.W.R. 688 (S.C.), came after *Sorenson* and was distinguished from it. The defendant sold the plaintiff land on which slag was piled. The defendant stated that the slag would make "excellent fill", omitting to mention that it was radioactive and that possession of it required a licence. The plaintiff spread the material over the property and built a warehouse on it. The Atomic Energy Control Board discovered the presence of the material, but concluded that it presented no health hazard. The plaintiff complained, however, that the adverse publicity had greatly diminished the value of his property.

The trial judge held that the statement was deliberately deceptive as a half-truth. Although a vendor may not be obligated "to decry his own wares unless he makes some positive assertion that becomes distorted by the failure", there can be deceit by incomplete disclosure. The Court of Appeal agreed with the trial judge's findings. Anderson J.A. supported the principle that "to knowingly represent only favourable aspects without disclosing the fact that those favourable aspects are substantially qualified by restrictions and unfavourable aspects, known to the person making the representation, amounts to fraud". In addition, Anderson J.A. founded liability on the principle that a failure to disclose the inherently dangerous nature of the radioactive waste was in itself fraudulent. The following rule was formulated: "The vendor of land on which is situate an inherently dangerous substance is guilty of fraud if he sells such land to a purchaser without warning the purchaser that, if the dangerous substance is not used or disposed of in a specified manner or in the manner prescribed by statute, the purchaser and/or strangers to the contract may suffer a serious risk of injury."

7. This principle was applied, and perhaps even extended, by Mr. Justice Oyen in *Sevidal v. Chopra* (1987), 64 O.R. (2d) 169, 41 C.C.L.T. 179 (H.C.J.). This case concerned

a couple who bought a house on land which was contaminated with radioactive soil. The vendors were aware, before the sale, that radioactive material had been discovered in the area, but they did not disclose this fact to the purchasers. The vendors also discovered before the closing, that there was radioactive material in their backyard, but they also concealed this from the purchasers. After an extensive review of both authorities and a lecture given by the late Chief Justice Laskin when he was a law professor, Mr. Justice Oyen held that the vendors were liable in fraud for having failed to disclose to the purchasers, prior to the agreement of purchase and sale, that there was radioactive material in the area. They also had a duty to disclose the fact that there was indeed radioactive material on their own lot, when they discovered this fact before closing. In an Annotation to this case at 41 C.C.L.T. 181, Professor Irvine notes that this judgment seems to extend the obligation to disclose discussed in *C.R.F. Holdings Ltd. v. Fundy Chemical, supra*, in two respects. First, the obligation to disclose is applied to cases of "unfit for habitation" as opposed to actual inherent danger. Second, it extends to defects known to be in the area, even though it is not certain whether the specific lot is affected. What has happened to the doctrine of *caveat emptor* in the light of these decisions? See *Crozman v. Ruesch,* [1994] 4 W.W.R. 116 (B.C.C.A.), where the court dismissed an action brought by purchasers who discovered structural defects in their home after they moved in. The court applied the principle of *caveat emptor*. There was no fraudulent intention on the part of the vendors, the defects were visible, and any latent defects were not knowingly concealed by the vendors. The vendors were not obliged to disclose the fact that they discovered cracks in the house when they were moving out.

8. Would the above principle apply to the sale of an automobile having a defect which might lead to a traffic accident? Would the seller be liable to all those injured in the traffic accident?

9. In order to succeed a plaintiff must have actually relied on the misrepresentation. Some cases have held, however, that once fraud has been proved, the onus reverts to the fraudulent party to prove that the plaintiff did not rely on the statement. See *System Contractors Ltd. v. 2349893 Manitoba Ltd.*, [1994] 4 W.W.R. 488 (Man. Q.B.) and *Sidhu Estate v. Bains, supra.* Other courts have held that all of the evidence must be considered and that "[w]here nothing else but the representation could have induced the contract, then a logical inference is that the representation did in fact induce the contract." See *473759 Alberta Ltd. v. Heidelberg Canada Graphic Equipment Ltd.*, [1995] 5 W.W.R. 214 at 223 (Alta. Q.B.). What is the difference between the two approaches? Why adopt the reverse onus approach?

10. How should damages be calculated when it is proved that a person was induced by fraud to enter into a contract of sale? Fleming, *The Law of Torts*, 9th ed., notes that there are two conceivable standards for measuring the damages. The first is to give the plaintiff the benefit of what was promised, *i.e.*, the difference between the actual value and the value it would have had if the representation had been true. The second is to put the plaintiff in the position the plaintiff would have been in had the misrepresentation not been made, *i.e.*, the difference between the purchase price and the value of the article at the time of sale. Fleming notes that the second approach has been adopted in Britain, and the first approach adopted in the U.S. Let us look at *C.R.F. Holdings Ltd. v. Fundy Chemical, supra*, to see how the assessment was handled in that case. The plaintiff paid $260,000 for the land. The court found that had the purchaser known about the radioactive slag, he would have paid $100,000. Using the second test, the plaintiff's loss on the purchase was assessed at $160,000. Complicating matters was the fact that after he purchased the land and thinking that the slag made "excellent fill", the plaintiff spent $318,000 on improvements. The court thus had to calculate how much the improvements were worth in view of the presence of radioactive slag, compare this with how much they would have been worth if there was no radioactive material, and award the plaintiff the difference.

Let us assume that the plaintiff paid $260,000 for the land. Because of the radioactive slag it was worth only $100,000. If the slag would have made "excellent fill", as promised by the vendor, assume that the land would have been worth $300,000. Under the Canadian approach, the plaintiff's damages are $160,000. Under the American approach, they are $200,000. Do you think that the American approach is more just?

11. An investor purchases shares in a company, relying upon false company records and a press release presenting a false picture of the company. He purchases the shares for $12.50 per share. When the dishonest conduct and news of the false reports become public, the share price drops and the investor sells his shares for $1.65 each. The investor successfully sues the wrongdoers for fraud and negligent misrepresentation. How should a court assess his damages? See *Dixon v. Deacon Morgan* (1993), 102 D.L.R. (4th) 1 (B.C.C.A.).

12. Are the civil actions for deceit and fraud the same thing? In *Harland v. Fancsali* (1993), 13 O.R. (3d) 103, 102 D.L.R. (4th) 577 (Gen. Div.), affirmed (1994), 121 D.L.R. (4th) 182 (Ont. Gen. Div.), D.S. Ferguson J. noted that the remedy for fraud is based in equity and is a broader remedy than the tort of deceit. It is not necessarily based upon a false representation, as is deceit, but on a dishonest act which deprives the plaintiff of something which the plaintiff is or would be entitled to but for the fraudulent act of the defendant. On the facts of the case, the plaintiff vendors had been dishonestly led to believe that there were two offers to purchase their house, whereas, in reality, the same vendors had made two different offers using different names. Since the judge was uncertain as to whether these facts strictly fit within the requirements of the tort of deceit, the broader action based upon fraud was used.

B. INDUCING BREACH OF CONTRACT

1. Direct Inducement

LUMLEY v. GYE

Queen's Bench. (1853), 118 E.R. 749, 2 E. & B. 216, 22 L.J.Q.B. 463.

Miss Johanna Wagner was a well-known opera singer. She agreed to perform for the season at the Queen's Theatre, which the plaintiff managed. The defendant Gye persuaded Miss Wagner to breach her contract with the plaintiff. As a result, she failed to perform at the Queen's Theatre, causing loss to the plaintiff, who sued Gye.

Erie J.: The authorities are numerous and uniform, that an action will lie by a master against a person who procures that a servant should unlawfully leave his service. ... If it is objected that this class of action for procuring; a breach of contract of hiring rests upon no principle, and ought not to be extended beyond the cases heretofore decided ... the answer appears to me to be, that the class of cases referred to rests upon the principle that the procurement of the violation of the right is a cause of action, and that, when this principle is applied to a violation of a right arising upon a contract of hiring, the nature of the service contracted for is immaterial. It is clear that the procurement of the violation of a right is a cause of action in all instances where the violation is an actionable wrong, as in violations of a right to property, whether real or personal, or to personal security: he who procures the wrong is a joint wrong-doer, and may be sued, either alone or jointly with the agent, in the appropriate action for the wrong complained of. Where a right to the performance of a contract has been violated by a breach thereof, the remedy is upon the contract against the contracting party; and, if he is made to indemnify for such breach, no further recourse is allowed; and, as in case of the procurement of a breach of contract the action is for a wrong and cannot be joined with the action on the contract, and as the act itself is not likely to be of frequent occurrence nor easy of proof, therefore the action for this wrong, in respect of other contracts than those of hiring, are not numerous; but still they seem to me sufficient to shew that the principle has been recognized. ...

He who maliciously procures a damage to another by violation of his right ought to be made to indemnify; and that, whether he procures an actionable wrong or a breach of contract. He who procures the nondelivery of goods according to contract may inflict an injury, the same as he who procures the abstraction of goods after delivery; and both ought on the same ground to be made responsible. The remedy on the contract may be inadequate, as where the measure of damages is restricted; or in the case of non-payment of a debt where the damage may be bankruptcy to the creditor who is disappointed, but the measure of damages against the debtor is interest only; or, in the case of the non-delivery of the goods, the disappointment may lead to a heavy forfeiture under a contract to complete a work within a time, but the measure of damages against the vendor of the goods for non-delivery may be only the difference between the contract price and the market value of the goods in question at the time of the breach. In such cases, he who procures the damage maliciously might justly be made responsible beyond the liability of the contractor. ...

The result is that there ought to be, in my opinion, judgment for the plaintiff.

NOTES

1. In a companion case, *Lumley v. Wagner* (1852), 1 De GM & G. 604, 42 E.R. 687, an injunction was granted preventing Miss Wagner from singing for Gye and prohibiting Gye from accepting her services.

2. The principle of *Lumley v. Gye* does not depend upon malice. This was established by the House of Lords in *Allen v. Flood*, [1898] A.C. 1, [1895-9] All E.R. Rep. 52 (H.L.) and *Quinn v. Leathem*, [1901] A.C. 495, [1900-3] All E.R. Rep. 1 (H.C.). In *Quinn v. Leathem*, Lord Macnaghten said:

   > The decision was right, not on the ground of malicious intention — that was not, I think, the gist of the action — but on the ground that a violation of legal right committed knowingly is a cause of action, and that it is a violation of legal right to interfere with contractual relations recognized by law if there be no sufficient justification for the interference.

3. In order to be liable, the defendant must have intended to induce a breach of the contract. This requirement implies two things: first, that the defendant knew there was a contract in existence, and second, that the defendant's conduct would lead to its breach. Although closely related, these two elements are not the same. In terms of knowledge, is it sufficient that the defendant knows in a general way that there is a contract, or must the defendant know its precise terms? In *Ed Miller Sales & Rentals Ltd. v. Caterpillar Tractor Co.,* [1996] 9 W.W.R. 449, 30 C.C.L.T. (2d) 1 (Alta. C.A.), the court reviewed the authorities on this point and concluded that the defendant must at least have known of enough of the terms of the contract "to have known that his acts would probably interfere with performance...". Logically, one could not intend to induce a breach of a contract, if one is unaware that one exists.

4. It has been held that as long as a party had "the means of knowledge" to determine whether a legitimate contract existed but deliberately disregarded this, the element has been made out. See *Royal Bank v. Wilton*, [1995] 6 W.W.R. 285 (Alta. C.A.).

5. In *Yellow Submarine Deli v. AGF Hospitality Associates Inc.*, [1998] 2 W.W.R. 701 (Man. C.A.), a lawyer was sued for inducing breach of contract, because he wrote a letter on behalf of his client to third parties informing them not to continue to deal with the plaintiff. The Court of Appeal dismissed the action on the basis that the solicitor had no reason to believe that there were valid subsisting contracts between the third parties and the plaintiff. It left open the question whether a solicitor should be liable at any event when he or she writes a letter on the instructions of his or her client. Should it be? See discussion on defences, *infra.*

6. There must also be the intention to induce breach. In what sense is the word "intention" being used here — desiring to induce breach, knowing with substantial certainty that there will be a breach, or simply foreseeing the probability or even possibility of a breach? What should the test be for an intentional tort? See *Parks West Mall Ltd. v. Jennett* (1995), 28 C.C.L.T. (2d) 1, [1996] 4 W.W.R. 87 (Alta. C.A.) and *Atcheson v. College of Physicians & Surgeons (Alberta)* (1994), 21 C.C.L.T. (2d) 166 (Alta. Q.B.).

7. Is there a difference between "inducing" a breach and "advising" someone not to perform? Klar, *Tort Law*, 2nd ed., p. 504 argues that the distinction between inducement and advice is a subtle one, which should be avoided. He suggests that any action taken to encourage another party not to perform should *prima facie* be actionable as long as the other elements of the tort are made out. See *Royal Bank v. Wilton, supra.*

8. Liability for inducing breach of contract can arise when a person deals with a third party in a way known to be inconsistent with the terms of a contract between the third party and the plaintiff. In *Soroka v. Skjoth* (1997), 37 C.C.L.T. (2d) 197 (Alta. Master), the plaintiff had an eight-year lease on land owned by the first defendant. The second defendant knowing of the lease and knowing that it was not registered and therefore would not be valid against him if he purchased the land, bought the land expressly free from the lease. The plaintiff sued both the vendor and purchaser. The purchaser argued that he could not be liable for acting in a way which was inconsistent with the contractual rights of the plaintiff since it was perfectly legal for him to buy the land free from the lease, if the lease was not registered. The lessee in fact knew that there might be an impending sale, yet still decided not to register the lease. Should the purchaser be liable for inducing breach of contract?

9. See Stevens, "Interference with Economic Relations — Some Aspects of the Turmoil in the Intentional Torts" (1974), 12 Osgoode Hall L.J. 595; Burns, "Tort Injury to Economic Interests: Some Facets of Legal Response" (1980), 58 Can. Bar Rev. 103; Richardson, "Interference with Contractual Relations: Is Torquay Hotel the Law in Canada?" (1983), 41 U. Toronto Fac. L. Rev. 1.

2. Indirect Inducement

D.C. THOMSON & CO. LTD. v. DEAKIN ET AL.

Court of Appeal. [1952] Ch. 646, [1952] 2 All E.R. 361.

The plaintiffs were printers and publishers of periodicals employing non-union labour. They obtained their paper under a contract with Bowaters Sales Ltd. Because of the plaintiffs' anti-union activity, the defendants asked union workers who worked for Bowaters to refuse to deliver paper to the plaintiffs. As a result Bowaters informed the plaintiffs that it could not deliver paper to it as contracted.

The plaintiffs sought an injunction to restrain the defendants who were officers of the unions concerned, to do any act with a view to procuring any breach by Bowaters of their contract with the plaintiffs to supply paper.

Evershed M.R.: It was suggested in the course of argument … that the tort must … be properly confined to … direct intervention, that is, to cases where the intervener or persuader uses by personal intervention persuasion on the mind of one of the parties to the contract so as to procure that party to break it.

I am unable to agree that any such limitation is logical, rational or part of our law. In such cases where the intervener (if I may call him such) does so directly act upon the mind of a party to the contract as to cause him to break it, the result is, for practical purposes, as though in substance he, the intervener, is breaking the contract, although he is not a party to it. Such a statement of the matter I take from Pollock's Law of Torts, 15th ed., p. 251, where reference is made to Street's Foundations of Legal Liability. At any rate, it is clear that, when there is such a direct intervention by the intervener, the intervention itself is thereby considered wrongful.

I cannot think that the result is any different if the intervener, instead of so acting upon the mind of the contracting party himself, by some other act tortious in itself, prevents the contracting party from performing the bargain. A simple case is where the intervener, for example, physically detains the contracting party so that the contracting party is rendered unable by the detention to perform the contract. …

What is the situation if he attains the same result, indirectly, by bringing his persuasion or procuration to bear upon some third party, commonly a servant of the contracting party, but possibly an independent third person? In my judgment, it is reasonably plain (and the result, as it seems to me, would otherwise be highly illogical and irrational) that, if the act which the third party is persuaded to do is itself an unlawful act or a wrongful act (including in that phrase a breach of contract) and the other elements are present (namely, knowledge and intention to do the damage which is in fact suffered), then the result is the same and the intervener or procurer will be liable for the loss or damage which the injured party sustains.

Jenkins L.J.: I see no distinction in principle for the present purpose between persuading a man to break his contract with another, preventing him by physical restraint from performing it, making his performance of it impossible by taking away or damaging his tools or machinery, and making his performance of it impossible by depriving him, in breach of their contracts, of the services of his employees. All these are wrongful acts, and if done with knowledge of and intention to bring about a breach of a contract to which the person directly wronged is a party, and, if in fact producing that result, I fail to see why they should not all alike fall within the sphere of actionable interference with contractual relations delimited by Lords Macnaghten and Lindley in *Quinn v. Leathem*. But, while admitting this form of actionable interference in principle, I would hold it strictly confined to cases where it is clearly shown, first, that the person charged with actionable interference knew of the existence of the contract and intended to procure its breach; secondly, that the person so charged did definitely and unequivocally persuade, induce or procure the employees concerned to break their contracts of employment with the intent I have mentioned; thirdly, that the employees so persuaded, induced or procured did in fact break their contracts of employment; and, fourthly, that breach of the contract forming the alleged subject of interference ensued as a necessary consequence of the breaches by the employees concerned of their contracts of employment.

[The Court of Appeal did not find that these elements were made out in the existing case and accordingly refused the injunction].

---

3. Interferences Short of Breach

TORQUAY HOTEL CO. LTD. v. COUSINS ET AL.
Court of Appeal. [1969] 2 Ch. 106, [1969] 1 All E.R. 522.

Due to a labour dispute, a contract between the plaintiff hotel and a fuel company for delivery of fuel oil could not be carried out. The contract contained a *force majeure* clause by which neither party would be liable if fulfilment of any term was hindered by any circumstance not within their immediate control including strikes and labour disputes. The plaintiff attempted to get fuel from another supplier, but this was also stopped as a result of threats from the union. The plaintiff sought an injunction.

Lord Denning M.R.:
The principles of law

The principle of *Lumley v. Gye* (1853) 2 E. & B. 216 is that each of the parties to a contract has a "right to the performance" of it: and it is wrong for another to procure one of the parties to break it or not to perform it. That principle was extended a step further by Lord Macnaghten in *Quinn v. Leathem* [1901] A.C. 495, so that each of the parties has a right to have his "contractual relations" with the other duly observed. "It is," he said at p. 510, "a violation of legal right to interfere with contractual relations recognised by law if there be no sufficient justification for the interference." That statement was adopted and applied by a strong board of the Privy Council in *Jasperson v. Dominion Tobacco Co.* [1923] A.C. 709. It included Viscount Haldane and Lord Sumner. The time has come when the principle should be further extended to cover "deliberate and direct interference with the execution of a contract without that causing any breach". That was a point left open by Lord Reid in *Stratford (J.T.) & Son Ltd. v. Lindley* [1965] A.C. 269, 324. But the common law would be seriously deficient if it did not condemn such interference. It is this very case. The principle can be subdivided into three elements:

First, there must be *interference* in the execution of a contract. The interference is not confined to the procurement of a *breach* of contract. It extends to a case where a third person *prevents* or *hinders* one party from performing his contract, even though it be not a breach.

Second, the interference must be deliberate. The person must know of the contract or, at any rate, turn a blind eye to it and intend to interfere with it: see *Emerald Construction Co. v. Lowthian* [1966] 1 W.L.R. 691.

Third, the interference must be *direct*. Indirect interference will not do. Thus, a man who "corners the market" in a commodity may well know that it may prevent others from performing their contracts, but he is not liable to an action for so doing. A trade union official, who calls a strike on proper notice, may well know that it will prevent the employers from performing their contracts to deliver goods, but he is not liable in damages for calling it. *Indirect* interference is only unlawful if unlawful means are used. I went too far when I said in *Daily Mirror Newspapers*

Ltd. v. Gardner [1968] 2 Q.B. 762, 782 that there was no difference between direct and indirect interference. On reading once again *Thomson (D.C.) & Co. Ltd. v. Deakin* [1952] Ch. 646, with more time, I find there is a difference. Morris L.J., at p. 702, there draws the very distinction between "*direct* persuasion to breach of contract" which is unlawful in itself: and "the intentional bringing about of a breach by *indirect* methods involving wrong-doing." This distinction must be maintained, else we should take away the right to strike altogether. Nearly every trade union official who calls a strike — even on due notice, as in *Morgan v. Fry* [1968] 2 Q.B. 710 — knows that it may prevent the employers from performing their contracts. He may be taken even to intend it. Yet no one has supposed hitherto that it was unlawful: and we should not render it unlawful today. A trade union official is only in the wrong when he procures a contracting party *directly* to break his contract, or when he does it indirectly by *unlawful means*. On reconsideration of the *Daily Mirror* case, [1968] 2 Q.B. 762, I think that the defendants there interfered directly by getting the retailers as their agents to approach the wholesalers.

I must say a word about unlawful means, because that brings in another principle. I have always understood that if one person deliberately interferes with the trade or business of another, and does so by unlawful means, that is, by an act which he is not at liberty to commit, then he is acting unlawfully, even though he does not procure or induce any actual breach of contract. If the means are unlawful, that is enough. Thus in *Rookes v. Barnard* [1964] A.C. 1129 (as explained by Lord Reid in *Stratford v. Lindley* [1965] A.C. 269, 325 and Lord Upjohn, at p. 337) the defendants interfered with the employment of Rookes — and they did it by unlawful means, namely, by intimidation of his employers — and they were held to be acting unlawfully, even though the employers committed no breach of contract as they gave Rookes proper notice. And in *Stratford v. Lindley* [1965] A.C. 269, the defendants interfered with the business of Stratford — and they did it by *unlawful means*, namely, by inducing the men to *break their contracts* of employment by refusing to handle the barges — and they were held to be acting unlawfully, even in regard to *new business* of Stratford which was not the subject of contract. Lord Reid said, at p. 324:

> The respondents' action made it practically impossible for the appellants to do any new business with the barge hirers. It was not disputed that such interference is tortious if any unlawful means are employed.

So also on the second point in *Daily Mirror v. Gardner*, [1968] 2 Q.B. 762, the defendants interfered with the business of the "Daily Mirror" — and they did it by a collective boycott which was held to be *unlawful* under the *Restrictive Trade Practices Act, 1956* — and they were held to be acting unlawfully.

NOTES

1. Lord Denning's extension of the tort was a radical departure from the traditional requirement that for the tort to be established there must have been a breach of an existing contract. For a review of the case law leading up to the new formulation, see Richardson, "Interference with Contractual Relations: Is Torquay Hotel the Law in Canada?" (1983), 41 U. Toronto Fac. L. Rev. 1.

2. Has *Torquay* been accepted into Canadian law? This is a controversial matter. Professor Burns, "Tort Injury to Economic Interests: Some Facets of Legal Response" (1980), 58 Can. Bar Rev. 103, has no doubt that it has. He cites five cases to support this proposition. Richardson, *supra,* denies this and attempts to refute Professor Burns. It is apparent that this debate will only be settled by a Supreme Court of Canada decision.

3. One court has expressly refused to accept *Torquay*. See *Mintuck v. Valley River Band No. 63A* (1977), 75 D.L.R. (3d) 589, 2 C.C.L.T. 1 (Man. C.A.).

4. Should Canadian courts accept *Torquay*? Here again there is disagreement. Burns and Stevens have cautiously welcomed it. Richardson is strongly opposed to it and views it as an attempt by anti-labour courts to intrude into areas where they have been clearly excluded by legislation.

5. Assuming that a breach of contract is necessary, what would happen if it is proved that the contract which was breached was unenforceable due to a technicality? See *Unident Ltd. v. DeLong et al.* (1981), 50 N.S.R. (2d) 1, 98 A.P.R. 1, 131 D.L.R. (3d) 225 (S.C.).

6. What are the two conflicting interests at stake here? The desire to maintain robust competition balanced against the desire to keep things "above board" creates the tension. Viewed in this way, did *Torquay* go too far?

7. In *Torquay*, could the plaintiff hotel have sued the fuel supplier for refusing to supply it with fuel? The answer is "no" since the parties had agreed that the inability of the fuel supplier to supply fuel due to a labour disruption would not constitute a breach of contract. What damages then did the plaintiff suffer when the defendant's activity prevented the supply of fuel? See Richardson, *supra*, for an elaboration of this crucial point.

8. C induces B to breach its employment contract with A. B breaches. A sues B for wrongful dismissal and receives damages. A sues C for inducing breach of contract. What damages is A entitled to in the suit against C? See *Vale v. Intl. Longshoremen's & Warehousemen's Union, Local 508*, [1979] 5 W.W.R. 231, 9 C.C.L.T. 262 (B.C.C.A.).

9. The context of the economic torts has frequently been labour relations disputes, an arena which pits the idea of the sanctity of contract against the value of free collective bargaining. A recent judgment in this area which has extensively dealt with the issues discussed in this chapter is *Garry v. Sherritt Gordon Mines Ltd.*, [1988] 1 W.W.R. 289, 42 C.C.L.T. 241 (Sask. C.A.). The case involved a legal strike against a subcontractor involved in the construction of a large fertilizer plant in Saskatchewan. Picketing eventually brought all work on the site to a standstill, allegedly disrupting the contractual activities of other parties who were involved in the project, although not parties to the labour dispute. Injunctions were sought to restrain picketing, on the basis that this conduct constituted the tort of intentional inducement of breach of contract and interference by unlawful means with the performance of a contract. An interlocutory injunction was granted, and the union appealed. Even though the dispute was resolved, the Saskatchewan Court of Appeal, *per* Cameron J.A. and Bayda C.J.S., delivered full and considered judgments because of the importance of the issues. In his judgment, Cameron J.A. stated that the tort of direct procurement of breach of contract did not occur merely because the picketers advised or informed other workers not to cross picket lines. There must have been an "inducement" and "procurement" of the contractual breaches. In terms of the "indirect" form of the tort, Cameron J.A. held that since no unlawful means were used, the action could not be made out. Bayda C.J.S. held that the torts could be committed even if the interferences induced fell

short of actual breaches of contract. He disagreed with Cameron J.A. on whether there was a direct interference, deciding that there was. Bayda C.J.S. also found that the "indirect" tort had been committed. The judgments provide an *excellent* discussion of these torts. See also *Thorvaldson v. Saskatchewan* (1991), 82 D.L.R. (4th) 537, 9 C.C.L.T. (2d) 205, where the Saskatchewan Court of Appeal again looked at these issues, particularly with regard to the acceptability of the *Torquay* principle.

4. Justification

BRIMELOW v. CASSON

Chancery Division. [1924] 1 Ch. 302, 93 L.J.Ch. 256, 130 L.T. 725.

The plaintiff was the owner of a burlesque troupe — the King Wu Tut Tut Revue — which was on tour fulfilling engagements at various theatres. The defendants were members of an actors' Joint Protection Committee which was making attempts to obtain better wages for chorus girls since it had been shown that the lack of a living wage had driven many girls to prostitution. The Committee had fixed a minimum wage of 2*l.* 10*s* per week. The plaintiff paid his girls 1*l.* 10*s*. It was proved that one of the plaintiff's chorus girls, in order to obtain a living, was living, to the plaintiff's knowledge, in immorality with an abnormal, deformed dwarf.

In order to improve the lot of this troupe, the defendants persuaded the proprietors of several theatres not to permit the plaintiff the use of their buildings and to break existing contracts or refuse to make contracts until higher wages were paid. The plaintiff brought action against the defendants for an injunction. ...

Russell J.: In my opinion, it is true to say that the evils which the Joint Protection Committee and the associations represented by it anticipate as the result of a company being run by a manager paying insufficient salaries are to be found in the plaintiff's company. *Prima facie* interference with a man's contractual rights and with his right to carry on his business as he wills is actionable; but it is clear on the authorities that interference with contractual rights may be justified; *a fortiori* the inducing of others not to contract with a person may be justified. ...

My task here is to decide whether, in the circumstances of this case, justification existed for the acts done. Let me summarize the salient facts of the present case. The plaintiff is carrying on a business which involves the employment for wage of persons engaged in the theatrical calling, a calling in which numberless persons of both sexes are engaged in different classes of work throughout the country. The unions, or associations, formed for the purpose of representing and advancing the interests of those persons in connection with their different classes of work, and the interests of the calling as a whole, have ascertained by experience, and no one could doubt the fact, that it is essential for the safeguarding of those interests that there should be no sweating by employers. They have found by experience that the payment of less than a living wage to chorus girls frequently drives them to supplement their insufficient earnings by indulging in misconduct for the purpose of gain, thus ruining themselves in morals and bringing discredit on the theatrical calling. With the object of protecting those girls and of safeguarding the interests of the theatrical calling and its various members they have fixed standards of minimum wages, the minimum wage for chorus girls being fixed by the Actors Association at the sum of 2*l.* 10*s*. a week. They find that the plaintiff is paying to his chorus girls wages on which no girl could with decency feed, clothe, and lodge herself, wages far below the minimum fixed by the Actors' Association. They have had previous experience of the plaintiff, and they cause fresh inquiries to be made, with the result that they are satisfied that many, if not all, the results anticipated by them to flow from such underpayment are present in the plaintiff's company. They desire in the interest of the theatrical calling and the members thereof to stop such underpayment with its evil consequences. The only way they can do so is by inducing the proprietors of theatres not to allow persons like the plaintiff the use of their theatres, either by breaking contracts already made or by refusing to enter into contracts. They adopt this course as regards the plaintiff as the only means open to them of bringing to an end his practice of underpayment which, according to their experience, is fruitful of danger to the theatrical calling and its members. In these circumstances, have the defendants justification for their acts? That they would have the sympathy and support of decent men and women I can have no doubt. But have they in law justification for those acts? As has been pointed out, no general rule can be laid down as a general guide in such cases, but I confess that if justification does not exist here I can hardly conceive the case in which it would be present. These defendants, as it seems to me, owed a duty to their calling and to its members, and, I am tempted to add, to the public to take all necessary peaceful steps to terminate the payment of this insufficient wage, which in the plaintiff's company had apparently been in fact productive of those results which their past experience had led them to anticipate. "The good sense" of this tribunal leads me to decide that in the circumstances of the present case justification did exist.

NOTES

1. Do you agree that this conduct was justified in the circumstances?

2. What if parents persuade their child to break an engagement to marry a person of bad moral character? *Gunn v. Barr*, [1926] 1 D.L.R. 855 (Alta. C.A.).

3. In *Babcock v. Carr; Babcock v. Archibald* (1981), 34 O.R. (2d) 65, 127 D.L.R. (3d) 77 (S.C.), a daughter induced her mother to breach a contract of sale that the latter had entered into with the plaintiff. The daughter was unhappy with the sale price which she considered too low. Justification?

4. In *Thermo King Corp. v. Provincial Bank of Canada* (1981), 34 O.R. (2d) 369, 130 D.L.R. (3d) 256 (C.A.); leave to appeal to S.C.C. refused 42 N.R. 352*n*, a bank wrongfully refused to issue a draft on its customer's instructions, knowing that the effect of this refusal would result in a breach of the contract entered into between the bank's customer and the plaintiff. The bank's motive was not to damage the plaintiff but to protect its own interests. Liability? Also see *Edwin Hill & Partners v. First National Finance Corp. Plc.*, [1988] 3 All E.R. 801 (C.A.), for a good review of this issue.

5. Suppose a lawyer advises a client that he or she can legally terminate a contract that the client has with another party. This advice, although honest, turns out to be mistaken, and the termination constitutes a breach of contract. Can the lawyer be sued for inducing breach of contract? In *Spectra Architectural Group Ltd. v. Eldred Sollows Consulting Ltd.* (1991), 80 Alta. L.R. (2d) 361, 7 C.C.L.T. (2d) 169 (Alta. Q.B.), the Master in Chambers decided that "professional advice givers" have a privilege which protects them in such circumstances from an action for inducing breach of contract. What if the lawyer knows that termination constitutes a breach but still feels that it is in the client's best financial interest to terminate? Is this protected?

6. Directors or officers of companies are also protected from liability for inducing breach of contract, as long as their decisions to have their companies sever contractual relations with third parties are made in good faith, in the interests of their companies. If their dominating motive, however, is to damage the third party, or to benefit themselves personally, they will lose the protection of this defence. For such a case, see *Jackson v. Trimac Industries Ltd.*, [1993] 2 W.W.R. 209 (Alta. Q.B.), varied, [1994] 8 W.W.R. 237 (Alta. C.A.). In another case, *Levi v. Charters of Canada Inc.*, [1995] 2 W.W.R. 279 (Man. Q.B.), the court held that not only must the officer not be acting *bona fide*, but the dominating purpose of the actions must have been to injure the plaintiff, in order for there to be liability.

7. The College of Physicians or Surgeons told a physicians' clinic that a nurse employed by it could not continue to perform certain functions as it was contrary to law to allow her to do so. The clinic fired the nurse and she sued the College for inducing breach of contract. Defence? See *Atcheson v. College of Physicians & Surgeons, supra.* What if the College was incorrect in its interpretation of the rules?

5. Extension to Negligence

NICHOLLS v. TOWNSHIP OF RICHMOND

British Columbia Court of Appeal. (1983), 145 D.L.R. (3d) 362, 24 C.C.L.T. 253; leave to appeal to S.C.C. refused (1983), 51 N.R. 397*n*.

The plaintiff solicitor was dismissed from his job with the defendant municipality. He sued the defendant municipality for wrongful dismissal and joined various servants of the municipality pleading, among other things, that because of their negligence he was dismissed. The defendants moved to strike out this allegation.

Lambert J.A.: The second question, and the real issue in this appeal, relates to the allegation of a breach by the personal defendants of a duty of care arising from their relationships with the plaintiff. Counsel for the defendants said that this was an allegation of "negligently inducing a breach of contract" and that there was no such cause of action.

The historical development of the nominate tort of inducing breach of contract has restricted that tort to acts that are intended to cause the breach, though it now seems that knowledge of the precise terms of the contract may not be necessary. But I do not think that the intention is in itself the central element of the tort. Rather, intention has been the key to unlocking the issue of remoteness of damage: see, particularly, the reasons of Crompton J. at p. 212 and Wightman J. at p. 215 in *Lumley v. Gye*, [1843-60] All E.R. Rep. 208.

Meanwhile, there has been a new perception of the theoretical foundation of the law of negligence. *M'Alister (or Donoghue) v. Stevenson, supra*, is now seen to have established that the duty of care does not grow from specific relationships, such as occupier and licensee, or bailor and bailee, where it has been found to have existed before, but rather from proximity of relationship and foreseeability of harm. It is a law of general application and not a law of specific instances.

Where, then, does liability end? First, the general law has its own boundary dictated by absence of proximity or of foreseeability. But, second, there are particular situations where, as a matter of legal policy, there is no liability, notwithstanding proximity and foreseeability, because there is a paramount social interest that must be protected, as, for example, in policy decisions of government on the allocation of public funds.

In short, the law of negligence is now seen as a general law, with exceptions, and not as a law of specific instances. I draw this conclusion from the speeches of Lord Reid at p. 1026 in *Home Office v. Dorset Yacht Co. Ltd.*, [1970] A.C. 1004; Lord Wilberforce at p. 751 in *Anns et al. v. Merton London Borough Council*, [1978] A.C. 728, and Lord Roskill at p. 490 in *Junior Books Ltd. v. Veitchi Co. Ltd.*, [1982] 3 W.L.R. 477. I do not think that the jurisprudential underpinning of the law of negligence is different in Canada than it is in England.

So the question in this case becomes: Is there a legal policy that denies recovery, as a matter of principle, where, in a relationship of proximity that may exist between officers and employees of a corporation, an act, omission or misstatement occurs, and the perpetrator should reasonably have foreseen that it would result directly in economic loss to a fellow employee, as, for example, by dismissal from employment? I am not persuaded that there is or should be such a general legal policy. In particular cases recovery may be denied as a matter of policy, but the policy would be a narrower one, applicable on the basis of facts that are not as yet revealed in this case. I reach no conclusion now as to the existence or scope of such a narrower policy.

In my opinion such cases as *Cattle v. Stockton Waterworks Co.* (1875), L.R. 10 Q.B. 453, and *Weller & Co. v. Foot & Mouth Disease Research Institute*, [1965] 3 All E.R. 560, should be seen as specific examples of a denial of recovery on the basis of absence of proximity, or remoteness of damage, or both, and not as establishing a principle that damages can never be recovered for economic loss if the loss arises from the breach of a contractual relationship between one victim who suffers economic loss and another victim who suffers physical injury. The answer to such problems lies not in a uniform denial of recovery but in an application of the customary and sometimes difficult questions relating to proximity, foreseeability, causation and remoteness.

Suppose an airline has a policy of discharging pilots who suffer from a medical disability and requires its pilots to undergo a medical examination each year by a doctor, selected by the airline, who knows the purpose of the examination. Suppose the doctor carelessly and incorrectly diagnoses a disability and the pilot is discharged. Would the pilot, as a matter of legal policy be denied a cause of action against the doctor? I do not think so. Yet the loss suffered by the pilot would be economic loss arising from the doctor's negligent interference with the pilot's contractual relations with the airline. I leave unanswered the question of what difference it would make, if any, if the doctor was a salaried employee of the airline.

And, of course, the action for loss of services, where it lies, extends to an action arising from a negligent act which injures the employee and at the same time interferes with the contractual relations between the employee and the employer, and so causes economic loss to the employer: see *A.-G. Can. v. Nykorak* (1962), 33 D.L.R. (2d) 373, [1962] S.C.R. 331, 37 W.W.R. 660.

So it is my opinion that in appropriate circumstances an action may be sustained by a former employee against another employee of his employer, or against a corporate or municipal officer, based on an act, omission or misstatement, in breach of a duty of care, that results in economic loss to the former employee through discharge from employment. It follows that I consider *McLaren v. British Columbia Institute of Technology et al.*, *supra*, was wrongly decided.

NOTES

1. In reaching this decision, the B.C. Court of Appeal overruled an earlier decision of the B.C. trial court in *McLaren v. B.C. Institute of Technology* (1978), 94 D.L.R. (3d) 411, 7 C.C.L.T. 192 (S.C.). In that case, Taylor J. stated (C.C.L.T., at 201):

   > In a society which grants its members freedom of contract, the opportunity for creation of contractual rights and obligations is, of course, unlimited. The existence of a right of action for damages for negligent interference in contractual relations would enable those who exercise the freedom of contract to impose an equally limitless variety of duties of care on third parties. This does not appear to be another step in the extension of the concept of actionable negligence which would flow logically from the existence of a duty of care on those who choose to exercise special skills in their own business. The movement is not a step but a leap in quite a different direction. This is not the manner in which the law has historically made its progress.

2. Do you agree with the Court of Appeal's "leap"? Is there not a danger that the tort of negligence will become so extended and vague as to emasculate other well-defined torts?

3. Whether there is an action for negligently inducing breach of contract is still an open question. In *ACL Holdings Ltd. v. St. Joseph's Hospital of Estevan,* [1996] 6 W.W.R. 207 (Sask. Q.B.), the court refused an application for summary judgment in favour of an architect who had advised his client, a hospital, not to enter into a construction contract with the plaintiff, the lowest bidder on a tender. The court left open the possibility that the architect could be liable for negligently inducing breach of contract. Klar, *Tort Law,* (2nd ed.) argues that inducing breach of contract should be strictly an intentional tort. Do you think there is scope for negligence here?

4. If a person's negligence leads to the wrongful dismissal of an employee by the employer, why not restrict the employee to an action for wrongful dismissal?

5. Is wrongful dismissal a tort or a breach of contract? See McDonald, "Wrongful Dismissal: Tortious Breach of Contract", in Law Society of Upper Canada Special Lectures, *New Developments in Torts* (1973).

C. INTIMIDATION

ROOKES v. BARNARD

House of Lords. [1964] A.C. 1129, [1964] 1 All E.R. 367.

The plaintiff was dismissed from his employment at B.O.A.C. when the defendants, union members and a union official, threatened to go on an illegal strike, in violation of their collective agreement, if the plaintiff was not let go. The House of Lords permitted recovery, holding that it was unlawful to threaten a breach of contract.

Lord Devlin: My Lords, in my opinion there is a tort of intimidation of the nature described in chapter 18 of *Salmond on the Law of Torts*, 13th ed. (1961), p. 697. The tort can take one of two forms which are set out in Salmond as follows:

> (1) *Intimidation of the plaintiff himself*
>
> Although there seems to be no authority on the point, it cannot be doubted that it is an actionable wrong intentionally to compel a person, by means of a threat of an illegal act, to do some act whereby loss accrues to him: for example, an action will

doubtless lie at the suit of a trader who has been compelled to discontinue his business by means of threats of personal violence made against him by the defendant with that intention. ...

(2) *Intimidation of other persons to the injury of the plaintiff*

In certain cases it is an actionable wrong to intimidate other persons with the intent and effect of compelling them to act in a manner or to do acts which they themselves have a legal right to do which cause loss to the plaintiff: for example, the intimidation of the plaintiff's customers whereby they are compelled to withdraw their custom from him, or the intimidation of an employer whereby he is compelled to discharge his servant, the plaintiff. Intimidation of this sort is actionable, as we have said, in certain classes of cases; for it does not follow that, because a plaintiff's customers have a right to cease to deal with him if they please, other persons have a right as against the plaintiff to compel his customers to do so. There are at least two cases in which such intimidation may constitute a cause of action: —

(i) When the intimidation consists in a threat to do or procure an illegal act;

(ii) When the intimidation is the act, not of a single person, but of two or more persons acting together in pursuance of a common intention.

As your Lordships are all of opinion that there is a tort of intimidation and on this point approve the judgments in both courts below, I do not propose to offer any further authorities or reasons in support of my conclusion. I note that no issue on justification was raised at the time and there is no finding of fact upon it. So your Lordships have not to consider what part, if any, justification plays in the tort of intimidation.

Your Lordships are here concerned with the sort of intimidation which Salmond puts into the second category, and with the first of Salmond's two cases. The second case is, so Salmond later observed, "one form of the tort of conspiracy." That form is the *Quinn v. Leathem* type, so that it is no use to the appellant here. He relies upon "a threat to do or procure an illegal act", namely, a breach of contract. Doubtless it would suit him better if he could rely on the procuring of a breach of contract, for that is a tort; but immunity from that is guaranteed in terms by section 3. So he complains only of the threat to break the service contracts and the breach would undoubtedly be an act actionable by B.O.A.C. though it is neither tortious nor criminal. He does not have to contend that in the tort of intimidation, as in the tort of conspiracy, there can be, if the object is injurious, an unlawful threat to use lawful means. I do not think that there can be. The line must be drawn according to the law. It cannot be said that to use a threat of any sort is per se unlawful; and I do not see how, except in relation to the nature of the act threatened, *i.e.*, whether it is lawful or unlawful, one could satisfactorily distinguish between a lawful and an unlawful threat.

This conclusion, while not directly in point, assists me in my approach to the matter to be determined here. It is not, of course, disputed that if the act threatened is a crime, the threat is unlawful. But otherwise is it enough to say that the act threatened is actionable as a breach of contract or must it be actionable as a tort? My Lords, I see no good ground for the latter limitation. I find the reasoning on this point of Professor Hamson (which Sellers L.J. sets out in his judgment though he does not himself accept it) very persuasive. The essence of the offence is coercion. It cannot be said that every form of coercion is wrong. A dividing line must be drawn and the natural line runs between what is lawful and unlawful as against the party threatened. If the defendant threatens something that that party cannot legally resist, the plaintiff likewise cannot be allowed to resist the consequences; both must put up with the coercion and its results. But if the intermediate party is threatened with an illegal injury, the plaintiff who suffers by the aversion of the act threatened can fairly claim that he is illegally injured.

Accordingly, I reach the conclusion that the respondents' second point fails and on the facts of this case the tort of intimidation was committed.

NOTES

1. In *Morgan v. Fry et al.*, [1968] 2 Q.B. 710, [1968] 3 All E.R. 452 (C.A.), Lord Denning, M.R., said at 724:

> According to the decision in *Rookes v. Barnard* [1964] A.C. 1129, [1964] 2 W.L.R. 269, [1964] 1 All E.R. 367, the tort of intimidation exists, not only in threats of violence, but also in threats to commit a tort or a breach of contract. The essential ingredients are these: there must be a threat by one person to use unlawful means (such as violence or a tort or a breach of contract) so as to compel another to obey his wishes; and the person so threatened must comply with the demand rather than risk the threat being carried into execution. In such circumstances the person damnified by the compliance can sue for intimidation.

2. In *J.T. Stratford & Son Ltd. v. Lindley*, [1965] A.C. 269, 307, [1964] 3 All E.R. 102 (H.L.), Lord Denning outlined his views of the tort of intimidation as follows:

> The fifth point is whether the defendants were guilty of the tort of intimidation. Such a tort has long been known in cases of threats of violence. If one man says to another, "I will hit you unless you give me £5" or "unless you give the cook notice," or "unless you stop dealing with your butcher"; and the party so threatened submits to the threat by paying over the £5, or by giving notice to the cook, or by ceasing to deal with the butcher, then the party damnified by the threat — the payer of the £5, or the cook or the butcher, as the case may be — has a cause of action for intimidation against the person who made the threat. But it is essential to the cause of action that the person threatened should comply with the demand. If he has the courage to resist it and replies saying, "You can do your worst. I am not going to pay you £5," or, "I am not going to give notice to the cook," or "I am not going to stop dealing with the butcher," then the party threatened has no cause of action for intimidation. Nor has the cook. Nor the butcher. For they have suffered no damage by the threat. But in that case, if the threatener carries out his threat — if he commits his act of violence — the party threatened can sue for the unlawful act. He can sue for assault. He need not, however, wait for it. He can sue in advance for an injunction to prevent the threat being carried out. Another thing that is essential to the cause of action is that the threat should be a coercive threat. It must be coupled with a demand. It must be intended to coerce a person into doing something that he is unwilling to do or not doing something that he wishes to do. It must be capable of being expressed in the form, "I will hit you *unless* you do what I ask," or "if you do what I forbid you to do." A bare threat without a demand does not to my mind amount to the tort of intimidation. If a man says to another, "I am going to hit you when I get you alone," it is undoubtedly a threat; and an injunction can be obtained to restrain him from carrying out his threat. But the threat itself does not give rise to a claim for damages. It is only when he delivers the blow that it is actionable: and then as an assault, not as intimidation.

> Very recently it has become clear that the tort of intimidation exists not only in threats of violence, but also in threats to commit a tort or a breach of contract. The essential ingredients are the same throughout: there must be a coercive threat to use unlawful means, so as to compel a person into doing something that he is unwilling to do, or not doing something that he wishes to do: and the party so threatened must comply with the demand rather than risk the threat being carried into execution. In such case the party damnified by the compliance can sue for damages for intimidation.

3. In England, *Rookes v. Barnard* has been abrogated by statute. See *Trade Union and Labour Relations Act*, 1974, c. 52, s. 13(1)(b). Its principle survives in Canada, however.

4. In *Central Canada Potash Co. Ltd. v. Attorney-General for Saskatchewan* (1975), 57 D.L.R. (3d) 7, [1975] 5 W.W.R. 193; revd 79 D.L.R, (3d) 203, [1977] 1 W.W.R. 487 (Sask. C.A.); revd in part, [1979] 1 S.C.R. 42, 6 C.C.L.T. 265. Mr. Justice Disbery, at trial, imposed liability for the tort of intimidation in the amount of $1,500,000. On appeal this was reversed. The Supreme Court affirmed the dismissal of the civil action, but reversed on the constitutional issue.

   The plaintiff company was in the mining business in Saskatchewan and had an agreement to supply potash to its United States-based shareholder. As a result of overproduction of potash and a drastic drop in world prices, the potash industry in New Mexico, which had been the major producer in the past, became depressed. A deal was made between the Government of Saskatchewan and the Government of New Mexico to control the production and sale of potash. Under the scheme, each producer in Saskatchewan was allowed, under a licence from the Minister, to sell a certain amount of potash, The object was to limit the supply of potash in world markets and to control its price. The scheme was changed to some extent in 1971 to control, through an export association, all exports of potash.

   The plaintiff company objected to this scheme on the ground that it interfered with its contractual obligations with its United States-based shareholder. An application for a licence permitting it to comply with its contract was refused, and the Deputy Minister, by letter to the plaintiff company, threatened to cancel its existing licence because it was exceeding its quota in order to meet its contractual obligation. The plaintiff company yielded to the threat and then, commenced this action for declarations that the regulations passed under the Act were *ultra vires* the provincial legislature and that all actions pursuant to them were null and void. In addition, the plaintiff sought damages for intimidation.

   The trial judge declared the marketing scheme *ultra vires* and awarded $1,500,000 damages for the tort of intimidation against the Government of Saskatchewan. During the course of his lengthy judgment, Mr. Justice Disbery remarked:

   > It is quite clear from the cases that the threat complained of must be a threat to do an act which is in itself illegal. So to make a coercive threat to sue on an overdue promissory note or to disinherit a child of the intimidator would not be actionable because the intimidator has the legal right to sue or to disinherit. On the other hand where a debtor threatened his creditor that he would pay no part of his debt unless the creditor accepted a lesser sum in full satisfaction, such threat was illegal: *D. & C. Builders Ltd. v. Rees*, [1966] 2 Q.B. 617 at p. 625. *Salmond on Torts*, 15th ed. (1969), p. 488, states that "The wrong of intimidation includes all those cases in which harm is inflicted by the use of unlawful threats whereby the lawful liberty of others to do as they please is interfered with."

> Lord Reid pointed out in the *Rookes* case that [at p. 374] "Threatening a breach of contract may be a much more coercive weapon than threatening a tort, particularly when the threat is directed against a company or corporation ...".

Again, in the *Rookes* case at p. 375, Lord Reid said:

> Intimidation of any kind appears to me to be highly objectionable. The law was not slow to prevent it when violence and threats of violence were the most effective means. Now that subtler means are at least equally effective I see no reason why the law should have to turn a blind eye to them. We have to tolerate intimidation by means which have been held to be lawful, but there I would stop.

> The Courts are always open to do justice according to the law as given to them by the people's representatives in Parliament and the Legislatures. The Courts have always been opposed to persons seeking "to do their own justice" in whatever way they themselves desire to adopt. The cult of the heaviest clout, which is too often seen in the world today, is, of course, the very antithesis of the rule of law. ...

> Two-party intimidation exists where the intimidator for some purpose of his own threatens his victim with an unlawful act unless the victim does (or refrains from doing) an act in such a way as to cause damage to himself, in order to avoid what, in the eyes of the victim, would be a greater evil to himself if he refused and the intimidator carried out his threat.

The Saskatchewan Court of Appeal reversed this decision and the Supreme Court of Canada affirmed, even though the scheme was found by the Supreme Court to be *ultra vires* the provincial government. Mr. Justice Martland, on the issue of civil liability, explained:

> If the course of conduct which the person making the threat seeks to induce is that which the person threatened is obligated to follow, the tort of intimidation does not arise. ... Here the Deputy Minister was seeking to induce conformity with the prorationing plan which had been created by legislation which it was his duty to enforce. ... It would be unfortunate, in a federal state such as Canada, if it were to be held that a government official, charged with the enforcement of legislation, could be held to be guilty of intimidation because of his enforcement of a statute whenever a statute whose provisions he is under a duty to enforce is subsequently held *ultra vires.*

5. In *Mintuck v. Valley River Band No. 63A* (1977), 75 D.L.R. (3d) 589, 2 C.C.L.T. 1 (Man. C.A.), the plaintiff was prevented from working part of the farm, which he leased from the federal government, as a result of harassment by the defendants including vehicles on the road blocking his access, stray cattle roaming on the farm damaging the crops, the defendants driving trucks over the farm under the pretext they were hunting game and, occasionally, he was threatened in person, over the telephone and even by firearms. The objective of all of this was to get him to abandon his lease rights. He did not. His action was successful at trial on the basis of inducing breach of contract. This was affirmed on appeal, but on different grounds. Mr. Justice Matas rested the liability on "the tort of intimidation and unlawful interference with economic interests". O'Sullivan J.A. said that there was no breach of any contract caused by the acts of the defendant, but the band was "guilty of the two-party torts of intimidation and unlawful interference with economic interests". See also *Gershman v. Manitoba Vegetable Producers' Marketing Bd.* (1976), 69 D.L.R. (3d) 114, [1976] 4 W.W.R. 406 (Man. C.A.).

6. The threatened act must be unlawful. Thus, it is not an intimidation for a lawyer to threaten that the plaintiff's logs will be seized unless he signs a settlement agreement, if the seizure would be legal. See *Sandy Ridge Sawing Ltd. v. Norrish*, [1996] 4 W.W.R. 528 (Sask. Q.B.).

7. For an analysis of the tort of intimidation see Burns, "Tort Injury to Economic Interests: Some Facets of Legal Response" (1980), 58 Can. Bar Rev. 103, at 126-40.

D. CONSPIRACY

CANADA CEMENT LAFARGE LTD. v. BRITISH COLUMBIA LIGHTWEIGHT AGGREGATE LTD.

Supreme Court of Canada. (1983), 145 D.L.R. (3d) 385, 24 C.C.L.T. 111.

The plaintiff company produced a lightweight aggregate for use in the production of concrete and concrete products. The appellants manufactured and supplied cement and concrete products. The plaintiff and defendants had entered into agreements whereby the plaintiff agreed not to compete with the defendants and the defendants agreed to purchase certain amounts of the plaintiff's product. After the agreements had expired, the defendants decided to purchase a lightweight aggregate from companies other than the plaintiff. Shortly after, the plaintiff ceased production due to a significant loss of sales. At about the same time, the defendants pleaded guilty to charges under the *Combines Investigation Act*, R.S.C. 1970, c. C-23, relating to their agreement to lessen competition unduly. The plaintiff sued the defendants for Conspiracy to injure and won both at trial and on appeal. The Supreme Court reversed these judgments.

Estey J.: The law concerning the tort of conspiracy is far from clear with respect to conduct of the defendants which is itself unlawful. The tort of conspiracy to injure is complete. ... where the predominant purpose of the conspiracy is to injure the plaintiff and damage in fact results. Thus the concerted action to give effect to the intent completes the tort, and if an unlawful object is necessary (assuming damages have been suffered by the plaintiff), it is but the object to injure the plaintiff. As Lord Cave said in *Sorrell v. Smith*, [1925] A.C. 700 at 712, [1925] All E.R. Rep. 1 (H.L.):

> A combination of two or more persons wilfully to injure a man in his trade is unlawful and, if it results in damage to him, is actionable.

The conspiracy to commit an unlawful act in the criminal law is, in this respect, differently structured. The question which must now be considered is whether the scope of the tort of conspiracy in this country extends beyond situations in which the defendants' predominant purpose is to cause injury to the plaintiff, and includes cases in which this intention to injure is absent but the conduct of the defendants is by itself unlawful, and in fact causes damage to the plaintiff. The causative problems common to the second and third submissions of the appellants will be discussed mainly in connection with the latter. Statements made in a number of English cases decided prior to *Lonrho*, *supra*, appeared to endorse this latter aspect of the tort and led the learned author of *Salmond on Torts*, *op. cit.*, at p. 379 to conclude:

> A second form of actionable conspiracy exists when two or more combine to injure a third person by unlawful means — *e.g.* the commission of a crime or tort, or the infringement of a guaranteed constitutional right. ... In such case it is irrelevant that the object of the conspirators in using those means may be legitimate. Combinations of this kind must be contrasted with what might be called *Quinn v. Leathem* conspiracies, where the means are legitimate but the object is not ... Hence a conspiracy may be actionable if either the end or the means, or both, are unlawful.

Lord Diplock declined to accept this analysis, however, observing in his judgment in *Lonrho*, *supra*, [at p. 189 A.C., p. 464 All E.R.] that:

> [I]n none of the judgments in decided cases in civil actions for damages for conspiracy does it appear that the mind of the author of the judgment was directed to a case where the damage-causing acts although neither done for the purpose of injuring the plaintiff nor actionable in his suit if they had been done by one person alone, were nevertheless a contravention of some penal law.

As a result, Lord Diplock concluded that the House of Lords had an "unfettered choice" in defining the scope of the tort of conspiracy, and elected to limit the civil action to acts done in combination for the predominant purpose of injuring the interests of the plaintiff.

The history of this tort in the United States has been quite different. While there are cases to the contrary, the Courts generally have for many years concluded that the tort of conspiracy to injury forms no part of the law. This has been said to be due to the unreality of the tort of conspiracy when the underlying act is not tortious when committed by an individual; and because of the development of the actions of unfair competition and prima facie tort in the field of commercial regulations: see Prosser, *Law of Torts* (4th ed., 1971), p. 291; "Civil Conspiracy", L.S.U.C. Special Lectures (1973), p. 502.

Canadian law concerning the tort of conspiracy displays the same lack of definition which characterized the law of England prior to the *Lonrho* decision. The subject of the tort of conspiracy has been comprehensively and critically examined in 16 U.B.C.L. Rev. 229 by Peter Burns. I agree with respect to his conclusion [at p. 254] that:

> The main effect of a finding that a conspiracy by unlawful means has been made out is to exclude the negative defence of predominant legitimate interests.

See as well p. 247.

It is important to bear in mind, when considering this explanation of the tort of conspiracy by unlawful means, the prior finding of fact that the defendants knew that their conduct, which was directed towards the plaintiff, would injure it. The presence of this element appears to be common to all the Canadian cases in which the tort of conspiracy by unlawful means has been applied.

Although the law concerning the scope of the tort of conspiracy is far from clear, I am of the opinion that whereas the law of tort does not permit an action against an individual defendant who has caused injury to the plaintiff, the law of torts does recognize a claim against them in combination as the tort of conspiracy if:

(1) Whether the means used by the defendants are lawful or unlawful, the predominant purpose of the defendants' conduct is to cause injury to the plaintiff; or
(2) Where the conduct of the defendants is unlawful, the conduct is directed towards the plaintiff (alone or together with others), and the defendants should

know in the circumstances that injury to the plaintiff is likely to and does result.

In situation (2) it is not necessary that the predominant purpose of the defendants' conduct be to cause injury to the plaintiff but, in the prevailing circumstances, it must be a constructive intent derived from the fact that the defendants should have known that injury to the plaintiff would ensue. In both situations, however, there must be actual damage suffered by the plaintiff: [Estey J. dismissed the plaintiff's action on the basis that the plaintiff's business failure was not shown to have been caused by the defendants' unlawful conduct. His Lordship further questioned the legitimacy of the plaintiff's claim in view of its own illegal participation in the defendants' scheme.]

NOTES

1. The House of Lords took a different approach in *Lonrho Ltd. v. Shell Petroleum Co. Ltd. (No. 2)*, [1982] A.C. 173, [1981] 2 All E.R. 456 (H.L.). The plaintiff owned and operated an oil pipeline. The defendants owned and operated an oil refinery. The parties had an agreement that oil supplied to the defendants would be transported by means of the plaintiff's pipeline. As a result of Southern Rhodesia's declaration of independence, Britain made it illegal to ship oil into Southern Rhodesia. The plaintiff alleged that despite the order, the defendants continued to supply oil into Southern Rhodesia through associated companies which they controlled. The plaintiff alleged that as a result of this, the illegal declaration of independence by Southern Rhodesia was prolonged preventing the plaintiff from operating its pipeline and causing it losses. The plaintiff claimed that this was an actionable conspiracy, since the defendants agreed to use unlawful means resulting in injury to the plaintiff. Lord Diplock held that there had been no actionable conspiracy and explained:

> Question 5(b), to which I now turn, concerns conspiracy as a civil tort. Your Lordships are invited to answer it on the assumption that the purpose of Shell and B.P. in entering into the agreement to do the various things that it must be assumed they did in contravention of the sanctions Order, was to forward their own commercial interests; *not* to injure those of Lonrho. So the question of law to be determined is whether an intent by the defendants to injure the plaintiff is an essential element in the civil wrong of conspiracy, even where the acts agreed to be done by the conspirators amount to criminal offences under a penal statute. It is conceded that there is no direct authority either way upon this question to be found in the decided cases; so if this House were to answer it in the affirmative, your Lordships would be making new law. ...
>
> My Lords, in none of the judgments in decided cases in civil actions for damages for conspiracy does it appear that the mind of the author of the judgment was directed to a case where the damage-causing acts although neither done for the purpose of injuring the plaintiff nor actionable at his suit if they had been done by one person alone, were nevertheless a contravention of some penal law. I will not recite the statements in those judgments to which your Lordships have been referred by the appellants as amounting to dicta in favour of the view that a civil action for conspiracy does lie in such a case. Even if the authors' minds had been directed to the point, which they were not, I should still find them indecisive. This House, in my view, has an unfettered choice whether to confine the civil action of conspiracy to the narrow field to which alone it has an established claim or whether to extend this already

anomalous tort beyond those narrow limits that are all that common sense and the application of the legal logic of the decided cases require.

My Lords, my choice is unhesitatingly the same as that of Parker J. and all three members of the Court of Appeal. I am against extending the scope of civil tort of conspiracy beyond acts done in execution of an agreement entered into by two or more persons for the purpose not of protecting their own interests but of injuring the interests of the plaintiff. So I would answer Question 5(b): "No."

Which view is preferable for a dynamic and competitive economy?

2. In a subsequent case, *Lonhro plc v. Fayed*, [1991] 3 W.L.R. 188, [1991] 3 All E.R. 303, the House of Lords clarified their position. The court held that defendants can be liable for a conspiracy, even where their predominant purpose was to further their own interest and not to injure the plaintiff, if they used unlawful means and their intention was to injure the plaintiff. Lord Bridge stated that the earlier decision did not change the law as significantly as some have suggested. It now appears, therefore, that the English and Canadian stands are fairly similar.

3. The Supreme Court of Canada has recently considered the tort of conspiracy in a completely "non-business" context. In *Frame v. Smith*, [1987] 2 S.C.R. 99, 42 C.C.L.T. 1, a father sued his ex-wife and her husband alleging, among other things, that they had conspired together to deprive him of access to his three children. The Supreme Court refused to extend this anomalous tort, outside of the business context, to the area of family relations. In arriving at this decision, both La Forest and Wilson JJ. continued to express doubt about the utility and wisdom of the tort even in the commercial setting.

4. Do you agree with those who criticize the continued existence of this tort? Should it be tortious for two or more persons to combine together with the predominant object of injuring another even when their acts are otherwise lawful? If Safeway, by using lawful conduct, acts with the predominant purpose being to drive a small grocer out of business, is this tortious? If two small corner stores combine together in the same way to drive a third store out of business, is this tortious? Should there be a difference depending on how many entities are involved?

5. If the acts of the conspirators are actionable in themselves, what is gained by the plaintiff also suing for conspiracy? Should the tort of conspiracy simply be subsumed in the other actions? Some courts have allowed both claims — see, for example, *Wallace Construction Specialities Ltd. v. Manson Insulation Inc.* (1993), 106 D.L.R. (4th) 169 (Sask. C.A.). Others have dismissed the conspiracy claim and considered only the underlying wrong — see, for example, *G. (R). v. Christison*, [1997] 1 W.W.R. 641 (Sask. Q.B.); and *Normart Management Ltd. v. West Hill Redevelopment Co.* (1996), 140 D.L.R. (4th) 550 (Ont. Gen. Div.), affd (1998), 155 D.L.R. (4th) 627 (Ont. C.A.).

6. If the acts of the conspirators are not unlawful, they can only be liable for conspiracy if their predominant purpose was to cause injury to the plaintiff as opposed to acting in their own interests. The test of intent is a subjective one, and is difficult to prove. See, for example, *Ontario (A.G.) v. Dieleman* (1994), 117 D.L.R. (4th) 449 (Ont. Gen. Div.), where the court held that the purpose of anti-abortion picketers was not to harm patients or doctors, but to further their own cause.

7. There are numerous cases dealing with the tort of conspiracy. A history of the tort is reviewed in *McKinnon v. F.W. Woolworth Co. Ltd. et al.* (1968), 70 D.L.R. (2d) 280,

66 W.W.R. 205 (Alta. C.A.). Many of these cases relate to trade and labour disputes, although the tort is not limited to these situations.

8. See Hughes, "The Tort of Conspiracy" (1952), 15 Mod. L. Rev. 209; Charlesworth, "Conspiracy as a Ground of Liability in Tort" (1920), 36 L.Q. Rev. 38; Christie, *The Liability of Strikers in The Law of Tort* (1967); Burns "Civil Conspiracy: An Unwieldy Vessel Rides a Judicial Tempest" (1982), 16 U.B.C.L. Rev. 229.

E. INTERFERENCE WITH ADVANTAGEOUS BUSINESS RELATIONS

TUTTLE v. BUCK

Supreme Court of Minnesota. (1909), 119 N.W. 946.

The plaintiff alleged that the defendant banker opened a rival barber shop in order to destroy the plaintiff's barber shop business. The plaintiff contended that the defendant, who was influential and wealthy, was not serving any purpose of his own but was maliciously seeking to put the plaintiff out of business and drive him out of town. The defendant influenced many of the plaintiff's former customers not to patronize the plaintiff any longer. It was alleged that, as a result the plaintiff's business was ruined. A demurrer by the defendant was overruled at trial and the defendant appealed.

Elliott J.: It has been said that the law deals only with externals, and that a lawful act cannot be made the foundation of an action because it was done with an evil motive. In *Allen v. Flood*, [1898] A.C. 1, Lord Watson said that except with regard to crimes the law does not take into account motives as constituting an element of civil wrong. In *Mayor of Bradford v. Pickles*, [1895] A.C. 587, Lord Halsbury stated that if the act was lawful "however ill the motive might be, he had a right to do it." In *Raycroft v. Tayntor*, 68 Vt. 219; 35 A. 53; 33 L.R.A. 225; 54 Am. St. Rep 882, the court said that, "when one exercises a legal right only, the motive which actuates him is immaterial." In *Jenkins v. Fowler*, 24 Pa. 308, Mr. Justice Black said that "malicious motives made a bad act worse, but they cannot make that wrong which, in its own essence is lawful." ...

Such generalizations are of little value in determining concrete cases. They may state the truth but not the whole truth. Each word and phrase used therein may require definition and limitation. Thus, before we can apply Judge Black's language to a particular case, we must determine what act is "in its own essence lawful". What did Lord Halsbury mean by the words "lawful act"? What is meant by "exercising a legal right"? It is not at all correct to say that the motive with which an act is done is always immaterial, providing the act itself is not unlawful. Numerous illustrations of the contrary will be found in the civil as well as the criminal law.

We do not intend to enter upon an elaborate discussion of the subject or become entangled in the subtleties connected with the words "malice" and "malicious". We are not able to accept without limitations the doctrine above referred to, but at this time content ourselves with a brief reference to some general principles.

It must be remembered that the common law is the result of growth and that its development has been determined by the social needs of the community which it governs. It is the resultant of conflicting social forces, and those forces which are for the time dominant leave their impress upon the law. It is of judicial origin, and seeks to establish doctrines and rules for the determination, protection, and enforcement of legal rights. Manifestly it must change as society changes and new rights are recognized. To be an efficient instrument, and not a mere abstraction, it must gradually adapt itself to changed conditions. Necessarily its form and substance have been greatly affected by prevalent economic theories.

For generations there has been a practical agreement upon the proposition that competition in trade and business is desirable, and this idea has found expression in the decisions of the courts as well as in statutes. But it has led to grievous and manifold wrongs to individuals, and many courts have manifested an earnest desire to protect the individual from the evil which results from unrestrained business competition. The problem has been to so adjust matters as to preserve the principle of competition and yet guard against its abuse to the unnecessary injury to the individual. So the principle that a man may use his own property according to his own needs and desires, while true in the abstract, is subject to many limitations in the concrete. Men cannot always, in civilized society, be allowed to use their own property as their interests or desires may dictate without reference to the fact that they have neighbours whose rights are as sacred as their own. The existence and well-being of society require that each and every person shall conduct himself consistently with the fact that he is a social and reasonable person. The purpose for which a man is using his own property may thus sometimes determine his rights. ...

Many of the restrictions which should be recognized and enforced result from a tacit recognition of principles which are not often stated in the decisions in express terms. Sir Frederick Pollock notes that not many years ago it was difficult to find any definite authority for stating as a general proposition of English law that it is wrong to do a wilful wrong to one's neighbour without lawful justification or excuse. But neither is there any express authority for the general proposition that men must perform their contracts. Both principles, in this generality of form and conception, are modern, and there was a time when neither was true. After developing the idea that law begins, not with authentic general principles, but with the enumeration of particular remedies, the learned writer continues: "If there exists, then, a positive duty to avoid harm, much more must there exist the negative duty of not doing wilful harm, subject, as all general duties must be subject, to the necessary exceptions. The three main heads of duty with which the law of torts is concerned, namely, to abstain from wilful injury, to respect the property of others, and to use due diligence to avoid causing harm to others, are all alike of a comprehensive nature." Pollock, *Torts* (8th ed.), p. 21. He then quotes with approval the statement of Lord Bowen that "at common law there was a cause of action whenever one person did damage to another, wilfully and intentionally, without just cause or excuse."

In *Plant v. Woods*, 176 Mass. 492; 57 N.E. 1011; 51 L.R.A. 339; 79 Am. St. Rep. 330, Mr. Justice Hammond said: "It is said also that, where one has the lawful right to do a thing, the motive by which he is actuated is immaterial. One form of this statement appears in the first headnote in *Allen v. Flood*, as reported in [1898] A.C. 1, as follows: "An act lawful in itself is not converted by a malicious or bad motive into an unlawful act so as to make the doer of the act liable to a civil action." If the meaning of this and similar expressions is that where a person has the lawful right to do a thing irrespective of his motive, his motive is immaterial, the proposition is a mere truism. If, however, the meaning is that where a person, if actuated by one kind of a motive, has a lawful right to do a thing, the act is lawful when done under any conceivable motive, or that an act lawful under one set of circumstances is therefore lawful under every conceivable set of circumstances, the proposition does not commend itself to us as either logically or legally accurate."...

It is freely conceded that there are many decisions contrary to this view; but, when carried to the extent contended for by the appellant, we think they are unsafe, unsound, and ill-adapted to modern conditions. To divert to one's self the customers of a business rival by the offer of goods at lower prices is in general a legitimate mode of serving one's own interest, and justifiable as fair competition. But when a man starts an opposition place of business, not for the sake of profit to himself, but regardless of loss to himself, and for the sole purpose of driving his competitor out of business, and with the intention of himself retiring upon the accomplishment of his malevolent purpose, he is guilty of a wanton wrong and an actionable tort. In such a case he would not be exercising his legal right, or doing an act which can be judged separately from the motive which actuated him. To call such conduct competition is a perversion of terms. It is simply the application of force without legal justification, which in its moral quality may be no better than highway robbery.

Nevertheless, in the opinion of the writer this complaint is insufficient. It is not claimed that it states a cause of action for slander. No question of conspiracy or combination is involved. Stripped of the adjectives and the statement that what was done was for the sole purpose of injuring the plaintiff, and not for the purpose of serving a legitimate purpose of the defendant, the complaint states facts which in themselves amount only to an ordinary every day business transaction. There is no allegation that the defendant was intentionally running the business at a financial loss to himself, or that after driving the plaintiff out of business the defendant closed up or intended to close up his shop. From all that appears from the complaint he may have opened the barber shop, energetically sought business from his acquaintances and the customers of the plaintiff, and as a result of his enterprise and command of capital obtained it, with the result that the plaintiff, from want of capital, acquaintance, or enterprise, was unable to stand the competition and was thus driven out of business. The facts thus alleged do not, in my opinion, in themselves, without reference to the way in which they are characterized by the pleader, tend to show a malicious and wanton wrong to the plaintiff.

A majority of the justices, however, are of the opinion that, on the principle declared in the foregoing opinion, the complaint states a cause of action, and the order is therefore affirmed.

NOTES

1. There are several well-known early cases which established this principle. In *Keeble v. Hickeringill* (1706), 11 East 574, 103 E.R. 1127, a defendant was held liable for maliciously firing guns to frighten ducks away from the plaintiff's pond, preventing the plaintiff from taking them.

2. Another famous old decision is *Tarleton v. M'Gawley* (1794), Peake 270, 170 E.R. 153, where the defendant fired on some African natives with whom the plaintiff was hoping to trade. This frightened them away, causing economic loss to the plaintiff. The plaintiff was awarded damages.

3. In *Temperton v. Russell*, [1893] 1 Q.B. 715, [1891-4] All E.R. Rep. 724 (C.A.), the court recognized that an action could lie for interference with economic relations which were merely prospective or potential, as well as for inducing actual breaches of contracts. See Lord Esher, at 728.

4. Someone buys a radio from a department store. It is defective. The purchaser gets a picket sign saying "X Co. cheated me. Will they cheat you?" and parades around in front of the store. The store's business suffers. Actionable? Should an injunction be issued. See *Canadian Tire Co. Ltd. v. Desmond*, [1972] 2 O.R. 60, 24 D.L.R. (3d) 642 (H.C.J.). See also *Hubbard v. Pitt*, [1976] Q.B. 142, [1975] 3 All E.R. 1 (C.A.), where Lord Denning allowed picketing to continue to communicate information, as long as the picketing was peaceful and the words on the placards were true.

5. An important recent case in this area is *Daishowa Inc. v. Friends of the Lubicon* (1998), 39 O.R. (3d) 620, 158 D.L.R. (4th) 699, 52 C.R.R. (2d) 7, 18 C.P.C. (4th) 272, 41 C.C.L.T. (2d) 193 (Ont. Gen. Div.); supp. reasons, unreported, April 14, 1998, Doc. No. 95-CQ-59707, MacPherson J. (Ont. Gen. Div.). In order to put pressure on Daishowa Inc. to stop logging lands claimed by the Lubicon Cree, the Friends of the Lubicon organized a consumer boycott of Daishowa products. The boycott involved activities such as issuing press releases condemning Daishowa, and urging companies which purchased Daishowa paper products to stop buying from Daishowa. About 50 companies were contacted. If these customers did not comply and stop buying from Daishowa, they were threatened with public boycotts of their own premises. "Pizza Pizza" was one such customer who did not comply and whose restaurants were boycotted. Demonstrations occurred outside of "Pizza Pizza", with the public being urged to boycott "Pizza Pizza". Ultimately "Pizza Pizza" complied and joined the boycott. Daishowa sued to restrain the Friends from continuing with this pressure campaign on its customers. After a series of legal proceedings involving requests for interim and interlocutory injunctions, McPherson J. rendered his judgment on the granting of a permanent injunction.

   The request for a permanent injunction was denied, subject to some minor conditions. McPherson J. relied on the constitutional guarantee of freedom of expression to protect the Friends' right to communicate their message to the public *as long as they did so without committing any unlawful acts*. In this respect the picketing and demonstrations which occurred outside of the premises of "Pizza Pizza", and other customers of Daishowa were lawful. McPherson J. distinguished between "secondary picketing" which occurs within a labour dispute, and this type of consumer boycott which is for ideological or political reasons, in arriving at his decision that this type of "secondary picketing" was lawful. No other torts were committed during the course of these demonstrations. McPherson J. considered the torts of interference with economic interests, inducing breach of contract, intimidation, conspiracy, misrepresentation, and defamation.

6. Would liability be imposed if an officer of a company, without proper authorization, instructs the company's bank to stop honouring cheques signed by the plaintiff? See *Volkswagen Canada Ltd. v. Spicer* (1978), 28 N.S.R. (2d) 496, 91 D.L.R. (3d) 42 (C.A.).

7. See generally Holmes, "Privilege, Malice and Intent" (1894), 8 Harv. L. Rev. 1; Ames, "How Far an Act May Be a Tort Because of Wrongful Motive of the Actor" (1905), 18 Harv. L. Rev. 411; Gutteridge, "Abuse of Rights" (1933), 5 Camb. L.J. 22.

8. To launch a totally unfounded lien claim as a form of "legal blackmail" to obtain a settlement is actionable and punitive damages may be awarded against the defendant. See *Guilford Industries Ltd. v. Hankinson Management Services Ltd.* (1973), 40 D.L.R. (3d) 398, [1974] 1 W.W.R. 141 (B.C.S.C.). There is also an action called slander of title. See *White v. Mellin*, [1895] A.C. 154, 64 L.J. Ch. 308 (H.L.); see also *Ontario Libel and Slander Act*, R.S.O. 1990, c. L.12. See Wood, "Disparagement of Title and Quality" (1942), 20 Can. Bar Rev. 296, 430. Actions for infringement of copyright and passing off are beyond the scope of this book. See *Canadian Shredded Wheat Co. Ltd. v. Kellogg Co. of Canada Ltd.*, [1938] 2 D.L.R. 145, [1938] 1 All E.R.

618 (P.C.); Fox, *Canadian Law of Copyright*, 2nd ed. (1967); Fox, *Canadian Law of Trade Marks and Unfair Competition*, 3rd ed. (1972).

9. The defendant, an ex-employee of the plaintiff, formed a company and solicited the plaintiff's customers. Tortious? See *W.J. Christie & Co. Ltd. v. Greer et al.* (1980), 3 Man. R. (2d) 431; varied (1981), 9 Man. R. (2d) 269, [1981] 4 W.W.R. 34 (Q.B.).

10. Is there an emerging tort of "causing harm by unlawful means" or "unlawful interference with economic interests"? Some writers and courts think that such a generalized tort action is developing. Various dicta in the following cases lend support to this view: *J.T. Stratford & Son v. Lindley*, [1965] A.C. 269, [1964] 3 All E.R. 102 (H.L.); *Torquay Hotel Co. Ltd. v. Cousins*, [1969] 2 Ch. 106, [1969] 1 All E.R. 522 (C.A.); *Gershman v. Manitoba Vegetable Producers' Marketing Bd.* (1976), 69 D.L.R. (3d) 114, [1976] 4 W.W.R. 406 (Man. C.A.), *Mintuck v. Valley River Band No. 63A* (1977), 75 D.L.R. (3d) 589, 2 C.C.L.T. 1 (Man. C.A.); *Cheticamp Fisheries Co-op. v. Canada* (1995), 26 C.C.L.T. (2d) 40 (N.S.C.A.). There are some very good articles which analyze these developments and attempt to formulate the elements of this developing tort. See Burns, "Tort Injury to Economic Interests: Some Facets of Legal Response" (1980), 58 Can. Bar Rev. 103; Mitchell, "Liability in Tort for Causing Economic Loss by the Use of Unlawful Means and Its Application to Australian Industrial Disputes" (1973-76), 5 Adel. L. Rev. 428; Stevens, "Interference with Economic Relations — Some Aspects of the Turmoil in the Intentional Torts" (1974), 12 Osgoode Hall L.J. 595.

11. In *Beaudesert Shire Council v. Smith* (1966), 40 A.L.J.R. 211, a landowner took water for irrigation from a pool in a river. The defendant destroyed the pool by removing gravel from the riverbed and thereby damaged the landowner's crops. He sued and recovered, the court explaining "independently of trespass, negligence or nuisance, but by an action upon the case, a person who suffers harm or loss as the inevitable consequence of the unlawful intentional and positive acts of another is entitled to recover damages from that other". This judgment has not been followed subsequently, in fact this is Lord Diplock's reaction to it in *Lonrhro v. Shell*, *supra*:

> *Beaudesert Shire Council v. Smith*, 120 C.L.R. 145 is a decision of the High Court of Australia. It appeared to recognise at p. 156 the existence of a novel innominate tort of the nature of an "action for damages upon the case" available to "a person who suffers harm or loss as the inevitable consequence of the unlawful, intentional and positive acts of another." The decision, although now 15 years old, has never been followed in any Australian or other common law jurisdiction. In subsequent Australian cases it has invariably been distinguished — most recently by the Privy Council in *Dunlop v. Woollahra Municipal Council* [1982] A.C. 158, on appeal from the Supreme Court of New South Wales. It is clear now from a later decision of the Australian High Court in *Kitano v. Commonwealth of Australia* (1974) 129 C.L.R. 151 that the adjective "unlawful" in the definition of acts which give rise to this new action for damages upon the case does not include *every* breach of statutory duty which in fact causes damage to the plaintiff. It remains uncertain whether it was intended to include acts done in contravention of a wider range of statutory obligations or prohibitions than those which under the principles that I have discussed above would give rise to a civil action at common law in England if they are contravened. If the tort described in *Beaudesert* was really intended to extend that range, I would invite your Lordships to declare that it forms no part of the law of England.

12. American courts have recognized what is known as the *prima facie* tort doctrine. This stems from *Tuttle v. Buck*, *supra*, and *Keeble v. Hickeringill*, *supra*. Its basic principle is that the intentional infliction of damage is actionable unless justified. Burns, *supra*,

discusses this doctrine and notes that it is unfortunate that it has not been accepted into English law since "it has the potential for providing a broad tort principle that could accommodate a variety of situations that legitimately call for legal support and yet do not fit into any of the recognized economic torts". Do you agree?

13. On the *prima facie* tort doctrine see, Forkosch, "An Analysis of the 'Prima Facie' Tort Cause of Action" (1957), 42 Cornell L. Rev. 465; Hale, "Prima Facie Torts, Combination and Non-Feasance" (1946), 46 Colum. L. Rev. 196; Brown, "The Rise and Threatened Demise of the Prima Facie Tort Principle" (1959), 54 Nw. U.L. Rev. 563. These references, *inter alia*, are noted by Burns, *supra*.

CHAPTER 16

DEFAMATION

KLAR, TORT LAW
2nd ed. (1996)

The law of defamation plays a distinctive and fascinating role within the tort law family. Unlike most of tort law, defamation law has little to do with protecting the security of persons or their property and, in most respects, has no interest in notions of fault or wrongdoing. Based almost entirely on rules of strict liability, defamation law seeks to protect the reputation of individuals against unfounded and unjustified attacks. What troubles the law of defamation, however, is that the protection of reputation comes only at a very high cost — the need to restrict freedom of speech.

The material that follows introduces some of the main issues in the field, but it is by no means complete. Each jurisdiction has its own unique legislative provisions and its own distinct procedural requirements. There is literally an avalanche of cases, all of which cannot be included in a work such as this.

A. THE VALUES AT STAKE

HILL v. CHURCH OF SCIENTOLOGY OF TORONTO
Supreme Court of Canada. (1995), 126 D.L.R. (4th) 129, 25 C.C.L.T. (2d) 89

The plaintiff was a lawyer with the Crown Law Office, Criminal Division of the Attorney General for the Province of Ontario. In the course of lengthy legal proceedings between the Crown and the Church of Scientology, an application for criminal contempt against the plaintiff was brought by the Church of Scientology through its lawyer Morris Manning. At a press conference held before the application was heard, details concerning the contempt proceedings, including *verbatim* passages from the notice, were made public. The application for contempt was ultimately dismissed and, as a result of the publications made at the press conference and other publications, the Church of Scientology and Manning were sued for defamation.

In the following passage, Cory J. discussed the values in issue in defamation actions:

...

Cory J.: Although a *Charter* right is defined broadly, generally without internal limits, the *Charter* recognizes, under s. 1, that social values will at times conflict and that some limits must be placed even on fundamental rights. As La Forest J. explained in *Cotroni c. Centre de Prevention de Montréal*, (sub nom. *United States v. Contronі; United States v. El Zein),* [1989] 1 S.C.R. 1469, at p. 1489, this court has adopted a flexible approach to measuring the constitutionality of impugned provisions wherein "the underlying values [of the *Charter* are] sensitively weighed in a particular context against other values of a free and democratic society."

In *R. v. Keegstra*, [1990] 3 S.C.R. 697, for example, s. 319(2) of the *Criminal Code* was found to be justified as a reasonable limit on the appellant's freedom to spread falsehoods relating to the Holocaust and thus to promote hatred against an identifiable group. Dickson C.J.C. adopted the contextual approach to s. 1 and concluded that, since hate propaganda contributed little to the values which underlie the right enshrined under s. 2(*b*), namely, the quest for truth, the promotion of individual self-development, and participation in the community, a restriction on this type of expression might be easier to justify than would be the case with other kinds of expression.

In *R. v. Butler*, [1992] 1 S.C.R. 452, the obscenity provisions of the *Criminal Code,* R.S.C. 1985, c. C-46, s. 163, were questioned. It was held, under the s. 1 analysis, that pornography could not stand on an equal footing with other kinds of expression which directly engage the "core" values of freedom of expression. Further, it was found that the fact that the targeted material was expression motivated by economic profit more readily justified the imposition of restrictions.

Certainly, defamatory statements are very tenuously related to the core values which underlie s. 2(*b*). They are inimical to the search for truth. False and injurious statements cannot enhance self-development. Nor can it ever be said that they lead to healthy participation in the affairs of the community. Indeed, they are detrimental to the advancement of these values and harmful to the interests of a free and democratic society. This concept was accepted in *Boland v. Globe and Mail Ltd.* [1960] S.C.R. 203, at pp. 208-209, where it was held that an extension of the qualified privilege to the publication of defamatory statements concerning the fitness for office of a candidate for election would be "harmful to that 'common convenience and welfare of society.'" Reliance was placed upon the text *Gatley on Libel and Slander in a Civil Action,* 4th ed. by Richard O'Sullivan (London: Sweet & Maxwell, 1953), at p. 254, wherein the author stated the following:

> It would tend to deter sensitive and honourable men from seeking public positions of trust and responsibility, and leave them open to others who have no respect for their reputation. ...

(ii) The reputation of the individual

The other value to be balanced in a defamation action is the protection of the reputation of an individual. Although much has very properly been said and written about the importance of freedom of expression, little has been written of the importance of reputation. Yet to most people, their good reputation is to be cherished above all. A good reputation is closely related to the innate worthiness and dignity of the individual. It is an attribute that must, just as much as freedom of expression, be protected by society's laws. In order to undertake the balancing required by this case, something must be said about the value of reputation.

Democracy has always recognized and cherished the fundamental importance of an individual. That importance must, in turn, be based upon the good repute of a person. It is that good repute which enhances an individual's sense of worth and value. False allegations can so very quickly and completely destroy a good reputation. A reputation tarnished by libel can seldom regain its former lustre. A democratic society, therefore, has an interest in ensuring that its members can enjoy and protect their good reputation so long as it is merited.

From the earliest times, society has recognized the potential for tragic damage that can be occasioned by a false statement made about a person. This is evident in the Bible, the Mosaic Code, and the Talmud. As the author Carter-Ruck, in *Carter-Ruck on Libel and Slander*, 4th ed. by Peter F. Carter-Ruck, Richard Walker, and Harvey N.A. Starte (London: Butterworths, 1992), explains, at p. 17:

> The earliest evidence in recorded history of any sanction for defamatory statements is in the Mosaic code. In *Exodus* XXII 28 we find "Thou shalt not revile the gods nor curse the ruler of thy people" and in *Exodus* XXIII 1 "Thou shalt not raise a false report: put not thine hand with the wicked to be an unrighteous witness". There is also a condemnation of rumourmongers in *Leviticus* XIX 16 "Thou shalt not go up and down as a talebearer among thy people".

To make false statements which are likely to injure the reputation of another has always been regarded as a serious offence. During the Roman era, the punishment for libel varied from the loss of the right to make a will, to imprisonment, exile for life, or forfeiture of property. In the case of slander, a person could be made liable for payment of damages.

It was decreed by the Teutons in the *Lex Salica* that if a man called another a "wolf" or a "hare", he must pay the sum of three shillings; for a false imputation of unchastity in a woman the penalty was forty-five shillings. In the Norman Costumal, if people falsely called another "thief" or "manslayer," they had to pay damages and, holding their nose with their fingers, publicly confess themselves a liar.

With the separation of ecclesiastical and secular courts by the decree of William I following the Norman conquest, the Church assumed spiritual jurisdiction over defamatory language, which was regarded as a sin. The Church "stayed the tongue of the defamer at once *pro custodia morum* of the community and *pro salute animae* of the delinquent." See Van Vechten Veeder, "The History and Theory of the Law of Defamation" (1903) 3 Colum. L. Rev. 546, at p. 551.

By the 16th century, the common law action for defamation became commonplace. This was in no small measure due to the efforts of the Star Chamber to eradicate duelling, the favoured method of vindication. The Star Chamber even went so far as to punish the sending of challenges. However, when it proscribed this avenue of recourse to injured parties, the Star Chamber was compelled to widen its original jurisdiction over seditious libel to include ordinary defamation.

The modern law of libel is said to have arisen out of the *Case de Libellis Famosis* (1605), 5 Co. Rep. 125a, 77 E.R. 250. There, the late Archbishop of Canterbury and the then Bishop of London were alleged to have been "traduced and scandalized" by an anonymous person. As reported by Coke, it was ruled that all libels, even those against private individuals, ought to be sanctioned severely by indictment at common law or in the Star Chamber. The reasoning behind this was that the libel could incite "all those of the same family, kindred, or society to revenge, and so tends *per consequens* to quarrels and breach of the peace" [at p. 251 E.R.]. It was not necessary to show publication to a third person and it made no difference whether the libel was true or whether the plaintiff had a good or bad reputation. Eventually, truth was recognized as a defence in cases involving ordinary defamation.

It was not until the late 17th century that the distinction between libel and slander was drawn by Chief Baron Hale in *King v. Lake* (1670), Hardres 470, 145 E.R. 552, where it was held that words spoken, without more, would not be actionable, with a few exceptions. Once they were reduced to writing, however, malice would be presumed and an action would lie.

The character of the law relating to libel and slander in the 20th century is essentially the product of its historical development up to the 17th century, subject to a few refinements, such as the introduction and recognition of the defences of privilege and fair comment. From the foregoing we can see that a central theme through the ages has been that the reputation of the individual is of fundamental importance. As Professor Raymond E. Brown writes in *The Law of Defamation in Canada*, 2nd ed. (Scarborough, Ont.: Carswell, 1994) [looseleaf], at p. 1-4:

> "[N]o system of civil law can fail to take some account of the right to have one's reputation untarnished by defamation." Some form of legal or social constraints on defamatory publications "are to be found in all stages of civilization, however imperfect, remote, and proximate to barbarism." [Footnotes omitted]

Though the law of defamation no longer serves as a bulwark against the duel and blood feud, the protection of reputation remains of vital importance. As M. David Lepofsky suggests in "Making Sense of the Libel Chill Debate: Do Libel Laws "Chill" the Exercise of Freedom of Expression?" (1994) 4 N.J.C.L. 169, at p. 197, reputation is the "fundamental foundation on which people are able to interact with each other in social environments." At the same time, it serves the equally or perhaps more fundamentally important purpose of fostering our self-image and sense of self-worth. This sentiment was eloquently expressed by Stewart J. in *Rosenblatt v. Baer*, 383 U.S. 75 (1966), who stated, at p. 92:

> The right of a man to the protection of his own reputation from unjustified invasion and wrongful hurt reflects no more than our basic concept of the essential dignity and worth of every human being — a concept at the root of any decent system of ordered liberty.

In the present case, consideration must be given to the particular significance reputation has for a lawyer. The reputation of a lawyer is of paramount importance to clients, to other members of the profession, and to the judiciary. A lawyer's practice is founded and maintained upon the basis of a good reputation for professional integrity and trustworthiness. It is the cornerstone of a lawyer's professional life. Even if endowed with outstanding talent and indefatigable diligence, a lawyer cannot survive without a good reputation. In his essay entitled "The Lawyer's Duty to Himself and the Code of Professional Conduct" (1993) 27 L. Soc. Gaz. 119, David Hawreluk described the importance of a reputation forintegrity. At p. 121, he quoted Lord Birkett on the subject:

> "The advocate has a duty to his client, a duty to the Court, and a duty to the State; but he has above all a duty to himself and he shall be, as far as lies in his power, a man of integrity. No profession calls for higher standards of honour and uprightness, and no profession, perhaps, offers greater temptations to forsake them; but whatever gifts an advocate may possess, be they never so dazzling, without the supreme qualification of an inner integrity he will fall short of the highest..."

Similarly, Esson J. in *Vogel v. Canadian Broadcasting Corp.*, [1982] 3 W.W.R. 97 (B.C. S.C.), at pp. 177-178, stated:

> The qualities required of a lawyer who aspires to the highest level of his profession are various, but one is essential. That is a reputation for integrity. The programs were a massive attack upon that reputation. The harm done to it can never be wholly undone, and therefore the stigma so unfairly created will always be with the plaintiff.
>
> When the details of the Vogel affair have faded from memory, what will remain in the minds of many people throughout Canada is a lurking recollection that he was the centre of a scandal which arose out of his conduct in office.

Although it is not specifically mentioned in the *Charter*, the good reputation of the individual represents and reflects the innate dignity of the individual, a concept which underlies all the *Charter* rights. It follows that the protection of the good reputation of an individual is of fundamental importance to our democratic society.

Further, reputation is intimately related to the right to privacy which has been accorded constitutional protection. As La Forest J. wrote in *R. v. Dyment*, [1988] 2 S.C.R. 417, at p. 427, privacy, including informational privacy, is "[g]rounded in man's physical and moral autonomy" and "is essential for the well-being of the individual." The publication of defamatory comments constitutes an invasion of the individual's personal privacy and is an affront to that person's dignity. The protection of a person's reputation is indeed worthy of protection in our democratic society and must be carefully balanced against the equally important right of freedom of expression. …

NOTE

1. Do you think that Cory J.'s balance between free speech and reputation is properly drawn in Canadian defamation law? Does Cory J. indicate a preference for one over the other in the above extract? Where would you draw the line?

B. WHAT IS DEFAMATORY?

MURPHY v. LAMARSH ET AL.

British Columbia Court of Appeal. [1971] 2 W.W.R. 196,
18 D.L.R. (3d) 208; affg (1970), 73 W.W.R. 114, 13 D.L.R. (3d) 484.
leave to appeal to the S.C.C. refused, [1971] S.C.R. ix.

Wilson C.J.S.C. [at trial]: The plaintiff Murphy was formerly employed as a radio newsman in the press gallery at Ottawa reporting for his radio station the doings of Parliament and the Government of Canada and general political news, including the public and private actions of politicians who were in the public eye.

The defendant Julia (more usually called Judy) LaMarsh is the author of, and the defendant McClelland and Stewart Limited is the publisher of, a book of political reminiscences called *Memoirs of a Bird in a Gilded Cage*, first published in 1968.

The first edition of this book, 10,000 copies, contained statements about the plaintiff which he says are defamatory and upon which this lawsuit is based. It is necessary to cite the impugned passage. …

> A brash young radio reporter, named Ed Murphy (heartily detested by most of the Press Gallery and the members), had somehow learned that Maurice Lamontagne (then Secretary of State, and a long-time friend and adviser of the Prime Minister) had purchased furniture but had not paid for it. …

In subsequent editions (25,000 copies) the words "heartily detested by most of the Press Gallery and the members" were deleted and they are also omitted from a paperback edition of which 50,000 copies are being circulated by another publisher.

The passage just cited ("heartily detested by most of the Press Gallery and the members") is alleged to be libellous. The plaintiff also claims that the latter part of the extract cited [omitted here] considered in its context, imputes to the plaintiff a disreputable action, the hounding of Mr. Lamontagne out of office, and is therefore libellous.

Miss LaMarsh was Member of Parliament for Niagara Falls from 1960 to 1968, and was, from 1963 to 1968, a Minister in a Government headed by Mr. Lester Pearson as Prime Minister and consisting of members of the Liberal political party.

Miss LaMarsh's memoirs were, her publisher tells me, expected to be a lively and colourful account of her political career. A good deal of the book fits readily into that definition and if Mr. Murphy's head is left bloody it is not the only one.

The first question is whether or not it is libel to say of a man in Mr. Murphy's occupation that he was "heartily detested" by most of colleagues and by most Members of Parliament.

Plaintiff's counsel has not argued that the word "brash" is defamatory. I have given some thought to this conception — that the word "brash" is the governing word in the sentence and that the words "heartily detested by most of the Press Gallery and the members" are only inserted to reflect the reaction of those persons to Mr. Murphy's brashness. I have come to the conclusion that this interpretation of what Miss LaMarsh has said will not stand analysis — the statement, in parenthesis, that Mr. Murphy was heartily detested is an independent clause, emphasized by the parenthesis, and not clearly related to the quality of brashness. I do not say that brashness cannot arouse detestation. "Brash", in Canada bears, I think, more the American meaning stated in *Webster's Dictionary*, 1966 of "bumptious", "tactless", "loudly assertive", rather than the English meaning given in the *Oxford Dictionary* of "bold", "rash" or "impudent". But I do not think Miss LaMarsh has asserted that Mr. Murphy is detested because of his brashness; I think she has merely said he is detested by majorities of two groups of people.

These are the people best placed to know and value him, his associates in the press gallery and the Members of Parliament with whom he must associate and about whom he writes.

Ordinarily a libel is more specific than the one alleged here. A shameful action is attributed to a man (he stole my purse), a shameful character (he is dishonest), a shameful course of action (he lives on the avails of prostitution), a shameful condition (he has the pox). Such words are considered defamatory because they tend to bring the man named, according to the classic definition, into hatred, contempt or ridicule. The more modern definition, given by Lord Atkin, in *Sim v. Stretch* 52 T.L.R. 669, 80 Sol. J. 703, [1936] 2 All E.R. 1237, at 1240, is words tending "to lower the plaintiff in the estimation of right-thinking members of society generally". Perhaps "words likely to cause a man to be detested" might also, although not an all-inclusive definition, fit into the class of defamatory words.

The difference between this and other cases I have read or tried is that no shameful action or characteristic or condition is directly attributed to Mr. Murphy. It is only said of him that he is heartily detested. A fairly careful search of authority has revealed to me no case in which the libel alleged has been couched in such terms — an allegation of bad repute without some direct supporting charge of wrongdoing or bad character.

It is obvious that any decision as to whether or not such words as were used here are libellous must be approached with care. Under proper circumstances I think it must generally be open to writers to express of certain persons opinions as to their popularity or unpopularity, perhaps to say they are by some classes of people liked or disliked. The words used, the circumstances, the person who comments, the person upon whom the comment is made, must all be considered. It may be permissible, for instance, in certain circumstances, to say of a politician that he is losing his popularity, even though such words will certainly not help him in his career and may well hurt him.

The first thing to consider is the nature of the operative word "detested" and this was much discussed at the trial. The *Oxford Dictionary* gives to the word "detests" the meanings "hate", "abominate", "abhor", "dislike intensely". *Webster's Dictionary*, I think, is more up to date in its definitions when it says, "Detest indicates very strong aversion but may lack the actively hostile male-violence associated with hate."

I would say, for instance, that Hamlet hated, or thought he ought to hate Claudius, the murderer of his father and the defiler, as Hamlet thought, of his mother but that he detested Polonius as a sycophant and a tedious moralizing bore ("These tedious old fools": Act II scene 2).

But "detest" remains a strong word. While it may express the feeling one has toward a boor, a bore or a braggart, it may also express the feeling one has toward an unscrupulous reporter, a reporter whose actions have displayed bad character. I do not think that the reasoning in *Capital & Counties Bank v. Henty* (1882), 7 App. Cas. 741, 52 L.J.Q.B. 232, applies here. The words used are not, as in that case, capable of a harmless meaning and alternatively and rather vaguely of a bad meaning, so that the harmless meaning should be preferred. They are disparaging in any sense, more disparaging in one sense than the other and it seems to me that in those circumstances, where it is clear that right-thinking persons can and probably will properly interpret them as defamatory, there must be liability. The tendency to defame is there.

No wrong or evil is directly attributed to Mr. Murphy but it is said of him that most men who have most to do with him in his occupation heartily detest him. I have no doubt that the ordinary reader, who is not perhaps inclined to such an analysis of words as I have here attempted would, after reading this, think "There must be something wrong or bad about this man Murphy to make these people detest him." Since I think this is the test to be applied, I think the words are defamatory. The effect is the same as would have resulted if it had been said, "He bears a bad reputation among his associates."

...

Maclean J.A. in the Court of Appeal (**Taggart J.A.** concurring):

In my view the learned trial Judge was correct when he held that the words are defamatory and that the effect is the same as would have resulted if it had been said, "He bears a bad reputation among his associates." It must be remembered too that his associates were the members of the Press Gallery, and that the members of the House of Commons were persons with whom Murphy was in daily contact.

In my view any reasonable reader, on reading the words complained of, would conclude that there must be something very wrong with a person when his associates hold him in such poor regard.

The learned trial Judge was correct when he found that the "tendency" to defame was present.

[**McFarlane J.A.** agreed.]

Appeal dismissed.

NOTES

1. Chief Justice Wilson relied on at least three verbal formulations of the test for defamation. What are they? What do you think of each of them? Which is the broadest and which the narrowest?

2. Two other word formulae were used in *Youssoupoff v. Metro-Goldwyn-Mayer Pictures Ltd.* (1934), 50 T.L.R. 581, 78 Sol. Jo. 617 (*sub nom. Princess Alexandrovna v. Metro-Goldwyn-Mayer Pictures Ltd.*) (C.A.). The defendants produced a film depicting the influence of a person called Rasputin, allegedly a monk, on the Czar and Czarina of Russia that led to the destruction of that country. In the film, Rasputin seduced a Princess Natasha. The plaintiff, Princess Irina Alexandrovna of Russia, sued for libel on the ground that she would be reasonably taken to be the ravaged woman. She succeeded before a jury and the defendant's appeal was dismissed. Scrutton L.J. explained as follows:

> There have been several formulae for describing what is defamation. The learned Judge at the trial uses the stock formula "calculated to bring into hatred, ridicule, or contempt" and because it has been clearly established some time ago that that is not exhaustive because there may be things which are defamatory which have nothing to do with hatred, ridicule, or contempt, he adds the words "or causes them to be shunned or avoided". I, myself, have always preferred the language which Mr. Justice Cave used in *Scott v. Sampson*, 8 Q.B.D. 491, a false statement about a man to his discredit. I think that satisfactorily expresses what has to be found. It has long been established that, with one modification, libel or no libel is for the jury and the Court very rarely interferes with a finding by the jury that a particular statement is libel or no libel. The only exception is that it has been established with somewhat unfortunate results that a Judge may say: "No reasonable jury could possibly think this is a libel, and consequently I will not ask the jury the question whether it is libel or not."...

What are the two other formulae used here? What do you think of them? What are the respective roles of judge and jury?

3. A good review of the judicial definitions of the word "defamatory" is found in the English case, *Berkoff v. Burchill*, [1996] 4 All E.R. 1008 (C.A.). The plaintiff, a well-known actor, director and writer was described as "notoriously hideous-looking" by a film reviewer. Do you think that to describe a person in this way is defamatory, or is it mockery which should be ignored by the courts as merely being "chaff and banter"?

4. Professor Fleming has suggested that defamation "tends to lower a person in the estimation of his fellows by making them think less of him": *The Law of Torts*, 9th ed. (1998), p. 528. What is your view of this test?

5. Can the Attorney-General seek an injunction to restrain the defamation of doctors on the basis that the harassment of physicians is harmful to the public interest? In *Ontario (Attorney-General) v. Dieleman* (1994), 117 D.L.R. (4th) 449 (Ont. Gen. Div.) the court, while conceding that the action for defamation is personal, held that it could in these exceptional circumstances be enforced by the Attorney General "in her capacity as *parens patriae* in pursuit of regulating a public nuisance".

6. In *Warren v. Green* (1958), 15 D.L.R. (2d) 251, 25 W.W.R. 563 (Alta. T.D.), Mr. Justice Cairns held that calling a doctor a "quack" is defamatory. His Lordship stated:

> There are many instances where words used would not be defamatory, which if used in another setting would be so, such as the using of words which might

> reflect on a person's ancestry, or other words which might be considered terms of endearment, but it depends on the manner in which these expressions are voiced, and the circumstances under which they are expressed. ... It is also most important to consider what persons hearing such words would, or might reasonably be expected to, understand from them, apart from a deliberate intention of the utterer.

Is it defamation if a doctor is called a "quack", in jest, by another doctor, who is an old friend?

7. Is it defamatory of doctors who perform abortions to carry signs saying: "Abortion Kills Children" or "Abortion, Canada's Holocaust"? What if the sign is more specific and says that "Dr. X. kills (by abortion) unborn babies"? What if the doctor is called an "Abortion Butcher"? See *Ontario (A.G.) v. Dieleman, supra.*

8. Is it defamation to call a lawyer a "shyster"? See *Nolan v. Standard Publishing Co.*, 67 Mont. 212, 216 P. 571 (1923). What if another lawyer jokingly says to the plaintiff, "You old shyster, you"?

9. Is it defamatory to call someone a liar in the presence of a third party? (See *Penton v. Calwell*, [1945] A.L.R. 262, 70 C.L.R. 219). What if the mayor of a city publicly charges a lawyer and the lawyer's developer clients with "deception" and a "breach of faith"? (See *Fraser v. Sykes*, [1974] S.C.R. 526). Is a newspaper cartoon libellous if it depicts a politician pulling the wings off flies with obvious enjoyment? (See *Vander Zalm v. Times Publishers et al.*, [1979] 2 W.W.R. 673 (B.C.S.C.), *per* Munroe J.; revd (1980), 109 D.L.R. (3d) 531, 12 C.C.L.T. 81 (C.A.).) Is it libellous to call someone, who permanently left the Soviet Union, a "defector" and a "traitor"? (See *Gouzenko v. Harris et al.* (1976), 13 O.R. (2d) 730, 1 C.C.L.T. 37 (H.C.), *per* Goodman J.)

10. The standard of measurement in defamation cases is sometimes said to be the "right-thinking members of society generally". (See Lord Atkin in *Sim v. Stretch*, [1936] 2 All E.R. 1237, 52 T.L.R. 669 (H.L.).) This has been somewhat diluted, however, for a person may be defamed in the eyes of citizens who are not "right-thinking" at all. The courts look at what people of "fair average intelligence" would think (see *Slayter v. Daily Telegraph* (1908), 6 C.L.R. 1 (H.C. of Aust.)) or what "ordinary decent folk in the community, taken in general" would feel. (See *Gardiner v. John Fairfax & Sons Pty. Ltd.* (1942), 42 S.R. (N.S.W.) 171.) Another standard suggested by Holmes J. and adopted by the *Restatement of Torts, Second* §559 is this: "If the advertisement obviously would hurt the plaintiff in the estimation of an important and respectable part of the community, liability is not a question of majority vote." (See *Peck v. Tribune Co.*, 214 U.S. 185, at 190 (1909).) It has been held that "the hypothetical sensible reader is not one who is 'avid for scandal'". Thus, to write of a brother and sister that they are "very defensive about their close relationship" and that "like a long married couple... finish one another's sentences" would not, to the reasonable person, suggest an incestuous relationship. See *Pollock v. Winnipeg Free Press* (1996), [1997] 2 W.W.R. 216, 34 C.C.L.T. (2d) 203 (Man. Q.B.).

11. In *Grant v. Reader's Digest Assoc. Inc.*, 1 F. 2d 733 (2nd Cir. C.A. 1945), a statement that the plaintiff, a lawyer, "recently was a legislative representative for the Massachusetts Communist Party", was held capable of a defamatory meaning in that it implied the plaintiff was in sympathy with the Party's objects and methods. L. Hand J. said that people may value their reputations among those who do not embrace "the prevailing moral standards". Whether "right-thinking" people might shun, despise or condemn a lawyer acting for the Communist Party was not the issue. "It is enough if there be some, as there certainly are, who would feel so, even though they would be 'wrong-thinking' people if they did."

12. Is it defamatory to say that the plaintiff informed the police about a crime and it leads to the plaintiff being shunned and avoided by certain criminal elements? See *Mawe v. Pigott* (1869), Ir. Rep. 4 C.L. 54. See also *Byrne v. Deane*, [1937] 1 K.B. 818, [1937] 2 All E.R. 204 (C.A.), a golf club member told police about illegal gambling machines, causing other members to think less of him. Is it defamatory to say that a professional gambler cheats at poker? See *Caldwell v. McBride* (1988), 45 C.C.L.T. 150 (B.C.S.C.).

13. Donald calls Peter a "scab". Peter is a member of a union. Defamatory? See *Murphy v. Plasterers' Union*, [1949] S.A.S.R. 98. Would it make any difference if Peter was a general manager or a supervisor, and not a union member?

14. In *Silver v. Dominion Telegraph Co.* (1882), 10 S.C.R. 238, it was held defamatory to have said of the plaintiffs, wholesale clothiers, that their business had "failed" and that their "liabilities [were] heavy". Is it actionable to say that X is in "dire financial straits"? See *Katapodis v. Brooklyn Spectator*, 287 N.Y. 17, 38 N.E. 2d 112 (1941). What about stating that Y refuses to pay just debts? See *Thompson v. Adelberg and Berman*, 181 Ky. 487, 205 S.W. 558 (1918).

15. If one accuses a kosher butcher of selling bacon, is this actionable? See *Braun v. Armour & Co.*, 173 N.E. 845 (N.Y. 1930). What if someone calls a retailer a price-cutter? See *Meyerson v. Hurlburt*, 98 F.2d 232 (1938).

16. Is it actionable to call someone a "Communist" or a "Communist rubber stamp"? See *Dennison et al. v. Sanderson et al.*, [1946] O.R. 601, [1946] 4 D.L.R. 314 (C.A.). What if it is alleged that the plaintiff is a "near-Communist" or that the plaintiff takes the side of the Communist Party? See *Braddock v. Bevins*, [1948] 1 K.B. 580, [1948] 1 All E.R. 450 (C.A.). Is it defamatory to be called a Red? A Pinko? A fellow-traveller? A Socialist? See *Slayter v. Daily Telegraph* (1908), 6 C.L.R. 1 (H.C. of Aust.). A radical? Does it matter if the plaintiff is a professor, a lawyer or a business-person? Does the place and time of the utterance make any difference?

17. Is it defamatory to say that someone is a Nazi? A Fascist? An arch-reactionary? A member of the Ku Klux Klan?

18. Can it ever be actionable to say that someone is a member of the Liberal Party of Canada? The Progressive Conservative Party? The N.D.P.? Reform? The Bloc Québecois?

19. Is it defamatory to say that someone is suffering from mental illness? From cancer? From venereal disease? See *French (Oscar) v. Smith* (1923), 53 O.L.R. 28, [1923] 3 D.L.R. 902 (H.C.).

20. Is it possible to defame someone without using words at all? What if a picture of the plaintiff is printed alongside a picture of a gorilla to indicate the resemblance between the two pictures? See *Zbyszko v. New York American*, 228 App. Div. 277, 239 N.Y. Supp. 411 (1930).

21. In *Burton v. Crowell Publishing Co.*, 82 F.2d 154 (U.S.C.A. 2d Cir. 1936), the defendant published an ad for Camel cigarettes featuring a photograph of the plaintiff, which, because of a blurring, made it appear that he was indecently exposed. Although the plaintiff had agreed to the ad generally, he had not approved of this particular picture. In allowing the plaintiff's claim, Learned Hand J. said:

> The gravamen of the wrong in defamation is not so much the injury to reputation, measured by the opinion of others, as the feelings, that is, the repulsion or light esteem, which those opinions engender … [B]ecause the picture …

> was calculated to expose the plaintiff to more than trivial ridicule, it was prima facie actionable [even though] it did not assume to state a fact or an opinion. ...

See also *Mazatti v. Acme Products Ltd.*, [1930] 4 D.L.R. 601, [1930] 3 W.W.R. 43 (Man. K.B.), where the plaintiff was alleged to have given a testimonial in an advertisement for a product called Keeno, a patent medicine, which was supposed to have cured him of constipation, dizzy spells and indigestion. Liability was imposed since this was "humiliating to the plaintiff, and tended to and did subject him to ridicule".

22. In his book, *The Acquisitors*, Peter Newman wrote the following:

> The condo in Maui or Miami, the stretch Learjet, the new house with its mandatory conversation pit, bathtub skylights, and colour co-ordinated French Impressionists — these and other constantly upgraded possessions become essential to their psychic survival. Their aptitude for self-gratification knows few bounds.
>
> In the spring of 1980, for instance, Carol Rapp, the wife of a Toronto millionaire, ordered a new set of bright blue uniforms for her chauffeur, which she insisted be colour-cued to the hue on the bottom of her swimming pool.

(See 34 O.R. (2d) 452 at 453).

If you were Carol Rapp would you consider these words defamatory? See *Rapp v. McClelland & Stewart Ltd.* (1981), 34 O.R. (2d) 452, 128 D.L.R. (3d) 650, 19 C.C.L.T. 68 (S.C.).

23. In *Pearlman v. C.B.C.* (1981), 13 Man. R. (2d) 1 (Q.B.), the plaintiff, a barrister and solicitor, was described as a "slum landlord" without "morals, principles, or conscience". The court dismissed the action upholding the defence of "fair comment". If damages were awarded, the court would have decided upon a sum of $1 because on the evidence as a whole the defendants were justified in referring to the plaintiff in those terms. Does this case not indicate the danger in jumping into a defamation action too impulsively? Do you think that the plaintiff was damaged more by the comments or by the unfavourable judgment in this case?

24. Is it defamatory to publish a congratulatory notice in a newspaper announcing the pregnancy of a single woman, who had wished to keep the matter confidential? Do you think that the nature and context of the notice could affect this question? See *Bordeleau v. Bonnyville* (1993), 97 D.L.R. (4th) 764, [1993] 1 W.W.R. 634 (Alta. Q.B.).

25. Is it defamatory to call someone a "son of a bitch"? This is what Spencer J. had to say about this in *Ralston v. Fomich* (1992), 66 B.C.L.R. (2d) 166, [1992] 4 W.W.R. 284 (B.C.S.C.), at 287:

> In my opinion, the words "son of a bitch" by themselves are not capable of any defamatory meaning. They are peculiar, in that they take their meaning either from the tone of voice used or from whatever adjective accompanies them. They are a translucent vessel waiting to be filled with colour by their immediate qualifier. Thus, one has sympathy for a poor son of a bitch, admiration for a brave son of a bitch, affection for a good old son of a bitch, envy for a rich son of a bitch and, perhaps incongruously, dislike for a proper son of a bitch. Why right thinking people should dislike anything that is proper is rather a mystery unless proper is used to mean "real," but I am confident that is the colour that adjective gives to the expression. It is perhaps a throw-back to an earlier use of the expression when the mere words themselves carried an

opprobrious meaning, see for example Kent's apostrophe to Oswald (Shakespeare, *King Lear*, Act II, Scene 2):

> ... [thou] art nothing but the composition of a knave, beggar, coward, pander and the son and heir of a mongrel bitch. ...

There are other early examples to be found of a stand alone meaning of the phrase, but in modern times the bare words are not capable of bearing a defamatory meaning. At most they insult. They are not likely to lower the object in the estimation of right thinking people. More probably they will demean the speaker, depending upon the company and the occasion. As an example of the modern neutrality of the phrase, I refer to Chapman, *New Dictionary of American Slang* (Harper and Row, 1986), where it means a person or thing that is remarkable, wonderful or superior, with reference to the phrase, "Their new album is a son of a bitch I tell you." One imagines that was not said on the Saturday afternoon Metropolitan Opera program but on some less formal occasion.

The words used in this case were "sick son of a bitch". Defamatory?

26. Is it defamatory of a professional dance band to say that when the band, which had been hired to play at a ball, switched their music to rock that they "cleared the floor sending many home before the 1 a.m. finish"? See *Murray Alter's Talent Associates Ltd. v. Toronto Star Newspapers Ltd.* (1995), 124 D.L.R. (4th) 105 (Ont. Div. Ct.).

27. Is the threshold test for determining whether material is defamatory too low? Professor Klar thinks so. In *Tort Law*, 2nd ed. (1996) at 555 he writes:

> the threshold which has been adopted by Canadian cases is *extremely minimal.* The cases indicate that virtually all critical comment, whether it be in the form of fact or opinion, which portrays a person in an uncomplimentary light will be considered to be defamatory.

As noted by Adams J. in *Ontario v. Dieleman, supra,* this shifts the focus to the defences which are "quite robust". In considering the defences below, do you think that they are adequate to counter the effect of the low threshold?

28. The defamatory statement must be spoken "of and concerning the plaintiff". And this must normally be pleaded and proved. Thus, if not specifically identified, the plaintiff must show that a sensible reader would reasonably understand that the plaintiff is the person being defamed. See *Morgan v. Odham's Press*, [1971] 1 W.L.R. 1239; *Youssoupoff v. M.-G.-M. Pictures* (1934), 50 T.L.R. 581, 78 Sol. Jo. 617 (*sub nom. Princess Alexandrovna v. Metro-Goldwyn-Mayer Pictures Ltd.*) (C.A.). A gossip columnist mistakenly writes that the "estranged wife of the Prime Minister was seen smoking pot". Could the Prime Minister's wife sue?

29. This problem of identifying the person defamed arises in cases of group defamation. If someone says "all lawyers are thieves", an individual lawyer could not say that this defamation was "of and concerning him [or her]". If the group being defamed, however, is a relatively small one, an individual member of the group may be allowed to recover. What if Donald says that X got one of the four Jones girls in trouble? Can any of them recover? See *Albrecht v. Burkholder* (1889), 18 O.R. 287. See also *Browne v. D.C. Thomson & Co.*, [1912] S.C. 359, 49 Sc. L.R. 285, one of seven people could sue; *Neiman-Marcus v. Lait* (1952), 13 F.R.D. 311, 15 salesmen could sue but not 382 saleswomen; *Ortenberg v. Plamondon* (1914), 35 Can. L.T. 262 (Que.), one of 75 families could sue; *Fraser v. Sykes*, [1974] S.C.R. 526, 39 D.L.R. (3d) 321, one of three can sue. In *A.U.P.E. v. The Edmonton Sun* (1986), 49 Alta. L.R. (2d) 141, 39 C.C.L.T. 143 (Q.B.), 25 prison guards from a group of 200 sued for defamation.

Do you think that when a group of 200 is defamed, any one individual member of that group can claim that his or her reputation has been damaged?

30. A fine explanation of the principles involved here was given in *Knupffer v. London Express Newspaper*, [1944] A.C. 116, [1944] 1 All E.R. 495 (H.L.), where some defamatory things were said of a group called Young Russia, a pro-Nazi organization, of which the plaintiff was a member. There were 2,000 other members in the world, 24 of whom were in Britain. The action was dismissed and Lord Atkin explained:

> I venture to think that it is a mistake to lay down a rule as to libel on a class, and then qualify it with exceptions. The only relevant rule is that in order to be actionable the defamatory words must be understood to be published of and concerning the plaintiff. It is irrelevant that the words are published of two or more persons if they are proved to be published of him, and it is irrelevant that the two or more persons are called by some generic or class name. There can be no law that a defamatory statement made of a firm, or trustees, or the tenants of a particular building is not actionable, if the words would reasonably be understood as published of each member of the firm or each trustee or each tenant. The reason why a libel published of a large or indeterminate number of persons described by some general name generally fails to be actionable is the difficulty of establishing that the plaintiff was, in fact, included in the defamatory statement, for the habit of making unfounded generalizations is ingrained in ill-educated or vulgar minds, or the words are occasionally intended to be a facetious exaggeration. Even in such cases words may be used which enable the plaintiff to prove that the words complained of were intended to be published of each member of the group, or, at any rate, of himself. Too much attention has been paid, I venture to think, in the textbooks and elsewhere to the ruling of Willes, J., in 1858 in *Eastwood v. Holmes*, 1 F. & F. 347, a case at nisi prius ... His words: "it only reflects on a class of persons" are irrelevant unless they mean "it does not reflect on the plaintiff", and his instance, "All lawyers were thieves" is an excellent instance of the vulgar generalizations to which I have referred. It will be as well for the future for lawyers to concentrate on the question whether the words were published of the plaintiff rather than on the question whether they were spoken of a class. I agree that in the present case the words complained of are, apparently, an unfounded generalization conveying imputations of disgraceful conduct, but not such as could reasonably be understood to be spoken of the appellant.

31. In *Booth v. B.C. Television Broadcasting Systems* (1982), 139 D.L.R. (3d) 88 (B.C.C.A.), 11 members of the Vancouver City Police Department sued the defendant broadcasting company for comments made by a prostitute during a television interview. The woman stated that two members of the Narc Squad "that are high up — right up on top" took payoffs. The trial judge gave judgment for the two detectives who headed the squad but dismissed the action brought by the other nine plaintiffs. In dismissing an appeal, Lambert J.A. stated that in considering whether words were defamatory of the plaintiffs what was relevant was not what the speaker subjectively meant to say but what "reasonable men would take from what was said". This depended on several factors — the kind of person that the speaker was, the kind of knowledge that people would anticipate that the speaker would have, the circumstances in which the words are used, the general audience to which the statement might be considered to be directed, and the special audience with special knowledge of the organization of the Vancouver Police Department. His Lordship also stated that merely because the statement may have cast suspicion on all the plaintiffs this does not in law link the statement to all the plaintiffs.

32. Does the existence of class action procedures change the group defamation issue? In *Elliott v. Canadian Broadcasting Corp.* (1995), 125 D.L.R. (4th) 534 (Ont. C.A.), one

of the 25,000 surviving ex-sevicemen of the British Bomber Command sued the C.B.C. for an allegedly defamatory film concerning their World War II service. The action was struck out on the basis that the servicemen had not been defamed by the show. Abella J.A. left open the possibility that the new class action procedures in Ontario might have otherwise allowed such a lawsuit to proceed.

33. Only living people can be defamed; accordingly, in most jurisdictions a defamation action cannot be brought by the personal representatives of a deceased person. What if the person was defamed while alive, commenced an action, but died before a judgment was rendered? Since the present law is that a defamation action dies with the death of the person defamed, the action could not succeed. In 1975, the Faulks Committee Report on Defamation, Cmnd. 5909, recommended changes to the existing law. The Report recommended that, where the person defamed has started an action but died prior to judgment, the personal representative should be entitled to carry on the action to the extent of recovering both general and special damages. Where the person defamed had not yet started an action, the Report recommended that only an injunction and actual or likely pecuniary damages suffered by the deceased or the deceased's estate should be recoverable. The most dramatic of the Report's recommendations was that a new action be given in the case of the defamation of a person already deceased. The majority of the Committee recommended that there be an action to restrain persons from telling defamatory falsehoods of a deceased for a period of five years after his death. Note that in Alberta a defamation action does not die with the death of the defamed person, although the estate is limited in its claim to the "actual financial loss" suffered by the deceased. See *Survival of Actions Act*, R.S.A. 1980, c. S-30.

    What are the policy problems regarding the survivability of defamation actions? Why should defamation be treated differently from all other tort claims for personal injury?

34. Words may appear innocent on the surface but may be defamatory to people who are aware of extrinsic facts. In such a case, the plaintiff must plead and prove this, which is called the "innuendo". See *Libel and Slander Act*, R.S.O. 1990, c. L.12, s. 19. An example of such a situation is the publication of the apparent good news that Mrs. M. has given birth to twins. Mrs. M. succeeds in libel when she pleads and proves that she was married only four weeks before, the innuendo being that she has given birth to illegitimate children. See *Morrison v. Ritchie & Co.* (1902), 4 F. (Ct. of Sess.) 645, 39 Scot. L.R. 432. Similarly, to publish a photograph identifying one woman as Mrs. X. becomes libellous when another woman proves that she is the real Mrs. X. and that she has been defamed because of the publication. *Cf.*, *Cassidy v. Daily Mirror Newspapers*, [1929] 2 K.B. 331, [1929] All E.R. Rep. 177 (C.A.).

35. Because of the lack of protection defamation law affords minority groups who are defamed, legislation has been enacted to furnish some protection to the victims of what has been called "hate propaganda".

    Under the *Criminal Code*, R.S.C. 1985, c. C-46, s. 319, "(1) Every one who, by communicating statements in any public place, incites hatred against any identifiable group [distinguished by colour, race, religion, or ethnic origin] where such incitement is likely to lead to a breach of the peace"; or "(2) Every one who, by communicating statements, other than in private conversation, wilfully promotes hatred against any identifiable group" is guilty of an offence. It is a defence for the accused to prove under s. (3) that the "statements communicated were true"; or "in good faith, he expressed or attempted to establish by argument an opinion on a religious subject"; or "the statements were relevant to any subject of public interest, the discussion of which was for the public benefit [and the accused believed] on reasonable grounds [that they were true]" or "in good faith, he intended to point out, for the purpose of removal, matters producing or tending to produce feelings of hatred toward an identifiable group in Canada". Do you think these provisions are a reasonable limitation on freedom of speech?

For a further discussion of the problem of group defamation, see Riesman, "Democracy and Defamation: Control of Group Libel" (1942), 42 Colum. L. Rev. 727; Fenson, "Group Defamation: Is the Cure Too Costly?" (1964), 1 Man. L.S.J. 255; Arthurs, "Hate Propaganda — An Argument against Attempts to Stop it by Legislation" (1970), 18 Chitty's L.J. 1; Cohen, "The Hate Propaganda Amendments: Reflections on a Controversy" (1971), 9 Alta. L. Rev. 103; Burns, "Defamatory Libel in Canada: A Recent Illustration of a Rare Crime" (1969), 17 Chitty's L.J. 213.

36. The *Criminal Code* also seeks to penalize "defamatory libel" against an individual. It states:

> **298(1)** A defamatory libel is matter published, without lawful justification or excuse, that is likely to injure the reputation of any person by exposing him to hatred, contempt or ridicule, or that is designed to insult the person of or concerning whom it is published.

And, following,

> **298(2)** A defamatory libel may be expressed directly or by insinuation or irony
> (*a*) in words legibly marked upon any substance; or
> (*b*) by any object signifying a defamatory libel otherwise than by words.

If the libeller knows the libel is false the libeller is subject to imprisonment for a maximum of five years; otherwise it is a two-year maximum penalty. See *R. v. Georgia Straight Publishing Ltd.* (1970), 4 D.L.R. (3d) 383, [1970] 1 C.C.C. 94 (B.C. Co. Ct.).

Can you discern any difference between the criminal definition of libel and that developed by tort law? Is it preferable to reduce libel by tort actions or by criminal prosecutions? See generally LaMarsh, "Abuse of Power by the Media" in Law Society of Upper Canada, Special Lectures, *Abuse of Power* (1979).

The Law Reform Commission of Canada has recommended the abolition of the crime of defamatory libel. See *Defamatory Libel* (1984). Is this a wise suggestion?

37. A corporation and a municipality may be defamed. See *City of Prince George v. B.C. Television* (1978), 85 D.L.R. (3d) 755, [1978] 3 W.W.R. 12 (B.C.S.C.); affd, 95 D.L.R. (3d) 577, [1979] 2 W.W.R. 404 (B.C.C.A.); but see *Church of Scientology of Toronto v. Globe and Mail* (1978), 19 O.R. (2d) 62, 84 D.L.R. (3d) 239 (H.C.); *Windsor R.C. Sep. School Bd. v. Southam Inc.* (1984), 46 O.R. (2d) 231, 9 D.L.R. (4th) 284 (H.C.J.) (school board).

38. Canadian politicians seem to resort to the action for defamation on a frequent basis. The following political figures have been plaintiffs in defamation actions: Alderman Cherneskey in *Cherneskey v. Armadale Publishers*, [1979] 1 S.C.R. 1067, [1978] 6 W.W.R. 618; Premier Lougheed in *Lougheed v. C.B.C.* (1979), 98 D.L.R. (3d) 264, [1979] 3 W.W.R. 334, 8 C.C.L.T. 120 (Alta. C.A.); M.P. Simma Holt in *Holt v. Sun Publishing* (1979), 100 D.L.R. (3d) 447 (B.C.C.A.); City Official Snyder in *Snyder v. Montreal Gazette* (1978), 87 D.L.R. (3d) 5, [1978] Que. S.C. 628 (S.C.); revd, 5 D.L.R. (4th) 206, [1983] C.A. 604 (Que.); revd, [1988] 1 S.C.R. 494, 49 D.L.R. (4th) 17; Federal Minister Munro in *Munro v. The Toronto Sun* (1982), 39 O.R. (2d) 100, 21 C.C.L.T. 261 (C.A.); Doug Christie in *Christie v. Geiger*, [1987] 1 W.W.R. 357, 38 C.C.L.T. 280 (Alta. C.A.); Minister Coates in *Coates v. The Citizen* (1986), 74

N.S.R. (2d) 143, 29 D.L.R. (4th) 523 (C.A.); Premier Getty in *Getty v. Calgary Herald* (1991), 47 C.P.C. (2d) 42 (Alta. Q.B.); and even one foreign politician, the Prime Minister of the Bahamas in *Pindling v. National Broadcasting Corp.* (1984), 14 D.L.R. (4th) 391, 31 C.C.L.T. 251 (Ont. H.C.J.). Do you think that Canadian attitudes to defamation law pose a danger to freedom of speech and dissent? How does the situation in Canada compare to that in the United States? Which system do you prefer? Has the *Canadian Charter of Rights and Freedoms* affected this situation?

39. The largest damage award given in a defamation case occurred in *Hill v. Church of Scientology of Toronto, supra.* The plaintiff received a total of $1.6 million, made up of compensatory, aggravated and punitive damages. What justified such a high award in that case?

40. When a person's goods are brought into discredit, rather than suing for defamation, the tort of injurious falsehood or slander of goods comes into play. For a discussion of this tort see *Flaman Wholesale Ltd. v. Firman et al.* (1982), 17 Sask. R. 305, 20 C.C.L.T. 246, 65 C.P.R. (2d) 152 (Q.B.) and Irvine, "Annotation" (1982), 20 C.C.L.T. 247. This tort, however, requires proof of actual monetary damages. See *Ferguson v. McBee Technographics Inc.*, [1988] 6 W.W.R. 716, 23 C.P.R. (3d) 47 (Man. Q.B.). Where the plaintiff is seeking an injunction in order to restrain a marketing campaign, proof that actual loss will occur is sufficient; see *Church & Dwight Ltd. v. Sifto Canada Inc.* (1994), 22 C.C.L.T. (2d) 304 (Ont. Gen. Div.).

41. Is a defamation suit a wise option for a person who feels defamed? A study into defamation cases was undertaken by Professor Marc Franklin in the United States. He examined all appellate court decisions reported over a three-year period. The purpose of the research was to determine the nature of defamation cases, the characteristics of the plaintiffs, defendants, and so on. One of the most interesting of the study's results was the demonstration that so few plaintiffs actually won defamation suits. Eighty-six per cent of reported defamation appeals were decided in the defendants' favour. This prompted Professor Franklin to speculate about the continued utility of defamation litigation in view of the low success rate and the high costs of suing. See Franklin, "Winners and Losers and Why: A Study of Defamation Litigation" [1980] A.B.F. Res. J. 457.

    Could one expect the same results if a Canadian study was done? It would be reasonable to speculate that plaintiffs are probably more successful in Canada where the law and our attitudes towards the conflicting interests involved are balanced more towards the plaintiffs. Professor Franklin's study points out the benefits obtained from conducting empirical research into how the law actually operates. Potential plaintiffs would learn, for example, that juries are more favourable to plaintiffs than are judges. Legislators and law reformers might also look at defamation law reform differently if they knew of the study's results.

42. See generally, Williams, *The Law of Libel and Slander in Canada,* 2nd ed. (1988); Gatley, *Libel and Slander*, 9th ed. (1998); Duncan and Neill, *Defamation,* 2nd ed. (1983); Brown, *The Law of Defamation in Canada,* 2nd ed. (1995).

C. LIBEL OR SLANDER?

Actionable defamation has long recognized a basic distinction between the written word (libel) and the spoken word (slander). The legal consequences of this distinction, originally emanating in the seventeenth century from the different functions of the common law courts which dealt with slander (a bequest from the Ecclesiastical Courts), and the Court of Star Chamber, which dealt with libel, have often led to unjust and anomalous results.

Libel, generally, includes writings, signs, pictures, statues, films, and even conduct implying a defamatory meaning. It is actionable without proof of damage since general damages are presumed. Libel is also a crime in many jurisdictions.

Slander is communicated orally and is not actionable *per se*, so that an action lies only if special damages are pleaded and proved. There are, however, four classes of slanderous statements that are actionable *per se* and do not require proof of special damages.

Although this "damage" rule is untenable on policy grounds and often generates unquestionably absurd results, the doctrine is well settled in the law and can only be changed by legislative reform. Because of its wholly arbitrary nature, the libel-slander distinction has led to a good deal of disrespect for the law of defamation in general.

Alberta, Manitoba, New Brunswick, Nova Scotia and Prince Edward Island have enacted legislation, suggested by the Uniformity Commissioners in 1944, that treats libel and slander alike. For example, s. 1(b) of the *Alberta Defamation Act*, R.S.A. 1980, c. D-6, states that "'defamation' means libel or slander". Section 2(2) of the Alberta Act states that "When defamation is proved, damage shall be presumed."

HERBERT, THE UNCOMMON LAW (1935)
CHICKEN v. HAM

Now, my Lords, you are aware that by the mysterious provisions of the English law a defamatory statement may be either a slander or a libel, a slander being, shortly, a defamation by word of mouth, and a libel by the written or printed word; and the legal consequences are in the two cases very different. A layman, with the narrow outlook of a layman on these affairs, might rashly suppose that it is equally injurious to say at a public meeting, "Mr. Chicken is a toad", and to write upon a postcard, "Mr. Chicken is a toad". But the unselfish labours of generations of British jurists have discovered between the two some profound and curious distinctions. For example, in order to succeed in an action for slander the injured party must prove that he has suffered some actual and special damage, whereas the victim of a written defamation need not; so that we have this curious result, that in practice it is safer to insult a man at a public meeting than to insult him on a postcard, and that which is written in the corner of a letter is in law more deadly than that which is shouted from the house-tops. My Lords, it is not for us to boggle at the wisdom of our ancestors, and this is only one of a great body of juridical refinements handed down to us by them, without which few of our profession would be able to keep body and soul together.

MELDRUM v. AUSTRALIAN BROADCASTING CO., LTD.

Supreme Court of Victoria. [1932] V.L.R. 425.

The plaintiff brought an action for defamation alleging in the statement of claim that the defendant "wrote a script" and "read out" the words on the script into a broadcasting apparatus. The words were capable of bearing a defamatory meaning and some of them might have been actionable without proof of special damage if they were a "slander"; others could not have been actionable as a "slander" without proof of special damage. No special damages were alleged. The defendant moved to strike out the statement of claim or to have it amended by striking out those parts which referred to a writing or script and those parts of the words which could not support an action of slander without proof of special damage.

McArthur J.: But for the decision of the Court of Appeal in 1893 in the case of *Forrester v. Tyrell* (1893), 1 T.L.R. 257, which plaintiff's counsel relied upon as being a decision directly in point, I would have had no hesitation in saying that in a civil action for damages the reading out to a third person or persons of written words defamatory of the person defamed constituted a slander and not a libel.

In that most accurate of text-books, the third edition of *Bullen and Leake's Precedents of Pleadings*, at p. 301, the distinction between libel and slander is as follows: "Libel consists in the publication by the defendant, by means of printing, writing, pictures, or the like signs, of matter defamatory to the plaintiff: 3 B1. Com. 125. Slander consists in the publication by the defendant, by means of words spoken, of matter defamatory to the plaintiff: 3 B1. Com. 123.". ...

It was suggested that *Forrester v. Tyrell* might be distinguished from the present case on the facts inasmuch as in that case it was clear that the hearers knew that the defendant was reading from a written document, whereas in the present case the hearers would not necessarily know whether the speaker was reading from a written document or not. In my opinion this distinction is quite immaterial. I cannot see how it can be said that when the hearers know that the speaker is reading from a written document it is a libel, and when they do not know it is a slander. ...

The distinction lies solely, in my opinion, in the mode of publication. Written defamatory words may, of course, be communicated to third persons by word of mouth; but, when so communicated, it is slander and not libel no matter whether the speaker openly reads out the written words, or whether he learns them off by heart and recites them or sings them; so long as the communication is by word of mouth it is, in my opinion, slander and not libel. If, on the other hand, the defamatory words are communicated to the third persons by means of printing, writing, pictures, signs, etc., it is libel and not slander.

It is suggested that this view will not stand the test when it is attempted to apply it to defamation by means of pictures, signs, sculptures, and the like so far at all events as the liability of persons other than those who produced such drawings, etc., is concerned. I do not agree with this. If the defendant showed to a third person, so that he could and did read them, written words defamatory of the plaintiff, though not written by the defendant, it would admittedly be a libel. Similarly, if the defendant showed to a third person a picture or sign or piece of sculpture which was defamatory of the plaintiff, though not painted or executed by the defendant, it would, in my opinion, be a libel. If, on the other hand, the defendant verbally described to a third person the defamatory picture, sign, or piece of sculpture, so as to communicate to a third person by word of mouth the defamatory nature thereof, it would, in my opinion, be a slander and not libel.

It is also said that curious results may be brought about if the law is as I have stated. One instance given is that no one can be "libelled", as distinguished from "slandered", to a blind man — except perhaps by means of Braille writing, which, however, for the purpose of this discussion we may leave out of account — and therefore in no case can the plaintiff recover damages from the publication to a blind man of defamatory matter, without proof of special damage (except, of course, for the publication of defamatory matter of a particular nature for which actions of slander may be brought without proof of special damage). The other instance given was this: showing a document containing written defamatory matter to a third person so that he can and does read it would be a libel, whereas merely reading it to him would be a slander, and not a libel. For the one an action may be brought without proof of special damage, whereas for the other it is necessary to prove special damage. But in each of these instances this peculiarity (if it be a peculiarity) is not due to the definition of libel and slander as such, or to the fundamental distinction between libel and slander as I have stated it, but to the distinction which the law has made between actionable libel and actionable slander — a distinction which some writers have thought unsatisfactory.

In the present case it is quite clear that the statement of claim alleges that the defamatory words complained of were published by means of words spoken, and not by means of writing; and therefore, if it discloses a cause of action at all, it discloses, in my opinion, a cause of action of slander and not libel. The allegation that prior to such publication the defendant's agent "wrote a script" from which he read out the alleged defamatory words is irrelevant and, I think, embarrassing, and should be struck out.

I agree with the order made by the learned Acting Chief Justice, and I am therefore of opinion that the appeal should be dismissed with costs.

[Judgments to the same effect of **Mann** and **Lowe JJ.**, are omitted.]

NOTES

1. In *Lawrence v. Finch* (1931), 66 O.L.R. 451, [1931] 1 D.L.R. 689 (C.A.), Riddell J.A., expressed his preference for the view that a person who dictates defamatory matter to a stenographer which is later transcribed, publishes a slander only.

2. In *Ostrowe v. Lee*, 256 N.Y. 505, 175 N.E. 505 (1931), Cardozo J., held that publication to a stenographer in such a case is libel.

> Many things that are defamatory may be said with impunity through the medium of speech. Not so, however, when speech is caught up on the wing and transmuted into print. What gives the sting to the writing is its permanence of form. The spoken word dissolves, but the written one abides and "perpetuates the scandal". ... There is a publication of a libel if a stenographer reads the notes that have been taken by another. Neither the evil nor the result is different when the notes that he reads have been taken by himself. ...

3. In *Youssoupoff v. Metro-Goldwyn-Mayer Pictures Ltd.* (1934), 50 T.L.R. 581, 78 Sol. Jo. 617 (*sub nom. Princess Alexandrovna v. Metro-Goldwyn-Mayer Pictures Ltd.*) (C.A.), a talking-moving-picture was held to be libel and not slander.

> So far as the photographic part of the exhibition is concerned, that is a permanent matter to be seen by the eye, and is the proper subject of an action for libel, if defamatory. I regard the speech which is synchronized with the photographic reproduction and forms part of one complex, common exhibition, as an ancillary circumstance, part of the surroundings explaining that which is to be seen.

4. How should television be treated?

5. In Ontario, the *Libel and Slander Act*, R.S.O. 1990, c. L.12 provides in s. 2 that "Defamatory words in a newspaper or in a broadcast shall be deemed to be published and to constitute libel." Section 1 provides:

(1) In this Act,

"broadcasting" means the dissemination of writing, signs, signals, pictures and sounds of all kinds, intended to be received by the public either directly or through the medium of relay stations, by the means of,

(*a*) any form of wireless radioelectric communication utilizing Hertzian waves, including radiotelegraph and radiotelephone, or

(*b*) cables, wires, fibre-optic linkages or laser beams,

and "broadcast" has a corresponding meaning.

This legislation reflects the belief that the potential for harm to reputation by means of radio and television is enormous and should be treated like the written word.

6. If defamatory, which of the following actions would be libel and which would be slander?

   (a) Speaking into a loudspeaker to a huge crowd at a public stadium.

   (b) Using sign language. See *Gutsole v. Mathers* (1836), 1 M. & W. 495, 501, 150 E.R. 530.

   (c) Hanging somebody in effigy. See *Eyre v. Garlick* (1878), 42 J.P. 68.

   (d) Meeting an unmarried couple with a charivari, consisting of guns being fired, bells being rung and shouting, according to a local custom for newly married people. See *Varner v. Morton* (1919), 52 N.S.R. 180, 46 D.L.R. 597 (C.A.).

   (e) Exhibiting a statue. See *Monson v. Tussauds, Ltd.*, [1894] 1 Q.B. 671, [1891-4] All E.R. Rep. 1051 (C.A.).

7. The Ontario *Libel and Slander Act*, s. 1(2) provides that "[a]ny reference to words in this Act shall be construed as including a reference to pictures, visual images, gestures and other methods of signifying meaning". Does this enactment affect your answers to any of the above questions?

8. The *Restatement of Torts, Second*, §568, reads as follows:

   (1) Libel consists of the publication of defamatory matter by written or printed words, or by its embodiment in physical form, or by any other form of communication which has the potentially harmful qualities characteristic of written or printed words.

   (2) Slander consists of the publication of defamatory matter by spoken words, transitory gestures, or by any form of communication other than those stated in Subsection (1).

   (3) The area of dissemination, the deliberate and premeditated character of its publication, and the persistence of the defamation are factors to be considered in determining whether a publication is a libel rather than a slander.

   What is your view of this suggestion?

9. The four types of slander actionable *per se* are the following:

   (1) *Imputation of the commission of a crime.* The crime must be a serious one, punishable by a prison term, and not merely a provincial offence. See *Conyd v. Brekelmans* (1971), 18 D.L.R. (3d) 366, [1971] 3 W.W.R. 107 (B.C.S.C.), saying someone would "pocket the money" from a grant is not an accusation

of crime. A general accusation of criminality may suffice; it is not necessary to specify, therefore, a particular crime. See *Curtis v. Curtis* (1834), 10 Bing. 477, 131 E.R. 980; *Webb v. Beavan* (1883), 11 Q.B.D. 609, 52 L.J.Q.B. 544.

(2) *Imputation of a loathsome disease.* To say that a person is suffering from a venereal disease is so likely to cause that person to be ostracized that it is actionable *per se.* See *French (Oscar) v. Smith* (1923), 53 O.L.R. 28, [1923] 3 D.L.R. 902 (H.C.); *Houseman v. Coulson*, [1948] 2 D.L.R. 62, [1947] 2 W.W.R. 1011 (*sub nom. X. v. Y.*) (Sask. K.B.). It is not actionable *per se*, however, to say that someone suffered from a venereal disease in the past. See *Halls v. Mitchell*, [1928] S.C.R. 125, [1928] 2 D.L.R. 97. Leprosy was among the loathsome diseases referred to here, because it seemed lasting and incurable. What about saying someone is incurably insane?

(3) *Imputation of unchastity to a woman.* In the past, to accuse a woman of unchastity has been considered serious enough to make it actionable *per se.* See *French (Elizabeth) v. Smith* (1922), 53 O.L.R. 31, [1923] 3 D.L.R. 904 (S.C.). It was not actionable *per se* to say of a man, however, that he is unchaste. See *Hickerson v. Masters*, 226 S.W. 1072 (1921). It was actionable *per se* to call a woman a lesbian. See *Kerr v. Kennedy*, [1942] 1 K.B. 409, 111 L.J.K.B. 367. So too, to say of a man that he is homosexual. See *Nowark v. Maguire*, 255 N.Y.S. 2d 318 (1964). Does any of this make sense in the 1990s?

(4) *Imputation of unfitness to practice one's trade or profession.* Slandering someone in relation to a trade, profession, office or other employment activity is actionable *per se* because it is clearly calculated to damage a person in a pecuniary way. This applies only to remunerative activities, however, and not to positions of honour that do not yield financial benefits. See *Alexander v. Jenkins*, [1892] 1 Q.B. 797, 71 L.J.Q.B. 634 (C.A.). The person being defamed must be in office at the time of the publication. At one time the words had to be in the way of the person's calling. See *Hopwood v. Muirson*, [1945] K.B. 313, [1945] 1 All E.R. 453 (C.A.). But this has now been abrogated by legislation both in the U.K. and Canada. The Ontario *Libel and Slander Act*, R.S.O. 1990, c. L.12, s. 16, provides that:

> In an action for slander for words calculated to disparage the plaintiff in any office, profession, calling, trade or business held or carried on by the plaintiff at the time of the publication thereof, it is not necessary to allege or prove special damage, whether or not the words are spoken of the plaintiff in the way of the plaintiff's office, profession, calling, trade or business, and the plaintiff may recover damages without averment or proof of special damage.

Is the test for whether the words were "calculated to disparage the plaintiff" in any calling an objective or subjective one?

10. With other types of slander the plaintiff must prove special damages. Often this is no easy matter. It is not enough to show damage to a reputation; there must also be demonstrated some pecuniary loss. The purpose of this requirement is to reduce the number of trivial slander claims. To prove that the plaintiff has lost the society of friends or was made ill as a result of the slander has been held not to amount to special damage. See *Palmer v. Solmes* (1880), 30 U.C.C.P. 481 (C.A.). This decision may, however, be open to review. See Fleming, *The Law of Torts*, 9th ed. (1998), p. 607.

D. PUBLICATION

MCNICHOL v. GRANDY

Supreme Court of Canada. [1931] S.C.R. 696, [1932] 1 D.L.R. 225.

The defendant and the plaintiff met in the dispensary of the plaintiff's drug store. In the course of the conversation the defendant spoke in a loud and angry tone and uttered words defamatory of the plaintiff. An employee of the plaintiff, Kathleen Wilson, went to the dressing room adjoining the dispensary, and her attention was attracted by the loud tones of the defendant which could be heard through the wall. She listened carefully and overheard the entire conversation by reason of a small hole (which had been cut by firefighters in a recent fire) in the wall between the two rooms.

At the trial on an action for slander, the trial judge withdrew the case from the jury on the ground that there was no evidence of publication. The Court of Appeal for Manitoba reversed this judgment and ordered a new trial. The defendant appealed.

Lamont J.: In an action of slander the onus is upon the plaintiff to prove publication in the fact by the defendant, in this sense, that it is publication for which the defendant is responsible. Where statements defamatory of a plaintiff have been uttered by a defendant and overheard by a third person the first inquiry in determining the defendant's responsibility is: Did he intend that anyone but the plaintiff should hear his defamatory utterances? In ascertaining his intention we must proceed in accordance with the fundamental principle referred to by Swinfen Eady, L.J., in the case of *Huth v. Huth*, [1915] 3 K.B. 32, that a man must be taken to intend the natural and probable consequences of his act in the circumstances. In that case the defendant sent through the post in an unclosed letter a written communication which the plaintiffs alleged was defamatory of them. The communication was taken out of the envelope and read by a butler who was a servant in the house at which the plaintiffs were staying. The butler did this out of curiosity and in breach of his duty. It was held that there was no publication by the defendant and that the case was properly withdrawn from the jury by the trial judge. The basis of the decision was that, although there had been publication to the butler, it was not publication for which the defendant was responsible, because there was no evidence that he knew or had reason to suspect or should have contemplated that a letter addressed to the plaintiffs and enclosed in an envelope "but unsealed and unstuck down" would, in the ordinary course, be likely to be opened by the butler or any other servant before being delivered to the defendant's wife. In his judgment Bray, J., said: "In my opinion it is quite clear that, in the absence of some special circumstances, a defendant cannot be responsible for a publication which was the wrongful act of a third person. He cannot be said, except in special circumstances, to have contemplated it. It was not the natural consequence of his sending the letter, or writing, in the way in which he did."...

On the other hand, there is a long line of authorities represented by *Delacroix v. Thevenot* (1817), 2 Starkie 63, and *Gomersall v. Davies* (1898), 14 Times L.R. 430, in which it has been held that, where a defendant, knowing that the plaintiff's letters were usually opened by his clerk, sent a libellous letter addressed to the plaintiff which was opened and read by the clerk lawfully and in the usual course of business, there was publication by the defendant to the plaintiff's clerk. In *Powell v. Gelston*, [1916] 2 K.B. 615, Bray, J., said: "Several cases were cited —

Delacroix v. Thevenot, *Gomersall v. Davies* and *Sharp v. Skues* (1909), 25 Times L.R. 336. They show that where to the defendant's knowledge a letter is likely to be opened by a clerk of the person to whom it is addressed the defendant is responsible for the publication to that clerk. As Lord Ellenborough said in *Delacroix v. Thevenot*, it must be taken that such a publication was intended by the defendant. On the other hand, in *Sharp v. Skues* (1909), 25 Times L.R. 336, Cozens-Hardy, M.R., said: 'It would be a publication if the defendant intended the letter to be opened by a clerk or some third person not the plaintiff, or if to the defendant's knowledge it would be opened by a clerk; but the jury had negatived this in the clearest terms, and under these circumstances it was impossible to hold that some act done by a partner or a clerk of the plaintiff by his direction and for his own convenience when absent from the office could be a publication'."

Then we have the further line of cases which show that where a letter containing defamatory matter concerning the plaintiff has been negligently dropped by the defendant and picked up and read by a third person, the defendant will be held responsible for publication to the person picking it up and reading it: *Weld-Blundell v. Stephens*, [1920] A.C. 956. Also where a letter intended for one person was by mistake sent to another *Thompson v. Dashwood* (1883), 11 Q.B.D. 43. The defendant in these cases was held responsible because the publication was directly due to his want of care.

The facts in the case at bar clearly distinguished it from the case of *Huth v. Huth*, [1915] 3 K.B. 32, upon which the appellant relied. There the publication to the butler resulted from a breach of duty on his part which the defendant could not reasonably be called upon to foresee; while in the case before us the publication to Kathleen Wilson took place while she was performing her duties in the usual course of business, and was not brought about by any improper act of hers.

Then can it be said that the defendant's ignorance (if he was ignorant, for he did not testify) of the presence of Miss Wilson in the dressing room, affords any answer to the plaintiff's claim? Applying the principles set out in the above authorities, we must take it that he intended the natural and probable consequences of his act. The natural and probable consequence of uttering the words used was that all persons of normal hearing who were within the carrying distance of his voice would hear what he said. When, therefore, it was established as a fact that Miss Wilson did overhear him utter the slanderous statements charged against him a *prima facie* case of publication by him was made out and, in order to displace that *prima facie* case the onus was on him to satisfy the jury, not only that he did not intend that anyone other than the plaintiff should hear him, but also that he did not know and had no reason to expect that any of the staff or any other person might be within hearing distance, and that he was not guilty of any want of care in not foreseeing the probability of the presence of someone within hearing range of the speaking tones which he used.

[The judgments of **Anglin C.J.C.**, and **Duff J.**, to the same effect are omitted. The appeal was dismissed.]

NOTES

1. Suppose the defendant was speaking in Greek to the plaintiff, who was also Greek, and the person listening knew no Greek at all, though actually hearing every word

spoken. Publication? See *Economopoulos v. A.G. Pollard Co.*, 105 N.E. 896 (Mass. 1914).

2. What if defamatory words are spoken to an individual in the presence of others, but they do not actually hear what was said? See *Sheffill v. Van Densen*, 13 Gray (Mass.) 304 (1859). What if a three-year-old child, who cannot understand the word, hears someone call his or her mother a "thief"? See *Sullivan v. Sullivan*, 48 Ill. App. 435 (1892).

3. The *Libel and Slander Act*, R.S.O. 1990, c. L.12, s. 2 states:

   > Defamatory words in a newspaper or in a broadcast shall be deemed to be published and to constitute libel.

   What is the effect of this section?

4. Which, if any, of the following are publications?
   (a) X. dictates a defamatory letter to a secretary, who types it up. X. then burns it. See *Osborn v. Thomas Boulter & Son*, [1930] 2 K.B. 226, [1930] All E.R. Rep. 154 (C.A.); *Pullman v. Hill & Co.*, [1891] 1 Q.B. 524, 60 L.J.Q.B. 299 (C.A.); *Simons v. Carr & Co.*, [1996] 10 W.W.R. 64 (Alta. Q.B.).
   (b) P., a 14-year-old boy, gets a letter accusing him of theft. He shows it to his older brother seeking his advice. See *Hedgepeth v. Coleman*, 111 S.E. 517 (S.C. of N.C. 1922). What if the recipient of the letter is a middle-aged woman? See *Hills v. O'Bryan*, [1949] 2 D.L.R. 716, [1949] 1 W.W.R. 985 (B.C.S.C.).
   (c) Perry, who is illiterate, receives a defamatory letter and asks his wife to read it to him. Would it make any difference if the defendant is aware or unaware of Perry's illiteracy? See *Jackson v. Staley* (1885), 9 O.R. 334 (C.A.).
   (d) Donald hears a defamatory statement being made by Dick. He repeats it to Ezra, saying, "Have you heard the rumour?" Publication by Donald? See *Houseman v. Coulson*, [1948] 2 D.L.R. 62, [1947] 2 W.W.R. 1011 (*sub nom. X. v. Y.*) (Sask. K.B.).
   (e) An author delivers his manuscript to a printer for printing and binding. The printer does its work and delivers copies of the completed book to the author. Publication by the printer? Does it matter whether the printer read the manuscript, edited it, or knew that it contained libellous statements? See *Menear v. Miguna* (1996), 32 C.C.L.T. (2d) 35 (Ont. Gen. Div.).
   (f) What if a newspaper prints a defamatory story that it picks up from the C.P. wire service? Publication by the newspaper? What if someone sells a magazine knowing it contains a defamatory article? What if several newspapers publish essentially the same story? Does each publication give rise to a new cause of action? See *Dickhoff v. Armadale Communications Ltd.*, [1994] 1 W.W.R 468 (Sask. C.A.).

5. In *Byrne v. Deane*, [1937] 1 K.B. 818, [1937] 2 All E.R. 204 (C.A.), some members of a golf club placed a poster containing material defamatory of the plaintiff on the wall of the club. The defendants, proprietors of the club, were held liable to the plaintiff since, having knowledge of the poster and the power to remove it, their failure so to do constituted publication. The Court of Appeal held that failure to remove defamatory matter may amount to publication where removal is simple and easy. On the other hand, it would be difficult, if not impossible, to draw an inference of "volition" from failure to remove deeply chiselled defamation from stonework of a building.

6. In *Duke of Brunswick v. Harmer* (1849), 14 Q.B. 185, 117 E.R. 75, the defendant's newspaper published a libel of the plaintiff. Seventeen years later an agent of the plaintiff purchased a copy of the newspaper at the newspaper office. In an action brought for libel seven months after such purchase, the defendant pleaded the Statute

of Limitations (21 Jac.I, c. 16, s. 3) which provided that an action for libel must be brought within six years from the date when the cause of action arose. The court held that the statute was no bar since, by the sale of a copy, the defendant had made a distinct and separate publication which gave rise to a separate cause of action. But *cf.*, *Thomson v. Lambert*, [1938] S.C.R. 253, [1938] 2 D.L.R. 545, limiting causes of action to one.

7. The American *Restatement of Torts* in §578, Comment (b) states the following rule:

> Each time a libellous article is brought to the attention of a third person, a new publication has occurred, and each publication is a separate tort. Thus, each time a libellous book or paper or magazine is sold, a new publication has taken place which … will support a separate action for damages against the seller.

An increasing number of American decisions (as well as those of the Supreme Court of Canada) now support the "single publication" rule to the effect that "where large distributions of published matter are involved, the cause of action accrues, for the purpose of the statute of limitations, upon the first publication, when the issue goes into circulation generally": *Hartmann v. Time, Inc.*, 64 F. Supp. 671 (Penn. D.C. 1946); *Winrod v. Time, Inc.*, 334 Ill. App. 59, 78 N.E. 2d 708 (C.A. 1948); *Ogden v. Association of U.S. Army*, 177 F. Supp. 498 (D.C. of D.C. 1959). There is now a Uniform Single Publication Act, which has been adopted by several states, including California and Pennsylvania.

8. Those who participate together in the publication of a defamation can be liable as "joint tortfeasors". They also will be liable for a subsequent republication if this is a "natural and logical consequence" of the first publication. See *Botiuk v. Toronto Free Press Publications Ltd.* (1995), 26 C.C.L.T. (2d) 109 (S.C.C.).

9. In Canada, several provinces provide by legislation for a short period of limitation in the case of libel in local newspapers or broadcasts. Thus, in Ontario, the *Libel and Slander Act*, R.S.O. 1990, c. L.12, provides in s. 5(1) that "[n]o action for libel in a newspaper or in a broadcast lies unless the plaintiff has, within six weeks after the alleged libel has come to the plaintiff's knowledge, given to the defendant notice in writing, specifying the matter complained of …".

By the Ontario Act, s. 6, actions for libel in a newspaper or a broadcast must be commenced within three months after the libel has come to the knowledge of the person defamed, but if an action is brought within that time, such action may include a claim for any other libel against the plaintiff by the defendant in the same newspaper or broadcast from the same station within a period of one year before the commencement of the action. Section 5(1) and s. 6 "apply only to newspapers printed and published in Ontario and to broadcasts from a station in Ontario" (s. 7).

E. BASIS OF LIABILITY

E. HULTON & CO. v. JONES

House of Lords. [1910] A.C. 20, 79 L.J.K.B. 198,
101 L.T. 831, 26 T.L.R. 128.

The plaintiff, Mr. Thomas Artemus Jones, a barrister practicing on the North Wales Circuit, brought the action to recover damages for the publication of an alleged libel concerning him contained in an article in the *Sunday Chronicle*, a newspaper of which the defendants were the printers, proprietors, and publishers. The article which was written by the Paris correspondent of the paper, purported to describe a motor festival at Dieppe, and the parts chiefly complained of ran thus: "Upon the terrace marches the world, attracted by the motor races — a world immensely pleased with itself, and minded to draw a wealth of inspiration — and, incidentally, of golden cocktails — from any scheme to speed the passing hour ... 'Whist! there is Artemus Jones with a woman who is not his wife, who must be you know — the other thing!' whispers a fair neighbour of mine excitedly into her bosom friend's ear. Really, is it not surprising how certain of our fellow-countrymen behave when they come abroad? Who would suppose, by his goings on, that he was a churchwarden at Peckham? No one, indeed, would assume that Jones, in the atmosphere of London would take on so austere a job as the duties of a churchwarden. Here, in the atmosphere of Dieppe, on the French side of the Channel, he is the life and soul of a gay little band that haunts the Casino and turns night into day, besides betraying a most unholy delight in the society of female butterflies." The defendants alleged that the name chosen for the purpose of the article was a fictitious one, having no reference to the plaintiff, and chosen as unlikely to be the name of a real person, and they denied that any officer or member of their staff who wrote or printed or published or said before publication the words complained of knew the plaintiff or his name or his profession, or his association with the journal or with the defendants, or that there was any existing person bearing the name of or known as Artemus Jones. They admitted publication, but denied that the words were published of or concerning the plaintiff. On the part of the plaintiff the evidence of the writer of the article and of the editor of the paper that they knew nothing of the plaintiff, and that the article was not intended by them to refer to them, was accepted as true. At the trial witnesses were called for the plaintiff, who said that they had read the article and thought that it referred to the plaintiff. The jury returned a verdict for the plaintiff with 1750*l* damages. The defendants' appeal to the Court of Appeal, and a further appeal to the House of Lords, were dismissed.

Lord Loreburn L.C.: Libel is a tortious act. What does the tort consist in? It consists in using language which others knowing the circumstances would reasonably think to be defamatory of the person complaining of and injured by it. A person charged with libel cannot defend himself by shewing that he intended in his own breast not to defame, or that he intended not to defame the plaintiff, if in fact he did both. He has none the less imputed something disgraceful and has none the less injured the plaintiff. A man in good faith may publish a libel believing it to be true, and it may be found by the jury that he acted in good faith believing it to be true, and reasonably believing it to be true, but that in fact the statement was false. Under those circumstances he has no defence to the action, however excellent his intention. If the intention of the writer be immaterial in considering whether the matter written is defamatory, I do not see why it need be relevant in considering whether it is defamatory of the plaintiff. The writing, according to the old form must be malicious, and it must be of and concerning the plaintiff. Just as the defendant could not excuse himself from malice by proving that he wrote it in the most benevolent spirit, so he cannot shew that the libel was not of and concerning the plaintiff by proving that he never heard of the plaintiff. His intention in both respects equally is inferred from what he did. His remedy is to abstain from defamatory words.

NOTES

1. The law on this point has been summed up as follows: "The question is not so much who was aimed at as who was hit." See *Corrigan v. Bobbs-Merrill Co.*, 126 N.E. 260 (N.Y. 1920), a case involving a supposedly fictitious book which referred to a New York City magistrate without realizing it. The court explained: "The fact that the publisher has no actual intention to defame a particular man or indeed to injure anyone does not prevent recovery of compensatory damages by one who connects himself with the publication."

2. It used to be that malice was required for slander, a carry-over from the ecclesiastical law. See Veeder, "History and Theory of the Law of Defamation" (1904), 4 Colum. L. Rev. 33. In 1825, however, the law began to imply malice, distinguishing between "malice in fact and malice in law". See *Bromage v. Prosser* (1825), 4 B. & C. 247, 107 E.R. 1051. Eventually, malice became a fiction only and defamation became strictly actionable without proof of intention or negligence. See *Morrison v. Ritchie & Co.*, 4 F. (Ct. of Sess.) 645, 39 Scot. L.R. 432 (1902), liability when birth of twins announced mistakenly, without knowledge of marriage four weeks before.

3. In *Newstead v. London Express Newspaper Ltd.*, [1940] 1 K.B. 377, [1939] 4 All E.R. 319 (C.A.), the defendant published a story about a bigamy trial and wrote that "Harold Newstead, 30-year old Camberwell man, who was jailed for nine months, liked having two wives at once". These words were true of a man called Henry Newstead, a barman of Camberwell, but the plaintiff, Harold Cecil Newstead, about 30 years of age, a hairdresser in Camberwell, sued, alleging the words were defamatory of him. During the course of the judgment Sir Wilfred Greene M.R. stated:

   > After giving careful consideration to the matter, I am unable to hold that the fact that defamatory words are true of A, makes it as a matter of law impossible for them to be defamatory of B, which was in substance the main argument on behalf of the appellants. At first sight this looks as though it would lead to great hardship. But the hardships are in practice not so serious as might appear, at any rate in the case of statements which are *ex facie* defamatory. Persons who make statements of this character may not unreasonably be expected, when describing the person of whom they are made, to identify that person so closely as to make it very unlikely that a judge would hold them to be reasonably capable of referring to someone else, or that a jury would hold that they did so refer. This is particularly so in the case of statements which purport to deal with actual facts. If there is a risk of coincidence it ought, I think, in reason to be borne not by the innocent party to whom the words are held to refer, but by the party who puts them into circulation. In matters of fiction, there is no doubt more room for hardship. Even in the case of matters of fact it is no doubt possible to construct imaginary facts which would lead to hardship. There may also be hardship if words, not on their faces defamatory, are true of A, but are reasonably understood by some as referring to B, and as applied to B are defamatory. But such cases must be rare. The law as I understand it is well settled, and can only be altered by legislation.

4. In *Lee v. Wilson and MacKinnon* (1935), 51 C.L.R. 276, [1935] V.L.R. 113, the defendant newspaper, in reporting a trial, stated that the prisoner had charged "detective Lee" of the local police force with taking a bribe. There were two constables, A.L. Lee and Clifford Lee, on the force, and both were known as "detective Lee". Both brought actions for libel, and the actions were tried together. At the trial, evidence was offered that the reference was to a third constable Lee of the motor vehicles department. The High Court of Australia held that the evidence was properly excluded and both plaintiffs could recover damages.

CASSIDY v. DAILY MIRROR NEWSPAPERS, LTD.

Court of Appeal. [1929] 2 K.B. 331, 98 L.J.K.B. 595, 141 L.T. 404, 45 T.L.R. 485.

Scrutton L.J.: The facts in this case are simple. A man named Cassidy, who for some reason also called himself Corrigan and described himself as a General in the Mexican Army, was married to a lady who also called herself Cassidy or Mrs. Corrigan. Her husband occasionally came and stayed with her at her flat, and her acquaintances met him. Cassidy achieved some notoriety in racing circles and in indiscriminate relations with women, and at a race meeting he posed, in company with a lady, to a racing photographer, to whom he said he was engaged to marry the lady and the photographer might announce it. The photographer, without any further inquiry, sent the photograph to the *Daily Mirror* with an inscription: "Mr. M. Corrigan, the race horse owner, and Miss X" — I omit the name — "whose engagement has been announced," and the *Daily Mirror* published the photograph and inscription. This paper was read by the female acquaintances of Mrs. Cassidy or Mrs. Corrigan, who gave evidence that they understood from it that the lady was not married to Mr. M. Corrigan and had no legal right to take his name, and that they formed a bad opinion of her in consequence. Mrs. Cassidy accordingly brought an action for libel against the newspaper setting out these words with an innuendo, meaning thereby that the plaintiff was an immoral woman who had cohabited with Corrigan without being married to him.

At the trial counsel for the defendants objected that the words were not capable of a defamatory meaning. McCardie, J., held that they were; the jury found that they did reasonably bear a defamatory meaning and awarded the plaintiff 500*l.* damages. ...

The real questions involved were: (1) Was the alleged libel capable of a defamatory meaning? (2) As the defendants did not know the facts which caused the friends of Mrs. Cassidy to whom they published the words to draw defamatory inferences from them about the plaintiff, were they liable for those inferences?

Now the alleged libel does not mention the plaintiff, but I think it is clear that words published about A may indirectly be defamatory of B. For instance, "A is illegitimate". To persons who know the parents those words may be defamatory of the parents. Or again, "A has given way to drink; it is unfortunately hereditary"; to persons who know A's parents these words may be defamatory. Or "A holds a D. Litt. degree of the University at X, the only one awarded". To persons who know B, who habitually describes himself (and rightly so) as "D. Litt. of X", these words may be capable of a defamatory meaning. Similarly, to say that A is a single man or a bachelor may be capable of a defamatory meaning if published to persons who know a lady who passes as Mrs. A and whom A visits. ...

In my view the words published were capable of the meaning "Corrigan is a single man", and were published to people who knew the plaintiff professed to be married to Corrigan; it was for the jury to say whether those people could reasonably draw the inference that the so-called Mrs. Corrigan was in fact living in immoral cohabitation with Corrigan, and I do not think their finding should be interfered with.

But the second point taken was that the defendants could not be liable for the inference drawn, because they did not know the facts which enabled some persons to whom the libel was published, to draw an inference defamatory of the plaintiff. This was rested on some dicta of Brett, L.J., in *Henty's* case, 5 C.P.D. 539, that the evidence which made apparently innocent statements defamatory must be, "known both to the person who wrote the document and to the persons to whom it was published." This, I think, was originally obiter, and, since the decision in *E. Hulton & Co. v. Jones*, is no longer law. ...

In my view, since *E. Hulton & Co. v. Jones*, it is impossible for the person publishing a statement which, to those who know certain facts, is capable of a defamatory meaning in regard to A, to defend himself by saying: "I never heard of A and did not mean to injure him." If he publishes words reasonably capable of being read as relating directly or indirectly to A and, to those who know the facts about A, capable of a defamatory meaning, he must take the consequences of the defamatory inferences reasonably drawn from his words.

It is said that this decision would seriously interfere with the reasonable conduct of newspapers. I do not agree. If publishers of newspapers, who have no more rights than private persons, publish statements which may be defamatory of other people, without inquiry as to their truth, in order to make their paper attractive, they must take the consequences, if on subsequent inquiry, their statements are found to be untrue or capable of defamatory inferences. No one could contend that "M. Corrigan, General in the Mexican Army", was "a source in whom we have full confidence." To publish statements first and inquire into their truth afterwards, may seem attractive and up to date. Only to publish after inquiry may be slow, but at any rate it would lead to accuracy and reliability.

In my opinion the appeal should be dismissed with costs. ...

NOTES

1. Professor Fleming has summarized the law regarding fault in this area as follows: "There is no liability for intentionally defamatory matter published accidentally, unlike accidentally defamatory matter published intentionally." *Law of Torts*, 9th ed. (1998), p. 599. Does this distinction make any sense at all?

2. What do you think about Professor Weiler's comments in "Defamation, Enterprise Liability and Freedom of Speech" (1967), 17 U. Toronto L.J. 278, at 285:

> If any distinction, for purposes of fault as opposed to strict liability, is possible in this area, it should be between those statements which are defamatory of the plaintiff on their face, and those which are innocent on their face and defamatory only by reason of extrinsic facts that are not reasonably knowable to the defendant. Such a distinction is the present basis of the developing doctrine of libel per quod in the United States. This doctrine limits the incidence of liability for libellous statements innocent on their face by requiring the proof of "special" damages as a condition of liability. Although this is an indirect and rather irrational way of achieving the result of a lesser incidence of defamatory liability (and perhaps justified only in terms of a somewhat misconceived deference for precedent), there is a real basis in fact to the distinction. Those statements which are defamatory on their face (and for which liability depends on their truth) can be seen by the defendant "publisher" to be a dangerous and harmful instrumentality as far as the plaintiff's reputation is concerned. It may not be unfair to require the defendant, who can fairly know the risk he is running, to bear the responsibility for the harm he causes if his (reasonable) belief that the statement is true proves unfounded. This is of course subject to the caveat that the issue of fault regarding the truth of the statement will become privileged if the interests of the parties concerned make it imperative that the statement be made (and thus the occasion becomes privileged). On the other hand, with regard to statements which are innocent on their face, the defendant

> is in no position to decide whether he will run the risks in making the particular statement, if it should prove to be untrue. Surely we ought not to be required to run this risk as to all statements we make, however innocent they seem, and thus another rationale must be found for strict liability.

American legal commentators have not been silent on this subject and alternative doctrines have been suggested and occasionally accepted by their courts. See Prosser, "Libel Per Quod" (1960), 46 Va. L. Rev. 389; Eldredge, "The Spurious Rule of Libel Per Quod" (1966), 79 Harv. L. Rev. 733; Prosser, "More Libel Per Quod", *ibid.*, at 1629.

VIZETELLY v. MUDIE'S SELECT LIBRARY, LTD.

Court of Appeal. [1900] 2 Q.B. 170, 69 L.J.Q.B. 645, 16 T.L.R. 352.

A book published in October, 1898, by Messrs. Archibald Constable & Co., called *Emin Pasha: his Life and Work*, contained a passage defamatory of the plaintiff. The latter brought action against the publishers for libel which action was settled by the publishers paying 100*l*. damages, apologizing and undertaking to withdraw the libel from circulation. In the issue of the Publishers' Circular for November 12, 1898, the publishers inserted a notice requesting that all copies of "The Life and Work of Emin Pasha" be returned immediately as they wished to cancel a page and insert another in its place. A similar note appeared on the same date in the *Athenaeum* newspaper.

In March, 1899, it came to the plaintiff's knowledge that the defendants, proprietors of a circulating library, were lending copies of the book as originally published and selling surplus copies. The plaintiff brought action for libel against the defendants.

At the trial it appeared that no one in the defendants' business had seen the notices which the publishers had circulated although the defendants took both papers in which the notices appeared. A managing director of the defendants testified that it was impossible for the defendants to have all books that they circulated read. On cross-examination he said there was no one other than himself and his co-directors who exercised any supervision over the books; they did not employ a reader and although on one or two occasions they had books which contained a libel they had never before been subject to an action; it was cheaper for them to run an occasional risk of an action than to have a reader.

Grantham, J., in summing up, directed the jury to consider whether, having regard to the evidence, the defendants had used due care in the management of their business. The jury found a verdict for the plaintiff, damages 100*l*. The defendants appealed.

Romer L.J.: The law of libel is in some respects a very hard one. In the remarks which I am about to make I propose to deal only with communications which are not privileged. For many years it has been well settled law that a man who publishes a libel is liable to an action, although he is really innocent in the matter, and guilty of no negligence. That rule has been so long established as to be incapable of being altered or modified, and the Courts, in endeavouring to mitigate the hardship resulting from it in many cases, have only been able to do so by holding that, under the circumstances of cases before them, there had been no publication of the libel by the defendant. The result, in my opinion, has been that the decisions on the subject have not been altogether logical or satisfactory on principle. The decisions in some of the earlier cases with which the Courts had to deal are easy to understand. Those were cases in which mere carriers of documents containing libels, who had nothing to do with and were ignorant of the contents of what they carried, have been held not to have published libels. Then we have the case of *Emmens v. Pottle*, in which vendors of newspapers in the ordinary course of their business sold a newspaper which contained a libel. It was clear that selling a document which contained a libel was prima facie a publication of it, but the Court then held that there was no publication of the libel under the circumstances which appeared from the special findings of the jury, those findings being (1.) that the defendants did not know that the newspapers at the time they sold them contained libels on the plaintiff; (2.) that it was not by negligence on the defendants' part that they did not know that there was any libel in the newspapers; and (3.) that the defendants did not know that the newspaper was of such a character that it was likely to contain libellous matter, nor ought they to have known so. Lord Esher M.R. in this Court was of opinion that, though the vendors of the newspapers, when they sold them, were prima facie publishers of the libel, yet, when the special findings of the jury were looked at, the result was that there was no publication of the libel by the defendants. Bowen L.J. put his judgment on the ground that the vendors of the newspapers in that case were really only in the same position as an ordinary carrier of work containing a libel. The decision in that case, in my opinion, worked substantial justice; but, speaking for myself, I cannot say that the way in which that result was arrived at appears to me altogether unsatisfactory; I do not think that the judgments very clearly indicate on what principle Courts ought to act in dealing with similar cases in future. That case was followed by other cases, more or less similar to it, namely, *Ridgway v. Smith & Son*, *Mallon v. W.W. Smith & Son*, and *Martin v. Trustees of the British Museum*. The result of the cases is I think that, as regards a person who is not the printer or the first work or main publisher of a work which contains a libel, but has only taken, what I may call, a subordinate part in disseminating it, in considering whether there has been publication of it by him, the particular circumstances under which he disseminated the work must be considered. If he did it in the ordinary way of his business, the nature of the business and the way in which it was conducted must be looked at; and, if he succeeds in shewing (1.) that he was innocent of any knowledge of the libel contained in the work disseminated by him, (2.) that there was nothing in the work or the circumstances under which it came to him or was disseminated by him which ought to have led him to suppose that it contained a libel, and (3.) that, when the work was disseminated by him, it was not by any negligence on his part that he did not know that it contained the libel, then, although the dissemination of the work by him was prima facie publication of it, he may nevertheless, on proof of the before-mentioned facts, be held not to have published it. But the onus of proving such facts lies on him, and the question of publication or non-publication is in such a case one for the jury. Applying this view of the law to the present case, it appears to me that the jury, looking at all the circumstances of the case, have in effect found that the defendants published the libel complained of, and therefore the defendants are liable, unless that verdict is disturbed. Looking at the special circumstances of the case which were brought to the attention of the jury, I cannot say that they could not reasonably find as they did. The only remaining question is whether the summing-up and direction of the learned judge were such as would justify us in sending down the case for a new trial. I find no misdirection in point of law, and though, with great respect to the learned judge, I do not think that all he said was correct, or justified by the evidence, the jury had the facts fully put before them, and on the whole I do not think that there was anything in the summing-up which caused the jury to come to an erroneous conclusion, or which would justify us in granting a new trial. For these reasons I think the application must be dismissed.

Application dismissed.

NOTES

1. Does this case make sense to you? Why treat libraries differently than newspapers or book publishers? How about book printers? See *Menear v. Miguna* (1996), 32 C.C.L.T. (2d) 35 (Ont. Gen. Div.) and the accompanying "Annotation" by R. Harris and P. Bujold. The case held that the defence of "innocent dissemination" is available to a printer of a book.

2. In *Bottomley v. F. W. Woolworth & Co. Ltd.* (1932), 48 T.L.R. 521 (C.A.), the defendant sold many copies of an American magazine called *Detective Story Magazine*, which contained material defamatory to the plaintiff. The action was dismissed at trial and on appeal Strutton L.J. relying on *Vizetelly* stated:

   > There was no evidence to justify the jury's finding that there was anything in the magazine which ought to have led the defendants to suppose that it contained libel.

3. In *Balabanoff v. Fossani*, 81 N.Y.S. 2d 732 (1948), the court stated:

   > It is a good defense to a libel action for a vendor or distributor of a newspaper or other periodical to show that he had no knowledge of the libelous matter and that there were no extraneous facts which should have put him on guard. Such vendor or distributor is liable, however, if he had knowledge that the newspaper or periodical contained libelous matter.

4. How should local radio or T.V. stations be treated when they merely broadcast what is supplied to them by national networks without checking the material? What if they rent their facilities to someone who defames the plaintiff? See *Kelly v. Hoffman*, 61 A. 2d 143 (N.J. 1948), where Burling J. stated:

   > The defendant-respondent as a radio broadcasting company which leased its facilities is not liable for a defamatory statement during a radio broadcast by the person hired by the lessees and not in the employ of the radio broadcasting company, the words being carried to the radio listeners by its facilities, if it could not have prevented publication by the exercise of reasonable care.

   Wachenfeld J. dissented and explained:

   > The defamation when transmitted by radio cannot effectively be eradicated by retraction or any other procedure. The utterance once made, the damage ensues. It could not have been made except for the use of the facilities and the equipment owned, maintained and provided by the broadcasting company. Its responsibility to the party injured should be definite, clear and absolute.

   See also *Summit Hotel Co. v. N.B.C.*, 8 A. 2d 302 (Pa. 1939).

5. Some relief has been afforded the media for publishing defamatory material in error. The Ontario *Libel and Slander Act*, R.S.O. 1990, c. L.12, s. 5(2), for example, allows recovery only of "actual damages" if an alleged libel was "published in good faith", that it "took place in mistake or misapprehension of the facts" and a "full and fair re-

traction" is published immediately. Pursuant to s. 9, newspapers and broadcasters may also plead in mitigation of damage that the libel was done "without actual malice and without gross negligence" and that a "full apology" was made "at the earliest opportunity". See *Munro v. Toronto Sun Publishing Corp.* (1982), 39 O.R. (2d) 100, 21 C.C.L.T. 261 (H.C.J.). The question of retractions and apologies has been in issue in the following cases. In *Tait v. New Westminister Radio* (1984), 15 D.L.R. (4th) 115, 31 C.C.L.T. 189, the B.C. Court of Appeal held that the trial judge was correct in taking the defendant's apology into account in quantifying damages, even though the requirements of the *Libel and Slander Act,* R.S.B.C. 1979, c. 234, *i.e.*, that there be an absence of malice and gross negligence, were not met. As to what constitutes a proper apology, for the purpose of Alberta's *Defamation Act,* R.S.A. 1980, c. D-6, see *Snider v. Calgary Herald* (1985), 41 Alta. L.R. (2d) 11, 34 C.C.L.T. 27 (Q.B.). On the question of "full and fair retraction" under Ontario's legislation, see *Wiley v. Toronto Star Newspapers Ltd.* (1988), 65 O.R. (2d) 31, 51 D.L.R. (4th) 439 (Ont. H.C.J.); vard (1990), 74 O.R. (2d) 100, 69 D.L.R. (4th) 448 (C.A.). The timing of an apology can even aggravate damages; see *Good v. North Delta-Surrey Sentinel*, [1985] 1 W.W.R. 166 (S.C.); affd, [1986] 3 W.W.R. 333 (B.C.C.A.).

6. As to defamation by a telegraph company, see *Silver v. Dominion Telegraph Co.* (1882), 10 S.C.R. 238; *Kahn v. Gt. Northwestern Telegraph Co.* (1930), 39 O.W.N. 11; affd, 39 O.W.N. 143 (C.A.). See Smith, "Liability of a Telegraph Company for Transmitting a Defamatory Message" (1920), 20 Colum. L. Rev. 30, 369; also 29 Mich. L. Rev. 339.

7. In *Allan v. Bushnell T.V. Co. Ltd.*, [1969] 2 O.R. 6, 4 D.L.R. (3d) 212, the Ontario Court of Appeal ruled that, in the absence of any relationship analogous to that of principal and agent, a television station is not bound by the malice or gross negligence of a news agency that supplies the station with reports.

8. In Canada, liability for a defamatory statement published either intentionally or negligently is strict. There are no exceptions to this fundamental proposition. As a result of the landmark decision in *New York Times v. Sullivan*, 376 U.S. 254 (1964), the situation in the United States is significantly different. In that case, the plaintiff claimed he had been libelled by an advertisement carried by the *New York Times*. The *Times* was found liable by the Supreme Court of Alabama. The United States Supreme Court, however, held that the constitutional protection of freedom of speech and the press, prevented liability for critical attacks on public figures, even if these attacks were factually inaccurate and defamatory. In order to be successful, the plaintiff must establish that the defendant made the statements with knowledge that they were false or with a reckless disregard for whether they were true or false. Since the decision, there have been many cases refining the principle. The most important element has been to define what was meant by the notion of a "public" figure. In *Gertz v. Robert Welch Inc.*, 418 U.S. 323 (1974), first amendment protection was refused in a case involving a private complainant. For a good discussion of this problem, especially as it relates to libellous material in a fictional work, see Wilson, "The Law of Libel and The Art of Fiction" (1981), 44 Law & Contemp. Probs. 27.

   Also see, Kaminsky, "Defamation Law: Once a Public Figure Always a Public Figure?" (1982), 10 Hofstra L. Rev. 803; "Determination of Public Figure Status in Libel Actions" (1982), 6 Am. J. Trial Advoc. 204.

9. Should Canadian defamation law move towards the American position or remain with the English? For a comparison of the two, and an assessment, see Zillman, "The American Approach to Defamation" (1980), 9 Anglo-Am. L. Rev. 316.

10. Since the introduction of the *Canadian Charter of Rights and Freedoms*, the question as to what effect the Charter has on defamation law has been discussed in numerous

cases. It has generally been held that defamation laws should not be changed by the Charter, either because the Charter is inapplicable at all to common law litigation between private parties, or because the principles of defamation law are consistent with Charter values in any event. See, for example, *Bank of British Columbia v. Canadian Broadcasting Corp.* (1993), 18 C.C.L.T. (2d) 149 (B.C.S.C.); affd (1995), 25 C.C.L.T. (2d) 229 (B.C.C.A.); *Hill v. Church of Scientology of Toronto* (1994), 114 D.L.R. (4th) 1; affd, (1995), 126 D.L.R. (4th) 129, 25 C.C.L.T. (2d) 89 (S.C.C.); and *Moises v. Canadian Newspaper Co.* (1996), 30 C.C.L.T. (2d) 145, [1997] 1 W.W.R. 337 (B.C.C.A.). In the *Hill* case, Cory J. dealt extensively with this issue and held that:

> (1) The Charter does not apply to the common law of defamation, even if one of the parties suing happens to be a government employee;
>
> (2) Private litigants can argue that the common law of defamation is inconsistent with Charter values, although under this principle courts should only use the Charter as a guide and should not make far-reaching changes to the common law;
>
> (3) The party alleging that the common law is inconsistent with the Charter has the onus of proving both that the common law fails to comply with Charter values and that a balancing of the values requires a modification of the common law.

The Supreme Court held that the Canadian common law of defamation need not be modified since it adequately balances the values at stake and does comply with the underlying values of the Charter. The Court expressly rejected the adoption of the principle of *New York Times Co. v. Sullivan* in defamation actions between private litigants.

Does the *Hill* case effectively put an end to the use of the Charter in all defamation litigation? How about when defamation legislation is under scrutiny? In view of Cory J.'s judgment do you think it likely that the Supreme Court of Canada will change defamation laws due to the Charter in any case? See Ross, "The Common Law of Defamation Fails To Enter the Age Of the Charter" (1996), 35 Alta. L. Rev. 117; Boivin," Accomodating Freedom of Expression And Reputation In The Common Law Of Defamation" (1997), 22 Queens L.J. 229.

11. The issue of the Charter, defamation law, and the difference between the Canadian and American attitudes was discussed by Richard J. in *Coates v. The Citizen* (1988), 85 N.S.R. (2d) 146, 44 C.C.L.T. 286 (T.D.). Mr. Justice Richard held that the Charter applied to defamation law, at least insofar as the provincial statutes were involved. Are the provisions of these statutes which require defendants in defamation actions to prove truth, the absence of malice, and which presume damages, in violation of the Charter? The court did not think so. The trial judge drew special attention to the difference in "constitutional ambience" between Canada and the United States due to the presence of s. 1 of the Charter. In defending the Canadian position, Richards J. subscribed to the views of Brown, *Law of Defamation in Canada* (1987), vol. 1, pp. 5-6:

> Unlike their American colleagues, therefore, our judges have weighed more heavily the value of personal reputation over those of free speech and free press. Thus there occurs in many of their decisions a careful reminder that these freedoms are ones "governed by law" and that there is no "freedom to make untrue defamatory statements".
>
> The press in Canada, particularly, has received no special protection in the law of defamation. The courts have been unwilling to recognize any unique prerogatives on the part of the press to communicate matters of public interest or

> concern to the general public. Thus, Canadian courts have stated emphatically that the press enjoys no privilege of free speech greater than enjoyed by a private individual and that the liberty of the press is no greater than the liberty of every subject.
>
> This is not intended as an invidious comparison. Our judges cherish free speech and a free press no less than their American counterparts. They just happen to value personal reputation, particularly the reputation of their public servants, more.

Do you agree?

12. The potential impact of the Charter on Canadian defamation law is evident in the judgment of the B.C. Court of Appeal in *Westbank Band of Indians v. Tomat* (1992), 88 D.L.R. (4th) 401, 10 C.C.L.T. (2d) 1. In reversing a trial judgment which awarded the plaintiffs substantial damages in a defamation suit, Wood J.A. stated that previous authorities which suggested that public authorities defamed in connection with their public duties should be awarded higher damages than other claimants must now be questioned in light of the Charter values. According to Wood J.A., these common law rules belong "to an earlier and very different era". Wood J.A. also referred to Iacobucci J.'s statement in *R. v. Salituro*, [1991] 3 S.C.R. 654, 68 C.C.C. (3d) 289, that "[w]here the principles underlying a common law rule are out of step with the values enshrined in the Charter, the courts should scrutinize the rule closely".

    Do you think that the common law of defamation is out of step with the Charter?

F. DEFENCES

1. Truth

FLEMING, THE LAW OF TORTS
9th ed. (1998)

At common law, truth is a complete answer to a civil action for defamation and the only defence known generally by the name of "justification". It is not that libel must be false but that truth is in all the circumstances an interest paramount to reputation." The law will not permit a man to recover damages in respect of an injury to a character which he either does not, *or ought not*, to possess."

Truth is a matter of defence or, alternatively expressed, the falsity of defamation is presumed until dispelled by the defendant. Casting the burden on him rather than the plaintiff has the effect, if not the purpose, of inhibiting defamatory speech. For in practice, it acts not only as a serious deterrent against dissemination of falsehoods but, in view of the difficulties of adducing legal proof of truth in all particulars or unwillingness to reveal confidential sources of information, constitutes also a powerful brake on public debate and the flow of information by underscoring the wisdom of caution and self-censorship.

NOTE

1. The Ontario *Libel and Slander Act*, R.S.O. 1990, c. L.12, s. 22 reads:

> In an action for libel or slander for words containing two or more distinct charges against the plaintiff, a defence of justification shall not fail by reason only that the truth of every charge is not proved if the words not proved to be true do not materially injure the plaintiff's reputation having regard to the truth of the remaining charges.

2. Absolute Privilege

On grounds of public policy, the common law has recognized that certain occasions require that an absolute privilege be granted to participants so that they may speak freely, without fear of any liability for defamation. In many jurisdictions the legislature has enshrined these immunities in legislation.

The doctrine of absolute privilege is justified on the ground that there are occasions when society is best served by individuals speaking and writing without restraint, even at the expense of another's reputation and good name. Because of the potential for abuse of such blanket privileges, the law has been loathe to permit reliance on them and has interpreted their scope narrowly.

(a) Judicial Proceedings

An absolute privilege to speak and write without legal liability for defamation flows to judges, juries, witnesses, and parties while participating in judicial proceedings. This is because "... the law takes the risk of their abusing the occasion and speaking maliciously as well as untruly ... in order that their duties may be carried on freely and without fear of any action being brought against them ...". (*More v. Weaver*, [1928] 2 K.B. 520, 140 L.T. 15 (C.A.)).

A witness's testimony is absolutely privileged, however, only if it is relevant to the issues before the bar. Although relevance has been interpreted rather expansively lest a witness withhold evidence out of fear of uttering defamatory words, if, in an aside, the witness says "Have you heard that Jones has run off with Mrs. Brown", that statement will not be privileged. See *More v. Weaver*, *supra*. Communications made within the solicitor and client relationship are absolutely privileged, provided they are reasonably related to the preparation of a case for trial, on the ground that a solicitor must have full disclosure of all the facts within the client's knowledge. *Watson v. M'Ewan*, [1905] A.C. 480, [1904-7] All E.R. Rep. 1 (H.L.); *Nixon v. O'Callaghan* (1927), 60 O.L.R. 76, [1927] 1 D.L.R. 1152 (C.A.). But *cf.*, *Minter v. Priest*, [1930] A.C. 558, 99 L.J.K.B. 391 (H.L.).

A statutory board or tribunal which has "similar attributes" to a court is included within the absolute privilege. *Royal Aquarium and Summer & Winter Garden Society v. Parkinson*, [1892] 1 Q.B. 431, [1891-4] All E.R. Rep. 429 (C.A.). Thus, a hearing before the Ontario Worker's Compensation Board was held to be a judicial proceeding within the meaning of the rule (*Halls v. Mitchell*, [1928] S.C.R. 125, [1928] 2 D.L.R. 97), while a petition to a board of licence commissioners regarding a licence application was not (*Wilhocks v. Howell* (1884), 5 O.R. 360 (C.A.)). In *O'Connor v. Waldron*, [1935] A.C. 76, [1935] 1 D.L.R. 260, the Privy Council held that an inquiry under the Combines Investigation Act of Canada [now the Competition Act] was not an absolutely privileged occasion as it was not a "judicial" proceeding. "The question ... in every case is whether the tribunal in question has similar attributes to a court of justice or acts in a manner similar to that in which such courts act." Apparently, the fact that the inquiry determined "no rights, nor the guilt or innocence of anyone" was considered as determinative, even though it might have the powers of a court regarding summoning witnesses and administering oaths, etc. See also *Perry v. Heatherington* (1972), 24 D.L.R. (3d) 127, [1971] 5 W.W.R. 670 (B.C.S.C.); *Duquette v. Belanger*, [1973] F.C. 868, 38 D.L.R. (3d) 613.

This absolute privilege extends to the reporting of judicial proceedings. The *Libel and Slander Act*, R.S.O. 1990, c. L.12, s. 4(1) states that:

> A fair and accurate report without comment in a newspaper or in a broadcast of proceedings publicly heard before a court of justice, if published in the newspaper or broadcast contemporaneously with such proceedings, is absolutely privileged unless the defendant has refused or neglected to insert in the newspaper in which the report complained of appeared or to broadcast, as the case may be, a reasonable statement of explanation or contradiction by or on behalf of the plaintiff.

This privilege, however, does not cover reports of pleadings filed in lawsuits. In *The Gazette Printing Company v. Shallow* (1909), 41 S.C.R. 339, 6 E.L.R. 348, the plaintiff sued the defendant, newspaper publishers, for a libel contained in certain pleadings filed in the course of an action instituted in the Superior Court of Quebec, and published in the defendant's newspaper. The defendant claimed the publication was privileged within the rule governing the fair report of judicial proceedings. The Supreme Court of Canada held the publication was not made under any privilege and the reasons for subjecting the interests of individuals to the public interest in the administration of justice, which found expression in the privilege to report public judicial proceedings, did not extend to preliminary statements formulated by the parties themselves, and upon which no judicial action has been, or may ever be, taken. "It is obviously undesirable that, by the simple expedient of commencing an action and filing a claim, anybody should be able to secure to himself the protection of the law in the dissemination of the most outrageous libel."

The defence of absolute privilege has been raised in the following cases. In *Razzell v. Edmonton Mint Ltd.* (1981), 29 A.R. 285, [1981] 4 W.W.R. 5 (Alta. Q.B.), absolute privilege covered defamatory statements in a statement of claim and examination for discovery. In *MacKenzie v. McArthur*, [1981] 4 W.W.R. 692 (B.C.S.C.), the Court stated that, although the defence applies without exception to a court of superior jurisdiction, it does not apply to a court of inferior jurisdiction which exceeds its authority. Therefore, a claim that the Chief Coroner had defamed the plaintiff in an inquest was permitted to go to trial in order to determine whether the Coroner had exceeded his authority in making the defamatory statement. In *Boyachyk v. Dukes* (1982), 136 D.L.R. (3d) 28, [1982] 5 W.W.R. 82 (Alta. Q.B.), the Court held that a written complaint made by a citizen to the Chief of Police concerning the conduct of a police officer was protected by an absolute privilege. The Court stated that the procedure established by statute concerning complaints created "a judicial proceeding in its broadest sense". In *Stark v. Auerbach et al.* (1979), 98 D.L.R. (3d) 583, [1979] 3 W.W.R. 563 (B.C.S.C.), the Court held that defendants, acting as members of a board of review established under worker's compensation legislation, were entitled to an absolute privilege. The absolute privilege does not extend beyond the formal initiation of the judicial process. Thus cries of "rape" and untrue accusations made on the scene before the police arrived were not protected by absolute privilege: *Canada v. Lukasic* (1985), 37 Alta. L.R. (2d) 170, 18 D.L.R. (4th) 425 (Q.B.). Even a draft statement of claim and a letter sent in conjunction with it are absolutely privileged if sent to lawyers or others who are intimately involved in the action or inter-connected litigation: *Dingwall v. Lax* (1988), 63 O.R. (2d) 336, 47 D.L.R. (4th) 604 (H.C.J.). Reports made by a counsellor for the purposes of custody hearings are absolutely privileged but the privilege is lost if the reports are published outside the boundaries of the court proceedings; see *G. (R.) v. Christison*, [1997] 1 W.W.R. 641, 31 C.C.L.T. (2d) 263 (Sask.).

(b) Parliamentary Proceedings

In order to foster frank and vigorous debate in our democratic institutions, an absolute privilege surrounds all statements by Members of Parliament made on the floor of the House of Commons in the exercise of their duties.

Reports of these debates are also protected but to a lesser extent. The *Libel and Slander Act*, R.S.O. 1990, c. L.12, s. 3(1), provides that "A fair and accurate report in a newspaper or in a broadcast of … proceedings … open to the public …" of any legislative or administrative body or any commission of inquiry in the British Commonwealth "is privileged, unless it is proved that the publication thereof was made maliciously."

It appears that only a qualified privilege attaches to statements by members of lesser legislative bodies, including local city councils. See *Royal Aquarium v. Parkinson, supra.*

There is considerable controversy whether absolute privilege protects communications between senior members of the executive arm of government. Although it appears that such a privilege protects Ministers of the Crown (*Chatterton v. Secretary of State for India*, [1985] 2 Q.B. 189, [1895-99] All E.R. Rep. 1035 (C.A.)), it is not clear how far down the chain it extends (*Isaacs (M.) & Sons Ltd. v. Cook*, [1925] 2 K.B. 391, 94 L.J.K.B. 886; *Jackson v. Magrath* (1947), 75 C.L.R. 293, [1947] A.L.J. 542). See generally Becht, "The Absolute Privilege of the Executive in Defamation" (1962), 15 Vand. L. Rev. 1127. See also Veeder, "Absolute Immunity in Defamation: Legislative and Executive Proceedings" (1910), 10 Colum. L. Rev. 131.

(c) Other

The common law protects communication between husband and wife with an absolute immunity. Whether this proposition is supported on the technical grounds of want of publication, because of the fiction that the husband and wife are one person, or on grounds of social policy, the rule is well embedded in the law and reflects a healthy respect for the sanctity of confidentiality in the marital relationship.

The common law flounders in confusion and the legislature hesitates to decide whether an absolute immunity attaches to members of the army, police, and national security agencies for their secret and less than secret reports about their own members and other individuals. See Fleming, *The Law of Torts*, 9th ed. (1998), p. 621.

A plaintiff who consents to the publication of defamatory material about himself or herself will be barred from recovery. See *Jones v. Brooks* (1974), 45 D.L.R. (3d) 413, [1974] 2 W.W.R. 729 (Sask. Q.B.). This defence, however, is narrowly construed and must be given for each publication separately. Thus, someone who agrees to discuss on a radio programme certain information that is defamatory of himself or herself, does not thereby consent to defamatory comment on the programme afterwards. See *Syms v. Warren* (1976), 71 D.L.R. (3d) 558 (Man. Q.B.).

3. Qualified Privilege

Qualified privilege is a partial immunity that attaches to certain occasions. Thus, communications that pertain to the legitimate purpose of the occasion, made without malice, are excused from liability for defamation.

Qualified privilege usually arises "where the person who makes [the] communication has an interest or a duty, legal, social or moral, to make it to the person to whom it is made, and the person to whom it is so made has a corresponding interest or duty to receive it". See *Adam v. Ward*, [1917] A.C. 309, at 334, [1916-17] All E.R. Rep. 157 (H.L.), *per* Lord Atkinson.

Another general description is that a publication is privileged when it is "fairly made by a person in the discharge of a public or private duty, whether legal or moral, or in the conduct of his own affairs, in matters where his interest is concerned". See *Toogood v. Spyring* (1834), 1 Cr. M. & R. 181, 149 E.R. 1044, *per* Baron Parke.

There are several broad areas of qualified privilege:

(a) Protection of One's Own Interest

SUN LIFE ASSURANCE CO. OF CANADA ET AL. v. DALRYMPLE

Supreme Court of Canada. [1965] S.C.R. 302, 50 D.L.R. (2d) 217.

Spence J.: This is an appeal from the judgment of the Court of Appeal for Ontario pronounced on November 5, 1964, on an appeal from the judgment of Richardson J. at trial dismissing the plaintiff's action.

This is an action against the Sun Life Assurance Company of Canada and three employees thereof, W.G. Attridge, the director of agencies, and A.G. Dennis and Blythe Moore, two supervisors of agencies, for damages for alleged slander uttered by the three employees on the 13th, 14th and 15th of January 1960 in the course of their duties for their employer.

At the close of the plaintiff's evidence at the trial, the defendant moved to dismiss the action on the ground that the alleged slanders were uttered on an occasion of privilege and that there was no evidence of express malice. After a very lengthy argument, the trial judge held that the alleged slanders were uttered on occasions of qualified privilege and that the plaintiff had failed to adduce sufficient evidence of express malice to justify sending the case to the jury.

The Court of Appeal for Ontario in an oral judgment given at the close of the argument, presumed without deciding that the trial judge had been correct in holding that the occasions were occasions of qualified privilege but differed with the trial judge in holding that there was both extrinsic and intrinsic evidence of express malice giving a sufficient probability to warrant the question of malice or not being put to the jury. The defendants appealed to this Court.

Considerable argument in this Court was concerned with the question of whether the alleged slanders were or were not spoken on occasions of qualified privilege. The occasion advanced by counsel for the appellant was that the individual defendants as company officers were concerned with what they believed to be a wholesale resignation of agents in the Peterborough branch territory including the district offices in Peterborough, Trenton and Oshawa. That situation was one with which they could validly be concerned as it was said in evidence that a very large sum of money must be expended to establish a branch agency of the company and train the agents. Statements which are fairly made by a person in the conduct of his own affairs in matters where his own interest is concerned are *prima facie* privileged: *Toogood v. Spyring*, at p. 193; *Halls v. Mitchell*, *per* Duff J. at p. 132; Gatley on Libel and Slander, 5th ed., p. 253.

...

There is a further grave question whether the statements made by the three individual defendants were so irrelevant to the proper protection of their employer's interest that the privilege was lost. Certainly, statements irrelevant to protecting the interests will result in loss of privilege: *Adam v. Ward*, *per* Lord Loreburn, at pp. 320-1, Lord Dunedin, pp. 326-7, and Gatley, *op. cit.*, pp. 267ff.

Were the comments irrelevant? The comments may be generally described as being an attempt to show to the agents that their loyalty to the plaintiff was one not justified in their own interests. ...

I am, in summary, of the view that the alleged slanders were all uttered on occasions of qualified privilege. However, it would seem that the Court of Appeal were, with respect, correct in their view that there was both extrinsic and intrinsic evidence of malice.

"Malice" of course does not necessarily mean personal spite or ill-will; it may consist of some indirect motive not connected with the privilege: . ...

Firstly, it must be determined what evidence of malice is sufficient to go to the jury. Whether the defendant was actuated by malice is, of course, a question of fact for the jury but whether there is any evidence of malice fit to be left to the jury is a question of law for the judge to determine. ...

Although upon an occasion held to be one of qualified privilege the court will not look too narrowly on the language used in the alleged slander. ... the slander if utterly beyond and disproportionate to the facts may provide evidence of express malice: . ...

Moreover, as Lord Porter pointed out in the judgment quoted and adopted by Cartwright J. in *Jerome v. Anderson*, *supra*, at p. 299, one piece of evidence tending to establish malice is sufficient evidence on which a jury could find for the plaintiff and therefore if more than a mere scintilla, it should be submitted to the jury for its finding of fact.

Express malice must be found against each one of the three defendants: *Egger v. Viscount Chelmsford et al.*, *per* Lord Denning M.R., at p. 412:

> It is a mistake to suppose that, on a joint publication, the malice of one defendant infects his co-defendant. Each defendant is answerable severally, as well as jointly, for the joint publication; and each is entitled to his several defence, whether he be sued jointly or separately from the others. If the plaintiff seeks to rely on malice to aggravate damages, or to rebut a defence of qualified privilege, or to cause a comment, otherwise fair, to become unfair, then he must prove malice against each person whom he charges with it. A defendant is only affected by express malice if he himself was actuated by it: or if his servant or agent concerned in the publication was actuated by malice in the course of his employment.

Of course, the express malice which actuated any of the three individual defendants will make the corporate defendant liable since the statement was made by the employee in the course of his employer's business.

The Court of Appeal for Ontario in its judgment said, in part:

> Because as a result of this unanimous view, there must, in the opinion of this Court, be a new trial, we refrain from more specific comment on the evidence so that the matter may in fairness to both parties be left at large for disposition in the new trial.

I have come to the conclusion, with respect, that such a course is a proper one under the circumstances and, therefore, I shall only state that I am convinced that there is both extrinsic and intrinsic evidence of express malice on the part of each of the three individual defendants. ...

For these reasons, I would dismiss the appeal with costs.

NOTES

1. A qualified privilege attaches to statements made in defence of one's own interests, both economic and personal. One is entitled, therefore, to defend oneself against attacks on one's own character. One is also permitted to protect the financial interests of one's employer, for presumably one has a personal stake in the employer's well-being. See *Penton v. Calwell*, [1945] A.L.R. 262, 70 C.L.R. 219.

2. The privilege is limited to information that is reasonably related to a refutation of the original attack. See *Loveday v. Sun Newspaper* (1958), 59 C.L.R. 503. As in self-defence, one cannot abuse the occasion of an attack to completely destroy another person's reputation. See *Douglas v. Tucker*, [1952] 1 S.C.R. 275, [1952] 1 D.L.R. 675. Some latitude is allowed, however, so that if a third person's character is besmirched incidentally, in the defence of one's own reputation, the privilege is still available to the publisher. See *Loveday v. Sun Newspaper*, *supra*; *Mowlds v. Fergusson* (1940), 64 C.L.R. 206.

3. The privilege protects the communication as long as it is made only to those who have an interest or duty to receive it, but the law has not "restricted the right ... within any narrow limits". See *Adam v. Ward*, [1917] A.C. 309, at 328, [1916-17] All E.R. Rep. 157 (H.L.).

4. In *Pleau v. Simpson-Sears Ltd.* (1976), 15 O.R. (2d) 436, 2 C.C.L.T. 28 (C.A.), the plaintiff's wallet was stolen and, shortly thereafter, forged cheques began appearing in his name. The defendant posted notices to its employees near the cash registers, which were visible to customers, to detain Pleau and call security if he presented a cheque. A friend of the plaintiff saw one of these notices and told the plaintiff, who sued. The action was dismissed by a jury and this was affirmed on appeal. Evans J.A. said:

> As to privilege, there is no doubt on the facts that there was a reciprocity of interest between the management of the defendant company and its employees to safeguard the defendant against loss from the passing of cheques bearing the forged name of the plaintiff. The defendant company had an interest to protect, an interest which would be sterile without a consequential interest to pass on to its employees the complaint received from the police.

As to the abuse of privilege Lacourciere J.A. observed:

> In my view, the only question in this appeal is whether the publication complained of went beyond the exigencies of the privileged occasion so as to constitute "publicity incommensurate to the occasion". ...
>
> ... publication of the impugned notice on a large placard exposed to public view would undoubtedly have removed the qualified privilege of the occasion. One can think of many such excesses. But this was not the case: the photographs exhibited indicate a typewritten slip attached to a cash register, obviously for the private information of the cashier. The notices were of reasonable size, unlikely to attract the public's attention. It was not an uncommon

> practice, as appears from the evidence of the operating superintendent of the store. …
>
> While the burden was on the respondent company in the first instance to establish the existence of a qualified privilege for the publication, once established, the burden was on the appellant as plaintiff to prove that it had been abused by excessive publication (Prosser, *Law of Torts*, 3rd ed. (1964), p. 823). I am of opinion that the number and size of the notices and their location on the cash registers were reasonable in the circumstances and did not exceed the privilege of the occasion.

Brooke J.A. dissented and remarked:

> Perhaps the notice was a convenient way to remind its staff, but one wonders why a list to be consulted before cheques were accepted would not have been just as convenient, and assure some privacy to the individual concerned. The communication was not restricted by this method of publication to staff alone, but was, on the contrary, publicly displayed and a notice to all who looked at it in a place where so many were intended to look when they purchased goods in this large store, or likely to look when simply passing by the area of the cash register. The evidence was that some 800 customers a day made their way through the store. There is, of course, the added dimension that the occasion was really a continuing one. This was a continuing publication in the sense that, unlike a letter to an individual or words spoken privately but overheard, it was a notice continuously displayed in 37 locations in this busy place.
>
> The rule is that if the occasion is privileged the communication may be protected. An occasion of the publication of words found to be defamatory of the plaintiff may be privileged if the publication was made as a result of a private or public duty or made in the conduct of one's own affairs: *Adam v. Ward*, [1917] A.C. 309, and *Toogood v. Spyring* (1834), 1 Cr.M. & R. 181, 149 E.R. 1044 at 1048. But to be privileged the communication is one that is made to another to whom there is a duty to publish or who has an interest in receiving the communication. …

Which side do you prefer? Would you have sued if you were Pleau? What do you think motivated Pleau to bring this action?

5. On the question of the onus of proof of malice, see also *Netupsky v. Craig*, [1973] S.C.R. 55, 28 D.L.R. (3d) 742, onus on the plaintiff.

6. Two Supreme Court of Canada cases dealt with the problem of malice in respect to qualified privilege.

   In *McLoughlin v. Kutasy,* [1979] S.C.R. 311, 97 D.L.R. (3d) 620, the plaintiff alleged that he was defamed by a company's physician, in the physician's report to the company concerning the plaintiff. At trial, the jury had found that although it was a qualified privilege situation, the defendant had been actuated by malice. Both the Ontario Court of Appeal and a majority of six in the Supreme Court held that the jury's finding could not be supported. Three members of the Supreme Court dissented. The learned justices were of the opinion that an appellate court ought not to interfere with a jury's findings except in extreme circumstances.

   In *Davies and Davies Ltd. v. Kott* (1979), 27 N.R. 181, 9 C.C.L.T. 249 (S.C.C.), a jury again found malice. This time, both the Ontario Court of Appeal and the Supreme Court held that the question of malice ought not to have been put to the jury because the evidence did not raise a "probability" of malice.

For a comment on these cases and the general issue of the right of appellate courts to interfere with jury findings, see Klar, "Developments in Tort Law: The 1978-79 Term" (1980), 1 Supreme Court L.R. 330-346.

7. Not having an honest belief in the impugned material is conclusive proof of malice. An issue which arises, however, is whether the honest belief must have been formed reasonably. There is disagreement on this point.

   In an Ontario Court of Appeal decision, *Korach v. Moore* (1991), 1 O.R. (3d) 275, 76 D.L.R. (4th) 506; leave to appeal to S.C.C. dismissed June 13, 1991, 91 B.S.C.C., p. 1489, the Court sided with the view that carelessness or negligence in forming the honest belief does not constitute malice.

   For a fuller discussion of this point see Brown, *The Law of Defamation in Canada,* 2nd ed. (1995), Vol 1., p. 743.

(b) Common Interest or Mutual Concern

BEREMAN v. POWER PUBLISHING CO.

Supreme Court of Colorado. (1933), 27 P. 2d 749.

Butler Justice: E.W. Bereman sued The Power Publishing Company, a corporation, Earl Hoage, C.A. Magnuson, Casey's Superior Laundry Company, a corporation, and Sam J. Kortz for damages for an alleged libel. The court non-suited him and rendered judgment dismissing the action. He seeks a reversal of that judgment.

The alleged libel was published in the Colorado Labor Advocate, the official publication of the Colorado State Federation of Labor and other labor organizations. ...

[The article accused the plaintiff, and two other members of the Laundry Drivers Union, of having turned traitor to the union by leaving the only union laundry in the city and taking employment with a non-union one; and further, with soliciting former customers without advising them that they were now working for a non-union laundry. The tone and temper of the article are represented by the statement: "These three labor spies have sold their manhood, if they ever possessed any, for a paltry few dollars."]

The trial court held that the publication was qualifiedly privileged. We are in accord with that holding. The article complained of appeared in the official publication of the labor organizations. The Labor Advocate is published weekly in the interests of organized labor, to keep union members informed concerning matters affecting their interests. The publishers of the article and those to whom it was addressed had a common interest in the matters to which it related. The article, therefore, was qualifiedly privileged. ...

The law on this branch of the case is settled in this state. In *Melcher v. Beeler*, ... we said at page 241 of 48 Colo., 110 P. 181, 184: "... A communication made bona fide upon any subject-matter in which the party communicating has an interest, or in reference to which he has a duty, is privileged, if made to a person having a corresponding interest or duty, although it contains incriminatory matter, which, without this privilege, would be slanderous and actionable; and this, though the duty be not a legal one, but only a moral or social duty of imperfect application [obligation]."

The communication being qualifiedly privileged, no right of action arose unless the publishers were actuated by express malice, and the burden of proving express malice was on the plaintiff. The presumption is that the communication was made in good faith and without malice. ...

In considering the extent of the publication in the present case, we must bear in mind the nature of the Colorado Labor Advocate and of the communication published therein.

The very life of labor unions depends upon the loyalty of their members. Unions have the power and the right to expel disloyal members, and before the trial that power and right were exercised in this very case. Nothing could be of greater practical interest to labor union members than information concerning acts of disloyalty. It is necessary that they be informed thereof in some manner in order that they may protect themselves against conduct injurious to the cause of organized labor and that, if not exposed, might tend to disrupt a union. Due to the number of labor unions and the large number of their members, it is impracticable to send sealed communications to all. Obviously, it was necessary to adopt some other method of communicating information of interest to organized labor. The Labor Advocate was established to furnish that information. It is not a newspaper of general circulation, its circulation being confined almost exclusively to members of labor unions.

That communications published in papers devoted to particular organizations are not to be treated the same as communication in newspapers of general circulation, is attested by the authorities. Thus, in *Redgate v. Roush*, 61 Kan. 480, 59 P. 1050, it was held, quoting from the syllabus: "Where the officers of a church, upon inquiry, find that their pastor is unworthy and unfit for his office, and thereupon, in the performance of what they honestly believe to be their duty towards other members and churches of the same denomination, publish, in good faith, in the church papers, the result of their inquiry, and there is a reasonable occasion for such publication, it will be deemed to be privileged and protected under the law. Where the publication appears to have been made in good faith, and for the members of the denomination alone, the fact that it incidentally may have been brought to the attention of others than members of the church will not take away its privileged character. In such case, and where the plaintiff seeks damages, it devolves upon him to establish actual malice". ...

The publication in the present case did not go beyond the reasonable requirements of the occasion. The case presents a situation wholly unlike that in *Bearman v. People*, 91 Colo. 486, 16 P.2d 425. There, a communication reflecting on a doctor on a hospital staff was directed to the president of the hospital association, but 10,000 printed copies were delivered or mailed to persons having no connection with or interest in the hospital. ... The following example illustrates the dividing line between what is permissible and what is not: Where an inquiry is made as to the responsibility of another, an answer properly communicated is qualifiedly privileged. See *Melcher v. Beeler*, *supra*. But a publication of the answer in a newspaper of general circulation would be an excessive publication, and would deprive the communication of its qualifiedly privileged character.

A communication may lose its qualifiedly privileged character by the use of language of a defamatory nature not warranted by the occasion that called forth the publication. [Citation omitted.] Some of the words in the article in question are in bad taste, no doubt. Less offensive words might have been selected. But we must not overlook the fact that disloyalty to a union is fraught with such possibilities of disaster to the union cause that loyal union members may be excused for referring to it in strong terms of condemnation. The conduct of the plaintiff not unnaturally suggested to the minds of union members such words as "traitor," "spies," and "despicable." Instances are not wanting where disloyalty to secret societies and organizations, both political and nonpolitical, has been condemned in language not less forceful. The condemnatory words in the article before us were applied to the drivers in connection with the facts stated; they were not intended to apply to the drivers generally or in connection with any other matter. Discussing the question when defamatory words in a communication may be considered as affording, by themselves, evidence of malice, Odgers, in his work on Libel and Slander (5th Ed.), says at page 254: "But the test appears to be this. Take the facts as they appeared to the defendant's mind at the time of publication; are the terms used such as the defendant might have honestly and bona fide employed under the circumstances? If so the judge should stop the case. For if the defendant honestly believed the plaintiff's conduct to be such as he described it, the mere fact that he used strong words in so describing it is no evidence of malice to go to the jury."

In view of all the circumstances, we do not believe that the qualifiedly privileged character of the article in question was lost by reason of the language used.

The action of the trial court in dismissing the suit was right.

The judgment is affirmed.

NOTES

1. This qualified privilege extends to members of a church to discuss church affairs (see *Slocinski v. Radwan*, 144 A. 787 (N.H. 1929), and to members of a lodge, social club or fraternity (see *Hayden v. Hasbrouck*, 84 A. 1087 (R.I. 1912). In *Chapman v. Lord Ellesmere et al.*, [1932] 2 K.B. 431, it was held that because a Jockey Club was obliged to publish notice of the plaintiff's suspension in their own racing periodical, the occasion was privileged. However, several newspapers which had printed the story were not privileged, since there was "no general interest to the public or duty owed to the public to publish matters which concern a section of the public only". But see *Libel and Slander Act*, R.S.O. 1990, c. L.12, s. 3(4).

2. People who share a common business interest may discuss amongst themselves matters of mutual economic concern in a privileged setting. Shareholders, for example, are privileged to exchange information about employees or customers freely without attracting tort liability unless they are malicious. See *Telegraph Newspaper v. Bedford* (1934), 50 C.L.R. 632.

3. Several lawyers, defending actions for different clients being sued by the same plaintiff regarding the same subject matter, are privileged to exchange information. See *Speilberg v. A. Kuhn & Bros.*, 116 P. 1027 (Utah 1911). Similarly, creditors of the same debtor have a qualified privilege to consult together in furtherance of their common interest. See *Smith Brothers & Co. v. W.C. Agee & Co.*, 59 So. 647 (Ala. 1912).

4. Members of professional associations may discuss matters of joint concern as long as they do so fairly and amongst themselves. See *Thompson v. Amos* (1949), 23 A.L.J. 98; *Guise v. Kouvelis* (1947), 74 C.L.R. 102, 21 A.L.J.R. 71. Here, as in the other privileged situations, there must be an interest *both* in the recipient of the information and the disseminator of it. A hospital can distribute a list of names of persons with infectious blood or fluids to its labs and emergency rooms; see *Peters-Brown v. Regina District Health Board,* [1996] 1 W.W.R. 337 (Sask. Q.B.).

5. Communications made by family members to each other or to therapists concerning allegations of sexual abuse by other members of the family are protected by qualified privilege. It has been said that "parents will be held to the highest moral, legal and social duty to receive information from their children regarding incidents or allegations of sexual abuse and that their interest in receiving communications of this nature are common with the interest of their children who make such communications."; see *C. (L.G.) v. C. (V.M.)* (1996), 33 C.C.L.T. (2d) 286 at 289-90 (B.C.S.C.).

6. In Britain, there was once recognized a common interest among voters in elections to communicate under the protection of a qualified privilege (see *Braddock v. Bevins*, [1948] 1 K.B. 580, [1948] 1 All E.R. 450 (C.A.)), but this was abrogated by statute. See *Defamation Act, 1952*, c. 66, s. 10, which provided:

> A defamatory statement published by or on behalf of a candidate in any election to a local government authority to the Scottish Assembly or to Parliament shall not be deemed to be published on a privileged occasion on the ground that it is material to a question in issue in the election, whether or not the person by whom it is published is qualified to vote at the election.

7. The Canadian law did not recognize such a privilege. In *Bureau v. Campbell*, [1928] 3 D.L.R. 907, [1928] 2 W.W.R. 535 (Sask. C.A.); affd, [1928] S.C.R. 576, [1929] 2 D.L.R. 205, Martin, J.A., at 931, 3 D.L.R. said:

> The contention that a political meeting is a privileged occasion is one which is too broad for consideration. ... There is no reciprocity of interest between the candidate and the hearers at the public meeting. The candidate and those who speak for him are endeavouring by what they say to procure as many votes as possible, and may very well have a motive for attacking opponents and in making defamatory statements about them: but it cannot be said that there is any duty, legal, social or moral, to make such defamatory statements.

8. In *Hanly v. Pisces Productions Inc.*, [1980] 1 W.W.R. 369 (B.C.S.C.), a letter to a union, detailing the reasons for a union member not having been hired, was protected by a qualified privilege. The Supreme Court of British Columbia also held that the defence of "consent" prevailed, in that the plaintiff had consented to the union board's request for reasons.

(c) Moral or Legal Duty to Protect Another's Interest

WATT v. LONGSDON

Court of Appeal. [1930] 1 K.B. 130, 98 L.J.K.B. 711,
142 L.T. 4, 45 T.L.R. 619.

The plaintiff, Watt, sued the defendant, Longsdon, *inter alia*, for sending his wife, who was in England, a letter which indicated that he had had "immoral relations" with his housemaid while living in Casablanca, Morocco. Longsdon, a friend of the wife, had done business with the plaintiff in Casablanca. The plaintiff's wife sued him for divorce as a result. The trial judge held that the publication was privileged and the plaintiff appealed.

Scrutton L.J.:

... By the law of England there are occasions on which a person may make defamatory statements about another which are untrue without incurring any legal liability for his statements. These occasions are called privileged occasions. A reason frequently given for this privilege is that the allegation that the speaker has "unlawfully and maliciously published", is displaced by proof that the speaker had either a duty or an interest to publish, and that this duty or interest confers the privilege. But communications made on these occasions may lose their privilege: (1) they may exceed the privilege of the occasion by going beyond the limits of the duty or interest, or (2) they may be published with express malice, so that the occasion is not being legitimately used, but abused. ...

It will be seen that the learned judge requires: (1) a public or private duty to communicate, whether legal or moral; (2) that the communication should be "fairly warranted by any unreasonable occasion or exigency"; (3) or a statement in the conduct of his own affairs where his interest is concerned. Parke, B., had given several other definitions in slightly varying terms. For instance, in *Cockayne v. Hogkisson* (1833), 5 C. & P. 543, 548, he had directed the jury: "Where the writer is acting on any duty, legal or moral, towards the person to whom he writes, or where he has, by his situation, to protect the interests of another, that which he writes under such circumstances is a privileged communication." This adds to the protection of his own interest, spoken of in *Toogood v. Spyring*, the protection of the interests of another where the situation of the writer requires him to protect those interests. This, I think, involves that his "situation" imposes on him a legal or moral duty. The question whether the occasion was privileged is for the judge, and so far as "duty" is concerned, the question is: Was there a duty, legal, moral, or social, to communicate? As to legal duty, the judge should have no difficulty; the judge should know the law; but as to moral or social duties of imperfect obligation, the task is far more troublesome. The judge has no evidence as to the view the community takes of moral or social duties. All the help the Court of Appeal can give him is contained in the judgment of Lindley, L.J., in *Stuart v. Bell*, [1891] 2 Q.B. 341, 350: "The question of moral or social duty being for the judge, each judge must decide it as best he can for himself. I take moral or social duty to mean a duty recognized by English people of ordinary intelligence and moral principle, but at the same time not a duty enforceable by legal proceedings, whether civil or criminal. My own conviction is that all or, at all events, the great mass of right-minded men in the position of the defendant would have considered it their duty, under the circumstances, to inform Stanley of the suspicion which had fallen on the plaintiff." Is the judge merely to give his own view of moral and social duty, though he thinks a considerable portion of the community hold a different opinion? Or is he to endeavour to ascertain what view "the great mass of right-minded men" would take? It is not surprising that with such a standard both judges and text-writers treat the matter as one of great difficulty in which no definite line can be drawn.

...

I have no intention of writing an exhaustive treatise on the circumstances when a stranger or a friend should communicate to husband or wife information he receives as to the conduct of the other party to the marriage. I am clear that it is impossible to say he is always under a moral or social duty to do so; it is equally impossible to say he is never under such a duty. It must depend on the circumstances of each case, the nature of the information, and the relation of speaker and recipient. It cannot, on the other hand, be the duty even of a friend to communicate all the gossip the friend hears at men's clubs or women's bridge parties to one of the spouses affected. On the other hand, most men would hold that it was the moral duty of a doctor who attended his sister in law, and believed her to be suffering from a miscarriage, for which an absent husband could not be responsible, to communicate that fact to his wife and the husband. ... If this is so, the decision must turn on the circumstances of each case, the judge being much influenced by the consideration that as a general rule it is not desirable for any one, even a mother in law, to interfere in the affairs of man and wife.

Using the best judgment I can in this difficult matter, I have come to the conclusion that there was not a moral or social duty in Longsdon to make this communication to Mrs. Watt such as to make the occasion privileged, and that there must be a new trial so far as it relates to the claim for publication of a libel to Mrs. Watt. ...

[The judgments of **Greer** and **Russell L.JJ.**, are omitted.]

NOTES

1. One of the leading cases in this area is *Adam v. Ward*, [1917] A.C. 309, [1916-17] All E.R. Rep. 157 (H.L.), where an M.P. made certain charges against a senior army officer. The Army Council made an official investigation, exonerated the officer, and, incidentally, made remarks defamatory of the M.P. The Council's report was found to be privileged since it had been made in the discharge of a public duty. Although the Council released the information to the public press, this was held not to be an abuse, having regard to the fact that the accusation had been made in the Parliament. See also *Lacarte v. Board of Education of Toronto*, [1959] S.C.R. 465, 17 D.L.R. (2d) 609.

2. Courts are more inclined to find a qualified privilege where statements are made in response to specific inquiries than when they are volunteered. For example, if a previous employer gives a character reference regarding a discharged employee at the request of a prospective employer, the former employer is more likely to be protected than if volunteering the information. See *Toogood v. Spyring* (1834), 1 Cr. M. & R. 181, 149 E.R. 1044. Similarly, a businessperson who comments on the financial standing of a buyer at the request of another stands in a better position than if the comments were unsolicited. See *Robshaw v. Smith* (1878), 38 L.T. 423.

3. An inquiry is not always required, however. Certain relationships generate a duty to inform even without any request to do so. For example, defamatory statements by a father to his daughter about a prospective husband are privileged because of his moral obligation as a father. See *Bordeaux v. Jobs* (1913), 6 Alta. L. Rev. 440, *per* Harvey C.J. An employer may also tell an employee certain things related to work. See *Cooke v. Wildes* (1855), 5 E. & B. 328, 119 E.R. 504. The police may explain to the plaintiff's mother that her son was accused of theft. See *Chrispen v. Novack*, [1995] 5 W.W.R. 752 (Sask Q.B.).

4. Mercantile agencies that collect and sell credit information for profit to their customers are denied qualified privilege on the ground that it is not in the public interest to protect those who trade for profit in the characters of other people. See *Macintosh v. Dun*, [1908] A.C. 390, [1908-10] All E.R. Rep. 664 (P.C.). This view has been much criticized and has been accordingly modified in *London Assoc. for Protection of Trade v. Greenlands Ltd.*, [1916] 2 A.C. 15, [1916-17] All E.R. Rep. 452 (H.L.), where a qualified privilege was accorded to credit reports by a mutual trade protective society, which was a co-operative service, rather than a business run for profit. See also *Howe v. Lees* (1910), 11 C.L.R. 361; *Todd v. Dun* (1888), 15 O.A.R. 85 (H.C.); *Robinson v. Dun* (1897), 24 O.A.R. 287 (H.C.). How would you handle the dissemination of information about the creditworthiness of consumers?

(d) Public Interest

THE GLOBE AND MAIL LTD. v. BOLAND
Supreme Court of Canada. [1960] S.C.R. 203, 22 D.L.R. (2d) 277.

Cartwright J.: The respondent was a candidate for election in Parkdale riding in the general election held in Canada on June 10, 1957. The words complained of appeared on May 27, 1957, as an editorial in all issues of *The Globe & Mail*, Toronto, a daily newspaper published by the appellant. They read as follows:

SHABBY TACTICS

One of the less creditable episodes of the election campaign occurred on Thursday evening in Parkdale constituency, in Toronto, when Mr. John Boland, self-styled independent Conservative candidate, introduced an issue which does not exist in this election. McCarthy-style, he put forward an ex-Communist in an attempt to show the Liberals are "Soft on Communism". The results were far from edifying.

The reason for this disgusting performance was undoubtedly to mislead the so-called New Canadian vote in that riding, in the hope that their anti-Communist fears might be translated into an anti-Liberal anti-Conservative prejudice. An election won by such tactics would be a degradation to the whole democratic system of Government in Canada. Let us have no more of that sort of thing, this time or ever.

In the statement of claim it is alleged that the defendant falsely and maliciously published this editorial of and concerning the plaintiff and that in its plain and ordinary meaning it is defamatory of him. In paras. 6 to 15 inclusive a number of innuendoes are alleged.

In the statement of defence publication is admitted. The defences pleaded are, (i) that the words complained of in their natural and ordinary meaning are no libel, (ii) that the said words do not bear and were not understood to bear and are incapable of bearing or being understood to bear the meanings alleged in paras. 6 to 15 of the statement of claim, (iii) a plea of qualified privilege, and (iv) the defence of fair comment, pleaded in the form of the "rolled-up" plea.

To hold that during a Federal election campaign in Canada any defamatory statement published in the press relating to a candidate's fitness for office is to be taken as published on an occasion of qualified privilege would be, in my opinion, not only contrary to the great weight of authority in England and in this country but harmful to that "common convenience and welfare of society" which Baron Parke described as the underlying principle on which the rules as to qualified privilege are founded. (See *Toogood v. Spyring* (1834), 1 C.M. & R. 181 at p. 193, 149 E.R. 1044). It would mean that every man who offers himself as a candidate must be prepared to risk the loss of his reputation without redress unless he be able to prove affirmatively that those who defamed him were actuated by express malice. I would like to adopt the following sentence from the judgment of the Court in *Post Pub. Co. v. Hallam* (1893), 59 Fed. 530 at p. 540: "We think that not only is such a sacrifice not required of every one who consents to become a candidate for office, but that to sanction such a doctrine would do the public more harm than good." And the following expression of opinion by the learned author of Gatley (*op. cit.*), p. 254: "It is, however, submitted that so wide an extension of the privilege would do the public more harm than good. It would tend to deter sensitive and honourable men from seeking public positions of trust and responsibility, and leave them open to others who have no respect for their reputation."

The passages just quoted recall the words of Cockburn, C.J., in *Campbell v. Spottiswoode* (1863), 3 B. & S. 769 at p. 777, 122 E.R. 288: "It is said that it is for the interest of society that the public conduct of men should be criticized without any other limit than that the writer should have an honest belief that what he writes is true. But it seems to me that the public have an equal interest in the maintenance of the public character of public men; and public affairs could not be conducted by men of honour with a view to the welfare of the country, if we were to sanction attacks upon them, destructive of their honour and character, and made without any foundation." The interest of the public and that of the publishers of newspapers will be sufficiently safeguarded by the availability of the defence of fair comment in appropriate circumstances. ...

At the new trial, in view of the state of the pleadings it should be taken that, as a matter of law, the defence of qualified privilege is not open to the defendant. I would dismiss the appeal with costs.

NOTES

1. For an account of the second trial and subsequent appeal, ordering a third trial, see *Boland v. Globe and Mail Ltd.*, [1961] O.R. 712, 29 D.L.R. (2d) 401 (C.A.).

2. In *Banks v. The Globe and Mail Ltd.*, [1961] S.C.R. 474, 28 D.L.R. (2d) 343, the trial judge and the Ontario Court of Appeal held that the publication in a newspaper of statements concerning a director of a labour union which had called a strike affecting eight Canadian-owned vessels, was made on an occasion of qualified privilege. The strike had lasted many months and before it was settled the eight ships had been transferred to a foreign registry. The existence of a subject matter of such wide public interest was held by the lower courts to support a plea of qualified privilege. "There is no more efficient organ for informing the public and for disseminating to the public intelligent comment on such matters of public interest, than a great metropolitan newspaper. ... The members of the public have a real, a vital — I might go so far as to say — a paramount interest in receiving those comments." The Supreme Court of Canada, however, pointed out that the Ontario courts had confused the *right* of any individual, or newspaper, to comment fairly upon matters of public interest, with a *duty* of the sort which gives rise to an occasion of privilege. No such duty existed here and there was, as explained in the *Boland* case, no qualified privilege.

3. The principle that there is in Canada no special protection given to the media has been reaffirmed in recent cases, the *Canadian Charter of Rights & Freedoms* having had no effect on this aspect of Canadian defamation law. See, for example, *Bank of British Columbia v. Canadian Broadcasting Corp.* (1993), 18 C.C.L.T. (2d) 149 (B.C.S.C.); affd, (1995), 25 C.C.L.T. (2d) 229 (B.C.C.A.).

4. In *Jones v. Bennett*, [1969] S.C.R. 277, 2 D.L.R. (3d) 291, Premier W.A.C. Bennett of B.C., at a public meeting of some of his Social Credit supporters in Victoria, B.C., sought to justify his government's suspension of Jones, a member of a provincial commission. During the course of his speech, which was covered by the press, the Premier uttered some defamatory remarks about Jones, implying that he was unfit for office because of dishonesty. Jones sued. The defence sought to invoke the defence of qualified privilege. The Supreme Court, however, held that privilege could not be relied on, even though the subject was clearly one of public interest. Cartwright C.J.C. stated:

> It is, of course, a perfectly proper proceeding for a member of the Legislature to address a meeting of his supporters at any time but if in the course of addressing them he sees fit to make defamatory statements about another which are in fact untrue, it is difficult to see why the common convenience and wel-

> fare of society requires that such statements should be protected and the person defamed left without a remedy unless he can affirmatively prove express malice on the part of the speaker.

His Lordship indicated that, even if there were a qualified privilege, the defendant had lost it because he was aware of the presence of reporters in the audience, who would publicize his remarks to the general public. The defence of fair comment was also rejected because the "sting of the words" were held not to be comment at all. Do you agree with this disposition of the matter?

5. Compare with *Stopforth v. Goyer* (1979), 97 D.L.R. (3d) 369, 8 C.C.L.T. 172 (Ont. C.A.), where Jean-Pierre Goyer, then a Minister of the federal Crown, said of one of his civil servants that he gave him "misinformation" and that he was "grossly negligent". The Ontario Court of Appeal, without citing *Jones v. Bennett*, held that "the electorate, as represented by the media, has a real and *bona fide* interest in the demolition of a senior civil servant for an alleged dereliction of duty ... and the appellant had a corresponding public duty and interest in satisfying that interest of the electorate". How would you handle such a situation if you had your choice? For similar decisions which protect the public's right to know and the politician's right to tell, see *Parlett v. Robinson* (1986), 30 D.L.R. (4th) 247, 37 C.C.L.T. 281 (B.C.C.A.); leave to appeal to S.C.C. dismissed 74 N.R. 240*n*; *Loos v. Robbins* (1987), 37 D.L.R. (4th) 418, [1987] 4 W.W.R. 469 (Sask. C.A.); and *Milgaard v. Saskatchewan (Minister of Justice)*, [1997] 3 W.W.R. 82 (Sask. Q.B.).

6. What do you think of this principle? In the United States, there is a constitutionally protected privilege to discuss matters of public concern. As long as there is no malice, one may, therefore, criticize public officials (*New York Times v. Sullivan*, 376 U.S. 254 (Ala. 1964)), or public figures (*Curtis Publishing v. Butts*, 388 U.S. 130 (1967)), without attracting liability for defamation. See also *Gertz v. Welsh*, 418 U.S. 323 (1974). Should such a concept be imported into Canada?

7. Much of the evil of this rule has been minimized by legislation. Several Canadian provinces permit recovery against newspapers and broadcasting stations that is limited to actual damage if the statement complained of was published in "good faith" and under "mistake" and a full retraction is published. This privilege does "not apply to the case of a libel against any candidate for public office unless the retraction of the charge is made in a conspicuous manner, at least five days before the election." See the *Libel and Slander Act*, R.S.O. 1990, c. L.12, s. 5(3). Similarly, the defence of fair comment may be available to the publisher. See *infra*. For a recent case, see *Ungaro v. Toronto Star Newspapers Ltd.* (1997), 144 D.L.R. (4th) 84 (Ont. Gen. Div.).

8. In addition to statutory protections for fair and accurate reporting of judicial and legislative proceedings, there is a common law defence of qualified privilege for fair and accurate reporting of public documents. It has been held that this qualified privilege applies to public records obtained under the disclosure requirements of Freedom of Information legislation; see *Fletcher-Gordon v. Southam Inc.*, [1997] 6 W.W.R. 155 (B.C.S.C.). In view of the increasing importance of freedom of information provisions, this qualified privilege is very significant.

9. A privilege is recognized, in the interest of the general public, to report crime to the police. See *Foltz v. Moore-McCormack Lines Inc.*, 189 F.2d 537 (U.S.C.A. 2nd Cir. 1951). Similarly, one can report the conduct of public officers to their superiors (see *Nuyen v. Slater*, 127 N.W. 2d 369 (Mich. 1964)), or to one's M.P. (*R. v. Rule*, [1937] 2 K.B. 375, [1937] 2 All E.R. 772 (C.A.)). So too, a teacher can be reported to a school board in a privileged context, *Fuson v. Fuson*, 57 S.W. 2d 42 (1933). But one is not privileged to write in a book called *The Children's Crusade*, an account of the Company of Young Canadians, which defames someone, merely because the public

would be interested in such an account, there being no "valid social reasons" to do so. See Dubin J.A. in *Littleton v. Hamilton* (1974), 4 O.R. (2d) 283, 47 D.L.R. (3d) 663 (C.A.); leave to appeal to S.C.C. refused, 4 O.R. (2d) 289*n*, 47 D.L.R. (3d) 663*n*.

10. Should a defendant be liable for mistakenly reporting defamatory information to the wrong authority, believing honestly and reasonably that it was the proper agency to receive it? In *Hebditch v. MacIlwaine*, [1894] 2 Q.B. 54, [1891-4] All E.R. Rep. 444 (C.A.), it was held that no privilege protected a group of ratepayers who complained about certain election irregularities to the wrong body, which had no duty or interest in receiving the information. Compare with *McIntire v. McBean* (1856), 13 U.C.Q.B. 534 (C.A.), where parents who complained to the wrong authority about a teacher's moral character were excused from liability since it was found commendable to do this as long as the information was "well-founded, or that they had good reason to believe it was, and that they acted in sincerity and good faith, not maliciously and without just cause or excuse". Similarly, in *Kerr v. Davison* (1873), 9 N.S.R. 354 (C.A.), it was held that a privilege exists if a communication is made to a person "not in fact having such interest or duty, but who might reasonably be and is supposed by the party making the communication to have such an interest or duty". In *Leverman v. Campbell Sharp Ltd.* (1987), 36 D.L.R. (4th) 401, 40 C.C.L.T. 73 (B.C.C.A.), it was held that as long as one had an honest belief in the material published, even if it was carelessly formed, the defence of qualified privilege will survive. However, should the material be carelessly published, so that it does not express the honest belief, or shows that the honest belief was never formed, the defence will be defeated.

11. Should a plaintiff be able to get around the defences by framing the action as one of "negligent reporting" or "negligent research"? In *Fulton v. The Globe & Mail* (1996), 32 C.C.L.T. (2d) 69, [1997] 3 W.W.R. 200 (Alta. Q.B.), vard in part, [1998] 1 W.W.R. 684, 152 D.L.R. (4th) 377 (Alta. Q.B.), such a claim was struck out as being essentially an action for defamation. As stated by Master Funduk "putting a business suit on a chimpanzee and calling it a businessman does not make it so". A loss of reputation claim is a defamation action, no matter how it is dressed up.

4. Fair Comment

Fair comment on matters of public concern or interest is protected from liability for defamation provided it is based on fact. These matters fall within two main categories; first, those in which the public has a legitimate interest, such as government activity, political debate, and proposals by public figures, and public affairs generally; second, works of art displayed in public such as theatrical performances, music and literature. In a democratic and culturally vibrant society, a discussion of these matters must be unfettered.

Fair comment must be based on fact. The facts must be included in the communication, or they must be indicated with sufficient clarity to lay a proper foundation for the comment being made. See *Kemsley v. Foot*, [1952] A.C. 345, at 357, [1952] 1 T.L.R. 532 (H.L.).

The comments cannot be presented so that they appear to be allegations of fact. The ordinary unprejudiced reader must take them to be comments based on facts for the defence to hold. See *Clarke v. Norton*, [1910] V.L.R. 494. Thus, if the "sting of the words complained of do not appear to be comment at all", the defence will fail. *Jones v. Bennett*, [1969] S.C.R. 277, 2 D.L.R. (3d) 291. In other words, to say that someone did something dishonourable is a fact, whereas to say that someone did a particular thing and that that was dishonourable is a statement of fact and a comment.

It is a question of fact for the jury to decide whether the communication is fact or comment, unless the judge withdraws the question from them. See *Jones v. Skelton*, [1963] 1 W.L.R. 1362, [1963] 3 All E.R. 952 (P.C.).

Unless the facts upon which the comment is based are true and undistorted, the comment cannot be "fair". The truth of the facts, therefore, is essential, not to prove that the statements were justified, but that the comment was a fair one.

Although the comment must be fair, this does not necessarily mean that it must be reasonable. Even the unreasonable are allowed to express their views. The test for the jury is whether they might reasonably regard the opinion as one that no fair-minded person could possibly have promulgated. The jury must not substitute their own opinion on the subject. See *McQuire v. Western Morning News Co. Ltd.*, [1903] 2 K.B. 100, [1900-3] All E.R. Rep. 673 (C.A.); *Masters v. Fox* (1978), 85 D.L.R. (3d) 64 (B.C.S.C.), fair comment defence fails because no fair-minded person could draw the inference from the facts. In other words, as long as the comment represents a legitimate opinion honestly held, it will be protected.

MCQUIRE v. WESTERN MORNING NEWS CO.

Court of Appeal. [1903] 2 K.B. 100, 72 L.J.K.B. 612, 88 L.T. 757, 19 T.L.R. 471.

The statement of claim stated that the plaintiff was an actor and theatrical manager, and the defendants were the owners of a newspaper called the *Western Morning News*; that on June 24, 1901, the plaintiff and a travelling company under his management appeared at the Theatre Royal, Plymouth, in a musical play written and composed by the plaintiff, entitled "The Major"; that, in the edition of the defendant's newspaper dated June 25, 1901, the defendants falsely and maliciously caused to be printed and published of and concerning the plaintiff, and of him as such actor and manager, and also as such author and composer as aforesaid, the words following: "A three act musical absurdity entitled 'The Major', written and composed by Mr. T.C. McQuire, was presented last evening before a full house by the author's company. It cannot be said that many left the building with the satisfaction of having seen anything like the standard of play which is generally to be witnessed at the Theatre Royal. Although it may be described as a play, 'The Major' is composed of nothing but nonsense of a not very humorous character, whilst the music is far from attractive. This comedy would be very much improved had it a substantial plot, and were a good deal of the sorry stuff taken out of it which lowers both the players and the play. No doubt the actors and actresses are well suited to the piece, which gives excellent scope for music-hall artists to display their talent. Among Mr. McQuire's company there is not one good actor or actress, and, with the exception of Mr. Ernest Braime, not one of them can be said to have a voice for singing. The introduction of common, not to say vulgar, songs does not tend to improve the character of the performance, and the dancing, which forms a prominent feature, is carried out with very little gracefulness"; and that by the said words the defendants meant, and were understood to mean, and the meaning of the said words was, that the said play was dull, vulgar, and degrading, that the members of the plaintiff's company were incompetent as actors, singers, and dancers, that they were music-hall artists, and that the plaintiff was himself incompetent both as an actor and composer as aforesaid.

The defence admitted the publication by the defendants of the matter complained of, but pleaded that it was published by them in the ordinary course of their business as public journalists, and without any malice to the plaintiff, and that it was a fair and bona fide criticism upon the play referred to in the statement of claim and its performance, which were matters of public interest, and was therefore no libel.

Evidence was given at the trial on both sides with regard to the nature of the play in question and its performance. … There was no evidence of any personal malice towards the plaintiff, or of any indirect motive, on the part of the writer of the criticism or anyone responsible for the management of the defendant's newspaper. The learned judge left the question whether the criticism complained of was or was not a libel to the jury, who found a verdict for the plaintiff with 100*l.* damages. Defendants appealed.

Collins M.R.: This raises a very important question as to what are the limits of "fair comment" on a literary work, and as to what are the respective provinces of the judge and jury with respect thereto. One thing, however, is perfectly clear, and that is that the jury have no right to substitute their own opinion of the literary merits of the work for that of the critic, or to try the "fairness" of the criticism by any such standard. "Fair", therefore, in this collocation certainly does not mean that which the ordinary reasonable man, "the man on the Clapham omnibus", as Lord Bowen phrased it, the juryman common or special, would think a correct appreciation of the work; and it is of the highest importance to the community that the critic should be saved from any such possibility. In principle, therefore, there would be nothing to leave to the jury unless there was some element in the criticism which might support an inference of unfairness in some other sense. No doubt this element might be, and has been, described in various ways and different instances of it given; but, broadly, I think Mr. Duke is right in contending that, in the case of a literary work at all events, it is something that passes out of the domain of criticism itself. Criticism cannot be used as a cloak for mere invective, nor for personal imputations not arising out of the subject-matter or not based on fact. "If," says Lord Ellenborough in *Carr v. Hood*, 1 Camp. 354; 10 R.R. 701, reported in a note to *Tabbart v. Tiffer*, 1 Camp. 350; 10 R.R. 698, "the commentator does not step aside from the work or introduce fiction for the purpose of condemnation he exercises a fair and legitimate right. … Had the party writing the criticism followed the plaintiff into domestic life for the purposes of slander that would have been libellous;" and, in another passage: "Shew me an attack on the moral character of this plaintiff, or any attack upon his character unconnected with his authorship, and I shall be as ready as any judge who ever sat here to protect him." In *Merivale v. Carson*, 20 Q.B.D. 275, Bowen, L.J., says: "In the case of literary criticism it is not easy to conceive what would be outside that region" — *i.e.* of fair comment — "unless the writer went out of his way to make a personal attack on the character of the author of the work which he was criticizing. In such a case the writer would be going beyond the limits of criticism altogether, and therefore beyond the limits of fair criticism. … Still, there is another class of cases in which, as it seems to me, the writer would be travelling out of the region of fair criticism — I mean if he imputes to the author that he has written something which in fact he has not written. That would be a misdescription of the work." I think "fair" embraces the meaning of honest and also of relevancy. The view expressed must be honest and must be such as can fairly be called criticism. I am aware that the word "moderate" has been used in this connection — *Watson v. Walter*, L.R. 4 Q.B. 73 — with reference to comment on the conduct of a public man; but I think it is only used to express the idea that invective is not criticism. It certainly cannot mean moderate in the sense that that which is deemed by a jury, in the case of a literary criticism, extravagant, and the outcome of prejudice on the part of an honest writer is necessarily beyond the limit of fair comment: see *Merivale v. Carson*, 20 Q.B.D. 275. No doubt in most cases of this class there are expressions in the impugned document capable of being interpreted as falling outside the limit of honest criticism, and, therefore, it is proper to leave the question to the jury, and in all cases where there may be a doubt it may be convenient to take the opinion of a jury. But it is always for the judge to say whether the document is capable in law of being a libel. It is, however, for the plaintiff, who rests his claim upon a document which on his own statement purports to be a criticism of a matter of public interest, to shew that it is a libel — *i.e.*, that it travels beyond the limit of fair criticism; and therefore it must be for the judge to say whether it is reasonably capable of being so interpreted. If it is not, there is no question for the jury, and it would be competent for him to give judgment for the defendant. ... The comment, in order to be within the protection of the privilege, had to be fair — *i.e.*, not such as to disclose in itself actual malice. It also had to be relevant; otherwise it never was within it, and the judge could hold as a matter of law that the privilege did not extend to it ... and in such case the only defence was truth. These factors were, I think, intended to be covered compendiously by the epithet "fair". In other words, it was intended to exclude those elements which took the comment out of, or prevented it from falling within, the privilege of the occasion. The result is that the question of "fair comment" is no more exclusively for the jury in one view of the nature of the right than in the other. In my opinion, there is in this case no evidence on which a rational verdict for the plaintiff can be founded, and the defendants are therefore entitled to have judgment entered for them. In this view it is not necessary to consider the grounds on which a new trial is asked for; but if there was any evidence fit to be considered by a jury, I am clearly of opinion that the verdict was against the weight of evidence.

[**Stirling** and **Mathew L.JJ.**, concurred, and judgment was entered for defendants.]

NOTES

1. In *Cherneskey v. Armadale Publishers Ltd.*, [1979] 1 S.C.R. 1067, 7 C.C.L.T. 69 (S.C.C.), two law students wrote a letter to the editor, which the *Saskatoon Star-Phoenix* published, complaining about the racist attitude of a local alderman. He sued the newspaper for libel. The law students did not testify at the trial and the newspaper staff testified that they did not agree with the contents of the letter. The trial judge withheld from the jury the defence of fair comment; this was reversed by the Saskatchewan Court of Appeal; the Supreme Court of Canada affirmed the trial judge, with Dickson, Spence and Estey JJ. dissenting:

   Mr. Justice Ritchie, for the majority, explained:

   > ... each publisher in relying on the defence of fair comment is in exactly the same position as the original writer. ...
   >
   > ... the newspaper and its editor cannot sustain a defence of fair comment when it has been proved that the words used in the letter are not an honest expression of their opinion and there is no evidence as to the honest belief of the writers.

   This was a reaffirmation of the traditional scope of the defence, which is available in discussion of matters of public interest, if (1) the facts upon which the comment is based are true, (2) the comment is fair, and (3) the person making the statement honestly believes it.

Mr. Justice Dickson disagreed fundamentally. He expresses his concern as follows:

> The important issue raised in this appeal is whether the defence of fair comment is denied a newspaper publishing material alleged to be defamatory unless it can be shown that the paper honestly believed the views expressed in the impugned material. It does not require any great perception to envisage the effect of such a rule upon the position of a newspaper in the publication of letters to the editor. An editor receiving a letter containing matter which might be defamatory would have a defence of fair comment if he shared the views expressed, but defenceless if he did not hold those views. As the columns devoted to letters to the editor are intended to stimulate uninhibited debate on every public issue, the editor's task would be an unenviable one if he were limited to publishing only those letters with which he agreed. He would be engaged in a sort of censorship, antithetical to a free press. One can readily draw a distinction between editorial comment or articles, which may be taken to represent the paper's point of view, and letters to the editor in which the personal opinion of the paper is, or should be, irrelevant. No one believes that a newspaper shares the views of every hostile reader who takes it to task in a letter to the editor for error of omission or commission, or that it yields assent to the views of every person who feels impelled to make his feelings known in a letter to the editor. Newspapers do not adopt as their own the opinions voiced in such letters, nor should they be expected to. …
>
> It is not only the right but the duty of the press, in pursuit of its legitimate objectives, to act as a sounding board for the free flow of new and different ideas. It is one of the few means of getting the heterodox and controversial before the public. Many of the unorthodox points of view get newspaper space through letters to the editor. It is one of the few ways in which the public gains access to the press. By these means, various points of view, old and new grievances and proposed remedies get aired. The public interest is incidentally served by providing a safety valve for people.
>
> Newspapers will not be able to provide a forum for dissemination of ideas if they are limited to publishing opinions with which they agree. If editors are faced with the choice of publishing only those letters which espouse their own particular ideology, or being without defence if sued for defamation, democratic dialogue will be stifled. Healthy debate will likely be replaced by monotonous repetition of majoritarian ideas and conformity to accepted taste. In one-newspaper towns, of which there are many, competing ideas will no longer gain access. Readers will be exposed to a single political, economic and social point of view. In a public controversy, the tendency will be to suppress those letters with which the editor is not in agreement. This runs directly counter to the increasing tendency of North American newspapers generally to become less devoted to the publishers' opinions and to print, without fear or favour, the widest possible range of opinions on matters of public interest. The integrity of a newspaper rests not on the publication of letters with which it is in agreement, but rather on the publication of letters expressing ideas to which it is violently opposed.
>
> I do not wish to overstate the case. It is my view, however, that anything which serves to repress competing ideas is inimical to the public interest. I agree that the publisher of a newspaper has no special immunity from the application of general laws, and that in the matter of comment he is in no better position than any other citizen. But he should not be in any worse position. That, I fear, will be the situation if one fails to distinguish between the writer of a letter to the editor, and the editor, or if one compresses into one statement

> the several steps in the requisite process of analysis of the defence of fair comment.

Mr. Justice Dickson preferred to adopt a new, more liberal test, from *Duncan and Neill on Defamation* (1978), for the scope of fair comment:

> (a) the comment must be on a matter of public interest;
>
> (b) the comment must be based on fact;
>
> (c) the comment, though it can include inferences of fact, must be recognisable as comment;
>
> (d) the comment must satisfy the following *objective* test: could any man honestly express that opinion on the proved facts?
>
> (e) even though the comment satisfies the objective test the defence can be defeated *if the plaintiff proves that the defendant was actuated by express malice.*

His Lordship explained further:

> ... If the analysis set out in Duncan and Neill is accepted, and I suggest it should be, it is readily apparent that newspapers need not be in any different position from the rest of the population. Once a comment which is defamatory (in the sense of lowering the subject's reputation) is shown to be objectively fair, the only question is whether it was published with malice. This will depend on whether there is appropriate evidence of malice, which will be different depending upon whether the newspaper, or its staff, writes the comment, or whether the newspaper publishes comments written by others.

In response to this concern Mr. Justice Ritchie had this to say:

> This does not mean that freedom of the press to publish its views is in any way affected, nor does it mean that a newspaper cannot publish letters expressing views with which it may strongly disagree. Moreover, nothing that is here said should be construed as meaning that a newspaper is in any way restricted in publishing two diametrically opposite views of the opinion and conduct of a public figure. On the contrary, I adopt as descriptive of the conclusion which I have reached, the language used by Brownridge J.A., in the following excerpt from his reasons for judgment in the Court of Appeal where he said at p. 192 of the Report:
>
>> What it does mean is that a newspaper cannot publish a *libellous* letter and then disclaim any responsibility by saying that it was published as fair comment on a matter of public interest but it does not represent the honest opinion of the newspaper.

2. The reaction to the majority's decision was most unfavourable and has led to legislative changes in various provincial defamation statutes. Ontario, Alberta, New Brunswick and Manitoba have amended their acts to make it clear that a defendant who publishes opinions expressed by another will not lose the defence of fair comment by virtue of the fact that the publisher did not share the opinions published. The legislation generally requires good faith on the part of the publishers.

For example, Ontario enacted the following new provision:

> Where the defendant published defamatory matter that is an opinion expressed by another person, a defence of fair comment shall not fail for the reason only

that the defendant or the person who expressed the opinion, or both, did not hold the opinion, if a person could honestly hold the opinion.

See the *Libel and Slander Act*, R.S.O. 1990, c. L.12, s. 24. See also the *Defamation Amendment Act*, R.S.A. 1980, c. D-6, s. 9; *An Act to Amend the Defamation Act*, S.N.B. 1980, c. 16, s. 8.1(1); the *Defamation Act*, R.S.M. 1987, c. D.20, s. 9. Is it a good thing to have different legislation in each province covering an issue as fundamental as this one? Will a national newspaper have to publish different "Letters to the Editor" material in different provinces? Should newspapers be protected when they print defamatory material in a letter to the editor?

3. In *Barltrop v. Canadian Broadcasting Corp.* (1978), 86 D.L.R. (3d) 61, 5 C.C.L.T. 88 (N.S.C.A.), the radio show "As It Happens" broadcasted some information about a doctor who was alleged to have "sold" his evidence, which was said to be contrary to public health, to an inquiry. Because the facts upon which the comment were based were found to be false, it was held not to be fair comment and $20,000 damages were awarded.

4. In *Slim v. Daily Telegraph*, [1968] 2 Q.B. 157, [1968] 1 All E.R. 497 (C.A.), Denning M.R., though holding defendants liable because of false facts, had this to say:

> The right of fair comment is one of the essential elements which go to make up our freedom of speech. We must even maintain this right intact. It must not be whittled down by legal requirements. When a citizen is troubled by things going wrong, he should be free to write to the newspaper; and the newspaper should be free to publish this letter. It is often the only way to get things put right. The matter must, of course, be one of public interest. The writer must get his facts right; and he must honestly state his real opinion. But that being done, both he and the newspaper should be clear of any liability. They should not be deterred by fear of libel actions.

See also *Holt v. Sun Publishing Co.* (1978), 83 D.L.R. (3d) 761; affd (1979), 100 D.L.R. (3d) 447 (B.C.C.A.), former M.P. Simma Holt collected $5,000 because comments about her were not based on facts.

5. Is the control of the media through defamation law a valuable contribution by tort law to Canadian society in the 1990s? What alternative methods of supervision exist?

CHAPTER 17

DAMAGES

The assessment of damages is one of the most important aspects of tort law and has received, until recently, only scant attention from scholars. Due however to important Supreme Court of Canada decisions in the area of damage assessment, there has been a surge of interest in the topic. And of course, as always, damage assessment cases dominate the reported tort law cases. As will be seen, the basic aim of the law of damages is to measure and provide compensation for the unique loss suffered by each individual claimant. As noble as this attempt may be, problems are created. It is a costly and time-consuming process. Moreover, it is impossible to achieve any precision. In recent years, the complexities have multiplied with the advent of tax laws, liability insurance and widespread social legislation. Many tough questions are being asked about the future of tort damages. Should the jury be involved? Should lump sums be continued? Should pain and suffering be compensated for? Underlying all of these questions relating to the details of damage assessment, of course, lies the main question: can society afford to continue to compensate tort victims *in full* for their losses while leaving non-tort victims to other, and in many cases less adequate, sources?

This chapter provides an introduction to the damage assessment process by looking at its major elements.

A. THE PURPOSE OF DAMAGES

CHARLES, "JUSTICE IN PERSONAL INJURY AWARDS"

in Klar (ed.), *Studies in Canadian Tort Law* (1977), p. 37

The general objectives of the law in the area of personal injuries can be stated without too much difficulty or disagreement. It is readily agreed that the injured person should be compensated for the loss he has suffered, and where he has died from his injuries, his dependants should be compensated for their loss. There is also public agreement that the law in this area, as in others, should operate uniformly and produce predictable results, while at the same time being fair to both plaintiff and defendant. The average citizen would probably think it reasonable that where the loss suffered by the victim can be quantified in monetary terms with reasonable accuracy, the plaintiff should be compensated to the full extent of his loss. In situations where the loss is of such a nature that it cannot be objectively determined, the plaintiff should nevertheless be awarded damages on the basis of principles which can be rationally supported and which can produce results considered by the public to be generally fair and just.

But while such broad objectives can be enunciated and agreed upon without too much difficulty, their very general nature provides little guidance when a court is required to place a dollar value on particular kinds of personal injuries in specific circumstances. Is it possible for a court, using the existing rules for the assessment of damages, to arrive at a monetary figure which accurately reflects the loss? There is obviously a need for more specific rules or principles, the application of which by the court will enable the law to reach the broad objectives previously suggested. How far have our courts progressed in developing a scientific statement of the law of damages? What are the new problems with which they are forced to cope in their assessment of the amount of compensation to which the plaintiff is entitled? The answers to these questions form the basis of the following discussion of the law of damages.

Although it is necessary for the plaintiff in a personal injury case to establish the liability of the defendant before the question of damages can be considered by the court, the calculation of losses suffered by the plaintiff is of equal, if not greater, importance to both the plaintiff and the defendant. Yet in spite of this obvious truism, most law teachers, students and lawyers, spend relatively little time studying the many problems involved in the calculation of damages, or the rules and principles used by the court in their assessment of the loss suffered. It has been said that "Questions of damages 151— and particularly their magnitude — do not lend themselves so easily to discourse. Professors dismiss them airily as matters of trial administration. Judges consign them uneasily to juries with a minimum of guidance, occasionally observing loosely that there are no rules of assessing damages in personal injury cases."

In personal injury cases, as with other torts situations, the law, by virtue of the principle of *restitutio in integrum*, seeks to place the victim in the same position he was in before the accident occurred. Since perfect compensation in the sense of physical reconstruction of the victim to his pre-accident condition is generally impossible, the initial premise upon which damage awards are based is that damages should be computed so that the dollars awarded will be an adequate compensation for the loss which was suffered by the injured party. To the extent that money damages can make the victim whole again, the award of compensation is considered to be the fairest solution to both plaintiff and defendant. The plaintiff recovers his losses to a reasonable extent and the defendant is penalized only to the extent that he has to compensate the plaintiff, either personally or through his insurance company. As a matter of practical policy the courts refuse to determine compensation on the basis of the amount of money the plaintiff would have been willing to pay himself in order to avoid the injury or be relieved of it. Such damages, even if measurable and accepted as adequate by the plaintiff, would be so high as to be socially unacceptable.

If it is considered important that justice be done between the parties in relation to the liability question, it is equally important that justice also be done insofar as the assessment of damages is concerned. The generally declining use of juries in personal injury cases in Canada means that the task of awarding proper damages falls more often on the shoulders of the judge. As plaintiffs' counsel present more detailed and sophisticated evidence of losses suffered by their clients as a result of the defendant's acts, judges are forced to think more and more about the principles upon which their damage awards are to be determined. Faced with arguments relating to collateral benefits, inflation, income tax, cost of future case [sic], loss of amenities and loss of expectation of life in complex cases involving severe loss, Canadian judges have been forced in recent years to articulate more clearly than ever before the principles governing the proper assessment of personal injury losses. Such an undertaking raises the question whether the assessment of damages as a process is susceptible to a rational analysis. Perhaps it is so elusive that it must be left to the individual judge to decide, on the basis of his own personal institution, what level of compensation is fair to both parties. Is it even possible for our judges to formulate principles which can be articulated in an open manner?

The degree to which they are, or will be, successful in creating socially acceptable guidelines may be an important factor the overall public evaluation and acceptance of the tort system as the primary instrument for the provision of compensation to injured persons.

NOTES

1. Professor Charles' cry "for more specific rules or principles" was answered by the Supreme Court of Canada in its famous 'trilogy': *Andrews v. Grand & Toy Alta. Ltd.*, [1978] 2 S.C.R. 229, 3 C.C.L.T. 225; *Thornton v. Board of School Trustees of School District No. 57 (Prince George) et al.*, [1978] 2 S.C.R. 267, 3 C.C.L.T. 257; *Arnold v. Teno*, [1978] 2 S.C.R. 287, 83 D.L.R. (3d) 609, 3 C.C.L.T. 272. A fourth important case, a fatal accident assessment, was decided at the same time: *Keizer v. Hanna et al.*, [1978] 2 S.C.R. 342, 3 C.C.L.T. 316. See *infra*.

2. In its trilogy, the Supreme Court reaffirmed that the purpose of an award of damages, particularly in the area of pecuniary losses, is to fully compensate the victim by restoring him or her, as much as money will allow, to his or her former position. Mr. Justice Dickson acknowledged however that a plaintiff "must be reasonable in making a claim".

3. What is the test of "reasonableness"? In *Thornton*, the plaintiff, who was a quadriplegic, asked that he be awarded enough money to provide him with his own home. Was this reasonable? Mr. Justice Dickson stated:

   > ... before denying a quadriplegic home care on the ground of "unreasonable" cost something more is needed than the mere statement that the cost is unreasonable. There should be evidence which would lead any right-thinking person to say: "That would be a squandering of money — no person in his right mind would make any such expenditure".

   Is this a useful test?

4. In assessing damages for *future* care, what is reasonable and feasible is a matter of speculation. Things may not actually turn out as expected. This is what apparently happened in the *Andrews* case. Although his damages were based upon his desire to live in his own home, it is reported that this type of accommodation did not suit Andrews and he moved into an auxiliary hospital. See Bissett-Johnson, "Damages for Personal Injury — The Supreme Court Speaks" (1978), 24 McGill L.J. 316, at 328, fn. 50a. In such a case, is the plaintiff entitled to keep all the money received to set up his or her own home?

5. What is reasonable also depends upon the evidence presented. Although an individual home might have been accepted by the court as being reasonable in the case of one quadriplegic plaintiff, the decision for other quadriplegics might very well be different. See Charles, "A New Handbook on the Assessment of Damages in Personal Injury Cases from the Supreme Court of Canada" (1977-78), 3 C.C.L.T. 344. For a recent case where the court decided that a group home would be better, see *Lusignan v. Concordia Hospital*, [1997] 6 W.W.R. 185 (Man. Q.B.).

6. Although plaintiffs are not required to settle for damages which do not represent their "real" loss, they are expected to take reasonable steps to ensure that their losses are as low as possible. Does this mean that a plaintiff is required to have an operation to correct a medical condition, if an operation has a reasonable chance of success with low

risk? See *Dominey v. Sangster and Sangster* (1980), 38 N.S.R. (2d) 403, 69 A.P.R. 403 (S.C.) and *Emeny v. Butters* (1982), 36 O.R. (2d) 328 (Co. Ct.). If a plaintiff unreasonably refuses to undergo surgery which has a 75 per cent chance of success and which would have the effect of completely repairing the plaintiff's disability, should the plaintiff's damages for loss of future income be reduced by 75 per cent or entirely eliminated? See *Ippolito v. Janiuk et al.* (1981), 34 O.R. (2d) 151, 126 D.L.R. (3d) 623, 18 C.C.L.T. 39 (C.A.). Also see *Engel v. Kam-Ppelle*, [1993] 1 S.C.R. 306, [1993] 2 W.W.R. 373.

7. What if plaintiffs cannot take steps to mitigate their losses because they do not have the resources to do so? Who should bear the consequences of a plaintiff's "impecuniosity"? In the House of Lords' decision in *The Liesboch v. The Edison*, [1933] A.C. 449, it was decided that the defendant should not be held responsible for damages which could have been prevented but for the plaintiff's impecuniosity. That rule now seems to have been replaced by the reasonable foreseeability test. That is, if the plaintiff's situation and damages are reasonably foreseeable consequences of the defendant's wrongdoing, the full damages are recoverable. See *Amar Cloth House Ltd. v. La Van & Co.* (1997), 35 C.C.L.T. (2d) 99 (B.C.S.C.) for a good review of this issue. For a very strong criticism of the principle of *The Liesboch,* see *Rollinson v. R.* (1994), 20 C.C.L.T. (2d) 92 (Fed. Ct.), and Wexler, "The Impecunious Plaintiff: Liesboch Reconsidered" (1987), 66 Can. Bar Rev. 129.

B. GENERAL PRINCIPLES

1. The Heads of Damage

CHARLES, "JUSTICE IN PERSONAL INJURY AWARDS"
in Klar (ed.), *Studies in Canadian Tort Law* (1977), p. 37

To establish a cause of action the plaintiff must first prove that he or she suffered injury that was not too remote or, in other words, an injury that was reasonably foreseeable. Damages, on the other hand, are awarded on the basis of losses which result from that injury. Compensability depends, not upon the severity of the injury, but on the consequences to the individual affected by the tortious act. Courts have recognized the fact that different kinds of consequences can ensure from a tortious act. They have done so by establishing several distinct heads of damage:

(a) the physical injury itself and the pain and suffering associated with it up to the time of trial;
(b) disability and loss of amenities before trial;
(c) loss of earnings before trial;
(d) expenses incurred before trial;
(e) pain and suffering expected to be suffered in the future (after trial) either temporarily or permanently;
(f) loss of amenities after trial;
(g) loss of life expectancy;
(h) loss of earnings to be suffered after the trial and into the foreseeable future, and
(i) cost of future care and other expenses.

In the case of personal injury actions resulting in the death of the victim, the law permits an action by the dependants as a class, as well as by the estate, against the wrongdoer. In an action by the dependants, the loss suffered is in most cases primarily financial, but it can also include, as in the case of the death of parent, loss of guidance and education as well. The common law does not presently recognize loss in the form of grief or *solatium*.

a) SPECIAL AND GENERAL DAMAGES

Some of the damages or losses suffered by the plaintiff will have manifested themselves prior to trial and thus will be capable of precise calculation by the court. Expenses such as physician fees, hospital bills, payment for housekeeping assistance, and lost wages can be easily pinpointed. They are usually agreed to by counsel and designated as special damages. The bulk of the plaintiff's loss, however, might well extend far into the future and be incapable of precise calculation. Pecuniary loss, involving loss of future wages and costs of future medical care, are dealt with separately by the court under the heading of general damages. Losses incurred between the date of the writ and the date of the trial have caused some difficulty. The practice of the courts does not appear to be uniform, with some tribunals treating lost wages as special damages, while others have added them to lump sum awards as general damages.

NOTES

1. In the past courts used to assess damages by presenting a "global" award. As a result of the trilogy, however, courts now classify damages into four heads: (1) special damages, (2) loss of earnings, (3) cost of future care, and (4) non-pecuniary losses. See Cooper-Stephenson, *Personal Injury Damages in Canada*, 2nd ed. (1996), p. 102.

2. Special damages are, by definition, calculable into exact monetary terms, tend not to be very large, and do not pose great difficulties for the parties. They are, in many cases, agreed to without requiring judicial determination. Problems sometimes do arise however.

3. On occasion a court may hold that a claimant is trying to recoup costs that are too extravagant. The claim must be a "reasonable" one. In *Alexandroff v. R. in Right of Ontario*, [1967] 2 O.R. 625, 64 D.L.R. (2d) 673 (H.C.); affd [1970] S.C.R. 753, 14 D.L.R. (3d) 66, a claim of $3,844.55 for a two-month holiday in Hawaii on the recommendation of a doctor, while undoubtedly "salubrious" was found to be "asking too much of the defendant" and was reduced by $2,000. Similarly, a claim for $1,295, the cost of seven suits at $185 that were prematurely worn because of a brace the plaintiff had to wear, was reduced by $700.

4. The characterization of pre-trial wage loss is not uniform. It is now generally regarded as an item of special damages, although still treated as general damages by some courts. See Cooper-Stephenson, *supra*, and *Baart v. Kumar and Kumar* (1983), 45 B.C.L.R. 233, [1983] 4 W.W.R. 419 (S.C.), which support the special damages approach and *Trache v. Can. Nor. Ry.*, [1929] 2 D.L.R. 32, [1929] 1 W.W.R. 100 (Sask. C.A.), for the general damages view. What practical difference may it make if the head is considered special as opposed to general damages?

5. Difficulties are encountered when relatives or friends expend money or provide services for injured persons without expecting to be recompensed for these expenses. Are these expenses claimable? By whom — the injured person or the person who provided

the service? Ontario has legislation dealing specifically with this issue. It permits relatives to recover expenses; see *Family Law Act*, R.S.O. 1990, c. F.3. There are also cases dealing with this issue. See, for example, *Dziver et al. v. Smith* (1983), 41 O.R. (2d) 385, 146 D.L.R. (3d) 314 (C.A.); *Feng v. Graham*, [1988] 5 W.W.R. 137, 44 C.C.L.T. 52 (B.C.C.A.); and *Crane v. Worwood*, [1992] 3 W.W.R. 638 (B.C.S.C.). An interesting case on this issue is *Kroeker v. Jansen* (1995), 24 C.C.L.T. (2d) 113, 123 D.L.R. (4th) 652, [1995] 6 W.W.R. 5 (B.C.C.A.); leave to appeal to S.C.C. refused (1995), 27 C.C.L.T. (2d) 209*n*. The plaintiff was injured in a car accident and as a result was unable to do household chores. Her sister assisted her, but after the plaintiff married, her husband did the household tasks. The trial judge awarded the plaintiff $23,000 for the loss of her ability to perform household tasks. On appeal, the majority recognized the claim but reduced the award to $7,000. Two dissenting judges held that since the plaintiff was married, it was expected that her spouse would do a normal amount of housework and that there should be no award made in these circumstances. The husband was in fact doing the vacuuming, ironing, washing and waxing the floors, and so forth. With which judgment do you agree? What if the husband refused to do the chores, or was too busy to do them, and the plaintiff tried her best to do them? What if they hired outside help? Do you think that the award should be based on such factors?

6. For an excellent discussion of other problems relating to the assessment of special damages, see Cooper-Stephenson, *supra*, Chapter 4.

2. The Role of the Jury

With the increasing use of jury trials in tort actions come difficult questions. Although juries are asked to fix damage awards, what they can be told about the assessment process is not altogether clear. What can a jury be told about the damage assessment process? Can it be told how much the plaintiff is asking? Can it be given guidance by counsel or the trial judge as to "conventional" or comparable awards? In the leading Ontario case of *Gray v. Alanco Developments Ltd.*, [1967] 1 O.R. 597, at 601, 61 D.L.R. (2d) 652 (C.A.), it was held that the Trial Judge had erred in suggesting lower and upper limits to a reasonable award of general damages. The Court of Appeal stated that these suggestions are not evidence and that the parties "are entitled to the jury's verdict uninfluenced by anything extraneous to the evidence, proper submissions of council thereon, the instructions of the Judge as to the law and his summing up of the evidence together with his comments thereon and the credit to be given to it". The Court followed the reasoning in *Ward v. James*, [1966] 1 Q.B. 273, [1965] 1 All E.R. 563 (C.A.), where Lord Denning held that juries cannot be informed of either comparable cases or conventional figures. Another effort to permit evidence for juries was also prevented in Ontario, see *Howes v. Crosby* (1984), 6 D.L.R. (4th) 698, 29 C.C.L.T. 60 (Ont. C.A.). It is interesting to note that Mr. Justice Osborne has recently recommended that trial judges, in their discretion, should be permitted to express opinions to the jury as to a range of compensation for both pecuniary and non-pecuniary damages.

The Saskatchewan Court of Appeal has taken a different approach. In two cases, *Rieger v. Burgess*, [1988] 4 W.W.R. 577, 45 C.C.L.T. 56, and *Quintal v. Datta* (1988), 68 Sask. R. 104, [1988] 6 W.W.R. 481, at 517; leave to appeal to S.C.C. refused (1989), 76 Sask. R. 80*n* (S.C.C.), the Court held that it was proper for a trial judge to give "meaningful guidance to the jury's deliberations by giving guidelines on the reasonable range of awards for pecuniary and non-pecuniary losses". The Court felt that if judges trying the case alone are entitled to receive full submissions on the range of appropriate awards, the jury should be entitled to the same assistance. Also, see *McGrath v. Pendergras* (1988), 60 Alta. L.R. (2d) 276, 45 C.C.L.T. 186; leave to appeal to S.C.C. refused, December 15, 1988, where the Alberta Court of Appeal left it up to the trial judge to decide whether the jury should be told about the rough, upper limit for non-pecuniary awards. Even in Ontario, juries are told about this rough, upper limit. The Supreme Court of Canada has recently affirmed that in cases where there is a conventional figure or an upper limit, at least, "judges are permitted, and indeed required, to give the jury guidance as to the proper conventional figure." See *ter Neuzen v. Korn* (1995), 127 D.L.R. (4th) 577 at 612-613 (S.C.C.)

Once made, it is extremely difficult to upset a jury's damage award. To overturn a jury's award it is not enough that the appellate court merely feels it is too high or too low. A jury assessment may be upset only if the appellate tribunal believes that no 12 people acting reasonably could have given it, if the jury took into account matters they ought not to have considered, or if the jury misunderstood or disregarded its duty. See generally *Davey et al. v. McManus Petroleum Ltd.*, [1949] O.R. 374, [1949] 3 D.L.R. 715 (C.A.); affd [1950] 1 D.L.R. 303 (*sub nom. Donnelly v. McManus Petroleum Ltd.*) (S.C.C.). If an assessment of damages is made by a trial judge alone, a court of appeal may interfere with it if the trial judge applied a wrong principle of law or if the award is so inordinately high or low that it must be a wholly erroneous estimate of the damage. It is sometimes said that there should be no interference unless the award "shocks the conscience". (See *Alexandroff v. R.*, [1970] S.C.R. 753, at 770, 14 D.L.R. (3d) 66.) The Supreme Court has expressed its reluctance to interfere with the assessments by provincial courts of appeal except in the most exceptional circumstances (as where there has been an error in principle), because it is felt that they are in a better position to decide on the basis of the local environment.

For an eloquent defence of the jury see Haines, "The Future of the Civil Jury" in Linden (ed.), *Studies in Canadian Tort Law* (1968), p. 10. See also *Special Lectures of the Law Society of Upper Canada*, "Jury Trials" (1959); Joiner, *Civil Justice and the Jury* (1962); Devlin, *Trial by Jury* (1956); Cornish, *The Jury* (1968).

3. Lump Sum or Periodic Payments?

CHARLES, "JUSTICE IN PERSONAL INJURY AWARDS"

in Klar (ed.), *Studies in Canadian Tort Law* (1977), p. 37

(b) LUMP SUM OR PERIODIC PAYMENTS

Canadian courts have adopted the traditional view that an award of periodic payments is not possible unless both parties consent or it is authorized by statute. The accepted practice is to award a lump sum, in spite of the fact that many of the difficulties encountered by the courts in the determination of damages stem from the necessity of awarding a once-and-for-all payment. Courts are thus forced in many cases to look far into the future and to struggle with a host of unknown factors such as the degree of improvement or deterioration in the victim's physical condition, the economic future the victim might have expected insofar as this relates to loss of future earnings, as well as future costs, particularly medical costs.

Although modern no-fault compensation schemes show a decided preference for a plan based upon periodic payments, the United Kingdom Law Commission has recently concluded that periodic payments should not be introduced into the existing fault system as an alternative mode of compensation. This decision was arrived at after consultation with the public and interested groups and left the Commission in no doubt that "the introduction of a system of periodic payments would meet with vehement opposition" from insurance interests, organizations representing plaintiffs' interests, the Bar Council and the Law Society itself.

The lump sum award procedure appears to have developed without a conscious regard for alternatives, but it appears to have certain attractions for the plaintiff, insurance companies, and courts alike. Even in those countries where choice is possible, claimants appear to prefer a lump sum award. Not only does it give them more flexibility in planning their future, but psychologically a bird in the hand appears to be more satisfying than one in the bush. From the court's point of view the desire to determine disputes with a degree of finality, and to avoid the increased administrative load associated with supervision of periodic payments tends to discourage the use of such payments. For the same reason insurance companies prefer to close their books on a claim and avoid the need to carry cash reserves to cover future payments or increases in awards. There would probably also be some difficulty establishing insurance rates on a short-term basis as well.

Those who advocate periodic payments do so not only because this mode of payment permits a more accurate determination of damages over a long period of time, but in addition such a system eliminates the chance that the victim will not invest his award wisely but will dissipate it and become a charge on society. Unfortunately, little is known about how victims spend their damage awards. If the lump sum awarded is to be retained, one way to protect the successful claimant from his own weakness would be to establish some form of trusteeship to invest, manage and dispurse [sic] funds as required by the victim. Periodic payments should be variable, if the effects of inflation are to be adequately countered. This may well require a detailed judicial statement of the assumptions underlying the awards, particularly the future variables such as the degree of disability and the wage rates to be applied. Although much has been written about the difficulties created by the present lump sum award procedure, there is little evidence of a desire within the judiciary or the profession to adopt a periodic payment plan within the existing tort fault system.

NOTES

1. There has been strong judicial criticism of the lump sum approach. See Dickson J., in *Andrews v. Grand & Toy*, *infra*, and consider the following comments by Lord Scarman in *Lim Poh Choo v. Camden and Islington Area Health Authority*, [1980] A.C. 174, [1979] 2 All E.R. 910 (H.L.):

> It cannot be said that any of the time judicially spent on these protracted proceedings has been unnecessary. The question, therefore, arises whether the state of the law which gives rise to such complexities is sound. Lord Denning M.R. in the Court of Appeal [1979] Q.B. 196, 216, declared that a radical reappraisal of the law is needed. I agree. But I part company with him on ways and means. The Master of the Rolls believes it can be done by the judges, whereas I would suggest to your Lordships that such a reappraisal calls for social, financial, economic and administrative decisions which only the legislature can take. The perplexities of the present case, following upon the publication of the report of the Royal Commission on Civil Liability and Compensation for Personal Injury (1978) (Cmnd. 7054) ('the Parson report'), emphasize the need for reform of the law.

> The course of the litigation illustrates, with devastating clarity, the insuperable problems implicit in a system of compensation for personal injuries which (unless the parties agree otherwise) can yield only a lump sum assessed by the court at the time of judgment. Sooner or later — and too often later rather than sooner — if the parties do not settle, a court (once liability is admitted or proved) has to make an award of damages. The award, which covers past, present, and future injury and loss, must, under our law, be of a lump sum assessed at the conclusion of the legal process. The award is final; it is not susceptible to review as the future unfolds, substituting fact for estimate. Knowledge of the future being denied to mankind, so much of the award as is to be attributed to future loss and suffering — in many cases the major part of the award — will almost surely be wrong. There is really only one certainty: the future will prove the award to be either too high or too low.
>
> Lord Denning appeared, however, to think — or at least to hope — that there exists machinery in the Rules of the Supreme Court which may be adapted to enable an award of damages in a case such as this to be "regarded as an interim award" [1979] Q.B. 196, 220. It is an attractive, ingenious suggestion — but, in my judgment, unsound. For so radical a reform can be made neither by judges nor by modification of rules of court. It raises issues of social, economic and financial policy not amenable to judicial reform, which will almost certainly prove to be controversial and can be resolved by the legislature only after full consideration of factors which cannot be brought into clear focus, or be weighed or assessed, in the course of the forensic process. The judge — however wise, creative, and imaginative he may be — is 'cabin'd, cribb'd, confin'd, bound in' not, as was Macbeth, to his "saucy doubts and fears" but by the evidence and arguments of the litigants. It is this limitation, inherent in the forensic process, which sets bounds to the scope of judicial law reform.

2. Do you agree with Mr. Justice Dickson and Lord Scarman that the courts are unable, on their own, to do anything about the lump sum approach? Who devised this method in the first place?

3. Critics of tort law who opt for "no-fault" schemes always point to the lump sum approach as an indictment of the common law action. Is this criticism fair? Is the lump sum approach a necessary element of the common law? Could a system of periodic payments and review not be part of a fault-based compensation law?

4. The choice between lump sums or periodic payments is a difficult one, since there are a great number of arguments, pro and con, for each option. Waddams, *The Law of Damages*, 3rd ed. (1997), extensively reviews the arguments. The main arguments against the lump sum approach are that it produces unreliable and inaccurate assessments, it creates delay in assessment and award which has a number of undesirable side effects for plaintiffs, it has tax disadvantages, and it creates the possibility that the money may be squandered. On the other side, critics of periodic payments note that this approach requires costly review procedures, review itself has a number of undesirable consequences for plaintiffs, the lack of finality has undesirable consequences for defendants, and evidence indicates that plaintiffs prefer lump sums when given the choice. It is not surprising, in view of the controversy, that a system of periodic payments has not been implemented which operates without consent of the parties. For such a suggestion see Ontario Committee on Tort Compensation (1980), discussed by Waddams, *supra*. Also see Bruce, "Four Techniques for Compensating Tort Damages" (1983), 21 U.W.O.L. Rev. 1, and a long list of articles cited by Bruce, at n. 1, p. 1, which have recommended use of periodic payments.

5. A thorough discussion of these problems and a new suggestion for assisting victims has been presented by Bale, "Encouraging the Hearse Horse Not to Snicker: A Tort Fund Providing Variable Periodic Payments for Pecuniary Loss", Steel and Rodgers-

Magnet (ed.) *Issues in Tort Law* (1983), p. 91. Professor Bale suggests that lump sum judgments for future loss of earnings, for future medical and health care not covered by the health insurance scheme, and for future loss of support by dependants in fatal accident cases be paid directly into a tort fund. Tort law victims would then receive from the fund variable, periodic payments for their pecuniary losses. Professor Bale believes that this system would eliminate many of the defects of periodic payments while providing victims with security against changing conditions which alter their needs.

6. There are legislative provisions in some jurisdictions providing for periodic payments. See, for example, *Court of Queen's Bench Act*, S.M. 1988-89, c. 4, C.C.S.M. c. C820, s. 80, which allows the court upon application by any party in court proceedings for damages for personal injuries or death to order that damages be paid by periodic payments. For a recent case applying this provision, see *Lusignan v. Concordia Hospital*, [1997] 6 W.W.R. 185 (Man. Q.B.). Also see *Webster v. Chapman* (1996), 30 C.C.L.T. (2d) 164 (Man. Q.B.) for a discussion of the new provisions, including the suggestion that they in reality change vey little about the damage assessment process.

7. An alternative to both the lump sum and periodic payment is the "structured settlement". The parties settle on the amount of damages initially, but agree that it will be paid out over a period of time.

   A structured settlement was approved of in *Yepremian v. Scarborough General Hospital* (1981), 15 C.C.L.T. 73 (Ont. H.C.). The plaintiff received increasing annual payments as long as the plaintiff was still alive. In approving the settlement, Mr. Justice R.E. Holland stated:

   > Since structured settlement is a relatively new method of settling personal injury cases it is appropriate for me to make certain comments on the system of structured settlements and on this particular settlement. Structured settlements are a means whereby all or part of the damages are paid to a claimant by means of periodic payments rather than by means of a lump sum. Perhaps the prime advantage of a structured settlement is that payments are received tax free in the hands of the plaintiff whereas if the plaintiff had used the lump sum to purchase an annuity the interest portion of the annuity payment would be subject to income tax.
   >
   > It apparently has been the experience of many solicitors that lump sum payments, even in the case of substantial payments resulting from serious personal injury or death, are often dissipated within months or a few years of the payment being received.
   >
   > The structural settlement proposed in this case is particularly suitable to the circumstances of the case because Tony, as a result of brain injury sustained in the hospital, is not mentally competent to manage his own affairs. Tony will receive a guaranteed income for life indexed at 3% and tax free. He is better looked after, in my view, under the terms of the settlement than he would have been under my judgment at trial or even under the increased award of the Court of Appeal.

   See, Henderson, "Periodic Payments of Bodily Injury Awards" (1980), 66 A.B.A.J. 734; Cave, "Structured Settlements: An Alternate Resolution of Claims Involving Death or Substantial Personal Injury" (1979), 27 Chitty's L.J. 234.

8. Can a court order a structured settlement on its own? In *Watkins v. Olafson* (1989), 61 D.L.R. (4th) 577, [1989] 6 W.W.R. 481; revg [1987] 5 W.W.R. 193, 40 C.C.L.T. 229, the Supreme Court of Canada held that in the absence of either enabling legislation or the consent of all parties, a plaintiff cannot be deprived of the right to a lump sum payment.

C. THE ASSESSMENT OF GENERAL DAMAGES FOR PERSONAL INJURIES

As a result of the "trilogy" the principles for assessing general damages for personal injuries have been carefully reviewed. As indicated above, the category of "general damages" includes numerous sub-categories, with differing objectives, rules, and methods of assessment. Before looking at these sub-categories separately, let us first look at the significant portions of the Supreme Court judgments.

ANDREWS v. GRAND & TOY ALBERTA LTD. ET AL.

Supreme Court of Canada. (1978), 3 C.C.L.T. 225, [1978] 2 S.C.R. 229.

Dickson J.: This is a negligence action for personal injury involving a young man rendered a quadriplegic in a traffic accident for which the respondent Anderson and his employer, Grand & Toy Alberta Ltd., have been found partially liable. Leave to appeal to this court was granted on the question whether the Appellate Division of the Supreme Court of Alberta erred in law in the assessment of damages. At trial Kirby J. awarded $1,022,477.48 [[1974] 5 W.W.R. 675, 54 D.L.R. (3d) 85]; the Appellate Division reduced that sum to $516,544.48 [[1976] 2 W.W.R. 385, 64 D.L.R. (3d) 663].

The amounts awarded in each court under each of the several heads of damages are set out below:

Pecuniary Loss

	Trial	Appellate Division
(a) Cost of Future Care		
— special equipment	$ 14,200	$ 14,200
— monthly amount	4,135	1,000
— contingencies	20%	30%
— capitalization rate	5%	5%
— life expectancy	45 years	45 years
	$735,594	$164,200
(b) Loss of Prospective Earnings		
— level of earnings	$ 830	$ 1,200
— basic deduction to avoid duplication between the award for future care and that part of the lost earnings that would have been spent on living expenses	440	—
Net	$ 390	$1,200
— contingencies	20%	20%
— work span	30.81	30.81
— capitalization rate	5%	5%
Total	$ 59,539	$175,000

Non-Pecuniary Loss		
— pain and suffering — loss of amenities — loss of expectation of life...............	$150,000	$100,000
Special Damages	$ 77,344	$ 77,344

Liability is not an issue. The trial judge found that the fault was entirely that of the respondents. The Appellate Division (McDermid J.A. dissenting on this issue) found the appellant James Andrews 25 per cent contributorily negligent. Those findings do not arise for discussion in this appeal. Nor does the question of special damages.

This court is called upon to establish the correct principles of law applicable in assessing damages in cases such as this where a young person has suffered wholly incapacitating injuries and faces a lifetime of dependency on others. The question of "million-dollar" awards has not arisen in Canada until recently, but within the past several years four such cases have been before the courts, namely, (i) the case at bar; (ii) *Thornton v. Bd. of School Trustees of School District No. 67 (Prince George)*, in which the award at trial was $1,534,058.93, reduced on appeal to $649,628.86; (iii) *Arnold v. Teno*, also under appeal to this court, in which the award for general damages at trial was $950,000, reduced on appeal to $875,000; (iv) *McLeod v. Hodgins* (not reported), in which Robins J. of the Ontario High Court awarded at trial an amount of $1,041,197, of which $1,000,000 was general damages.

Let me say in introduction what has been said many times before, that no appellate court is justified in substituting a figure of its own for that awarded at trial simply because it would have awarded a different figure if it had tried the case at first instance. It must be satisfied that a wrong principle of law was applied, or that the overall amount is a wholly erroneous estimate of the damage: *Nance v. B.C. Electric Ry. Co.*, [1951] A.C. 601, 2 W.W.R. (N.S.) 665, [1951] 3 D.L.R. 705, [1951] 2 All E.R. 448.

The method of assessing general damages in separate amounts, as has been done in this case, in my opinion, is a sound one. It is the only way in which any meaningful review of the award is possible on appeal and the only way of affording reasonable guidance in future cases. Equally important, it discloses to the litigants and their advisers the components of the overall award, assuring them thereby that each of the various heads of damage going to make up the claim has been given thoughtful consideration.

The subject of damages for personal injury is an area of the law which cries out for legislative reform. The expenditure of time and money in the determination of fault and of damage is prodigal. The disparity resulting from lack of provision for victims who cannot establish fault must be disturbing. When it is determined that compensation is to be made, it is highly irrational to be tied to a lump-sum system and a once-and-for-all award.

The lump-sum award presents problems of great importance. It is subject to inflation; it is subject to fluctuation on investment; income from it is subject to tax. After judgment new needs of the plaintiff arise and present needs are extinguished; yet, our law of damages knows nothing of periodic payment. The difficulties are greatest where there is a continuing need for intensive and expensive care and a long-term loss of earning capacity. It should be possible to devise some system whereby payments would be subject to periodic review and variation in the light of the continuing needs of the injured person and the cost of meeting those needs. In making this comment I am not unaware of the negative recommendation of the British Law Commission (Law Com. 56 — Report of Personal Injury Litigation — Assessment of Damages) following strong opposition from insurance interests and the plaintiffs' bar.

The apparent reliability of assessments provided by modern actuarial practice is largely illusionary, for actuarial science deals with probabilities, not actualities. This is in no way to denigrate a respected profession; but it is obvious that the validity of the answers given by the actuarial witness, as with a computer, depends upon the soundness of the postulates from which he proceeds. Although a useful aid and a sharper tool than the "multiplier-multiplicand" approach favoured in some jurisdictions, actuarial evidence speaks in terms of group experience. It cannot and does not purport to speak as to the individual sufferer. So long as we are tied to lump-sum awards, however, we are tied also to actuarial calculations as the best available means of determining amount.

In spite of these severe difficulties with the present law of personal injury compensation, the positive administrative machinery required for a system of reviewable periodic payments and the need to hear all interested parties in order to fashion a more enlightened system both dictate that the appropriate body to act must be the legislature, rather than the courts. Until such time as the legislature acts, the courts must proceed on established principles to award damages which compensate accident victims with justice and humanity for the losses they may suffer.

I proceed now to a brief recital of the injuries sustained by the appellant James Andrews in the present case. He suffered a fracture with dislocation of the cervical spine between the fifth and sixth cervical vertebrae, causing functional transection of the spinal cord but leaving some continuity; compound fracture of the left tibia and left humerus; fracture of the left patella. The left radial nerve was damaged. The lesion of the spinal cord left Andrews with paralysis involving most of the upper limbs, spine and lower limbs. He has lost the use of his legs, his trunk, essentially his left arm and most of his right arm. To add to the misery, he does not have normal bladder, bowel and sex functions. He suffers from spasticity in both upper and lower limbs. He has difficulty turning in bed and must be re-positioned every two hours. He needs regular physiotherapy and should have someone in close association with him at all times, such as a trained male orderly. The only functioning muscles of respiration are those of the diaphragm and shoulders. There is much more in the evidence but it need not be recited. Andrews is severely if not totally disabled. Dr. Weir, a specialist in neurosurgery, said of Andrews' condition that "there is no hope of functional improvement." For the rest of his life he will be dependent on others for dressing, personal hygiene, feeding and, indeed, for his very survival. But, of utmost importance, he is not a vegetable or a piece of cordwood. He is a man of above average intelligence and his mind is unimpaired. He can see, hear and speak as before. He has partial use of his right arm and hand. With the aid of a wheelchair he is mobile. With a specially-designed van he can go out in the evening to visit friends, or to the movies, or to a pub. He is taking driving lessons and proving to be an apt pupil. He wants to live as other human beings live. Since 31st May 1974 he has resided in his own apartment with private attendant care. The medical long-term care required is not at a sophisticated level, but rather at a practical care level.

Andrews was 21 years of age and unmarried on the date of the accident. On that date he was an apprentice carman employed by the Canadian National Railways in the City of Edmonton.

I turn now to consider assessment of the damages to which Andrews is entitled.

1. Pecuniary Loss

(a) Future Care

(i) Standard of Care

While there are several subsidiary issues to be decided in this case, there is one paramount issue: in a case of total or near-total disability, should the future care of the victim be in an institutional or a home-care environment? The trial judge chose home care. The Appellate Division agreed that home care would be better but denied it to him. McGillivray C.J.A., who delivered the judgment of the court on this issue, said [pp. 422-23]:

> All the evidence called supports the proposition that psychologically and emotionally Andrews would be better in a home of his own, where he could be lord of the manor, as it were.

Some evidence even indicated the medical superiority of a home environment.

The trial judge found that it would take $4,135 per month to provide care for Andrews in a home environment. The Appellate Division considered that this standard of care was unreasonably and unrealistically high. Without giving any reason for selecting the particular figure chosen, the Appellate Division substituted $1,000 per month. Obviously, here is the heart of the controversy. On other matters there was substantial agreement between the lower courts.

In my opinion, the court of appeal erred in law in the approach it took. After the statement quoted above, that Andrews would be better psychologically and emotionally in a home of his own, McGillivray C.J.A. referred to some of the evidence supporting that proposition. He quoted the following passage from the evidence of Dr. Weir:

> Well, I think that the greatest problem they have and the greatest burden of their affliction is the fact that they are all depressed because not only have they lost the potential for many normal and enjoyable human activities, in fact up until the present they pretty well have been converted into life-long inhabitants of a hospital institution; and an institution is an institution, it is virtually a life sentence and has been to this date. I would say that if you really, you know, if you wanted to give him the optimal potential it would be in a home environment in which he had some, in which he had the control of it to the same extent that the rest of us have control over our own homes and dwelling places. I don't really think that any hospital or medical institution has the potential to give someone that same feeling that they are in fact the lords and masters of their own castle.

[The justice noted that Andrews had said he would not live in an institution, and quoted excerpts from the evidence.]

With respect, I agree that a plaintiff must be reasonable in making a claim. I do not believe that the doctrine of mitigation of damages, which might be applicable, for example, in an action for conversion of goods, has any place in a personal injury claim. In assessing damages in claims arising out of personal injuries, the ordinary common law principles apply. The basic principle was stated by Viscount Dunedin in *Admiralty Commrs. v. S.S. Susquehanna*, [1926] A.C. 655 at 661 (cited with approval in *H. West & Son v. Shephard*, [1964] A.C. 326 at 345, [1963] 2 All E.R. 625), in these words:

> ... the common law says that the damages due either for breach of contract or for tort are damages which, so far as money can compensate, will give the injured party reparation for the wrongful act.

The principle was phrased differently by Lord Dunedin in the earlier case of *Admiralty Commrs. v. S.S. Valeria (No. 2)*, [1922] 2 A.C. 242 at 248, but to the same effect:

> ... in calculating damages you are to consider what is the pecuniary sum which will make good to the sufferer, so far as money can do so, the loss which he has suffered as the natural result of the wrong done to him.

The principle that compensation should be full for pecuniary loss is well established: see McGregor on Damages, 13th ed. (1972), pp. 738-39, para. 1097:

> The plaintiff can recover, subject to the rules of remoteness and mitigation, full compensation for the pecuniary loss that he has suffered. This is today a clear principle of law.

To the same effect, see Kemp and Kemp, Quantum of Damages, 3rd ed. (1967), vol. 1, at p. 4: "The person suffering the damage is entitled to full compensation for the financial loss suffered." This broad principle was propounded by Lord Blackburn at an early date in *Livingstone v. Rawyards Coal Co.* (1880), 5 App. Cas. 25 at 39, in these words:

> I do not think there is any difference of opinion as to its being a general rule that, where any injury is to be compensated by damages, in settling the sum of money to be given for reparation of damages you should as nearly as possible get at that sum of money which will put the party who has been injured, or who has suffered, in the same position as he would have been in if he had not sustained the wrong for which he is now getting his compensation or reparation.

In theory a claim for the cost of future care is a pecuniary claim for the amount which may reasonably be expected to be expended in putting the injured party in the position he would have been in if he had not sustained the injury. Obviously, a plaintiff who has been gravely and permanently impaired can never be put in the position he would have been in if the tort had not been committed. To this extent, restitutio in integrum is not possible. Money is a barren substitute for health and personal happiness, but to the extent, within reason, that money can be used to sustain or improve the mental or physical health of the injured person it may properly form part of a claim.

Contrary to the view expressed in the Appellate Division of Alberta, there is no duty to mitigate, in the sense of being forced to accept less than real loss. There is a duty to be reasonable. There cannot be "complete" or "perfect" compensation. An award must be moderate and fair to both parties. Clearly, compensation must not be determined on the basis of sympathy or compassion for the plight of the injured person. What is being sought is compensation, not retribution. But, in a case like the present, where both courts have favoured a home environment, "reasonable" means reasonableness in what is to be provided in that home environment. It does not mean that Andrews must languish in an institution which on all evidence is inappropriate for him. ...

An award must be fair to both parties, but the ability of the defendant to pay has never been regarded as a relevant consideration in the assessment of damages at common law. The focus should be on the injuries of the innocent party. Fairness to the other party is achieved by ensuring that the claims raised against him are legitimate and justifiable. ...

In reducing the monthly amount to $1,000 the Appellate Division purported to apply a "final test", which was expressed in terms of the expenses that reasonably-minded people would incur, assuming sufficient means to bear such expense. It seems to me difficult to conceive of any reasonably-minded person of ample means who would not be ready to incur the expense of home care, rather than institutional care, for himself or for someone in the condition of Andrews for whom he was responsible. No other conclusion is open upon the evidence adduced in this case. If the test enunciated by the Appellate Division is simply a plea for moderation then, of course, no one would question it. If the test was intended to suggest that reasonably-minded people would refuse to bear the expense of home care, there is simply no evidence to support that conclusion.

The Appellate Division, seeking to give some meaning to the test, said that it should be open to consider "standards of society as a whole as they presently exist" [p. 146]. As instances of such standards the court selected the daily allowances provided under *The Workers' Compensation Act, 1973* (Alta.), c. 87, s. 56, and the *Federal Pension Act*, R.S.C. 1970, c. P-7, s. 28. The standard of care expected in our society in physical injury cases is an elusive concept. What a legislature sees fit to provide in the cases of veterans and in the cases of injured workers and the elderly is only of marginal assistance. The standard to be applied to Andrews is not merely "provision", but "compensation", *i.e.*, what is the proper compensation for a person who would have been able to care for himself and live in a home environment if he had not been injured? The answer must surely be home care. If there were severe mental impairment or [if this were a case of] an immobile quadriplegic, the results might well be different; but, where the victim is mobile and still in full control of his mental facilities, as Andrews is, it cannot be said that institutionalization in an auxiliary hospital represents proper compensation for his loss. Justice requires something better.

Other points raised by the Appellate Division in support of its reversal of the trial judge may be briefly noted:

(a) "It seems to me probable that ... there will be, at government expense, people employed to look after quadriplegics. In the United States there are now a few institutions which have special apartments as part of the hospital setting, where patients can receive attention and at the same time have privacy" [p. 429]. There is no evidence that the government of Alberta at present has any plans to provide special care or institutions for quadriplegics. Any such possibility is speculation.

(b) "... will the respondent, in fact, operate from a home of his own?" [p. 430]. The court expressed the fear that Andrews would take the award, then go into an auxiliary hospital and have the public pay. It is not for the court to conjecture upon how a plaintiff will spend the amount awarded to him. There is always the possibility that the victim will not invest his award wisely but will dissipate it. That is not something which ought to be allowed to affect a consideration of the proper basis of compensation within a fault-based system. The plaintiff is free to do with that sum of money as he likes. Financial advice is readily available. He has the flexibility to plan his life and to plan for contingencies. The preference of our law to date has been to leave this flexibility in the plaintiff's hands: see Fleming, "Damages: Capital or Rent?" (1969), 19 U. of T. Law Jour. 295. Save for infants and the mentally incompetent, the

> courts have no power to control the expenditure of the award. There is nothing to show that the dangers the Appellate Division envisaged have any basis in fact.

In its conclusion, the Appellate Division held that the damages awarded by the trial judge were "unreasonably and unrealistically high" [p. 430], and that an award which would result in the appellant receiving approximately $1,000 a month for cost of care would be entirely adequate and would constitute a generous award. The Appellate Division further reduced the award by 30 per cent for potential contingencies. Why $1,000?

The main issue at trial was the choice between home care and institutional care. There is no question but that Andrews could be taken care of in an auxiliary hospital, but both courts below concluded that home care was the appropriate standard. The trial judge made an award reflecting the cost of home care. The Appellate Division made an award related neither to home care nor to institutional care. The effect is to compel a youthful quadriplegic to live the rest of his life in an auxiliary hospital. In my opinion, the Appellate Division failed to show that the trial judge applied any wrong principle of law or that the overall amount awarded by him was a wholly erroneous estimate of the damage. With great respect, the irrelevant considerations which the Appellate Division took into account were errors in law.

Is it reasonable for Andrews to ask for $4,135 per month for home care? Part of the difficulty of this case is that 24-hour orderly care was not directly challenged. Counsel never really engaged in consideration of whether, assuming home care, such care could be provided at lesser expense. Counsel wants the court, rather, to choose between home care and auxiliary hospital care. There are unanimous findings below that home care is better. Although home care is expensive, auxiliary hospital care is so utterly unattractive and so utterly in conflict with the principle of proper compensation that this court is offered no middle ground.

The basic argument, indeed, the only argument, against home care is that the social cost is too high. In these days the cost is distributed through society through insurance premiums. In this respect, I would adopt what was said by Salmon L.J. in *Fletcher v. Autocar and Transporters Ltd.*, [1968] 2 Q.B. 322, [1968] 1 All E.R. 726 at 750, where he stated:

> Today, however, virtually all defendants in accident cases are insured. This certainly does not mean compensation should be extravagant, but there is no reason why it should not be realistic. ... It might result in some moderate increase in premium rates, which none would relish, but of which no-one, in my view, could justly complain. It would be monstrous to keep down premiums by depressing damages below their proper level, *i.e.*, a level which ordinary men would regard as fair — unprejudiced by its impact on their own pockets.

I do not think the area of future care is one in which the argument of the social burden of the expense should be controlling, particularly in a case like the present, where the consequences of acceding to it would be to fail in large measure to compensate the victim for his loss. Greater weight might be given to this consideration where the choice with respect to future care is not so stark as between home care and an auxiliary hospital. Minimizing the social burden of expense may be a factor influencing a choice between acceptable alternatives. It should never compel the choice of the unacceptable.

(ii) Life Expectancy

At trial, figures were introduced which showed that the life expectancy of 23-year-old persons in general is 50 years. As McGillivray C.J.A. said in the Appellate Division, it would be more useful to use statistics on the expectation of life of quadriplegics. A statistical average is helpful only if the appropriate group is used. At trial, Dr. Weir and Dr. Gingras testified that possibly five years less than normal would be a reasonable expectation of life for a quadriplegic. The Appellate Division accepted this figure. On the evidence I am willing to accept it.

(iii) Contingencies of Life

The trial judge did, however, allow a 20 per cent discount for "contingencies and hazards of life". The Appellate Division allowed a further 10 per cent discount. It characterized the trial judge's discount as being for "life expectancy" or "duration of life", and said that this ignored the contingency of "duration of expense", *i.e.*, that despite any wishes to the contrary, Andrews in the years to come may be obliged to spend a great deal of time in hospital for medical reasons or because of the difficulty of obtaining help. With respect, the Appellate Division appears to have misunderstood what the trial judge did. The figure of 20 per cent as a discount for contingencies was arrived at first under the heading of "Prospective Loss of Earnings" and then simply transferred to the calculation of "Costs of Future Care". It was not an allowance for a decreased life expectancy, for this had already been taken into account by reducing the normal 50-year expectancy to 45 years. The "contingencies and hazards of life" in the context of future care are distinct. They relate essentially to duration of expense and are different from those which might affect future earnings, such as unemployment, accident, illness. They are not merely to be added to the latter so as to achieve a cumulative result. Thus, so far as the action taken by the Appellate Division is concerned, in my opinion, it was an error to increase by an extra 10 per cent the contingency allowance of the trial judge.

This whole question of contingencies is fraught with difficulty, for it is in large measure pure speculation. It is a small element of the illogical practice of awarding lump-sum payments for expenses and losses projected to continue over long periods of time. To vary an award by the value of the chance that certain contingencies may occur is to ensure either over-compensation or under-compensation, depending on whether or not the event occurs. In light of the considerations I have mentioned, I think it would be reasonable to allow a discount for contingencies in the amount of 20 per cent, in accordance with the decision of the trial judge.

(iv) Duplication with Compensation for Loss of Future Earnings

It is clear that a plaintiff cannot recover for the expense of providing for basic necessities as part of the cost of future care while still recovering fully for prospective loss of earnings. Without the accident, expenses for such items as food, clothing and accommodation would have been paid for out of earnings. They are not an additional type of expense occasioned by the accident.

When calculating the damage award, however, there are two possible methods of proceeding. One method is to give the injured party an award for future care which makes no deduction in respect of the basic necessities for which he would have had to pay in any event. A deduction must then be made for the cost of such basic necessities when computing the award for loss of prospective earnings, *i.e.*, the award is on the basis of net earnings and not gross earnings. The alternative method is the reversal, *i.e.*, to deduct the cost of basic necessities when computing the award for future care and then to compute the earnings award on the basis of gross earnings.

The trial judge took the first approach, reducing loss of future earnings by 53 per cent. The Appellate Division took the second. In my opinion, the approach of the trial judge is to be preferred. This is in accordance with the principle which I believe should underlie the whole consideration of damages for personal injuries: that proper future care is the paramount goal of such damages. To determine accurately the needs and costs in respect of future care, basic living expenses should be included. The costs of necessaries when in an infirm state may well be different from those when in a state of health. Thus, while the types of expenses would have been incurred in any event, the level of expenses for the victim may be seen as attributable to the accident. In my opinion, the projected cost of necessities should, therefore, be included in calculating the cost of future care, and a percentage attributable to the necessities of a person in a normal state should be reduced from the award for future earnings. For the acceptability of this method of proceeding see the judgment of this court in *Regina v. Jennings*, [1966] S.C.R. 532 at 540-41, 57 D.L.R. (2d) 644, affirming [1965] 2 O.R. 285, 50 D.L.R. (2d) 385 at 418 (*sub nom. Jennings v. Cronsberry*), and also *Bisson v. Powell River* (1967), 62 W.W.R. 707 at 720-21, 66 D.L.R. (2d) 226, affirmed without written reasons 64 W.W.R. 768, 68 D.L.R. (2d) 765n (Can.).

(v) Cost of Special Equipment

In addition to his anticipated monthly expenses, Andrews requires an initial capital amount for special equipment. Both courts below held that $14,200 was an appropriate figure for the cost of this equipment. In my opinion, this assessment is correct in principle, and I would therefore accept it.

(b) Prospective Loss of Earnings

We must now gaze more deeply into the crystal ball. What sort of a career would the accident victim have had? What were his prospects and potential prior to the accident? It is not loss of earnings but, rather, loss of earning capacity for which compensation must be made: *Regina v. Jennings*, supra. A capital asset has been lost: what was its value?

(i) Level of Earnings

The trial judge fixed the projected level of earnings of Andrews at $830 per month, which would have been his earnings on 1st January 1973. The Appellate Division raised this to $1,200 per month, a figure between his present salary and the maximum for his type of work of $1,750 per month. Without doubt the value of Andrews' earning capacity over his working life would have been higher than his earnings at the time of the accident. Although I am inclined to view even that figure as somewhat conservative, I would affirm the holding of the Appellate Division that $1,200 per month represents a reasonable estimate of Andrews' future average level of earnings.

(ii) Length of Working Life

Counsel for the appellants objected to the use of 55 rather than 65 as the projected retirement age for Andrews. It is agreed that he could retire on full pension at 55 if he stayed with his present employer, Canadian National Railways. I think it is reasonable to assume that he would, in fact, retire as soon as it was open for him to do so on full pension.

One must then turn to the mortality tables to determine the working life expectancy for the appellant over the period between the ages of 23 and 55. The controversial question immediately arises whether the capitalization of future earning capacity should be based on the expected working life span prior to the accident, or the shortened life expectancy. Does one give credit for the "lost years"? When viewed as the loss of a capital asset consisting of income-earning capacity rather than a loss of income, the answer is apparent: it must be the loss of that capacity which existed prior to the accident. This is the figure which best fulfils the principle of compensating the plaintiff for what he has lost: see Mayne and McGregor on Damages, 12th ed. (1961), at p. 659; Kemp and Kemp, Quantum of Damages, vol. 1 (Supp.), c. 3, p. 28; *Skelton v. Collins* (1966), 39 A.L.J.R. 480, 115 C.L.R. 94. In the instant case, the trial judge refused to follow the *Oliver v. Ashman*, [1962] 2 Q.B. 210, [1961] 3 All E.R. 323, approach, the manifest injustice of which is demonstrated in the much-criticized case of *McCann v. Sheppard*, [1973] 1 W.L.R. 540, [1973] 2 All E.R. 881, and in this I think the judge was right. I would accept his decision that Andrews had a working life expectancy of 30.81 years.

(iii) Contingencies

It is a general practice to take account of contingencies which might have affected future earnings, such as unemployment, illness, accidents and business depression. In the *Bisson* case, *supra*, which also concerned a young quadriplegic, an allowance of 20 per cent was made. There is much support for the view that such a discount for contingencies should be made: see, *e.g.*, *Warren v. King*, [1964] 1 W.L.R. 1, [1963] 3 All E.R. 521; *McKay v. Bd. of Govan School Unit No. 29*, 64 W.W.R. 301, [1968] S.C.R. 589, 68 D.L.R. (2d) 519. There are, however, a number of qualifications which should be made. First, in many respects, these contingencies implicitly are already contained in an assessment of the projected average level of earnings of the injured person, for one must assume that this figure is a projection with respect to the real world of work, vicissitudes and all. Second, not all contingencies are adverse, as the above list would appear to indicate. As is said in *Bresatz v. Przibilla*, 108 C.L.R. 541, [1963] A.L.R. 218, in the Australian High Court, at p. 544: "Why count the possible buffets and ignore the rewards of fortune?" Finally, in modern society there are many public and private schemes which cushion the individual against adverse contingencies. Clearly, the per centage deduction which is proper will depend on the facts of the individual case, particularly the nature of the plaintiff's occupation; but generally it will be small: see J.H. Prevett, "Actuarial Assessment of Damages: The Thalidomide Case — I" (1972), 35 Modern Law Rev. 140 at 150.

In reducing Andrews' award by 20 per cent Kirby J. gives no reasons. The Appellate Division also applied a 20 per cent reduction. It seems to me that actuarial evidence could be of great help here. Contingencies are susceptible to more exact calculation than is usually apparent in the cases: see A.T. Traversi, "Actuaries and the Courts" (1956), 29 Australian Law Jour. 557. In my view, some degree of specificity, supported by evidence, ought to be forthcoming at trial.

The figure used to take account of contingencies is obviously an arbitrary one. The figure of 20 per cent which was used in the lower courts (and in many other cases), although not entirely satisfactory, should, I think, be accepted.

(iv) Duplication of the Cost of Future Basic Maintenance

As discussed, since basic needs such as food, shelter, and clothing have been included in the cost of future care, a deduction must be made from the award for prospective earnings to avoid duplication. The injured person would have incurred expenses of this nature even if he had not suffered the injury. At trial evidence was given that the cost of basics for a person in the position of Andrews prior to the accident would be approximately 53 per cent of income. I would accept this figure and reduce his anticipated future monthly earnings accordingly to a figure of $564.

(c) Considerations Relevant to Both Heads of Pecuniary Loss

(i) Capitalization Rate: Allowance for Inflation and the Rate of Return on Investments

What rate of return should the court assume the appellant will be able to obtain on his investment of the award? How should the court recognize future inflation? Together these considerations will determine the discount rate to use in actuarially calculating the lump sum award.

The approach at trial was to take as a rate of return the rental value of money which might exist during periods of economic stability, and consequently to ignore inflation. This approach is widely referred to as the Lord Diplock approach, as he lent it his support in *Mallett v. McMonagle*, [1970] A.C. 166, [1969] 2 All E.R. 178. Although this method of proceeding has found favour in several jurisdictions in this country and elsewhere, it has an air of unreality. Stable, non-inflationary economic conditions do not exist at present, nor did they exist in the recent past, nor are they to be expected in the foreseeable future. In my opinion, it would be better to proceed from what known factors are available rather than to ignore economic reality. Analytically, the alternate approach to assuming a stable economy is to use existing interest rates and then make an allowance for the long-term expected rate of inflation. ...

The approach which I would adopt, therefore, is to use present rates of return on long-term investments and to make some allowance for the effects of future inflation. Once this approach is adopted, the result, in my opinion, is different from the 5 per cent discount figure accepted by the trial judge. While there was much debate at trial over a difference of a half to one per centage point, I think it is clear from the evidence that high quality long-term investments were available at time of trial at rates of return in excess of 10 per cent. On the other hand, evidence was specifically introduced that the former head of the Economic Council of Canada, Dr. Deutsch, had recently forecast a rate of inflation of 3½ per cent over the long-term future. These figures must all be viewed flexibly. In my opinion, they indicate that the appropriate discount rate is approximately 7 per cent. I would adopt that figure. It appears to me to be the correct result of the approach I have adopted, *i.e.*, having regard to present investment market conditions and making an appropriate allowance for future inflation. I would, accordingly, vary to 7 per cent the discount rate to be used in calculating the present value of the awards for future care and loss of earnings in this case. The result in future cases will depend upon the evidence adduced in those cases.

(ii) Allowance for Tax

In *Regina v. Jennings*, *supra*, this court held that an award for prospective income should be calculated with no deduction for tax which might have been attracted had it been earned over the working life of the plaintiff. This results from the fact that it is earning capacity and not lost earnings which is the subject of compensation. For the same reason, no consideration should be taken of the amount by which the income from the award will be reduced by payment of taxes on the interest, dividends, or capital gain. A capital sum is appropriate to replace the lost capital asset of earning capacity. Tax on income is irrelevant either to decrease the sum for taxes the victim would have paid on income from his job, or to increase it for taxes he will now have to pay on income from the award.

In contrast with the situation in personal injury cases, awards under *The Fatal Accidents Act*, R.S.A. 1970, c. 138, should reflect tax considerations, since they are to compensate dependants for the loss of support payments made by the deceased. These support payments could only come out of take-home pay, and the payments from the award will only be received net of taxes: see the contemporaneous decision of this court in *Keizer v. Hanna*. ...

One subsidiary point should be affirmed with respect to the determination of the present value of the cost of future care. The calculations should provide for a self-extinguishing sum. To allow a residual capital amount would be to overcompensate the injured person by creating an estate for him. This point was accepted by the lower courts and not challenged by the parties.

2. Non-Pecuniary Loss

Andrews used to be a healthy young man, athletically active and socially congenial. Now he is a cripple, deprived of many of life's pleasures and subjected to pain and disability. For this, he is entitled to compensation. But the problem here is qualitatively different from that of pecuniary losses. There is no medium of exchange for happiness. There is no market for expectation of life. The monetary evaluation of non-pecuniary losses is a philosophical and policy exercise more than a legal or logical one. The award must be fair and reasonable, fairness being gauged by earlier decisions; but the award must also of necessity be arbitrary or conventional. No money can provide true restitution. Money can provide for proper care: this is the reason that I think the paramount concern of the courts when awarding damages for personal injuries should be to ensure that there will be adequate future care.

However, if the principle of the paramountcy of care is accepted, then it follows that there is more room for the consideration of other policy factors in the assessment of damages for non-pecuniary losses. In particular, this is the area where the social burden of large awards deserves considerable weight. The sheer fact is that there is no objective yardstick for translating non-pecuniary losses, such as pain and suffering and loss of amenities, into monetary terms. This area is open to widely extravagant claims. It is in this area that awards in the United States have soared to dramatically high levels in recent years. Statistically, it is the area where the danger of excessive burden of expense is greatest.

It is also the area where there is the clearest justification for moderation. As one English commentator has suggested, there are three theoretical approaches to the problem of non-pecuniary loss (A.I. Ogus, "Damages for Lost Amenities: For a Foot, a Feeling or a Function?" (1972), 35 Modern Law Rev. 1). The first, the "conceptual" approach, treats each faculty as a proprietary asset with an objective value, independent of the individual's own use or enjoyment of it. This was the ancient "bot", or tariff system, which prevailed in the days of King Alfred, when a thumb was worth 30 shillings. Our law has long since thought such a solution unsubtle. The second, the "personal" approach, values the injury in terms of the loss of human happiness by the particular victim. The third, or "functional" approach, accepts the personal premise of the second, but rather than attempting to set a value on lost happiness it attempts to assess the compensation required to provide the injured person "with reasonable solace for his misfortune". "Solace" in this sense is taken to mean physical arrangements which can make his life more endurable rather than "solace" in the sense of sympathy. To my mind, this last approach has much to commend it, as it provides a rationale as to why money is considered compensation for non-pecuniary losses such as loss of amenities, pain and suffering, and loss of expectation of life. Money is awarded because it will serve a useful function in making up for what has been lost in the only way possible, accepting that what has been lost is incapable of being replaced in any direct way. As Windeyer J. said in *Skelton v. Collins*, supra, at p. 131:

> He is, I do not doubt, entitled to compensation for what he suffers. Money may be a compensation for him if having it can give him pleasure or satisfaction. ... But the money is not then a recompense for a loss of something having a money value. It is given as some consolation or solace for the distress that is the consequence of a loss on which no monetary value can be put.

If damages for non-pecuniary loss are viewed from a functional perspective, it is reasonable that large amounts should not be awarded once a person is properly provided for in terms of future care for his injuries and disabilities. The money for future care is to provide physical arrangements for assistance, equipment and facilities directly related to the injuries. Additional money to make life more endurable should then be seen as providing more general physical arrangements above and beyond those relating directly to the injuries. The result is a coordinated and interlocking basis for compensation, and a more rational justification for non-pecuniary loss compensation.

However one may view such awards in a theoretical perspective, the amounts are still largely arbitrary or conventional. As Denning L.J. said in *Ward v. James*, [1966] 1 Q.B. 273, [1965] 1 All E.R. 563, there is a great need in this area for assessability, uniformity and predictability. In my opinion, this does not mean that the courts should not have regard to the individual situation of the victim. On the contrary, they must do so to determine what has been lost. For example, the loss of a finger would be a greater loss of amenities for an amateur pianist than for a person not engaged in such an activity. Greater compensation would be required to provide things and activities which would function to make up for this loss. But there should be guidelines for the translation into monetary terms of what has been lost. There must be an exchange rate, albeit conventional. In *Warren v. King*, supra, at p. 528, the following dictum of Harman L.J. appears, which I would adopt, in respect of the assessment of non-pecuniary loss for a living plaintiff:

> It seems to me that the first element in assessing such compensation is not to add up items as loss of pleasures, of earnings, of marriage prospects, of children and so on, but to consider the matter from the other side, what can be done to alleviate the disaster to the victim, what will it cost to enable her to live as tolerably as may be in the circumstances?

Cases like the present enable the court to establish a rough upper parameter on these awards. It is difficult to conceive of a person of his age losing more than Andrews has lost. Of course, the figures must be viewed flexibly in future cases in recognition of the inevitable differences in injuries, the situation of the victim, and changing economic conditions.

The amounts of such awards should not vary greatly from one part of the country to another. Everyone in Canada, wherever he may reside, is entitled to a more or less equal measure of compensation for similar non-pecuniary loss. Variation should be made for what a particular individual has lost in the way of amenities and enjoyment of life, and for what will function to make up for this loss, but variation should not be made merely for the province in which he happens to live.

There has been a significant increase in the size of awards under this head in recent years. As Moir J.A., of the Appellate Division of the Alberta Supreme Court, has warned: "To my mind, damages under the head of loss of amenities will go up and up until they are stabilized by the Supreme Court of Canada": *Hamel v. Prather*, [1976] 2 W.W.R. 742 at 748, 66 D.L.R. (3d) 109. In my opinion, this time has come.

It is customary to set only one figure for all non-pecuniary loss, including such factors as pain and suffering, loss of amenities and loss of expectation of life. This is a sound practice. Although these elements are analytically distinct, they overlap and merge at the edges and in practice. To suffer pain is surely to lose an amenity of a happy life at that time. To lose years of one's expectation of life is to lose all amenities for the lost period, and to cause mental pain and suffering in the contemplation of this prospect. These problems, as well as the fact that these losses have the common trait of irreplaceability, favour a composite award for all non-pecuniary losses.

There is an extensive review of authorities in the court of appeal judgment in this case as well as in the *Thornton* and *Teno* cases, to which I have referred. I need not review these past authorities. What is important is the general picture. It is clear that until very recently damages for non-pecuniary losses, even from very serious injuries such as quadriplegia, were substantially below $100,000. Recently, though, the figures have increased markedly. In *Jackson v. Millar*, [1976] 1 S.C.R. 225, 59 D.L.R. (3d) 246, this court affirmed a figure of $150,000 for non-pecuniary loss in an Ontario case of a paraplegic. However, this was done essentially on the principle of non-interference with awards allowed by provincial Courts of Appeal. The need for a general assessment with respect to damages for non-pecuniary loss, which is now apparent, was not as evident at that time. Even in Ontario, prior to these recent cases, general damages allocable for non-pecuniary loss, such as pain and suffering and loss of amenities, were well below $100,000.

In the present case, $150,000 was awarded at trial, but this amount was reduced to $100,000 by the Appellate Division. In *Thornton* and *Teno*, $200,000 was awarded in each case, unchanged in the provincial Courts of Appeal.

I would adopt as the appropriate award in the case of a young adult quadriplegic like Andrews the amount of $100,000. Save in exceptional circumstances, this should be regarded as an upper limit of non-pecuniary loss in cases of this nature.

Total Award

This is largely a matter of arithmetic. Of course, in addition, it is customary for the court to make an overall assessment of the total sum. This, however, seems to me to be a hangover from the days of global sums for all general damages. It is more appropriate to make an overall assessment of the total under each head of future care, prospective earnings, and non-pecuniary loss, in each case in light of general considerations such as the awards of other courts in similar cases and an assessment of the reasonableness of the award.

In the result I would assess general damages for the appellant Andrews as follows:

1. PECUNIARY LOSS	
(a) Cost of future care	
— special equipment	$ 14,200
— amount of monthly payments (monthly amount $4,135; life expectancy 45 years; contingencies 20 per cent; capitalization rate 7 per cent)	557,232
(b) Prospective loss of earnings	
(monthly amount $564; work span 30.81 years: contingencies 20 per cent; capitalization rate 7 per cent)	69,981
2. NON-PECUNIARY LOSS	
compensation for physical and mental pain and suffering endured and to be endured, loss of amenities and enjoyment of life, loss of expectation of life	100,000
Total General Damages	$741,413
Rounded off at	$740,000

To arrive at the total damages award, the special damages of $77,344 must be added to give a final figure of $817,344.

The appellant Andrews will have judgment for 75 per cent of that amount, that is, $613,008.

The appellants should have their costs in this court and in the trial court. The respondents should have their costs in the court of appeal as they achieved substantial success in that court in respect of the finding of contributory negligence on the part of Andrews.

Appeal allowed.

NOTES

1. The second case of the trilogy was *Thornton v. Board of School Trustees of School District No. 57 (Prince George) et al.*, [1978] 2 S.C.R. 267, 3 C.C.L.T. 257, where a 15-year-old student in B.C. was rendered quadriplegic when he fractured his back doing gymnastics at school. The principles enunciated by Dickson J. in *Andrews* were applied by His Lordship to the facts of this case and an award of $810,000 in general damages was made.

2. The third case of the trilogy was *Arnold v. Teno; J.B. Jackson v. Teno*, [1978] 2 S.C.R. 287, 83 D.L.R. (3d) 609, 3 C.C.L.T. 272. This case differed from the other two in that the plaintiff was 4½ years-old when injured, and her injuries involved not quadriplegia, but injuries to the brain resulting in physical disability and mental

impairment. The Court applied the principles enunciated in the other two judgments recognizing, however, that their application to this case needed to recognize the factual differences between the victims' positions.

3. The trilogy had an important and immediate impact on damage judgments which followed. Certain aspects of the Supreme Court's judgments were causing some confusion, however, especially relating to the use of a discount rate, the role of contingencies, the use of expert evidence, and the role of non-pecuniary damages. The Supreme Court accordingly took advantage of two subsequent damage assessment cases to clarify its principles. See *Lewis v. Todd et al.; Canadian Provincial Insurance Co. (third party)*, [1980] 2 S.C.R. 694, 14 C.C.L.T. 294; and *Lindal v. Lindal*, [1981] 2 S.C.R. 629, 19 C.C.L.T. 1.

4. A useful summary of the three cases is provided by Charles, "A New Handbook on the Assessment of Damages ..." (1977-78), 3 C.C.L.T. 344:

> (1) The judge should assess damages using an itemization approach rather than a global approach.
>
> (2) Courts should continue to use actuarial evidence as long as lump sum payments are made, but with the realization that actuarial predictions are not as accurate in relation to individual cases as they might seem to be.
>
> (3) General principles:
>
> > (a) The mitigation of damage principle has no place in personal injury cases.
> >
> > (b) There should be full compensation for pecuniary loss.
> >
> > (c) The law cannot provide perfect or complete compensation and the plaintiff has a duty to be reasonable in his claim.
> >
> > (d) The award must be moderate and fair to both parties.
> >
> > (e) Compensation must not be determined on the basis of sympathy for the victim but neither should the court try to punish the defendant.
>
> (4) The primary or guiding principle in total disability cases is to ensure that the injured plaintiff should be adequately cared for during the rest of his or her life.
>
> (5) A lump sum should be awarded to cover all non-pecuniary losses such as (i) pain and suffering, (ii) loss of amenities, and (iii) loss of enjoyment of life. The upper limit in most total disability cases will be $100,000 unless exceptional circumstances exist.
>
> (6) In computing lost future earnings, the court should take into account various factors that might increase or decrease the plaintiff's earning capacity. This will, in most cases, result in a reduction of the amount computed, but, in most cases, the per centage reduction will be small.
>
> (7) When capitalizing to present value, courts should recognize the effects of inflation upon damage awards and the fact of high interest rates. This can best be done by adopting a discount rate of 7 per cent in relation to sums awarded for cost of future care and loss of future earnings.
>
> (8) Allowance for tax:
>
> > (a) In non-fatal injury cases the effect of taxation is not to be considered in computing loss of future earnings or in relation to taxation of the award.

(b) In fatal injury cases the effect of taxation upon the lost dependency is to be taken into account.

(9) Credit should be given for the "lost years". Capitalization of future earning capacity should be based on the expected working life span prior to the accident rather than the shortened life span.

(10) In computing the future loss earnings of a very young child, it is not proper to assume that the child will necessarily adopt the vocation of the parent and to calculate lost future earnings on this basis.

(11) In cases where the plaintiff is mentally incapable of handling his or her own affairs, it is proper to add a management fee to the damage award.

(12) The cost of providing basic necessities should be deducted from the award for loss of future income rather than from the award for cost of future care.

It is clearly the intention of the Supreme Court of Canada that the principles and rules concerning assessment of damages in personal injury cases, which it has taken pains to lay down in the four cases under review, should form the basis upon which lower courts can, and should, approach the problem of personal injury claims.

5. The Supreme Court's attempts to rationalize the damage assessment process have not alleviated the grave concerns of many of tort law's critics concerning the present system.

Consider the following comments by Hall J.A. of the Manitoba Court of Appeal in *MacDonald v. Alderson et al.* (1982), 15 Man. R. (2d) 35, [1982] 3 W.W.R. 385, 20 C.C.L.T. 64, 14 M.V.R. 212:

> Before considering these various heads of damages, it is appropriate to refer with emphasis to what was stated by Dickson J., in delivering the judgment of the Supreme Court of Canada in *Andrews v. Grand & Toy (Alta.) Ltd.*, [1978] 2 S.C.R. 229, 3 C.C.L.T. 225, [1978] 1 W.W.R. 577, 8 A.R. 182, 83 D.L.R. (3d) 452, 19 N.R. 50. At p. 236 of the [S.C.R.] report, he stated:
>
>> The subject of damages for personal injury is an area of the law which cries out for legislative reform. The expenditure of time and money in the determination of fault and of damage is prodigal, the disparity resulting from lack of provision for victims who cannot establish fault must be disturbing. When it is determined that compensation is to be made, it is highly irrational to be tied to a lump sum system and a once-and-for-all award.
>
> I agree entirely and only wish to add that, in my opinion, it makes no sense at all to have in place a modest and predictable system of compensation for injured workers and victims of crime while, at the same time, tolerate a risky, difficult and wholly irrational system of Court sponsored assessments for persons injured by reason of a motor vehicle upon a highway. It is all the more nonsensical when such persons may receive no compensation at all or compensation away out of proportion to that received by injured workers and victims of crime. In addition, there is in place in each province universal health care services and welfare plans.
>
> The Legislature needs to address the broad question of accident and sickness compensation in Manitoba, and a good starting point would be 'A Government White Paper' on that subject published in May of 1977. I commend that paper to the government for early consideration.

In his judgment, Mr. Justice O'Sullivan expressed great reservations concerning the process of assessment introduced by the Supreme Court. His Lordship was critical of the need for "mathematical precision", the use of actuaries and economists in the trial whom he likened to "fortune tellers" and "futurologists", the method of arriving at lump sums which are designed to exhaust themselves at the end of the projected period, and the conscious decision to ignore the effects of taxation.

What do you think of these criticisms? Would a system of compensation based on a fixed schedule without regard to non-pecuniary losses, as suggested by Hall J.A., be preferable?

6. The Supreme Court reaffirmed its support for the functional approach in *ter Neuzen v. Korn* (1995), 127 D.L.R. (4th) 577 (S.C.C.). The jury had awarded the plaintiff $460,000 in non-pecuniary damages. In agreeing with the Court of Appeal's holding that the award could not exceed the limit, Sopinka J. reiterated that the award for non-pecuniary loss (at 611 D.L.R.):

> ...acts as a substitute for the pleasure and enjoyment which has been lost and endeavours to alleviate, as far as possible, the pain and suffering that the plaintiff has endured and will have to endure in the future.
>
> *The amount of the award depends on the ability of money to ameliorate the condition of the victim in his or her particular situation. Non-pecuniary damaes should only be awarded to the extent that they can serve a useful purpose by providing an alternative source of satisfaction.*

(Emphasis added.)

Do you think that the courts have been following this guideline?

7. Despite the Supreme Court's efforts to clarify the reasons for awarding non-pecuniary losses and to explain the "functional" approach, this aspect of the damage assessment process remains one of the most troublesome for courts to deal with. There is no clear idea as to how one uses the functional approach to assess the plaintiff's entitlement, nor when a court can legitimately exceed the upper limit, which due to inflation, has now risen to approximately $260,000 (see, for example, *Roberts v. Morana* (1997), 38 C.C.L.T. (2d) 1 (Ont. Gen. Div.)). For a detailed look at these problems see Osborne, "Annotation" (1982), 19 C.C.L.T. 9; McLachlin, "What Price Disability? A Perspective on the Law of Damages for Personal Injury" (1981), 59 Can. Bar Rev. 1, at 46; Cooper-Stephenson, *Personal Injury Damages in Canada*, 2nd ed. (1996), p. 550; Klar, "Developments in Tort Law: The 1981-82 Term": (1983), 5 S.C.L.R. 273.

8. How does the functional approach affect the problem of the unconscious plaintiff? Recall that the purpose of the award for non-pecuniary losses is to set up a fund which can then usefully be used by the plaintiff to ameliorate his or her condition in life. Before the Supreme Court's trilogy, there were two competing views with regard to the awarding of general damages to an unconscious plaintiff. The "objective" view, adopted by the majority of the House of Lords in *H. West & Son Ltd. v. Shephard*, [1964] A.C. 326, [1963] 2 All E.R. 625 (H.L.), was to award the plaintiff compensation without regard to the fact that the plaintiff's physical or mental state prevented the plaintiff from using the money. The "subjective" approach, adopted by the minority, was to award the plaintiff much less, a "moderate" amount, if the plaintiff could not enjoy the award. Prior to the trilogy, the Supreme Court of Canada in *R. in the Right of the Province of Ontario v. Jennings*, [1966] S.C.R. 532, 57 D.L.R. (2d) 644, adopted the objective approach. It is now unclear whether, as a result of the trilogy, this position has changed. In *Knutson v. Farr*, [1984] 5 W.W.R. 315, 30 C.C.L.T. 8 (B.C.C.A.), the court reversed a trial judgment ([1982] 5 W.W.R. 114) which had awarded a plaintiff $77,000 for non-pecuniary losses even though the plaintiff's prognosis was that he would never regain consciousness. Hinkson J.A. stated that the

Jennings decision "has been implicitly overruled by the decisions of the Supreme Court of Canada in the trilogy and Lindal". Do you agree?

9. In *Roberts v. Morana* (1997), 38 C.C.L.T. (2d) 1 (Ont. Gen. Div.) the court agreed with the defence counsel's submission that "the maximum should be awarded only in those cases where there is no longer any meaningful life activity for an injured plaintiff". Is this a correct application of the functional approach?

10. What about a plaintiff who has only a few years to live? In *Crocker v. Sundance Northwest Resorts Ltd.* (1983), 43 O.R. (2d) 145, 25 C.C.L.T. 201 (H.C.J.), the trial judge accepted evidence that indicated the plaintiff's life expectancy to be two years. Despite this, the court, without comment, assessed the plaintiff's non-pecuniary losses at $155,000! Does this not show that the "functional" approach to non-pecuniary damages is in great difficulty?

11. In *Penso v. Solowan and Public Trustee* (1982), 35 B.C.L.R. 250, [1982] 4 W.W.R. 385, 22 C.C.L.T. 161, the British Columbia Court of Appeal attempted to use a functional approach in its assessment of damages for non-pecuniary losses. The Court stated that the first step in this assessment is to compare awards made in previous cases for similar injuries. The second step is to adjust this conventional award to meet the specific circumstances of the individual case having regard to the plaintiff's "need for solace". In doing this, however, the Court stated that evidence as to the need for particular kinds of "solace" and the cost of meeting such need will, as a general rule, be irrelevant. Does this sound like the functional approach to you?

12. Questions relating to the appropriate discount rate, the effect of taxation, and the reduction for contingencies have frequently been raised since the Supreme Court judgments. The Court made it clear that the appropriate discount rate was to be established by the evidence in each case. Certain jurisdictions, *e.g.*, Ontario, have eliminated the problem of having different discount rates in different cases, by prescribing a standard discount rate. Courts in other jurisdictions have been critical of the absence of a uniform rate; see, *e.g.*, Monnin J.'s judgment in *McLeod v. Palardy* (1981), 10 Man. R. (2d) 181, 124 D.L.R. (3d) 506, 17 C.C.L.T. 62 (C.A.). There has also been some confusion regarding the problem of contingencies. See, *e.g.*, the B.C. Court of Appeal's decision in *Lan v. Wu* (1980), 21 B.C.L.R. 216, 14 C.C.L.T. 282 (C.A.), where the use of a deduction for contingencies was treated as being fairly automatic. Finally, the Court's decision to assess loss of earning capacity based upon a person's gross income in personal injury cases, and upon a person's net income in fatal accident cases, and to ignore the impact of taxation on the income produced by the lump sum awarded to personal injury claimants has provoked controversy. In *Watkins v. Olafson* (1989), 61 D.L.R. (4th) 577, [1989] 6 W.W.R. 481, and *Scarff v. Wilson*, [1989] 2 S.C.R. 776, 61 D.L.R. (4th) 749, the Supreme Court of Canada held that the impact of taxation on the award for cost of future care can be taken into consideration. Is this consistent with the approach taken in the trilogy?

13. As stressed by the Supreme Court, each case of damage assessment depends upon its own facts. What happens, however, where there are few, if any, available facts on which to base an assessment? This happens in the case of injury to a young child, where the court attempts to assess damages for loss of future earning capacity. In *Houle v. City of Calgary; Houle (Thivierge) et al. (Third Parties)* (1983), 26 Alta. L.R. (2d) 34, 24 C.C.L.T. 275 (Q.B.); vard (1985), 38 Alta. L.R. (2d) 331 (C.A.); leave to appeal to S.C.C. refused (1985), 39 Alta. L.R. (2d) xlvi*n* (S.C.C.), the court was forced to assess the future prospects for a nine-year-old child with an amputated arm. Based on his background, intelligence and so on, they predicted that the boy, before his injury, would have amounted to no more than an unskilled labourer. Is this fair? For a criticism of the case see Klar, "Annotation" (1983), 24 C.C.L.T. 275, at 276. For a contrary view, see Alexander (1984), 22 Alta. L. Rev. 291.

14. When assessing damages for loss of future earnings, should the court take into account the gender of the victim and apply statistical tables which show that women on average earn less than men? What are the arguments, for and against, this approach? See *Terracino v. Etheridge* (1997), 36 C.C.L.T. (2d) 92 (B.C.S.C.), and *McCabe v. Westlock Roman Catholic Separate School District No. 110*, unreported, October 5, 1998, Doc. No. 9303 05787, Johnstone J. (Alta. Q.B.) where this gender approach was rejected as perpetuating inequality. In *Toneguzzo-, Norvell v. Burnaby Hospital* (1994), 18 C.C.L.T. (2d) 209 (S.C.C.), the issue was raised but not dealt with by the Supreme Court due to the evidence presented by the parties. What is the role of tort law in this context?

15. A new head of damage which has emerged since the trilogy is the plaintiff's inability to perform housekeeping duties. This is akin to loss of earning capacity. But how is it to be assessed? In *Fobel v. Dean* (1991), 83 D.L.R. (4th) 385, 9 C.C.L.T. (2d) 87 (Sask. C.A.), Vancise J.A. stated that the best way of approaching the assessment for loss or impairment of housekeeping ability was to recognize the "catalogue of services" provided by the homemaker. The homemaker acts as "chef, nurse, counsellor etc.". The work is divided up into direct labour and management. Direct labour includes things such as food preparation, cleaning, clothing and linen care, maintenance, gardening, and physical child care. Management includes items such as marketing, food planning, tutorial child care, activity co-ordination and organization, health care and counselling. Evidence as to the replacement costs for such services, as well as the use of economic models, can assist the courts in arriving at fair and just compensation. Despite this approach, arriving at the assessment can be very difficult. Also see Picard J.'s judgment in *McLaren v. Schwalbe*, [1994] 4 W.W.R. 532 (Alta. Q.B.).

16. What happens if after a judgment is rendered new evidence is brought to light which, if known, would have altered the assessment? What happens if the plaintiff is cured miraculously? dies? or remarries? See *Maitland v. Drozda* (1983), 22 Sask. R. 1, [1983] 3 W.W.R. 193 (Q.B.), where, in a fatal accident claim, an application to hear evidence regarding the remarriage of the plaintiff was admitted. Also see *Mulholland v. Mitchell*, [1971] A.C. 666, [1971] 1 All E.R. 307. The House of Lords allowed the Court of Appeal to exercise its discretion to hear new evidence in order to reassess damages in personal injury cases. In this case the plaintiff's condition had deteriorated after trial, resulting in significantly higher costs for future care. See Kidd, "Damages for Personal Injuries: Taking Account of the Vicissitudes of Life" (1982), 56 A.L.J. 389. For a more recent decision discussing the conditions upon which the court will exercise its discretion and allow new evidence to be introduced see *Leenstra v. Miller* (1993), [1994] 3 W.W.R. 751 (B.C.C.A.).

17. What is the burden of proof in damage assessment cases? In *Schrump v. Koot* (1977), 18 O.R. (2d) 337, 82 D.L.R. (3d) 553 (C.A.), an expert testified, in a back injury case, that there was a 25 to 50 per cent probability that future surgery would be required. The trial judge allowed this to go to the jury. Counsel for the defendant argued on appeal that this was evidence of a mere possibility and that the jury ought to have been told to exclude it from their consideration. Mr. Justice Lacourciere disagreed and explained:

> In this area of the law relating to the assessment of damages for physical injury, one must appreciate that though it may be necessary for a plaintiff to prove, on the balance of probabilities, that the tortious act or omission was the effective cause of the harm suffered, it is not necessary for him to prove, on the balance of probabilities, that future loss or damage *will* occur, but only that there is a reasonable chance of such loss or damage occurring. The distinction is made clear in the following passages in 12 Hals., 4th ed., pp. 437, 483-4:
>
> > 1137. *Possibilities, probabilities and chances.* Whilst issues of fact relating to liability must be decided on the balance of probability, the law

> of damages is concerned with evaluating in terms of money, future possibilities and chances. In assessing damages which depend on the court's view as to what will happen in the future, or would have happened in the future if something had not happened in the past, the court must make an estimate as to what are the chances that a particular thing will happen or would have happened and reflect those chances, *whether they are more or less than even*, in the amount of damages which it awards.
>
> ...
>
> 1199. *Proof of damage.*
>
> ...
>
> The plaintiff must prove his damage on a balance of probabilities. In many cases, however, the court is called upon to evaluate chances, such as the chances of a plaintiff suffering further loss or damage in the future; in these cases the plaintiff need only establish that he has a *reasonable*, as distinct from a *speculative*, chance of suffering such loss or damage, and the court must then assess the value of that chance. (Emphasis added.)

The principle concisely stated in the passage quoted is directly applicable in this case. Speculative and fanciful possibilities unsupported by expert or other cogent evidence can be removed from the consideration of the trier of fact and should be ignored, whereas substantial possibilities based on such expert or cogent evidence must be considered in the assessment of damages for personal injuries in civil litigation. This principle applies regardless of the percentage of possibility, as long as it is a substantial one, and regardless of whether the possibility is favourable or unfavourable. Thus, future contingencies which are less than probable are regarded as factors to be considered, provided they are shown to be substantial and not speculative: they may tend to increase or reduce the award in a proper case.

18. The problem of compensation for loss of expectation of life traditionally created many difficulties. The loss of the right to a normal life span was recognized by the House of Lords in *Rose v. Ford*, [1937] A.C. 826, [1937] 3 All E.R. 359 (H.L.), when Lord Wright stated: "A man has a legal right that his life should not be shortened by the tortious act of another." The award, however, was a moderate one. In *Crosby v. O'Reilly*, [1974] 6 W.W.R. 475, 2 N.R. 338, the Supreme Court rejected the Court of Appeal's position that the award should be set at a maximum of $10,000. Now after the "trilogy", however, the position of the past may no longer be relevant. There is no longer a separate calculation for loss of expectation of life, but rather it forms part of the non-pecuniary damage award. In view of the upper limit and the adoption of a "functional" approach, the problem of assessing damages for loss of expectation of life may have disappeared.

D. A NOTE ON COLLATERAL SOURCES

Accident victims now have available to them several sources of compensation in addition to the tortfeasor. They may receive money from a variety of public and private schemes that reimburse them for their hospital, medical, wage and other losses. In Canada, we have a plethora of federal and provincial programs such as Canada Pension Plan, Employment Insurance, Workers' Compensation, O.H.I.P. and general welfare. In addition, there are an assortment of private sources of aid to accident victims. Needless to say, these various sources of payment have created many problems for the courts in assessing damages.

There are three possible methods of handling these collateral benefits:

(1) Accumulation, which allows the injured person to keep the collateral source funds and to collect in full from the wrongdoer as well. This, of course, permits double recovery, something that many people object to.
(2) Subrogation, which provides for the reimbursement of the collateral source by the wrongdoer. Under this method, the claimant receives only one payment, the tortfeasor pays for the loss, but the fund receives a type of windfall.
(3) Set-off or deduction, under which the collateral payment is deducted from what the defendant has to pay. This technique avoids double recovery, but it gives the defendant a windfall and denies the plaintiff the benefits of the plaintiff's own insurance.

All three treatments of collateral sources have their deficiencies, yet all of them are used in different situations. The first, accumulation, is now the most popular in Canada and the United States. (See *Boarelli v. Flannigan*, [1973] 3 O.R. 69, 36 D.L.R. (3d) 4 (C.A.); and *Gill v. C.P.R.*, [1973] S.C.R. 654, [1973] 4 W.W.R. 593 (*sub nom. Canadian Pacific Ltd. v. Gill*).) The second, subrogation, is frequently provided for in legislation. (See, for example, R.R.O. 1990, O. Reg. 552, s. 39, under the *Health Insurance Act*, R.S.O. 1990, c. H.6, which grants subrogation rights to the Commission. See also *Ledingham v. Di Natale*, [1973] 1 O.R. 291, 3 D.L.R. (3d) 18 (C.A.), noted by Fleming in (1974), 52 Can. Bar Rev. 103. Often, insurance companies contract for subrogation rights in the policies they issue. The third, deduction, still has a following in the United Kingdom and among many scholars, but it is wanting in popularity. Deduction may be provided for in legislation or by contract (see material on no-fault insurance, Chapter 18, *infra*).

The Supreme Court of Canada carefully reviewed the issue of collateral benefits in *Ratych v. Bloomer* (1990), 69 D.L.R. (4th) 25, 107 N.R. 335. The plaintiff, an injured police officer, received his full salary even though he was unable to work for several months. He did not lose any of his accumulated "sick credits". Could he claim loss of wages from the wrongdoer, or would they be deducted from his award? The majority of the Supreme Court held that the benefits should be deducted from the award. The Court wished to avoid the problem of "double recovery" and in view of the fact that the plaintiff could not prove that he had paid for his benefits, they did not fall within the collateral benefits rule. There was a strong dissent based on the view that the benefits received had been directly or indirectly paid for by the workers. For a comment, see Klar, "Recent Developments in Canadian Law: Tort Law" (1991), 23 Ottawa L. Rev. 265.

The Supreme Court revisited the issue of collateral benefits in *Cunningham v. Wheeler*, [1994] 4 W.W.R. 153 (S.C.C.). Three separate appeals with different facts dealt with the deductibility of disability benefits. The majority of the Court held that where a person has in some way paid for the disability benefits, there is no deductibility. The types of payments can be very wide and varied. They can arise from trade-offs which occurred in the collective bargain, actual money foregone by the worker, direct contributions by the worker, or included in the wage package provided to the worker. If, on the other hand, the payments were totally gratuitous, there still seems to be no deductibility (see, for example, *Kask v. Tam*, [1996] 7 W.W.R. 494 (B.C.C.A.)). In view of this, when, if ever, will disability benefits be deducted?

The dissenting justices approached the issue from the presumption of deductibility, whether or not the employee contributed to the disability plan. For the dissent, only where there is subrogation, should the wrongdoer be required to pay for the benefits, and in this case the employee would be given an award to be held in trust for the party with the right of subrogation. Does the majority's decision in

Cunningham v. Wheeler effectively undermine the whole thrust of *Ratych v. Bloomer?* What do you think is the better policy: allowing double recovery or letting a wrongdoer off the hook due to the foresight of the victim?

E. POST-ACCIDENT EVENTS

JOBLING v. ASSOCIATED DAIRIES LTD.

House of Lords. [1981] 2 All E.R. 752, [1981] 3 W.L.R. 155.

Lord Bridge of Harwich: My Lords, on 15th January 1973 the appellant injured his back in a fall at the premises where he was employed by the respondents. He sustained a prolapsed intervertebal disc which produced low back pain. In 1976 he developed cervical myelopathy. This condition was wholly unrelated to the 1973 injury. It has also been treated as common ground in the courts below and in your Lordships' House, that the condition of cervical myelopathy was not present in any latent or dormant form at the date of the appellant's accident, but developed subsequently. The effect of the myelopathy was of itself such as to render the appellant totally unfit to work from the end of September 1976 onwards.

The appellant's claim for damages against the respondent was tried by Reeve J. who, on 26th March 1979, gave judgment for the appellant, awarded him £6,000 for general damages (reduced in the Court of Appeal to £4,000) and awarded him special damages representing his loss of earnings from the date of the accident to the end of September 1976. No issue is raised as to any of these matters in your Lordships' House. The judge went on to consider the extent to which the appellant's earning capacity would have been impaired by the accident injury if the myelopathy had not supervened. He assessed this impairment at 50%, held that he was bound by authority to disregard the supervening myelopathy in assessing the damages resulting from the accident, and accordingly awarded further special damages to represent half the appellant's lost earnings from October 1976 to the date of the trial, and a sum in respect of future loss of earnings calculated by applying a multiplier of seven to a figure representing half the appellant's annual earning capacity. The respondents appealed against the inclusion of these elements of damage in the award on the ground that the supervening incapacity of the appellant attributable to myelopathy put an end to their legal liability for any loss of earnings which, but for myelopathy, would have resulted from the appellant's accident injury in 1973. The Court of Appeal (Stephenson, Ackner LJJ. and Dame Elizabeth Lane), in a unanimous judgment delivered by Ackner LJ., so held and reduced the damages accordingly. The appellant invites your Lordships to restore the award of the judge.

The authority by which the judge held himself bound, and that which is the linchpin of the argument for the appellant before your Lordships is the decision of this house in *Baker v. Willoughby*, [1969] 3 All ER 1528, [1970] AC 467. The plaintiff in that case sustained, by the negligence of the defendant, an injury to his left leg which caused a stiff and painful left ankle, liability to future arthritis, diminished mobility and loss of earning capacity. Subsequently, but before the trial, he was shot in the left leg in the course of a robbery and as a result the leg had to be amputated above the knee. The trial judge held that he should not take into account in his assessment of the damages the amputation of the left leg, since the appellant's actual and prospective loss flowing from the respondent's negligent act had not been reduced by the subsequent loss of the leg. The Court of Appeal reduced the damages to such as were appropriate to compensate the plaintiff for the effects of the injury up to the date of the subsequent amputation but no longer, holding that the subsequent consequences of the plaintiff's disability were in law attributable not to the original injury but to the subsequent amputation. This House reversed that decision and restored the award of the trial Judge.

It is significant that the argument for the plaintiff in *Baker's* case was put by counsel on the ground that special considerations governed the assessment of damages in the case of a plaintiff suffering successive injuries, such as those suffered by Mr. Baker, where both were caused tortiously. Counsel appears to have conceded, by implication if not expressly, that, if the amputation of the plaintiff's leg had been caused by disease or non-tortious accident, the Court of Appeal's view of its effect on the assessment of damages for the previous injury would have been correct. He argued that the trial judge's basis of assessment was necessary in the case of successive tortious injuries to ensure that the plaintiff should recover in the sum of the awards against both tortfeasors the aggregate loss he had sustained from both injuries. This he would not do if the first tortfeasor's liability was reduced by the effect of the second injury, and the second tortfeasor was entitled to take the plaintiff as he found him, *i.e.* as an already injured man. The Court of Appeal rejected this argument as fallacious on the ground that the second tortfeasor would be liable to compensate the plaintiff not only for the loss of his injured leg, but also for the diminution of his entitlement to damages against the first tortfeasor attributable to the loss of the leg.

Notwithstanding the course taken by the argument, in the speech of Lord Reid in this House (with which Lord Guest, Viscount Dilhorne and Lord Donovan agreed) there is no reference at all to the circumstance that the amputation of the plaintiff's leg was the result of a tort as a factor relevant to the decision. On the contrary, the reasoning in the speech applies equally to the effect of a supervening disability arising from illness or non-tortious accident, as the following passage amply demonstrates ([1969] 3 All E.R. 1528 at 1532-1534, [1970] A.C. 467 at 492-494):

> A man is not compensated for the physical injury; he is compensated for the loss which he suffers as a result of that injury. His loss is not in having a stiff leg; it is in his inability to lead a full life, his inability to enjoy those amenities which depend on freedom of movement and his inability to earn as much as he used to earn or could have earned if there had been no accident. In this case the second injury did not diminish any of these. So why should it be regarded as having obliterated or superseded them? If it were the case that in the eye of the law an effect could only have one cause then the respondent might be right. It is always necessary to prove that any loss for which damages can be given was caused by the defendant's negligent act. But it is commonplace that the law regards many events as having two causes; that happens whenever there is contributory negligence, for then the law says that the injury was caused both by the negligence of the defendant and by the negligence of the plaintiff. And generally it does not matter which negligence occurred first in point of time. I see no reason why the appellant's present disability cannot be regarded as having two causes, and if authority be needed for this I find it in *Harwood v. Wyken Colliery Co.* ([1913] 2 KB 158). That was a *Workmen's Compensation Act 1906* case. But causation cannot be different in tort. There an accident made the man only fit for light work. And then a heart disease supervened and it also caused him only to be fit for light work. The argument for the employer was the same as in the present case. Before the disease supervened the workman's incapacity was caused by the accident. Thereafter it was caused by the disease and the previous accident became irrelevant; he would have been equally incapacitated if the accident had never happened. But Hamilton, L.J., said (at 169): "... he is not disentitled to be paid compensation by reason of the supervention of a disease of the heart. It cannot be said of him that partial incapacity for work has not resulted and is not still resulting from the injury. All that can be said is that such partial incapacity is not still result-

> ing 'solely' from the injury." ... If the later injury suffered before the date of the trial either reduces the disabilities from the injury for which the defendant is liable, or shortens the period during which they will be suffered by the plaintiff then the defendant will have to pay less damages. But if the later injuries merely become a concurrent cause of the disabilities caused by the injury inflicted by the defendant, then in my view they cannot diminish the damages. Suppose that the plaintiff has to spend a month in bed before the trial because of some illness unconnected with the original injury, the defendant cannot say that he does not have to pay anything in respect of that month; during that month the original injuries and the new illness are concurrent causes of his inability to work and that does not reduce the damages.

In the speech of Lord Pearson there are references to the tortious causation of the supervening injury, but it is certainly not clear that Lord Pearson was treating this as the critical factor and thus adopting the narrow ground for decision advanced by counsel in argument. In any event, the ratio decidendi must be collected from the reasons adopted by the majority and, according to the strict doctrine of precedent, I think Reeve J. was right to treat the wide principle expressed in the passages from the speech of Lord Reid which I have cited as binding him to decide the present case as he did.

Counsel for the appellant has naturally relied on *Baker's* case as binding authority supporting the judge's assessment of the damages, but, recognising that it is open to your Lordships to examine critically and, if thought right, to differ from Lord Reid's reasoning, he has sought to reconcile it with those principles of law which the Court of Appeal in the instant case treated as justifying them in reaching a different conclusion from the judge.

The first principle is that, in assessing damages for future loss of earnings, the court makes a discount for the possibility that, apart from the injury in respect of which he claims, the plaintiff's earning capacity may be diminished by some independent cause ('the vicissitudes principle').

The second principle is that, since the court does not speculate when it knows, damages for loss of earnings, if the plaintiff's earning capacity has before trial been actually diminished by some independent cause of the kind to which the court would have had regard in applying the vicissitudes principle, must be reduced accordingly.

Counsel does not dispute the existence of either of these principles, but he contends that the scope of the vicissitudes principle must be confined to consideration of those future possibilities which arise from factors which can be shown at the date of trial to have been already inherent in some way in the plaintiff's physical make-up, or in his situation at the date of the tort, such as a latent but symptomless arthritis or a particular liability to injury by accident arising from the hazardous nature of his occupation.

Naturally, when such factors are shown to have been present, they will materially affect the extent of the discount to be made in assessing damages, but the judgment of the Court of Appeal has drawn attention to the absurdities which would flow from the adoption of any such absolute limitation of the vicissitudes principle as that suggested. The limitation would, moreover, be contrary both to authority and to the underlying theory of legal causation on which the vicissitudes principle itself depends.

In the classic words cited by the Court of Appeal from the judgment of Brett LJ in *Phillips v. London and South Western Railway Co.* (1879), 5 CPD 280 at 291; *cf* [1874-80] All ER Rep 1176 at 1180-1181:

> ... if no accident had happened, nevertheless many circumstances might have happened to prevent the plaintiff from earning his previous income; he may be disabled by illness, he is subject to the *ordinary* accidents and vicissitudes of life; and if all these circumstances of which no evidence can be given are looked at, it will be impossible to exactly estimate them; yet if the jury wholly pass them over they will go wrong, because these accidents and vicissitudes ought to be taken into account. (Emphasis added.)

In delivering the judgment of the Privy Council (in *Paul v. Rendell* (1981), 34 A.L.R. 569 (P.C.)) on the very day your Lordships concluded the hearing of the appeal in this case, Lord Diplock said:

> Where, as in the present case, the plaintiff's disability is permanent, it is, their Lordships are informed, the common practice in Australia to use actuarial tables for calculating the present capital value of future annual economic loss resulting from the reduction in the plaintiff's annual earnings which the judge considers that he will suffer for the remainder of his working life. From this figure as a starting point the judge makes such adjustments as he thinks appropriate. Some adjustment downwards would be needed to take account of all those contingencies such as unemployment, ill-health or any other disability short of premature death, for which allowance is not made in the actuarial tables but which might have deprived the plaintiff of his earning power or reduced it below the figure adopted for the purpose of the actuarial calculation.

The vicissitudes principle itself, it seems to me, stems from the fundamental proposition of law that the object of every award of damages for monetary loss is to put the party wronged so far as possible in the same position, no better and no worse, as he would be in if he had not suffered the wrong in respect of which he claims. To assume that an injured plaintiff, if not injured, would have continued to earn his full wages for a full working life, is very probably to overcompensate him. To apply a discount in respect of possible future loss of earnings arising from independent cases may be to under-compensate him. When confronted by future uncertainty, the court assesses the prospects and strikes a balance between these opposite dangers as best it can. But, when the supervening illness or injury which is the independent cause of loss of earning capacity has manifested itself before trial, the event has demonstrated that, even if the plaintiff had never sustained the tortious injury, his earnings would now be reduced or extinguished. To hold the tortfeasor, in this situation, liable to pay damages for a notional continuing loss of earnings attributable to the tortious injury is to put the plaintiff in a better position than he would be if he had never suffered the tortious injury. Put more shortly, applying well-established principles for the assessment of damages at common law, when a plaintiff injured by the defendant's tort is wholly incapacitated from earning by supervening illness or accidental injury, the law will no longer treat the tort as a continuing cause of any loss of earning capacity.

...

[**Lords Wilberforce, Edmund-Davies, Russell**, and **Keith** concurred.]

Appeal dismissed.

NOTES

1. Prior to the *Jobling* decision, the leading case on this problem of post-accident events was *Baker v. Willoughby*, [1970] A.C. 467, [1969] 3 All E.R. 1528, [1970] 2 W.L.R. 50 (H.L.). In that case the plaintiff's leg was injured in a car accident. Later, during a robbery, he was shot in the same leg, and the leg had to be amputated. At trial for the first accident the defendant argued that the plaintiff's damages for his injured leg ought to be assessed keeping in mind that the injured leg was amputated because of the robbery. The House of Lords rejected this. Lord Reid stated:

   > If the later injury suffered before the date of the trial either reduces the disabilities from the injury for which the defendant is liable, or shortens the period during which they will be suffered by the plaintiff, then the defendant will have to pay less damages. But if the later injuries merely become a concurrent cause of the disabilities caused by the injury inflicted by the defendant, then in my view they cannot diminish the damages. Suppose that the plaintiff has to spend a month in bed before the trial because of some illness unconnected with the original injury, the defendant cannot say that he does not have to pay anything in respect of that month: during that month the original injuries and the new illness are concurrent causes of his inability to work and that does not reduce the damages.

2. What was the factual difference between *Jobling* and *Baker*? Does this justify the different approaches? Is *Baker v. Willoughby* still good law or has it now been overruled?

3. In *Penner v. Mitchell*, [1978] 5 W.W.R. 328, 6 C.C.L.T. 132 (Alta. C.A.), the plaintiff would have missed three months of work, even if he had not been injured, because of an illness unconnected with the accident. The court did not allow recovery for this period. Is this consistent with *Baker*? with *Jobling*?

4. *Baker* was followed in *Hicks v. Cooper; Hicks v. Can. Petrofina Ltd.* (1973), 1 O.R. (2d) 221, 41 D.L.R. (3d) 454 (C.A.); and *Berns v. Campbell* (1974), 8 O.R. (2d) 680, 59 D.L.R. (3d) 44 (H.C.). These cases involved successive, unrelated accidents in which the plaintiffs were able to recover all their damages from the various parties on the *Baker* principle. According to this approach, the plaintiff receives all the damages that would have been received from the first defendant disregarding the fact of the second accident. If the second accident has worsened the plaintiff's position, the plaintiff receives this added amount from the second defendant.

5. In *Bourque v. Wells* (1991), 118 N.B.R. (2d) 394, 82 D.L.R. (4th) 574 (C.A.); application for leave to appeal to S.C.C. dismissed March 12, 1992, 92 B.S.C.C., p. 672, a second traffic accident exacerbated injuries which the plaintiff suffered in a prior traffic accident. Rather than applying the method laid down in *Baker v. Willoughby*, *supra*, the court apportioned the total damages suffered by the plaintiff between the two accidents. The court stated that this was a case of aggravated damages rather than a "thin skull" case. In your opinion, what is the best way to treat these cases of successive injuries?

6. The principle that "you take your victim as you find him" sometimes works to the financial advantage of defendants.

   In *Dillon v. Twin State Gas & Electric Co.*, 85 N.H. 449, 163 A. 111 (1932), a 14-year-old boy was killed in strange circumstances. While he was playing on a bridge he lost his balance and reached for a wire to save himself. The electrical current in the wire killed the boy. If he had not grabbed the wire, he would have fallen, either to his death, or to serious injury below. Mr. Justice Allen of the Supreme Court of New

Hampshire stated that the boy had not been deprived of a normal life expectancy but only of a few moments of life, "too short to be given pecuniary allowance". If it were shown that he would only have been injured in the fall, he should be awarded just the value of the loss to the earning capacity he would have had in his crippled or maimed condition.

7. The plaintiff is dying from an incurable disease. The defendant negligently kills the plaintiff. What loss has the defendant caused?

8. The deceased, who suffered from cirrhosis of the liver and cancer, incurred minor injuries in an accident caused by the defendant's negligence. The deceased's life expectancy prior to the accident was about two and one-half years but death ensues three months after the accident. The evidence shows that death was hastened by the accident. Is the defendant liable to the heirs for the hastening of death? How could one go about assessing damages in such a case? See *Windrim v. Wood* (1974), 7 O.R. (2d) 211, 54 D.L.R. (3d) 667 (H.C.J.).

9. One of the most difficult issues in the damage assessment process involves pre-existing conditions or post-accident events. Frequently, a plaintiff's disability arises from multiple factors, such as a pre-existing susceptibility to a medical problem, the exacerbation of an existing medical problem, or the interaction of several causes, some tortious, others not. Courts generally analyze this issue from the perspective of "causation", and ask whether the defendant's conduct was a necessary cause of the plaintiff's injury. See Chapter 4, *infra,* and the leading case of *Athey v. Leonati* (1997), 31 C.C.L.T. (2d) 113 (S.C.C.).

F. FATAL ACCIDENTS

TRUSTEE ACT

R.S.O. 1990, c. T.23, s. 38

38. — (1) Except in cases of libel and slander, the executor or administrator of any deceased person may maintain an action for all torts or injuries to the person or to the property of the deceased in the same manner and with the same rights and remedies as the deceased would, if living, have been entitled to do, and the damages when recovered shall form part of the personal estate of the deceased but if death results from such injuries no damages shall be allowed for the death or for the loss of the expectation of life, but this proviso is not in derogation of any rights conferred by Part V of the *Family Law Act.*

(2) Except in cases of libel and slander, if a deceased person committed or is by law liable for a wrong to another in respect of his or her person or to another person's property, the person wronged may maintain an action against the executor or administrator of the person who committed or is by law liable for the wrong.

FAMILY LAW ACT

R.S.O. 1990, c. F.3, ss. 61-63

61. — (1) If a person is injured or killed by the fault or neglect of another under circumstances where the person is entitled to recover damages, or would have been entitled if not killed, the spouse, as defined in Part III (Support Obligations), children, grandchildren, parents, grandparents, brothers and sisters of the person are entitled to recover their pecuniary loss resulting from the injury or death from the person from whom the person injured or killed is entitled to recover or would have been entitled if not killed, and to maintain an action for the purpose in a court of competent jurisdiction.

(2) The damages recoverable in a claim under subsection (1) may include,

(a) actual expenses reasonably incurred for the benefit of the person injured or killed;

(b) actual funeral expenses reasonably incurred;

(c) a reasonable allowance for travel expenses actually incurred in visiting the person during his or her treatment or recovery;

(d) where, as a result of the injury, the claimant provides nursing, housekeeping or other services for the person, a reasonable allowance for loss of income or the value of the services; and

(e) an amount to compensate for the loss of guidance, care and companionship that the claimant might reasonably have expected to receive from the person if the injury or death had not occurred.

(3) In an action under subsection (1), the right to damages is subject to any apportionment of damages due to contributory fault or neglect of the person who was injured or killed.

(4) No action shall be brought under subsection (1) after the expiration of two years from the time the cause of action arose.

62. — (1) The defendant may make an offer to settle for one sum of money as compensation for his or her fault or neglect to all plaintiffs, without specifying the shares into which it is to be divided.

(2) If the offer is accepted and the compensation has not been otherwise apportioned, the court may, on motion, apportion it among the plaintiffs.

(3) The court may direct payment from the fund before apportionment.

(4) The court may postpone the distribution of money to which minors are entitled.

63. In assessing damages in an action brought under this Part, the court shall not take into account any sum paid or payable as a result of the death or injury under a contract of insurance.

NOTES

1. These two statutes have their counterparts in each of the provinces of Canada. The purpose of the *Trustee Act* is to permit tort actions both by and against the estate of a deceased person. According to the early common law, personal actions died with the deceased so that the estate could neither sue nor be sued. By virtue of the *Trustee Act*, which was first enacted in 1886 in Ontario, this is no longer the case.

2. The purpose of the *Family Law Act* is to create a legal right of action by the dependants of the deceased for their individual losses as a result of the death. At common law, if someone was wrongfully killed, no tort liability arose. See *Baker v. Bolton* (1808), 1 Camp. 493; *Admiralty Commrs. v. S.S. Amerika*, [1917] A.C. 38, [1916-17] All E.R. Rep. 177 (H.L.). In 1846, however, Lord Campbell's Act granted limited protection to some dependants of the deceased. The *Family Law Act* is a successor statute, upon which dependants of the deceased now sue.

3. Damages awarded under the *Trustee Act*, or its equivalent, are usually quite low. This is especially so in view of legislative changes which do not permit an estate to sue for

anything but the pecuniary losses of the deceased. This rules out such items as loss of expectation of life and pain and suffering. But see the Manitoba case: *Gallant et al. v. Boklaschuk et al.* (1978), 7 C.C.L.T. 302 (Man. Q.B.). In Alberta, the *Survival of Actions Act,* R.S.A. 1980, c. S-30, s. 5 states:

> If a cause of action survives under section 2, only those damages that resulted in actual financial loss to the deceased or his estate are recoverable and, without restricting the generality of the foregoing, punitive or exemplary damages or damages for loss of expectation of life, pain and suffering, physical disfigurement or loss of amenities are not recoverable.

See also *Cromwell v. Dave Buck Ford Lease Ltd.* (1980), 109 D.L.R. (3d) 82, [1980] 4 W.W.R. 322 (B.C.S.C.), for an example in British Columbia.

4. In the trilogy, the Supreme Court viewed loss of future earnings as a pecuniary loss. It also assessed it on the basis of pre-accident working life. Does this mean that even in Alberta and other provinces which have restricted an estate's claim to pecuniary losses, that estates can claim for loss of future earnings of the deceased? Or would this be contrary to the intention of the legislative reforms? In Alberta, the issue was recently resolved in *Duncan Estate v. Baddeley* (1997), 36 C.C.L.T. (2d) 156 (Alta. C.A.). The deceased was a 16-year-old boy. His estate claimed for damages for the loss of the boy's future earnings, under the *Survival of Actions Act*, R.S.A. 1980, c. S-30, s. 5. The majority of the Court of Appeal held that the loss of ability to earn a livelihood is an actual financial loss and is recoverable by the estate. The dissenting judge held that it was the intention of the legislation to eliminate these speculative losses. Appeal to the Supreme Court of Canada was refused. Do you think that this judgment will have an impact on other provinces with similar legislative provisions? The issue is now being examined by the Alberta Law Reform Institute. What are the arguments for and against allowing such recovery? In awarding loss of future earnings to an estate, how should this award be calculated? How will this award affect an award to dependants under the *Fatal Accidents Act*?

5. The *Fatal Accidents Act*, R.S.A. 1980, c. F-5, s. 8(2), am. 1994, c. 16, s. 5 gives damages to certain relatives of the deceased for grief and loss of guidance, care and companionship. For example, the spouse is entitled to $40,000; the parents of a minor child or an unmarried child under 26 years of age are entitled to $40,000 in total, and each minor child or unmarried child under 26 years of age to $25,000. Why do you think these provisions were enacted? Now that there is also a claim by the estate for the loss of future earnings of the deceased, do you think these awards are unnecessary?

6. Legislation dealing with fatal accident claims, whether by the deceased's estate or the deceased's dependants, is not uniform across Canada. For example, where Ontario permits claims to be made by dependants in the case of an *injury* to the person on whom they depend, other jurisdictions do not.

7. See Cooper-Stephenson, *Personal Injury Damages in Canada*, 2nd ed. (1996), Chapters 10 and 11.

KEIZER v. HANNA ET AL.

Supreme Court of Canada. (1978), 3 C.C.L.T. 316,
[1978] 2 S.C.R. 342.

Dickson J. (**Laskin C.J.C.**, **Martland**, **Ritchie**, **Beetz** and **Pigeon JJ.** concurring): ... There are two issues: (i) the deductibility of income tax in arriving at an award of damages; and (ii) quantum. Although as a member of the court I shared in the decision in *Gehrmann v. Lavoie*, [1976] 2 S.C.R. 561, 59 D.L.R. (3d) 634, I have concluded, upon reading the reasons for judgment to which I have referred, and upon further reflection, that de Grandpré J. is correct in law and that the impact of income tax should be taken into account in assessing a damage award under *The Fatal Accidents Act*, R.S.O. 1970, c. 164.

On point (ii), however, "quantum", I have come to a conclusion other than that arrived at by my brother de Grandpré. I would allow the appeal, and like my brother Spence, award the amount of $100,000 claimed in the statement of claim but deduct therefrom the amount of $6,500 for insurance benefits already received by the appellant under the accident and death benefits provision found in Sched. E of the deceased's insurance policy. In the result, the award of general damages would amount to $93,500.

The accident in which Mr. Keizer was killed occurred on 16th July 1973. At that date he was 33 years of age with a life expectancy of 38.55 years. He was a tool room foreman for the town of Renfrew, capable, conscientious, industrious and in good health. He had been married for 9 years to the appellant, who at the date of his death was 27 years of age with a life expectancy of 49.60 years. Mr. and Mrs. Keizer had one child, an infant of six months.

The trial judge projected average earnings of $15,000 for a working expectancy of 31 years [7 O.R. (2d) 327, 55 D.L.R. (3d) 171]. From this figure he deducted $3,200 for income tax, $1,800 for personal use and $3,000 for personal support leaving disposable income for dependants in the amount of $7,000. The judge made a deduction for income tax with which the Court of Appeal agreed [10 O.R. (2d) 597, 64 D.L.R. (3d) 193] and which, in my view, was proper. The Court of Appeal did not question the judge's finding that the deceased would expend $1,800 for his personal use and $3,000 for his personal support. Thus, as a result, $7,000 would be available as disposable income for dependants. The evidence was that he contributed his pay cheque weekly to his family, reserving only nominal sums and odd-job earnings for his own use. Having concluded that $7,000 per year would have been available to the appellant and her child each year, the judge said [p. 336]:

> Actuarial tables filed as ex. 1 herein at 9% and 10% compound interest show the present value of $1 to age 65 for the male as $9.9375 and $9.1381 respectively. I believe a more realistic interest rate would be the approximate amount of 6½% which would materially inflate these figures; for example, at 4% the factor is 18.66461. One must consider income tax as a reality of modern life and its depreciating impact along with the contingencies herein-before alluded to is reflected in my assessment. Under the provisions of the *Fatal Accidents Act* I award the plaintiff the sum of $120,000, of which sum I apportion $17,500 for the infant Mitchel Stephen.

It is difficult, if not impossible, to know what use, if any, the trial judge made of actuarial tables to which he was referred. It would seem, however, that he proceeded on an exhausting fund basis, with a discount rate of approximately 6½ per cent. He made an allowance in respect of the income tax which the deceased would have had to pay on his earnings had he lived, and he further reduced the award by a contingency allowance. He referred to the contingencies which might bear on assessment, as follows [pp. 333-34]:

> (a) Possibility of remarriage;
> (b) Possibility of widow's death before expiry of joint expectancy period;

(c) Possibility of deceased's dying under other circumstances prior to expiry of said joint expectancy period;
(d) Possibility of deceased husband's retiring before expiry of joint expectancy period;
(e) Acceleration of inheritance to widow — bearing in mind likelihood of increased inheritance in event death had not occurred;
(f) Possibility the infant child may not be a burden to the father or require additional benefits for the full period of his calculated working life.

On the question of prospects of remarriage, the judge adopted the apt comments of Phillimore J. in *Buckley v. John Allen & Ford (Oxford) Ltd.*, [1967] 2 Q.B. 637, [1967] 1 All E.R. 539, including the statement that judges should act on evidence rather than guesswork, and, there being no evidence of any existing interest or attachment, he concluded [p. 335]: "I therefore accord no material significance to this prospect by way of deduction." He did not say that he is according no weight to the contingency.

As to the possibility of the early demise of either husband or wife, the judge said [p. 335]:

> All of the evidence indicates excellent health prospects and I rule that relatively little real significance can be attached to this contingency by way of reduction.

Again, it is not a question of refusing to consider a particular contingency. The judge considered the contingency but decided it merited little significance. I do not think he can be faulted on this account.

With respect to the possibility of acceleration of the inheritance to the appellant, the judge had this to say [p. 335]:

> So far as the acceleration of her inheritance is concerned, I am readily satisfied that same should have no reducing effect as in these circumstances. I am assured it is more than offset by the substantial loss she has suffered in future realization from this source.

Finally, the possibility that the infant child might not be a burden during his father's working life — on this point, the judge said that he would give this fact material consideration in considering his award. These are his words [p. 335]:

> Unquestionably, there is the probability that the child Mitchel Stephen would not have been a burden to his father for anything like the 30 years or so of his working expectancy and I give this fact material consideration in considering this award.

The quantum of the award came before the Court of Appeal for Ontario. In that court, reference was made by Arnup J.A., for the court, to the six contingencies to which the trial judge referred. Arnup J.A. observed that the trial judge might have added [p. 604]: "Possibility of incapacity to earn, occasioned by industrial or other accident, or by illness." He then continued:

> Having listed these contingencies, the trial Judge decided he should make no deduction for any of them. In so doing, he erred. A contingency, in the context of damages under the *Fatal Accidents Act*, is obviously an event that may or may not happen. A defendant is entitled to have contingencies taken into account by way of reduction from the result that would be reached if every contingency turned out favourably to the dependants, although due weight must be given in each case to the probability, or otherwise, of the contingent event actually happening.

I have been unable to find in the trial judgment any statement by the trial judge that he had decided he should not make any deduction for any of the contingencies. The evidence, as I read it, is to the contrary. It is true that the trial judge might have considered the possibility of the deceased husband becoming unable to earn, but I do not think it can be said that failure to express himself on this point amounts to reversible error. The award of $120,000 exceeded the amount claimed of $100,000 but that does not preclude an award of $100,000.

In making a gross award of $65,000 the Court of Appeal was content with the following cryptic statement [p. 604]:

> In my view, the appropriate award of general damages in all of the circumstances of this case, as disclosed by the evidence, would have been $65,000.

The judgment does not assist us, or the parties, by explaining why $65,000 should be considered to be the appropriate award. From this amount the Court of Appeal deducted the $6,500, to which I have referred, and directed that $10,000 be paid into court for the infant. In the result, the widow would receive from the defendants for her support and maintenance for the next 50 years the sum of $48,500. This, plus $6,500 already received, totals $55,000.

It is, of course, true that a trial judge must consider contingencies tending to reduce the ultimate award and give those contingencies more or less weight. It is equally true that there are contingencies tending to increase the award, to which a judge must give due weight. At the end of the day the only question of importance is whether, in all the circumstances, the final award is fair and adequate. Past experience should make one realize that if there is error in the amount of an award it is likely to be one of inadequacy.

In my opinion, in the circumstances of this case, an award of $55,000 to the appellant can only be described as niggardly. The appellant is entitled to an award of such amount as will ensure her the comforts and station in life which she would have enjoyed but for the untimely death of her husband. If one is speaking of contingencies, I think it is not unreasonable to give primary attention to the contingencies, and they are many, the occurrence of which would result in making the award, in the light of events, entirely inadequate. An assessment must be neither punitive nor influenced by sentimentality. It is largely an exercise of business judgment. The question is whether a stated amount of capital would provide, during the period in question, having regard to contingencies tending to increase or decrease the award, a monthly sum at least equal to that which might reasonably have been expected during the continued life of the deceased.

The proper method of calculating the amount of a damage award under *The Fatal Accidents Act* is similar to that used in calculating the amount of an award for loss of future earnings, or for future care, in cases of serious personal injury. In each, the court is faced with the task of determining the present value of a lump sum which, if invested, would provide payments of the appropriate size over a given number of years in the future, extinguishing the fund in the process. This matter has been discussed in detail in the decisions of this court in *Andrews v. Grand & Toy Alta. Ltd.*, *Thornton v. Bd. of School Trustees of School District No. 57 (Prince George)* and *Arnold v. Teno*, which are being delivered with the decision in the present case.

The object here is to award a sum which would replace present day payments of $7,000 per year for a future period of 31 years, with some reduction for contingencies. The trial judge used a discount rate of 6½ per cent without explaining this choice except to say that it was a "more realistic" rate than 9 or 10 per cent. As I have said in *Andrews* and *Thornton*, in my opinion the discount rate should be calculated on the basis of present rates of return on long-term investments with an allowance for the effects of future inflation. Evidence on these matters was not introduced at trial in the present case. However, the 6½ per cent rate chosen by the judge can be tested by the fact that present day investment rates reach about 10½ per cent, and Dr. Deutsch of the Economic Council of Canada forecasted an inflation rate of about 3½ per cent over the long-term future. These two figures suggest that an appropriate discount rate is approximately 7 per cent. This is only marginally different from the rate used by the trial judge. Ignoring, for the moment, the other factors to be taken into consideration, the sum required to produce $7,000 per year for 31 years, payable monthly, discounted at 6½ per cent, is slightly less than $95,000. The award should be reproduced somewhat to account for contingencies although, as I have mentioned, this amount would probably not be large. On the other hand, in order to yield the sum required net of taxes a greater sum would obviously be called for. The resulting amount would not reach the figure of $120,000 which the trial judge chose. However, the sum of $100,000, the amount claimed, can be justified with reasonable allowance made for income tax impact and contingency deduction.

I would allow the appeal, set aside the judgment of the Court of Appeal and direct that the appellant recover from the defendants the sum of $93,500. Out of that sum there should be paid to Marilyn E. Keizer the sum of $78,500, and there should be paid into court to the credit of the infant, Mitchel Stephen Keizer, the sum of $15,000, to be paid out to the said infant when he attains the age of 18 years, or upon further order of a judge of the County Court of the county of Renfrew. The appellant is also entitled to her award of $1,600 under the provisions of *The Trustee Act*, R.S.O. 1970, c. 470, in respect of funeral expenses and the value of an automobile.

I would allow the appellant her costs at trial against both defendants and her costs in this court and in the Court of Appeal against the defendant Buch.

Appeal allowed.

NOTES

1. *Keizer v. Hanna* was the fourth Supreme Court decision, rendered at the same time as the trilogy. It was the only one which dealt with the assessment in the case of a fatal accident, and like the others, clarified the principles to be applied.

2. Why did the Supreme Court treat the question of the effect of income tax on the assessment differently in fatal accident cases than in personal injury cases? Is this logical?

3. There are two elements to a fatal accident claim. The major one is for the pecuniary losses suffered by the dependants as a result of the death of a wage earner. The second is for the intangible losses. Even though many statutes speak only of pecuniary or financial losses, *Vana v. Tosta*, [1968] S.C.R. 71, 66 D.L.R. (2d) 97, affirmed that damages can be awarded for the loss of guidance, care and comfort provided by a loved one.

4. As for the meaning of "guidance, care and companionship", Linden J. in *Thornborrow v. MacKinnon* (1981), 32 O.R. (2d) 740, 16 C.C.L.T. 198 (*sub nom. Re Schmidt; Thornborrow v. MacKinnon*) (H.C.), explained:

> In considering these words initially, it appears as though the guidance and care concepts are ones which generally flow from parents and older relatives to the younger members of the family. To a large extent that is true. But it is not uncommon in some situations for young people to guide and care for older members of the family.
>
> As for guidance, most of the guidance, that is, things such as education, training, discipline, moral teaching, etcetera, usually goes from older members to younger members of the family, but that is not universally so. Often it is the child who acquires some skill or knowledge which he imparts to the parents. Not infrequently parents are taught by their children about such things as modern music, for example rock and roll, modern styles, modern activities, modern morals. It is not a rarity that a child introduces a parent to a new sports activity such as skiing or tennis and gives guidance and instruction to the parent in mastering that sport. Of course, this is especially the case as a parent grows older and loses touch with some of the developments in the modern world. Children then are extremely important as teachers of their parents as well as vice versa. Where the evidence supports it, therefore, an award can include a sum for the guidance that a child can give to a parent as well as that which a parent can give to a child.
>
> As for the word care, I think a child can also give care to a parent. The *Mason v. Peters* case is an example of that, where a young boy who was killed had helped to care for his mother who was a paraplegic in a wheelchair and in need of his care. Thus, when a parent is ill, a child, even a small one, may assist in giving care. Care, I think, includes such things as feeding, clothing, cleaning, transporting, helping and protecting another person. This is especially important in relation to parents who are elderly, whose children often help them with the daily tasks of living, such as shopping, getting around, attending at various medical advisors and other events. Care, then, is a concept that can apply, on proper evidence, among all the members of a family, regardless of age.
>
> In relation to the notion of companionship, age differences are totally irrelevant. Members of a family enjoy the companionship of other members of that family no matter what their ages. People of the same age welcome the company of the others in their age bracket, of course, but older people enjoy being with the young and younger people enjoy companionship of older people as well.
>
> The companionship of a parent and child is a truly unique pleasure. The joy of sharing experiences with one's child is hard to surpass, whether it be sports, culture, conversation or play. There are not many activities more enjoyable for a parent than to participate with one's child in the celebration of birthdays, graduations, weddings, the births of grandchildren and all of the other landmark events in their lives. What greater joy is there than to be with one's child on religious holidays, such as Christmas or Easter or Chanukkah? What could be a greater pleasure than to accompany one's child to a movie, a circus or a hockey game? What can be more marvellous than to hear one's child laugh, to cuddle it before bed or to watch it play with a dog? To see the enthusiasm for life in one's children often helps to restore one's own faltering commitment to a better world. Yes, companionship with one's children is one of the most prized of human experiences. To lose that is one of life's greatest losses. It was to provide compensation for that loss of companionship that the Ontario

> Legislature inserted that language into the *Family Law Reform Act*. It was not meant to be treated as a trivial loss, for it is not.
>
> Thus, loss of guidance, care and companionship can be suffered by each member of a family as a result of the death or injury of any other member of that family. Age is irrelevant. It is always an individual matter that must be established on the evidence in each case. This may differ in every family and with each individual in the family. It may be that a parent may consider one of his children a "pain in the neck" and will avoid its company. If that is the case, then there would not be very much evidence of loss. The figure awarded would be low. But in most cases, I would expect that the evidence would show that parents do receive much in the way of guidance, care and companionship from their children, as well as the other way around. There is still no compensation allowed, however, for grief or solatium.

5. Why allow a claim at all for non-pecuniary losses? Does the following explanation by Linden J. in *Thornborrow, supra*, provide a satisfactory answer?:

> In my view the Legislature intended, by s. 60, to go further than merely codify the old law under *The Fatal Accidents Act* which limited damages for the death of children to pecuniary loss, that is, the potential economic gain that parents may receive from their children by way of support in old age or before. Under that inhuman principle we have seen situations where, because there was no pecuniary loss, nothing at all was awarded for the death of very small children. (*Barnett v. Cohen*, [1921] 2 K.B. 461, 90 L.J.K.B. 1307; a six-year-old was killed, no award at all given.) We have also seen cases where insultingly small sums were awarded for older children. (*Courtemanche v. McElwain*, [1962] 1 O.R. 472, 37 D.L.R. (2d) 595 (Ont. C.A.).) It was no credit to the law that a wrongdoer, who injured a child, paid more damages than one who killed a child. It was said, in a kind of macabre jest that was a stain on our law, that it was better to kill a child than to injure one. This was a sickening situation, which embarrassed anyone who had anything to do with the law in this country. It was an affront to Canadians, who expect their law to be the embodiment of rational and civilized thought. Such low damage awards were barbaric, and did not reflect the prevailing views of our society which recognizes that children have a special value that transcends the pecuniary benefits they may some day bestow on their parents.

6. The opposite of "wrongful death" is "wrongful life". What damages, if any, should be assessed for "wrongful life"? Suppose, for example, a sterilization procedure is done improperly and a pregnancy and unplanned birth of a child ensues. Should the cost of raising such child be recoverable? See *Doiron v. Orr* (1978), 20 O.R. (2d) 71, 86 D.L.R. (3d) 719 (H.C.), where Garrett J. denied compensation for this because he found such a claim "grotesque". Also see *Kealey v. Berezowski* (1996), 136 D.L.R. (4th) 708 (Ont. Gen. Div.), where there were no damages awarded for the birth of a healthy baby in case of failed sterilization. See, however, *Cherry (Guardian) v. Borsman* (1992), 94 D.L.R. (4th) 487, [1992] 6 W.W.R. 701, 12 C.C.L.T. (2d) 137 (B.C.C.A.); leave to appeal to S.C.C. refused (1993), 99 D.L.R. (4th) vii*n* (S.C.C.), where a child and mother received damages following a failed abortion. What about recovery for the pain and suffering undergone by the mother? See *Cryderman v. Ringrose* (1978), 89 D.L.R. (3d) 32, [1978] 3 W.W.R. 481 (Alta. C.A.), where $5,000 was awarded, and *Doiron v. Orr, supra,* where $1,000 was assessed but not awarded because no negligence was found. Compare with the position under the civil law of Quebec, *Cataford v. Moreau* (1978), 114 D.L.R. (3d) 585, 7 C.C.L.T. 241 (Que. S.C.), where Deschênes C.J. permitted damages to the mother for the equivalent of pain and suffering, but did not allow anything to the child. What if there is an allegation that there was a negligent failure to counsel the parents concerning a genetic illness? See *H. (R.) v. Hunter* (1996), 32 C.C.L.T. (2d) 44 (Ont. Gen. Div.). See

Rodgers-Magnet, "Action for Wrongful Life" (1979), 7 C.C.L.T. 242; Tedeschi, "On Tort Liability for Wrongful Life" (1979), 7 C.C.L.T. 242; Tedeschi, "On Tort Liability for Wrongful Life", [1966] Israel L. Rev. 513. *Cf., Troppi v. Scarf*, 18 N.W. 2d 511 (Mich. 1971), where damages were allowed for cost of rearing child. See also Ashman, "Wrongful Life — Measuring Damages" (1982), 68 A.B.A.J. 1313.

CHAPTER 18

ALTERNATIVES TO TORT LAW: AUTOMOBILE ACCIDENT COMPENSATION AND BEYOND

Obtaining compensation for personal injury or death by means of a tort claim is a recourse available to only a few of society's disabled persons. It is the "exclusive" nature of tort law which has led many of its opponents to argue for its abolition and replacement by a universal, social insurance program. It is said that in view of the limited numbers who obtain tort compensation and its high cost of operation, paid for in part by many of those who will never receive tort benefits, that tort law is a luxury which we can no longer afford.

In recent years the focus of the debate has primarily been on automobile accident compensation. This has been a logical starting point for the reformer. With tort law having long been supplanted by workers' compensation schemes for work-related accidents, automobile accident victims were clearly the next priority. Not only is the devastation on our roads particularly appalling, but also the fact that compulsory liability insurance is already a feature of automobile accident compensation makes the transition from fault to no-fault particularly easy in this field. In addition tort law probably works least effectively in this area in attempting to achieve its goals of justice, deterrence, and education.

It has become clear, however, that the reformer's goal is not to stop at automobile accident compensation, but to replace tort law virtually entirely by universal, social insurance programs. In terms of personal injury and death cases, this has been more or less accomplished already in New Zealand. It is here that the arguments become more complex — what may be true of automobile accident cases is not necessarily true in the other areas in which tort law operates.

This chapter briefly reviews the debate which has led to the implementation of no-fault automobile accident compensation. The various schemes which are in effect will be highlighted. Suggested proposals will be noted.

It is obvious, however, that tort law compensation is only one part — and a relatively small part — of the total compensation package presently available in Canadian jurisdictions for disabled persons. This is often ignored. These other "non-tort" compensation systems, in particular, workers' compensation, criminal injuries compensation, and social security, play an important role. Only when one has a realistic appreciation of what compensation is available, to whom, and for how much, can one make meaningful judgments about where society's priorities should lie and what society can afford.

A. AUTOMOBILE ACCIDENT COMPENSATION: THE DEBATE OVER NO-FAULT

DUFF AND TREBILCOCK, EXPLORING THE DOMAIN OF ACCIDENT LAW

(1996, Oxford University Press)

Injuries stemming from automobile accidents are the most numerous and costly of all personal injuries in North America. They are also one of the most fertile areas of current experience and debate regarding the role of the tort system and its alternatives. In 1989, roughly 5 million Americans experienced auto-related injuries, 47,000 of which were fatal. In Canada, more than 200,000 people were injured in motor vehicle accidents in 1985 and more than 6000 died. To put these figures in perspective, between 1945 and 1985 more Canadians died as a result of automobile accidents (168,319) than the combined total of Canadians killed in both world wars (102,703).

The costs of these injuries are enormous. In 1985, the economic costs (medical expenses, wage losses, and other out-of-pocket expenses) of automobile injuries in the United States are estimated to have totaled $50 billion, and another estimate assessed the 1986 costs at $74.2 billion. Further, despite steady decreases in the annual number of traffic fatalities in Canada and the United States since the mid-1970s, injury insurance costs have risen sharply during this period, increasing by about 140% in the United States from 1977 to 1987.

KEETON AND O'CONNELL, BASIC PROTECTION FOR THE TRAFFIC VICTIM

(1969), p. 1.

Serious shortcomings beset the automobile claims system operating in each of our states. In each there is need for re-examination and reform of the whole set of laws, institutions, insurance arrangements, and customary practices currently used in determining who among the hundreds of thousands of annual traffic victims will receive compensation and how much each will receive. The most striking of the shortcomings can be stated in five points.

First, measured as a way of compensating for personal injuries suffered on the roadways, the system fails grievously short. Some injured persons receive no compensation. Others receive far less than their economic losses. Partly this gap is due to the role of fault in the system — to the need for the injured person to assert that another was at fault in causing the accident, and was legally blameless. In advancing these contentions a traffic victim faces severe problems of proof. Nearly always he finds it difficult to show what actually happened, and occasionally he cannot even identify the person responsible, because the accident was hit and run. Another major factor contributing to the gap between amounts of loss and amounts of compensation is that a person legally responsible for an injury may be financially irresponsible — uninsured and with inadequate assets of his own available to satisfy a claim. ...

Second, the present system is cumbersome and slow. Prompt payments of compensation for personal injuries are extraordinary indeed. And delays of several years before final payment — or determination that no payment is due — are common, especially in metropolitan areas. The backlog of automobile personal injury cases presents a serious community problem of delay in the courts, affecting other kinds of cases as well. And often justice delayed is justice denied. An injured person needing money to pay his bills cannot wait, as can an insurance company, through the long period necessary to press and recover his claim, and he may be forced to settle for an inadequate amount in order to obtain immediate recovery.

Third, the present system is loaded with unfairness. Some get too much — even many times their losses — especially for minor injuries. To avoid the expenses and risks of litigation insurance companies tend to make generous settlements of small claims. This largesse comes out of the pockets of all who are paying premiums as insured motorists. Others among the injured, as we have just suggested, get nothing or too little, and most often it is the neediest (those most seriously injured) who get the lowest per centage of compensation for their losses. Their larger claims are more vigorously resisted, and their more pressing needs induce them to give up more in return for prompt settlement. This disparity between losses and compensation is not explained by differences in fault in different cases. It is true that under the theory of the present system, in general, only an injured person innocent of fault is entitled to recover, and then only against a motorist who was at fault. But the practical results are more often inconsistent with this theory than consistent. In short, the results are branded unfair by the theory of the system itself, and one searches in vain for any substitute standard of fairness that gives these results a clean bill of health.

Fourth, operation of the present system is excessively expensive. It is burden enough to meet the toll of losses that are inescapable when injuries occur. It is intolerable to meet the toll of losses that are inescapable when injuries occur. It is intolerable to have to meet the additional burden of administrative waste built into our methods of shouldering inescapable costs. To some extent, it is true, costs of administration are part of the inescapable burden. But because of the role of fault in the present system, contests over the intricate details of accidents are routine. Often these contests are also exercises in futility, since all drivers must continually make split-second judgments and many accidents are caused by slight but understandable lapses occurring at unfortunate moments. Such contests, and all the elaborate preparations that precede them, wastefully increase the costs of administration. In cases of relatively modest injury, the expense of the contest often exceeds the amount claimed as compensation. All this expense, of course, is added to automobile insurance costs and, together with mark-up for the insurers through whose treasuries the premium dollars must pass, is reflected in the premium of every insured.

Fifth, the present system is marred by temptations to dishonesty that lure into their snares a stunning per centage of drivers and victims. To the toll of physical injury is added a toll of psychological and moral injury resulting from pressures for exaggeration to improve one's case or defense and indeed for outright invention to fill its gaps or cure its weaknesses. These inducements to exaggeration and invention strike at the integrity of driver and injured alike, all too often corrupting both and leaving the latter twice a victim — injured and debased. If one is inclined to doubt the influence of these debasing factors, let him compare his own rough-and-ready estimates of the per centage of drivers who are at fault in accidents and the per centage who admit it when the question is put under oath. Of course the disparity is partly accounted for by self-deception, but only partly. And even this self-deception is an insidious undermining of integrity, not to be encouraged.

This, in capsule, is the way the present automobile claims system looks when we stand back and view its performance in gross. It provides too little, too late, unfairly allocated, at wasteful cost, and through means that promote dishonesty and disrespect for law.

NOTES

1. The most prominent Canadian critic of the tort law system is Professor T.G. Ison. His book *The Forensic Lottery* (1966) is a leading work on the subject of the replacement of the tort law system by no-fault compensation schemes. The main criticisms levelled by Professor Ison against tort law are the following:

   (a) It is inappropriate to determine questions of compensation by resort to the fault principle. Fault frequently arises in the absence of any real negligence. Decisions as to fault are frequently based on considerations not related to moral precepts.
   (b) There are serious evidentiary problems in attempting to determine questions of fault.
   (c) Various factors combine to produce unsatisfactory damage assessments.
   (d) Proving causation produces insoluble difficulties.
   (e) Even if successful, the plaintiff might have difficulty executing judgment.
   (f) It takes too long to process claims.

   Professor Ison has recommended a reform plan — see Ison, "Human Disability and Personal Income" in Klar (ed.), *Studies in Canadian Tort Law* (1977), at 425.

2. New Zealand's Royal Commission of Inquiry into Compensation for Personal Injury (1967) (the "Woodhouse Inquiry") agreed with Professor Ison's criticisms. The report criticized the fault principle for ignoring the plight of innocent plaintiffs, for failing to assess damages according to fault, for ignoring the subjective qualities of the defendant, and stated that the community is not concerned with fault-based compensation. It also attacked the adversary basis of tort compensation noting problems of delays, uncertainties, and especially costs.

3. One of the most impressive and influential works on the whole question of compensation is Atiyah, *Accidents, Compensation and the Law*, 5th ed. (1993). Professor Atiyah is committed to comprehensive reform, and regrets "piecemeal" approaches which focus on particular claimants, such as victims of road accidents. In this comprehensive book, not only is the tort system examined, but as well, Professor Atiyah examines other compensation systems such as, first party insurance, criminal injuries compensation, and state provisions. In Chapter 7, "An Appraisal of the Fault Principle", Atiyah indicts the fault principle on the following counts:

   (a) the compensation payable bears no relation to the degree of fault;
   (b) the compensation payable bears no relation to the means of the defendant;
   (c) a defendant may be negligent without being morally culpable and vice versa;
   (d) fault is defined objectively;
   (e) the distinction between negligence and error is blurred;
   (f) the fault principle pays insufficient attention to the conduct or the needs plaintiff;
   (g) justice may require payment of compensation without fault; and
   (h) difficulties of adjudicating questions of fault.

   Do you have answers for Professor Atiyah on any of these points?

Also see Atiyah, "Personal Injuries In The Twenty First Century: Thinking The Unthinkable" in *Wrongs and Remedies in the Twenty First Century*, Birks ed., 1996 (Oxford, Clarendon Press).

4. In their book *Exploring the Domain of Accident Law, supra*, Dewees, Duff and Trebilcock looked at the empirical evidence concerning the efficacy of tort and alternatives to tort in five major accident areas: automobile, medical malpractice, products, environment, and workplace. The authors examined tort law's approach to each of these areas in terms of the goals of deterrence, compensation, and corrective justice, and looked at penal and regulatory alternatives to tort law and no-fault compensation schemes as well. The "Summary and Implications" of their analysis was expressed in the following way:

> Over the past 20 years or so, tort scholarship has been dominated by theoretical debates about the appropriate normative goals of the tort system and the doctrinal implications that each entails. These debates have centered around three major goals: deterrence, compensation, and corrective justice. We believe that these debates cannot be resolved in the abstract, but require close attention to empirical evidence on how the tort system, and alternatives to it, actually perform. We believe that the central normative question should not be which of these goals, or values, is superior to which other, but rather which legal or policy instruments are best equipped to vindicate which values. In other words, we accept the legitimacy of all of these goals and focus our analysis on identifying the means that best achieve each goal.
>
> In this respect, the empirical evidence has convinced us that a single instrument, the tort system, cannot successfully achieve all three of the major goals claimed for it, and attempting to use it in pursuit of objectives for which it is not well suited is both costly and damaging to its ability to perform well with respect to other goals that it is better able to realize. Almost a century ago, the tort system was abandoned for workplace accidents and replaced by an administrative workers' compensation system to perform the compensation function with a regulatory system emerging to deter some types of hazardous workplace behavior. Since the middle of this century, no-fault compensation systems have been adopted in various jurisdictions to compensate victims of automobile accidents, complementing regulatory systems for reducing risks to motorists. We endorse these moves and propose extensions of them with three caveats: compensation schemes must be separately funded in each of the accident areas; premiums for compensation schemes must be risk-rated to preserve deterrence incentives; and tort should not be entirely displaced, but should have a residual role in cases of egregious behavior causing serious harm. However, we do not see these compensation schemes operating in the area of product or environmental injuries.
>
> . . .
>
> We believe that the systems performing the three normative objectives that we have focused on in this study have become seriously unbalanced in the United States during the last three decades, and that the solution is to bring them back into balance. Balance will be achieved not by turning back the clock, but by moving forward to replace tort with new systems that perform better and more efficiently. Canada has already taken some of the steps that we recommend, providing useful experience as to their performance. We believe that our recommendations would provide substantial net benefits for Americans.
>
> Our substantive conclusions also lead us to some reflections on the activity of economists, lawyers, and other analysts who have written about these problems over the last two decades. As noted in these chapters, many assertions in the academic literature about the efficacy of the tort system have been supported principally by theory and assumption with little or no empirical

analysis. We have tried to redress this balance by assembling the available empirical evidence and testing the theoretical hypotheses. The great disappointment that the deterrent effect of tort is limited and uneven or cannot be established by existing studies suggests that considerable intellectual effort has been expended on models that omit some crucial facts about the real world, including high transactions costs and imperfect information. The implication for academics is that theory can only take us so far; at some point it is essential to gather data to test the most basic parameters of the systems in which we are interested — that is, to take the facts seriously.

For the legal profession there is another lesson. The tort system expanded in response to powerful demands for victim compensation and a belief that large corporations and insurance companies are appropriate risk-spreaders. The result has largely been a failure: compensation remains very uneven. It is time to admit that tort does not and cannot perform this general compensation function well and to turn to other instruments that are more appropriate for compensation, leaving tort to focus more directly on its traditional corrective justice objective.

5. In another interesting article, "Do We Really Know Anything about the Behavior of the Tort Litigation System — And Why Not?" (1992), 140 U. Pa. L. Rev. 1147, Professor Michael Saks argues that "much of what we think we know about the behavior of the tort litigation system is untrue, unknown, or unknowable". The article reviews the data available concerning how tort laws operate in practice.

BLUM AND KALVEN, "PUBLIC LAW PERSPECTIVES ON A PRIVATE LAW PROBLEM — AUTO COMPENSATION PLANS"

(1965) printed in (1964), 31 U. Chi. L. Rev. 646

We turn to consider fault as a criterion of liability. We do so with only the most modest of expectations. The whole concept of fault, even in our torts system, is so closely tied to views on personal responsibility — and hence to values that have deep cultural and religious roots — that we must limit our discussion of it here to very narrow confines. We have no intention of developing an adequate brief on its behalf. Our purpose is merely to counteract the fashionable tendency to dismiss it out of hand as being an untenable principle.

There have been various objections to fault as a criterion for liability, but in oversimplified fashion they can be schematized as three general points: (1) We can never get enough facts about a particular accident to know whether fault was present or not; (2) even if we had a full history of the event we would be unable to rationally apply the fault criterion because it is unintelligible; and (3) even if we knew the history of the event and understood what fault meant, we would be deciding cases on the basis of an unsound and arbitrary criterion.

The objection based on the difficulties of proof is a familiar one in all litigation, but it is urged as presenting special and decisive difficulties for the auto accident. There is the threat of evidence deteriorating because of the time it may take to get to trial. There is the sheer absence of competent witnesses at the crucial time of the event. And there is the emphasis under the fault criterion on split-second time sequences which place extra burdens on the capacity of witnesses to perceive, recall and narrate. These difficulties cumulate, we are told, so that the actual trial almost necessarily involves an imperfect and ambiguous historical reconstruction of the event, making a mockery of the effort to apply so subtle a normative criterion to the conduct involved. An impenetrable evidentiary screen thus makes fault unworkable as a criterion whatever its merits as a concept.

But does not this objection run the risk of proving too much? All adjudication is vulnerable to the inadequacies of evidence and the consequent exploitation of the situation by the skill of counsel. From prosecutions for murder to adjudications of the validity of family partnerships for income tax purposes, the law has had to wrestle with these difficulties. Auto accidents are at least more public than many other legal situations and they almost invariably do leave physical traces.

The witness to an auto accident is asked for observations likely to be well within his daily experience. The law can tolerate a goodly margin of error, and the threshold of distortion which this line of attack on liability for fault must establish before it becomes a persuasive reason for throwing over the system is high. We remain skeptical that the evidentiary aspects of the auto accident are so peculiar as to be set apart from the evidentiary aspects of all other controversies that are brought to law.

The objections to fault as being an unintelligible concept also run the risk of proving too much. One needs a generous view of the meaning of a legal principle. We should be at least as charitable toward negligence as we are toward procedural due process, fraud or gross income. All the big ideas of law are imprecise and have a core meaning which moves toward ambiguity at the margin. Except intuitively, there seems no way of measuring the relative clarity of such ideas. When we place negligence in the context of law's other big ideas, it looks at home. A simple test of its intelligibility is whether we can put easy cases so as to compel virtually complete agreement on the presence or absence of fault. We would all readily recognize that the negligence concept could pass this test were it not for the fact that our impressions of it are derived so much from the reading of appellate decisions with their marginal fact situations. The negligence concept, after all, has been employed by generations of lawyers and judges as though it makes sense. They were able to argue in terms of it and to array cases inside and outside the line. The decades of apparently rational discussion at the bar are paralleled by the decades of law school teaching. Every law student has been exposed to the experience of locating the relevant variables involved and of ranking the cases through varying a fact in one direction or the other.

But the critic can rightly say that law students do not decide cases, while juries do. The negligence concept is too vague, asserts the critic, to guide the judgment of juries. The result is that juries allocate liability on the basis of all kinds of legally irrelevant but humanly sympathetic grounds, and that the legal criterion in fact evaporates at the level of actual jury behavior.

Normally on a point such as this there is little evidence other than lawyer anecdotes. However, in this instance the University of Chicago Law School Jury Project does have some directly relevant data. In an extensive survey of the way judge and jury would decide the same personal injury case, the project found that in 80% of all cases the judge and jury agreed on liability or no liability. In 10% of the cases the jury found for the plaintiff where the judge would have found for the defendant. And, surprisingly, in the remaining 10% of the cases the judge would have found for the plaintiff where the jury found for the defendant. In brief, the jury would have found for the plaintiff in precisely the same number of cases as the judge. The upshot seems to be that whatever hidden rules the jury is in fact following when it operates under the negligence formula, its rules must be very similar to those governing the judge. It is thus difficult to make any special argument about the failure of this negligence criterion to control the jury.

This, however, does not dispose of the issue completely since the critic may now press his final objection to the intelligibility of the fault principle — the difficulty of controlling even the behavior of judges by so expansible a standard as negligence. In fact he may well say that our Jury Project evidence confirms his worst fears that fault is inherently a quixotic criterion that is infinitely expansible and is constantly changing its meaning. He will tell us that what is now regarded as negligence would have astonished judges and juries of a century ago. The challenge is that within established and apparently unchanging doctrine, the concept of negligence has greatly expanded its boundaries and will continue to do so.

The difficulty with this line of objection is that it presupposes that where a jury instructed under negligence has found negligence and the judge concurs there is available the judgment of some third party bystander who fails to find negligence and who over time would increasingly be in disagreement with the official results. Without this ideal bystander how can one say that negligence was found by the law and the community when negligence does not exist? At a deep level all that the negligence formula ever required was that the actor be held liable only when the community judged that the risk he took was not a reasonable one. It is possible, although there is no evidence here, that the community is gradually becoming more stringent in its judgments about the reasonableness of risks in the operation of autos. In a formal sense no matter how harsh these judgments become the system would remain essentially a negligence system. In a realistic sense, however, it is conceivable that a point could be reached where negligence in auto accidents became only a fiction. Whatever might lie in the future, it seems clear to us that we are not approaching such a point today.

The third objection, that even the fault theory is an unsound criterion, has several facets. The first is that the law exaggerates the contribution of the actor's fault to an accident. On a larger view the actor's role is frequently dwarfed by other causally contributing factors, such as road engineering, traffic density, car design, traffic regulations, and the performance of other cars just before the accident. The precise challenge is whether an admitted flaw in the actor's conduct, looked at in the context of other causes, is a sufficient basis for determining whether the accident victim is to get compensation.

This challenge appears to mirror the proposition sometimes advanced in criminal law that the individual actor's contribution to the crime is overshadowed by such other contributing factors as poor education, poverty, broken home, and so forth. The difficulty with this approach either in tort or in crime is that it is hard to see what else the law could do but single out the conduct of the individual actor. Speaking statistically, we can of course say that road engineering or broken homes are significant causes of accidents or crimes. But this does not help dispose of the individual case, and the law is charging the actor for a flaw in conduct that the mass of mankind — including those who come from broken homes or drive on poorly engineered highways — could have avoided. Although never philosophical about causation, the law has clearly recognized that any actor is but one of an infinity of causes of a particular event. It has dealt with the actor because he was a reachable cause and because his contribution to the event was relevant and decisive. Even if we conceded that the law always overrates the contribution of the actor, there is nothing in the auto accident field that gives this perception any special force.

The critic of the fault criterion might shift his emphasis and follow another line in pressing the point about the incommensurability of the actor's flaw and the consequences the law attaches to it. Negligence covers a multitude of sins, ranging from the grave to the trivial; and the critic can stress that there is no correlation whatsoever between the gravity of the sin and the magnitude of the damage caused. If tort damages were viewed as a system of fines, everyone would agree that the incidence of sanctions would be absurd, and it would be the rare case in which the punishment fits the crime. The difference in conduct between the negligent and the non-negligent drivers is too slight to support the huge difference in consequences that the fault principle attaches.

Does it matter for tort law that the punishment does not fit the crime? A sufficient answer is that the purpose of tort law is to compensate and not to punish; and this is well understood throughout the community and by the typical defendant. But the critic's point probably overestimates the lack of correlation between risk and damage. On the average we are likely to find that the magnitude of harm caused correlates fairly well with the magnitude of the risk taken — in fact, the magnitude of the potential harm bears a direct relationship to the magnitude of the risk taken. The critic's point in any event is especially weak in the case of auto accidents inasmuch as virtually everyone is well aware that an auto in motion can maim or kill. It is true that on occasion the law has recognized the point as when it limited liability for a slip of the pen in the *Ultramares* case. The fact that no such limitation has been imposed in auto accident situations suggests that the law deliberately declines to follow the policy in the case of the auto. Be that as it may, it is improper to invert the process of judgment and argue that a small amount of harm somehow indicates a small degree of negligence. The key concept for the law here is risk; and what is constant in these situations is the amount of negligent risk taken — and this is a factor which, as Holmes noted almost a century ago, is independent of the harm that actually occurs.

Another facet of the objection to fault as a principle builds on the not implausible assumption that all drivers are at some time or other clearly negligent. Most negligent conduct, however, is not actionable inasmuch as it does not cause harm. Whether a given negligent act causes harm seems to be largely a matter of chance. Since all drivers are in the same boat morally and only chance distinguishes them, it has been urged that all drivers ought to pay for the damages inflicted by drivers as a class, and that it is unjustifiable to place the burden solely on those whom chance did not favor.

The popular impression that all drivers are alike in being occasionally negligent is very likely an overestimation, for it fails to take account of the many minor adjustments in conduct which are made when men engage in what seems to be essentially the same risky behavior. Driving eighty miles an hour is not a constant risk, and presumably all recognize that such a speed in the city entails a markedly higher risk than in open country. But driving eighty miles an hour in the city does not represent a constant risk either, and those who drive at this speed under similar conditions might well do so with differing degrees of reserve or caution. It is not unlikely that there are grades of prudence even among the negligent risk takers. These minor differentiations in all probability partially account for which of the negligent drivers in fact get into accidents. And even if we grant that there is a large factor of chance as to which of the negligent drivers do cause accidents, it does not follow that the recruitment of drivers to accidents is a random process. Under the laws of chance, the drivers who take relatively more risks of a given magnitude are more likely to become involved in accidents than their fellow drivers who take relatively fewer risks of the same magnitude.

The last challenge to fault as a principle echoes the recurring suggestion in much contemporary writing about tort law that a proper criterion for choice between competing rules is the sheer number of losses that would be shifted. We should always prefer, we are told, the rule that results in shifting the largest number of losses off victims. Using this criterion at the most general level, it could be said that the basic difficulty with the common law fault rule in the world of the auto is that it leaves too many victims of auto accidents uncompensated. And we are offered empirical studies to prove that this is indeed the case.

If the earlier objections to fault run the risk of proving too much, this one runs the risk of begging the question. It should be abundantly clear that the common law never has had information about the incidence of recovery which would follow from the application of its liability rules. What is more important, it has had no expectations about incidence of recovery, and could not have cared less. Its commitment to fault as a basis for shifting losses is independent of any estimates of how many losses will thus be shifted.

No empirical study of gaps in loss shifting, insofar as they rest on the absence of liability, can be relevant. The striking point is that under the common law system it is intended that some victims will have to bear their own losses.

As familiar as all this is, it marks a critical point of departure. The question frequently now heard is: "By what arrangement can we most expeditiously maximize the shift of losses?" There is a profound difference between this and the old-fashioned question: "What losses should be shifted and what losses should the victim bear?" Under the logic of the common law, there is no meaningful way of answering the first question unless the second question has already been answered. We agree with that logic.

AMERICAN BAR ASSOCIATION, AUTOMOBILE NO-FAULT INSURANCE, A STUDY BY THE COMMITTEE ON AUTOMOBILE INSURANCE LEGISLATION

(1978), p. 9

A. MISCHARACTERIZATION OF THE FAULT SYSTEM

The most common criticism of the fault system is that it is an inadequate and inequitable system of compensation for losses sustained in automobile accidents. But this criticism incorrectly assumes that the purpose of negligence liability is to compensate accident victims and that, therefore, the appropriate criteria for evaluating the system's success are those that are used to evaluate schemes of compensation. Under this view, the fault system is a scheme for insuring automobile accident victims which has been complicated by the injection of a fault criterion for recovery of compensation under the scheme. This ignores the fact that negligence liability in accident cases long predated widespread private insurance, let alone the contemporary interest in social insurance. Negligence liability is rooted in age-old notions of corrective justice, in concepts of moral responsibility, and (according to a newer analysis) in the concept of economic efficiency, which is closely related to the intuitive notion of due care. Negligence liability creates rights against that form of wrongful conduct which consists of carelessly injuring another. Its purpose never was to insure people against mishaps. That idea was rejected in the formative years of the negligence concept.

Insurance became an aspect of fault only because potential injurers bought insurance to protect themselves from the consequences of a legal judgment for negligence. This was insurance for injurers, not for victims. Potential victims could, of course, insure themselves against accident injury, whether caused by careless driving or anything else, but this right existed independently of the fault system. The traditional purpose of the fault system, in short, is to provide remedies for wrongful acts rather than to insure victims of accidents.

To this it may be answered that what society needs in the accident area is not remedies for wrongful conduct but an effective system of compensation. This assumes, however, that there are no social benefits to providing remedies against wrongful conduct in this area, and this assumption, as we shall see, is incorrect. It also assumes incorrectly that the voluntary first-party and voluntary or compulsory third-party insurance that is associated with (and in part motivated by) the fault system is not capable of providing adequate compensation to victims of automobile accidents.

Contrary to widespread belief, universal compensation is not incompatible with the fault system. A fact overlooked by critics of the system is that people who are concerned that they might be injured in an automobile accident in which, for one reason or another, they might not receive adequate compensation through a tort claim, have always been free to take out first-party insurance. Life, disability, accident, collision, and medical insurance policies are widely available at reasonable cost and have the added advantage, compared to a scheme of compensation limited to automobile accidents alone, that they protect the insured against a much broader range of potential mishaps. They also enable the insured to choose the precise amount of coverage that is appropriate to his needs. And the voluntary character of this kind of first-party insurance is a positive feature in a society which values individual freedom of choice.

The combination of tort liability (and liability insurance, which naturally accompanies it) and voluntary first-party insurance constitutes a "system" of sorts, but it is not a system of automobile accident compensation which can be meaningfully compared with workers' compensation or social security or health care plans. The fault principle creates a common-law remedy for certain types of wrongful injury and leaves it to the private insurance market to provide potential accident victims with comprehensive compensation if they want it. If this market is deemed to work inadequately, for one reason or another, that is an argument for reform of the insurance market rather than for abrogation of the fault principle.

Once the fault "system" is viewed in its proper light, not only the criticism of its adequacy as a compensation scheme but also the criticism that it costs too much to operate become largely irrelevant. Of course a judicial determination of negligence and contributory negligence, and a judicial assessment of common-law damages, will seem a cumbersome and costly method of determining entitlement to insurance benefits compared to the methods used in other forms of insurance. The purpose of a tort proceeding is not, however, to determine eligibility for an insurance benefit, but to determine common law rights and liabilities. Since the same method is used to determine these rights and liabilities in automobile accident cases as in other common law cases involving other tortious invasions, breach of contract, property right infringements, and the like, there is no basis for concluding that the procedures used are unduly costly — unless it is proposed to do away with the entire system of private law in this country.

Those who advocate sweeping curtailment of automobile accident liability on grounds of cost and court congestion would be shocked to see similar measures proposed in other areas of law. For example, in the criminal law, procedural shortcuts are sometimes advocated to cut costs and relieve the pressures on the courts arising from the efforts of criminal defendants to vindicate their rights. Perhaps the reason why those who oppose this position on criminal rights do not defend the substantive and procedural rights of automobile tort claimants with comparable vigor is that they do not perceive the issue in automobile tort litigation as one of rights at all, but as one of reforming an insurance scheme unaccountably administered by the common-law courts. This, however, is a misconception of the nature of the tort remedy in automobile accident cases. It is not a claim for insurance, but an assertion of a fundamental common-law right to be free from certain wrongful invasions of personal integrity and property.

NOTES

1. Until relatively recently, arguments about the adequacy of tort law as a compensation device for victims of road and other accidents were largely based on impression and general principles. There were very few studies which actually tested the assertions being made. For example, the Woodhouse Report, *supra*, which led to the extinction of common law rights on action in New Zealand contained very little empirical evidence to support its claims. As Geoffrey Palmer has stated, the Woodhouse attack on the common law "was largely based on principle. There were almost no empirical data in New Zealand on who got what, when, and how from the common law system." See Palmer, *Compensation for Incapacity: A Study of Law and Social Change in New Zealand and Australia* (1979), p. 26. Fortunately, because of some studies, we are now in a better position to assess the arguments. See for example, the *Report of the Osgoode Hall Study on Compensation for Victims of Automobile Accidents*, 1965; the *Report of the Royal Commission on Civil Liability and Compensation for Personal Injury*, 1978 (the "Pearson Report"); and the *Report of the Ontario Task Force on Insurance*, 1988 (the "Osborne Report"). Although these reports do not agree on all things, a few common findings which bear upon the fault/no-fault debate emerge. First, it is clear that for most accident victims there is a considerable amount of non-tort compensation for which they are eligible, in addition to whatever tort compensation they may receive. Nevertheless, there remain losses that are not reimbursed by either source. Second, only a small fraction, in the order of one to two per cent, of all automobile accident claims, ever proceed to trial and judgment. The rest are settled. Third, delay is a problem, not only for plaintiffs but for defendant insurers. Fourth, the present system is costly, but it is hard to tell what, if any, the savings would be if a switch to no-fault were made. How would all of these findings affect your decision whether to stay with tort or abandon it for no-fault?

2. One of the most compelling arguments for the retention of civil liability is that ordinary people believe that a wrongdoer should compensate the victim for the injurious consequences of the wrongdoing. Do ordinary people really believe this? There is at least one study which indicates that many accident victims do share this view. See Lloyd-Bostock, "Common Sense, Morality and Accident Compensation" [1980] Ins. L.J. 331. The argument used to discount this is that even if this value is widely held it is misguided, especially in the case of motor vehicle accidents, where insurance is compulsory and it is the liability insurer and not the wrongdoer who pays the judgment. One area which has not been explored, however, is to examine whether it is that important to victims that the compensation actually comes from the wrongdoer, as long as the wrongdoer is adjudged to be the guilty party. Might there not be important symbolic values behind the common law right of action, notwithstanding liability insurers? If you were involved in an automobile accident, would you be concerned about whose fault the accident was? Why have many victims in New Zealand attempted to sue their wrongdoer in court to obtain punitive damages despite the fact that they were compensated by accident compensation? See Klar, "New Zealand's Accident Compensation Scheme: A Tort Lawyer's Perspective" (1983), 33 U. Toronto L.J. 80. For an opposing view as to how New Zealanders have reacted to the scheme see Ison, *Accident Compensation: A Commentary on the New Zealand Scheme* (1980), p. 179.

3. Is fault a concept which is difficult to understand and to prove? A person associated with an insurance company conducted research into the matter. His opinion was "that a large proportion of all automobile accidents are uncomplicated events in which the fault determination is very easy and that many of the more complex accidents can be accurately analyzed, by people trained to do such work, on the basis of the physical facts, even when the impressions of the witnesses are confused." Three hundred and fifty-two insurance files were consulted. The result was that fault was questionable in only 7.4 per cent of the cases, and clearly attributable to one of the parties in 92.6 per cent of the cases. See Marryott, "Testing the Criticisms of the Fault Concept" in *Justice and the Adversary System* (1968). One way in which insurers handle questions of fault which eliminates any dispute is by the use of "fault charts". These charts determine questions of fault according to the way in which the accident occurred. The parties agree to be bound by the chart and eliminate the issue of fault.

4. The argument that tort law deters wrongful conduct seems particularly weak in the automobile accident field. It is persuasively argued that if the threat of serious personal injury and criminal sanctions does not deter someone from driving recklessly, a tort law judgment will have little effect. How about the effect of adverse tort judgments on a person's liability insurance premiums, however? Careless drivers who cause accidents pay significantly higher premiums than safe drivers. If the premiums are too high, careless drivers might be forced off the roads. Would this improve road safety? Under a no-fault scheme, do careless drivers receive disincentives? How are "careless" drivers determined? Do you agree with the following argument by Posner, *Economic Analysis of Law*, 3rd ed. (1987)?

   > Criticisms of the operation of the negligence system in the automobile field have led to a number of proposals for no-fault automobile accident compensation. Many states have now passed statutes based on such proposals. A surprising feature of these measures, at least from an economic standpoint, is that they are not concerned with creating better incentives for accident avoidance. They do not seek to make the tort system a better deterrent of unsafe conduct. They seek to increase the coverage of the system and to reduce the cost of insurance. These goals are inconsistent with each other as well as with the goal of reducing the number of accidents.

5. In Posner, *Tort Law: Cases and Economic Analysis* (1982), the author makes the following observation, at p. 851, n. 1:

   > Since the publication of the ABA Special Committee's report, there has been an interesting empirical study of the effect of state no-fault statutes (and hence, implicitly, of the fault system itself) on the automobile accident rate. The study, utilizing statistical techniques to hold constant the effect of other variables on the accident rate besides the legislation, finds that the adoption of no-fault laws raises the accident rate — and the more stringent the law (*e.g.*, Michigan versus Delaware), the greater this effect. See E.M. Landes, Insurance, Liability and Accidents: A Theoretical and Empirical Investigation of the Effect of No-Fault on Accidents (Center for the Study of the Economy and the State, University of Chicago, May 1980). The study finds that states that place relatively moderate restrictions on tort liability experience between two and five per cent more fatal accidents as a result, while states with highly restrictive laws experience as many as 10-15 per cent more fatal accidents. This result may seem extremely surprising, if only because no-fault laws leave tort liability intact in death cases. However, as Landes points out, if restricting tort liability results in less care in driving, there will be more accidents, some fraction of which result in death. For other empirical evidence on the operation of no fault, see All-Industry Research Advisory Comm., Automobile Injuries and Their Compensation in the United States (1979).

6. When all is said and done, is the following not the crux of the fault/no-fault debate: as a question of values, is it justifiable to treat victims of wrongs differently from wrongdoers, innocent victims where there has been no wrong, or others disabled by illness, ageing, or otherwise disadvantaged? If it is justifiable, then serious efforts can be made to improve the existing defects in the tort system, which can to a very large measure be successful. If it is not justifiable, of course, then the common law cause of action ought to be abandoned. In many respects, endless arguments about costs, delays, difficulties of proof, and so on, only serve as smoke screens to camouflage the real issue. Do you agree with this view or is it an oversimplification?

B. ARE THE VICTIMS OF AUTO ACCIDENTS DIFFERENT?

LINDEN, "PEACEFUL COEXISTENCE AND AUTOMOBILE ACCIDENT COMPENSATION"

(1966), 9 Can. Bar J. 5

... [W]hy single out motor accident victims for special treatment over other victims of adversity? Injuries resulting from automobile accidents are worthy of special treatment because, as Judge Marx, a dedicated proponent of reform, has written, "The automobile accident victim ... is a very marked social problem, both because of his number and because of the source of his injury." Indeed automobile accidents kill almost 50,000 people and injure over a million each year in North America. Governments have long recognized this by the enactment of special legislation making owners of automobiles responsible for the negligence of their drivers, creating unsatisfied judgment funds, requiring compulsory liability insurance and the like. Criminal and quasi-criminal legislation has been passed regulating traffic, enacting rules of the road and requiring certain equipment on motor vehicles. Moreover, the legal profession bears a special responsibility because it is already heavily committed to participation in both civil and criminal cases arising from automobile accidents. Accordingly, it is looked to for leadership in this field, while it plays no role in the economic or social treatment of bathtub or cancer victims. Another factor which distinguishes automobile victims is that the machinery for loss-distribution and loss-spreading is already available in the almost universal liability insurance that is prevalent in Canada. No longer are we forced to choose one of the two *individuals* involved in an accident to bear the total losses produced; we are now able to allocate all of the costs generated by an activity to a *group* of persons selected in advance through the insurance device.

ISON, "TORT LIABILITY AND SOCIAL INSURANCE"

(1969), 19 U.T.L.J. 614

There are two possible explanations of why motor vehicle compensation plans have come to be advocated. First, the sudden drama of the event, the exposure to public view, the system of prosecutions, tort claims, the availability of statistical data, traffic safety campaigns, rising casualty figures, and increasing insurance premiums have all combined to focus public attention on road accidents. Hence motor vehicle accidents feature in the press and in political debate, and any proposal for a motor vehicle compensation plan is assured of a sympathetic audience. Second, a plan of motor vehicle accident compensation can be administered by insurance companies whereas a more comprehensive plan of sickness and injury compensation can only be implemented efficiently by the development of a social insurance system administered by government. Hence the advocates of a compensation plan limited to motor vehicle accidents can hope for support from the insurance industry. In the United States, this support is already coming. In other words, the advocacy of compensation plans limited to motor vehicle accidents seems to be justified by nothing more virtuous than a timid concession to predictions of political feasibility.

Of course it can be argued that for good social cost accounting, the cost of accident compensation should be charged on those who engage in accident-causing activities. But, as I will try to show, this can be achieved more efficiently by an advanced system of social insurance than by a proliferation of separate plans, each of which compensates a different category of misfortunes classified according to their cause.

Furthermore, there is really no rational ground for distinguishing between deaths and disabilities caused by accidents and those resulting from sickness or disease.

So far in Canada we have dealt with compensation for disablement and death by a proliferation of separate plans involving separate administrative structures. Thus we have Workmen's Compensation, the Canada Pension Plan, compensation for the victims of crimes of violence, the Saskatchewan Automobile Insurance Plan, sick pay, life insurance, personal accident insurance, and welfare. Expensive enquiries into complex issues of causation are often required to determine under which plan, if any, the victim is entitled to compensation. There is surely no point in aggravating these problems by adding to the list another plan and another administrative structure.

BLUM AND KALVEN, "PUBLIC LAW PERSPECTIVES ON A PRIVATE LAW PROBLEM — AUTO COMPENSATION PLANS"

(1965), printed in (1964), 31 U. Chi. L. Rev. 641

Nor will we do more than mention several differences, which some observers have urged as critical, between the industrial accident situation and the auto accident situation. It is said that while the industrial accident is relatively fixed and easy to investigate, the auto accident is more transient and difficult to investigate. The result is that there are likely to be great differences in the opportunities for policing fraudulent claims in the two areas. It is also said that damages are more amenable to scheduling in the one case than in the other, both because the range and variety of physical injuries is more restricted in the industrial accident and because the injured personnel are drawn from a fairly homogeneous economic group. These are acute observations, and they do point up specific difficulties which would be encountered in administering a compensation plan, but they do not cut deep enough to put to rest Jeremiah Smith's challenge of fundamental inconsistency.

There are three residual differences which lead us to deny the analogy to workmen's compensation. First, there is a great difference between the common law system for industrial accidents which workmen's compensation was created to replace and the common law system for auto accidents which exists today. Under the law of fifty years ago, we are told, the ability of the injured employee to recover was greatly circumscribed by the well-known trilogy of employer defenses — assumption of risk, contributory negligence, and the fellow servant rule. The old law has looked to some like a conspiracy to throw the losses of industrial accidents onto employees as a class at a time when they were conspicuously less well off than their employers. There is no comparable harshness in the law which confronts the auto accident claimant today. In the same vein, the whole "welfare" support for workmen's compensation is considerably diluted today in the auto accident area. First party insurance and social legislation have come on the scene and have greatly reduced the likelihood that the auto accident victim and his family will bear the full brunt of the accident.

A second difference is that the enterprise situation made possible a popular myth as to how the cost of workmen's compensation was to be borne. The widespread image was that by placing the cost of workmen's compensation on employers the cost would be passed on to consumers of their products through operation of market forces. The result was thought to be that not only social justice but economic justice would be accomplished; and this view of the matter was crystalized in the slogan that the cost of products should reflect the blood of workmen. Although there are good reasons today for doubting whether consumers do bear the cost of workmen's compensation, for our immediate purposes it is enough that there is no one in the auto situation who occupies a role which the employer was popularly thought to play in the industrial accident situation — no one, that is, who could be regarded as being in a position to pass on the costs to consumers via the market.

A third difference challenges the view that workmen's compensation offers a competing doctrine of tort liability. There is no doubt that this is the traditional view; workmen's compensation was enacted to repeal and replace common law tort rules, and it was challenged and ratified in court on that premise. We wish to suggest here a considerably different view of the history and rationale. In retrospect, we are impressed that workmen's compensation can best be understood as a kind of "fringe benefit" incorporated by law into the basic employment contract. The law in effect compelled the employer to provide, as a term of employment, an industrial accident policy for his employees.

BLUM AND KALVEN, "PUBLIC LAW PERSPECTIVES ON A PRIVATE LAW PROBLEM — AUTO COMPENSATION PLANS"

(1965) printed in (1964), 31 U. Chi. L. Rev. 641

From the very beginning the proponents of plans have insisted that the auto accident be viewed as an instance of human misfortune calling for a welfare remedy. When the situation is looked at in this manner, it immediately becomes apparent that the problem is bigger than that which the proponents started out to solve. The welfare universe is not limited to victims of auto accidents but includes victims of all other kinds of human misfortune. We can think of no ground for singling out the misfortune of auto victims for special welfare treatment.

The social security perspective also has the merit of bringing to the surface the profound question of why the state should do anything about human misfortune. We infer that those who urge the state to intervene have mixed motives. To some extent they favor sumptuary legislation in behalf of prudence. They are willing to restrict the power of the individual to choose because they distrust every man's capacity to make prudent judgments about privately carrying accident insurance. But more important, they are concerned over the financial ability of people to absorb misfortune. They see that by no means is everyone prosperous enough to buy adequate insurance against misfortune. The attraction of financing protection through the tax mechanism is that the necessary funds can be collected on some progressive tax basis, so that the richer will pay the costs for the poorer. Intervention by the state thus is sought in order to mitigate the evils of poverty. We are tempted to hazard the grand generalization that at the root of most of our major social issues lies the concern with what is thought to be poverty. The automobile compensation plan is no exception... .

The old common law issue of justice apart, the social security approach to the problem of the auto accident victim has some distinctive disadvantages of its own. If economic considerations have a bearing on accident-causing behavior, this approach would seem to run the greatest risk of lessening deterrence. Neither drivers nor pedestrians would perceive any relationship between their taxes and their conduct in respect to automobiles. The approach also has the disadvantage of supplanting the private insurance industry in a major sector of its activities, and replacing it with taxation and government administration of welfare benefits. Such a development would add to the power of the government and weaken what is now an important private pool of power. Finally, the approach calls for one more — and perhaps an irreversible — reduction in the area of individual autonomy.

It is not comfortable for us to end by repeating all the well-aired objections to social security. We are aware that we are a long way from home. And it is no accident that we have travelled so far from the tort world from which we began. Private law cannot borrow goals from public law fields without accepting the obligation to make a proper public law analysis. In the case of automobile compensation plans, such an analysis shows that the special problem cannot be solved adequately without solving a larger problem. This much, at least, we have learned from this venture in applying public law perspectives to an important private law problem.

NOTES

1. Are those pressing to reform the auto accident system too limited in their objectives? Should they be urging compensation for all accident victims? All sickness and injury victims? All victims of misfortune in society? All poor people?

2. Are there any good logical reasons for limiting their objectives? Economic reasons? Political reasons?

3. The studies have indicated that up to 70 per cent of motor vehicle accident victims receive tort compensation while as few as 10 per cent of those not injured at work or on the road receive any compensation from any source. Further many of those who receive tort compensation as a result of a motor vehicle accident have other sources of compensation available to them. In view of these figures, do you think that automobile accident victims ought to be the first priority for new social insurance schemes?

4. In order to move to pure no-fault schemes with no common law rights, the reformer must convince the community that the common law action is no longer worthy of retention. This is more easily done in relation to motor vehicle accident cases than in the other areas in which tort law operates. Compulsory liability insurance weakens arguments relating to the moral precepts of tort law, "fault" is often attributable to ordinary human error, and the legal system already has in place other ways to deter and punish wrongdoers. This is probably the main reason that no-fault auto schemes are easier to sell to the public and why law reform groups usually start off here.

C. WHO SHOULD PAY THE COSTS OF AUTO ACCIDENTS?

CALABRESI, "THE DECISION FOR ACCIDENTS: AN APPROACH TO NON-FAULT ALLOCATION OF COSTS"
(1965), 78 Harv. L. Rev. 713

Many recent writers have tended to focus on compensation as the main purpose of accident law. Were this emphasis proper, that would be no justification for limiting compensation to accidents and not spreading it across the board to illness, old age, and all the troubles of this planet. Of course, we do spread compensation beyond accidents to some extent, but it is the fact that we only do it "to some extent" that is crucial. Why is compensation for illness — even in highly welfaristic countries — much less complete than compensation for accidents? And why is the accident field kept a separate entity, where methods that achieve a fair degree of compensation spreading are used, but which would be woefully inefficient if compensation spreading were the only aim? Surely, if the type of cost reduction with which we are concerned is solely or principally that accomplished by diminishing secondary costs — social and economic dislocations — then a generalized system of social insurance covering all types of severe injuries would be the only efficient system.

The answer is that accidents are not the same as diseases. There are ways to reduce the primary cost of accidents — their number and severity — that can, indeed must, be an important aim of whatever system of law that governs the fields. One way is to discourage those activities that result in accidents and to substitute safer ones for them. Another is to encourage care in the course of an activity. "Activity" and "care" are not, of course, mutually exclusive categories. If "activity" is defined narrowly or if "care" is broadly viewed, the concepts tend to merge. The activity of driving is not thought to be careless although a predictable number of accidents result from it. Driving through a busy intersection without brakes is careless and not an activity. Between these relatively clear cases the distinction becomes more difficult, as, for example, navigating without radar. In addition, an activity may properly be defined as the doing of something by an actuarial class, which may tend to do it carelessly. Treating the problems of accident law in terms of activities rather than in terms of careless conduct is the first step toward a rational system of resource allocation. The question is to what extent an economically rational system is our goal. ...

Our society is not committed to preserving life at any cost. In its broadest sense, this rather unpleasant notion should be obvious. Wars are fought. The University of Mississippi is integrated. But what is more interesting to the study of accident law, though perhaps equally obvious, is that lives are used up when the *quid pro quo* is not some great moral principle but "convenience". Ventures are undertaken that, statistically at least, are certain to cost lives. Thus, we build a tunnel under Mont Blanc because it is essential to the Common Market and cuts down the traveling time from Rome to Paris, though we know that about a man per kilometre of tunnel will die. We take planes and cars rather than safer, slower means of travel. And perhaps most telling, we use relatively safe equipment rather than the safest imaginable because — and it is not a bad reason — the safest costs too much.

Of course, it is rarely known who is to die. Indeed, in the uncustomary case of an individual — a known individual rather than a statistical unknown — in a position of life or death, we are apt to spend very much more to save him than in any conceivable money sense he is worth. And while I do not doubt this is as it should be, it seems odd that we should refuse to apply the same standards of "value beyond any price" when we deal with the same man's life as part of a statistic. But odd or not, it is the case.

A decision balancing lives against money or convenience when made in the broadest terms is not purely an economic one. The decision whether the Mont Blanc tunnel is worth building is not based solely on whether the revenue received from tolls through the completed tunnel will pay for the construction costs, including compensation of the killed and maimed. Neither is the decision whether to allow prostitution based solely on whether it can pay its way. Such a pure free enterprise solution has never been acceptable. It was in fact rejected by even the most classical of classical economists, though they felt it necessary to explain the rejections in terms of a theory that is as narrow or broad as any society, welfaristic or free enterprise, cares to make it. The real issue, whether or not expressed in terms of these economists' "hidden social costs" or "hidden social savings" theory, is how often a decision for or against an activity is to be allowed regardless of whether it can pay its way. Such decisions operate, on the one hand, to create subsidies for some activities that could not survive in the market place, and on the other, to bar some activities that can more than pay their way. The frequency with which decisions to ignore the market are made tells something about the nature of a society — welfare or *laissez-faire*. What is clear is that in virtually all societies such decisions to overrule the market are made, but are made only sometimes.

Characteristically, in the field of accident law the decision whether or not to take lives in exchange for money or convenience is sometimes made politically or collectively without a balancing of the money value of the lives taken against the money price of the convenience, and sometimes made through the market on the basis of such a value. The reasons for this varying approach are not entirely reasons of principle. Great moral issues lend themselves to political determination. These questions must necessarily be decided in whatever political way our society chooses to decide moral questions. But "rotary mowers versus reel mowers", "one method of making steel as against another" are questions difficult of collective decision. For one thing, they occur too frequently. Every choice of product and use hides within it a decision regarding safety and expense. The dramatic cases we resolve politically. We ban the general sale of fireworks regardless of the ability or willingness of the manufacturer to pay for all of the injuries that result. But we cannot deal with all issues involved in all activities through the political process. For most, the market place serves as the tough testing ground. A manufacturer is free to employ a process even if it occasionally kills or maims if he is able to show that consumers want his product badly enough to enable him to compensate those he injures and still make a profit. Economists would say that except in those few areas of collective decision, this is the best way to decide if the activity is worth having.

All this is just saying, in a slightly different way, that one of the functions of accident law is to reduce the cost of accidents, by reducing those activities that are accident prone. Activities are made more expensive, and thereby less attractive, to the extent of the accidents they cause. In the extreme cases they are priced out of the markets: the market mechanism may thus eliminate an otherwise useful activity because it maims too many.

CALABRESI, THE COSTS OF ACCIDENTS
(1970), p. 73

The general deterrence approach operates in two ways to reduce accident costs. The first and more obvious one is that it creates incentives to engage in safer activities. Some people who would engage in a relatively dangerous activity at prices that did not reflect its accident costs will shift to a safer activity if accident costs *are* reflected in prices. The degree of the shift will depend on the relative difference in accident costs and on how good a substitute the safer activity is. Whatever the shift, however, it will reduce accident costs, since a safer activity will to some degree have been substituted for a dangerous one.

The second and perhaps more important way general deterrence reduces accident costs is that it encourages us to make activities safer. This is no different from the first if every variation in the way an activity is carried out is considered to be a separate activity, but since that is not how the term activity is used in common language, it may be useful to show how general deterrence operates to cause a given activity to become safer. Taney drives a car. His car causes, on the average, $200 per year in accident costs. If a different kind of brake were used in the car, this would be reduced to $100. The new kind of brake costs the equivalent of $50 per year. If the accident costs Taney causes are paid either by the state out of general taxes or by those who are injured, he has no financial incentive to put in the new brake. But if Taney has to pay, he will certainly put the new brake in. He will thus bear a new cost of $50 per year, but it will be less than the $100 per year in accident costs he will avoid. As a result, the cost of accidents to society will have been reduced by $50.

NOTES

1. Professor Calabresi's work triggered a remarkable debate in the law reviews with Professors Blum and Kalven of the University of Chicago, all of which is rewarding reading. See Blum and Kalven, "Public Law Perspectives on a Private Law Problem — Auto Compensation Plans" (1965), reprinted in (1964), 31 U. Chi. L. Rev. 641; Calabresi, "Fault Accidents and the Wonderful World of Blum and Kalven" (1965), 75 Yale L. J. 216; Blum and Kalven, "The Empty Cabinet of Dr. Calabresi: Auto Accidents and General Deterrence" (1967), 34 U. Chi. L. Rev. 239; Calabresi, "Views and Overviews" (1967), U. Ill. L. F. 600; Blum and Kalven, "A Stopgap Plan for Compensating Auto Accident Victims", [1968] Ins. L.J. 661; Calabresi, *The Costs of Accidents* (1970); Blum and Kalven, "Ceilings, Costs and Compulsion in Auto Compensation Legislation" (1973), Utah L. Rev. 341. See also Posner, *Economic Analysis of Law* (1972), p. 84.

2. Professors Blum and Kalven argue in their article "The Empty Cabinet of Dr. Calabresi: Auto Accidents and General Deterrence", *supra*:

> The difficulty with general deterrence as a justification for shifting non-fault auto accident losses to motorists is that it is too fragile to carry the weight that would be put on it. Where the burdens are clear, certain, and not trivial, something more that conjecture about possible patterns of behavior is needed as a countervalue. To put the disagreement in a nutshell: when we know as little as we appear to know now about the prophecies of general deterrence, it is unjust to tax motorists on behalf of it.

KEETON AND O'CONNELL, BASIC PROTECTION FOR THE TRAFFIC VICTIM
(1965), pp. 257 *et seq.*

When we recognize that the law may distribute losses rather than merely shift them, one significant possibility that is presented is to place the burden of bearing an assigned share of the losses resulting from accidents on those who benefit most from motoring; that is, to adopt explicitly the principle that motoring should be required to pay its way in society.

a. *Fairness.* One ground of support for such a requirement is an unabashed appeal to one's sense of fairness. Is it not fair that the burdens and costs of an activity be borne by those who benefit from it and, insofar as feasible, in proportion to the benefit each receives? Occasionally society subsidizes some activity instead of requiring it to pay its way. For example, our society commonly subsidizes municipal transit systems. In this example, however, a subsidy seems fair because all the citizens of the community, including nonusers of public transportation, benefit directly or indirectly from its availability; moreover, experience has demonstrated that a subsidy may be essential if the system is to function at all.

It can be argued, of course, that motoring also indirectly benefits the whole community and is often indirectly subsidized. To the extent that gasoline taxes do not cover the costs of building and maintaining roads, and to the extent that tax-supported activities of the police and the courts are devoted to the consequences of motoring, such an indirect subsidy does exist. Our society's treatment of automobiles does not, however, simply underwrite a definite and definable loss as it does in the case of municipal transportation; we expect motoring to pay its own way, at least to the extent that the costs of purchasing and operating cars are to be borne by motorists themselves. Should not the costs of damage caused by cars also be treated as part of the costs of operating them? In answering this question consider first losses resulting from unavoidable accidents — unavoidable in the sense that they occur without substandard conduct either of the victim or of anyone against whom he might claim. It has been implicit in our automobile law that losses caused by non-negligent motoring are to be borne by the victims. Yet it is not the theory that the victims deserve to bear these losses. Leaving the loss on the victim in a particular case is rather an incidental consequence of finding no sufficient reason to shift the loss to another. The harshness of this result becomes especially evident once it is recognized that the alternatives include not only the unpalatable shifting of the whole loss to another equally blameless party but also the distribution of the loss among a larger group, all of whom are potentially victims of mischance. No one can know where or when any particular accident will occur, but we do know that there will be unavoidable accidents if we permit motoring to continue. The cost of compensating losses from such accidents can be allocated to motoring generally by requiring drivers, as part of their motoring costs, to pay insurance premiums from which a pool of funds can be drawn to compensate victims of these accidents. In cases of this type, the imposition of this relatively slight burden on many motorists seems much fairer than causing some particular motorist or victim to bear the whole burden.

Somewhat different considerations are raised by avoidable accidents brought about by the substandard conduct of one or both of the parties involved. It may be argued that it is unfair to treat such accidents as part of the costs of motoring, as opposed to treating them as part of the costs of engaging in sub-standard conduct. For example, it may seem unfair to add to the costs borne by every motorist in order to provide a fund for compensation of a loss caused by the exceptional conduct of a motorist who uses his vehicle as a weapon, deliberately running another down. The loss caused by such an intentional injury, it may be argued, should be treated as a cost of the particular motorist's deliberate misconduct and not as a cost of motoring in general. It might be thought to follow that loss caused by a motorist's careless driving should also be treated as a cost of his carelessness and not as a cost of motoring. The extent to which this argument is persuasive depends to a considerable degree on the standard of carelessness applied. If the standard is one that drivers generally can meet if they try, then the analogy between cases of careless injury and cases of intentional injury is rather close. If, on the other hand, the standard is one that drivers generally cannot hope to meet, then the analogy to intentional injury is weak and the analogy to injuries caused without substandard conduct is strong. As the definition of negligence is broadened to include instances of conduct not morally blameworthy, the argument becomes stronger for treating such losses as costs of motoring to be distributed equitably among motorists through insurance, rather than to be borne by either of the parties to the particular accident. In fact, the standard of negligence has been broadened beyond a standard that drivers can meet if only they will try. And as this trend continues, the argument becomes more cogent that the judgment against a motorist ought not to end the matter but rather should be one step in a system that treats losses sustained by accident victims as inevitable costs of motoring and distributes them generally through insurance. ...

We propose a new allocation of the burden of motoring injuries. It is an allocation guided by the two principles that motoring should pay its way and that negligent motorists should pay their way. It is not a sacrifice of one principle to the other, but an accommodation of the two. Motorists generally will pay a share of the burden, and negligent motorists will pay a somewhat larger share. We do not argue that this is the only allocation one might reach under the general direction of these principles. We do believe that one who accepts these principles must be dissatisfied with present automobile claims systems and that commitment to these principles will move one in the general direction we have gone, if not to our proposed solution in all its details. One who believes that motoring generally ought to bear at least a part of the cost of motoring accidents, and yet also believes that fault has a place in an automobile claims system, will in all likelihood end up somewhere near our proposal.

NOTE

1. In 1946, Saskatchewan adopted what Linden has named a "peaceful coexistence" plan, pursuant to which no-fault benefits were paid by a government-operated scheme to all auto accident victims without interfering with their right to sue. (See Lang, "The Nature and Potential of the Saskatchewan Insurance Experiment" (1942), 14 U. Fla. L. Rev. 352]. It took over 20 years for the other common-law provinces to adopt similar schemes, which were operated not by governments but by private insurers. By the 1980s, however, all common-law provinces (and a few states), had enacted what some have called "add-on" schemes. These plans were praised by Linden in "Peaceful Coexistence and Automobile Accident Compensation" (1966), 9 Can. Bar J. 5:

   > It is now possible, however, to provide basic compensation for all accident victims without discarding the jury trial, without the necessity of creating another board, and without submitting to "creeping socialism". Further, there is no need to jettison the present system with its reliance on the fault doctrine. In

> other words, an accommodation is possible — let there be peaceful coexistence between tort law and the automobile accident compensation plan. The best features of both systems could be retained and the worst of both mitigated. Full and immediate compensation may be provided to all injury victims for medical, rehabilitation, and burial costs and subsistence income regardless of fault. At the same time, the tort system would remain available to those who wished to press their claims against negligent motorists to secure additional reparation.

See also Blum and Kalven, "The Empty Cabinet", *supra*. The voices of reform, however, were not stilled and more radical changes were urged. Several provinces have maintained their "peaceful coexistence" plans, but others have gone further. See Table 1, at the end of this chapter, for the current schemes in force.

D. NEW SCHEMES: THE REDUCTION OR ELIMINATION OF TORT RIGHTS

Rather than allowing tort law to co-exist with no-fault schemes, some jurisdictions have taken an even larger and bolder step — severely reducing or even eliminating altogether tort law rights. This has permitted the introduction of no-fault schemes with benefits which are much more generous than those offered under the mixed systems discussed above. The question whether the benefits justify the elimination of tort is, of course, the controversial point.

NOTES

1. In the Province of Quebec, a "pure" no-fault scheme has been in effect since March 1, 1978. Pursuant to the *Report of the Committee of Inquiry on Automobile Insurance* (Gauvin Committee) 1974, the Parti Québecois government created a new agency, called Régie de l'Assurance Automobile du Québec to supply compensation to all Québec victims of auto accidents regardless of fault.

   The right to sue in tort (or delict) was completely abolished and replaced by a no-fault compensation system. Some of the benefits payable under this system are reproduced in Table 1, *infra*.

   As for appeal rights, there is a right of reconsideration by the Régie. Following that, a dissatisfied claimant may appeal to the Commission des Affaires Sociales.

   Compensation funds are also established for accidents involving hit-and-run drivers, certain accidents off the highway and for unsatisfied judgments up to a maximum of $50,000.

   Quebec citizens are covered by the plan if they are involved in accidents while outside their home province. Non-residents of Quebec are covered for collisions that occur in Quebec but benefits are provided to them only to the extent that they are not responsible for the accident. The decision of the Régie about the per centage of responsibility may be contested in the courts. See *What Non-Residents Should Know About Quebec Auto Insurance* (1979).

   The fund is financed from contributions from automobile owners, automobile drivers, interest earned from the investment of accumulated funds and a portion of the taxes collected under the *Fuel Tax Act*.

See Quebec Government, *General Guide to Quebec Auto Insurance* (1979), Projet de loi No 67, Dec. 22/77.

Also see Perret, "La nouvelle Loi sur l'assurance automobile du Québec" (1978), 9 Rev. Gen. De Droit 7; Perret, "Le regime de 'No-fault integral de la nouvelle loi sur l'assurance", in Steel and Rodgers-Magnet (ed.), *Issues In Tort Law* (1983), p. 51.

2. The province of Ontario has experimented with several variations of no-fault. These developments are explained in *Ontario Motor Vehicle Insurance Practice* (Butterworths) :

> **§1.13** Ontario, influenced by these criticisms and studies, undertook four major overhauls of its auto accident compensation system in the last three decades. The first major overhaul was the introduction of what has been described as the "peaceful coexistence plan" on January 1, 1969. For the first five years, it was offered on a voluntary basis, and on January 1, 1974 it was made a mandatory part of all auto insurance policies. Inspired by the *Final Report of the Select Committee of the Legislative Assembly of Ontario* (1963), and a statistical study entitled the *Osgoode Hall Study on Compensation for Victims of Automobile Accidents* (1965), this reform, which was a private enterprise version of the famous Saskatchewan plan, provided for limited accident benefits to be paid to all the victims of auto accidents on a no-fault basis. However, it allowed the right to sue in tort to survive intact, except for a set-off of any amount received from the no-fault plan. Not long after, following a further report by a Select Committee the no-fault benefits were enriched as of July 1, 1978, liability insurance was made compulsory in 1980, and coverage for underinsured and hit-and-run accidents was mandatorily included as of March 1, 1980. This peaceful coexistence plan was an ingenious scheme; a major achievement for the province of Ontario, placing it in the forefront of auto insurance reform around the world. It provided relatively generous benefits, at reasonable cost, without interfering with the historic right to sue in tort. In other words, Ontarians had the best of both worlds — tort and non-tort — while avoiding the shortcomings of both.
>
> **§1.14** The next major renovation of the auto accident compensation system was effectuated as of June 22, 1990. This followed two further inquiries — one under the chairmanship of Dr. Philip Slater of York University and another under Mr. Justice Coulter Osborne — established to deal with what was perceived by some as an "insurance crisis". In the mid-1980s, the amounts of tort awards appeared to soar, as the economy boomed and inflation raged. This, in turn, drove insurance premiums up and caused some insurance companies to withdraw from certain types of coverage. The antidote was thought to be a new auto compensation scheme, the main features of which were the elimination of the smaller tort claims and the enrichment of the no-fault benefits. There were also some changes made in the property damage claim system. The main purpose of this reform seems to have been the containment of the cost of auto insurance premiums which, it was felt, necessitated the sacrificing of tort recovery for smaller claims. This was achieved by creating what was commonly called a "threshold", which should more properly be called an "immunity from tort liability", subject to certain exceptions. These exceptions will be more fully discussed later but, briefly, they permitted tort recovery in fatal accident cases, in "permanent serious disfigurement" cases, and where there had been "permanent serious impairment of an important bodily function caused by a continuing injury which is physical in nature". This scheme, which was severely criticized, was in effect for only three years before it was replaced by another system.

§1.15 The third major repair to the Ontario auto compensation system came into effect on January 1, 1994. This plan, described in detail later, altered the no-fault benefits provided, as well as the so-called "threshold". Under this scheme, there is immunity from tort liability, for all pecuniary losses. Tort suits are preserved, however, for the exceptional situations of non-pecuniary loss in cases of death, "serious disfigurement", or "serious impairment of an important physical, mental or psychological function". In addition, there is a deductible of $10,000 per plaintiff for all tort claims that qualify under the exceptions, so that every successful tort claimant will receive $10,000 less than the actual non-pecuniary loss. It will be seen that this plan appears to countenance more tort cases than its predecessor would have in certain situations, in all likelihood increasing its cost, but also fewer in other situations, like the absence of pecuniary claims, perhaps moderating its cost. There were also major alterations to the property loss regime.

§1.16 A fourth plan has now been put into effect for accidents occurring after November 1, 1996. The "threshold" is slightly altered to permit tort suits for death, "*permanent* serious disfigurement" or "*permanent* serious impairment of an important physical, mental or psychological function".

There is also a deductible of $15,000 for injury claims and $7,500 for claims under the *Family Law Act*. These figures are deducted after damages are reduced because of any contributory negligence that may have been proven. One major change is that income loss claims, which had been largely abolished under the January 1, 1994 scheme, have been resurrected, but only up to 80% of net loss prior to trial. Another significant change is that the no-fault benefit for loss of wages was reduced from a maximum of $1000 per week to $400 per week.

3. The latest province to go pure no-fault in automobile insurance is Manitoba. On March 1, 1994, Manitoba put into effect a Quebec-style no-fault scheme which completely eliminates the right to sue in tort. Benefits are paid to all, regardless of fault, but as compared to tort, these benefits appear to be quite modest. The maximum amount for non-pecuniary losses, for example, is $100,000, and wage losses are capped at $40,000 per annum. Students who are permanently disabled are entitled to prospective wage losses based on average industrial wages. Do you think this is fair for a law or medical student?

   Saskatchewan has also adopted a no-fault scheme. The scheme eliminates the right to sue for pain and suffering, while maintaining the right to sue for economic losses. See Table 1, *infra*.

4. An even more ambitious no-fault scheme is New Zealand's Accident Compensation program. This is a comprehensive scheme which deals not only with automobile accidents, but with *all* accidents. It virtually eliminates tort law rights. For a description of the scheme see Ison, *Accident Compensation: A Commentary on the New Zealand Scheme*, 1980.

5. High costs have forced the New Zealand government to rethink its scheme. After almost 20 years of operation, proposals have now been put forward to convert the scheme into more of an insurance scheme. Some benefits have been eliminated, and the minor costs of accidents have been shifted back onto victims. The right to sue in tort, however, has not been reintroduced.

6. Canadian provinces have had non-tort compensation schemes in other areas for many years. Medical and hospital bills are paid for. Workers' Compensation schemes, which provide no-fault benefits and eliminate tort rights, have existed in Canada starting with the Ontario scheme in 1914. For a description of these schemes see Ison, *Workers' Compensation in Canada*, 2nd ed. (1989).

7. There are also criminal injuries compensation schemes, which compensate victims of violent crimes on a no-fault basis. For a description of these schemes see Burns, *Criminal Injuries Compensation*, 2nd ed. (1992).

8. Canadians receive significant amounts of benefits from a host of other public and private sources. See Weiler, *Protecting the Worker from Disability: Challenges for the Eighties*, 1983, a Report to the Ontario Ministry of Labour.

9. Where are we going with our myriad of compensation programs and schemes? Do we need to rationalize this entire area? Professor Weiler estimated that in Ontario in 1981 roughly $2.5 billion was expended in group programs of one kind or another to compensate the victims of disabling or fatal injuries. Can we continue to afford this in the current economic climate? What, if any, is the role of tort in the 21st Century?

10. One dramatic suggestion by Patrick Atiyah, a respected torts scholar, is to abolish all tort claims for personal injury, leaving private insurance and social welfare schemes to handle compensation. See "Thinking the Unthinkable" in Birks (ed.) *Wrongs and Remedies in the Twenty-first Century* (1996).

> It is one of the functions of the academic lawyer from time to time to think the unthinkable, and to challenge some of the most fundamental assumptions of our legal system. Few assumptions are more basic than the idea that if someone wrongfully does you an injury you should be entitled to sue him, and to think of abolishing this right without providing any real replacement is to go about as far as one can in thinking the unthinkable. Yet I want in all seriousness to float the suggestion that the action for damages for personal injuries should largely be abolished, and its replacement left to the free market. I shall also offer some reasons for thinking that the next century may well see some moves in this direction. ...
>
> I do not expect to make many immediate converts to these proposals or anything remotely like them. Practising lawyers will naturally condemn them unreservedly. Many academic lawyers who still hanker after Woodhouse-type schemes will probably regard me as a traitor to the cause. Other academic lawyers who delight in the apparently constantly expanding frontiers of legal liability will hardly welcome the disappearance of an entire legal subject with which they are familiar. Politicians on the left will be aghast at the idea of little old ladies not being allowed to sue the drug companies, and doubtless most politicians on the right will feel equally unhappy at the idea of discarding tort law, which they were told by Margaret Thatcher was a system of personal responsibility. The media will presumably express shock and horror at the very idea of abolition of an important source of copy for them, and the public will undoubtedly be outraged at the idea of having their right to sue taken away, and being expected to pay for some alternative.
>
> And yet ... and yet ... For the reasons I have given I do believe that the next century will see massive pressure to expand private insurance against many of those risks presently covered by the welfare state, and movement in that direction must surely put on the agenda some of the issues I have raised here.

See also Sugarman, "Doing Away with Tort Law" (1985), 73 Calif. L. Rev. 555; Abel, *A Critique of Torts* (1994); Huber, *Liability: The Legal Revolution and its Consequences* (1988); Ison, *Compensation Systems for Injury and Disease: The Policy Choices* (1994); and Atiyah, *The Damages Lottery* (1997).

11. As this book goes to print, Canada is embroiled in a debate about compensation for victims of hepatitis C transmitted by tainted blood. There have been many lawsuits filed. The federal government has agreed to compensate all persons with HIV or

AIDS contracted from tainted blood regardless of any fault. However, as for hepatitis C victims, it has so far sought to limit the compensation it would pay to these individuals who were infected between January 1, 1986 and July 1, 1990 on the ground that fault might be proved and tort liability imposed for these victims. Over $1 billion has been allocated for this. As for the others, since the federal government's fault, and hence tort liability, is doubtful, it has refused to pay. It is estimated that between 14,000 and 40,000 people may have been infected with hepatitis C before 1986 and after 1990. Some provinces have criticized the federal government and urged it to pay all these victims, regardless of fault. Justice Horace Krever, who headed a Royal Commission on the issue, recommended that all victims of tainted blood be paid on a no-fault basis. On what theory can we distinguish between those people who have contracted hepatitis C through no-one's negligence, and any other person who suffers an accident or disease through no other person's fault? Is the tort law solution appropriate one here? If it is not the proper solution in this case, can it ever be the appropriate method of deciding these matters? Does it make a difference that there are many sufferers and much publicity? If you were the federal health minister how would you handle the problem? Is this a political opportunity which might allow for the implementation of a comprehensive insurance scheme covering all the victims of sickness and injury on a no-fault basis? Or is it better to let tort law take its ordinary course? Remember, all these victims are entitled, like all other Canadians, to medical and hospital care, as well as income support under E.I., C.P.P., and social welfare, if they are qualified.

Table 1
Canadian automobile insurance plans — Compulsory minimum insurance coverage for private passenger vehicles
(Accident benefits coverage is compulsory everywhere in Canada *except* in Newfoundland.)

Province	Compulsory minimum 3rd-party liability	Medical Payments	Funeral Expense Benefits	Disability Income Benefits
Newfoundland	$200,000 is available for any one accident; however, if a claim involving both bodily injury and property damage reaches this figure, payment for property damage would be capped at $20,000.	$25,000/person, including rehabilitation, excluding health insurance plans; time limit 4 years	$1,000	104 weeks partial disability; lifetime if totally disabled; maximum $140/week; 7-day wait; unpaid housekeeper $70/week, maximum 12 weeks
Nova Scotia	$200,000 is available for any one accident; however, if a claim involving both bodily injury and property damage reaches this figure, payment for property damage would be capped at $10,000.	$25,000/person, including rehabilitation, excluding health insurance plans; time limit 4 years	$1,000	104 weeks partial disability; lifetime if totally disabled; maximum $140/week; 7-day wait; unpaid housekeeper $70/week, maximum 12 weeks
New Brunswick	$200,000 is available for any one accident; however, if a claim involving both bodily injury and property damage reaches this figure, payment for property damage would be capped at $20,000.	$50,000/person, including rehabilitation, excluding health insurance plans; time limit 4 years	$2,500	104 weeks partial disability; lifetime if totally disabled; maximum $250/week; 7-day wait; unpaid housekeeper $100/week, maximum 52 weeks
Prince Edward Island	$200,000 is available for any one accident; however, if a claim involving both bodily injury and property damage reaches this figure, payment for property damage would be capped at $10,000.	$25,000/person, including rehabilitation, excluding health insurance plans; time limit 4 years	$1,000	104 weeks partial disability; to age 65 if totally disabled; maximum $140/week, 7-day wait; unpaid housekeeper $70/week, maximum 12 weeks
Quebec[1]	$50,000; liability limits relate to property damage claims within Quebec and to personal injury and property damage claims outside Quebec.	No time or amount limit; includes rehabilitation	$3,650	90% on net wages; maximum income gross $50,000/year; temporary 3 years; permanent life-time; 7-day wait, indexed
Ontario[2]	$200,000 is available for any one accident; however, if a claim involving both bodily injury and property damage reaches this figure, payment for property damage would be capped at $10,000.	$100,000/person ($1-million if injury "catastrophic") ,including rehabilitation, excluding health insurance plans; attendant care $72,000 ($1-million if injury "catastrophic")	$6,000	80% of net wages up to $400/week; $185/week for those not employed (104 weeks maximum; longer if victim is unable to pursue *any* suitable occupation); 7-day wait for employed persons, otherwise 26 weeks

[1] Lawsuits are not permitted with respect to injuries sustained in automobile accidents in Quebec. Victims and their dependants resident in Quebec are compensated by their government insurer for their injuries whether or not the accident occurs in Quebec. Accident victims who do not reside in Quebec are entitled to compensation only to the extent that they are not responsible for the accident, unless otherwise agreed between the Société de l'assurance automobile du Québec and authorities of the victims' place of residence; additional compensation may be available from their own insurers.
[2] Ontario "insureds" involved in accidents in Quebec can receive from their own insurer the equivalent to the benefits available to Quebec residents from the Société de l'assurance automobile du Québec. Policyholders may purchase coverage for economic loss greater than maximum accident benefits.

Table 1
Canadian automobile insurance plans — Compulsory minimum insurance coverage for private passenger vehicles
(Accident benefits coverage is compulsory everywhere in Canada *except* in Newfoundland.)

Death benefits	Impairment benefits	Right to sue for pain and suffering	Right to sue for economic loss in excess of no-fault benefits	Administration
Death within 2 years; head of household $10,000 plus $1,000 each for all dependants beyond first; spouse $10,000; dependent child $2,000		Yes	Yes	Private insurers
Death within 2 years; head of household $10,000 plus $1,000 each for all dependants beyond first; spouse $10,000; dependent child $2,000		Yes	Yes	Private insurers
Death within 2 years; head of household $50,000 plus $1,000 each for all dependants beyond first; spouse $25,000; dependent child $5,000		Yes	Yes	Private insurers
Death within 2 years; head of household $10,000 plus $1,000 each for all dependants beyond first; spouse $10,000; dependent child $2,000		Yes	Yes	Private insurers
Death anytime; depends on wage and age; minimum $48,683; maximum $250,000 plus $23,123-$45,198 to dependants according to age; if no dependants — $18,256 to parents	Scheduled up to $137,210	No	No	Bodily injury: government; property damage: private insurers
Death within 3 years; $25,000 for spouse, $10,00 for surviving dependant or for loss of dependant		Yes, if injury meets verbal threshold; deductible applies. Lawsuit allowed only if injured person dies, or sustains "permanent serious" disfigurement and/or impairment of important physical, mental or psychological function; the court is directed to assess damages, then deduct $15,000 ($7,500 if *Family Law Act* claim)	Yes. Injured person may sue for 80% of net income loss before trial, 100% of gross after trial; also for medical, rehabilitation and related costs when injury is catastrophic.	Private insurers

Table 1 continued on page 756

Table 1
Canadian automobile insurance plans — Compulsory minimum insurance coverage for private passenger vehicles
(Accident benefits coverage is compulsory everywhere in Canada *except* in Newfoundland.)

Province	Compulsory minimum 3rd-party liability	Medical Payments	Funeral Expense Benefits	Disability Income Benefits
Manitoba[3]	$200,000 is available for any one accident; however, if a claim involving both bodily injury and property damage reaches this figure, payment for property damage would be capped at $20,000.	No time or amount limit; includes rehabilitation	$3,803	90% of net wages; maximum income gross $58,500/year; 7-day wait; indexed
Saskatchewan[4]	$200,000 is available for any one accident; however, if a claim involving both bodily injury and property damage reaches this figure, payment for property damage would be capped at $10,000.	$526,970/person; includes rehabilitation	$5,270	90% of net wages; maximum income gross $54,893/year; 7-day wait; indexed
Alberta[5]	$200,000 is available for any one accident; however, if a claim involving both bodily injury and property damage reaches this figure, payment for property damage woul be capped at $10,000.	$10,000/person, rehabilitation included, amounts from medical and hospital plans excluded; chiropractors $500/person per occurrence; time limit 2 years	$2,000	80% gross wages; maximum $300/week; 104 weeks temporary or total disability; 7-day wait; unpaid housekeeper $100/week, maximum 26 weeks
British Columbia	$200,000 is available for any one accident; however, if a claim involving both bodily injury and property damage reaches this figure, payment for property damage would be capped at $20,000.	$150,000/person, rehabilitation included, excludes amounts payable under surgical, dental, hospital plan or other insurer.	$2,500	75% gross wages; maximum $300/week; 104 weeks temporary disability, lifetime total and permanent; 7-day wait; homemaker up to $145/week; maximum 104 weeks
Northwest Territories	$200,000 is available for any one accident; however, if a claim involving both bodily injury and property damage reaches this figure, payment for property damage would be capped at $10,000.	$25,000/person, excluding medical and hospital plans; time limit 4 years	$1,000	80% gross wages; maximum $140/week; 104 weeks temporary disability; lifetime if totally disabled; 7-day wait; unpaid housekeeper $100/week, maximum 12 weeks
Yukon	$200,000 is available for any one accident; however, if a claim involving both bodily injury and property damage reaches this figure, payment for property damage would be capped at $10,000.	$10,00/person, rehabilitation included, amounts from medical and hospital plans excludedd; time limit 2 years	$2,000	80% gross wages; maximum $300/week; 104 weeks temporary or total disability; 7-day wait; unpaid housekeeper $100/week, maximum 26 weeks

[3] Residents of Manitoba involved in accidents in Quebec can receive from their own insurer the equivalent to the benefits available to Quebec residents from the Société de l'assurance automobile du Québec. First party all-perils insurance is compulsory in Manitoba (deductibles vary according to type of vehicle). Policyholders may purchase coverage for economic loss greater than maximum accident benefits. Lawsuits are not permitted with respect to injuries sustained in automobile accidents in Manitoba. Victims and their dependants resident in Manitoba are compensated by their government insurer for their injuries whether or not the accident occurs in Manitoba.
[4] First party all-perils insurance is compulsory in Saskatchewan (deductibles vary according to type of vehicle).
[5] Alberta "insureds" involved in accidents in Quebec can receive from their own insurer the equivalent to the benefits available to Quebec residents from the Société de l'assurance automobile du Québec. Similar arrangements were implemented in June 1998 for accidents involving Alberta "insureds" in Saskatchewan and Manitoba.

Table 1
Canadian automobile insurance plans — Compulsory minimum insurance coverage for private passenger vehicles
(Accident benefits coverage is compulsory everywhere in Canada *except* in Newfoundland.)

Death benefits	Impairment benefits	Right to sue for pain and suffering	Right to sue for economic loss in excess of no-fault benefits	Administration
Death anytime; depends on wage and age; minimum $43,466; maximum $292,500 plus $20,646-$38,032 to dependants according to age	Scheduled up to $108,664	No	No	Government (government and private insurers compete for optional and excess coverage)
$47,427 minimum with spouse or dependants, otherwise $10,539; educational benefit $31,618.	Scheduled up to $131,743	No	Yes; injured persons may sue for economic losses that exceed no-fault benefits. However, in regard to loss of income, they may recover only with respect to gross income losses that exceed $52,058/year; award is net of income taxes.	Government (government and private insurers compete for optional and excess coverage)
Death anytime; head of household $10,000 plus $2,000 each dependant after first and 1% of total principal sum for 104 weeks, no limit; spouse $10,000; dependent child according to age, maximum $3,000		Yes	Yes	Private insurers
Death anytime; head of household $5,000 and $145/week for 104 weeks to first survivor plus $1,000 and $35/week for 104 weeks for each survivor after first, no limit; spouse $2,500; dependent child according to age, maximum $1,500		Yes	Yes	Government (government and private insurers compete for optional and excess coverage)
Death within 2 years; head of household $10,000; spouse $10,000; each survivor after first $2,500; one survivor, spouse or dependant, principal sum increased by $1,500		Yes	Yes	Private insurers
Death anytime; head of household $10,000 plus $2,000 each dependant after first and 1% of total principal sum for 104 weeks, no limit; spouse $10,000; dependent child according to age, maximum $3,000		Yes	Yes	Private insurers

Courtesy of the Insurance Council of Canada

INDEX

A

Absolute liabilitiy. *See* Strict liability
Abuse of power, 481-84
Abuse of process
  false imprisonment and, 73
Accidental conduct
  intentional conduct, vs., 38-42
  negligent conduct, vs., 38-42
Act of God, 511
Animals, liabiltiy for, 516-19
Appropriation of one's personality, tort of, 93
Arrest
  false arrest, 143, 148-49
  meaning of, 70-71
  police powers of, 145-47, 149-51, 152-53
  private citizen, by, 147-48
Assault
  Criminal Code provisions, 50, 51, 53
  generally, 48-53
  road rage as, 52
  sufficiency of acts, 50-51, 52
  words alone, 50
Automobile accident compensation
  civil liability, arguments for retention of, 738
  coexistence schemes, 748-53
  compensation issues discussed, 730-32
  costs of accidents, who should pay, 749
  criticisms of tort law system, 730
  deterrence factor, 739
  fault concept, 739, 743
  generally, 727
  no-fault insurance
    debate over, 728-40
    variety of schemes re, 749-53
  plans by provinces, charts re, 754-57
  studies re, 738
  tort rights, reduction or elimination of, 749
  victims of auto accidents as different, 740-43

B

Battery
  conduct amounting to, 54-55, 58
  criminal and civil liability for, 58
  generally, 53-59
  kiss as, 55
  limits of liability, 58
  mental state required for, 46
  motive and, 55
  negligent battery, 34
  transmission of sexual disease, 55
Breach of contract, inducing
  direct inducement, 595-97
  extension to negligence, 604-606
  indirect inducement, 597-99
  interferences short of breach, 599-602
  justification, 602-604
Business relations, interference with
  consumer boycott, 618
  early cases, 617
  generally, 615-20
  prima facie tort doctrine, 619-20
  prospective business relations, 617
  unfounded lien claim, 618
  unlawful interference with
    economic interests, emerging tort of, 619
Business torts
  business relations. *See* Business
    relations, interference with
  conspiracy. *See* Conspiracy, tort of
  deceit. *See* Deceit, tort of
  generally, 589
  inducing breach of contract. *See*
    Breach of contract, inducing
  intimidation. *See* Intimidation, tort of

C

Capacity
  children, 39
  volition and, 42-48
Causation
  burden of proof re, 160
  "but for" test, 159, 161
  inferring, 262-67
  lack of proof of, 160
  multiple causes, 160-62
  negligence liability requirement, as, 158-59
Charter of Rights and Freedoms
  damages for breaches of, 487-88
  defamation, effect on, 653-55
  invasion of privacy and, 93
Chattels, interference with
  conversion. *See* Conversion
  detinue, 84
  trespass to goods. *See* Trespass to goods
Children
  medical consents, 124-27
  mental suffering, tort of
    intentional infliction of, 65
  pre-natal injuries, 293-94
  seat belt defence and, 406
  standard of care re. *See* Young
    persons, standard of care re
  tort liability of, 44-45
  unborn child as unforeseeable
    plaintiff, 292
Consent
  fighting and, 114-15

Consent — *cont'd*
- fraud as vitiating, 111
- medical context, in. *See* Medical consents
- nature of, 101-12
- onus of proof, 102
- sexual acts, 110-11
- sexually transmissible disease and, 111
- sporting context, 112-15
- voluntary assumption of risk and, 409
- vulnerability, 111

Conspiracy, tort of
- generally, 611-15
- intention, proof of, 614
- non-business context, 614

Constitutional torts
- breach of statute, 484-87
- Charter violation, damages for, 487-88
- generally, 484-88
- motives for bringing actions, 488
- U.S. practice, 488

Contributory negligence
- breach of contract, application to, 393
- causation and, 274-76
- defendant in violation of penal statute, 392
- historical perspective, 383-85
- intentional torts, application to, 392-93
- intermediate inspection and, 375-76
- jury vs. non-jury trials, 395-96
- last clear chance doctrine, 385-86, 388-92
- *Negligence Act* and, 386-87
- plaintiff's conduct and, 388
- procedural and mathematical problems re, 394-95
- rescuer and, 365
- thin-skull rule and, 331

Conversion
- detinue vs., 89
- generally, 85-89

Criminal conduct
- battery as, 58
- recovery of tort damages for, 58
- restitution order, 59
- victim compensation schemes, 58-59

Crown. *See* Public authorities, tort liability of

Crumbling skull doctrine, 330-31

Custom
- community practices, 181-82
- generally, 181-84
- guideline, as, 184
- importance of, 183
- reasonableness of, 183
- rejection by courts, 183

D

Damage
- loss and, 157
- limitation periods, 157-58
- meaning of in negligence law, 157
- negligence liability requirement, as, 156
- psychiatric damage, foreseeability of, 295-96

Damages
- aggravated, 96
- Charter violations, for, 487-88
- collateral benefits and, 709-11
- fatal accidents. *See* Fatal accidents, damage assessment
- future care, for, 681
- generally, 679
- global approach, 683
- heads of damage, 682-88
- intentional torts, for, 94-98
- jury, role of, 684-85
- loss of a chance doctrine, 267
- lump sum vs. periodic payments, 685-88
- mitigation of losses, 681-2
- personal injuries. *See* Personal injuries, damage assessment
- post-accident events, 711-16
- purpose of, 679-81
- punitive. *See* Punitive damages
- reasonableness and, 681
- services provided, damages for, 683-84
- special and general damages, 683
- structured settlement, 688

Deceit, tort of
- diminished importance of, 591
- fraud vs., 592-95
- generally, 589-94
- prospectus cases, 589-91
- reliance on misrepresentation, 591-95

Defamation
- Charter, effect of, 653-55
- class action procedures and, 634
- damage awards for, 636
- defamatory libel, criminal provision re, 635
- defences to. *See* Defences to defamation
- definitions of, 628
- described, 625-36
- error, 652-53
- examples of, 629-36
- fair comment defence, 631
- free speech vs. reputation, 621-25
- generally, 621
- hate propaganda legislation, 634-35
- identity of person defamed, 632-33
- innuendo, 634
- intention irrelevant, 647
- liability for, basis of, 645-55
- libel, 636-42
- live persons only, 634
- malice requirement, 647
- public nuisance and, 628
- publication, 642-45
- slander, 636-42, 647
- standard of measurement, 629
- strict liability re intentional defamation, 653
- study re, 636
- threshold test for determining, 632
- values at stake, 621-25

Defective products and structures. *See* Products liability

Defences
- consent. *See* Consent
- defamation, to. *See* Defences to defamation
- legal authority. *See* Legal authority
- necessity. *See* Necessity

Defences — *cont'd*
negligence action, to. *See* Defences to negligence action
property. *See* Property, defence of
self-defence. *See* Self-defence
third persons, defence of, 130-31
trespass, 34-38
Defences to defamation
absolute privilege, 656-58
common interest or mutual concern, 663-66
fair comment, 672-78
judicial proceedings, 656-58
moral or legal duty to protect another's interest, 666-68
parliamentary proceedings, 658
protection of one's own interest, 659-63
public interest, 669-72
qualified privilege, 659-72
truth, 655-56
Defences to negligence action
contributory negligence. *See* Contributory negligence
illegality. *See* Illegality
seat belt defence. *See* Seat belt defence
voluntary assumption of risk. *See* Voluntary assumption of risk
Detinue, 84
Disabled persons, standard of care re
criminal law insanity standard, 209
drugs, 210
generally, 207-11
physical disabilities generally, 211
intoxication, 210
mental vs. physical disabilities, 209
Quebec civil code re, 210-11
Discrimination, tort of, 317-19
Doctor/patient relationship
fiduciary responsibilities, 239-40
sexual wrongdoing and, 60
Doctors, disclosure duty
cosmetic operations, 233
generally, 223
informed consent, 223-29
malpractice actions. *See* Medical malpractice actions
malpractice crisis and, 235-37
material risk, meaning of, 229
modified objective test of causation, 233-34
objective standard of, 230
professional negligence, 216-45
Reibl v. Hughes, 223-29, 230-32, 235
unusual or special risks, 230
Doctors, standard of care re
child abuse, reporting of, 221
city vs. rural, 221
disclosure duty. *See* Doctors, disclosure duty
error in judgment, 220
expert evidence requirement, 222
follow-up, 221
generally, 216-23
inexperienced doctor, 221
informed consent, duty re. *See* Doctors, disclosure duty
proof problems in malpractice actions, 222
Quebec civil law, 220
specialists, 221
statement of, 219-20
third person, liability re, 221
Drunkenness
volition and, 42
Duty
Donoghue v. Stevenson principle, 277-81
extensions of, 287
failure to act. *See* Failure to act
foreseeability of risk, 283
generally, 277-90
Good/Bad Samaritan, 296-301
neighbour principle, 280, 283
prima facie duty of care doctrine, 282
probability of harm giving rise to, 284
public authorities, 469-84
remoteness and, 288-89
rescue. *See* Rescue
risk and, 277, 288
standard of care issues, 288
statutory duties, 314-17
use of to limit liability, 277
unforeseeable plaintiff. *See* Unforeseeable plaintiff

E

Economic analysis of nuisance
application of, 573-74
assumptions re human behaviour, 571-73
economic approach to law, generally, 570-71
generally, 570
opportunity costs, 573
transaction costs, 574
Economic losses
defective products and structures. *See* Products liability
generally, 415
negligent performance of services. *See* Negligent performance of services
negligent statements, liability for. *See* Negligent statements, liability for
public authorities, tort liability of, 474, 476-79
relational economic losses. *See* Relational economic losses
Employer
action *per quod servitium amisit*, abolishment of, 463
liability for employee's negligent statement, 438
vicarious liability of, 519-22

F

Failure to act
generally, 296-97
Good/Bad Samaritan, 296-301
nonfeasance and misfeasance, 297-301
rescue duty, 300
False imprisonment
abuse of process and, 73
acts constituting, 67-68, 72

False imprisonment — *cont'd*
"arrest", meaning of, 70-71
consciousness of confinement, requirement of, 71
generally, 66-73
legal authority defence, 143, 148-49
malicious prosecution vs., 72-73
negligent false imprisonment, 72
police officers, actions against, 70
U.S. practice, 70
Fatal accidents, damage assessment
Family Law Act provisions, 716-17
grief and loss of guidance, 718, 722-24
loss of future earnings, 718
non-pecuniary losses, 724
S.C.C. decision re, 718-22
Trustee Act provisions, 716
wrongful life claim, 724
Fiduciary duty
doctor/patient relationship, 239-40
sexual wrongdoing as breach of, 59, 60
Fighting
consent to, 114-15
Fires, liabilty for, 515-16
Foreseeability of risk
duty and, 283
private nuisance and, 556
thin-skull rule and, 329
Fraud
deceit vs., 592-95
vitiating consent, 111

G

Good/Bad Samaritan, 296-301

H

Hate propaganda legislation, 634-35

I

Illegality
application to torts, 413
compensation for personal injuries and, 413
contributory negligence and, 413
generally, 410-13
Informed consent. *See* Doctors, disclosure duty
Injurious falsehood, tort of, 636
Inspection, intermediate
cars, 377
contrasting cases re, 375
contributory negligence and, 375-76
generally, 373-78
guns, 377
Intentional conduct, *see also* Volition
accidental conduct vs., 38-42
ambiguity in concept, 41
constructive intention, 40
motive and, 42
negligent conduct vs., 38-42
transferred intent, doctrine of, 41
Intentional torts
damages for, 94-98
defences to. *See* Defences
historical context, 33-38
Intervening forces
dangerous products, 353
duty-to-protect relationships, 353
fire, 354
generally, 351-5
medical error, 371-73
stolen cars, 252
Intimidation, tort of
Canadian cases, 609-10
generally, 606-10
requirement that threatened act be unlawful, 611
Invasion of privacy
alternative remedies for, 92-93
appropriation of one's personality, tort of, 93
Charter rights and, 93
development of tort re, 92
generally, 90-94
statutory protection, 94

J

Judges
immunity for tort liabiltiy, 244
Jury
damages assessment, role of, 684-85

L

Lawyers, negligence of. *See* Negligent performance of services, liability for; Negligent statements, liability for
Lawyers, standard of care re
concurrent liability in contract and tort, 241
generalist vs. specialist, 242
generally, 240-45
judges, immunity of, 244
litigation immunity of English barristers, 242-44
mental suffering, liability for, 244
third persons, liability to, 244
Legal authority
arrest by police and, 145-47, 149-51
arrest by private citizen, 147-48
Criminal Code provisions re, 142-43
false arrest/imprisonment actions and, 143, 148-49
generally, 141-53
police powers, 152-53
use of force and, 144
Liability insurance
punitive damages and, 97
Libel. *See* Defamation
Limitation periods
damage and, 157-58
sexual wrong-doing torts, for, 60

M

Malicious prosecution
false imprisonment vs., 72-73
Market share liability, 270-76

Medical consents
children, 124-26
eugenics and, 127
form, 124
generally, 115-27
incapacity, 123
informed consent. *See* Doctors, disclosure duty
Jehovah's Witness cases, 115-19, 127
parent's rights re children, 126-27
right to die, 120
right to refuse treatment, 119-20
sterilization of mentally retarded patients, 127
Medical malpractice actions
"crisis" re, 235-37
general discussion, 238-39
jury trial, 237
no-fault insurance and, 237
tainted blood and, 239
Mental disability
capacity and, 47-48
standard of care. *See* Disabled persons, standard of care re
Mental suffering, damages for
liability of lawyers for, 244
thin-skull rule and, 329-30
Mental suffering, tort of intentional infliction of
children and, 65
examples of, 64
generally, 61-66
harm requirement, 64
medical criticism of, 63
sexual wrongdoing and, 60
U.S. position, 64
workplace harassment and, 65
Mitigation of losses, 681-82
Motive
intention vs., 42

N

Necessity
Crown, actions by, 136
generally, 134-41
killing as, 139-40
ship cases, 136-39
Negligence
causation. *See* Causation
damage. *See* Damage
contributory. *See* Contributory negligence
defences to action. *See* Defences to negligence action
duty. *See* Duty
inducing breach of contract and, 604-606
introduction to, 155-62
proof of. *See* Proof
punitive damages and, 95
remoteness. *See* Remoteness
standard of care. *See* Standard of care
strict liability. *See* Strict liability
trespass and, 37
Negligent conduct
accidental conduct vs., 38-42
intentional conduct vs., 38-42
Negligent performance of services, liability for
generally, 438-41
negligent advice, similarity to, 438
Negligent statements, liability for
basis of, 416
Canadian leading cases re, 417-32
contract and tort, concurrent liability in, 432-8
disclosure omission, 421
employer's liability for employee, 438
generally, 415-38
Hedley Byrne case, 416
narrowing of, 432
origins of, 415-16
reliance requirement, 420-21
special relationship requirement, 420
Neighbour principle, 280, 283
No-fault insurance. *See* Automobile accident compensation
Nuisance
economic analysis of. *See* Economic analysis of nuisance
generally, 531-32
private. *See* Private nuisance
public. *See* Public nuisance

O

Occupiers' liability
common law re, 575-82
generally, 575
statutory law re, 582-87

P

Personal injuries, damage assessment
approach to, 704
burden of proof, 708
criticisms of S.C.C. approach, 705
discount rate, 707
functional approach, 706
future earnings, 708
housekeeping duties, assessment of, 708
loss of expectation of life, 709
non-pecuniary loss, 700-703
particular facts as determinant, 707
pecuniary loss, 692-700
subsequent change of circumstances, 708
"trilogy" S.C.C. judgments, 689-703
unconscious plaintiff problem, 706
Picketers, trespass by, 76-77, 78
Police
arrest by, 145-7, 149-51
false imprisonment actions against, 70, 143, 148-49
powers of, 152-53
statutory duties, 314-17
unreasonable risk and, 173-74
Pre-natal injuries, 293-94
Prima facie tort doctrine, 619-20
Privacy, invasion of. *See* Invasion of privacy
Private nuisance
criteria for assessing, 549-50

Private nuisance — *cont'd*
examples of, 558, 560
foreseeability and, 556
generally, 531, 543-69
injunction for, 560
material damage vs. amenity interference, 549
motive of defendant, 560-61
purpose of tort re, 555
remedy for, 560
scope of tort re, 555
statutory authority defence, 562-70
TV reception, interference with, 550-55
utility of defendant's activity, 559
Products liability
economic losses. *See* Products liability, economic losses
intermediate inspection, 373-78
strict liability and, 522-29
warnings, 378-82
Products liability, economic losses
danger requirement, 448-51
generally, 442
leading case re, 442-47
Professional negligence
doctors. *See* Doctors, disclosure duty
lawyers. *See* Lawyers, negligence of
Proof of negligence
causation, inferring, 262-67
contributory negligence, 274-76
generally, 247
inferring negligence, 249-55
market share liability, 270-76
multiple defendants, 255-60
multiple defendants; one cause of action, 267-70
onus of proof, 247-49
problems of, 247
res ipsa loquitur. *See Res ipsa loquitur*
statutory onus shifts, 260-61
Property, defence of, *see also* Occupier's liability
generally, 131-34
killing or wounding in, 131-33
permissible acts in, 133-34
recapture of property, privilege of, 134
warning signs, 133
Provocation
self-defence vs., 129-30
Psychiatric damage
foreseeability of, 295-96
thin-skull rule, 330
Public authorities, tort liability of
abuse of power, 481-84
B.C. practice, 479-80
building supervision, negligence in, 479
constitutional torts. *See* Constitutional torts
Crown, proceedings against, 467-69
duty owed, 469-84
economic loss case, 474, 476-79
English practice, 475
history of, 467
legislative and quasi-judicial action, 480-81
non-delegable duty on Crown, 472
policy vs. operations, 472-75
provision of services vs. governing, 472-74
Public nuisance
defamation and, 628
discharge of oil, 536, 537
future of tort re, 538
generally, 531-42
highways, use of, 539-42
noise pollution, 537
protesters, 538
street prostitution, 537-38
Punitive damages
aggravated damages in alternative, 96
criminal sentence, in addition to, 97
English practice, 96
estate of deceased, award to, 97
liability insurance re, 97
negligence actions, in, 95
novel situations and, 95
purpose of, 94
vicarious liability and, 97

R

Reasonable person
accident prone, the, 176
activities covered by, 181
beginners, 179
description of, 178-79
disabled persons, 179
enquiries, obligation to make, 179
gender issues, 180
generally, 175-81
inclusion issues, 180
objective standard re, 176-77
Recurring situations and remoteness
rescue situations, 355-67
second accident, 367-71
Relational economic losses
action *per quod servitium amisit*, abolishment of, 463
development of liability, 451
exclusionary rule approach, 452-53
known plaintiff test, 463
leading case, 454-62
proximity approach, 452
Remoteness
alternative formulations of issue, 348
causation approach, 349-51
duty and, 288-89
foreseeability test, 326-27, 349-51
general principle of, 321-27
"instinctive feeling" test, 351
intermediate inspection, 373-78
intervening forces. *See* Intervening forces
intervening medical error, 371-73
learned intermediary, 378-82
possibility of damage test, 337-43
proximity as synonymous, 321
rescue situations, 355-67
recurring situations. *See* Recurring situations and remoteness
retreat from *The Wagon Mound (No. 1)* case, 327-51

Remoteness — *cont'd*
second accident situations, 367-71
The Wagon Mound (No. 1) case, 321-27
The Wagon Mound (No. 2) case, 337-43
thin-skull rule. *See* Thin-skull rule, 327-31
use to limit liability, 321
warnings, 378-82
type of damage, 331-36
Res ipsa loquitur
generally, 249-55
multiple defendants and, 255-60
statutory onus shifts and, 260-61
U.S. malpractice cases, 259
vehicle collision claims, 258
Rescue
contributory negligence and, 365
control or supervision relationships, 307-308
danger, creation of, 308-309
duty re, 300
economic benefit relationships and, 301-307
futile attempt, 364
relationships requiring, 301
reliance relationships and, 310-14
rescued person's duty to rescuer, 365
professional rescuers, 367
statutory duties, 314-17
Risk
assumption of. *See* Voluntary assumption of risk
duty and, 277, 288
Road rage
assault, as, 52

S

Seat belt defence
benefit of wearing seat belts, 403
children and, 406
criticism of, 402
generally, 396-406
mandatory legislation, 405
reasonableness question, 404-405
proof problems associated with, 405
Self-defence
generally, 127-30
killing in, 129
onus of proof, 128
permissible actions in, 129
provocation vs., 129-30
Sexual acts
consent, 110-11
Sexual battery, 59
Sexual harassment, 60
Sexual wrongdoing, 59-61
doctor/patient relationship, 60
feminist legal theory re, 61
fiduciary duty, as breach of, 59, 60
institutional liability, 60
intentional infliction of mental suffering and, 60
limitation periods, 60
sexual battery, 59
sexual harassment, 60
torts involved, 59
tort remedy, usefulness of, 61
Slander. *See* Defamation
Slander of goods, tort of, 636
Sports
consents, 112-15
voluntary assumption of risk, 408
Standard of care
custom. *See* Custom
disabled persons. *See* Disabled persons, standard of care re
doctors. *See* Doctors, standard of care re
duty and, 288
elderly persons, 216
generally, 163
lawyers. *See* Lawyers, standard of care re
mentally disabled persons. *See* Disabled persons
physically disabled persons. *See* Disabled persons
professional negligence. *See* Professional negligence
reasonable person. *See* Reasonable person
statutory standards. *See* Statutory standards
unreasonable risk. *See* Unreasonable risk
young persons. *See* Young persons, standard of care re
Statutory authority defence
private nuisance, to, 562-70
Statutory standards
compliance with statute, 202-206
criminal statutes, reliance on re civil liability, 195
criticism of, 195
examples, 200-202
generally, 184-206
gross negligence and, 198
industrial safety statutes, 196
landlord and tenant statutes, 197
legislative direction, 197-98
limitations on statutory use, 198-202
motor vehicle legislation, use in tort cases, 195-96, 197-98
pre-*Saskatchewan Wheat Pool* law, 194
specialized regulatory statutes, 196
Strict liability
act of God, meaning of, 511
animals, liability for, 516-19
escape situations, 501-507
defences to, 507-15
employer, vicarious liability of, 519-22
fires, liability for, 515-16
generally, 489
heightened-danger activity, 498
intentional discharge of offensive substance, 507
non-natural user, 494-501
normal usage, 498
origin and scope of, 489-507
products liability and, 522-29
public sewerage and drainage systems, 496-97
reviews of rule in *Rylands v. Fletcher*, 505
statutory authorization, 513-14

Strict liability — *cont'd*
ultra-hazardous uses, 497
vicarious liability, 519-22
Structured settlement, 688

T

Thin-skull rule
contributory negligence and, 331
crumbling skull doctrine vs., 330-31
foresight principle and, 329
generally, 327-31
mental suffering and, 329-30
personality changes and, 330
Tort law
aims of, 15-19
alternatives to. *See* Automobile accident compensation
class action suit and, 28
compensation purpose of, 20
critiques of, 28, 730
definitions of, 3-4
deterrent role of, 20-21
empowerment, as, 28-29
expansion in role of, 28-29
fault concept, 739, 743
general deterrence theory of, 11-12
moral aspect of, 6, 9
multi-facted nature of, 19
nature and function of, 1-31
new rationale for, 28
ombudsman, as, 22-28
psychological function of, 14-15
reduction in role of, 29-30
Transferred intent, doctrine of, 41
Trespass
case, distinction between, 37
defences to. *See* Defences
directness requirement, 34
negligence and, 37
onus shifts, 37
survival of action in, 38
writs of, 34
Trespass to goods
generally, 83-84
possession requirement, 84
Trespass to land
absolute right of landowner, 78
air space, 82-83
damages for, 75
examples of actions, 74, 76, 79
generally, 73-83
government-owned property, 77-78
Ontario statute re, 74-75
overhanging branches, 78
overhanging buildings, 78
picketers, 76-77, 78
possession requirement, 79
power transmission line, errection of, 79
subsurface invasions, 82

U

Unforeseeable plaintiff
generally, 290-96
pre-natal injuries, 293-94
psychiatric damage, foreseeability of, 295-96
unborn child, 292
wrongful birth, action for, 294
wrongful life, action for, 294
wrongful pregnancy, action for, 295
Unlawful interference with economic interests
emerging tort of, 619
Unreasonable risk
economic test of, 166-68
generally, 163-75
meaning of, 166-67
medical shortages, 175
police liability and, 173-74

V

Vicarious liability
punitive damages and, 97
strict liability and, 519-22
Victim compensation schemes, 58-59
Volition
capacity and, 42-48
drunkenness and, 42
insanity and, 46-47
intention vs., 42
mental disability, 46
mental incapacity, 47-48
Voluntary assumption of risk
consent and, 409
contractual waiver, 407
generally, 406-409
judicial attitude to, 407
proof of, 407-408
sports cases and, 408
waiver of liability, 407

W

Waiver of liability, 407
Workplace harassment, 65
Wrongful birth, action for, 294
Wrongful death. *See* Fatal accidents, damage assessment
Wrongful life, action for, 294, 724
Wrongful pregnancy, action for, 295

Y

Young persons, standard of care re
children, 213
children of tender age, 214
generally, 211-16
liability to children, 215-16
parental liability, 215
subjective/objective test re, 213-14
young person engaged in adult activity, 214-15